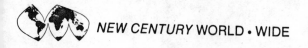
NEW CENTURY WORLD · WIDE

FRENCH
DICTIONARY

FRENCH-ENGLISH/ENGLISH-FRENCH

(American English)

Compiled by
RICHARD SWITZER, Ph.D.
Associate Professor of French, University of Wisconsin

and
HERBERT S. GOCHBERG, Ph.D.
Associate Professor of French, University of Wisconsin

with a
TRAVELER'S CONVERSATION GUIDE
Containing hundreds of expressions and items of information
useful to tourists, students, and business people

NEW CENTURY PUBLISHERS, INC.

Printing Code
16   17   18   19   20   21

Library of Congress Catalog Card Number: 82-81060

ISBN 0-8329-9682-3 Paper
ISBN 0-8329-9681-4 Thumb Indexed, Cloth

Printed in the United States of America

A PRACTICAL TOOL OF COMMUNICATION

For many years the French language has been a favorite subject of study in high school and college throughout the English-speaking world. Today it is more than a subject of study; it is a practical tool of communication in almost every corner of the globe. It is second only to English itself as a universal tongue.

Whether one travels abroad as a tourist, an exchange student, a business agent or an employee of the government, a good speaking acquaintance with the French language is an asset of great personal value. Even for the stay-at-home whose travels are purely literary, the ability to read French may become an unfailing source of profit and enjoyment.

For a thorough, up-to-date mastery of the language, nothing can be more useful than a thoroughly up-to-date French-English, English-French Dictionary. That is exactly what is provided here. Within the covers of this book are all the translated words and phrases needed to understand, read, and speak both languages. Many of the new words have never before appeared in any French-English dictionary.

Features of special value to every user of this dictionary are a complete guide to French pronunciation and a brief but comprehensive guide to French grammar.

Also included is another extra feature, a **Traveler's Conversation Guide,** which lists in English and translates into good idiomatic French hundreds of the most commonly used questions, phrases, expressions, and road signs of practical value to tourists. With the help of this Guide, one can travel with greater convenience and enjoyment wherever the French language is spoken.

CONTENTS

PRONUNCIATION GUIDES

1. **Ordinary Vowels.** French vowels are pronounced much more precisely and cleanly than English vowels. This is due, in part, to the fact that in English the muscles involved in speech are usually very relaxed. In French these muscles are markedly tense during articulation. While it is impossible to give faithful comparisons between the sounds of English and French, the following examples provide useful approximations of French sound patterns.

French Spelling	Examples	English Sound
a, a + s, à, â	pas, là, âme	f*a*ther, b*a*h
è, ê, ai, ei, -ais, e followed by two consonants	père, bête, peine, laid, selle, parlais	s*e*nd
é, final er, -et, -ez, -ai	été, aller, palet, donnez, parlai	p*ay*
e	le, petit	p*er*
i, y	mine, y	mach*i*ne
i (as semi-vowel)	rien	*y*ear
o, ô, -ot, au, eau	rose, vôtre, complot, gauche, beau	*o*pen
o, au	donner, auto	l*o*ve
œ, œu, eu, ue	œil, bœuf, heure, orgueil	h*u*rt
oi	loi	s*wa*t
ou	vous	s*oo*n
u	vu, puis	*No example

2. **Nasal Vowels.** Nasalization occurs during speech when sound is accompanied by air being expelled through the mouth *and* nose. In general, vowels followed by *n* or *m* are nasalized, except when followed by a vowel or another *n* or *m*. In French the words pin and pain are nasalized, but not peine and penne.

French Spelling	Examples	English Sound
an, am, en, em	pan, champ, enfant, emploi	t*o*ng
in, im, ain, aim, ein, yn, ym, en	pin, impie, pain, faim, ceinture, syndicat, sympathie, bien	t*a*ng
on, om	bon, pompier	*o*nly
un, um	un, parfum	l*u*ng

* Vowel may be reproduced by uttering the sound of *ee*, as in *seen*, with the lips rounded.

3. Consonants. Listed below are French consonants which differ from English in one or more respects.

French Spelling	Examples	English Sound
c (before a, o, u)	**canne, corps, cube**	*can*
c (before e, i, y)	**cent, cire, cygne**	*ceiling*
ç	**français**	*ceiling*
ch	**chien**	*share*
g (before a, o, u)	**garçon, gober, légume**	*gone*
g (before e, i, y)	**gens, gifler, gyroscope**	*azure*
gn	**cogner**	*onion*
gu (before e, i)	**guerre, gui**	*gone*
h	**halte**	Always silent

Although all **h**'s are silent in French, a distinction is made between the *mute* **h** and the *aspirate* **h**. The latter is indicated by an asterisk (*h) in this dictionary. *Aspirate* **h** prevents linking and elision. *Mute* **h**: **l'heure**; aspirate **h**: **le haut monde.**

il (final), ill (between vowels)	**travail, travailler**	*player*
j	**juger**	*azure*
q (final)	**coq**	*cock*
qu	**quel**	*kill*
r	**raison, carotte**	*No example
s (between vowels)	**raison**	*pose*
s (other cases)	**seigneur, masseur, censure, pasteur**	*sing, missile*
th	**théâtre**	*test*
ti (before vowels)	**patience, nation**	*missile*
w	**wagon, watt**	*very, watt*
y	**fuyant**	*yes*

SILENT LETTERS

e is sient when its elimination does not form a group of three consonants; **-ent** is silent when it is final in a third person plural verb. Final consonants are usually silent.

---

* The trilled *r*, formed in the front of the mouth with the tip of tongue, is heard in some parts of France. The Parisian French *r*, in contrast, comes from well back in the mouth. The sound is caused by friction between the back of the tongue and the soft palate, accompanied by vibration of the vocal chords.

ELISION

Monosyllables ending in **e** and the word **la** elide to **l'** before a word beginning with a vowel or a silent *h*. **si** contracts before **il**.

si plus **il = s'il**   **le** plus **homme = l'homme**

LINKING

An otherwise silent final consonant is pronounced in careful speech when the following word begins with a vowel and is closely linked grammatically.

STRESS

The syllables in French words are pronounced with almost equal force, with a very light stress on the last pronounced vowel.

INTONATION

The voice tends to rise on the accentuated syllable in a given word group, and on the next-to-last syllable of a sentence. It then falls on the last syllable.

USEFUL FRENCH GRAMMAR GUIDES

ARTICLES

1. Definite Article

Masc. **le** (**l'** before vowel)
  le garçon the boy
  l'arbre the tree

Fem. **la** (**l'** before vowel)
  la dame the lady
  l'école the school

Pl. **les**
  les pommes (the) apples

2. Indefinite Article

Masc. **un**
  un homme a man

Fem. **une**
  une fête a holiday

Pl. **des**
  des amis (some) friends

3. Partitive Construction. In French the definite article is often used with the preposition **de** to express the partitive. In some cases, **de** alone signifies a partitive construction. The definite article used by itself may refer to specific objects or to a whole category of objects. The following examples will be helpful:

Avez-vous du pain?	Have you any bread?
Je n'ai pas de pain.	I haven't any bread.
Il a des amis.	He has (some) friends.
L'homme est riche.	The man is rich.
Le lait est blanc.	Milk is white.
Les hommes sont des animaux.	Men are animals.

4. Contractions with Articles

à plus *le* = **au**   *à* plus *les* = **aux**   *de* plus *le* = **du**   *de* plus *les* = **des**

GENDER OF NOUNS AND ADJECTIVES

Nouns in French are masculine or feminine. The gender of a noun is predetermined by history and usage. Modifying words will be of the same gender and number as the noun.

Un bon ami (*m.*)   A good friend
La main droite (*f.*)   The right hand

Some nouns, because of the nature of the reference, may be either masculine or feminine.

Un élève, une élève a pupil   **Un enfant** a child, a boy
Une enfant a child, a girl

The feminine of most adjectives and nouns is indicated by adding **-e** to the masculine form.

grand, grande   **ami, amie**

Most adjectives ending in **-e** in the masculine remain invariable in the feminine.

Un champ fertile   **Une terre fertile**

Other regular patterns of gender are as follows:

Masculine	Feminine	Masculine	Feminine
beau	belle	lion	lionne
chameau	chamelle	ancien	ancienne
heureux	heureuse	pieux	pieuse
sec	sèche	blanc	blanche
danseur	danseuse	reveur	reveuse
acteur	actrice	moteur	motrice
neuf	neuve	veuf	veuve

PLURALS

Most words add **-s** to indicate the plural.

Singular **le grand garçon**   *Plural* **les grands garçons**
la petite fille   **les petites filles**

Masculine words ending in **-s** or **-x** remain unchanged in the plural.

Singular **le chapeau gris**   *Plural* **les chapeaux gris**
le moment heureux   **les moments heureux**

Most words ending in **-al, -au, -eu,** and **-eau** form the plural ending in **-x.**

Singular	Plural	Singular	Plural
cheval	chevaux	beau	beaux
feu	feux	château	châteaux

8

UNSTRESSED PRONOUNS

1. Direct Object Pronouns

me	me; myself	la	her; it
te	you; yourself	nous	us; ourselves
se	himself; herself; themselves	vous	you; yourself; yourselves
le	him; it	les	them

2. Indirect Object Pronouns

me	to me; to myself	lui	to him, her
te	to you; to yourself	nous	to us; to ourselves
se	to himself, herself; to themselves; to each other	vous	to you; to yourself; yourselves
	leur	to them	

3. The unstressed words **y** (to it, to them, there) and **en** (of it, of them, from it, some, any) appear in the same part of the sentence as the unstressed pronouns.

The position of pronouns in normal French word order is at times similar to English usage. In many instances, however, the position varies, particularly in the use of the unstressed pronouns. In declarative, interrogative and all negative sentences, these pronouns appear *before* the verb. The examples below will be helpful:

Je vous parle.	I am speaking to you.
Il le voit.	He sees him.
Y êtes-vous allé?	Did you go there?
Je n'en vois pas.	I don't see any.
Nous nous habillons.	We are dressing (ourselves).
Elles se sont parlé.	They spoke to each other.
Je lui ai donné le livre.	I gave him the book. (her)
Je le lui ai donné.	I gave it to him. (to her.)
Les avez-vous?	Do you have them?
Je leur en parlerai.	I'll speak to them about it.
Elle me l'a vendu.	She sold it to me.
Nous les y verrons.	We'll see them there.

ADVERBS

Most adverbs are derived from corresponding adjective forms by adding the suffix **-ment** to the feminine form of the adjective.

Adjective	*Adverb*
heureux	**heureusement**
cruel	**cruellement**
final	**finalement**

Some adverbs follow a variant of the above pattern.

Adjective	*Adverb*
négligent	**négligemment**
évident	**évidemment**
constant	**constamment**

9

INTERROGATION

Interrogation is indicated in French in several ways, just as in English. The use of the interrogative pronouns, adjectives, and adverbs; the inversion of verb and subject; the addition of a questioning phrase at the beginning or end of the sentence; a simple change in the inflection of the voice—all are signs of interrogation.

Qui êtes-vous?	Who are you?
Quel est son nom?	What is his name?
Qu'a-t-elle fait?	What has she done?
Comment le sait-il?	How does he know (it)?
Qu'est-ce qui est tombé?	What fell?
Pourquoi ne me parlez-vous pas?	Why don't you speak to me?
Est-ce que c'est vrai?	Is it true?

NEGATION

Verbs are made negative in French by the use of **ne** before the verb and one of several negative words after the verb. In some cases, **ne** may appear without an accompanying sign of negation, but for the most part both signs are found.

Je ne sais pas.	I don't know.
Je ne sais danser.	I don't know how to dance.
Il ne lui écrit jamais.	He never writes to her.
Il n'a rien vu.	He saw nothing.
Je ne la verrai plus.	I won't see her any more.
Elle n'aime personne.	She loves no one.

When negative signs such as **personne** and **rien** are used as subjects of the sentence, the following order is found:

Personne ne le sait.	No one knows it.

The use of **ne . . . que** (only) follows the same pattern as the above.

Je ne vois que deux choses.	I only see two things.

REGULAR VERBS

In each of these conjugations, the endings refer to 1st, 2nd, and 3rd person, singular and plural.

1. -er Verbs. Example: **donner**

Present participle, donnant; *Past participle,* donné
Present donne, -es, -e, -ons, -ez, -ent
Future donnerai, -as, -a, -ons, -ez, -ont
Conditional donnerais, -ais, -ait, -ions, -iez, -aient
Present subjunctive donne, -es, -e, -ions, -iez, -ent
Imperfect donnais, -ais, -ait, -ions, -iez, -aient
Past definite donnais, -as, a, -âmes, -âtes, -èrent

2. -ir Verbs. Example: **finir**

Present participle finissant; *Past participle* fini
Present finis, -is, -it, -issons, -issez, -issent
Future finirai, -as, -a, -ons, -ez, -ont
Conditional finirais, -ais, -ait, -ions, -iez, -aient
Present subjunctive finisse, -es, -e, -ions, -iez, -ent
Imperfect finissais, -ais, -ait, -ions, -iez, -aient
Past definite finis, -is, -it, -îmes, -îtes, -irent

3. -re Verbs. Example: **rendre**

Present participle rendant; *Past participle* rendu
Present rends, -ds, -d, -dons, -dez, -dent
Future rendrai, -as, -a, -ons, -ez, -ont
Conditional rendrais, -ais, -ait, -ions, -iez, -aient
Present subjunctive rende, -es, -e, -ions, -iez, -ent
Imperfect rendais, -ais, -ait, -ions, -iez, -aient
Past definite rendis, -is, -it, -îmes, -îtes, -irent

4. Examples of Compound Verb Tenses

Present Perfect	**J'ai donné**	I gave, have given
(Past Indefinite)	**Il a fini**	He finished, has finished
	Il est allé	He went, has gone
Past Perfect	**Nous avions vendu**	We had sold
(Pluperfect)	**Ils avaient parlé**	They had spoken
	Elle etait arrivée	She had arrived
Future Perfect	**Vous aurez obéi**	You will have obeyed
	Je serai venu	I will have come
	Tu auras rendu	You will have given back
Past Conditional	**Elles auraient pleuré**	They would have cried
	Vous auriez beni	You would have blessed
	Elle serait devenue	She would have become
Past Anterior	**Il eut fendu**	He had split
	Vous eûtes étudié	You had studied
	Je fus tombé	I had fallen
Perfect Subjunctive	**Elle ait bondi**	She jumped, has jumped
	Nous ayons tordu	We twisted, have twisted
	Vous soyez resté	You remained, have remained

IRREGULAR VERB FORMS

The following list deals with the frequently used irregular verbs. Only the basic pattern of irregularity is given. Where forms and tenses do not deviate from regular patterns, they are not listed; it may be assumed that they are like regular forms.

absoudre like **résoudre**; *p.p.* **absous**
accueiller like **cueillir**
acquérir *p.p.* **acquis**; *pres.* **acquiers -s, -t**, acquérons, -ez, acquièrent *fut.* acquerrais; *pres. subj.* acquières, -es, -e, acquérions, -iez, acquièrent
admettre like **mettre**
aller *pres.* **vais, vas, va, allons, -ez, vont**; *fut.* **irai**; *pres. subj.* **aille, -es, -e, allions, -iez, aillent**
apercevoir like **recevoir**
apparaître like **connaître**
appartenir like **tenir**
apprendre like **prendre**
asseoir *p.p.* **assis**; *pres.* **assieds, -ds, -d, asseyons, -ez, -ent**; *fut.* **assiérai**
assortir like **sortir**
atteindre like **craindre**

11

avoir *pres. p.* ayant; *p.p.* eu; *pres.* ai, as, a, avons, -ez, ont; *fut.* aurai; *pres. subj.* aie, -es, -e, aient

battre *pres.* bats, -ts, -t, -ttons, -ttez, -ttent

boire *p.p.* bu; *pres.* bois, -s, -t, buvons, -ez, boivent; *pres. subj.* boive, -es, -e, buvions, -iez, boivent

bouillir *pres. p.* bouillant; *pres.* bous, -s, -t, -illons, -illez, -illent

commettre like **mettre**

comprendre like **prendre**

concevoir like **recevoir**

conclure *p.p.* conclu; *pres.* conclus, -s, -t, -ons, -ez, -ent

concourir like **courir**

conduire *p.p.* conduit; *pres.* conduis, -s, -t, -sons, -sez, -sent; *past def.* conduisis

confire like **suffire**

connaître *p.p.* connu; *pres.* connais, -aît, -aissons, -aissez, -aissent

conquérir like **acquérir**

consentir like **mentir**

construire like **conduire**

contenir like **tenir**

contredire like **dire**

convaincre like **vaincre**

convenir like **venir**

coudre *pres. p.* cousant; *p.p.* cousu; *pres.* couds, -ds, -d, -sons, -sez, -sent

courir *p.p.* couru; *pres.* cours, -s, -t, -ons, -ez, -ent; *fut.* courrai

couvrir like **ouvrir**

craindre *p.p.* craint; *pres.* crains, -s, -t, craignons, -ez, -ent

croire *p.p.* cru; *pres.* crois, -s, -t, croyons, -ez, croient; *pres. subj.* croie, -es, -e, croyions, -iez, croient

croître *p.p.* crû; *pres.* croîs, -s, -t, croissons, -ez, -ent, *past def.* crûs; *imp. subj.* crusse

cueillir *pres.* cueille, -es, -e, ons, -ez, -ent; *fut.* cueillerai

cuire like **conduire**

decevoir like **recevoir**

découvrir like **ouvrir**

décrire like **écrire**

dédire like **dire**

déduire like **conduire**

défaire like **faire**

dépeindre like **craindre**

détruire like **conduire**

devoir *p.p.* dû; *pres.* dois, -s, -t, devons, -ez, doivent; *fut.* devrais *pres. subj.* doive, -es, e, devions, diez, doivent; *past def.* dus

dire *p.p.* dit; *pres.* dis, -s, -t, -sons, -tes, -sent

discourir like **courir**

disparaître like **connaître**

dissoudre like **résoudre**; *p.p.* dissous

dormir *pres.* dors, -s, -t, -mons, -mez, -ment

écrire *p.p.* écrit; *pres.* écris, -s, -t, -vons, -vez, -vent; *past def.* écrivis

élire like **lire**

endormir like **dormir**

entreprendre like **prendre**

envoyer *pres.* envoie, -es, -e, envoyons, -ez, envoient; *fut.* enverrai; *pres. subj.* envoie, -es, -e, envoyions, -iez, envoient

être *pres. p.* étant; *p.p.* été; *pres.* suis, es, est, sommes, ètes, sont; *fut.* serai; *pres. subj.* sois, -s, -t, soyons, ez, soient

étreindre like **craindre**

exclure like **conclure**

faire *p.p.* fait; *pres.* fais, -s, -t, -sons, -tes, font; *fut.* ferai; *pres. subj.* fasse; *past def.* fis

falloir *p.p.* fallu; *pres.* (3rd per. sing. only) faut; *fut.* faudra; *pres. subj.* faille

feindre like **craindre**

frire *p.p.* frit; *pres.* fris, -s, -t, -ons, -ez, -ent

fuir *pres.* fuis, -s, -t, fuyons, -ez, fuient; *pres. subj.* fuie, -es, -e, fuyions, -iez, fuient

geindre like **craindre**

haïr *p.p.* haï; *pres.* hais, -s, -t, haïssons, -ez, -ent

inscrire like **écrire**

instruire like **conduire**

joindre like **craindre**

lire *p.p.* lu; *pres.* lis, -s, -t, -sons, -sez, -sent

maintenir like **tenir**

mentir *pres.* mens, -s, -t, -tons, -tez, -tent

mettre *p.p.* mis; *pres.* mets, -ts, -t, -ttons, -ttez, -ttent

moudre *pres. p.* moulant, *p.p.* moulu; *pres.* mouds, -ds, -d, -lons, -les, -lent

mourir *p.p.* mort; *pres.* meurs, -s, -t, mourons, -ez, meurent; *fut.* mourrai; *pres. subj.* meure, -es, -e, mourions; -iez, meurent; *past def.* mourus

mouvoir *p.p.* mû; *pres.* meus, -s, -t, mouvons, -ez, meuvent; *fut.* mouvrai; *pres. subj.* meuve; *past def.* mus

naître *p.p.* né; *pres.* nais, naît, naissons, -ez, -ent; *past def.* naquis

nuire like conduire

obtenir like tenir

offrir like ouvrir

ouvrir *p.p.* ouvert; *pres.* ouvre, -es, -e, -ons, -ez, -ent; *past def.* ouvris

paître like connaître

paraître like connaître

parcourir like courir

partir *pres.* pars, -s, -t, -tons, -tez, -tent

parvenir like venir

peindre like craindre

permettre like mettre

plaindre like craindre

plaire *p.p.* plu; *pres.* plais, -ais, -aît, -aisons, -aisez, -aisent

pleuvoir *pres. p.* pleuvant; *p.p.* plu; *pres.* (3rd. per. sing. only) pleut; *fut.* pleuvra

poursuivre like suivre

pouvoir *p.p.* pu; *pres.*. peux, -x, -t, pouvons, -ez, peuvent; *fut.* pourrai; *pres. subj.* puisse

prédire like dire

prendre *p.p.* pris; *pres.* prends, -ds, -d, prenons, -ez, -nent; *pres. subj.* prenne, -es, prenions, -iez, prennent

prescrire like écrire

produire like conduire

promettre like mettre

recevoir *p.p.* reçu; *pres.* reçois, -s, -t, recevons, -ez, reçoivent; *fut.* recevrai; *pres. subj.* reçoive, -es, -e, recevions, -iez, reçoivent

reconnaître like connaître

réduire like conduire

repentir like mentir

résoudre *pres. p.* résolvant; *p.p.* résolu, résous; *pres.* résous, -s, -t, résolvons, -ez, -ent; *pres. subj.* résolve

rire *p.p.* ri; *pres.* ris, -s, -t, -ons, -ez, -ent

rompre *pres.* romps, -s, -t, -ons, -ez, -ent

satisfaire like faire

savoir *p.p.* su; *pres.* sais, -s, -t, savons, -ez, -ent; *fut.* saurai; *pres. subj.* sache

secourir like courir

séduire like conduire

sentir like mentir

servir *pres.* sers, -s, -t, -vons, -vez, -vent

sortir *pres.* sors, -s, -t, -tons, -tez, -tent

souffrir like ouvrir

soumettre like mettre

sourire like rire

soutenir like tenir

suffire *pres.* suffis, -s, -t, -sons, -sez, -sent

suivre *pres.* suis, -s, -t, -vons, -vez, -vent

surprendre like prendre

taire like plaire (without circumflex)

teindre like craindre

tenir *p.p.* tenu; *pres.* tiens, -s, -t, tenons, -ez, tiennent; *fut.* tiendrai; *pres. subj.* tienne, -es, -e, tenions, -iez, tiennent

traduire like conduire

tressaillir like cueillir

vaincre *p.p.* vaincu; *pres.* vaincs, -cs, -c, vainquons, -ez, -ent; *past def.* vainquis

valoir *p.p.* valu; *pres.* vaux, -x, -t, valons, -ez, -ent; *fut.* vaudrai; *pres. subj.* vaille, -es, -e, valions, -iez, vaillent

venir like tenir (compound tenses conjugated with être as auxiliary verb)

vêtir *p.p.* vêtu; *pres.* vêts, -ts, -t, -tons, -tez, -tent; *past def.* vêtis

vivre *p.p.* vécu; *pres.* vis, -s, -t, -vons, -vez, -vent

voir *p.p.* vu; *pres.* vois, -s, -t, voyons, -ez, voient; *fut.* verrai; *pres. subj.* voie, -es, -e, voyions, -iez, voient; *past def.* vis

vouloir *p.p.* voulu; *pres.* veux, -x, -t, voulons, -ez, veulent; *fut.* voudrais; *pres. subj.* veuille, -es, -e, voulions, -iez, veuillent

ABBREVIATIONS

a.	adjective	math.	mathematics
adv.	adverb	mech.	mechanics
agr.	agriculture	med.	medicine
anat.	anatomy	mil.	military art
arch.	architecture	min.	mining
art.	article	mus.	music
ast.	astronomy	*n.*	noun
auto.	automobile	naut.	nautical
avi.	aviation	*past def.*	past definite
biol.	biology	phot.	photography
bot.	botany	phy.	physics
chem.	chemistry	*pl.*	plural
coll.	colloquial	poet.	poetry
com.	commerce	pol.	politics
cond.	conditional	*p.p.*	past participle
conj.	conjunction	*prep.*	preposition
dent.	dentistry	*pres.*	present
eccl.	ecclesiastic	*pres. p.*	present participle
elec.	electricity	print.	printing
ent.	entomology	*pron.*	pronoun
f.	feminine	rad.	radio
fig.	figuratively	rail.	railway
fut.	future	rhet.	rhetoric
geol.	geology	*sing.*	singular
gram.	grammar	*subj.*	subjunctive
imp.	impersonal	theat.	theatre
imper.	imperfect	*v.*	verb
infin.	infinitive	vet.	veterinary
interj.	interjection	*vi.*	verb intransitive
interr.	interrogative	*vt.*	verb transitive
m.	masculine	zool.	zoology

FRENCH-ENGLISH

A

à *prep.* to, at, in, with

abaisse-langue *m.* tongue depressor

abaissement *m.* lowering, falling; drop; abasement

abaisser *vt.* to lower; abase; **s'—** to humble oneself; resort, stoop, cringe

abandon *m.* abandonment, neglect; abandon; **à l'—** uncared for, at random

abandonner *vt.* to abandon, give up; **s'—** to resign oneself; give way, yield

abasourdi *a.* astounded, amazed; **-ssement** *m.* bewilderment, consternation

abasourdir *vt.* astound, stupefy, amaze

abat *m.* sudden shower; **pluie d'—** drenching rain

abâtardir *vt.* corrupt, debase, bastardize

abat-jour *m.* lamp shade; shutter, blind, skylight

abattage *m.* slaughter; (coll.) reprimand; felling (trees)

abattant *m.* flap; **— a.** depressing

abattement *m.* prostration; dejection

abattis *m.* giblets, feet; slaughtered animals; felling

abattoir *m.* stockyard; slaughterhouse

abattre *vt.* to fell; demolish; slaughter; depress; **s'—** to alight; (avi.) crash; calm down, abate; become depressed

abattu *a.* depressed, humbled

abbaye *f.* abbey

abbé *m.* abbot; priest, superior; ecclesiastic

abbesse *f.* abbess

abcéder *vi.* to abscess

abcès *m.* abscess

abdication *f.* abdication

abdiquer *vt.* to abdicate; resign

abdomen *n.* abdomen

abdominal *a.* abdominal

abécédaire *m.* child's first speller, reader or primer

abeille *f.* bee

aberration *f.* aberration, alienation

abêtir *vt.* to stupefy, blunt

abhorrer *vt.* to abhor, detest, loathe

abîme *m.* abyss, chasm

abîmer *vt.* to damage, ruin, spoil; **s'—** to spoil; be engulfed

abject *a.* abject

abjuration *f.* abjuration, renunciation

abjurer *vi.* to abjure, renounce

ablatif *m.* ablative

ablution *f.* ablution, purification

abnégation *f.* abnegation, sacrifice

aboiement *m.* barking, baying

abois *m. pl.*, **aux —** at bay; **mettre aux —** to make desperate

abolir *vt.* to abolish, repeal, suppress

abolition *f.* abolition; **-iste** abolitionist

abomination *f.* abomination

abominer *vt.* to abominate, detest

abondamment *adv.* abundantly

abondance *f.* abundance, wealth; **parler d'—** to speak extemporaneously

abondant *a.* plentiful, abundant, abounding

abonder *vi.* to abound, be plentiful

abonné *m.* subscriber

abonnement *m.* subscription; (rail.) commuter ticket; season ticket

abonner *vt.* to enter a subscription (for someone); **s'— a** to subscribe to

abonnir *vt.* to improve, correct

abonnissement *m.* improvement

abord *m.* approach; **-s** *pl.* outskirts; **d'—** at first abordable *a.* accessible, receptive, approachable

aborder *vt.* to approach, accost; undertake; — *vi.* (naut.) to land

aborigène *a. & m.* aboriginal, native

abortif *a.* abortive

abot *m.* hobble; fetter for horse

aboucher *vt.* s'— confer; bring together

about *m.* end of wood piece (to be added to another), butt end

aboutement *m.* abutment; placing end to end

abouter *vt.* to place end to end

aboutissement *m.* result, outcome; (med.) heading of an abcess

aboyer *vi.* to bark, yelp

abrasion *f.* abrasion

abrégé *m.* resumé, digest, abridgment; en — briefly

abrégement *m.* abridgment; abridging

abreger *vt.* to shorten; abbreviate

abreuer *vt.* to water; soak; flood

abreuvoir *m.* trough for water

abri *m.* shelter; protection; à l'— de under cover of, sheltered from; sans — homeless

abricot *m.* apricot; –ier *m.* apricot tree

abriter *vt.* to shelter, protect

abri-voûte *m.* bomb shelter

abroger *vt.* to abrogate

abruti *m.* stupid person, fool; — *a.* stupid

abrutir *vt.* to stupefy

abrutissement *m.* stupefaction, degradation

absent *a.* absent; absent-minded

absentéisme *m.* absenteeism

absenter *v.*, s'— to be away, step out

abside *f.* apse

absinthe *f.* (liqueur) absinthe; wormwood

absolu *a.* absolute, unlimited

absolument *adv.* absolutely; completely

absolution *f.* absolution

absolutisme *m.* absolutism

absorbant *a.* absorbing; absorbent

absorber *vt.* to absorb; s'— to be absorbed

absorption *f.* absorption

absoudre *vt.* to absolve; forgive; remit

abstenir *v.*, s'— to abstain

abstention *f.* abstention

abstinence *f.* abstinence; abstention

abstinent *a.* abstinent, abstemious

abstraction *f.* abstraction

abstractionnisme *m.* (art) abstractionism

abstraire *vt.* to abstract, consider separately

abstrait *a.* abstract; engrossed; inattentive

absurde *a.* absurd; silly; preposterous

absurdité *f.* absurdity; nonsense

abus *m.* abuse, misuse; mistake; breach

abuser *vi.* to take advantage, impose; misuse; — *vt.* to deceive; s'— to be mistaken

abusif *a.* abusive; contrary to rule or law; improper

Abyssinie *f.* Abyssinia

abyssinien *a.* Abyssinian

acacia *m.* acacia

académicien *m.* academician

académie *f.* academy; school; university; learned society

académique *a.* academic

acajou *m.* mahogany

acariâtre *a.* quarrelsome; nagging

accablant *a.* overwhelming; annoying

accablement *m.* dejection, discouragement

accablé *a.* worn out; overwhelmed; (fig.) weighed down

accabler *vt.* to discourage; wear out; crush, overwhelm

accalmie *f.* (naut.) calm, lull, respite

accaparer *vt.* to corner (the market); monopolize

accéder *vi.* to agree; accede; to have access to

accélérateur *m.* accelerator; — *a.* accelerative

accélération *f.* acceleration

accélérer *vi.* to accelerate

accent *m.* accent; tone; emphasis, stress

accentuer *vt.* to accent, accentuate, stress

acceptabilité *f.* acceptability

acceptable *a.* acceptable

acceptation *f.* acceptance

accepter *vt.* to accept, agree

acception *f.* meaning, acceptation

accès *m.* approach; access; attack, fit; par — by fits and starts

accessible *a.* accessible

accession *f.* accession, adhesion, union

accessoire *m. & a.* accessory

accident *m.* accident; — de terrain unevenness of ground

accidenté *a.* rough, uneven; varied

accidentel *a.* accidental, unexpected

accidenter *vt.* (coll.) to involve in an accident; to make uneven

accise *f.* excise tax

acclamation *f.* acclamation

acclamer *vt.* to acclaim, hail

acclimatation *f.* acclimation

acclimater *vt.* to acclimate

accointance *f.* acquaintance; familiarity

accointer *vt.* to make acquainted; s'— to become friendly

accolade *f.* embrace; accolade; knighting; (print.) bracket, brace

accoler *vt.* to fasten; join, link

accommodage *m.* preparation *or* dressing; hairdressing

accommodant *a.* accommodating, easy-going, obliging; courteous

accommodement *m.* agreement, compromise, settlement; reconciliation

accommoder *vt.* to adjust; fix up; fix over; arrange; s'— to adjust, adapt; make oneself comfortable; compromise; come to terms with

accompagnateur *m.* accompanist

accompagnement *m.* accompaniment; tir d'— *m.* (mil.) covering-fire

accompagner *vt.* to accompany, be with, come with, go with

accompli *a.* accomplished; fulfilled; perfect

accomplir *vt.* to accomplish, do; complete

accomplissement *m.* accomplishment, achievement; completion

accord *m.* accord; agreement; (mus.) chord; harmony, tune; d'— in agreement; agreed, all right; être d'— to agree; **tomber d'**— to come to an agreement, agree

accordé *m.* bridegroom, fiancé

accordéon *m.* accordion

accorder *vt.* to reconcile; accord; tune; s'— agree, be in agreement; be in tune, harmonize

accore *a.* abrupt, sheer; vertical (coast); — *m.* (naut.) prop used during boat construction

accort *a.* gracious, compliant

accoster *vt.* to approach; accost

accoter *v.*, s'— à to lean against

accotoir *m.* support; prop; stanchion

accouchement *m.* delivery (birth); lying-in

accoucher *vi.* to give birth; — *vt.* to attend someone giving birth; deliver (baby)

accoucheur *m.* obstetrician

accoucheuse *f.* midwife

accoudoir *m.* armrest, sill; (arch.) rail

accouplement *m.* coupling; joining; pairing

accoupler *vt.* to couple, join, pair

accourcie *f.* shortcut

accourcir *vt.* to shorten; hasten

accourir *vi.* to rush up to, flock together

accoutrement *m.* bizarre attire; garb

accoutrer *vt.* to dress up ridiculously, to rig out

accoutumance *f.* habit, custom

accoutumé *a.* accustomed; customary, usual

accoutumer *vt.* to accustom; s'— get used to, become accustomed to

accréditer *vt.* to accredit; give credence to

accroc *m.* tear, rip; difficulty; hindrance, hitch

accrocher *vt.* to hang up; bump; catch (by hook), hook; embarrass; s'— hold on, cling, grab; clinch (in boxing)

accroire (faire) *vt.* to believe; **enfaire** — impose on; **s'en faire** — be self-conceited

accroissement *m.* growth, increase

accroître *vi.* to grow; — *vt.* to increase, enhance

accroupir *v.*, s'— to crouch, squat

accroupissement *m.* crouching, cowering

accueil *m.* reception; welcome

accueillant *a.* cordial, hospitable, gracious

accueillir *vt.* to receive, welcome, greet

accul *m.* blind alley

acculer *vt.* to drive back, corner

accumulateur *m.* battery, cell

accumulation *f.* accumulation

accumuler *vt.* to accumulate

accusateur *a.* accusing; — *m.* **accuser**; — public *m.* attorney-general

accusatif *a. & m.* accusative

accusation *f.* accusation, indictment

accusé *m.* accused; defendant; notice; — de réception receipt; — *a.* accentuated, marked

accuser *vt.* to accuse; reveal; announce; accentuate, heighten

acerbe *a.* bitter, sour, sharp, astringent

acerbité *f.* acerbity; bitterness, sharpness

acéré *a.* sharp, keen

acescent *a.* becoming acid

acétique *a.* acetic

acétone *f.* acetone

acétylène *m.* acetylene

achalander *vt.* to supply *or* attract customers; to stock, supply

acharné *a.* stubborn, tenacious, persistant; desperate

acharnement *m.* tenacity, obstinacy, rancor

acharner *v.*, s'— to be tenacious; persist

achat *m.* purchase; — *vt.* faire des —s to buy

achée *f.* worms used for bait

acheminement *m.* progress; direction

acheminer *vt.* to send, forward; s'— to go ahead, move

acheter *vt.* to buy, purchase

acheteur *m.* purchaser, buyer

achevé *a.* finished; perfect; accomplished

achèvement *m.* finish(ing), completion; finished quality

achever *vt.* to finish, complete; finish off, dispatch

achoppement *m.* obstacle; **pierre d'**— *f.* stumbling block

achopper *v.*, s'— to stumble

acide *n. & a.* acid

acidité *f.* acidity

acidulé *a.* acid, acidulated; **bonbon —** *m.* drop; fruit-flavored hard candy

acier *m.* steel; **— fondu** cast steel; **— trempé** tempered steel; **cœur d'—** hard heart; **fil d'—** steel wire

aciérer *vt.* to convert to steel

aciérie *f.* steel mill

acmé *f.* acme

acné *f.* acne

acompte *m.* part payment, payment on account, installment

à-coup *m.* jerk, jolt

acoustique *a.* acoustic(al); **cornet — *m.*** ear trumpet; **— *f.*** acoustics; **— *m.*** speaking-tube

acquéreur *m.* purchaser

acquérir *vt.* to acquire, win

acquiescement *m.* acquiescence, consent

acquiescer *vi.* to acquiesce, consent, agree

acquis *a.* acquired; **— *m.*** acquired knowledge *or* experience

acquisition *f.* acquisition

acquit *m.* receipt; release; **par — de conscience** to ease one's conscience; **pour — paid**

acquittement *m.* (com.) payment in full; legal acquittal

acquitter *vt.* to acquit, discharge; (com.) receipt; **s'—** discharge, fulfill

acre *m.* acre

âcre *a.* acrid, sharp, bitter

âcreté *f.* bitterness, sharpness

acrimonie *f.* acrimony

acrimonieux *a.* acrimonious

acrobate *m. & f.* acrobat; rope-dancer

acrobatie *f.* acrobatics; stunt

acrobatique *a.* acrobatic

acropole *f.* acropolis

acrostiche *m.* acrostic

acrylique *a.* acrylic

acte *m.* act, action; title; deed; certificate; **— de naissance** birth certificate; **—s** *pl.* proceedings

acteur *m.* actor

actif *a.* active; **— *m.*** credit side of a ledger; asset; (gram.) active voice

actinique *a.* actinic

actinium *m.* actin

action *f.* action; act; lawsuit; (mil.) engagement; (com.) share of stock

actionnaire *m. & f.* stockholder

actionné *a.* active, busy

actionner *vt.* to put in motion; begin a court action, sue

activer *vt.* to activate; make active

activeur *m.* activator

activité *f.* activity; **en — active**

actrice *f.* actress

actuaire *m.* actuary; Roman scribe

actualité *f.* something real; present, thing of the moment; **—s** *pl.* newsreel; news items

actuel *a.* present, current

actuellement *adv.* at present, now, today, really

acuité *f.* acuteness, keenness

adaptateur *m.* adaptor

adapter *vt.* to adapt, adjust; **s'—** adapt oneself

addenda *m.* addition(s)

additif *m. & a.* additive

addition *f.* addition; (restaurant) check

additionnel *a.* additional

additionner *vt.* to add up; adulterate, cut (with water)

adénoïde *a.* adenoids; **végétations —s** *f. pl.* adenoids

adent *m.* notch, groove; dovetail, mortise

adepte *n.* partisan; expert; adept

adéquat *a.* equivalent; adequate

adhérence *f.* adherence

adhérent *a.* adherent; adhesive; **— *m.*** supporter; adherent; subscriber to a belief

adhérer *vi.* to adhere, stick, cling; subscribe, belong

adhésif *a. & m.* adhesive

adhésion *f.* adhesion; adherence

adieu *m.* farewell

adipeux *a.* adipose

adjacent *a.* adjacent, adjoining

adjectif *a.* adjectival, adjective; **— *n.*** adjective

adjectivement *adv.* adjectively

adjoindre *vt.* to adjoin, join on, add

adjoint *a. & m.* assistant, deputy, adjunct

adjonction *f.* addition, annex

adjudant-chef *m.* master sergeant, sergeant-major

adjudicataire *m. & f.* highest bidder; beneficiary of adjudication

adjudication *f.* adjudication; knocking down (at auction sale); contract; **mettre en — contract for**

adjuger *vt.* to adjudicate, award, knock down at auction

adjurer *vt.* to adjure; entreat; bind *or* command under oath

admettre *vt.* to admit, allow

administrateur *m.* administrator; director

administratif *a.* administrative

administration *f.* administration; management; direction

administrer *vt.* to administer, manage, direct

admirateur *a.* admiring; **— *n.*** admirer

admiratif *a.* admiring

admiration *f.* admiration

admirer *vt.* to admire; wonder
admissibilité *f.* admissibility
admissible *a.* admissible
admission *f.* admission
admonestation *f.* admonition
admonester *vt.* to admonish
adolescence *f.* adolescence
adolescent *a. & m.* adolescent
adonner *v.* s'— à to devote oneself to
adopter *vt.* to adopt
adoption *f.* adoption
adorateur *m.* adorer
adoration *f.* adoration, worship
adorer *vt.* to adore, worship
adosser *vt.* to place back to back, lean
  back against; s'— to lean (back)
adoucir *vt.* to soften, moderate; relieve,
  ease; s'— to become mild, soften
adoucisseur *m.* water softener
adrénaline *f.* adrenalin
adresse *f.* address; skill; adroitness
adresser *vt.* to address; s'— (à) to address
  oneself to; apply to; speak to
adroit *a.* skillful, clever, adroit
aduler *vt.* to adulate
adulte *m. & a.* adult
adultération *f.* adulteration
adultère *m.* adultery; — *a.* adulterous
adultérer *vt.* to adulterate
advenir *v.* to happen, come about; become
adverbe *m.* adverb
adverbial *a.* adverbial
adversaire *m.* adversary, opponent
adverse *a.* contrary; adverse
adversité *f.* adversity, affliction
aération *f.* aeration, renewal of air
aéré *a.* airy, well-aired
aérer *vt.* to air, ventilate; aerate
aérien *a.* aerial; ligne –ne *f.* airline
aérodrome *m.* airport
aérodynamique *f.* aerodynamics; — *a.*
  aerodynamic
aérofrein *m.* airbrake
aérogare *f.* airline terminal
aérogramme *m.* airletter
aérographe *m.* airbrush
aéronaute *m.* aeronaut
aéronautique *f.* aeronautics; — *a.* aero-
  nautic
aéronef *n.* airship, aircraft
aéroplane *m.* airplane
aéroport *m.* airport
aéroporté *a.* airborne
aéropostal *a.* relating to airmail
aérostat *m.* balloon
aérothermodynamique *f.* aerothermodynamics
aérotransporté *a.* airborne
affabilité *f.* affability, kindness
affable *a.* affable, courteous

affadir *vt.* to dull; make insipid
affadissement *m.* state of becoming faded;
  dulling, loss of taste
affaiblir *vt.* to weaken; s'— to grow weak;
  droop
affaiblissement *m.* weakening
affaire *f.* business, lawsuit; matter, deal;
  -s belongings; business; chiffre d'—s *m.*
  receipts (total business); homme d'-s
  m. business man; avoir — à to have to
  deal with
affairé *a.* busy
affairement *m.* activity, bustle
affairer *v.* s'— to be busy, hustle and
  bustle
affaissement *m.* collapse, depression,
  weakness
affaisser *v.* s'— to collapse, sink
affaîter *vt.* to train falcons
affamé *a.* starved, famished; greedy
affamer *vt.* to starve
affectation *f.* affectation; pretense; designation
affecter *vt.* to affect; feign; assume; (mil.)
  draft; designate; s'— to be moved
affectif *a.* affective; emotional
affection *f.* affection; mental state; (med.)
  ailment; -né *a.* affectionate
affectionner *vt.* to be fond of; take an
  interest in
affecteux *a.* affectionate
affermer *vt.* to rent by lease
affermir *vt.* to strengthen; harden; s'— to
  become firmer
affété *a.* affected
affichage *m.* posting on billboards
affiche *f.* poster, bill; -r *vt.* to post,
  advertise; make a show of
afficheur *m.* bill poster
affidavit *m.* affidavit
affidé *a.* trustworthy; — *m.* confederate;
  spy
affier *vt.* give one's word
afilé *a.* sharp; avoir la langue bien –e to
  have a sharp tongue, gossip; d'—e *adv.*
affiler *vt.* to sharpen
affilier *vt.* to affiliate, associate closely
affiloir *m.* hone; steel; knife sharpener
affiner *vt.* to refine; improve
affinité *f.* affinity; tendency to combine
affiquets *m. pl.* gew-gaws; knickknacks
affirmatif *a.* affirmative, positive
affirmation *f.* affirmation; assertion
affirmer *vt.* to affirm, assert; s'— assert
  oneself
affleurer *vt.* to make even; be even with
affliction *f.* affliction
affligé *a.* afflicted; sad; vexed
affligeant *a.* sad, distressing, bad (news)

affliger *vt.* to afflict; grieve, sadden, trouble

affluence *f.* affluence; abundance; crowd; **heures d'—** *f. pl.* rush hours

affluent *m. & a.* tributary

affluer *vi.* to flow; abound

afflux *m.* influx

affolement *m.* panic, distress; infatuation

affolé *a.* maddened, panic-stricken; infatuated

affoler *vt.* to madden, panic; infatuate; **s'—** to be panic-stricken; be madly in love with

affouiller *vt.* to undermine; wash away

affranchir *vt.* to emancipate, free; to stamp (letter)

affranchissement *m.* postage; liberation, emancipation

affres *f. pl.* anguish; dread

affrètement *m.* chartering, freighting

affréter *vt.* to charter, freight

affreux *a.* frightful; horrible

affriander *vt.* to make appetizing; lure; entice

affrioler *vt.* to attract; allure

affront *m.* insult; disgrace; reproach

affronter *vt.* to face; brave; **s'—** be in opposition

affubler *vt.* to fit out bizarrely; muffle

affût *m.* gun carriage; hunting post; **être à l'—** be on watch; lie in wait

affûter *vt.* to sharpen tools

affûtiau *m.* trifle; knickknack

Afghan *m. & a.* Afghan

afin, **— que** *conj.* so that, in order that; **— de** *prep.* in order to

Africain *m. & a.* African

Afrique *f.* Africa

afro-asiatique *a.* Afro-Asian

agaçant *a.* irritating, annoying

agacement *m.* annoyance, irritation

agacer *vt.* to irritate, annoy; egg on

âge *m.* age; period, epoch; **— viril** manhood; **d'un certain —** middle-aged; **bas —** infancy; **eutre deux –s** of middle age; **fleur de l'—** prime of life; **moyen — Middle Ages**; **quel — avez-vous?** how old are you?

âgé *a.* old, aged; of age

agence *f.* agency; bureau

agencement *m.* arrangement; **–s** *pl.* fixtures

agencer *vt.* to adjust, arrange; equip

agenda *m.* memorandum book; appointment book

agenouillé *a.* kneeling

agenouiller *v.*, **s'—** to kneel

agenouilloir *m.* kneeling stool, kneeler

agent *m.* agent; **— de change** stockbroker; **— de police** policeman

agglomération *f.* agglomeration; settlement (of people)

aggloméré *m.* briquette, compressed fuel

agglutiner *vt.* to unite; **s'—** agglutinate, to cake

aggraver *vt.* to aggravate, worsen

agile *a.* agile, nimble

agilité *f.* agility

agioteur *m.* (com.) speculator

agir *vi.* to act; operate; (com.) manage; prosecute; **il s'agit de** it is a question of

agitateur *m.* agitator; stirrer, stirring-rod

agitation *f.* agitation

agité *a.* agitated; upset; restless

agiter *vt.* to agitate, shake, stir; disturb; debate

agneau *m.* lamb

agneler *vi.* to lamb

agnelin *m.* lamb's skin (with wool)

agnès *f.* innocent girl, ingénue

agnostique *m. & a.* agnostic

agonie *f.* agony, death throes

agonir *vt.* abuse; (coll.) insult highly

agonisant *a. & m.* dying; dying person

agoniser *vi.* to lie dying; be at death's door

agrafe *f.* clasp, hook, clip, clamp; **— et porte** hook and eye

agrafer *vt.* to clasp, hook, fasten

agrafeuse *f.* stapler

agraire *a.* agrarian

agrandir *vt.* to enlarge; **s'—** to grow, expand

agrandissement *m.* enlargement; aggrandizement

agrandisseur *m.* (phot.) enlarger

agrarien *m. & a.* agrarian

agréable *a.* pleasant, agreeable

agréer *vt.* to accept; approve; allow; **— vi.** to suit, be acceptable

agrégation *f.* degree required for teaching in a lycée; aggregation, aggregate

agrégé *m.* holder of the agrégation

agréger *vt.* to admit (to a society); accept; incorporate

agrément *m.* charm; ornamentation; pleasure; **note d'— *f.*** (mus.) grace-note

agrémenter *vt.* to embellish, adorn; trim

agrès *m. pl.* gymnasium equipment; (naut.) gear; rigging

agresser *vt.* to attack, commit aggression on

agresseur *m.* aggressor

agressif *a.* aggressive

agression *f.* aggression

agressivité *f.* aggressiveness

agreste *a.* rustic; rural

agricole *a.* agricultural; **comices –s** *m. pl.* county fairs

agriculteur *m.* farmer

agriculture f. agriculture
agriffer v., s'— to hang, grip by claws
agripper vt. to snatch, grab; s'— to clutch at; come to grips
agronomie f. agronomy
agrouper vt. to group
aguerrir vt. to train in war, season, inure
aguet m. watch, watching; —s pl., être aux —s to be on the lookout
ahaner vi. to groan, pant; sigh
aheurtement m. stubbornness, obstinacy
ahuri a. astounded
ahurir vt. to astound, amaze
ahurissement m. stupefaction
aiche, éche f. bait
aide f. help, aid; — m. & f. helper, aide, assistant; à l'—! interj. help!; à l'— de by means of
aide-mémoire m. reminder; memory aid
aider vt. to aid, help, assist
aïeul m. grandfather; -e f. grandmother; —s m. pl. grandfathers, grandparents
aïeux m. pl. ancestors
aigle m. eagle
aiglefin m. haddock
aiglon m. eaglet
aigre a. sour; sharp; harsh; — m. sourness, mustiness
aigre-doux a. bittersweet; sweet and sour
aigrefin m. adventurer, swindler; haddock
aigrelet a. somewhat bitter
aigrette f. aigrette; crest; cluster of feathers, diamonds, etc.
aigreur f. bitterness; (med.) heartburn
aigrir vt. to embitter; turn sour; make ill-humored
aigu a. acute, sharp; bitter, intense; piercing, shrill
aiguillage m. (rail.) switch; switching
aiguille f. needle; (clock) hand; pointer, indicator; (rail.) switch; magnetic needle
aiguiller vt. (rail.) to switch; direct
aiguilleur m. switchman
aiguillon m. goad; stinger; thorn; stimulus
aiguiser vt. to sharpen, stimulate
ail m. garlic
aile f. wing; blade; (auto.) fender
ailé a. winged
aileron m. wing tip; (avi.) aileron; fin
ailette f. wing; fin; blade
ailleurs adv. elsewhere; d'— besides, furthermore; par — besides; otherwise
aimable a. pleasant, kind, amiable
aimant m. magnet
aimanter vt. to magnetize
aimer vt. to love, like; — bien to like, be fond of
aine f. groin
aîné a. elder, eldest

aînesse f. seniority; primogeniture
ainsi adv. & conj. so, thus; — que just as; et — de suite and so forth
air m. air; tune, melody, appearance; manner; avoir l'— to seem; au grand —, en plein — outdoors, open air
airain m. bronze, brass
aire f. area; floor; surface; eyrie; wind direction
airelle f. cranberry
aisance f. ease; lieu d' — m. toilet
ais m. stave, board
aise f. comfort, ease; à l'— comfortable; mal à l'— uncomfortable; indisposed; — a. happy, content
aisé a. easy; well-off
aisselle f. armpit
aisément adv. easily
ajour m. opening; openwork
ajournement m. (mil.) deferment; postponement; legal summons
ajourner vt. to adjourn, postpone, defer
ajouter vt. to add; supply; interpolate
ajuster vt. to adjust; fix; ornament, dress
alambic m. (chem.) still
alambiquer vt. to distill; (fig.) make overly subtle
alanguir vt. to make languid, feeble
alarme f. alarm
alarmer v., s'— de to become alarmed at
alarmiste m. & a. alarmist
Albanais n. & a. Albanian
Albanie f. Albania
albâtre m. alabaster
albatros m. albatros
album m. album, scrapbook; coloring book
albumen m. albumen
albumine f. albumen, egg white
alcaloïde m. alkaloid
alchimie f. alchemy
alchimiste m. alchemist
alcool m. alcohol; -ique m. & a. alcoholic
alcoolisme m. alcoholism
alcôve f. alcove
aléa m. chance, hazard
aléatoire a. risky; contingent (law); -ment adv. by chance
alène f. awl
à l'entour adv. in the vicinity; around
alentours m. pl. vicinity, neighborhood
alerte f. alarm, warning; — d'avions (avi. mil.) scramble; — a. alert, brisk, watchful
alerter vt. to alert, warn
aléser vt. to bore (tube, gun, etc.), grind
alevin m. fish fry; young fish
aleviner vt. to stock with young fish
algarade f. unmotivated attack; insult
algèbre f. algebra

algébrique *a.* algebraic
Alger *m.* Algiers
Algérie *f.* Algeria; −n *m. & a.* Algerian
algue *f.* seaweed; alga
aliboron *m.* jackass
aliéné *m.* deranged person, lunatic; — *a.* mad
aliéner *vt.* to give over, transfer; alienate
alignée *f.* line, row
alignement *m.* alignment
aligner *vt.* to align; (com.) balance an account
aliment *m.* food, nourishment
alimentaire *a.* alimentary; subsistance; pension — *f.* alimony; régime — *m.* diet
alimentation *f.* feeding; nourishment; provisionment
alimenter *vt.* to feed; maintain
alinéa *m.* indentation, paragraph
alité *a.* bedridden, confined to bed
allaitement *m.* nursing, nourishing on milk
allaiter *vt.* to suckle, nurse
allant *a.* active; — *m. pl.* activities, comings and goings
allécher *vt.* to entice; attract
allée *f.* walk, alley, path; going
allégation *f.* allegation; statement
alléger *vt.* to lighten; relieve
allègre *a.* gay, lively
alléguer *vt.* to allege
alléluia *m.* hallelujah
Allemagne *f.* Germany
Allemand *n. & a.* German
aller *vi.* to go, ride; — à to fit, suit; — bien to be well; — mal to be ill; billet d'— et retour *m.* round-trip ticket; s'en — to go away, go off
allergène *m.* (med.) allergen
allergie *f.* allergy
allergique *a.* allergic
alliage *m.* alloy; mixture
alliance *f.* alliance; union; wedding ring
allié *a.* allied; — *m.* ally; in-law, relative by marriage
allier *vt.* to alloy; ally; join; mix
alligator *m.* alligator
allitération *f.* alliteration
allocation *f.* allowance, subsidy; item
allocution *f.* address, speech
allonge *f.* extension; elongating piece; hook for hanging meat; boxing reach
allonger *vt.* to lengthen; extend; s'— to lie down; grow longer
allongement *m.* lengthening
allouer *vt.* to allocate, allow
allumage *m.* lighting; ignition, spark
allume-gaz *m.* gas stove lighter
allumer *vt.* to light; fire; ignite; turn on;

s' — catch fire
allumette *f.* match
allure *f.* gait; bearing; speed
allusif *a.* allusive, containing an allusion
allusion *f.* allusion
alluvial *a.* alluvial
almanach *m.* almanac, calendar
aloès *m.* aloes
aloi *m.* purity, quality
alors *adv.* then; — que *conj.* while, whereas; — même que even though, even when
alose *f.* shad
alouette *f.* lark
alourdir *vt.* to make heavy; s'— to become heavy
alourdissant *a.* oppressive
alourdissement *m.* heaviness; dullness
aloyau *m.* sirloin of beef
alpaga *m.* alpaca
alpage *m.* mountain pasture
Alpes *f. pl.* Alps
alpestre *a.* Alpine
alphabet *m.* alphabet
alphabétique *a.* alphabetical
alpin *a.* Alpine
alpinisme *m.* mountain climbing
alpiniste *m.* mountain climber
Alsace *f.* Alsace
Alsacien *n. & a.* Alsatian
altérable *a.* alterable
altération *f.* alteration, falsification
altercation *f.* altercation; dispute
altérer *vt.* to spoil; tamper with, distort; make thirsty
altéré *a.* altered; avid
alternance *f.* alternation
alternatif *a.* alternating
alternation *f.* alternation; succession
alternative *f.* alternative
alterner *vi.* to alternate
altesse *f.* (titre) highness
altier *a.* haughty
altièrement *adv.* haughtily, proudly
altimètre *m.* altimeter
altitude *f.* altitude; — absolue (avi.) absolute altitude
alto *m.* alto; viola; alto horn
altruisme *m.* altruism
altruiste *n.* altruist; — *a.* altruistic
alumelle *f.* plane (tool)
aluminium *m.* aluminum
alun *m.* alum
alvéole *m.* cell of honeycomb; socket of tooth; compartment, pigeonhole
alvéolé *a.* honey-combed
alvin *a.* abdominal; flux — *m.* diarrhea
amabilité *f.* amiability; kindness
amadou *m.* tinder
amadouer *vt.* to wheedle, coax

amaigrir vt. to make thin; — vi. to become thin

amaigrissant a., **régime** — m. weight-reducing diet

amaigrissement m. reducing, dieting; emaciation

amalgamation f. amalgamation

amalgame m. amalgam, mixture

amalgamer vt. to amalgamate; blend

amande f. almond

amandier m. almond tree

amant m. lover

amarrage m. (naut.) mooring

amarre f. (naut.) hawser, painter, cable

amarrer vt. to moor; make fast

amaryllis f. amaryllis

amas m. heap, pile, accumulation

amasser vt. to heap up, pile up, amass

amateur m. amateur, fan; devotee; connoisseur

Amazone f. Amazon; horsewoman; riding habit; **monter en** — ride side-saddle

ambages f. pl., **parler sans** — to stop beating around the bush

ambassade f. embassy

ambassadeur m. ambassador

ambassadrice f. ambassador's wife

ambiance f. atmosphere, environment

ambiant a. surrounding

ambidextre a. ambidextrous

ambigu a. ambiguous; — m. cold buffet; — **comique** comic play

ambiguïté f. ambiguity

ambitieux a. ambitious

ambitionner vt. to have ambitions to

ambivalence f. ambivalence

amble m. trot, amble

ambre m. amber; — **gris** ambergris

ambré a. amber-colored

ambulance f. ambulance

ambulancier m. ambulance attendant

ambulant a. itinerant; traveling; **marchand** — peddler; — m. railway post office

ambulatoire a. ambulatory; movable

âme f. soul, spirit, life

amélioration f. improvement, amelioration

améliorer vt. to improve, ameliorate

aménagement m. arrangement; preparation; furnishings

aménager vt. to prepare; fix up; arrange; outfit

amende f. fine, penalty; **faire** — **honorable** apologize courteously

amendement m. amendment; improvement; fertilizer

amender vt. to improve; amend; **s'**— reform

amène a. affable

amener vt. to bring; introduce, bring in; lead to

aménité f. amenity, pleasantness

amenuiser vt. to thin, make thin

amer a. bitter; — m. landmark

américain a. & m. American

américaine f. bicycle relay race; surrey

américaniser vt. Americanize

américanisme m. Americanism; American studies

Amérindien m. & a. Indian (of America)

Amérique f. America

amerrir vi. to land on the water

amertume f. bitterness

améthyste f. amethyst

ameublement m. furniture

ameuter vt. to gather hunting hounds; stir up

ami m. friend; sweetheart; — a. friendly

amiable a. amicable; **à l'**— adv. amicably

amiante m. abestos

amibe f. amoeba

amibiase f. amoebic dysentery

amibien a. amoebic

amical a. friendly

amicale f. club, group

amict m. amice

amidon m. starch

amidonnage m. starching

amidonner vt. to starch

amincir vt. to make thin

aminé a. amino

amiral m. admiral

amirauté f. admiralty

amitié f. friendship; liking; **-s** pl. regards

ammoniaque f. ammonia

amnésie f. amnesia

amnésique m. & f. amnesia victim

amnistie f. amnesty, pardon

amnistier vt. to amnesty, pardon

amoindrir vt. to lessen, reduce, diminish

amollir vt. to soften; weaken; **s'**— to grow softer

amollissement m. softening

amonceler vt. to heap up, pile up

amoncellement m. heap, pile

amont m. upper portion of a river; **en** — upstream

amorce f. fuse, detonator; bait; beginning

amorcer vt. to prime a gun; bait; start

amorphe a. amorphous

amortir vt. to deaden, muffle, dull; amortize, redeem

amortissable a. redeemable

amortissement m. amortization; deadening, damping; depreciation; (arch.) finial, crowning ornament; **caisse d'**— f. sinking fund

amortisseur m. shock absorber

amour m. love; passion

amouracher v., s'— (de) to become infatuated (with)
amourette f. love affair
amoureux a. in love; amorous; — m. lover; suitor
amour-propre m. self-esteem, pride, vanity
amovible a. movable; removable
ampère m. ampere; —mètre m. ammeter
amphibie a. amphibious; — m. amphibian
amphibologique a. ambiguous, equivocal
amphigouri m. hodge-podge; nonsense
amphithéâtre m. amphitheater; lecture hall
amphore f. amphora
ample a. wide, vast; ample, full; roomy, spacious; —ur f. fullness
ampliation f. amplification, expansion; duplicate
amplificateur m. amplifier; (phot.) enlarger; — a. enlarging, amplifying
amplification f. amplification; enlarging
amplifier vt. to amplify; enlarge; magnify
amplitude f. amplitude, extent
ampoule f. blister; sealed phial; ampule; (elec.) light bulb
ampoulé a. pompous, high-flown; blistered
amputé m. amputee
amputer vt. to amputate
amulette f. amulet, charm
amusement m. amusement, fun, entertainment
amuser vt. to entertain; amuse; s'— to have a good time
amusette f. plaything; toy; small amusement
amygdale f. tonsil
amygdalite f. tonsilitis
an m. year; jour de l'— New Year's day; par — yearly
ana m. collection of ancedotes and sayings
anachorète m. hermit
anachronique a. anachronistic
anachronisme m. anachronism
anagramme f. anagram
anal a. anal
analogie. f analogy
analogique a. analogical
analogue a. analogous; — m. analogue
analphabète n. & a. illiterate
analphabétisme m. illiteracy
analysable a. analysable
analyse f. analysis; résumé, summary
analyser vt. to analyse
analytique a. analytical
ananas m. pineapple
anarchie f. anarchy
anarchique a. anarchical
anarchiste m. & f. anarchist

anathématiser vt. to curse, anathematize
anathème m. anathema
anatomie f. anatomy
anatomique a. anatomical
anatoxine f. antitoxin
ancêtre m. ancestor
anche f. (mus.) reed
anchois m. anchovy
ancien a. old; former; ancient; — élève m. alumnus; —nement adv. formerly
ancienneté f. seniority; age, antiquity
ancrage m. anchorage
ancre f. anchor; —r vt. to anchor
Andalou m. & a. Andalusian
Andalousie f. Andalusia
Andes f. pl. Andes
Andorre f. Andorra
andouille f. pork, tripe sausage; (coll.) idiot, fool
andouiller m. antler
andouillette f. small pork or tripe sausage
androgène m. (biol.) androgen
âne m. ass, donkey; fool
anéantir vt. to destroy, annihilate
anéantissement m. destruction, annihilation
anémie f. anemia
anémié a. anemic
anémique a. anemic
anémomètre m. anemometer
anémone f. anemone
ânerie f. huge blunder; gross ignorance
anesthésie f. anesthesia
anesthésier vt. anesthetize
anesthésique a. & m. anesthetic
anesthésiste m. anesthetist
ange m. angle; être aux —s to be delighted
angélique a. angelic; — f. angelica
angélus m. angelus
angine f. quinsy, tonsillitis; angina
anglais m. the English language; — basique basic English; -es f. pl. long curls; — a. English; filer à l'—e to take French leave; pommes à l'—e boiled potatoes
Anglais m. Englishmen
angle m. corner; angle
Angleterre f. England
anglican a. Anglican
angliciser vt. Anglicize
anglophile m. & a. Anglophile
Anglo-Saxon m. & a. Anglo-Saxon
angoisse f. anguish, agony
angoisser vt. to anguish; afflict
anguille f. eel; nœud d'— m. slipknot
angulaire a. angular; pierre — f. cornerstone
anguleux a. angular
anicroche f. small obstacle, snag

ânier *m.* mule driver, muleteer
animadversion *f.* reproof, blame
animal *m.* animal, beast; — *a.* animal
animateur *m.* animator; organizer
animation *f.* animation; movement, life
animé *a.* animated; lively; **dessin** — *m.* cartoon (movies)
animer *vt.* to animate, enliven; move, encourage
animosité *f.* animosity
anion *m.* anion
anis *m.* anise; **–ette** *f.* (liqueur) anisette
ankylose *f.* stiffness of the joints
ankylosé *a.* stiff
ankyloser *vt.* to stiffen; **s'—** to stiffen; rust
annales *f. pl.* annals
anneau *m.* ring; link
année *f.* year
annelé *a.* ringed, annulated
annexe *f.* annex; supplement
annexer *vt.* to annex; append
annexion *f.* annexation
annihilation *f.* annihilation
annihiler *vt.* to annihilate
anniversaire *m.* birthday; anniversary
annonce *f.* advertisement; announcement
annoncer *vt.* to announce; predict; **s'—** to give promise of being
annonceur *m.* advertizer, sponsor
Annonciation *f.* Annunciation
annotateur *m.* annotator
annotation *f.* annotation
annoter *vt.* to annotate
annuaire *m.* directory (phone); yearbook; annual
annuel *a.* yearly, annual
annuité *f.* annuity; yearly payment
annulaire *a.* annular
annulation *f.* annulment
annuler *vt.* to annul, cancel
anoblir *vt.* to ennoble
anodin *a.* soothing; harmless; — *m.* anodyne
anomal *a.* irregular, abnormal
anomalie *f.* anomaly, irregularity
ânonner *vi.* to speak haltingly; stutter
anonymat *m.* anonymity
anonyme *a.* anonymous; — *n.* anonymity
anophèle *m.* **anoph**eles, mosquito
anorak *m.* hooded jacket; rainproof sport jacket
anormal *a.* abnormal
anse *f.* handle; inlet, bay
antagonisme *m.* antagonism
antagoniste *n.* antagonist; — *a.* antagonistic; opposite
antan *m.* yore, yesteryear
antarctique *a.* antarctic
antécédent *a.* previous, prior, antecedent; — *m.* antecedent; **–s** *pl.* past

history
Antéchrist *m.* Antichrist
antediluvien *a.* antediluvian
antenne *f.* antenna; aerial
antérieur *a.* anterior; front; previous, earlier
anthologie *f.* anthology
anthracite *f.* anthracite, hard coal
anthropoïde *n. & a.* anthropoid
anthropologie *f.* anthropology
anthropologue *m.* anthropologist
anthropophage *m.* cannibal; — *a.* cannibalistic
anthropophagie *f.* cannibalism
antiaérien *a.* antiaircraft
antibiotique *m.* antibiotic
antibrouillard *a.* anti-fog; **phare** — *m.* fog light
antichambre *f.* antichamber, waiting room
antichar *a.* (mil.) antitank
anticipation *f.* anticipation
anticiper *vt.* to anticipate, forestall
anticlérical *a.* anticlerical
anticorps *m.* antibody
antidater *vt.* to antedate
antienne *f.* anthem
antigel *m.* antifreeze
antihistaminique *m.* antihistamine
Antilles *f. pl.* West Indies
antilope *f.* antelope
antimite *m.* moth repellant
antimoine *m.* antimony
antimoral *a.* immoral
antinomie *f.* antinomy, contradiction
antinomique *a.* contradictory
antiparticule *f.* (phys.) antiparticle
antipathie *f.* antipathy, repugnance
antipathique *a.* antipathetic
antiproton *m.* antiproton
antiquaille *f.* rubbish, junk
antiquaire *m.* antiquary; antique dealer
antique *a.* antique, ancient
antiquité *f.* antiquity; antique
antirabique *a.* antirabies
antiradar *a.* anti-radar
antirouille *m.* rust preventative
antisémite *m. & f.* antisemite
antisémitisme *m.* antisemitism
antiseptique *m. & a.* antiseptic
antisocial *a.* antisocial
antithèse *f.* antithesis
antitoxine *f.* antitoxin
antivol *m.* antitheft device, burglar alarm
antonyme *m.* antonym
antre *m.* cavern, lair, den
anus *m.* anus
Anvers *m.* Antwerp
anxiété *f.* anxiety
anxieux *a.* anxious, concerned, uneasy

aorte *f.* aorta

août *m.* August

apaiser *vt.* to appease; calm; **s'—** to abate, calm down

apanage *m.* lot, portion

aparté *m.* (theat.) aside

apathie *f.* apathy

apathique *a.* apathetic

apatride *a.* stateless

apercevoir *vt.* to perceive, see; **s'—** de to discover, realize

aperçu *m.* brief account; first glimpse; **par — rough guess**

apéritif *m.* apéritif, appetizer, small, before-dinner drink

apeuré *a.* frightened

aphasie *f.* aphasia

aphone *a.* soundless, voiceless

aphonie *f.* aphony, loss of speech

aphorisme *m.* aphorism

aphte *m.* mouth canker; cold sore

aphteux *a.* cankerous; **fièvre aphteuse** *f.* hoof and mouth disease

apiculteur *m.* beekeeper

apitoiement *m.* pity, compassion

apitoyer *vt.* to cause pity, move to pity; **s'— sur** to sympathize with

aplanir *vt.* to level, smoothe; plane

aplatir *vt.* to flatten; **s'—** to become flat; lie flat, fall flat

aplomb *m.* balance, poise; plumb; assurance; **d'—** level, even, plumb

apocalypse *f.* Apocalypse, Revelations; (fig.) obscure text *or* allegory

apocalyptic *a.* obscure; allegorical; apocalyptic

apocope *f.* (gram.) apocope, elision; (med.) amputation

apocryphe *a.* apocryphal

apode *a.* apodal, footless

apogée *m.* apogee, zenith

apologétique *a.* apologetic

apologie *f.* justification, defense, apology

apologue *m.* apologue, fable

apoplectique *a.* apopleptic

apoplexie *f.* stroke; apoplexy

apostasie *f.* apostasy; back sliding

apostat *m. & a.* apostate

aposter *vt.* to station; place in ambush

apostille *f.* annotation, postscript, endorsement

apostiller *vt.* to annotate, endorse; add postscript

apostolique *a.* apostolic

apostrophe *f.* apostrophe

apothéose *f.* apotheosis

apothicaire *m.* apothicary, pharmacist

apôtre *m.* apostle

apparaître *vi.* to appear; become apparent

apparat *m.* pomp, show

apparaux *m. pl.* fittings (of a ship)

appareil *m.* appliance, machine; apparatus; telephone; **— photographique** camera; **— plâtré** (med.) cast

appareiller *vi.* to set sail; prepare to leave; **— *vt.*** to equip; match (with); cut

apparemment *adv.* apparently

apparence *f.* appearance, semblance

apparent *a.* apparent; **-é** *a.* related

apparenter *v.*, **s'—** to be related

apparier *vt.* to match, pair (off)

apparition *f.* apparition; appearance

appartement *m.* apartment

appartenance *f.* appurtenance

appartenant *a.* belonging, pertaining to

appartenir *vi.* to belong; appertain

appas *m. pl.* charms

appât *m.* bait, lure, attraction

appâter *vt.* to lure; fatten; feed (baby or invalid)

appauvrir *vt.* to impoverish; **s'—** to become poor

appauvrissement *m.* impoverishment

appeau *m.* bird call; lure, decoy

appel *m.* appeal; call; roll call; telephone buzzer

appelant *m.* decoy; appellant (law)

appelé *m.* draftee

appeler *vt.* to call; call up; invoke, summon; **— *vi.*** appeal (law); **s'—** to be named; **je m'appelle** my name is

appellation *f.* appellation; brand name; **— contrôlée** registered trademark

appendice *m.* appendix

appendicite *f.* appendicitis

appentis *m.* lean-to

appesantir *vt.* to make heavy; **s'—** to insist

appétissant *a.* appetizing

appétit *m.* appetite; desire

applaudir *vt.* to applaud; approve

applaudissements *m. pl.* applause

application *f.* application; diligence

applique *f.* ornamentation; wall candlestick, wall bracket

appliqué *a.* diligent, studious

appliquer *vt.* to apply; adapt; **s'—** to apply; apply oneself

appoint *m.* (com.) balance

appointements *m. pl.* salary

appointer *vt.* to pay a salary; sharpen; settle a case at law

appontage *m.* landing (on the deck of an aircraft carrier)

appontement *m.* crane; dock

apponter *vi.* to land on the deck of an aircraft carrier

apport *m.* contribution, share

apporter *vt.* to bring; procure, use

apposer *vt.* to apply, affix, put
appréciable *a.* appreciable
appréciation *f.* appreciation; appraising, estimate, evaluation
apprécier *vt.* to appreciate; appraise, value, evaluate, estimate
appréhender *vt.* to apprehend; dread, fear
appréhension *f.* apprehension
apprendre *vt.* to learn; find out, hear; teach, show
apprenti *m.* apprentice
apprentissage *m.* apprenticeship
apprêt *m.* preparing, cooking and seasoning; affectation; —s *pl.* preparation
apprêter *vt.* to prepare; s'— prepare oneself
appris *a.*, mal — ill-bred
apprivoiser *vt.* to tame; make sociable
approbateur *a.* approving
approbation *f.* approval, approbation
approchable *a.* accessible
approchant *a.* somewhat like, approximately
approche *f.* approach; –s *pl.* access
approché *a.* approximate
approcher *vt.* to bring near; — *vi.* to come close; s'— to approach
approfondi *a.* thorough, deep
approfondir *vt.* to deepen; examine thoroughly; s'— to deepen
appropriation *f.* appropriation
approprier *vt.* to make appropriate, conform; s'— to appropriate
approuver *vt.* to approve (of); agree to
approvisionnement *m.* supply, provisions; provisioning
approvisionner *vt.* to provision; s'— to buy provisions; take in supplies
approximatif *a.* approximate
approximation *f.* approximation
appui *m.* support; prop; ledge, sill
appui-bras *m.* armrest
appui-livres *m.* bookends
appui-tête *m.* headrest
appuyer *vt. & vi.* to press; lean; support; s'— to lean, depend; insist
âpre *a.* rough, harsh; bitter, sharp; eager
après *prep.* after; next to; d'— according to; from, after; — *adv.* afterward, later, et —? so?, so what?; then what?
après-demain *m.* day after tomorrow
après-dîner *m.* period after dinner, evening
après-guerre *f.* postwar period
après-midi *m. or f.* afternoon
âpreté *f.* bitterness; harshness, roughness
à-propos *m.* opportuneness; aptness
apte *a.* apt, proper, suited, suitable
aptitude *f.* aptitude, capacity, qualification

apurement *m.* audit, verification
apurer *vt.* to verify, audit
apyre *a.* fireproof
aquafortiste *m.* etcher
aquaplane *m.* aquaplane, surfboard
aquapoumon *m.* aqualung
aquarelle *f.* watercolor
aquarelliste *n.* water-color artist
aquatique *a.* aquatic
aqueduc *m.* aqueduct
aqueux *a.* aqueous, watery
aquifère *a.* water-bearing
aquilin *a.* aquiline
aquilon *m.* north wind; cold blast
ara *m.* macaw
Arabe *m.* Arabian; — *a.* Arabian, Arabic
Arabie *f.* Arabia; — Soudite, — Saoudite, — Séoudite Saudi Arabia
arable *a.* arable
arachide *f.* peanut
araignée *f.* spider; toile d'— *f.* spider web
araser *vt.* to level
aratoire *a.* agricultural
arbalète *f.* crossbow
arbalétier *m.* crossbowman; rafters
arbitrage *m.* arbitration
arbitraire *a.* arbitrary
arbitre *m.* arbiter; umpire, referee; libre — free will (philosophy)
arbitrer *vt.* to arbitrate; referee
arborer *vt.* show off; — un drapeau hoist a flag
arbousier *m.* arbutus
arbre *m.* tree; (mech.) shaft; — moteur driveshaft; — à cames camshaft
arbrisseau *m.* shrub
arbuste *m.* shrub, bush
arc *m.* bow; arch; arc
arcade *f.* archway; série d'–s *f.* arcade
arcane *m.* mystery
arcature *f.* blind arcade; row of arcades
arc-boutant *m.* flying buttress
arceau *m.* arched opening; small arch
arc-en-ciel *m.* rainbow
archaïque *a.* archaic
archange *m.* archangel
arche *f.* arch; ark
archéologie *f.* archeology
archéologue *m.* archeologist
archer *m.* bowman, archer
archet *m.* (mus.) bow
archevêché *m.* archdiocese; archbishop's palace
archevêque *m.* archbishop
archi- *prefix* arch-
archipel *m.* archipelago
architecte *m.* architect
architectural *a.* architectural
architecture *f.* architecture
archives *f. pl.* archives

archiviste *m. & f.* archivist
arçon *m.* saddle bow; saddle; wool carder
arctique *a.* arctic
ardemment *adv.* ardently
ardent *a.* ardent; burning; fiery
ardeur *f.* ardor; heat; fire; zeal
ardillon *m.* tongue of a belt buckle
ardoise *f.* slate; score
ardu *a.* arduous; steep; difficult
are *m.* 100 square meters (about 120 square yards)
arène, –s *f. s. or pl.* arena, bull ring
aréner *vi.* to sink, settle
aréneux *a.* sandy
arête *f.* fishbone; ridge; edge; angle; — **du nez** bridge of the nose
argent *m.* silver; money
argenté *a.* silver; silver-plated; silvery
argenter *vt.* to plate with silver
argenterie *f.* silver plate, silverware
argentifère *a.* silver-bearing
argentin *a.* silvery; tinkling
argenture *f.* silvering; **l'— des glaces** silvering on mirrors
argile *f.* clay
argileux *a.* of clay, clayey
argonaute *m.* argonaut; nautilus
argot *m.* slang; **–ique** *a.* slangy
argousin *m.* prison guard
arguer *vt.* to infer; — *vi.* to argue
argument *m.* argument, summary, reasoning
argumentation *f.* argumentation; arguing
argumenter *vt.* to argue
argus *m.* spy; argus
argutie *f.* subtlety; quibbling
aride *a.* arid, dry, barren
aridité *f.* aridity
ariette *f.* air, song
aristocrate *m. & f.* aristocrat; — *a.* aristocratic
aristocratie *f.* aristocracy
aristocratique *a.* aristocratic
aristotélicien *a.* Aristotelian
arithméticien *m.* arithmetician
arithmétique *f.* arithmetic; — *a.* arithmetical
arlequin *m.* Harlequin
arlésien *a.* from Arles
armagnac *m.* brandy of Armagnac
armateur *m.* ship outfitter, shipowner
armature *f.* armature; (arch.) steel framework, iron braces; (mus.) signature
arme *f.* arm, weapon; **–s portatives** small arms; **maître d'—s** *m.* fencing master; **place d'—s** *f.* parade ground; **salle d'—s** *f.* fencing school
armé *a.* armed; **béton —** reinforced concrete
armée *f.* army

armement *m.* armament; arming; weaponry; equipment; loading; cocking
Arménie *f.* Armenia; **–n** *m. & a.* Armenian
armer *vt.* to arm; (naut.) to fit out; commission; reinforce; equip, outfit; load; cock; — *vi.* arm oneself
armistice *m.* armistice
armoire *f.* wardrobe; cupboard
armoiries *f. pl.* arms (heraldic), coat of arms
Armor *m.* (Celtic) Brittany
armorial *m.* armorial, book of heraldry
Armoricain *m. & a.* Breton
armure *f.* armor; (mus.) signature
armurier *m.* armorer, gunsmith
aromate *m.* aromatic substance
aromatique *a.* aromatic
aromatiser *vt.* to perfume; flavor
arôme *m.* aroma, flavor
aronde *f.* swallow; **queue d'—** *f.* dovetail
arpège *m.* arpeggio
arpent *m.* acre (= approximately 1½ American acres); **–er** *vt.* to survey, measure
arpenteur *m.* surveyor
arqué *a.* arched; bowed
arquebuse *f.* musket
arquer *vt.* to arch, bend, bow; curve; — *vi.* bend, sag
arrache-clou *m.* claw hammer
arrache-pied, d'— *adv.* uninterruptedly
arracher *vt.* to tear out; uproot, pull a tooth
arracheuse *f.* digger (potatoes, sugar beets)
arrangement *m.* arrangement; settlement; **–s** *m.* terms
arranger *vt.* to arrange, fix, settle; **s'—** to manage; agree, come to an agreement
arrangeur *m.* arranger
arrérages *m. pl.* arrears; money due
arrestation *f.* arrest, custody
arrêt *m.* stop; decree; verdict (law), sentence; arrest; **mandat d'—** *m.* arrest warrant; **chien d'—** *m.* hunting dog, pointer
arrêté *m.* decree, order; police decision
arrêter *vt.* to arrest; stop; settle; close (an account); determine, fix; engage; point (dog); **s'—** to stop
arrêtoir *m.* stop, catch
arrhes *f. pl.* deposit, security
arrière *m.* back; stern; rear; **vent —** *m.* tail wind; **en —** *adv.* back, backwards; behind; **en — de** *prep.* behind
arrière- *prefix* rear-; after-; great- (relationship by blood)
arriéré *m.* arrears; — *a.* backward; overdue
arriéré *m.* arrearage; — *a.* deferred; be-

hind

arriere-ban *m.* reserve

arriere-bouche *f.* pharynx

arrière-boutique *f.* back room of a shop

arrière-garde *f.* rear guard

arrière-goût *m.* aftertaste

arrière-pays *m.* hinterland, back country

arrière-pensée *f.* ulterior motive

arrière-plan *m.* background

arrièrer *vt.* to delay; **s'—** stay behind

arrière-saison *f.* end of autumn

arrière-train *m.* rear; hindquarters

arrimer *vt.* to stow away

arrimeur *m.* stevedore

arrivage *m.* arrival of goods *or* ships

arrivée *f.* arrival, coming, approach

arriver *vi.* to arrive; happen; succeed; **— à** to reach, attain; manage to

arrivisme *m.* social climbing

arrogamment *adv.* arrogantly

arrogant *a.* arrogant

arroger *v.*, **s'—** to claim, assume with presumption

arrondir *vt.* to round off, make round; enlarge

arrondissement *m.* administrative district; ward

arrosage *m.* sprinkling; watering; basting; **tuyau d'—** *m.* garden hose

arroser *vt.* to water; baste; drain an area

arroseur *m.* sprinkler

arrosoir *m.* watering can; shower head

arrondir *vt.* to make round; increase; double

arsenic *m.* arsenic

art *m.* art; cunning; **beaux —s** fine arts

artère *f.* artery

artérial *a.* arterial

artériosclérose *f.* hardening of the arteries

artésian *a.* artesian; from Artois

arthrite *f.* arthritis

arthritique *a. & n.* arthritic

artichaut *m.* artichoke

article *m.* article; item; **— de fond** editorial

articulation *f.* articulation; joint; enumerated legal facts

articulé *a.* articulated; articulate

articuler *vt.* to affirm, declare; articulate

artifice *m.* artifice, trick; **feu d'—** *m.* fireworks

artificiel *a.* artificial

artificier *m.* maker of fireworks

artificieux *a.* sly, artful, full of artifice

artillerie *f.* artillery; ordnance

artilleur *m.* artilleryman

artisan *m.* craftsman, artisan

artiste *m. & f.* artist; **— a.** artistic

artistique *a.* artistic

arum *m.* calla lily; arum

aryen *a.* Aryan

as *m.* ace; expert

ascendant *m.* influence; **—s** *pl.* ancestry, lineage; **— a.** ascending

ascenseur *m.* elevator

ascension *f.* ascent; Assumption

ascète *m. & f.* ascetic

ascétique *a.* ascetic

ascétisme *m.* asceticism

asdic *m.* sonar, submarine detector

aseptique *a.* aseptic

Asiatique *m. & f. & a.* Asiatic

Asie *f.* Asia; **— Mineure** Asia Minor

asile *m.* asylum, refuge, shelter

aspect *m.* aspect, appearance, sight; look

asperge *f.* asparagus

aspergès *m.* sprinkler for holy water; time of sprinkling with such water

asperger *vt.* to sprinkle

aspérité *f.* asperity, roughness

asphalte *m.* asphalt

asphalter *vt.* to asphalt

asphyxie *f.* asphyxia

asphyxier *vt.* to asphyxiate

aspirant *m.* officer candidate; candidate

aspirateur *m.* vacuum cleaner; aspirator; **— de buée** *f.* ventilator

aspiration *f.* aspiration; intake

aspiré *m.* aspirate; **— a.** aspirated

aspirer *vi.* to aspire; **— vt.** to aspirate: take in; inhale

aspirine *f.* aspirin

assaillant *m.* assailant; aggressor

assaillir *vt.* to assail, attack

assainir *vt.* to make healthy, purify

assaisonnement *m.* seasoning, condiment; dressing

assaisonner *vt.* to season, flavor

assassin *m.* murderer; **— a.** murderous

assassinat *m.* assassination, murder

assassiner *vt.* to assassinate, murder

assaut *m.* assault, attack; bout

assécher *vt.* to drain, dry up

assemblage *m.* collection; assembly, assemblage; joining, joint (in carpentry)

assemblée *f.* assembly; meeting

assembler *vt.* to assemble; join; gather; **s'—** to meet, assemble

asséner *vt.* to strike a blow

assentiment *m.* assent, agreement, approval

asseoir *vt.* to seat; place, lay; **s'—** to sit down, be seated

assermenté *a.* sworn

assertion *f.* assertion

asservir *vt.* to enslave; **s'— à** to obey

asservissement *m.* slavery

assez *adv.* enough; rather; sufficiently

assidu *a.* assiduous; **—ité** *f.* assiduity

assidûment *adv.* assiduously; punctually

assiéger *vt.* to besiege

assiette *f.* plate; dish; position

assignation *f.* assignation; (com.) assignment; summons

assigner *vt.* to summon; assign; subpoena

assimiler *vt.* to assimilate; compare

assis *a.* seated, sitting; **place -e** *f.* seat

assise *f.* layer, stratum; **-s** *pl.* criminal court sessions

assistance *f.* audience; spectators; aid, assistance; — **judiciare** public defender's office; — **sociale** social work, welfare work

assistant *m.* assistant; bystander; **-s** *pl.* audience; **-e sociale** *f.* social worker

assister *vt.* to help; — **à** *vi.* to attend, be present at

association *f.* association; partnership

associé *m.* associate, partner

associer *vt.* to associate; **s'**— to enter into partnership; join in; be associated with

assoiffé *a.* thirsting, greedy

assolement *m.* crop rotation

assoler *vt.* to rotate crops

assombrir *vt.* to darken; **s'**— to get gloomy

assommant *a.* boring; crushing, telling

assommer *vt.* to knock down; kill; bore

assommoir *m.* blunt instrument, bludgeon; (coll.) bar, dive

Assomption *f.* Assumption

assorti *a.* matching

assortiment *m.* assortment; set; matching

assortir *vt.* to match

assoupir *vt.* to make sleepy; lull; **s'**— to doze off, fall asleep

assouplir *vt.* to make supple

assouplissement *m.* suppleness, docility

assourdir *vt.* to deafen; muffle

assourdissant *a.* deafening

assouvir *vt.* to gratify, satiate, surfeit

asujettir *vt.* subdue, subjugate; oblige; **s'**— to submit

asujettissement *m.* submission; subduing, subjugation

assumer *vt.* to assume, take on oneself

assurance *f.* assurance; insurance; — **par groupe** group insurance; **-s sociales** *pl.* social security

assuré *a.* assured; confident; secure; firm, steady; insured

assurément *adv.* certainly, assuredly; confidently

assurer *vt.* to assure; secure; insure; **s'**— to make sure

Assyrie *f.* Assyria; **-n** *m. & a.* Assyrian

astérie *f.* starfish

astérisque *m.* asterisk

astéroïde *m.* asteroid

asthmatique *m. & a.* asthmatic

asthme *m.* asthma

asticot *m.* maggot, worm

astigmatisme *m.* astigmatism

astiquer *vt.* to polish; clean up

astrakan *m.* Persian lamb

astre *m.* star

astreindre *vt.* to oblige, force, compel; **s'**— (à) to force oneself

astringent *a. & m.* astringent

astrologie *f.* astrology

astrologue *m.* astrologer

astronaute *m.* astronaut

astronautique *f.* space travel, astronautics

astronef *f.* space ship; space capsule

astronome *m.* astronomer

astronomie *f.* astronomy

astronomique *a.* astronomical

astrophysigne *f.* astrophysics

astuce *f.* astuteness, guile, wile

astucieux *a.* astute, crafty

asymétrique *a.* asymetrical

atavique *a.* atavistic

atelier *m.* workshop; studio

atermoyer *vi.* to stall, delay

athée *m.* atheist; — *a.* atheistic

athéisme *m.* atheism

athénée *m.* secondary school

athlète *m.* athlete

athlétique *a.* athletic

athlétisme *m.* track, athletics (sports)

Atlantide *f.* Atlantis

atlantique *a.* Atlantic

atmosphère *f.* atmosphere

atmosphérique *a.* atmospheric

atome *m.* atom; iota, speck

atomique *a.* atomic

atomiser *vt.* to atomize; subject to radiation; destroy with an atomic bomb

atomiseur *m.* atomizer

atomiste *m. & f.* atom scientist

atonal *a.* atonal

atonalité *f.* atonality

atone *a.* atonic, unaccented; atonal; dull

atours *m. pl.* women's finery

atout *m.* trump; **sans** — no trump

âtre *m.* hearth, fireplace

atroce *a.* atrocious

atrocité *f.* atrocity

atrophie *f.* atrophy

atrophier *vt.* to atrophy, waste away

attabler *v.*, **s'**— to sit down at the table

attache *f.* fastener, tie, clip; leash; tether

attaché *m.* attaché

attacher *vt.* to attach, fasten, join, tie; **s'**— (à) to grow fond (of); apply oneself (to)

attaquant *m.* attacker; aggressor

attaque *f.* attack; fit; **-r** *vt.* to attack

attardé *a.* late; behind; delayed

attarder *vt.* to delay; **s'**— to linger

atteindre vt. to reach, attain; strike, hit; wound

atteinte f. attack; blow; reach; injury

attelage m. team; pair; harnessing; coupling

atteler vt. to harness, yoke; hitch; couple

attelle f. splint

attenant a. adjoining, next

attendant adv., **en —** meanwhile; for the moment; **en — que** conj. until

attendre vt. to wait for, expect; **s'— (à)** to expect

attendrir vt. to make tender; move, affect; touch; **s'—** to be moved

attendu prep. in view of; **— que** conj. since, whereas

attentat m. criminal attack or attempt; outrage

attente f. expectation; waiting; hope

attenter vi. to make an attempt

attentif a. attentive; careful

attention f. attention, care; **—!** interj. watch out!; **faire —** to pay attention, be careful

atténuant a. extenuating; attenuating

atténuer vt. to attenuate; diminish, reduce

atterrage m. (naut.) landfall; landing

atterrer vt. to crush, overwhelm; demolish

atterrir vi. (avi.) to land

atterrissage m. (avi.) landing

atterrissement m. alluvion; descent (balloon)

attestation f. attestation, testimony

attester vt. to attest (to); witness

attiédir vt. to make lukewarm; **s'—** to become lukewarm

attifer vt. to deck out, ornament

attirail m. paraphernalia, gear

attirance f. attraction, temptation

attirant a. attracting, attractive

attirer vt. to attract, lure; **s'—** to bring upon oneself

attiser vt. to stir up; excite

attitré a. official

attitude f. posture, attitude, position

attractif a. attractive

attraction f. attraction; **—s** pl. shows, entertainment

attrait m. charm, attraction

attrape f. snare; trick

attrape-mouches m. flypaper; flycatcher (bird)

attrape-nigaud m. booby trap

attraper vt. to catch; take in; trick

attrayant a. attractive

attribuer vt. to attribute, ascribe

attribut m. attribute

attribution f. attribution; sphere, power

attrister vt. to sadden; **s'—** to become sad

attrouper vt. to assemble

aubaine f. windfall

aube f. dawn; board; paddle; (eccl.) **alb**; **roue à —s** f. paddlewheel

aubépine f. hawthorn

auberge f. inn; **— de la jeunesse** youth hostel

aubergine f. eggplant

aubergiste m. & f. innkeeper

aucun pron. & a. no one, none; no; any

aucunement adv. not at all, by no means, in no way

audace f. boldness, audacity

audacieux a. audacious, bold; impudent

au-dehors adv. outside

au-delà adv. beyond; **— de** prep. beyond

au-dessous adv. below, under; **— de** prep. below, under

au-dessus adv. above, over; **— de** above, over

au-devant adv., **aller —** to go, meet; anticipate

audience f. hearing, audience

audiologie f. audiology

audio-visuel a. audio-visual

auditeur m. listener, hearer; **—s** pl. audience

auditif a. audial, auditory, auditive

audition f. hearing; audition

auditionner vt. to listen to; audition

auditoire m. audience

auge f. trough; hod

augmentation f. increase; salary raise

augmenter vt. to augment; increase; **raise**; enlarge; **— vi.** increase; rise

augure m. omen; **de bon —** auspicious

augurer vt. to augur; foresee

auguste a. august

aujourd'hui adv. today, nowadays; **d'—** **en huit** in a week, a week from today

aumône f. alms, charity

aumônier m. chaplain

aune f. ell (= 45 inches); measure, standard; **— m.** alder

auparavant adv. before, previously

auprès prep., **— de** near, close to; next to, with; compared with; **— adv.** nearby

auquel pron. to whom, to which

auréole f. halo; glory, aureola

auréomycine f. aureomycin

auriculaire a. aural, auricular; **doigt — m.** little finger

auricule f. auricle; outer ear

aurifier vt. to fill a tooth with gold

aurore f. dawn; **— boréale** aurora borealis

ausculter vt. (med.) to auscultate

aussi adv. also, too; **— ... que as ... as**; **— conj.** therefore, so

aussitôt adv. immediately; **— que as** soon as

austère a. austere, stern, severe

austérité *f.* austerity

austral *a.* southern

Australie *f.* Australia; **–n** *m. & a.* Australian

autan *m.* south wind; storm

autant *adv.* as much, as many; **d'—** as much as; **d'— plus, (moins)** all the more (less); **d'— plus que** all the more because

autel *m.* altar

auteur *m.* author; creator; cause

authenticité *f.* authenticity

authentifier *vt.* to authenticate

authentique *a.* authentic; sincere

auto *f.* automobile, auto, car

autobiographie *f.* autobiography

autobus *m.* bus

autocar *m.* intercity bus, sightseeing bus

autochenille *f.* caterpillar-tread vehicle

autochtone *a.* native

autoclave *m.* pressure cooker; sterilizer

autocopier *vt.* to duplicate, ditto

autocrate *m.* autocrat

autocratie *f.* autocracy

autocratique *a.* autocratic

autocritique *f.* self-criticism

autocuiseur *m.* pressure cooker

autodestruction *f.* self-destruction

autodétermination self-determination

autodidacte *a.* self-taught

autodrome *m.* race track (auto.)

auto-école *f.* driving school

autogène *a.* welded

autogire *m.* autogiro

autographe *m. & a.* autograph

autographier *vt.* to autograph

automate *m.* automaton

automatique *a.* automatic; **—** *f.* automation

automatiser *vt.* to introduce automation in

automatisme *m.* automation

automnal *a.* autumnal

automne *m.* or *f.* autumn

automobilisme *m.* driving, motoring

automobiliste *m.* motorist

automoteur *a.* self-propelling; **train —** *m.* diesel-powered train

autonome *a.* autonomous

autonomie *f.* autonomy

autoplastie *f.* skin grafting

autoportrait *m.* self-portrait

autopropulsion *f.* self-propulsion

autopsie *f.* autopsy

autopsier *vt.* to perform an autopsy on

autorail *m.* railway diesel car

autorisation *f.* authorisation

autoriser *vt.* to authorize, empower

autoritaire *a. & m.* authoritarian

autoroute *f.* highway; expressway

autorité *f.* authority; **–s** *pl.* officials, authorities

auto-stop *m.* hitchhiking; **faire l'—** to hitchhike

autostrade *f.* superhighway, expressway

autour *adv.* about, around; **— de** *prep.* about, around

autre *a.* other, another; different; **—part** elsewhere; **d'— part** on the other hand; **de temps à** — from time to time, occasionally; **l'un et l'—** both; **l'un ou l'—** either; **ni l'un ni l'—** neither

autrefois *adv.* formerly, once

autrement *adv.* otherwise; differently

Autriche *f.* Austria

autrichien *a. & m.* Austrian

autruche *f.* ostrich

autrui *pron.* others

auvent *m.* shed; cover, roof; penthouse

auvergnat *a.* from Auvergne

auxiliaire *a. & n.* auxiliary

avachir *v.,* **s'—** to become deformed; become flabby

aval *m.* guarantee; downstream portion of a river; **en —** downstream

avaler *vt.* to swallow

avaliser *vt.* to guarantee, co-sign

avaliseur *m.* co-signer

à-valoir *m.* part-payment

avance *f.* head start, lead; advance; loan; **d'—** in advance; **en —** early

avancé *a.* advanced; **heure -e** *f.* late hour

avancement *m.* advancement, advancing; furthering; progress; projection

avancer *vt.* to advance; hasten; further; promote; extend, put out; **—** *vi.* advance, move forward, progress; to be fast (clock)

avanie *f.* public insult; affront

avant *prep. & adv.* before; **— (de)** before; **en —** forward; **— que** *conj.* before; **—** *m.* front portion; (naut.) bow

avantage *m.* advantage; profit

avantager *vt.* to favor; give an advantage

avantageux *a.* profitable, advantageous; vain

avant-bras *m.* forearm

avant-coureur *m.* forerunner

avant-dernier *f.* next-to-last

avant-garde *f.* vanguard

avant-goût *m.* foretaste

avant-guerre *f.* prewar period; **d'—** *a.* prewar

avant-hier *adv.* day before yesterday

avant-port *m.* outer port

avant-poste *m.* outpost

avant-projet *m.* preliminary consideration (of a plan or project)

avant-propos *m.* foreward

avant-scène *f.* proscenium; stagebox

avant-veille *f.* second day previous, two days before

avare *a.* miserly, stingy

avaricieux *a.* avaricious, stingy, miserly

avarie *f.* damage; loss; deterioration

avarié *a.* spoiled, damaged

avec *prep.* with; **d'—** from

aveline *f.* filbert

avenant *a.* coming; becoming; in keeping

avènement *m.* succession; coming; advent

avenir *m.* future; **à l'—** henceforth

avent *m.* (eccl.) Advent

aventure *f.* adventure, intrigue; **bonne —** fortune telling; **à l'—** *adv.* at random

aventurer *vt.* to venture, risk; **s'—** to venture

aventureux *a.* adventurous; risky

aventurier *m.* adventurer

avérage *m.* average

avéré *a.* verified, established

avérer *v.*, **s'—** to appear, prove

averse *f.* shower, downpour

averti *a.* informed; on guard; experienced

avertir *vt.* to warn; inform, notify

avertissement *m.* warning; notice; preface

avertisseur *a.* warning; **— m.** warning device; horn; alarm

aveu *m.* confession, avowal, admission

aveugle *a.* blind; **— m. & f.** blind person

aveuglement *m.* blinding; (fig.) blindness

aveuglément *adv.* blindly

aveugler *vt.* to blind

aveuglette, à l'— *adv.* blindly, gropingly; at random

aveulir *vt.* to weaken; enervate

aviateur *m.* aviator

aviation *f.* aviation; air force

avide *a.* greedy; eager, avid

avidité *f.* avidity, eagerness

avilir *vt.* to vilify; lower in value; **s'—** to lower oneself, stoop to; become lower in value

avilissement *m.* vilification

aviné *a.* drunk (from wine)

avion *m.* airplane; **par —** by air mail

aviron *m.* oar; rowing; **donner un coup d'—** lend a helping hand

avis *m.* advice; opinion; notice; **à mon —** in my opinion; **changer d'—** to change one's mind

avisé *a.* prudent; shrewd, wary

aviser *vt.* to notify; warn; notice; **— à** *vi.* to take care of, see to; **s'— (de)** to take into one's head (to)

avivage *m.* polishing, brightening; revival

aviver *vt.* to sharpen; irritate; make brighter

avocat *m.* lawyer; advocate; **poire d'— f.** avocado

avocatier *m.* avocado tree

avoine *f.* oats

avoir *vt.* to have; get; **— chaud (froid, raison, tort)** to be hot (cold, right, wrong); **qu'avez-vous?** what's the matter?; **y — v.**, **il y a** there is, there are, it is; **ago**; **— m.** property, possessions; credit (ledger)

avoisiner *vt.* to neighbor, be near, border on

avorter *vi.* to miscarry; go wrong, fail

avorton *m.* miscarriage; abortion; abortive offspring

avoué *m.* attorney, lawyer

avouer *vt.* to avow, confess, admit

avril *m.* April

axe *m.* axis; axle; Axis

axillaire *a.* axillary

axiomatique *a.* axiomatic

axiome *m.* axiom

axonge *f.* lard

azalée *f.* azalea

azotate *m.* nitrate

azote *m.* nitrogen; **–ux** *a.* nitrous

azotique *a.* nitric

aztèque *a.* Aztec

azur *m.* azure

azuré *a.* azure, bluish

azyme *a.* unleavened

B

baba *m.* rumcake

babeurre *m.* buttermilk

babil *m.* babble, babbling; baby talk

babillard *a.* babbling; talkative; **— m.** chatterbox; tattler

babiller *vi.* to babble, chatter about nothing

babine *f.* heavy lip; chop; **se lécher les –s** to lick one's chops

babiole *f.* bauble, toy, trinket

bâbord *m.* (naut.) port side

babouche *f.* heelless slipper

babouin *m.* baboon

Babylone *n.* Babylon

Babylonien *m. & a.* Babylonian

baby-parc *m.* playpen

bac *m.* ferry; vat, tank; box, bin; (coll.) bachelor's degree

baccalauréat *m.* bachelor's degree

baccara *m.* baccarat

bâche *f.* tarpaulin; tank; hotbed frame

bachelier *m.* lycée graduate

bachot *m.* small boat; (coll.) bachelor's degree

bacillaire *a.* caused by a bacillus

bacille *m.* bacillus

bâcle *f.* bolt, bar of a door

bâcler *vt.* to botch, patch together; bolt,

bar; block, obstruct
bactérie f. microbe, bacterium
bactériologie f. bacteriology
bactériologue m. bacteriologist
badaud m. loafer; stroller
badigeon m. whitewash
badigeonner vt. to whitewash; fill with plaster; (med.) paint the throat
badin a. playful, joking, fooling
badinage m. banter, fooling, playfulness
badine f. switch, wand, rod
badiner vi. to joke, play, be playful; trifle, fool; — vt. tease
badminton m. badminton
bafouer vt. to make fun of; scoff at; ridicule without pity
bafouiller vi. & vt. (coll.) to stammer; (fig.) speak disconnectedly
bâfrer vt. & vi. (coll.) to devour, guzzle
bagage m. baggage; **plier — to pack up and go; -s** m. pl. baggage, luggage
bagarre f. riot, brawl, fight
bagatelle f. trifle; (fig.) something frivolous
bagnard m. prisoner, convict
bagne m. penitentiary; penal servitude
baguage m. banding (tree)
bague f. ring; **jeu de –s** merry-go-round
baguenauder vi. to trifle, waste time
baguer vt. to ring, band (tree); baste (cloth)
baguette f. switch, rod; drum stick; wand; long thin loaf of bread
baguier m. jewel box
bahut m. trunk, chest; (coll.) school
bai a. bay horse
baie f. berry; bay, gulf; (arch.) bay
baignade f. swimming; swimming place
baigner vt. to soak, bathe
baignoire f. bathtub; (theat.) orchestra box
bail m. (pl. **baux**) lease
bâillant a. yawning; open, ajar
bâillement m. yawn; opening; gap
bâilleur m. bondsman
bâiller vi. to yawn, gape; be ajar
bailli m. bailliff
bâillon m. gag
bâillonner vt. to gag; muzzle; (fig.) silence
bain m. bath; **costume de — bathing suit, swim suit; -s** pl. baths; spa, hot springs, resort
bain-marie m. water bath; double boiler
baïonnette f. bayonet
baisemain m. hand-kissing
baiser m. kiss; — vt. to kiss (hand, brow); (fig.) compliment
baissant a. setting (sun); falling; failing
baisse f. fall, decline, drop
baisser vt. to lower; — vi. to fall, drop,

go down; sink; **se — to stoop; bow down; — m.** fall, falling; setting (of sun)
bajoue f. jowl
Bakélite f. Bakelite (trademark)
bal m. ball, dance
balader v., **se — to wander, stroll**
baladeuse f. cart; trailer, portable light, trouble light
baladin m. buffoon; actor
balafre f. gash; slash; scar; **-r** vt. to gash; scar
balai m. broom; (elec.) brush; carpet sweeper; **manche à — m.** (avi.) control stick; **— à laver** mop
balance f. scales; balance; balance sheet
balancement m. rocking; hesitation; poising
balancer vt. to balance; swing, rock; weigh for and against — vi. to hesitate; fluctuate, waver; swing
balancier m. pendulum; beam; balance wheel; coin-press lever
balançoire f. seesaw, teeter-totter; swing
balayer vt. to sweep
balayette f. whisk broom
balayeur m. street cleaner, street sweeper
balayeuse f. carpet sweeper; street-cleaning truck
balayures f. pl. sweepings
balbutier vi. to stutter, stammer, mumble
balbuzard m. buzzard
balcon m. balcony
baldaquin m. canopy, tester
baleine f. whale; whalebone, stay
baleinier m. whaling ship
baleinière f. whaleboat
balise f. buoy, marker, beacon
baliser vt. to mark with buoys or lights
balistique a. ballistic; — f. ballistics
baliverne f. nonsense, stupidity, humbug
balkanique a. Balkan
Balkans m. pl. Balkans
ballant a. swinging, slack (rope), dangling
ballast m. ballast
balle f. ball; bullet; husk; **— traçante** tracer bullet
ballerine f. ballerina
ballet m. ballet
ballon m. balloon; ball; **— d'essai** trial balloon
ballonner vi. to swell, puff up
ballot m. bundle; bale; package of merchandise
ballottage m. balloting; indecisive first ballot
ballotter vt. to agitate; — vi. to move about; to be shaken
ballottine f. chicken loaf
balnéaire a. bathing; **station — f.** resort
balourd a. dull, heavy; stupid,

balsa *m.* balsa wood
Balte, Baltique *n. & a.* Baltic
balustrade *f.* balustrade, railing
balustre *m.* baluster
bambin *m.* little child
bambou *m.* bamboo
ban *m.* proclamation; cheer; **-s** *pl.* (eccl.) banns
banal *a.* banal, trite, commonplace
banalité *f.* triviality, triteness; overused expression
banane *f.* banana
bananier *m.* banana tree
banc *m.* bench; seat; pew; shoal
bancal *a.* bow-legged, bandy-legged
bandage *m.* bandage, truss; winding
bande *f.* band; strip; group; cushion (billiards)
bandeau *m.* headband; blindfold; **en -x** hair parted in the middle
bandelette *f.* band, headband, fillet
bander *vt.* to bandage; bind; blindfold; wind; **se —** to band together, join together
banderole *f.* streamer, pennant
bandit *m.* bandit
bandoulière *f.* sling; bandoleer; **en —** *a.* over the shoulder
banian *m.* banyan tree
banlieue *f.* suburbs; **de —** *a.* suburban
banlieusard *m.* suburbanite
banne *f.* basket, hamper; tarpaulin; awning
bannière *f.* banner, flag
bannir *vt.* to banish, exile
bannissement *m.* banishment, exile
banque *f.* bank; **— du sang** blood bank
banqueroute *f.* bankruptcy
banqueroutier *m.* bankrupt person
banqueter *vi.* to banquet, feast
banquette *f.* seat (train, bus); bank (earth or sand)
banquier *m.* banker
banquise *f.* ice pack, floe
banquiste *m.* charlatan
baptême *m.* christening, baptism; **nom de —** christian name
baptiser *vt.* to christen, baptize
baptismal *a.* baptismal
baptiste *m. & f.* Baptist
baptistère *m.* baptistry
baquet *m.* tub, washtub
bar *m.* bar; bass, perch
baragouiner *vt. & vi.* (coll.) to jabber; pronounce badly
baraque *f.* hut, shack; hovel
baratte *f.* churn; **-r** *vt.* to churn
Barbade *f.* Barbados
barbare *a.* barbarous, cruel; barbaric; **—** *m.* barbarian

barbarie *f.* barbarity; **orgue de —** *m.* barrel organ, organ-grinder's organ
barbarisme *m.* barbarism
barbe *f.* beard; **se faire la —** to shave; **rire dans sa —** laugh up one's sleeve
barbelé *a.* barbed; **fil de fer —** *m.* barbed wire
barbet *m.* water spaniel
barbiche *f.* goatee
barbier *m.* barber
barbillon *m.* barb
barbiturique *m. & a.* barbiturate
barbon *m.* old man; greybeard; (coll.) old fogy
barbouiller *vt.* to daub, smear, dirty; mess up, bungle
barbu *a.* bearded
barbue *f.* brill
barde *m.* bard; **—** *f.* fat used for larding
bardeau *m.* shingle; lath
barder *vt.* to lard; armor
bardot *m.* mule; laughing stock
barème *m.* tables of figures
barguette *f.* flat boat used as a ferry
barguigner *vi.* to hesitate
baricant *m.* small barrel
baril *m.* barrel, small cask
barillet *m.* small barrel; revolver cylinder; spring case
bariolage *m.* medley of colors
bariolé *a.* speckled ; multicolored
barman *m.* bartender
baromètre *m.* barometer
barométrique *a.* barometric
baron *m.* baron; **-ne** *f.* baronness
baroque *a.* irregular; baroque
barque *f.* bark (small boat)
barrage *n.* (mil.) barrage; dam; barrier; (sports) play-off
barre *f.* bar; helm; stroke; dividing line
barreau *m.* bar; rung
barrer *vt.* to bar; cross out
barrette *f.* biretta; bar; barrette, slide; pin
barricade *f.* barricade; **-r** *vt.* to barricade
barrière *f.* barrier; starting gate; fence; **— du son** sound barrier
barrique *f.* cask; barrel
barrir *vi.* to trumpet (elephant)
baryton *m.* baritone; baritone horn
baryum *m.* barium
bas (basse) *a.* low; vulgar, cheap; **—** *m.* stocking, hose; lower part, bottom; foot; **—** *adv.* softly; down, low; **en —** downstairs, below
basalte *m.* basalt
basane *f.* sheep skin
basané *a.* tanned, sunburned, swarthy
bas-côté *m.* church side aisle; highway shoulder
bascule *f.* scale; balance; seesaw

basculer *vi.* to swing, rock, seesaw; dim (headlights)

base *f.* base, basis, foundation

baser *vt.* to base, found

bas-fond *m.* hole; hollow; shoal; **-s** *pl.* dregs

basilic *m.* sweet basil

basilique *f.* basilica

basique *a.* basic

Basque *m. & f. & a.* Basque

bas-relief *m.* bas-relief

basse *f.* (mus.) bass; tuba

basse-cour *f.* poultry yard; backyard

basse-fosse *f.* dungeon

bassesse *f.* baseness, lowness, meanness

bassin *m.* basin; dock; (anat.) pelvis

bassine *f.* pan (round and shallow)

bassiner *vt.* to sprinkle, water; warm; (coll.) bore, weary

bassinet *m.* small basin

bassinoire *f.* bedwarmer; (coll.) bore

basson *m.* bassoon, bassoonist

bastille *f.* fort, fortress

bastion *m.* bastion

bastonnade *f.* beating

bas-ventre *m.* abdomen

bat *m.* bat

bât *m.* pack saddle

bataclan *m.* paraphernalia

bataille *f.* battle, fight

batailler *vi.* to battle

batailleur *a.* quarrelsome, fighting

bataillon *m.* battalion

bâtard *m.* bastard; medium-sized loaf of bread — *a.* not pure bred; inferior

bâtarde *f.* cursive writing

bâtardeau *m.* temporary dam

bateau *m.* boat

bateau-maison *m.* houseboat

bateau-mouche *m.* Parisian excursion boat

batelée *f.* boatload

bateler *vt.* to transport by boat; — *vi.* to perform tricks, juggle

bateleur *m.* trickster, juggler, tumbler

batelier *m.* boatman

bâter *vt.* to saddle (a pack animal)

bâti *m.* frame; basted garment; basting thread

bâtiment *m.* building; ship

bâtir *vt.* to build; baste (clothing)

bâtisse *f.* masonry; building

bâtisseur *m.* builder

batiste *f.* batiste

bâton *m.* stick, cudgel; baton

bâtonner *vt.* to beat; cross out

bâtonnier *m.* dean of lawyers (in France)

battage *m.* beating, threshing; churning

battant *m.* bell clapper; part of door or furniture that swings on a hinge; **porte**

à deux —s double door; — *a.* pelting, driving; **porte —** swinging door

batte *f.* bat; mallet

battement *m.* beating; throbbing, pulsing, pulsation; shuffling (cards)

batterie *f.* battery; (mus.) percussion; — **de cuisine** kitchen utensils

batteuse *f.* threshing machine

battoir *m.* paddle

battre *vt.* to beat, strike; mint; defeat; clap; shuffle cards; **se —** to fight

baudet *m.* donkey, ass; sawhorse; (fig.) idiot

baudrier *m.* shoulder belt, sword belt

bauge *f.* lair, den

baume *m.* balm, balsam

bauxite *f.* bauxite

bavard *a.* talkative, gossipy

bavarder *vi.* to chatter, gossip

Bavarois *m. & a.* Bavarian

bave *f.* slobber, drool; drivel

baver *vi.* to drool, slobber

bavette *f.* bib; **tailler une —** to chat

Bavière *f.* Bavaria

bavocher *vi.* to be smeared, poorly printed

bavoir *m.* bib

bavure *f.* seam (of a mold)

bayer *vi.* to gape, stare

bazar *m.* bazaar; variety store

béant *a.* agape, gaping, yawning

béat *a.* smug, complacent, sanctimonious

béatification *f.* beatification

béatifier *vt.* to beatify

béatitude *f.* beatitude

beau, bel (belle) *a.* fine, fair, beautiful, handsome; **vous avez — faire** no matter what you do

beaucoup *adv.* much, many; **de —** by far

beau-fils *m.* son-in-law; stepson

beau-frère *m.* brother-in-law

beau-père *m.* father-in-law; stepfather

beauté *f.* beauty

beaux-arts *m. pl.* fine arts

beaux-parents *m. pl.* father-in-law and mother-in-law; (coll.) in-laws

bébé *m.* baby

bec *m.* beak, bill; spout; point

bécane *f.* old locomotive, switch engine

bécarre *m.* (mus.) natural

bécasse *f.* woodcock

bécassine *f.* snipe

bec-de-cane *m.* door handle; door bolt (like a beak)

bec-de-corbeau *m.* wire cutters

bec-de-lièvre *m.* harelip

bêche *f.* spade; **-r** *vt. & vi.* to dig, spade

bêchoir *m.* hoe

becqueter *vt.* to peck (at)

bedeau *m.* beadle

Bédouin *m. & a.* Bedouin

bée *a.* open; **bouche** — **agape**; flabbergasted; — *f.* large opening
beffroi *m.* belfry
bégayer *vi.* to stutter; stammer
bégaiement *m.* stammering
bégonia *m.* begonia
begue *a.* stuttering, stammering
bégueter *vi.* to bleat
béguin *m.* hood, cap; infatuation
beige *a.* beige; unbleached
beignet *m.* fritter; doughnut
béjaune *m.* novice, beginner; one having no knowledge of a matter at hand
bêler *vi.* to bleat
belette *f.* weasel
Belge *n. & a.* Belgian
Belgique *f.* Belgium
bélier *m.* ram
bélitre *m.* scoundrel
belladone *f.* belladonna
belinogramme *m.* wire photo
belinographe *m.* wire photo transmitter
belle *adv.* **l'échapper** — to have a narrow escape
belle-de-jour *f.* morning glory
belle-fille *f.* daughter-in-law; stepdaughter
belle-mère *f.* mother-in-law; stepmother
belle-sœur *f.* sister-in-law
belliciste *m.* warmonger
belligérance *f.* belligerance
belligérant *m. & a.* belligerant
belligueux *a.* warlike
bémol *m.* (mus.) flat
bémoliser *vt.* (mus.) to flat
bénédicité *m.* grace before meals
bénédictin *m.* (liquer) benedictine; **-e** *f.* benedictine nun
bénédiction *f.* benediction
bénéfice *m.* benefice; profit; advantage
bénéficiaire *a.* beneficiary
bénéficier *vi.* to benefit, profit
benêt *a.* stupid; — *m.* simpleton
bénévole *a.* kind; well-intentioned
Bengale *m.* Bengal
Bengali *n. & a.* Bengal
bénignité *f.* benignness; kindness; mildness
bénin (bénigne) *a.* benign; benignant; mild, gentle; kind
bénir *vt.* to bless, consecrate
bénitier *m.* holy-water font
benjamin *m.* youngest child, favorite child
benne *f.* hamper; hopper; body (dump truck); mine elevator
benoît *a.* indulgent
benzine *f.* benzine
benzoate *m.* benzoate
béquille *f.* crutch; **-r** *vi.* to walk with

crutches
béquillon *m.* cane, crutch
bercail *m.* (eccl.) fold
berceau *m.* cradle; arbor; (arch.) tunnel vault; (mech.) motor support
bercelonnette *f.* cradle, bassinet
bercer *vt.* to rock; soothe; (fig.) lull to sleep
berceuse *f.* lullaby; rocking chair; rocking cradle
béret *m.* beret
berge *f.* steep bank, edge
berger *m.* shepherd
bergère *f.* shepherdess; armchair
bergerie *f.* fold, sheepfold; pastoral poetry
béribéri *m.* beri-beri
berlingot *m.* hard candy (caramel)
berkélium *m.* berkelium
berline *f.* carriage; sedan; mine truck
berne *f.* banter; **en** — at half mast
berner *vt.* to toss in a blanket; fool; haze
bernacle, bernache *f.* barnacle
berrichon *a.* from Berry
béryl *m.* beryl
béryllium *m.* beryllium
besace *f.* beggar's bag; wallet
besicles *f. pl.* spectacles
besogne *f.* work, task; **-r** *vi.* to work
besogneux *a.* needy
besoin *m.* need, want; necessity; misery; **avoir** — **de** have need of; **au** — if necessary
bessemer *m.* Bessemer converter
bestialité *f.* bestiality
bestiaux *m. pl.* cattle, livestock
bestiole *f.* little animal
bétail *m.* cattle, livestock
bêtatron *m.* betatron
bête *f.* animal; beast; — *a.* stupid, foolish
bêtifier *vt.* to make stupid
bêtise *f.* stupidity; nonsense
béton *m.* concrete; — **armé** reinforced concrete
bétonner *vt.* to make of concrete
bétonnière *f.* cement mixer
bette *f.* beet
betterave *f.* beet; — **sucrière** sugar beet
betting *m.* odds (racing)
beuglement *m.* bellow, bellowing; lowing
beugler *vi.* to low, bellow
beurre *m.* butter; **-r** *vt.* to butter
beurrée *f.* slice of bread and butter
beurrier *m.* butter dish
beuverie *f.* drinking party
bévatron *m.* bevatron
bévue *f.* blunder, big mistake, gaff
biais *m.* bias, slant; — *a.* oblique; **en** — at an angle, askew
biaiser *vi.* to go at an angle; hedge
bibelot *m.* knicknack, trinket

biberon *m.* nursing bottle; drinker

Bible *f.* Bible

bibliobus *m.* mobile library

bibliographe *m.* bibliographer

bibliographie *f.* bibliography

bibliographique *a.* bibliographical

bibliophile *m.* bibliophile

bibliothécaire *m. & f.* librarian

bibliothèque *f.* library; book shelves, bookcase

biblique *a.* Biblical

bicamérisme *m.* (pol.) two-house system

bicéphale *a.* two-headed

biceps *m.* biceps

biche *f.* hind, darling

bichlamar *m.* pidgin English

bichon *m.* lapdog

bichonner *vt.* to curl; (fig.) caress

bicoque *f.* shack, hut

bicorne *a.* two-cornered

bicyclette *f.* bicycle

bidet *m.* nag, horse; sawhorse; sitz-bath

bidon *m.* can (for liquids); canteen

bief *m.* millrace; section of a canal (between two locks)

bielle *f.* (mach.) connecting rod, tie rod

bien *adv.* well; rightly; indeed; properly; quite; much, many; — que although; si — que so that; tant — que mal indifferently, so-so; — *m.* good; fortune; estate; welfare

bien-aimé *m.* beloved

bein-être *m.* well-being

bienfaisance *f.* charity, beneficence

bienfaisant *a.* charitable; beneficial

bienfait *m.* benefit, favor

bienfaiteur *m.* benefactor

bien-fonds *m.* real property, real estate

bienheureux *a.* very happy; blessed

biennal *a.* biennial

bienséance *f.* propriety, convention

bienséant *a.* proper, appropriate, fitting

bientôt *adv.* soon; shortly; à — goodbye, see you soon

bienveillance *f.* kindness, benevolence

bienveillant *a.* kind, benevolent

bienvenu *a.* welcome; -e *f.* welcome

bière *f.* coffin; bier

biffer *vt.* to cross out; cancel

bifteck *m.* beefsteak

bifurcation *f.* fork in a road; (rail.) junction; turnoff

bifurquer *vt. & vi.* to fork; bifurcate

bigame *a.* bigamous; — *m.* bigamist

bigamie *f.* bigamy

bigarreau *m.* white-heart cherry

bigarrer *vt.* to speckle

bigarrure *f.* mixture of colors or designs

bigle *f.* beagle hound; — *a.* squint-eyed

bigler *vi.* to squint

bigot *a.* bigotted, excessively devout; hypocritical; — *m.* bigot; hypocrite

bigoterie *f.* bigotry

bigoudi *m.* small hair curler

bijou *m.* jewel, gem, stone

bijouterie *f.* jewelry; jeweler's shop

bijoutier *m.* jeweler

bilan *m.* balance sheet

bilatéral *a.* bilateral

bile *m.* bile, gall; (fig.) anger

biliaire *a.* biliary, bilious

bilieux *a.* bilious; choleric

bilingue *a.* bilingual

billard *m.* billiards; billiard table; billiard parlor

bille *f.* billiard ball; child's marble; log; block of wood; rolling pin; (mech.) ball; stylo à — *m.* ballpoint pen

billet *m.* note; bill; ticket; card; — d'aller et retour round-trip ticket; — simple one-way ticket; — de correspondance transfer

billevesée *f.* nonsense; fantasy

billon *m.* copper coin

billot *m.* block; chopping block

bimensuel *a.* semi-monthly

bimestriel *a.* bimonthly

bimoteur *a.* bimotor, two-engine

binaire *a.* binary

bine, binette *f.* hoe

binocle *m.* pince-nez, eye glasses (nose)

biochimie *f.* biochemistry

biogenèse *f.* biogenesis

biogénétique *f.* biogenetics

biographe *m.* biographer

biographique *a.* biographical

biologie *f.* biology; — moléculaire molecular biology

biologique *a.* biological

biologiste *m.* biologist

biophysique *a.* biophysical

biopsie *f.* biopsy

bipède *a.* two-footed; — *n.* biped

biplace *m. & f. & a.* two-seater

biplan *m.* biplane

Birman *m. & a.* Burmese; -ie *f.* Burma

bis *adv.* encore; (mus.) repeat, twice; house numbers(A,½)

bis aïeul *m.* great-grandfather; -e *f.* great-grandmother

bisannuel *a.* biennial

biscornu *a.* two-horned; odd; (fig.) bizarre

biscotte *f.* rusk

biscuit *m.* cooky, wafer, cracker; unglazed porcelain

bise *f.* cold wind; north wind

biseau *m.* beveled edge; bevelling tool

biseauter *vt.* to bevel; mark cards (to cheat)

biser *vt.* redye; — *vi.* spoil, degenerate;

get brown (cereals)
bismuth *m.* bismuth
bisque *f.* rich, creamy soup
bissac *m.* bag, wallet
bisser *vt.* to give or ask for an encore
bissextile *a.*, **année —** *f.* leap year
bistouri *m.* scalpel
bistre *a.* bistre, black-brown; **-r** *vt.* to brown
bisulfite *m.* bisulfate
bisut(h) *m.* freshman
bitume *m.* asphalt; bitumen; **—** *vt.* to asphalt
bitumineux *a.* bituminous
bivouac *m.* bivouac, bivouac area
bizarre *a.* odd; strange, bizarre
bizarrerie *f.* oddness, whim; oddity
blackbouler *vt.* to blackball
blafard *a.* pale, pasty
blague *f.* tobacco pouch; joke; **sans —?** really?
blaguer *vi.* to joke; hoax
blagueur *m.* jokester, joker
blaireau *m.* badger; shaving brush
blâmable *a.* censurable, blameworthy
blâme *m.* blame; disapproval
blâmer *vt.* to find fault with; blame
blanc (blanche) *a.* white; blank; innocent; clean; (print.) space free of type; **fer —** *m.* tin; **—** *m.* white, whiteness (linen); **— de chaux** whitewash
blanchâtre *a.* whitish
blanche *f.* (mus.) half note
blancheur *f.* whiteness
blanchir *vt. & vi.* to whiten, bleach; wash; scald (raw food)
blanchissage *m.* laundering, washing
blanchisserie *f.* laundry
blanchisseuse *f.* laundress
blanc-manger *m.* blancmange pudding
blanquette *f.*, **— de veau** veal in white sauce
blasé *a.* bored
blason *m.* coat of arms; heraldry
blasphématoire *a.* blasphemous
blasphème *m.* blasphemy
blasphémer *vi.* to blaspheme
blatte *f.* cockroach
blé *m.* wheat; grain; **— noir** buckwheat
blême *a.* wan, livid, pale
blêmir *vi.* to turn pale
blèse *a.* lisping
bléser *vi.* to lisp
blessant *a.* offensive, mortifying; injurious
blesser *vt.* to wound, hurt, offend; injure
blessure *f.* wound; injury
blet *a.* overripe
blettir *vi.* to overripen
bleu *a.* blue: **—** *m.* blue; bruise; coveralls;

(coll.) draftee; bluing; **petit —** letter sent by pneumatic tube
bleuâtre *a.* bluish
bleuet *m.* cornflower
bleuir *vt.* to make blue; **—** *vi.* to become blue
bleuté *a.* bluish
blindage *m.* armor plate
blindé *a.* armor-plated, armored
bloc *m.* block; lump; tablet, pad of paper; bloc; **en —** in a lump, in large quantities
blocaille *f.* rubble
blockhaus *m.* blockhouse
bloc-notes *m.* writing pad, note pad
blocus *m.* blockade
blond *a.* blond; fair
bloquer *vt.* to blockade; block, obstruct
blottir *v.*, **se —** to nestle; crouch; huddle
blouse *f.* blouse; smock; jacket
blouson *m.* jacket (sport or military)
bluette *f.* spark, flash
bluffer *vt. & vi.* to bluff
blutage *m.* act of bluing
bluter *vt.* to sift flour
blutoir *m.* sifter
boa *m.* boa
bobine *f.* bobbin; spool; reel; coil; roll
bobiner *vt.* to roll, spool, wind
bocage *m.* grove, small woods
bocager *a.* wooded
bocal *m.* bottle (druggist's), jar; fishbowl
bock *m.* beer, glass of beer
bœuf *m.* ox; beef; steer; **— bourguignon** beef in wine sauce
boggie *m.* (rail.) truck, bogie
Bohême *m.* Bohemia
bohème *f.* (fig.) Bohemia; **—** *a. & n.* bohemian, person living from day to day; beatnik; gypsy
bohémien *a.* Bohemian; **—** *m.*; gypsy; vagabond; unconventional person
Bohémien *m.* Bohemian
boire *vt.* to drink; swallow an insult; absorb; **— un coup** to have a drink; **—** *m.* drink, drinking
bois *m.* wood; forest; antlers; **— de lit** bedstead; **— contreplaqué** plywood; **— fondu** plastic wood
boisé *a.* wooded; panelled
boiserie *f.* woodwork; panelling, wainscoting
boisseau *m.* bushel
boisson *f.* beverage, drink
boîte *f.* box; can, tin; **— de nuit** night club
boiter *vi.* to limp
boiteux *a.* lame
boîter *m.* watch case
boitte *f.* fish bait
bol *m.* bowl; bolus, large pill
bolchevisme *m.* Bolshevism

boléro *m.* bolero; bolero jacket

bolide *m.* meteorite; (fig.) racing car

Bolivie *f.* Bolivia; **–n** *m. & a.* Bolivian

bombance *f.* feasting

bombarde *f.* mortar; ancestor of oboe

bombarder *vt.* to bombard, bomb

bombardier *m.* bomber (plane); bombardier

bombe *f.* bomb, shell; feast; **— de cobalt** cobalt bomb; **—glacée** molded ice cream; **faire la —** to have a gay time

bombé *a.* arched, rounded

bomber *vt.* to make round; **— vi.** to become round

bon *a.* good; kind; sound; wholesome; valid; fir; **à quoi —?** what's the use (of)?; **à la –ne heure!** fine!; well done; **de –ne heure** early; **— m.** (com.) bond, coupon

bonace *f.* calm sea; calm

bonasse *a.* simple; innocent; good-natured; **–ment** *adv.* simply; simple-mindedly

bonbec *m.* gossip

bonbon *m.* candy

bonbonne *f.* demijohn

bonbonnière *f.* candy dish

bond *m.* bound, leap; bounce

bonde *f.* bung hole; bung; plug; sluice gate

bondé *a.* crowded, jammed

bondir *vi.* to bound, leap; bounce

bondon *m.* bung; plug

bonheur *m.* happiness; good fortune, luck; **par —** luckily

bonhomie *f.* kindness; credulity

bonhomme *m.* fellow, good-natured man

boni *m.* surplus; bonus

bonification *f.* improvement; discount

bonifier *vt.* to improve; give a discount to

boniment *m.* misleading talk, empty talk; quack's show

bonite *f.* bonito

bonjour *m.* good day, good morning, hello

bonne *f.* maid, servant girl

bonnement *adv.* honestly; truly; **tout —** simply; plainly

bonnet *m.* cap; woman's hat; **gros —** (fig. & coll.) important person

bonneterie *f.* hosiery, knitwear

bonsoir *m.* good evening; good night

bonté *f.* goodness, kindness

borborygme *m.* growling of the stomach

bord *m.* edge, brink; shore; **à — on board; — de la mer** seashore; **faux — m.** (naut.) list; **hors — outboard**

bordage *m.* boards, planking; bulwarks; curb

bordeaux *m.* Bordeaux wine, claret

bordée *f.* (naut.) broadside, volley; tack; watch

bordel *m.* brothel

bordelais *a.* from Bordeaux; **sauce –e** *f.* Bordeau wine sauce

border *vt.* to border, edge; tuck in (bed); **— un lit** make a bed

bordereau *m.* itemized account; memorandum, note

bordure *f.* border; curb

bore *m.* boron

boreal *a.* northern

borgne *a.* one-eyed; suspicious (in appearance)

borinage *m.* soft coal mining *or* miner

borique *a.* boric

borne *f.* boundary, limit, milestone

borné *a.* limited, narrow

borner *vt.* to bound, limit

bosquet *m.* small wood, grove

bosse *f.* hump, bump, hunch

bosseler *vt.* to emboss

bossu *a.* hunchbacked

bot *a.,* clubfooted; **— m.** clubfooted person; **pied — m.** clubfoot

botanique *f.* botany; **— a.** botanical

botte *f.* boot; bunch, bundle; sword thrust

botteler *vt.* to bunch, tie in bunches

botter *vt.* to shoe, put on shoes; to boot, kick

bottier *m.* bootmaker (to order)

bottine *f.* high shoe (with buttons or elastic)

boubouler *vi.* to hoot like an owl

bouc *m.* billy goat; **— émissaire** scapegoat

boucan *m.* smokehouse; (coll.) noise, tumult; **–er** *vt.* to smoke meat

boucanier *m.* buccaneer

boucharde *f.* roller; hammer (having points on the head)

bouche *f.* mouth; muzzle of a gun; opening; **— d'incendie** fire hydrant

bouchée *f.* mouthful; patty filled with creamed food

boucher *m.* butcher

boucher *vt.* to cork; block, stop up

boucherie *f.* butcher shop; slaughter, butchery

bouche-trou *m.* stopgap

bouchon *m.* cork, stopper

boucle *f.* buckle; curl; bend; loop, bow; **— d'oreille** earring

boucler *vt.* to buckle; curl, loop; tie; **— vi.** to curl; buckle

bouclier *m.* shield

bouddhisme *m.* Buddhism

bouddhiste *m.* Buddhist

bouder *vi.* to pout, sulk

boudeur *a.* pouting

boudin *m.* blood sausage; spring (coach); flange

boudiner *vt.* to twist

boudoir *m.* boudoir
boue *f.* mud, filth; (fig.) humiliation, abjection
bouée *f.* buoy; — **de sauvetage** life preserver
boueur *m.* garbage collector
boueux *a.* muddy
bouffant *a.* puffed
bouffe *a.* comical; **opéra** — light opera
bouffée *f.* puff; gust
bouffer *vt.* to puff; (coll.) gulp down food; — *vi.* to swell, puff
bouffette *f.* bow of ribbon; tassel (on harness)
bouffi *a.* swollen, puffed, bloated
bouffir *vt. & vi.* to expand, swell, bloat
bouffissure *f.* swelling; extreme vanity
bouffon *m.* clown; — *a.* comic, burlesque
bouffonnerie *f.* buffoonery, burlesque
bouge *m.* (coll.) burlesque; den; evil place; bulge
bougeoir *m.* short candlestick
bouger *vi.* to budge, stir, move
bougie *f.* candle; sparkplug; probe
bougran *m.* buckram
bouillabaisse *f.* fish stew
bouillant *a.* boiling; (fig.) ardent
bouilleur *m.* still (liquor); small nuclear reactor
bouilli *m.* boiled meat
bouillie *f.* cooked cereal, pap; pulp
bouillir *vi.* to boil; bubble
bouilloire *f.* teakettle
bouillon *m.* broth; **à gros** —**s** at a rolling boil
bouillonnement *m.* boiling; (fig.) agitation
bouillonner *vi.* to boil up
bouillotte *f.* hot-water bottle
boulanger *m.* baker; — *vi.* to bake bread
boulangerie *f.* bakery
boule *f.* ball
bouleau *m.* birch
bouledogue *m.* bulldog
bouler *vt.* to roll like a ball; (coll.) to muff, fail at; send (someone) packing
boulet *m.* cannon ball
boulette *f.* little ball, pellet; — **de viande** meatball
bouleversement *m.* upset, upheaval
bouleverser *vt.* to overthrow; upset
boulier *m.* kind of abacus
boulingrin *m.* lawn (edged with trees); bowling green
boulodrome *m.* bowling alley, bowling green
boulon *m.* metal bolt; —**ner** *vt.* to bolt
boulot *a.* fat, round; — *m.* (coll.) work; cylindrical loaf of bread
bouquet *m.* bunch, bouquet; clump; aroma (of wine); large shrimp; hare

bouquetier *m.* vase
bouquetière *f.* flower seller
bouquiner *vi.* to shop for old books
bouquiniste *m.* dealer in old books
bourbe *f.* mire, mud, slush
bourbeux *a.* muddy
bourbier *m.* mire; difficulty
bourde *f.* fib; sham; (coll.) error, stupidity
bourdon *m.* bumblebee; great bell; bourdon; pilgrim's staff; **faux** — drone
bourdonnement *m.* buzz, buzzing
bourdonner *vi.* to buzz, hum
bourg *m.* large village, small town
bourgade *f.* little village
bourgeois *m.* bourgeois; commoner; — *a.* middle-class
bourgeoisie *f.* middle class, bourgeoisie
bourgeon *m.* bud; pimple; —**ner** *vi.* to bud
bourgeonnement *m.* budding
bourgeron *m.* smock
bourguignon *a.* from Burgundy
Bourgogne *f.* Burgundy; — *m.* Burgundy wine
bourlinguer *vi.* to roll (ship); (coll.) gad about, travel
bourrade *f.* sharp blow; poke
bourrage *m.* stuffing; cramming
bourrasque *f.* squall; fit, attack, spasm
bourre *f.* wad; stuffing
bourreau *m.* executioner
bourreler *vt.* to torment, torture
bourrelet *m.* pad; weather stripping
bourrer *vt.* to stuff, pad, cram; beat, drub
bourrique *f.* she-ass; (coll.) stupid person
bourru *a.* rough; brusque; unfermented (wine)
bourse *f.* purse, bag; scholarship; stock exchange; —**s** *pl.* scrotum
boursier *m.* scholarship student; purse maker; stock dealer
boursouflé *a.* swollen, puffed up; bombastic
boursoufler *vt.* to swell, bloat, puff up
bousculer *vt.* to jostle; throw into disorder
bouse *f.* dung
bousiller *vt.* to bungle
boussole *f.* compass
boustifaille *f.* feasting; good food
bout *m.* end, tip; bit, piece; **pousser à** — to push to the limit; **être à** — to be exhausted; **venir à** — **de** to succeed in
boutade *f.* outburst, fit; whim
boutefeu *m.* firebrand; (fig.) trouble maker
bouteille *f.* bottle; — **isolante** vacuum bottle
boutique *f.* shop
boutiquier *m.* shopkeeper
bouton *m.* button, knob, handle; bud; pimple; — **d'or** buttercup

boutonner *vt.* to button; — *vi.* to bud

boutonneux *a.* pimply

boutonnière *f.* buttonhole

bouture *f.* cutting (from a plant)

bouturer *vi.* to take root; — *vt.* to root (cuttings)

bouvier *m.* cowherd

bouvillon *m.* young steer

bouvreuil *m.* bullfinch

bovin *a.* bovine

bow-window *m.* bay window

boxe *f.* boxing; —**r** *vi.* to box; —**ur** *m.* boxer

boy *m.* houseboy

boyau *m.* gut, intestine, bowel; narrow passage; tube

boycotter *vt.* to boycott

bracelet *m.* bracelet; — **de caoutchouc** rubber band

bracelet-montre *m.* wristwatch

braconnage *m.* poaching

braconner *vi. & vt.* to poach

braconnier *m.* poacher

braguette *f.* fly (pants); codpiece

Brahmane *m.* Brahman

brai *m.* resin, pitch

braille *m.* Braille

brailler *vi.* to bawl, yell

braiment *m.* bray

braire *vi.* to bray

braise *f.* embers, coals

braiser *vt.* to braise

brancard *m.* stretcher; shaft

brancardier *m.* stretcher-bearer

branche *f.* branch, bough

brancher *vt.* to connect, plug in; — *vi.* perch

branchies *f. pl.* gills

brande *f.* broom (plant); brand

brandebourg *m.* braid; facing

brandevin *m.* brandy

brandir *vt.* to brandish; wave

brandon *m.* torch; firebrand

branlant *a.* shaking, tottering; loose

branle *m.* impetus; oscillation; **mettre en** — to put in motion; —**r** *vt. & vi.* to shake, oscillate

braquer *vt.* to aim, point

bras *m.* arm; shaft; handle; — **dessus** — **dessous** arm in arm

braser *vt.* to braise, solder

brasero *m.* brazier, charcoal burner

brasier *m.* brazier; very hot charcoal fire

brasiller *vt.* to grill over charcoal; — *vi.* to spark, sparkle

brassage *m.* brewing; mixing

brassard *m.* brassard, armband

brasse *f.* (naut.) fathom; breast stroke (swimming)

brassée *f.* armful; stroke (swimming)

brasser *vt.* to brew; mix completely;

(naut.) brace

brasserie *f.* brewery; bar, café

brasseur *m.* brewer; — **d'affaires** (fig.) one with many irons in the fire

brassière *f.* baby shirt; shoulder strap; breast support; — **de sauvetage** life-jacket

bravache *m.* braggart; bold front, false bravery; bully

bravade *f.* bravado

brave *a.* worthy; honest; courageous, brave

braver *vt.* to brave, face, defy

bravoure *f.* bravery; intrepidity

brebis *f.* ewe; — **galeuse** black sheep

brèche *f.* breach; gap

brèche-dent *a.* snaggle-toothed; missing one front tooth

bréchet *m.* breastbone (of a bird)

bredouille *f.* (fig.) sheepishness (as a result of returning empty-handed)

bredouiller *vi.* to stutter, sputter

bref (**brève**) *a.* brief, short; — *adv.* in short; — *m.* (eccl.) pastoral letter of the Pope

brelan *m.* three-of-a-kind; gaming house

breloque *f.* trinket, watch charm; **battre la** — to work irregularly; (fig.) go off the track

brème *f.* bream; flat calm-water fish

Brésil *m.* Brazil

Brésilien *m. & a.* Brazilian

Bretagne *f.* Brittany

bretelle *f.* sling, strap; (mil.) line of defense; —**s** *pl.* suspenders

Breton *m. & a.* Breton

bretzel *m.* pretzel

breuvage *m.* brew, potion; beverage

brevet *m.* diploma; license; patent

brevetable *a.* patentable

breveté *a.* certified, approved, licensed

breveter *vt.* to patent

bréviaire *m.* (eccl.) breviary

bribe *f.* scrap, bit; oddments

bric-à-brac *m.* bric-a-brac, odds and ends

brick *m.* brig (ship)

bricole *f.* trifle; strap, harness; something without importance

bricoler *vi.* to putter; — *vt.* (coll.) to cook up

bricoleur *m.* putterer

bride *f.* bridle; strap; clamp; **à** — **abattue** at full speed

brider *vt.* to bridle, check

bridge *m.* bridge (cards, teeth)

bridger *vi.* to play bridge

bridgeur *m.* bridge player

brièvement *adv.* briefly

brièveté *f.* brevity

brigade *f.* brigade; **général de** — *m.* briga-

dier general
brigadier *m.* corporal (cavalry)
brigand *m.* robber, brigand
brigue *f.* plot; **—r** *vt.* to plot to obtain
brigueur *m.* plotter, schemer
brillamment *adv.* brilliantly
brillant *a.* brilliant; sparkling; **—** *m.* brilliance; diamond
brillantine *f.* brilliantine
briller *vi.* to shine, sparkle, glitter
brimade *f.* hazing
brimborion *m.* small object of little value
brimer *vt.* to haze
brin *m.* bit, sprig; **— d'herbe** blade of grass
brindille *f.* twig; sprig
brio *m.* spirit
brioche *f.* brioche; rich, light roll
brique *f.* brick
briquet *m.* lighter; **pierre à —** *f.* flint
briquetage *m.* brickwork
briqueteur *m.* bricklayer
briquetier *m.* brickmaker
briquette *f.* fuel briquette
brisant *m.* breakers, reef
brise *f.* breeze
brisé *a.* broken; folding; jagged; **chaise —e** *f.* folding chair; **pâte —e** *f.* puff paste
brise-bise *m.* weather stripping; café curtains
brise-glace *m.* ice breaker
brise-jet *m.* deflector
brise-lames *m.* breakwater
briser *vt.* to break, shatter, crush
brisque *f.* service stripe (army)
bristol *m.* cardboard
brisure *f.* break; joint
britannique *a.* British
broc *m.* jug
brocanteur *m.* secondhand dealer
brocard *m.* taunt, gibe
brocart *m.* brocade
brocatelle *f.* imitation brocade; variegated marble
broche *f.* brooch (jewelry); spit; spindle; peg
broché *a.* brocaded; **livre —** *m.* paper-bound book
brocher *vt.* to brocade; bind in paper; sew a binding; be slipshod (in working); nail the shoe of a horse
brochet *m.* pike (fish)
brochette *f.* skewer
brocheuse *f.* stapler
brochure *f.* pamphlet, brochure
brocoli *m.* broccoli
brodequin *m.* buskin; torture boot
broder *vt.* to embroider; **—ie** *f.* embroidery
brome *m.* bromine
bromure *f.* bromide

broncher *vi.* to stumble, falter; flinch; budge
bronches *m. pl.* bronchial tubes
bronchite *f.* bronchitis
bronzer *vt.* to tan; bronze
brook m. brook; waterjump (steeplechase
broque *m.* broccoli
broquette *f.* tack
brossage *m.* brushing
brosse *f.* brush; **—r** *vt.* to brush
brou *m.* walnut shell
brouet *m.* thin broth, stew
brouette *f.* wheelbarrow
brouillage *m.* radio jamming
brouillard *m.* fog, mist
brouille *f.* quarreling, falling out
brouillé *a.* confused, mixed up; on the outs with; **œufs —s** *m. pl.* scrambled eggs
brouiller *vt.* to mix up, tangle, confuse; **se —** to have a falling out, quarrel; become confused
brouillon *m.* mischief-making; rough draft; muddled person; **—** *a.* muddled
broussailles *f. pl.* brush, underbrush
broussailleux *a.* overgrown; thick, heavy
brousse *f.* brush
brouter *vt.* to graze
broyer *vt.* to grind, crush, pulverize
bru *f.* daughter-in-law
brucelles *f. pl.* tweezers
brugnon *m.* clingstone peach
bruine *f.* drizzle; **—r** *vi.* to drizzle
bruire *vi.* to sound, make a confused noise, rustle
bruissement *m.* rustling
bruit *m.* noise; rumor; uproar; fuss, ado
brûlé *a.* burned; **—** *m.* smell of something burned
brûle-gueule *m.* short pipe
brûle-parfums *m.* incense burner
brûle-pourpoint *adv.* **à —** point-blank; (fig.) brusquely
brûler *vt.* to burn; singe; sting; **—** *vi.* to burn; **se — la cervelle** to blow out one's brains
brûleur *m.* burner
brûloir *m.* roaster
brûlure *f.* burn; scald
brumailleux *a.* misty
brume *f.* mist, fog; **—r** *vi.* to be foggy
brumeux *a.* misty, foggy
brun *a.* brown; dark; **—** *m.* brown; **—e** *f.* twilight
brunâtre *a.* brownish
brunet *a.* brownish; **—te** *f.* brunette
bruni *a.* burnished; **—** *m.* polish
brunir *vt.* to burnish; brown, tan; **—** *vi.* become dark; tan
brusque *a.* abrupt, brusque, blunt

brusquer *vt.* to treat roughly; be abrupt with
brut *a.* rough, raw; rude; crude; dry
brutal *a.* brutal, brutish; coarse
brutaliser *vt.* to treat roughly
brutalité *f.* brutality, brutishness; cruelty
Bruxelles, Brussels; choux de — *m. pl.* Brussels sprouts
bruyamment *adv.* noisily; clamorously
bruyant *a.* noisy, loud
bruyère *f.* heath; (bot.) heather; briar
buanderie *f.* laundry room
buandière *f.* laundress
bubonique *a.* bubonic; **peste —** *f.* bubonic plague
bûche *f.* firewood, log; (fig.) stupid person; **— de Noël,** log-shaped Christmas cake
bûcher *vi.* to chop wood; work hard; **—** *m.* woodshed; stake; pyre
bûcheron *m.* woodcutter
bûchette *f.* stick of wood
bûcheur *m.* hard worker, eager beaver (U.S. coll.)
bucolique *a.* bucolic
budgétaire *a.* budgetary
buée *f.* steam; mist, vapor
buffet *m.* buffet; refreshment room; sideboard
buffle *m.* buffalo
building *m.* very large, modern building
buis *m.* boxwood
buisson *m.* bush; thicket
buissonier *a.* hidden in bushes; (fig.) **faire l'école —ère** to play hooky
bulbe *f.* bulb
bulbeux *a.* bulbous
Bulgare *n. & a.* Bulgarian
Bulgarie *f.* Bulgaria
bulle *f.* bubble; (eccl.) papal bull; **papier — ** *m.* wrapping paper
bulletin *m.* bulletin; ballot; **— de bagages** baggage check; **— scolaire** report card
bure *f.* monk's cloth; mine shaft
bureau *m.* office; writing desk; bureau; officers
bureaucrate *m.* bureaucrat
bureaucratie *f.* bureaucracy
bureaucratique *a.* bureaucratic
burette *f.* cruet; burette; oilcan
burin *m.* engraving; burin, engraving tool
burlesque *a.* comical
busc *m.* metal stay, whalebone
buse *f.* buzzard; millrace; shaft, tube
business *m.* work; complicated business
busqué *a.* arched; aquiline
buste *m.* bust (sculpture)
but *m.* mark, aim, purpose, design; goal; **de — en blanc** *adv.* abruptly; point-blank

butane *m.* butane
buté *a.* obstinate, unmoving, set
butée *f.* abutment
buter *vi.* to abut; **— contre** bump into, stumble on; **—** *vt.* to prop, support
butin *m.* booty; prize
butiner *vi.* to pillage; **—** *vt.* to gather nectar
butoir *m.* buffer
butor *m.* (fig.) lout, good-for-nothing
butte *f.* bluff; hill; **en — à** exposed to
butter *vt.* to heap earth around (asparagus, celery)
buvable *a.* drinkable
buvard *m.* blotter
buvette *f.* bar; taproom
buveur *m.* drinker; drunkard
Byzance *f.* Byzantium
Byzantin *m. & a.* Byzantine

C

ça *pron.* (coll.) that; **c'est —** that's it
çà *adv.* here; **— et là** here and there
cabale *f.* plot, cabal
cabaler *vi.* to plot, cabal
cabalistique *a.* cabalistic; mysterious
cabane *f.* cabin; hut; kennel
cabanon *m.* cabin; padded cell
cabas *m.* basket
cabestan *m.* capstan
cabillaud *m.* fresh cod
cabine *f.* boat cabin; booth; beach cabana
cabinet *m.* closet; study; lawyer's office; cabinet; collection; **-s** *pl.* toilets, bathrooms
câble *m.* cable
câbler *vi.* to twist; cord; send a cable
câblier *m.* cable-layer
câblogramme *m.* cable
cabochard *a.* obstinate
caboche *f.* hobnail; (coll.) big head
cabochon *m.* upholstery nail
cabot in *m.* strolling comedian; ham actor
cabrer *vt.* put into a passion; **se —** *vi.* to rear up
cabri *m.* kidskin
cabriole *f.* caper
cabrioler *vi.* to caper
cabriolet *m.* gig; **place de —** *m.* cabstand
cacao *m.* cocoa
cacaouète, cacaouette, cacauète *f.* peanut
cache *f.* cache, hiding place
cache-cache *m.* hide-and-go-seek
cachemire *m.* cashmere
cache-nez *m.* scarf, muffler
cacher *vt.* to hide, conceal
cache-radiateur *m.* radiator cover
cache-sexe *m.* loin cloth, shorts
cachet *m.* seal, distinctive mark; fee

cacheter vt. to seal; close an envelope
cachette f. hiding place; **en — ** adv. secretly
cachot m. dungeon; cell
cacophonie f. cacophony
cadastre m. land-survey register
cadavre m. cadaver, corpse
cadeau m. gift, present
cadenas m. padlock; **–ser** vt. to padlock
cadencer vt. to cadence; put into rhythm
cadet a. younger, junior; **— ** m. younger son; caddie (golf)
cadmium m. cadmium
cadrage m. framing
cadran m. dial; **— solaire** sundial
cadre m. frame; limit(s); (mil.) cadre
cadrer vi. to conform, agree, tally
caduc a. old, decrepit; null and void
caducée m. (med.) caduceus, symbol of Hermes
caducité f. decrepitude
cafard m. hypocrite; (coll.) melancholy; cockroach
café m. coffee; coffee shop, café
caféier m. coffee plant
caféière f. coffee plantation
caféine f. caffeine
cafetière f. coffeepot
cage f. cage; stair well; casing
cagnard a. indolent, lazy
cagneux a. knock-kneed
cagot m. & a. bigot; bigoted
cagoule f. hood, cowl
cahier m. notebook
cahot m. jerk, bump, jolt
cahoter vi. to jerk, bump, jolt
cahoteux a. bumpy
cahute f. hut
caille f. quail
caillé m. curdled milk, curds
caillebotis m. (mil.) duckboard; wooden trellis
cailler vt. & vi. to curdle, clot
caillot m. blood clot
caillou m. pebble
cailloutage m. paving with pebbles, gravelling
caillouteux a. pebbly
cailloutis m. mass of broken stones, gravel
caiman m. crocodile
caisse f. chest; till; cashier's desk; chassis, body; **— d'épargne** savings bank; **grosse —** bass drum
caissier m. cashier
caisson m. caisson, ammunition wagon; **maladie des –s** f. (med.) the bends
cajoler vt. to wheedle, cajole
cajolerie f. wheedling, cajolery
calamine f. calamine; sludge
calamiteux a. calamitous

calandre f. mangle, roller
calcaire a. calcarious, chalky; **— ** m. limestone; **eau — ** f. hard water
calcédoine f. chalcedony
calciner vt. to burn, reduce to powder
calcium m. calcium
calcul m. calculation; calculus; (med.) stone
calculateur m. calculator; **— ** a. calculating
calculatrice digitale f. digital computer
calculer vt. to calculate; **machine à — ** f. adding machine
cale f. wedge; (naut.) hold; **— sèche** dry dock
calé a. smart
calebasse f. gourd
calèche f. old-style open carriage
caleçon m. undershorts; swimming trunks
calembour m. pun
calendrier m. calendar
caler vt. to prop up; give in; stop; stall, jam
calfater vt. to caulk
calfeutrer vt. to stop up; **se — ** to shut oneself up
calibre m. caliber, quality; cylinder diameter (gun)
calibrer vt. to calibrate
calice m. chalice; calyx
calicot m. calico
calife m. caliph
californium m. californium
califourchon, (à) adv. astride, astraddle
câlin a. coaxing, cajoling
câliner vt. to coax; cajole
calleux a. callous; callused
calligraphie f. calligraphy, penmanship
callosité f. callus
calmant m. (med.) sedative
calmar m. squid
calme a. & n. calm, calmness
calmer vt. to calm, appease, quiet; **se — ** to calm down
calomnie f. calumny, slander
calorifère m. radiator; heater
calorifuge a. heat-retaining; insulating
calot m. cap, policeman's hat
calotte f. skullcap; (coll.) blow on the head
calotter vt. to hit on the head
calquer vt. to trace, copy
calumet m. pipe, peace pipe
calvados m. applejack
calvaire m. Calvary; Stations of the Cross
calviniste n. & a. Calvinist
calvitie f. baldness
camarade m. & f. comrade, friend
camaraderie f. companionship
camard a. snub-nosed
Cambodge m. Cambodia
cambouis m. sludge; axle grease

cambrer *vt.* to curve, arch
cambrioler *vt.* to burgle
cambrioleur *m.* burglar
cambrure *f.* arch; curve
cambuse *f.* (naut.) storeroom; canteen
came *f.* cam
camée *m.* cameo
caméléon *m.* chameleon
camélia *m.* camellia
camelot *m.* peddler; paper boy
camelote *f.* junk, rubbish
camembert *m.* cheese of Camembert
caméra *f.* camera (movies, pictures) television camera
camion *m.* truck; paint bucket
camion-citerne *m.* tank truck
camionnage *m.* trucking
camionnette *f.* light truck; — sanitaire mobile health unit
camionneur *m.* truck driver, teamster
camisole *f.* camisole; — de force strait jacket
camomille *f.* camomile
camouflage *m.* camouflage
camoufler *vt.* to camouflage
camp *m.* camp; camp site; ficher le — (coll.) to clear out
campagnard *m.* country dweller; —*a.* rustic
campagne *f.* country; countryside; campaign
campé *a.* built, constructed; established
campement *m.* encampment
camper *vt. & vi.* to encamp
campeur *m.* camper
camphre *m.* camphor
camus *a.* flat-nosed
Canada *m.* Canada
Canadien *n. & a.* Canadian
canadienne *f.* mackintosh, jacket; canoe with raised ends
canaille *f.* rabble; scoundrel
canal *m.* canal; irrigation drain
canalisation *f.* canalization; canal system
canapé *m.* sofa; canapé
canard *m.* duck; rumor; newspaper; sugar soaked in alcohol
canari *m.* canary
cancan *m.* can-can (dance); gossip
cancaner *vi.* to quack; gossip
cancer *m.* cancer; —eux *a.* cancerous
candélabre *m.* candelabrum; sconce
candeur *f.* candor, innocence
candi *m.* rock candy; — *a.* candied
candidat *m.* candidate
candidature *f.* candidacy
candide *a.* naïve, innocent
candir *v.*, se — to crystallize; go to sugar
cane *f.* female duck
caneton *m.* duckling

canette *f.* cane; beer bottle
canevas *m.* canvas
canezou *m.* lace blouse, usually sleeveless
caniche *f.* poodle
canicule *f.* dog days
canif *m.* penknife
canin *a.* canine; dent –e *f.* canine tooth
cannaie *f.* sugar-cane plantation
canne *f.* cane; reed; — à pêche fishing rod
canneler *vt.* to flute (a column)
cannelle *f.* cinnamon; spigot
cannelure *f.* fluting (of a column)
canner *vt.* to cane a chair
cannibale *n.* cannibal
canoë *m.* canoe
canon *m.* cannon; barrel of a gun; — *m.* (eccl.) decree; — *a.* canon; droit — *m.* canon law
cañon *m.* canyon
canonial, canonique *a.* canonical
canoniser *vt.* to canonize
canonnade *f.* volley, barrage
canonner *vt.* to fire cannons on
canonnier *m.* cannoneer
canonnière *f.* popgun; gunboat
canot *m.* rowboat, dinghy; — de sauvetage lifeboat
canotier *m.* rower; sailor hat, straw hat
cantaloup *m.* cantaloupe
cantate *f.* cantata
cantatrice *f.* professional singer
cantine *f.* canteen
cantique *m.* canticle, hymn
canton *m.* canton, district
cantonade *f.*, à la — *adv.* (theat.) in (to) the wings
cantonnement *m.* cantonment, billet(ing)
cantonner *vt.* to billet; district
canular *m.* practical joke
canule *f.* tube of a syringe
caoutchouc *m.* rubber
caoutchoutier *a.* rubber
cap *m.* cape, headland; (naut.) course
capacité *f.* capacity; ability; aptitude
cape *f.* cape; rire sous — to laugh up one's sleeve
capillaire *a.* capillary; vaisseau — *m.* capillary
capitaine *m.* captain
capital *m.* capital; stock; — *a.* capital; main, principal
capitale *f.* chief city, capital; capital letter
capitaliste *m.* capitalist; — *a.* capitalistic
capitation *f.* poll tax
capiteux *a.* heady wine or beer
capitonner *vt.* to stuff, upholster
capitulation *f.* capitulation, surrender
capituler *vt.* to capitulate
capon *a.* shameful, bashful; — *m.* coward, sneak

caporal *m.* corporal; shag (tobacco)
capot *m.* (auto.) hood; cover; casing; — *a.* trickless (cards); confused
capotage *m.* (auto.) overturning
capote *f.* hooded cloak; (mil.) greatcoat; (auto.) top of convertible
capoter *vi.* (auto.) to turn over; (naut.) capsize
câpre *f.* (bot.) caper
caprice *m.* caprice, whim
capricieux *a.* capricious
capsule *f.* capsule; bottle cap; pod; percussion cap
capsuler *vt.* to cap a bottle; — *vi.* to misfire
capter *vt.* to obtain, get hold of insidiously; to tap, bring in a water supply; (rad.) to tune in
captieux *a.* insidious; specious
captif *a.* & *n.* captive
captivant *a.* captivating
captiver *vt.* to captivate
captivité *f.* captivity
capture *f.* capture; —r *vt.* to capture
capuchon *m.* hood; cover; cap
capucine *f.* nasturtium; Capuchin nun
caque *f.* keg, barrel
caquet *m.* cackling; gossip, slander
caquetage *m.* cackling; gossiping
caqueter *vi.* to cackle; gossip
car *conj.* for, because; — *m.* sightseeing bus
carabe *m.* beetle
carabine *f.* carbine, rifle
carabinier *m.* cavalryman, rifleman; Italian policeman
caraco *m.* loose bodice; jacket
caractère *m.* character; feature; nature
caractériser *vt.* to characterize; distinguish
carafe *f.* decanter, bottle, carafe
carafon *m.* small carafe
Caraïbe *n.* & *a.* Carib; Mer — *f.* Caribbean Sea
carambolage *m.* jostling, bumping
caramboler *vi.* to carom (billiards)
caramel *m.* drop, chewy candy; — mou caramel
caraméliser *vt.* to caramelize
carapace *f.* turtle shell, carapace
caravane *f.* caravan; convoy; house trailer
caravansérail *m.* caravansary
caravelle *f.* (naut.) caravel
carbonate *m.* carbonate
carbonation *f.* carbonation
carbone *m.* carbon; — 14 (chem.) carbon 14; papier — *m.* carbon paper
carboné *a.* carbonated
carbonique *a.* carbonic

carboniser *vt.* to carbonize
carbonnade *f.* stew, pot roast
carborundum *m.* carborundum
carburant *m.* motor fuel
carburateur *m.* (auto.) carburetor
carbure *m.* carbide
carburéacteur *m.* jet fuel
carcasse *f.* carcass; skeleton
carcinogénique *a.* (med.) carcinogenic
cardamome *m.* cardamon
cardan *m.* (mech.) universal joint
carder *vt.* to card wool or flax
cardiaque *a.* cardiac; — *n.* heart patient
cardinal *m.* & *a.* cardinal
cardiographe *m.* cardiograph; — électrique electrocardiograph
carême *m.* Lent
carême-prenant *m.* Shrovetide
carence *f.* lack; failure
carène *f.* hull
caréner *vt.* to careen
caresse *f.* caress; endearment
caresser *vt.* to caress, fondle
cargaison *f.* cargo, shipload
cargo *m.* freighter, cargo ship
cari *m.* curry powder
caricature *f.* caricature
caricaturer *vt.* to caricature
caricaturiste *m.* caricaturist
carie *f.* caries, decay; —r *vt.* to decay
carillonner *vi.* to chime
carlingue *f.* (avi.) cockpit
carmin *m.* & *a.* carmine
carnage *m.* carnage
carnassier *a.* carniverous
canassière *f.* bag for game
carnation *f.* flesh coloring; flesh color
carnaval *m.* carnival
carné *a.* flesh-colored; meaty
carnet *m.* notebook; ticket book; — de chèques checkbook
carnier *m.* hunting sack
carnivore *a.* carnivorous
carolingien *a.* Carolingian
carotide *f.* & *a.* carotid
carotte *f.* carrot; sampling (of rock from a mine)
carpe *f.* carp
carpette *f.* rug, mat
carquois *m.* quiver (for arrows)
carre *f.* shape; crown; breadth
carré *a.* square; sensible; firm; obstinate; — *m.* square; patch; — de papier slip of paper
carreau *m.* tile; flagstone; diamond (at cards); pane of glass; à —x checked;
carrefour *m.* crossroads
carrelage *m.* tiling, flooring
carreler *vt.* to tile
carrément *adv.* squarely; frankly

carrer *vt.* to square

carrier *m.* quarry worker

carrière *f.* career, course; race; quarry; open-pit mine

carriole *f.* cart

carrossable *a.* passable for vehicles

carrosse *m.* coach, carriage

carrosserie *f.* (auto.) body

carrousel *m.* cavalry parade; carousel

carrure *f.* width (of shoulders)

cartable *m.* cardboard portfolio; briefcase

carte *f.* card; map; chart; menu; **jeu de —s** *m.* deck of cards; **— blanche** free hand; **— grise** automobile registration

cartel *m.* wall clock; cartel, monopoly, trust; challenge

carte-lettre *f.* correspondence card

carter *m.* case, casing; (auto.) crankcase; bicycle-chain guard

cartésien *a.* cartesian, relative to Descartes

cartilagineux *a.* cartilagenous

cartographe *m.* cartographer, mapmaker

cartomancie *f.* fortune telling with cards

carton *m.* cardboard; cardboard box; cartoon

carton-pâte *m.* papier-mâché

cartonnage *m.* cardboard construction; cardboard binding

cartonner *vt.* to bind in cardboard

cartonnier *m.* cardboard file; chest of cardboard drawers

cartouche *f.* cartridge; cartouche; **— chargée à balle** rifle cartridge; **— chargée à plomb** shotgun shell

cartouchière *f.* cartridge bag

cas *m.* case, circumstance; matter; **en tout — in** any case, in any event; **faire peu de — de** to pay little attention to; consider unimportant

casanier *m.* homebody; **— a.** retired, domestic

casaque *f.* jacket; jockey's jacket

cascade *f.* cascade, waterfall

cascader *vt.* to cascade

case *f.* compartment; square, box; hut, cabin; **— postale** post-office box

caséine *f.* caseine

casemate *f.* underground fortification

caser *vt.* to get someone settled in a job; to put in order; **se — to** get settled, be established

caserne *f.* (mil.) barracks

caserner *vt.* to lodge in barracks

casier *m.* set of pigeonholes; cabinet of small drawers; **— judiciaire** police record

casque *m.* helmet; headpiece, headphones

casquette *f.* cap

cassant *a.* brittle; rigid

cassation *f.* reversal of a court decision; breaking of a noncommissioned officer; **cour de — f.** supreme court

casse *f.* breakage; type case; cassia

cassé *a.* broken, broken-down; hesitant voice

casse-cou *m.* daredevil; dangerous point in a road

casse-croûte *m.* snack

casse-noisette, casse-noix *m.* nutcracker

casser *vt.* to break, crack; reverse; reduce in rank

casserole *f.* saucepan

casse-tête *m.* club; cudgel; (fig.) work requiring close application

cassette *f.* strongbox

cassis *m.* black currant; black-currant liqueur; dip in a road

cassolette *f.* incense burner

cassonade *f.* brown sugar

cassoulet *m.* stew with white beans

cassure *f.* fracture, crack

castagnettes *f. pl.* castanets

caste *f.* caste, class

castor *m.* beaver

castrat *m.* something castrated

castration *f.* castration

castrer *vt.* to castrate

casuel *a.* chance, accidental; **— m.** supplementary income

casuiste *m.* casuist

cataclysme *m.* cataclysm

catacombes *f. pl.* catacombs

catafalque *m.* bier

catalepsie *f.* catalepsy

cataleptique *a.* cataleptic

catalogue *m.* catalog

cataloguer *vt.* to catalog

catalyse *f.* catalysis

catalyseur *m.* catalyst

catalytique *a.* catalytic

cataplasme *m.* poultice

catapulte *f.* catapult

cataracte *f.* cataract, waterfall

catarrhe *m.* catarrh

catastrophique *a.* catastrophic

catch *m.* wrestling

catcheur *m.* wrestler

catéchisme *m.* catechism

catégorie *f.* category

catégorique *a.* categorical

caterpillar *m.* caterpillar tread

cathartique *a.* cathartic

cathédrale *f.* cathedral

cathode *f.* cathode

catholique *m. & a.* Catholic

cati *m.* glaze, gloss

catir *vt.* to glaze

Caucasien *m. & a.* Caucasian

cauchemar *m.* nightmare

cause *f.* cause; source; reason; **à — de** on account of (law), for the sake of
causer *vt.* to cause; **— *vi.*** chat
causerie *f.* chat, talk; gossiping; unpretentious conference, informal lecture
causeur *a.* chatty, having art of conversation
causeuse *f.* love seat
caustique *m. & a.* caustic
cautérisation *f.* cauterization
cautériser *vt.* to cauterize
caution *f.* bail, security; (fig.) guarantee
cautionnement *m.* bail
cautionner *vt.* to provide bail for, bail out
cavalcade *f.* cavalcade; parade
cavalerie *f.* cavalry
cavalier *m.* horseman, rider; cavalier; gentleman; knight (chess); **— *a.*** cavalier; unceremonious; **piste cavalière** *f.* bridle path
cave *f.* cellar; crypt
caveau *m.* cellar
caver *vt.* to dig, excavate
caverne *f.* cavern; cave, den
caverneux *a.* cavernous
caviar *m.* caviar
caviarder *vt.* to cross out; censor
cavité *f.* cavity, hollow
cawcher, kasher *a.* kosher
ce, (cet) *a. m.* this, that; **— *pron.*** it, that, this; he, she; **— qui, — que** what, that which
céans *adv.* herein
ceci *pron.* this; the latter
cécité *f.* blindness
céder *vt. & vi.* to cede, yield, give up
cédille *f.* (gram.) cedilla
cédrat *m.* citron, citron tree
cèdre *m.* cedar
cédule *f.* rate, schedule
ceindre *vt.* to buckle on, gird; encircle
ceinture *f.* belt; waist, waistline; circle
cela *pron.* that, it; this; the former
célébrant *m.* priest officiating at Mass
célébration *f.* celebration; solemn commemoration
célèbre *a.* celebrated, famous
célébrer *vt.* celebrate; commemorate
célébrité *f.* celebrity
celer *vt.* to hide, conceal
céleri *m.* celery root; celery; **— en branches** celery stalks
célérité *f.* rapidity, promptness
céleste *a.* celestial, heavenly; **mécanique — *f.*** celestial mechanics
célibat *m.* celibacy; bachelorhood
célibataire *a.* unmarried; **— *m.*** bachelor
celle *pron.* the one, she; **-ci** this one; the latter; **-là** that one; the former
cellier *m.* storeroom; wine cellar

cellulaire *a.* cellular
cellule *f.* cell, cellule; **— photo-électrique** (phot.) exposure meter
celluloïd *m.* celluloid
celte *a. & m.* celt; celtic
celui *pron. m.* he, the one; **— -ci** the latter, this one; **— -là** the former; that one
cénacle *m.* group, club, circle
cendre *f.* ashes; **couleur de —** ashen
cendrée *f.* shot, buckshot; cinder track
cendrier *m.* ash tray
Cendrillon *f.* Cinderella
Cène *f.* Last Supper
cénobite *m.* cenobite
cénotaphe *m.* cenotaph
cens *m.* census; minimum tax for voting qualification
censé *a.* supposed, reputed; **-ment** *adv.* supposedly, reputedly
censeur *m.* censor, censurer; auditer
censurable *a.* censurable; blameworthy
censure *f.* censorship; censure; audit (govt.)
censurer *vt.* to censor; censure, criticize, find fault with
cent *a. & m.* one hundred; **pour — per cent**
centenaire *m.* centenary
centennal *a.* centennial
centiare *m.* 1/100 are, 1 square meter
centième *a. & m.* hundredth
centigramme *m.* centigram
centilitre *m.* centiliter
centime *m.* centime
centimètre *m.* centimeter
centipède *m.* centipede
central *a.* central; middle; main, principal; **— *m.*** center
centraliser *vt.* to centralize
centre *m.* center; middle
centrer *vt.* to center; focus, adjust
centrifuge *a.* centrifugal
centripète *a.* centripetal
centuple *m.* hundredfold (100 times); **au — *adv.*** a hundredfold
cep *m.* vine, vine stock
cèpe *m.* edible mushroom
cependant *adv.* meanwhile; **— *conj.*** however; but; still, yet
céramique *a.* ceramic; **— *f.*** ceramics; ceramic piece; ceramic tile
cerbère *m.* watchdog; guard
cerceau *m.* hoop, ring; **-x** *m. pl.* pin feathers
cercle *m.* circle, ring; club, group; dial
cercler *vt.* to ring, encircle
cercueil *m.* coffin
céréale *a. & f.* cereal plant
cérébral *a.* cerebral
cérémonial *a.* ceremonial; **— *m.*** ceremo-

nial, ceremony

cérémonie *f.* ceremony, formality; **faire des –s** to stand on ceremony

cérémonieux *a.* ceremonious; formal

cerf *m.* stag

cerf-volant *m.* kite

cerisaie *f.* cherry orchard

cerise *f.* cherry; — *a. & m.* cherry-colored, cerise

cerisier *m.* cherry tree

cerne *m.* annual ring (of a tree); circle, ring

cerner *vt.* to surround, ring, encircle; **avoir les yeux cernés** to have rings under one's eyes

certain *a.* certain, sure; some; **–ement** *adv.* certainly; of course

certes *adv.* indeed; certainly

certificat *m.* certificate

certification *f.* certification

certifier *vt.* to certify; authenticate

certitude *f.* certainty

cérumen *m.* ear wax

céruse *f.* lead carbonate, white lead

cerveau *m.* brain; mind

cervelet *m.* cerebellum

cervelle *f.* brain, brains; mind

cervical *a.* cervical, of the neck

ces *a. pl.* these, those

césar *m.* Caesar, occidental emperor

césarienne *a.* (med.) Caesarean (operation)

cesse *f.* cessation, rest; **sans —** unceasingly, incessantly, continually

cesser *vt. & vi.* to cease, stop, discontinue (com.) stop payment

cession *f.* relinquishing, giving up

cessez-le-feu *n.* cease-fire

c'est-à-dire *conj.* that is to say, in other words

césure *f.* caesura

cette *a. f.* this, that

ceux *pron., m. pl.* these, those, the ones

Ceylan *m.* Ceylon

chablis *m.* Chablis wine

chacal *m.* jackal

chacun *pron.* each; everyone

chadburn *m.* public address system (ship)

chagrin *m.* grief, sorrow; worry; goat leather; sheepskin; **–é** *a.* sad, worried, upset

chagriner *vt.* to grieve; worry

chah *m.* shah

chaîne *f.* chain; (naut.) cable; mountain range; fabric warp

chaînette *f.* small chain; **point de —** chainstitch

chaînon *m.* link of a chain

chair *f.* flesh; pulp; meat; **— de poule** goose flesh

chaire *f.* pulpit; professorship, chair

chaise *f.* chair, seat; **— longue** reclining chair

chaland *n.* river *or* canal barge

Chaldée *f.* Chaldea

Chaldéen *m. & a.* Chaldean

châle *m.* shawl

chalet *m.* cottage, chalet; **— de nécessité** public toilet

chaleur *f.* heat, warmth; zeal

chaleureux *a.* warm, heated

châlit *m.* bedstead

chaloupe *f.* launch

chalumeau *m.* straw, reed; **— oxyacétylénique** acetylene torch

chalut *m.* seine, net

chalutier *m.* trawler

chamailler *v., se* **—** to squabble

chamarrer *vt.* to deck, ornament

chambellan *m.* chamberlain

chambre *f.* room; chamber; **— à coucher** bedroom; **— à air** (auto.) inner tube

chambré *a.* at room temperature (wine); chambered; honeycombed

chambrée *f.* roommates (army)

chameau *m.* camel

chamois *m.* chamois, shammy; **—** *a.* buff, chamois

champ *m.* field; ground; scope; range; subject; **— de courses** race track; **— de tir** firing range; **— libre** clear field

Champagne *f.* (province) Champagne; **—** *m.* champagne

champêtre *a.* rural

champignon *m.* mushroom (edible *or* inedible)

champignonner *vi.* to mushroom

championnat *m.* championship

chance *f.* chance; luck, good luck, good fortune; **avoir de la —** to be lucky, be fortunate

chancelant *a.* staggering; wavering; unsteady

chanceler *vi.* to stagger, waver

chancelier *m.* chancellor

chancellerie *f.* chancery; chancellery

chanceux *a.* risky; lucky

chancre *m.* canker

chandail *m.* sweater

chandelier *m.* candlestick

chandelle *f.* candle, taper; prop, stay; **— de glace** icicle

change *m.* exchange; **agent de —** stockbroker; **cours du —** rate of exchange; **donner le — à** to throw off the track

changeable *a.* changeable; exchangeable

changeant *a.* changing, changeable

changement *m.* change; turn; alteration

changer *vt.* to change; exchange; turn; alter; **—** *vi.* change; **— d'avis** change

one's mind
changeur *m.* changer
chanoine *m.* (eccl.) canon
chanson *f.* song
chansonnier *m.* song writer; song book
chant *m.* singing, song; chant; canto; crowing (rooster)
chantage *m.* blackmail
chanter *vt. & vi.* to sing; praise
chanteur *m.*, **chanteuse** *f.* singer, vocalist; blackmailer
chantier *m.* workshop; woodyard; shipyard
chantonner *vt. & vi.* to sing softly; hum
chantoung *m.* shantung
chantourner *vt.* to cut out; cut in profile, silhouette
chantre *m.* singer; poet
chanvre *m.* hemp; **couleur de —** flax color
chaos *m.* chaos, confusion, disorder
chaotique *a.* chaotic
chape *f.* cover, covering; coping; (eccl.) cope; cap; tire tread
chapeau *m.* hat; cap; cover
chapelet *m.* rosary, beads
chapelier *m.* hatmaker, hat seller, hatter
chapelle *f.* chapel; choir
chapellerie *f.* hat trade, hats; hat shop
chapelure *f.* bread crumbs
chaperon *m.* hood, riding hood; chaperon; coping
chaperonner *vt.* to chaperon
chapiteau *m.* capital of a column; top
chapitre *m.* chapter; item, subject
chapitrer *vt.* to reprimand, lecture someone
chapon *m.* capon; head of garlic
chaque *a.* each, every
char *m.* chariot; cart; (mil.) tank
charabia *m.* gibberish
charançon *m.* weevil
charbon *m.* coal, ember; (med.) carbuncle; **— de bois** charcoal; carbon
charbonnage *m.* coal mining; coal mine
charbonnier *m.* charcoal-burner; coaldealer
charcuter *vt.* to butcher, botch; mangle
charcuterie *f.* delicatessen
charcutier *m.* owner of a delicatessen; pork shop
chardon *m.* thistle
chardonneret *m.* goldfinch
charge *f.* load, burden; charge; commission; duty, responsibility; **— prep. à —** de provided that
chargé *a.* loaded, laden; full; overcast; **lettre —e** *f.* registered letter; **— m.** assistant, deputy; **— d'affaires** diplomatic representative
chargement *m.* loading, lading; charging; cargo

charger *vt.* to load, burden; entrust; charge; **se — de** to be responsible for, to take it upon oneself to
chargeur *m.* loader; stoker; shipper
chariot *m.* wagon; baby walker; typewriter carriage; **— élévateur** fork-lift; **le grand —** Ursa Major; **le petit —** Ursa Minor
charitable *a.* charitable
charité *f.* charity, love of neighbor
charivari *m.* noise; cacophony
charlatan *m.* charlatan, quack
charlatanisme *m.* charlatanism, quackery
charlemagne *m.*, king (cards); **faire — to** quit while winning
charmant *a.* charming
charme *m.* charm, spell
charmer *vt.* to charm, bewitch; delight
charmeur *m.* charmer
charmille *f.* bower, arbor
charnel *a.* carnal; sensual
charnière *f.* hinge
charnu *a.* fleshy, pulpy; plump
charogne *f.* carrion
charpente *f.* framework; **bois de — m.** lumber
charpenter *vt.* to square (off); construct; frame; shape, cut
charpenterie *f.* carpentry
charpentier *m.* carpenter
charpie *f.* lint
charretée *f.* cartload
charretier *m.* driver of a cart
charrette *f.* cart
charriage *m.* cartage
charrier *vt.* to cart, haul
charroi *m.* cartage
charron *m.* cartmaker
charrue *f.* plow
charte *f.* charter
chartiste *m. & f.* student of the École des Chartes
chartreuse *f.* chartreuse liqueur; Carthusian monastery
chas *m.* eye of a needle
chasse *f.* hunting; chase; pursuit; **— d'eau** flush of water
châsse *f.* shrine; reliquary; (coll.) frame of eyeglasses
chasse-clou *m.* tool for countersinking; nail puller
chasse-mouches *m.* fly swatter
chasse-neige *m.* snowplow
chasse-pierres *m.* cowcatcher (train)
chasser *vt.* to hunt; put to flight, drive out; discharge, dismiss, fire; **— vi.** hunt
chasseresse *f.* huntress
chasseur *m.* hunter; bellhop; busboy; fighter plane; fighter pilot; **— a.** hunting

châssis *m.* frame, chassis; window frame; hotbed

châssis-presse *m.* (phot.) printing frame

chasteté *f.* chastity

chasuble *f.* chasuble

chat *m.*, **chatte** *f.* cat; darling; — **en poche** pig-in-a-poke

châtaigne *f.* chestnut

châtaignier *m.* chestnut tree

châtain *a.* chestnut color, brown

château *m.* castle, fort; estate, manor; palace

chateaubriand, châteaubriant *m.* grilled beef steak

châtelain *m.* lord of a manor; **–e** *f.* lady of a manor; decorative chain

châtelet *m.* small chateau

chat-huant *m.* screech owl

châtier *vt.* to chastise, punish

châtiment *m.* punishment, chastisement

chatoiement *m.* sparkle; play of colors

chaton *m.* kitten; setting; set stone; (bot.) catkin

chatouillement *m.* tickling

chatouiller *vt.* to tickle

chatouilleux *a.* ticklish; sensitive, touchy

chatoyer *vi.* to shine, glisten like cat's eye

châtrer *vt.* to castrate

chatterie *f.* cajoling, coaxing

chatterton *m.* friction tape, insulating tape

chaud *a.* hot, warm; **il fait** — it is warm (weather); — *m.* heat, warmth; **avoir** — to be warm (of body)

chaud-froid *m.* jellied poultry (chicken) covered with jellied mayonnaise

chaudière *f.* large kettle, steam boiler

chaudron *m.* caldron, boiler

chaudronnier *m.* boilermaker

chauffage *m.* fuel; heating; stoking

chauffe *f.* heating; stoking

chauffe-assiette *m.* hot plate

chauffe-bain *m.* bathroom water heater

chauffe-eau *m.* water heater

chauffe-lit *m.* bed warmer

chauffe-pieds *m.* foot warmer

chauffe-plat *m.* dish warmer

chauffer *vt.* to heat, warm; — *vi.* get warm; overheat

chaufferette *f.* chafing dish; car heater; foot warmer

chauffeur *m.* driver, chauffeur; stoker

chaume *m.* stubble; thatch

chaumière *f.* thatched cottage

chausse *f.* professor's robe insignia; **–s** *pl.* breeches

chaussée *f.* causeway; road, pavement

chausse-pied *m.* shoehorn

chausser *vt.* to put on footwear; **se** — put on one's shoes

chaussette *f.* sock

chausson *m.* slipper, pump; gym shoe; stocking; savate, French boxing; — **aux pommes** apple turnover

chaussure *f.* shoes, footwear; shoe

chauve *a.* bald

chauve-souris *f.* (zool.) bat

chauvin *a.* chauvinist(ic); — *m.* chauvinist

chaux *f.* lime; **blanchir à la** — to whitewash; **lait de** —, **blanc de** — whitewash; **pierre à** — *f.* limestone

chef *m.* chief, head, leader; chef; (mus.) conductor; sports captain; — **de gare** stationmaster

chef-d'œuvre *m.* masterpiece

chef-lieu *m.* chief town of a department

cheik *m.* sheik

chelem (schelem) *m.* slam (at cards)

chemin *m.* way, path, road; means; — **de fer** railroad, railway; — **de traverse** crossroad

chemineau *m.* tramp, vagabond, vagrant

cheminée *f.* fireplace; mantelpiece; chimney

cheminer *vi.* to walk, trudge, tramp

cheminot *m.* railway employee

chemise *f.* shirt; chemise; cover, folder; book jacket; **–tte** *f.* short-sleeved shirt

chemisier *m.* shirtmaker; tailored blouse

chenal *m.* channel

chenapan *m.* bandit, good-for-nothing

chêne *m.* oak

chéneau *m.* rain spout

chêne-liège *m.* cork oak

chenet *m.* andiron

chenil *m.* dog kennel

chenille *f.* caterpillar; chenille; caterpillar tread

chenillé *a.* with a caterpillar tread

chenu *a.* hoary; white with age

chèque *m.* check; **toucher un** — to cash a check

chéquier *m.* checkbook

cher (chère) *a.* dear; beloved; expensive; high; — *adv.* dear(ly), a great deal

chercher *vt.* to look for, seek; try; **aller** — to go and get; **envoyer** — to send for

chercheur *m.* seeker; researcher

chère *f.*, **faire bonne** — to live well

chéri (chérie) *a.* cherished, dear; — *n.* dear, darling

chérir *vt.* to cherish

cherté *f.* dearness, expensiveness

chérubin *m.* cherub

chétif *a.* puny, sickly; poor; wretched

cheval *m.* (*pl.* **chevaux**) horse; **à** — on horseback; — **de course** race horse; — **de race** thoroughbred

chevaleresque *a.* chivalrous

chevalerie *f.* chivalry; knighthood

chevalet *m.* sawhorse; easel; frame, stand; violin bridge

chevalier *m.* knight; rider; — **d'industrie** adventurer; swindler

chevalière *f.* signet ring

chevalin *a.* horse; **boucherie –e** *f.* horse-meat shop

cheval-vapeur *m.* horsepower

chevauchée *f.* ride on horseback; cavalcade

chevaucher *vi.* to ride a horse; overlap, cross; — *vt.* ride, straddle

chevelu *a.* hairy; long-haired

chevelure *f.* head of hair

chevet *m.* headboard; bolster; **livre de —** *m.* favorite book, constant reference; **table de —** *f.* bedside table

cheveu *m.* (*pl.* **cheveux**) hair of the head

cheville *f.* ankle; peg; pin, bolt; skewer

cheviller *vt.* to pin, bolt together

chèvre *f.* goat; derrick

chevreau *m.* kid, kidskin

chèvrefeuille *m.* honeysuckle

chevrette *f.* kid, goat; andiron; tripod

chevreuil *m.* roebuck; **peau de —** *f.* buckskin

chevron *m.* stripe, chevron; rafter

chevronné *a.* experienced; chevroned

chevrotant *a.* trembling, tremulous

chevrotine *f.* buckshot

chez *prep.* at, to, in one's house; among, with; — **soi** at home

chez-soi *m.* home

chiasse *f.* metal scum, dross; flyspecks

chic *m.* style; — *a.* stylish, smart, fashionable; **un —** type a good egg (U.S. coll.)

chicane, chicanerie *f.* chicanery; quibbling, quarrel

chicaner *vt. & vi.* to quibble (with)

chiche *a.* stingy; lacking; **pois — ** *m.* chickpea; dwarf pea

chichon *m.* romaine lettuce

chicorée *f.* chicory; curly endive

chicot *m.* stump, stub

chien *m.* dog; gun hammer; — **d'arrêt** pointer; — **couchant** setter; — **de garde** watchdog; **temps de —** *m.* bad weather

chienlit *m.* mask; disguise

chien-loup *m.* wolf hound

chienne *f.* bitch

chienner *vi.* to whelp

chiffe *f.* rag; (fig.) man without character

chiffon *m.* rag; scrap; chiffon

chiffonnade *f.* shredded greens

chiffonner *vt.* to crimple, rumple, wrinkle; to ruffle, anger

chiffonnier *m.* ragpicker; chest of drawers

chiffre *m.* figure, number; total; code; monogram

chiffrer *vt.* to number, mark; code, put into code; — *vi.* to calculate

chignole *f.* punch; (coll.) jalopy

chignon *m.* chignon, bun of hair

Chili *m.* Chile

chimère *f.* chimera, fancy

chimérique *a.* chimerical; fancied, fanciful

chimie *f.* chemistry; — **polymère** polymer chemistry

chimique *a.* chemical; **produit —** *m.* chemical

chimiste *m.* chemist

chimpanzé *m.* chimpanzee

Chine *f.* China; **encre de —** *f.* India ink

Chinois *m. & a.* Chinese

chinoiserie *f.* oriental objet d'art; -s *pl.* complications

chiot *m.* pup

chiquenaude *f.* flip, flick

chiromancie *f.* palm reading

chirurgical *a.* surgical

chirugie *f.* surgery; -**n** *m.* surgeon

chiure *f.* flyspeck

chlorate *m.* chlorate

chlore *m.* chlorine

chlorer *vt.* to chlorinate

chlorhydrique *a.* hydrochloric

chloroformer, chloroformiser *vt.* to chloroform

chlorophylle *f.* chlorophyll

chlorose *f.* anemia; (med.) chlorosis, green sickness; yellowing of plant leaves

chlorure *m.* chloride

chlorurer *vt.* to chlorinate, chlorinize

choc *m.* shock, collision; clash; clink of glasses

chocolat *m.* chocolate

chocolaterie *f.* chocolate factory

chocolatière *f.* chocolate pot

chœur *m.* choir; chorus

choir *vi.* to fall

choisi *a.* choice, select

choisir *vt.* to choose, select, pick

choix *a.* choice, option, selection; — *a.* **de** — choice, prime, best, first-class

choléra *m.* cholera; (coll.) evil person

cholestérol *m.* cholesterol

chômage *m.* unemployment; **en —** unemployed

chômé *a.* nonworking

chômer *vi.* to be unemployed

chômeur *m.* unemployed worker

chope *f.* beer mug, stein

chopine *f.* small mug; half-liter measure

chopper *vi.* to stumble; blunder

choquant *a.* shocking

choquer *vt.* to shock; strike against, knock; clink; **se —** to collide; be shocked

choral *a.* choral; — *m.* religious chant; -**e**

f. choral group, chorus
chorégraphie *f.* choreography
choriste *m. & f.* member of the chorus
chorus *m.* chorus; **faire —** to repeat in chorus
chose *f.* thing; matter, case; **autre —** something else, another thing, another matter; **quelque —** something
chou *m.* cabbage; cream puff; dear, darling; **— de Bruxelles** Brussels sprout
chou-fleur *m.* cauliflower
chou-rave *m.* kohlrabi
choucroute *f.* sauerkraut; **— garnie** sauerkraut with sausages, ham
chouette *f.* owl
chow-chow *m.* chow dog
choyer *vt.* to pamper
chrême *m.* holy oil
chrestomathie *f.* anthology
chrétien (chrétienne) *a. & n.* Christian
chrétienté *f.* Christianity, Christendom
Christ *m.* Christ; Christus; crucifix
christianiser *vt.* to christianize
christianisme *m.* Christianity
chromatique *a.* chromatic
chrome *m.* chromium; chrome
chromer *vt.* to chrome-plate
chromosome *m.* chromosome
chronique *f.* chronicle; **— a.** chronic
chroniqueur *m.* chronicler; reporter
chronologique *a.* chronological
chronomètre *m.* chronometer; stop watch
chronométrer *vt.* to time
chronométreur *m.* timekeeper
chrysalide *f.* chrysalis, pupa
chrysanthème *m.* chrysanthemum
chuchotement *m.* whisper, whispering
chuchoter *vt. & vi.* to whisper
chuchoterie *f.* whispering; gossip
chuchoteur *m.* whisperer; **— a.** whispering
chut! *interj.* sh!, quiet!
chute *f.* fall, downfall; drop; **— d'eau** cataract
chuter *vt.* to quiet; shush
Chypre *f.* Cyprus
ci *adv.* here; **par —, par là** here and there
ci-après *adv.* hereafter
ci-bas *adv.* below
cible *f.* target
ciboire *m.* ciborium
ciboule *f.* scallion; **-tte** *f.* chive
cicatrice *f.* scar
cicatriser *vt. & vi.* to scar; heal
cicérone *m.* guide
ci-dessous *adv.* hereafter; underneath
ci-dessus *adv.* aforesaid
ci-devant *a.* former; **— adv.** formerly
cidre *m.* cider; **— bouché, — mousseux** sparkling cider
ciel *m.* (*pl.* cieux) sky, heaven

cierge *m.* wax candle, church candle
cigale *f.* grasshopper; cicada
cigare *m.* cigar
cigogne *f.* stork
ciguë *f.* hemlock
ci-inclus *a.* enclosed
ci-joint *a.* herewith, enclosed
cil *m.* eyelash
cilice *m.* hair shirt
ciller *vt. & vi.* to blink, wink
cime *f.* top, summit
ciment *m.* cement; concrete; **-er** *vt.* to cement
cimeterre *m.* scimitar
cimetière *m.* cemetery
ciné *m.* movies
cinéaste *m.* movie technician
ciné-club *m.* film group, film club
cinégraphiste *m.* scenarist
cinéma *m.* movie theater; movies; cinema
cinémascope *m.* cinemascope
cinémathèque *f.* film library
cinématographique *a.* film, motion-picture, cinematographic
cinéphile *m. & f.* movie lover, movie fan
cinéprojecteur *m.* motion-picture projector
cinérama *m.* cinerama
cinétique *a.* kinetic; **— f.** kinetics
Cingalais *m. & a.* Cingalese, of Ceylon
cinglant *a.* biting, cutting; scathing
cingler *vt.* to cut, bite, sting; lash; **— vi.** to sail
cinq *a. & m.* five
cinquantaine *f.* fifty, about fifty; **avoir la —** be fifty years old
cinquante *a.* fifty
cinquantenaire *m.* fiftieth (golden) anniversary
cinquantième *a. & m.* fiftieth
cinquième *a. & m.* fifth
cintre *m.* arch, curve; hanger
cintrer *vt.* to arch, bend, curve
cirage *m.* shoe polish; wax; polishing, waxing
circoncire *vt.* to circumcise
circoncision *f.* circumcision
circonférence *f.* circumference
circonflexe *a.* circumflex
circonlocution *f.* circumlocution
circonscription *f.* circumscription, district
circonscrire *vt.* to circumscribe, circle; limit
circonspect *a.* circumspect, cautious
circonspection *f.* circumspection, caution, prudence
circonstance *f.* circumstance; case, situation; **— a. de —** occasional; improvised
circonstancié *a.* detailed
circonstanciel *a.* circumstantial; (gram.)

adverbial

circonvenir *vt.* to circumvent

circuit *m.* circuit; lap (sports)

circulaire *a. & f.* circular

circulation *f.* circulation; traffic; movement; action

circulatoire *a.* circulatory

circuler *vi.* to circulate; move about; pass from one to another

circumnavigation *f.* circumnavigation

cire *f.* wax; **-r** *vt.* to wax; polish

ciré *a.* waxed, polished; **toile -e** *f.* oilcloth

cireur *m.* polisher, waxer; bootblack

cireuses *f.* (mech.) floor waxer

cireux *a.* waxy

ciron *m.* mite, tiny animal infesting food

cirque *m.* circus

cirrhose *f.* cirrhosis

cirrus *m.* cirrus cloud

cisaille(s) *f.* (*pl.*) shears (for metal, branches); cuttings, metal shearings

cisailler *vt.* to shear

ciseau *m.* chisel; **-x** *pl.* scissors, shears, chisels

ciseler *vt.* to chisel; cut, carve; chase; emboss, tool

citadelle *f.* citadel

citadin *m.* townsman, citizen

citation *f.* citation; quotation; summons

cité *f.* city; fortified city; group of apartment buildings; **—** universitaire university dormitories; **-s ouvrières** housing project

citer *vt.* to quote; cite; summon, subpoena

citerne *f.* cistern

cithare *f.* zither

citoyen *m.*, **citoyenne** *f.* citizen

citoyenneté *f.* citizenship

citrate *m.* citrate

citrique *a.* citric

citron *m.* lemon; **—** *a.* lemon-colored **— pressé**, lemonade

citronnade *f.* lemonade, lemon drink

citronnelle *f.* citronella

citronnier *m.* lemon tree

citrouille *f.* gourd; pumpkin

cive *f.* scallion

civet *m.* stew; **—** de lièvre jugged hare

civette *f.* civet cat

civière *f.* stretcher, litter; bier

civil *a.* civil; civic; polite; **droit —** *m.* civil rights, common law; **—** *m.* civilian

civilisateur *a.* civilizing

civilisation *f.* civilization

civiliser *vt.* to civilize; **se —** to become civilized

civilité *f.* civility, politeness

civique *a.* civic; civil

civisme *m.* civic pride, civic duty

clabauder *vi.* to clamor, bawl

claie *f.* wicker work; trellis; screen

clair *a.* clear, bright; evident, plain; light; pale; **—** *m.* light, brightness, highlight; **— de lune** moonlight

clairet *a.* light; pale

claire-voie *f.* skylight; lattice; (arch.) clerestory

clairière *f.* clearing

clair-obscur *m.* chiaroscuro (art)

clairon *m.* bugle; bugler

claironner *vi.* to sound the bugle; **—** *vt.* to announce

clairsemé *a.* scattered; sparse, thin

clairvoyance *f.* clairvoyance, second sight

clairvoyant *a.* clear-sighted; clairvoyant

clamer *vt.* to cry out

clameur *f.* clamor, outcry

clamp *m.* surgical clamp

clan *m.* clan, tribe

clandestin *a.* clandestine; secret

clapet *m.* (mech.) valve

clapier *m.* rabbit warren; hutch

clapotement *m.* lapping, splashing

clapoter *vi.* to lap, splash (water)

claque *f.* (theat.) claque; slap; **—** *m.* opera hat

claquemurer *vt.* to shut up, confine; **s'—** to shut oneself up at home

claquer *vi.* to clap; slap; bang; click; crack; snap; chatter (teeth); **—** *vt.* slap; applaud

claqueur *m.* member of the claque

clarifier *vt.* to clarify; **se —** become clear

clarine *f.* cowbell

clarinette *f.* clarinet

clarté *f.* clearness, clarity, brightness; light

classe *f.* class, order, rank; school

classement *m.* classification; filing

classer *vt.* to class, classify; sort; file; **— selon le groupe sanguin** to blood-type

classeur *m.* sorter; file, filing cabinet

classification *f.* classification

classifier *vt.* to classify; sort

classique *a.* classic(al); **livre —** *m.* schoolbook, textbook; **—** *m.* classic; classicist

claudication *f.* limp, limping

clause *f.* clause, stipulation

claustration *f.* confinement; cloistering

clavecin *m.* harpsichord

claveciniste *m. & f.* harpsichordist

clavette *f.* (mech.) retaining pin

clavicule *f.* clavicle, collarbone

clavier *m.* keyboard; key ring

clayère *f.* oyster bed

clé, clef *f.* key; wrench; clue; (mus.) clef; **donner un tour de —** à to lock; **fermer à —** to lock; **sous —** locked, under lock and key

clémence *f.* clemency, leniency, mercy

clément a. lenient, merciful; mild

clenche, clenchette f. latch

cleptomane m. & f. kleptomaniac

cleptomanie f. kleptomania

clerc m. cleric; clergyman; clerk; scholar

clergé m. clergy

clérical a. (eccl.) clerical

cléricalisme m. clericalism

cliché m. stencil; negative; (print.) cut; cliché; photograph, picture; (coll.) banality

clicher vt. to stereotype

client m. client; customer; patient

clientèle f. customers, clientele; practice

clignement m. blinking; wink, winking

cligner vt. & vi. to wink; blink

clignotant m. (auto.) direction signal

clignotement m. twinkling, flickering; blinking

clignoter vi. to twinkle; flicker; wink; blink

climat m. climate

climatisation f. air-conditioning

climatisé a. air-conditioned

climatiser vt. to air-condition

clin d'œil m. twinkling of an eye

clinicien m. clinician

clinique a. clinical; — f. hospital

clinquant m. tinsel; foil; gaudiness, showiness

clip m. clip, pin (jewelry)

clique f. group, band, clique; drum and bugle corps; -s pl. wooden shoes

cliquet m. pawl, ratchet

cliqueter vi. to click; clink; jingle

cliquetis m. click(ing); clink(ing); jingling

clisse f. draining rack; wicker bottle-wrapping

cliver vt. to cleave, cut a gem

cloaque f. cesspool; sewer

cloche f. bell; glass-bell; blister (skin); — de sauvetage escape hatch (submarine)

clochement m. limp, limping

clocher vi. to limp

clocher m. steeple; bell tower, belfry

cloche-pied adv. à — hopping

clocheton m. small steeple, spire

clochette f. small bell

cloison f. partition, wall; — étanche ship's watertight door

cloisonner vt. to partition

cloître m. cloister; monastery

cloîtrer vt. to cloister; confine

clopiner vi. to limp

cloque f. blister

cloquer vt. & vi. to blister

clore vt. to close, shut; enclose; conclude, end

clos a. closed; concluded; — m. closing, end; enclosure

clôture f. fence, enclosure; cloture; closure; conclusion

clôturer vt. to fence, enclose; conclude

clou m. nail; boil; highlight; — de girofle clove

clouer vt. to nail, tack; pin, hold down

clouter vt. to trim with nails; passage clouté m. crosswalk

club m. club, society

clystère m. enema

coadjuteur m. coadjutor

coagulation f. coagulation

coaguler vt. to coagulate, congeal; se — to clot, coagulate, congeal

coaliser v., se — to form a coalition

coalition f. coalition; combination

coasser vi. to croak

coauteur m. coauthor

coaxial a. coaxial; câble — m. coaxial cable

cobalt m. cobalt

cobaye m. guinea pig

cobra m. cobra

cocaïne f. cocaine

cocaïnomane m. & f. cocaine addict

cocarde f. cockade

cocasse a. funny, ridiculous

coccinelle f. wood louse; lady bug (U.S.)

coche m. coach, stagecoach, 2-door sedan; barge; — f. notch

cocher m. coachman, driver; — vt. to check; notch; tally

cochère, porte — f. carriage entrance

cochon m. hog, pig; (fig.) swine; — de lait suckling pig; — d'Inde guinea pig

cockpit m. (avi.) cockpit

cocktail m. cocktail; cocktail party

coco m., noix de — f. coconut

cocon m. cocoon

cocotier m. coconut palm

cocotte f. saucepan, casserole; (coll.) hussy, streetwalker

code m. code; law; — postale d'arrondissement zip code number; — de district area code number

codéine f. codeine

codicille m. codicil

codifier vt. to codify; code

coefficient m. coefficient; factor

coercitif a. coercive

coercition f. coercion

cœur m. heart; feeling(s); courage; center, middle; à contre — against one's will; avoir mal au — to be sick to one's stomach; donner mal au — to nauseate

coffre m. chest, box, trunk, coffer

coffre-fort m. safe, strongbox

coffrer vt. to place in safety; (coll.) lock up, jail

coffret m. small box; — à bijoux jewel case

cognac *m.* brandy from Cognac
cognassier *m.* quince tree
cognée *f.* axe, hatchet
cogner *vt.* to hammer, knock; bump; — *vi.* knock; bump
cohérence *f.* coherence
cohérent *a.* coherent
cohéritier *m.* joint heir
cohésion *f.* cohesion, cohesiveness
cohorte *f.* cohort
cohue *f.* crowd, throng
coi, (coite) *a.* calm, quiet, peaceful
coiffer *vt.* to put on a head covering; cap; to dress the hair; se — to arrange one's hair or hat
coiffeur *m.* hairdresser; barber
coiffeuse *f.* hairdresser; dressing table
coin *m.* corner; nook; quiet place, spot; wedge
coincer *vt.* to wedge; se — *vi.* to jam, stick
coïncidence *f.* coincidence
coïncider *vi.* to coincide
coing *m.* quince
col *m.* collar; neck; (geog.) mountain pass
coléoptère *m.* beetle
colère *f.* anger; en — angry; mettre en — to anger; se mettre en — become very angry, lose one's temper
coléreux *a.* quick-tempered
colibri *m.* hummingbird
colifichet *m.* trinket
colimaçon *m.* snail; en — spiral
colin-maillard *m.* blindman's buff
colique *f.* colic
colis *m.* package, parcel
côlite *f.* colitis
collaborateur *m.*, **collaboratrice** *f.* collaborator; contributor; associate
collaboration *f.* collaboration
collaborer *vi.* to collaborate; contribute
collage *m.* pasting, gluing, mounting; collage; sizing; (coll.) common-law marriage
collant *a.* tight-fitting; sticky
collatéral *a. & m.* collateral
collation *f.* light meal; collation; conferring
collationner *vi.* to have a snack; — *vt.* to collate; confer
colle *f.* glue, paste
collecteur *m.* collector; (elec.) commutator; tuyau — sewage collector
collectif *a.* collective; joint, cooperative
collection *f.* collection, collecting
collectionner *vt.* to collect
collectionneur *m.* collector
collectivisme *m.* collectivism
collectivité *f.* collectivity
collège *m.* secondary school; college
collégial *a.* collegiate; (eccl.) of the chapter (canon); –e *f.* collegiate church
collègue *m.* colleague
coller *vt.* to paste, glue; stick; press; — *vi.* stick; cling
collerette *f.* cloth collar; metal flange; ring, pipe joint
collet *m.* collar; flange; neck; snare
colleter *vt.* to collar; s'— wrestle, scuffle with
collier *m.* necklace; harness collar; metal ring; (fig.) coup de — great effort
colline *f.* hill
collision *f.* collision
colonnade *f.* collonade
colloque *m.* conversation; conference
collusion *f.* collusion
colocataire *m. & f.* co-tenant
colombe *f.* dove
colombophile *m. & f.* pigeon raiser, pigeon fancier
colon *m.* colonist; settler
côlon *m.* (anat.) colon
colonial *a. & m.* colonial; soldier of colonial army
colonialisme *m.* colonialism
colonie *f.* colony; settlement
colonisation *f.* colonization
coloniser *vt.* to colonize; settle
colonne *f.* column, pillar
colophane *f.* colophony, rosin
coloration *f.* color, coloring
coloré *a.* colored; ruddy
colorer, colorier *vt.* to color
coloris *m.* coloring
colossal *a.* colossal, huge
colosse *m.* colossus, giant
colporter *vt.* to peddle; spread news
colporteur *m.* peddler
columbarium *m.* columbarium
comateux *a.* comatose
combat *m.* battle, fight, combat, struggle; hors de — out of action
combattant *m.* combatant
combattre *vt. & vi.* to fight
combien *adv.* how much, how many
combinaison *f.* combination; coveralls; (chem.) compound; machination; — s *f. pl.* lady's undergarment
combiné *m.* compound; — *a.* combined, joint
combiner *vt.* to combine, unite; contrive
comble *m.* top, summit; roofing; limit, end; — *a.* full, packed
combler *vt.* to fill; heap; overwhelm
combustible *a.* inflammable; — *m.* fuel; — exotique exotic fuel
combustion *f.* combustion
comédie *f.* comedy
comédien *m.* actor; –ne *f.* actress
comédon *m.* blackhead

comestible *m.* food, provision; — *a.* edible

comète *f.* comet

comique *a.* comic(al), funny; — *m.* comic, comedian; comic author; comedy

comité *m.* committee

commandant *m.* commander; major; commanding officer

commande *f.* order for goods; control, lever; control panel; **fait sur** — made to order

commandement *m.* command, order; commandment

commander *vt. & vi.* to command, order; control

commandeur *m.* (mil.) cavalry commander

commanditaire *m.* backer, financier

commandite *f.* joint-stock company

commanditer *vt.* to back, finance

commando *m.* (mil.) detachment, detail; commando group

comme *adv.* as, like; how; sort of; — *conj.* as, since

commémoraison *f.* commemoration (of a saint)

commémoratif *a.* commemorative; memorial

commémoration *f.* commemoration

commémorer *vt.* to commemorate

commençant *m.* beginner

commencement *m.* beginning

commencer *vt. & vi.* to begin, commence

comment *adv.* how; —! *interj.* what!

commentaire *m.* comment, commentary; —s *pl.* memoirs

commentateur *m.* commentator; author of commentaries

commenter *vt.* to comment on; annotate

commérage *m.* gossip

commerçant *m.* merchant, businessman; — *a.* commercial, business

commercer *vi.* to deal, trade, do business

commercial *a.* commercial, business; -e *f.* station wagon

commère *f.* gossip, busybody

commettre *vt.* to commit; do, make

commis *m.* clerk; **grand** — **de l'État** high official; — **voyageur** traveling salesman

commisération *f.* commiseration, pity

commissaire *m.* commissioner; commissar; purser

commissaire-priseur *m.* appraiser; auctioneer

commissariat *m.* commissariat; function of a commissioner; — **de police** police station

commission *f.* commission; committee, board; errand; (com.) payment for selling

commissionnaire *m.* factor; agent; messenger

commissionner *vt.* to delegate; authorize

commode *f.* chest of drawers; — *a.* convenient, comfortable, spacious; accommodating

commodité *f.* comfort, convenience, accommodation

commotion *f.* concussion (brain); commotion; shock

commuer *vt.* to commute (law)

commun *a.* common, ordinary, usual; commonplace; **en** — in common; cooperative(ly)

communal *a.* common; communal

communauté *f.* community

commune *f.* township, commune

communiant *m.* (eccl.) communicant

communicant *a.* communicating

communicatif *a.* communicative

communication *f.* communication; message; phone call; **fausse** — wrong number

communier *vi.* to take communion; commune

communiqué *m.* press release; official communication

communiquer *vt. & vi.* to communicate

communisant *m.* communist sympathizer

communisme *m.* communism

communiste *m. & f.* communist

commutation *f.* commutation

commutateur *m.* (elec.) switch, commutator

commutatrice *f.* (elec.) transformer

compact *a.* compact, solid

compagne *f.* female companion; spouse

compagnie *f.* company

compagnon *m.* companion, associate; worker, co-worker

comparable *a.* comparable

comparaison *f.* comparison

comparaître *vi.* (law) to appear

comparatif *a. & m.* comparative

comparé *a.* comparative; compared

comparer *vt.* to compare

comparoir *vi.* to appear in court

comparse *m. & f.* (theat.) supernumerary

compartiment *m.* compartment; division

comparution *f.* court appearance

compas *m.* compass; calipers; (fig.) standard

compassé *a.* stiff, set; formal; regularized

compasser *vt.* to measure with compass; weigh, consider

compatible *a.* compatible; — *f.* compatability

compatir *vi.* to sympathize

compatissant *a.* compassionate; sympathetic

compatriote *m.* fellow countryman

compensateur *a.* compensating; equalizing; — *m.* compensator; equalizer

compensation *f.* compensation; equalization; adjustment; **chambre de** — *f.* clearing house

compenser *vt.* to compensate, make up for; equalize; adjust

compérage *m.* gossip; plotting

compétence *f.* competence; competency; (fig.) jurisdiction

compétent *a.* competent; reliable

compilateur *m.* compiler

compilation *f.* compilation, compiling

compiler *vt.* to compile

complainte *f.* lament

complaire *vi.* to please; **se** — **à** take pleasure in, delight in

complaisance *f.* kindness, goodness, obligingness; complacency

complaisant *a.* obliging; compliant; complacent

complément *m.* complement

complémentaire *a.* complementary

complet (complète) *a.* complete; full; — *m.* man's suit; **au** — full; **au grand** — in force; at full strength

compléter *vt.* to complete; finish

complexe *a.* complex, complicated; (math.) compound; — *m.* complex

complexion *f.* constitution, disposition

complexité *f.* complexity

complice *m. & f.* accomplice, accessory

complicité *f.* complicity

compliment *m.* compliment

complimenter *vt.* to compliment; congratulate

compliqué *a.* complicated, intricate

compliquer *vt.* to complicate; **se** — become complicated

complot *m.* plot, conspiracy

comploter *vt.* to plot, conspire

comploteur *m.* plotter, conspirator

componction *f.* compunction

comportement *m.* behavior

comporter *vt.* to permit; comprise; **se** — to behave

composant *a. & m.* component

composé *a.* composed; compound, composite; — *m.* compound

composer *vt. & vi.* to compose; compound; write; set (type); **se** — **de** consist of, be composed of

compositeur *m.* composer; compositor

composition *f.* composition; composing; compound; typesetting

compost *m.* compost

composteur *m.* (print.) composing stick

compotier *m.* compote dish; dish for sauce

compréhensible *a.* comprehensible

compréhensif *a.* comprehensive; understanding

compréhension *f.* comprehension, understanding

comprendre *vt.* to understand; include, comprise; **se faire** — make oneself understood

compresse *f.* compress

compresseur *m.* compressor; **rouleau** — *m.* steam roller

compression *f.* compression; repression

comprimé *m.* tablet, pill; — *a.* compressed

comprimer *vt.* to compress; repress

compris *a.* understood, included; **y** — including

compromettre *vt. & vi.* to compromise; expose, put in embarrassment *or* peril

compromis *m.* compromise, mutual agreement

comptabilité *f.* accounting, bookkeeping

comptable *m.* accountant, bookkeeper; — *a.* accountable

comptant *a.* counted on, prompt; **argent** — *m.* ready money, cash

compte *m.* account, computation; value; profit; **à** — on account; **à bon** — cheap; — **rendu** *m.* report; review; **se rendre** — **de** to realize, be aware of; **tenir** — **de** take into account; bear in mind

compte-fils *m.* magnifier

compte-gouttes *m.* medicine dropper

compter *vt.* to count; number; expect; — *vi.* count, rely; **sans** — to say nothing of, not to mention, not counting

compte-tours *m.* revolution counter

compteur *m.* meter; speedometer; counter; comptometer

comptoir *m.* counter; cashier's desk

compulser *vt.* to subpoena records; **to examine records**

computation *f.* computation

computer *vt.* to compute

comte *m.* count, earl

comté *m.* county, earldom

comtesse *f.* countess

concasser *vt.* to crush

concasseur *m.* stone crusher, crushing machine

concéder *vt.* to concede, grant, admit

concentration *f.* concentration

concentré *a.* concentrated; (fig.) **taciturn**

concentrer *vt.* to concentrate, condense, repress; **se** — concentrate

concentrique *a.* concentric

concept *m.* concept, idea

conception *f.* conception; idea; image

concernant *prep.* concerning, about

concerner *vt.* to concern

concert *m.* concert; harmony; **de** — **avec** together with, hand in hand with

concertant *a.* performing together

concerté *a.* concerted
concerter *vt.* to plan, concert
concession *f.* concession; grant
concevable *a.* conceivable
concevoir *vt.* to conceive; imagine, understand
concierge *m. & f.* doorkeeper, janitor
concile *m.* (eccl.) council
conciliateur *a.* conciliating, conciliatory
conciliation *f.* conciliation; reconciliation
concilier *vt.* to conciliate; reconcile
concis *a.* concise, short
concision *f.* conciseness, brevity
concitoyen *m.* fellow citizen
conclave *m.* conclave
concluant *a.* conclusive
conclure *vt.* to conclude; decide; end, finish; drive or strike a bargain
conclusif *a.* conclusive
conclusion *f.* conclusion; decision; end, ending
concombre *m.* cucumber
concordance *f.* concordance; (gram.) agreement
concordat *m.* concordat, agreement
concorde *f.* harmony, concord, agreement
concorder *vi.* to agree
concourir *vi.* to compete; converge; co-operate
concours *m.* competitive examination; concourse; assistance, aid; concurrence
concret *a.* concrete
concupiscence *f.* lust
concurremment *adv.* concurrently; jointly
concurrence *f.* competition; concurrence
concurrencer *vt.* to rival; compete with
concurrent *a.* competitive; — *m.* competitor
concussion *f.* extortion, embezzlement
condamnable *a.* blameworthy
condamnation *f.* condemnation; blame, censure; legal sentence *or* judgment
condamner *vt.* to condemn, sentence; blame, censure, criticize
condensateur *m.* condenser
condensation *f.* condensation; gas liquidation; condensing
condensé *m.* resumé
condenser *vt.* to condense, liquify gas; se — condense (fig.) to group, assemble
condenseur *m.* condenser
condescendance *f.* condescension
condescendre *vi.* to condescend
condiment *m.* condiment, seasoning, spice
condisciple *m.* fellow student
condition *f.* condition, state; circumstance(s); position; rank; status; station; à — on approval; à — que on condition that; sans — unconditional
conditionnel *a.* conditional; — *m.* (gram.)
conditional
conditionner *vt.* to condition
condoléance *f.* condolence
conducteur *m.*, **conductrice** *f.* leader; driver; motorman; (elec.) conductor; overseer, foreman; — *a.* conducting; driving
conduire *vt.* to conduct, lead; drive; se — to behave; **permis de** — *m.* driver's license
conduit *m.* conduit, pipe, main
conduite *f.* conduct, behavior; driving; direction, supervision; flue; main; tubing; pipeline
cône *m.* cone
confection *f.* making; manufacturing; ready-made clothes
confectionner *vt.* to make; manufacture
confédération *f.* confederation, confederacy
confédérer *vt.* to confederate
conférence *f.* lecture; conference
conférencier *m.* lecturer
conférer *vt.* to compare; confer, bestow; — *vi.* confer, discuss
confesser *vt.* to confess; se — (eccl.) to confess
confesseur *m.* (eccl.) confessor
confession *f.* confession
confiance *f.* confidence; reliance; trust; (digne) de — reliable, trustworthy
confiant *a.* confiding; confident
confidamment *adv.* confidently, in confidence
confidence *f.* confidence, trust; secrecy; secret
confident *m.*, **confidente** *f.* trusted friend, confidant
confidentiel *a.* confidential
confier *vt.* to confide; trust, entrust; se — à to put one's trust in
configuration *f.* configuration
confiner *vt.* to confine; — *vi.* to border, verge on
confins *m. pl.* confines, limits
confire *vt.* to preserve, pickle, candy
confirmation *f.* confirmation
confirmer *vt.* to confirm
confiserie *f.* confectionary
confiseur *m.* confectioner
confisquer *vt.* to confiscate
confit *a.* preserved; candied
confiture *f.* jam, preserve(s)
confiturière *f.* jam dish; dealer in preserves
conflagration *f.* conflagration
conflit *m.* conflict, clash, struggle
confluence *f.* confluence
confluer *vi.* to meet, come together
confondre *vt.* to confound, mingle, con-

fuse, mistake; disconcert, upset; se — to mix, blend

conformation *f.* conformation

conforme *a.* conformable, consistent; — à corresponding to; according to; copie — *f.* true copy

conformément *adv.* in conformity; — à in accordance with, according to

conformer *vt.* to form; conform; se — to conform, comply

conformiste *m. & f.* conformist

conformité *f.* conformity; similarity

confort *m.* comfort

confortable *a.* comfortable

confrère *m.* colleague

confrérie *f.* brotherhood

confronter *vt.* to confront, compare

confus *a.* confused; embarassed; blurred; overcome

confusément *adv.* confusedly; vaguely

confusion *f.* confusion; embarrassment

congé *m.* leave, furlough; dismissal; vacation; jour de — *m.* holiday

congédiement *m.* dismissal

congédier *vt.* to discharge, dismiss

congélation *f.* freezing; congealing, coagulation

congeler *vt.* to congeal, freeze

congère *f.* snowdrift

congestion *f.* congestion; accumulation in blood vessels

congestionné *a.* flushed face

congestionner *vt.* to congest; se — to become congested

conglomérat *m.* conglomerate

conglomérer *vt.* to conglomerate

congre *m.* conger eel

congrégation *f.* congregation

congrès *m.* congress

congressiste *m.* delegate

congru *a.* precise; sufficient; suitable

conifère *a.* coniferous; — *m.* conifer

conique *a.* conic(al)

conjecturer *vt.* to conjecture, guess

conjoindre *vt.* to join in marriage; unite

conjoint *a.* joined, joint; married

conjoncteur *m.* automatic switch

conjonctif *a.* (gram.) conjunctive; relative; (anat.) connective

conjonction *f.* conjunction; connection, joining, union

conjoncture *f.* contingency, conjuncture, juncture

conjugaison *f.* conjugation

conjugal *a.* conjugal; vie -e *f.* marriage, married life

conjuguer *vt.* to join; (gram.) to conjugate

conjurateur *m.* conjurer

conjuration *f.* conspiracy, plot; exorcism

conjuré *m.* conspirator, plotter

conjurer *vt.* to implore, beg, beseech; conspire, plot

connaissance *f.* knowledge; acquaintance; consciousness; faire la — de to meet, become acquainted with a person; perdre — to lose consciousness; sans — unconscious

connaissement *m.* bill of lading

connaisseur *m.* connoisseur, judge, expert

connaître *vt.* to know; be acquainted with; se — à, se — en be an expert in, be a good judge of

connecter *vt.* (elec.) to connect

connecteur *m.* (elec.) connector

connexe *a.* connected; related

connexion *f.* connection; relation

connexité *f.* relationship, connection

connivence *f.* connivance

connu *a.* known, well-known

conque *f.* conch; conch shell; (anat.) concha

conquérant *a.* conquering; — *m.* conqueror

conquérir *vt.* to conquer; gain

conquête *f.* conquest; acquired property, acquisition

consacré *a.* consecrated; hallowed, sacred; time-honored

consacrer *vt.* to consecrate; ordain; sanctify; dedicate, devote

consanguin *a.* related on the father's side

consciemment *adv.* consciously

conscience *f.* conscience, consciousness; conscientiousness; avoir — de to be aware of, be conscious of; avoir de la — be conscientious; en — *adv.* in truth

consciencieux *a.* conscientious

conscient *a.* conscious, aware

conscrit *m.* recruit, conscript, draftee

consécration *f.* consecration; dedication

consécutif *a.* consecutive

conseil *m.* counsel, advice; council, committee; — d'administration board of directors; — d'Etat legislative advisory group; — de guerre court-martial; — de révision draft board; — de prud'hommes labor-management arbitration committee; — des ministres cabinet; — général local (departmental) legislature

conseiller *m.* counsellor; councillor; adviser

conseiller *vt.* to counsel, advise, recommend

consensus *m.* consensus

consentement *m.* consent; approval

consentir *vi.* to consent, agree; approve; — *vt.* to grant; approve

conséquemment *adv.* consequently

conséquence *f.* consequence, conclusion,

result; importance; inference

conséquent a. consistent; (coll.) important; **par —** consequently

conservateur a. preserving; conservative; **— m.** keeper; curator; librarian; conservative

conservation f. conservation, preservation; keeping

conservatisme m. conservatism

conservatoire m. conservatory, school of music

conserve f. preserved food, canned food; **de —** preserved; canned; **—s** pl. preserves, canned goods

conserver vt. to conserve, preserve; keep, hold, maintain; **se —** to keep, remain preserved

conserverie f. canning factory or industry

considérable a. considerable; extensive, large; important

considérant m. motive

considération f. consideration; regard, respect

considérer vt. to consider; regard

consignataire m. (com.) consignee; legal trustee

consignation f. (com.) consignment

consigne f. (mil.) order, instructions; password; (rail.) checkroom

consigner vt. to consign; confine; deposit money; check baggage

consistance f. consistency; stability

consistant a. firm, set

consister vi. to consist

consolateur a. consoling; **— m.** consoler

console f. bracket; console table

consoler vt. to console, comfort

consolidation f. consolidation; (med.) buildup

consolider vt. to consolidate; **se —** to heal

consommateur m. consumer; café customer

consommation f. consummation; consumption; drink, beverage

consommé a. consummate, perfect; **— m.** consommé

consommer vt. to consummate; consume

consomptif a. consumptive

consonance f. consonance

consonne f. (gram.) consonant

consort a. consort; **prince — m.** prince consort; **—s** m. pl. interested parties

consortium m. association, company, group

conspirateur m. conspirator, plotter

conspirer vt. & vi. to conspire, plot

constable m. constable, policeman

constamment adv. constantly

constance f. constancy; perseverance

constant a. constant; unchanging, steady;

uniform; (math.) invariable

constat m. official declaration, examination

constatation f. proof; statement, declaration; authentication

constater vt. to declare; take note of; certify; establish

constellé a. spangled, star-spangled

consteller vt. to bespangle

consterner vt. to consternate, dismay

constipant a. constipating

constipation f. constipation

constituant a. constituent, component; **— m.** voter, constituent

constituer vt. to constitute, set up; make, take; **— prisonnier** to take prisoner, take into custody

constitutif a. constituant

constitution f. constitution; composition

constitutionnalité f. constitutionality

constitutionnel a. constitutional

constricteur a. & m. constrictor

constriction f. constriction; compression of diameter

constructeur m. constructor; builder, engineer

constructif a. constructive

construction f. construction, building; **— mécanique** mechanical engineering

construire vt. to construct; build; (gram.) to construe

consulaire a. consular

consulat m. consulate; consulship

consultant a. consulting; **— m.** consultant

consultation f. consultation

consulte f. (pol. & eccl.) consultation

consulter vt. to consult

consumer vt. to consume, destroy; use up

contact m. contact; touch; connection; switch

contacter vt. to contact, come in contact with

contagieux a. contagious

container m. case

contamination f. contamination

contaminer vt. to contaminate

conte m. tale, story

contemplateur m. contemplator

contemplatif a. contemplative

contemplation f. contemplation; meditation, thought

contempler vt. to contemplate; meditate

contemporain a. & m. contemporary

contempteur a. contemptuous

contenance f. countenance; content(s), capacity

contenant m. container

contenir vt. to contain; restrain

content a. content, satisfied, happy, glad

contentement m. contentment, satisfac-

tion
contenter *vt.* to content, satisfy; **se — de** to be content with, be satisfied with
contentieux *a.* contentious
contention *f.* contention; contest
contenu *m.* contents
conter *vt.* to relate, tell
contestable *a.* disputable, debatable
contestation *f.* dispute
conteste, sans — *adv.* incontestably
contester *vt. & vi.* to dispute, contest
conteur *m.* storyteller
contexte *m.* context
contexture *f.* structure, arrangement
contigu (contiguë) *a.* adjoining, adjacent, contiguous
contiguïté *f.* contiguity
continence *f.* continence
continent *m.* continent; **–al** *m.* continental
contingence *f.* contingency
contingent *a.* contingent; **—** *m.* contingent; quota
continu *a.* continual, continuous
continuel *a.* continual; continuous
continûment *adv.* continually; continuously
continuer *vt. & vi.* to continue
continuité *f.* continuity
contondant *a.* blunt
contorsion *f.* contortion
contortionner *vt.* to contort
contortionniste *m. & f.* contortionist
contour *m.* outline, contour
contourné *a.* twisted; affected
contournement *m.* detour, bypass
contourner *vt.* to outline, shape; bypass, skirt; twist, distort; **— la loi** to get around the law
contractant *m.* person contracting; **—** *a.* contracting
contracte *a.* contracted, agreed
contracté *a.* contracted (made shorter)
contracter *vt.* to contract; acquire; **se —** to contract, narrow
contractuel *a.* contractual; stipulated by contract
contradiction *f.* contradiction
contradictoire *a.* contradictory
contraindre *vt.* to compel, restrain, constrain, force
contraint *a.* constrained, forced
contrainte *f.* restraint; force, constraint
contraire *a.* contrary, opposite; against; **au —** on the contrary
contrarier *vt.* to thwart; vex, annoy; go against
contrariété *f.* contrariness; annoyance
contraste *m.* contrast
contraster *vt. & vi.* to contrast
contrat *m.* contract, agreement

contravention *f.* violation, misdemeanor; traffic ticket
contre *prep.* against; contrary to; near by; **—** *adv.* against; near by; **—** *m.* counter, opposite; **le pour et le —** the pros and cons; **par —** on the other hand
contre-amiral *m.* rear admiral
contre-appel *m.* second appeal
contre-attaque *f.* counterattack
contre-attaquer *vt.* to counterattack
contre-avions *a.* antiaircraft
contrebalancer *vt.* to counterbalance
contrebande *f.* contraband; smuggling
contrebandier *m.* smuggler
contrebas, en — *adv.* downwards
contrebasse *f.* double bass; tuba; double bass player
contrebassiste, contrebassier *m.* double bass player
contrebasson *m.* contrabassoon
contre-boutant *m.* buttress
contre-bouter, contre-buter *vt.* to buttress
contrecarrer *vt.* to foil, thwart; oppose
contre-chant *m.* counter theme
contrecœur *m.* back of a fireplace; fireplace plaque; (rail.) guard rail; **à —** *adv.* unwillingly, reluctantly
contrecoup *m.* rebound; backfire; result
contredanse *f.* contredanse, country dance
contrée *f.* country, region
contre-écrou *m.* lock nut
contre-épaulette *f.* epaulette without fringe
contre-espion *m.* counterspy
contre-espionnage *m.* counterespionnage
contrefaçon *f.* counterfeit; forgery; counterfeiting; plagiarism
contrefacteur *m.* forger, counterfeiter
contrefaction *f.* counterfeiting
contrefaire *vt.* to counterfeit, forge, imitate; disguise
contre-feu *m.* reverse fire (fire fighting)
contre-fil *m.* opposite direction
contrefort *m.* buttress; spur; foothill(s); reinforcement
contre-haut, en — *adv.* up, upwards, above
contre-jour *m.* (photo.) light from opposite side of an object; **à —** *adv.* against the light
contremaître *m.* foreman; (naut.) petty officer
contremander *vt.* to countermand
contremarque *f.* countersign; pass-out check
contrepartie *f.* counterpart; return match (sports)
contre-pas *m.* rapid half-step; change in step (marching)
contre-plaqué *a.* laminated; **bois —** *m.*

plywood
contre-plaquer *vt.* to laminate, manufacture plywood
contrepoids *m.* counterweight, counterbalance
contre-poil *m.* opposite direction; **à —** *adv.* against the grain
contrepoint *m.* (mus.) counterpoint
contre-pointer *vt.* to quilt
contrepoison *m.* antidote
contrer *vt.* to counter; **—** *vi.* to double (at cards)
contre-rail *m.* guard rail
contre-révolution *f.* counterrevolution
contre-révolutionnaire *a. & m. & f.* counterrevolutionary
contresens *m.* misinterpretation
contresigner *vt.* to countersign
contretemps *m.* mishap; delay; (mus.) syncopation; **à —** inopportunely
contre-torpilleur *m.* destroyer (navy)
contrevenant *m.* lawbreaker; nonconformer
contrevenir *vt.* to break a law; act contrarily
contrevent *m.* window shutter
contribuable *m. & f.* taxpayer
contribuer *vi.* to contribute
contribution *f.* contribution; tax
contrister *vt.* to sadden
contrit *a.* contrite, grieved
contrôle *m.* inspection, verification; auditing; ticket-taking
contrôler *vt.* to supervise; check; inspect-audit; verify; control, restrain
contrôleur *m.* ticket collector; auditor; inspector; comptroller
controuvé *a.* made-up, invented, imagined
controversable *a.* controversial
controverse *f.* controversy; discussion
controverser *vt.* to debate; controvert
contumace *f.* contempt of court; nonappearance; default
contus *a.* bruised; **–ion** *f.* contusion, bruise
contusionner *vt.* to bruise
convaincant *a.* convincing
convaincre *vt.* to convince; convict
convalescent *a. & m.* convalescent
convenable *a.* suitable, proper, appropriate, becoming
convenance *f.* suitability; expediency; propriety, convention; conformity
convenir *vi.* to agree; fit, suit
convention *f.* convention; agreement; **de — conventional**
conventionnel *a.* conventional
convenu *a.* agreed, arranged, settled
convergeance *f.* convergence
converger *vi.* to converge
conversation *f.* conversation

converser *vi.* to converse, talk
converti *m.* convert
convertibilité *f.* convertibility
convertible *a.* (law) convertible
convertir *vt.* to convert; **se — (en)** to become converted; turn into, change into
convertissable *a.* convertible
convertisseur *m.* converter; transformer
convexe *a.* convex
convexité *f.* convexity
conviction *f.* conviction; belief
convié *m.* one guest
convier *vt.* to invite
convive *m.* guest; table companion
convocation *f.* convocation; convening
convoi *m.* funeral procession; convoy
convoiter *vt.* to covet, want, desire
convoiteur *a.* covetous
convoitise *f.* covetousness; cupidity; immoderate desire
convoquer *vt.* to convoke; summon
convoyer *vt.* to convoy
convoyeur *a.* convoying, escorting; **—** *m.* escort, convoy; conveyor
convulser *vt.* to convulse
convulsif *a.* convulsive
convulsionner *vt.* to convulse
coopérateur *m.* co-operator; member of a co-operative
coopératif *a.* co-operative
coopération *f.* co-operation
coopérer *vi.* co-operate
coordination *f.* co-ordination
coordonnateur *m.* co-ordinator; **—** *a.* co-ordinating
coordonné *a.* co-ordinate; co-ordinated; **–es** *f. pl.* co-ordinates
copeau *m.* chip, wood shaving
copie *f.* copy; imitation; reproduction; **— conforme** true copy, authenticated copy
copier *vt.* to copy, imitate; reproduce
copieux *a.* copious; hearty
copilote *m.* copilot
copiste *m.* copyist; copier; clerk; **faute de — ** *f.* clerical error
coposséder *vt.* to own jointly
copra(h) *m.* copra
copte *m. & f.* Copt; **—** *a.* coptic
copulatif *a.* co-ordinating
coq *m.* rooster, cock; weathervane; sea cook; **— de bruyère** grouse; **poids —** bantamweight (boxing)
coq-à-l'âne *m.* confused speech; farce, cock-and-bull story
coque *f.* shell; cocoon; hull; **œuf à la — ** *m.* soft-boiled egg
coquelicot *m.* (bot.) poppy
coqueluche *f.* whooping cough

coquerie *f.* galley, ship's kitchen
coqueriquer *vi.* to crow
coquet *a.* coquettish; natty
coqueter *vi.* to flirt
coquetier *m.* egg cup; egg and chicken wholesaler
coquetière *f.* egg cooker
coquette *f.* coquette, flirt
coquetterie *f.* flirtation, coquetry
coquillage *m.* shellfish; shell
coquille *f.* shell; case, casing; typographical error; — **Saint-Jacques** creamed scallops; **huîtres en** — *f. pl.* scalloped oysters
coquin *m.* rogue, rascal; — *a.* roguish
cor *m.* horn; French horn; corn (foot); — **de chasse** hunting horn
corail *m.* coral
corbeau *m.* raven; crow
corbeille *f.* basket; wedding presents; — **à papier** wastepaper basket
corbillard *m.* hearse
cordage *m.* rope; string
corde *f.* cord, rope, line; string; thread; wire; chord
cordé *a.* heart-shaped
cordeau *m.* string, lace
cordée *f.* cord (of wood); group of mountain climbers (roped together)
cordelier *m.* Franciscan friar
corder *vt.* to cord; make into rope; string
cordial *a.* cordial, warm, hearty; stimulating; — *m.* cordial; stimulant
cordialité *f.* cordiality
cordier *m.* ropemaker
cordon *m.* strand; cord; ribbon; tape; door pull; cordon; — **bleu** expert chef; — **de soulier** shoelace
cordonnerie *f.* shoemaking; shoe repairing
cordonnier *m.* shoemaker
Corée *f.* Korea; **-n** *m. & a.* Korean
coriace *a.* tough, leathery
Corinthe *f.* Corinth; **raisin de** — *m.* currant
corinthien *a.* Corinthian
cormoran *m.* cormorant
cornac *m.* elephant boy; guide
corne *f.* horn; dog-ear a page; — **à souliers** shoehorn
corné *a.* horny
cornée *f.* cornea
corneille *f.* crow
cornemuse *f.* bagpipes
corner *vt. & vi.* to blare out; (auto.) to blow the horn
cornet *m.* horn; trumpet; cornet; paper cone; — **acoustique** ear trumpet; — **à pistons** cornet with valves; **glace en** — ice-cream cone
cornette *f.* nun's headdress

corniche *f.* cornice; ledge
cornichon *m.* gherkin, pickle
Cornouailles *f. pl.* Cornwall
cornouiller *m.* dogwood
cornu *a.* horned
cornue *f.* (chem.) retort
corollaire *m.* corollary
coronaire *a.* coronary
corporatif *a.* corporate
corporel *a.* corporal; corporeal; bodily
corps *m.* body; substance; corpse; corps; font (type); — **à** — hand-to-hand; — **simple** (chem.) element; — **composé** (chem.) compound; **prendre** — to develop, take shape; **saisir au** — to arrest (law)
corps-à-corps *m.* hand-to-hand combat; clinch (boxing)
corpulent *a.* corpulent, fat
corpuscule *m.* corpuscle
correct *a.* correct; accurate; right; proper
correcteur *m.* corrector; proofreader
correctif *a.* corrective
correction *f.* correction, correcting; correctness, propriety; proofreading; punishment; reprimand
correctionnel *a.* relating to a misdemeanor; **-le** *f.* misdemeanor court
corrélatif *a.* correlative
corrélation *f.* correlation
correspondance *f.* correspondence; interchange, transfer
correspondant *a.* corresponding; — *m.* correspondent
correspondre *vi.* to correspond; communicate
corriger *vt.* to correct; proofread; punish
corroborer *vt.* to corroborate
corrodant *a. & m.* corrosive
corroder *vt.* to corrode
corrompre *vt.* to corrupt; spoil; bribe
corrompu *a.* corrupt; spoiled
corrosif *a. & m.* corrosive
corroyer *vt.* to plane (wood); solder, weld; prepare (leather)
corrupteur *a.* corrupting; — *m.* corrupter
corruption *f.* corruption; corruptness; bribery
corsage *m.* bust, bodice; blouse
corsaire *m.* corsair, pirate
Corse *f.* Corsica; — *m. & f. & a.* Corsican
corsé *a.* full-bodied; (fig.) scabrous
corselet *m.* bodice
cortege *m.* cortege, train, retinue, procession; funeral
cortisone *f.* cortizone
corvée *f.* drudgery; unpleasant task; hard labor; **tenue de** — *f.* (mil.) fatigues
corvette *f.* corvette; **capitaine de** — lieutenant commander

cosignataire *m. & f.* cosigner
cosinus *m.* (math.) cosine
cosmétique *a. & m.* cosmetic
cosmique *a.* cosmic
cosmopolite *a.* cosmopolitan
cosmos *m.* cosmos
cosse *f.* pod, husk, shell
costume *m.* costume, dress, suit
costumer *vt.* to costume
cosy *m.* cosy corner; studio bed
cote *f.* number; quota; mark; classification; (com.) price, quotation
côte *f.* rib; seacoast; hill; chop; — à — side by side
côté *m.* side; way; à — near, by, on one side; à — de beside, next to; d'un — on one hand; de l'autre — on the other hand; on the other side; across; de — aside, to one side; du — de in the direction of
coteau *m.* hill, hillside; slope
côtelé *a.* ribbed cloth; corded; corduroy
côtelette *f.* chop, cutlet
coter *vt.* to mark; number; classify; quote a price; assess
coterie *f.* group, set, coterie
cothurne *m.* buskin
côtier *a.* coastal
cotisation *f.* share; dues, fee; assessment
cotiser *vi.* to pay one's share
coton *m.* cotton
cotonnade *f.* cotton goods
cotonner *vt.* to pad, stuff with cotton; (se) — *vi.* to become fluffy, downy
cotonnerie *f.* cotton field; cotton raising; cotton factory
cotonneux *a.* fluffy; downy
cotonnier *a.* cotton; relating to cotton; — *m.* cotton plant
côtoyer *vt.* to border on; stay close to, hug (the shore)
cotre *m.* (naut.) cutter
cotte *f.* short skirt; — à bretelles overalls; — de mailles coat of mail
cou *m.* neck; couper le — à to behead
couard *a.* cowardly; — *m.* coward
couardise *f.* cowardice
couchage *m.* bedding; coating; sac de — *m.* sleeping bag
couchant *a.* setting; — *m.* sunset, west; decline
couche *f.* bed; confinement; layer, coat; fausse — miscarriage
couché *a.* lying; in bed
coucher *vt.* to put to bed; put down, lay down; — en joue to aim at; se — to go to bed; lie down; — *m.* setting of sun; going to bed; bed, lodging
couchette *f.* berth; crib
coucou *m.* cuckoo; (bot.) daffodil

coude *m.* elbow; bend; angle; coup de — *m.* nudge, poke
cou-de-pied *m.* instep
couder *vt.* to bend like an elbow
coudoyer *vt.* to elbow, jostle
coudre *vt. & vi.* to sew; machine à — *f.* sewing machine
couenne *f.* rind; skin; birthmark
couette *f.* (coll.) feather bed; grating (on escape valve); strainer
couguar *m.* cougar
coulage *m.* pouring; leaking; (naut.) scuttling; waste
coulant *a.* flowing, smooth; nœud — *m.* slipknot
coulé *a.* cast *or* poured metal
coulée *f.* flow; casting; pouring
couler *vi.* to flow, run; leak; founder, sink; — *vt.* pour; sink, scuttle
couleur *f.* color; paint; complexion; suit at cards
couleuvre *f.* snake, serpent
coulisse *f.* groove; slide; (theat.) wing à — sliding
coulisseau *m.* slide, runner
couloir *m.* passage, corridor; lobby
coup *m.* blow, throw, stroke; knock, tap, rap; thrust; shot; attempt, coup; — de feu gun shot; — de froid chill, cold; — d'œil glance, look; — de sang (med.) stroke; — de téléphone telephone call; — de tête butt; rash action; — de vent gust of wind; encore un — once again; en venir aux —s to come to blows; sur le — on the spot, right off, outright; tout à — suddenly, all of a sudden; tout d'un — at one shot; at once
coupable *a.* guilty; culpable; sinful, wrong; — *m. & f.* culprit, guilty one
coupant *a.* sharp, cutting; — *m.* sword edge
coup-de-poing *m.* brass knuckles (U.S.); fist blow
coupe *f.* cut, cutting; haircut; cross section; cup, champagne glass
coupé *a.* cut, broken; — *m.* (auto.) coupe
coupe-circuit *m.* circuit-breaker; fuse
coupe-coupe *m.* machete
coupe-feu *m.* fire break
coupe-fil *m.* wirecutters
coupe-gorge *m.* hazard, danger spot
coupe-jarret *m.* assassin
coupe-légumes *m.* vegetable cutter
coupe-ongles *m.* nail clippers
coupe-papier *m.* paper knife
couper *vt.* to cut; cross; interrupt, cut off, break; turn off; trump cards; cut wine, water down; se — to cut oneself; intersect
couperet *m.* chopper, cleaver; guillotine

blade

couperose *f.* (med.) acne; (chem.) blue vitriol

coupeur *m.* cutter

coupe-vent *m.* windbreaker

couple *m.* couple, pair; — *f.* couple; yoke; brace

coupler *vt.* to couple, connect, join

couplet *m.* stanza, verse

coupleur *m.* coupler

coupoir *m.* cutter, cutting tool

coupole *f.* cupola

coupon *m.* remnant, cutting; coupon

coupure *f.* cut, slit; cutting, clipping; banknote (under 1000 francs)

cour *f.* court; yard; courtship; **faire la —** **à** to court

courage *m.* courage, bravery, valor; (fig.) heart, spirit

courageux *a.* courageous, brave

courailler *vi.* to run around, run from side to side

couramment *adv.* fluently; easily; currently

courant *a.* current, running; present; **prix** **—** *m.* price list; — *m.* current, flow, stream; course; **— d'air** draft; **être au** **—** **de** to know about, be informed about

courbature *f.* aching, stiffness

courbaturé *a.* aching, stiff

courbe *f.* curve; — *a.* curved, crooked, bent

courber *vt.* to bend, bow; curve; — *vi.* to bend, sag, droop; **se —** to bend, stoop

courbure *f.* curve, curvature, bend

courette *f.* small courtyard

coureur *m.* runner, racer; wanderer; adventurer; **— de spectacles** playgoer

courge *f.* gourd, squash

courgette *f.* zucchini

courir *vi.* to run; race; — *vt.* to run, run after, hunt, pursue; run, take a risk

courlis *m.* plover

couronne *f.* crown; coronet; wreath

couronnement *m.* coronation; crowning

couronner *vt.* to crown; cap; (fig.) honor, pay

courrier *m.* courier; mail; column, section of a newspaper

courriériste *m.* columnist, feature editor

courroie *f.* strap; drive-belt

courroucer *vt.* to irritate; anger

courroux *m.* anger, wrath

cours *m.* course; current, stream; way; price, rate; lecture; **au — de** during, in the course of; **— du change** rate of exchange; **en — de route** on the way, along the way

course *f.* running; racing; race; trip; errand; flight, course, path; **champ de —s**

racetrack; **faire des —s** to go shopping

coursier *m.* messenger; steed

coursive *f.* passageway to ship cabin

court *a.* short; concise; brief; — *adv.* short; **à —** de short of; — *m.* tennis court

courtage *m.* brokerage; fee, commission

courtaud *a.* short, stocky

court-circuit *m.* short circuit

courtepointe *f.* quilt

courtier *m.* broker; jobber; agent

courtisan *m.* courtier; **-e** *f.* courtesan

courtiser *vt.* to court; woo

courtois *a.* courteous, polite; courtly

courtoisie *f.* courtesy, politeness

couru *a.* sought after; (fig. & coll.) sure thing

couseuse *f.* seamstress; sewing machine

cousin *m.*, **cousine** *f.* cousin; **—germain(e)** first cousin

cousinage *m.* relatives

coussin *m.* cushion

coussinet *m.* small cushion; (mech.) bearing

coût *m.* cost, price

couteau *m.* knife

coutelas *m.* cutlass

coutellerie *f.* cutlery

coûter *vi.* to cost; **— cher** to be expensive

coûteux *a.* costly, expensive

coutil *m.* twill, duck; mattress ticking

coutume *f.* custom, habit; common law

coutumier *a.* customary, usual; **droit —** *m.* common law

couture *f.* sewing; seam; suture; scar

couturer *vt.* to seam, scar

couturier *m.* designer of women's clothes

couturière *f.* seamstress, dressmaker

couvaison *f.* incubation period

couvée *f.* brood of chickens; group of eggs under brood hen; (coll.) all the family

couvent *m.* convent; monastery

couver *vt.* to hatch; sit on; — *vi.* to smolder; brew; develop

couvercle *m.* cover, lid, cap

couvert *m.* table place setting; cover charge; shelter, cover; **mettre le —** to set the table; **ôter le —** to clear the table; — *a.* covered; shady, wooded; clothed, clad; overcast (weather)

couverture *f.* cover; wrapper; blanket

couveuse *f.* brood hen; incubator

couvre-feu *m.* curfew

couvre-lit *m.* bedspread, coverlet

couvre-pieds *m.* bedspread; quilt

couvreur *m.* roofer

couvrir *vt.* to cover; clothe; **se —** to put one's hat on; clothe oneself

coyote *m.* coyote

crabe *m.* crab

crachat *m.* spit; sputum

cracher *vt. & vi.* to spit out
crachin *m.* light drizzle
crachoir *m.* spittoon
crachoter *vi.* to spit frequently
craie *f.* chalk
craindre *vt.* to fear, be afraid of
crainte *f.* fear; **de — de** for fear of; **de — que** for fear that
craintif *a.* timid; fearful
cramoisi *a.* crimson
crampe *f.* cramp
crampillon *m.* small hook
crampon *m.* clamp; crampon; stud
cramponner *vt.* to clamp; (coll.) to pester, bother
cran *m.* cog, tooth, catch; notch
crâne *m.* skull; **—** *a.* bold, swaggering
crâner *vi.* to swagger
crânerie *f.* bravado; daring
cranien *a.* cranial
cranter *vt.* to notch, tally; cog
crapaud *m.* toad
crapule *f.* mob, rabble; lewdness; filth
crapuleux *a.* lewd; foul, filthy
craqueler *vt.* to crack
craquelure *f.* crack
craquement *m.* cracking, snapping
craquer *vi.* to crack; creak; crackle; crunch
crasse *f.* filth; squalor; stinginess; **—** *a.* crass
crasseux *a.* dirty, filthy; stingy
cratère *m.* crater
cravacher *vt.* to whip
cravate *f.* necktie; cravat, scarf
crayeux *a.* chalky
crawl(e) *m.* crawl (swimming stroke)
crayon *m.* pencil; crayon; stick; **— hémo-statique** styptic pencil
crayonnage *m.* pencil sketch, pencil drawing
crayonner *vt.* to draw, sketch
créance *f.* trust, credit; credence; debt
créancier *m.* creditor
créateur *m.*, **créatrice** *f.* creator; inventor, author; **—** *a.* creative
création *f.* creation, creating; establishment, establishing
créature *f.* creature; creation
crécelle *f.* rattle
crèche *f.* crib, manger; nursery school
crédence *f.* credenza, buffet
crédibilité *f.* credibility; probability
crédit *m.* credit; credence; prestige, repute; **à —** on credit
créditer *vt.* to credit
créditeur *m.* creditor
credo *m.* creed, belief
crédule *a.* credulous
crédulité *f.* credulity

créer *vt.* to create; produce; engender
crémaillère *f.* pothook; **pendre la —** to have a housewarming
crémation *f.* cremation
crématoire *a.* pertaining to cremation
crème *f.* cream; custard, pudding; cream soup; **— fouettée** whipped cream
crémer *vt.* to cremate
crémerie *f.* dairy; grocery; creamery
crémeux *a.* creamy
crémier *m.* dairyman, grocer
crénelé *a.* notched (as coin edge), toothed; crenate; crenellated; milled
créneler *vt.* to crenelate; cog; notch
créole *a. & n.* creole, French-colonial born
créosol *m.* creosol
créosote *f.* creosote
crêpe *f.* pancake; **—** *m.* crepe, crape; mourning band
crépitation *f.*, **crépitement** *m.* crepitation; crackling
crépiter *vi.* to crackle
crépu *a.* fuzzy, frizzy; crinkled
crépusculaire *a.* twilight, crepuscular
crépuscule *m.* twilight
cresson *m.* watercress
crête *f.* crest, comb; ridge
crétin *m.* cretin; idiot
crétois *a. & n.* Cretan
creuser *vt.* to dig, excavate; look deeply into, study carefully; **se — la tête** to rack one's brains
creuset *m.* crucible; melting pot
creux (creuse) *a.* hollow; deep; sunken; **—** *m.* hollow; pit; hole
crevaison *f.* bursting; (auto.) puncture, blowout
crevasse *f.* crevice, chink, crack, crevasse
crevasser *vt.* to crack; to chap hands
crève-cœur *m.* heartbreak
crever *vi.* to break; burst; (coll.) die; **—** *vt.* to burst; puncture
crevette *f.* shrimp; prawn
cri *m.* cry, shout; **dernier —** latest thing, latest style
criaillement *m.* shrill sound; shouting, shrieking
criailler *vi.* to shout; bawl; whine; nag
criaillerie *f.* shouting; bawling; whining; nagging
criant *a.* outrageous, crying
criard *a.* noisy, shrill; loud color
crible *m.* sieve; screen
criblé *a.* riddled; pitted face; saddled with debts
cribler *vt.* to sift; riddle
cribleur *m.*, **cribleuse** *f.* sifter (machine)
cricri *m.* cricket; chirping
criée *f.* auction, public selling
crier *vi.* to proclaim; shout, cry out;

scream; squeal; chirp; creak; — *vt.* shout, cry; peddle

crieur *m.* shouter, crier; peddlar; town crier

crime *m.* crime

criminalité *f.* crime rate; criminality

criminel *a.* criminal; guilty; — *m.* criminal

criminologie *f.* criminology

crin *m.* horsehair

crinière *f.* mane

crinoline *f.* crinoline, hoop skirt

crique *f.* cove; creek

criquet *m.* locust; cricket

crise *f.* crisis; attack, fit; problem

crispant *a.* irritating, annoying

crispation *f.* puckering, shriveling; tic, twitching; clenching; fidgeting

crisper *vt.* to contract; clench; make fidgety

crissement *m.* grating, rasping, grinding; squeaking

crisser *vt. & vi.* to grate, rasp, grind; squeak

cristal *m.* crystal; glass; — **taillé** cut glass

cristallin *a.* crystalline; clear, transparent

cristallisation *f.* crystalization

cristalliser *vt. & vi.* to crystallize

critère, critérium *m.* criterion; standard; test

critiquable *a.* censurable

critique *f.* criticism, critique; — *m.* critic; — *a.* critical

critiquer *vt.* to criticize

croasser *vi.* to croak; caw

croate *a. & n.* Croatian

Croatie *f.* Croatia

croc *m.* hook; fang; tusk

croc-en-jambe *m.* trip, fall; **faire un — à** to trip

croche *f.* (mus.) eighth-note

crocher *vt.* to hook

crochet *m.* small hook; (print.) square bracket; sharp turn; fang; pick, key

crocheter *vt.* to pick a lock; crochet

crochu *a.* hooked; crooked

crocodile *m.* crocodile

crocus *m.* crocus

croire *vt. & vi.* to believe, think; — **à** to believe in; **en —** to take someone's word for it

croisade *f.* crusade

croisé *a.* crossed; twilled; double-breasted; **mots –s** *m. pl.* crossword puzzle; — *m.* crusader; twill

croisée *f.* crossing; casement window; crossed filaments in a bomb sight

croisement *m.* crossing; cross; intersection

croiser *vt.* to cross; to fold arms; meet; pass; — *vi.* to cruise; **se — to** cross, meet, intersect

croisette *f.* small cross

croiseur *m.* cruiser

croisière *f.* cruise

croissance *f.* growth

croissant *a.* growing; increasing; — *m.* crescent moon; crescent roll

croître *vi.* to grow; increase

croix *f.* cross, crucifix; — **ou pile** heads or tails

croquant *a.* crisp, crunchy; tasty

croque-mitaine *m.* bugaboo, bugbear, bogyman

croque-mort *m.* funeral attendant

croquer *vt. & vi.* to crunch, munch; sketch

croquette *f.* croquette

croquis *m.* rough sketch; draft, outline

crosse *f.* crook, club, stick; gun butt; crozier

crotale *m.* rattlesnake

crotte *f.* mud; dung

crotter *vt.* to dirty; cover with mud

crottin *m.* horse manure

croulant *a.* crumbling, falling, tottering

crouler *vi.* to crumble, totter; collapse

croupe *f.* croup, crupper, rump

croupetons, à — *adv.* squatting

croupier *m.* croupier

croupion *m.* rump

croupir *vi.* to stagnate; wallow

croustade *f.* crusty food

croustillant *a.* crisp, crusty

croustiller *vi.* to crunch

croustilleux *a.* risqué

croûte *f.* crust; rind; scab; **casser la —** to have a snack; **faire —** to form a crust

crouton *m.* piece of crust; crouton

croyable *a.* credible, believable

croyance *f.* belief

croyant *a.* believing; — *m.* believer

cru *m.* place of origin of a wine; vintage; — *a.* raw; rough; crude

cruauté *f.* cruelty

cruche *f.* pitcher, jug

cruchon *m.* small pitcher

crucial *a.* cruciform; crucial

cruciefiement *m.* crucifixion

crucifier *vt.* to crucify

crucifix *m.* crucifix

crucifixion *f.* crucifixion

cruciforme *a.* cross-shaped, cruciform

crudité *f.* crudeness; crudity; rawness; roughness, coarseness

crue *f.* rise, rising, flood

cruel *a.* cruel

cruellement *adv.* cruelly

crûment *adv.* roughly; crudely; harshly

crustacé *m.* crustacean

cryogénique *f.* cryogenics

crypte *f.* crypt

cryptogénétique *a.* of unknown origin
cryptogramme *m.* cryptogram
cryptographie *f.* cryptography
Cuba *m.* Cuba
cubage *m.* cubic volume, capacity, space
Cubain *n. & a.* Cuban
cube *m.* cube; block
cuber *vt.* (math.) to cube
cubique *a.* cubic, cubical
cubisme *m.* cubism
cubital *a.* cubital
cubitus *m.* (anat.) ulna
cueillage *m.* gathering, picking; harvest time
cueillaison *f.* gathering, picking
cueilleur *m.* gatherer, picker, fruitpicker
cueillir *vt.* to gather, pluck, pick; (coll.) grab, take
cuiller, cuillère *f.* spoon; ladle; scoop; — à bouche tablespoon; — à café teaspoon
cuillerée *f.* spoonful
cuilleron *m.* bowl of a spoon
cuir *m.* leather, hide; — chevelu scalp; — verni patent leather; — vert untanned leather; rawhide
cuirasse *f.* armor, plate; cuirass
cuirassé *m.* battleship
cuirasser *vt.* to armor; protect; se — to steel oneself
cuire *vt. & vi.* to cook
cuisant *a.* biting, stinging, smarting
cuisine *f.* kitchen; cuisine, cooking; food; faire la — to do the cooking
cuisiner *vt.* to cook; (coll.) doctor, falsify; question, grill
cuisinier *m.* cook
cuisinière *f.* cook; stove, range
cuisse *f.* thigh; drumstick
cuisseau *m.* leg of veal
cuisson *f.* cooking; firing; burning
cuissot *m.* leg of game
cuistre *m.* (coll.) pedant
cuite *f.* firing (ceramics)
cuivre *m.* copper; — jaune brass
cuivré *a.* copper-colored; bronzed; brassy
cuivrer *vt.* to copper; bronze; — *vi.* to blare, sound
cuivreux *a.* cuprous
cuivrique *a.* cupric
cul *m.* posterior, bottom; rump
culasse *f.* gun breech; bolt; (mech.) cylinder head
culbute *f.* fall, tumble; somersault
culbuter *vt.* to overturn, overthrow, knock over — *vi.* to tumble; somersault
cul-de-sac *m.* dead-end street
culée *f.* abutment
culinaire *a.* culinary
culminant *a.* culminating, culminant;

point — *m.* height, zenith
culminer *vi.* to culminate
culot *m.* base, bottom; dottle; (coll.) youngest child
culotte *f.* breeches; panties; shorts; rump meat
culotter *vt.* to color; — une pipe to cure a pipe
culpabilité *f.* guilt, culpability
culte *m.* worship; cult; religion
cultivable *a.* suitable for farming; arable
cultivateur *m.* farmer; grower; plow, cultivator
cultivé *a.* cultivated; cultured person
cultiver *vt.* to cultivate; grow; farm; raise
cultural *a.* agricultural
culture *f.* cultivation, tillage; culture
culturel *a.* cultural
cumin *m.* cumin
cumul *m.* accumulation
cumulatif *a.* cumulative
cumuler *vt.* to accumulate
cumulus *m.* cumulus
cunéiforme *a.* cuneiform
cupide *a.* greedy
cupidité *f.* greed, cupidity
Cupidon *m.* Cupid
cuprifère *a.* copper-bearing
curable *a.* curable
curaçao *m.* curaçao, orange-peel liqueur
curage *m.* cleansing
curare *m.* curare
curatelle *f.* guardianship, trusteeship
curateur *m.* guardian, trustee
curatif *a.* curative
cure *f.* care; (med.) treatment; ministry; presbytery, rectory
curé *m.* parish priest
cure-dent *m.* toothpick
curée *f.* quarry (hunting); spoils
cure-pipe *m.* pipe cleaner
curer *vt.* to cleanse; pick; dredge
curieux *a.* curious; interested; indiscreet; inquisitive; odd
curiosité *f.* curiosity; inquisitiveness; curio; oddness; -s *pl.* sights; visiter les -s to go sightseeing
curium *m.* curium
curseur *m.* slide, runner
cursif *a.* cursory; handwritten
cursive *f.* handwriting
cutané *a.* cutaneous; pertaining to the skin
cuticule *f.* cuticle
cuve *f.* vat, tank for fermenting grapes
cuveau *m.* small vat or tank
cuver *vt. & vi.* to ferment wine
cuvette *f.* basin, pan
cuvier *m.* washtub
cyanose *f.* (med.) cyanosis

cyanure *m.* cyanide
cybernétique *f.* cybernetics
cyclable *a.* piste — *f.* bicycle path
cycle *m.* cycle; bicycle
cyclique *a.* cyclic, cyclical
cyclisme *m.* cycling, bicycling
cycliste *m. & f.* cyclist, bicyclist
cycloïde *f.* cycloid
cyclomoteur *m.* motorbike
cyclone *m.* cyclone
cyclope *m.* cyclops; giant
cyclotron *m.* cyclotron
cygne *m.* swan
cylindre *m.* cylinder; drum; roller
cylindrer *vt.* to roll; mangle
cylindrique *a.* cylindrical
cymbale *f.* cymbal
cynique *a.* cynical; — *m.* cynic
cynisme *m.* cynicism
cyprès *m.* cypress
cyste *m.* cyst
cytologie *f.* cytology
cytoplasme *m.* cytoplasm

D

dactyle *m.* dactyl
dactylique *a.* dactylic
dactylo, dactylographe *m. & f.* typist
dactylographie *f.* typing, typewriting
dactylographié *a.* typed, typewritten
dactylographier *vt.* to typewrite
dada *m.* hobbyhorse; (coll.) hobby; obsession
dadais *m.* idiot, stupid fellow
dague *f.* dagger
daguerréotype *m.* daguerrotype
dahlia *m.* dahlia
daigner *vt.* to deign, condescend
daim *m.* deer; buckskin; suede
dais *m.* canopy
dallage *m.* floor tile; flagstone surface
dalle *f.* flagstone, slab of marble, tile
daller *vt.* to tile, pave
dalmate *a. & n.* Dalmatian
dalot *m.* scupper
daltonien *a.* color-blind
daltonisme *m.* color blindness
Damas *m.* Damascus
damas *m.* damask; damson plum
damassé *a.* damask; Damascus steel
dame *f.* lady; queen (at cards); jeu de —s *pl.* game of checkers; pion du jeu de —s checkers man
damier *m.* chessboard, checkerboard
damnation *f.* damnation
damné *a.* damned
damner *vt.* to damn
damoiseau *m.* dandy; fop
dancing *m.* dance hall; public dance, ball

dandiner *vt.* to dandle; (fig.) pamper; se — to waddle
Danemark *m.* Denmark
danger *m.* danger; risk, peril
dangereux *a.* dangerous
danois *a.* Danish; — *m.* Dane; Danish language
dans *prep.* in, into, at, within; from, out of
dansant *a.* dancing; soirée -e *f.* dance; thé — *m.* tea dance
danse *f.* dance, dancing
danser *vt. & vi.* to dance
danseur *m.*, danseuse *f.* dancer, ballet dancer
dard *m.* dart; forked tongue; pain, sting
darder *vt.* to shoot, throw, flash
dardillon *m.* small dart
darne *f.* slice of fish
datation *f.* dating
date *f.* calendar date; sans — undated
dater *vt. & vi.* to date
datif *a. & m.* (gram.) dative
datte *f.* (bot.) date
dattier *m.* date palm
daube *f.* braising; bœuf en — braised beef
dauber *vt. & vi.* to braise; make fun of
dauphin *m.* dolphin; Dauphin
davantage *adv.* more, any more; more time
davier *m.* (naut.) davit; (dent.) forceps
de *prep.* of; from; by; with; in; — *art.* some, any
dé *m.* thimble; die; domino; golf tee; -s *m. pl.* dice
déambuler *vi.* to stroll, saunter
débâcle *m.* debacle, disaster, rout; collapse, downfall
déballer *vt.* to unpack
déballeur *m.* peddler
débandade *f.* dispersal; à la — in disorder
débander *vt.* to unbend, relax; unbandage; se — to disband, disperse
débaptiser *vt.* to change the name of
débarbouiller *vt.* to wash someone's face; se — to wash one's face; clear up (weather)
débarcadère *m.* landing place; wharf
débardage *m.* unloading
débarder *vt.* to unload
débardeur *m.* stevedore
débarquement *m.* landing; arrival; unloading
débarquer *vt.* to land, disembark; unload; — *vi.* to land, disembark, get off
débarras *m.* riddance
débarrasser *vt.* to clear; rid, disencumber; relieve; se — de to get rid of
débarrer *vt.* to unbar

débat *m.* debate; discussion; dispute

débattre *vt.* to discuss; debate; **se — to** struggle

débauche *f.* debauchery

débauché *a.* debauched

débaucher *vt.* to debauch; corrupt; lead astray

débile *a.* weak, sick

débilitant *a.* debilitating

débilité *f.* debility, weakness

débiliter *a.* to debilitate

débit *m.* debit; sale; store, shop; flow, output

débitant *m.* retailer

débiter *vt.* to retail, sell; deliver; produce; speak, pronounce, utter; debit

débiteur *m.* debtor; teller, speaker

déblayer *vt.* to clear away

débloquer *vt.* to unblock

déboire *m.* unpleasant aftertaste

déboisement *m.* deforestation

déboiser *vt.* to deforest

déboîtement *m.* (med.) dislocation

déboîter *vt.* to disconnect; dislocate

débonnaire *a.* easy-tempered, kind, good-natured, weak

débordant *a.* overflowing; blooming; protruding

debordé *a.* overflowing; (coll.) rushed, busy, snowed under

débordement *m.* overflowing; outburst

déborder *vt. & vi.* to overflow, run over; protrude; trim (adorn)

débouché *m.* outlet, exit

déboucher *vt.* to uncork; open; clear; — *vi.* to flow; open on; emerge

déboucler *vt.* to unbuckle; uncurl

débourser *vt.* to disburse, lay out

debout *adv.* standing up, upright; alive; **à dormir —** boring; **se tenir —** to stand

déboutonner *vt.* to unbutton

débraillé *a.* untidy, unkempt; loose

débrayage *m.* (auto.) clutch

débrayer *vt.* to disengage from gear; disconnect

débrider *vt.* to unbridle; stop

débris *m. pl.* remains; ruins; debris

débrouillard *a. & m.* resourceful, (coll.) smart person

débrouiller *vt.* to disentangle; clear up; decipher; **se — to** clear up; get along, manage

début *m.* beginning; debut; coming out

débutant *m.* beginner; new performer **—e** *f.* beginner in society

débuter *vi.* to begin; do, appear for the first time

deçà *prep. & adv.* on this side

décacheter *vt.* to unseal

décadence *f.* decay, decline, decadence

décadent *a.* decadent

décaféiné *a.* decaffeinated, caffeine-free

décaisser *vt.* to uncrate; pay out, disburse

décalcomanie *f.* decalcomania, transfer

décaler *vt.* to change, shift

décalitre *f.* decaliter

décalogue *m.* Ten Commandments

décalque *m.* tracing, transfer

décalquer *vt.* to trace, transfer

décamètre *m.* ten meters

décamper *vi.* to decamp

décanat *m.* office of dean, deanship

décanter *vt.* to decant, pour (off)

décaper *vt.* to scour, clean

décapitation *f.* decapitation

décapiter *vt.* to behead, decapitate

décapotable *a.* (auto.) convertible

décatir *vt.* to remove cloth shine by steaming

décathlon *m.* decathlon

décavé *a.* (coll.) broke, ruined, cleaned out

décédé *a.* deceased, departed

décéder *vi.* to decease, die

déceler *vt.* to disclose, betray

décélération *f.* deceleration

décembre *m.* December

décemment *adv.* decently

décence *f.* decency; propriety

décennal *a.* decennial

décent *a.* decent; proper

décentralisation *f.* decentralization

décentraliser *vt.* to decentralize

déception *f.* disappointment; deception

décerner *vt.* to award, confer

décès *m.* decease, death; **acte de —** *m.* death certificate

décevant *a.* disappointing; deceptive

décevoir *vt.* to disappoint; to deceive

déchaînement *m.* unchaining; outburst, wave

déchaîner *vt.* to unchain; let loose; **se —** to break out

décharge *f.* discharge; discharging, unloading; rebate; release; acquittal (at law)

déchargement *m.* discharging, unloading

décharger *vt.* to unload, discharge; unburden; fire a gun; **se — to** discharge; go off; **se — de** to get rid of; relieve oneself of

déchargeur *m.* unloader

décharné *a.* skinny; emaciated; gaunt

déchaussé *a.* barefoot

déchausser *vt.*, **se — to** take off one's shoes

déchéance *f.* forfeiture; downfall; term, expiration

déchet *m.* loss; waste

déchiffrable *a.* legible, readable, decipherable

déchiffrer vt. to decipher; decode; read, make out

déchiqueté a. jagged, torn

déchirant a. heartrending

déchirement m. tearing; rift; sorrow

déchirer vt. to tear; rend

déchirure f. tear, rip, rent

déchloruré a. salt-free

déchoir vi. to fall; go down; decline in condition

déchu a. fallen; forfeited; expired

décibel m. decibel

décidé a. decided; resolved, determined

décidément adv. decidedly, positively; firmly, resolutely

décider vt. to decide; persuade; determine; se — to resolve, decide

décigramme m. ½ gram

décilitre m. ¹⁄₁₀ liter

décimal a. decimal; —e f. decimal

décimer vt. to decimate

décisif a. decisive; positive, firm; critical, crucial

décision f. decision; resolution

déclamation f. declamation; declaiming

déclamer vt. to declaim; rant, harangue

déclaration f. declaration; affadavit; statement; announcement

déclarer vt. to declare, proclaim; state, assert; notify

déclassé m. social outcast; — a. socially lowered; obsolete

déclasser vt. to lower in rank, class; demote; make obsolete; disarrange; declassify

déclencher vt. to unleash; (fig.) set in motion, release; trigger (mech.) disengage

déclic m. catch; trigger

déclin m. decline, decay; wane; ebb; fall

déclinaison f. (gram.) declension; (ast.) declination

décliner vt. to decline; shun, refuse; — vi. decline, diminish, fall, wane

déclive a. sloping; —f. slope

décliver vi. to slope, incline

déclivité f. slope, incline

décoder vt. to decode

décoiffer vt. to undo, disarrange (the hair)

décollage m. unsticking; (avi.) take-off

décollation f. decapitation, beheading

décoller vt. to unstick; loosen; — vi. (avi.) to take off

décolleté a. in a low-cut dress

décolorer vt. to fade; bleach; discolor

décombres m. pl. rubbish, refuse, debris

décommander vt. to cancel, countermand

décomposer vt. to decompose; se — to become decomposed; decay, rot; become distorted

décomposition f. decomposition

décompression f. decompression

décomprimer vt. to decompress

décompter vt. to deduct

déconcertant a. disconcerting

déconcerter vt. to disconcert; baffle, confound; upset

déconfit a. baffled, confused

décongeler vt. to defrost, thaw

déconseiller vt. to dissuade; advise against

déconsidérer vt. to discredit

décontenancer vt. to discountenance, upset, mortify

déconvenue f. disappointment

décor m. decoration; scenery, setting

décorateur m. decorator; (theat.) designer

décoratif a. decorative

décoration f. decoration; scenery; medal, ribbon

décorer vt. to decorate, adorn

décorum m. decorum; propriety, decency

découdre vt. to unsew, unstitch, rip; gore

découler vi. to flow, proceed; drip, trickle

découper vt. to carve; cut up; couteau à — m. carving knife; scie à — f. jigsaw; se — sur to stand out against

découpler vt. to uncouple

découpure f. cutting out; clipping, cutout; indentation

découragé a. discouraged

décourageant a. discouraging

découragement m. discouragement

décourager vt. to discourage; se — to become discouraged

découronner vt. to dethrone; untop a tree

décours m. wane, ebb, decline

décousu a. unsewed, unstitched, ripped; rambling, incoherent; disjointed; loose

découvert m. deficit; overdraft; mettre à — to reveal, expose; — a. uncovered; open

découverte f. discovery

découvreur m. discoverer

découvrir vt. to uncover; discover; disclose; expose; show; se — to take off one's hat; be discovered, be revealed; come to light

décrasser vt. to scour, cleanse; (auto.) remove carbon

décréditer vt. to discredit

décrépi a. dilapidated

décrépit a. decrepit; dilapidated

décret m. decree

décréter vt. to decree

décri m. disrepute

décrier vt. to decry, disparage

décrire vt. to describe

décrocher vt. to unhook; lift the receiver (telephone); disconnect

décroiser vt. to uncross

décroissance f. decrease; decline

décroître vi. to decrease; decline; diminish

décrotter vt. to clean; scrape clean

décrotteur m. bootblack

décrottoir m. scraper; doormat

décrue f. fall, drop, subsiding

décuple a. tenfold

dédaigner vt. to disdain, scorn

dédaigneux a. disdainful, scornful

dédain m. disdain, scorn

dédale m. labyrinth, maze, confusion

dedans adv. in, within; — m. inside

dédicace f. dedication

dédicacer vt. to dedicate; autograph a book

dédicatoire a. dedicatory

dédier vt. to dedicate; inscribe

dédire v., se — de to take back, go back on, retract

dédit m. retraction; forfeit

dédommagement m. indemnity, damages, compensation

dédommager vt. to indemnify, compensate

dédouaner vt. to clear through customs

dédoublement m. dividing, sectioning into two parts; duality; duplication

dédoubler vt. to divide; remove lining; unfold; se — to divide; unfold

déduction f. deduction; discount

déduire vt. to deduct; discount; deduce

déesse f. goddess

défaillance f. failing; failure; weakness; lapse; faint

défaillant a. failing; weakening; faint

défaillir vi. to fail, faint; grow weak

défaire vt. to unmake, undo; defeat; rid of; untie; unpack; se — de to get rid of

défait a. lean; worn; pale

défaite f. defeat

défaitiste a. & n. defeatist

défalquer vt. to deduct, take away

défaut m. defect; fault, failing; default; lack, want; à — de, au — de for want of

défaveur f. disfavor

défavorable a. unfavorable

défavoriser vt. to handicap, put at a disadvantage

défectif a. (gram.) defective verb

défection f. defection; faire — to defect

défectueux a. defective

défectuosité f. defectiveness; defect

défendeur m. defendant (at law)

défendre vt. to defend; protect; prohibit; se — to defend oneself; protect oneself

défense f. defense; prohibition; — civile civil defense; — de fumer no smoking, smoking prohibited; légitime — self-defense (at law); -s pl. tusks

défenseur m. defender; protector; defense counsel (law)

défensif a. defensive

déférence f. deference; consideration, respect

déférent a. deferent; respectful

déférer vt. to confer, award; hand over (at law); refer; swear (in); — vi. to defer, comply

déferler vt. to unfurl; set sail; — vi. to break (waves)

défeuiller vt. to remove the leaves from

défi m. defiance; challenge

défiance f. diffidence; distrust, mistrust

défiant a. mistrustful, distrustful; suspicious

déficeler vt. to untie

déficit m. deficit

déficience f. lack, deficiency

déficitaire a. unbalanced, with a deficit

défier vt. to defy; challenge; se — de to mistrust, distrust, be suspicious of, beware of

défigurer vt. to disfigure, deform

défilé m. defile, narrow passage; pass; parade, procession; — de voitures autocade, motorcade

défiler vi. to parade, march by

défini a. definite; well-defined

définir vt. to define; se — to become clear

définissable a. definable

définitif a. definitive; final; permanent; definite

définition f. definition

définitivement adv. finally; permanently; once and for all, for good; definitely

déflatation f. deflation; deflating

défloraison f. time of falling of flowers, falling of petals

défoncé a. battered; crumpled; bumpy

défoncer vt. to smash in; break up

déformation f. deformation; warping

déformer vt. to deform, distort; warp; se — to become deformed, lose shape; warp

défraîchi a. shopworn; faded

défrayer vt. to defray

défricher vt. (agr.) to clear ground

défriser vt. to uncurl

défroncer vt. remove the wrinkles from

défunt a. deceased, late

dégagé a. disengaged, free; nonchalant

dégagement m. disengagement; clearing, freeing from obligation; release; relief; redeeming (pawned article); exit

dégager vt. to disengage, free; clear; release; relieve; redeem; se — to free oneself; clear oneself; appear, emerge, come out

dégaine f. (coll.) gait; ridiculous attitude

dégainer *vt.* to draw a sword; unsheathe

déganter *vt.* to unglove; **se —** to take off one's gloves

dégarnir *vt.* to strip, take apart; remove, take away; **se —** to lose (hair, leaves); be depleted, emptied, stripped

dégâts *m. pl.* damage

dégauchir *vt.* to straighten

dégel *m.* thaw; **—er** *vt. & vi.* to thaw

dégénération *f.* degeneration; deterioration

dégénéré *a.* degenerate

dégénérer *vi.* to degenerate; decline

dégivrer *vt.* to deice; defrost

dégivreuse *f.* defroster

déglacer *vt.* to thaw; defrost

dégonfler *vt.* to deflate; reduce; **se —** to lose air, go flat; diminish, subside

dégorger *vt.* to disgorge; clear, open; scour; **— vi.** to flow into; overflow

dégourdi *a.* lively; sharp, alert

dégourdir *vt.* to revive, quicken; warm, take the chill from; **se —** to stretch one's limbs; get warm

dégoût *m.* disgust; dislike

dégoûtant *a.* disgusting; disagreeable, unpleasant

dégoûter *vt.* to disgust; **se — de** to become disgusted with; be fed up with

dégouttant *a.* trickling; dripping

dégoutter *vi.* to drip, trickle

dégradation *f.* degradation; erosion; defacement; wear; damage

dégrader *vt.* to degrade; damage, deface; **se —** to degrade oneself, lower oneself; become dilapidated

dégrafer *vt.* to unhook, unclasp, undo

dégraisser *vt.* to remove fat from; scour, clean, dry-clean

dégraisseur *m.* cleaner, dry cleaner

degré *m.* degree; stair step

dégriser *vt.* to sober up; (fig.) to disillusion

déguenillé *a.* ragged, in rags

déguerpir *vi.* to move out; clear out; **faire — ** to evict

déguisement *m.* disguise

déguiser *vt.* to disguise; hide, conceal

dégustation *f.* tasting, art of tasting

déguster *vt.* to taste; sip, savor

dehors *adv.* out, outdoors, outside; **— m.** outside; external appearance

déifier *vt.* to deify

déisme *m.* deism

déité *f.* deity

déjà *adv.* already

déjeter *vt.* to warp; make uneven

déjeuner *m.* lunch; **petit —** breakfast; **— vi.** to breakfast; lunch

déjouer *vt.* to baffle; frustrate, foil

delà *prep. & adv.* beyond, on the other side; **au — (de)** beyond

délabré *a.* broken, dilapidated

délabrer *vt.* to ruin, dilapidate

délacer *vt.* to unlace

délai *m.* delay; interval; respite; (com.) time extension; **sans —** immediately

délaissement *m.* legal abandonment, desertion; loneliness; helplessness

délassement *m.* rest, relaxation

délaisser *vt.* to abandon, forsake; relinquish

délasser *vt.* to rest, relax

délavé *a.* faded, washed out; soaked

délayer *vt.* to dilute, thin, water

délébile *a.* erasable

délectable *a.* delectable

délectation *f.* delight, pleasure

délecter *vt.* to delight; **se — à** to delight in, enjoy

délégation *f.* delegation

délégué *m.* delegate

déléguer *vt.* to delegate

délester *vt.* to unburden, relieve

délétère *a.* deleterious; harmful; poisonous

délibération *f.* deliberation

délibéré *a.* deliberate

délibérer *vt. & vi.* to deliberate; resolve

délicat *a.* delicate; sensitive; fine; difficult; dainty; touchy; tactful

délicatesse *f.* delicacy; daintiness; nicety; fineness; difficulty

délice *m.* delight; **-s** *f. pl.* delight, pleasure

délicieux *a.* delicious; delightful

délié *a.* slender, slim; sharp; glib

délier *vt.* to untie, release; **se —** to come loose

délinéer *vt.* to delineate

délinquant *m.* delinquent, offender

délirant *a.* delirious

délire *m.* delirium, frenzy

délirer *vi.* to be delirious; rave

délit *m.* offense, wrong; misdemeanor

délivrance *f.* deliverance, rescue; delivery

délivre *m.* afterbirth, placenta

délivrer *vt.* to deliver, free; rescue; **se — de** to free oneself from; get rid of

déloger *vi.* to move out; go away; **— vt.** to eject, dislodge, drive out

déloyal *a.* disloyal, unfaithful; unfair; foul, unsporting

déloyauté *f.* disloyalty; treachery; foul play

déluge *m.* deluge, flood

déluré *a.* lively

démagnétiser *vt.* to demagnetize

démagogie *f.* demagogy

démagogue *m.* demagog

démailler *vt.* to undo links *or* mesh

démailloter *vt.* to unswathe

demain *adv. & m.* tomorrow; **à —** good-by, until tomorrow, see you tomorrow

demande *f.* question, claim; request; demand; application; petition; proposal, offer

demander *vt.* to ask, ask for; claim; request; want, require, need; demand

demandeur *m.* plaintiff (at law)

démangeaison *f.* itch, itching; desire

démanger *vi.* to itch

démarcation *f.* demarcation

démarche *f.* step, pace; gait; measure; procedure

démarquer *vt.* to remove the mark; imitate; reduce, put on sale

démarrer *vt. & vi.* (naut.) to cast off; (auto.) start; (coll.) leave

démarreur *m.* (auto.) starter

démasquer *vt.* to unmask

démêlé *m.* dispute, strife

démêler *vt.* to disentangle, separate comb out; clear up; make out, see

démembrement *m.* dismemberment

démembrer *vt.* to dismember; divide up

déménagement *m.* moving, removal; **voiture de — f.** moving van

déménager *vi.* to move, change residence; (fig.) (coll.) to become childish

déménageur *m.* mover of household goods

démence *f.* insanity, madness

démener *v.,* **se —** to struggle, be agitated

dément *a. & m.* lunatic

démenti *m.* denial, contradiction

démentir *vt.* to deny; contradict; belie

démérite *m.* lack of merit

démériter *vi.* to lose esteem, lose favor

démesure *f.* lack of measure, lack of moderation, excess

démesuré *a.* excessive; immoderate; inordinate

démettre *vt.* to dislocate; **se — (de)** to resign (from)

démeubler *vt.* to remove the furniture from

demeurant *adv.,* **au —** furthermore, besides, moreover

demeure *f.* dwelling, residence; delay (law)

demeurer *vi.* to live; stay, remain; delay

demi *a.* half; **— m.** half; football halfback; **à — half,** by half

demi-cercle *m.* semicircle

demi-dieu *m.* demigod

demi-finale *f.* semi-final (sports)

demi-frère *m.* half brother; stepbrother

demi-heure *f.* half hour

demi-jour *m.* half-light; gray; twilight

démilitarisé *a.* demilitarized

demi-lune *f.* half-moon

demi-mesure *f.* half measure

demi-monde *m.* shady society

demi-mot *m. adv.,* **entendre à —, comprendre à —** to take a hint

déminer *vt.* to demine, clear of mines

demi-pension *f.* partial board (two meals per day)

demi-pensionnaire *m. & f.* boarder (for breakfast and supper)

demi-place *f.* half price; half fare

demi-saison *f.* periods between winter and summer (spring *and* fall); **vêtements de — m. pl.** spring *or* fall clothing

demi-sœur *f.* half sister; stepsister

demi-solde *f.* army pension; **— m.** pensioned officer

démission *f.* resignation

démissionner *vi.* to resign

demi-tasse *f.* small coffee cup (after-dinner size)

demi-teinte *f.* medium shade (color)

demi-ton *m.* (mus.) half tone

demi-tour *m.* half turn; about-face; **faire — to** turn back, turn around

démobilisation *f.* demobilization

démobiliser *vt.* to demobilize

démocrate *m. & f.* democrat

démocratie *f.* democracy

démocratique *a.* democratic

démodé *a.* out of style; obsolete, old-fashioned

demoiselle *f.* young lady; dragonfly; **— d'honneur** bridesmaid; **nom de — m.** maiden name

démolir *vt.* to demolish

démolition *f.* demolition

démon *m.* demon, devil

démonétiser *vt.* to devalue, depreciate

démoniaque *a.* demoniac(al), devilish

démonstrateur *m.* demonstrator

démonstratif *a.* demonstrative

démonstration *f.* demonstration

démontable *a.* collapsible; detachable; portable

démonter *vt.* to dismantle; unhorse; upset

démontrable *a.* demonstrable

démontrer *vi.* to demonstrate

démoralisant, démoralisateur *a.* demoralizing

démoraliser *vt.* to demoralize

démuni *a.* out, sold out; unprovided; deprived

dénationaliser *vt.* to denationalize

dénaturer *vt.* to denature; make unnatural; pervert

dénégation *f.* denial

déni *m.* denial at law, refusal

dénicher *vt.* to dislodge; discover

denier *m.* money; penny, denier (of

fibers); interest money

dénier *vt.* to deny, refuse

dénigrer *vt.* to disparage

dénombrement *m.* enumeration; census

dénombrer *vt.* to enumerate, count

dénominateur *m.* denominator

dénomination *f.* denomination; name

dénommer *vt.* to name

dénoncer *vt.* to denounce

dénonciateur *m.* denouncer; informer; — *a.* revealing

dénonciation *f.* denunciation

dénoter *vt.* to denote

dénouement *m.* untying; end, ending, outcome, result

dénouer *vt.* to untie, undo, clear up

denrée *f.* commodity, product; —s *pl.* provisions; produce

dense *a.* dense; thick; close

densité *f.* density

dent *f.* tooth; notch; cog; prong; **coup de** — *m.* bite; —s **de lait** baby teeth; **mal de** —s *m.* toothache; **avoir mal aux** —s to have a toothache

dentaire *a.* dental

dental *a.* dental (phonetics)

dent-de-lion *f.* dandelion

denté *a.* notched; cogged; toothed

dentelle *f.* lace, lacework

dentelure *f.* notching; perforation

dentier *m.* row of teeth; denture

dentifrice *m.* dentifrice; **pâte** — *f.* toothpaste

dentine *f.* dentine

dentiste *m.* dentist

dénuder *vt.* to strip, denude

dénué *a.* devoid, lacking; out, without

dénuement *m.* destitution; want, poverty

dénuer *vt.* to deprive, strip

déodoriser *vt.* to deodorize

dépannage *m.* repair service

dépanner *vt.* to repair a breakdown

dépanneur *m.* (auto.) repair man

dépanneuse *f.* wrecker, tow truck

dépaqueter *vt.* to unpack; unwrap

dépareiller *vt.* to remove one of a pair; spoil a pair

déparer *vt.* to strip; remove adornment from

départ *m.* departure; start; division, separation

département *m.* department, administrative department

départemental *a.* departmental

départir *vt.* to divide; **se** — **de** to depart from; part with, to cease, desist

dépasser *vt.* to go beyond, overreach, overstep; overtake; transcend; exceed

dépaysé *a.* out of place

dépecer *vt.* to carve, cut in pieces

dépêche *f.* dispatch; telegram

dépêcher *vt.* to dispatch; **se** — to hurry, hasten

dépeindre *vt.* to paint, portray, depict

dépendance *f.* dependence, dependency

dépendant *a.* dependent

dépendre *vi.* to depend on; result; belong; — *vt.* to unhang, take down

dépens *m. pl.* (com.) cost; costs (law); **aux** — **de** at the expense of

dépense *f.* expense, expenditure; pantry

dépenser *vt.* to spend, expend

dépensier *a. & m.* extravagant; spendthrift

dépérir *vi.* to waste away; pine; decline; die out

dépeupler *vt.* to depopulate; unstock

dépilatoire *a.* hair-removing, depilatory

dépiler *vt.* to remove hair from

dépister *vt.* to track, hunt down

dépit *m.* spite; vexation

dépiter *vt.* to vex; spite

déplacé *a.* misplaced, out of place

déplacement *m.* moving; travelling; displacement

déplacer *vt.* to move; displace; transfer

déplaire *vi.* to displease; offend

déplaisant *a.* unpleasant

déplaisir *m.* displeasure

déplanter *vt.* to dig up for transplanting

dépliant *m.* folder, brochure

déplier *vt.* to unfold

déplisser *vt.* to remove the pleats *or* wrinkles from

déploiement *m.* deployment; unfolding

déplorable *a.* deplorable

déplorer *vt.* to deplore

déployé *a.* unfolded; **rire à gorge** —**e to** laugh heartily

déployer *vt.* to unfold; display; deploy

déplumer *vt.* to pluck the feathers of

dépolariser *vt.* to depolarize

dépolarisation *f.* depolarization

dépolir *vt.* to take off the polish; **verre dépoli** *m.* frosted glass

dépopulation *f.* depopulation

déportation *f.* deportation

déportements *m. pl.* misdeeds

déporter *vt.* to deport; — *vi.* to swerve

déposant *m.* depositor; deponent (law), witness; — *a.* testifying

dépose *f.* removal

déposer *vt. & vi.* to depose; deposit; give testimony

dépositaire *m. & f.* depository

déposition *f.* deposition

déposséder *vt.* to dispossess

dépôt *m.* deposit; storehouse, warehouse, trust

dépouille *f.* spoil; remains; cast-off skin;

—s *pl.* booty

dépouiller *vt.* to strip, skin an animal; examine, study

dépourvu *a.* unprovided for, destitute, lacking; **au —** *adv.* unawares

dépravation *f.* depravity, corruption

dépraver *vt.* to deprave

déprécier *vt.* to depreciate, disparage

déprédation *f.* depradation, pillage

déprendre *v.*, **se —** to separate, detach oneself

dépression *f.* depression

déprimer *vt.* to depress; disparage

depuis *prep.* since, for; **— longtemps** for a long time; **—** *adv.* since; **— que** *conj.* since

dépurer *vt.* to purify

députation *f.* deputation

député *m.* deputy

députer *vt.* to send as representative

déraciner *vt.* to root out, uproot

dérailler *vi.* to be derailed; go off the track

déraison *f.* unreasonableness, folly

déraisonnable *a.* unreasonable

déraisonner *vi.* to be unreasonable

dérangement *m.* derangement; breakdown

déranger *vt.* to derange; put out of order; disturb

déraper *vi.* to detach; skid; aweigh (anchor)

dératé *m.* lively individual; **courir comme un —** to run like a deer

derechef *adv.* again, anew

déréglé *a.* out of order; disorderly

dérèglement *m.* disorder; irregularity

dérégler *vt.* to put out of order

dérider *vt.* to unwrinkle; (fig.) to cheer up

dérision *f.* derision; **tourner en —** to ridicule, deride

dérisoire *a.* derisive, ridiculous

dérivatif *m. & a.* derivative

dérivation *f.* derivation; drift; diversion

dérive *f.* drift; **à la —** adrift

dérivé *m.* derivative

dériver *vi.* to derive; **—** *vt.* to divert

dermatologie *f.* dermatology

dermatologiste *m.* dermatologist

dernier *a.* last; preceding; final

dernièrement *adv.* recently, lately

dernier-né *m.* youngest (in a family)

dérobée *f.*, **à la —** secretly

dérober *vt.* to rob, steal; hide, conceal; **se —** to steal away; disappear; hide

dérogation *f.* derogation

déroger *vi.*, **— à** to depart from, not conform to; detract from

dérouiller *vt.* to remove the rust from;

limber up; polish

dérouler *vt.* to unroll, unfold

déroute *f.* rout, disorder

dérouter *vt.* to rout

derrière *prep. & adv.* behind; **—** *m.* back, rear; behind

derviche *m.* dervish

dès *prep.* from, since, starting with; **— que** *conj.* as soon as

désabonner *v.*, **se —** to cancel a subscription

désabuser *vt.* to disabuse, undeceive

désaccord *m.* disagreement, discord

désaccorder *vt.* to cause discord in

désaffecter *vt.* to deconsecrate, eliminate the original function of

désaffection *f.* loss of affection

désagréable *a.* disagreeable, unpleasant

désagrégation *f.* dissolution, separation; breaking up

désagréger *vt.* to separate, break up

désagrément *m.* unpleasantness

désaltérer *vt.* to quench one's thirst

désamorcer *vt.* to disarm a bomb; (elec.) cut the current

désappointement *m.* disappointment

désappointer *vt.* to disappoint; dull

désapprendre *vt.* to unlearn, forget

désapprobateur *a.* disapproving

désapprobation *f.* disapproval

désapprouver *vt.* to disapprove (of)

désarçonner *vt.* to unsaddle, unseat, throw from horse; (fig. & coll.) to disconcert; confuse in a discussion

désarmement *m.* disarmament

désarmer *vt.* to disarm; appease

désarroi *m.* disorder, confusion

désastre *m.* disaster

désastreux *a.* disastrous

désavantage *m.* disadvantage

désavantager *vt.* to put at a disadvantage, handicap

désavantageux *a.* disadvantageous

désaveu *m.* disavowal, denial

désavouer *vt.* to disavow

desceller *vt.* to unseal

descendance *f.* descent, descendants

descendant *a.* descending; **—** *m.* descendant

descendre *vi.* to descend, come downstairs; **— à un hotel** stay at a hotel; **—** *vt.* to bring down; (coll.) depose; (avi.) bring down an enemy plane

descente *f.* descent; decline; hernia; **— de lit** bedside rug

descriptible *a.* describable

descriptif *a.* descriptive

désemballer *vt.* to unpack, unwrap

désemparé *a.* disconcerted

désemparer *vi.*, **sans —** immediately;

continuously

désenchanter *vt.* to disillusion, disenchant

désencombrer *vt.* to free, disencumber

désengager *vt.* to release from a commitment

désennuyer *vt.* to divert, cheer

désensabler *vt.* to free from the sand

désensibiliser *vt.* to desensitize

désentortiller *vt.* to straighten; sort

déséquilibrer *vt.* to unbalance

désert *m.* desert, wilderness; — *a.* deserted, solitary, abandoned

déserter *vt. & vi.* to desert

déserteur *m.* deserter

désertion *f.* desertion

désespérance *f.* despair, loss of hope

désespéré *a.* desperate, hopeless

désespérer *vi.* to despair; — *vt.* to be the despair of

désespoir *m.* despair

déshabillé *m.* housecoat

déshabiller *vt.* to undress

déshérité *a.* disinherited; downtrodden

déshériter *vt.* to disinherit

déshonnête *a.* improper, unseemly

déshonneur *m.* dishonor, disgrace

déshonorer *vt.* to dishonor

déshydratant *m.* dehumidifier

déshydrater *vt.* to dehydrate

désignation *f.* designation

désigner *vt.* to designate; appoint

désillusion *f.* disappointment, disillusion

désillusionner *vt.* to disillusion

désinence *f.* (gram.) ending of word

désinfecter *vt.* to disinfect

désinfection *f.* disinfection

désintégrable *a.* fissionable

désintégration *f.* disintegration; fission

désintégrer *vt.* to disintegrate

désintéressé *a.* disinterested; unselfish

désintéressement *m.* impartiality; unselfishness

désintéresser *vt.* to indemnify; buy out

désinviter *vt.* to withdraw an invitation

désinvolte *a.* unconstrained; impertinent

désinvolture *f.* ease, gracefulness

désir *m.* desire, wish

désirable *a.* desirable

désirer *vt.* to desire, wish for

désireux *a.* desirous, anxious

désister *v., se* — to desist; se — de to waive, renounce

désobéir *vi.* to disobey

désobéissance *f.* disobedience; — civile civil disobedience

désobligeant *a.* disobliging

désobliger *vt.* to displease

désodorisant *m.* deodorant

désodoriser *vt.* to clear of odor, deodorize

désœuvré *a.* idle, unoccupied

désœuvrement *m.* idleness, lack of occupation

désolant *a.* distressing, sad

désolation *f.* desolation; desolateness; grief

désolé *a.* very sorry; desolate

désoler *vt.* to desolate, ruin, destroy

désopilant *a.* very funny, hilarious

désordonné *a.* disordered; disorderly

désordonner *vt.* to disorder

désordre *m.* disorder, confusion

désorganiser *vt.* to disorganize

désorienter *vt.* to mislead; cause to become lost

désormais *adv.* henceforth

désoxyder *vt.* to deoxidize

despote *m.* despot; — *a.* despotic

despotisme *m.* despotism

dessaisir *vt.* to dispossess

dessécher *vt.* to dry; wither

dessein *m.* design, purpose; scheme, plan; à — on purpose; sans — unintentionally; aimlessly

desserrer *vt.* to loosen

dessert *m.* dessert

desserte *f.* sideboard

dessertir *vt.* to remove a gem from its setting

desservant *m.* parish priest

desservir *vt.* to serve; clear the table; harm, be of disservice to

dessiller *vt.* to open the eyes

dessin *m.* drawing; plan; pattern; — de vol (avi.) flight pattern

dessinateur *m.* designer; draftsman

dessiner *vt.* to draw, design, sketch

dessouler *vt. & vi.* to sober up

dessous *prep. & adv.* under, below; underneath, undermost; au — (de) below; — *m.* underpart; wrong side

dessus *prep. & adv.* on, upon, uppermost; au — (de) above, beyond; — *m.* upper part; advantage

destin *m.* destiny, fate

destinataire *m.* receiver, addressee, consignee

destinée *f.* destiny, doom, fate

destiner *vt.* to destine; intend

destitué *a.* destitute, devoid

destituer *vt.* to dismiss, discharge

destitution *f.* destitution, dismissal

destrier *m.* charger, war horse

destructeur *a.* destructive; — *m.* destroyer

destructif *a.* destructive

désuet *a.* obsolete

désuétude *f.* obsolescence, disuse

désunion *f.* lack of harmony, discord; misunderstanding

désunir *vt.* to separate, unjoin

détaché *a.* loose, indifferent, detached

détachement *m.* detachment

détacher *vt.* to detach, loosen; clean, remove spots from

détail *m.* detail; (com.) retail; **au —** (com.) at retail

détaillant *m.* retailer

détailler *vt.* to cut up; detail; retail

détartrer *vt.* remove tartar from teeth

detaxer *vt.* to remove the tax from, exempt from tax

détecter *vt.* to detect

détecteur *m.* detector

détective *m.* detective; (phot.) box camera

déteindre *vi.* to fade *or* run (colors)

dételer *vt.* to unharness; give up, cease

détendre *vt.* to relax, loosen; take down

détenir *vt.* to detain, withhold; hold, possess

détente *f.* trigger; (fig.) relaxation; expansion

détention *f.* detention, custody

détenu *m.* prisoner

déterger *vt.* to clean

détérioration *f.* deterioration

détériorer *vt.* to deteriorate

déterminant *a.* determining; — *m.* determinant

déterminatif *a.* determining

détermination *f.* determination

déterminé *a.* determined; definite

déterminer *vt.* to determine, settle, decide; cause

déterminisme *m.* determinism

déterrer *vt.* to disinter; unearth, discover

détersif *m.* detergent

détestable *a.* detestable

détestation *f.* detestation

détester *vt.* to detest, abhor, hate

détonant *a. & m.* explosive

détonateur *m.* detonating cap

détonation *f.* detonation, explosion

détoner *vi.* to explode

détonner *vi.* to sing *or* play off key; to clash

détordre *vt.* to untwist

détorquer *vt.* to distort, misrepresent

détorsion *f.* distortion

détortiller *vt.* to untwist

détour *m.* turning, roundabout way; evasion, excuse, subterfuge; turn, bend; **prendre des —s** to beat about the bush

détourné *a.* off the beaten track; isolated; secret

détournement *m.* diverting, turning away; embezzlement

détourner *vt.* to turn aside; divert, change; avert

détracteur *m.* detractor; — *a.* detracting

détraquer *vt.* to lead astray, distract,

divert; break, put out of commission; **se —** to break down

détrempe *f.* distemper (art)

détremper *vt.* to dilute; soften, remove the temper

détresse *f.* distress; danger

détriment *m.* detriment

détritus *m.* waste, rubbish, debris

détroit *m.* strait, channel

détromper *vt.* to undeceive

détrôner *vt.* to dethrone

détrousser *vt.* to undo; rob

détruire *vt.* to destroy, ruin

dette *f.* debt

deuil *m.* mourning, mourning clothes

deutérium *m.* deuterium

deux *a.* two; **tous les —** both

deuxième *a.* second

deux-points *m.* colon

dévaler *vi.* to go down(ward)

dévaliser *vt.* to rob

dévaloriser *vt.* to devaluate

dévaluation *f.* devaluation

dévaluer *vt.* to devaluate

devancer *vt.* to go before, precede; anticipate

devancier *m.* predecessor; **—s** *pl.* ancestors

devant *m.* front, forepart; **aller au — de** to go and meet; — *prep. & adv.* in front of, before

devanture *f.* store window; window display

dévastateur *m.* devastator; — *a.* devastating

dévastation *f.* devastation

dévaster *vt.* to devastate

déveine *f.* bad luck

développement *m.* development

développer *vt.* to develop; unfold

devenir *vi.* to become; grow, turn

dévergondage *m.* shamelessness; excesses

dévergonder *v.*, **se —** to become dissolute, commit excesses, be shameless

dévernir *vt.* to remove the varnish

déverrouiller *vt.* to unbolt

devers *prep.* towards; **par —** in the possession of; in the eyes of

dévers *a.* out of alignment

déverser *vt.* to slope, bank; pour, divert; — *vi.* lean; become lopsided

dévêtir *vt.* to undress; divest

déviation *f.* deviation, deflection; detour

dévider *vt.* to wind onto

dévier *vt.* to turn aside; — *vi.* to make a detour; deviate

deviner *vt.* to divine, guess

devinette *f.* riddle

dévisager *vt.* to stare at

devise *f.* motto; **—s** *pl.* foreign currency

deviser *vi.* to chat

dévisser *vt.* to unscrew
dévoiler *vt.* to unveil, discover
devoir *vt. & vi.* to owe, be indebted to; be bound, be obliged; must, ought; be necessary; — *m.* duty, obligation, task
dévorateur *a.* devouring
dévorer *vt.* to devour; (fig.) consume
dévot *a.* devout; pious; bigoted
dévouement *m.* devotion; religious devotion
dévouer *vt.* to devote, dedicate
dévoyé *m. & a.* stray
dextérité *f.* dexterity
diabète *m.* (med.) diabetes
diabétique *a. & n.* diabetic
diable *m.* devil; hand truck for baggage
diablerie *f.* deviltry
diablotin *m.* little devil
diabolique *a.* diabolic(al)
diaconesse *f.* deaconess
diacre *m.* deacon
diacritique *a.* diacritic(al)
diadème *m.* diadem
diagnose *f.* (med.) diagnosis
diagnostique *a.* diagnostic
diagnostiquer *vt.* to diagnose
diagramme *m.* diagram
dialectal *a.* dialectical
dialecte *m.* dialect
dialectique *a.* dialectic; — *f.* dialectics
dialogue *m.* dialog
dialoguer *vi.* to converse
diamant *m.* diamond
diamantaire, diamantin *a.* diamond-like
diamétral *a.* diametrical
diamètre *m.* diameter
diane *f.* (mil.) reveille
diantre *interj.* devil, dickens
diapason *m.* diapason
diaphane *a.* transparent
diaphragme *m.* diaphragm
diapositif *m.*, diapositive *f.* (phot.) transparency
diaprer *vt.* to ornament, color with many hues
diarrhée *f.* diarrhea
diastolique *a.* (med.) diastolic
diathermie *f.* diathermy
diatomée *f.* diatom
diatonique *a.* (mus.) diatonic
dichromatique *a.* dichromatic
dictateur *m.* dictator
dictatorial *a.* dictatorial
dictature *f.* dictatorship
dictée *f.* dictation
dicter *vt.* to dictate
diction *f.* diction
dictionnaire *m.* dictionary
dicton *m.* saying, proverb
didactique *a.* didactic

diérèse *f.* diaeresis
dièse *a. & m.* (mus.) sharp
diesel *m.* diesel engine
diéser *vt.* (mus.) to sharp
diète *f.* diet
diéticien *m.* dietician
diététique *f.* dietetics
Dieu *m.* God; — merci! thank God!; plût à —! God grant it!; à — ne plaise! God forbid!
diffamation *f.* defamation
diffamatoire *a.* defamatory
diffamer *vt.* to defame, slander; libel
différemment *adv.* differently
différence *f.* difference
différenciation *f.* differentiation
différencier *vt.* to distinguish
différend *m.* difference, source of argument
différentiel *a. & m.* differential
différer *vt.* to defer, put off; — *vi.* to differ
difficile *a.* difficult; hard
difficulté *f.* difficulty
difficultueux *a.* difficult
difforme *a.* deformed
difformité *f.* deformity
diffracter *vt.* to diffract
diffraction *f.* diffraction
diffus *a.* diffuse; wordy
diffuser *vt.* to diffuse, spread
diffusion *f.* diffusion; spreading
digérer *vt. & vi.* to digest; stomach; simmer
digest *m.* digest, abridgment, résumé
digestif *m.* (med.) digestive; liqueur, brandy; — *a.* digestive
digestion *f.* digestion
digitaline *f.* (med.) digitalis
digne *a.* worthy (of); dignified
dignitaire *m.* dignitary
dignité *f.* dignity, title, rank
digression *f.* digression
digue *f.* dike
dilacérer *vt.* to lacerate
dilapidation *f.* dilapidation
dilapider *vt.* to dilapidate; embezzle; squander
dilation *f.* dilation, expansion
dilater *vt.* to dilate, expand, widen
dilatoire *a.* dilatory
dilemme *m.* dilemma
dilettante *m.* dilettante, amateur
diligemment *adv.* diligently
diligence *f.* diligence; haste; stagecoach
diluer *vt.* to dilute
diluvien *a.* diluvian; diluvial
dimanche *m.* Sunday
dîme *f.* tithe
diminuer *vt. & vi.* to diminish

diminutif *a.* diminutive

dinde *f.* hen turkey; (fig.) goose; foolish woman

dindon *m.* tom turkey; —neau *m.* young turkey

dîner *m.* dinner; — *vi.* to dine

dînette *f.* family supper; children's evening meal

dîneur *m.* dinner guest; diner

dinosaure, dinosaurien *m.* dinosaur

diocèse *m.* diocese

diphthérie *f.* diphtheria

diphthongue *m.* diphthong

diphtonguer *vt.* to diphthongize

diplomate *m.* diplomat

diplomatie *f.* diplomacy

diplomatique *a.* diplomatic

diplôme *m.* diploma

diplômé *a.* graduate, licensed

dipsomanie *f.* compulsive drinking

dire *vt.* to tell, say, relate; think; mean; pour ainsi — as it were; vouloir — to mean; — *n.* words, statement

directeur *m.* director, manager

direction *f.* direction; management; steering gear

directionnel *a.* directional

directive *f.* directive

directoire *m.* directory

directorat *m.* directorship

dirigeable *m.* dirigible

diriger *vt.* to direct, manage, guide, lead — par radio (avi.) to vector

discernable *a.* discernible, perceptible

discernement *m.* discernment

discerner *vt.* to discern

disciple *m.* disciple

disciplinaire *a.* disciplinary; — *m.* disciplinarian

discipliner *vt.* to discipline

discobole *m.* discus thrower

discontinu *a.* discontinuous

discontinuation *f.* discontinuation

discontinuer *vt.* to interrupt, discontinue

discontinuité *f.* interruption, discontinuity

disconvenance *f.* disproportion, disparity; unsuitableness

disconvenir *vi.* to disagree

discophile *m. & f.* amateur record collector *or* maker

discordant *a.* discordant

discorde *f.* discord

discorder *vi.* to be out of harmony, not to harmonize; clash

discothèque *f.* collection of phonograph records, record library

discourir *vi.* to discourse

discours *m.* discourse; speech

discourtois *a.* discourteous

discourtoisie *f.* discourtesy, impoliteness

discrédit *m.* discredit; disfavor

discréditer *vt.* to discredit

discret *a.* discreet; prudent; quiet

discrétion *f.* discretion

discrétionnaire *a.* discretionary

discrimination *f.* discrimination

disculper *vt.* to clear, exonerate

discussion *f.* argument, debate; discussion

discutable *a.* moot, debatable

discuter *vt.* to discuss, argue, debate

disert *a.* fluent, eloquent

disette *f.* want, poverty; famine

diseur (diseuse) *m. & f.* speaker, teller; — de bonne aventure fortune teller

disgrâce *f.* disgrace, disfavor

disgracié *a.* fallen from favor

disgracieux *a.* ungraceful, awkward; disagreable; rude

disjoindre *vt.* to disjoin, disjoint

disjoncteur *m.* circuit breaker

disjonctif *a.* disjunctive

disloquer *vt.* to dislocate

disparaître *vi.* to disappear

disparate *a.* incongruous; unmatched; — *f.* incongruity, sharp contrast

disparité *f.* disparity

disparition *f.* disappearance

dispendieux *a.* costly, expensive

dispensaire *m.* dispensary, clinic

dispensation *f.* dispensing, dispensation

dispense *f.* dispensation; exemption

dispenser *vt.* to dispense; excuse, exempt

disperser *vt.* to disperse, scatter

dispersion *f.* dispersion, dispersal

disponibilités *f. pl.* available funds

disponible *a.* available; free, unoccupied

dispos *a.* well-disposed; in good condition

disposé *a.* disposed, inclined

disposer *vt. & vi.* to dispose; — de to have at one's disposal

dispositif *m.* apparatus; terms; assembly of machinery pieces

disposition *f.* disposition; arrangement; –s *pl.* preparation; — de vol flight pattern

disproportionné *a.* disproportionate

dispute *f.* dispute, quarrel

disputer *vt. & vi.* to dispute, quarrel, argue

disqualification *f.* disqualification

disquaire *m.* record seller, record dealer

disqualifier *vt.* to disqualify

disque *m.* disk, discus; phonograph record; (rail.) safety signal; — lorgue durée long-playing record

dissection *f.* dissection

dissemblable *a.* unsimilar, different

dissémination *f.* dissemination

disséminer *vt.* to disseminate

dissension *f.* dissension, discord

dissentiment *m.* difference of opinion

disséquer *vt.* to dissect
dissertation *f.* dissertation; essay on a certain subject
disserter *vi.* to expound
dissident *a.* dissident
dissimulateur *m.* dissembler; — *a.* dissembling, hiding
dissimulation *f.* dissimulation, dissembling
dissimulé *a.* secretive, deceptive
dissimuler *vt. & vi.* to conseal; hide; dissemble
dissipation *f.* dissipation
dissiper *vt.* to dissipate; disperse
dissociation *f.* dissociation
dissocier *vt.* to dissociate, separate
dissolu *a.* dissolute
dissolution *f.* dissolution; dissoluteness; dissolving
dissonance *f.* disssonance
dissonant *a.* dissonant
dissoudre *vt.* to dissolve
dissuder *vt.* to dissuade
distance *f.* distance; interval
distancer *vt.* to outdistance; to stagger (racing); to disqualify (racing)
distant *a.* distant
distendre *vt.* to distend
distension *f.* distension
distillat *m.* distillate
distillateur *m.* distiller
distillation *f.* distillation
distiller *vt.* to distill; –ie *f.* distillery
distinct *a.* distinct, clear
distinctif *a.* distinctive
distinction *f.* distinction
distingué *a.* distinguished
distinguer *vt.* to distinguish; single out
distordre *vt.* to distort, twist
distors *a.* distorted, twisted
distorsion *f.* distortion
distraction *f.* distraction, abstraction; absent-mindedness; amusement
distraire *vt.* to distract, divert
distrait *a.* inattentive, absent-minded
distribuer *vt.* to distribute
distributeur *a.* distributing; — *m.* distributor
distribution *f.* distribution; (theat.) cast
district *m.* district
dit *a.* said, appointed, fixed; prendre pour — to take for granted; — *m.* saying
dito *adv.* ditto
diurétique *a. & m.* diuretic
diurne *a.* daily; day-blooming; active in daylight
divaguer *vi.* to go astray, wander, ramble
divan *m.* divan, couch
divergence *f.* divergency, divergence
divergent *a.* divergent

diverger *vi.* to diverge
divers *a.* diverse; various; different
diversifier *vt.* to diversify, vary
diversion *f.* diversion
diversité *f.* diversity
divertir *vt.* to divert, entertain; se — to have a good time
divertissement *m.* recreation, pastime, diversion
dividende *f.* dividend
divin *a.* divine; heavenly
divination *f.* divination, soothsaying
diviniser *vt.* to deify
divinité *f.* divinity
diviser *vt.* to divide; separate
diviseur *m.* divider; (math.) divisor, factor
divisible *a.* divisible
division *f.* division; dividing; section; disagreement; hyphen
divorcer *vi.* to divorce, be divorced
divulguer *vt.* to divulge
dix *a.* ten
dix-huit *a.* eighteen
dixième *a.* tenth
dix-neuf *a.* nineteen
dix-sept *a.* seventeen
dizaine *f.* about ten
djinn *m.* jinni, genie
do *m.* (mus.) do; first scale syllable; French key of C
docile *a.* docile, submissive
docilité *f.* docility
dock *m.* dock
docker *m.* dock worker
docte *a.* learned, scholarly
docteur *m.* doctor
doctorat *m.* doctor's degree, doctorate
doctrinal *a.* doctrinal
doctrine *f.* doctrine, dogma
document *m.* document; written proof
documentaire *a. & m.* documentary; documentative, educational film
documentation *f.* documentation
documenter *vt.* to document
dodeliner *vi.* to sway, rock; — *vt.* to dandle a baby, balance gently
dogmatique *a.* dogmatic
dogmatiser *vi.* to pontificate; speak in a pre-emptory tone
dogmatisme *m.* dogmatism
dogme *m.* dogma, tenet
dogue *m.* bulldog; watchdog
doigt *m.* finger; — du pied toe; montrer du — to point at
doigter *vt.* to finger, strum, play
doigtier *m.* finger guard
doit *m.* (com.) debit
doléance *f.* complaint; grievance
dolent *a.* sad, doleful; painful

dolmen *m.* dolmen (archeology)

domaine *m.* domain; estate; property

dôme *m.* dome; — **géodésique** geodesic dome

domestication *f.* domestication

domesticité *f.* domesticity

domestique *m. & f.* domestic, servant; — *a.* domestic

domestiquer *vt.* to tame, domesticate

domicilier *vt.* to domicile; **se** — to establish residence

dominant *a.* dominant; —**e** *f.* dominant trait

dominateur *a.* dominant, dominating

dominer *vt.* to dominate, rule, control; overlook; — *vi.* to rule, prevail

dominical *a.* dominical; Sunday; **oraison** —**e** *f.* Lord's prayer

domino *m.* domino; robe; disguise

dommage *m.* damage, loss; **c'est** — it is a pity

dommageable *a.* damaging; damageable

domptable *a.* conquerable; tamable, trainable

dompter *vt.* to tame; subdue, vanquish, conquer

dompteur *m.* conqueror; animal trainer

don *m.* gift, present; (fig.) knack, talent

donataire *m. & f.* recipient, beneficiary

donateur *m.* donor

donation *f.* donation, gift

donc *conj.* then, thus, therefore, so

donjon *m.* castle keep; isolated tower for castle watchman; tiered metal tower (modern battleship)

donne *f.* card deal

donnée *f.*, —**s** *pl.* information; data

donner *vt. & vi.* to give; impart; grant; deal cards; — **sur** to open onto, look out on

donneur *m.* donor; dealer at cards

dont *pron.* whose, of which, of whom

donzelle *f.* woman of easy virtue

dorade, daurade *f.* goldfish

dorénavant *adv.* henceforth

dorer *vt.* to gild; to glaze pastry

doreur *m.* gilder

dorique *a.* Doric

dorlotement *m.* coddling, pampering

dorloter *vt.* to pamper, coddle

dormant *a.* sleeping; dormant

dormeur *m.* sleeper

dormir *vi.* to sleep; **à** — **debout** boring

dortoir *m.* dormitory

dorure *f.* gilding; application of pastry glaze

dos *m.* back; — **du nez** bridge of the nose

dosage *m.* dose, dosage

dossier *m.* chair back; file, folder; dossier

dot *f.* dowry

dotation *f.* endowment

doter *vt.* to endow; furnish with a dowry

douaire *m.* widow's dowry

douairière *f.* dowager

douane *f.* custom house, duty, customs

douanier *m.* customs officer; — *a.* concerning customs

doublage *m.* lining; doubling; dubbing (movie film)

double *m.* double; spare; copy; — *a.* double

doublé *m.* plated metal; metal plating (gold *or* silver); bank shot (billiards); — *a.* lined

doublement *adv.* doubly

doubler *vt.* to double; line; pass (a car); hasten; begin over; dub (a film)

doublon *m.* doubloon

doublure *f.* lining; (theat.) understudy

doucement *adv.* softly; slowly

doucereux *a.* unpleasantly sweet

douceur *f.* sweetness; softness, gentleness; docility

douche *f.* shower bath; (med.) douche

doucir *vt.* to polish, rub

doué *a.* gifted, endowed

douer *vt.* to bestow, endow

douille *f.* socket; cartridge shell; casing

douillet *a.* soft, delicate; (fig.) oversensitive

douleur *f.* pain, sorrow

douloureux *a.* painful; sorrowful

doute *m.* doubt; suspicion; skepticism; **mettre en** — to doubt, question; **sans** — without doubt, probably; of course

douter *vi.* to doubt; **se** — **de** to suspect

douteur *a.* doubting

douteux *a.* doubtful; dubious, suspicious

douve *f.* moat; plank, stave

doux (douce) *a.* sweet; soft, smooth; fresh; quiet; mild; timid

douzaine *f.* dozen

douze *a.* twelve

douzième *a.* twelfth

doxologie *f.* doxology

doyen *m.* dean

doyenneté *f.* seniority

dragée *f.* Jordan almond; buckshot; sugar-coated pill

drageon *m.* (bot.) sucker, shoot (tree root)

dragon *m.* dragon; (mil.) dragoon

drague *f.* dredge; seine; minesweeping apparatus; — **à vapeur** steam shovel

draguer *vt.* to dredge

dragueur *m.* dredge (boat); minesweeper

drain *m.* drain pipe; (med.) drain

drainage *m.* drainage

drainer *vt.* to drain

dramatique *a.* dramatic

dramatiser *vt.* to dramatize

dramaturge *m.* dramatist
drame *m.* drama, play
drap *m.* cloth; bed sheet; **–ie** *f.* drapery
drapeau *m.* flag
draper *vt.* to drape
drapier *m.* cloth merchant, cloth manufacturer; draper
drelin *m.* sound of ringing, ting-a-ling (bell)
dressage *m.* training of animals
dresser *vt.* to raise; build; train animals; set up; trim; — **les oreilles** prick up ears; **se** — **to stand**, straighten up, rise; sit up
dresseur *m.* animal trainer
dressoir *m.* sideboard, buffet; dresser
drisse *f.* halyard, rope
drogue *f.* drug; chemical
droguer *vt.* to drug; physic
droguerie *f.* drug business
droguiste *m.* druggist
droit *m.* right, justice; prerogative, privilege; law; tax; **de** — by rights, rightfully; — *a.* right; straight; just; honest; upright; — *adv.*, **tout** — straight ahead
droite *f.* right; **à** — to the right
droitier *a.* right-hand(ed)
droiture *f.* integrity
drolatique *a.* droll, funny, amusing
drôle *a.* droll, funny; odd, peculiar
drôlesse *f.* wench, hussy
dromadaire *m.* dromadary
dru *a.* vigorous, heavy; — *adv.* thickly, heavily
dû *a. & m.* due; what is owed
dualisme *m.* dualism
dualité *f.* duality
duc *m.* duke; horned owl
duché *m.* duchy
duchesse *f.* duchess; (coll.) woman with airs; 18th century couch; Duchess pear
ductile *a.* ductile
duègne *f.* duenna, chaperon
duel *m.* duel
duelliste *m.* duelist
dulcifier *vt.* to sweeten; neutralize
dûment *adv.* duly
dune *f.* dune
dunette *f.* (naut.) poop
duo *m.* (mus.) duet
duodécimal *a.* duodecimal
duodénum *m.* duodenum
dupe *f.* dupe; — *a.* duped
duper *vt.* to dupe; fool
duperie *f.* deception, trickery
duplicata *m.* duplicate
duplicateur *m.* duplicator, duplicating machine
duplication *f.* duplication
duplicité *f.* duplicity

duquel *pron.* of which, of whom, whose
dur *a. & adv.* hard; tough; difficult
durabilité *f.* durability
durable *a.* durable, lasting
durant *prep.* during
durcir *vt. & vi.* to harden
durcissement *m.* hardening; stiffening
durée *f.* duration
durer *vi.* to last, endure
dureté *f.* hardness, toughness; cruelty
durillon *m.* callus, corn
duvet *m.* down; fuzz
duveté *a.* downy
duveteux *a.* downy
dynamique *a.* dynamic
dynamisme *m.* dynamism
dynamite *f.* dynamite; **–r** *vt.* to dynamite
dynamo *f.* dynamo
dynastie *f.* dynasty
dynastique *a.* dynastic
dyne *f.* dyne
dysenterie *f.* dysentery
dyspepsie *f.* dispepsia, indigestion

E

eau *f.* water; — **de Cologne** cologne; — **douce** soft water; fresh water; **cours d'** — *m.* stream; **jet d'** — *m.* fountain
eau-de-vie *f.* brandy; spirits
eau-forte *f.* nitric acid; etching
ébahir *vt.* to stupify, amaze
ébahissement *m.* astonishment, amazement
ébats *m. pl.* frolics, revels
ébattre *v.*, **s'** — to frolic, revel
ébaubir *v.*, **s'** — to be astonished
ébauche *f.* rough draft, sketch
ébaucher *vt.* to sketch, make a rough draft of
ébène *f.* ebony
ébenier *m.* ebony tree
ébéniste *m.* cabinetmaker
éberluer *vt.* to astonish
éblouir *vt.* to dazzle; bewitch
éblouissement *m.* dazzlement; glare
ébouillanter *vt.* to scald
éboulement *m.* landslide; cave-in (earth)
ebouler *vt.* to cause to fall; to crumble; **s'** — to tumble down
ébouriffant *a.* amazing
ébouriffer *vt.* to disorder, mess up; amaze
ébrancher *vt.* to prune
ébranlement *m.* shaking; shock
ébranler *vt.* to shake, shock; set in motion; **s'** — to waver, shake
ébrécher *vt.* to breach; notch; — **sa fortune** cut into one's fortune
ébriété *f.* inebriation
ébroer *v.* **s'** — to snort

ébruiter *vt.* to spread about; make public

ébullition *f.* boiling; boiling point

éburnéen *a.* ivory

écaille *f.* scale, shell; tortoise shell

écailler *vt. & vi.* to scale fish

écale *f.* shell, hull

écaler *vt.* to shell, hull

écarlate *f. & a.* scarlet

écarquiller *vt.* to spread, open wide

écart *m.* stepping aside; swerving; discard; digression; **à l' —** *adv.* aside; secluded; aloof **à l' — de** *prep.* far from

écarté *a.* lonely, secluded

écartèlement *m.* quartering

écarteler *vt.* to quarter

écartement *m.* removal, separation

écarter *vt.* to put aside; separate; avert

ecchymose *f.* bruise, black-and-blue mark

ecclésiastique *a. & m.* ecclesiastic

écervelé *a.* brainless, flighty; **— *m.*** scatterbrain

échafaud *m.* scaffold; platform

échafaudage *m.* scaffolding

échafauder *vt.* to put up a scaffold; plan, set up, build up

échalote *f.* (bot.) shallot

échancrer *vt.* to hollow out; indent

échange *m.* exchange; **libre —** free trade

échanger *vt.* to exchange, barter

échanson *m.* cupbearer

échantillon *m.* sample, specimen

échappatoire *f.* way out; loophole

échappée *f.* escape; space, short period; **à l' —** stealthily

échappement *m.* escapement (watch); leak, leakage, escape; exhaust

échapper *vt.* to escape; avoid; **s' —** to escape; leave

écharde *f.* splinter

écharpe *f.* scarf; sash; sling; **en —** *adv.* diagonally

écharper *vt.* to slash, cut up

échasse *f.* stilt

échauder *vt.* to scald

échauffement *m.* heating; overexcitement

échauffer *vt.* to warm; excite; **s' —** to get warm; grow angry

échauffourée *f.* blunder; riot; rash project

échéance *f.* expiration, falling due; **tomber à —** to fall due

échéant *a.* falling due; **le cas —** if such should be the case

échec *m.* check; failure; **-s** *pl.* chess; chessmen; **— et mat** checkmate

échelle *f.* ladder, scale; stocking run; **—**

échelon *m.* rung; echelon

échelonnement *m.* spreading out

échelonner *vt.* to spread out; space out; (mil.) arrange in echelon

écheniller *vt.* to exterminate caterpillars

écheveau *m.* skein

échevelé *a.* dishevelled, tangled

écheveler *vt.* to dishevel

échine *f.* spine; backbone

échiner *vt.* to break the back of; beat; **s' —** to tire oneself out

échiquier *m.* chessboard; exchequer

écho *m.* echo

échoir *vi.* to fall due; happen

échopper *vt.* to gouge, scoop out

échotier *m.* gossip columnist, newsmonger

échouer *vt. & vi.* (naut.) to run aground, strand; be stranded; fail; **faire —** to wreck

échu *a.* expired

éclabousser *vt.* to splash, splatter

éclaboussure *f.* splash, splatter

éclair *m.* lightning flash; eclair (pastry)

éclairage *m.* lighting, lamps; (fig.) point of view

éclaircie *f.* bright spot (sky); clearing (forest)

éclaircir *vt.* to clear, thin, brighten; explain, elucidate

éclaircissement *m.* clearing up; explanation

éclairer *vt. & vi.* to light, illuminate, enlighten

éclaireur *m.* scout

éclaireuse *f.* girl scout

éclat *m.* splinter; brightness; splendor; explosion; peal of thunder; (fig.) glory

éclatant *a.* glittering, brilliant

éclatement *m.* explosion, bursting

éclater *vi.* to split, burst; sparkle, glitter; break out, blow up

éclectique *a. & n.* eclectic

éclectisme *m.* eclecticism

éclipser *vt.* to eclipse; **s' —** to be eclipsed, vanish

éclisse *f.* splinter; (med.) splint

éclisser *vt.* (med.) to use a splint

éclopé *a.* lame, crippled

éclore *vi.* to be hatched; blossom; open

éclosion *f.* blooming; manifestation; advent; hatching

écluse *f.* floodgate; canal lock

écluser *vt.* to close by a lock; **— un bateau** to take a boat through a lock

écœurer *vt.* to sicken; dishearten; cause aversion

école *f.* school; **— maternelle** nursery school; **— mixte** school for boys *and* girls

écolier *m.* schoolboy

écolière *f.* schoolgirl

écologie *f.* ecology

éconduire *vt.* to show out; get rid of

économat *m.* treasurer's office; bureau of economies

économe *a.* economical; — *m. & f.* house-keeper; accounts keeper; treasurer

économie *f.* economy; saving; — **domestique** home economics

économique *a.* economic; economical

économiser *vt.* to economize, save

économiste *m.* economist

écope *f.* (naut.) bailing scoop

écoper *vt.* (naut.) to bail out

écorce *f.* bark (tree), rind, peel; outside

écorcer *vt.* to peel

écorcher *vt.* to flay; scrape; scorch

écorchure *f.* scrape, abrasion

écorner *vt.* to dog-ear; curtail, reduce

écornifleur *m.* parasite, moocher

écossais *a.* Scotch, Scottish; — *n.* Scot, Scotsman

Ecosse *f.* Scotland

écosser *vt.* to shell

écot *m.* share, part, portion; tree stump

écoulement *m.* drain, discharge; sale

écouler *vt.* to sell; s' — to flow out, drain off; elapse, go by

écourter *vt.* to shorten; crop

écoute *f.* listening post; monitor; être aux —s to be listening (in), be eavesdropping

écouter *vt.* to listen (to); pay attention

écouteur *m.* listener; telephone receiver

écoutille *f.* hatch

écran *m.* fire screen; (phot.) filter

écrasant *a.* crushing

écrasement *m.* crushing; defeat, disaster

écraser *vt.* to crush; s' — to crash; flock over

écrémer *vt.* to skim milk

écrémeuse *f.* cream separator

écrevisse *f.* crayfish

écrier *v.*, s' — to cry out, exclaim

écrin *m.* jewel box, casket

écrire *vt.* to write, compose; write down

écrit *m.* writing, written word, written examination; — *a.* written

écriteau *m.* sign, placard

écritoire *f.* writing set; desk set

écriture *f.* handwriting; document; account

Ecriture *f.*, l' — sainte Scriptures

écrivailleur *m.* scribbler, hack writer

écrivain *m.* writer, author of books

écrou *m.* screw nut; lever l' — to liberate

écrouelles *f. pl.* scrofula

écrouer *vt.* to imprison

écroulement *m.* fall, collapse; (fig.) complete ruin

écrouler *v.*, s' — to collapse, crumble

écroûter *vt.* to remove the crust from

écru *a.* unbleached; raw silk

ectoplasme *m.* ectoplasm

écu *m.* shield; crown (coin); —s *pl.* (fig.) money

écueil *m.* reef, rock

écuelle *f.* bowl, basin

éculer *vt.* to wear down a heel

écumant *a.* foaming; fuming

écume *f.* foam; froth; scum; (fig.) dregs (of humanity); — de mer meerschaum

écumer *vt.* to skim; — *vi.* to foam

écumeux *a.* scummy; foamy, frothy

écumoire *f.* skimmer

écurage *m.* scouring

écurer *vt.* to scour, cleanse

écureuil *m.* squirrel

écurie *f.* stable; string of horses (same owner)

écusson *m.* shield (heraldry); escutcheon; bud (grafting)

écuyer *m.* horseman, squire

écuyère *f.* horsewoman

eczéma *m.* eczema

éden *m.* Garden of Eden; paradise

édenté *a.* toothless

édicule *m.* small building on the street, shelter

édifiant *a.* edifying

édification *f.* erecting, building; edification

édifier *vt.* to edify; build, found

édile *m.* town councillor

édit *m.* edict

éditer *vt.* to edit; publish

éditeur *m.* editor, publisher; — *a.* publishing

édition *f.* edition; publishing

éditorial *a. & m.* editorial

édredon *m.* eiderdown; feather quilt

éducation *f.* upbringing; education; breeding

édulcorer *vt.* to sugar-coat; water down; make inoffensive

éduquer *vt.* to rear, bring up

effacement *m.* effacement, erasing, obliteration

effacer *vt.* to efface, erase; s' — to be obliterated; stand aside; (fig.) to bow to superiority

effarement *m.* fright

effarer *vt.* to frighten

effaroucher *vt.* to scare away; frighten, alarm

effectif *m.* effective force; (mil.) complement; manpower; size; — *a.* effective, actual

effectivement *adv.* actually, in fact

effectuer *vt.* to effect, accomplish

efféminé *a.* effeminate

effervescence *f.* effervescence, excitement

effervescent *a.* effervescent

effet *m.* effect, result; impression; —s *pl.* belongings; —s publics public bonds; en — indeed

effeuillaison *f.* falling of leaves
effeuiller *vt.* to strip of leaves, petals
efficace *a.* effective, efficacious
efficacité *f.* efficiency, effectiveness, efficacy
efficience *f.* effectiveness; efficiency
effigie *f.* effigy
effilé *a.* slender; — *m.* fringe
effiler *vt.* to unravel; taper
effilocher *vt.* to unravel
efflanqué *a.* lean, skinny, thin
effleurer *vt.* to graze, touch lightly
effluve *m.* effluvium, emanation
effondrement *m.* collapse, collapsing, destruction
effondrer *vt.* to break open; break up ground s' — to sink down, cave in
efforcer *v.*, s' — to strive, try to do one's best
effort *m.* effort, work; stress, strain
effraction *f.* housebreaking, burglary
effranger *vt.* to unravel the edges
effrayant *a.* frightful, dreadful
effrayer *vt.* to frighten; s' — to be frightened
effréné *a.* unbridled; frantic
effroi *m.* fright, terror
effronté *a.* bold, shameless, impudent
effronterie *f.* impudence, insolence, effrontery
effroyable *a.* frightful
effusion *f.* effusion; outpouring; — de sang bloodshed
égal *a.* equal; alike; indifferent; even, level; — *m.* equal; cela m'est — it's all the same to me, I don't care, all right
egaler *vt.* to equal, match, value the same
égalisation *f.* equalisation, equalizing
égaliser *vt.* to equalize, make even
égalitaire *a.* equalitarian
égalité *f.* equality; evenness
égard *m.* respect, consideration; à l' — de in reference to, toward; en — à considering that
égaré *a.* stray, lost
égarement *m.* losing, misplacing; deviation; straying, wandering; mental disorder
égarer *vt.* to mislead; mislay; bewilder; s' — to go astray, wander
égayer *vt.* to cheer up; s' — to make merry
égéen *a.* Aegean
églantier *m.* (plant), églantine *f.* (flower) eglantine; sweetbrier, wild rose
église *f.* church
égocentrique *a.* egocentric
égoïne *f.* handsaw
égoïsme *m.* selfishness
égoïste *a.* selfish; — *m.* egotist
égorger *vt.* to cut the throat (of), slaughter

égotisme *m.* egotism
égotiste *m.* & *f.* egotist
égout *m.* drainage; sewer
égoutier *m.* sewer worker
égoutter *vt.* & *vi.* to drain
égouttoir *m.* draining rack
égratigner *vt.* to scratch
égratignure *f.* scratch
égrener *vt.* to shell; pick off (grapes); gin
égrillard *a.* fancy-free
égrugeoir *m.* mortar
égruger *vt.* to pound, pulverize
égueuler *vt.* to break the neck of
Égypte *f.* Egypt
égyptien *m.* & *a.* Egyptian
égyptologie *f.* Egyptology
éhonté *a.* shameless
éjaculation *f.* ejaculation
éjaculer *vt.* to ejaculate
éjecter *vt.* to eject
éjection *f.* ejection
élaboration *f.* elaboration
élaborer *vt.* to elaborate
élaguer *vt.* to prune, trim; (fig.) to curtail (literary work)
élan *m.* impetus, impulse; bound; outburst; elk
élancé *a.* slender, slim
élancement *m.* twinge; yearning
élancer *vi.* to throb; dart; s' — to rush upon; shoot forward *or* up
élargir *vt.* to widen; free
élasticité *f.* elasticity
élastique *a.* elastic; — *m.* elastic, rubber band
électeur *m.* elector, voter
électif *a.* elective
élection *f.* election
électoral *a.* electoral
électricien *m.* electrician
électricité *f.* electricity
électrification *f.* electrification
électrifier *vt.* to electrify
électrique *a.* electric, electrical
électriser *vt.* to electrify
électro-aimant *m.* electromagnet
électrocardiogramme *m.* cardiogram
électrochoc *m.* shock treatment
électrocuter *vt.* to electrocute
électrocution *f.* electrocution
électrode *f.* electrode
électrodynamique *a.* electrodynamic; —*f.* electrodynamics
électro-encéphalogramme *m.* electroencephalogram
électrolyse *f.* electrolysis
électromagnétique *a.* electromagnetic
électromètre *m.* electrometer
électron *m.* electron
électronique *a.* electronic

électroscope *m.* electroscope
électrostatique *a.* electrostatic
élégamment *adv.* elegantly
élégance *f.* elegance
élégant *a.* elegant, stylish
élégie *f.* elegy
élément *m.* element; (elec.) cell —s *pl.* natural forces
élémentaire *a.* elementary, basic
éléphant *m.* elephant
éléphantesque *a.* enormous
élevage *m.* animal husbandry; ranching
élévation *f.* elevation
élève *m. & f.* pupil
élevé *a.* high; brought up; **bien —** well-bred, well-mannered; **mal —** ill-bred
élever *vt.* to raise, bring up; **s' —** to rise, arise
éleveur *m.* animal raiser
elfe *m.* elf
élider *vt.* to elide
éligibilité *f.* eligibility
éligible *a.* eligible
élimer *vt.* to wear out
élimination *f.* elimination
éliminatoire *a.* preliminary (sports)
éliminer *vt.* to eliminate; cancel
élire *vt.* to elect
élisabéthain *a.* Elizabethan
élision *f.* elision
élite *f.* élite; choice
élixir *m.* elixir
elle *pron.* she, her, it; —s *pl.* they
elle-même *pron.* herself, itself
ellipse *f.* ellipse
elliptique *a.* elliptical
élocution *f.* elocution
éloge *m.* eulogy, praise
élogieux *a.* full of praise
éloigné *a.* distant, faraway, remote; removed
éloignement *m.* absence, remoteness; aversion; postponement
éloigner *vt.* to remove; drive away; defer; **s' —** to move off, away, deviate
élongation *f.* elongation
éloquemment *adv.* eloquently
éloquence *f.* eloquence
éloquent *a.* eloquent
élu *n.* chosen one; —s *pl.* elect
élucidation *f.* elucidation
élucider *vt.* to elucidate
éluder *vt.* to elude
émaciation *f.* emaciation
émacié *a.* emaciated
émail *m.* enamel, glaze
émailler *vt.* to enamel
émailleur *m.* enameller
émanation *f.* emanation
émancipation *f.* emancipation

émanciper *vt.* to emancipate
émaner *vi.* to emanate
émarger *vt.* to note in the margin, initial to prove reading; trim; receive pay
émasculer *vt.* to emasculate
emballage *m.* packing, crating
emballer *vt.* to pack, wrap; crate; excite
emballeur *m.* packer
embarcadère *m.* wharf; (rail.) platform
embarcation *f.* small boat, launch
embardée *f.* lurch; (naut.) yaw; (auto.) swerve
embarquement *m.* embarcation; shipment
embarquer *vt. & vi.* to embark
embarras *m.* obstruction; difficulty; perplexity; confusion
embarrasser *vt.* to trouble; perplex; confuse; embarass
embaucher *vt.* to hire
embauchoir *m.* shoe tree
embaumement *m.* embalming
embaumer *vt.* to embalm; perfume
embellir *vt. & vi.* to embellish; become beautiful
embellissement *m.* embellishment
embêtement *m.* annoyance
embêter *vt.* (coll.) to bother, annoy
emblée, d' — *adv.* first, on the spot; without difficulty
emblématique *a.* emblematic
emblème *m.* emblem
embobiner *vt.* to wind (up), put on a spool *or* reel
emboîter *vt.* to fit in; copy, take after; set a bone; **— le pas à** to fall into step with
embonpoint *m.* plumpness
embouche *f.* pasture
embouché *a.*, **mal —** foulmouthed
embouchoir *m.* (mus.) instrument mouthpiece
embouchure *f.* mouth of a river; mouthpiece
embourber *vt.* to stick in the mud, implicate
embout *m.* handle (cane, umbrella)
embouteillage *m.* bottling up; bottleneck; traffic jam
embouteiller *vt.* to bottle up; (fig.) to block
embranchement *m.* branch, division; road junction
embrasement *m.* conflagration, burning
embraser *vt.* to set on fire
embrassade *f.* embrace
embrasse *f.* curtain tieback; armrest
embrassement *m.* embrace; kiss
embrasser *vt.* to embrace; kiss
embrasure *f.* opening; port
embrayage *m.* clutch; coupling, engaging
embrayer *vt.* to connect, engage; (auto.)

to let in the clutch

embrocher *vt.* to spit (meat cookery)

embrouiller *vt.* to tangle, mix up; **s'** — to get confused; become intricate

embroussaillé *a.* bushy; complex, tangled

embrumé *a.* misty, hazy

embrun *m.* spray; fog

embryologie *f.* embryology

embryon *m.* embryo

embryonnaire *a.* embryonic

embûche *f.* trap

embuscade *f.* ambush

embusqué *m.* soldier at the rear; person lying in ambush

embusquer *vt.* to ambush, trap

émeraude *f.* emerald

émergence *f.* emergence

émerger *vi.* to emerge

émeri *m.* emery

émerillonné *a.* lively

émérite *a.* eminent, experienced; emeritus

émerveillement *m.* wonderment

émerveiller *vt.* to astonish, amaze

émétique *m.* emetic

émetteur *m.* radio transmitter

émettre *vt.* to emit, issue; transmit, broadcast

émeute *f.* riot

émietter *vt.* to crumble

émigration *f.* emigration

émigré *m.* emigrant; refugee; emigrated nobleman (history)

émigrer *vt.* to emigrate

émincé *m.* minced meat, mincemeat

émincer *vt.* to slice thinly; hash

éminemment *adv.* eminently

éminence *f.* eminence

éminent *a.* eminent; distinguished

émissaire *m.* emissary

émission *f.* emission, issue; transmission, broadcast; — **transmise en direct** live broadcast; — **de télévision transmise en couleurs** colorcast

emmagasiner *vt.* to store up, stockpile

emmailloter *vt.* to swathe, swaddle

emmêler *vt.* to entangle, mat; disturb

emménagement *m.* moving in, installation

emménager *vi.* to move into

emmener *vt.* to take away, lead away

emmitoufler *vt.* to muffle up

emmurer *vt.* to wall up

émoi *m.* emotion, agitation, turmoil

émoluments *m. pl.* emoluments

émonder *vt.* to prune, trim

émotif *a.* emotive; emotional

émotion *f.* emotion, feeling; excitement

émotionnable *a.* emotional

émotionner *vt.* to move, thrill; **s'** — to get excited

émouchoir *m.* fly swatter

émoudre *vt.* to sharpen, grind

émoulage *m.* grinding, sharpening

émoulu *a.* sharpened; **frais** — **de** fresh from, just out of

émousser *vt.* to dull (senses), blunt; weaken

émouvoir *vt.* to move, affect; rouse; **s'** — to be moved

empailler *vt.* to cover, stuff, pack

empailleur *m.* taxidermist

empaler *vt.* to impale

empan *m.* span (measure)

empanacher *vt.* to plume

empaqueter *vt.* to package

emparer *v.,* **s'** — **de** to take possession of, seize

empâter *vt.* to make sticky; destroy harmony

empattement *m.* foundation, platform; (auto.) wheelbase

empaumer *vt.* to take in hand; overcome

empêchement *m.* obstacle, hindrance

empêcher *vt.* to hinder, prevent; **s'** — **de** to keep from, help, refrain from

empêcheur *m.* preventer; — **de danser en rond** (coll.) wet blanket

empeigne *f.* top leather of shoes

empennage *m.* stabilizing fins; feathers on an arrow

empenné *a.* plumed, feathered

empereur *m.* emperor

empeser *vt.* to starch

empester *vt.* to infect, make foul; — *vi.* to reek, smell

empêtrer *vt.* to bind, involve, hinder

emphase *f.* overemphasis; bombast

emphatique *a.* emphatic, bombastic

emphysème *m.* emphysemia

empiècement *m.* yoke (clothing)

empierrer *vt.* to pave with stone (road); ballast (tracks, roads, etc.)

empiétement *m.* incursion, usurpation

empiéter *vi.,* — **sur** to usurp; encroach on

empiler *vt.* to pile up, stack

empire *m.* empire, rule; mastery

empirer *vt.* to make worse; aggravate; — *vi.* grow worse

empirique *a.* empirical

empirisme *m.* empiricism

emplacement *m.* place, location, site

emplâtre *m.* (med.) plaster, salve; (fig.) apathetic person

emplette *f.* purchase; **aller faire des** —**s** to go shopping

emplir *vt.* to fill up

emploi *m.* use; employment; — **du temps** schedule; **mode d'** — instructions for use

employé *m.* employee; clerk; white-collar

worker

employer *vt.* to employ; use; **s' —** to occupy oneself

employeur *m.* user, employer

empocher *vt.* to pocket

empoigner *vt.* to grasp; seize; arrest

empois *m.* starch

empoisonnement *m.* poisoning

empoisonner *vt.* to poison; ruin; make bitter; (coll.) bore, annoy

empoisonneur *m.* poisoner, (coll.) bore, annoying person

empoissonner *vt.* to stock with fish

emporté *a.* quick-tempered, hasty

emporte-pièce *m.* punch tool

emportement *m.* temper, anger

emporter *vt.* to take away, carry away; prevail; **s' —** to lose control of oneself

empoter *vt.* to pot (plant)

empourprer *v.*, **s' —** to turn crimson; flush

empreindre *vt.* to imprint, stamp

empreinte *f.* imprint; **— digitale** fingerprint

empressé *a.* bustling, eager

empressement *m.* eagerness, zeal, readiness

empresser *v.*, **s' —** to be eager; hasten

emprise *f.* seizure; influence

emprisonnement *m.* imprisonment

emprisonner *vt.* to imprison

emprunt *m.* loan, borrowing

emprunté *a.* feigned; constrained

emprunter *vt.* to borrow; (fig.) plagiarize

emprunteur *m.* borrower

ému *a.* moved; affected

émulation *f.* emulation

emule *m.* emulator; rival

émulsion *f.* emulsion

émulsionner *vt.* to emulsify

en *prep.* in, into; at; by; **— pron.** of him, of her, of it, of them; some, any; **— adv.** from it, thence

enamourer *v.*, **s' — (de)** to fall in love (with)

encadrement *m.* frame, framework

encadrer *vt.* to frame

encager *vt.* to cage

encaisse *f.* cash in hand; cash balance

encaissé *a.* banked, with high banks

encaissement *m.* taking in of money; boxing, crating; embankment

encaisser *vt.* to pack, box; deposit; take in

encan *m.* auction

encanailler *vt.* to degrade; **s' —** to lose caste

encapuchonner *vt.* to hood

encart, encartage *m.* insert

encarter *vt.* to insert

en-cas *m.* snack, potluck meal; emergency supply

encastrement *m.* groove; fitting

encastrer *vt.* to fit in, imbed

encaustique *f.* furniture wax, floor wax

encaustiquer *vt.* to wax

encaver *vt.* to put away, store (in a cellar)

enceindre *vt.* to surround, gird, encircle; enclose

enceinte *f.* enclosure; **— a.** pregnant

encens *m.* incense

encenser *vt.* to incense, perfume

encensoir *m.* incense burner

encéphalite *f.* encephalitis

encerclement *m.* encirclement

encercler *vt.* to encircle

enchaînement *m.* chain(ing); series

enchaîner *vt.* to chain; connect

enchanter *vt.* to enchant, delight; charm

enchanteur *a.* enchanting; **— m.** enchanter

enchâsser *vt.* to enclose; fit in; enshrine; set a jewel

enchère *f.* bid, bidding; **vente aux —s** *f.* auction sale

enchérir *vt.* to raise prices; **— vi.** go up in price; **— sur** outdo, exceed

enchevêtrer *vt.* to bind; entangle

enchifrener *vt.* to stop up, stuff up (with a cold)

enclave *f.* enclave; enclosed land

enclaver *vt.* to enclose; dovetail

enclin *a.* inclined, prone

enclos *m.* enclosure

enclume *f.* anvil

encoche *f.* notch; **—s** *pl.* thumb index

encocher *vt.* to notch, nick

encoignure *f.* corner building; corner furniture

encollage *m.* size (glue); sizing

encoller *vt.* to size

encolure *f.* neck opening; collar size; horse collar

encombre, encombrement *m.* encumbrance; hindrance; cumbersomeness; congestion

encombrer *vt.* to encumber, clog

encontre, à l' — *prep.* counter to

encore *adv.* yet; still; **— une fois** again

encorner *vt.* to horn; gore

encourageant *a.* encouraging

encourager *vt.* to encourage

encourir *vt.* to incur

encrasser *vt.* to make dirty, soil; clog

encre *f.* ink; **— de Chine** India ink

encrer *vt.* to ink

encroûter *vt.* to crust; plaster (walls); (fig.) make stupid

encrier *m.* inkwell

encyclique *f.* encyclical

encyclopédie *f.* encyclopedia

encyclopédique *a.* encyclopedic

endémique *a.* endemic
endenter *vt.* to tooth, cog; mesh
endetter *vt.* to put into debt; **s' —** to go into debt
endiablé *a.* bedeviled
endimancher *v.,* **s' —** to put on Sunday clothes; get dressed up
endive *f.* French endive
endocrinologie *f.* endocrinology
endoctrinement *m.* indoctrination
endoctriner *vt.* to indoctrinate
endolorir *vt.* to make painful, cause pain in
endommagement *m.* damage
endommager *vt.* to damage, injure
endormi *a.* asleep, sleepy
endormir *vt.* to put to sleep; lull; **s' —** to fall asleep
endos, endossement *m.* endorsement
endosser *vt.* to endorse; take on
endosseur *m.* endorser
endroit *m.* place, spot; right side of cloth
enduire *vt.* to spread, cover, coat
enduit *m.* layer, coat, plastering
endurable *a.* endurable, bearable, tolerable
endurant *a.* patient
endurci *a.* hardened, inveterate, calloused
endurcir *vt.* to harden
endurcissement *m.* hardening
endurer *vt.* to endure, suffer, bear, tolerate
en entier *adv.* fully, in detail
énergie *f.* energy
énergique *a.* energetic
énergumène *m. & f.* enthusiast, avid fanatic, madman
énervant *a.* weakening, debilitating; nerve-racking
énervement *m.* enervation
énerver *vt.* to enervate
enfance *f.* childhood; children; dotage; première **—** infancy
enfant *m. & f.* child; **— naturel** illegitimate child; **— trouvé** foundling
enfantement *m.* childbirth; (fig.) creation
enfanter *vt.* to give birth to
enfantillage *m.* childishness
enfantin *a.* childish; juvenile; infantile
enfariner *vt.* to flour, cover with flour
enfer *m.* hell
enfermé *m.* mustiness
enfermer *vt.* to shut up, lock up; enclose
enferrer *vt.* to pierce; **s' —** to be caught
enfiévrer *vt.* to make feverish; inflame
enfilade *f.* file, string, series
enfiler *vt.* to thread (needle); string (beads); (fig.) put on (clothes); pierce; start down a street
enfin *adv.* after all, at last, finally; in short
enflammer *vt.* to inflame; **s' —** to catch fire; become inflamed
enfler *vt. & vi.* to swell, bloat; (fig.) exaggerate
enflure *f.* swelling
enfoncé *a.* sunken, deep
enfoncement *m.* hollow; recess; breaking down; breaking in
enfoncer *vt. & vi.* to thrust, drive in; break open; sink; **s' —** to plunge; sink
enfouir *vt.* to bury; hide
enfourcher *vt.* to climb on; straddle
enfourchure *f.* crotch (tree *or* trousers)
enfourner *vt.* to put in the oven
enfreindre *vt.* to violate, break, infringe on
enfuir *v.,* **s' —** to run away; elope
enfumé *a.* smoked; smoky
enfumer *vt.* to smoke, blacken
engagé *m.* (mil.) volunteer, enlisted man
engageant *a.* engaging, prepossessing
engagement *m.* commitment, obligation; pawning; promise; hiring; enlistment; (mil.) engagement
engager *vt.* to pawn; pledge; hire; (mech.) engage; enter into; **s' —** to commit oneself; enlist
engainer *vt.* to sheathe, envelop
engazonner *vt.* to sod
engeance *f.* breed; race
engelure *f.* chilblain
engendrer *vt.* to engender
engin *m.* engine; machinery; device
englober *vt.* to unite; comprise
engloutir *vt.* to swallow up, engulf
engloutissement *m.* swallowing (up)
engluer *vt.* to glue; lime; catch; take in
engorgement *m.* obstruction
engorger *vt.* to obstruct; block
engouement *m.* infatuation
engouer *v.,* **s' —** to become infatuated
engouffrer *vt.* to engulf
engourdi *a.* dull, numbed
engourdir *vt.* to numb; lull
engourdissement *m.* numbness
engrais *m.* fertilizer, manure; enriched fodder
engraisser *vt.* to fatten; fertilize; **— vi.** to grow fat
engramme *m.* engram
engrenage *m.* gear, system of gears
engrener *vt.* to engage gears
engueuler *vt.* (coll.) to bawl out; insult
enhardir *vt.* to make bold; **s' —** to venture, be bold enough
enharnacher *vt.* to harness; (fig.) to deck out
énigmatique *a.* enigmatic
énigme *f.* riddle; enigma
enivrant *a.* intoxicating
enivrement *m.* intoxication
enivrer *vt.* to intoxicate; (fig.) carry away;

s' — to get drunk
enjambée f. stride
enjamber vt. & vi. to stride over, straddle; encroach
enjeu m. stake, bet
enjoindre vt. to enjoin, call on; order
enjôler vt. to coax, cajole, wheedle
enjôleur a. coaxing, cajoling
enjoliver vt. to make pretty, ornament, embellish
enjoué a. cheerful, lively, playful
enjouement m. cheerfulness
enlacer vt. to entwine; clasp; hem in
enlaidir vt. to make ugly; disfigure; — vi. to grow ugly
enlèvement m. removal; kidnapping; elopement
enlever vt. to remove; take away; abduct
enliser vt. to swallow up in sand, suck in
enluminer vt. to illuminate a manuscript
ennemi m. enemy; — a. hostile
ennoblir vt. to make noble, ennoble, dignify
ennui m. boredom, worry
ennuyeux a. annoying; boring, tiresome
ennuyer vt. to annoy; worry; bore; s' — to be bored, weary
énoncé m. terms, data; statement
énoncer vt. to state, announce
énonciation f. enunciation; stating, announcing
enorgueillir vt. to make proud; s' — de to pride oneself on
énorme a. enormous
énormément adv. enormously; a great deal
énormité f. enormity
enquérir v., s' — de to inquire about
enquête f. inquiry, investigation
enquêter (sur) vi. to investigate
enraciner vt. to implant s' — to take root
enragé m. enthusiast; madman; — a. mad; enthusiastic; inveterate
enrager vt. to madden; — vi. to be mad
enrayer vt. to halt, stop, brake; suspend
enrégimenter vt. to regiment
enregistrement m. recording, registering, transcribing; transcription
enregistrer vt. to register, record
enrhumer v., s' — to catch cold
enrichir vt. to enrich; adorn; develop
enrichissement m. enrichment
enrober vt. to cover, coat; wrap
enrôler vt. to enroll; enlist
enrouement m. hoarseness
enrouer v., s' — to become hoarse
enrouler vt. to roll up
ensabler vt. to cover with sand; run aground
ensacher vt. to bag

ensanglanter vt. to stain with blood
enseignant a. teaching; — m. teacher
enseigne f. distinctive sign; insignia designating particular firm; ensign; — m. ensign (rank)
enseignement m. teaching; education
enseigner vt. to teach, show
ensemble adv. together; — m. whole, entirety; d' — comprehensive; combined
ensemencer vt. to sow
ensevelir vt. to bury; shroud
ensevelissement m. burial, interment
ensiler vt. to put in a silo
ensoleillé a. sunny
ensommeillé a. sleepy
ensorceler vt. to bewitch
ensorcellement m. enchantment, charm, spell; sorcery
ensuite adv. afterwards, then, after
ensuivre v., s' — to result; follow; be the consequence
entacher vt. to soil, stain, taint
entailler vt. to notch, nick, gash
entamer vt. to cut; open; begin
entassement m. heaping, piling up, accumulation
entasser vt. to heap up, accumulate
ente f. plant graft; handle
entendement m. understanding, judgment
entendre vt. to hear; understand; mean; s' — to be heard; understand each other; get along
entendu a. heard, understood; c'est — all right, agreed
entente f. understanding; agreement
enter vt. to graft; s' — to be related by blood
entériner vt. to ratify
entérique a. enteric
entérite f. enteritis
enterrement m. funeral, burial, interment
enterrer vt. to bury, inter
en-tête m. heading, headline; letterhead
entêté a. obstinate, headstrong
entêtement m. obstinacy
entêter v., s' — to persist, be obstinate
enthousiasme m. enthusiasm
enthousiasmer vt. to fill with enthusiasm; s' — to be enthusiastic about
enthousiaste m. & f. enthusiast; fanatic; — a. enthusiastic
entichement m. infatuation
enticher v., s' — to become infatuated
entier a. entire, whole, intact; — m. totality
entièrement adv. completely, entirely, wholly
entité f. entity

entomologie *f.* entomology

entomologiste *m.* entomologist

entonner *vt.* to intone; begin to sing

entonnoir *m.* funnel

entorse *f.* sprain

entortiller *vt.* to twist, wind; warp, deform

entour *m.* à l' — (de) around, in the vicinity (of); -s *pl.* vicinity, surrounding area

entourage *m.* surroundings; set, circle, associates

entourer *vt.* to surround

entraccuser *v.*, s' — to accuse each other, accuse one another

entracte *m.* intermission, interval

entradmirer *v.*, s' — to admire each other, admire one another

entraide *f.* mutual aid

entraider *v.*, s' — to help one another

entrailles *f. pl.* entrails, bowels; feeling

entr'aimer *v.*, s' — to love each other, love one another

entrain *m.* spirit, gusto

entraînement *m.* carrying away; enthusiasm; training

entraîner *vt.* to drag, carry away; lead astray; entail

entraîneur *m.* trainer

entrave *f.* shackle; hindrance

entraver *vt.* to shackle; hinder

entre *prep.* between, among

entre- *prefix* inter-; partially; reciprocally, mutually

entrebâiller *vt.* to open partially, open slightly

entrebâilleur *m.* doorstop

entrecôte *f.* ribsteak, beef rib

entrecouper *vt.* to interrupt; intersect

entre-deux *m.* space between; partition

entrée *f.* entry, entrance, admission; course (usually fish or eggs) preceding main course; porte d' — *f.* front door

entrefaites *f. pl.*, sur ces — meanwhile

entrefermer *vt.* to close partially

entrefilet *m.* note, item in a newspaper

entregent *m.* tact, confidence; resourcefulness

entrejambes *m.* crotch; longueuer d' — length from crotch to heel

entrelacer *vt.* to interlace

entrelarder *vt.* to lard

entre-ligne *m.* space between the lines

entremêler *vt.* to mix, mingle; intersperse

entremets *m.* dessert, sweet

entremetteur *m.* go-between

entremetteuse *f.* B-girl

entremettre *v.* s'— to intervene

entremise *f.* intervention, mediation

entrepont *m.* (naut.) between decks

entreposer *vt.* to place in a warehouse

entrepôt *m.* warehouse

entreprenant *a.* enterprising

entreprendre *vt.* to undertake; contract for

entrepreneur *m.* contractor

entreprise *f.* enterprise, contract(ing)

entrer *vi.* to enter, come in

entreregarder *v.*, s' — to look at each other, look at one another

entresol *m.* mezzanine floor

entre-temps *adv.* meanwhile; — *m.* interval

entretenir *vt.* to maintain, support; entertain, converse with

entretien *m.* maintenance; conversation

entre-tuer *v.*, s' — to kill each other, kill one another

entrevoir *vt.* to glimpse; foresee

entrevue *f.* interview

entrouvrir *vt.* to open partially

énumérer *vt.* to enumerate

envahir *vt.* to invade

envahissement *m.* invasion

envaser *vt.* to fill with mud

enveloppe *f.* envelope, wrapper, casing

enveloppement *m.* enveloping

envelopper *vt.* to envelop, wrap up

envenimer *vt.* to poison, ruin

envergure *f.* wingspread; spread; scope, power

envers *m.* wrong side, reverse; à l' — inside out; upside down; — *prep.* towards

envi, à l' — (de) *adv.* vying (with)

envie *f.* desire, longing; envy; birthmark, hangnail; avoir — de to feel like, want to

envier *vt.* to envy, be jealous of; covet

envieux *a.* envious

environ *adv.* about, approximately; -s *m. pl.* outskirts, vicinity

environner *vt.* to surround

envisager *vt.* to envisage

envoi *m.* dispatch; consignment, shipment; envoy (poetry)

envol *m.*, **envolée** *f.* flight; take-off

envoler *v.*, s' — to fly away, take off

envoûtement *m.* voodoo, spell

envoûter *vt.* to dominate; to harm by a wax image used to cause a person to suffer (voodoo)

envoyé *m.* envoy

envoyer *vt.* to send

enzyme *m.* enzyme

épagneul *m.* spaniel

épais *a.* thick

épaisseur *f.* thickness

épaissir *vt. & vi.* to thicken

épanchement *m.* pouring out; effusion

épancher *vt.* to pour out, pour forth; s' —

to open up, overflow
épandre *vt.* to scatter, spread
épanouir *v.*, s' — to bloom; beam
épanouissement *m.* blossoming
épargne *f.* saving, thrift; **caisse d'** — *f.* savings bank
épargner *vt.* to spare, save
éparpillement *m.* scattering
éparpiller *vt.* to scatter
épars *a.* scattered, sparse
épatant *a.* amazing; (coll.) wonderful
épaté *a.* flattened; flat-nosed
épaule *f.* shoulder
épaulement *m.* breastworks
épauler *vt.* to help; put against the shoulder; put behind breastworks
épaulette *f.* epaulette; shoulder strap
épave *f.* wreck, wreckage; stray; (fig.) debris in general
épée *f.* sword
épéiste *m.* fencer, swordsman
épeler *vt.* to spell
épellation *f.* spelling
éperdu *a.* distracted; desperate
éperdument *adv.* desperately, wildly, madly
éperlan *m.* smelt
éperon *m.* spur
éperonner *vt.* to spur
épervier *m.* sparrow hawk; fishnet
épeuré *a.* fearful, frightened
éphémère *a.* ephemeral; — *m.* May fly
épi *m.* ear, head of grain; tuft, cowlick; cluster
épice *f.* spice; **pain d'** — gingerbread
épicer *vt.* to spice
épicerie *f.* grocery
épicier *m.* grocer
épicurien *a.* Epicurean
épidémie *f.* epidemic
épidémique *a.* epidemic
épiderme *m.* epidermis
épier *vt.* to watch, spy on
épieu *m.* pike
épiglotte *f.* epiglottis
épigramme *f.* epigram
épigraphe *f.* **epigraph**; quotation, motto
épilepsie *f.* epilepsy
épileptique *m. & f. & a.* epileptic
épiler *vt.* to pluck hair; depilitate
épilogue *m.* epilogue
épiloguer *vi.* to criticize, harp (on); split hairs
épinard *m.* spinach
épine *f.* thorn; spine
épinette *f.* spinet, clavichord
épineux *a.* thorny; difficult
épingle *f.* pin; — **de sûreté** safety pin
épingler *vt.* to pin; (fig., coll.) to pin down
épinière *a. & f.* spinal

Épiphanie *f.* Epiphany
épique *a.* epic
épiscopal *a.* episcopal, of the bishop
épiscopal *m.* bishopric; body of bishops; episcopacy
épisode *m.* episode
épisodique *a.* episodic
épisser *vt.* to splice
épissure *f.* splice
épistémologie *f.* epistemology
épistolaire *a.* epistolary
épistolier *m.* letter writer
épitaphe *f.* epitaph
épithète *f.* epithet
épitoge *f.* shoulder band (equivalent of French doctor's hood)
épitomé *m.* digest, abridgment
épître *f.* epistle, letter
éploré *a.* weeping, sad
éployé *a.* outspread
éplucher *vt.* to peel, pare, clean; (fig.) examine closely
épluchoir *m.* paring knife
épluchure *f.* peeling, waste
épode *f.* epode
épointer *vt.* to dull the point of
éponge *f.* sponge
éponger *vt.* to sponge
épopée *f.* epic poem, epic
époque *f.* epoch, period, era; — **de l'espace** air age, space age
épouiller *vt.* to delouse
épousailles *f. pl.* wedding
épouse *f.* wife, spouse
épouser *vt.* to marry; espouse
époussetage *m.* dusting
épousseter *vt.* to dust
époussette *f.* duster
épouvantable *a.* dreadful, frightful
épouvantail *m.* scarecrow
épouvante *f.* fright, terror
épouvanter *vt.* to terrify, frighten
époux *m.* husband; — *pl.* married couple
éprendre *v.*, s' — **de** to fall in love with
épreuve *f.* trial, proof, test; (phot.) print
épris (de) *a.* in love (with)
éprouver *vt.* to try; experience
éprouvette *f.* test tube, gauge
epsomite *f.* Epsom salts
épucer *vt.* to deflea
épuisant *a.* exhausting
épuisement *m.* exhaustion
épuiser *vt.* to exhaust; drain; wear out; use up
épuration *f.* purification, purifying, refining
épurer *vt.* to purify, filter
équanimité *f.* equanimity
équarrir *vt.* to square off; cut up, quarter
équateur *m.* equator

Équateur *m.* Ecuador
équation *f.* equation
équatorial *a.* equatorial
Equatorien *m. & a.* Ecuadorian
équerre *f.* T-square, angle iron
équestre *a.* equestrian
équidistant *a.* equidistant
équilatéral *a.* equilateral
équilibrage *m.* balancing
équilibre *m.* equilibrium; balance
équilibrer *vt.* to poise, balance
équilibriste *m. & f.* acrobat, tight-rope performer
équin *a.* equine
équinoxe *m.* equinox
équipage *m.* (naut.) crew; retinue; apparel, equipment
équipe *f.* team; travail d' — *m.* teamwork
équipée *f.* wild time, mad frolic
équipement *m.* equipment
équiper *vt.* to equip, fit out, man
équipier *m.* member of a team
équitable *a.* equitable
équitation *f.* horseback riding
équité *f.* equity, justice
équivalence *f.* equivalent, equivalence
équivalent *a.* equivalent
équivaloir *vt.* to be equivalent to
équivoque *f.* ambiguity; misunderstanding; — *a.* ambiguous; doubtful
équivoquer *vi.* to be ambiguous, be equivocal
érable *m.* maple; sucre d' — maple sugar
érafler *vt.* to graze, scratch
éraflure *f.* graze, scratch
éraillé *a.* bloodshot; frayed
ère *f.* era, epoch
érectile *a.* erectile
érection *f.* erection
éreinter *vt.* to exhaust; break from fatigue
érémitique *a.* ascetic, pertaining to hermits
erg *m.* erg
ergot *m.* rooster's spur; (agr.) ergot
ergotage *m.*, ergoterie *f.* quibbling, hairsplitting
ergoter *vi.* to quibble
ériger *vt.* to erect, raise
ermitage *m.* hermitage
ermite *m.* hermit
éroder *vt.* to erode
érosif *a.* erosive
érosion *f.* erosion
érotique *a.* erotic
érotisme *m.* eroticism
errant *a.* wandering; stray; errant
erratique *a.* erratic
errements *m. pl.* erring ways, habits
errer *vi.* to wander
erreur *f.* error, mistake; delusion

erroné *a.* erroneous
éructation *f.* belch
éructer *vi.* to belch
érudit *a.* learned; — *m.* scholar
érudition *f.* erudition
éruptif *a.* eruptive
éruption *f.* eruption
ès *prep.* in; docteur — lettres *m.* doctor of letters
escabeau *m.* stool; stepladder
escabelle *f.* stool; stepstool
escadre *f.* (navy) squadron
escadrille *f.* escadrille; small squadron
escadron *m.* (army) squadron
escalade *f.* scaling
escalader *vt.* to scale
escale *f.* (naut., avi.) port of call, stop; vol sans — *m.* nonstop flight
escalier *m.* staircase, stairs
escalope *f.* cutlet
escamotable *a.* concealable; retractable
escamoter *vt.* to hide, conceal; make away with; (fig.) side step a question
escarbille *f.* cinder, clinker
escarboucle *f.* carbuncle
escarcelle *f.* purse
escargot *m.* snail
escarmouche *f.* skirmish
escarmoucher *vt.* to skirmish
escarole *f.* escarole
escarpe *f.* scarp, escarpment; — *m.* thief, cutthroat
escarpé *a.* steep
escarpement *m.* escarpment; steep incline
escarpin *m.* pump (shoe)
escarpolette *f.* swing
escarre *f.* scab
esche *f.* bait
escient, à bon — with full knowledge
esclaffer *v.*, s' — to burst out laughing
esclandre *m.* scandal
esclavage *m.* slavery; bondage
esclave *m. & f.* slave
escompte *m.* (com.) discount; rebate
escompter *vt.* (com.) to discount
escopette *f.* blunderbuss
escorte *f.* escort; (naut.) convoy
escorter *vt.* to escort, convoy
escouade *f.* squad
escrime *f.* fencing
escrimer *vi.* to fence
escrimeur *m.* fencer
escroc *m.* crook, swindler
escroquer *vt.* to swindle, cheat
escroquerie *f.* swindle, fraud
ésotérique *a.* esoteric
espace *m.* space, room; interval; time lapse; — interplanétaire aerospace
espacer *vt.* to space; separate
espadon *m.* swordfish

espadrille *f.* tennis shoe; beach sandal
Espagne *f.* Spain
Espagnol *m.* Spaniard
espagnol *a.* Spanish
espagnolette *f.* window catch
espalier *m.* row of espaliered trees
espèce *f.* species, kind; **-s** *pl.* cash
espérance *f.* hope, expectation
espéranto *m.* esperanto
espérer *vt. & vi.* to hope, expect
espiègle *a.* mischievous; — *m. & f.* mischievous person
espièglerie *f.* prank, mischievousness
espionnage *m.* espionage, spying
espionner *vt.* to spy (on)
esplanade *f.* esplanade, promenade
espoir *m.* hope
esprit *m.* spirit; mind; wit, intelligence
esquif *m.* skiff
esquimau *a. & n.* Eskimo
esquisse *f.* sketch; outline, rough plan
esquisser *vt.* to sketch, outline
esquiver *vt.* to avoid; — **de la tête** to duck; **s'** — to steal away
essai *m.* test, trial; assaying metal; attempt
essaim *m.* swarm; host, multitude
essaimage *m.* swarming
essaimer *vt.* to swarm
essarter *vt.* to clear
essarts *m. pl.* clearing(s)
essayage *m.* fitting; testing; trying on, trying out
essayer *vt.* to try, attempt; try on; try out, test
essayiste *m.* essayist
essence *f.* essence; gasoline
essentiel *a.* essential; most important, basic, fundamental; — *m.* most important thing; gist
esseulé *a.* left alone, abandoned
essieu *m.* axle
essor *m.* flight; soaring; (fig.) development
essorer *vt.* to dry; wring
essoreuse *f.* dryer; wringer
essoufflé *a.* breathless
essoufflement *m.* breathlessness
essuie-glace *m.* windshield wiper
essuie-main(s) *m.* towel
essuie-pieds *m.* doormat
essuie-plume *m.* penwiper
essuyer *vt.* to wipe, dry; suffer, endure, undergo
est *m.* east
estacade *f.* stockade
estafette *f.* runner, messenger
estafier *m.* armed servant; bully
estaminet *m.* bar, café
estampe *f.* print, engraving

estampille *f.* trademark; seal; impression; tax stamp
ester *vi.* to appear in court
esthète *m.* esthete
esthéticienne *f.* beauty shop attendant
esthétique *a.* esthetic; — *f.* esthetics
estimateur *m.* estimator, appraiser
estimation *f.* evaluation; estimation
estime *f.* esteem, estimation
estimer *vt.* to esteem; estimate; value; deem
estival *a.* summer
estivant *m.* summer resident
estiver *vi.* to spend the summer
estomac *m.* stomach
Estonie *f.* Esthonia
estrade *f.* platform for chairs
estragon *m.* tarragon
estropié *a.* crippled
estropier *vt.* to cripple
estuaire *m.* estuary
estudiantin *a.* student, pertaining to students
esturgeon *m.* sturgeon
et *conj.* and; — ... — both ... and
étable *f.* cattle shed; sty
établer *vt.* to stable; place in a stall
établi *m.* workbench
établir *vt.* to establish; create
établissement *m.* establishment; institution
étage *m.* story, floor; stage; condition
étagère *f.* set of shelves; whatnot
étai *m.* prop, stay, support
étain *m.* tin
étal *m.* butcher's block
étalage *m.* display, show
étalagiste *m.* window dresser, window trimmer
étaler *vt.* to display, show
étalon *m.* standard; stallion
étalonner *vt.* to verify, control, test; standardize; scale, graduate, calibrate
étamer *vt.* to tin; tin-plate; silver (a mirror)
étamine *f.* stamen; cheesecloth; etamine
étampe *f.* punch, stamp, die
étamper *vt.* to punch, stamp
étanche *a.* watertight
étancher *vt.* to stop; appease
étang *m.* pond
étape *f.* stage, stop
état *m.* state, condition; estate; — **civil** vital statistics
étatiser *vt.* to nationalize, put under state control
étatisme *m.* state control
état-major *m.* staff, headquarters
étau *m.* vise
étayer *vt.* to prop, stay

été *m.* summer
éteignoir *m.* candle snuffer
éteindre *vt.* to extinguish, put out; calm; fade; s' — to go out; become extinct
éteint *a.* extinguished, out, extinct
étendard *m.* standard, flag
étendoir *m.* clothesline, drying room
étendre *vt.* to extend, spread, stretch; s' — to stretch out; extend
étendu *a.* extended; stretched (out); adulterated, watered; vast, extensive
étendue *f.* extent, expanse, range, scope
éternel *a.* eternal
éterniser *vt.* to drag out, make last a long time
éternité *f.* eternity
éternuement *m.* sneeze, sneezing
éternuer *vi.* to sneeze
étêter *vt.* to top, remove the top of
éteule *f.* stubble
éther *m.* ether
éthéré *a.* ethereal
Ethiopie *f.* Ethiopia
éthiopien *a. & m.* Ethiopian
éthique *a.* ethical; — *f.* ethics
ethnique *a.* ethnic
ethnographie *f.* ethnography
ethnologie *f.* ethnology
ethnologue *m. & f.* ethnologist
éthyle *m.* ethyl
éthylène *m.* ethylene
étiage *m.* low-water point; low water
étincelant *a.* sparkling, glittering
étinceler *vi.* to sparkle, glitter
étincelle *f.* spark, flash
étincellement *m.* sparkling, glittering; twinkling
étioler *v.*, s' — to wither away
étique *a.* lean, emaciated
étiqueter *vt.* to label, ticket, mark
étiquette *f.* label; etiquette
étirer *vt.* to lengthen, elongate
étoffe *f.* material, fabric
étoile *f.* star
étoiler *vt.* to bespangle
étole *f.* stole
étonnamment *adv.* astonishingly
étonnant *a.* astonishing
étonnement *m.* astonishment
étonner *vt.* to astonish; s' — to be astonished
étouffant *a.* stifling; sweltering
étouffée *f.* cuire à l' — to braise
étouffement *m.* suffocation; choking
étouffer *vt. & vi.* to stifle, suffocate, choke, smother
étouffoir *m.* piano damper; stuffy room
étoupe *f.* oakum, hemp fiber
étourderie *f.* inadvertance; oversight, stupidity

étourdi *a.* thoughtless, scatterbrained
étourdir *vt.* to stun, daze; deaden
étourdissement *m.* dizziness; numbing
étourneau *m.* starling
étrange *a.* strange
étranger *m.* foreigner; stranger, outsider; à l' — abroad; — *a.* strange, foreign
étrangeté *f.* strangeness
étrangler *vt. & vi.* to strangle; choke; strangulate
étrangleur *m.* strangler
être *vi.* to be, exist; — à belong to; y — understand; *m.* being, existence
étreindre *vt.* to embrace; grip
étreinte *f.* grasp; embrace
étrenner *vt.* to use for the first time
étrier *m.* stirrup
étrille *f.* currycomb
étriller *vt.* to curry; thrash; ransom
étriper *vt.* to gut, clean
étriquer *vt.* to make too narrow
étroit *a.* narrow; strict
étroitement *adv.* closely, intimately; strictly
étroitesse *f.* narrowness; closeness; — d'esprit narrow-mindedness
Étrusque *m. & f. & a.* Etruscan
étude *f.* study, research; study hall; lawyer's office; (mus.) etude
étudiant *m.* student
étudié *a.* studied, calculated
étudier *vt.* to study
étui *m.* case, box
étuve *f.* steam room; drying oven; sterilizer
étuver *vt.* to stew; steam; heat
étymologie *f.* etymology
étymologique *a.* etymological
étymologiste *m.* etymologist
eucalyptus *m.* eucalyptus
eucharistie *f.* eucharist
eugénique *f.*, eugénisme *m.* eugenics
eunuque *m.* eunuch
euphémisme *m.* euphemism
euphonie *f.* euphony
eurasien *a. & m.* Eurasian
Europe *f.* Europe
Européen *m. & a.* European
euthanasie *f.* euthanasia
eux *pron.*, *m. pl.* them, they
évacuation *f.* evacuation
évacuer *vt.* to evacuate; vacate
évader *v.*, s' — to escape; break loose
évaluation *f.* evaluation
évaluer *vt.* to value, appraise
évangélique *a.* evangelical
évangéliser *vt.* to evangelise
évangeliste *m.* evangelist
évangile *m.* Gospel
évanouir *v.*, s' — to faint; vanish

evanouissement *m.* faint; disappearance; (rad.) fading
évaporation *f.* evaporation
évaporé *a.* flighty, fickle
évaporer *vt.* to evaporate
évaser *vt.* to enlarge, widen
évasif *a.* evasive
évasion *f.* escape, evasion; (fig.) distraction
évêché *m.* bishopric, diocese; bishop's palace
éveil *m.* alertness; warning; awakening; wakefulness
éveillé *a.* awake, alert
éveiller *vt.* to awaken, wake up
événement *m.* event; outcome
évent *m.* vent
éventail *m.* fan
éventer *vt.* to fan, ventilate, air; sense, suspect; s' — to get stale; fan oneself
éventrer *vt.* to disembowel; rip open
éventualité *f.* eventuality
éventuel *a.* possible; eventual
évêque *m.* bishop
évertuer *v.*, s' — to strive, exert oneself
évidement *m.* hollowing out; hollowness
évidemment *adv.* evidently, obviously
évidence *f.* evidence
évident *a.* obvious, evident
évider *vt.* to hollow out
évier *m.* kitchen sink
évincer *vt.* to evict; oust
éviter *vt.* to avoid; dodge
évocateur *a.* evocative
évocation *f.* evocation; recollection
évocatoire *a.* evocative
évoluer *vi.* to evolve; revolve
évolution *f.* evolution
évoquer *vt.* to evoke
exacerber *vt.* to exacerbate
exact *a.* exact; correct; punctual
exaction *f.* exacting; exaction
exactitude *f.* exactness, correctness; punctuality
exagération *f.* exaggeration
exagérer *vt.* to exaggerate
exalté *a.* exalted
exalter *vt.* to exalt; excite
examen *m.* examination; survey; — de conscience self-examination
examinateur *m.* examiner
examiner *vt.* to examine
exaspérant *a.* exasperating
exaspération *f.* exasperation
exaspérer *vt.* to exasperate
exaucer *vt.* to grant prayer *or* request; — un vœu to fulfill a desire
excavateur *m.* steam shovel
excaver *vt.* to excavate
excédant *a.* excessive

excédent *m.* excess, surplus
excéder *vt.* to exceed; wear out
excellemment *adv.* excellently
excellence *f.* excellence; Excellency
exceller *vt.* to excel
excentricité *f.* eccentricity
excentrique *a.* eccentric
excepté *prep.* except, save
excepter *vt.* to except
exceptionnel *a.* exceptional
excès *m.* excess; abuse; (phot.) — de pose overexposure
excessif *a.* excessive; unreasonable
exciper (de) *vi.* to allege; take exception to
exciser *vt.* to excise, cut off
excitabilité *f.* excitability
excitant *m.* stimulant; — *a.* stimulating
excitateur *a.* exciting
excitation *f.* excitement
exciter *vt.* to excite, arouse, stimulate
exclamation *f.* exclamation; point d'— *m.* exclamation point
exclamer *v.*, s' — to exclaim
exclure *vt.* to reject; exclude; (fig.) to be incompatible
exclusif *a.* exclusiveness
exclusivité *f.* exclusivity, exclusiveness; en — first-run movies
excommunier *vt.* to excommunicate
excorier *vt.* to excoriate
excrément *m.* excrement
excréter *vt.* to excrete
excrétion *f.* excretion
excroissance *f.* growth, tumor
excursionner *vi.* to take a trip, go on an excursion
excuse *f.* excuse; —s *pl.* apology; faire ses —s to apologize
excuser *vt.* to excuse; apologize for; s'— excuse oneself, apologize
exécrable *a.* execrable
exécration *f.* execration
exécrer *vt.* to execrate
exécutant *m.* performer
exécuter *vt.* to execute, perform
exécuteur *m.* executor
exécutif *a.* executive
exécution *f.* execution
exégèse *f.* exegesis
exemplaire *m.* copy, sample; — *a.* exemplary
exemple *m.* example; precedent; par — for example; indeed!
exempter *vt.* to exempt
exemption *f.* exemption
exercé *a.* practiced, experienced
exercer *vt.* to exercise; train; exert; s'— to practice
exercice *m.* exercise, practice; drill
exfolier *vt.* to scale, exfoliate

exhalaison *f.* exhalation, vapor

exhalation *f.* exhalation, exhaling

exhaler *vt.* to exhale; breathe out; give off

exhaussement *m.* raising; rise

exhausser *vt.* to raise; s'— to rise

exhaustif *a.* exhaustive

exhaustion *f.* exhaust

exhiber *vt.* to exhibit, display, show

exhibition *f.* exhibition; show, showing, exposition, display

exhibitionniste *m. & f.* exhibitionist

exhorter *vt.* to exhort, urge, encourage

exhumation *f.* exhumation

exhumer *vt.* to exhume, disinter; unearth, dig up

exigeant *a.* exacting, hard to please, demanding

exigence *f.* exigence, exigency, requirement, demand

exiger *vt.* to exact, require, demand

exigible *a.* required, due, exigible

exigu *a.* very small, tiny; slim, scanty

exiguïté *f.* smallness; scantiness; relative poverty

exil *m.* exile, banishment

exilé *m.* exiled person

exiler *vt.* to exile, banish

existant *a.* existent, existing, extant; living; present; available

existence *f.* existence; life, living; being; (com.) stock, inventory

existentialiste *m. & f.* existentialist

existentiel *a.* existential; pertaining to existence

exister *vi.* to exist, be; live

exode *m.* exodus

exonération *f.* exoneration; exemption

exonérer *vt.* to exonerate; exempt

exorable *a.* exorable, flexible

exorciser *vt.* to exorcize

exorcisme *m.* exorcism; exorcizing

exotique *a.* exotic

expansif *a.* expansive

expansion *f.* expansion; expansiveness

expatrié *m.* expatriate, exile

expatrier *vt.* to expatriate

expectant *a.* expectant

expectative *f.* expectancy, expectation; prospect

expectoration *f.* expectoration; sputum

expectorer *vt.* to expectorate

expédient *a.* expedient; — *m.* expedient; resource; device

expédier *vt.* to expedite; send off; dispatch; clear, get through

expéditeur *m.* sender, shipper

expéditif *a.* expeditious

expédition *f.* expedition; shipment, consignment; dispatch; copy

expéditionnaire *a.* expeditionary; — *m.*

sender; shipper; forwarding agent

expérience *f.* experience; experiment

expérimental *a.* experimental

expérimentateur *m.* experimenter

expérimentation *f.* experimentation

expérimenté *a.* experienced; peu — inexperienced

expérimenter *vt.* to try, test; — *vi.* to experiment

expert *a.* expert; trained; skilled; competent; — *m.* expert; appraiser

expert-comptable *m.* certified public accountant

expertise *f.* expert appraisal or evaluation

expertiser *vt.* to appraise

expiable *a.* expiable

expiation *f.* expiation, atonement

expier *vt.* to expiate, atone for

expirant *a.* expiring, dying

expiration *f.* expiration; termination

expirer *vi.* to expire; die; terminate; exhale

explétif *a. & m.* expletive

explicable *a.* explainable, explicable

explicatif *a.* explanatory

explication *f.* explanation, interpretation; accounting

explicite *a.* explicit

expliciter *vt.* to make explicit

expliquer *vt.* to explain; comment on, interpret; account for; s'— to explain oneself; have an argument

exploit *m.* exploit, deed, (law), writ summons

exploitable *a.* exploitable, workable

exploitant *m.* operator of an enterprise; cultivator; developer; — *a.*, huissier — *m.* process server

exploitation *f.* exploitation; working, cultivation; improvement; development

exploiter *vt.* to exploit; operate; work; cultivate; develop

explorateur *m.* explorer; — *a.* exploratory

exploratif *a.* exploratory

exploration *f.* exploration, exploring

explorer *vt.* to explore; examine; probe; — au scaphandre autonome to skin-dive

exploser *vi.* to explode, blow up

explosible *a.* explosive

explosif *a. & m.* explosive

explosion *f.* explosion, exploding, blowing up; outburst

exportateur *m.* exporter

exporter *vt.* to export

exposant *m.* exhibitor; petitioner; (math.) exponent

exposé *a.* exposed; open; subject to, liable; — *m.* statement, account

exposer *vt.* to expose; exhibit, display, show; explain

exposition f. exposition; exhibition, display, showing; exposure; **salle d'—** f. showroom

exprès (expresse) a. express, explicit; **par — special delivery; —** adv. on purpose, intentionally, expressly

express m. local-express train

expressément adv. expressly, clearly

expressif a. expressive

expression f. expression; show, display; term, language, words; squeezing, extracting

expressivement adv. expressively

exprimable a. expressible

exprimer vt. to express; show; squeeze out, extract

expropriation f. expropriation

exproprier vt. to expropriate

expugnable a. pregnable

expulser vt. to expel; evict; eject, throw out

expulsion f. expulsion; eviction; ejection; deportation

expurger vt. to expurgate

exquis a. exquisite; of extreme beauty

exsangue a. bloodless, anemic

exsuder vt. & vi. to exude

extase f. ecstasy, rapture; trance

extasier v., **s'—** to go into ecstasy, go wild, be wild

extatique a. ecstatic

extenseur m. stretcher, expander; extensor muscle

extensible a. extendable, expandable

extensif a. extensive; tensile

extension f. extension; stretching; spread, expansion; extent

exténuation f. extenuation; exhaustion

exténuant a. extenuating, exhausting

exténuer vt. to extenuate; exhaust; **s'— to exhaust oneself**

extérieur a. exterior, external; outside; foreign; **—** m. exterior, outside; outward appearance; surface

extérieurement adv. externally; outwardly; superficially, on the surface

exterminateur m. exterminator

extermination f. extermination

exterminer vt. to exterminate; wipe out

externat m. day school

externe a. external, exterior, outside; **—** m. nonresident pupil; (med.) nonresident assistant interne

extincteur m. fire extinguisher

extinction f. extinction; extinguishing; slaking; abolition; loss

extirpateur m. uprooter, extirpator; remover

extirpation f. uprooting, extirpation; removal

extirper vt. to extirpate, uproot; remove

extorquer vt. to extort

extorqueur m. extortionist

extorsion f. extortion

extra adv. extra, additional; **—** m. (pl.) extra(s)

extracteur m. extractor

extraction f. extraction; pulling out; origin, ancestry, birth

extrader vt. to extradite

extradition f. extradition

extra-fin a. superfine, very fine

extraire vt. to extract, draw out; pull out; pull a tooth

extrait m. extract, excerpt; abstract

extra-légal a. extralegal

extraordinaire a. extraordinary, out of the ordinary

extrapoler vt. to extrapolate

extra-sensoriel a. extrasensory

extravagance f. extravagance; **exorbitance**; foolishness

extravagant a. extravagant; **exorbitant**; foolish

extravaguer vi. to rave, talk nonsense

extrême a. extreme; excessive; severe; farthest; **—** m. extreme

extrêmement adv. extremely, very highly

extrême-onction f. (eccl.) extreme unction

Extrême-Orient m. Far East

extrémist m. & f. extremist

extrémité f. extremity; tip, end; urgency; dying moment; extreme

extrinsèque a. extrinsic

extroverti m. extrovert

exubérance f. exuberance

exubérant a. exuberant, luxuriant

exultation f. exultation

exulter vi. to exult, rejoice

ex-voto m. (eccl.) votive offering; **ex-voto**

F

fable f. fable, story; laughing stock

fablier m. collection of fables

fabricant m. manufacturer

fabricateur m. fabricator; forger

fabrication f. manufacturing, **manufacture**; fabrication; forging

fabrique f. manufacture; factory; **paper** mill

fabriquer vt. to manufacture, **produce**, make; fabricate; forge

fabuleux a. fabulous

façade f. façade, front

face f. front, face; aspect; side; **en — de** opposite; **faire — à** to face, confront, meet; **pile ou —** heads or tails

face-à-main m. lorgnette

facétie f. prank, joke, trick

facétieux *a.* facetious

facette *f.* facet

facetter *vt.* to cut in facets

fâché *a.* angry; sorry

fâcher *vt.* to anger; afflict, grieve; **se —** to get angry; be offended

fâcheux *a.* tiresome, annoying; troublesome; unfortunate

faciès *m.* facies; appearance, facial aspect

facile *a.* easy; facile; glib

facilité *f.* facility; ease, easiness; aptitude; glibness

faciliter *vt.* to facilitate

façon *f.* fashion; fashioning, making, creation; way, manner; fuss, ceremony; **à la — de** like; **de — que** so that; **de cette — in** this way, thus; **de toute — in** any event, in any case; **faire des —s** to stand on ceremony; **sans —(s)** without fuss or ceremony; unceremoniously

faconde *f.* glibness, fluency

façonner *vt.* to fashion, make; shape, form

façonnier *a.* overly fussy

facsimilé *m.* facsimile, reproduction, duplicate

factage *m.* delivery, delivery service

facteur *m.* (math.) factor; mailman, postman; agent; maker, manufacturer

factice *a.* imitation, factitious

factieux *a.* factious

factionnaire *m.* sentry; picket

factorielle *f.* (math.) factorial

factotum *m.* factotum; jack-of-all-trades; handyman

facturation *f.* billing, invoicing

facture *f.* (com.) invoice, bill; workmanship, make; making, manufacture

facturer *vt.* to invoice

facturier *m.* invoice book; billing clerk

facultatif *a.* optional

faculté *f.* faculty; ability, capacity; option; school within a university

fadaise *f.* silliness, foolishness, nonsense

fade *a.* insipid, tasteless, flat

fadeur *f.* insipidity; lack of taste, flatness

fagot *m.* faggot, bundle of sticks

fagotin *m.* small faggot, small bundle

faible *a.* feeble, weak; faint; poor; low; thin; — *m.* foible, weakness

faiblesse *f.* weakness; feebleness; failing, frailty; faint

faiblir *vi.* to weaken, fail; abate, diminish

faïence, (faïencerie) *f.* earthenware, pottery

faille *f.* (geol.) fault, crack, break

faillibilité *f.* fallibility

faillible *a.* fallible

faillir *vi.* to fail; go bankrupt; be on the point of; **— faire quelque chose** almost to do something

faillite *f.* failure, bankruptcy; **faire — to** go bankrupt

faim *f.* hunger; **avoir — to** be hungry; hunger

fainéant *a.* lazy; — *m.* loafer, idler; good-for-nothing

fainéanter *vi.* to idle, loaf, do nothing

fainéantise *f.* laziness, loafing, idleness

faire *vt.* to make; do; perform, execute, accomplish; be, come to, amount to; say, remark; play (music), act, pretend; matter, be of importance; see to, attend to, arrange; cause something to be done, have someone do something; have something done; **— le mort** play dead; **— le tour de** circumnavigate; round; **— son droit** study law; **— une malle** pack a trunk; **— une pièce** clean a room; **— une promenade** take a walk, go for a walk; **cela ne fait rien** it doesn't matter, never mind; **il fait beau** it's nice out (weather); **il fait chaud** it's warm, hot; **il fait froid** it's cold; **il fait mauvais** the weather is bad; **il fait du soleil** it's sunny; **il fait du vent** it's windy; **se — become,** grow; develop, be formed; get used to, adjust to; be, happen

faire-part *m.* notification, notice

faisable *a.* feasible, practical

faisan *m.,* **—(de)** *f.* pheasant

faisceau *m.* bundle, bunch, cluster

faiseur *m.* maker, doer

fait *a.* made, done; matured, ripe; — *m.* fact; feat, act, deed; **mettre au — to** inform, bring up to date; **sur le — in** the act

fait-divers *m.* news item

faîte *m.* top, summit; ridge; (fig.) in highest point

faix *m.* load, burden, weight

falaise *f.* cliff

fallacieux *a.* fallacious

falloir *v.* to be necessary; to be lacking; **il faut — it** is necessary, one must, one should; it takes; **il me faut** I must, I have to; I need; **comme il faut** proper, properly; **il s'en faut de beaucoup, tant s'en faut** far from it; **peu s'en faut** almost, nearly

falot *a.* pale, colorless; quaint; — *m.* lamp, lantern, light

falsificateur *m.* falsifier, forger

falsifier *vt.* to falsify; adulterate; forge

famé *a.* noted; **bien — of** good repute

famélique *a.* famished, starving, starved

fameux *a.* famous; distinguished; wonderful, excellent

familial *a.* of the family; domestic

familiariser *vt.* to familiarize; **se — avec**

to become accustomed to, familiarize oneself with; become familiar with
familiarité *f.* familiarity; intimacy
familier *a.* familiar, intimate; of the family, domestic; colloquial
familièrement *adv.* familiarly, in a familiar manner
famille *f.* family; **soutien de —** *m.* bread-winner
famine *f.* famine; starvation
fanal *m.* light, lantern, beacon; headlight
fanatique *a. & n.* fanatic
fanatiser *vt.* to make fanatic, make a fanatic of
fanatisme *m.* fanaticism
fanchon *f.* scarf, kerchief
faner *vt.* to fade; pitch (hay); **se —** to fade, wither
fanfare *f.* fanfare, flourish; brass band, military band
fanfaron *a.* boasting, bragging; **—** *m.* braggart
fanfaronnade *f.* boasting, bragging
fanfaronner *vi.* to boast, brag, swagger
fanfreluche *f.* frill; trifle
fange *f.* mire, mud, dirt, filth; vice
fangeux *a.* muddy, dirty, filthy
fanion *m.* pennant, flag
fanon *m.* fetlock, dewlap, wattle; pendant; whalebone; (eccl.) maniple; **-s** *pl.* streamers of a bishop's mitre
fantaisie *f.* fantasy; fancy, imagination; whim, caprice; vagary; **de —** fancy; imaginary
fantaisiste *a.* fanciful, whimsical, imaginary
fantasmagorique *a.* fantastic, grotesque, weird
fantasque *a.* whimsical; temperamental; odd
fantassin *m.* foot soldier
fantastique *a.* fantastic; fanciful; unbelievable; weird
fantoche *m.* puppet, marionette
fantôme *m.* phantom, spectre, ghost, spirit
faon *m.* fawn
faonner *vi.* to fawn
faquin *m.* rascal, scoundrel
farce *f.* farce; trick, joke; stuffing (for food)
farceur *m.* joker, buffoon
farcir *vt.* to stuff (in cooking)
fard *m.* rouge; cosmetics, makeup; embellishment; pretense
fardeau *m.* burden, load, weight
farder *vt.* to make up; disguise, mask; **se —** to put on make-up
farfouiller *vt. & vi.* to search, look around, rummage
farine *f.* flour, meal; **— lactée** malted milk

farineux *a.* starchy, mealy; covered with flour
farouche *a.* wild, savage; cruel; timid, shy
fascicule *m.* cluster, bunch; section, part of a publication
fascinant, fascinateur *a.* fascinating
fasciner *vt.* to fascinate; charm; bewitch
fascisme *m.* Fascism
fasciste *m. & f.* Fascist
faste *m.* pomp; ostentation
fastidieux *a.* tedious, tiresome; dull
fastueux *a.* ostentatious; pompous; sumptuous
fat *a.* conceited, vain
fatal *a.* fatal; mortal; inevitable
fatalisme *m.* fatalism
fataliste *a.* fatalistic; **—** *m. & f.* fatalist
fatalité *f.* fatality, fate
fatidique *a.* fateful
fatigant *a.* fatiguing, tiring, tiresome
fatigue *f.* fatigue, weariness; strain, wear
fatiguer *vt.* to fatigue, tire; strain, overwork; **—** *vi.* to labor, strain; **se —** to get tired
fatras *m.* rubbish, trash, jumble
fatuité *f.* conceitedness
faubourg *m.* suburb
faubourien *a.* suburban; **—** *m.* suburbanite
faucher *vt.* to mow, cut down; reap
faucheuse *f.* harvester, mower, reaper
faucille *f.* sickle
faucon *m.* falcon; hawk
fauconnerie *f.* falconry
faufil *m.* thread for basting
faufiler *vt.* to baste, tack; weave in and out; slip in; **se —** thread one's way; slip in *or* out, sneak in *or* out; curry favor
faune *m.* faun; **—** *f.* (zool.) fauna
faussaire *m. & f.* forger
faussement *adv.* falsely
fausser *vt.* to falsify; bend, warp; force (a lock); **se —** to bend, warp, crack, break down
fausset *m.* falsetto
fausseté *f.* falseness, falsehood, untruth
faute *f.* fault; error, mistake; blame; fowl (in sports); lack, need, want; **faire —** to be lacking; **— de** for lack of, for want of; **sans —** without fail
fauteuil *m.* armchair; chair; (theat.) seat
fauteur *m.* instigator, agitator
fautif *a.* faulty; offending
fauvette *f.* warbler
faux *f.* scythe
faux *m.* falsehood, lie; forgery, imitation; **— (fausse)** *a.* false, untrue; imitation, counterfeit, forged; wrong
faux-col *m.* removable collar

faux-filet *m.* steak
faux-fuyant *m.* evasion, subterfuge
faux-monnayeur *m.* counterfeiter
faux-semblant *m.* pretext
faveur *f.* favor; preference; liking, good graces; **billet de —** *m.* complimentary ticket, pass
favori *m.* favorite; **-s** *m. pl.* side whiskers; **— (favorite)** *a.* favorite
favoriser *vt.* to favor; encourage, promote; like
favoritisme *m.* favoritism
fébrile *a.* feverish, febrile
fébrilité *f.* feverishness
fécal *a.* fecal
fèces *f. pl.* feces, stool
fécond *a.* fecund, fertile, productive, fruitful; rich
féconder *vt.* to fecundate, impregnate
fécondité *f.* fecundity, fertility; richness
fécule *f.* flour-like consistency; **— de maïs** cornstarch
féculent *a.* starchy; **—** *m.* starchy food
fédéral *a.* federal
fédéraliser *vt.* to federalize
fédéraliste *a. & n.* federalist
fédératif *a.* federated, confederate
fédération *f.* federation
fédérer *vt.* to federate
fée *f.* fairy; **conte de —s** *m.* fairy tale
féerie *f.* fairyland; enchantment; fantasy
féerique *a.* fairy; magic
feindre *vt.* to feign, pretend, simulate
feinte *f.* feint, pretense, pretending; limp
feinter *vi.* to feint
feldspath *m.* felspar
fêlé *a.* cracked; crazy
fêler *vt.* to crack
félicitations *f. pl.* congratulations
félicité *f.* felicity, happiness
féliciter *vt.* to congratulate
félin *a. & m.* feline
félonie *f.* treason
fêlure *f.* crack, chink; break, fracture
femelle *f. & a.* female
féminin *a.* feminine; **—** *m.* (gram.) feminine
féminisme *m.* feminism
femme *f.* woman, wife; female; **— de charge** housekeeper; **— de chambre** chambermaid
fémur *m.* femur
fenaison *f.* harvesting of hay
fendille *f.* crack, break, fissure
fendiller *vt.* to crack; **se —** to crack, peel
fendoir *m.* cleaver, chopper
fendre *vt.* to split; crack; cleave; rend
fenêtre *f.* window
fenil *m.* hayloft
fenouil *m.* fennel

fente *f.* crack, split, crevice, fissure; slot; lunge
féodal *a.* feudal
féodalité *f.* feudalism
fer *m.* iron; (fig.) sword, blade; **coup de —** *m.* pressing, ironing; **— à cheval** horseshoe; **— à friser** curling iron; **— à marquer** branding iron; **— à repasser** flatiron; **— à souder** soldering iron; **— de fonte** cast iron; **— forgé** wrought iron; **marquer au —** to brand; **-s** irons, chains
ferblanterie *f.* tinware
ferblantier *m.* tinsmith
férié *a.*, **jour —** *m.* public holiday
férir *vt.* to strike; **se — de** be struck with, stricken with; fall in love with
ferler *vt.* to furl
fermage *m.* tenant farming
ferme *a.* firm, fixed, steady; **—** *adv.* fast; hard; firmly; with assurance
ferme *f.* farm; (theat.) flat (scenery mounted on frame)
fermé *a.* closed; exclusive, restricted
fermentation *f.* fermentation, ferment
fermenter *vi.* to ferment
fermer *vt.* to shut, close; turn off; **—** *vi.* shut, close; **— à clef** to lock
fermeté *f.* firmness, steadiness
fermeture *f.* closing; shutting; fastening, lock; bolt of a gun; lockout; **— éclair** zipper
fermier *m.* farmer
fermoir *m.* fastener, snap, clasp
féroce *a.* ferocious, savage, wild
férocité *f.* ferocity, wildness
ferraille *f.* scrap iron; junk
ferrailler *vi.* to rattle
ferré *a.* ironclad, ironshod; hobnailed (shoe sole); (coll.) good, well versed; **route —e** *f.* paved road; **voie —e** *f.* railway
ferrer *vt.* to shoe (horse); equip, fit with iron; pave
ferret *m.* tab, tag
ferreux *a.* ferrous
ferrique *a.* ferric
ferronnerie *f.* wrought iron; ironworks
ferroviaire *a.* railroad, railway, train
ferrure *f.* iron fittings
fertilisant *a.* fertilizing; **—** *m.* fertilizer
fertiliser *vt.* to fertilize; enrich
fertilité *f.* fertility, fruitfulness; richness
féru *a.* in love with; wrapped up, obsessed
férule *f.* stick, cane, rod
fervent *a.* fervent, ardent; **—** *m.* devotee
ferveur *f.* fervor; ardor
fesse *f.* buttock
fessée *f.* spanking
fesse-mathieu *m.* miser, skinflint; usurer

fesser *vt.* to spank
festin *m.* feast, banquet
festiner *vt. & vi.* to feast
festivité *f.* festivity
feston *m.* festoon; scallop (sewing, edging)
festonner *vt.* to festoon; scallop
festoyer *vt. & vi.* to feast
fête *f.* feast, festival; holiday; saint's day; birthday; festivity; **jour de — ** *m.* holiday
fête-Dieu *f.* (eccl.) Corpus Christi
fêter *vt.* to celebrate; entertain
fétiche *m.* fetish
fétide *a.* fetid, repulsive
fétidité *f.* fetidness
fétu *m.* straw; (fig.) something of no value
feu *m.* (*pl.* **feux**) fire, burning; flame; match, light; **— de joie** bonfire; **— d'artifice** fireworks; **— rouge** red light; **au —!** fire!; **à petit —** on a slow fire; by inches; **armes à — ** *f. pl.* firearms; **coup de — ** *m.* gunshot; **mettre — à** to set fire to; **prendre — ** to catch fire; **faire — ** to fire; **faire du — ** to make a fire; **faire long — ** hang fire
feu *a.* late, defunct
feudataire *m.* vassal
feuillage *m.* foliage
feuillaison *f.* appearance of leaves
feuille *f.* leaf; sheet; page; paper, newspaper
feuillée *f.* foliage; **—s** *pl.* (mil.) latrine
feuiller *vi.* to produce leaves
feuilleté *a.* laminated, foliated; **— ** *m.* puff pastry
feuilleter *vt.* to leaf through; turn the pages of; foliate, form into leaves *or* thin layers
feuilleton *m.* serial; **roman — ** serialized novel
feuillette *f.* small leaf; leaflet
feuillu *a.* leafy; **— ** *m.* foliage
feutre *m.* felt; felt hat
feutré *a.* soft, quiet, velvet-like; muffled
feutrer *vt.* to cover with felt; make into felt
fève *f.* lima bean
février *m.* February
fi *interj.* fie! for shame!; **— ** *m.*, **faire — de** dislike, scorn
fiacre *m.* horse-drawn cab, hack
fiançailles *f. pl.* engagement, betrothal
fiancé *a.* engaged, betrothed; **— ** *m.* fiancé, bridegroom; **—e** *f.* fiancée, bride
fiancer *v.*, **se — ** to become engaged
fibre *f.* fiber, grain, thread
fibreux *a.* fibrous; stringy
ficeler *vt.* to tie (up); wrap and tie
ficelle *f.* string, cord, twine

fiche *f.* index card, note card; case history; (elec.) plug; pin; microscope slide
ficher *vt.* to drive, thrust in; (coll.) cheat, trick; throw out; **se — de** to laugh at, make fun of; care nothing about
fichier *m.* file, card file; filing cabinet
fichu *m.* scarf, shawl, kerchief
fictif *a.* fictitious, invented, imaginary
fiction *f.* fiction; invention; story; **— interplanétaire** space fiction
fidéicommis *m.* trust (law)
fidèle *a.* faithful, true, loyal
fidélité *f.* fidelity, faithfulness; loyalty
fiduciaire *a.* fiduciary; paper money; **— ** *m.* fiduciary, trustee
fief *m.* fief, fee
fiel *m.* gall; bitterness, malice
fielleux *a.* galling, bitter
fiente *f.* droppings, manure, dung
fier (fière) *a.* proud; haughty
fier *vt.* to entrust; **se — à** to rely upon, trust, depend on, count on
fier-à-bras *m.* braggart, swaggerer
fièrement *adv.* proudly
fierté *f.* pride; dignity
fièvre *f.* fever; heat; temperature
fiévreux *a.* feverish, fevered
figement *m.* clotting, coagulation, congealing
figer *vt.* to coagulate, congeal; curdle; thicken, solidify; **se — ** to clot, coagulate; become frozen
figue *f.* fig; **— de Barbarie** prickly pear
figuier *m.* fig tree
figurant *n.* (theat.) extra; **-e** *f.* ballet dancer
figuratif *a.* figurative
figuration *f.* figuration; (theat.) extras
figure *f.* face; figure, form, shape
figuré *a.* figured; figurative
figurer *vt.* to represent; portray; **— ** *vi.* to figure; **se — ** to imagine
fil *m.* thread; line; cutting edge; grain (of wood); **— de fer** wire; **— de l'eau** current, stream
filasse *f.* tow; oakum
filature *f.* spinning
file *f.* file, row, line; **à la — ** in file; in succession, on end
filé *m.* thread
filer *vt.* to spin; draw out, prolong; follow, shadow; **— ** *vi.* pass, go by; move along, get going; leave; **— à l'anglaise** to take French leave
filet *m.* net; fillet; thread; bit, small amount, trickle; snaffle (harness part)
fileter *vt.* to stretch, draw metal; thread a screw
fileur *m.* spinner
filial *a.* filial; **-e** *f.* branch, subsidiary

filiation *f.* filiation; relationship; ancestry

filigrane *m.* filigree; watermark

fille *f.* daughter; girl; (eccl.) sister; fille d'honneur bridesmaid; maid of honor; jeune — girl; vieille — old maid, spinster

fillette *f.* young girl, little girl

filleul *m.* godson; -e *f.* goddaughter

film *m.* film; — fixe filmstrip

filmer *vt.* to film

filoche *f.* netting

filon *m.* vein, lode, strike

filou *m.* pickpocket; cheat, thief

filouter *vt.* to rob, cheat

fils *m.* son; junior (after a name); the younger

filtrant *a.* filtering; filterable; bout — *m.* filter tip

filtrat *m.* filtrate

filtration *f.* filtration, filtering

filtre *m.* filter; strainer; individual coffeemaker (strainer type)

filtrer *vt.* to filter, strain; — *vi.* to filter through; drip, leak

fin *f.* end, extremity, conclusion, close; aim, purpose; en — de compte in the end, as it turned out; to get to the point; sans — endless

fin *a.* fine; delicate, small, thin; clear, pure; ingenious; clever, subtle

final *a.* final, last, concluding

finalement *adv.* finally, lastly

finaliste *m. & f.* finalist

finalité *f.* finality

financement *m.* financing

financer *vt.* to finance, back

financier *a.* financial; — *m.* financier

finasser *vi.* to finesse, use finesse

finasserie *f.* finesse, shrewdness

finaud *a.* clever, shrewd, cunning

finesse *f.* fineness; finesse; delicacy, artifice; artfulness; ingenuity, subtlety; shrewdness

fini *a.* finished, ended, over, done, concluded; skilled, experienced; finite

finir *vt.* to finish, end, conclude; — *vi.* finish, end; en — avec be done with, get something over with; — de finish, stop

finissage *m.* finishing, final step, finishing touch

finisseur *m.* finisher

finlandais *a.* Finnish; — *m.* Finn

Finlande *f.* Finland

fiole *f.* phial, flask, bottle

fioriture *f.* flourish, curlicue

firmament *m.* firmament, heavens, sky

firme *f.* firm, house, company; imprint

fisc *m.* treasury, internal revenue

fiscal *a.* fiscal; pertaining to revenue

fiscaliser *vt.* to tax, make subject to tax

fiscalité *f.* tax collecting

fissurer *vt.* to fissure, split, cleave

fistule *f.* fistula

fixatif *m.* fixative

fixation *f.* fixation; fixing, setting, placing; determining

fixe *a.* fixed, steady, set; prix — set price; — *m.* regular salary

fixer *vt.* to fix; make firm, set, hold; stare at

fixité *f.* fixity

flaccidité *f.* flaccidity; flabbiness

flacon *m.* flask, bottle, decanter; flagon

flagellant *m.* flagellant

flagellation *f.* flagellation; flogging, whipping

flagelier *vt.* to flagellate; flog, whip

flageoler *vi.* to quiver, tremble, buckle

flageolet *m.* (mus.) flageolet, flute; kidney bean

flagorner *vt.* to flatter, be obsequious toward

flagrance *f.* flagrancy

flagrant *a.* flagrant; en — délit in the act

flair *m.* scent; perspicacity; flair, knack

flairer *vt.* to smell, scent, sniff; sense

flamand *a. & m.* Flemish

flamant *m.* flamingo

flambant *a.* flaming

flambé *a.* flamed with brandy

flambeau *m.* torch, brand; light; candle; candlestick

flambée *f.* fire, blaze

flambement *m.* collapse, buckling

flamber *vi.* to flame, blaze; collapse, buckle, fall in; — *vt.* to singe, char

flamboyant *a.* flaming; flamboyant

flamboyer *vi.* to blaze

flamme *f.* flame; love

flammèche *f.* spark, ember

flan *m.* custard

flanc *m.* flank, side; (fig.) womb

flanchet *m.* meat flank

Flandre *f.* Flanders

flanelle *f.* flannel

flâner *vi.* to stroll; idle, loiter

flânerie *f.* idling, loitering; strolling

flâneur *m.* idler; loiterer; stroller

flanquer *vt.* to flank; throw; — à la porte throw out, kick out

flaque *f.* puddle

flash *m.* (photo.) flash attachment, flash bulb

flasque *a.* flaccid; flabby; — *f.* powder flask

flatter *vt.* to flatter, caress; please

flatterie *f.* flattery

flatteur *a.* flattering; pleasing; — *m.* flatterer

flatueux *a.* flatulent
flatulence *f.* flatulence
fléau *m.* scourge; flail; (fig.) plague
flèche *f.* arrow; church spire; pole; rise; (avi.) direction indicator
fléchette *f.* dart
fléchir *vt. & vi.* to bend; submit; give way
flegmatique *a.* phlegmatic; stolid
flegme *m.* phlegm
flet *m.* flounder
flétan *m.* halibut
flétrir *vt.* to fade, wither; tarnish, stain; se — to fade, wither
flétrissure *f.* fading; withering; tarnish; stigma
fleur *f.* flower; blossom; prime; à — de level with
fleuraison *f.* flowering, blooming
fleuret *m.* fencing foil
fleurette *f.* little flower
fleuri *a.* in bloom; flowery; florid
fleurir *vt.* to decorate with flowers; — *vi.* to flower, bloom; flourish
fleuriste *m. & f.* florist
fleuve *m.* river
flexibilité *f.* flexibility
flexible *a.* flexible; pliant, pliable
flexion *f.* bending, flexion; inflexion
flibuster *vt.* to rob; — *vi.* to steal; commit piracy
flibustier *m.* buccaneer, pirate
flirt *m.* flirting, flirtation
flirter *vi.* to flirt
flocon *m.* snowflake; tuft; fleece
floconner *vi.* to form flakes; become fleecy
floconneux *a.* fleecy, fluffy
floraison *f.* blossoming, flourishing
flore *f.* flora
florentin *a.* Florentine; à la —e served with spinach
florissant *a.* flourishing
flot *m,* wave; flood, tide; floating; raft; à — floating, afloat
flottabilité *f.* buoyancy
flottable *a.* buoyant
flottant *a.* floating; vacillating, undecided
flotte *f.* fleet; float
flottement *m.* vacillation, wavering; undulation; flapping, waving
flotter *vt.* to float;— *vi.* to float; vacillate, waver; wave
flotteur *m.* float; buoy
flottille *f.* flotilla
flou *a.* light and soft; blurred, hazy; fluffy
fluctuer *vi.* to fluctuate
fluer *vi.* to flow
fluet *a.* thin, slender
fluide *m. & a.* fluid; liquid
fluidifier *vt.* to liquefy
fluidité *f.* fluidity

fluor *m.* fluorine
fluorescent *a.* fluorescent
fluoridation *f.* fluoridation
fluorure *m.* fluoride
flûte *f.* flute; tube, shaft
flûter *vi.* to play the flute
flux *m.* flow; flux; ebb
fluxion *f.* fluxion; — de poitrine pneumonia
foc *m.* (naut.) jib
foetal *a.* foetal
foetus *m.* foetus
foi *f.* faith; fidelity; belief; trust, confidence; de bonne — sincere, honest; digne de — trustworthy, reliable
foie *m.* liver; — gras goose liver paste
foin *m.* hay
foire *f.* fair, market
fois *f.* time; à la — at once, simultaneously, at a time; une — que once; encore une — once again; une — pour toutes definitely
foison *f.* abundance
foisonnant *a.* plentiful, abundant
folâtre *a.* frisky, playful
folâtrer *vi.* to play, frolic, romp
folie *f.* folly; insanity, madness
folié *a.* foliated
folio *m.* folio; page number
folklorique *a.* concerning folklore
follement *adv.* madly, foolishly
follet *a.* merry, gay
follicule *m.* follicle
fomentateur *m.* fomenter, agitator
fomenter *vt.* to foment
foncé *a.* dark, deep, somber (color)
foncer *vt.* to drive (in); deepen, darken — *vi.,* — sur to charge, rush
foncier *a.* pertaining to land or property; (fig.) fundamental; biens — *m. pl.* real property, real estate
foncièrement *adv.* fundamentally, basically
fonction *f.* function, duty, office
fonctionnaire *m. & f.* civil servant, petty official
fonctionnarisme *m.* bureaucracy
fonctionnel *a.* functional
fonctionnement *m.* functioning; order
fonctionner *vi.* to function, work, run
fond *m.* bottom; foundation; back; end; à — thoroughly; au — basically; de — fundamental, main, most important; sans — bottomless
fondamental *a.* fundamental, (fig.) essential
fondant *a.* melting; — *m.* flux for soldering; candy, bonbon
fondateur *m.* founder
fondation *f.* founding; foundation

fondé *a.* founded; justified; — *m.* agent; manager

fondement *m.* foundation; basis, base

fonder *vt.* to found; lay the foundation of; establish

fonderie *f.* foundry; casting; smelting

fondre *vt.* to melt, dissolve; smelt (iron); cast; — *vi.* to melt

fondrière *f.* quagmire; mud hole

fonds *m.* land; landed property; capital; funds

fondu *a.* melted, molten; — *m.* fadeout (films)

fontaine *f.* fountain, spring, well, source

fonte *f.* melting; cast iron; casting; smelting; alloy; (print.) font, type of one style and size

footing *m.* walk, hike, walking

forage *m.* drilling, boring

forain *a.*, **fête** — *f.* fair

forban *m.* pirate

forçat *m.* galley slave; convict, one condemned to hard labor

force *f.* force, strength, power; à — de by means of, by dint of; —s *f. pl.* shears (for metal, hedges, etc.)

forcé *a.* forced

forcément *adv.* necessarily

forcement *m.* forcing

forcené *a.* frantic, mad

forcer *vt.* to force, compel; break into; break out of

forer *vt.* to drill, bore

forestier *a.* of the forest; — *m.* forest ranger

foret *m.* drill

forêt *f.* forest; — **pluvieuse** rain forest

foreuse *f.* drilling machine, drill, borer

forfaire *vt.* to forfeit; — à to be remiss in

forfait *m.* crime; forfeit; contract

forfaitaire *a.* contractual

forfanterie *f.* bragging, boasting

forgé *a.* forged; **fer** — *m.* wrought iron

forgeage *m.* forging

forger *vt.* to forge; (fig.) invent, imagine

forgeron *m.* blacksmith

forgeur *m.* forger, inventor

formaldéhyde *m.* formaldehyde

formaliser *v.*, **se** — to be offended

formaliste *m. & f.* formalist

formalité *f.* formality; form, ceremony

format *m.* size, format

formatif *a.* formative

formation *f.* formation; forming

forme *f.* form, shape; formality; politeness; **sous la** — **de** in the form of

formel *a.* formal; express; strict

formellement *adv.* formally; strictly

former *vt.* to form; formulate; model; bring up, train, educate

formidable *a.* formidable; tremendous

formique *a.* formic

formulaire *m.* set of rules *or* regulations

formule *f.* formula; form, blank

formuler *vt.* to formulate

forniquer *vi.* to fornicate

forsythia *m.* forsythia

fort *a.* strong, vigorous; high (wind); loud; heavy (sea); large, great; — *adv.* very, extremely; loudly; strongly; — *m.* strong point; strong man; fort

forteresse *f.* fortress

fortifiant *a.* fortifying; — *m.* tonic

fortification *f.* fortification

fortifier *vt.* to fortify, strengthen

fortuit *a.* chance, casual, fortuitous

fortune *f.* fortune; chance; destiny; **faire** — to become rich

fortuné *a.* fortunate, happy; well-off

forum *m.* forum

fosse *f.* pit, hole; grave

fossé *m.* ditch; moat

fossette *f.* dimple

fossile *a. & m.* fossil

fossilisation *f.* fossilization

fossiliser *vt.* to fossilize

fossoyeur *m.* gravedigger

fou *m.* fool; madman; jester; bishop (chess)

fou, fol (folle) *a.* mad, foolish; in love

foucade *f.* impulse, whim

foudre *f.* thunderbolt; thunder; lightning; **coup de** — *m.* love at first sight

foudroyant *a.* crushing, overwhelming

foudroyer *vt.* to strike with lightning; strike down; blast; dumbfound

fouet *m.* whip

fouettement *m.* whipping

fouetter *vt.* to whip, flog; — *vi.* to whip, lash; flap

fougère *f.* fern

fougue *f.* spirit, fire, mettle

fougueux *a.* firery, impetuous, spirited

fouille *f.* digging, excavation

fouiller *vt.* to dig, excavate; search, look through; — *vi.* search

fouillis *m.* jumble, disorder

fouiner *vi.* to pry, ferret

fouir *vt.* to burrow, dig

foulard *m.* scarf, foulard cloth

foule *f.* crowd; pressing, milling

foulée *f.* tread; stride; track, spoor

fouler *vt.* to tread on; press; crush, trample; sprain; **se** — **la cheville** to sprain one's ankle

foulure *f.* sprain

four *m.* oven; kiln; **faire** — to fail; **petit** — **cooky**, pastry; — **soufflé** blast furnace

fourbe *m.* deceiver, cheat; — *a.* deceitful

fourberie *f.* deceit; cheating
fourbir *vt.* to furbish, polish
fourbissage *m.* polishing, furbishing
fourbu *a.* exhausted
fourche *f.* fork, pitchfork
fourcher *vt. & vi.* to fork
fourchetée *f.* forkful of food
fourchette *f.* fork
fourchon *m.* prong, tine
fourchu *a.* forked; cloven
fourgon *m.* wagon, van; baggage car; truck; poker
fourmi *f.* ant; — **blanche** termite
fourmilier *m.* anteater
fourmilière *f.* ant hill
fourmillement *m.* swarming; pricking sensation
fourmiller *vi.* to swarm, teem
fournaise *f.* furnace
fourneau *m.* cooking stove; furnace; **haut** — blast furnace
fournée *f.* batch, ovenful
fourni *a.* bushy, thick
fournir *vt.* to furnish, provide, supply; produce
fournisseur *m.* contractor, supplier, caterer
fourniture *f.* furnishing; -s *pl.* supplies
fourrage *m.* fodder; foraging
fourrager *vi.* to forage; search; — *vt.* to ravage
fourreau *m.* scabbard, sheath; case
fourré *a.* fur-lined, furry; densely wooded; — *m.* thicket
fourrer *vt.* to put in; stuff, cram, poke
fourre-tout *m.* duffel bag
fourreur *m.* furrier
fourrière *f.* dog pound
fourrure *f.* fur; hair; skin; lining
fourvoyer *vt.* to lead astray
foyer *m.* hearth; home; center, source, seat; foyer, lobby; focus
frac *m.* dress coat
fracas *m.* bustle, noise
fracasser *vt.* to break in pieces, shatter
fraction *f.* fraction
fractionner *vt.* to split, divide
fracture *f.* fracture; breaking
fracturer *vt.* to fracture; break open
fragilité *f.* fragility; frailty
fragment *m.* fragment
fragmentaire *a.* fragmentary
fragmenter *vt.* to break into fragments
fraîchement *adv.* freshly; coolly; recently, lately
fraîcheur *f.* freshness; coolness; chill
fraîchir *vi.* to freshen; become cooler
frais (fraîche) *a.* fresh; cool; recent; — *m.* fresh air; cool(ness)
frais *m. pl.* expenses; cost

fraise *f.* strawberry
framboise *f.* raspberry
franc (franche) *a.* free; frank; open; sincere; — *adv.* frankly
franc (franque) *a.* Frankish, of the Franks
franc *m.* franc (currency)
français *m.* the French language; — *a.* French; **à la** —**e** in the French fashion
Français *m.* Frenchman
France *f.* France
franchement *adv.* frankly, sincerely
franchir *vt.* to leap over; clear; overcome; cross
franchise *f.* frankness, sincerity; immunity, exemption; — **académique** academic freedom
franchissement *m.* crossing
francique *a.* Frankish
franciscain *a. & m.* Franciscan
franciser *vt.* to gallicize
francium *m.* francium
franc-maçon *m.* freemason
franc-maçonnerie *f.* freemasonry
franco *adv.* postpaid
franco-bord *m. & adv.* free on board (F.O.B.)
franc-parler *m.* frankness
franc-tireur *m.* sniper
frange *f.* fringe; -r *vt.* to fringe
frangible *a.* breakable, fragile
frappant *a.* striking, surprising
frappe *f.* minting, striking of coins
frappé *a.* cooled, chilled (wine)
frapper *vt.* to strike, hit; knock; mint stamp; ice
frasque *f.* escapade
fraternel *a.* fraternal; brotherly
fraternisation *f.* fraternizing
fraterniser *vi.* to fraternize
fraternité *f.* fraternity, brotherhood
fratricide *m. & f.* fratricide
fraude *f.* deceit, imposture; fraud; — **fiscale** tax evasion
frauder *vt.* to defraud, cheat
fraudeur *m.* cheat, defrauder
frauduleux *a.* fraudulent
frayer *vt.* to scrape; open, clear, trace; — *vi.* to associate with; spawn (fish)
frayeur *f.* fright, terror
fredaine *f.* frolic, prank
fredonner *vt. & vi.* to hum
frégate *f.* frigate
frein *m.* brake; bit; bridle; **sans** — unbridled, unchecked
freiner *vt.* to brake, apply the brakes; check
frelater *vt.* to adulterate
frêle *a.* frail, weak
frelon *m.* hornet
frémir *vi.* to shudder, tremble, quiver

frémissement *m.* shivering, shuddering, quivering
frêne *m.* (bot.) ash
frénésie *f.* frenzy
frénétique *a.* frantic; frenzied
fréquemment *adv.* frequently
fréquence *f.* frequency
fréquent *a.* frequent
fréquentation *f.* frequenting; association, company
fréquenter *vt.* to frequent, haunt; associate with
frère *m.* brother
fresque *f.* fresco
fret *m.* (naut.) freight, cargo; chartering; (naut.) charge for freight transportation by boat
fréter *vt.* (naut.) to load freight; charter
frétillant *a.* brisk, lively; frisky; wagging; wriggling
frétiller *vi.* to wriggle; fidget
fretin *m.* menu — small fish thrown back; small fry
frette *f.* hoop, iron ring; fret
freudien *a.* Freudian
freudisme *m.* Freudianism
friable *a.* friable, capable of being pulverized
friand *a.* dainty, nice; fond
friandise *f.* daintiness; –s *pl.* dainties, delicacies
fricassée *f.* fricassee
fricasser *vt.* to fricassee; squander
fricatif *a.* fricative (phonetics)
friche *f.* fallow land; en — fallow
friction *f.* rub, massage; friction
frictionner *vt.* to rub, massage
frigide *a.* frigid
frigidité *f.* frigidity
frigorification *f.* refrigeration
frigorifier *vt.* to refrigerate
frigorifique *a.* refrigerating
frimas *m.* rime, hoarfrost
fringale *f.* hunger pang
fringant *a.* frisky, lively; dapper
fringuer *vi.* to frisk, frolic
fripé *a.* rumpled, mussed
friper *vt.* to rumple, wrinkle
friperie *f.* secondhand clothes; rubbish
fripier *m.* secondhand clothier, ragman
fripon *m.* rogue
friponnerie *f.* roguery
frire *vi.* to fry
frise *f.* frieze
frisé *a.* curly, crisp
friser *vt. & vi.* to curl
frisoir *m.* hair curler
frisson *m.* shivering, shaking; thrill
frissonnement *m.* shiver; thrill
frissonner *vi.* to shiver, shudder; be

thrilled
frisure *f.* curliness
frit *a.* fried; –es *f. pl.* French fried potatoes
friture *f.* frying; fritter; any fried food; fat for frying; radio static
frivole *a.* frivolous, trifling
frivolité *f.* frivolity
froc *m.* frock (of a monk)
froid *m.* coldness, chilliness; **il fait** — it is cold (weather); **avoir** — to be cold (person); — *a.* cold; cool
froideur *f.* coldness; coolness
froidure *f.* coldness; frostbite
froissant *a.* hurting, hurtful, injurious
froissement *m.* rumpling; rustling; clash, jostling
froisser *vt.* to bruise; rumple; jostle; hurt (feelings); se — to take offense
frôlement *m.* rustling sound
frôler *vt.* to touch lightly, brush
fromage *m.* cheese
froment *m.* wheat
fronce *f.* crease, fold, pucker
froncement *m.* frown, frowning; wrinkling
froncer *vt.* to pucker, wrinkle; — **le sourcil** to frown
frondaison *f.* foliage; foliation
fronde *f.* slingshot; (bot.) frond
fronder *vt.* to sling
front *m.* forehead, brow, face, head; front; boldness, impudence, nerve
frontal *a.* frontal
frontière *f.* frontier, border
frontispice *m.* frontispiece
fronton *m.* façade
frottement *m.* rubbing, friction; chafing
frotter *vt.* to rub, polish; — *vi.* to rub
frotteur *m.* polisher
frottoir *m.* polisher; brush; sandpaper on a matchbox
froufrou *m.* swish, rustling; pomp, show
fructifère *a.* fruit-bearing
fructification *f.* fruition
fructifier *vi.* to bear fruit
fructueux *a.* fruitful, profitable
frugal *a.* frugal
frugalité *f.* frugality
fruit *m.* fruit; profit; **sans** — fruitless(ly)
fruiterie *f.* fruit dealer's, fruit and vegetable store
fruitier *m.* fruit dealer
frumentaire *a.* pertaining to wheat
fruste *a.* rough; worn
frustration *f.* frustration; cheating
frustrer *vt.* to frustrate, disappoint; cheat
fugace *a.* fleeting
fugitif *a.* fugitive; transitory, fleeting; — *m.* fugitive
fugue *f.* fugue; flight

fuir vi. to flee; leak; — vt. to avoid
fuite f. flight; avoiding; leak
fulgurant a. flashing
fulgurer vi. to flash, shine
fuligineux a. sooty, smoky
fulminant a. fulminating
fulminer vt. & vi. to fulminate
fumage m. smoking (of meat)
fumage, fumaison m. manuring, fertilizing
fumant a. smoking, steaming
fume-cigarette m. cigarette holder
fumée f. smoke, steam; fumes
fumer vt. to smoke; fertilize, manure; — vi. to smoke, steam; fume
fumet m. bouquet (of wine); aroma; scent
fumeur m. smoker
fumeux a. smoky; heady
fumier m. dung, manure
fumigation f. production of smoke or steam; treatment using a vaporizer
fumiger vt. to fumigate
fumoir m. smoking room, smoker; smoke house
funambule m. & f. tightrope artist
funambulesque a. fantastic
funèbre a. funeral; dismal, funereal
funerailles f. pl. funeral ceremony
funéraire a. funereal, funeral urn
funeste a. fatal
funiculaire a. & m. (rail.) funicular
fur m., au — et à mesure que as, in proportion to
furet m. ferret; (coll.) busybody
fureter vi. to ferret, pry about, search
fureur f. fury, rage, craze, passion
furibond a. furious
furie f. fury; rage
furieux a. furious, wild, raging
furoncle m. (med.) boil, furuncle
furtif a. furtive
furtivement adv. furtively, stealthily
fusain m. art charcoal; charcoal drawing
fuseau m. spindle; time zone
fusée f. rocket; fuse; axle; **avion à — m.** rocket plane
fuselage m. fuselage
fuselé a. tapered; streamlined
fuseler vt. to taper
fuser vi. to fuse, melt; run (color)
fusible m. (elec.) fuse; — a. fusible
fusil m. gun, rifle; whetstone; **— à deux coups** double-barreled gun; **coup de — m.** gunshot, report; **pierre à — f.** flint
fusillade f. rifle fire, fusillade, volley
fusiller vt. to shoot; execute by firing squad
fusion f. fusion, melting; (com.) merger
fusionner vt. & vi. to unite, blend; (com.) to merge

fustiger vt. to beat, whip, thrash
fût m. stock of a gun; bole of a tree; cask, barrel; shaft of a column, stem
futaie f. forest of tall trees
futaille f. cask, barrel
futé a. smart, cunning, shrewd
futile a. futile
futilité f. futility
futur a. future; — m. (gram.) future; fiancé, husband-to-be
fuyant a. fleeing; fleeting
fuyard m. runaway, fugitive

G

gabare f. barge, lighter
gabarit m. mold; model; gauge
gabelle f. salt tax (history)
gâche f. catch; notch; clip; staple
gâcher vt. to spoil; bungle; squander
gâchette f. catch, pawl; trigger
gâcheur a. & m. spoiling, bungling; bungler
gâchis m. slush; mud; unhardened cement; (coll.) mess
gaélique a. & m. Gaelic
gaffe f. boat hook; blunder; **faire une —** to put one's foot in it
gaffer vt. to hook; — vi. to put one's foot in it
gage m. pawn, pledge; token; **mettre en —** to pawn; **—s** pl. wages; **prêteur sur —** pawnbroker
gagé a. salaried
gager vt. to hire, pay wages to; bet, wager
gageur m. bettor, wagerer
gageure f. bet, wager
gagiste m. pledger (law); (theat.) bit player, extra
gagnant m. winner
gagne-pain m. livelihood, living; breadwinner
gagner vt. to gain; win, earn; reach; — vi. gain, improve
gai a. gay, lively, cheerful
gaité f. gaiety
gaillard a. hearty; fresh; strong; ribald; — m. (naut.) quarterdeck; fellow; strong, attractive man; quick-witted man
gaillardise f. cheerfulness; risqué remark
gain m. gain, earnings, profit
gaine f. sheath, casing; holster
gainer vt. to sheath, cover
gala m. gala, celebration, festivity
galamment adv. gallantly; politely
galant a. gallant; gay; elegant; — m. wooer, suitor, lover
galanterie f. politeness; gallant talk; escapade, love affair

galaxie *f.* galaxy; Milky Way

galbe *m.* curve; curving shape, outline

gale *f.* itch; scab; mange

galère *f.* (naut.) galley; (fig.) labor

galerie *f.* gallery; (theat.) balcony; arcade; cornice

galérien *m.* galley slave; convict

galet *m.* pebble; shingle; roller

galetas *m.* garret; hovel

galette *f.* flat thin cake; pancake

galeux *a.* mangy

galimatias *m.* nonsense, jumble

galion *m.* galleon

galle *f.* gall

Galles *f.* Wales

gallois *a.* Welsh; — *m.* Welshman; Welsh language

galoche *f.* clog; overshoe

galon *m.* braid, stripe, chevron

galonner *vt.* to braid, trim with braid

galop *m.* gallop; petit — canter

galopade *f.* gallop, galloping

galoper *vt. & vi.* to gallop

galopin *m.* rascal; (coll.) mischievous child

galuchat *m.* sharkskin

galvanique *a.* galvanic

galvaniser *vt.* to galvanize; electroplate

galvanomètre *m.* galvanometer

galvanoplastie *f.* electroplating

galvauder *vt.* (coll.) to smear; botch; — *vi.* roam

galvaudeux *m.* (coll.) tramp

gambade *f.* gambol, frolic, caper

gambader *vi.* to gambol, frolic, caper

gambit *m.* gambit

gamelle *f.* mess kit

gamin *m.* street urchin, rascal, youngster

gaminer *vt.* to play in the streets

gaminerie *f.* urchin's prank

gamme *f.* gamut; scale; range

ganglion *m.* ganglion

gangrène *f.* gangrene; (bot. *and* med.) canker

gangrener *vt.* to gangrene

ganse *f.* braid, piping, cord

gant *m.* glove

gantelet *m.* gauntlet

ganter *vt.* to glove; se — to put on one's gloves

ganterie *f.* glovemaking; glove department; glove shop

gantier *m.* glover

garage *m.* garage; parking place; boathouse; docking, dock; (rail.) siding

garagiste *m.* garageman; auto mechanic

garant *m.* guarantee; surety; security

garantie *f.* guarantee; warranty; deposit, security; underwriting

garantir *vt.* to guarantee, vouch for; insure, protect

garce *f.* trollop

garçon *m.* boy; fellow, young man; bachelor; waiter; — d'honneur best man

garçonnière *f.* tomboy; bachelor's apartment

garde *m.* guard, watchman; — *f.* keeping; guard; guarding; care, custody; watch; watching; fly-leaf; chien de — *m.* watchdog; prendre — (de) to be careful (not to)

garde-à-vous *m.* (mil.) attention

garde-barrière *m.* gatekeeper; crossing guard

garde-boue *m.* mudguard

garde-chasse *m.* gamekeeper

garde-corps *m.* railing, guardrail; parapet, barrier; (naut.) life line

garde-côte *m.* coast guardsman; coast guard cutter

garde-feu *m.* fire screen

garde-fou *m.* guardrail; parapet

garde-frein *m.* (rail.) brakeman

garde-magasin *m.* warehouseman

garde-malade *m. & f.* nurse

garde-manger *m.* pantry, larder

garde-meuble *m.* furniture warehouse

garde-nappe *m.* table mat, place mat

gardénia *m.* gardenia

garde-pêche *m.* fishing warden

garde-phare *m.* lighthouse keeper

garde-place(s) *m.* (rail.) reservations office

garder *vt.* to keep; guard; protect, watch over; preserve; — le lit to stay in bed, be confined to bed, be ill; se — de to beware of, take care not to

garderie *f.* nursery school

garde-robe *f.* wardrobe

gardeur *m.* keeper; herder

garde-vue *m.* eyeshade; lamp shade

gardien *m.* guardian, keeper; prison guard; policeman; goal tender

gare *f.* railway station; chef de — *m.* stationmaster

gare *interj.* watch out!, look out!

garer *vt.* to dock; shunt; put in the garage; se — to get out of the way

gargariser *v.*, se — to gargle

gargarisme *m.* gargle

gargote *f.* ordinary, cheap restaurant (in lower-class area)

gargouille *f.* spout of a gutter; drainpipe; (arch.) gargoyle

gargouiller *vi.* to gurgle; rumble

garnement *m.* scamp, rogue

garni *a.* garnished; served with parsley or watercress; plat — *m.* main dish with potatoes or vegetable; chambre —e *f.* furnished room; choucroute —e *f.* sauerkraut with frankfurters; — *m.* furnished room

garnir *vt.* to furnish; strengthen; trim; garnish; line; (mil.) garrison

garnison *f.* garrison

garniture *f.* garnish, ornaments, trimming; lining; complete set; — **de lit** bedding; — **de feu,** — **de foyer** set of fire irons; — **de frein** brake lining

garrot *m.* (med.) tourniquet; withers of a horse

garrotte *f.* garrote; garroting, strangling

garrotter *vt.* to garrote, strangle; secure, pinion

garrulité *f.* garrulity, garrulousness, loquacity

Gascogne *f.* Gascony; **Golfe de** — *m.* Bay of Biscay

gascon *a. & m.* Gascon

gasconner *vi.* (coll.) boast, brag

gasoil *m.* Diesel fuel

gaspiller *vt.* to waste, squander

gastrique *a.* gastric

gastrite *f.* gastritis

gastronome *m.* epicure, gourmet

gastronomie *f.* gastronomy

gastronomique *a.* gastronomical

gâté *a.* spoiled; pampered

gâteau *m.* cake; honeycomb

gâte-papier *m.* hack writer; scribbler

gâter *vt.* to spoil, harm, damage; pamper, overindulge

gâterie *f.* spoiling, overindulgence

gâtisme *m.* senility

gauche *a.* left; crooked; awkward; **à** — **to the left;** — *m.* left; left wing

gaucher *a.* left-handed; leftist, left-wing

gaucherie *f.* awkwardness; blunder; left-handedness

gauchir *vt.* to warp; — *vi.* to warp, buckle; flinch

gaufrage *m.* fluting; embossing; corrugating

gaufre *f.* honeycomb; waffle, wafer

gaufrer *vt.* to flute; emboss; corrugate

gaufrette *f.* wafer

gaufrier *m.* waffle iron

gaule *f.* pole, rod, stick

Gaule *f.* Gaul

gaulois *a.* Gallic

gauloiserie *f.* risqué joke *or* story

gausser *vt. & vi.,* **se** — to scoff; jest, banter

gaver *vt.* to cram; forcefeed; **se** — to gorge with food

gaz *m.* gas; **compteur à** — gas meter

gaze *f.* gauze

gazéifier *vt.* to carbonate; ærate

gazelle *f.* gazelle

gazer *vt.* to gas; cover with gauze; gloss over

gazeux *a.* gaseous; fizzy, carbonated

gazon *m.* turf, lawn, sod

gazonner *vt.* to cover with sod

gazouillement *m.* warbling; babbling

gazouiller *vi.* to warble; babble

gazouillis *m.* warbling

geai *m.* jay

géant *m.* giant; — *a.* gigantic

geignard *a.* (coll.) whining; — *m.* habitual whiner

geignement *m.* whine, whining, whimpering

geindre *vi.* to whine, whimper

gel *m.* frost, freezing

gélatine *f.* gelatin

gélatineux *a.* gelatinous

gelé *a.* frozen; frostbitten

gelée *f.* frost; jelly

geler *vt. & vi.* to freeze; jelly

gélose *f.* agar-agar

gelure *f.* frostbite

géminé *a.* twin

gémir *vi.* to groan, moan

gémissement *m.* groan, moan; groaning, moaning

gemme *f.* gem, precious stone; resin; **sal** — *m.* rock salt

gemmer *vi.* to bud; — *vt.* to cut, tap for resin

gênant *a.* troublesome, embarrassing

gencive *f.* (anat.) gums

gendarme *m.* policeman

gendarmer *vt.* to arouse, stir up

gendarmerie *f.* police; police headquarters; gendarmes

gendre *m.* son-in-law

gêne *f.* discomfort, embarrassment; **sans** — unconstrained

gêné *a.* embarrassed, troubled; having difficulty; short of money

généalogie *f.* genealogy; pedigree

généalogique *a.* genealogical; **arbre** — *m.* family tree

gêner *vt.* to pinch; obstruct; hinder, inconvenience, embarrass

général *a.* general; **en** — generally, in general; — *m.* general; **-e** *f.* general alert, general quarters

généralement *adv.* generally, in general

généralisateur *a.* generalizing; — *m.* generalizer

généralisation *f.* generalization

généraliser *vt.* to generalize

généralissime *m.* generalissimo

généralité *f.* generality

générateur (génératrice) *a.* generating; — *n.* generator

génératif *a.* generative

génération *f.* generation

générer *vt.* to generate

généreux *a.* generous, liberal
générique *a.* generic
générosité *f.* generosity, liberality
Gênes *f.* Genoa
genèse *f.* genesis, origin
genêt *m.* (bot.) broom plant
génétique *f.* genetics
genevois *a.* of Geneva
genévrier *m.* juniper
génial *a.* brilliant, ingenious
génie *m.* genius; spirit; genie; engineering; (mil.) engineers
genièvre *m.* (bot.) juniper; **gin**
génisse *f.* heifer
génital *a.* genital
géniteur *m.* sire, father
génitif *m.* (gram.) genitive
génocide *m.* genocide
génois *a.* of Genoa
genou *m.* knee; (mech.) joint; ball and socket
genouillère *f.* knee guard, knee pad, knee-cap
genre *m.* genus; (gram.) gender; kind, type, manner; style; genre; **— humain** man, mankind
gens *m. pl.* people, men; servants; **jeunes — ** young people; young men
gentil (gentille) *a.* nice; pretty; *m.* gentile
gentilhomme *m.* gentleman, nobleman
gentilité *f.* pagans
gentillesse *f.* graciousness, kindness
gentillet *a.* rather nice
gentiment *adv.* nicely; gracefully
génuflexion *f.* (eccl.) kneeling, genuflexion
géocentrique *a.* geocentric
géodésique *a.* geodetic; geodesic
géographie *f.* geography
géographique *a.* geograph...c(al)
geôle *f.* jail
geôlier *m.* jailor
géologie *f.* geology
géologique *a.* geological
géologue *m.* geologist
géométrie *f.* geometry
géomètrique *a.* geometric(al)
géophysique *a.* geophysical; **— *f.*** geophysics
gérance *f.* management; board of directors
géranium *m.* geranium
gérant *m.* manager; director; **— d'une publication** managing editor
gerbe *f.* sheaf; column, cone
gerbée *f.* straw (rye *or* corn)
gerber *vt.* to bind in sheaves; stack
gerce *f.* crack, split; chap; clothes moth
gercer *vt.* to crack, split; chap
gerçure *f.* crack, cracking; chap, chapping
gérer *vt.* to manage, operate, run

gériatrie *f.* geriatrics
germain *a.* german; **cousin — *m.*** first cousin
germain *a. & m.* German
germanique *a.* Germanic
germanium *m.* germanium
germe *m.* germ, seed; sprout, shoot
germer *vi.* to germinate, sprout
germicide *a. & m.* germicide
germination *f.* germination
gérondif *m.* (gram.) gerundive
gérontologie *f.* geriatrics; gerontology
gésier *m.* gizzard
gésir *vi.* to lie; lie dead
gesse *f.* (bot.) vetch; **— odorante** sweet pea
gestation *f.* gestation
geste *m.* gesture, movement, motion; wave, waving
geste *f.* heroic exploit; **chanson de — *f.*** medieval French epic
gesticuler *vi.* to gesticulate
gestion *f.* management, administration
gestionnaire *m. & f.* manager
geyser *m.* geyser
gibbeux *a.* hunchbacked; humped
gibecière *f.* game bag; satchel
gibelotte *f.* rabbit stew
giberne *f.* cartridge pouch; satchel
gibet *m.* gibbet; gallows
gibier *m.* game; **gros — ** big game; **— de potence** jailbird
giboulée *f.* shower, squall of sleet or hail
gicelée *f.* spurt of liquid; squirt
giclement *m.* spurting
gicler *vi.* to squirt, spurt
gicleur *m.* jet, nozzle; sprayer; **carburetor** opening
gifle *f.* slap, smack; humiliation
gifler *vt.* to slap, smack; affront
gigantesque *a.* gigantic
gigone *a.,* **table — *f.*** stack-table (nested tables)
gigot *m.* leg of lamb
gigue *f.* jig
gilet *m.* vest, cardigan, waistcoat; **— de force** strait jacket; **— de sauvetage** life jacket
gingembre *m.* ginger
gingivite *f.* gingivitis
girafe *f.* giraffe
girandole *f.* cluster; centerpiece, candelabrum; earring
giration *f.* gyration
giratoire *a.* turning, gyratory
girofle *m.* clove
giron *m.* lap; **— de l'Eglise** bosom of the church
girouette *f.* weather vane
gisant *a.* lying; lying dead

gît (*from* gésir), ci-gît here lies
gitan a. Gypsy
gîte m. lodging, resting place; refuge, lair; stratum, layer, (mining)
gîte f. (naut.) list, heeling
gîter vt. to shelter, lodge; — vi. to lie; perch; (naut.) list; run aground
givre m. hoarfrost
givrer vt. to frost
glabre a. smooth shaven, beardless; (fig.) smooth
glace f. ice; plate glass; mirror; windshield; glaze; icing; ice cream
glacé a. frozen; cold; iced; icy; chilled; glazed; glossy
glacer vt. to freeze; glaze; frost; ice
glacerie f. glass factory
glaciaire a. glacial
glacial a. icy, cold, freezing, frigid
glacier m. (geol.) glacier; ice-cream vendor
glacière f. icehouse; refrigerator, icebox
glacis m. slope; colorless glaze (art); tacking (sewing)
glaçon m. ice floe; icicle
glaçure f. ceramic glaze, glazing
gladiateur m. gladiator
glaïeul m. gladiolus
glaire f. white of egg; mucus
glaise f. clay; potter's earth
glaisière f. clay pit
glaive m. sword
gland m. acorn; tassel
glande f. gland
glandulaire, glanduleux a. glandular
glaner vt. to glean
glanure f. gleaning
glapir vi. to yelp; scream
glas m. knell
glaucome m. glaucoma
glauque a. blue-green
glèbe f. clod, sod; soil
glène f. (naut.) coil of rope; (anat.) socket
glissade f. slip, slide, sliding; glide
glissant a. slippery; sliding; unstable
glissement m. slipping, sliding; landslide
glisser vt. & vi. to slip, slide; skid; glide; se — to glide, steal, slip
glisseur m. glider; slider
glissière f. slide, groove; shoot; porte à —s f. sliding door
glissoir m. icy slide
glissoire f. sliding, slide on ice
global a. global; total; lump (sum)
globe m. globe, ball, sphere
globulaire a. globular
globuleux a. globular
globulin m. globulin
gloire f. glory; halo; pride; vanity
gloria m. coffee with brandy

gloriette f. arbor, summerhouse
glorieux a. glorious; proud; vain
glorification f. glorification
glorifier vt. to glorify; se — to boast
gloriole f. vainglory, vanity
glose f. gloss; commentary
gloser vt. to gloss, comment on; — vi. to find fault; criticize
glossaire m. glossary
glotte f. (anat.) glottis; coup de — m. glottal stop (phonetics)
glouglou m. gurgle, gurgling sound; coo, cooing; gobble
glouglouter vi. to gurgle; gobble; coo
glousser vi. to cluck; (coll.) chuckle
glouton m. glutton; — a. gluttonous
gloutonnerie f. gluttony
glu f. birdlime; glue; (fig.) trap, snare
gluant a. sticky, viscous; (fig.) tenacious
glucose f. glucose
glutineux a. glutinous
glycérine f. glycerin
glycine f. wistaria
go (tout de) adv. at once; easily; at one shot; suddenly
goal m. goal tender, goalie
gobelet m. goblet, cup, tumbler
gobe-mouches m. flycatcher (bird) (fig.) gullible person
gober vt. to swallow greedily, gulp down; (fig.) believe credulously se — to be conceited
gobeter vt. to plaster; fill in cracks
gobeur a. & m. easily fooled person
goder vi. to wrinkle, pucker
godet m. mug; bowl; basin; pan; scoop; flare of a skirt
godille f. oar, scull
godiller vi. to scull
goéland m. sea gull
goélette f. (naut.) schooner
goguenard a. jeering, mocking
goguenarder vi. to mock; banter
goitre m. goiter
golf m. golf; terrain de — golf course
golfe m. gulf
gomme f. gum; — élastique gum eraser; — laque shellac
gommelaquer vt. to shellac
gommer vt. to gum; erase; — vi. to stick, become stuck
gommeux a. gummy
gommier m. gum tree
gonade f. gonad
gond m. door hinge; sortir de ses —s to fly off the handle
gondole f. gondola
gondoler vi. to warp, buckle
gondolier m. gondolier
gonfalon m. gonfalon, pennant

gonflage *m.* inflating

gonflement *m.* inflating, inflation

gonfler *vt.* to inflate; fill with air; pump up; bulge; puff up; swell; — *vi.* to be inflated, become inflated

gonfleur *m.* (auto.) air pump

goret *m.* young pig; (coll.) dirty person

gorge *f.* throat; bosom; bust; gorge; avoir mal à la — to have a sore throat

gorgée *f.* mouthful, gulp

gorger *vt.* to gorge, stuff

gorille *m.* gorilla

gosier *m.* throat; gullet

gosse *m. & f.* (coll.) youngster; child

gothique *a. & m.* Gothic

gouape *f.* (coll.) good-for-nothing person; hoodlum

gouaper *vi.* to loaf, idle

goudron *m.* tar

goudronner *vt.* to tar

gouffre *m.* gulf, abyss; whirlpool

gouge *f.* gouge, chisel

gouger *vt.* to gouge

goujat *m.* lout, boor

goujon *m.* gudgeon; (fig.) bait

goulasch *m.* goulash

goule *f.* ghoul

goulet *m.* (naut.) channel, narrows

goulot *m.* neck of a bottle

goulu *a.* gluttonous; greedy

goupille *f.* peg, pin, bolt

goupillon *m.* brush; (eccl.) holy water sprinkler

gourd *a.* benumbed, numb

gourde *f.* gourd; metal flask

gourdin *m.* club, bludgeon

gourmand *m.* greedy person; glutton; — *a.* greedy, gluttonous

gourmander *vi.* to guzzle; — *vt.* rebuke

gourmandise *f.* greediness, gluttony; sweets

gourme *f.* rash; impetigo

gourmé *a.* formal, stiff; stuck up (U.S. coll.)

gourmet *m.* connoisseur of food and drink; epicure

gourmette *f.* curb (of a harness); watch chain

gousse *f.* pod, husk; — d'ail clove of garlic

gousset *m.* watch pocket, vest pocket

goût *m.* taste; flavor; aroma; liking; style

goûter *vt.* to taste, like, enjoy; — *m.* afternoon snack

goutte *f.* drop; speck, spot, bit; nothing, anything; (med.) gout

gouttelette *f.* droplet

goutteux *a.* gouty

gouttière *f.* gutter; rainspout; —s *pl.* eaves

gouvernail *m.* rudder; helm, steering wheel

gouvernante *f.* housekeeper; governess; governor's wife

gouverne *f.* guidance; —s *pl.* (avi.) controls

gouvernement *m.* government; management; control; steering

gouvernemental *a.* governmental

gouverner *vt.* to govern, manage; direct; control; (naut.) to steer

gouverneur *m.* governor

grabat *m.* pallet, litter; sickbed

grâce *f.* grace; gracefulness; favor; pardon; mercy; thanks; actions de — *f. pl.* thanksgiving; avec — gracefully; de —! please!, I beg of you!; de bonne — graciously, willingly; — à thanks to; faire — to pardon, reprieve

graciable *a.* pardonable

gracier *vt.* to pardon, reprieve

gracieusement *adv.* graciously; gracefully; gratuitously

gracieuseté *f.* graciousness, kindness

gracieux *a.* gracious; graceful; à titre — free, gratis; as a favor

gracile *a.* slender, svelte

gracilité *f.* slenderness

gradation *f.* gradation

grade *m.* grade, rank, degree

gradé *m.* noncommissioned officer

gradient *m.* gradient, variation

gradin *m.* tier, row; tiered seating

gradué *a.* graduated, measured, graded

graduel *a.* gradual (eccl.) verse between epistle and gospel

graduellement *adv.* gradually

graduer *vt.* to graduate, scale; grade

graillement *m.* hoarseness, huskiness

grailler *vi.* to speak in a hoarse manner; cough up phlegm

grain *m.* grain; berry, bean; bead; particle, iota, speck; (naut.) squall; — de beauté beauty mark

grain-d'orge *m.* (coll.) sty of the eye

graine *f.* seed

grainer *vt.* to grain; granulate

graissage *m.* greasing, lubrication

graisse *f.* grease, fat; — de rôti meat drippings

graisser *vt.* to grease, oil, lubricate

graisseux *a.* greasy, oily; fatty

grammaire *f.* grammar

grammairien *m.* grammarian

grammatical *a.* grammatical

gramme *m.* gram

grand *a.* great; large, tall, high; important, big; main, chief, principal; — *m.* great person; grownup; grandee

grand-chose *m.* something important; something significant

Grande-Bretagne *f.* Great Britain

grandelet *a.* rather big

grandeur *f.* greatness, tallness, largeness, magnitude; size; nobility; grandeur
grandiloquence *f.* (eccl.) grandiloquence
grandiose *a.* grandiose, impressive
grandir *vi.* to grow, grow up; — *vt.* to increase; magnify
grandissant *a.* growing
grandissement *m.* growth, growing; magnification
grand-livre *m.* ledger
grand'mère *f.* grandmother
grand-messe *f.* (eccl.) high mass
grand-oncle *m.* great-uncle
grand-père *m.* grandfather
grand'route *f.* main highway
grand'rue *f.* main street
grands-parents *m. pl.* grandparents
grand-tante *f.* great-aunt
grange *f.* barn; building for keeping straw *or* hay
granit *m.* granite
granulaire *a.* granular
granuler *vt.* to granulate
granuleux *a.* granular
graphique *a.* graphic; — *m.* graph
graphite *m.* graphite
graphologue *m.* graphologist
grappe *f.* bunch, cluster of fruit
grappillon *m.* little bunch *or* cluster
grappin *m.* grapnel, grappling hook
gras (grasse) *a.* fat, stout; fatty, greasy; thick; containing meat; caractères — *m. pl.* bold-faced type; jours — *m.* (eccl.) carnival days (pre-lenten) temps — *m.* foggy weather; — *m.* fat
gras-double *m.* tripe
grassement *adv.* comfortably; generously
grassouillet *a.* plump, chubby
gratification *f.* tip; bonus; reward
gratifier *vt.* to confer, bestow
gratin *m.* breading, crust; au — served *or* cooked with cheese and bread crumbs
gratiné *a.* au gratin; breaded
gratis *adv.* gratis, free
gratitude *f.* gratitude
gratte-ciel *m.* skyscraper
gratte-papier *m.* (coll.) hack writer; copyist
gratte-pieds *m.* doormat; scraper for shoes
gratter *vt.* to scrape, scratch; scratch out, erase
grattoir *m.* scraper; eraser
gratuit *a.* gratuitous; free; unmotivated à titre — free of charge
gratuité *f.* gratuitousness
grave *a.* grave, serious, important; (phy.) heavy; (mus.) flat; (gram.) accent grave
graveler *vt.* to gravel
graveleux *a.* gravelly, gritty

gravelle *f.* gravel
gravement *adv.* gravely, seriously
graver *vt.* to engrave; carve; — à l'eau forte etch
graveur *m.* engraver; etcher
gravier *m.* gravel; grit
gravir *vt.* to climb with effort
gravité *f.* gravity; graveness; seriousness; (mus.) lowness, flatness
graviter *vi.* to gravitate
gravure *f.* engraving, etching; print; carving
gré *m.* will, liking; de bon — willingly; bon — mal — willy-nilly; de son propre — freely, of one's own free will; savoir (bon) — de to be grateful for; — *adv.* de — à — amiably; de son pleine — voluntarily
grec (grecque) *a.* Greek, Grecian; — *m.* Greek
Grèce *f.* Greece
gredin *m.* scoundrel
gréement *m.* (naut.) rig, rigging
gréer *vt.* (naut.) to rig
greffe *f.* (med., bot.) graft, grafting; — épidermique *f.* skin graft
greffer *vt.* to graft
greffier *m.* recorder, clerk of the court
grégaire *a.* gregarious
grégorien *a.* Gregorian
grêle *f.* hail; hailstorm; — *a.* shrill
grêlé *a.* pock-marked
grelin *m.* (naut.) hawser
grêlon *m.* large hailstone
grelot *m.* little bell
grelotter *vi.* to shiver, tremble; jingle
grenade *f.* pomegranate; grenade
grenadier *m.* grenadier; pomegranate tree
grenadine *f.* grenadine syrup
grenailler *vt.* to granulate
grenat *a. & m.* garnet
grené *a.* stippled (art); — *m.* stipple
grenier *m.* granary; hayloft; attic
grenouille *f.* frog
grenouillère *f.* swamp, marsh
grenu *a.* granular, grainy, rough-grained
grès *m.* sandstone; stoneware
grésil *m.* sleet
grésiller *vi.* to crackle; sizzle; patter
grève *f.* sandy shore, beach; strike (labor); faire — to strike, go out on strike
grever *vt.* to entail legally, encumber
gréviste *m. & f.* worker on strike, striker
gribouillage *m.* scribble, scrawl
gribouiller *vt.* to scribble, scrawl
grief *m.* grievance; injury, wrong
grièvement *adv.* grievously, seriously, gravely
griffe *f.* claw, talon; clamp, clip; coup de — *m.* scratch; — à papiers paper clip;

marteau à — claw hammer
griffer *vt.* to claw, scratch
griffonnage *m.* scribble, scribbling, scrawl
griffonner *vt.* to scrawl, scribble
grignoter *vt.* to pick at, nibble
gril *m.* grill, gridiron
grillade *f.* grilled meat
grillage *m.* grating, latticework; grilling, toasting
grille *f.* iron bars; gate, grate; grid
grille-pain *m.* toaster
griller *vt. & vi.* to grill; toast; broil; bar, grate
grillon *m.* cricket
grimacer *vi.* to grimace
grimacier *a.* grimacing; affected
grimer *vt.* (theat.) to apply makeup, make up
grimper *vt. & vi.* to climb up; scale
grimpeur *a.* climbing; — *m.* climber
grincement *m.* gnashing
grincer *vi.* to gnash; grind; scratch; — des dents grit one's teeth in anger
grincheux *a.* grumpy, crabby; — *m.* grumbler, crab
gringalet *m.* weakling, runt
grippe *f.* influenza; (fig.) dislike
grippé *a.* having influenza; stuck together
gripper *vt.* to grab, seize; — *vi.* to grab, stick, jam
grippe-sou *m.* miser, skinflint
gris *a.* gray; gray-haired; drunk, tipsy; cloudy, overcast (weather)
grisailler *vt.* to daub with gray; — *vi.* to turn gray (hair)
grisâtre *a.* grayish
griser *vt.* to intoxicate; se — to become intoxicated
griserie *f.* intoxication, drunkenness, tipsiness
grisonner *vi.* to become gray (hair)
grive *f.* thrush
grivelé *a.* speckled
grivois *a.* risqué, off-color
grizzly *m.* grizzly bear
Groenland *m.* Greenland
grog *m.* grog, toddy
grognard *a.* grumbling; — *m.* grumbler
grognement *m.* grumbling, growling; grunt, grunting
grogner *vi.* to grunt, grumble, growl
grognerie *f.* grumbling, growling
grognon *a.* grumbling; — *m.* grumbler
grognonner *vi.* to grumble, complain, whine
groin *m.* snout of a pig
grommeler *vi.* to grumble, mutter
grondement *m.* rumbling, roaring; growling; — sonique sonic boom
gronder *vt.* to scold; — *vi.* to grumble,

growl; rumble
gronderie *f.* scolding
grondeur *a.* grumbling; scolding; — *m.* grumbler
grondeuse *f.* nag, shrew
gros (grosse) *a.* big, bulky, large; rich; heavy; thick; loud; coarse; vulgar; pregnant, swollen; — sel *m.* coarse salt; — jeu *m.* high stakes; — temps *m.* bad weather; — *m.* bulk, main part; — *adv.* en — in bulk, wholesale; rough, roughly
gros-bec *m.* grosbeak
groseille *f.* currant; gooseberry
grosse *f.* (com.) gross, twelve dozen
grossesse *f.* pregnancy
grosseur *f.* size; bulk; swelling; largeness
grossier *a.* coarse, rough; rude; vulgar
grossièreté *f.* grossness, coarseness, rudeness, vulgarity
grossir *vt. & vi.* to enlarge, increase
grossissant *a.* growing, increasing, swelling; verre — *m.* magnifying glass
grossissement *m.* increase, growth, swelling; enlargement; magnification
grossiste *m.* wholesaler
grotte *f.* grotto; cavern
grouiller *vi.* to swarm, teem, crawl
groupe *m.* group; unit; set, section; — sanguin blood type
groupement *m.* group, grouping; coupling
grouper *vt.* to group; bring together; couple; se — to form a group
gruau *m.* oatmeal; fine flour; small crane
grue *f.* crane
grumeler *v.*, se — to curdle, clot
grumeleux *a.* curdled; gritty, grainy
gruyère *m.* variety of Swiss cheese; crème de — *f.* processed gruyère cheese
gué *m.* ford, crossing
guéable *a.* fordable
guéer *vt.* to ford; water
guelte *f.* (com.) commission, percentage, fee
guenille *f.* ragged garment, tatters
guenilleux *a.* ragged, in rags
guenipe *f.* whore, trollop
guenon *f.* monkey
guépard *m.* cheetah
guêpe *f.* wasp
guêpier *m.* wasps' nest; (fig.) hornets' nest
guère *adv.*, not much; not long; but little; ne . . . — hardly
guéret *m.* (agr.) unsown land
guéridon *m.* small table
guérilla *f.* guerilla warfare; guerilla army
guérillero *m.* guerilla, guerilla fighter
guérir *vt.* to cure, heal; — *vi.* to recover, be cured, healed
guérison *f.* cure, recovery; healing

guérissable *a.* curable
guérisseur *a.* healing; — *m.* healer; quack
guérite *f.* turret, sentry box; shack, hut (for watchman); (rail.) signal box; — **téléphonique** call box
guerre *f.* war, warfare; struggle, strife; **en —** at war
guerrier *a.* warlike; — *m.* warrior
guerroyant *a.* warlike, bellicose
guerroyer *vi.* to make war
guerroyeur *a.* fighting; — *m.* fighter
guet *m.* watch, lookout; **au —** on the lookout
guet-apens *m.* ambush; (fig.) premeditation
guêtre *f.* gaiter; legging; (auto.) tire patch
guetter *vt.* to watch for; (coll.) lie in wait for
guetteur *m.* lookout
gueulard *m.* furnace mouth, gun muzzle; powerful loudspeaker
gueule *f.* mouth; muzzle; **avoir la — de bois** to have a hangover
gueule-de-loup *f.* snapdragon
gueuse *f.* beggar; hussy; **fer en —** *m.* pig iron
gueuser *vi.* to beg in the streets
gueuserie *f.* begging; wretchedness
gueux (gueuse) *a.* beggarly, wretched, poor; — *m.* beggar
gui *m.* mistletoe; (naut.) guy; boom
guichet *m.* grilled window; ticket window; box-office window
guide *m.* guide, guidebook; — *f.* rein
guide-âne *m.* manual, set of instructions; travel guide
guider *vt.* to guide, lead; steer; drive
guidon *m.* handlebar; gun sight *or* bead; (naut.) pennant
guigne *f.* white-heart cherry; (coll.) bad luck
guigner *vt.* to ogle; eye
guignol *m.* Punch and Judy show; puppet theater
guignolet *m.* cherry liqueur
guillemeter *vt.* to put in *or* between, quotation marks
guillemets *m. pl.* quotation marks
guiller *vi.* to ferment
guilleret *a.* gay, lively
guillotine *f.* guillotine; **fenêtre à —** sash window
guillotiner *vt.* to guillotine
guindé *a.* stiff, affected, stuck-up
guindeau *m.* windlass; hoist
guinder *vt.* to hoist; **se —** to act superior
Guinée *f.* Guinea
guingan *m.* gingham
guingois (de) *adv.* askew
guipage *m.* wrapping, covering, winding; tape, taping
guiper *vt.* to wrap, cover; wind; tape
guipure *f.* lace
guirlande *f.* garland, wreath
guirlander *vt.* to garland
guise *f.* manner, fashion, wax; **en — de** by way of
guitare *f.* guitar
guppy *m.* guppy
gustation *f.* taste, tasting; eating
Guyane *f.* Guiana
gymnase *m.* gymnasium
gymnaste *m. & f.* gymnast
gymnastique *a.* gymnastic; — *f.* gymnastics
gynécologie *f.* gynecology
gynécologue, gynécologiste *m.* gynecologist
gypse *m.* gypsum; plaster of Paris
gyrocompas *m.* gyrocompass
gyroscope *m.* gyroscope

H

* Indicates a word which allows neither elision nor linking
habile *a.* clever, skilful; capable
habileté *f.* cleverness; skill, ability
habilité *f.* ability (law), title
habillé *a.* dressed
habillement *m.* clothing, clothes
habiller *vt.* to dress; clothe; put together; **s' —** to get dressed
habit *m.* suit, full-dress suit; evening clothes; (eccl.) habit; frock; **-s** *pl.* clothes; **prendre l' —** to become a nun *or* monk
habitabilité *f.* habitability
habitable *a.* habitable
habitacle *m.* cockpit; (naut.) binnacle
habitant *m.* inhabitant, dweller
habitat *m.* habitat
habitation *f.* habitation; housing; dwelling
habiter *vt. & vi.* to inhabit; live in
habitude *f.* habit, custom; **avoir l' — de** to be used to; be in the habit of; **d' —** usually; **comme d' —** as usual
habitué *m.* regular customer, frequenter
habituel *a.* habitual; usual, regular
habituer *vt.* to habituate, accustom; **s' — à** to get used to
*hâbler *vi.* to brag
*hâblerie *f.* bragging
*hâbleur *m.* braggart
*hache *f.* axe, hachet
*haché *a.* chopped; choppy, jerky
*hacher *vt.* to hash, chop, mince; hack
*hachette *f.* hatchet
*hachis *m.* hash, minced meat
hachisch *m.* hashish, hasheesh

*hachoir *m.* chopper; cleaver; chopping board
*hachurer *vt.* (art) to shade
*hagard *a.* haggard, drawn
*haie *f.* hedge; hurdle
*haillon *m.* rag, tatter
*haillonneux *a.* ragged, in rags
*haine *f.* hate, hatred
*haineux *a.* full of hate
*haïr *vt.* to hate; loathe; feel repugnance for
*haïssable *a.* hateful; odious
*halage *m.* towing
halcyon *m.* kingfisher
*hâle *m.* sunburn, tan; searing wind
*hâlé *a.* sunburned, tanned
haleine *f.* breath, wind
halenée *f.* whiff
*haler *vt.* to tow; (naut.) heave; — *vi.* to heave, haul
*hâler *vt.* to burn, tan; se — to be burned by the sun, become tanned
*haletant *a.* breathless, out of breath, panting
halètement *m.* breathlessness, panting
*haleter *vi.* to pant; puff
*hall *m.* hall, hallway; lounge; shop in a factory
*halle *f.* covered market place
*hallier *m.* thicket
hallucination *f.* hallucination
halluciner *vt.* to hallucinate, delude
*halo *m.* halo (meteorology)
*halte *f.* halt, stop; faire — to halt, come to a halt; —! (mil.) *interj.* halt! stop!
haltère *m.* dumbbell (gymnastics)
*hamac *m.* hammock
*hameau *m.* hamlet
hameçon *m.* hook, fishhook; (fig.) bait
*hamman *m.* Turkish bath(s)
*hampe *f.* pole, shaft; stem
*hamster *m.* hamster
*hanche *f.* hip, haunch; (naut.) lee quarter
*hanché *a.* (mil.) at ease
*handicap *m.* handicap
*handicaper *vt.* to handicap (sports)
*hangar *m.* shed; boathouse; (avi.) hangar
*hanter *vt.* to haunt, frequent; obsess
*hantise *f.* obsession
*happe *f.* tongs; staple
*happer *vt.* to grab, snatch, seize; — *vi.* to stick
*harangue *f.* speech, harangue
*haranguer *vt.* to harangue
*harasser *vt.* to harass; exhaust
*harceler *vt.* to harass, harry; torment; nag, pester
*harde *f.* flock, herd; dog leash

*hardes *f. pl.* ordinary clothes
*hardi *a.* hardy, bold, daring
*hardiesse *f.* boldness, daring, audacity
*harem *m.* harem
*hareng *m.* herring; — saur smoked herring
*harenguet *m.* sprat
*hargne *f.* irritation, peevishness, ill temper
*hargneux *a.* surly, snapping; ill-tempered, cross; nagging
*haricot *m.* bean; — vert string bean; — de mouton mutton stew
*haricot-beurre *m.* butter bean
harmonie *f.* harmony; accord
harmonieux *a.* harmonious; melodious
harmonique *a. & m.* harmonic
harmonisation *f.* harmonizing, harmonization
harmoniser *vt.* to harmonize; s'— to harmonize; blend; agree
*harnachement *m.* harness, harnessing; saddlery
*harnacher *vt.* to harness; rig, deck out
*harnais *m.* harness, armor; gears
harpagon *m.* miser
*harpe *f.* harp
*harpie *f.* harpy
*harpin *m.* boat hook
*harpiste *m. & f.* harpist
*harpon *m.* harpoon
*harponner *vt.* to harpoon
*hasard *m.* hazard, chance, luck, accident; au — at random; coup de — *m.* stroke of luck; par — by chance, accidentally
*hasardé *a.* risky, hazardous; rash; indiscreet
*hasarder *vt.* to risk, hazard, venture
*hasardeux *a.* risky, hazardous
*hâte *f.* haste, speed; à la — hastily; avoir — de to be in a hurry to; be anxious to, be eager to
*hâter *vt.* to hasten, hurry, quicken; se — to hurry oneself
*hâtif (hâtive) *a.* hasty; early, premature
*hâtivement *adv.* hastily, hurriedly
*hauban *m.* (naut.) shroud; stay
*haubert *m.* coat of mail, hauberk
*hausse *f.* rise, increase; (mil.) elevation, range
*haussement *m.* raising; — d'épaules shrug
*hausser *vt.* to raise, lift, elevate; — *vi.* to rise; — les épaules shrug
*haussier *m.* bull stock
*haussière *f.* hawser
*haut *a.* high; tall; elevated; great; loud; upper, higher; — *adv.* high, up; loud(ly); aloud; back (in time); — *m.* height; top; au — de at the top of; de — en

bas from top to bottom; condescendingly; en — above; upstairs
*hautain a. haughty, proud, arrogant
*hautbois m. oboe
*hautboïste m. & f. oboist
*haut-de-chausses m. breeches
*haut-de-forme m. top hat
*hautement adv. highly; nobly; loudly
*hauteur f. height, elevation; rise; hill; haughtiness, scorn; (mus.) pitch; à la — de level with
*haut-fond m. shallows, shoal
*haut-fourneau m. blast furnace
*haut-le-cœur m. nausea
*haut-le-corps m. start, jump
*haut-parleur m. speaker, loudspeaker
*havana m. Havana cigar
la Havane f. Havana
*hâve a. gaunt, sunken; pale and sickly
*havre m. haven, harbor
*havresac m. bag, kit; knapsack
hawaiien a. & m. Hawaiian
la Haye f. the Hague
hebdomadaire a. weekly; — m. weekly paper
héberger vt. to lodge, shelter
hébété a. dazed, bewildered
hébètement m. daze, bewilderment, stupor
hébéter vt. to dull, blunt; daze, stupefy
hébraïque a. Hebrew, Hebraic
hébreu a. Hebrew
hectare m. hectare (about 2½ acres)
hédonisme m. hedonism
hégémonie f. hegemony
*hein interj. what?; right?
*hélas interj. alas!
*héler vt. to hail, call
hélianthe m. sunflower
hélice f. (naut.) screw; helix, spiral; (avi.) propeller; — en drapeau feathered propeller
hélicoptère m. helicopter
hélio f. heliogravure
héliocentrique a. heliocentric
héliothérapie f. sun-lamp treatment
héliotrope m. heliotrope
héliport m. heliport
hélium m. helium
hélix m. helix
hellène a. Hellenic
hellénique a. Hellenic, Hellenistic
hellénisme m. Hellenism
hellénistique a. Hellenistic
helvétique a. Swiss
hématie f. red blood corpuscle
hémisphère m. hemisphere
hémisphérique a. hemispherical
hémistiche m. hemstitch
hémoglobine f. hemoglobin

hémophile a. & n. hemophiliac
hémophilie f. hemophilia
hémorragie f. hemorrhage
hémorroïdes f. pl. hemorrhoids
hémostatique a. styptic
*henné m. henna
*hennir vi. to neigh, whinny
*hennissement m. neigh, whinny
hépatique a. hepatic
hépatite f. hepatitis
heptagone a. heptagonal; — m. heptagon
heptemètre m. heptameter
héraldique a. heraldic; — f. heraldry
*héraut m. herald; sign, harbinger
herbacé a. (bot.) herbaceous
herbage m. grass; pasture, meadow
herbe f. grass; herb; weed; en — budding; green (unripe); mauvaises –s pl. weeds; fines –s seasoning herbs
herbeux a. grassy
herbivore a. herbivorous
herbu a. grassy
herculéen a. Herculean
*hère m. wretch
héréditaire a. hereditary
hérédité f. inheritance; heredity
hérésie f. heresy
hérétique a. heretical; — m. & f. heretic
*hérissé a. bristling; brushy, shaggy
*hérisser vt. to bristle
*herisson m. hedgehog; series of bristles or spikes; bottle brush; pinwheel; — de mer sea urchin
heritable a. inheritable
héritage m. heritage, inheritance, legacy
hériter vt. & vi. to inherit
héritier m., héritière f. heir, heiress
hermétique a. hermetic, tight; hermetically sealed
hermine f. ermine
herminette f. adze
hermite m. hermit, recluse
*herniaire a. hernial; bandage — m. truss
*hernie f. (med.) hernia, rupture
*hernieux a. ruptured
héroïne f. heroine; (chem.) heroin
héroïque a. heroic
héroïsme m. heroism
*héron m. heron
*héros m. hero
hésitant a. hesitant, hesitating
hésitation f. hesitation
hésiter vi. to hesitate; falter
hétéroclite a. unusual, odd; eccentric
hétérodoxe a. heterodox
hétérogène a. heterogeneous
*hêtre m. beech tree
heur m. luck, good luck
heure f. hour; time; moment; à l'— on time; de bonne — early; à la bonne —!

well!, fine!; **tout à l'**— in a little while; a little while ago; **à tout à l'**— see you soon!, see you later!, so long!

heureusement adv. fortunately

heureux a. happy, fortunate, lucky, successful

*__heurt__ m. blow, bump, shock; **sans** — without a hitch

*__heurtement__ m. shock, clash

*__heurter__ vt. & vi. to strike against, hit against, knock; bump into; conflict with

*__heurtoir__ m. bumper, stop; knocker of a door

hexagone a. hexagonal; — m. hexagon

hiatus m. hiatus; gap, break

hibernant a. hibernating

hiberner vi. to hibernate

hibiscus m. hibiscus

*__hibou__ m. owl

*__hideur__ f. hideousness, ugliness

*__hideux__ a. hideous, ugly

hiémal a. pertaining to winter

hier adv. yesterday; — **soir** last night

*__hiérarchie__ f. hierarchy

*__hiérarchique__ a. hierarchical

hiéroglyphe m. hieroglyph; **-s** pl. hieroglyphics

hilarant a. producing laughter; **gaz** — m. laughing gas

hilare a. hilarious

hilarité f. hilarity, laughter

hindou a. & m. Hindu

hippique a. equine; pertaining to horses

hippisme m. horse racing

hippocratique a. Hippocratic

hippodrome m. race track; hippodrome

hippopotame m. hippopotamus

hirondelle f. swallow

hirsute a. hirsute, hairy

hispanique a. Hispanic, Spanish

hispano-américain a. Spanish-American

*__hisser__ vt. (naut.) to hoist; raise, pull up

histoire f. history; story

histologie f. histology

historien m. historian

historier vt. to illuminate a book; illustrate

historiette f. short story, anecdote

historique a. historic(al)

histrion m. histrion, actor

histrionique a. histrionic

hiver m. winter

hivernage m. winter quarters; winter season

hivernal a. of the winter

hiverner vi. to hibernate; winter

*__hoche__ f. notch, cut, nick

*__hochement__ m. head shaking, affirmative nod

*__hocher__ vt. to shake, nod; notch, nick

*__hochet__ m. toy, teething ring

*__holà__ interj. stop!; hello!

*__holding__ m. (com.) holding company

*__hollandais__ a. & m. Dutch

*__Hollande__ f. Holland

holocauste m. holocaust

*__homard__ m. lobster

homélie f. homily

homérique a. Homeric, epic

homicide m. homicide (person or the act); — **involontaire** manslaughter; — a. homicidal; murderous

hommage m. homage; present; testimony; tribute; **-s** pl. respects

homme m. man; — **d'affaires** businessman

homogène a. homogeneous

homologation f. probating

homologuer vt. confirm (law); probate

homonyme m. homonym

homosexuel a. & m. homosexual

*__hongre__ m. gelding, castrated horse

*__hongrer__ vt. to geld

*__Hongrie__ f. Hungary

*__hongrois__ a. & m. Hungarian

honnête a. honest, sincere; respectable; gentlemanly; proper, decent, mannerly; reasonable

honnêteté f. honesty, integrity; respectability; courtesy; decency

honneur m. honor; respect

honorabilité f. respectability

honorable a. honorable, respectable

honoraire a. honorary; — m. honorarium, fee; royalty

honorer vt. to honor, respect

honorifique a. honorary

*__honte__ f. shame, dishonor, disgrace; **avoir** — to be ashamed

*__honteux__ a. shameful; disgraceful; shamefaced

hôpital m. hospital

*__hoquet__ m. hiccup; gasp

*__hoqueter__ vi. to hiccup, have the hiccups

horaire m. timetable, schedule

horizon m. horizon

horizontal a. horizontal

horloge f. timeclock

horloger m. watchmaker, clockmaker

horlogerie f. clocks, watches; watch business; watch factory; watch and clock shop

*__hormis__ prep. except, save, but

hormone f. hormone

horoscope m. horoscope

horreur f. horror, terror; abhorrence; **avoir** — **de** to abhor; **faire** — **à** to horrify

horrible a. horrible; horrid

horrifier vt. to horrify

horrifique a. horrific

horripilant *a.* hair-raising
horripilation *f.* goose flesh
*hors *prep.* except, out of; — de out of,
outside of; — de combat out of action;
— de soi beside oneself
*hors-bord *m.* outboard motorboat
*hors-caste *m. & f.* untouchable, outcast
*hors-d'œuvre *m.* outwork; digression;
first course, hors d'œuvres
*hors-jeu *m.* offside (sports)
*hors-la-loi *m.* outlaw
hortensia *m.* hydrangea
horticole *a.* horticultural
horticulture *f.* horticulture
hosanna *m.* hosanna, praise
hospice *m.* charitable institution; asylum,
home; poorhouse
hospitalier *a.* hospitable; pertaining to
charitable institutions
hospitalisation *f.* hospitalizing, hospitali-
zation, hospital care
hostie *f.* (eccl.) host
hostile *a.* hostile, inimical; opposed
hostilité *f.* hostility
hôte *m.* host; landlord; guest; table d'— *f.*
fixed menu
hôtel *m.* hotel; mansion; building; — de
ville city hall; — meublé lodginghouse;
maître d' — head waiter
hôtel-Dieu *m.* main hospital
hôtelier *m.* innkeeper
hôtellerie *f.* hostelry; inn
hôtesse *f.* hostess; guest; — de l'air airline
stewardess
*hotte *f.* hod; basket; (chem.) hood
*houache *f.* (naut.) wash, wake
*houblon *m.* (bot.) hops
*houe *f.* hoe
*houer *vt.* to hoe
*houille *f.* coal; — blanche water power
*houillère *f.* coal mine
*houilleur *m.* coal miner
*houle *f.* surge; swell
*houlette *f.* crook, staff; trowel
*houleux *a.* stormy, surging
*houppe *f.* tuft; puff, powder puff; tassel;
crest on an animal
*houppelande *f.* overcoat, greatcoat
*houppette *f.* powder puff
*houspiller *vt.* to jostle; abuse
*housse *f.* cover; slipcover; dust cover;
(auto.) seat cover
*housser *vt.* to dust
*houssine *f.* furniture and rug beater;
switch (for punishment)
*houssoir *m.* brush, whiskbroom
*houx *m.* (bot.) holly
*hoyau *m.* pickax; hoe used to flatten
*hublot *m.* porthole; verre de — *m.* bull's-
eye

*huche *f.* bin; hopper; trough
*huer *vt. & vi.* to hoot, shout, boo
*huguenot *a. & m.* Huguenot
huile *f.* oil
huiler *vt.* to oil, grease
huileux *a.* oily; greasy
huilier *m.* oiler; oilcan; oil seller *or* maker
huis *m.* door
huisserie *f.* door frame
huissier *m.* usher; bailiff
*huit *a. & m.* eight; d'aujourd'hui en —
a week from today; — jours a week
*huitaine *f.* about eight; week
*huitième *a. & m.* eighth
huître *f.* oyster
*huit-reflets *m.* top hat
huîtrière *f.* oyster bed
humain *a.* human; humane; — *m.* human
being
humanisation *f.* humanization
humaniser *vt.* to humanize
humaniste *m.* humanist; classicist
humanitaire *a. & n.* humanitarian
humanité *f.* humanity; mankind; –s *pl.*
humanities
humble *a.* humble
humecter *vt.* to moisten
*humer *vt.* to suck in, breathe in
humérus *m.* (anat.) humerus
humeur *f.* humor; disposition, mood;
temper
humide *a.* humid, moist, damp
humidifier *vt.* to humidify, moisten
humidistat *m.* humidistat
humidité *f.* humidity, moisture, dampness;
— absolue absolute humidity; — relative relative humidity
humiliant *a.* humiliating
humiliation *f.* humiliation
humilier *vt.* to humiliate, humble
humilité *f.* humility
humoriste *m.* humorist; — *a.* humorous
humoristique *a.* humorous
humour *m.* comic irony, humor
humus *m.* humus
*hune *f.* (naut.) top; — de vigie crow's
nest
*hunter *m.* hunting horse, jumper
*huppé *a.* crested; well-dressed
*hurlement *m.* howl, howling, roar, yell
*hurler *vi.* to howl, roar, yell
*hurleur *a.* howling, yelling; — *m.* howler;
powerful loudspeaker
hurluburlu *m.* silly person, scatterbrain
*hussard *m.* hussar
*hussarde *f.* Hungarian dance; à la —
adv. roughly, unceremoniously
*hutte *f.* hut, cabin, shack
hyalin *a.* glassy
hybridation *f.* crossbreeding

hybride *a. & m.* hybrid
hybrider *vt.* to cross breeds *or* strains
hydratation *f.* hydration
hydrate *m.* hydrate; — de carbone carbohydrate; —r *vt.* to hydrate
hydraulique *a.* hydraulic; —*f.* hydraulics
hydravion *m.* seaplane
hydre *f.* hydra
hydrocarbure *m.* hydrocarbon
hydrodynamique *a.* hydrodynamic; — *f.* hydrodynamics; — **magnétique** magnetohydrodynamics
hydroélectrique *a.* hydroelectric
hydrofuge *a.* waterproof
hydrofuger *vt.* to make waterproof *or* watertight
hydrogène *m.* hydrogen; — **liquide** liquid hydrogen
hydroglisseur *m.* speedboat
hydrologie *f.* hydrology
hydrolyse *f.* hydrolysis
hydrophile *a.* absorbent
hydrophobie *f.* hydrophobia, fear of the water
hydropisie *f.* dropsy
hydrosphère *f.* hydrosphere
hydrothérapie *f.* hydrotherapy, water cure
hydrure *m.* hydride
hyène *f.* hyena
hygiène *f.* hygiene, health; sanitation
hygiènique *a.* hygienic; sanitary
hygiéniste *m. & f.* hygienist
hymnaire *m.* hymnal
hymne *m.* hymn; song, anthem
hyperbole *f.* hyperbole; (math.) hyperbola
hypercritique *a.* hypercritical
hypergolique *a.* hypergolic
hypersensibilité *f.* hypersensitivity
hypersensible *a.* hypersensitive
hypersonique *a.* hypersonic
hypertension *f.* hypertension
hypertrophie *f.* hypertrophy; (fig.) excessive development
hypnose *f.* hypnosis
hypnotique *a.* hypnotic
hypnotiser *vt.* to hypnotize
hypnotisme *m.* hypnotism
hypocondriaque *a. & n.* hypochondriac
hypocondrie *f.* hypochondria
hypocrisie *f.* hypocrisy
hypocrite *m.* hypocrite; — *a.* hypocritical
hypodermique *a.* hypodermic
hypotension *f.* (med.) hypotension
hypoténuse *f.* hypotenuse
hypothécable *a.* mortgageable
hypothécaire *a.* mortgage; —*n.* mortgagee
hypothèque *f.* mortgage
hypothéquer *vt.* to mortgage
hypothèse *f.* hypothesis
hypothétique *a.* hypothetical

hystérie *f.* (med.) hysterics
hystérique *a.* hysterical

ïambique *a.* iambic
ibère, ibérique *a. & n.* Iberian
ibis *m.* ibis
ichtyologie *f.* ichthyology
ichtyologiste *m.* ichthyologist
ici *adv.* here; d'— from hence, hence; **par** — this way; d'— là between now and then; jusqu'— until now; this far
ici-bas *adv.* here on earth
icone *f.* icon, ikon
iconoclaste *a.* iconoclastic; — *m.* iconoclast
ictère *m.* (med.) jaundice
idéal *m. & a.* ideal; —iser *vt.* to idealize
idéalisme *m.* idealism
idéaliste *m. & f.* idealist; — *a.* idealistic
idéation *f.* ideation
idée *f.* idea, thought, opinion; **changer** d'— to change one's mind; — **fixe** obsession
identification *f.* identification
identifier *vt.* to identify
identique *a.* identical
identité *f.* identity; **carte d'**— *f.* identification card
idéologie *f.* ideology
idéologique *a.* ideological
idéologue *m.* ideologist
ides *f. pl.* ides
idiomatique *a.* idiomatic
idiome *m.* language, speech, idiom, dialect
idiosyncrasie *f.* idiosyncrasy
idiot *a.* idiot; idiotic; — *m.* idiot; fool
idiotie *f.* idiocy; stupidity
idiotisme *m.* (gram.) idiom, idiomatic expression
idolâtre *a.* idolatrous; — *m.* idolater
idolâtrer *vt.* to worship, idolize
idole *f.* idol, god
idylle *f.* idyl
idyllique *a.* idyllic
if *m.* (bot.) yew
igname *f.* Chinese yam
ignare *a.* ignorant; uninstructed
igné *a.* igneous
ignifuge *a.* fireproof
ignoble *a.* ignoble, base
ignominie *f.* ignominy, shame
ignominieux *a.* ignominious, shameful
ignorance *f.* ignorance
ignorant *a.* ignorant; unaware; — *m.* ignoramus, dunce
ignoré *a.* unknown
ignorer *vt.* to be ignorant of, not to know
iguane *m.* iguana

il *pron.* he, it; — **y a** there is, there are; ago; —s they
île *f.* island
iléon *m.* (anat.) ileum
ilex *m.* holm oak
iliaque *a.* iliac
illégal *a.* illegal; unlawful
illégalité *f.* illegality
illégitime *a.* illegitimate; unlawful
illégitimité *f.* illegitimacy; unlawfulness
illettré *a.* illiterate
illicite *a.* illicit, illegal
illimité *a.* unlimited
illisibilité *f.* illegibility
illisible *a.* illegible, unreadable
illogique *a.* illogical
illuminant *a.* illuminating
illuminateur *m.* illuminator
illumination *f.* illumination; light; lighting
illuminer *vt.* to illuminate, enlighten
illusion *f.* illusion, delusion; self-deception
illusionner *vt.* to delude; deceive
illusionnisme *m.* conjuring, conjurer's art
illusionniste *m. & f.* conjurer
illusoire *a.* illusive; fallacious
illustrateur *m.* illustrator
illustration *f.* illustriousness; glorification; glory; explanation; illustration
illustre *a.* illustrious
illustré *m.* tabloid; — *a.* illustrated
illustrer *vt.* to make illustrious; illustrate
îlot *m.* small island, islet; block of houses
ilote *m.* helot
image *f.* picture; image; metaphor
imagé *a.* metaphorical
imager *vt.* to embellish with metaphors, images
imagerie *f.* imagery
imaginable *a.* imaginable
imaginaire *a.* imaginary
imaginatif *a.* imaginative
imagination *f.* imagination, fancy
imaginer *vt.* to imagine, conceive, contrive; picture; s'— imagine, think
imbattable *a.* unbeatable
imbattu *a.* unbeaten
imbécile *m. & f.* imbecile; idiot, fool
imbécillité *f.* imbecility; stupidity
imberbe *a.* beardless; very young
imbiber *vt.* to imbue, soak, steep; imbibe, absorb
imbrifuge *a.* waterproof
imbrisable *a.* unbreakable
imbrûlable *a.* fireproof
imbu *a.* imbued, steeped, soaked
imbuvable *a.* undrinkable
imitateur *m.* imitator; — *a.* imitative
imitatif *a.* imitative
imitation *f.* imitation; copy; forgery, counterfeit

imiter *vt.* to imitate; copy; forge, counterfeit
immaculable *a.* stainless
immaculé *a.* immaculate; (fig.) untarnished; stainless
immanent *a.* immanent
immangeable *a.* uneatable, inedible
immanquable *a.* infallible, inevitable
immatériel *a.* immaterial
immatriculation *f.* registration; enrollment
immatricule *f.* registration number
immatriculer *vt.* to matriculate; register; enroll
immaturité *f.* immaturity
immédiat *a.* immediate; imminent; urgent
immédiatement *adv.* immediately, right away
immémorial *a.* immemorial
immense *a.* immense; vast
immensément *adv.* immensely
immensité *f.* immensity
immensurable *a.* immeasurable
immerger *vt.* to immerse; (naut.) submerge
immérité *a.* undeserved
immersion *f.* immersion; plunging; submersion
immesurable *a.* immeasurable
immeuble *a.* real (law); biens —s *m. pl.* real estate; — *m.* real estate; building, apartment house
immigrant *a. & m.* immigrant
immigré *m.* immigrant
immigrer *vi.* to immigrate
imminence *f.* imminence
imminent *a.* imminent, impending
immiscer *vt.* to involve; mix up; s'— to meddle; intrude
immixtion *f.* interference, meddling
immobile *a.* immovable, motionless
immobilier *a.* pertaining to real property; agent — *m.* realtor
immobiliser *vt.* to immobilize
immobilité *f.* immobility
immodéré *a.* immoderate
immodeste *a.* immodest
immodestie *f.* immodesty
immolation *f.* immolation, sacrifice
immoler *vt.* to immolate, sacrifice
immonde *a.* unclean, foul
immondices *f. pl.* rubbish, refuse, filth
immoral *a.* immoral
immoralité *f.* immorality
immortaliser *vt.* to immortalize
immortalité *f.* immortality
immortel *a.* immortal, everlasting
immotivé *a.* unmotivated
immuable *a.* immutable, unchangeable

immunisation *f.* immunization
immuniser *vt.* to immunize
immunité *f.* immunity
immutabilité *f.* immutability
impact *m.* impact
impair *a.* odd, uneven; — *m.* blunder
impalpabilité *f.* impalpability
impalpable *a.* impalpable
impardonnable *a.* unpardonable, unforgivable
imparfait *a.* imperfect; incomplete; — *m.* (gram.) imperfect
imparité *f.* inequality; (math.) oddness
impartial *a.* impartial; without prejudice
impartialité *f.* impartiality
impartir *vt.* (law), to grant accord
impassable *a.* impassable
impasse *f.* dead end; deadlock
impassibilité *f.* impassibility
impassible *a.* impassible; impassive; without emotion
impatiemment *adv.* impatiently, eagerly
impatience *f.* impatience, eagerness
impatient *a.* impatient, eager
impatienter *vt.* to make impatient; s'— to fret, grow impatient
impavide *a.* fearless
impayable *a.* invaluable, inestimable, priceless
impayé *a.* unpaid
impeccabilité *f.* impeccability
impeccable *a.* impeccable; flawless
impécunieux *a.* impecunious
impédance *f.* impedance
impénétrabilité *f.* impenetrability, inscrutability
impénétrable *a.* impenetrable; inscrutable
impénitent *a.* unrepentant
impensable *a.* unthinkable
impératif *a.* imperative; — *m.* (gram.) imperative
impératrice *f.* empress
imperceptible *a.* imperceptible
imperfection *f.* imperfection; incompleteness
impérial *a.* imperial
impériale *f.* style of beard; upper deck of a two-decker bus
impérialisme *m.* imperialism
impérialiste *m.* imperialist
impérieux *a.* imperious; imperative
impérissable *a.* imperishable
impéritie *f.* incapacity, lack of experience
imperméabiliser *vt.* to waterproof
imperméable *a.* impervious, waterproof; — *m.* raincoat
impersonnel *a.* impersonal
impertinemment *adv.* impertinently
impertinence *f.* impertinence, impropriety; irrelevance

impertinent *a.* impertinent; rude; irrelevant
imperturbable *a.* imperturbable
impétueux *a.* impetuous, impulsive
impétuosité *f.* impetuosity, impulsiveness
impie *a.* impious, irreligious
impiété *f.* impiety; blasphemy
impitoyable *a.* unmerciful, merciless; pitiless
implacabilité *f.* implacability
implacable *a.* implacable, unforgiving
implanter *vt.* to implant, insert; graft; s'— to take root
implication *f.* implication; suggestion of contradiction
implicite *a.* implicit
impliquer *vt.* to implicate; imply
imploration *f.* imploring, beseeching
implorer *vt.* to implore, beseech
imployable *a.* unyielding, unbending, inflexible
impoli *a.* impolite, rude, discourteous
impolitesse *f.* impoliteness, rudeness, discourtesy
impolitique *a.* ill-advised
impondérable *a.* imponderable
impopulaire *a.* unpopular
impopularité *f.* unpopularity
importable *a.* unbearable; importable
importance *f.* importance, consequence; seriousness; authority; social standing, self-conceit
important *a.* important; having authority; — *m.* essential point
importateur *m.* importer
importer *vt.* to import; — *v.* to be of importance; be of consequence, to concern; **n'importe** it does not matter; **n'importe qui** no matter who, anyone; **n'importe quoi** no matter what, anything; **qu'importe?** what does it matter?
importun *a.* importunate; annoying, bothersome
importuner *vt.* to importune; annoy, bother
imposable *a.* taxable
imposant *a.* imposing, impressive
imposé *m.* taxpayer
imposer *vt.* to impose; inspire, command; tax; — *vi.* to command respect; — **à** impose on; deceive; s'— command, inspire; assert oneself; force oneself on someone
imposition *f.* imposition; imposing; tax; assessment
impossibilité *f.* impossibility
impossible *a.* impossible
imposte *f.* transom; (arch.) impost
imposteur *m.* imposter

imposture *f.* imposture; swindle

impôt *m.* tax, duty; **— sur le revenu** income tax

impotence *f.* impotence, infirmity, helplessness

impotent *a.* impotent; infirm, crippled; **— m.** cripple

impraticable *a.* impracticable, impractical; impassable

impratiqué *a.* unused, out-of-the-way

imprécation *f.* curse, imprecation

imprécis *a.* not precise, indefinite

imprécision *f.* lack of precision

imprégner *vt.* to impregnate

imprenable *a.* impregnable

impréparation *f.* lack of preparation

imprésario *m.* impresario

impression *f.* impression; printing process; print; mark; edition; **faute d'— f.** typographical error, misprint

impressionnable *a.* impressionable; sensitive

impressionnant *a.* impressive

impressionner *vt.* to impress; make an impression upon; **s'— to** get excited; be moved

impressionniste *m.* impressionist

imprévisible *a.* unpredictable, unforeseeable

imprévision *f.* lack of foresight

imprévoyable *a.* unpredictable, unforeseeable

imprévoyance *f.* improvidence; lack of foresight

imprévoyant *a.* improvident

imprévu *a.* unforeseen, unexpected; **— m.** contingency

imprimé *m.* printed paper; **-s** *p.* printed matter

imprimer *vt.* to print, stamp; impart

imprimerie *f.* printing; print shop; typography

imprimeur *m.* printer

imprimeuse *f.* printing press

improbabilité *f.* improbability

improbable *a.* improbable, unlikely

improbatif *a.* disapproving

improbation *f.* lack of approval, disapproval

improbité *f.* lack of probity; dishonesty

improductif *a.* unproductive

improductivité *f.* unproductiveness

impromptu *m. & a.* impromptu; **à l'—** extemporaneously

imprononçable *a.* unpronounceable

impropre *a.* improper; incongruous; unfit

impropriété *f.* impropriety

improuvable *a.* unprovable

improvisateur *m.* improviser

improviser *vt. & vi.* to extemporize, improvise

improviste *adv.*, **a l'—** unawares, unexpectedly

improvoqué *a.* unprovoked

imprudemment *adv.* imprudently

imprudence *f.* imprudence, indiscretion

imprudent *a.* imprudent; indiscreet; unwise

impubliable *a.* unpublishable; not fit for publication

impudemment *adv.* impudently

impudence *f.* impudence

impudent *a.* impudent; immodest; shameless

impudeur *f.* shamelessness, immodesty; lewdness

impudicité *f.* lack of chastity; act of lust

impudique *a.* immodest, unchaste

impuissance *f.* impotence, inability; vainness

impuissant *a.* impotent, powerless; vain

impulsif *a.* impulsive, without deliberation

impulsion *f.* impulse, impetus, urge

impulsivité *f.* impulsiveness

impunément *adv.* with impunity

impuni *a.* unpunished

impunité *f.* impunity

impur *a.* impure, tainted; (fig.) unchaste

impureté *f.* impurity; (fig.) immorality

impurifié *a.* unpurified

imputable *a.* attributable, imputable; (com.) chargeable; creditable

imputation *f.* imputation, charge; (com.) deduction

imputer *vt.* to impute, attribute, charge; deduct; (com.) credit; debit

inabondance *f.* scarcity, short supply

inabordable *a.* inaccessible; too costly

inabrité *a.* unsheltered

inaccentué *a.* unaccented, unstressed

inacceptable *a.* unacceptable

inacceptation *f.* nonacceptance, refusal

inaccessible *a.* inaccessible; unattainable

inaccompagné *a.* unaccompanied

inaccompli *a.* unaccomplished, unfulfilled

inaccordable *a.* irreconcilable; untunable; inadmissible

inaccoutumé *a.* unaccustomed, unused; unusual

inachevé *a.* unfinished, not completed

inachèvement *m.* state of incompletion

inactif *a.* inactive; inert

inaction *f.* inaction; lack of business activity

inactivité *f.* inactivity; inertness

inadéquat *a.* inadequate

inadmissibilité *f.* inadmissibility

inadmissible *a.* inadmissible; nonqualifying

inadvertance *f.* oversight, inadvertance, carelessness

inadvertant *a.* inadvertent

inaliénable *a.* inalienable

inaliéné *a.* unalienated

inaltérabilité *f.* unchanging nature; permanence

inaltérable *a.* unchangeable; incorruptible; unalterable

inamical *a.* unfriendly, hostile; discourteous

inamovible *a.* irremovable; permanent

inanimé *a.* inanimate, lifeless; unconscious

inanité *f.* inanity; inane remark

inapaisable *a.* inappeasable, unquenchable

inapaisé *a.* unappeased, unquenched

inapercevable *a.* unperceivable

inaperçu *a.* unperceived, unnoticed, unseen

inapparent *a.* unapparent

inappétence *f.* lack of appetite

inapplication *f.* lack of application

inappliqué *a.* unapplied; lacking in application

inappréciable *a.* invaluable, inestimable; unperceivable; inappreciable

inapprécié *a.* unappreciated

inapprivoisable *a.* untamable

inapprivoisé *a.* untamed

inapte *a.* inapt, inept; unfit

inaptitude *f.* lack of aptitude

inarticulé *a.* inarticulate; inarticulated

inassociable *a.* incompatible, unmixable

inassouvi *a.* unsatisfied, unquenched

inassouvissable *a.* insatiable

inattaquable *a.* unquestionable; unassailable

inattendu *a.* unexpected; unforeseen

inattentif *a.* inattentive

inattention *f.* carelessness; lack of attention

inauguration *f.* inauguration; unveiling

inaugurer *vt.* to inaugurate; unveil a monument; (fig.) mark a beginning

inauthenticité *f.* lack of authenticity

inauthentique *a.* unauthentic

inautorisé *a.* unauthorized

inaverti *a.* uninformed; unwarned

inavouable *a.* shameful

inavoué *a.* unconfessed; unacknowledged

incalculable *a.* incalculable

incandescence *f.* incandescence

incandescent *a.* white-hot, incandescent

incapable *a.* incapable, unable, unfit

incapacité *f.* incapacity, incapability, inability, unfitness; disability

incarcération *f.* incarceration

incarcérer *vt.* to incarcerate

incarnadin *a.* pink, rosy

incarnat *m.* flesh color; — *a.* rosy, pink

incarné *a.* incarnate; ingrown

incarner *vt.* to incarnate; s'— to become incarnate; grow into, embody

incartade *f.* tirade; prank

incassable *a.* unbreakable

incendiaire *m.* arsonist; (coll.) firebug

incendie *m.* fire, arson, conflagration; pompe à — *f.* fire engine

incendié *m.* victim of a fire

incendier *vt.* to burn, set fire to

incertain *a.* uncertain; doubtful, undecided

incertitude *f.* uncertainty, doubt, indecision

incessamment *adv.* incessantly, continually; shortly, without delay

incessant *a.* incessant, unceasing

incessible *a.* inalienable

inceste *m.* incest

incestueux *a.* incestuous

inchangé *a.* unchanged

incidemment *adv.* incidently

incidence *f.* (phy.) incidence

incident *a.* incidental; parenthetical; — *m.* incident; difficulty

incinérateur *m.* incinerator

incinération *f.* incineration; cremation

incinérer *vt.* to incinerate; cremate

incirconcis *a.* uncircumcized

inciser *vt.* to cut, make an incision in

incisif *a.* incisive

incisive *f.* (dent.) incisor

incision *f.* incision, cut, cutting

incitant *a.* stimulating; — *m.* tonic, stimulant

incitation *f.* incitement, inciting

inciter *vt.* to incite; urge

incivil *a.* uncivil, rude

incivilisé *a.* uncivilized

incivilité *f.* incivility, rudeness

incivique *a.* uncivil

inclassable *a.* unclassifiable

inclémence *f.* inclemency

inclément *a.* inclement

inclinaison *f.* inclination; incline, slope; tilt, slant

inclination *f.* inclination; bowing, stooping; love; mariage d'— *m.* love match

incliné *a.* inclined; bowed

incliner *vt. & vi.* to incline, bow; tilt, slant; s'— bow, yield; slope, slant; (avi.) bank; (naut.) heel

inclure *vt.* to enclose; insert

inclus *a.* enclosed

inclusif *a.* inclusive

inclusion *f.* enclosing; inclusion; enclosure

inclusivement *adv.* inclusively
incohérence *f.* incoherence
incohérent *a.* incoherent, unconnected
incohésion *f.* lack of cohesion
incolore *a.* colorless
incomber *vi.* to be incumbent
incombustible *a.* fireproof
incomestible *a.* inedible
incommensurable *a.* incommensurate; immeasurable
incommodant *a.* disagreeable, annoying
incommode *a.* uncomfortable, inconvenient
incommodé *a.* indisposed
incommoder *vt.* to annoy, trouble, inconvenience; upset
incommodité *f.* inconvenience; discomfort
incommunicable *a.* incommunicable
incommutable *a.* nontransferable (at law)
incomparablement *adv.* incomparably
incompatibilité *f.* incompatibility
incompatible *a.* incompatible
incompétence *f.* incompetency, lack of authority
incompétent *a.* incompetent; unauthorized, unqualified
incomplaisant *a.* disobliging
incomplet *a.* unfinished, incomplete
incomplètement *adv.* incompletely
incompréhensibilité *f.* incomprehensibility
incompréhensible *a.* incomprehensible
incompréhension *f.* lack of understanding
incompris *a.* not understood; unappreciated
inconcevable *a.* inconceivable
inconciliable *a.* irreconcilable
inconditionnel *a.* unconditional
inconduite *f.* misconduct (law); misbehavior
inconfort *m.* lack of comfort
inconfortable *a.* uncomfortable
incongru *a.* incongruous; inappropriate
incongruité *f.* incongruity; impropriety
inconnu *a.* unknown; strange; — *m.* unknown; unknown person, stranger
inconsciemment *adv.* unconsciously, unknowingly
inconscience *f.* unconsciousness, unawareness
inconscient *a.* unconscious, unaware
inconséquence *f.* inconsequence
inconséquent *a.* inconsequent, inconsistent; inconsequential
inconsidération *f.* lack of consideration
inconsidéré *a.* inconsiderate; thoughtless; ill-considered
inconsistance *f.* inconsistency; lack of solidity
inconsistant *a.* inconsistent; loose, soft

inconsolable *a.* inconsolable; disconsolate
inconstance *f.* inconstancy; fickleness; changeability
inconstant *a.* inconstant, changeable, fickle
inconstitutionnalité *f.* unconstitutionality
inconstitutionnel *a.* unconstitutional
incontestable *a.* incontestable, indisputable
incontesté *a.* uncontested, undisputed
incontinence *f.* incontinence
incontinent *a.* incontinent; — *adv.* at once, immediately
incontrôlable *a.* impossible to check *or* verify
incontrôlé *a.* unchecked, unverified
incontroversé *a.* uncontroverted, undisputed
inconvaincu *a.* unconvinced
inconvenance *f.* impropriety; indecency; lack of suitability
inconvenant *a.* unbecoming, improper; indecent
inconvénient *m.* inconvenience; disadvantage, objection
inconvertissable *a.* beyond conversion
inconvié *a.* uninvited
incoordination *f.* lack of co-ordination
incorporel *a.* incorporeal
incorporer *vt.* to incorporate
incorrect *a.* incorrect; wrong; unseemly, improper
incorrection *f.* incorrectness; mistake, error; inaccuracy
incorrigibilité *f.* incorrigibility
incorruptibilité *f.* incorruptibility
incrédibilité *f.* incredibility
incrédule *a.* incredulous; unbelieving; — *m. & f.* infidel, unbeliever
incrédulité *f.* incredulity; disbelief
incrément *m.* increment
increvable *a.* puncture-proof
incrimination *f.* incrimination; indictment; accusation
incriminer *vt.* to incriminate; indict; accuse
incrochetable *a.* burglarproof
incroyable *a.* incredible, unbelievable
incroyant *a.* unbelieving; — *m.* unbeliever
incrustation *f.* incrustation; inlaying; scale, crust
incruster *vt.* to incrust; inlay
incubateur *m.* incubator
incubation *f.* incubation; hatching
incuber *vt.* to incubate (eggs)
incuit *a.* uncooked
inculpabilité *f.* blamelessness, innocence; liability to indictment (law)
inculpable *a.* liable to indictment (law)
inculpation *f.* indictment, charge

inculpé *m.* defendant (law), accused
inculper *vt.* to accuse, charge; indict
inculquer *vt.* to inculcate
inculte *a.* uncultivated, untilled
incultivé *a.* uncultivated, untilled; uncultured; rude
incurable *a. & n.* incurable
incurie *f.* lack of concern; negligence, carelessness
incurieux *a.* not curious
incuriosité *f.* lack of curiosity
incursion *f.* inroad, incursion
incurvé *a.* incurvated, concave
Inde *f.* India; —s *pl.* Indies
inde *m.* indigo plant, indigo blue
indébrouillable *a.* tangled
indécemment *adv.* indecently; immodestly; improperly
indécence *f.* indecency
indécent *a.* indecent; unbecoming, immodest; improper
indéchiffrable *a.* undecipherable; illegible
indéchirable *a.* untearable
indécis *a.* undecided; vague; hesitating, doubtful
indécisif *a.* indecisive
indécision *f.* indecision; irresolution
indéclinable *a.* not refusable; indeclinable
indécousable *a.* rip-proof
indécouvrable *a.* undiscoverable, hidden
indécrottable *a.* uncleanable
indédoublable *a.* indecomposable
indéfendable *a.* indefensible
indéfini *a.* indefinite; undefined
indéfinissable *a.* indefinable
indéformable *a.* not capable of losing shape *or* form
indéfrisable *a.* permanent (curls); — *f.* permanent wave
indélébile *a.* indelible
indélébilité *f.* indelibility
indélibéré *a.* undeliberated, unpremeditated
indélicat *a.* indelicate; tactless; unscrupulous
indélicatesse *f.* indelicacy; tactlessness; unscrupulousness
indémaillable *a.* run-proof
indemne *a.* undamaged, unhurt; without loss
indemnisable *a.* entitled to damages *or* compensation
indemnisation *f.* indemnification
indemniser *vt.* to indemnify, compensate, pay damages to
indemnité *f.* indemnity, compensation, damages; grant, benefit; expenses
indémontrable *a.* undemonstrable
indéniable *a.* undeniable

indénouable *a.* secure, fast, tight; not able to be untied
indépendamment *adv.* independently
indépendance *f.* independence
indépendant *a.* independent
indéracinable *a.* firmly rooted; not able to be uprooted; impossible to eradicate
indéréglable *a.* foolproof; impossible to upset
Indes *f. pl.* Indies
indescriptible *a.* indescribable
indésirable *a. & n.* undesirable
indesserrable *a.* self-locking (nut); very tight
indestructible *a.* indestructible
indéterminable *a.* indeterminable
indétermination *f.* indetermination, lack of determination; indefiniteness
indéterminé *a.* indeterminate, undetermined; indefinite; undecided
indevinable *a.* unguessable; mysterious
indévot *a.* undevout, irreligious
indévotion *f.* irreligion
index *m.* table of contents, index; index finger; indicator, pointer
indicateur *a.* indicatory; telltale; doigt — *m.* index finger; poteau — *m.* signpost; — *m.* indicator; gauge; speedometer; timetable; spy, informer
indicatif *a.* indicative, indicating, indicatory; — *m.* (gram.) indicative; (rad.) program theme music
indication *f.* indication, sign; information; —s *pl.* directions, instructions
indice *m.* sign, mark; clue; index; indication; (com.) trace
indicible *a.* unspeakable, indescribable
indien *a. & m.* Indian
indienne *f.* print; calico; chintz; overarm swimming stroke
indiennerie *f.* printed cotton fabric
indifféremment *adv.* indifferently, indiscriminately
indifférence *f.* indifference
indifférent *a.* indifferent, unconcerned; immaterial
indigence *f.* indigence, poverty
indigène *a. & m.* native
indigent *a.* indigent, poor, needy; — *m.* pauper; — s *pl.* the poor, needy, destitute
indigeste *a.* indigestible; undigested
indigestion *f.* indigestion
indignation *f.* indignation
indigne *a.* unworthy, undeserving; odious
indigné *a.* indignant
indigner *vt.* to make indignant, shock; s'— to be indignant
indignité *f.* indignity; unworthiness
indigo *m.* indigo dye *or* color

indigotier *m.* (bot.) indigo plant
indiquer *vt.* to indicate, point out, show; appoint
indirect *a.* indirect; underhand(ed); circumstantial (law)
indirectement *adv.* indirectly
indiscernable *a.* indistinguishable
indisciplinable *a.* intractable
indiscipliné *a.* undisciplined, unmanageable
indiscret *a.* indiscreet, tactless; — *m.* indiscreet, tactless person
indiscrètement *adv.* indiscreetly
indiscrétion *f.* indiscretion; tactlessness
indiscutable *a.* indisputable
indisponibilité *f.* unavailability
indisponible *a.* unavailable; inalienable (law)
indisposé *a.* indisposed, unwell; unfriendly, angry
indisposer *vt.* to indispose; make unwell; turn against
indisposition *f.* indisposition, mild illness
indisputable *a.* indisputable, unquestionable
indissolubilité *f.* indissolubility; insolubility
indissoluble *a.* indissoluble; insoluble
indistinct *a.* indistinct; vague, hazy, faint, blurred
indistinguible *a.* indistinguishable
individu *m.* individual; person, fellow; character
individualiser *vt.* to individualize
individualiste *a.* individualistic; — *m. & f.* individualist
individualité *f.* individuality
individuel *a.* individual; private, personal
indivisibilité *f.* indivisibility
indivisible *a.* indivisible
indivulgué *a.* undivulged, unrevealed
Indo-Chine *f.* Indo-China
indochinois *a. & m.* Indochinese
indocile *a.* indocile, intractable
indocilité *f.* indocility, intractability
indo-européen *a. & m.* Indo-European
indolemment *adv.* indolently, lazily
indolence *f.* indolence, laziness
indolent *a.* indolent, lazy
indolore *a.* painless
indomptable *a.* untamable, unmanageable, unconquerable; indomitable
indompté *a.* untamed, unconquered
Indonésie *f.* Indonesia
indonésien *a. & m.* indonesian
indu *a.* undue; unowed; not due
indubitable *a.* indubitable, unquestionable
inductance *f.* (elec.) inductance; inductance coil

inducteur *a.* (elec.) inductive; — *m.* inductor
inductif *a.* inductive
induire *vt.* to induce; infer; lead
induit *a.* (elec.) induced; — *m.* armature
indulgence *f.* indulgence
indulgent *a.* indulgent
indûment *adv.* unduly
indurer *vt.* to harden
industrialisation *f.* industrialization
industrialiser *vt.* to industrialize
industrialisme *m.* industrialism
industrie *f.* industry; ingenuity, skill
industriel *a.* industrial; — *m.* industrialist
industrieux *a.* industrious; skillful
inébranlable *a.* firm; unshakable; resolute
inéchangeable *a.* unexchangeable
inéclairci *a.* unexplained, unelucidated
inéclairé *a.* unlighted, unlit; unenlightened
inédit *a.* unpublished; new, latest, original
ineffaçable *a.* ineffaceable, unforgettable; indelible
inefficace *a.* ineffectual, unavailing
inefficacité *f.* inefficacy, inefficiency
inégal *a.* unequal; uneven; irregular
inégalité *f.* inequality; unevenness; irregularity, disparity
inélégance *f.* inelegance
inélégant *a.* inelegant
inéligibilité *f.* ineligibility
inéligible *a.* ineligible
inéluctable *a.* ineluctable; unescapable, irrevocable
inéludable *a.* unescapable, inevitable
inemployé *a.* unemployed, unused
inentamé *a.* uncut; whole, intact
inepte *a.* inept, unfit; foolish
ineptie *f.* ineptness, ineptitude
inépuisable *a.* inexhaustible
inépuisé *a.* unexhausted, unused, remaining
inéquitable *a.* inequitable, unfair, unjust
inerte *a.* inert; passive; dull
inertie *f.* inertia; dullness
inespéré *a.* unhoped for, unexpected
inessayé *a.* untried, untested
inestimable *a.* inestimable, invaluable
inétudié *a.* unstudied, natural
inévitable *a.* inevitable; unavoidable
inexact *a.* inexact, inaccurate; wrong, incorrect; careless, remiss; unpunctual
inexactitude *f.* inexactitude, inaccuracy; incorrectness; error, mistake; carelessness, remissness; unpunctuality
inexécutable *a.* impracticable; impossible to do
inexécuté *a.* undone, unfulfilled, unperformed; not carried out
inexecution *f.* inexecution; nonfulfillment

inexercé *a.* unexercised; unpracticed, untrained

inexistant *a.* nonexistent

inexistence *f.* nonexistence

inexpérience *f.* inexperience, lack of experience

inexpérimenté *a.* inexperienced; untested, untried

inexpiable *a.* unatonable, inexpiable

inexpié *a.* unatoned

inexplicable *a.* inexplicable, unaccountable

inexpliqué *a.* unexplained

inexploitable *a.* unexploitable; unworkable

inexploité *a.* unexploited, undeveloped; unworked

inexploré *a.* unexplored

inexplosible *a.* nonexplosive

inexpressif *a.* expressionless; inexpressive

inexprimable *a.* inexpressable; ineffable, unspeakable

inexprimé *a.* unexpressed

inexpugnable *a.* impregnable

in-extenso (en entier) *adv.* fully, in detail

inextinguible *a.* inextinguishable; unquenchable; irrepressible

infaillibilité *f.* infallibility

infaillible *a.* infallible; unfailing; certain

infaisable *a.* impracticable, not feasable

infamant *a.* dishonorable, defamatory

infâme *a.* infamous; vile, fowl, base

infamie *f.* infamy; infamous action

infanterie *f.* infantry

infantilisme *m.* infantilism

infatigable *a.* indefatigable, tireless

infatuation *f.* infatuation, self-satisfaction

infatué *a.* self-satisfied

infécond *a.* sterile, barren

infécondité *f.* sterilty

infect *a.* foul, filthy; smelly, noisome, stinking

infecter *vt.* to infect; taint, corrupt; pollute

infectieux *a.* infectious

infection *f.* infection; smell, stench

inférence *f.* inference

inférer *vt.* to infer

inférieur *a.* inferior, lower; of poor(er) quality; — *m.* subordinate, underling

infériorité *f.* inferiority

infertile *a.* sterile; infertile; unfruitful

infertilité *f.* sterility, infertility; unfruitfulness

infester *vt.* to infest

infidèle *a.* unfaithful; faithless; dishonest; inexact, incorrect; heathenish; — *m.* infidel, unbeliever

infidélité *f.* infidelity, unfaithfulness; faithlessness; dishonesty; inexactitude,

inaccuracy; unbelief

infiltration *f.* infiltration; filtering; seepage

infiltrer *vt.*, **s'** — to infiltrate; seep

infime *a.* lowest; smallest; infinitesimal, minute

infini *a.* infinite; endless; unlimited; — *m.* infinite; infinity; à l'— ad infinitum, to infinity; -té *f.* infinity

infiniment *adv.* infinitely

infinitésimal *a.* infinitesimal

infinitif *a. & m.* (gram.) infinitive

infinitude *f.* infiniteness

infirme *a.* infirm; frail, feeble; crippled — *m. & f.* cripple; invalid

infirmer *vt.* to weaken; invalidate; annul (law); set aside

infirmerie *f.* infirmary, sickroom

infirmier *m.* male nurse; hospital attendant

infirmière *f.* nurse

infirmité *f.* infirmity; disability

inflammabilité *f.* inflammability

inflammation *f.* inflammation; firing; igniting

inflammatoire *a.* inflammatory

inflation *f.* inflation

inflationniste *a.* inflationary; — *m.* inflationist

infléchir *vt.* to inflect, bend

infléchissable *a.* unbendable; unbending, inflexible

inflexibilité *f.* inflexibility

inflexible *a.* inflexible; unbending, unyielding

inflexion *f.* inflexion, inflection; modulation; bending

infliger *vt.* to inflict, impose

influençable *a.* able to be influenced

influence *f.* influence, sway; effect

influencer *vt.* to influence, sway

influent *a.* influential

influer (sur) *vi.* to influence

influx *m.* influx

informateur *m.* informant

informatif *a.* informative

information *f.* inquiry; information; news; legal investigation; proceedings; **prendre des —s** to make inquiries

informe *a.* shapeless, formless; unshapely; informal

informer *vt.* to inform, tell, apprise; — *vi.* to inform; investigate (law); **s'** — **to** make inquiries, ask

informulé *a.* unformulated

infortune *f.* misfortune

infortuné *a.* unfortunate, unhappy, unlucky

infraction *f.* infraction, violation; infringement

infranchissable *a.* impassable

infrangible *a.* unbreakable
infrarouge *a.* infrared
infrastructure *f.* substructure; undercarriage, underframe
infréquent *a.* infrequent, unusual, rare
infréquenté *a.* unfrequented
infructueux *a.* unfruitful, unprofitable; fruitless
infus *a.* infused, innate
infusé *m.* infusion
infuser *vt.* to infuse, steep; instill
infusion *f.* infusion, tea
ingambe *a.* active, alert, nimble
ingénier *v.*, s'— to tax one's ingenuity
ingénieur *m.* engineer
ingénieusement *adv.* ingeniously
ingénieux *a.* ingenious
ingéniosité *f.* ingenuity
ingénu *a.* ingenuous; naïve, artless; —e *f.* naïve girl; (theat.) ingénue
ingénuité *f.* ingenuousness
ingérence *f.* interference, meddling
ingérer *vt.* to ingest; s'— de to interfere in, meddle in
inglorieux *a.* inglorious
ingouvernable *a.* ungovernable, unmanageable
ingrat *a.* ungrateful; thankless; unpleasant; unproductive
ingratitude *f.* ingratitude, ungratefulness; thanklessness
ingrédient *m.* ingredient, component
inguéable *a.* unfordable
inguérissable *a.* incurable; chronic
ingurgitation *f.* swallowing, gulping
ingurgiter *vt.* to swallow
inhabile *a.* unfitted, unskilled, inept; clumsy, awkward; legally incompetent
inhabileté *f.* clumsiness, awkwardness; lack of skill *or* knack; incapability
inhabilité *f.* legal incompetency, incapacity
inhabitable *a.* uninhabitable
inhabité *a.* uninhabited
inhabitude *f.* lack of familiarity *or* experience
inhabitué *a.* accustomed, not used to
inhabituel *a.* not habitual, unusual
inhalateur *m.* inhalator
inhalation *f.* inhalation
inhaler *vt.* to inhale
inharmonieux *a.* inharmonious, unmelodious; discordant
inhérent *a.* inherent
inhiber *vt.* to inhibit
inhibiteur, inhibitif *a.* inhibiting, inhibitive
inhibition *f.* inhibition
inhospitalier *a.* inhospitable
inhumain *a.* inhuman

inhumanité *f.* inhumanity
inhumation *f.* inhumation, burial
inhumer *vt.* to inter, bury, inhume
inimaginable *a.* unimaginable, inconceivable
inimitable *a.* inimitable
inimitié *f.* emnity, hatred, hostility
inimprimé *a.* unprinted, unpublished
ininflammable *a.* fireproof; noninflammable
inintelligemment *adv.* unintelligently
inintelligence *f.* lack of intelligence
inintelligent *a.* unintelligent
inintelligibilité *f.* unintelligibility
inintelligible *a.* unintelligible
inintéressant *a.* uninteresting
ininterrompu *a.* uninterrupted, unbroken
inique *a.* unjust, iniquitous; sinful
iniquité *f.* iniquity
initial *a.* initial; — e *f.* first letter (name, word, person's name); -ement *adv.* originally
initiateur *m.* initiator
initiative *f.* initiative
initié *m.* initiate
initier *vt.* to initiate
injecté *a.* injected; bloodshot
injecter *vt.* to inject; s'— become bloodshot
injecteur *m.* injector
injection *f.* injection
injonction *f.* injunction, formal order
injouable *a.* unplayable
injudicieux *a.* injudicious, unwise
injure *f.* insult; wrong, injury; tort (law)
injurier *vt.* to insult, abuse
injurieux *a.* insulting, abusive, outrageous
injuste *a.* unjust, unfair
injustice *f.* injustice; wrong; unfairness
injustifiable *a.* unjustifiable
injustifié *a.* unjustified
inlassable *a.* untiring; tireless
innavigable *a.* unnavigable; unseaworthy
inné *a.* innate, inborn; -ité *f.* innateness
innocemment *adv.* innocently, foolishly
innocence *f.* innocence; simplicity
innocent *a.* innocent; harmless; simple; — *m.* simpleton
innocenter *vt.* to find innocent, clear; excuse
innocuité *f.* harmlessness, innocuousness
innombrable *a.* innumerable, numberless
innovateur *m.* innovator
innover *vi.* to innovate
inobservance *f.* nonobservance
inobservation *f.* nonobservance, disregard
inobservé *a.* unobserved; disregarded
inoccupation *f.* inoccupation, idleness, unemployment
inoccupé *a.* unoccupied; vacant; not busy,

idle; not in use

inoculer *vt.* to inoculate; infect

inodore *a.* odorless

inoffensif *a.* inoffensive, harmless

inondation *f.* flood, inundation

inondé *a.* flooded; deluged; — *m.* flood victim

inonder *vt.* to flood, inundate

inopérable *a.* inoperable

inopérant *a.* inoperative

inopiné *a.* unexpected, unforeseen

inopportun *a.* inopportune; not appropriate

inopportunité *f.* inopportuneness

inopposable *a.* unanswerable

inorganique *a.* inorganic

inoubliable *a.* unforgettable; memorable

inoublié *a.* unforgotten

inouï *a.* unheard of; unbelievable; fantastic

inoxydable *a.* rustproof; stainless (steel)

inqualifiable *a.* unqualifiable; unspeakable

inquiet (inquiete) *a.* uneasy, anxious, disturbed, nervous, restless, upset, concerned

inquiétant *a.* disturbing, upsetting

inquiéter *vt.* to disturb, upset, make uneasy; s'— to be anxious, worry, be uneasy

inquiétude *f.* uneasiness, anxiety, nervousness, concern

inquisiteur *m.* inquisitor; — *a.* inquisitive

inquisition *f.* inquisition

inrouillable *a.* rustproof, stainless

insaisissable *a.* unseizable, difficult to grasp; fleeting, imperceptible

insalubre *a.* unhealthy, unwholesome

insalubrité *f.* unhealthiness, unwholesomeness

insanité *f.* insanity

insatiabilité *f.* insatiability

insatiable *a.* insatiable

insatisfaction *f.* lack of satisfaction

insatisfait *a.* unsatisfied

insciemment *adv.* unknowingly, unwittingly

inscripteur *m.* recorder, recording apparatus

inscriptible *a.* inscribable

inscription *f.* inscription; inscribing; registration, enrolling; recording

inscrire *vt.* to inscribe; register, enroll; s'— to register, sign up

inscrutable *a.* inscrutable

insécable *a.* indivisible

insecte *m.* insect

insécurité *f.* insecurity

insémination *f.* insemination

insensé *a.* insane, mad, senseless; — *m.* madman

insensiabilisation *f.* local anesthesia, removal of sense of feeling

insensibiliser *vt.* to anesthetize

insensibilité *f.* lack of sensitivity, lack of feeling(s); insensibility; coldness, indifference

insensible *a.* insensitive; unfeeling; insensible; cold, indifferent; imperceptible

inséparable *a.* inseparable

inséparablement *adv.* inseparably

insérer *vt.* to insert; wedge, sandwich in

insertion *f.* insertion

inserviable *a.* not obliging, disobliging

insidieusement *adv.* insidiously

insidieux *a.* insidious

insigne *a.* notorious; unusual; distinguished; — *m.* sign of membership, authority, dignity

insignes *m. pl.* insignia

insignificance *f.* insignificance

insignifiant *a.* insignificant

insincère *a.* insincere

insincérité *f.* insincerity

insinuant *a.* insinuating

insinuation *f.* insinuation, implication; hint

insinuer *vt.* to insinuate; insert; s'— (dans) to steal (into); penetrate; insinuate oneself

insipide *a.* insipid; tasteless; uninteresting; flat

insipidité *f.* insipidity; lack of taste; flatness

insistance *f.* insistence

insistant *a.* insisting, insistent

insister *vt.* to insist; emphasize; persist

insobriété *f.* lack of sobriety, intemperance

insociabilité *f.* unsociableness

insociable *a.* unsociable

insolation *f.* sunstroke; insolation

insolemment *adv.* insolently

insolence *f.* insolence, impudence

insolent *a.* insolent, impudent; rude

insoler *vt.* to expose to the sun; s'— to sunbathe

insolite *a.* unusual

insolubilité *f.* insolubility

insoluble *a.* insoluble; unsolvable

insolvabilité *f.* insolvency

insolvable *a.* insolvent

insomnie *a.* insomnia

insondable *a.* unfathomable, mysterious; unsoundable

insonore *a.* soundproof

insonorisation *f.* soundproofing

insonoriser *vt.* to soundproof, insulate

insonorité *f.* lack of sonority

insouciance *f.* lack of care *or* concern, un-

concern; carelessness, thoughtlessness
insouciant *a.* unconcerned; careless; thoughtless
insoucieux *a.* unmindful, heedless
insoumis *a.* unsubdued, unruly
insoumission *f.* unruliness, lack of submissiveness; insubordination
insoupçonnable *a.* above suspicion
insoupçonné *a.* unsuspected
insoutenable *a.* untenable, unmaintainable; unbearable
inspecter *vt.* to inspect; survey
inspecteur *m.* inspector; examiner; surveyor, supervisor
inspection *f.* inspection; examining
inspirant *a.* inspiring
inspirateur *a.* inspiring; — *m.* inspirer
inspiration *f.* inspiration; prompting; inhaling
inspiré *a.* inspired
inspirer *vt.* to inspire; motivate; inhale, breathe in; s'— de be inspired by
instabilité *f.* instability; uncertainty
instable *a.* unstable, unsteady; uncertain
installation *f.* installation; arranging; setting up; moving in; equipment; plant, shop; apparatus, set
installer *vt.* to install; arrange; settle; set up; equip; s'— to install oneself; settle; move in; make oneself comfortable
instamment *a.* urgently, insistently; immediately
instance *f.* instance, instancy; request; immediacy, urgency; legal proceedings, action
instant *a.* urgent; — *m.* instant, moment; à l'— immediately, at once; just now, a moment ago
instantané *a.* instantaneous; — *m.* snapshot
instar, à l'— de in the manner of
instaurateur *m.* founder of an institution
instauration *f.* founding, establishment
instaurer *vt.* to found, establish
instigateur *m.* instigator
instigation *f.* instigation; suggestion
instiller *vt.* to instill, pour by drops
instinct *m.* instinct; d'— instinctively
instinctif *a.* instinctive
instinctivement *adv.* instinctively
instituer *vt.* to institute, establish, found; appoint
institut *m.* institute
instituteur *m.*, **institutrice** *f.* grade school teacher; tutor; founder
institution *f.* institution; establishment
institutionnel *a.* institutional
instructeur *m.* instructor
instructif *a.* instructive

instruction *f.* instruction; direction; training, education, schooling; lesson; legal investigation; **juge d'—** *m.* examining magistrate
instruire *vt.* to instruct, educate, teach, inform, train; investigate legally, examine
instruit *a.* educated; trained; learned; informed, aware
instrument *m.* instrument, tool
instrumentation *f.* instrumentation, orchestration
instrumenter *vt.* to score, orchestrate; — *vi.* to order proceedings (law)
instrumentiste *m.* instrumentalist
insu *m.*, **à l'— de** unknown to, without the knowledge of
insubmersible *a.* unsinkable
insubordonné *a.* insubordinate
insuccès *m.* lack of success; failure
insuffisamment *adv.* insufficiently
insuffisance *f.* insufficiency, deficiency; inadequacy; incapacity; — **de pose** (phot.) underexposure
insuffisant *a.* insufficient, inadequate; incapable
insuffler *vt.* to inflate, blow up; breathe in; insufflate; (med.) spray
insulaire *a.* insular; — *m. & f.* islander
insularité *f.* insularity
insuline *f.* insulin
insultant *a.* insulting
insulte *f.* insult, affront
insulter *vt.* to insult
insupportable *a.* unbearable; intolerable; insufferable
insurgé *a. & m.* insurgent
insurger *v.*, **s'—** to rebel
insurmontable *a.* insuperable, insurmountable
insurpassable *a.* unsurpassable; incomparable
insurrection *f.* insurrection, rebellion
intact *a.* intact, untouched; undamaged; whole
intangibilité *f.* intangibility
intarissable *a.* inexhaustible; endless
intégral *a.* integral; whole; full, in full, unexpurgated
intégrale *f.* (math.) integral
intégralement *adv.* wholly, fully, in full
intégralité *f.* wholeness, entireness
intégrant *a.* integral
intégration *f.* integration
intègre *a.* upright, honest; ethical; incorruptible
intégrer *vt.* to integrate
intégrité *f.* integrity, honesty; entirety, wholeness
intellect *m.* intellect

intellectualité *f.* intellectuality
intellectuel *a. & m.* intellectual
intellectuellement *adv.* intellectually
intelligemment *adv.* intelligently
intelligence *f.* understanding, intellect, intelligence, comprehension; être d'— to have an understanding together; —s *pl.* relations, connections, dealings
intelligent *a.* intelligent
intelligentsia *f.* intelligentsia, intellectuals
intelligibilité *f.* intelligibility
intelligible *a.* intelligible
intempérance *f.* intemperance
intempérant *a.* intemperate
intempéré *a.* immoderate, intemperate; inclement
intempérie *f.* inclement weather
intempestif *a.* untimely, inopportune
intemporel *a.* timeless, eternal
intenable *a.* untenable
intendance *f.* direction, management
intendant *m.* steward, manager; intendant
intense *a.* intense; intensive; severe; high; deep
intensément *adv.* intensely
intensif *a.* intensive
intensifier *vt.* to intensify
intensité *f.* intensity; strength; depth; force; severity
intensivement *adv.* intensively
intenter *vt.* to bring legal suit
intention *f.* intention; intent; purpose; wish; à l'— de for, for the sake of; designed for, destined for; in honor of; avoir l'— de to intend to
intentionné *a.* intentioned
intentionnel *a.* intentional, deliberate
intentionnellement *adv.* intentionally
interallié *a.* interallied, interrelated
interastral *a.* interstellar
interattraction *f.* mutual attraction
intercalaire *a.* interpolated
intercalation *f.* interpolation, intercalation
intercaler *vt.* to intercalate, interpolate
intercéder *vi.* to intercede
intercellulaire *a.* intercellular
intercepter *vt.* to intercept
intercepteur *m.* (avi.) interceptor
interception *f.* interception
intercesseur *m.* intercessor, mediator
intercession *f.* intercession
interchangeable *a.* interchangeable
intercontinental *a.* intercontinental
intercostal *a.* intercostal
interdépartemental *a.* interdepartmental
interdépendance *f.* interdependence
interdépendant *a.* interdependent
interdiction *f.* interdiction, prohibition
interdire *vt.* to forbid, ban, prohibit; bewilder

interdit *a.* speechless, taken aback; prohibited, forbidden; — *m.* (eccl.) interdict, prohibitory decree
intéressant *a.* interesting
intéressé *a.* interested; selfish; — *m.* interested party
intéresser *vt.* to interest; be interesting to; concern; s'— à to take an interest in
intérêt *m.* interest, concern, self-interest; share; advantage
intérieur *a.* interior; internal; inner; — *m.* interior, inside
intérieurement *adv.* internally; inwardly; inside
intérim *m.* interim
intérimaire *a.* temporary, provisional
interindividuel *a.* among individuals, group
injecter *vt.* to utter, ejaculate
interjection *f.* interjection
interjeter *vt.* to interject; — appel (law) lodge an appeal
interligne *f.* space between lines; (print.) leading
interligner *vt.* to interline; write between the lines
interlinéaire *a.* interlinear
interlocuteur *m.* interlocutor
interlocutoire *a.* interlocutory
interlope *a.* illegal; unauthorized; suspect
interloquer *vt.* to make speechless, confuse
intermède *m.* intermediary; (theat.) interlude
intermédiaire *a.* intermediate; — *m.* intermediary, agent, middleman
intermezzo *m.* (mus.) intermezzo
interminable *a.* interminable, endless
intermittence *f.* intermittency; par — intermittently
internat *m.* living-in, residing; internship; boarding school
international *a.* international
internationaliser *vt.* to internationalize
internationaliste *m. & f.* internationalist
internationalité *f.* internationality
interne *m.* resident student; intern; boarder; — *a.* internal, interior, inner
internement *m.* internement
interner *vt.* to intern; confine
internissable *a.* untarnishable
interpellation *f.* interpellation; question, challenge
interpeller *vt.* to challenge, demand an accounting; interpellate
interplanétaire *a.* interplanetary
interpolation *f.* interpolation
interpoler *vt.* to interpolate
interposer *vt.* to interpose; s'— to intervene

interposition *f.* intervention; interposition
interprétable *a.* interpretable
interprétateur *m.* commentator, interpreter (of a work of art)
interprétation *f.* interpretation
interprète *m. & f.* interpreter
interpréter *vt.* to interpret; render, perform; read, make out, translate
interrègne *m.* interregnum
interrogateur *a.* questioning, interrogatory; — *m.* questioner, interrogator
interrogatif *a.* interrogative
interrogation *f.* interrogation, questioning, examination; **point d'**— *m.* question mark
interrogatoire *m.* questioning, examination, cross-examination
interroger *vt.* to interrogate, question, examine
interrompre *vt.* to interrupt; break; break off; stop
interrupteur *m.* interrupter; (elec.) switch, circuit-breaker
interruption *f.* interruption; break, breaking; disconnecting
inter-saison *f.* offseason (sports)
intersecté *a.* intersecting
intersection *f.* intersection
intersession *f.* intersession, break, recess
intersidéral, interstellaire *a.* interstellar
interstitiel *a.* interstitial
interurbain *a.* interurban
intervalle *m.* interval; period; space, distance
intervenir *vi.* to intervene, interfere; happen
intervention *f.* intervention; interference
interventionniste *m.* interventionist
interversion *f.* inversion
intervertir *vt.* to invert, reverse, transpose
interviewer *vt.* to interview
intestat *a.* intestate
intestin *a.* internal, intestine; civil; — *m.* intestine, bowel
intestinal *a.* intestinal
intimation *f.* notice, notification
intime *a.* intimate, close; inner; — *n.* close friend
intimement *adv.* intimately, closely
intimer *vt.* to notify; summon at law
intimidant *a.* intimidating
intimidateur *a.* intimidating; — *m.* intimidator
intimidation *f.* intimidation; threat, threatening
intimider *vt.* to intimidate; threaten, frighten; **s'**— to become nervous
intimité *f.* intimacy, closeness, privacy; inner being

intitulé *m.* title, heading
intituler *vt.* to entitle
intolérable *a.* intolerable, unbearable
intolérance *f.* intolerance
intolérant *a.* intolerant
intouchable *a. & n.* untouchable
intoxicant *a.* toxic, poisonous
intoxication *f.* poisoning
intoxiquer *vt.* to poison
intraduisible *a.* untranslatable
intraitable *a.* intractable, unmanageable
intra-muros *a.* intramural
intransférable *a.* untransferable
intransigeance *f.* intransigence
intransigeant *a.* intransigent, uncompromising, inflexible
intransitif *a.* intransitive
intraveineux *a.* intravenous
intrépide *a.* intrepid, fearless, undaunted
intrépidité *f.* intrepidity
intrigant *a.* intriguing, scheming; — *m.* intriguer, schemer
intrigailler *vi.* to scheme, plot
intrigue *f.* intrigue, plot
intriguer *vt.* to perplex; intrigue; — *vi.* to intrigue, scheme, plot
intrinsèque *a.* intrinsic
introducteur *m.* introducer, usher
introductif *a.* introductory
introduction *f.* introduction; insertion; induction
introduire *vt.* to bring in, show in; insert, introduce; **s'**— to enter, penetrate
intronisation *f.* enthronement; founding, establishment
introniser *vt.* to enthrone; found, establish
introspectif *a.* introspective
introspection *f.* introspection
introuvable *a.* which cannot be found, undiscoverable; incomparable
introverti *a.* introverted; — *m.* introvert
intrus *a.* intruding; trespassing; — *m.* intruder; trespasser
intrusion *f.* intrusion; trespassing
intuitif *a.* intuitive
intuition *f.* intuition
inusable *a.* that will never wear out; everlasting
inusité *a.* not in use; unusual; obsolete
inutile *a.* useless, needless, vain, unavailing
inutilisable *a.* unusable, unserviceable
inutilisé *a.* unused, unutilized
inutilité *f.* uselessness, inutility
invaincu *a.* unvanquished, unconquered
invalidation *f.* invalidating, invalidation
invalide *a.* invalid; disabled; void; — *m.* invalid, disabled veteran
invalider *vt.* to invalidate

invalidité *f.* disability; ill-health; invalidism; invalidity
invariabilité *f.* invariability
invariable *a.* invariable
invariablement *adv.* invariably
invasion *f.* invasion
invective *f.* invective
invectiver *vi.* to inveigh; — *vt.* to insult, abuse
invendable *a.* unsaleable
invendu *a.* unsold
inventaire *m.* inventory, stock
inventer *vt.* to invent; make up
inventeur *m.* inventor, discoverer
inventif *a.* inventive
invention *f.* invention, discovery; inventiveness; lie
inventorier *vt.* to inventory, take stock of
invérifiable *a.* unverifiable
invérifié *a.* unverified
inverse *a. & m.* inverse, opposite, reverse
inversement *adv.* inversely
inverser *vt.* to reverse
inversion *f.* inversion; reversing
invertébré *a.* invertebrate
invertir *vt.* to reverse, invert
investigateur *a.* investigating; — *m.* investigator
investigation *f.* investigation
investir *vt.* to invest
investissement *m.* investment, investing
investiture *f.* investiture
invétéré *a.* inveterate, confirmed
invétérer *v.,* s'— to become inveterate
invincibilité *f.* invincibility
invincible *a.* invincible; insurmountable
inviolabilité *f.* inviolability
inviolable *a.* inviolable; sacred
invisibilité *f.* invisibility
invisible *a.* invisible
invitant *a.* inviting
invitation *f.* invitation
invite *f.* signal, cue (cards); discard conveying information to one's partner
invité *m.* guest
inviter *vt.* to invite
involontaire *a.* involuntary
involontairement *adv.* involuntarily
involuté *a.* involute(d)
involution *f.* involution
invoquer *vt.* to invoke
invraisemblable *a.* improbable, unlikely
invraisemblance *f.* unlikelihood, improbability
invulnérabilité *f.* invulnerability
invulnérable *a.* invulnerable
iode *m.* iodine
ioder *vt.* to iodize
iodure *m.* iodide
iodurer *vt.* to iodize

ion *m.* ion
ionien *a.* Ionian
ionique *a.* (arch.) Ionic; (phy.) ionic
ionisation *f.* ionization
ioniser *vt.* to ionize
ionosphère *f.* ionosphere
iota *m.* iota; bit, scrap, speck
iouler *vi.* to yodel
ipréau *m.* white poplar
Irak *m.* Iraq
irakien *a. & m.* Iraqi
Iran *m.* Iran
iranien *a. & m.* Iranian
irascibilité *f.* irascibility, irritability
irascible *a.* irascible, irritable
ire *f.* anger
iridescence *f.* iridescence
iridium *m.* iridium
iris *m.* iris; rainbow; halo; — *m. or f.* (bot.) iris
irisation *f.* iridescence
irisé *a.* iridescent; rainbow-colored
irlandais *a.* Irish; Erse
Irlande *f.* Ireland
ironie *f.* irony
ironique *a.* ironical
ironiser *vi.* to speak *or* write ironically
irraccommodable *a.* unrepairable, unmendable
irrachetable *a.* irredeemable
irradiation *f.* irradiation, radiation
irradier *vi.* to irradiate, radiate; spread, increase, advance
irraisonnable *a.* irrational
irrassasiable *a.* insatiable
irrationalisme *m.* irrationalism
irrationalité *f.* irrationality
irrationnel *a.* irrational
irréalisable *a.* unrealizable; impossible
irrecevable *a.* unacceptable, inadmissible
irréconciliable *a.* irreconcilable
irrécusable *a.* irrecusable, unimpeachable
irréductible *a.* irreducible; firm, unyielding, inflexible
irréel *a.* unreal
irréfléchi *a.* thoughtless, unthinking, hasty
irréflexion *f.* thoughtlessness, haste
irréfragable *a.* unimpeachable
irréfutable *a.* irrefutable
irréfuté *a.* unrefuted
irrégularité *f.* irregularity; unevenness; unpunctuality
irrégulier *a.* uneven; unpunctual; (gram.) irregular; — *m.* irregular, guerilla
irrégulièrement *adv.* irregularly
irréligieux *a.* irreligious
irréligion *f.* irreligion
irréligiosité *f.* irreligiousness
irrémédiable *a.* irremediable, incurable

irrémédiablement *adv.* irremediably, incurably
irremplaçable *a.* irreplaceable
irréparable *a.* irreparable
irrépréhensible *a.* not reprehensible, blameless
irrépressible *a.* irrepressible
irréprimable *a.* irrepressible
irréprochable *a.* irreprochable
irrésistible *a.* irresistible
irrésolu *a.* irresolute; uncertain; hesitant, undecided; unsteady; unsolved
irrésoluble *a.* irresolvable; unsolvable
irrésolution *f.* irresolution; hesitation; indecision
irrespect *m.* disrespect, lack of respect
irrespectueux *a.* disrespectful
irrespirable *a.* unbreathable
irresponsabilité *f.* irresponsibility
irresponsable *a.* irresponsible
irrévérence *f.* irreverence
irrévérencieusement *adv.* irreverently
irrévérencieux *a.* irreverent
irréversible *a.* irreversible
irrévocabilité *f.* irrevocability
irrévocable *a.* irrevocable
irrigateur *m.* watering hose
irrigation *f.* irrigation; watering; flooding; spraying
irriguer *vt.* to irrigate; water; flood; spray
irritabilité *f.* irritability; sensitivity
irritable *a.* easily irritable; sensitive
irritant *a.* irritating; — *m.* irritant
irriter *vt.* to irritate; s'— to become irritated; get angry
irruption *f.* irruption; inrush; inroad, invasion; bursting in; flooding
Islam *m.* Islam
islamique *a.* Islamic
islandais *a. & m.* Icelandic
Islande *f.* Iceland
isobare *f.* isobar
isocèle *a.* isosceles
isolant *a.* isolating; insulating; **bouteille —e** *f.* vacuum bottle, Thermos bottle
isolateur *a.* (elec.) insulating; — *m.* insulator
isolation *f.* insulating, insulation
isolationnisme *m.* isolationism
isolationniste *m. & f.* isolationist
isolé *a.* isolated; apart; lonely, desolate; insulated
isolement *m.* isolation, loneliness; (elec.) insulation
isolément *adv.* individually, singly, separately; solitarily
isoler *vt.* to isolate; segregate; (elec.) insulate
isoloir *m.* insulator; voting booth
isomère *m.* isomer

isométrique *f.* isometrics
isomorphe *m.* isomorph
isotherme *m.* isotherm
isotope *m.* isotope
isotrope *m.* isotrope
Israël *m.* Israel
israélien *a. & m.* Israeli
issu *a.* descended, born; (fig.) resulting
issue *f.* outlet, exit; conclusion; issue; —s *pl.* by-products
isthme *m.* isthmus
Italie *f.* Italy
italien *a. & m.* Italian
italique *a.* Italic; — *m.* italics
itération *f.* iteration, repetition
itinéraire *m.* itinerary, route; — *a.* pertaining to roads
itinérant *a.* itinerant
ivoire *m.* ivory
ivoirin *a.* resembling ivory
ivre *a.* inebriated, intoxicated, drunk
ivresse *f.* intoxication; (fig.) ecstasy
ivrogne *a.* drunken; — *m.* drunkard
ivrognerie *f.* chronic drunkenness

J

jabot *m.* bird's crop; ruffle, neck frill
jabotage *m.* chatter, talk, gossip
jaboter *vi. & vt.* to jabber; chatter; talk unintelligibly
jacasse *f.* gossip, chatterbox; magpie
jacasser *vi.* to jabber, chatter; gossip
jacasserie *f.* chatter, gossip
jachère *f.* fallow land
jacinthe *f.* (bot.) hyacinth
jack *m.* (elec.) jack
jacobée *f.* (bot.) ragwort
jacobin *m.* Dominican friar; Jacobin
Jacques (*m.*) James
jacquet *m.* backgammon
jactance *f.* boasting, bragging
jade *m.* jade
jadis *adv.* of old, formerly
jaguar *m.* jaguar
jaillir *vi.* to spout out, spurt, gush, squirt; fly up; flash; (fig.) show liveliness
jaillissant *a.* gushing, spurting; flying
jaillissement *m.* spurt, spurting, gushing
jais *m.* jet; **noir comme du —** jet-black
jalon *m.* marker (post, stake, rod, staff); landmark
jalonner *vt.* to mark; stake (out); blaze
jalouser *vt.* to envy, be jealous of
jalousie *f.* jealousy; chagrin; Venetian blind
jaloux *a.* jealous, envious; desirous
Jamaïque *f.* Jamaica
jamais *adv.* ever; **ne . . . —** never; **à —, pour —** for ever

jambage *m.* jamb of a door; side

jambe *f.* leg; shank; stem of a glass; brace, support; **à toutes –s** at full speed

jambière *f.* elastic stocking; **-s** *pl.* leggings; shin guards (sports)

jambon *m.* ham

jamboree *m.* jamboree, international scout meeting

janissaire *m.* janissary; 14th century Turkish soldier

jansénisme *m.* Jansenism

janséniste *a. & n.* Jansenist

jante *f.* rim of wheel

janvier *m.* January

Japon *m.* Japan

japonais *a. & m.* Japanese

japonaiseries *f. pl.* Japanese art objects

jappement *m.* yelp, yelping

japper *vi.* to yelp, yap

jaquemart *m.* jack, figure which strikes the hours

jaquette *f.* jacket, coat

jardin *m.* garden; — **d'enfants** kindergarten; — **des plantes** botanical garden(s); — **potager** vegetable garden; truck farm

jardinage *m.* gardening; gardening products; produce

jardiner *vi.* to garden

jardinet *m.* small garden

jardinier *m.* gardener

jardinière *f.* gardener; flower stand; **à la** — served with various vegetables

jardiniste *m.* landscape gardener

jargon *m.* jargon

jargonner *vi.* to speak in jargon; use jargon

jarre *f.* large jar

jarret *m.* shin; hock; knuckle; part of leg back of the knee joint

jarretelle *f.* garter

jarretière *f.* garter; rope

jars *m.* (zool.) gander

jaser *vi.* to prattle, chatter, talk; gossip

jaserie *f.* chatter, gossip, talk

jaseur *a.* talkative, gossipy; — *m.* talker, chatterbox; gossip

jasmin *m.* jasmine

jaspe *m.* jasper

jasper *vt.* to marble

jatte *f.* bowl, basin

jattée *f.* bowlful

jauge *f.* gauge; (naut.) tonnage

jaugeage *m.* gauging, measuring

jauger *vt.* to gauge, measure

jaunâtre *a.* yellowish

jaune *a.* yellow; — *m.* yellow; (coll.) non-union worker; — **d'œuf** egg yolk; **race** — yellow race

jaunir *vt.* to make yellow; — *vi.* grow yellow

jaunisse *f.* (mcd.) jaundice

javanois *a. & m.* Javanese

javeline *f.* javelin

javellisation *f.* chlorination

javelliser *vt.* to chlorinate; add bleach to

javelot *m.* javelin, spear

je, (j') *pron.* I

Jean (*m.*) John

Jeanne (*f.*) Jane, Joan, Jean

jeannette *f.* small gold crucifix (pendant)

jérémiade *f.* lament, complaint, jeremiad

jersey *m.* jersey material

jésuite *m.* Jesuit

Jésus *m.* Jesus depicted as infant

jet *m.* throwing, casting; jet, spurt, spout, gush; blast, burst; jettisoning; (bot.) shoot; **premier** — rough draft, first attempt; — **d'eau** fountain

jetée *f.* pier, jetty

jeter *vt.* to throw, cast, fling, toss, hurl; utter

jeton *m.* counter, chip, token

jeu *m.* (*pl.* **jeux**) play, game, sport, performance; acting; gambling; slack, play, looseness; set; **en** — at stake; in action; — **de cartes** pack of cards; — **d'esprit** witticism; — **de mots** pun; — **de paume** tennis court; **maison de** — *f.* gambling house; **table de** — *f.* card table; gambling table

jeudi *m.* Thursday

jeun, *adv.* **à** — fasting; without having eaten

jeune *a.* young, youthful; green (not ripe)

jeûne *m.* fast, fasting

jeûner *vi.* to fast

jeunesse *f.* youth, young people; youthfulness

jeunet *a.* (coll.) very young

joaillerie *f.* jewelry

joaillier *m.* jeweller

jobard *a. & m.* (coll.) easy mark, fool, dupe

jocrisse *m.* fool, dupe

jodler *vi.* to yodel

joie *f.* joy, gladness; **feu de** — *m.* bonfire

joindre *vt.* to join, put together, connect; meet; adjoin; add; combine; weld; **se** — to join; meet; adjoin

joint *a.* joined, united — *m.* joint

jointif *a.* joined

jointure *f.* joint; juncture

joker *m.* joker (cards)

joli *a.* pretty

joliment *adv.* nicely; very

jonc *m.* rush, rattan, reed

joncher *vt.* to strew, scatter; litter, be spread over

jonction *f.* junction; joining

jongler vi. to juggle
jonglerie f. juggling
jongleur m. juggler; jongleur
jonque f. (naut.) junk
jonquille f. jonquil
jouable a. playable
joue f. cheek; flange; coucher en — to aim at, point a gun at
jouer vt. to play; perform; act; bet on; feign; trick; — vi. to play; gamble; act, work; come into play, operate; faire — to bring into play
jouet m. plaything, toy
joueur m. player, gambler; performer; mauvais — poor sport
joug m. yoke; slavery
jouir vi. to enjoy; possess
jouissance f. enjoyment; possession
joujou m. plaything, toy
jour m. day, daylight, light; opening; du — au lendemain at any moment; soon; faire — to grow light; grand — broad daylight; mettre au — to bring to light; give birth to; petit — early dawn; plein — broad daylight; -s pl. days; life; de nos -s today, nowadays
Jourdain m. Jordan
journal m. (pl. journaux) journal, diary; log; newspaper
journalier a. daily, everyday; — m. day-laborer
journalisme m. journalism
journaliste m. & f. journalist; reporter
journalistique a. journalistic
journée f. daytime; day's work; day's pay; day's march; à la — by the day; toute la — all day long
journellement adv. daily
joute f. joust, jousting; competition, contest
jouter vi. to joust, fight
jouvence f. youth
jovialité f. joviality
joyau m. jewel
joyeusement adv. joyfully
joyeuseté f. prank, joke
joyeux a. joyful; glad, merry
jubilation f. jubilation
jubilé m. jubilee; golden anniversary
jubiler vi. to jubilate, be jubilant, exult
jucher vi. & vt. to perch
juchoir m. perch, roost
judaïque a. Judaic, Jewish
judaïsme m. Judaism
judas m. traitor; peephole
judéo-allemand a. & m. Yiddish
judiciaire a. judicial, judiciary
judicieusement adv. judiciously
judicieux a. judicious
juge m. judge; — d'instruction examining

magistrate
jugement m. judgment, understanding; trial; sentence, decision, verdict; opinion; sense
jugeotte f. (coll.) common sense
juger vt. to judge, try; pass sentence; think; consider, deem
jugoslave a. & n. Yugoslav(ian), Jugoslav
jugulaire a. jugular; — f. jugular vein; chin strap
juguler vt. to strangle; cut the throat of
juif (juive) a. Jewish
juillet m. July
juin m. June
Jules (m.) Julius
julien a. Julian
julienne f. consommé Julienne (made with herbs and vegetables)
jumeau (jumelle) a. & n. twin
jumelé a. paired, coupled; twin; dual
jumeler vt. to pair
jumelles f. pl. binoculars
jument f. mare
jumping m. steeplechase (racing)
jungle f. jungle
junior a. & m. junior
junte f. junta
jupe f. skirt
jupon m. petticoat
juré a. sworn; — m. juror; les -s pl. the jury
jurement m. cursing, swearing
jurer vt. to swear, vow; — vi. curse; to clash (color)
juridiction f. jurisdiction
juridictionnel a. jurisdictional
juridique a. judicial, juridical
jurisconsulte m. lawyer, law expert
jurisprudence f. jurisprudence
juriste m. jurist
juron m. oath, swear word
jury m. jury, board, panel
jus m. juice; gravy
jusant m. ebb tide
jusque, jusqu'à prep. until; as far as; even; jusqu'ici, jusqu'à present till now, hitherto; jusqu'à ce que conj. until
justaucorps m. doublet
juste a. just, equitable, right, fair; precise, exact; au — exactly, precisely; — adv. right, very, exactly; — m. just person; person in state of grace
juste-milieu m. moderation, golden mean
justesse f. exactness, accuracy; fairness
justice f. justice; law; faire — de to treat as one deserves; se faire — to punish oneself; avenge oneself
justiciable a., — de under the jurisdiction of
justicier m. officer of justice, judge; — vt.

to punish
justifiable *a.* justifiable
justificateur *a.* justifying
justicatif *a.* justificative
justification *f.* justification
justifier *vt.* to justify, vindicate; — **de to**
give proof of
juteux *a.* juicy
juvénile *a.* juvenile
juvénilité *f.* character of what is juvenile
juxtaposer *vt.* to juxtapose

K

kaki *a.* khaki-colored
kaléidoscope *m.* kaleidoscope
kangourou *m.* kangaroo
kaolin *m.* kaolin
kapok *m.* kapok
kayac *m.* kayak
keepsake *m.* album, scrapbook
képi *m.* military cap
kermesse *f.* village fair
kérosène *m.* kerosene
kitchenotte *f.* peasant's bonnet
kidnapper *vt.* to kidnap
kidnappeur *m.* kidnapper
kilo(gramme) *m.* kilogram
kilomètre *m.* kilometer
kilométrer *vt.* to mark off in kilometers
kilométrique *a.* kilometric
kilowatt *m.* kilowatt
kilt *m.* kilt
kimono *m.* kimono
kinescope *m.* kinescope; picture tube
kiosque *m.* kiosk; newsstand; conning
tower
kirsch *m.* Kirsch, cherry brandy
klaxon *m.* (auto.) horn
klaxonner *vi.* to blow the horn
kleptomanie (cleptomanie) *f.* kleptomania
knock-out *m.* boxing knockout
knockouter *vt.* to knock out
kodak *m.* camera
krach *m.* financial crash
krypton *m.* krypton
kyrie *m.* (eccl.) Kyrie eleison (invocation)
kyrielle *f.* (coll.) tirade, avalanche of
words
kyste *m.* (med.) cyst

L

la *art. f.* the; — *pron.* her, it; — *m.* (mus.)
French key of A; 6th note of a scale
là *adv.* there, that, that way; then
là-bas *adv.* over there; yonder
label *m.* guarantee; inspection mark
labeur *m.* labor, work
laborantine *f.* laboratory technician

laboratoire *m.* laboratory
laborieusement *adv.* laboriously
laborieux *a.* hard-working; painstaking,
difficult
labour *m.* tillage, plowing
labourable *a.* arable
labourage *m.* plowing
labourer *vt.* to till, plow
laboureur *m.* plower; farm hand
labyrinthe *m.* labyrinth, maze
lac *m.* lake
laçage *m.* lacing
lacer *vt.* to lace; se — to tie one's shoe-
laces, lace one's shoes
lacération *f.* laceration
lacérer *vt.* to lacerate
lacet *m.* shoelace; hairpin turn; snare;
route en −s winding road
lâche *a.* loose, lax; cowardly; — *m.* coward
lâcher *vt.* to release, loosen; let go, drop;
— prise to let go
lâcheté *f.* cowardice; cowardly action
lâcheur *m.* (coll.) quitter
lacis *m.* network
laconique *a.* laconic
lacrymal *a.* teary
lacrymogène *a.*, **gaz** — *m.* tear gas
lacs *m.* knotted cord; trap, snare
lacté *a.* lacteal, milky; **voie −e** *f.* Milky
Way
lactique *a.* lactic
lactose *m.* lactose, milk sugar
lacune *f.* gap, void, lacuna
lad *m.* stable boy
là-dessus *adv.* thereupon
ladre *a.* mean, stingy; leprous
lagon *m.* lagoon of an atoll
lagune *f.* lagoon
là-haut *adv.* up above, up there
lai *m.* lay, song; — *a.* lay; **frère** — *m.* lay
brother
laïc *a.* lay, secular
laid *a.* ugly
laideron *f.* ugly young woman
laideur *f.* ugliness
lainage *m.* wool goods
laine *f.* wool
laineux *a.* woolly, fleecy
lainier *a.* wool; — *m.* wool merchant
laïque *a.* laic, lay; — *m.* layman
laisse *f.* leash
laissé-pour-compte *m.* unsold item; unwanted thing
laisser *vt.* to let, allow; leave behind, leave
alone
laisser-aller *m.* unconstraint
laissez-passer *m.* pass, permit
lait *m.* milk; — **écrémé** skim milk; **cochon
de** — *m.* suckling pig; **dents de** — *f. pl.*
milk teeth, baby teeth; **petit** — whey

laitance *f.* milt
laiterie *f.* dairy, dairy store
laiteux *a.* milky
laitier *m.* milk seller, milkman; — *m.* vitrified slag
laitière *f.* milkmaid; dairy cow
laiton *m.* brass
laitue *f.* lettuce
laize *f.* cloth width
lamaserie *f.* lamasery
lambeau *m.* rag, tatter; shred
lambin *a.* slow; loitering
lambiner *vi.* to move slowly, dawdle
lambourde *f.* studding
lambrequin *m.* valence, hanging
lambris *m.* wainscoting, paneling, wall plaster
lame *f.* knife blade; slat; wave
lamentation *f.* lamentation
lamenter *v.*, se — to lament, complain
laminage *m.* laminating
laminer *vt.* to laminate
lampadaire *m.* lamppost; floor lamp
lampe *f.* lamp; light; bulb; (rad.) tube; — éclair photoflash bulb, flash bulb
lampion *m.* oil lamp; lantern
lampiste *m. & f.* lampmaker; lamp seller
lamproie *f.* lamprey
lampyre *m.* firefly
lance *f.* lance; lancer; nozzle
lance-flammes *m.* flame-thrower
lance-fusées *m.* rockèt launcher
lance-grenades *m.* grenade launcher
lancement *m.* throw, throwing; start, send-off
lance-pierres *m.* slingshot
lancer *vt.* to fling, hurl, throw, start; launch
lance-torpille *m.* torpedo tube
lancette *f.* lancet
lancier *m.* lancer
lanciner *vi.* to shoot (pain)
lande *f.* heath, moor
langage *m.* language, speech
lange *m.* swaddling cloth
langer *vt.* to swaddle
langoureux *a.* languishing, languid
langouste *f.* spiny lobster
langoustine *f.* very small lobster
langue *f.* tongue; speech, language
languette *f.* tongue, tab; (mus.) instrument reed
langueur *f.* languor
languir *vi.* to languish, pine; — pour to long for
languissant *a.* languishing
lanière *f.* strap
lanoline *f.* lanolin
lanterne *f.* lantern, light; projector
lanterner *vi.* to loaf, idle, waste time

lapement *m.* lapping
laper *vt. & vi.* to lap
lapereau *m.* young rabbit
lapidaire *m. & a.* lapidary
lapidation *f.* stoning, lapidation
lapider *vt.* to stone
lapin *m.* rabbit, (coll.) brave man, cunning man
lapis *m.* lapis lazuli
Laponie *f.* Lapland
lapsus *m.* error, slip of the tongue
laquais *m.* lackey; flunky
laque *f.* lac; — en feuilles shellac; — *m.* lacquer
laquelle *pron. f.* who, which, that
laquer *vt.* to lacquer
larcin *m.* larceny, theft
lard *m.* bacon; pork, fat
larder *vt.* to lard; interlard, sprinkle; pierce, riddle
lardon *m.* bit of fat
large *a.* wide, broad; liberal, generous; large; — *m.* room, space; width; open sea
largesse *f.* liberality, generosity
largeur *f.* breadth, width
largue *a.* slack; (naut.) on the quarter
larguer *vt.* to slacken
larme *f.* tear; drop
larmioement *m.* weeping, tears
larmoyant *a.* weeping, tearful
larmoyer *vt.* to weep constantly
larron *m.* thief, robber
larvaire *a.* larval
larve *f.* larva
laryngite *f.* laryngitis
laryngologiste *m.* throat specialist
las! *interj.* alas!
las (lasse) *a.* tired, weary
lascif *a.* lascivious
lasciveté *f.* lasciviousness
lassant *a.* tiring; tedious
lasser *vt.* to tire; se — to grow tired
lassitude *f.* weariness, fatigue, lassitude
latent *a.* latent
latéral *a.* lateral; –ement *adv.* on the side
Latin *m. & a.* Latin
latiniser *vt.* to latinize
latiniste *m. & f.* latinist
latino-américain *a. & m.* Latin-American
latrines *f. pl.* latrines
lattage *m.* lathwork
latte *f.* lath, slat
latter *vt.* to lath
lattis *m.* lathwork; latticework
latvien *a. & m.* Latvian
laudatif *a.* laudatory
lauré *a.* crowned with laurel, laureate
lauréat *m.* laureate, winner
Laurent(*m.*) Lawrence

laurier *m.* laurel
lavable *a.* washable
lavabo *m.* wash basin, sink; lavatory; (eccl.) priest's prayer
lavage *m.* washing
lavallière *f.* necktie with large flat knot
lavande *f.* lavender
lavandière *f.* washerwoman
lave *f.* lava
lavé *a.* washed out; water-color wash (art)
lavement *m.* washing; enema
laver *vt.* to wash
lavette *f.* dishcloth
laveur *m.* washer; **raton —** raccoon
laveuse *f.* washing machine
lavis *m.* wash (art)
lavoir *m.* wash house, laundry
laxatif *a. & m.* laxative
lazaret *m.* quarantine station
lazzi *m. pl.* (theat.) tricks, jokes
le *art. m.* the; **—** *pron. m.* him, it
leader *m.* political leader; editorial
lèche *f.* thin slice (food)
lèchefrite *f.* dripping pan
lécher *vt.* to lick; polish; polish excessively
lècherie *f.* gluttony
leçon *f.* lesson, assignment; reading, version
lecteur *m.* reader
lecture *f.* reading
légal *a.* legal
légalement *adv.* legally
légalisation *f.* legalization
légaliser *vt.* to legalize; authenticate
légalité *f.* legality
légat *m.* papal legate
légataire *m. & f.* heir, legatee; **— universel** residual heir
légation *f.* legation
légendaire *a.* legendary
légende *f.* legend
léger *a.* light; slight; active; agile; frivolous
légèrement *adv.* lightly
légèreté *f.* lightness, levity, triviality
légion *f.* legion
légionnaire *m.* legionary; member of the Foreign Legion; member of the Legion of Honor
législateur *m.* legislator
législatif *a.* legislative
législation *f.* legislation
législature *f.* legislature
légiste *m.* jurist, legist
légitime *a.* legitimate; lawful
légitimer *vt.* to recognize, legitimatize
légitimité *f.* legitimacy, lawfulness
legs *m.* legacy

léguer *vt.* to leave, bequeathe
légume *m.* vegetable; **—** *f.* (coll.) very important person
légumeuse *f.* legume
légumier *m.* vegetable dish; **—** *a.* vegetable; vegetable garden
légumineux *a.* leguminous
lendemain *m.* next day, tomorrow
lénifier *vt.* to mitigate, attenuate
lénitif *a.* soothing
lent *a.* slow
lente *f.* nit
lentement *adv.* slowly
lenteur *f.* slowness
lenticulaire *a.* lenticular
lentille *f.* lentil; lens; **—s** *pl.* freckles
léonin *a.* leonine; **part —e** *f.* lion's share
léopard *m.* leopard
léopardé *a.* spotted
lèpre *f.* leprosy
lépreux *a.* leprous; **—** *m.* leper
lequel *pron. m.* which, who, that
les *art.* (*pl. of* le, la); **—** *pron.* them
lès *prep.* near
lesbien *a.* Lesbian
lèse-humanité *f.* crime against humanity
lèse-majesté *f.* high treason
léser *vt.* to wrong, injure
lésine *f.* stinginess
lésiner *vi.* to be stingy, be niggardly
lésion *f.* wrong, damage, hurt; lesion
lessivage *m.* washing
lessive *f.* lye; laundry, washing powder
lessiver *vt.* to launder
lest *m.* (naut.) ballast
lestage *m.* ballasting
leste *a.* nimble, brisk, agile
lester *vt.* to ballast, weight
léthargie *f.* lethargy
léthargique *a.* lethargic
Lette *m. & f. & a.* Lett, Latvian
letton *a. & m.* Lett, Latvian
Lettonie *f.* Latvia
lettrage *m.* lettering
lettre *f.* letter; **à la —, au pied de la —** literally
lettré *a.* literate; learned
lettrine *f.* large initial capital letter; reference letter at head of dictionary column
leucémie *f.* leukemia
leucocyte *m.* leucocyte, white blood cell
leur *a.* their; **—** *pron.* to them, for them; **le —, la —** theirs
leurre *m.* lure, decoy
leurrer *vt.* to lure, trap, decoy
levain *m.* leaven, yeast; **poudre — f.** baking powder
levant *a.* rising; **—** *m.* east
Levantin *m. & a.* Levantine

levée *f.* raising, lifting; adjourning; harvesting; levying; mail collection; trick (at cards); removal; levee, dike

lever *m.* rising; — du soleil sunrise

lever *vt.* to lift, raise; collect; levy; remove; draw (a plan); — *vi.* to come up (plants); to rise (dough)

levier *m.* lever; crowbar; — articulé toggle switch

lévitation *f.* levitation

levraut *m.* young hare

lèvre *f.* lip; rim

lévrette *f.*, **lévrier** *m.* greyhound

levure *f.* yeast; — chimique baking powder

lexicographe *m.* lexicographer

lexicologie *f.* lexicology

lexique *m.* lexicon; glossary; vocabulary

lézard *m.* lizard

lézarde *f.* crevice, crack

lézarder *vt.* to crack

liaison *f.* binding, joining, relation; intimacy, affair

liane *f.* liana, vine

liant *a.* good-natured, engaging; flexible; — *m.* flexibility, affability

liard *m.* ¼ sou; tiny sum, cent; un rouge — a red cent

liasse *f.* bundle, wad, file

Liban *m.* Lebanon

Libanais *m. & a.* Lebanese

libation *f.* libation

libelle *m.* lampoon, satire; libel

libellé *m.* composition, wording (judiciary *or* administrative)

libeller *vt.* to draw up, compose, word

libelliste *m.* satirist

libellule *f.* dragonfly

libéral *a. & m.* liberal

libéralement *adv.* liberally

libéralisation *f.* liberalization

libéraliser *vt.* to liberalize

libéralisme *m.* liberalism

libéralité *f.* liberality, generosity

libérateur *m.* liberator

libération *f.* liberation

libérer *vt.* to free, liberate, discharge

libertaire *m. & f.* anarchist

liberté *f.* liberty, freedom

libertin *a.* libertine, licentious; — *m.* libertine; freethinker (history)

libertinage *m.* licentiousness, debauchery; libertinage

libidineux *a.* libidinous, lascivious

libraire *m. & f.* bookseller

librairie *f.* bookstore; book trade; publishing house

libre *a.* free; unoccupied

libre-échange *m.* free trade

librement *adv.* freely

libre-service *m.* self-service; restaurante de — cafeteria

librettiste *m.* librettist

Libye *f.* Libya

lice *f.* lists, jousting field; bitch; entrer en — to undertake, enter upon

licence *f.* license; Master's degree

licencié *m.* holder of a Master's degree

licenciement *m.* dismissal, firing

licencier *vt.* to dismiss, fire

licencieux *a.* licentious

lichen *m.* lichen

licitation *f.* sale at auction

licite *a.* lawful

liciter *vt.* to sell at auction

licorne *f.* unicorn

licou, licol *m.* halter (of a harness)

licteur *m.* lictor

lie *f.* lees, (dregs) — de vin wine dregs; red-violet color

lié *a.* tied, united; intimate

liège *m.* cork, cork oak; à bout(s) de — cork-tipped

lien *m.* tie, bond

lier *vt.* to tie, bind, fasten; establish; bind, thicken (cooking); se — to become close friends, become intimate; thicken

lierre *m.* ivy

liesse *f.* joy, gaiety

lieu *m.* place; cause, reason; — x *pl.* premises; au — de instead of; avoir — to take place; avoir — de to have reason to; — commun commonplace, banality; tenir — de to replace

lieue *f.* league (2 ½ miles)

lieutenance *f.* lieutenancy

lieutenant-colonel *m.* lieutenant-colonel

lièvre *m.* hare

liftier *m.* elevator operator

ligament *m.* ligament

ligaturer *vt.* to ligature, bind

lignage *m.* lineage

ligne *f.* line

lignée *f.* issue, stock; chien de bonne — *m.* pedigreed dog

ligneux *a.* ligneous

lignite *m.* lignite

ligoter *vt.* to bind, tie up

ligue *f.* league

liguer *vt.* to bind together, unite

ligueur *m.* member of the League (historical)

ligurien *a. & m.* Ligurian

lilas *m.* lilac; lilac color, light purple

lilliputien *a.* Lilliputian, tiny

limace *f.* (zool.) slug

limaçon *m.* snail

limande *f.* straight edge (carpentry)

limbe *m.* border; — s *pl.* limbo

lime *f.* file

limer *vt.* to file; (fig.) to polish, rework
limier *m.* bloodhound; sleuth
liminaire *a.* prefatory, introductory
limitable *a.* limitable
limitatif *a.* limiting
limitation *f.* limitation; — **sur la natalité** birth control
limite *f.* boundary, limit
limiter *vt.* to limit
limitrophe *a.* surrounding, bordering
limon *m.* lime; mud, slime; silt; shaft; support of a stair step
limonade *f.* lemon soda, lemonade
limoneux *a.* slimy; full of mud; silted
limousine *f.* limousine
limpide *a.* limpid
limpidité *f.* limpidness, clearness
lin *m.* flax; linen; **graine de** — *f.* linseed
linceul *m.* shroud
linéaire *a.* linear
linéal *a.* lineal
linéament *m.* feature; stoke; line; element
linette *f.* linseed
linge *m.* linen; table linen; underclothing; soiled clothes
lingerie *f.* linen goods; underclothing; linen closet; **vente de** — *f.* white-goods sale
lingot *m.* ingot
linguiste *m.* linguist
linguistique *a.* linguistic; — *f.* linguistics
liniment *m.* liniment
linoléum *m.* linoleum
linon *m.* batiste
linotype *f.* linotype machine
linotypiste *m. & f.* linotypist
linteau *m.* lintel
lion *m.* lion; — **ne** *f.* lioness
lionceau *m.* lion cub
lippe *f.* protruding lower lip; **faire la** — to pout
liquéfaction *f.* liquefying, liquefaction
liquéfier *vt.* to liquefy
liqueur *f.* liqueur; liquor, liquid; (chem.) solution
liquidation *f.* settlement, liquidating of debts
liquide *a.* liquid; — *m.* liquid; — *f.* liquid consonant
liquider *vt.* to liquidate; settle
liquoriste *m.* dealer in liqueurs
lire *vt.* to read
lire *f.* lira
lis, lys *m.* (bot.) lily; (fig.) **teint de** — very white
Lisbonne *f.* Lisbon
lise *f.* quicksand
liséré *m.* piping; a sewed-on border
lisérer *vt.* to edge, border
liseur *m.* reader; bookmark

liseuse *f.* reader; protective cover of a book
lisibilité *f.* legibility
lisible *a.* legible, readable
lisière *f.* selvage; border, edge; support
lisse *a.* sleek, smooth, glossy
lisser *vt.* to smoothe, make glossy
lisseuse *f.* polishing machine
liste *f.* list
listel *m.* edging, frame
lit *m.* bed; layer; — **de sangle** folding bed
litanie *f.* litany
litée *f.* litter of young animals
literie *f.* bedding
lithium *m.* lithium
lithographe *m.* lithographer
lithographie *f.* lithograph; lithography
lithographier *vt.* to lithograph
litière *f.* litter
litige *m.* litigation
litigieux *a.* litigious; contentious (law)
litre *m.* liter
lit-sac *m.* sleeping bag
littéraire *a.* literary
littéral *a.* literal
littéralement *adv.* literally
littérateur *m.* literary man, man of letters
littérature *f.* literature
littoral *m. & a.* coast; littoral
Lituanie *f.* Lithuania
Lituanien *m. & a.* Lithuanian
liturgie *f.* liturgy
liturgique *a.* liturgical
livarot *m.* livarot cheese
livide *a.* livid
lividité *f.* lividness, lividity
Livourne *f.* Leghorn
livrable *a.* deliverable
livraison *f.* delivery; part, installment (of book)
livre *f.* pound (weight *or* Eng. money)
livre *m.* book, register; **grand** — ledger
livrée *f.* livery; colors
livrer *vt.* to deliver; hand over; betray; **se** — **à** to give oneself over to; devote oneself to; go in for, indulge in; surrender to
livresque *a.* relating to books
livret *m.* small book; passbook; libretto
livreur *m.* delivery man
livreuse *f.* delivery truck
lobaire *a.* lobar
lobe *m.* lobe
local *m.* premises; — *a.* local
localisation *f.* localization
localiser *vt.* to localize
localité *f.* locality
locataire *m. & f.* tenant
locatif *m.* (gram.) locative
location *f.* renting; **bureau de** — *m.* box

office
loch *f.* (naut.) log; **table de —** *f.* log book
locomoteur *a.* locomotive
locomotion *f.* locomotion
locuste *f.* locust
locution *f.* locution; phrase
logarithme *m.* logarithm
logarithmique *a.* logarithmic
loge *f.* (theat.) box; dressing room; janitor's apartment; loggia
logement *m.* lodging, housing
loger *vt.* to lodge, house; **—** *vi.* to reside
logeur *m.* landlord
logicien *m.* logician
logique *a.* logical; **—** *f.* logic
logis *m.* home, dwelling
logistique *f.* logistics
loi *f.* law
loin *adv.* far, far off, at a distance
lointain *a.* far, remote, distant; **—** *m.* distance
loir *m.* dormouse
loisible *a.* permissible
loisir *m.* leisure; time-off
lombago *m.* lumbago
lombaire *a.* lumbar
lombes *m. pl.* lumbar region
lombric *m.* earthworm
londonien *m.* Londoner; **—** *a.* of London
Londres *m.* London
long (longue) *a.* long, lengthy; **à la — ue** in the long run; **—** *m.* length; **de — en** large up and down, back and forth; **le — de** *prep.* along
longanimité *f.* longanimity; forbearance
long-courrier *m.* ocean-going ship
longe *f.* tether; loin
longer *vt.* to go along, skirt
longeron *m.* crossbeam; boom (avi.)
longévité *f.* longevity
longitudinal *a.* longitudinal
longtemps *adv.* a long time
longue *f.* long vowel
longuement *adv.* for a long time, at length
longuet *a.* rather long; **—** *m.* long roll
longueur *f.* length
longue-vue *f.* telescope
looping *m.* (avi.) loop
lopin *m.* bit, piece
loquace *a.* loquacious
loquacité *f.* loquaciousness
loque *f.* rag, tatter
loquet *m.* latch
loqueteau *m.* small latch
loqueteux *a.* ragged, dressed in rags
loquette *f.* scrap, waste
lorgner *vt.* to ogle, stare at
lorgnette *f.* opera glasses
lorgnon *m.* lorgnette
loriot *m.* oriole

lorrain *a.* Lorraine
lors *adv.* at the time; **dès —** from that time; **— de** at the time of
lorsque *conj.* when
losange *f.* lozenge
lot *m.* lot, part, share; jack pot; prize (gambling)
loterie *f.* lottery
loti *a.* favored; divided
lotion *f.* lotion; hair tonic
lotionner *vt.* to lotion, bathe
lotir *vt.* to divide into lots; sort out; provide for
loto *m.* lotto
lotus *m.* lotus
louable *a.* praiseworthy
louage *m.* letting out; hiring
louange *f.* praise
louanger *vt.* to praise
louangeur *a.* praising, laudatory
louche *f.* soup ladle; **—** *a.* cross-eyed, squinting; shady, suspect, unwholesome
loucher *vi.* to squint; be cross-eyed
louchet *m.* spade
louer *vt.* to praise; hire, rent; **se — de** to be pleased with
loufoque *m.* crank
lougre *m.* (naut.) lugger
louis *m.* 20-franc gold piece
loulou *m.* Pomeranian dog
loup *m.* wolf; evil person; mask; defect
loupe *f.* magnifying glass; cyst, wen, tree gnarl
louper *vt.* to botch
loup-garou *m.* werewolf
lourd *a.* heavy, weighty, dull
lourdaud *a.* clumsy
lourdement *adv.* heavily
lourdeur *f.* heaviness; dullness; sultriness
loutre *f.* otter
louveteau *m.* wolf cub
louveterie *f.* wolf hunt; hunting gear
louvoyer *vi.* dodge, be evasive; (naut.) to tack
lover *vt.* to coil
loyaliste *a. & n.* loyalist
loyauté *f.* loyalty
loyer *m.* rent, rental
lubie *f.* whim, fancy
lubricité *f.* lewdness, inclination toward obscenity
lubrifiant *m.* lubricant; **—** *a.* lubricating
lubrificateur *a.* lubricating
lubrifier *vt.* to lubricate
lubrique *a.* lewd
Luc (*m.*) Luke
lucarne *f.* skylight, dormer window
lucide *a.* lucid
lucidité *f.* lucidity

luciole *f.* firefly
lucratif *a.* lucrative
lucre *m.* profit, love of profit
luette *f.* uvula
lueur *f.* gleam, glimmer
luge *f.* sled
lugubre *a.* lugubrious, gloomy
lui *pron.* he, him, to him, to her, to it
luire *vi.* to shine, gleam
luisance *f.* shininess, glossiness
luisant *a.* shining, gleaming; glossy
lumière *f.* light, illumination
lumignon *m.* small light; wick
luminaire *m.* luminary; lights, lighting
luminescent *a.* luminescent
lumineux *a.* luminous
luminosité *f.* luminosity
lunaire *a.* lunar
lunaison *f.* lunation, lunar month
lunatique *a.* fantastic; — *m. & f.* lunatic
luncher *vi.* to have lunch
lundi *m.* Monday
lune *f.* moon; clair de — *m.* moonlight; — de miel honeymoon
luné *a.* crescent-shaped
lunetier *m.* optician
lunette *f.* glass, telescope; hole; — de tir telescopic gunsight; — s *pl.* eyeglasses
lunetterie *f.* optician's trade
lustre *m.* luster, gloss; chandelier; 5-year period, lustrum
lustrer *vt.* to gloss; glaze
lustrine *f.* cotton satin
luth *m.* lute
Luthérien *m.* Lutheran
luthier *m.* maker of stringed instruments
lutin *m.* sprite, elf
lutiner *vt.* to tease, torment
lutrin *m.* lectern
lutte *f.* struggle, wrestling
lutter *vi.* to wrestle, struggle
lutteur *m.* wrestler
luxation *f.* dislocation
luxe *m.* luxury
luxer *vt.* to dislocate
luxmètre *m.* light meter
luxueux *a.* luxurious
luxure *f.* lewdness, lust
luxuriant *a.* luxuriant
luxurieux *a.* lustful, lewd
luzerne *f.* alfalfa
lycée *m.* secondary school, junior college
lycéen *m.* schoolboy, student, lycée student
lymphatique *a.* lymphatic
lymphe *f.* lymph
lynchage *m.* lynching
lyncher *vt.* to lynch
lynx *m.* lynx
lyonnais *a.* from Lyons

lyre *f.* lyre
lyrique *a.* lyrical

M

ma *a. f.* my
macabre *a.* macabre, deathly; danse — *f.* dance of death
macadamiser *vt.* to pave with macadam
macaron *m.* macaroon
macaronis *m. pl.* macaroni
macédoine *f.* mixed salad; mixed vegetables
Macédonie *f.* Macedonia
Macédonien *m. & a.* Macedonian
macération *f.* maceration
macérer *vt.* to macerate; se — to mortify the flesh
mâchefer *m.* clinker, dross, slag
mâchelier *a.* molar
mâcher *vt.* to chew
machette *f.* machete
machin *m.* thing, gadget
machinal *a.* mechanical; instinctive
machinalement *adv.* mechanically
machine *f.* machine, engine; — à coudre sewing machine; — à écrire typewriter
machiner *vt.* to machinate, put together, prepare; to handle scenery
machinerie *f.* machinery; machine works; engine room
machiniste *m.* bus driver; (theat.) stagehand
mâchoire *f.* jaw, jawbone
mâchonner *vt.* to munch, chew slowly; mutter, mumble
mâchure *f.* bruise; defect in cloth
mâchurer *vt.* to daub, blacken
macis *m.* mace (spice)
maçon *m.* mason, bricklayer
maçonnage *m.* masonry
maçonner *vt.* to construct with masonry
maçonnerie *f.* masonry; free-masonry
maçonnique *a.* masonic
macrocosme *m.* macrocosm, the Universe
maculation, maculature *f.* macule; spotted sheet; poorly printed sheet
macule *f.* spot, stain
maculer *vt.* to spot, stain
Madagascar *m.* Madagascar
madame *f.* madam, Mrs.
madécasse *a.* Malagasy
Madeleine (*f.*) Magdalen
madeleine *f.* small sponge cake
mademoiselle *f.* miss
Madère *f.* Madeira; — *m.* Madeira wine
madone *f.* madonna
madras *m.* madras
madré *a.* cunning, sly
madrier *m.* thick plank

madrigal *m.* madrigal

madrilène *a.* of Madrid, from Madrid

magasin *m.* store; warehouse; magazine of a rifle; **grand** — department store

magasinage *m.* warehousing

magasinier *m.* warehouse clerk; stock clerk; library stack boy

mage *m.* magus, wizard; **les** — **s, les rois** — **s** the Magi, the Wise Men

magicien *m.* magician

magie *f.* magic

magique *a.* magic

magister *m.* country teacher

magistère *m.* mastery; teaching

magistral *a.* imposing; authoritative; magisterial

magistrat *m.* magistrate

magistrature *f.* magistrate's position; the bench; magistrates

magnanarelle *f.* silkworm raiser; mulberry-leaf picker

magnanerie *f.* silkworm house

magnanime *a.* magnanimous

magnanimité *f.* magnanimity

magnat *m.* magnate

magnésie *f.* magnesia

magnésium *m.* magnesium

magnétique *a.* magnetic

magnétisation *f.* magnetization, magnetizing

magnétiser *vt.* to magnetize

magnétisme *m.* magnetism

magnéto *f.* magneto; **–hydrodynamique** magnetohydrodynamics

magnétophone *m.* tape or wire recorder

magnificat *m.* Magnificat

magnificence *f.* magnificence

magnifier *vt.* to glorify, magnify

magnifique *a.* magnificent

magnitude *f.* magnitude

magnolia *m.* magnolia

magnum *m.* magnum, two-liter bottle

magot *m.* ape, monkey; treasure; grotesque figurine

Mahométan *m. & a.* Mohammedan

mahométisme *m.* Mohammedanism

mai *m.* May

maie *f.* kneading trough

maigre *a.* thin, lean; meager; **jour** — *m.* fast day, meatless day

maigrelet *a.* somewhat thin

maigreur *f.* thinness; meagerness

maigrir *vt.* to make thin; — *vi.* to grow thin, lose weight

mail *m.* mall; public walk

maille *f.* stitch; mesh; link mail; **avoir** — **à partir** to have a disagreement, have a bone to pick (U.S. coll.)

maillechort *m.* German silver

maillet *m.* mallet

mailloche *f.* large mallet

maillon *m.* link of a small chain

maillot *m.* swaddling clothes; tights; swim suit; jersey

main *f.* hand; handwriting; **coup de** — *m.* aid, **de longue** — for a long time; **battres des** — **s** to applaud; **en venir aux** — **s** to come to blows

main-d'oeuvre *f.* manual labor, manpower

main-forte *f.* help, assistance

mainmise *f.* legal seizure

mainmorte *f.* mortmain, perpetual possession

maint *a.* many, undetermined number; **–es fois** on many occasions, often

maintenant *adv.* now, at present

maintenir *vt.* to maintain, support

maintien *m.* maintenance, support

maire *m.* mayor; — **sse** *f.* mayor's wife

mairie *f.* town hall

mais *conj.* but

maïs *m.* corn

maison *f.* house, home

maisonnée *f.* household, houseful

maisonnette *f.* small house

maître *m.* master, teacher; lawyer's title; — **d'hôtel** head waiter

maître-autel *m.* high altar

maîtresse *f.* mistress

maîtrise *f.* mastery; lectureship; choir school; choir boys; master's degree

maîtriser *vt.* to master, control

majesté *f.* majesty

majestueusement *adv.* majestically

majestueux *a.* majestic

majeur *a.* major; of age; *f.* **force** — **e** absolute necessity; — *m.* middle finger; — **e** *f.* major premise

major *m.* (mil.) executive officer of a regiment; medical officer

majoration *f.* increase in price

majordome *m.* majordomo, butler

majorer *vt.* to increase the price

majoritaire *a.* majority, of the majority

majorité *f.* majority

Majorque *f.* Majorca

majuscule *f.* capital letter

mal *m.* (*pl.* **maux**) evil, harm, wrong; pain, ailment; — **de tête,** — **à la tête** headache; — **de mer** seasickness; — **du pays** homesickness; — *adv.* ill, badly; **pas** — **de** (coll.) many, a great deal of

malade *a.* sick, ill

maladie *f.* sickness, illness

maladif *a.* sickly

maladresse *f.* awkwardness, clumsiness

maladroit *a.* awkward

malaga *m.* Malaga wine

malaire *a.* (anat.) of the cheek

Malais *m. & a.* Malay

malaise *m.* uneasiness; indisposition
malaisé *a.* difficult
Malaisie *f.* Malaya
malandrin *m.* vagabond
malappris *a.* ill-bred
malavisé *a.* ill-advised
malaxer *vt.* to mix, knead
malaxeur *m.* mixer; concrete mixer
malbâti *a.* ill-formed; ill-shaped
malchance *f.* bad luck, mishap
malchanceux *a.* unlucky
maldonne *f.* misdeal (at cards)
mâle *a.* male, manly; — *m.* male
malédiction *f.* curse
maléfice *m.* witchcraft
maléfique *a.* harmful, malignant
malemort *f.* violent death, tragic death
malencontre *f.* mishap
malencontreux *a.* unfortunate, unlucky
malendurant *a.* impatient
mal-en-point *a.* in a bad way, badly off
malentendu *m.* misunderstanding
malfaçon *f.* defect
malfaire *vi.* to do evil
malfaisance *f.* evil-doing
malfaisant *a.* harmful; evil-minded
malfaiteur *m.* malefactor, evildoer, criminal
malfamé *a.* ill-famed, infamous, notorious
malgache *a.* from Madagascar
malgracieux *a.* ungraceful
malgré *prep.* in spite of, notwithstanding; — que *conj.* in spite of the fact that
malhabile *a.* awkward
malheur *m.* misfortune; ill luck, bad luck
malheureusement *adv.* unfortunately
malheureux *a.* unhappy, unfortunate, unlucky
malhonnête *a.* dishonest; rude; indecent
malhonnêteté *f.* dishonesty; rudeness
malicieusement *adv.* maliciously
malicieux *a.* malicious
malignité *f.* malignity
malin (maligne) *a.* malicious, malignant; shrewd, sharp; — *m.* devil
malingre *a.* sickly
malintentionné *a.* ill-disposed, evil-intentioned
mal-jugé *m.* miscarriage of justice
malle *f.* trunk; faire une — to pack a trunk
malléabilité *f.* malleability
malléable *a.* malleable
malle-poste *f.* mail coach
mallette *f.* small trunk
malmener *vt.* to mistreat, abuse
malodorant *a.* malodorous, foul-smelling
malotru *m.* uncouth individual
malpropre *a.* slovenly; dirty; improper
malpropreté *f.* dirtiness; impropriety; dishonesty

malsain *a.* unhealthy, unwholesome
malséance *f.* unseemliness; inopportuneness
malséant *a.* unbecoming, unseemly
malsonnant *a.* clashing; unseemly
malt *m.* malt
maltais *a. & m.* Maltese
Malte *f.* Malta
malthusianisme *m.* theory of birth control
maltose *m.* maltose
maltraiter *vt.* to mistreat
malveillamment *adv.* malevolently
malveillance *f.* ill will, malevolence
malveillant *a.* malevolent
malvenu *a.* uncalled for, unwarranted
malversation *f.* embezzlement of public funds
maman *f.* mama, mother
mamelle *f.* breast; udder
mamelon *m.* nipple; hillock
mammaire *a.* mammary
mammouth *m.* mammoth
manager *m.* trainer, athlete's manager
manant *m.* peasant; uncouth individual
manche *f.* sleeve; hose; air shaft; channel; (avi.) wind sock — *m.* handle; — à balai broomstick; (avi.) control stick
Manche, La *f.* English Channel
manchette *f.* cuff; marginal note; headline
manchon *m.* muff; casing, sleeve; mantle of gas light
manchot *a.* one-armed, one-handed — *m.* penguin
mandarine *f.* mandarin orange; tangerine
mandat *m.* mandate; warrant; power of attorney; proxy; order; — poste postal money order; — lettre money order with space for message
mandataire *m. & f.* representative, agent, proxy
Mandchourie *f.* Manchuria
mandement *m.* mandamus; bishop's charge
mander *vt.* to send for; send word
mandibule *f.* mandible
mandoline *f.* mandolin
manège *m.* horsemanship; riding school; mill, treadmill; merry-go-round, carousel; intrigue
mânes *m. pl.* manes, dead souls (Roman history)
manette *f.* handle, lever
manganèse *m.* manganese
mangeable *a.* eatable
mangeoire *f.* manger, crib
mangeotter *vt.* to pick at one's food
manger *vt. & vi.* to eat, eat up; — *m.* food

mange-tout *m.* bean, pea with which pods are eaten

mangeur *m.* eater; wastrel

mangouste *f.* mongoose

mangue *f.* mango

manguier *m.* mango tree

maniabilité *f.* maneuverability; suppleness

maniable *a.* tractable, pliable; supple; maneuverable

maniaque *m. & f.* maniac; — *a.* maniacal

manie *f.* mania; passion

maniement *m.* handling; maneuvering

manier *vt.* to handle; feel; manage; work, use, drive, activate

manière *f.* manner, way; **de — que** so that; **de — à** so as to

maniéré *a.* affected

maniérisme *m.* mannerism, affectedness

manieur *m.* handler, manager

manifestant *m.* demonstrator

manifestation *f.* manifestation

manifeste *m.* manifesto; — *a.* obvious, evident, manifest

manifester *vt.* to manifest, show; — *vi.* to make a demonstration

manifold *m.* notebook; sales book

manigance *f.* intrigue, plot, trick

manigancer *vt.* to plot, scheme, be up to something

Manille *f.* Manila

manille *f.* link; manilla (card game); — *m.* cigar originating in Manila; hat of manilla straw

manioc *m.* manioc, source of tapioca

manipulateur *m.* manipulator

manipule *m.* (eccl.) maniple

manipuler *vt.* to manipulate; wield

manivelle *f.* handle, crank; winch

manne *f.* manna; two-handled basket

mannequin *m.* model, mannequin; fashion model; — **de couturière** dressmaker's dummy

manœuvrabilité *f.* maneuverability

manœuvrable *a.* maneuverable

manœuvre *f.* working, handling (boat); maneuver; (mil.) drill, maneuvers; — *m.* common laborer

manœuvrer *vt.* to maneuver, work; — *vi.* to maneuver

manœuvrier *m.* tactician; able seaman

manoir *m.* manor

manomètre *m.* pressure gauge

manqué *a.* which has failed, who has failed; inadequate; defective; short of the mark

manquement *m.* failing; infraction

manquer *vt.* to miss, fail; — *vi.* want, lack; — **à quelqu'un** to be missed by someone

mansarde *f.* mansard roof; attic; dormer

mansardé *a.* with dormers, dormered

mansuétude *f.* mildness, gentleness, indulgence

mante *f.* mantle; mantis

manteau *m.* coat, overcoat, cloak; mantle

mantelet *m.* short coat

mantille *f.* mantilla

manucure *f.* manicurist

manuel *a.* manual, hand; — *m.* manual

manuellement *adv.* manually, by hand

manufacture *f.* factory; manufacture

manufacturer *vt.* to manufacture

manufacturier *a.* manufacturing; — *n.* factory owner

manumission *f.* manumission, freeing of slaves

manutention *f.* maintenance; handling; manipulation; administration; (mil.) bakery

manutentionner *vt.* to handle, manipulate

mappemonde *f.* world map (global projection)

maquereau *m.* mackerel; pimp

maquette *f.* sketch, design; model; **d'après la — de** designed by

maquignon *m.* horse dealer; (fig.) go-between

maquignonner *vt.* to deal underhandedly

maquillage *m.* make-up

maquiller *vt.* to put on make-up

maquilleur *m.* make-up man

maquis *m.* underbrush, scrub; (pol.) underground unit *or* movement

maquisard *m.* member of the underground

maraîcher *m.* truck farmer; — *a.* of truck farming

marais *m.* marsh, bog, swamp; truck-garden land; — **salants** saltern, salt bed

marasme *m.* apathy; atrophy

marasque *f.* maraschino cherry

marasquin *m.* maraschino liqueur

marâtre *f.* stepmother; cruel mother

maraud *a.* rascal

maraude *f.* marauding; petty thievery from gardens; **taxi en —** cruising taxi

marauder *vi.* to maraud; prowl

maraudeur *m.* marauder

marbre *m.* marble

marbré *a.* marbled, veined

marbrer *vt.* to marble, vein

marbrière *f.* marble quarry

marc *m.* marc, residue; dregs (from wine making); — **de café** coffee grounds; **eau-de-vie de —** brandy made from marc

marcassin *m.* young boar

marchand *m.* merchant, shopkeeper, dealer

marchander *vt. & vi.* to bargain, haggle

marchandise *f.* merchandise

marche *f.* step; march; functioning, running (machine); (mus.) march (fig.) progress **se mettre en —** to start out; **— arrière** reverse motion

marché *m.* market, market place; bargain; deal; shopping, marketing; **bon —** cheapness; **— noir** black market **bon —** *a.* cheap, inexpensive, low-cost

marchepied *m.* stepladder; running board; step of a carriage; (fig.) stepping stone

marcher *vi.* to march, walk; move, function

marcheur *m.* walker

mardi *m.* Tuesday; **— gras** Shrove Tuesday

mare *f.* stagnant pond

marécage *m.* marsh, swamp

marécageux *a.* swampy

maréchal *m.* (mil.) marshal; **— des logis** master sergeant (cavalry, artillery)

maréchale *f.* marshal's wife

maréchal-ferrant *m.* blacksmith

maréchaussée *f.* constabulary, state police

marée *f.* tide; salt-water fish

marelle *f.* hopscotch

marémoteur *a.* tide-powered

mareyeur *m.* wholesale fishmonger

marge *f.* page margin; edge, rim; leeway

margelle *f.* stone rim around a well

marger *vt.* to feed into a press

Margot (*f.*) Marjorie

marguerite *f.* daisy

Marguerite (*f.*) **Margaret**

marguillier *m.* churchwarden, deacon

mari *m.* husband

mariable *a.* marriageable

mariage *m.* marriage, wedding

marial *a.* pertaining to the Virgin Mary

Marie (*f.*) Mary

marié *a.* married; **— m.** bridegroom; **— e f.** bride; **nouveaux — s** *m. pl.* newlyweds

marier *vt.* to marry off; wed, unite; match; **se — (avec)** to get married (to), marry

marin *a.* marine, nautical; **— m.** sailor, seaman

marine *f.* navy

mariner *vt.* to marinate, pickle

marinier *a.* marine; **— m.** sailor, bargeman

marinière *f.* middy, blouse

marionnette *f.* marionette, puppet

maritime *a.* maritime; **gare — f.** boatside railway terminal

maritorne *f.* (coll.) slut, wench

marivaudage *m.* banter, witty patter

marjolaine *f.* marjoram

mark *m.* German mark

marmaille *f.* (coll.) brood of children

marmelade *f.* marmelade, preserves

marmite *f.* pot, pan; **— norvégienne** fireless cooker; **petite —** vegetable soup

marmitée *f.* potful

marmiton *m.* kitchen boy, apprentice cook

marmonner *vt.* to mutter, mumble

marmoréen *a.* marble, marblelike

marmot *m.* lad; youngster

marmotte *f.* marmot; babushka; sample case

marmottement *m.* mumbling

marne *f.* marl; chalk and clay mixture used as fertilizer

Maroc *m.* Morocco

marocain *a.* Moroccan

maroquinerie *f.* leather goods

maroquinier *m.* dealer in Morocco leather goods

marotte *f.* whim, hobby; fool's sceptre; dummy head

maroufle *m.* rascal

marquage *m.* marking process

marque *f.* mark; trademark, brand; score; **— déposée** registered trademark

marquer *vt.* to mark, stamp, brand

marqueter *vt.* to splatter; inlay

marqueterie *f.* marquetry, inlay work

marquisat *m.* marquisate, marquis' lands

marquise *f.* marchioness; marquee

marquoir *m.* sampler; marker

marraine *f.* godmother; sponsor

marri *a.* sorry, grieved

marron *m.* chestnut; **— a.** maroon, brown; **— a. & m.** runaway, fugitive

marronnier *m.* chestnut tree

mars *m.* March

marseillais *a. & m.* of Marseilles, from Marseilles

Marseillaise *f.* Marseillaise, French national anthem

marsouin *m.* porpoise

marteau *m.* hammer; **— pneumatique** air-pressure hammer

marteau-pilon *m.* pile driver

martelage *m.* hammering operation

martèlement *m.* hammering, result of hammering

marteler *vt.* to hammer, pound; (fig.) to torment

martien *a.* martian

martinet *m.* trip hammer; cat-o'-nine-tails, lash; swift

martingale *f.* martingale; **jouer à la —** to play double or nothing

martin-pêcheur *m.* kingfisher

martre *f.* marten

martyr *m.*, **martyre** *f.* martyr

martyre *m.* martyrdom

martyriser *vt.* to martyr, martyrize

marxisme *m.* Marxism

marxiste *m. & f.* Marxist
maryland *m.* Maryland tobacco
mas *m.* farmhouse, country house (southern France)
mascarade *f.* masquerade
mascotte *f.* charm, mascot
masculin *a.* masculine, male
masculinité *f.* masculinity
masochisme *m.* masochism
masochiste *m. & f.* masochist
masque *m.* mask; masked person
masquer *vt.* to mask, conceal
massacrant *a.* disagreeable
massacrer *vt.* to massacre
massage *m.* massage
masse *f.* mass, lump; sledge hammer; mace; group; fund; en — in a body, all at once
massepain *m.* marzipan
masser *vt.* to mass; massage
massette *f.* bullrush; sledge hammer
massier *m.* mace-bearer; seargeant-at-arms
massif *a.* massive, massy; solid; **argent —** *m.* solid (sterling) silver
massivement *adv.* massively
massivité *f.* massiveness
massue *f.* club
mastic *m.* putty
mastiquer *vt.* to masticate; putty
mastoc *m.* heavy metal
mastodonte *m.* mastodon
mastoïdien *a.* mastoid
mastoïdite *m.* mastoid infection
masure *f.* hut: house in ruins
mat *a.* unpolished, dull; — *m.* mate (chess); **être —** to be in check
mât *m.* (naut.) mast
matador *m.* matador
matamore *m.* braggart
match *m.* match, game
matelas *m.* mattress
matelasser *vt.* to pad, stuff
matelassure *f.* stuffing
matelot *m.* seaman, sailor
matelote *f.* fish stew using red wine
mater *vt.* to check (chess); (fig.) to check, overcome
matérialisation *f.* materialization, realization
matérialiser *vt.* to materialize
matérialisme *m.* materialism
matérialiste *m.* materialist; — *a.* materialistic
matérialité *f.* materiality, reality
matériaux *m. pl.* materials
matériel *a.* material, corporeal; — *m.* materials; apparatus; equipment
matériellement *adv.* materially
maternel *a.* maternal; **école –le** *f.* kindergarten

maternellement *adv.* maternally
maternité *f.* maternity; lying-in hospital
mathématicien *m.* mathematician
mathématique *a.* mathematical; **–s** *f. pl.* mathematics
matière *f.* matter, materials, body, subject
matin *m.* morning; — *adv.* early
mâtin *m.* mastiff
matinal *a.* morning, early
mâtiné *a.* crossbred
matinée *f.* morning, forenoon; morning's occupation; afternoon performance; morning dress; **faire la grasse —** to sleep late
mâtiner *vt.* to crossbreed (dogs)
matines *f. pl.* Matins
matineux *a.* early-rising
matinière *a. f.* morning; **étoile —** morning star
matité *f.* dullness
matois *a.* sharp, cunning, foxy
matoiserie *f.* cunning
matou *m.* tomcat
matraque *f.* bludgeon
matraquer *vt.* to club, bludgeon
matriarcal *a.* matriarchal
matrice *f.* matrix; womb
matricide *m. & f.* matricide
matricule *f.* matriculation; — *m.* (auto.) license number; serial number
matriculer *vt.* to register, matriculate
matrimonial *a.* matrimonial
matrone *f.* matron
mâture *f.* (naut.) masts
maturité *f.* maturity, ripeness
matutinal *a.* morning, of the morning
maudire *vt.* to curse
maudit *a.* cursed; very bad
maugréer *vi.* to fume, be angered, grumble
Maure *m. & f.* Moor; — *a.* Moorish
mauresque *a.* Moorish
mausolée *m.* mausoleum
maussade *a.* sulky, sullen
maussaderie *f.* sullenness
mauvais *a.* bad, ill, evil; **il fait — (temps)** the weather is bad
mauve *f.* mallow; — *f. & a.* mauve
mauviette *f.* lark
maxillaire *a.* maxillary
maxima *a. & f.* maximum
maximal *a.* maximal
maxime *f.* maxim
maximum *m. & a.* maximum
Mayence *f.* Mainz
mazout *m.* oil residue
me *pron.* me, to me
méandre *m.* meander; winding
mécanicien *m.* mechanic, machinist;

(rail.) engineer

mécanique *f.* mechanics; — *a.* mechanical

mécaniquement *adv.* mechanically

mécanisation *f.* mechanization

mécaniser *vt.* to mechanize

mécanisme *m.* mechanism

mécène *m.* patron

méchamment *adv.* wickedly, maliciously

méchanceté *f.* wickedness, malice

méchant *a.* wicked, bad; poor, sad, worthless

mèche *f.* wick; fuse; bit, drill; cloth filter; plot; — **de cheveux** lock of hair

mécompte *m.* miscalculation, mistake

méconnaissable *a.* unrecognizable

méconnaissance *f.* lack of appreciation, lack of recognition, lack of awareness

méconnaître *vt.* not to know; disown; ignore

méconnu *a.* unappreciated, unrecognized

mécontent *a.* dissatisfied

mécontentement *m.* discontent

mécontenter *vt.* to discontent

Mecque *f.* Mecca

mécréant *m.* miscreant

médaille *f.* medal

médaillé *a.* decorated; — *m.* decorated soldier, decorated individual

médailler *vt.* to decorate

médaillier *m.* medal collection

médaillon *m.* medallion

médecin *m.* physician, doctor, medic

médecine *f.* medicine; — **aérienne** aero-medicine

médial *a.* median, middle

médian *a.* median; —e *f.* median

médianoche *f.* midnight supper; midnight supper following a meatless day

médiateur *m.* mediator

médiation *f.* mediation

médical *a.* medical

médicament *m.* medicine

médicamenter *vt.* to dose, administer medicine to

médicamenteux *a.* medicinal

médicastre *m.* quack doctor, charlatan

médication *f.* medication

médicinal *a.* medicinal

médiéval *a.* medieval

médiévisme *m.* Medieval studies

médiéviste *m. & f.* medievalist

médiocre *a.* mediocre, moderate; indifferent

médiocrité *f.* mediocrity

médire *vi.* to slander

médisance *f.* slander, scandal

méditatif *a.* meditative

méditation *f.* meditation

méditer *vt. & vi.* to meditate

Méditerranée, Mer — *f.* Mediterranean Sea

méditerranéen *a.* Mediterranean

médium *m.* medium, spiritualist; (mus.) middle voice

médius *m.* middle finger

médoc *m.* Medoc (a Bordeaux wine)

médullaire *a.* medullar

médulle *f.* medulla

méduse *f.* jellyfish

meeting *m.* political meeting, sports meet

méfaire *vi.* to do wrong

méfait *m.* misdeed

méfiance *f.* mistrust, distrust

méfiant *a.* distrustful, suspicious

méfier *v.*, **se** — **(de)** to mistrust, distrust

mégacycle *m.* megacycle

mégalithique *a.* megalithic

mégalomanie *f.* megalomania

mégaphone *m.* megaphone

mégarde *f.* inadvertency; **par** — inadvertently

mégère *f.* shrew, vixen

mégisserie *f.* leather dressing

mégissier *m.* leather dresser

mégot *m.* cigarette butt; cigar stump

méhari *m.* camel

méhariste *m.* camel-mounted soldier

meilleur *a.* better; **le** — best

méjuger *vi.* to misjudge, be mistaken

mélancolie *f.* melancholy

mélancolique *a.* melancholy

mélanésien *a. & m.* Melanesian

mélange *m.* mixture; —s *pl.* miscellany

mélanger *vt.* to mix

mélangeur *m.* mixer

mélasse *f.* molasses

mêlée *f.* conflict; scuffle

mêler *vt.* to mix, mingle; **se** — to mingle, blend; **se** — **de** to meddle in; pay attention to

méli-mélo *m.* (coll.) combination, jumble

mélinite *f.* melinite

mélisse *f.* balm

mellifue *a.* mellifluous

mélodie *f.* melody

mélodieusement *adv.* melodiously

mélodieux *a.* melodious

mélodique *a.* melodic

mélodiste *m. & f.* melodist, composer of melodies

mélodramatique *a.* melodramatic

mélodrame *m.* melodrama

mélomane *m.* music lover

melon *m.* melon; — **d'eau** watermelon; **chapeau** — *m.* derby

melonnière *f.* melon patch

membrane *f.* membrane

membre *m.* member; limb

membru *a.* long-legged, long-armed; with large arms and legs

même *pron.* same, self, itself; — *adv.* same, like; very; even, also; **de** — in the same way; **tout de** — all the same; **de** — **que** as well as; **à** — **de** in a position to

mémento *m.* notebook, memorandum book; résumé, compendium; memento

mémoire *f.* memory, remembrance; — *m.* memorandum; memorial; bill, statement; report, monograph, dissertation; —**s** *pl.* proceedings, reports; memoirs

mémorable *a.* memorable

mémorandum *m.* memorandum, notebook

mémoratif *a.* memorative

mémorial *m.* report; memorabilia

mémorialiste *m.* author of memoirs

mémorisation *f.* memorization, memorizing

menacer *vt.* to menace, threaten

ménage *m.* household; housekeeping; married couple; family; **femme de** — *f.* cleaning woman, maid

ménagement *m.* care, prudence

ménager *vt.* to spare; handle, treat with tact; humor; arrange

ménager *a.* household; sparing, prudent; **arts** —**s** *m. pl.* home economics

ménagère *f.* housekeeper

ménagerie *f.* menagerie

mendiant *m.* beggar; — *a.* begging, mendicant

mendicité *f.* begging; beggars (collectively)

mendier *vt. & vi.* to beg

meneau *m.* (arch.) mullion

menée *f.* plot, intrigue

mener *vt.* to lead, conduct, govern; steer; manage (an enterprise); treat

ménestrel *m.* minstrel

ménétrier *m.* country fiddler

meneur *m.* leader; head, chief

méningite *f.* meningitis

ménopause *m.* menopause

menotter *vt.* to handcuff

menottes *f. pl.* handcuffs

mensonge *m.* lie, falsehood

mensonger *a.* lying, deceitful

menstruation *f.* menstruation

mensualité *f.* monthly payment

mensuel *a.* monthly

mensuellement *adv.* monthly, by the month

mensurabilité *f.* mensurability

mensurer *vt.* to measure

mental *a.* mental

mentalement *adv.* mentally

mentalité *f.* mentality; state of mind

menterie *f.* lie, lying

menteur *m.* liar; — *a.* deceitful, false

menthe *f.* mint

menthol *m.* menthol

mentholé *a.* mentholated

mentionner *vt.* to mention

mentir *vi.* to lie

menton *m.* chin

mentonnet *m.* catch of a lock

mentonnière *f.* chin strap

mentor *m.* mentor, guide

menu *m.* menu; table d'hote, fixed menu; — *a.* small, thin; — **peuple** *m.* lowest class; —**s plaisirs** *m. pl.* pocket money, mad money (U.S. coll.); — *adv.* fine, in small pieces

menuet *m.* minuet

menuiser *vi.* to do woodworking

menuiserie *f.* woodwork; carpentry

menuisier *m.* carpenter, cabinet maker

méplat *a.* thicker on one side

méprendre *v., se* — to be mistaken

mépris *m.* contempt, scorn, disdain

méprisable *a.* despicable, contemptible

méprise *f.* mistake

mépriser *vt.* to despise, scorn, slight

mer *f.* sea; **pleine** —, **haute** — high seas; **basse** — low tide; **d'outre** — oversea; **mal de** — *m.* seasickness

mercanti *m.* dishonest businessman

mercantile *a.* mercantile, commercial

mercenaire *m. & a.* mercenary

mercerie *f.* notions, knick-knacks

merceriser *vt.* to mercerize

merci *m.* thanks; — *f.* mercy; —! thank you; **no thank you;** — **bien!** thank you very much!

mercier *m.* notions salesman

mercredi *m.* Wednesday; — **des Cendres** Ash Wednesday

mercure *m.* mercury

mercuriale *f.* grain market prices; reprimand, rebuke

mercuriel *a.* mercurial

mercurique *a.* mercuric

merde *f.* excrement

mère *f.* mother

méridien *a. & n.* meridian

méridional *a.* southern

mérinos *m.* merino sheep; merino wool

merisier *m.* wild cherry tree

méritant *a.* worthy, meritorious

mérite *m.* merit

mériter *vt.* to merit, deserve; — *vi.* to be deserving

méritoire *a.* meritorious

merlan *m.* whiting

merle *m.* blackbird

merlin *m.* cleaver; club

merluche *f.* dried cod

Mérovingien *m. & a.* Merovingian

merrain *m.* stave; clapboard

merveille *f.* marvel; **à** — wonderfully

merveilleusement *adv.* marvelously, wonderfully

merveilleux *a.* marvellous; wonderful
mes *a. pl.* my
mésalliance *f.* misalliance
mésallier *v.,* **se —** to marry beneath one's station
mésange *f.* titmouse, tomtit
mésaventure *f.* misadventure
mesdames *f. pl.* ladies, women
mesdemoiselles *f. pl.* young ladies; misses
mésentente *f.* misunderstanding
mésestime *f.* poor opinion of someone, lack of consideration, scorn
mésestimer *vt.* to underrate, scorn
mésintelligence *f.* incompatibility, lack of understanding
mésinterpréter *vt.* to misinterpret
mesmérisme *m.* mesmerism
mésopotamien *a. & m.* Mesopotamian
mesquin *a.* stingy, shabby, low, mean
mesquinerie *f.* stinginess, meanness
messager *m.* messenger
messagerie *f.* steamship line; transport line; parcel delivery service
messe *f.* (eccl.) Mass
messianique *a.* Messianic
Messie *m.* Messiah
messieurs *m. pl.* gentlemen, sirs
mesurable *a.* measurable
mesurage *m.* measuring
mesure *f.* measure, proportion; restraint; mean(s); **à — que** *conj.* in proportion as; **sur —** made to order
mesuré *a.* measured, cautious
mesurer *vt.* to measure, consider, calculate; **se — avec** to compete with; compare oneself with
métabolisme *m.* metabolism; **— basal** basal metabolism
métairie *f.* farm of a sharecropper
métal *m.* metal
métallifère *a.* metal-bearing
métallique *a.* metallic
métalliser *vt.* to plate, metallize
métallurgie *f.* metallurgy
métallurgique *a.* metallurgical
métallurgiste *m.* metallurgist
métamorphique *a.* metamorphic
métamorphisme *m.* metamorphism
métamorphose *f.* metamorphosis
métamorphoser *vt.* to transform, metamorphose
métaphore *f.* metaphor
métaphorique *a.* metaphorical
métaphysicien *m.* metaphysician
métaphysique *f.* metaphysics
métapsychique *f.* psychic research
métastase *f.* metastasis
métatarse *m.* metatarsus
métatarsien *a.* metatarsal
métathèse *f.* metathesis

métayage *m.* tenant farming, sharecropping
métayer *m.* tenant farmer, sharecropper
méteil *m.* mixture of wheat and rye
métempsycose *f.* metempsychosis, transmigration of souls
météore *m.* meteor
météorique *a.* meteoric
météoriser *vt.* to distend
météorisme *m.* gas, flatulence
météorite *f.* meteorite
météorologie *f.* meteorology
météorologique *a.* meteorological
météorologiste, météorologue *m.* meteorologist
métèque *m.* foreigner
méthane *m.* methane
méthode *f.* method, system
méthodique *a.* methodical
méthodisme *m.* methodism
méthodiste *m.* Methodist
méthodologie *f.* methodology
méthyle *m.* methyl
méthylène *m.* methylene; (com.) methyl or wood alcohol
méthylique *a.* methyl
méticuleusement *adv.* meticulously
méticuleux *a.* meticulous
méticulosité *f.* meticulousness
métier *m.* trade, profession; loom
métis *a. & m.* half-breed, half-caste
métissage *m.* crossbreeding
métisser *vt.* to cross, crossbreed
métrage *m.* measuring by the meter
mètre *m.* meter; yardstick
métrer *vt.* to measure out by the meter
métreur *m.* surveyor; measurer
métrique *a.* metrical; metric; **tonne —** metric ton (1000 kg.); **—** *f.* metrics
Métro *m.* Paris subway
métromanie *f.* mania for writing verse
métronome *m.* metronome
métropole *f.* metropolis; continental France
métropolitain *a.* metropolitan; **chemin de fer — m.** Paris subway
mets *m.* dish; cooked or prepared food
mettable *a.* wearable
metteur *m.* one who places; **— en pages** (print.) make-up man; **— en scène** (theat.) director
mettre *vt.* to put, place; put on; suppose; **— en drapeau** (avi.) to feather (an engine); **— en vedette** to highlight; **se — à** to begin to
meuble *m.* piece of furniture; **–s** *pl.* furniture
meubler *vt.* to furnish; stock
meuglement *m.* bellow
meugler *vi.* to bellow

meule *f.* millstone; haystack; round, wheel of cheese
meulière *f.* flint
meunier *m.* miller
meunière *f.* miller's wife; **à la —** sautéed in butter
meurtre *m.* murder
meurtrier *m.* murderer; **—** *a.* murderous, dangerous
meurtrière *f.* gun slit
meurtrir *vt.* to bruise
meurtrissure *f.* bruise
meute *f.* pack, band
mévendre *vt.* to sell at a loss
mévente *f.* sale at a loss
Mexicain *m. & a.* Mexican
Mexico *m.* Mexico City
Mexique *m.* Mexico
miasme *m.* miasma, evil odor
miaulement *m.* mew, meow
miauler *vi.* to mew, meow
miche *f.* round loaf of bread
Michel (*m.*) Michael
micheline *f.* (rail.) diesel car *or* train
mi-chemin, à — *adv.* halfway, at the halfway point
micro *m.* microphone
microbiologie *f.* microbiology
microcircuit *m.* microcircuit
microcosme *m.* microcosm
microfilm *m.* microfilm
microfilmer *vt.* to microfilm
micrographie *f.* micrography
micromètre *m.* micrometer
micron *m.* micron, 1-millionth meter
micro-organisme *m.* micro-organism
microphone *m.* microphone
microphotographie *f.* microphotography
microphysique *f.* microphysics
microscope *m.* microscope; **— électronique** electron microscope
microscopique *a.* microscopic
microsillon *m.* record microgroove; long-playing record
midi *m.* noon; south
midinette *f.* seamstress, shop girl
mie *f.* inside part of bread; **pain de — ** *m.* sandwich bread, American-style bread; **ma —** (coll.) my dear, my darling; **—** *adv.* not at all
miel *m.* honey
mielleux *a.* honeyed, honey-like
mien *pron.*, le **—**, la **—**ne mine
miette *f.* bread crumb, bit
mieux *adv.* better, rather; le **—** best; de **— en —** better and better; aimer **—** prefer
mièvre *a.* affected; roguish
mièvrerie *f.* affectedness; roguishness
mignard *a.* nice, delicate, sweet

mignarder *vt.* to indulge, coddle; be over-nice to
mignardise *f.* delicacy, daintiness
mignon *a.* delicate, cute, nice, slight; **—** *m.* favorite
mignonnerie *f.* niceness; cuteness; delicateness
migraine *f.* headache
migraineux *a.* migraine
migrateur *a.* migrating
migratoire *a.* migratory
mijaurée *f.* finicky woman; **faire la —** to be finicky
mijoter *vi.* to simmer
mil *a.* thousand; **—** *m.* millet
milady *f.* lady, wife of a lord; my lady (salutation)
milan *m.* kite (bird)
milanais *a.* of Milan, from Milan
milice *f.* militia
milicien *m.* militiaman
milieu *m.* middle; environment; area; **au — de** in the middle of; **au beau —** in the very middle
militaire *m.* soldier; **—** *a.* military
militariser *vt.* to militarize
militarisme *m.* militarism
militariste *m. & f.* militarist
militer *vi.* to militate, work, fight
mille *m.* mile; **—** *a.* thousand
mille-feuille *f.* napoleon (pastry); milfoil
millénaire *m.* 1000 years; 1000th anniversary; **—** *a.* 1000-year-old
millésime *m.* date
milliaire *a.*, **pierre —** *f.* milestone
milliard *m.* billion
milliardaire *m. & f. & a.* billionaire
millibar *m.* millibar
millième *m. & a.* thousandth
millier *m.* about a thousand; **-s** *pl.* thousands
milligramme *m.* milligram
millimètre *m.* millimeter
millionnaire *m. & f. & a.* millionnaire
milord *m.* lord; my lord (salutation)
mime *m.* mime, pantomime
mimer *vt. & vi.* to mime, mimic
mimi *m.* kitty, pussycat (baby **talk**); darling
mimique *a.* mimetic; **—** *f.* mimicry; pantomime
mimodrame *m.* pantomime play
mimosa *m.* acacia
minable *a.* pitiful, shabby
minaret *m.* minaret
minauder *vi.* to mince, be or act affected, smirk
minauderie *f.* mincing manner; affectedness
minaudier *a.* mincing

mince *a.* thin, slender

minceur *f.* thinness, slenderness, scantiness

mine *f.* look, appearance; mine, excavation; mina (Greek coin); pencil lead; (mil.) mine; **avoir bonne (mauvaise)** — to look well (bad)

miner *vt.* to mine; wear away, undermine

minerai *m.* ore

minéral *a. & m.* mineral

minéralisation *f.* mineralization

minéraliser *vt.* to mineralize

minéralogie *f.* mineralogy

minéralogique *a.* mineralogical

minéralogiste *m.* mineralogist

minestrone *m.* minestrone soup

minet *m.*, minette *f.* (coll.) kitty, pussy

mineur *m.* minor; miner; — e *f.* minor premise

miniature *f.* miniature

miniaturer *vt.* to paint in miniature

minier *a.* mining

minimal *a.* minimal

minime *a.* insignificant, trifling

minimiser *vt.* to minimize

minimum *m.* minimum

ministère *m.* ministry, office; cabinet

ministériel *a.* of the ministry, of the cabinet, pro-government

ministre *m.* minister, secretary (government)

minium *m.* red lead

minoritaire *a.* minority, belonging to the minority

minorité *f.* minority

Minorque *f.* Minorca

minoterie *f.* flour milling

minotier *m.* miller

minuit *m.* midnight

minuscule *a.* tiny; — *f.* lower-case letter

minute *f.* minute, moment; rough draft; original copy

minuter *vt.* to take minutes; limit

minuterie *f.* (elec.) time-switch (which stays on for only a short time)

minutie *f.* minutia; minuteness

minutieusement *adv.* minutely

minutieux *a.* minute; detailed

mioche *m. & f.* (coll.) brat; young child

mi-parti *a.* half

mi-partition *f.* dividing in half

mirabelle *f.* small yellow plum; mirabelle liqueur

miracle *m.* miracle

miraculeusement *adv.* miraculously

miraculeux *a.* miraculous

mirador *m.* watchtower

mirage *m.* mirage

mire *f.* gun sight; aim

mirer *vt. & vi.* to aim at; se — to look at

oneself

mirliton *m.* reed flute; **vers de** — doggerel

mirmillon *m.* gladiator

miroir *m.* mirror, looking glass

miroitant *a.* reflecting, sparkling

miroitement *m.* mirroring, reflection, sparkling

miroiter *vi.* to shine, glisten

miroitier *m.* dealer in mirrors

miroton *m.* onion stew

misaine *f.* (naut.) foremast

misanthrope *m. & f.* misanthrope

misanthropie *f.* misanthropy

miscellanées *f. pl.* miscellanea, miscellany

miscible *a.* miscible, which can be mixed

mise *f.* putting, placing; dress, clothing, appearance; game stake; investment; bid; — **en plis** finger wave; — **en scène** (theat.) direction

miser *vt.* to bet; bid

misérable *a.* miserable; wretched; wicked; poverty-stricken

misérablement *adv.* miserably, wretchedly

misère *f.* misery, poverty

miséreux *m.* pauper

miséricorde *f.* mercy, pardon

miséricordieux *a.* merciful

misogyne *m.* mysogynist

missel *m.* missal

missionnaire *m.* missionary

missive *f.* missive, letter

mistral *m.* cold north wind of Provence

mitaine *f.* mitten, mitt

mite *f.* clothes moth

mité *a.* moth-eaten

miteux *a.* pitiful

mitigation *f.* mitigation

mitiger *vt.* to mitigate, soften

mitonner *vi.* to simmer; — *vt.* to coddle

mitoyen *a.* intermediate, joint, dividing (line)

mitraille *f.* (mil.) grapeshot, canister shot

mitrailler *vt.* to machine gun

mitraillette *f.* tommy gun

mitrailleur *m.* machine gunner

mitrailleuse *f.* machine gun

mitre *m.* miter

mitré *a.* mitered

mitron *m.* baker's boy

mi-voix, à — *adv.* in a low voice

mixte *a.* mixed; école — *f.* coeducational school

mixtion *f.* mixture

mixtionner *vt.* to mix

mnémonique *a.* mnemonic

mnémotechnie *f.* memory training

mobile *m.* spring; motive; — *a.* movable; quick

mobilier *m.* furniture

mobilisation *f.* mobilization, mobilizing
mobiliser *vt.* to mobilize
mobilité *f.* mobility
mocassin *m.* moccasin
moche *f.* skein, hank
modal *a.* (gram.) modal
modalité *f.* modality
mode *m.* (gram.) mood; mode; — *f.* fashion, custom, way; –s *pl.* millinery; **à la** — in fashion; **à la** — **de** . . . in the . . . fashion
modelage *m.* modelling
modèle *m.* model
modeler *vt.* to model
modeleur *m.* modeller
modéliste *m. & f.* model designer
modérantisme *m.* (pol.) moderation in political matters
modérantiste *m. & f.* (pol.) moderate
modérateur *m.* moderator; governor
modération *f.* moderation
modéré *a.* moderate
modérer *vt.* to moderate, regulate, reduce
moderne *a.* modern
modernisation *f.* modernization
moderniser *vt.* to modernize
modernisme *m.,* **modernité** *f.* modernity
moderniste *m. & f.* modernist
modeste *a.* modest
modestement *adv.* modestly
modestie *f.* modesty
modicité *f.* smallness, lowness
modifiable *a.* modifiable
modification *f.* modification
modifier *vt.* to modify
modique *a.* moderate, small in importance, low in price
modiste *f.* milliner, modiste
module *m.* modulus; module; diameter of coins; thickness of bells
moduler *vt. & vi.* to modulate
moelle *f.* marrow; pith
moelleux *a.* pithy; soft, mellow
moellon *m.* small stone used in walls
mœurs *f. pl.* manners, morals, customs, mores
mofette *f.* poison gas
mogol *m.* mogul
moi *pron.* I, me; — *m.* self, ego
moignon *m.* stump, stub
moindre *a.* less, lesser; **le** — least, slightest
moine *m.* monk, friar; warming pan
moineau *m.* sparrow
moins *adv.* less; minus; **au** —, **pour le** —, **du** — at least; **à** — **que** *conj.* unless; — **le** — least; **à** — at a lower price; *prep.* minus, less
moins-perçu *m.* underpayment
moins-value *f.* depreciation, loss of value
moire *f.* watered silk, moire

moirer *vt.* to water silk
mois *m.* month; monthly salary, monthly payment
moïse *m.* cradle, baby basket
Moïse (*m.*) Moses
moise *f.* tie beam, brace
moisi *a.* moldy, musty; — *m.* mustiness
moisir *vt. & vi.* to mildew
moisissure *f.* mold, mildew
moisson *f.* harvest
moissonnage *m.* reaping, harvesting
moissonner *vt.* to reap, harvest
moissonneur *m.,* **moissonneuse** *f.* reaper; (person)
moissonneuse *f.* reaper, harvester (machine)
moite *a.* moist, clammy
moiteur *f.* moistness
moitié *f. & a.* half; **à** — **prix** *adv.* half-price
moitir *vt.* to moisten
moka *m.* mocha coffee; mocha cake
mol *a.* soft
molaire *a. & n.* molar
môle *m.* mole, pier
moléculaire *a.* molecular
molécule *f.* molecule
moleskine *f.* leatherette
molestation *f.* molesting, molestation
molester *vt.* to molest
molette *f.* roller; serrated roller; rowel; trimming tool; edging tool; **clé à** — *f.* adjustable wrench
mollesse *a.* apathetic, flabby
mollesse *f.* softness; flabbiness
mollet *m.* calf of the leg; — *a.* soft; **œuf** — *m.* soft-boiled egg
molletière *f.* legging
molleton *m.* flannel
mollification *f.* mollification, mollifying
mollir *vt. & vi.* to soften, grow soft; give way, slacken
mollusque *m.* mollusk
molosse *m.* mastiff, watchdog
molybdène *m.* molybdenum
momentané *a.* momentary
momentanément *adv.* momentarily
momie *f.* mummy
momification *f.* mummification
momifier *vt.* to mummify
mon *a. m.* my
monacal *a.* monkish
monarchie *f.* monarchy
monarchique *a.* monarchical
monarchisme *m.* monarchism
monarchiste *m. & f. & a.* monarchist
monarque *m.* monarch
monastère *m.* monastery; convent
monastique *a.* monastic
monceau *m.* heap, pile

mondain *a.* worldly; mundane; society; — *m.* society person

mondanité *f.* mundaneness, mundanity, worldliness; **-s** *pl.* social events (newspaper)

monde *m.* world; society; people; **tout le** — everybody

monder *vt.* to clean; husk

mondial *a.* worldwide

monégasque *a.* from Monaco

monétaire *a.* monetary

Mongol *m. & a.* Mongol; **purée -e** *f.* tomato and pea soup

Mongolie *f.* Mongolia

mongolien *a.* (med.) Mongolian

Mongoloïde *a.* Mongoloid

moniteur *m.* monitor

monnaie *f.* money, coin; mint; change; — **légale** legal tender

monnayage *m.* coinage, minting

monnayer *vt.* to coin, mint

monnayeur *m.* coiner, minter

monobloc *a.* in one piece

monochrome *a.* monochromatic

monoculture *f.* one-crop farming

monodie *f.* (mus.) unaccompanied solo

monogame *a.* monogamous

monogamie *f.* monogamy

monogramme *m.* monogram

monographie *f.* monograph

monolithe *a.* monolithic

monologue *m.* monologue

monologuer *vi.* to talk to oneself; soliloquize

monomane, monomaniaque *m. & f.* monomaniac

monomanie *f.* monomania

monôme *m.* student parade, demonstration, snake dance; (math.) monomial

monophasé *a.* (elec.) single-phase

monoplace *a.* in one place; **voiture** — *f.* one-seater

monoplan *m.* monoplane

monopole *m.* monopoly

monopolisation *f.* monopolization

monopoliser *vt.* to monopolize

monosyllabe *m.* monosyllable

monosyllabique *a.* monosyllabic

monothéisme *m.* monotheism

monothéiste *m. & f.* monotheist; — *a.* monotheistic

monotone *a.* monotonous

monotonie *f.* monotony

monotype *f.* (print.) typesetting machine

monovalent *a.* univalent

monseigneur *m.* highness; monsignor; lock pick

monsieur *m.* sir, gentleman; Mister, Mr.

monstre *m.* monster

monstrueux *a.* monstrous

monstruosité *f.* monstruousness; monstrosity

mont *m.* mount, mountain

montage *m.* carrying up; layout; (elec.) wiring; editing (movie film)

montagnard *m.* mountaineer

montagne *f.* mountain

Montagnes Rocheuses *f. pl.* Rocky Mountains

montagneux *a.* mountainous

montant *m.* amount, sum; goal post; upright; side piece of a ladder; odor, taste; — *a.* rising, uphill; high-cut (dress)

mont-de-piété *m.* municipal pawn shop

monte-charge *m.* freight elevator

montée *f.* rise, ascent

monte-plats *m.* dumb waiter

monter *vt. & vi.* to go up, climb, rise; carry up, take up; mount, sit on a horse; to set up; arouse, excite

monteur *m.* mounter

montgolfière *f.* hot-air balloon

monticule *m.* hillock

montmorency *f.* variety of sour cherry

montoir *m.* stepping-stone for mounting a horse

montrable *a.* showable

montre *f.* watch; display, shop window

montre-bracelet *m.* wristwatch

montrer *vt.* to show, exhibit

montreur *m.* displayer; showman

montueux *a.* hilly

monture *f.* mount; setting; frame

monument *m.* monument; curiosity, sight; **visiter les -s** to sightsee

moquer *v.,* **se** — **de** to mock, laugh at; not to care

moquerie *f.* mockery, derision

moquette *f.* velvet carpet, carpeting

moqueur *a.* mocking; — *m.* mocker

moral *a.* moral, ethical; — *m.* state of mind; morale

morale *f.* morals, ethics; morale

moralement *adv.* morally

moralisateur *a.* moralizing

moraliser *vi. & vt.* to moralize; lecture

moraliste *m. & f.* moralist

moralité *f.* morality, morals; moral; morality play

morasse *f.* (print.) final proof

moratoire *m.* moratorium

morave *a. & n.* Moravian

morbide *a.* morbid

morbidesse *f.* morbidezza; suppleness, delicacy of skin (fine arts)

morbidité *f.* morbidness

morceau *m.* bit, piece

morceler *vt.* to break, divide into pieces

morcellement *m.* fragmentation, breaking-up

mordacité *f.* bitterness; corrosiveness
mordancer *vt.* to size, varnish
mordant *a.* biting; corrosive; — *m.* sizing, varnish; bitterness
mordicus *adv.* stoutly, tenaciously
mordiller *vt.* to nibble
mordorer *vt.* to give a russet color to
mordre *vt.* to bite, corrode; — *vi.* to engage, take hold
morfondre *vt.* to chill, freeze, benumb
morganatique *a.* morganatic
morgue *f.* haughtiness; morgue
moribond *a.* moribund
moricaud *a.* black, dark-skinned
morigéner *vt.* to reprimand
morille *f.* morel (edible mushroom)
morne *a.* gloomy, dull, dejected
morosité *f.* moroseness
morphine *f.* morphine
morphinomane *m. & f.* morphine addict
morphologie *f.* morphology
morphologique *a.* morphological
mors *m.* curb, bit
morse *m.* walrus
morsure *f.* bite
mort *f.* death; — *a. & m.* dead, deceased; dummy (at cards)
mortadelle *f.* large Italian sausage
mortaise *f.* dovetail
mortaiser *vt.* to dovetail
mortalité *f.* mortality; death rate
mort-aux-rats *f.* rat poison
mort-bois *m.* deadwood
mortel *a.* mortal, fatal
mortellement *adv.* mortally
morte-saison *f.* off-season
mortier *m.* mortar
mortifère *a.* death-dealing
mortifiant *a.* mortifying
mortification *f.* mortification
mortifier *vt.* to mortify
mort-né *a.* stillborn
mortuaire *a.* mortuary
morue *f.* codfish
morve *f.* nasal discharge; glanders
morveux *a.* one with a clogged or running nose; sick with glanders; — *m.* brat
mosaïque *f.* mosaic
mosaïquer *vt.* to decorate with mosaic tile
Moscou *m.* Moscow
Moscovite *m. & f. & a.* Muscovite
mosquée *f.* mosque
mot *m.* word; **bon** — witticism; **en un** — *a.* briefly
moteur *m.* motor, engine; moving force; (fig.) instigator; — *a.* motivating
moteur-fusée *m.* rocket motor
motif *m.* motive, reason, motif, theme
motion *f.* parliamentary motion
motivation *f.* motivation

motiver *vt.* to motivate, justify
motoculture *f.* mechanized farming
motocyclette *f.* motorcycle
motocycliste *m. & f.* motorcyclist
motorcade *f.* autocade, motorcade
motorisation *f.* motorization
motoriser *vt.* to motorize
mots-croisiste *m. & f.* crossword-puzzle fan
motte *f.* clod; mound; butter pat
motus! *interj.* quiet!
mou, (**mol**, **molle**) *a.* soft, mellow; weak; (fig.) effeminate; limp; muggy; — *m.* edible animal lungs
mouche *f.* fly; speck, stain; bull's-eye; beauty spot; vandyke beard; secret policeman; — **à miel** bee
moucher *vt.* to wipe the nose; **se** — to blow one's nose
moucheron *m.* fly
moucheter *vt.* to spot; polka dot
mouchette *f.* candle snuffer
moucheture *f.* spot; polka dot
mouchoir *m.* handkerchief
mouchure *f.* nasal mucus
moudre *vt.* to grind, mill
moue *f.* pout; **faire la** — to pout
mouette *f.* sea gull
mouffette *f.* skunk
moufle *f.* mitten; block and tackle; — *m.* kiln, furnace
mouflon *m.* wild sheep, moufflon
mouillage *m.* wetting; watering, adulterration with water; (naut.) anchor, anchorage
mouiller *vt.* to wet, soak; water, adulterate; (naut.) heave (anchor); lay (mine)
mouilleur *m.* moistener; — **de mines** minelayer
mouillure *f.* wetting; water spot; wet spot
moulage *m.* molding, casting; grinding
moule *m.* mold, cast; — *f.* mussel
moulé *a.* well-molded, well-made; tight-fitting; — *m.* printed letter, printing
mouler *vt.* to mold, cast
mouleur *m.* molder, caster
moulin *m.* mill; — **à vent** windmill; — **à café** coffee grinder
moulinet *m.* wheel; paddle wheel; reel; turnstile; winch
moulu *a.* ground, powdered
moulure *f.* molding
mourant *a.* dying; fading
mourir *vi.* to die; **se** — to be dying
mousquet *m.* musket
mousquetaire *m.* musketeer
mousqueton *m.* carbine
mousse *f.* (bot.) moss; foam, lather; whipped dessert; — *m.* cabin boy; — *a.*

dull, calm

mousseline *f.* muslin; **pommes —** mashed potatoes

mousser *vi.* to foam, lather, whip; sparkle

mousseux *a.* mossy; foamy; **—** *m.* sparkling wine

moussoir *m.* beater, whipper, eggbeater

mousson *f.* monsoon

moussu *a.* mossy

moustache *f.* mustache

moustiquaire *f.* mosquito net

moustique *m.* mosquito

moût *m.* grape juice, unfermented fruit juice

moutarde *f.* mustard

moutardier *m.* mustard pot; mustard maker

mouton *m.* sheep; mutton; sheepskin; pile driver, rammer, **–s** *pl.* (naut.) whitecaps

moutonné *a.* fleecy; frizzy

moutonner *vt.* to curl; **—** *vi.* to form whitecaps

moutonneux *a.* fleecy; (naut.) whitecapped

moutonnier *a.* sheeplike

mouture *f.* grinding, milling; mixture of wheat, rye, barley

mouvant *a.* moving; shifting; **sable —** *m.* quicksand

mouvement *m.* motion, movement

mouvementé *a.* agitated, animated; hilly, undulating

mouvoir *vt.* to move, propel

moyen *m.* means, way; **au —** de by means of; **—** *a.* middle, intermediate; average, mean; **le — âge** Middle Ages

moyenâgeux *a.* medieval

moyennant *prep.* on condition that, in return for; by means of

moyenne *f.* average

moyennement *adv.* to an average degree

moyeu *m.* hub

muable *a.* mutable, changeable

mucilagineux *a.* mucilaginous

mucosité *f.* mucosity, mucus

mue *f.* moulting, moulting time; adolescent change of voice

muer *vi.* to moult; have an adolescent change of voice

muet *a.* mute, dumb, speechless; **—** *m.* mute

mufle *m.* snout; (fig.) cad, coarse individual

muflerie *f.* coarseness

muge *m.* mullet

mugir *vi.* to bellow, low (cattle); roar; howl (wind)

mugissant *a.* roaring

mugissement *m.* roaring, bellowing; of cattle; howling of wind

muguet *m.* lily of the valley

muid *m.* hogshead

mulâtre *a. & n.* mulatto

mule *f.* mule; backless slipper

mulet *m.* mule; mullet

muletier *m.* mule driver

mulot *m.* field mouse

mulsion *f.* milking

multicolore *a.* multicolored

multiforme *a.* multiform, many-formed

multimillionnaire *m. & f.* multimillionaire

multiplicande *m.* multiplicand

multiplicateur *m.* multiplier

multiplication *f.* multiplication

multiplicité *f.* multiplicity

multiplier *vt.* to multiply

multitude *f.* multitude

municipalité *f.* municipality

munificence *f.* munificence

munificent *a.* munificent

munir *vt.* to provide, furnish; **se — de** to procure, provide oneself with

munitionnaire *m.* commissary

munitions *f. pl.* munitions, stores, supplies

muqueuse *f.* mucous membrane

muqueux *a.* mucous

mur *m.* wall

mûr *a.* ripe, mature

murage *m.* walling, walling up

muraille *f.* outer wall

mural *a.* mural, wall

mûre *f.* blackberry

murène *f.* marine eel

murer *vt.* to wall in, wall up, block up

muret *m.,* **murette** *f.* small wall

muriatique *a.* muriatic

mûrier *m.* blackberry bush; mulberry tree

mûrir *vt. & vi.* to ripen, mature

murmurant *a.* murmuring

murmure *m.* murmur

murmurer *vi.* to murmur; grumble

musaraigne *f.* shrew mouse

musard *a.* dawdling; **—** *m.* dawdler

musarder *vt.* to dawdle

musc *m.* musk

muscade *f.* nutmeg; **fleur de —** *f.* mace

muscadier *m.* nutmeg tree

muscat *m.* muscatel wine, muscatel grape

muscle *m.* muscle

musclé *a.* muscled

muscler *vt.* to develop the muscles of

musculaire *a.* muscular

musculature *f.* musculature

musculeux *m.* muscular, brawny

muse *f.* muse

museau *m.* animal snout, muzzle

musée *m.* museum

museler *vt.* to muzzle

muselière *f.* muzzle
muser *vi.* to loiter, loaf
musette *f.* bagpipe; bag, musette bag; **bal** — dance, small dance, country dance, dance to accordion
muséum *m.* museum, natural history museum
music-hall *m.* vaudeville theater
musicien *m.* musician
musique *f.* music; band
musqué *a.* musk-scented; **rat** — *m.* muskrat
Musulman *m. & a.* Moslem
mutabilité *f.* mutability
mutable *a.* mutable
mutation *f.* mutation
muter *vt.* to transfer; transform
mutilateur *m.* mutilator
mutilation *f.* mutilation
mutiler *vt.* to mutilate
mutin *a.* disobedient, unruly; mutinous
mutiner *v.*, se — to mutiny; be disobedient
mutinerie *f.* mutiny
mutisme *m.* muteness
mutualité *f.* mutualness; mutuality; mutual-aid society
mutuel *a.* mutual
mutuellement *adv.* mutually
myope *a.* nearsighted
myopie *f.* myopia; near-sightedness
myosotis *m.* forget-me-not
myriade *f.* myriad
myriapode *m.* myriapod, millipede
myrrhe *f.* myrrh
myrte *m.* myrtle
myrtille *f.* blueberry
mystère *m.* mystery; mystery play
mystérieusement *adv.* mysteriously
mystérieux *a.* mysterious
mysticisme *m.* mysticism
mystificateur *a.* mystifying; — *m.* mystifier
mystification *f.* mystification, hoax
mystifier *vt.* to mystify, hoax
mystique *a. & n.* mystic
mythe *m.* myth
mythique *a.* mythical
mythologie *f.* mythology
mythologique *a.* mythological

N

nabab *m.* nabob
nabot *m.* small person
nacelle *f.* small boat; (avi.) nacelle
nacre *f.* mother-of-pearl
nacré *a.* pearl-colored, pearly
naevus *m.* birthmark
nage *f.* swimming; rowing; **à la** — by

swimming; **être tout en** — to be soaking with perspiration
nageoire *f.* fin of a fish
nager *vi.* to swim, float; row
naguère *adv.* a short time ago
naïade *f.* naiad, water nymph
naïf *a.* artless, ingenuous, innocent, inexperienced
nain *m. & a.* dwarf
naissance *f.* birth, origin, beginning; **acte de** — *m.* birth certificate
naissant *a.* dawning; incipient
naître *vi.* to be born; arise, come about
naïvement *adv.* naively
naïveté *f.* artlessness, ingenuousness
naja *m.* cobra
nanan *m.* goodies (baby talk); delight; something exquisite
nantir *vt.* to give as security, pledge; provide
nantissement *m.* pledge, security
naphte *m.* naphtha
napoléon *m.* gold 20-franc piece
napoléonien *a.* Napoleonic
napolitain *a. & m.* Neapolitan
nappe *f.* tablecloth, cloth, cover; sheet
napper *vt.* to cover with a cloth
napperon *m.* tea-table cloth; **petit** — doily
narcisse *m.* narcissus
narcose *f.* narcosis
narcotique *a. & m.* narcotic
narguer *vt.* to harrass; flout; jeer at
narguilé *m.* Turkish water pipe
narine *f.* nostril
narquois *a.* sly, cunning; mocking
narrateur *m.* narrator
narratif *a.* narrative
narration *f.* narration, narrative
narrer *vt.* to narrate, tell of
narthex *m.* narthex, vestibule
nasal *a.* nasal; -e *f.* nasal consonant
nasaliser *vt.* to nasalize
nasarde *f.* blow on the nose; affront
naseau *m.* animal nostril
nasillard *a.* nasal
nasiller *vi.* to speak through the nose
nasonnement *m.* nasal voice, nasal speech
nasse *f.* fish trap
natal *a.* native; **jour** — *m.* birthday; **pays** — *m.* native country
natalité *f.* birth rate
natation *f.* swimming
natatoire *a.* pertaining to swimming
natif *a.* native; natural
national *a.* national
nationaliser *vt.* to nationalize
nationaliste *m. & f.* nationalist; — *a.* nationalistic
nationalité *f.* nationality
nativement *adv.* natively, by nature

nativité f. nativity; (eccl.) celebration of the birthday of a saint
Nativité f. Christmas
natte f. mat; braid
natter vt. to weave, braid
naturalisation f. naturalization
naturaliser vt. to naturalize
naturaliste m. naturalist; naturalist author; — a. naturalistic
nature f. nature; character; kind; **d'après** — from nature, from life; **contre** — unnatural; — **morte** still life; **café** — m. black coffee
naturel m. nature, disposition; — a. natural; **au** — plain; **enfant** — illegitimate child
naturellement adv. naturally
naufrage m. shipwreck
naufrager vi. to be wrecked, sink
nauséabond a. nauseating
nausée f. nausea
nauséeux a. nauseous
nautique a. nautical, aquatic
navarin m. mutton stew prepared with turnips and potatoes
navet m. turnip
navette f. shuttle; **faire la** — to shuttle back and forth; — **hélicoptère** helibus
navigabilité f. navigability
navigable a. navigable
navigateur m. navigator
navigation f. navigation
naviguer vi. & vt. to navigate, sail
navire m. ship, vessel
navrant a. heartrending
navrer vt. to grieve, break the heart of
ne adv. no, not; — . . . . **pas** not
né a. born
néanmoins conj. nevertheless, still, yet
néant m. nothingness, nothing
nébuleux a. nebulous, cloudy
nébulosité f. nebulousness, nebulosity
nécessaire a. necessary; — m. necessities of life; kit, set
nécessairement adv. necessarily
nécessité f. necessity
nécessiter vt. to necessitate
nécessiteux a. needy
nécrologie f. necrology, obituary
nécromancie f. necromancy
nécromancien m. necromancer
nécrose f. necrosis
nectar m. nectar
néerlandais a. Dutch
nef f. nave of a church
néfaste a. ill-fated, fatal, harmful
négatif a. negative; — m. (phot.) negative
négative f. negative side (debating)
négation f. negation
négativement adv. negatively

négligé a. neglected, careless, informal
négligeable a. negligeable
négligemment adv. negligently, indifferently
négligence f. negligence
négligent a. negligent; indifferent
négliger vt. to neglect
négoce m. negotiation
négociable a. negotiable
négociant m. merchant, dealer, trader
négociateur m. negotiator
négociation f. negotiation
négocier vt. & vi. to negotiate; trade; deal
nègre, négresse n. & a. Negro; ghost writer; **petit** — m. pidgin French
négrier m. slave ship; slave dealer
négroïde a. negroid
neige f. snow; **battre en** — to beat stiff
neiger vt. to snow
neigeux a. snowy
ne-m'oubliez-pas m. forget-me-not
nénuphar m. water lily
Néo-caledonien m. & a. New Caledonian
néolithique a. neolithic
néon m. neon
neophyte m. & f. neophyte
Néo-zélandais m. New Zealander; — a. of New Zealand
néphrite f. nephritis
néo-platonicien a. neo-Platonic; — m. neo-Platonist
néo-platonisme m. neo-Platonism
népotisme m. nepotism
neptunien a. Neptunian
néréide f. Nereid
nerf m. nerve; sinew, (coll.) tendon; leaf vein
nerveusement adv. nervously
nerveux a. nervous, high-strung; sinewy, vigorous
nervosité f. nervousness
nervure f. leaf rib; nervure, cording of a book binding
net a. clean; clear, clear-cut; net; — adv. flatly, outright; **s'arrêter** — to stop dead; — m., **mettre au** — to put in final form
nettement adv. cleanly; clearly; flatly
netteté f. cleanness, clearness; neatness
nettoiement, nettoyage m. cleaning, cleansing; **nettoyage au sec** dry-cleaning
nettoyer vt. to clean, cleanse, scour
nettoyeur m. cleaner
neuf a. nine; new, fresh
neurasthénie f. neurasthenia
neurasthénique a. neurasthenic
neurologie f. neurology
neurologue, neurologiste m. neurologist
neurone m. neuron

neutralisation *f.* neutralization
neutraliser *vt.* to neutralize
neutraliste *m. & f.* neutralist
neutralité *f.* neutrality
neutre *a.* neuter; neutral
neutron *m.* neutron
neuvaine *f.* novena
neuvième *a.* ninth
neveu *m.* nephew
névralgie *f.* neuralgia
névrite *f.* neuritis
névropathie *f.* nervous disorders
névrose *f.* neurosis
névrosé *a.* neurotic
nez *m.* nose; cape of land; prow; — à — face to face; piquer du — to nose-dive
ni *conj.* neither, nor
niable *a.* deniable
niais *a.* silly; foolish
niaiserie *f.* silliness
niche *f.* prank, trick; niche; — à chien doghouse
nichée *f.* nestful
nicher *vi.* to nestle
nickel *m.* nickel
nickelage *m.* nickel-plating
nickeler *vt.* to nickel-plate
nicotine *f.* nicotine
nid *m.* nest
nidifier *vi.* to make a nest
nièce *f.* niece
nielle *m.* enamel inlay; cereal blight; cockleweed
nier *vt.* to deny
nigaud *a.* simple; — *m.* simpleton, idiot
nigauderie *f.* stupidity
nihilisme *m.* nihilism
nihiliste *m. & f.* nihilist; — *a.* nihilistic
Nil *m.* Nile
nimbe *f.* halo, nimbus
nimber *vt.* to halo
nimbus *m.* numbus cloud
nippes *f. pl.* things, old clothes, possessions
nippon *a.* Nipponese
nique *f.* gesture of scorn; faire la — à to make fun of, scorn
nirvanâ *m.* nirvana
nitouche *f.* apparently *or* falsely innocent person
nitrate *m.* nitrate
nitre *m.* saltpeter, niter
nitreux *a.* nitrous
nitrique *a.* nitric
nitrite *m.* nitrite
nitroglycérine *f.* nitroglycerin
niveau *m.* level; — de vie standard of living; passage à — *m.* level crossing
nivelage *m.* leveling
niveler *vt.* to level

nivellement *m.* leveling
nobiliaire *a.* of the nobility
noble *a. & m. & f.* noble
noblesse *f.* nobility
noce, noces *f.* wedding; faire la — (coll.) to be living it up, living riotously
nocif *a.* harmful
nocivité *f.* noxiousness, harmfulness
noctambule *m. & f.* sleepwalker; person active at night
nocturne *a.* nocturnal
nocuité *f.* noxiousness
nodal *a.* nodal
nodosité *f.* node; knot
nodule *m.* nodule
Noé (*m.*) Noah
Noël *m.* Christmas; veille de — *f.* Christmas Eve
nœud *m.* knot
noir *a.* black, dark
noirâtre *a.* blackish
noiraud *a.* black-haired, dark
noirceur *f.* blackness, darkness
noircir *vt. & vi.* to blacken, darken
noircissement *m.* blackening
noircissure *f.* black spot
noire *f.* (mus.) quarter note
noise *f.* quarrel
noisetier *m.* hazelnut tree
noisette *f.* hazelnut
noix *f.* nut, walnut; — de veau veal shoulder
noliser *vt.* to charter, rent
nom *m.* name; surname; (gram.) noun; au — de in the name of; petit — given name; nickname; — et prénoms full name
nomade *a.* nomadic, wandering; — *m. & f.* nomad
nombrable *a.* countable
nombre *m.* number
nombrer *vt.* to number, count
nombreux *a.* numerous, many
nombril *m.* navel
nomenclature *f.* nomenclature, list
nominal *a.* nominal
nominalement *adv.* nominally
nominatif *m. & a.* nominative
nomination *f.* nomination
nommer *vt.* to name; se — to be called
non *adv.* no, not
nonagénaire *m. & f.* nonagenarian
non-agression *f.* nonaggression
nonante *a.* ninety (in Belgium and Switzerland)
nonce *m.* nuncio, papal legate
nonchalamment *adv.* nonchalantly
nonchalance *f.* nonchalance
nonchalant *a.* negligent, unconcerned
non-combattant *a. & m.* noncombattant

non-conformisme *m.* non-conformity, non-conformism
non-conformiste *a. & n.* nonconformist
non-être *m.* (phil.) non-existence
non-intervention *f.* non-intervention
non-lieu *m.* no grounds for prosecution
nonne *f.* nun; pet de — *m.* apple turnover
nonobstant *prep. & adv.* notwithstanding
non-paiement *m.* nonpayment
nonpareil *a.* peerless, without equal
non-pesanteur *f.* weightlessness
non-réussite *f.* failure
non-sens *m.* nonsense
non-syndiqué *a.* nonunion
non-violence *f.* nonviolence
nord *m.* north
nord-africain *a.* North African
nord-américain *a.* North American
nord-est *m.* northeast
nordique *a.* Nordic
nord-ouest *m.* northwest
normal *a.* normal; école —e *f.* teachers' college
normalement *adv.* normally
normalien *m.* normal school student
normalisation *f.* normalization
normand *a.* Norman
Normandie *f.* Normandy
norme *f.* norm, standard
Norvège *f.* Norway
norvégien *a. & m.* Norwegian
nos *a. pl.* our
nostalgie *f.* homesickness; nostalgia
notabilité *f.* notability; notable
notable *a. & m. & f.* notable
notaire *m.* notary
notamment *adv.* especially
notarié *a.* notarized
notation *f.* notation
note *f.* note, memorandum; mark, grade; bill, invoice
noter *vt.* to note, mark; signify
notice *f.* account, review
notification *f.* notification
notifier *vt.* to notify
notion *f.* notion, acquaintance, slight knowledge
notoire *a.* notorious, well-known
notoriété *f.* notoriety
notre *a.* our
nôtre *pron.*, le (la) — ours
notule *f.* gloss, short note
nouer *vt.* to tie, knot; stiffen; se — to kink, twist; knit
noueux *a.* knotty, gnarled
nouilles *f. pl.* noodles
nourrice *f.* wet nurse
nourricier *a.* nutritive; père — *m.* foster father
nourrir *vt. & vi.* to nourish; nurse; feed; bring up; foster
nourrissant *a.* nourishing
nourrisseur *m.* cattle feeder
nourrisson *m.* infant at the breast
nourriture *f.* nourishment, food
nous *pron. pl.* we, us, to us
nouveau (nouvel, nouvelle) *a.* new, recent; novel, different; de — again, anew
nouveau-né *a. & m.* new-born child
nouveauté *f.* novelty, newness; something new
nouvelle *f.* news; short story
Nouvelle-Écosse *f.* Nova Scotia
nouvellement *adv.* lately, recently
nouvelliste *m.* short-story writer
novateur *m.* innovator
novembre *m.* November
novice *m. & f.* novice
noviciat *m.* noviciate
noyade *f.* drowning
noyau *m.* pit, core, stone; nucleus; (pol.) cell, unit
noyautage *m.* forming of political units
noyauter *vt.* to form political cells
noyer *vt.* to drown; inundate; — *m.* walnut tree
nu *a.* naked, bare, nude; mettre à — to expose; — *m.* nude; nudity
nuage *m.* cloud; — artificiel smoke screen
nuageux *a.* cloudy
nuance *f.* shade, tinge; suggestion
nuancer *vt.* to shade, blend, vary
nubile *a.* nubile, marriageable
nucléaire *a.* nuclear
nucléé *a.* having a nucleus
nucléique *a.* nucleic
nucléon *m.* nucleon
nudisme *m.* nudism
nudiste *m. & f.* nudist
nudité *f.* nudity
nuée *f.* cloud; (fig.) swarm
nuer *vt.* to shade colors in embroidery
nuire *vi.* to injure, harm, wrong, prejudice
nuisible *a.* detrimental, injurious
nuit *f.* night; darkness; (fig.) — blanche sleepless night
nuitamment *adv.* by night, at night
nul *a.* null, void; no, not one; match —, partie —e *f.* tie game, draw
nullement *adv.* not at all, by no means
nullifier *vt.* to nullify
nullité *f.* nullity, nothing, negative quantity
nûment *adv.* openly, frankly
numéraire *m.* coin, coined money, cash
numéral *a.* numeral
numérateur *m.* numerator
numération *f.* numbering
numérique *a.* numerical
numéro *m.* number; issue of a periodical

numérotage *m.* numbering
numéroter *vt.* to number; (print.) page
numéroteur *m.* numbering stamp
numismate *m.* numismatist, coin collector
nuptualité *f.* marriage rate
nuque *f.* nape of the neck
nurse *f.* child's nurse
nutritif *a.* nutritive
nutrition *f.* nutrition
nymphe *f.* nymph
nymphéa *m.* water lily

O

oasis *m.* oasis
obéir(à) *vi.* to obey, comply
obéissance *f.* obedience; compliance
obéissant *a.* obedient
obélisque *m.* obelisk
obérer *vt.* to burden with debt
obèse *a.* obese
obésité *f.* obesity
obi *f.* Japanese sash
obit *m.* memorial service
obituaire *a. & m.* obituary
objecter *vt.* to object
objecteur *m.* objector; — de conscience conscientious objector
objectif *a.* objective; — *m.* lens; objective
objection *f.* objection
objectivement *adv.* objectively
objectiver *vt.* to make objective
objectivité *f.* objectivity
objet *m.* object; subject; (gram.) complement
objurgation *f.* objurgation
oblat *m.* oblate
obligataire *m. & f.* bondholder
obligation *f.* obligation; bond
obligatoire *a.* obligatory, compulsory
obligé *a.* obliged, compelled
obligeamment *adv.* obligingly
obligeance *f.* kindness
obligeant *a.* kind, obliging
obliger *vt.* to oblige, compel; bind
oblique *a.* oblique, slanting
obliquer *vi.* to strike at an angle; go off at an angle, swerve
oblitération *f.* obliteration; cancellation
oblitérer *vt.* to obliterate; cancel (stamp); obstruct
obole *f.* obole, bit; (fig.) penny, red cent
obscène *a.* obscene, smutty
obscénité *f.* obscenity
obscur *a.* obscure; abstruse; of humble birth
obscurcir *vt.* to obscure, darken; s'— to become dark, cloud over
obscurcissement *m.* obscuring, darkening

obscurément *adv.* obscurely, dimly
obscurité *f.* obscurity, darkness
obséder *vt.* to obsess
obsèques *f.* funeral, obsequies
obséquieusement *adv.* obsequiously
obséquieux *a.* obsequious
obséquiosité *f.* obsequiousness
observable *a.* observable
observance *f.* observance
observateur *m.* observer
observation *f.* observation
observatoire *m.* observatory; observation post
observer *vt.* to observe; s'— to be careful, watch one's step
obsession *f.* obsession
obsolète *a.* obsolete
obstacle *m.* obstacle
obstétrical *a.* obstetric(al)
obstétrique *f.* obstetrics
obstination *f.* obstinacy
obstiné *a.* obstinate
obstinément *adv.* obstinately
obstiner *v.*, s'— (à) to persist in
obstruction *f.* obstruction
obstructionnisme *m.* obstructionism
obstructionniste *m. & a.* obstructionist
obstruer *vt.* to obstruct
obtempérer *vi.* to obey, yield
obtenir *vt.* to obtain
obtention *f.* attainment, obtaining
obturateur *m.* (phot.) shutter
obturer *vt.* to close, stop
obtus *a.* obtuse
obus *m.* (mil.) shell
obusier *m.* howitzer
obvier *vi.*, — à to obviate
oc *m.*, langue d'— southern-French dialect, old Provençal
ocarina *m.* ocarina
occasion *f.* occasion, opportunity; bargain; d'— secondhand
occasionnel *a.* occasional; chance
occasionner *vt.* to occasion, cause, bring about, result in
occident *m.* Occident
occidental *a.* Western, Occidental
occipital *a.* occipital
occis *a.* killed
occlure *vt.* to occlude
occlusif *a.* occlusive
occlusion *f.* occlusion
occulte *a.* occult
occupant *m.* occupant; — *a.* occupying
occupé *a.* busy, occupied
occuper *vt.* to occupy; busy; s'— to keep busy; be interested in
occurrence *f.* occurrence; chance happening
océan *m.* ocean

océanide *f.* sea nymph
Océanie *f.* Oceania
océanien *a.* of Oceania, from Oceania
océanique *a.* oceanic
océanographie *f.* oceanography
ocelot *m.* ocelot
ocre *f.* ochre
ocré *a.* ochre-colored
octaèdre *m.* octahedron
octante *a.* eighty (in Belgium and Switzerland)
octave *f.* (mus., poet.) octave; week following a festival
Octave (*m.*) Octavius
octobre *m.* October
octogénaire *m.* octogenarian
octogonal *a.* octagonal
octogone *a.* octagonal; — *m.* octagon
octroi *m.* grant, granting; city tariff; city customs
octroyer *vt.* to grant, accord
oculaire *a.* ocular; — *m.* eye piece of microscope; témoin — *m.* eyewitness
oculiste *m.* & *f.* oculist, ophthalmologist
odalisque *f.* odalisk
ode *f.* ode
odelette *f.* short ode
odeur *f.* odor, smell, scent
odieux *a.* odious, hateful; heinous; — *m.* odiousness, hatefulness
odomètre *m.* odometer, mileage meter
odontalgie *f.* toothache
odorant *a.* odorous, fragrant
odorat *m.* sense of smell
odorer *vt.* to smell
odoriférant *a.* sweet-smelling
odyssée *f.* odyssey
œdème *m.* edema
œdipe *m.* œdipus
œil *m.* (*pl.* yeux) eye; sight; à vue d'— visibly; coup d'— *m.* glance, look
œil-de-boeuf *m.* (arch.) bull's-eye window; oxeye daisy
œillade *f.* ogling, ogle, glance
œillère *f.* eyecup; horse blinder
œillet *m.* carnation; eyelet
œsophage *m.* esophagus
œuf *m.* egg; — à la coque soft-boiled egg; — brouillé scrambled egg; — sur le plat fried egg
œuvre *m.* & *f.* work, working; literary production
œuvrer *vi.* to produce, turn out
offensant *a.* offensive
offense *f.* offense
offenser *vt.* to offend; s'— de to take offense at
offenseur *m.* offender
offensif *a.* offensive
offensivement *adv.* offensively

offertoire *m.* offertory
office *m.* office, function; church service; d'— officially; — *f.* pantry
officiant *m.* officiating priest
officiel *a.* official
officiellement *adv.* officially
officier *m.* officer; — *vt.* to officiate; — *vi.* to say a divine service
officieusement *adv.* officiously
officieux *a.* officious
offrande *f.* offering; (eccl.) offertory
offrant *adj.* & *m.*, au plus — to the highest bidder
offre *f.* offer
offrir *vt.* to offer
offset *m.* offset printing
offusquer *vt.* to cloud; dazzle; offend
ogival *a.* (arch.) Gothic
ogive *f.* Gothic arch; warhead
ogre *m.* ogre
ohé! *interj.* hey!
ohm *m.* ohm
oie *f.* goose
oignon *m.* onion; bunion
oïl *adv.*, langue d'— *f.* Northern French
oindre *vt.* to anoint; (eccl.) to consecrate sacramental oil
oint *a.* anointed; consecrated; — *m.* something that has been consecrated
oiseau *m.* bird; à vol d'— *a.* in a straight line, as the crow flies; vue à vol d'— *f.* bird's eye view
oiseau-mouche *m.* hummingbird
oiseleur *m.* bird trapper
oiselier *m.* bird seller
oisellerie *f.* bird store; bird farm
oiseux *a.* idle, useless
oisif *a.* lazy; idle, unemployed
oisillon *m.* little bird
oisiveté *f.* idleness
oison *m.* gosling
oléagineux *a.* oleaginous, oily
oléandre *m.* oleander
olfactif *a.* olfactory
oligarchie *f.* oligarchy
oligophrénie *f.* mental retardation
olivacé *a.* olive-colored
olivaie *f.* olive orchard
olivâtre *a.* olive-colored, greenish
olive *f.* olive
olivette *f.* olive orchard
olivier *m.* olive tree
Olivier Oliver
olographe *a.* holographic, handwritten by testator
Olympe *m.* Olympus; — *f.* Olympia
olympiade *f.* Olympiad
olympique *a.* Olympic
ombilic *m.* navel
ombilical *a.* umbilical

omble *m.* fresh-water salmon
ombrage *m.* shade; umbrage, suspicion
ombrager *vt.* to shade
ombrageux *a.* skittish; umbrageous, suspicious
ombre *f.* shadow; shade; darkness; ghost; sienna
ombrelle *f.* parasol
ombrer *vt.* to shade
ombreux *a.* shaded, shadowed
omelette *f.* omelet
omettre *vt.* to omit; neglect
omission *f.* omission, oversight
omnibus *a.*, train — *m.* local train
omnipotence *f.* omnipotence
omniprésence *f.* omnipresence
omniprésent *a.* omnipresent
omniscience *f.* omniscience
omniscient *a.* omniscient
omnivore *a.* omnivorous
omoplate *f.* shoulder blade
on *pron.* one, we, they, people
onagre *m.* wild ass
onanisme *m.* onanism
once *f.* ounce
oncle *m.* uncle
onction *f.* unction, annointing
onctueusement *adv.* unctuously
onctueux *a.* unctuous; oily
onctuosité *f.* unctuousness
onde *f.* wave; — ultracourte microwave
ondé *a.* waved, wavy, with wavy lines
ondée *f.* shower, passing storm
ondoiement *m.* undulation; baptism
ondoyer *vi.* to undulate, billow
ondulant *a.* undulant, undulating
ondulation *f.* wave; undulation; — permanente permanent wave
ondulatoire *a.* undulating
onduler *vt. & vi.* to wave the hair; undulate
onéreux *a.* onerous, burdensome
ongle *m.* nail; claw; coup d'— *m.* scratch
onglé *a.* nailed
onglée *f.* numbness, frostbite of the fingers
onglet *m.* tab; boîte à –s miter box
onglier *m.* manicure set; –s *pl.* nail scissors
onguent *m.* ointment
ongulé *a.* having hoofs, nails
oniromancie *f.* dream interpretation
ontologie *f.* ontology
O.N.U. *f.* United Nations
onyx *m.* onyx
onze *a.* eleven
onzième *a.* eleventh
opacifier *vt.* to make opaque
opacité *f.* opaqueness
opale *f.* opal

opalescence *f.* opalescence
opalescent *a.* opalescent
opalin *a.* opaline
opaque *a.* opaque
opéra *m.* opera, grand opera; opera house
opéra-comique opera with alternate songs and spoken dialogue
opérable *a.* operable
opérateur *m.* operator
opération *f.* operation
opérationnel *a.* operational
opercule *m.* cover, lid
opérer *vt.* to operate, effect, perform; s'— to take place; se faire — to undergo an operation
opérette *f.* operetta, musical comedy
ophtalmie *f.* ophthalmy
ophtalmologue, ophtalmologiste *m.* ophthalmologist
opiacé *a.* containing opium
opiner *vi.* to be of the opinion; — de la tête to nod approval
opiniâtre *a.* obstinate, stubborn
opiniâtrer *v.*, s'— to be obstinate
opinion *f.* opinion
opiomane *m. & f.* opium addict
opium *m.* opium
opossum *m.* opossum
oppidum *m.* fortified city
opportun *a.* opportune
opportunément *adv.* opportunely
opportunisme *m.* opportunism
opportuniste *m. & f.* opportunist
opportunité *f.* opportuneness
opposable *a.* opposable
opposant *a.* opposing; — *m.* opponent
opposé *a.* opposing, opposite; — *m.* opposite
opposer *vt.* to oppose; s'— to be against
opposite *m.* opposite
opposition *f.* opposition
oppresser *vt.* to oppress; weigh on
oppresseur *m.* oppressor
oppressif *a.* oppressive
oppression *f.* oppression
opprimer *vt.* to oppress
opprobre *m.* shame, disgrace
opter *vi.* to choose, make a choice
opticien *m.* optician
optimisme *m.* optimism
optimiste *m. & f.* optimist; — *a.* optimistic
optimum *a. & m.* optimum
option *f.* option
optique *a.* optical; — *f.* optics
optométrie *f.* optometry
opulence *f.* opulence
opulent *a.* opulent
opuscule *m.* short work; pamphlet, booklet

or *m.* gold; — *conj.* now
oracle *m.* oracle
orage *m.* electrical storm
orageux *a.* stormy, violent
oraison *f.* oration; prayer
oral *a.* oral
oralement *adv.* orally
orange *f.* orange; — **pressée** orangeade; — *m.* orange color
orangé *a.* orange-colored
orangeade *f.* orange drink
oranger *m.* orange tree
orangeraie *f.* orange grove
orangerie *f.* hothouse for orange trees
orang-outan *m.* orangutang
orateur *m.* orator
oratoire *a.* oratorical; — *m.* oratory, chapel
orbe *m.* orb; sphere
orbital *a.* orbital; **décrire une courbe** **-e** to orbit
orbite *f.* orbit; **décrire une** — to orbit
orchestral *a.* orchestral
orchestration *f.* orchestration
orchestre *m.* orchestra
orchestrer *vt.* to orchestrate
orchidée *f.* orchid
ordalie *f.* ordeal, trial by ordeal
ordinaire *a.* ordinary, common, usual; — *m.* custom, practice; **d'**— *adv.* usually
ordinairement *adv.* ordinarily
ordinal *a.* ordinal
ordination *f.* ordination
ordonnance *f.* order; class; ordinance; prescription; (mil.) orderly
ordonner *vt.* to order, put in order; ordain
ordre *m.* order; **numéro d'**— *m.* serial number; **de premier** — first-class, first-rate; **billet à** — *m.* promissory note
ordure *f.* filth, dirt; excrement; garbage
ordurier *a.* filthy
orée *f.* border, edge
oreille *f.* ear; hearing
oreiller *m.* pillow
oreillette *f.* auricle
oreillons *m. pl.* mumps
ores *adv.*, **d'**— **et déjà** from now on
orfèvre *m.* goldsmith, silversmith
orfèvrerie *f.* jewelry; goldsmith's shop; goldsmith's trade
orfraie *f.* osprey
organdi *m.* organdy
organe *m.* organ
organique *a.* organic
organisateur *m.* organizer
organisation *f.* organization
organiser *vt.* to organize
organisme *m.* organism
organiste *m. & f.* organist
orge *f.* barley; **sucre d'**— *m.* barley sugar

orgelet *m.* (med.) sty on the eye
orgie *f.* orgy
orgue *m.* (mus.) organ; — **de barbarie** barrel organ, hand organ
orgueil *m.* pride
orgueilleusement *adv.* proudly
orgueilleux *a.* proud
Orient *m.* Orient, East
oriental *a.* oriental, eastern
orientation *f.* orientation
orienter *vt.* to orient, direct; **s'**— to become oriented; get one's bearings
orifice *m.* orifice
origan *m.* marjoram
originaire *a.*, — **(de)** native (to)
original *a.* original; eccentric
originalité *f.* originality; eccentricity
origine *f.* origin
originel *a.* original, inherited
orignal *m.* moose
orillon *m.* handle, ear, grip of a bowl
oripeau *m.* tinsel; trash
ormaie *f.* elm grove
orme *m.* elm
orne *m.* ash tree
ornement *m.* ornament
ornemental *a.* ornamental
ornementation *f.* ornamentation
ornementer *vt.* to ornament
orner *vt.* to adorn, ornament
ornière *f.* rut, groove
ornithologie *f.* ornithology
ornithologue *m.* ornithologist
orpailleur *m.* prospector who pans for gold
orphelin *m.* orphan
orphelinat *m.* orphanage
orteil *m.* toe; **gros** — big toe
orthodentiste *m.* orthodontist
orthodoxe *a.* orthodox
orthodoxie *f.* orthodoxy
orthographe *f.* spelling
orthographier *vt.* to spell
orthographique *a.* orthographic, spelling
orthopédie *f.* orthopedics
orthopédique *a.* orthopedic
orthopediste *m.* orthopedist
ortie *f.* nettle
os *m.* bone
oscillation *f.* oscillation
oscillatoire *a.* oscillating
osciller *vi.* to oscillate; hesitate
osé *a.* bold, daring
oseille *f.* sorrel
oser *vt. & vi.* to dare, venture
oseraie *f.* willow grove
oseur *a.* daring
osier *m.* (bot.) willow; wicker work
osmium *m.* osmium
osmose *f.* osmosis
ossature *f.* bones, bone structure; frame

osselet *m.* little bone, osselet; knuckle-bone

ossements *m. pl.* bones

osseux *a.* bony

ossification *f.* ossification

ossifier *vt.* to ossify

ossu *a.* bony

ossuaire *m.* ossuary; bone pile

ostensible *a.* ostensible

ostensoir *m.* monstrance

ostentateur *a.* ostentatious

ostentation *f.* ostentation

ostéomyélite *f.* osteomyelitis

ostracisme *m.* ostracism

ostréiculture *f.* oyster farming

otage *m.* hostage; guarantee

otalgie *f.* earache

otarie *f.* sea lion

ôter *vt.* to take away, take off; remove

otique *a.* pertaining to the ear

ottoman *m. & a.* ottoman

ou *conj.* or; **ou . . . ou** either . . . or

où *adv.* where, on which, when; **d'—** whence, from where; **par —** which way; **— que** wherever

ouaille *f.* member of a spiritual flock

ouate *f.* cotton batting

ouater *vt.* to stuff with cotton batting; pad

oubli *m.* oblivion, forgetfulness, neglect

oubliable *a.* forgettable

oublier *vt.* to forget

oubliette *f.* dungeon, cell

oublieux *a.* forgetful

ouest *m.* west

oui *adv.* yes

ouï-dire *m.* hearsay

ouïe *f.* hearing

ouïr *vt.* to hear

ouragan *m.* hurricane

ourdir *vt.* to plot; weave (intrigue)

ourler *vt.* to hem; **— à jour** to hemstitch

ourlet *m.* hem

ours *m.* bear

Ourse, la Grande — Ursa Major; **la Petite —** Ursa Minor

oursin *m.* sea urchin

ourson *m.* bear club

out *adv.* out; out of bounds (sports)

outarde *f.* bustard

outil *m.* tool, implement

outillage *m.* tools, tool kit; apparatus

outiller *vt.* to tool; furnish, supply

outrage *m.* outrage, abuse, insult

outrageant *a.* insulting, abusive

outrager *vt.* to outrage

outrageusement *adv.* insultingly; outra-geously

outrageux *a.* outrageous; insulting

outrance *f.* excess

outrancier *a.* excessive

outre *adv.* further, beyond; **en —** more-over, besides; **— prep.** beyond; **— f.** goatskin waterbag

outré *a.* overdone, exaggerated

outrecuidance *f.* presumption, conceit

outrecuidant *a.* conceited, self-satisfied

outremer *m.* ultramarine; lapis lazuli

outre-mer *adv.* overseas

outrepasser *vt.* to overtake, go beyond

outrer *vt.* to overdo, exaggerate; anger

ouvert *a.* open; candid; sincere

ouvertement *adv.* openly, frankly

ouverture *f.* opening; beginning; overture

ouvrable *a.* workable, capable of being worked; working; **jour — m.** working day

ouvrage *m.* work, piece of work

ouvrager *vt.* to work on, work over

ouvre-boîtes *m.* can opener

ouvrer *vt.* to work

ouvreuse *f.* (theat.) usher

ouvrier *m.* laborer, worker

ouvrir *vt.* to open

ouvroir *m.* workroom

ovaire *m.* ovary

ovale *a. & m.* oval

ovarien *a.* ovarian

ovation *f.* ovation

ovationner *vt.* to applaud, give an ovation to

ove *m.* egg, egg-shaped ornament; ovum

ové *a.* egg-shaped

oviducte *m.* oviduct

ovin *a.* ovine

ovipare *a.* oviparous

ovoïde *a.* ovoid

ovulation *f.* ovulation

ovule *m.* ovule

oxalide *f.* oxalis

oxalique *a.* oxalic

oxhydrique *a.* oxyhydric

oxyacétylénique *a.* oxyacetylene

oxydant *a.* oxidizing; **— m.** oxidizer

oxygène *m.* oxygen

oxyure *f.* tapeworm

P

pacage *m.* pasture

pacager *vt.* to put to pasture

pachyderme *m.* pachyderme

pacificateur *m.* pacifier; **— a.** pacifying

pacification *f.* pacifying

pacifier *vt.* to pacify, appease

pacifique *a.* peaceful; mild

pacifisme *m.* pacifism

pacifiste *m.* pacifist; **— a.** pacifistic

pacotille *f.* cheap merchandise, trash

pacte *m.* pact

pactiser *vi.* to make a pact; compromise

pactole *m.* source of great wealth

padou *m.* narrow tape

Padoue *f.* Padua

pagaie *f.* paddle

pagaille, pagaye *f.* disorder, confusion

paganisme *m.* paganism

pagayer *vt. & vi.* to paddle

pagayeur *m.* paddler

page *f.* page; (fig.) epoch; **à la —** up to date; **— m.** page boy (court)

pagination *f.* pagination

paginer *vt.* to paginate

pagne *m.* loincloth

pagode *f.* pagoda

paie *f.* pay; paying off; salary

paiement *m.* payment, paying

païen *m. & a.* pagan, heathen

paierie *f.* paymaster's office

paillard *a.* lecherous

paillasse *f.* straw mattress; **— m.** pagliaccio, clown

paillasson *m.* straw mat

paille *f.* straw; flaw; **— de fer** steel wool; **tirer à la courte —** to draw straws

pailler *vt.* to cover with straw

pailleté *a.* spangled, sequined

pailleter *vt.* to spangle

paillette *f.* sequin, spangle; gold nugget; flake

paillon *m.* spangle; straw basket; straw wrapping (of a bottle); large gold nugget

pain *m.* bread, loaf; **petit —** roll

pair *m.* peer, equal; equality; **au —** at par; without salary, with board and lodging in exchange for services; **— a.** even, equal; **nombre — m.** even number; **de — adv.** on the same level

paire *f.* pair

pairesse *f.* peeress

paisible *a.* peaceable; peaceful, calm

paître *vi.* to browse; **— vt.** to put to pasture

paix *f.* peace, quiet

pal *m.* stake; pale

palabre *f.* talk, conference

paladin *m.* paladin, knight

palais *m.* palace; (anat.) palate; **— de justice** courthouse

palan *m.* block of a pulley; tackle

palanche *f.* yoke

palanque *f.* stockade

palanquin *m.* palanquin

palatalisation *f.* palatalization

pale *f.* post, stake, pale; (mech.) blade

pâle *a.* pale, wan, pallid

palefrenier *m.* horse's groom

palefroi *m.* palfrey; parade horse (Middle Ages)

paléographie *f.* paleography

paléolithique *a.* paleolithic

paleron *m.* part of an animal's shoulder; cut of meat

palestinien *a. & m.* Palestinian

palet *m.* quoit

paletot *m.* topcoat, overcoat

palette *f.* pallette; paddle; oar blade

palétuvier *m.* mangrove

pâleur *f.* paleness, pallor

palier *m.* landing of a staircase; (fig.) level; degree

palindrome *m.* palindrome

palinodie *f.* retraction

pâlir *vi.* to turn pale, wane: fade; **— vt.** make pale

palis *m.* picket; picket fence; pale, enclosure

palissade *f.* fence, fencing; palisade; stockade

palissader *vt.* to fence in, enclose; palisade

palliatif *a. & m.* palliative

pallier *vt.* to palliate, alleviate

palmarès *m.* list of honors and awards

palme *f.* palm; palm tree; **-s** *pl.* honors *or* insignia

palmé *a.* palmate; web-footed

palmeraie *f.* palm grove

palmette *f.* (arch.) palm-leaf design

palmier *m.* palm tree

palmiste *m.* palmetto

palombe *f.* wood pigeon

palourde *f.* clam

palpable *a.* palpable, obvious

palpe *f.* feeler, palp of an insect

palper *vt.* to feel with the hand

palpitation *f.* palpitation

palpiter *vi.* to palpitate; flutter; thrill

paludéen *a.* pertaining to marshes or swamps; **fièvre -ne** *f.* malaria

paludisme *m.* malaria

pâmer *v.,* **se —** to be overcome, faint; be excessively happy

pâmoison *f.* faint, fainting

pamphlet *m.* lampoon, satire

pamphlétaire *m.* lampooner, pamphleteer

pamplemousse *f.* grapefruit

pampre *m.* branch of a fruit vine

pan *m.* section, piece; flap; wall panel; **— interj.** bang!

panacée *f.* panacea

panache *m.* decorative plume, stripe; swagger

panaché *a.* plumed; streaky; varied

panacher *vt.* to plume; decorate with different colors

panais *m.* parsnip

Panama *m.* Panama; Panama hat

panaméricain *a.* Pan-american

pancarte *f.* placard, sign, folder

panchromatique *a.* panchromatic
pancréas *m.* pancreas
panda *m.* panda
pandémonium *m.* pandemonium
pandit *m.* pundit
pané *a.* breaded
panégyrique *m.* panegyric, eulogy
paner *vt.* to bread
panerée *f.* basketful
panier *m.* basket; hoop skirt
panique *f.* panic
panne *f.* breakdown, failure; lard; plush;
   être en — to be out of order, not to
   work
panneau *m.* wood panel; trap, snare;
   (naut.) hatch
panneton *m.* window catch
panoplie *f.* suit of armor; panoply
panoramique *a.* panoramic
panse *f.* paunch, (coll.) belly
pansement *m.* bandage, dressing
panser *vt.* to bandage, dress
pantalon *m.* pair of pants, trousers
panteler *vi.* to pant
panthéisme *m.* pantheism
panthéiste *m.* pantheist; — *a.* pantheistic
panthéon *m.* pantheon
panthère *f.* panther, leopard, jaguar
pantin *m.* puppet; jumping jack
pantographe *m.* pantograph
pantomime *f.* pantomime; — *m.* pantomimist
pantoufle *f.* house slipper
panure *f.* bread crumbs
paon *m.* peacock
paonner *vi.* to strut
papal *a.* papal
papauté *f.* papacy
pape *m.* pope
paperasse *f.* old paper
paperasserie *f.* red tape
papeterie *f.* paper mill; stationery; stationery store
papetier *m.* stationer; papermaker
papier *m.* paper; — à lettres stationery;
   — hygiénique toilet tissue; — peint
   wallpaper; — de soie tissue paper; —
   de verre sandpaper
papier-cuir *m.* imitation leather, leatherette
papille *f.* papilla
papillon *m.* butterfly; leaflet; amendment;
   — de nuit moth; nœud — *m.* bow tie
papillonner *vi.* to flit, flutter
papillote *f.* curlpaper
papillotement *m.* fluttering, flickering
papilloter *vi.* to flicker, twinkle; glitter
papoter *vi.* to talk, chatter, gossip
paprika *m.* paprika
papule *f.* papule, rash, blemish

papyrus *m.* papyrus
Pâque *f.* Passover
paquebot *m.* liner, ship; mail boat
Pâques *f. pl.* Easter
paquet *m.* bundle, parcel, pack
paquetage *m.* packaging
paqueter *vt.* to bale, package, tie up
par *prep.* by, through; by means of; per;
   in; on; finir — (faire quelque chose) to
   end up doing something; — ici this way;
   — là that way; — où? which way?
   — trop much too much
parabole *f.* parable; parabola
parachever *vt.* to complete to perfection
parachutage *m.* parachuting, air-drop
parachute *m.* parachute; — de traînage
   drogue
parachuter *vt.* to parachute
parachutiste *m.* parachutist, paratrooper;
   — du corps médecin paramedic
parade *f.* display, show, pomp; parade
parader *vi.* to display, show off; parade
paradis *m.* paradise; (theat.) gallery
paradisier *m.* bird of paradise
paradoxe *m.* paradox
paradoxal *a.* paradoxical
parafe *m.* initials; flourish
parafer *vt.* to initial; sign
paraffine *f.* paraffin
paraffiner *vt.* to coat with paraffin
parage *m.* trimming, paring; lineage, birth
   –s *m. pl.* ocean localities, vicinity
paragraphe *m.* paragraph
paraître *vi.* to appear, seem; be apparent;
   be published
parallèle *a. & m.* parallel
parallélogramme *m.* parallelogram
paralogisme *m.* fallacy
paralysant *a.* paralyzing
paralyser *vt.* to paralyze
paralysie *f.* paralysis; — agitante shaking
   palsy; — cérébrale cerebral palsy
paralytique *a. & n.* paralytic
paramécie *f.* (zool.) paramecium
paramètre *m.* parameter
paramilitaire *a.* paramilitary
parangon *m.* paragon, model, example
paranoïa *f.* paranoia
parapet *m.* parapet
paraphrase *f.* paraphrase
paraphraser *vt.* to paraphrase; stretch
paraplégique *a.* paraplegic
parapluie *m.* umbrella
parapsychologie *f.* parapsychology
parasite *m.* parasite; –s *pl.* (coll.) static
parasitaire, parasitique *a.* parasitic
parasol *m.* parasol
paratonnerre *m.* lightning rod
paravent *m.* folding screen
parc *m.* park; grounds; parking space;

parcage *m.* parking
parcelle *f.* piece; plot, parcel, lot; bit, scrap
parceller *vt.* to divide into parcels
parce que *conj.* because
parchemin *m.* parchment
parcimonie *f.* parsimony
parcimonieux *a.* parsimonious; sparing; stingy
parcourir *vt.* to travel over; (fig.) run through, read over
parcours *m.* trip, distance; route, course
par-dessous *adv. & prep.* under, underneath
pardessus *m.* overcoat, topcoat
par-dessus *adv. & prep.* over, on top of
pardon *m.* pardon, forgiveness
pardonnable *a.* pardonnable, forgivable
pardonner *vt.* to pardon, forgive
paré *a.* dressed up; adorned
pare-boue *m.* mudguard
pare-brise *m.* windshield
pare-bruit *m.* (auto.) muffler
pare-chocs *m.* (auto.) bumper
pare-étincelles *m.* fire-screen
parégorique *a. & m.* paregoric
pareil (pareille) *a.* like, alike; equal, same; similar; such; — *m.* equal, peer, like; **sans** — without equal, peerless
pareillement *adv.* similarly; in the same way; also
parement *m.* adornment, ornament; ornamentation; curb; facing of outer wall
parent *m.* relative, relation; **-s** *pl.* parents; family, relatives
parentage *m.* parentage, lineage; family, relatives
parenté *f.* relationship; relatives
parenthèse *f.* parenthesis, parenthetical phrase; **en -s** *adv.* parenthetically
parer *vt.* to adorn; trim; prepare; parry, avoid; **se** — to adorn oneself; dress up
pare-soleil *m.* visor, shade
paresse *f.* laziness
paresseux *a.* lazy; sluggish, slow
parfaire *vt.* to perfect
parfait *a.* complete, perfect; absolute; — *m.* (gram.) perfect tense
parfaitement *a.* completely, perfectly; absolutely, certainly
parfois *adv.* sometimes
parfum *m.* perfume, scent, fragrance
parfumer *vt.* to perfume, scent
pari *m.* wager, bet
paria *m.* pariah, outcast
parier *vt.* to bet, wager
parieur *m.* bettor
Paris *m.* Paris
parisien *a. & m.* Parisian
parité *f.* parity, equality

parjure *a.* perjured; — *m.* perjury; perjurer
parjurer *vt.*, **se** — to perjure oneself, commit perjury
parking *m.* garage, parking place
parlant *a.* speaking; expressive
parlé *a.* spoken
parlement *m.* parliament; court
parlementaire *a.* parliamentary; **drapeau** — *m.* flag of truce
parlementer *vi.* to confer, parley
parler *vi.* to speak, talk; **entendre** — **de** to hear about; — *m.* speech, language
parleur *m.* speaker, talker
parloir *m.* parlor
Parme *f.* Parma
parmesan *a.* from Parma; — *m.* Parmesan cheese
parmi *prep.* among
parnassien *a. & m.* Parnassian
parodie *f.* parody
parodier *vt.* to parody
paroi *f.* partition, wall; (anat.) lining
paroisse *f.* parish
paroissial *a.* parochial, parish
paroissien *m.* parishioner; prayer-book
parole *f.* word, spoken word, parole, promise; speech, speaking; **avoir la** — to be speaking, have the floor
paroxysme *m.* paroxysm
Parque *f.*, **les -s** *pl.* the Fates
parquer *vt.* to pen up; park
parquet *m.* floor, flooring; court, bar of justice; pit, trading floor
parqueter *vt.* to parquet a floor
parqueterie *f.* parquet floor, inlaid floor
parrain *m.* godfather; sponsor
parricide *m. & f.* parricide
parsemer *vt.* to strew, scatter; intersperse
part *f.* portion, share; **à** — aside; peculiar; **autre** — elsewhere; **de** — **et d'autre** on both sides; **nulle** — nowhere; **quelque** — somewhere; **de ma** — from me; for me; **de la** — **de** on behalf of; **d'une** — on one hand; **d'autre** — on the other hand; **faire** — **de** to announce; inform, notify
partage *m.* share, portion; sharing, dividing
partager *vt.* to share, divide
partance *f.* (naut.) leaving, departure, sailing; **en** — **pour** bound for
partant *conj.* therefore; consequently
partenaire *m. & f.* partner
parterre *m.* flower bed; (theat.) orchestra, rear of orchestra, audience
parti *m.* party, faction, cause; decision; profit; match, prospective husband or wife; **du** — **de** on the side of; **prendre son** — to make up one's mind; — **pris**

prejudice; closed mind; **prendre le —
de** to take the side of; to decide to;
tirer — de to take advantage of
partialement adv. partially, in a prejudiced manner
partialité f. prejudice, partiality
participant m. participant
participation f. participation; sharing
participe m. participle
participer vi. to participate, share
participial a. participial
particulariser vt. to specify; go into detail
about
particularité f. particularity; peculiarity;
particular, detail
particule f. particle; **— bêta** beta particle
particulier a. particular; special; peculiar; characteristic; private, personal;
en — privately; **— m.** individual, private party
particulièrement adv. particularly, especially
partie f. part, portion; game, match; party
(law); **— civile** plaintiff; **en —** in part,
partly; **en grande —** for the most part
partiel a. partial, part, incomplete
partiellement adv. partially, in part
partir vi. to depart, leave, go away; start,
come, emanate; come off; go off (gun);
à — d'aujourd'hui from this day on;
— à l'anglaise to take French leave
partisan m. partisan; believer, follower
partitif a. partitive
partition f. division; (mus.) score
partout adv. everywhere; **— ailleurs** anywhere else
parure f. dress, ornament; decoration;
necklace
parution f. appearance of a published
work
parvenir vi. to arrive, reach; manage, succeed
parvenu m. upstart
parvis m. church square
pas m. step, footstep, pace; threshold;
narrow passage; defile; (fig.) precedence; **faux —** stumble, slip, mistake;
mauvais — scrape, difficulty; **— de
ce —** immediately; **à — de loup**
stealthily; **— à —** step by step, slowly
pas adv. no, not, none; **— du tout** not at
all; **— mal de** many, quite a few
Pas de Calais m. Straits of Dover
pascal a. (eccl.) Paschal
passable a. passable, fair
passage m. passage; passing; voyage;
crossing; **droit de — m.** right of way;
— clouté crosswalk
passager a. transient, transitory, fleeting,

momentary; migratory (bird); **— m.**
passenger
passant m. passer-by
passavant m. (naut.) gangway; pass,
permit
passe f. pass; passing; permit; fencing
thrust; **mauvaise —** difficult situation
passé a. past, over, gone by; **— m.** past
time; (gram.) past tense
passement m. braid, lace
passementerie f. braid or lace trimming
passe-partout m. skeleton key, master key
passe-passe m. sleight of hand, magic
passepoil m. braid, braiding
passeport m. passport
passer vi. to pass, go by; go over; go
through; pass away; pass on; **— vt.** to
pass; exceed, go beyond; strain; go
over, pass over, cross; hand, give; put;
put on; spend time; sign an agreement;
se — to happen, occur, go on; go by;
pass away; **se — de** to do without
passereau m. sparrow
passerelle f. foot bridge
passe-temps m. pastime
passe-thé m. tea strainer
passeur m. ferryman
passible a. liable, subject
passif a. passive; **— m.** passive; (com.)
liabilities, debt
passion f. passion
passionnant a. exciting, moving, thrilling
passionnel a. pertaining to passion(s);
crime — m. crime committed in the
heat of jealousy
passionner vt. to excite; impassion; thrill
passivité f. passivity
passoire f. strainer
pastel m. pastel color or drawing
pastèque f. watermelon
pasteur m. shepherd; pastor, minister
pasteuriser vt. to pasteurize
pastiche m. parody, pastiche, imitation
pasticher vt. to parody, imitate
pastille f. drop, candy; cough drop; rubber patch
pastoral a. pastoral
pat m. stalemate
patate f. sweet potato; (coll.) potato
pataud a. & m. clumsy person
pataugeage, pataugement m. floundering
patauger vi. to flounder; splash, wade
pâte f. paste, dough; pasta, spaghetti products; **— dentifrice** toothpaste
pâté m. pâté of meat; ink blot; clump;
block of houses
pâtée f. mash for animals
patelinage m. glib talk, smooth talk
patenôtre f. Lord's prayer
patent a. patent, obvious, clear

patente *f.* license, permit, certification, authorization
patenter *vt.* to license, authorize
patère *f.* clothing peg; curtain hook
paterne *a.* benevolent, kindly
paternel *a.* paternal; fatherly
paternité *f.* paternity, fatherhood
pâteux *a.* pasty; thick
pathétique *a.* pathetic; — *m.* pathos
pathologie *f.* pathology
pathologiste *m.* pathologist
patiemment *adv.* patiently
patience *f.* patience; jeu de — *m.* jigsaw puzzle; solitaire (cards)
patient *a.* patient; — *m.* patient
patienter *vi.* to have patience, be patient
patin *m.* skate; runner; brake shoe; –s à roulettes roller skates
patine *f.* patina
patiner *vi.* to skate; slip
patinette *f.* child's scooter
patineur *m.* skater
patinoire *f.* skating rink
pâtir *vi.* to suffer
pâtis *m.* pasture
pâtisser *vi.* to make pastry
pâtisserie *f.* pastry; pastry shop
pâtissier *m.* pastry cook, baker of cake and pastry
patois *m.* dialect; jargon
patouiller *vi.* to flounder in mud
pâtre *m.* shepherd
Patrice (*m.*) Patrick
patricien *a. & m.* patrician
patrie *f.* native country
patrimoine *m.* patrimony
patrimonial *a.* patrimonial
patriote *a.* patriotic; — *n.* patriot
patriotique *a.* patriotic
patriotisme *m.* patriotism
patron *m.* patron; employer, boss, chief, proprietor; skipper; pattern; — à jour stencil
patronage *m.* patronage; church social group
patronal *a.* pertaining to employers; pertaining to a patron saint
patronne *f.* patroness; owner, proprietress
patronner *vt.* to patronize, support; pattern; stencil
patrouiller *vi.* to patrol
patrouilleur *m.* soldier on patrol; patrol boat
patte *f.* paw, foot; tab, strap; à quatre –s four-footed; on all fours
patte-d'oie *f.* wrinkle, crow's foot
pâturage *m.* pasture, grazing
pâture *f.* feed, fodder; pasture
pâturer *vi. & vt.* to graze, feed
paume *f.* palm of the hand; jeu de — *m.*

tennis court (history)
paumer *vt.* to strike, slap with the palm
paupière *f.* eyelid
pause *f.* pause, stop, respite, interval; (mus.) rest
pauser *vi.* to pause
pauvre *a.* poor; wretched, unfortunate; — *n.* poor person
pauvresse *f.* poor woman, beggar
pauvreté *f.* poverty, poorness
pavage *m.* pavement; paving
pavaner *v.*, se — *vi.* to strut, parade
pavé *m.* pavement; slab, block of paving stone; street; sidewalk
paver *vt.* to pave
pavillon *m.* pavillion; lodge; flag; — de golf golf clubhouse
pavoiser *vt.* to trim, adorn with bunting
pavot *m.* poppy
payable *a.* payable
payant *a.* paying; — *m.* payer
paye *f.* wages, pay
payement *m.* payment
payer *vt.* to pay, pay for, pay back; treat; se — to treat oneself to
payeur *m.* payer; bursar; bank teller; paymaster
pays *m.* country, land, region; avoir le mal du — to be homesick
paysage *m.* landscape; scenery; countryside
paysagiste *m. & f.* landscape painter
paysan *m.* peasant
paysannerie *f.* peasantry
Pays-Bas *m. pl.* Netherlands
péage *m.* toll; pont à — *m.* toll bridge
péan *m.* paean
peau *f.* skin, hide; pelt; peel; à fleur de — skin-deep
Peau-Rouge *m.* Indian, redskin
pécari *m.* peccary
pechblende *f.* pitchblende
pêche *f.* peach; fishing
pêcher *vt.* to fish, fish up, catch; — *m.* peach tree
pécher *vi.* to sin
pécheress *f.* sinner; trespasser; — *a.* sinning
pêcherie *f.* fishery
pêcheur *m.* angler, fisherman; fishing boat
pécheur *m.* sinner
pectine *f.* pectin
pectoral *a. & m.* pectoral
péculat *m.* embezzlement
péculateur *m.* embezzler
pécule *m.* nest egg, savings
pécuniaire *a.* pecuniary
pédagogique *a.* pedagogic(al)
pédagogue *m.* pedagogue
pédale *f.* pedal; frein à — *m.* foot brake;

— **d'embrayage** (auto.) clutch
pédaler *vi.* to pedal
pédaleur *m.* bicyclist
pédant *a.* pedantic; — *m.* pedant
pédanterie *f.*, **pédantisme** *m.* pedantry
pédantesque *a.* pedantic
pédestre *a.* pedestrian
pédiatre *m.* pediatrician
pédiatrie *f.* pediatrics
pédicure *m.* chiropodist
pedigree *m.* pedigree
peigne *m.* comb
peigné *a.* combed; **bien** — well-groomed; **mal** — unkempt
peigner *vt.* to comb, card wool; (coll.) beat, thrash; **se** — to comb one's hair
peignoir *m.* dressing gown, wrapper
peindre *vt.* to paint, portray, depict
peine *f.* pain, punishment, penalty; difficulty; trouble; **à** — hardly, scarcely; **faire de la** — à to trouble, disturb, distress; **se donner (de) la** — to take the trouble
peiner *vt.* to pain, trouble, distress; — *vi.* to work hard, struggle, labor
peintre *m.* painter; artist; — **en bâtiments** house painter
peinture *f.* painting; paint; picture
peinturer *vt.* to paint, coat with paint
péjoratif *a.* pejorative
péjorativement *adv.* pejoratively
pekinois *m.* Pekinese
pelage *m.* fur, coat of an animal; skinning
pelé *a.* hairless; skinless; peeled
pêle-mêle *adv.* pell-mell; hastily; in confusion; — *m.* jumble, disorder
peler *vt.* to peel, pare, skin; remove the hair from; — *vi.* to peel; **se** — peel; lose hair
pèlerin *m.* pilgrim
pèlerinage *m.* pilgrimage
pèlerine *f.* cape, tippet
pélican *m.* pelican
pelisse *f.* pelisse, cloak
pellagre *f.* pellagra
pelle *f.* shovel, scoop; blade of a paddle
pelletée *f.* shovelful
pelleter *vt.* to shovel
pelleterie *f.* furs, fur trade
pelletier *m.* furrier
pellicule *f.* skin, film; (phot.) film; **-s** *pl.* dandruff
pelote *f.* wad, ball; pincushion; pelota
peloter *vt.* to wind into a ball
peloton *m.* group; (mil.) platoon; wad, ball; cluster
pelotonner *v.*, **se** — to group together; huddle; roll up, curl up
pelouse *f.* lawn, grass, a green
peluche *f.* plush, shag

pelucher *vi.* to shed the nap (fabric), become nappy
pelucheux *a.* fluffy
pelure *f.* paring, peel; rind; **papier** — *m.* onionskin paper
pelvien *a.* pelvic
pénal *a.* penal
pénalisation *f.* sports penalty
pénaliser *vt.* to penalize
pénalité *f.* penalty
penaud *a.* sheepish, crestfallen
penchant *a.* sloping, inclined; — *m.* slope; inclination, leaning, bent
penché *a.* bent, leaning
pencher *vt. & vi.* to incline, tilt, lean over; **se** — bend, stoop; lean out
pendable *a.* deserving of hanging
pendaison *f.* hanging on the gallows
pendant *a.* hanging; pending; — *m.* pendant; match, one of a pair; — *prep.* during, for; — **que** *conj.* while
pendeloque *f.* earring; crystal of a chandelier
pendiller *vi.* to dangle, hang
pendre *vt. & vi.* to hang, hang up
pendule *f.* clock with pendulum; — *m.* pendulum
pêne *m.* bolt of a lock
pénétrabilite *f.* penetrability
pénétrable *a.* penetrable
pénétrant *a.* penetrating, sharp, keen, searching, deep, profound
pénétration *f.* penetration; insight
pénétrer *vt.* to penetrate, pierce; fill; — *vi.* penetrate, enter, get into
pénible *a.* painful; difficult, hard, rough
péniblement *adv.* painfully
péniche *f.* canalboat, barge
pénicilline *f.* penicillin
péninsulaire *a.* peninsular
péninsule *f.* peninsula
pénis *m.* penis
pénitence *f.* penitence, penance; repentance
pénitencier *m.* penitentiary
pénitent *a. & m.* penitent
pénitentiaire *a.* penitentiary
penne *f.* feather, plume
pennon *m.* pennant
pénombre *f.* semidarkness, half-light
pensant *a.* thinking
pensée *f.* thought, idea; (bot.) pansy
penser *vi.* to think; remember; — *vt.* to think, believe, conceive, imagine
penseur *m.* thinker
pensif *a.* pensive, thoughtful, thinking
pension *f.* pension; boardinghouse, boarding school; room and board; — **alimentaire** alimony
pensionnaire *m. & f.* boarder; pensioner;

inmate
pensionnat *m.* boarding school
pensionner *vt.* to pension
pensivement *adv.* pensively
pensum *m.* task, chore (as punishment)
pentagone *m.* pentagon; — *a.* pentagonal
pentamètre *m.* pentameter
pentathlon *m.* pentathlon
pente *f.* slope, incline, grade
Pentecôte *f.* Pentecost
pénultième *a. & f.* penultimate, last but one
pénurie *f.* penury, poverty; scarcity
pépiement *m.* cheeping, chirping
pépin *m.* pip, seed
pépinière *f.* nursery garden
pépite *f.* nugget
pepsine *f.* pepsin
percale *f.* percale
perçant *a.* piercing; penetrating; biting, sharp; shrill
perce *f.* drill, punch; boring implement
perce-bois *m.* teredo, ship worm, borer
percée *f.* opening, break
percepteur *m.* tax collector; — *a.* discerning
perceptible *a.* perceptible
perception *f.* perception; revenue collection
percer *vt.* to pierce; go through, penetrate; bore, drill, sink; — *vi.* to pierce, come through
perceur *m.* driller, borer
perceuse *f.* drill, drilling machine
percevable *a.* perceivable; collectable
percevoir *vt.* to perceive; collect taxes
perche *f.* fresh-water perch; pole
percher *vi.* to perch, roost; se — to come to rest, alight
percheron *m.* percheron
perchoir *m.* perch, roost
perclus *a.* stiff-jointed, crippled
perçoir *m.* awl; punch; borer
percolateur *m.* percolator
percussion *f.* percussion
percutant *a.*, **fusée** –e *f.* percussion fuse
percuter *vt.* to percuss, tap
percuteur *m.* hammer of a gun
perdant *a.* losing; — *m.* loser
perdition *f.* perdition; (naut.) sinking
perdre *vt.* to lose; ruin, destroy; waste time; — *vi.* lose; lose value; fall; leak; se — be lost; get lost
perdrix *f.* partridge
perdu *a.* lost, ruined; wasted
père *m.* father
pérégrination *f.* peregrination
péremptoire *a.* peremptory
perfection *f.* perfection
perfectibilité *f.* perfectibility

perfectionnement *m.* improvement; perfecting
perfectionner *vt.* to perfect; improve
perfide *a.* perfidious, treacherous
perfidie *f.* perfidy, treachery
perforateur *m.* drill, punch
perforation *f.* perforation; drilling; puncture
perforer *vt.* to perforate; drill; puncture
pergola *f.* pergola
péri *m. & f.* genie, peri
péricarde *m.* pericardium
périclitant *a.* risky, shaky
péricliter *vi.* to be in danger
perigée *f.* perigee
péril *m.* peril, risk, danger
périlleusement *adv.* perilously
périlleux *a.* perilous, dangerous
perimé *a.* overdue; expired; out of date
périmer *vi.* to lapse, expire
périmètre *m.* perimeter
période *f.* period; age, era; (elec.) cycle
périodicité *f.* periodicity
périodique *a. & m.* periodical
périodiquement *adv.* periodically
péripatétique *a.* peripatetic
péripétie *f.* sudden turn of fortune; –s *pl.* vicissitudes, up and downs
périphérie *f.* periphery; circumference
périphérique *a.* peripheral
périr *vi.* to perish, die
périscope *m.* periscope
périscopique *a.* periscopic
périssable *a.* perishable
péristyle *m.* peristyle
péritoine *m.* peritoneum
péritonite *f.* peritonitis
perle *f.* pearl, bead
perlé *a.* pearled; pearly; beaded
perler *vt.* to husk; — *vi.* to bead
permanence *f.* permanence; en — permanent; without cessation; permanently
permanent *a.* permanent; lasting; open continuously; open day and night; spectacle — *m.* continuous performance
permanganate *m.* permanganate
perméable *a.* permeable; porous
permettre *vt.* to permit, allow
permis *a.* permitted; — *m.* permit, license; — **de conduire** *m.* driver's license
permission *f.* permission; (mil.) leave, pass
permissionnaire *m.* soldier on leave
permutable *a.* interchangeable
permutation *f.* permutation; transfer, exchange of positions
permutatrice *f.* (elec.) rectifier, commutator

pernicieusement *adv.* perniciously
pernicieux *a.* pernicious, harmful, injurious
perniciosité *f.* perniciousness
péroné *m.* fibula
péroraison *f.* peroration
pérorer *vi.* to harangue
Pérou *m.* Peru
peroxyde *m.* peroxide
perpendiculaire *a.* perpendicular
perpétration *f.* perpetration
perpétrer *vt.* to perpetrate
perpétuel *a.* perpetual; endless; for life
perpétuellement *adv.* perpetually
perpétuer *vt.* to perpetuate
perpétuité *f.* perpetuity; à — for life, forever
perplexe *a.* perplexed; perplexing
perplexité *f.* perplexity
perquisition *f.* search; **mandat de** — *m.* search warrant
perquisitionner *vi.* to search, conduct a search
perron *m.* flight of steps to a house
perroquet *m.* parrot
perruche *f.* parakeet
perruque *f.* wig
pers *a.* gray-green
persan *a. & m.* Persian
perse *f.* chintz
Perse *f.* Persia; — *n. & a.* Persian
persécuter *vt.* to persecute; harass; annoy
persécuteur *m.* persecutor
persécution *f.* persecution
persévérance *f.* perseverance
persévérant *a.* persevering
persévérer *vi.* to persevere, persist
persienne *f.* outside shutter
persiflage *m.* persiflage, banter
persifler *vt.* to treat lightly, banter
persil *m.* parsley
persillé *a.* marbled, streaked
persique *a.* Persian
persistance *f.* persistence, persistency
persistant *a.* persistent
persister *vi.* to persist
personnage *m.* personage, important person; (theat.) character, role
personnalité *f.* personality; personage; individuality
personne *f.* person; en — in person, personified; — *pron.* nobody, no one; anybody, anyone
personnel *a.* personal; — *m.* personnel
personnellement *adv.* personally
personnifier *vt.* to personify; impersonate
perspective *f.* perspective; prospect; view
perspicacité *f.* perspicacity
persuadant *a.* persuasive, convincing
persuadé *a.* positive, convinced, sure

persuader *vt.* to persuade, convince
persuasif *a.* persuasive, convincing
persuasion *f.* persuasion, conviction
persuasivement *adv.* persuasively, convincingly
perte *f.* loss, damage, ruin; leakage; falling off, drop; (med.) discharge; à — de vue as far as the eye can see
pertinence *f.* pertinence, relevance
pertinent *a.* pertinent, relevant
pertuis *m.* channel, narrows; opening; narrow pass, passage; sluice
perturbateur *a.* disturbing; — *m.* disturber
perturbation *f.* perturbation; disturbance
perturber *vt.* to perturb; disturb
péruvien *a. & m.* Peruvian
pervenche *f.* periwinkle
pervers *a.* perverse
perversement *adv.* perversely
perversion *f.* perversion
perversité *f.* perversity
pervertir *vt.* to pervert; se — to become perverted
pesage *m.* weighing in
pesamment *adv.* heavily
pesant *a.* heavy, weighty; — *m.* weight
pesanteur *f.* weight; gravity; heaviness
pèse-alcool *m.* alcometer
pèse-bébé *m.* baby scale(s)
pesée *f.* weighing; leverage
pèse-lettres *m.* postal scale(s)
peser *vt.* to weigh, consider; measure; — *vi.* to weigh; press
pessimisme *m.* pessimism
pessimiste *m. & f.* pessimist; — *a.* pessimistic
peste *f.* plague, pestilence
pester *vi.* to rage, storm; curse
pestiféré *a.* stricken with the plague
pétale *m.* petal
pétarade *f.* backfire
pétard *m.* firecracker; detonator
pétarder *vt.* to blast; — *vi.* backfire
péter *vi.* to backfire, explode, pop
pétillant *a.* sparkling; crackling
pétillement *m.* crackling sound
pétiller *vi.* to sparkle; crackle; bubble
petit *a.* small, little; young; petty; minor, of humble origin, lesser; — à — little by little; — *m.* child; little boy; -e *f.* little girl; -s *m. pl.* children, little ones; en — *adv.* shortened
petit-cheval *m.* donkey engine
petit-cousin *m.* second cousin
petite-fille *f.* granddaughter
petitesse *f.* smallness, littleness; pettiness
petit-fils *m.* grandson
pétition *f.* petition
pétitionnaire *m. & f.* petitioner

pétitionner *vi.* to petition
petit-lait *m.* whey
petit-maître *m.* fop
petit-neveu *m.* grandnephew
petite-nièce *f.* grandniece
petits-enfants *m. pl.* grandchildren
petit-suisse *m.* cream cheese
pétoire *f.* popgun
pétoncle *m.* scallop
pétrel *m.* petrel
pétri *a.* kneaded, shaped; full of
pétrifier *vt.* to petrify
pétrin *m.* container for dough (bakery); (coll.) in trouble, difficulty
pétrir *vt.* to knead; shape
pétrole *m.* petroleum, oil
pétrolier *m.* (naut.) tanker
pétrolifère *a.* oil-yielding, oil-bearing
pétulance *f.* friskiness, vivacity
pétulant *a.* frisky, vivacious
pétunia *m.* petunia
peu *adv.* little; not very; — **de** few; — **à** — gradually; **depuis** — lately; **quelque** — somewhat; — *m.* small quantity; **un** — **(de)** a little
peuplade *f.* tribe, people
peuple *m.* people, nation; masses, lower class
peuplé *a.* populated
peupler *vt.* to people, populate, settle; stock with fish
peuplier *m.* poplar
peur *f.* fear, fright; **avoir** — to be afraid; **de** — **de** for fear of; **de** — **que** for fear that; **faire** — **à** to frighten; **prendre** — become afraid
peureux *a.* fearful; timid, shy
peut-être *adv.* perhaps, maybe
phalange *f.* phalanx
phalène *f.* moth
pharaon *m.* Pharaoh; faro
phare *m.* lighthouse, beacon; (auto.) headlight
pharisien *m.* pharisee
pharmacie *f.* pharmacy
pharmacien *m.* pharmacist, druggist
pharyngite *f.* pharyngitis
pharynx *m.* pharynx
phase *f.* phase, stage
Phénicie *f.* Phoenicia
phénicien *a. & m.* Phoenician
phénique *a.* carbolic
phénix *m.* phoenix
phénol *m.* phenol; carbolic acid
phénoménal *a.* phenomenal
phénomène *m.* phenomenon
philanthrope *m.* philanthropist
philanthropie *f.* philanthropy
philanthropique *a.* philanthropic
philatéliste *m. & f.* philatelist, stamp collector

philharmonique *a.* philharmonic
Philippe (*m.*) Philip
philistin *a. & m.* Philistine
philologie *f.* philology
philologue *m.* philologist
philosophe *m.* philosopher; — *a.* philosophical
philosopher *vi.* to philosophize
philosophie *f.* philosophy
philosophique *a.* philosophical
philtre *m.* philter, magic potion
phlébite *f.* phlebitis
phlogistique *m.* phlogiston
phlyctène *f.* blister, vesicle
phobie *f.* phobia, dread
phonème *m.* phoneme
phonétique *a.* phonetic; — *f.* phonetics
phonique *a.* acoustic, phonic
phonographe *m.* phonograph
phonologie *f.* phonology
phoque *m.* (zool.) seal
phosphate *m.* phosphate
phosphore *m.* phosphorus
phosphorescence *f.* phosphorescence
phosphorescent *a.* phosphorescent
phosphure *m.* phosphide
photo *f.* photo, photograph
photocalque *m.* blueprint
photocopie *f.* photocopy
photo-électrique *a.* photoelectric
photogénique *a.* photogenic
photographe *m.* photographer
photographie *f.* photography; photograph; — **aérienne** aerial photography
photographier *vt.* to photograph
photographique *a.* photographic
photogravure *f.* photoengraving
photostat *m.* photostat
photosynthèse *f.* photosynthesis
phrase *f.* sentence; phrase
phraséologie *f.* phraseology
phrénologie *f.* phrenology
phrénologiste *m.* phrenologist
phtisie *f.* pulmonary tuberculosis
phtisique *a.* tubercular, consumptive
physicien *m.* physicist
physico-chimie *f.* physical chemistry
physiologie *f.* physiology
physiologique *a.* physiological
physiologiste *m.* physiologist
physionomie *f.* face, features, character
physique *a.* physical; — *f.* physics; — *m.* physique; — **plasmatique** plasma physics
physiquement *adv.* physically
piaffer *vi.* to step, prance, paw the ground
piaillard *a.* bawling, crying; chirping
piailler *vi.* to bawl, squall, cry; chirp
piaillerie *f.* bawling, crying; whining;

chirping
pianiste *m. & f.* pianist
piano *m.* piano; — à **queue** grand piano;
— à **demi-queue** baby grand piano
piaulard *a.* crying, whining; chirping
piauler *vi.* to whine, cry; chirp
piaulis *m.* chirping
pic *m.* pickax; mountain peak; woodpecker; à — precipitous, sheer, abrupt
picard *a. & m.* native of Picardy
Picardie *f.* Picardy
picaresque *a.* picaresque
piccolo *m.* piccolo
pichet *m.* pitcher, jug
picorer *vi.* to peck, pick up food (birds)
picot *m.* splinter; picot
picotement *m.* pricking sensation, prickle;
pins and needles (coll. U.S.)
picoter *vt.* to prick; pick at, peck at; —
vi. sting, smart, burn
picrique *a.* picric
pictural *a.* pictorial
pie *f.* magpie; (coll.) chatterbox; — *a.*
piebald
pièce *f.* piece; patch; room in a house;
(theat.) play; coin; cask; part; — **de**
rechange spare part
piécette *f.* one-act play; small coin
pied *m.* foot; footing; base; leg of a chair;
support, stand; tripod; à — on foot; **an**
— **de la lettre** literally; **coup de** — *m.*
kick; **en** — full-length (portrait) **mettre**
— à **terre** to dismount; step down from,
get out of a vehicle; — **de laitue** head
of lettuce; **lâcher** — to turn tail
pied-bot *m.* clubfooted person
pied-d'alouette *m.* larkspur, delphinium
pied-de-biche *m.* forceps; nail claw; bell
pull
piédestal *m.* pedestal
piège *m.* snare, trap, pitfall
piéger *vt.* to trap
pie-grièche *f.* shrike
Piémont *m.* Piedmont
pierraille *f.* rubble, stones; ballast
pierre *f.* stone; flint; — à **fusil** flint; —
d'achoppement stumbling block; — **de**
touche touchstone
Pierre (*m.*) Peter
pierreries *f. pl.* precious stones, jewels
pierrette *f.* small stone
pierreux *a.* stony; gritty; gravelly
piété *f.* piety; devotion
piétinement *m.* trampling; treading
piétiner *vt.* to trample, tread on; — *vi.* to
stamp
piéton *m.* pedestrian, person on foot
piètre *a.* poor, miserable, paltry
pieu *m.* stake, post, pile
pieusement *adv.* piously

pieuvre *f.* octopus
pieux *a.* pious, devoted, reverent
pige *f.* measuring stick
pigeon *m.* pigeon, dove; — **voyageur**
homing pigeon
pigeonneau *m.* squab
pigeonnier *m.* dovecote, pigeon roost
piger *vt.* to measure, check; (coll.) nab,
grab
pigmentation *f.* pigmentation
pigne *f.* pine cone
pignon *m.* house gable; chain-sprocket;
pine seed
pilaf *a.* pilaf
pilastre *m.* pilaster, newel
pilau *m.* rice, pilaf
pile *f.* pile, heap; battery; — **ou face**
heads or tails
piler *vt.* to pound, grind by pounding
pilet *m.* pintail duck
pileux *a.* hairy
pilier *m.* pillar, column
pillage *m.* pillage, plunder, sacking, looting; pilfering, stealing
pillard *a.* pillaging, looting; pilfering,
stealing; — *m.* pillager, looter; pilferer,
thief
piller *vt.* to pillage, plunder, sack, loot,
steal from; plagiarize
pilleur *a.* pillaging; pilfering; — *m.* pillager
pilon *m.* hammer, rammer; pestle; crushing implement
pilonner *vt.* to ram, pound, crush
pilori *m.* pillory
pilot *m.* bridge pile
pilotage *m.* piloting; flying; pile driving
pilote *m.* pilot
piloter *vt.* to pilot, fly
pilotis *m.* piling
pilou *m.* cotton flannel
pilule *f.* pill
piment *m.* red pepper, allspice; — **vert**
green pepper
pimenter *vt.* to spice, season with red
pepper
pin *m.* pine tree; fir tree
pinacle *m.* pinnacle
pince *f.* pincers, tweezers, tongs; pliers;
forceps; clip, clamp; lever, crowbar;
claw of a lobster; hand grip; — à **linge**
clothespin
pincé *a.* pinched; wry; — *m.* pizzicato
pinceau *m.* paint brush; beam of light
pincée *f.* pinch, small quantity
pincement *m.* pinching, pinch
pince-monseigneur *m.* jimmy
pince-nez *m.* pince-nez, nose glasses
pincer *vt.* to pinch; (mus.) pluck; clip;
hold, grip; catch, nab

pincettes *f. pl.* pincers, tongs, tweezers
pingouin *m.* penguin; auk
pingre *a.* miserly, stingy; — *m.* miser
pinière *f.* pine forest
pinson *m.* finch
pintade *f.* guinea hen
pinte *f.* pint
pioche *f.* pickax
piocher *vt.* to dig; — *vi.* work hard
piocheur *m.* digger; (with a pick); plodder hard worker
piolet *m.* ice axe; piolet
pion *m.* checker; pawn; monitor (coll.) school disciplinary officer
pionnier *m.* pioneer
pipe *f.* pipe
pipeau *m.* (mus.) pipe
pipée *f.* snaring birds with artifical bird calls
pipe-line *m.* pipeline
piper *vi.* to chirp, cheep, peep; — *vt.* to snare; lure birds; decoy
piquant *a.* sharp; spicy; witty; interesting; pricking, stinging; — *m.* sharpness; pointedness; best part, main point (of a story)
pique *f.* pike, lance; pique; — *m.* spade (at cards)
piqué *a.* piqued; stung, pricked, stuck; spotted, dotted; quilted; (mus.) staccato; (avi.) nose dive
pique-assiette *m.* parasite, sponger (person)
pique-nique *m.* picnic
pique-niquer *vi.* to picnic
piquer *vt.* to prick, sting; stick; inject; quilt; stimulate; irritate, pique; — *vi.* (avi.) to nose dive; se — prick oneself; be irritated, be offended; pride onself; become pitted
piquet *m.* picket, post, stake; piquet (at cards)
piqueter *vt.* to picket; stake out; spot, dot
piqueur *m.* machine sewer, stitcher; outrider; digger
piqûre *f.* puncture, sting; prick; injection; shot (U.S.); quilting, stitching; — de rappel (med.) booster shot
pirater *vi.* to pirate
piraterie *f.* piracy
pire *a.* worse; le — the worst
pirogue *f.* pirogue, canoe
pirouette *f.* pirouette, whirling
pirouetter *vi.* to pirouette; whirl
pis *adv.* worse; le — the worst; de — en — worse and worse
pis *m.* udder
pis-aller *m.* worst alternative, last resort
pisan *a.* of Pisa, from Pisa
piscine *f.* pool, swimming pool

pissenlit *m.* dandelion
pisser *vi.* to urinate
pissoir *m.* urinal
pistache *f.* pistachio nut
piste *f.* path; track; trail; — d'atterrissage airstrip, landing strip; — cavalière bridle path; — cyclable bicycle path
pister *vt.* to track, trail; follow; shadow
pisteur *m.* tracker, follower
pistolet *m.* pistol; (naut.) davit
piston *m.* piston; influence, pull; (mus.) cornet valve
pistonner *vt.* to use one's influence to help another; sponsor, back
pitance *f.* pittance, allowance, bare living
piteusement *adv.* piteously
piteux *a.* piteous, pitiable
pithécanthrope *m.* pithecanthropus
pitié *f.* pity, compassion, mercy
piton *m.* ring bolt; screw eye
pitoyable *a.* pitiful, pitiable
pitre *m.* clown
pittoresque *a.* picturesque
pituitaire *a.* pituitary
pivert *m.* woodpecker
pivoine *f.* peony
pivot *m.* pivot, fulcrum, axis; à — revolving, swivel
pivoter *vi.* to pivot, revolve, turn
placage *m.* veneering; plating
placard *m.* placard; poster; closet; cupboard; (print.) proof
placarder *vt.* to post a bill, placard
place *f.* square; seat; place, room, space; job, employment; — d'armes parade ground; faire — à to make room for; — marchande shopping plaza
placement *m.* investment; placement; bureau de — employment agency
placer *vt.* to place; sell; invest
placeur *m.* placer; usher; seller
placide *a.* placid, calm
placidité *f.* placidity, calmness
placier *m.* traveling salesman; agent
plafond *m.* ceiling; limit, maximum; top
plafonner *vt.* to equip with a ceiling
plage *f.* beach
plagiat *m.* plagiarism
plagier *vt.* to plagiarize
plaid *m.* plaid
plaider *vt. & vi.* to plead a case
plaideur *m.* party in a lawsuit, litigant
plaidoirie *f.* legal plea, pleading
plaidoyer *m.* legal plea, remarks by defense attorney
plaie *f.* wound
plaignant *m.* plaintiff at law
plain-chant *m.* (mus.) plainsong
plaindre *vt.* to pity; se — to complain

plaine *f.* plain, field

plain-pied *m.*, **de —** *adv.* on a level; even; smoothly, evenly

plainte *f.* complaint; moan

plaintif *a.* plaintive

plaintivement *adv.* plaintively

plaire *vi.* to please; **s'il vous plaît** please; **plût à Dieu!** would to God!; **à Dieu ne plaise!** God forbid!; **se —** enjoy oneself, take pleasure, be pleased

plaisamment *adv.* pleasantly, agreeably

plaisance *f.* pleasure; **maison de —** *f.* country home

plaisant *a.* amusing, funny; **—** *m.* joker; **mauvais —** practical joker

plaisanter *vi.* to joke, fool; **—** *vt.* to make fun of, tease

plaisanterie *f.* joke; trick

plaisir *m.* pleasure; enjoyment; **faire — à** to please

plan *m.* plane; plan; map, diagram; project; **— de vol** flight plan; **gros —** movie closeup; **premier —** foreground; **—** *a.* flat, even, plane

planage *m.* planing; smoothing

planche *f.* plank, board; plate, illustration; **faire la —** to float on one's back; **— à repasser** ironing board; **— de bord** dashboard; **-s** *pl.* (theat.) stage

planchéier *vt.* lay a wooden floor

plancher *m.* floor; flooring; planking

planchette *f.* small plank

plancton *m.* plankton

plane *m.* plane tree

plané *m.* glide, gliding; rolled gold

planer *vt.* to plane, smooth; **—** *vi.* to glide soar; hover, hang

planétaire *a.* planetary; **—** *m.* planetarium

planète *f.* planet

planeur *m.* glider

planquer *vt.*, **se —** to fall flat on the ground; take cover

plant *m.* sapling, seedling; grove, clump

plantage *m.* planting

plantain *m.* plantain

plantation *f.* plantation; planting

plante *f.* plant; sole of the foot

planter *vt.* to plant; place, put; stick

planteur *m.* planter

plantoir *m.* dibble

plantureux *a.* abundant, fertile; plump

planure *f.* wood shaving(s)

plaque *f.* plate; metal sheet; badge; tag

plaqué *a.* plated

plaquemine *f.* persimmon

plaquer *vt.* to plate; veneer; cover; cake; plaster; tackle (sports); **se —** to lie flat, fall flat

plaquette *f.* small plate or sheet; brochure

plasticité *f.* plasticity

plastique *a.* plastic; **matière —** *f.* plastic

plastron *m.* breastplate, protective pad; front of a shirt, dickey; butt of a joke

plat *a.* flat; smooth; level; dull; **à —** flat; tired, run down; **—** *m.* flat surface, flat part; dish, course; plate

platane *m.* plane tree

plat-bord *m.* (naut.) gunwale

plateau *m.* tray; plateau; platform; plate; stage

plate-bande *f.* border, bed of flowers or grass

platée *f.* plateful, dishful

plate-forme *f.* platform

platine *m.* platinum; **—** *f.* gun lock; platen

platiner *vt.* to coat, plate with platinum

platitude *f.* platitude, dullness

Platon *m.* Plato

platonique *a.* platonic (love)

platonisme *m.* Platonism

plâtrage *m.* plastering

plâtras *m.* plaster rubbish

plâtre *m.* plaster; plaster cast

plâtrer *vt.* to plaster; cover over, smooth over

plâtrier *m.* plasterer

plausibilité *f.* plausibility

plausible *a.* plausible

plèbe *f.* common people, masses

plébéien *a.* & *m.* plebeian

plébiscite *m.* plebiscite

plein *a.* full, filled; complete; **en — . . .** in the middle of; **en — air** in the open air, out of doors; **en — jour** in broad daylight; **—** *m.* fullness, fill, plenum

pleinement *adv.* fully

plénière *a.* & *f.* plenary, full; complete

plénipotentiaire *a.* & *m.* plenipotentiary

plénitude *f.* plenitude, fullness

pléonasme *m.* pleonasm

pléthore *f.* plethora

pleur *m.* tear; **-s** *pl.* tears, crying

pleurard *a.* whimpering; **—** *m.* whimperer, whiner

pleurer *vi.* to cry, weep; run, water (eyes); drip, leak; **—** *vt.* to cry for, mourn

pleurésie *f.* pleurisy

pleureur *m.* whimperer, weeper; **—** *a.* whimpering, weeping

pleurnicher *vi.* to whine, whimper

pleuviner *v.* to drizzle

pleuvoir *vi.* to rain

plexus *m.* plexus

pli *m.* fold; wrinkle; crease; wave; tuck; pleat; cover, envelope; bend; **sous ce —** enclosed herewith

pliable *a.* pliable; folding

pliant *a.* pliant; tractable; folding; **—** *m.* folding chair

plier *vt.* to fold, bend; warp; discipline;

— vi. to bend; yield, give in, submit;
se — yield; obey

plinthe f. (arch.) plinth

plissement m. folding, pleating; creasing; wrinkling

plisser vt. to pleat; crease; wrinkle

ploiement m. folding, bending

plomb m. lead; plumb line; shot; (elec.) fuse; à — vertical, plumb

plombage m. leading; (dent.) filling

plombagine f. graphite, black lead

plombé a. leaden; lead-coated; livid

plomber vt. to lead, cover with lead; plumb; se — to become leaden

plomberie f. plumbing

plombier m. plumber; — a. leaden, about lead

plombières f. ice cream with glacé fruit

plongée f. plunge, dive; dip

plongement m. plunging

plongeoir m. diving board

plongeon m. dive, plunge

plonger vt. to plunge, immerse; — vi. to plunge, dive; dip; submerge

plongeur m. diver; washer of dishes; — a. diving

ploutocrate m. plutocrat

ployable a. pliable, tractable

pluie f. rain

plume f. feather; pen; quill

plumeau m. feather duster

plumer vt. to pluck; — vi. to feather oars

plumet m. plume

plumeux a. feathery

plupart f. most, majority; **pour la —** mostly

pluralité f. plurality, majority

pluriel a. & m. (gram.) plural

plus adv. more; plus; **ne** — no more, no longer; **au** — at most, maximum; — **tôt** sooner; **le** — the most; **de** — besides, moreover; more, additional, extra; **de — en** — more and more; **non** — either, neither; — m. more; most, best; greatest number; (math.) plus sign

plusieurs a. pl. several

plus-que-parfait m. (gram.) pluperfect

plutonium m. plutonium

plutôt adv. rather; better, preferably

pluvial a. rainy; pertaining to rain

pluvieux a. rainy

pluviosité f. precipitation, rainfall

pneu m. tire

pneumatique a. pneumatic; — m. tire; letter sent by pneumatic tube

pneumonie f. pneumonia

pochade f. work done hastily

pochard m. drunk, drunkard

poche f. pocket; pouch; sac; bag, sack; ladle

pochée f. pocketful, contents of a pocket

pocher vt. to bruise, blacken; poach; sketch; stencil

pochetée f. pocketful

pochette f. small pocket; pouch

podagre f. gout; — a. gouty

podium m. podium

podomètre m. pedometer

poêle f. frying pan, pan; — m. stove, cooker; pall

poêlée f. panful

poêlette f. small frying pan

poêlon m. saucepan

poème m. poem

poésie f. poetry; poem

poète m. poet

poétique a. poetical, poetic; — f. poetics

poids m. weight; load, burden; consequence, importance; — utile payload

poignant a. poignant, gripping

poignard m. dagger

poignarder vt. to stab

poigne f. grip, hold, grasp

poignée f. handful; handle; grip, hold; hilt, haft; — de main handshake

poignet m. wrist; cuff

poil m. hair; bristle; nap; down; (coll.); à — a. naked; bareback; **être de mauvais —** bad humored

poilu a. hairy; — m. soldier of the First World War

poinçon m. punch; awl; die, stamp; hallmark

poinçonner vt. to stamp; punch

poinçonneuse f. punch, punching machine, hole punch

poindre vi. to appear, come into view; dawn; sprout

poing m. fist, hand; **coup de** — m. punch, blow; **menacer du** — to shake a fist at

point m. point; period, dot; mark; (med.) stitch; à — cooked to a turn, medium; à — apropos; **au** — ready, in shape; in tune; in focus; **deux** –s (gram.) colon; — **d'appui** fulcrum; basis; (mil.) bridge-head; — **d'interrogation** question mark; — **du jour** dawn, daybreak; — **et virgule** semicolon; **sur le** — **de** on the point of; — adv. no, not

pointage m. checking, checking off, ticking off; scoring; timing; aiming, pointing

pointe f. point; pointed tool; promontory; tip; diaper, kerchief; (fig.) sharpness

pointer vt. to sharpen; prick; check a list; aim, point; — vi. to appear; rise; sprout

pointeur m. checker, scorer; **chien** — m. pointer (dog)

pointiller vt. to stipple, dot; harass; — vi. quibble

pointillerie *f.* quibbling
pointilleux *a.* fastidious; finicky; touchy
pointu *a.* pointed; sharp
pointure *f.* size, fit
poire *f.* pear
poireau *m.* leek
poirier *m.* pear tree
pois *m.* pea; — **chiche** chick pea; **petits —** *pl.* green peas
poison *m.* poison
poissard *a.* common, vulgar speech
poisser *vt.* to cover with a sticky substance; make sticky; pitch, tar
poisseux *a.* sticky, gummy
poisson *m.* fish; — **rouge** goldfish
poissonnerie *f.* fish market
poissonneux *a.* full of fish
poissonnier *m.* fishmonger, operator of a fish market
Poitevin *m. & a.* native of Poitou
poitrail *m.* breast of a horse
poitrinaire *a. & m.* consumptive, tubercular person
poitrine *f.* chest; breast, bust, bosom; brisket
poivre *m.* pepper; **grain de — m.** peppercorn; — **de Cayenne** red pepper
poivré *a.* peppered; peppery, spicy
poivrer *vt.* to pepper, season, spice
poivrier *m.* pepperbox; pepper plant
poivrière *f.* pepper shaker
poivron *m.* green pepper; allspice
poix *f.* pitch, resin
polaire *a.* polar
polarisateur *a.* polarizing; — *m.* polarizer
polarisation *f.* polarization
polariser *vt.* to polarize
polarité *f.* polarity
pôle *m.* (elec., geog.) pole
polémique *f.* polemic; — *a.* polemical
poli *a.* polished; polite; — *m.* polish
police *f.* police; policy; — **d'assurance** insurance policy; **agent de — m.** policeman; **bonnet de — m.** overseas cap
policer *vt.* to regulate, organize, police
polichinelle *m.* Punch, buffoon; **théâtre de — m.** Punch and Judy show
policier *a.* police; **roman — m.** detective novel; — *m.* detective, policeman
poliment *adv.* politely
poliomyélite *f.* poliomyelitis, infantile paralysis
polir *vt.* to polish; refine
polisseur *m.* one who polishes, buffer
polisseuse *f.* polishing machine, buffing machine
polissoir *m.* polishing implement, buffer
polisson *m.* rascal; mischievous child
polissonnerie *f.* mischief, mischievousness; lewdness

politesse *f.* politeness, courtesy
politicien *m.* politician
politique *a.* political; politic; diplomatic; — *f.* policy; politics; — *m.* politician
polka *f.* polka
polker *vi.* to polka
pollinisation *f.* pollinization
polluer *vt.* to pollute
pollution *f.* pollution
Pologne *f.* Poland
polonais *a. & m.* Polish; — *m.* Pole
poltron *m.* coward; — *a.* cowardly
poltronnerie *f.* cowardice
polycopier *vt.* to duplicate, reproduce
polyèdre *m.* polyhedron; — *a.* polyhedral
polygame *a.* polygamous; — *m.* polygamist
polygamie *f.* polygamy
polyglotte *a.* polyglot
polygone *m.* polygon; — *a.* polygonal
polygraphe *m. & f.* versatile author, writer on varied subjects
polymorphe *a.* polymorphous
Polynésie *f.* Polynesia
Polynésien *m. & a.* Polynesian
polynôme *m.* polynomial
polype *m.* polyp
polyphasé *a.* multi-phase
polyphonique *a.* polyphonic
polysoc *m.* gangplow
polysyllabe *a.* polysyllabic
polytechnicien *m.* student at the École Polytechnique
polytechnique *a.* polytechnic
polythéiste *m. & f.* polytheist; — *a.* polytheistic
polyvalent *a.* polyvalent, multivalent
pommade *f.* pomade; salve, ointment
pommader *vt.* to pomade
pomme *f.* apple; knob; — **d'arrosoir** sprinkler; — **de pin** pine cone; — **de terre** potato; **–s à l'huile** potato salad; **–s frites** French fried potatoes; **–s en purée, purée de –s** mashed potatoes; **–s vapeur** boiled potatoes; **–s rissolées** roast potatoes
pommé *a.* round; consummate
pommeau *m.* knob; pummel of a sword
pommelé *a.* dappled, mottled
pommelle *f.* grating
pommeraie *f.* apple orchard
pommette *f.* cheekbone; knob
pommier *m.* apple tree
pompadour *m.* flowered cloth
pompe *f.* pump; pomp, splendor; **–s funèbres** *pl.* funeral
pomper *vt.* to pump
pompeux *a.* pompous
pompier *m.* fireman
pompon *m.* pompon; puff

pomponner *vt.* to ornament, adorn, deck out, festoon
ponant *m.* Occident
ponce *f.* pumice
ponceau *m.* culvert; corn poppy, red poppy
poncer *vt.* to sand, sandpaper; rub with pumice
poncho *m.* poncho
ponction *f.* (med.) opening, pricking; puncture
ponctualité *f.* punctuality
ponctuation *f.* punctuation
ponctué *a.* punctuated; having dotted line
ponctuel *a.* punctual
ponctuer *vt.* to punctuate; accentuate
pondaison *f.* egg laying
pondérable *a.* ponderable, weighable
pondérateur *a.* stabilizing
pondération *f.* ponderation; poise, balance
pondéré *a.* well-balanced; collected, cool
pondérer *vt.* to balance, stabilize
pondeuse *f.* laying hen
pondre *vt.* to lay (eggs)
poney *m.* pony
pongé *m.* pongee
pont *m.* bridge; deck of a ship; axle, shaft; platform; **— aérien** airlift; **— élévateur** (auto.) grease rack; **tête de — ** *f.* bridge-head
ponte *f.* egg laying
ponté *a.* equipped with a deck
pontée *f.* deck cargo
ponter *vt.* to lay a deck (on a ship); **—** *vi.* play against the bank (at cards)
pontet *m.* trigger guard
pontife *m.* pontiff; pope
pontifical *a.* pontifical
pontificat *m.* pontificate
pontifier *vi.* to pontificate
pont-levis *m.* drawbridge
ponton *m.* pontoon; hulk
popeline *f.* poplin
populace *f.* populace, mob, rabble
populacier *a.* vulgar, common, low
populaire *a.* of the people; popular; **chanson —** *f.* folk song
populariser *vt.* to popularize
popularité *f.* popularity
population *f.* population
populeux *a.* populous
poquet *m.* hole for seeds
porc *m.* hog, pig; pork
porcelaine *f.* porcelain, china
porcelet *m.* piglet; wood louse
porc-épic *m.* porcupine
porche *m.* porch
porcher *m.* swineherd
poreux *a.* porous

pornographie *f.* pornography
pornographique *a.* pornographic
porosité *f.* porosity
porphyre *m.* porphyry
port *m.* port, harbor; postage; charge for transportation; carriage, deportment
portable *a.* portable; wearable
portage *m.* portage; transport, transporting; (mech.) bearing
portail *m.* portal, front gate
portant *a.* bearing; **bien —** in good health; **mal —** not well; **—** *m.* support; handle
portatif *a.* portable
porte *f.* door, gate; doorway; entrance; **— cochère** *f.* carriage entrance, gate at beginning of a driveway; **— d'entrée** front door
porté *a.* inclined; carried; worn; **— à** inclined to
porte-à-faux *m.* overhang; **en —** in a dangerous position
porte-affiches *m.* bulletin board; billboard
porte-aiguilles *m.* needle case
porte-allumettes *m.* matchbox
porte-amarre *m.* gun for shooting mooring lines
porte-avions *m.* aircraft carrier
porte-bagages *m.* baggage rack, luggage carrier
porteballe *m.* peddlar
porte-bannière *m. & f.* standard bearer
porte-bât *m.* pack animal
porte-billets *m.* billfold
porte-bonheur *m.* good luck charm
porte-cartes *m.* card case
porte-chapeaux *m.* hat rack
porte-cigarette *m.* cigarette holder
porte-clefs *m.* guard, turnkey
porte-copie *m.* copy stand
porte-couteau *m.* knife rest
porte-documents *m.* zippered portfolio
porte-drapeau *m.* flag bearer
portée *f.* brood, litter; scope, range, reach, extent; comprehension; implication, meaning; (mus.) staff
portefaix *m.* porter; stevedore
porte-fenêtre *f.* French door, French window
portefeuille *m.* portfolio; billfold, wallet
portemanteau *m.* coat rack; suitcase; saddlebag
porte-mine *m.* automatic pencil
porte-monnaie *m.* coin purse, change purse
porte-musique *m.* music case
porte-objet *m.* microscope slide
porte-parapluies *m.* umbrella stand
porte-parole *m.* spokesman
porte-pipes *m.* pipe rack

porte-plat *m.* trivet, hot pad; hot-pan holder

porte-plume *m.* penholder

porter *vt.* to carry, bear; raise, lift; indicate, mark; bring; take; wear; — *vi.* to bear, have an effect; **se — bien** to be well

porte-serviettes *m.* towel rack

porteur *m.* porter, carrier, bearer

porte-vent *m.* wind tunnel, air duct

porte-vêtement(s) *m.* clothes hanger

porte-voix *m.* megaphone; speaking tube

portier *m.* doorman; porter; janitor

portière *f.* door of a vehicle

portillon *m.* gate, barrier

portionner *vt.* to apportion

portique *m.* portico

portland *m.* Portland cement

Porto *m.* port wine

portrait *m.* portrait

portraitiste *m. & f.* portrait painter

portraiturer *vt.* to paint the portrait of

Portugais *m. & a.* Portuguese

Portugal *m.* Portugal

pose *f.* pose, posing, posture; (phot.) exposure; — **instantanée** snapshot

posé *a.* steady, even, sedate

posemètre *m.* (phot.) exposure meter

poser *vt.* to put, place; — *vi.* to pose; — **une question** to ask a question; **se —** (avi.) to land; **se — en** set oneself up as

poseur *a.* posing, putting on airs, affected; — *m.* affected person; — **de mines** (naut.) minelayer

positif *a.* positive

position *f.* position, location; standing, status; stance; post, job

positivisme *m.* positivism

possédé *a.* possessed; — *m.* person possessed by the devil

posséder *vt.* to possess, have, own

possesseur *m.* possessor

possessif *a. & m.* possessive

possession *f.* possession, ownership; property

possibilité *f.* possibility

possible *a.* possible; — *m.* everything possible, utmost

postage *m.* packing for mailing; mailing

postdater *vt.* to postdate

poste *f.* post, mail; post office; **mettre (une lettre) à la poste** to mail a letter; — **recommandée** *f.* registered mail; — **restante** general delivery; — *m.* post; station; job, position; entry in a ledger; — **de TSF** radio set

poster *vt.* to post, station

postérieur *a.* posterior; back, hind; later; — *m.* posterior

postérité *f.* posterity

posthume *a.* posthumous

postiche *a.* false, imitation

postier *m.* postal worker

postillon *m.* postilion

postopératoire *a.* post-operative

postscolaire *a.* postgraduate; after-school

post-scriptum *m.* postscript

postsynnchronisation *f.* dubbing

postsynchroniser *vt.* to dub movies

postulant *m.* candidate, applicant

postulat *m.* postulate

postuler *vt.* to apply for

posture *f.* posture, position

pot *m.* pot; jug, jar; — **d'échappement** (auto.) muffler; — **pourri** stew; mixture

potable *a.* drinkable; **eau — ** *f.* drinking water

potage *m.* soup

potager *a.* culinary; **jardin — ** *m.* vegetable garden; truck farm

potasse *f.* potash

potassium *m.* potassium

pot-au-feu *m.* boiled or pot-roasted beef and vegetables

pot-de-vin *m.* tip; bribe

poteau *m.* post, stake, pole; — **indicateur** signpost

potée *f.* potful, jugful

potelé *a.* plump, chubby

potence *f.* gallows; bracket, support

potentat *m.* potentate

potentiel *a.* potential; — *m.* potential, potentialities

poter *vt. & vi.* to putt (in golf)

poterie *f.* pottery

poterne *f.* postern

potiche *f.* porcelain vase

potier *m.* potter

potin *m.* pewter; (coll.) talk, gossip; ado, fuss

potion *f.* potion

potiron *m.* pumpkin

pou *m.* louse, tick

pouah! *interj.* ugh!

poubelle *f.* garbage can, refuse can

pouce *m.* thumb; big toe; inch; (fig.) very small quantity

poucettes *f. pl.* thumbscrew

poudre *f.* powder; gunpowder; **en — ** powdered, ground; — **de riz** face powder

poudrer *vt.* to powder

poudreux *a.* dusty, powdery

poudrière *f.* powder magazine; powder horn

poudrin *m.* spindrift, sea spray, fine spray

poudroyant *a.* dusty

poudrier *m.* powder box; compact

poudroyer *vt.* to cover with dust; — *vi.* to raise dust

pouf *m.* pouf, ottoman; — *interj.* phew! plop!

pouffer *vi.* to burst out laughing

pouillerie *f.* place infested with lice; hovel; poverty

pouilleux *a.* lousy, lice-ridden; wretched, filthy

poulailler *m.* henhouse; poulterer

poulain *m.* colt, foal

poulaine *f.* (naut.) latrine

poularde *f.* chicken

poule *f.* hen; gambling pool

poulet *m.* chicken

poulette *f.* pullet

pouliche *f.* filly

poulie *f.* pulley; block

pouliner *vi.* to foal

poulinière *f.* brood mare

pouliot *m.* windlass

poulpe *m.* octopus

pouls *m.* pulse

poumon *m.* lung

poupard *m.* baby; doll; — *a.* baby-like; chubby

poupe *f.* poop, stern

poupée *f.* doll; puppet

poupin *a.* baby-like, pink, rosy

pouponnière *f.* nursery school, day nursery

pour *prep.* for, in order to; for the sake of; because of; with regard to; — **ainsi** — **dire** so to speak; — **que** *conj.* in order that; — *m.* pros, advantages; le — et le contre pros and cons

pourboire *m.* gratuity, tip

pourceau *m.* hog, pig

pour-cent *m.* per cent; —**age** percentage

pourchasser *vt.* to pursue; harass

pourfendre *vt.* to attack, tilt with

pourlécher *v.*, **se** — to lick one's lips

pourparlers *m. pl.* parleys, conferences, negotiations

pourpier *m.* (bot.) purslane

pourpre *m.* dark red; —*f.* purple, symbol of royalty

pourpré *a.* dark red

pourquoi *adv.* why

pourri *a.* rotten; putrid

pourrir *vt. & vi.* to rot

pourriture *f.* rot, decay; rottenness

poursuite *f.* pursuit; —**s** *pl.* legal action

poursuivant *m.* plaintiff at law

poursuivre *vt.* to pursue, chase; prosecute; continue

pourtant *adv.* however, still, nevertheless

pourtour *m.* circumference, periphery

pourvoi *m.* appeal at law

pourvoir *vt.* to provide, supply, furnish

pourvoyeur *m.* provider; purveyor; caterer

pourvu que *ccnj.* provided

pousse *f.* shoot, sprout; growth

poussé *a.* deep; comprehensive; elaborate

poussée *f.* push, thrust, shove; growth, sprouting; buoyancy

pousse-pousse *m.* rickshaw

pousser *vt.* to push, urge, drive; utter; — *vi.* push; grow; sprout

poussier *m.* coal dust

poussière *f.* dust; spray

poussiéreux *a.* dusty

poussin *m.* spring chicken; baby chick

poussinière *f.* incubator for chicks; chicken coop

poussoir *m.* push button

poutrage *m.* beams, rafters

poutre *f.* beam, girder

poutrelle *f.* small beam

pouvoir *vt.* to be able; be possible; — *m.* power, authority

pragmatique *a.* pragmatic

prairie *f.* meadow; grassland, prairie

pralin *m.* kind of fertilizer; burnt-sugar frosting

praline *f.* burnt almond candy, praline

praliner *vt.* to brown (in sugar)

praticabilité *f.* practicability, feasibility

praticable *a.* practicable, feasible; sociable, easy-going

praticien *m.* practitioner

pratiquant *a.* practicing, (eccl.) orthodox

pratique *f.* practice, exercise, use; application; custom; experience; — *a.* practical

pratiquer *vt.* to practice, use, exercise; effect; frequent

pré *m.* meadow

préalable *a.* previous; preliminary; **au** — previously, beforehand

préambule *m.* preamble

préau *m.* yard, playground, recreation area

préavis *m.* advance notice

préaviser *vt.* to give advance notice to

prébendier *m.* (eccl.) prebendary

précaire *a.* precarious

précaution *f.* precaution, caution, care

précautionner *vt.* to warn, caution; **se** — to take precautions

précautionneux *a.* cautious, careful

précédemment *a.* before, previously

précédence *f.* precedence, priority

précédent *a.* preceding, previous, having priority; — *m.* precedent

précéder *vt.* to precede; have precedence of

précellence *f.* superiority

précepte *m.* precept

précepteur *m.* tutor

préceptoral *a.* tutorial, preceptorial

préchauffage m. preheating
prêche f. sermon
prêcher vt. to preach
prêcheur m. (coll.) preacher; — a. preaching, sermonizing
précieux a. precious; affected
préciosité f. affectation; preciosity
précipice m. precipice
précipitamment adv. headlong, in haste, precipitately
précipitation f. precipitation, haste; rain, rainfall
précipité a. precipitate; precipitous, hasty; hurried, rushed; headlong; — m. (chem.) precipitate
précipiter vt. to precipitate, hurry; se — to rush upon, rush into
précis a. precise, exact; — m. brief summary
précisément adv. precisely, just, exactly
préciser vt. to specify
précision f. precision, preciseness, exactness; specification, detail
précité a. above, aforementioned
précoce a. precocious; maturing early
précocité f. precociousness, precocity
préconception f. preconception
préconcevoir vt. to preconceive
préconiser vt. to advocate
préconnaissance f. prior knowledge, foreknowledge
précurseur m. precursor, forerunner
prédateur a. predatory
prédécéder vi. to die first
prédécesseur m. predecessor
prédestination f. predestination
prédestiner vt. to predestine
prédéterminer vt. to predetermine
prédicat m. predicate
prédicateur m. preacher
prédicatif a. predicative
prédiction f. prediction, forecast
prédilection f. predilection; de — favorite
prédire vt. to predict, foretell
prédisposer vt. to predispose; prejudice
prédisposition f. predisposition; prejudice
prédominance f. predominance
prédominant a. predominant, prevailing
prédominer vt. & vi. to predominate
prééminence f. pre-eminence
prééminent a. pre-eminent
préemptif a. pre-emptive
préemption f. pre-emption
préétabli a. pre-established
préétablir vt. to pre-establish
préexister vi. to pre-exist
préfabrication f. prefabrication
préfabriqué a. prefabricated
préface f. preface
préfacer vt. to preface

préfecture f. prefecture; police headquarters in Paris; administrative headquarters of a Department
préférable a. preferable, better
préféré a. preferred; — m. favorite
préférence f. preference; de — preferential; (com.) preferred; preferably
préférer vt. to prefer
préfet m. prefect; — de police chief of police
préfixe m. prefix
préfixer vt. to prefix; determine in advance
préhenseur a. prehensile
préhistorique a. prehistoric
préjudice m. prejudice, wrong, detriment
préjudiciable a. prejudicial, injurious
préjudicier vi. to be injurious, be prejudicial
préjugé m. prejudice, bias; presumption; legal precedent
préjuger vt. to prejudge
prélart m. tarpaulin
prélasser v., se — to act important
prélat m. prelate
prélèvement m. deduction; sample
prélever vt. to deduct, take off
préliminaire a. preliminary
prélude m. prelude
prématuré a. premature, inopportune
préméditation f. premeditation
préméditer vt. to premeditate
prémices f. pl. first fruits; (fig.) beginnings
premier a. first; — ministre m. Prime Minister, premier; le — venu anyone
première f. first performance, opening night
premièrement adv. first, in the first place
premier-né a. & m. first-born
premier-paris m. lead article in newspaper
prémisse f. premise
prémonition f. premonition
prémunir vt. to forewarn; se — contre be prepared for
prenable a. pregnable, accessible
prenant a. attractive; adhesive; — m. taker
prénatal a. prenatal
prendre vt. to take; seize, grab; get; acquire; take on; catch; pick up, call for; take in; influence, gain, win; — vi. to take, set; be effective, work; succeed; freeze; — corps take form; — le change be mistaken; — le large flee; se — to catch, be caught; s'en — à to blame; s'y — to go about it, manage
preneur m. taker; purchaser; catcher
prénom m. first name
prénommé a. above-named

préoccupation *f.* preoccupation, care, concern; absent-mindedness

préoccupé *a.* preoccupied; absentminded

préoccuper *vt.* to preoccupy, concern; **se** — be preoccupied, be busy

préopiner *vi.* to speak *or* vote first

préordonné *a.* preordained

préparateur *m.* preparer; coach

préparation *f.* preparation

préparatoire *a.* preparatory

préparer *vt.* to prepare, get ready; **se** — to get ready; be in the process, be developing

prépondérance *f.* preponderance

prépondérant *a.* preponderant, major, key

préposé *m.* person in charge

préposer *vt.* to name, appoint

prépositif *a.* (gram.) prepositive, prepositional

préposition *f.* preposition

prérogative *f.* prerogative

près *adv.* near, close; **à cela** — except for that; **à peu** — almost, nearly; roughly, approximately; — **de** *prep.* near; nearly; ready to, about to

présage *m.* presage, omen, foreboding

présager *vt.* to forebode, presage, predict

presbyte *a.* far-sighted

presbytère *m.* parsonage, rectory

prescience *f.* prescience

prescient *a.* prescient

prescription *f.* regulation(s); direction(s); prescription (at law)

prescrire *vt.* to prescribe, call for, ordain

préséance *f.* priority, precedence

présence *f.* presence; — **d'esprit** presence of mind

présent *a.* present; — *m.* present time; (gram.) present tense; **à** — at present, right now

présentable *a.* presentable

présentateur *m.* introducer, presenter

présentation *f.* presentation, introduction

présentement *adv.* at the moment, right now

présenter *vt.* to present; introduce; **se** — to present oneself; appear; introduce oneself; arise, come about

préservateur *a.* preservative

préservatif *a. & m.* preservative; preventive; contraceptive; — oral *m.* oral contraceptive

préservation *f.* preservation, conservation, saving

préserver *vt.* to preserve, save, protect

présidence *f.* presidency, chairmanship

président *m.* president, chairman, presiding officer

présidentiel *a.* presidential

présider *vt. & vi.* to preside over

présomptif *a.* presumptive

présomption *f.* presumption

présomptueux *a.* presumptuous

presque *adv.* almost, nearly

presqu'île *f.* peninsula

pressant *a.* pressing, urgent

presse *f.* press; crowd; haste; impressment (history)

pressé *a.* pressed; crowded; squeezed; **in a hurry**; **citron** — lemonade

presse-citron *m.* lemon squeezer

presse-fruits *m.* fruit press

pressentiment *m.* presentiment, feeling, foreboding

pressentir *vt.* to have a presentiment of, sense in advance

presse-papiers *m.* paperweight

presse-purée *f.* vegetable masher

presser *vt. & vi.* to press, squeeze; urge; hurry; **se** — to hurry; crowd

pressier *m.* pressman

pression *f.* pressure; (elec.) tension

pressoir *m.* wine press; push button

pressurer *vt.* to press, extract, squeeze

prestance *f.* bearing, carriage of a person

prestation *f.* prestation; oath; lending, loaning

preste *a.* quick, nimble, agile

prestesse *f.* nimbleness, quickness, agility

prestidigitateur *m.* prestidigitator, magician

prestige *m.* prestige, renown; wonder, marvel

prestigieux *a.* marvelous, amazing

présumer *vt.* to presume, assume; allege

présupposer *vt.* to presuppose

prêt *a.* ready, prepared; — *m.* loan

prétendant *m.* aspirant, candidate, applicant

prétendre *vt.* to claim, maintain; aspire

prétendu *a.* so-called, alleged; — *n.* (coll.) future spouse, intended

prête-nom *m.* figurehead, front

prétentieux *a.* pretentious

prétention *f.* pretension, claim

prêter *vt.* to lend; attribute; — **attention** to pay attention; — **serment** to take an oath; **se** — **à** to lend oneself to, agree to; indulge in

prétérit *m.* preterite

prétexte *m.* pretext, excuse; **sous** — **de** supposedly, presumably

prétexter *vt.* to offer as a pretext

prétoire *m.* courtroom

prêteur *m.* lender; — **sur gages** pawnbroker

prêtre *m.* priest; —**sse** *f.* priestess

prêtrise *f.* priesthood

preuve *f.* proof, evidence

preux *a.* valiant, courageous

prévaloir *vi.* to prevail; **se — ** to avail oneself

prévaricateur *a.* dishonest public official

prévarication *f.* malfeasance, dishonesty

prévenance *f.* kind attention, consideration

prévenant *a.* considerate, attentive; engaging, prepossessing

prévenir *vt.* to anticipate; prevent; prejudice; warn, inform

préventif *a.* preventive; pre-emptive (cards)

prévention *f.* prejudice; custody

prévenu *a.* prejudiced, accused (at law)

prévision *f.* forecast, estimate

prévoir *vt.* to foresee; forecast; provide for, anticipate

prévôt *m.* provost

prévoyance *f.* foresight, precaution

prévoyant *a.* foreseeing, looking ahead, farsighted

prie-dieu *m.* prayer desk

prier *vt.* to pray; ask; invite; **je vous (en) prie** please, if you please

prière *f.* prayer; request

prieuré *m.* priory

primaire *a.* primary

primauté *f.* priority; primacy

prime *f.* premium; bonus, gift; (eccl.) prime; **— ** *a.* first, earliest; **de — abord** first of all

primer *vt.* to surpass; give a prize to

primerose *f.* hollyhock

primesaut *m.* first impulse

prime-sautier *a.* impulsive; quick

primeur *f.* newness, earliness; early crop

primevère *f.* (bot.) primrose; cowslip

primitif *a.* primitive; primary; early; earliest; crude

primo *adv.* first of all, firstly

primogéniture *f.* primogeniture

primordial *a.* primordial, primeval

prince *m.* prince; ruler, monarch

princeps *a.*, **édition — ** *f.* first edition

princesse *f.* princess

princier *a.* princely, royal

principal *a.* principal, main, chief; **— ** *m.* principal; main point, main thing

principauté *f.* principality

principe *m.* principle

printanier *a.* spring, springlike

printemps *m.* spring, springtime

priorité *f.* priority, precedence

pris *a.* taken, caught; busy, occupied; **bien — ** having a good figure *or* shape

prise *f.* taking, capture; hold, grip; setting, hardening; engaging of gears; valve, intake; (naut.) prize; **en venir aux –s** to come to blows, come to grips; **hors de — ** out of gear; **lâcher — **

to let go; **— de corps** arrest; **— de courant** (elect.) plug, outlet; **— de tabac** pinch of snuff; **— de vue** viewfinder

prisée *f.* evaluation, appraisal

priser *vt.* to appraise, value, prize; to take snuff

priseur *m.* appraiser; auctioneer; user of snuff

prismatique *a.* prismatic

prisme *m.* prism

prisonnier *m.* prisoner

privation *f.* privation; deprivation; poverty; hardship

privautés *f. pl.* familiarity, liberties

privé *a.* private; privy; tame

priver *vt.* to deprive; **se — ** to do without, stint

privilège *m.* privilege; authorization, license

privilégié *a.* privileged; authorized, licensed; preferred (stock)

privilégier *vt.* to privilege; authorize, license

prix *m.* price, value, cost; prize, award; **à tout — ** at any price; **au — de** at the price of; compared with, in comparison with; **— dirigé** (econ.) price control; **hors de — ** prohibitive; **— fixe** set price

prix-courant *m.* price list, catalog

probable *a.* probable, likely

probabilité *f.* probability, likelihood

probe *a.* honest, upright, of integrity

problème *m.* problem

procède *m.* proceeding, procedure; process

procéder *vi.* to proceed

procédure *f.* procedure; proceedings

procès *m.* lawsuit; trial; ceremony, formality, ado; process

processif *a.* pertaining to courtroom procedure

processionnel *a.* processional

processionner *vi.* to file by (as in a procession)

processus *m.* process; development

procès-verbal *m.* report, record, minutes

prochain *a.* next; neighboring, nearest; imminent; **— ** *m.* neighbor, fellow man

prochainement *adv.* in the near future, shortly, soon

proche *a.* near, close; **–es** *m. pl.* relatives

proclamation *f.* proclamation

proclamer *vt.* to proclaim

proconsul *m.* proconsul

procréateur *a.* procreative; **— ** *m.* procreator

procréation *f.* procreation

procréer *vt.* to procreate

procurable *a.* procurable, obtainable

procuration *f.* power of attorney; proxy

procurer *vt.* to procure, obtain

procureur *m.* attorney; prosecuting attorney, prosecutor

prodigalité *f.* prodigality; extravagance

prodige *m.* prodigy, marvel

prodigieux *a.* prodigious

prodigue *a. & m.* prodigal; spendthrift

prodiguer *vt.* to waste, squander; lavish

producer *m.* movie producer

producteur *a.* productive; — *m.* producer

productif *a.* productive

production *f.* production; producing; yield; product

productivité *f.* productivity

produire *vt.* to produce; yield, give, bear; se — to happen, take place, occur

produit *m.* product; proceeds

proéminence *f.* prominence; protuberance

proéminent *a.* prominent; protuberant

profanateur *m.* profaner

profanation *f.* profanation, desecration

profane *a.* profane; sacrilegious; secular, lay; — *m.* layman, uninitiated person; something profane

profaner *vt.* to profane, desecrate

proférer *vt.* to utter

professer *vt.* to profess; teach

professeur *m.* professor, teacher

profession *f.* profession; occupation, business

professionnel *a. & m.* professional

professoral *a.* professorial

professorat *m.* professorship

profil *m.* profile, side view; outline, shape, contour

profilé *a.* in sections, sectional; streamlined

profilée *f.* side view

profiler *vt.* to profile; shape; se — to be silhouetted, be outlined

profitable *a.* profitable, advantageous

profiter *vi.* to profit, be profitable; gain by; grow, develop

profiteur *m.* profiteer

profond *a.* profound; deep; — *m.* deepest part, depth(s)

profondeur *f.* profundity, depth

profus *a.* profuse

profusion *f.* profusion, abundance

progéniture *f.* progeny, offspring

prognostique *a.* prognostic

programme *m.* program; plan; curriculum

progrès *m.* progress

progresser *vi.* to progress

progressif *a.* progressive

progressiste *a. & m. & f.* (pol.) progressive

progression *f.* progress, progression

prohiber *vt.* to prohibit, forbid

prohibitif *a.* prohibitive

proie *f.* prey; en — à prey to; subject to; affected by

projecteur *m.* projector; searchlight

projectile *a. & m.* projectile; — balistique ballistic missile

projection *f.* projection; (phot.) slide; beam, shaft of light

projecture *f.* projection

projet *m.* project, plan; — de vol flight plan

projeter *vt.* to project; plan

prolétaire *a. & m.* proletarian

prolétariat *m.* proletariate

prolifération *f.* proliferation

prolifère *a.* proliferous

prolifique *a.* prolific

prolixe *a.* prolix, verbose

prolixité *f.* prolixity, verbosity

prolongateur *m.* extension cord

prolongation *f.* prolongation; extension of time

prolongé *a.* prolonged, long

prolongement *m.* prolongation; extension

prolonger *vt.* to prolong, extend, lengthen

promenade *f.* walking, walk, stroll; promenade; faire une — take a walk; — en auto auto ride; — en bateau boat ride

promener *vt.* to take for a walk; se — to take a walk

promeneur *m.* walker

promenoir *m.* promenade; (theat.) standing room

promesse *f.* promise

prometteur *a.* promising

promettre *vt. & vi.* to promise

promis *a.* promised; — *m.* fiancé; -e *f.* fiancée

promiscuité *f.* promiscuity

promontoire *m.* promontory, cape

promoteur *m.* promoter

promotion *f.* promotion

promouvoir *vt.* to promote

prompt *a.* prompt, ready, quick minded

promptitude *f.* promptitude; readiness, quickness

promu *a.* promoted

promulgation *f.* promulgation

promulguer *vt.* to promulgate, publish

pronation *f.* prone position

prône *m.* sermon

prôner *vt.* to praise; preach

pronom *m.* pronoun

pronominal *a.* pronominal; verbe — *m.* reflexive verb

prononçable *a.* pronounceable

prononcé *a.* pronounced, marked, decided, definite; — *m.* decision, verdict

prononcer *vt.* to pronounce; deliver; declare

prononciation *f.* pronunciation

pronostic *m.* prognostic, prognostication; (med.) prognosis

pronostiquer *vt.* to prognosticate, predict

propagande *f.* publicity, advertising, propaganda

propagandiste *m. & f.* propagandist

propagateur *a.* propagating; — *m.* propagator

propager *vt.* to propagate; se — to spread; be propagated

propédeutique *f.* first year of university studies

propension *f.* propensity

prophétie *f.* prophecy

prophétique *a.* prophetic

prophétiser *vt.* to prophesy; forecast

prophylactique *a.* prophylactic

prophylaxie *f.* prophylaxis

propice *a.* propitious, auspicious

propitiatoire *a.* propitiatory, conciliatory

proportionné *a.* proportioned; proportionate

proportionnel *a.* proportional

proportionner *vt.* to proportion

propos *m.* discourse, talk, words; design; purpose; subject; à — suitable, appropriate; by the way; à — de on the subject of; hors de — inopportune, out of place

proposer *vt.* to propose, present, recommend, suggest

proposition *f.* proposition, proposal, motion; clause

propre *a.* one's own; clean; proper; fit, suitable

proprement *adv.* properly; cleanly; appropriately

propreté *f.* cleanliness, neatness

propriétaire *m. & f.* proprietor, owner; landlord

propriété *f.* property; ownership; propriety; quality, characteristic

propulser *vt.* to propel

propulseur *a.* propelling; — *m.* propellant

propulsion *f.* propulsion; — à réaction jet propulsion

prorata *m.* share; au — pro rata

proroger *vt.* to extend, prolong; adjourn

prosaïque *a.* prosaic

prosateur *m.* prose writer

proscenium *m.* (theat.) proscenium

proscription *f.* proscription, proscribing

proscrire *vt.* to proscribe, outlaw; abolish, forbid

proscrit *a.* proscribed, outlawed; — *m.* proscript, outlaw

prosélyte *m. & f.* proselyte

prospecter *vt.* to prospect

prospecteur *m.* prospector

prospectus *m.* prospectus; leaflet, handbill

prospérer *vi.* to prosper, thrive

prospérité *f.* prosperity

prostate *f.* prostate

prosternation *f.* prone position; prostration; bowing

prosterné *a.* prone, prostrate

prosternement *m.* prone position, prostration; bowing

prosterner *vt.*, se — to prostrate oneself; bow down

prostituée *f.* prostitute, call girl

prostitution *f.* prostitution

prostration *f.* prostration, exhaustion, breakdown; prone position

prostré *a.* prostrate, exhausted

protagoniste *m.* protagonist

protane *m.* methane

protase *f.* (theat.) protasis, exposition

protecteur *m.* protector, guard; patron; — *a.* protective

protection *f.* protection, patronage

protectionisme *m.* protectionism

protectionniste *m. & f.* protectionist

protectorat *m.* protectorate

protéger *vt.* to protect, guard; patronize

protège-vue *m.* eyeshade

protéine *f.* protein

protestant *a. & m.* Protestant

protestantisme *m.* Protestantism

protestateur *m.* protestor

protestation *f.* protest; protestation

protester *vt. & vi.* to protest

protêt *m.* legal protest

prothèse *f.* prosthesis, artificial limb *or* part

protocolaire *a.* pertaining to protocol

protocole *m.* protocol, etiquette

proton *m.* proton

protoplasme *m.* protoplasm

prototype *m.* prototype

protozoaire *m.* protozoan

protubérance *f.* protuberance; bump; knob

protubérant *a.* protuberant

proue *f.* (naut.) prow, bow

prouesse *f.* prowess; feat

prouver *vt.* to prove, establish

provenance *f.* origin, source; production; en — de coming from

provençal *a.* Provençal, of Provence; — *m.* Provençal

Provence *f.* Provence

provende *f.* fodder, provender

provenir *vi.* to proceed, arise, come, result, issue

proverbe *m.* proverb

providence *f.* providence

providentiel *a.* providential

province *f.* province; country; de — provincial

provincial *a. & m.* provincial
proviseur *m.* school principal
provision *f.* provision; supply; stock; deposit; reserve; funds
provisoire *a.* provisional, temporary, acting
provocant *a.* provocative
provocateur *a.* provocative; — *m.* provoker, instigator
provocatif *a.* provocative
provoquer *vt.* to provoke, instigate; arouse; challenge
proximité *f.* proximity, nearness
prude *a.* prudish; — *f.* prude
prudemment *adv.* prudently
prudence *f.* prudence, caution, discretion
prudent *a.* prudent, cautious, discreet
pruderie *f.* prudery, prudishness
prud'homme *m.* elected arbiter
prune *f.* plum
pruneau *m.* prune
prunelle *f.* pupil of the eye; sloe
prunier *m.* plum tree
prurit *m.* itching
Prusse *f.* Prussia
Prussien *m. & a.* Prussian
psalmiste *m.* psalmist
psalmodier *vt. & vi.* to intone
psaume *m.* psalm
psautier *m.* psalm book, Psalter
pseudonyme *m.* pseudonym
pseudopode *n.* pseudopod
psychanalyse *f.* psychoanalysis
psychanalyser *vt.* to psychoanalyze
psychanalyste *m. & f.* psychoanalyst
psychiatre *m.* psychiatrist
psychiatrie *f.* psychiatry
psychique *a.* psychic
psychologie *f.* psychology; — industrielle industrial psychology
psychologique *a.* psychological
psychologue *m. & f.* psychologist
psychose *f.* psychosis
psychosomatique *a.* psychosomatic
psychothérapie *f.* psychotherapy
ptomaïne *f.* ptomaine
P.T.T.: Postes Télégraphes Téléphones postal and telegraph service
puant *a.* smelly, stinking
pubère *a.* in puberty, pubescent
puberté *f.* puberty
public (publique) *a.* public; open; — *m.* public, the people
publication *f.* publication, publishing
publiciste *m.* publicist, newspaperman
publicitaire *m.* (com.) adman
publicité *f.* advertising
publier *vt.* to publish
puce *f.* flea
pucelle *f.* maid, virgin

puceron *m.* aphid
pudeur *f.* decency, modesty
pudibond *a.* prudish, excessively modest
pudibonderie *f.* prudishness
pudique *a.* chaste
puer *vi.* to stink, smell
puériculture *f.* raising, rearing of children
puéril *a.* childish, puerile
puérilité *f.* puerility
puffisme *m.* publicity, boosting
puffiste *m.* booster
pugilat *m.* pugilism, boxing
pugiliste *m.* pugilist, boxer
puiné *a.* younger
puis *adv.* then, afterwards; moreover, besides
puisage *m.* pumping; droit de — *m.* water rights
puisard *m.* cesspool; sump
puisatier *m.* well digger
puisette *f.* scoop, ladle
puisoir *m.* large industrial scoop
puisque *conj.* since, as; but
puissamment *adv.* powerfully
puissance *f.* power, force, strength; authority, control
puissant *a.* powerful, strong, potent
puits *m.* well; shaft; hole
pullman *m.* luxury car; parlor car
pulluler *vi.* to multiply; swarm; pullulate
pulmonaire *a.* pulmonary
pulmonie *f.* lung disease
pulpe *f.* pulp
pulper *vt.* to pulp
pulpeux *a.* pulpy
pulsatif *a.* throbbing
pulsation *f.* pulsation, throbbing
pulvérisateur *m.* pulverizer; atomizer
pulvérisation *f.* pulverization
pulvériser *vt.* to pulverize, crush, grind; atomize
pulvériseur *m.* disc plow
puma *m.* puma
punaise *f.* bedbug; thumbtack
punch *m.* punch (beverage)
punir *vt.* to punish
punition *f.* punishment, punishing; penalty
pupe *f.* pupa, chrysalis
pupille *m. & f.* legal ward; — *f.* pupil of the eye
pupitre *m.* desk; lectern; music stand
pur *a.* pure; simple; clear
purée *f.* thick soup; mashed vegetable
pureté *f.* purity, pureness
purgatif *a. & m.* purgative
purgation *f.* purgation, purging
purge *f.* purge; purgative; purging; draining; cleaning; redeeming, paying off
purger *vt.* to purge, cleanse; clear; redeem,

pay off; drain
purificateur *a.* purifying; — *m.* purifier
purification *f.* purification
purifier *vt.* to purify, refine; clean
puriste *m.* purist
purpurin *m.* crimson, dark red
pur-sang *m.* thoroughbred, race horse
purulent *a.* purulent
pus *m.* pus
pusillanime *a.* pusillanimous
pusillanimité *f.* pusillanimity
pustule *f.* pustule
putatif *a.* putative, supposed
putois *m.* skunk, polecat
putréfaction *f.* putrefaction
putréfier *vt.* to putrify
putride *a.* putrid, rotten
puzzle *m.* jigsaw puzzle
pygmée *m. & f.* pygmy
pyjama *m.* pajamas
pylône *m.* pylon, tower
pylore *m.* pyloris
pyorrhée *f.* pyorrhea
pyramidal *a.* pyramidal
pyramide *f.* pyramid
Pyrénées *f. pl.* Pyrenees
pyrite *f.* pyrite
pyrotechnie *f.* pyrotechnics
pyrotechnique *a.* pyrotechnic
python *m.* python

Q

Quadragésime *f.* old name of Lent; **dimanche de la** — *m.* first Sunday in Lent
quadrangulaire *a.* quadrangular
quadratique *a.* quadratic
quadrature *f.* squaring
quadriennal *a.* quadrennial
quadrilatéral *a.* quadrilateral
quadrilatère *m.* quadrilateral
quadrillage *m.* squaring, checkering, cross-ruling
quadrillé *a.* squared, checked, cross-ruled
quadriller *vt.* to cross-rule
quadrimoteur *a.* four-engined
quadrupède *m.* quadruped
quadrupler *vt. & vi.* to quadruple
quai *m.* quay, wharf; embankment; (rail.) platform
qualificatif *a.* qualifying
qualification *f.* qualification; qualifying; character; naming, calling, designating
qualifier *vt.* to qualify; call, designate; **se** — to qualify; call oneself
qualitatif *a.* qualitative
qualité *f.* quality; rank; characteristic, property; qualification; occupation

quand *adv.* when; **depuis** — how long; — *conj.* when; although, though, even if; — **même** even though; in spite of all; just the same
quant à *prep.* as to, as for
quant-à-moi, quant-à-soi *m.* reserve, aloofness
quantième *m.* a day of the month
quantitatif *a.* quantitative; (gram.) quantity
quantité *f.* quantity, amount
quantum *m.* quantum; amount
quarantaine *f.* forty, around forty, two score; quarantine
quarante *a.* forty
quarantième *a.* fortieth
quart *m.* quarter, fourth; (naut.) watch; ¼ liter; — **d'heure** quarter-hour, fifteen minutes
quarte *f.* quart; (mus.) fourth
quarteron *a. & m.* quadroon
quartier *m.* quarter, district; piece, part, portion; barracks, camp; — **commerçant** shopping plaza; — **général** headquarters
quarto *adv.* fourthly; in fourth place
quartz *m.* quartz
quasi *adv.* almost
quatorze *a.* fourteen; fourteenth
quatorzième *a.* fourteenth
quatrain *m.* quatrain
quatre *a.* four; fourth
quatre-saisons *f.* strawberry plant bearing very small fruit; **marchand des** — *m.* pushcart vendor of seasonal fruits and vegetables
quatre-vingts *a.* eighty
quatrième *a.* fourth
quatuor *m.* quartet
que *conj.* that; if, when, as, than, till, until, whether, than; **afin** —, **de sorte** — so that; **ne . . . .** — only; — *pron.* that, whom, which; — *interr. pron.* what; how; — **de** how many, how much; **ce** — that which, what; which; (with exclamations)
quel (quelle) *a. interr.* which, what; what (a) (in exclamations); — *pron.* whatever
quelconque *a.* any, whatever, any at all; mediocre
quelque *a.* some, any; a few; — **chose** something, anything; — **part** somewhere; — *adv.* however; — *pron.* whatever
quelquefois *adv.* sometimes
quelqu'un, quelqu'une *indefinite pron.* one; somebody, someone; **quelques-uns, quelques-unes** *pl.* some
quémander *vi. & vt.* to beg for, solicit
quenelle *f.* meatball, fishball

quenouille *f.* distaff; bedpost; bulrush

querelle *f.* quarrel, row, feud

quereller *vt.* to quarrel with; **se —** to quarrel; have a strong difference of opinion; have a falling out

querelleur *a.* quarrelsome; **—** *m.* quarreler

quérir *vt.* to find, get, bring, fetch

qu'est-ce que *interr. pron.* what (as object of verb)

qu'est-ce qui *interr. pron.* what (as subject of verb)

question *f.* question; matter; **poser une —, faire une —** to ask a question

questionnaire *m.* questionnaire; questions

questionner *vt.* to question, interrogate

questionneur *a.* inquisitive; **—** *m.* interrogator

quetsche *f.* purple plum

quête *f.* quest, search; (eccl.) collection

quêter *vt.* to collect; look for

queue *f.* tail; line; handle; stalk; train of a garment; **piano à —** *m.* grand piano; **faire la —** to line up

queue-d'aronde *f.* dovetail

queue-de-chat *f.* cat-o'-nine-tails; cirrus cloud

queue-de-rat *f.* round *or* rat-tail file

qui *interr. pron.* who, whom; **à —** whose, to whom; **de —** whose, of whom; **—** *rel. pron.* who, which, that; the one who, he who; **ce —** that which, what; **which; — que** whoever; **— que ce soit** anyone

quiconque *pron.* whoever; anyone

quidam *m.* unidentified person, someone; unknown party (law)

qui est-ce que *interr. pron.* whom

qui est-ce qui *interr. pron.* who

quiétude *f.* quietude

quignon *m.* hunk, chunk

quille *f.* ninepin, tenpin; (naut.) keel; **jeu de –s** *m.* bowling

quincaillerie *f.* hardware, hardware store

quincaillier *m.* hardware dealer

quinconce *f.*, **en —** alternately; staggered, zigzag

quinine *f.* quinine

quinquennal *a.* quinquennial, five-year

quintal *m.* hundredweight, quintal

quinte *f.* (mus.) fifth; fit of coughing

quintette *f.* quintet

quinteux *a.* fitful, restive

quintuple *a.* quintuple

quintupler *vt. & vi.* to quintuple

quintuplés *m. pl.* quintuplets

quinzaine *f.* about fifteen; two-week period, fortnight

quinze *a.* fifteen; fifteenth; **— jours** two weeks

quinzième *a.* fifteenth

quiproquo *m.* mistake, mistaken identity

quittance *f.* receipt

quitte *a.* free, clear; rid; quits, even; **jouer à — ou double** to play double or nothing

quitter *vt.* to leave; take off; abandon

qui-vive *m.* (mil.) challenge by a sentry, **être sur le —** to be on the watch, be alert

quoi *interr. pron.* what; **— de nouveau** what's new; **un je ne sais —** a certain something; **—** *rel. pron.* what; **de —** enough; wherewithal; reason, cause, justification; **il n'y a pas de —** you're welcome, don't mention it; **— que** whatever; **— qu'il en soit** be that as it may; **sans —** or else, otherwise

quoique *conj.* though, although

quolibet *m.* gibe, jeering remark

quote-part *f.* quota, share

quotidien *a.* daily; **—** *m.* daily newspaper

quotidiennement *adv.* every day, daily

quotient *m.* quotient; quota

R

rabâcher *vi.* to repeat, rehash

rabais *m.* reduction, discount, rebate

rabaisser *vt.* to lower, reduce, humiliate, deprecate

rabat *m.* flap

rabat-joie *m.* killjoy

rabattre *vt.* to turn down; lower; fold back; flatten; lower, reduce the price; **—** *vi.* to turn off; **se —** to fall back; fold

rabbin *m.* rabbi

râblé *a.* strong, strong-backed

rabonnir *vt. & vi.* to improve

rabot *m.* plane (tool)

raboter *vt.* to plane, smooth

raboteux *a.* rough, uneven; knotty

rabougrir *vt.* to stunt

rabouter *vt.* to place end to end

rabrouer *vt.* to snub; become very angry at, become surly toward

racaille *f.* rubbish, trash; social outcast

raccommodage *m.* mending, repairing; darning

raccommodement *m.* reconciliation

raccommoder *vt.* to mend, repair; darn; reconcile; **se —** to be reconciled, make up

raccord *m.* joint, coupling, connection; tieing together, joining

raccordement *m.* connecting, joining; junction

raccorder *vt.* to connect, join, tie together, link; **se —** to join, fit

raccourci *a.* abridged, shortened; **—** *m.* abridgment; short cut; book digest; **en**

— briefly

raccourcir *vt.* to shorten; abridge; — *vi.* to become shorter

raccourcissement *m.* shortening; shrinking

raccoutrer *vt.* to repair, mend

raccroc *m.* stroke of luck, fluke, chance

raccrocher *vt.* to hook up; hang up (telephone); **se** — to grab hold; regain, recover

race *f.* race, family, breed; **de** — thoroughbred

racé *a.* thoroughbred

rachat *m.* buying back, repurchase; redemption

rachetable *a.* redeemable

racheter *vt.* to buy back, repurchase; redeem; ransom

rachitisme *m.* rickets

racine *f.* root

raciste *m.* racist

racketter *m.* racketeer

raclage *m.* scraping

racle *f.* scraper

racler *vt.* to scrape; rake

raclette *f.* scraper; hoe

racloir *m.* scraping implement

raclure *f.* scrapings

racoler *vt.* to recruit, enlist, enroll

racoleur *m.* recruiter

racontage *m.* reccunting, telling; gossip

raconter *vt.* to relate, tell

raconteur *m.* storyteller

racornir *vt.* to harden, make horny

racquitter *v.*, **se** — to recoup

radar *m.* radar

radariste *m.* radar operator

rade *f.* (naut.) roadstead, basin, harbor

radeau *m.* raft, float

radiateur *m.* radiator; — *a.* radiating

radiation *f.* radiation; cancellation; erasure, crossing out; disbarment

radical *a. & m.* radical

radicelle *f.* (bot.) radicle

radier *m.* frame, foundation floor

radier *vi.* to radiate; — *vt.* to erase, cross out; strike off

radieux *a.* radiant, bright

radio *f.* radio; — *m.* radio operator

radio-actif *a.* radioactive

radio-activité *f.* radioactivity

radio-astronomie *f.* radioastronomy

radiobalisage *m.* (avi.) radio beam

radiocommunication *f.* radio communication

radiodiffuser *vt.* to broadcast

radiodiffusion *f.* radio program; broadcast

radio-émission *f.* broadcast; broadcasting

radiogoniomètre *m.* direction finder

radiogramme *m.* radiogram, radio message

radiographie *f.* X-ray photography, radiography

radiographier *vt.* to X-ray

radiographique *a.* X-ray, radiographic

radiojournal *m.* radio newscast

radiologie *f.* radiology

radiologique *a.* radiological, X-ray

radiologue *m. & f.* radiologist, X-ray technician

radioreportage *m.* radio report, program

radioreporter *m.* radio commentator

radioscopie *f.* radioscopy

radiotéléscope *m.* radio telescope

radiothérapie *f.* X-ray therapy

radium *m.* radium

radius *m.* (anat.) radius

radotage *m.* dotage; raving; nonsense

radoter *vi.* to be in one's dotage; talk nonsense

radoteur *m.* dotard

radoub *m.* (naut.) repair; **bassin de** — *m.* drydock

radouber *vt.* to repair; put in drydock

radoucir *vt.* to soften, appease; calm; **se** — to relent, soften; turn mild

rafale *f.* gust, flurry; burst, volley

raffermir *vt.* to strengthen, make firm(er), reinforce; harden; **se** — to become firmer, become stronger; harden

raffinage *m.* refining

raffiné *a.* refined

raffinement *m.* refinement

raffiner *vt.* to refine; **se** — to become refined

raffinerie *f.* refinery; refining

raffoler (de) *vi.* to be wild about; be infatuated with; dote on

raffûter *vt.* to sharpen, resharpen

rafistoler *vt.* to patch up

rafle *f.* raid; loot; looting; police roundup

rafler *vt.* to loot, clean out (a house); round up (criminals)

rafraîchir *vt.* to refresh, cool; renovate; touch up; remind; trim hair, **se** — to refresh oneself; drink; become cooler (weather)

rafraîchissant *a.* cooling, refreshing

rafraîchissement *m.* refreshment, cooling; touching up; brushing up

rage *f.* rage, madness; passion, mania; rabies; **à la** — *adv.* excessively

rager *vi.* (coll.) to rage, fume

ragot *a.* stocky, squat; — *m.* (coll.) gossip, talk

ragoût *m.* stew, ragout; relish

ragoûter *vt.* to revive the appetite

rai *m.* radius; beam of light; spoke

raid *m.* raid; endurance contest; (avi.) long flight, trip

raide *a.* stiff; inflexible; steep; firm; —

adv. quickly; on the spot

raideur *f.* stiffness; steepness

raidir *vt.* to stiffen; **se —** to get stiff, stiffen, become tight

raie *f.* line, stripe; part in the hair; furrow; ray, skate (fish)

raifort *m.* horseradish

rail *m.* rail

railler *vt.* to laugh at, make fun of; — *vi.* to joke

raillerie *f.* raillery, mockery, joking

railleur *a.* jeering, scoffing, joking; — *m.* scoffer, joker

rainer *vt.* to groove

rainette *f.* tree frog

rainure *f.* groove; channel

raiponce *f.* rampion

rais *m.* spoke

raisin *m.* grape, grapes; **grappe de —** *f.* bunch of grapes; **— sec** raisin; **— de Corinthe** currant

raison *f.* reason, cause, motive; justification; satisfaction, amends; (math.) ratio; **à —** de at the rate of; **à plus forte — all** the more; **avoir —** to be right; **en — de** by reason of, because of; **— d'être** rational explanation, justification

raisonnable *a.* reasonable, rational; just, fair

raisonné *a.* founded on reason, methodical

raisonnement *m.* reasoning; argument

raisonner *vi.* to reason; — *vt.* to think out, study

rajeunir *vt.* to make young again; rejuvenate; — *vi.* to grow young again; be rejuvenated

rajustement *m.* readjustment; setting in order

rajuster *vt.* to readjust, set in order again, straighten, fix

râle *m.* death rattle; rail

ralenti *a.* slow, slower, slowed down; — *m.* slow motion

ralentir *vt.* to slacken, lessen, slow down

ralentissement *m.* slackening, slowing down, abatement

râler *vi.* give the death rattle; grumble

ralliement *m.* rally, rallying

rallier *vt.* to rally; assemble, bring together

rallonge *f.* extension; table leaf

rallongement *m.* lengthening, extending

rallonger *vt.* to lengthen, extend; thin a sauce

rallumer *vt.* to light again, rekindle

ramage *m.* warbling of birds; prattle; flowering; floral pattern

ramas *m.* heap, accumulation, collection

ramassé *a.* stocky; compact

ramasse-miettes *m.* silent butler, crumb tray

ramasse-poussière *m.* dustpan

ramasser *vt.* to pick up, gather, collect; **se —** to gather together; pick oneself up; crouch

ramassis *m.* collection, accumulation

rambarde *f.* railing

rame *f.* oar; ream of paper; (rail.) train, string of cars; convoy; wooden support for plants

ramé *a.* supported by sticks

rameau *m.* bough, branch; **dimanche des Rameaux** *m.* Palm Sunday

ramée *f.* boughs, arbor

ramener *vt.* to bring back, lead back, take back; pull down one's hat; restore

ramequin *m.* filled pastry shell

ramer *vi.* to row; grow antlers

rameur *m.* rower, oarsman

rameux *a.* ramose, having many branches

ramification *f.* ramification; branch

ramifier *v.*, **se —** to ramify, branch out

ramille *f.* twig

ramoindrir *vt.* to lessen, diminish, reduce

ramollir *vt.* to soften; weaken; **se —** to become soft

ramollissement *m.* softening

ramonage *m.* chimney sweeping

ramoner *vt.* to sweep a chimney

ramoneur *m.* chimney sweep

rampant *a.* creeping, crawling; rampant (heraldry)

rampe *f.* flight of stairs; balustrade, banister, handrail; slope; ramp; footlights of a stage

ramper *vi.* to crawl, creep; grovel; toady

ramure *f.* branches; antlers

rance *a.* rancid

ranch *m.* ranch

rancidité *f.* rancidness

rancir *vi.* to become rancid

rancœur *f.* bitterness, rancor

rançon *f.* ransom

rançonner *vt.* to ransom

rancune *f.* grudge, ill-feeling, rancor, spite

rancunier *a.* rancorous, spiteful, vindictive

randonnée *f.* trip, outing, excursion

rang *m.* row, file, line; rank, standing

rangé *a.* ranged; steady, regular, orderly; pitched battle

rangée *f.* row, file, line

ranger *vt.* to range; rank, put in ranks; arrange, set in order; put away; **se —** to line up; pull up; take sides; settle down

ranimer *vt.* to restore, revive; rouse; **se —** to become animated again; enliven

Raoul (*m.*) Ralph

rapace *a.* rapacious; grasping; ravenous

rapacité *f.* rapacity

râpage *m.* grating, filing

rapatriement *m.* repatriation

rapatrier *vt.* to repatriate

râpe *f.* grater; file, rasp

râpé *a.* threadbare; grated

râper *vt.* to grate; file; wear out (clothing)

rapetasser *vt.* to patch up clothing; mend extensively

rapetisser *vt.* to make smaller, shorten; shrink; — *vi.* to become shorter, become smaller

raphia *m.* raffia

rapide *a.* rapid, swift, fast; — *m.* express train; –s *pl.* rapids in a river

rapidité *f.* rapidity, speed

rapiéçage *m.* patching, mending

rapiécer *vt.* to piece; patch, mend

rapière *f.* rapier

rapine *f.* pillage, pillaging

rapiner *vt. & vi.* to pillage

rappareiller *vt.* to match

rapparier *vt.* to pair, match

rappel *m.* recall; calling in; call to arms; (theat.) curtain call; reminder; revocation, repeal; back spacer of a typewriter

rappeler *vt.* to recall, call back; remind; se — to remember, recall

rapport *m.* report; return, profit; relation, connection; ratio; par — à, sous le — de with regard to, with respect to

rapportable *a.* attributable

rapporter *vt.* to bring back, carry back; return, produce, bring in; report, tell of; revoke; attribute; se — to refer, relate, have to do with; s'en — à to rely on

rapporteur *m.* reporter; tattletale; (math.) protractor; sponsor, introducer

rapprendre *vt.* to learn again; teach again

rapproché *a.* close, near; connected, related; close-set (eyes)

rapprochement *m.* reconciliation; bringing together; comparison, comparing; closeness

rapprocher *vt.* to draw near again, bring near; bring together; compare

rapsodie *f.* rhapsody

rapt *m.* abduction, kidnapping

râpure *f.* gratings, scrapings

raquette *f.* racket; snowshoe

rare *a.* rare; thin, sparse; unusual, uncommon

raréfaction *f.* rarefaction; scarcity

raréfier *vt.* to rarefy; make scarce

rareté *f.* rarity; scarcity; unusualness

rarissime *a.* very rare

ras *a.* short-haired, close-cut; smooth-shaven; bare; plain, smooth; open; flat; au — de on a level with; à — de level with; faire table –e start from scratch;

make a clean sweep

rasant *a.* grazing, skimming, staying close to; boring, dull

rase-mottes *m.* (avi.) low-level flying, hedge-hopping

raser *vt.* to shave; raze; graze, skim; stay close to; bore; se — to shave; be bored

raseur *m.* shaver; bore

rasoir *m.* razor; — à lame straight razor; cuir à — *m.* razor strop; — de sûreté safety razor

rassasiant *a.* satisfying, filling

rassasiement *m.* satisfying, satiety

rassasier *vt.* to satiate, fill, satisfy; se — to fill up, eat one's fill

rassemblement *m.* assembling; assemblage

rassembler *vt.* to collect, assemble; unite; se — to meet; assemble

rasseoir *vt.* to seat again

rasséréner *vt.* to calm; se — to brighten, clear up

rassir *vi.* to harden (bread)

rassis *a.* calm, sedate; stale (bread)

rassortir *vt.* (com.) to restock

rassurer *vt.* to reassure; strengthen; se — be reassured

rat *m.* rat; — musqué muskrat

rataplan *m.* roll of a drum

ratatiner *vt.* to dry up; shrink, shrivel

rate *f.* spleen

raté *a.* failed, missed; — *m.* failure; dud

râteau *m.* rake

râteler *vt.* to rake

rater *vi.* to miss; fail; misfire; — *vt.* miss, fail in

ratière *f.* rat trap

ratifier *vt.* to ratify

rationaliser *vt.* to rationalize

rationnel *a.* rational

rationner *vt.* to ration

ratisser *vt.* to scrape, rake

ratissoire *f.* rake; scraper

raton *m.* small rat; — laveur raccoon

rattacher *vt.* to tie again, attach, fasten; se — to be tied to, be connected with

ratteindre *vt.* to overtake; retake

rattraper *vt.* to catch again, retake; overtake, catch up with; get back, recover; se — to make up, recoup

rature *f.* erasure; scraping

raturer *vt.* to scratch out, erase

raucité *f.* hoarseness

rauque *a.* hoarse, harsh, raucous

ravager *vt.* to ravage, pillage, devastate; pit by smallpox

ravages *m. pl.* devastation; havoc

ravalement *m.* scraping, cleaning; resurfacing

ravaler *vt.* to reswallow; (fig.) hold back;

take back, retract; **se** — to debase oneself

ravaudage *m.* mending, patching; bungling

ravauder *vt.* to mend, patch

ravi *a.* delighted

ravier *m.* hors-d'œuvres dish

ravigote *f.* sauce with shallots

ravillir *vt.* to vilify

ravin *m.* ravine

raviner *vt.* to furrow

ravir *vt.* to ravish, abduct, steal; delight

raviser *v.*, **se** — to change one's mind

ravissant *a.* delightful, ravishing

ravissement *m.* ravishing, abduction: delight, rapture

ravisseur *m.* ravisher, abductor, kidnapper

ravitaillement *m.* supplying, provisioning, revictualing; refueling

ravitailler *vt.* to supply, provision; **se** — to take in fresh supplies

ravitailleur *m.* supply ship

raviver *vt.* to revive; renew, touch up; reopen a wound

ravoir *vt.* to have again; recover, get back

rayé *a.* striped; rifled; (fig.) suppressed; erased

rayer *vt.* to erase, cross out, strike out; rule, line; rifle a gun

rayon *m.* ray, beam; spoke; radius; furrow, row; shelf; department (in a store); **chef de** — floorwalker; — **X X** ray

rayonnant *a.* radiant, beaming; radiating

rayonne *f.* rayon

rayonnement *m.* radiation, radiancy

rayonner *vi.* to radiate, beam

rayure *f.* erasure, crossing out; scratch; stripe; groove, furrow; rifling

raz *m.* race, current; — **de marée** tidal wave

razzia *f.* raid

razzier *vt.* to raid

réabonnement *m.* renewal of a subscription

réabonner *vt.* **to** renew a subscription

réabsorber *vt.* to reabsorb

réaccoutumer *vt.* to reaccustom

réacteur *m.* reactor; — **nucléaire** nuclear reactor

réactif *m.* (chem.) reagent; — *a.* reactive

réaction *f.* reaction; **avion à** — *m.* jet plane; — **en chaîne** chain reaction; **fusée à** — *f.* jet-propelled missile; **moteur à** — *m.* jet engine

réactionnaire *m. & a.* reactionary

réadmettre *vt.* to readmit

réaffirmer *vt.* to reaffirm

réagir *vi.* to react

réalisable *a.* realizable; practicable, feasible

réalisation *f.* realization, fulfilling, execution; — **de** produced by (movie credit)

réaliser *vt.* to realize, fulfil, execute; convert into money; **se** — to be realized; come true

réalisme *m.* realism

réaliste *m. & f.* realist; — *a.* realistic

réalité *f.* reality

réapparaître *vi.* to reappear

réapparition *f.* reappearance

réapprovisionner *vt.* to restock; revictual

réarmer *vt.* to rearm; refit; recock

réassurer *vt.* to reinsure

rébarbatif *a.* surly, grim

rebâtir *vt.* to rebuild

rebattre *vt.* to beat again; (fig.) repeat uselessly

rebattu *a.* repeated; trite; **sentier** — *m.* beaten track

rebelle *m. & f.* rebel; — *a.* rebellious

rebeller *v.*, **se** — to rebel, resist

rébellion *f.* rebellion, revolt

rebobiner *vt.* to rewind

reboire *vt.* to drink again

reboisement *m.* reforestation, tree conservation

reboiser *vt.* to reforest

rebond *m.* rebound, bounce

rebondi *a.* plump, chubby

rebondir *vi.* to rebound, bounce

rebord *m.* edge, border, rim; ledge

reboucher *vt.* to stop up again; recork

rebours *m.* wrong side; reverse; **à** —, **au** — against the grain; backwards; the wrong way

rebouter *vt.* to set (a broken bone)

reboutonner *vt.* to rebutton

rebrousse-poil (à) *adv.* — against the grain

rebrousser *vt.* to turn back; — **chemin to** retrace one's steps

rebuffade *f.* rebuff, snub

rébus *m.* rebus, puzzle

rebut *m.* outcast; reject; scrap, **trash,** rubbish

rebutant *a.* discouraging, tedious; repellent

rebuter *vt.* to reject, repulse, refuse, rebuff; dishearten

récalcitrance *f.* recalcitrance

récalcitrant *a.* recalcitrant

récapitulation *f.* recapitulation, summary

récapituler *vt.* to recapitulate, summarize

recel, recèlement *m.* concealment (law); receiving of stolen goods

recéler *vt.* to conceal stolen goods; harbor

recéleur *m.* receiver of stolen goods, **fence**

récemment *adv.* recently, lately

recensement *m.* census

recenser *vt.* to make a census; tally, **count**

recenseur *m.* census taker (counter)

récent *a.* recent, new, late

récépissé *m.* receipt, acknowledgment

réceptacle *m.* receptacle

récepteur *m.* receiver; — *a.* receiving

réception *f.* reception; receiving; receipt; **accusé de** — *m.* receipt, acknowledgment

réceptionnaire *m.* (com.) consignee; — *a.* receiving

recette *f.* receipt of money; receiving, collection; recipe; **-s** *pl.* receipts

recevable *a.* acceptable, allowable, admissible

receveur *m.* receiver; tax collector; postmaster

recevoir *vt.* to receive; accept; entertain

rechange *m.* spare, replacement; **pièce de** — spare part; **pneu de** — *m.* spare tire

rechaper *vt.* to recap, retread a tire

réchappé *m.* survivor of a disaster

réchapper *vi.* to escape, survive

recharger *vt.* to recharge, reload

réchaud *m.* chafing dish; heater; stove; — **électrique** hot plate

réchauffer *vt.* to warm up *or* over, rekindle; **se** — to get warm, warm oneself

rechausser *vt.* to put footwear on again

rêche *a.* harsh, rough; bitter

recherche *f.* search, inquiry, investigation; finery, care; **à la** — **de** in search of; **-s** *pl.* research

recherché *a.* choice, rare; much in demand; affected; studied

rechercher *vt.* to seek again; search for; court

rechigné *a.* sulky, crabby

rechigner *vi.* to look unhappy; balk

rechuter *vi.* to relapse; have a relapse

récidive *f.* recurrence, relapse; second offense

récidiver *vi.* to recur; relapse (crime)

récif *m.* reef, shelf of rocks

récipient *m.* receptacle, container

réciprocité *f.* reciprocity

récit *m.* recital, relation, narrative, story; (mus.) solo

récital *m.* recital

récitant *m.* (mus.) solo, solo part

récitatif *m.* (mus.) recitative

récitation *f.* recitation

réciter *vt.* to recite

réclamant *m.* legal claimant

réclamation *f.* claim; protest; complaint

réclame *f.* advertising; **article de** — feature article

réclamer *vt.* to claim, call for, demand; — *vi.* to protest, complain

reclasser *vt.* to reclassify, rearrange

reclus *m.* recluse

réclusion *f.* reclusion; solitary confinement (penal)

récognition *f.* recognition (of a nature *or* quality)

recoin *m.* corner, nook, cranny

récoler *vt.* to verify, audit, check

recoller *vt.* to paste together again, put together again; **se** — to mend, knit, or heal (a fracture); cling together

récolte *f.* crop; harvest

récolter *vt.* to reap, gather, harvest

recommandable *a.* commendable, praiseworthy

recommandation *f.* recommendation; registration of mail

recommandé *a.* registered (mail)

recommander *vt.* to recommend; register a letter

recommencer *vt. & vi.* to recommence, begin again

récompense *f.* reward, recompense

récompenser *vt.* to reward, recompense

réconciliable *a.* reconcilable

réconciliation *f.* reconciliation

réconcilier *vt.* to reconcile; **se** — to be reconciled

reconduire *vt.* to lead back, see someone home, drive home; show out, usher out

réconfort *m.* consolation, comfort; relief

réconfortant *a.* comforting, consoling; stimulating

réconforter *vi.* to comfort, cheer; strengthen, refresh

reconnaissable *a.* recognizable

reconnaissance *f.* recognition; gratitude, thankfulness; recompense, reward; acknowledgment; note, pawn ticket; (mil.) reconnaissance

reconnaissant *a.* thankful, grateful

reconnaitre *vt.* to recognize, acknowledge; (mil.) to reconnoiter; **se** — to acknowledge; become oriented; (fig.) take one's bearings

reconquérir *vt.* to reconquer, regain

reconstituant *m.* tonic, stimulant, restorative

reconstituer *vt.* to reconstitute; restore

reconstruire *vt.* to rebuild

reconvention *f.* countersuit

recopier *vt.* to copy over, recopy

record *m.* sports record

recorder *vt.* to retie; restring

recordman *m.* record holder

recoucher *vt.*, **se** — to go back to bed, lie down again

recoudre *vt.* to sew in place again; sew up; (fig.) reunite

recoupement *m.* cross-check, verification

recouper *vt.* to cut again; mix, blend (wines)

recourber *vt.* to bend back
recourir *vi.* to run again; have recourse, resort to
recours *m.* recourse, resort
recouvrement *m.* recovery, getting back; recovering; cover
recouvrer *vt.* to recover, regain
recouvrir *vt.* to cover again, re-cover; cover
recracher *vt.* to spit out
récréatif *a.* recreational, entertaining
récréation *f.* recreation; recess
recréer *vt.* to create again, re-create
récréer *vt.* to entertain; please; **se** — to enjoy oneself, relax; be entertained
récrier *v.*, **se** — to exclaim; protest
récrimination *f.* recrimination
récriminer *vi.* to recriminate
récrire *vt.* to rewrite
recroqueviller *v.*, **se** — to retract; (fig.) to curl up, shrivel, wilt
recru *a.* worn out
recrû *m.* annual growth
recrue *f.* recruit, draftee
recruter *vt.* to recruit, enlist
rectal *a.* rectal
rectangle *m.* rectangle; — *a.* right-angled
rectangulaire *a.* rectangular
recteur *m.* rector; university president
rectificateur *m.* (elec.) rectifier; — **dentaire** dental brace
rectificatif *a.* rectifying; — *m.* correction
rectifier *vt.* to rectify, adjust, correct; straighten
rectifieuse *f.* rectifier
rectitude *f.* rectitude, uprightness; correctness; straightness
rectorat *m.* rectorate; university presidency
rectum *m.* rectum
reçu *m.* receipt; — *a.* received; usual; customary; **être** — to pass; graduate
recueil *m.* collection; anthology
recueillement *m.* contemplation, pious meditation
recueilli *a.* contemplative
recueillir *vt.* to gather, collect; shelter; **se** — to meditate
recuire *vt.* to recook, reheat; temper, anneal
recuit *a.* tempered, annealed
recul *m.* gun recoil; setback; backing up
reculade *f.* moving back; retreat
reculé *a.* remote, distant (in time); isolated
reculée *f.* space in which to move backward
reculement *m.* moving back, backing up; postponement
reculer *vi.* to move back; retreat; recoil;

— *vt.* to move back; postpone; hesitate
reculons, à — *adv.* backwards
récuperable *a.* recuperable
récupération *f.* recuperation, recovery
récupérer *vt.* to retrieve, recoup, recover; **se** — to recuperate, recover
récurage *m.* scouring, cleansing
récurer *vt.* to scour, cleanse
récurrence *f.* recurrence
récurrent *a.* recurrent, recurring
récusable *a.* exceptionable (at law)
récusation *f.* legal exception, objection
récuser *vt.* to object to, challenge; **se** — to disqualify oneself
rédacteur *m.* editor, compiler; writer; — **en chef** editor-in-chief
rédaction *f.* editorship, compiling; editorial staff; theme, composition
rédactionnel *a.* editorial
reddition *f.* surrender; rendering
redécouvrir *vt.* to rediscover
redemander *vt.* to ask again, ask return of something
rédempteur *m.* redeemer; — *a.* redeeming
rédemption *f.* redemption, redeeming
redescendre *vi.* to go down again; go back down; — *vt.* to bring down, take down
redevable *a.* indebted; bound by gratitude
redevance *f.* fee, tax; royalty
redevenir *vi.* to become again
rédiger *vt.* to phrase, draw up, write; edit
redingote *f.* frock coat
redire *vt.* to repeat, say again; **trouver à** — **à** to find fault with, criticize
redistribuer *vt.* to redistribute
redite *f.* repetition; redundancy
redondance *f.* redundancy
redondant *a.* redundant
redonner *vi.* to be redundant
redonner *vt.* to give again, give back
redorer *vt.* to re-gild
redoublé *a.* redoubled; **pas** — *m.* (marching) double-time, quick-step
redoublement *m.* doubling, redoubling
redoubler *vt.* to redouble; reline clothing; — *vi.* to redouble; increase
redoutable *a.* formidable, redoubtable; dreadful
redoute *f.* redoubt
redouter *vt.* to dread, fear; be afraid
redressé *a.* upright, erect
redressement *m.* making erect again, righting; straightening, rectifying; recovery
redresser *vt.* to make straight again; set upright; mend, correct; straighten, rectify; **se** — become upright again; sit up again
redresseur *m.* rectifier; righter

redû *m.* balance due

réducteur *m.* reducer; reducing agent; — *a.* reducing

réductible *a.* reducible

réduction *f.* reduction, reducing

réduire *vt.* to reduce, subdue, conquer

réduit *m.* redoubt; retreat; shack, hovel; — *a.* reduced, obliged

réduplication *f.* reduplication

rééditier *vt.* to rebuild

rééditer *vt.* to republish

réédition *f.* reprinting, republication

rééducatif *a.*, **thérapie rééducative** *f.* occupational therapy

rééducation *f.* rehabilitation

rééduquer *vt.* to re-educate; rehabilitate

réel *a.* real; — *m.* reality

réélection *f.* re-election

réélire *vt.* to re-elect

réellement *adv.* really, actually

réensemencer *vt.* to reseed

refaçonner *vt.* to refashion

réfaction *f.* (com.) allowance, rebate; repairs

refaire *vt.* to do again; remake; **se — to** recover, recuperate

réfection *f.* rebuilding; repairing, restoration

réfectoire *m.* refectory, dining room

refend *m.* (arch.) **pierre de —** *f.* cornerstone

refendre *vt.* to split

référence *f.* reference

référendum *m.* referendum

référer *vi.* to refer; — *vt.* to attribute; impute; **se — à** to refer to; **s'en —** to confide

refermer *vt.* to reclose, shut again

refiler *vt.* (coll.) to pass, pass off

réfléchi *a.* thoughtful; considered; premeditated; **peu —** hasty; **verbe —** *m.* reflexive verb

réfléchir *vt.* to reflect, reverberate; — *vi.* reflect, think; **se —** to be reflected

réfléchissement *m.* reflection, reflecting

réfléchissant *a.* reflecting

réflecteur *m.* reflector; — *a.* reflecting

reflet *m.* reflection

refléter *vt.* to reflect

refleurir *vi.* to flower again, flourish again

réflexe *a. & m.* reflex

réflexion *f.* reflection; thought; **toute —** **faite** all things considered

refluer *vi.* to ebb, flow back

reflux *m.* ebb, reflux, flowing back

refondre *vt.* to remelt, recast

refonte *f.* remelting, recasting

réformateur *m.* reformer

réformation *f.* reformation

réforme *f.* reform, reformation; (mil.)

discharge

réformé *m.* Protestant; rejected serviceman, soldier discharged for wounds or unfitness

reformer *vt.* to re-form, form again

réformer *vt.* to reform; (mil.) discharge, retire

refoulement *m.* forcing back; repression; output

refouler *vt.* to force back; repress

réfractaire *a.* refractory, rebellious; fire resistant

réfracter *vt.* to refract

réfracteur *m.* refractor

réfraction *f.* refraction

refrain *m.* refrain; song; chorus

réfranger *vt.* to refract

réfréner *vt.* to check, curb, bridle, restrain

réfrigérant *a.* refrigerating; cooling; — *m.* refrigerator; cooler

réfrigération *f.* refrigeration

réfrigérer *vt.* to refrigerate

refroidir *vt.* to cool, chill; — *vi.* to grow cool, grow cold

refroidissement *m.* cooling; chill

réfugié *m.* refugee

réfugier *v.*, **se —** to take refuge

refus *m.* refusal

refuser *vt.* to refuse, deny; reject; fail (a student); **se —** to object; refuse

réfutable *a.* refutable

réfutation *f.* refutation

réfuter *vt.* to refute

regagner *vt.* to regain, recover; reach again, return to

regain *m.* (agr.) aftergrowth; renewal

régal *m.* feast; treat

régalade *f.* regaling, feasting; treat

régalant *a.* entertaining, diverting

régale *a.*, **eau —** (chem.) aqua regia

régalement *m.* leveling

régaler *vt.* to treat, entertain; level, smooth out

régalien *a.* royal, regal

regard *m.* look, glance; eyes; aperture, opening; peephole; manhole

regardant *m.* onlooker; — *a.* particular, fussy; stingy

regarder *vt.* to look at; regard, concern; face

regarnir *vt.* to regarnish, restock, replenish

regate *f.* regatta, boat race

regel *m.* refreezing; new freeze

regeler *vt. & vi.* to refreeze, freeze again

régence *f.* regency

régénérateur *a.* regenerative; — *m.* hair restorer

régénération *f.* regeneration

régénérer *vt.* to regenerate

régent *m.* regent
régenter *vt.* to dominate
régicide *m.* regicide
régie *f.* administration, management; public corporation
regimbement *m.* recalcitrance
regimber *vi.* to balk, object
régime *m.* regime, administration; system; bunch of dates; diet; (gram.) object; être au — to be on a diet
régiment *m.* regiment
régimentaire *a.* regimental
région *f.* region, area
régional *a.* regional; local
régir *vt.* to govern, manage, supervise
régisseur *m.* administrator, manager; (theat.) stage manager
registre *m.* register, ledger, account book
réglable *a.* adjustable
réglage *m.* way of ruling paper; adjustment of machinery, tuning
règle *f.* rule, ruler; order; — à **calcul** slide rule; en — in order
réglé *a.* ruled, regular, orderly; vent — *m.* tradewind
règlement *m.* regulation; rule; adjustment, settlement; payment
réglementaire *a.* prescribed by law
réglementation *f.* regulating
réglementer *vt.* to regulate
régler *vt.* to rule; regulate; adjust, set; settle
réglet *m.* moulding
réglette *f.* small ruler; metal strip
régleur *m.* adjuster
réglisse *f.* licorice
réglure *f.* ruling of paper
règne *m.* reign; kingdom
régnant *a.* reigning; dominant
régner *vi.* to reign; prevail
regommer *vt.* to retread
regonfler *vt.* to pump up again, reinflate
regorgeant *a.* overflowing, brimming
regorger *vi.* to overflow, abound, be full, be packed; — *vt.* to regurgitate
regoûter *vt.* to taste again
regrat *m.* peddling used *or* retail articles
regrattage *m.* scraping
regratter *vi.* to peddle, hawk; — *vt.* re-scrape, scrape clean
régressif *a.* regressive
régression *f.* regression, retrogression; recession
regret *m.* regret; à — regretfully, reluctantly
regretter *vt.* to regret, be sorry; miss
régularisation *f.* regularizing
régulariser *vt.* to regularize
régularité *f.* regularity; evenness
régulateur *a.* regulating; — *m.* regulator;

governor
régulation *f.* regulating
régulier *a.* regular; even; steady; punctual
régurgitation *f.* regurgitation
régurgiter *vt.* to regurgitate
réhabilitation *f.* rehabilitation
réhabiliter *vt.* to rehabilitate; reinstate
réhabituer *vt.* to reaccustom
rehaussement *m.* raising; enhancing
rehausser *vt.* to raise; enhance, accentuate
réimperméabiliser *vt.* to waterproof again
réimposer *vt.* to reimpose
réimpression *f.* reprint, reprinting
réimprimer *vt.* to reprint
rein *m.* kidney; -s *pl.* lower part of back
réincarnation *f.* reincarnation
réincarner *v.*, se — to be reincarnated
réincorporer *vt.* to reincorporate
reine *f.* queen
reine-claude *f.* greengage plum
réinscrire *vt.* to reinscribe; re-enter
réintégrer *vt.* to reinstate
réitération *f.* reiteration
réitérer *vt.* to reiterate
rejaillir *vi.* to spurt out; rebound; be reflected
rejet *m.* rejection; plant shoot, sprout; throwing out; enjambement
rejeter *vt.* to throw back; reject; se — move back, fall back
rejeton *m.* offspring, shoot
rejetonner *vi.* to throw off shoots (plants)
rejoindre *vt.* to rejoin; overtake; se — to meet again
rejouer *vt.* to play again, replay
réjoui *a.* jovial, joyful, happy
réjouir *vt.* to gladden; entertain; se — to rejoice, be happy
réjouissance *f.* rejoicing, merrymaking
réjouissant *a.* pleasing, entertaining, giving pleasure
relâchant *a.* (med.) laxative
relâche *m.* rest, respite; (theat.) no performance; interruption; (naut.) port of call
relâché *a.* loose, slack; relaxed
relâchement *m.* relaxation, loosening; abatement
relâcher *vt.* to relax; release, slacken; — *vi.* (naut.) to put into port; se — to become loose, slacken; diminish, abate; become milder
relais *m.* relay, shift
relancer *vt.* to throw again, throw back; start again; hunt
relater *vt.* to relate, tell of, give, state
relatif *a.* relative; pertinent, relating
relation *f.* relation, connection; report, statement, account

relationné *a.* having contacts *or* connections

relativité *f.* relativity

relaxation *f.* legal release; lessening, reduction

relaxer *vt.* to release, discharge at law

relayer *vt.* to relieve, relay; — *vi.* to relay; se — to take turns, work in shifts

relégation *f.* life sentence to penal colony

relégué *m.* convict serving life sentence

reléguer *vt.* to relegate; sentence for life, transport

relent *m.* musty smell, staleness

relevage *m.* lifting, raising; collecting of letters from a mail box

relevant *a.* pertaining; dependent

relevé *a.* raised, high; highly seasoned; — *m.* abstract, summary, statement; survey; meter reading

relève *f.* (mil.) relief, changing of the guard

relevée *f.* afternoon

relèvement *m.* raising, lifting; increase; restoration, recovery; (mil.) relieving; (naut.) bearing; (com.) statement

relever *vt.* to raise again, lift up, turn up; increase; enhance, heighten; season; point out; (mil.) relieve; (naut.) take the bearings of; (com.) bill; read a meter; — *vi.* be dependent, be responsible; recover from illness; se — get up again; revive, recover

relief *m.* relief, embossing, enhancement; —s *pl.* left-over food

relier *vt.* to tie again; bind, connect, join

relieur *m.* bookbinder

religieux *a.* religious; — *m.* monk

reliquaire *m.* (eccl.) shrine, reliquary

reliquat *m.* left-over portion, remainder; aftereffects; balance due

relique *f.* relic

relire *vt.* to read again; reread

reliure *f.* binding of a book; bookbinding trade

relouer *vt.* to sublet, relet

reluctance *f.* (elec.) reluctance

reluire *vi.* to shine, glitter, gleam

reluisant *a.* shining, glittering, gleaming; glossy

reluquer *vt.* to look at sideways, look at from the corner of the eyes

remâcher *vt.* to chew again; mull over

remailler *vt.* to mend (knitted or meshed garments)

remaniement *m.* alteration; reshaping, rehandling

remanier *vt.* to handle again, alter; reshape

remarier *vt.*, **se** — to marry again, remarry

remarquable *a.* remarkable; noteworthy

remarque *f.* remark; **digne de** — noteworthy

remarquer *vt.* to observe, notice, remark; mark again; **se faire** — to be noticed, attract attention

remballer *vt.* to repack

rembarquer *vt. & vi.* to re-embark

remblai *m.* fill for construction; earth; embankment

remblaver *vt.* to reseed

remblayer *vt.* to fill; embank

rembobinage *m.* rewinding

rembobiner *vt.* to rewind

remboîter *vt.* to repack, recase; reassemble; (med.) set a bone

rembourrer *vt.* to stuff, wad; pad, upholster

rembourrure *f.* stuffing material

remboursable *a.* refundable

remboursement *m.* reimbursement, redemption; refund; **livraison contre** — *f.* C.O.D.

rembourser *vt.* to reimburse, repay, refund

rembrunir *vt. & vi.* to darken; make gloomy; **se** — grow dark

remède *m.* remedy, cure

remédiable *a.* remediable, curable

remédier *vt.* to remedy, cure

remêler *vt.* to mix again, remix

remembrer *vt.* to assemble, consolidate

remémoratif *a.* commemorative

remémorer *vt.* to remind; **se** — to remember

remerciement *m.* thanks

remercier *vt.* to thank; discharge, dismiss

réméré *m.* (com.) repurchase

remettant *m.* sender, remitter

remetteur *a.* remitting; — *m.* remitter

remettre *vt.* to put back; put on again; restore; hand over, remit; postpone; **se** — recover one's health; **se** — **à** to start again; **s'en** — **à** rely on, depend on

remeubler *vt.* to refurnish

réminiscence *f.* reminiscence

remise *f.* putting back; remitting, remittance; remission; rebate, discount; shed, garage, *or* coachhouse; — **en état** repair, restoration; **voiture de grande** — *f.* rentable limousine

remiser *vt.* to house; put back in a garage, shed, *or* coachhouse; (coll.) to pension

rémissible *a.* remissible

rémission *f.* remission

remmener *vt.* to lead back, take back

rémois *a.* from Rheims

remontant *a. & m.* tonic, stimulant

remonte *f.* remounting; return, ascent of salmon

remontée *f.* going up again, ascent, climb

remonter *vi.* to go up again; remount; reascend; go back; — *vt.* go up again, climb again; take up again; pull up; wind up; remount, reassemble; (theat.) perform again, put on again, redo; se — recover one's strength *or* spirit

remontoir *m.* watch winder

remontrance *f.* remonstrance

remontrer *vt.* to show again; indicate, point out; en — à to remonstrate with

remords *m.* remorse, conscience

remorquage *m.* towing

remorque *f.* towing, tow; tow rope; (auto.) trailer; à la — in tow

remorquer *vt.* to tow, pull

remorqueur *m.* tugboat; tractor

remoudre *vt.* to grind again, regrind

rémoudre *vt.* to resharpen, regrind

rémouleur *m.* knife grinder

remous *m.* eddy, swirl, backwash

rempailler *vt.* to repair, recane, replace chair reeds

rempailleur *m.* repairer of chairs

rempart *m.* rampart

remplaçable *a.* replaceable

remplaçant *m.* replacement, substitute

remplacement *m.* replacing, substitution

remplacer *vt.* to replace, substitute for

rempli *m.* fold, tuck

remplier *vt.* to make a fold *or* tuck in

remplir *vt.* to refill, fill in; fill out; fill up; fulfill, do, carry out

remployer *vt.* to use again

remplumer *v.*, se — to grow new feathers

rempoissonner *vt.* to stock with fish

remporter *vt.* to carry back, carry away; win, achieve, obtain

rempoter *vt.* to repot a plant

remuant *a.* moving; agitated

remue-ménage *m.* bustle, to-do, movement, agitation, stir, stirring

remuement *m.* movement, agitation, stir

remuer *vt.* to move, stir up; arouse, agitate; turn (earth); — *vi.* move, budge, stir

remugle *m.* musty odor, stale odor

rémunérateur *a.* remunerative, rewarding, profitable; — *m.* remunerator

rémunération *f.* remuneration

rémunérer *vt.* to remunerate, reward, pay for

renâcler *vi.* to snort; shirk; be hesitant, be reluctant

renaissance *f.* rebirth, revival

renaissant *a.* renascent

renaître *vi.* to be born again; revive; reappear

rénal *a.* renal, kidney

renard *m.* fox

renarde *f.* vixen

rencaisser *vt.* to recase, rebox; receive as a refund

renchaîner *vt.* to chain up again

renchéri *a.* fastidious

renchérir *vi.* to increase in price; — **sur** to outdo; outbid

renchérissement *m.* increase in price

renchérisseur *m.* one who outbids, highest bidder

rencogner *vt.* to drive into a corner; se — be pushed, retreat into a corner

rencontre *f.* meeting, encounter; occasion; aller à la — de to go to meet; de — chance, random, haphazard

rencontrer *vt.* to meet, come across, run into, encounter; se — meet, meet by chance; collide; come together, agree, check

rendement *m.* yield, profit, return; efficiency, output

rendez-vous *m.* appointment; meeting place, rendezvous

rendormir *vt.* to put back to sleep; se — to fall asleep again, go back to sleep

rendosser *vt.* to put on again

rendre *vt.* to give back; return; produce, yield; give up; vomit; render; make; se — to go, proceed; surrender

rendu *a.* tired out, exhausted, spent; — *m.* rendering; (com.) return of an article

rêne *f.* rein

renégat *m.* renegade

rêner *vt.* to rein in

renfaîter *vt.* to repair a roof

renfermé *a.* stuffy, close; uncommunicative

renfermer *vt.* to shut up, lock up, confine; contain, include, comprise; enclose; conceal

renflammer *vt.* to set fire to again, rekindle; se — catch fire again, be rekindled

renflement *m.* swelling, bulge

renfler *vt. & vi.* to swell

renflouer *vt.* to reinflate; refloat

renfoncé *a.* recessed; sunken

renfoncer *vt.* to drive in, hammer in; indent, recess

renforcé *a.* reinforced, strengthened, strong; absolute

renforcer *vt.* to reinforce, strengthen, brace; intensify; se — grow stronger

renfort *m.* reinforcement; backing, support

renfrogné *a.* frowning, scowling

renfrogner *v.*, se — to frown, scowl

rengager *vt.* to engage again; pawn again; — *vi.* to re-enlist

rengaine *f.* refrain, old story

rengainer *vt.* to sheathe, put back (a

sword)

rengorgement *m.* swagger, strutting

rengorger *v.*, se — to strut, swagger

reniement *m.* denial, repudiation, disavowal

renier *vt.* to deny, disown, disavow, repudiate, abjure

reniflard *m.* air valve; sniffer, sniffler

reniflement *m.* sniffing, snorting, snort; sniffle, sniffling

renifler *vi.* to sniff, snivel, snuffle, snort; — *vt.* to sniff

reniveler *vt.* to level again

renne *m.* reindeer

renom *m.* renown, fame, repute

renommé *a.* renowned, famous, famed, celebrated, well-known

renommée *f.* fame, reputation, renown, repute

renommer *vt.* to renominate, rename

renonce *f.* renege, revoke (at cards)

renoncement *m.* renunciation; renouncing; self-denial

renoncer *vi.* to renounce, give up, waive; renege, revoke (at cards); — *vt.* to renounce

renonciation *f.* renunciation

renoncule *f.* buttercup

renouer *vt.* to tie again, knot again; renew

renouveau *m.* revival, renewal; springtime

renouvelable *a.* renewable

renouveler *vt.* to renew; revive; repeat; change, alter; se — be renewed; renew again; happen again

rénover *vt.* to renew, give a new form

renseignement *m.* piece of information; –s *pl.* information; (mil.) intelligence; prendre des –s sur to inquire about

renseigner *vt.* to inform; se — to inquire, ask

rente *f.* income, revenue; annuity, pension

renté *a.* endowed; of independent means, having a private income

renter *vt.* to endow, provide with an income

rentier *m.* person of independent means, stockholder, bondholder

rentrant *m.* recess in a wall; new participant, new player

rentré *a.* hollow, sunken; suppressed

rentrée *f.* return, homecoming; reopening of school; gathering, collecting, bringing in

rentrer *vi.* to re-enter, return, come home; reopen; bring in, take in

renverse *f.* (naut.) turn, change in weather; tomber à la — to fall backwards

renversement *m.* reversing, reversal, inversion; turn, turning, change; overturning, overthrowing

renverser *vt.* to reverse, invert; knock over, turn over, overturn, upset; overthrow; — *vi.* to overturn; (naut.) capsize; se — to fall down; turn over; lean back; capsize

renvoi *m.* sending back, returning; throwing back; reflection; discharge, dismissal; postponement; reference mark; caret; belch; (mus.) repetition

renvoyer *vt.* to send back, return, throw back; reflect; discharge, dismiss; postpone; refer

réoccupation *f.* reoccupation

réoccuper *vt.* to reoccupy

réordonner *vt.* to reorder

réorganisation *f.* reorganization

réorganiser *vt.* to reorganize

réorientation *f.* reorientation

réorienter *vt.* to reorient

réouverture *f.* reopening

repaire *m.* lair, den

repaître *vt.* to feed, se — de to eat one's fill of; delight in

répandre *vt.* to spread; spill, shed; give off; strew, scatter; se — to spread, spill, spill over

répandu *a.* widespread; fashionable

reparaître *vi.* to reappear

réparation *f.* reparation; repairing; amends, satisfaction

réparer *vt.* to repair, fix, mend; make up for, make amends for

repartie *f.* repartee, reply, retort

repartir *vi.* to reply, retort; start out again, set out again

répartir *vt.* to divide, distribute; allocate, allot, apportion; assess

répartiteur *m.* distributor; assessor

répartition *f.* dividing, distribution; allocation, apportionment; assessment

repas *m.* meal

repassage *m.* ironing, pressing; sharpening

repasser *vi.* to pass by again; — *vt.* to pass again, pass over; go over; sharpen grind, strop; iron; planche à — *f.* ironing board

repasseur *m.* grinder, sharpener; finisher

repasseuse *f.* ironer

repavage *m.* repaving

repaver *vt.* to repave

repayer *vt.* to pay for again

repêcher *vt.* to fish out again, fish up; rescue

repeindre *vt.* to paint again, repaint

rependre *vt.* to hang up again

repenser *vt.* to think over again

repenti *a. & m.* repentant

repentir v., se — repent, be sorry about, rue; — m. repentance

repérable a. locatable, findable

repérage m. finding, locating

répercussion f. repercussion, reverberation; consequence, effect

répercuter vt. to reflect, reverberate; se — to have repercussions

reperdre vt. to lose again

repère m. reference mark; **point de —** point of reference, guidemark; landmark

repérer vt. to mark with points of reference (blaze a trail); fix, locate; se — to take one's bearings

répertoire m. index, list; directory; (theat.) stock, repertory

répertorier vt. to list; index; catalog

répéter vt. to repeat; rehearse; se — to repeat, be done again, recur

répétiteur m. tutor, helper, coach

répétition f. repetition; duplicate; rehearsal, practice; tutoring lesson; (TV) rerun

repeupler vt. to repopulate; restock

repiquer vt. to prick again; restitch; repair, mend; transplant

répit m. respite, delay

replacer vt. to put back, replace; reinvest

replanter vt. to replant

replâtrer vt. to replaster; patch up

replet a. plump, chubby

réplétion f. repletion; plumpness

repli m. fold; coil; bend; (mil.) retreat

replier vt. to fold again, fold up; tuck; coil cord; se — fold up; wind; (mil.) fall back, retreat

réplique f. answer, reply, retort, replica; (theat.) cue

répliquer vi. to reply, answer back, retort

replonger vt. to plunge again; — vi. dive again; sink again

repolir vt. to repolish

répondant m. guarantor, surety; (eccl.) server at mass

répondre vt. to answer, reply; — vi. to answer; respond; reciprocate; correspond

réponse f. answer, reply

report m. carry over, amount brought forward (bookkeeping)

reportage m. reporting, newspaper writing, commentary

reporter vt. to carry back, carry over; postpone; se — à refer to

repos m. rest, repose, tranquility; landing of a stairway; au — (mil.) at ease; en — resting, at rest

reposant a. restful

reposé a. rested; tranquil, calm; à tête

-e adv. calmly, coolly, deliberately

reposer vt. to put back, replace; rest; — vi. to rest, lie; se — rest, repose; come to rest, alight; se — sur rely on

reposoir m. resting place; (eccl.) temporary parade altar; repository

repoussage m. stamping of sheet metal

repoussant a. repulsive; offensive

repousse f. new growth

repoussé a. embossed; chased; — m. embossing; chasing

repoussement m. repulse, repulsing; rejecting, rejection; dislike; recoil

repousser vt. to repulse, repel, reject; deny; postpone; recoil; emboss; chase; — vi. produce new plant growths

repoussoir m. embossing punch; contrast, foil

répréhensible a. reprehensible

reprendre vt. to retake, take again, take back; resume; regain; reply; continue; reprove, criticize; — vi. return, come back; recover; se — take hold of oneself, regain composure; correct oneself

représailles f. pl. reprisals, retaliation

représentant a. & m. representative; — de commerce salesman

représentatif a. representative

représentation f. representation; agency; protest; (theat.) performance; — à grand spectacle (TV) spectacular

représenter vt. to represent; reintroduce; present again; show, depict; perform; point out; se — present oneself again; represent oneself; recur, reappear

répressif a. repressive

répression f. repression

réprimable a. repressible

réprimandable a. censurable, worthy of censure

réprimande f. reprimand

réprimander vt. to reprimand, censure

réprimer vt. to repress; hold back, check

repris m., — de justice habitual criminal

reprise f. retaking; recapture; renewal; recovery; repetition; mending, darning; (theatre) revival; (mus.) chorus, refrain; (auto.) trade-in; à plusieurs —s repeatedly

repriser vt. to darn, mend

réprobateur a. reproachful

réprobation f. reprobation, censure; rejection

reproche m. reproach, blame; —s pl. blame, criticism, censure

reprocher vt. to reproach, blame, find fault with; grudge, begrudge

reproducteur a. reproductive; — m. reproducer; stud, sire

reproductif a. reproductive

reproduction *f.* reproduction; — **en miniature** miniaturization
reproduire *vt.* to reproduce; **se** — to reproduce; recur, occur again
réprouvé *m.* reprobate
réprouver *vt.* to disapprove of; reject
reptation *f.* crawling
reptile *m. & a.* reptile
repu *a.* sated, satiated, full
républicain *a. & m.* republican
républicanisme *m.* republicanism
republier *vt.* to republish
république *f.* republic
répudiation *f.* repudiation
répudier *vt.* to repudiate, renounce
repue *f.* **franche** — free dinner
répugnance *f.* repugnance, loathing, aversion, dislike; reluctance
répugnant *a.* repugnant, loathsome; loath, reluctant
répugner *vi.* to feel repugnance; be repugnant; be reluctant
répulsif *a.* repulsive
répulsion *f.* repulsion
réputation *f.* reputation, repute, name, renown
réputé *a.* of repute, well-known, famous
réputer *vt.* to repute, consider, think
requérable *a.* demandable
requérant *m.* legal petitioner, plaintiff
requérir *vt.* to demand, petition; ask
requête *f.* request, petition
requin *m.* shark; **peau de** — *f.* shagreen
requis *a.* requisite, required
réquisition *f.* requisition; requisitioning
réquisitionner *vt.* to requisition
réquisitoire *m.* legal indictment, charge
rescapé *a.* rescued, delivered
rescinder *vt.* to rescind
rescousse *f.* rescue
réseau *m.* network; net; (rad., rail.) system
réséda *m.* mignonette
réservation *f.* reservation
réserve *f.* reserve, reservation; **à la** — **de** except for; **sans** — unqualified, without exception; **sous** — **de** subject to
réservé *a.* reserved; shy; guarded
réserver *vt.* to reserve, save
réservoir *m.* reservoir; tank; well
résidence *f.* residence; dwelling
résider *vi.* to reside, dwell; consist
résidu *m.* residue; (com.) balance
résiduel *a.* residual
résignation *f.* resignation; submission, submissiveness
résigné *a.* resigned; submissive
résigner *vt.* to resign; submit; give up; **se** — to resign oneself, submit
résiliation *f.* cancellation, termination of

an agreement
résilience *f.* resilience
résilier *vt.* to cancel, terminate an agreement
résille *f.* hair net, snood; lattice
résine *f.* resin
résiner *vt.* to resin; tap for resin
résineux *a.* resinous
résistance *f.* resistance; stamina, strength; **pièce de** — *f.* main dish, main course; highlight, main feature
résistant *a.* resistant, strong; — *m.* member of the resistance
résister *vi.* to resist, withstand, endure
résolu *a.* resolute, determined
résoluble *a.* solvable; terminable
résolument *adv.* resolutely, determinedly
résolution *f.* resolution; resolve; solution; termination, cancellation
résonance *f.* resonance
résonnement *m.* resonance, reverberation
résonner *vi.* to resound, reverberate
résorber *vt.* to absorb again, reabsorb; imbibe
résoudre *vt.* to resolve; solve; dissolve; terminate, cancel; **se** — to make up one's mind
respect *m.* respect; **rendre ses -s à** to pay one's respects to
respectabilité *f.* respectability
respecter *vt.* to respect, have respect for; **se** — to act in a seemly fashion
respectif *a.* respective
respectueux *a.* respectful
respirateur *m.* respirator
respiration *f.* respiration, breathing
respiratoire *a.* respiratory
respirer *vt. & vi.* to breathe; inhale; (fig.) to pause for breath
resplendir *vi.* to shine, glow, be resplendent
responsabilité *f.* responsibility; liability
responsable *a.* responsible; liable
ressac *m.* surf; undertow
ressaigner *vi.* to open, start bleeding again
ressaisir *vt.* to seize again; retake, recapture; **se** — to recover, regain one's composure
ressasser *vt.* to repeat incessantly
ressaut *m.* projection; rise
ressauter *vi.* to rise; jump again
ressayer *vt.* to try again
resseller *vt.* to resaddle
ressemblance *f.* resemblance, likeness
ressembler *vi.* to resemble, look alike; be like; **se** — to be the same, be alike
ressemeler *vt.* to resole
ressentiment *m.* resentment
ressentir *vt.* to resent; feel, experience
resserre *f.* storing, storage; storeroom;

shed

resserré *a.* tight, narrow, confined

resserrement *m.* tightening, contracting; oppression, heaviness; constipation

resserrer *vt.* to contract, constrict, tighten; confine; compress; lock up again; se — to become tighter; contract

resservir *vt. & vi.* to serve again

ressort *m.* spring; elasticity, resilience; motive; legal jurisdiction, competence; resort; (fig.) function

ressortir *vi.* to go out again, emerge again; stand out, appear, be evident; — à belong to legally, be under the jurisdiction of; **faire** — make evident, bring out, stress, emphasize

ressouder *vt.* to solder *or* weld again; **se** — to heal, mend, *or* knit bone

ressource *f.* resource; expedient, resort; —s *pl.* resources, means; funds

ressouvenance *f.* remembrance, recollection

ressouvenir *v.* **se** — to remember, recollect; — *m.* memory, remembrance

ressuer *vi.* to sweat

ressusciter *vt.* to ressuscitate, revive, restore; — *vi.* to ressuscitate, come back to life, revive

ressuyer *vt.* to dry

restant *a.* remaining; **poste -e** *f.* general delivery; — *m.* remainder, balance, residue

restaurant *m.* restaurant; — *a. & m.* restorative

restaurateur *m.* restorer; restaurant proprietor

restauration *f.* restoration, restoring

restaurer *vt.* to restore; refresh; **se** — take refreshment; refresh oneself (fig.) to regain strength

reste *m.* remainder, rest, remains; **au** —, **du** — besides; **de** — left over; **et le** — and so forth

rester *vi.* to remain, be left; stay

restituer *vt.* to restore; give back; rehabilitate

restreindre *vt.* to restrict, limit; **se** — to limit oneself, retrench

restreint *a.* restricted, limited

restrictif *a.* restrictive

restringent *a. & m.* astringent

résultant *a.* resulting, resultant

résultat *m.* result

résulter *vi.* to result, follow

résumé *m.* summary, résumé, abstract; **en** — in short, in brief

résumer *vt.* to sum up, summarize

résurgence *f.* resurgence, reappearance

résurgin *vi.* to rise, reappear

résurrection *f.* resurrection

retable *m.* retable, shelf or screen above an altar

rétablir *vt.* to re-establish, restore; recover, regain; **se** — to re-establish oneself; regain one's health

rétablissement *m.* re-establishment; restoration; recovery

retaille *f.* chip, portion removed

retailler *vt.* to cut again, recut; resharpen

retaillure *f.* cutting; sharpening

rétameur *m.* tinker

retaper *vt.* to fix, adjust, straighten; retype; **se** — to get well

retard *m.* delay; backwardness; slowness, lateness; **en** — late, behind, in arrears

retardataire *a.* late; backward; slow; in arrears; — *m. & f.* latecomer; person in arrears

retarder *vt.* to delay, retard; put back; defer; — *vi.* be late, be slow

reteindre *vt.* to dye again, redye

retendre *vt.* to stretch again; set (a trap) again

retenir *vt.* to retain, detain, keep back; hold back, withhold; restrain; **se** — to restrain oneself

rétenteur *a.* retaining

rétention *f.* retention, holding in

retentir *vi.* to resound, reverberate

retentissant *a.* resounding, loud

retentissement *m.* resounding, reverberation, effect, repercussion

retenu *a.* circumspect, prudent; reserved; booked; detained

retenue *f.* holding back; deduction; detention; reserve, modesty; restraint

réticence *f.* reticence

réticulaire *a.* reticular, netlike

réticule *m.* cross hairs in an eyepiece, reticle; reticule, bag, handbag

rétif *a.* restive, stubborn

rétiforme *a.* netlike, retiform

rétine *f.* retina

retirer *vt.* to withdraw, pull out; take off; take away; derive; reprint; **se** — to retire, withdraw; recede

rétivité *f.* stubbornness, obstinacy

retombant *a.* sagging, hanging, drooping

retomber *vi.* to fall again, sink again; hang down; droop

retordre *vt.* to twist again

rétorquer *vt.* to retort

retors *a.* wily, clever, crafty; twisted in weaving

retoucher *vt.* to retouch, touch up

retoucheur *m.* alterer; (phot.) retoucher

retour *m.* return; turn, twist; **billet d'aller et** — round-trip ticket; **billet de** — return ticket; **être de** — to be back

retournage *m.* turning, reversing

retourner *vt.* to turn, turn over; turn inside out; return; — *vi.* to return, go back; **se —** to turn around; **s'en —** return, be on the way back

retracer *vt.* to retrace

rétractation *f.* retraction, recantation

rétractable *a.* retractable

rétracter *vt.* to retract; recant; **se —** to retract

retrait *m.* withdrawal; shrinkage; recess, indentation

retraite *f.* retreat; retirement; refuge, lair; (mil.) **battre en —** to beat a retreat; **prendre sa —** to retire

retraiter *vt.* to pension off, retire

retranché *a.* entrenched, fortified

retranchement *m.* entrenchment; cutting off

retrancher *vt.* to retrench, entrench, fortify; cut off, cut out

retransmettre *vt.* to retransmit; broadcast

retransmission *f.* rebroadcast

retravailler *vt.* to rework

retraverser *vt.* to cross again, recross, cross back

rétréci *a.* narrow, shrunken

rétrécir *vt.* to narrow, contract; shrink; take in; — *vi.* grow narrow

retremper *vt.* to soak again; retemper; **se —** to be invigorated

rétribuer *vt.* to remunerate, reward, pay

rétribution *f.* remuneration, reward, pay

rétroactif *a.* retroactive

rétroaction *f.* (elec.) feedback; retroactivity

rétrogradation *f.* retrogression; reduction in rank

rétrograde *a.* retrograde, reverse(d)

rétrograder *vt.* to reduce in rank; — *vi.* to retrogress; shift to a lower gear

rétrogressif *a.* retrogressive

rétrogression *f.* retrogression

rétrospectif *a.* retrospective

retroussé *a.* turned up; snub-nosed

retroussement *m.* curling

retrousser *vt.* to turn up, tuck up; roll up; **se —** tuck up a dress; lift out of the mud

retrouver *vt.* to find again, recover; meet, rejoin; **se —** to recover oneself, find oneself again, meet again

rétroviseur *m.* rear-view mirror; reflector

rets *m.* net, snare

réunion *f.* bringing together, meeting, gathering; reunion

réunir *vt.* to reunite, unite, assemble; bring together; **se —** to meet, gather

réussi *a.* successful, well-done

réussir *vi.* to succeed, have a happy outcome; — *vt.* to carry out, succeed in, bring off

réussite *f.* success; result, outcome, issue

revacciner *vt.* to revaccinate

revaloir *vt.* to pay back, get even with

revaloriser *vt.* to revalue

revanche *f.* revenge; return; return match; **en —** on the other hand; in return

rêvasser *vi.* to dream, daydream, be lost in thought

rêvasserie *f.* dreaming, daydreaming

rêve *m.* dream

revêche *a.* rough, harsh; crabby, ill-tempered

réveil *m.* waking, awakening; alarm clock; (mil.) reveille; (eccl.) revival

réveille-matin *m.* alarm clock

réveiller *vt.* to awaken, wake up; **se —** wake up, awake

réveillon *m.* midnight supper (Christmas Eve and New Year's Eve)

réveillonner *vi.* to celebrate Christmas *or* the New Year at a midnight supper

révélateur *a.* revealing; — *m.* revealer; (phot.) developer

révélation *f.* revelation

révéler *vt.* to reveal, show, display, disclose; (phot.) develop; **se —** to be revealed, appear

revenant *a.* pleasing; — *m.* ghost

revendeur *m.* secondhand dealer; retailer

revendication *f.* claim, demand, petition

revendiquer *vt.* to claim, demand

revendre *vt.* to sell again, resell

revenir *vi.* to come back, return, go back; recover, get over; **s'en —** to return, be coming back

revente *f.* resale

revenu *m.* revenue, income; profit, yield

rêver *vt. & vi.* to dream

réverbération *f.* reverberation

réverbère *m.* reflector; street light

réverbérer *vt. & vi.* to reverberate, reflect

revercher *vt.* to patch, solder

reverdir *vi.* to become green again; — *vt.* to make green again

révéremment *adv.* reverently

révérence *f.* reverence; bow, curtsey

révérenciel *a.* reverential

révérencieux *a.* ceremonious, overly formal

révérendissime *a.* very reverend, most reverend

révérer *vt.* to revere

rêverie *f.* musing, dreaming, reverie

revernir *vt.* to revarnish

revers *m.* reverse, back; lapel; **coup de —** *m.* backhand stroke; (fig.) setback

reverser *vt.* to pour again, pour back; shift, assign blame

réversible *a.* reversible
réversion *f.* reversion
reversoir *m.* irrigation dam
revêtement *m.* covering, casing, coating
revêtir *vt.* to clothe, reclothe, dress; se — put on again; put on; cover, case
rêveur *a.* pensive, musing, dreaming, dreamy; — *m.* dreamer
revient *m.*, prix de — cost price
revigorer *vt.* to reinvigorate
revirement *m.* sudden change; reversal; (com.) assignment, transfer
réviser, reviser *vt.* to revise; audit; overhaul; re-examine
réviseur, reviseur *m.* reviser; auditor; proofreader
révision, revision *f.* revision; examination, inspection; proofreading; overhauling; conseil de — *m.* draft board
revisser *vt.* to screw tight, tighten
revivification *f.* revival
revivifier *vt.* to revive
revivre *vi.* to live again, come back to life
révocable *a.* revokable
révocation *f.* revocation, repeal; dismissal
revoir *vt.* to see again; revise, review; — *m.*, au — good-bye
revoler *vi.* to fly again, fly back
révolte *f.* revolt, rebellion, uprising
révolté *m.* rebel
révolter *vt.* to cause to revolt; shock; se — to rebel, revolt
révolu *a.* completed, accomplished
révolution *f.* revolution; revulsion
révolutionnaire *a. & n.* revolutionary
révolutionner *vt.* to revolutionize
revolver *m.* revolver
revomir *vt.* to vomit, throw up
révoquer *vt.* to revoke, repeal; dismiss
revue *f.* review, inspection; revue
rez-de-chaussée *m.* ground floor, street floor, first floor
rhabiller *vt.* to dress again, reclothe; repair, fix, mend; se — to get dressed again, put on one's clothes again
rhabilleur *m.* repairer
rhabituer *vt.* to reaccustom
rhapsodie *f.* rhapsody
rhénan *a.* pertaining to the Rhine, Rhenish
rhénium *m.* rhenium
rhéostat *m.* rheostat
rhésus *m.* rhesus monkey; facteur — *m.* RH factor
rhétorique *f.* rhetoric
Rhin *m.* Rhine
rhinite *f.* rhinitis
rhinocéros *m.* rhinoceros
rhodanien *a.* pertaining to the Rhone
rhodium *m.* rhodium

rhodedendron *m.* rhododendron
rhombe *m.* rhombus
rhomboïdal *a.* rhomboid
rhomboïde *m.* rhomboid
rhubarbe *f.* rhubarb
rhum *m.* rum
rhumatisant *a. & m.* rheumatic person
rhumatisme *m.* rheumatism
rhume *m.* (med.) cold
riant *a.* laughing, smiling
ribaud *a.* ribald
riblons *m. pl.* scrap metal
ricanement *m.* sneering, snickering, scoffing
ricaner *vi.* to sneer, laugh derisively
ricaneur *a.* derisive, snickering; — *m.* derider
riche *a.* rich, wealthy
richesse *f.* riches, richness, wealth
ricin *m.* castor-oil plant; huile de — *f* castor oil
ricocher *vi.* to rebound; ricochet
ricochet *m.* rebound; ricochet
ride *f.* wrinkle; ripple; (naut.) lanyard
ridé *a.* wrinkled, lined; corrugated
rideau *m.* curtain; screen; (phot.) shutter — de fer iron curtain
ridelle *f.* side panel of a truck, *or* cart
rider *vt.* to wrinkle, line; ripple; corrugate; se — become wrinkled, become lined
ridicule *a.* ridiculous, absurd, laughable; — *m.* ridicule, ridiculousness; tourner en — to ridicule, make fun of
ridiculiser *vt.* to ridicule
rien *pron.* nothing, anything; de — you're welcome, don't mention it; — que only, merely; ne . . . — nothing, not anything; — *m.* nothing; bagatelle, trifle
rieur *a.* laughing; — *m.* laughter
riflard *m.* file; plastering trowel; jackplane; (coll.) very large umbrella
rifler *vt.* to file; plane; pare
rigide *a.* rigid, stiff; fixed, in place; tense
rigidité *f.* rigidity, stiffness; — cadavérique rigor mortis
rigole *f.* trench, gutter, drain
rigoleur *a.* fun-loving; laughing; — *m.* laugher; gay person
rigorisme *m.* absolute strictness
rigoriste *a.* very strict, rigorous; — *m. & f.* very strict person
rigoureux *a.* rigorous, strict, severe; hard, harsh
rigueur *f.* rigor, strictness, severity, harshness; à la — strictly; if necessary; de — required, obligatory
rillettes *f. pl.* minced pork
rillons *m. pl.* greaves, fryings
rimailler *vi.* to write verse, write second-

rate poetry
rimailleur *m.* rhymester, writer of verse
rime *f.* rhyme, verse
rimer *vt. & vi.* to rhyme
rimeur *m.* rhymer, writer of verse
rinçage *m.* rinsing
rince-bouteilles *m.* bottle-washer
rince-doigts *m.* finger bowl
rincer *vt.* to rinse, wash
rinçure *f.* dirty water, waste water, wash water
ringard *m.* poker, fire iron
ripaille *f.* feast, celebration, party
ripailler *vi.* to feast, celebrate
ripe *f.* scraper
riper *vt. & vi.* to scrape, rub
ripolin *m.* enamel
ripoliner *vt.* to enamel
riposte *f.* retort; repartée; counter
riposter *vi.* to retort, counter, riposte
riquiqui *m.* little finger; tiny person
rire *vi.* to laugh; joke; — à smile at, smile upon; — de laugh at, laugh about; éclater de — burst out laughing; il n'y a pas de quoi — it's not at all funny; se — de laugh at, make fun of; — *m.* laugh, laughing, laughter
ris *m.* laugh; (naut.) reef in a sail; — de veau sweetbreads
risée *f.* mockery, laughing stock; (naut.) gust, squall
risette *f.* smile of a child, little smile
risible *a.* laughable, ludicrous
risque *m.* risk, peril, danger
risqué *a.* risqué, risky
risquer *vt.* to risk, chance, endanger; se — to dare, venture; take risks
risque-tout *m.* daredevil
rissoler *vt.* to brown
ristourne *f.* refund, rebate; kickback
ristourner *vt.* to refund, rebate
ritournelle *f.* (mus.) ritournelle, short instrumental passage; (coll.) same old story
ritualiste *a.* ritualistic; — *m. & f.* ritualist
rituel *a. & m.* ritual
rivage *m.* bank, shore
rivaliser (avec) *vi.* to rival, compete (with)
rivalité *f.* rivalry
rive *f.* bank, shore; edge, border, side
rivelaine *f.* pick (tool)
river *vt.* to rivet, clinch
riverain *a.* riparian; bordering on a water-way *or* road
riveraineté *f.* riparian rights
rivet *m.* rivet; clinch
rivetage *m.* riveting
riveter *vt.* to rivet
riveur *m.* riveter

riveuse *f.* riveting machine
rivière *f.* river, stream
rivoir *m.* riveting hammer
rivure *f.* riveting; riveted work
rixe *f.* scuffle, melee, brawl
riz *m.* rice; — au lait rice pudding; **poudre** de — face powder
rizière *f.* rice field
robe *f.* dress, gown, frock; robe; husk, animal coat; **gens de** — bar, legal profession
robinet *m.* spigot, faucet, tap
rob, robre *m.* rubber (at cards)
robuste *a.* robust, strong, sturdy
robustesse *f.* robustness, strength, sturdiness
roc *m.* rock
rocaille *f.* rocks; rubble; **jardin de** — *m.* rock garden
rocailleur *m.* ornamental stonemason
rocailleux *a.* rocky; rough, harsh
rocambolesque *a.* fantastic
roche *f.* rock, stone
rocher *m.* rock, crag; — *vi.* to froth
rochet *m.* ratchet
rocheux *a.* rocky
rochier *m.* rockfish
rococo *a. & m.* rococo, baroque
rodage *m.* grinding; polishing; wear, wearing away; breaking-in of an automobile motor
rodailler *vi.* to wander, loaf
roder *vt.* to grind, polish; break in (a motor)
rôder *vi.* to roam, prowl
rôdeur *a.* roaming, prowling, idling; — *m.* prowler, idler, loafer
rodoir *m.* grinder, grinding implement
rodomont *m.* boaster
rœntgenthérapie *f.* X-ray treatment
rogatons *m. pl.* scraps, bits of food
rogner *vt.* to pare, clip, trim
rognoir *m.* parer, paring implement
rognon *m.* edible animal kidney
rognures *f. pl.* cuttings, parings, trimmings; leftovers, scraps
rogue *a.* haughty
roi *m.* king
roide *a.* stiff; steep; firm
roideur *f.* stiffness
rôle *m.* roll, roster, list; (theat.) part, role; à tour de — in turn
Romain *m. & a.* Roman
romaine *f.* balance, scale; romaine lettuce
roman *m.* novel; romance; — *a.* Romance; (arch.) Romanesque
romance *f.* (mus.) ballad, song
romancier *m.* novelist
romand *a.*, **Suisse –e** *f.* French-speaking Switzerland

romanesque *a.* romantic
roman-feuilleton *m.* serialized novel
romanichel *m.* gypsy, wanderer
romaniste *m.* specialist in Romance languages; (eccl.) Romanist
romantique *a.* romantic (literature, art); — *m.* romanticist
romantisme *m.* romanticism
romarin *m.* rosemary
rompre *vt.* to break, break off, break up; break in, train; disrupt, interrupt; — *vi.* break; se — to break off, break up; break oneself in, become accustomed
rompu *a.* broken; broken in, trained, experienced; fatigued, worn out
romsteck *m.* rump steak
ronce *f.* bramble; blackberry bush
ronce-framboise *f.* loganberry
ronceux *a.* thorny, brambly
ronchonner *vi.* to grumble, complain
rond *a.* round; plump; straightforward; — *m.* round, circle, ring; — de serviette napkin ring
rondache *f.* round shield
rond-de-cuir *m.* (coll.) bureaucrat, petty official
ronde *f.* (mus.) round; patrol
rondeau *m.* (mus.) rondo; rondeau (literature)
rondelet *a.* round, roundish; plump
rondelle *f.* ring, washer; disk; circular piece; round
rondement *adv.* roundly; promptly; in a straightforward manner
rondeur *f.* roundness; rotundity; frankness, straightforwardness
rondin *m.* log; stick; beam
rond-point *m.* circular intersection, circus
ronflant *a.* snoring; booming; rumbling; pretentious
ronflement *m.* snoring, snore; buzzing; booming cannon; rumbling
ronfler *vi.* to snore; roar; whirr; boom; rumble
ronfleur *m.* snorer
rongeant *a.* gnawing, eating away; corroding
ronger *vt.* to gnaw, nibble, eat away; erode; corrode; torment
rongeur *a.* gnawing; corroding; tormenting; — *m.* rodent
ronron *m.* hum, purr
ronronner *vi.* to hum, purr
roquer *vt.* to castle (chess)
roquet *m.* mongrel, cur, dog
rosaire *m.* (eccl.) rosary, beads
rosâtre *a.* pinkish
rosbif *m.* roast beef
rose *f.* rose; — *a.* pink; rosy
rosé *a.* light red

roseau *m.* (bot.) reed
rosée *f.* dew
roselet *m.* ermine fur
roséole *f.* (med.) roseola; German measles
roseraie *f.* rose garden
rosette *f.* rosette; ribbon, bow
rosier *m.* rose bush
rosir *vi.* to turn pink *or* rosy
rossard *m.* good-for-nothing
rossée *f.* beating, thrashing, licking
rosser *vt.* to thrash, whip, beat
rossignol *m.* nightingale
rossinante *f.* nag, old horse
rôt *m.* roast
rotative *f.* rotary press
rotatoire *a.* rotary
roter *vi.* to belch, eructate
rôti *m.* roast
rôtie *f.* toast
rotin *m.* rattan
rôtir *vt. & vi.* to roast; toast
rôtissage *m.* roasting
rôtisserie *f.* roaster's shop
rôtissoire *f.* Dutch oven; roaster
rotonde *f.* rotunda
rotondité *f.* rotundity, roundness
rotor *m.* rotor
rotule *f.* kneecap; knee joint; (mech.) knuckle
roture *f.* low estate; commoners
roturier *m. & a.* plebeian, commoner
rouage *m.* wheels, gears, workings
rouan *a.* roan
roublard *a. & m.* shrewd, crafty person
roublardise *f.* skulduggery
roucouler *vi.* to coo
roue *f.* wheel
roué *m.* rake, profligate, roué; — *a.* clever, shrewd, crafty, sly
rouelle *f.* round piece, slice; filet of veal
rouennerie *f.* printed fabrics
rouer *vt.* to torture on a wheel; beat, thrash
rouerie *f.* cheating, trickery, sharping
rouet *m.* spinning wheel; pulley wheel
rouge *a.* red; — *m.* red; rouge; lipstick
rougeâtre *a.* reddish
rougeaud *a.* red-faced, ruddy
rouge-gorge *m.* robin
rougeole *f.* measles
rougeoyer *vi.* to turn red
rougeur *f.* redness; blush
rougir *vt.* to redden, turn red; heat, cause to glow; — *vi.* to grow red, turn red; blush
rouille *f.* rust; blight
rouillé *a.* rusty, rusted; blighted
rouiller *vt.* to rust, blight; se — to become rusty, rust
rouilleux *a.* rust-colored

rouillure *f.* rust, rustiness
roulade *f.* trill, roll
roulage *m.* rolling; hauling, transporting; traffic
roulant *a.* rolling; moving; smooth; **fauteuil — ** wheel chair
rouleau *m.* roll; roller; coil; cylinder; rolling pin; **— compresseur** steam roller
roulement *m.* rolling; functioning, running; rotation, alternation; **— à billes** ballbearing
rouler *vt.* to roll; roll up; carry, haul; consider, turn over; **— ** *vi.* roll; run; turn; move along; rove; rumble; rotate, alternate
roulette *f.* small wheel; roller; caster; roulette; **patins à —s** *m. pl.* roller skates
roulier *m.* hauler, trucker, carter
roulis *m.* (naut.) roll
roulotte *f.* caravan, house trailer
Roumain *m. & a.* Roumanian
Roumanie *f.* Roumania
roupie *f.* rupee
roussâtre *a.* reddish
rousselet *m.* russet pear
rousseur *f.* reddishness, redness; **tache de — ** freckle
roussi *a.* burned; burning; browned
roussin *m.* draft horse, plow horse
roussir *vt. & vi.* to redden; turn brown; singe, burn
routage *m.* newspaper delivery *or* distribution
route *f.* route, road, way; **grande — ** highway; **en — ** on the way; go on; let's go; **se mettre en — ** to start out, set out
router *vt.* to deliver, distribute
routier *a.* of roads; **— ** *m.* long-distance trucker; long-distance cyclist; **-s** *pl.* highwaymen; **carte routière** *f.* road map
routine *f.* routine, habit
routinier *a.* routine
rouvrir *vt.* to open again, reopen
roux (rousse) *a.* reddish, red-headed
royal *a.* royal; regal
royaliste *m. & f.* royaliste
royaume *m.* kingdom, realm
royauté *f.* royalty
ru *m.* streamlet
ruade *f.* attack; kicking of an animal
ruban *m.* ribbon; tape; band, strip; **— magnétique** magnetic recording-tape
rubané *a.* striped
rubaner *vt.* to adorn with ribbons; cut into strips
rubéole *f.* German measles
rubicond *a.* rubicund
rubiette *f.* robin
rubigineux *a.* rusty; rust-colored

rubis *m.* ruby; watch jewel
rubrique *f.* rubric; red chalk; category, heading
ruche *f.* beehive; frill, ruche, ruffle
ruché *m.* ruche, frilling
ruchée *f.* bees of a hive
rucher *m.* apiary; **— ** *vt.* to gather (sewing); trim with ruching
rude *a.* rough, rugged; hard, harsh; coarse; steep; brusque; primitive
rudement *adv.* roughly, harshly
rudesse *f.* roughness, ruggedness; harshness; coarseness; abruptness
rudiment *m.* rudiment
rudimentaire *a.* rudimentary, elementary
rudoyer *vt.* to treat roughly
rue *f.* street
ruée *f.* rush, stampede; attack, onslaught
ruelle *f.* narrow street, lane, alley
ruer *vi.* to kick; **se — (sur)** to rush upon, stampede
rufian *m.* ruffian
ruginer *vt.* to clean, scale teeth
rugir *vi.* to roar, bellow
rugissement *m.* roar, roaring, bellow, bellowing
rugosité *f.* roughness, ruggedness; wrinkle
rugueux *a.* rough, rugged; wrinkled, gnarled
ruine *f.* ruin; downfall; destruction
ruiner *vt.* to ruin, destroy; **se — ** to be ruined; go to ruin; fall to ruins
ruineux *a.* ruinous; disastrous
ruisseau *m.* stream, brook; gutter
ruisseler *vi.* to stream, gush out, run; drip, trickle
ruisselet *m.* little brook *or* stream
rumba *f.* rhumba
rumen *m.* first stomach of a ruminant
rumeur *f.* noise, din, sound; rumor
ruminant *a. & m.* ruminant
rumination *f.* rumination
ruminer *vt. & vi.* to ruminate
rumsteck *m.* rump steak
runes *f. pl.* runes
runique *a.* Runic
rupteur *m.* (elec.) circuit breaker
rupture *f.* breaking, rupture; fracture; breaking up; breaking in two; breaking off; breach
ruse *f.* ruse, trick
rusé *a.* sly, cunning, crafty
ruser *vi.* to use trickery
Russe *m. & a.* Russian
Russie *f.* Russia
rustaud *m.* boor; hick, bumpkin; **— ** *a.* boorish
rusticité *f.* rusticity
rustique *a.* rustic; strong, robust
rustre *m.* boor, lout; **— ** *a.* boorish, loutish

ruthénium *m.* ruthenium
rutilant *a.* glowing, gleaming, red
rutiler *vi.* to glow, gleam, redden
rythme *m.* rhythm
rythmé, rythmique *a.* rhythmic, rhythmical

S

sa *a. f.* his, her, its; one's
Saba *m.* Sheba
sabbat *m.* Sabbath
sabbatique *a.* sabbatical
sabin *a. & m.* Sabine
sable *m.* sand; — **mouvant** quicksand
sablé *a.* sanded, covered with sand *or* gravel; — *m.* shortbread cookie
sabler *vt.* to sand, gravel, cover with sand *or* gravel; sand-blast; drink dry
sableux *a.* sandy
sablier *m.* hourglass
sablière *f.* sandbox; sand pit, gravel pit; — *f.* beam, plate, templet
sablon *m.* sand for cleaning *or* scouring
sablonner *vt.* to clean, scour with sand
sablonneux *a.* sandy
sabord *m.* port hole, gun port
saborder *vt.* to hit below the water line; se — to scuttle
sabot *m.* wooden shoe; hoof; (auto.) brake shoe; **-s en caoutchouc** rubbers
sabotage *m.* sabotage; manufacture of sabots
saboter *vt.* to sabotage
sabotier *m.* maker of sabots
sabre *m.* saber, sword
sabrer *vt.* to saber, cut down
sac *m.* sack, sac, bag, pouch; sackcloth; sacking (a place); — **à main** handbag, purse
saccade *f.* jerk, jolt
saccadé *a.* by jerks; abrupt; irregular, uneven
saccader *vt.* to jerk, jolt
saccager *vt.* to plunder, sack, pillage; ransack
saccageur *m.* plunderer
saccharine *f.* saccharine
sacerdotal *a.* priestly
sachée *f.* sackful, bagful
sachet *m.* sachet; small sack *or* bag
sacoche *f.* bag; handbag; satchel; saddlebag; tool kit
sacre *m.* coronation; consecration
sacré *a.* sacred, holy; confounded; (anat.) sacral
sacrement *m.* sacrament
sacrer *vt.* to crown; consecrate
sacrificateur *m.* sacrificer
sacrificatoire *a.* sacrificial

sacrifice *m.* sacrifice; oblation
sacrifier *vt.* to sacrifice; devote
sacrilège *m.* sacrilege; — *a.* sacrilegious
sacristain *m.* sexton, sacristan
sacristie *f.* vestry
sacro-saint *a.* sacrosanct
sacrum *m.* (anat.) sacrum
sadique *a.* sadistic
sadisme *m.* sadism
sadiste *m. & f.* sadist
safran *m.* saffron, crocus
safrané *a.* saffron-colored
sagace *a.* sagacious
sagacité *f.* sagacity
sage *a.* wise; good, well-behaved; — *m.* sage, wise man
sage-femme *f.* midwife
sagesse *f.* wisdom; good behavior; discretion
sagittaire *m.* archer; (astrol., ast.) Sagitarius
sagittal *a.* arrow-shaped
sagou *m.* sago
Sahara *m.* Sahara
saharien *a.* of the Sahara
saie *f.* cape; hog-bristle brush
saignant *a.* bleeding, bloody; rare (meat)
saignée *f.* (med.) bleeding, bloodletting; drainage ditch; groove
saigner *vt. & vi.* to bleed
saigneux *a.* bloody
saillant *a.* projecting, prominent; salient; **dents -es** *f. pl.* buck teeth
saillie *f.* protrusion, projection; start; sally; spurt; gushing
saillir *vi.* to jut out, project; stand out, be prominent; spurt, gush; rush forth
sain *a.* sound, healthy; wholesome; sane; — **et sauf** safe and sound
sainfoin *m.* hay, forage
saindoux *m.* lard
saint *a.* saint; sacred, holy; saintly, godly; consecrated; — *m.* saint
saint-cyrien *m.* army cadet
Saint-Domingue *m.* Santo Domingo; Dominican Republic
Saint-Esprit *m.* (eccl.) Holy Ghost
sainte-nitouche *f.* hypocrite
sainteté *f.* sanctity, holiness
saint-frusquin *m.* possessions
Saint-Laurent *m.* St. Lawrence River
Saint-Marin *m.* San Marino
Saint-Père *m.* (eccl.) Pope, Holy Father
Saint-Siège *m.* (eccl.) Holy See
Saint-Sylvestre *m.* New Year's Eve
saisie *f.* seizure; attachment, foreclosure
saisie-arrêt *f.* legal garnishment, attachment
saisir *vt.* to seize, catch, grip, grasp; understand, apprehend; attach legally

saisissable *a.* perceptible

saisissant *a.* striking; startling; thrilling; gripping; keen, sharp

saisissement *m.* sudden shock, attack, seizure

saison *f.* season; de — in season; timely; opportune; hors de — out of season; untimely, inopportune

saisonnier *a.* seasonal

salacité *f.* salaciousness

salade *f.* salad

saladier *m.* salad bowl

salaire *m.* salary, wages, pay; fee; reward

salaison *f.* salting, curing; salted meat

salamandre *f.* salamander, newt

salanque *f.* salt marsh

salariat *m.* wage earners, salaried class

salarier *vt.* to pay, salary

sale *a.* dirty; foul; filthy; coarse

salé *m.* salt pork; petit — ham hock; — *a.* salted; risqué

saler *vt.* to salt; season; pickle, cure

saleté *f.* dirtiness, dirt, filth; obscenity

salicoque *f.* shrimp, prawn

salière *f.* salt cellar, salt shaker

salin *a.* saline, briny, salty

saline *f.* salt flats, salt mine

salinité *f.* salinity

salir *vt.* to soil, dirty; tarnish

salissure *f.* spot, stain, dirt mark

salivaire *a.* salivary

salive *f.* saliva

saliver *vi.* to salivate

salle *f.* hall, room; auditorium; audience; — à manger dining room; — d'attente waiting room; — de bain bathroom; — de conférences lecture hall

Salomon (*m.*) Solomon

salon *m.* living room, parlor; exhibition; — de thé tearoom; — de beauté beauty shop; — de coiffure barber shop

salopette *f.* dungarees, overalls

salpêtre *m.* saltpeter

salsepareille *f.* sarsaparilla

salsifis *m.* salsify, oysterplant

saltimbanque *m.* quack, charlatan; mountebank; tumbler

salubre *a.* salubrious, wholesome, healthy

salubrité *f.* salubrity, wholesomeness, healthiness; health, hygiene

saluer *vt.* to salute, greet, bow

salure *f.* saltiness, salinity

salut *m.* bow, greeting, salutation, salvation; safety; welfare; —! *interj.* hello!

salutaire *a.* salutary, beneficial

salve *f.* salvo, salute

samaritain *m.* samaritan

samedi *m.* Saturday

samovar *m.* samovar, tea urn

sanctifier *vt.* to sanctify, hallow

sanction *f.* sanction; approval, consent; penalty, punitive action

sanctionner *vi.* to sanction, approve; penalize

sanctuaire *m.* sanctuary

sandale *f.* sandal

sandaraque *f.* sandarac

sang *m.* blood; lineage; coup de — (med.) stroke; pur — thoroughbred

sang-froid *m.* composure, self-control, calmness, coolness

sanglant *a.* bloody, covered with blood; cutting, keen

sangle *f.* strap; lit de — *m.* cot, camp bed

sangler *vt.* to strap; whip, lash

sanglier *m.* wild boar

sanglot *m.* sob

sangloter *vi.* to sob

sangsue *f.* leech

sanguin *a.* sanguine, blood-red; of blood

sanguinaire *a.* sanguinary; bloody; bloodthirsty

sanguine *f.* blood orange; bloodstone; red chalk

sanguinelle *f.* dogwood

sanitaire *a.* sanitary; medical

sans *prep.* without; were it not for; free of; — doute without a doubt; probably; perhaps

sans-cœur *m.* heartless person

sanscrit, sanskrit *a.* & *m.* Sanskrit

sans-façon *m.* lack of formality, straightforwardness

sans-fil *m.* wireless, radio

sans-gêne *m.* excessive familiarity; lack of ceremony

sans-le-sou *m.* penniless person

sans-logis *m. pl.* homeless persons

sansonnet *m.* starling

sans-souci *m.* lack of concern; — *m.* & *f.* carefree person

sans-travail *m. pl.* unemployed persons

santal *m.* sandalwood

santé *f.* health

saoul *a.* (See soûl)

saouler *vt.* (See soûler)

sape *f.* (mil.) sap, sapping; undermining

saper *vt.* to sap, undermine

sapeur *m.* (mil.) sapper

sapeur-pompier *m.* fireman, fire fighter

saphir *m.* sapphire

sapide *a.* savory, flavorful

sapience *f.* wisdom

sapin *m.* fir tree; –ette *f.* spruce tree

sapine *f.* scaffolding; fir board; construction crane

sapinière *f.* fir forest

saponacé *a.* soapy

sarbacane *f.* blowpipe; pea shooter

sarcasme *m.* sarcasm
sarcastique *a.* sarcastic
sarcler *vt.* to weed; hoe
sarcleur *m.* weeder
sarcloir *m.* hoe
sarclure *f.* weeds
sarcome *m.* (med.) sarcoma
sarcophage *m.* sarcophagus
Sardaigne *f.* Sardinia
Sarde *m. & a.* Sardinian
sardinerie *f.* sardine cannery
sardinier *m.* sardine fishermen, cannery worker
sardoine *f.* sardonyx
sardonique *a.* sardonic
sargasse *f.* sargasso; **mer des –s** *f.* Sargasso Sea
S.A.R.L.: Société à Responsabilité Limi-tée incorporated
sarment *m.* shoot of a vine
sarracenique *a.* Saracen
sarrasin *m.* buckwheat
Sarrasin *m. & a.* Saracen
sarrasine *f.* portcullis
sarrau *m.* smock; overalls
Sarre *f.* Saar Basin
sariette *f.* savory
sas *m.* sifter, sieve, screen; lock of a dam
sasser *vt.* to sift, screen; (naut.) lock a vessel (in a canal)
Satan *m.* Satan, the Devil
satanique *a.* diabolical, devilish, satanic
satellite *m.* satellite
satiété *f.* satiety, repletion, fullness
satiné *a.* satin-like; glossy
satiner *vt.* to satin, gloss, glaze
satinette *f.* sateen
satire *f.* satire
satirique *a.* satirical; — *m.* satirist
satiriser *vt.* to satirize
satisfaction *f.* satisfaction; amends
satisfaire *vt.* to satisfy; please; make amends to; — *vi.* to satisfy, carry out, fulfil
satisfaisant *a.* satisfactory; satisfying
satisfait *a.* satisfied; pleased
satrape *m.* satrap
saturation *f.* saturation
saturer *vt.* to saturate
saturnin *a.* saturnine
saturnisme *m.* lead poisoning
satyre *m.* satyr
sauce *f.* sauce; gravy; dressing
saucer *vt.* to dip into sauce; soak, drench
saucière *f.* gravy boat; sauce dish
saucisse *f.* sausage; — **de Francfort** frankfurter
saucisson *m.* sausage, salami
sauf *prep.* except, except for, but; barring; — (sauve) *a.* safe

sauf-conduit *m.* safe conduct, pass, permit
sauge *f.* sage
saugrenu *a.* absurd, ridiculous
saule *m.* willow; — **pleureur** weeping willow
saumâtre *a.* brackish; salty; bitter
saumon *m.* salmon; ingot, bar; — **de fonte** pig iron; — *a.* salmon, pink
saumoné *a.* pink-fleshed; **truite –e** *f.* salmon trout
saumurage *m.* curing in brine
saumure *f.* brine
saupiquet *m.* spicy sauce
saupoudrer *vt.* to sprinkle; powder; dust with
saupoudroir *m.* shaker
saur *a.*, **hareng** — *m.* smoked red herring
saure *a.* sorrel
saurer *vt.* to smoke, cure fish
saut *m.* jump, leap; waterfall; — **à la perche** pole vault; — **d'obstacles** hurdles
saut-de-lit *m.* dressing gown; bedroom scatter rug
saut-de-mouton *m.* overpass, underpass
saute *f.* jump, leap; rise, increase
sauté *a.* fried; — *m.* food fried rapidly
saute-mouton *m.* leapfrog
sauter *vt.* to leap, jump; skip, omit; — *vi.* leap, jump; skip; explode, blow up; fail; — **au cou de** throw one's arms around; — **aux veux** to be very obvious; **faire** — to blow up, explode; pop open
sauterelle *f.* grasshopper
sauterie *f.* leaping, jumping; hopping, hop; dance, dancing
sauternes *m.* Sauterne wine
sauteur *a.* leaping, jumping; — *m.* leaper, jumper
sautiller *vt.* to skip, leap, hop
sautoir *m.* X-shaped cross; frying pan; sports hurdle; bar of a jump *or* vault; **en** — crosswise
sauvage *a.* wild; savage; barbarous, uncivilized; shy, unsociable
sauvagerie *f.* wildness, savagery; shyness, unsociability
sauvegarde *f.* safeguard, protection; bodyguard; safe-conduct; (naut.) lifeline
sauvegarder *vt.* to protect, safeguard
sauve-qui-peut *m.* wild flight, stampede
sauver *vt.* to save, preserve; rescue; **se** — to escape; run away, flee
sauvetage *m.* salvage; saving, rescue; **canot de** — lifeboat; **ceinture de** — *f.* life preserver
sauveteur *m.* saver, rescuer; salvager
sauvette; **à la** — *adv.* hastily
sauveur *m.* deliverer; saviour, redeemer
savamment *adv.* in a learned *or* scholarly

manner; knowingly

savane *f.* savanna

savant *a.* learned, scholarly, erudite; knowing; — *m.* scholar; scientist

savarin *m.* rum cake

savate *f.* old shoe; foot boxing (French style); (fig.) bungler

savetier *m.* cobbler, shoe repairer

saveur *f.* flavor, savor, taste

Savoie *f.* Savoy; **gâteau de** — *m.* sponge cake

savoir *vt.* to know, know how, be able, find out; **à** — namely, viz., to wit; **faire** — to inform; **reste à** — it remains to be seen; — *m.* knowledge, learning, erudition

savoir-faire *m.* skill, ability, know-how; tact

savoir-vivre *m.* manners, breeding, social poise

savoisien *a.* of Savoy

savon *m.* soap; **pain de** — *m.* cake of soap; **pierre de** — *f.* soapstone

savonnage *m.* soaping, washing

savonner *vt.* to soap; lather; wash

savonnette *f.* toilet soap

savonneux *a.* soapy

savourer *vt.* to relish, taste, savor, enjoy

savoureux *a.* savory, flavorful, tasty; spicy

Saxe *f.* Saxony; **porcelaine de** — *f.* Dresden china

saynète *f.* comic play, farce

Saxon *m. & a.* Saxon

saxophone *m.* saxophone

scabieux *a.* scabby

scabreux *a.* scabrous; risky, dangerous; risqué

scalpe *m.* scalp

scalper *vt.* to scalp

scandale *m.* scandal, disgrace

scandaleux *a.* scandalous, disgraceful, shocking

scandaliser *vt.* to scandalize

scander *vt.* to scan (poetry); stress, accentuate, measure

Scandinave *m. & a.* Scandinavian

Scandinavie *f.* Scandinavia

scansion *f.* scanning

scaphandre *m.* diving suit; aqualung

scaphandrier *m.* deep-sea diver

scapulaire *m.* (eccl.) scapular

scarabée *m.* beetle, scarab

scarlatine *f.* scarlet fever

scarole *f.* escarole

sceau *m.* seal; stamp, mark, imprint

scélérat *a.* villainous, wicked; sly, crafty; — *m.* villain, scoundrel

scélératesse *f.* villainy, wickedness

scellage *m.* sealing

scellé *m.* legal seal

scellement *m.* fixing in cement, plaster

sceller *vt.* to seal; fasten

scénario *m.* scenario, screenplay

scénariste *m. & f.* author of a screenplay

scène *f.* scene; stage; scenery; **metteur en** — *m.* director; **mettre en** — to direct, stage; **mise en** — *f.* direction, staging

scénique *a.* scenic; of the stage

scepticisme *m.* skepticism

sceptique *a.* skeptical; — *m. & f.* skeptic

sceptre *m.* scepter

schelem *m.* slam (in bridge)

schelling *m.* shilling

schéma *m.* plan, sketch, diagram

schématique *a.* schematic

schisme *m.* schism

schiste *m.* shale

schizophrène *a.* schizophrenic

schizophrénie *f.* schizophrenia

schnorchel *m.* snorkel

sciage *m.* sawing

sciatique sciatic; — *f.* sciatica

scie *f.* saw; — **à chantourner** jigsaw; — **à métaux** hack saw; — **à refendre** ripsaw; — **à ruban** band saw; — **de mer** sawfish

sciemment *adv.* knowingly; purposely

science *f.* science; knowledge, learning; — **des fusées** rocketry

scientifique *a.* scientific

scientiste *m.* scientist

scier *vt.* to saw

scierie *f.* sawmill

scinder *vt.* to split, divide

scintillant *a.* scintillating; twinkling

scintillation *f.* scintillation; twinkling; (phot.) flickering

scintiller *vi.* to scintillate; twinkle; flicker

scion *m.* scion, shoot, sprout

scission *f.* secession; division, split

sciure *f.* sawdust

sclérose *f.* sclerosis; — **multiple** multiple sclerosis

scléroser *vt.* (med.) to harden

scolaire *a.* scholastic, academic, school

scolarisation *f.* teaching; school attendance

scolarité *f.* length of study; **certificat de** — *m.* attendance certificate

scolastique *a.* scholastic

scolopendre *f.* centipede

scombre *m.* mackerel

scorbut *m.* scurvy

scorie *f.* slag, dross

scoutisme *m.* scouting, boy scout movement

scrofules *f. pl.* (med.) scrofula

scrupule *m.* scruple, qualm, doubt; **sans** —**s** unscrupulous

scrupuleux *a.* scrupulous

scruter *vt.* to scrutinize; examine at length

scrutin *m.* ballot, vote, voting

scrutiner *vi.* to vote, ballot

sculpter *vt.* to sculpt, sculpture, carve, chisel

sculpteur *m.* sculptor

scythe *a. & n.* Scythian

se *pron.* oneself, himself; herself, itself, themselves; each other, one another

séance *f.* sitting, session, meeting; showing, performance; **lever la —** to adjourn

séant *a.* sitting; in session; fitting, proper, becoming

seau *m.* pail, bucket

sébacé *a.* fatty

sébile *f.* wooden bowl

sec (sèche) *a.* dry, dried; lean; sharp, curt; barren; **argent —** *m.* hard cash; **coup —** *m.* snap; clean, hard blow; **à —** dry; aground; **mettre à —** to dry up, drain, pump out; **— adv.**, **boire —** to drink straight; **parler —** to speak plainly, in a straightforward manner

sèche-cheveux *m.* hair dryer

sécheresse *f.* dryness; leanness; curtness; drought

sécher *vt.* to dry; (coll.) cut a class; fail a student; **— vi.** dry

sécheur *m.* drier

séchoir *m.* drier; towel rack

second *a.* second; **en — lieu** secondly, in the second place; **sans —** peerless, unequalled; **— m.** second in command; first mate

secondaire *a.* secondary

seconde *f.* second; second class

seconder *vt.* to second, assist, support, promote

secouer *vt.* to shake, shake off

secourable *a.* helpful; ready to help

secourir *vt.* to succor, help, assist, aid

secours *m.* succor, aid, assistance, help; **crier au —** to call for help; **premiers —** *pl.* first aid

secousse *f.* shake, shock, jolt

secret *a.* secret; concealed, hidden; **— m.** secret; secrecy

secrétaire *m. & f.* secretary

secrétariat *m.* secretariat; secretary's office

sécréter *vt.* to secrete

sécréteur *a.* secreting

sécrétion *f.* secretion

sectaire *m.* sectarian

sectateur *m.* member of a sect

secte *f.* sect, party, faction

secteur *m.* sector; area, district; segment

sectionner *vt.* to divide into sections

séculaire *a.* century-old, secular

sécularisation *f.* secularization

séculariser *vt.* to secularize

séculier *a.* secular, worldly; **— m.** layman

sécurité *f.* security; safety

sédatif *a. & m.* sedative

sédentaire *a.* sedentary

sédiment *m.* sediment

séditieux *a.* seditious

sédition *f.* sedition

séducteur *a.* enticing, seductive; **— m.** enticer; seducer

séduction *f.* seductiveness, charm; bribery; seduction

séduire *vt.* to charm; bribe; seduce

séduisant *a.* charming; enticing, seductive

segment *m.* segment; **— de piston** piston ring

segmenter *vt.* to divide into segments

ségrégation *f.* segregation

ségrégationiste *m.* segregationist

seiche *f.* cuttlefish; floodwave

seigle *m.* rye; **pain de —** *m.* rye bread

seigneur *m.* lord, nobleman

seigneurie *f.* lordship; domain

seille *f.* wooden bucket

seillon *m.* shallow tub

sein *m.* breast; bosom

seing *m.* signature; **acte sous — privé** simple contract

séisme *m.* earthquake

seize *a.* sixteen

seizième *a.* sixteenth

séjour *m.* sojourn, stay; abode, dwelling

séjourner *vi.* to stay, sojourn; reside

sel *m.* salt; (fig.) wit; **— anglais** *m.* Epsom salts; **— blanc** table salt; **— gemme** rock salt

sélecteur *a.* selective; **— m.** selector

sélection *f.* selection, choice, choosing

sélectivité *f.* selectivity

sélénium *m.* selenium

selle *f.* saddle; stool

seller *vt.* to saddle

sellette *f.* stool; saddle

selon *prep.* according to, by

seltz *m.*, **eau de —** *f.* seltzer, soda water

semailles *f. pl.* sowing, seeding

semaine *f.* week; week's pay; week's work; **— anglaise** five and one-half-day week

semaison *f.* seeding time

sémantique *a.* semantic; **— f.** semantics

sémaphore *m.* semaphore

semblable *a.* like, similar; such; **— n.** like, equal, fellow man

semblablement *adv.* likewise, similarly

semblant *m.* semblance, appearance; **faire — (de)** to pretend (to)

sembler *vi.* to seem, appear, look

semelle *f.* sole of a shoe; **battre la —** to be on the move, be roving

semence *f.* seed

semer *vt.* to sow; seed; spread, scatter

semestre *m.* semester, term; six-month period

semestriel *a.* six months long; taking place every six months, semi-annual

semeur *m.* sower; spreader

semi-circulaire *a.* semicircular

sémillant *a.* sprightly; light, gay

sémi-mensuel *a.* bimonthly

séminaire *m.* seminary

semis *m.* sowing, seeding; seed bed

sémitique *a.* Semitic

semi-voyelle *f.* semivowel

semoir *m.* mechanical sower, seeder

semonce *f.* summons; warning; lecture, talking-to

semoncer *vt.* to lecture, reprimand

semoule *f.* semolina

sempiternel *a.* eternal

sénat *m.* senate

sénateur *m.* senator

sénatorial *a.* senatorial

séné *m.* senna

senestrorsum *adv.* counterclockwise

sénévé *m.* mustard seed

sénile *a.* senile

sénilité *f.* senility

sens *m.* sense; judgment; meaning; direction; consciousness; **bon —** common sense; **— interdit** one-way street

sensation *f.* sensation; feeling; excitement

sensationnel *a.* sensational, exciting

sensé *a.* sensible, aware

sensibilisateur *a.* sensitizing; **— m.** sensitizer

sensibiliser *vt.* to sensitize

sensibilité *f.* sensitiveness, feeling; sensibility

sensible *a.* sensitive; sympathetic; tender, painful, sore; perceptible

sensiblement *adv.* perceptibly, measurably

sensiblerie *f.* sentimentality

sensitif *a.* sensory; sensitive

sensualiste *a.* sensual; **— m.** sensualist

sensualité *f.* sensuality

sensuel *a.* sensuous, sensual

sentant *a.* sentient

sente *f.* path, footpath, trail

sentence *f.* maxim, saying; penal sentence; **— de mort** sentence of death

sentencieux *a.* sententious

senteur *f.* scent, perfume, fragrance; **pois de — m.** sweet pea

sentier *m.* path, track

sentiment *m.* septiment, feeling; sensation, sense

sentimentalité *f.* sentimentality

sentinelle *f.* sentinel; sentry

sentir *vt.* to feel; sense; smell; **— vi.** smell; smell of, reek of; **se —** feel

seoir *vi.* to suit, become; be located

sépale *m.* sepal

séparable *a.* separable

séparateur *m.* separator

séparatif *a.* separating, dividing

séparation *f.* separation; partition, division; parting

séparé *a.* separate; apart, separated

séparément *adv.* separately

séparer *vt.* to separate; divide; part; **se — to** separate, divide, part; break up; branch off

sépia *f.* sepia; cuttlefish

sept *a.* seven; seventh

septante *a.* seventy

septembre *m.* September

septicémie *f.* blood poisoning

septième *a.* seventh

septique *a.* septic; **fosse — f.** septic tank

sépulcral *a.* sepulchral

sépulcre *m.* sepulcher

sépulture *f.* burial; tomb; cemetery

séquence *f.* sequence

séquestration *f.* seclusion; sequestration (law)

séquestre *m.* sequestration (law); depository

séquestrer *vt.* to sequester; isolate, confine

sérail *m.* seraglio, harem

séraphin *m.* seraph

séraphique *a.* seraphic, angelic

Serbe *m. & f. & a.* Serb, Serbian

Serbo-Croate *m. & f. & a.* Serbo-Croatian

serein *a.* serene, calm, peaceful

sérénade *f.* serenade

sérénissime *a.* most serene

sérénité *f.* serenity, calm, calmness

sergent *m.* sergeant; **— de ville** policeman

sériculture *f.* silkworm raising

série *f.* series, succession, string, run; **fin de — f.** (com.) remainder, remnant

sérier *vt.* to arrange in series

sérieux *a.* serious, grave; genuine; **— m.** seriousness

sérigraphie *f.* (print.) silk screen process

serin *m.* canary

seringue *f.* syringe

seringuer *vt.* to syringe; squirt

serment *m.* oath; **faux —** perjury; **prêter — to** take an oath

sermonner *vi. & vt.* to sermonize, lecture

serpe *f.* billhook, pruning hook; rough work

serpent *m.* snake

serpenter *vi.* to wind, meander, twist

serpentin *a.* serpentine; — *m.* coil
serpette *f.* billhook, pruning hook
serpillière *f.* sacking; apron
serpolet *m.* thyme
serrage *m.* tightening, clamping
serre *f.* grip; bird claw; squeezing; forceps; greenhouse; — **chaude** hothouse
serré *a.* tight, compact, dense, close
serre-frein *m.* brakeman
serre-livres *m.* book ends
serrement *m.* squeezing, gripping; — **de cœur** pang; — **de main** handshake
serre-papiers *m.* paper clip; paperweight; file, folder
serrer *vt.* to squeeze, tighten, clasp, grip; lock up; keep close to, hug; — **la main (à)** to shake hands (with); — **les freins** to put on the brakes; **se —** tighten; press, mill, be close together
serre-tête *m.* headband; kerchief; crash helmet
serrure *f.* lock
serrurerie *f.* locksmith's establishment; works, workings of a lock; iron work
serrurier *m.* locksmith; ironworker
sertir *vt.* to set; mount (jewel)
sertissure *f.* bezel; setting
sérum *m.* serum
servage *m.* bondage, slavery, serfdom
servant *m.* server (sports)
servante *f.* servant; serving tray
serveur *m.* server; bartender; card dealer
serveuse *f.* waitress
serviabilité *f.* obligingness, usefulness
serviable *a.* obliging
service *m.* service; military service; **chef de — m.** department head; — **compris** service charge included; **être de —** be on duty
serviette *f.* napkin; towel; briefcase
servilité *f.* servility
servir *vi.* to serve, be useful; — **de** to serve as; — *vt.* serve, wait on; **se — de** to use, make use of
serviteur *m.* servant
servo-frein *m.* power brakes
servo-moteur *m.* servomotor
ses *a. pl.* his, her, its
sésame *m.* sesame
session *f.* session, sitting; term
set *m.* tennis, movies; set of games (tennis); (theat.) scenery
sétacé *a.* bristly
séton *m.*, **blessure en — f.** flesh wound
seuil *m.* sill, threshold
seul *a.* sole, single; only; alone
seulement *adv.* only; even; merely
sève *f.* sap, juice; vitality
sévère *a.* severe, hard, harsh; strict
sévérité *f.* severity

sévices *m. pl.* maltreatment (law)
sévir *vi.* to be severe; rage
sevrer *vt.* to wean
sexe *m.* sex
sextuor *m.* (mus.) sextet
sexualité *f.* sexuality
sexuel *a.* sexual
seyant *a.* becoming, suitable
shake-hand *m.* handshake
shaker *m.* cocktail shaker
shampooing *m.* shampoo; liquid shampoo
shantung *m.* shantung
short *m.* movie short subject; clothing shorts
shunter *vt.* (elec.) to shunt
si *conj.* if; whether; suppose, how about, what if; — *adv.* so; yes; — **... que** however, no matter how
siamois *a. & m.* Siamese
Sibérie *f.* Siberia
sibilant *a.* sibilant
sicaire *m.* hired cutthroat
siccatif *a.* siccative, drying; — *m.* siccative, dryer
siccité *f.* dryness
Sicile *f.* Sicily
Sicilien *m. & a.* Sicilian
sidéral *a.* sidereal
sidération *f.* apoplectic stroke; sideration
sidéré *a.* struck, killed by lightning *or* apoplexy; thunderstruck
siècle *m.* century; age, time, period
siège *m.* seat; chair; (eccl.) see; center, focus; — **social** (com.) central office
siéger *vi.* to sit, be seated; (com.) have a central office
sien *pron.*, **le —, la -ne** his, hers, its; **les -s** *m. pl.* one's family, one's close friends
Sienne Sienna; **terre de — f.** burnt Sienna
sieste *f.* siesta, nap
sifflant *a.* whistling, hissing, sibilant
sifflante *f.* sibilant, consonant
sifflement *m.* whistling, hissing; sizzling; wheezing
siffler *vi.* to whistle, hiss; sizzle; wheeze; — *vt.* to whistle; hiss, hoot
sifflet *m.* whistle; hiss, hoot
siffleur *a.* whistling, hissing; — *m.* whistler, hisser
siffloter *vi.* to whistle quietly, whistle to oneself
signalé *a.* conspicuous; notorious; signal; well-known
signalement *m.* description
signaler *vt.* to signal; signalize, point out, report; **se —** distinguish oneself
signaleur *m.* signalman

signalisateur *m.* traffic signal; burglar alarm; — **de direction** direction indicator
signataire *m. & f.* signer, subscriber
signe *m.* sign, mark, symbol, indication; omen; gesture; **faire** — **à** to signal to; motion to; — **de tête** nod; — **des yeux** wink
signer *vt.* to sign; mark
signet *m.* bookmark
significatif *a.* significant, meaningful
signification *f.* signification; meaning, sense; service of a legal writ
signifier *vt.* to signify, mean; declare, notify; serve a legal writ
silence *m.* silence; secrecy; (mus.) rest
silencieux *a.* silent, still, taciturn; — *m.* auto muffler
silex *m.* flint, silex
silhouette *f.* silhouette, outline
silhouetter *vt.* to silhouette, outline; **se** — be silhouetted, stand out
silicate *m.* silicate
silice *f.* silica
silicium *m.* silicon
sillage *m.* (naut.) wake, wash; headway; — **de fumée** (avi. coll.) contrail
sillon *m.* furrow; wrinkle, groove; wake, path
sillonner *vt.* to furrow, wrinkle; streak
simagrée *f.* affectation; **faire des** –s to make faces, fuss
simiesque *a.* simian, monkey-like
similaire *a.* similar, like
similarité *f.* similarity, likeness
similateur *m. & f.* pretender, malingerer
simili *m.* imitation
similicuir *m.* imitation leather
similigravure *f.* half-tone
similitude *f.* similitude; similarity, likeness; simile
similor *m.* imitation gold
simoun *m.* desert storm, sandstorm
simple *a.* simple; single; plain, ordinary; simple-minded; **corps** — *m.* (chem.) element
simplet *a.* ingenuous
simplicité *f.* simplicity; simpleness; ingenuousness
simplificateur *a.* simplifying; — *m.* simplifier
simplification *f.* simplification, simplifying
simpliste *a.* oversimple, simplistic
simulacre *m.* semblance, show; image
simulateur *m.* simulator, pretender; faker
simulation *f.* simulation, pretense
simulé *a.* simulated, pretended, feigned
simuler *vt.* to simulate, pretend, feign
simultané *a.* simultaneous

sinapisme *m.* mustard plaster
sincère *a.* sincere, genuine; frank
sincérité *f.* sincerity, genuineness; frankness
sinécure *f.* sinecure
singe *m.* monkey, ape; imitator
singer *vt.* to ape, imitate, mimic
singerie *f.* aping, imitation; monkey-like behavior; mimicry
singeur *a.* aping, imitating; — *m.* aper, imitator
singulariser *vt.* to singularize, make distinguished, make conspicuous; **se** — stand out, be conspicious
singularité *f.* singularity; oddness, peculiarity
singulier *a.* singular; peculiar; odd; conspicuous
sinistre *a.* sinister, threatening; dismal; fatal; — *m.* disaster, catastrophe
sinistré *m.* victim of a disaster
sinon *conj.* if not, otherwise; except; — **que** except that
sinueux *a.* sinuous, winding
sinuosité *f.* sinuosity; bending, winding
sinus *m.* sinus; sine
sinusite *f.* sinus infection, sinusitis
siphonner *vt.* to siphon
sire *m.* lord, sire
sirène *f.* siren, mermaid; horn
siroc *m.* sirocco
sirop *m.* syrup
siroter *vt. & vi.* to sip
sirupeux *a.* syrupy
sisal *m.* sisal (hemp)
sismique *a.* seismic
sismographe *m.* seismograph
site *m.* site, location
sitôt *adv.* immediately; **de** — soon; — **que** *conj.* as soon as
situation *f.* situation; position, location; condition; circumstances
situé *a.* situated, located
situer *vt.* to situate, locate
six *a.* six
sixième *a.* sixth
sketch *m.* short theatrical sketch
ski *m.* ski, skiing; **faire du** — to ski
skier *vi.* to ski
skieur *m.* skier
Slave *m.* Slav; — *a.* Slavic, Slavonic
sleeping *m.* Pullman sleeper
slip *m.* shorts, briefs; — **(de bain)** bathing trunks, bathing suit
Slovaque *m. & f.* Slovak; — *a.* Slovakian
slovène *a. & m. & f.* Slovenian
smoking *m.* dinner jacket
snow-boot *m.* overshoe
sobre *a.* temperate; restrained, sober
sobriété *f.* sobriety, temperance, modera-

tion, restraint
sobriquet *m.* nickname
soc *m.* plowshare
sociabilité *f.* sociability
sociable *a.* sociable, companiable
socialiser *vt.* to socialize
socialisme *m.* socialism
socialiste *m. & f.* socialist; — *a.* socialistic
sociétaire *m. & f.* member; stockholder
société *f.* society; company; association, club; partnership; — **anonyme** corporation
sociologie *f.* sociology
sociologique *a.* sociological
sociologue *m.* sociologist
socle *m.* base, pedestal; stand
socque *m.* clog; (fig.) (theat.) sock; comedy
socquettes *f. pl.* bobby socks, anklets
socratique *a.* socratic
soda *m.* soda water
sodium *m.* sodium
sœur *f.* sister; nun
soi *pron.* himself, herself, oneself, itself
soi-disant *a.* so-called, supposed, self-styled; — *adv.* supposedly
soie *f.* silk; **papier de** — *m.* tissue paper
soierie *f.* silk goods; silk factory
soif *f.* thirst; **avoir** — to be thirsty
soigné *a.* carefully done; well cared for; neat, well-groomed
soigner *vi.* to look after, take care of; attend, nurse
soigneux *a.* careful; neat, tidy
soi-même *pron.* oneself
soin *m.* care; attention; **avec** — carefully; **premiers –s** *pl.* first aid; **aux bons –s de** in care of
soir *m.* evening, late afternoon; **hier** — last night
soirée *f.* evening; evening out; evening performance; party
soit *interj.* all right, so be it; — *conj.*, — **(que)** . . . — **(que)** either . . . or; **tant** — **peu** *adv.* very little
soixantaine *f.* about sixty
soixante *a.* sixty
soixante-dix *a.* seventy
soixantième *a.* sixtieth
soja *m.* soy bean
sol *m.* soil, ground, earth; (mus.) key of G; 5th note of a scale
solaire *a.* solar; **cadran** — *m.* sundial
soldat *m.* soldier
solde *m.* (com.) balance; surplus; **(en)** — at reduced prices; **vente de –s** *f.* clearance sale
solder *vt.* (com.) to settle, balance; sell, put on sale; (mil.) pay

sole *f.* sole; animal hoof
soleil *m.* sun; sunshine; **coucher du** — *m.* sunset; **coup de** — *m.* sunstroke; **il fait du** — it's sunny; **lever du** — *m.* sunrise; (coll.) **piquer un** — blush; **prendre du** — to sun oneself
solennel *a.* solemn; ceremonial, formal, official
solenniser *vt.* to solemnize; mark, celebrate
solennité *f.* solemnity; formality, ceremony
solidage *f.* goldenrod
solidaire *a.* responsible; integral; interlocked
solidariser *vt.* to make responsible; cause to interlock; se — join together in a common responsibility *or* cause
solidarité *f.* solidarity; joint responsibility
solide *a.* solid; strong; sound; reliable; — *m.* solid
solidification *f.* solidification, solidifying
solidifier *vt.* to solidify
solidité *f.* solidity; strength; soundness; reliability
soliloque *m.* soliloquy
soliloquer *vi.* to soliloquize
soliste *m. & f.* soloist
solitaire *a.* solitary, lonely; — *m.* solitaire; hermit
solitude *f.* solitude, loneliness
solive *f.* beam, joist, rafter, girder
soliveau *m.* small beam *or* joist
sollicitation *f.* solicitation, plea, request; pull of a magnet
solliciter *vt.* to solicit, canvass; request, beg, pull, attract
solliciteur *m.* canvasser; petitioner
sollicitude *f.* solicitude, concern, care
solubilité *f.* solubility; solvability
solution *f.* solution; solving; (med.) termination
solutionner *vt.* to solve
solvabilité *f.* solvency
solvable *a.* solvent
Somalie *f.* Somaliland
sombre *a.* dark, gloomy, somber; melancholy; overcast, cloudy; **faire** — to be dark
sombrer *vi.* to sink, go down
sommaire *a. & m.* summary
sommation *f.* legal summons, legal notice
somme *m.* sleep, nap; — *f.* sum, amount; **en** — in short; — **toute** all in all, on the whole; **bête de** — pack animal, beast of burden
sommeil *m.* sleep; **avoir** — to be sleepy
sommeiller *vi.* to slumber, doze, be dormant, lie dormant
sommer *vt.* to summon; sum up

sommet *m.* summit, top

sommier *m.* pack animal; transom; balance beam; mattress; register, file (law) — **élastique** spring mattress

sommité *f.* summit

somnambule *m.* somnambulist, sleep-walker

somnifère *a. & m.* soporific

somnolence *f.* somnolence, sleepiness

somnolent *a.* somnolent, sleepy

somnoler *vi.* to doze, drowse

somnose *f.* sleeping sickness; hypnotic sleep

somptuaire *a.* sumptuary

somptueux *a.* sumptuous

somptuosité *f.* sumptuousness

son *m.* sound; bran

son (sa) *a.* his, her, its

sonar *m.* sonar

sonate *f.* sonata

sondage *m.* (naut.) sounding; (med.) probing

sonde *f.* (naut.) lead; (med.) probe; (mining) boring apparatus

sonder *vt.* to probe; (naut.) sound; examine, explore

sondeur *m.* (naut.) sounder; prober; borer, driller

sondeuse *f.* drilling apparatus

songe *m.* dream

songe-creux *m.* dreamer, visionary

songer *vi.* to dream; think; imagine

songerie *f.* daydreaming

songeur *a.* dreamy, musing, pensive; — *m.* dreamer

sonique *a.* sonic; **vitesse —** *f.* speed of sound

sonnaille *f.* cow bell

sonnailler *m.* bellwether; — *vi.* to toll; ring incessantly

sonnant *a.* ringing, striking; hard (money); **à . . . . heures -es** at the stroke of . . .

sonné *a.* past; completed

sonner *vi. & vt.* to sound; ring; strike

sonnerie *f.* ringing; chimes; bell clapper

sonnette *f.* little bell; doorbell; **coup de —** *m.* ring, ringing; **serpent à -s** *m.* rattlesnake

sonneur *m.* sounder, ringer; bell-ringer; bugler

sonore *a.* sonorous, resonant; ringing; loud; voiced; **film —** *m.* sound film; **onde —** *f.* sound wave

sonoriser *vt.* to make resonant; add sound to

sonorité *f.* sonority, resonance

sophisterie *f.* sophistry

sophistication *f.* alteration, adulteration

sophistique *a.* sophistic; — *f.* sophistry

sophistiquer *vi.* to quibble; — *vt.* adulterate

soporatif *a. & m.* soporific

soporifique *a.* soporific, causing sleep

sopraniste *m.* male soprano, castrato

soprano *m. & f.* soprano

sorbet *m.* sherbet

sorbetière *f.* ice cream freezer

Sorbonne *f.* University of Paris

sorcellerie *f.* sorcery, witchcraft

sorcier *m.* sorcerer

sorcière *f.* sorceress, witch

sordide *a.* sordid; grubby; mean

sordidité *f.* sordidness

sornettes *f. pl.* foolishness, nonsense

sort *m.* fate, destiny, lot; spell, charm; **coup du —** *m.* stroke of fate; **tirage au —** *m.* drawing of a lottery; **tirer au —** to draw lots

sortable *a.* suitable

sortant *a.* outgoing, coming out, going out; **numéro —** *m.* winning number

sorte *f.* sort, kind; way, manner; **de la —** thus, in this manner; **de — que** so that; **en quelque —** in a certain way

sortie *f.* going out; exit; excursion; (com.) exporting; (mil.) sortie

sortilège *m.* spell, charm

sortir *vi.* to go out, come out, be out; leave; come from, issue; stand out; — *vt.* take out, bring out; pull out; put out; — *m.* coming out, going out, emerging

sosie *m.* double, image, twin

sot (sotte) *a.* stupid; silly; foolish; — *n.* fool

sottise *f.* foolishness, silliness; stupidity

sou *m.* sou, five-centime coin; cent, penny; **cent -s** five francs

soubresaut *m.* start, jolt; leap; gasp; **-s** *pl.* trembling

soubresauter *vi.* to jolt, start, leap

soubrette *f.* maid, chambermaid

souche *f.* stump; stub; shaft of a chimney; lineage, ancestry; founder of a family; **faire —** to found a family

souci *m.* care, anxiety, worry; marigold; **sans —** carefree

soucier *vt.* to trouble; **se — (de)** to concern oneself (about), care (for)

soucieux *a.* uneasy, concerned, anxious, worried

soucoupe *f.* saucer

soudain *a.* sudden; — *adv.* suddenly

Soudan *m.* Sudan

Soudanais *m. & a.* Sudanese

soude *f.* soda; **bicarbonate de —** *m.* bicarbonate of soda, baking soda

souder *vt.* to solder; weld; **lampe à —** *f.* blowtorch; **se —** to be welded; fuse,

join; mend, knit (bone)
soudoir *m.* soldering iron
soudoyer *vt.* to hire (for criminal purposes); bribe
soudure *f.* solder; soldering; welding
soue *f.* pigsty
soufflage *m.* blowing, blasting (of a furnace); glassblowing
souffle *m.* breath; breathing; blast, puff; à bout de — out of breath
soufflé *a.* puffed, puffy; unvoiced vowel; — *m.* soufflé
souffler *vi.* to blow; puff, pant, be short of breath; — *vt.* to blow, blow up, blow out; breathe; (theat.) prompt
soufflerie *f.* blower, bellows
soufflet *m.* bellows, blower; slap, box on ears; insult
souffleter *vt.* to slap; insult
souffleur *m.* blower; (theat.) prompter
soufflure *f.* air or gas blister, bubble
souffrance *f.* suffering, pain; abeyance
souffrant *a.* suffering, in pain; ailing, ill
souffre-douleur *m. & f.* butt, scapegoat
souffreteux *a.* suffering, poor, destitute; sickly
souffrir *vt.* to suffer, tolerate, endure, bear; allow; — *vi.* suffer, be in pain
soufre *m.* sulfur
souhait *m.* wish, desire; à — according to one's wish
souhaitable *a.* desirable
souhaiter *vt.* to wish, desire
souillarde *f.* laundry room
souiller *vt.* to dirty, stain; sully, taint
souillure *f.* stain, spot; blot, taint
soûl *a.* drunk; full, gorged, sated
soulagement *m.* relief, comfort, comforting
soulager *vt.* to ease, relieve, alleviate
soûler *vt.* to fill, gorge, stuff; make drunk; se — to get drunk; overeat, stuff oneself
soulèvement *m.* rising; uprising; — de cœur nausea
soulever *vt.* to lift, raise; stir up, arouse, excite; se — rise, swell; heave; revolt, rise up
soulier *m.* shoe, slipper
souligner *vt.* to underline, emphasize
soulte *f.* balance, balance due; settlement; difference between declared and actual value
soumettre *vt.* to submit; subdue
soumis *a.* submissive, compliant
soumission *f.* submission, obedience, compliance; tender, contract
soumissionner *vt.* to contract for, tender
soupape *f.* valve; plug; — de sûreté safety valve

soupçon *m.* suspicion; bit, tiny amount
soupçonner *vt.* to suspect; question
soupçonneux *a.* suspicious; suspecting
soupe *f.* soup; meal, mess
soupente *f.* attic, attic ceiling
souper *m.* supper; — *vi.* to eat supper
soupeser *vt.* to weigh, judge, heft
soupière *f.* soup tureen
soupir *m.* sigh; (mus.) quarter rest; dernier — last breath
soupirail *m.* vent; cellar window
soupirant *m.* suitor
soupirer *vi.* to sigh; — après to long for
souple *a.* supple
souplesse *f.* suppleness, flexibility
souquenille *f.* long smock
souquer *vi.* to strive, strain
source *f.* source, spring, fountain
sourcier *m.* dowser, user of a divining rod
sourcil *m.* eyebrow
sourciller *vi.* to knit the brow; frown
sourcilleux *a.* haughty, severe
sourd *a.* deaf; dull; dark; hollow; — *m.* deaf person
sourdine *f.* (mus.) mute; à la —, en — muted, soft; slyly
sourd-muet *a.* deaf and dumb; — *m.* deaf and dumb person
sourdre *vi.* to spring, well up, gush out (water)
souricier *m.* mouser, mouse catcher
souricière *f.* mousetrap; stake-out, police ambush; trap
sourire *vi.* to smile; be favorable
sourire, souris *m.* smile
souris *f.* mouse
sournois *a.* sly, cunning
sournoiserie *f.* cunning, slyness
sous *prep.* under, beneath, below; (in compound words) assistant, sub; — peu *adv.* shortly, soon, in a little while
sous-alimentation *f.* insufficient food supply
sous-bois *m.* underbrush
sous-chef *m.* assistant manager, second-in-command
souscripteur *m.* subscriber
souscription *f.* subscription; signature
souscrire *vt. & vi.* to subscribe
sous-cutané *a.* subcutaneous, under the skin
sous-développé *a.* underdeveloped
sous-diacre *m.* subdeacon
sous-directeur *m. or f.* assistant manager, assistant director
sous-entendre *vt.* to understand, leave unexpressed
sous-estimer *vt.* to undervalue
sous-évaluer *vt.* to undervalue
sous-garde *m.* trigger guard

sous-lieutenant *m.* second lieutenant
sous-locataire *m. & f.* subletter, sub-tenant
sous-location *f.* subletting, sublease
sous-louer *vt.* to sublet
sous-main *m.* desk blotter; **en —** *adv.* secretly
sous-marin *a. & m.* submarine
sous-marinier *m.* submarine crewman
sous-mentonnière *f.* chin strap
sous-nappe *m.* table pad
sous-officier *m.* noncommissioned officer
sous-préfecture *f.* subprefecture, second administrative capital of a department
sous-produit *m.* by-product
sous-secrétaire *m.* undersecretary, assistant secretary
sous-secretariat *m.* work of a undersecretary
soussigné *a.* undersigned
sous-sol *m.* subsoil; basement
sous-titre *m.* subtitle
soustraction *f.* subtraction; abstraction
soustraire *vt.* to subtract, deduct; remove, protect
sous-ventrière *f.* cinch, strap
sous-verre *m.* bound slide, bound picture, picture covered with glass but un-framed
sous-vêtements *m. pl.* underclothing
soutacher *vt.* to trim with braid
soutane *f.* cassock
soute *f.* magazine of a ship
soutenable *a.* supportable
soutenance *f.* oral exam covering a thesis, defense
soutènement *m.* retaining, support
souteneur *m.* upholder; white-slaver, pro-curer
soutenir *vt.* to support; bear
soutenu *a.* elevated, lofty; sustained
souterrain *a.* underground; **—** *m.* tunnel; underground passage, cave
soutien *m.* support
soutien-gorge *m.* brassière
soutirer *vt.* to draw off, obtain by deception
souvenance *f.* memory; remembrance
souvenir *m.* remembrance, memory; **—** *v.*, **se — (de)** to remember
souvent *adv.* often
souverain *m. & a.* sovereign
souveraineté *f.* sovereignty
soviétique *a.* Soviet
soya *m.* soybean
soyeux *a.* silky
spacieux *a.* spacious
spahi *m.* North African trooper
sparadrap *m.* adhesive plaster, adhesive tape

Sparte *f.* Sparta
Spartiate *m. & f. & a.* Spartan
spasme *m.* spasm
spasmodique *a.* spasmodic
spatule *f.* spatula; spoonbill
speaker *m.* radio announcer
speakerine *f.* woman radio announcer
spécial *a.* special
spécialisation *f.* specialization
spécialiser *vt.* to specialize
spécialiste *m. & f.* specialist; **—** *a.* specialized, specializing
spécialité *f.* speciality
spécieux *a.* specious
spécification *f.* specification
spécifier *vt.* to specify
spécifique *m.* medication, remedy; **—** *a.* specific
spécimen *m.* specimen; sample
spectacle *m.* spectacle, show
spectaculaire *a.* spectacular
spectateur *m.* spectator
spectral *a.* spectral
spectre *m.* apparition, ghost; spectrum
spectroscope *m.* spectroscope
spéculateur *m.* speculator
spéculatif *a.* speculative
spéculation *f.* speculation
spéculer *vi.* to speculate
spéléologie *f.* cave exploration
sphère *f.* sphere
sphéricité *f.* sphericity, roundness
sphérique *a.* spherical
sphéroïde *m.* spheroid
spider *m.* (auto.) rumble seat
sphincter *m.* sphincter
sphinx *m.* sphinx
spinelle *m.* spinel
spiral *a.* spiral; **—** *m.* watch hairspring
spirale *f.* spiral
spire *f.* spiral line, helix
spirée *f.* spiraea
spirite *m. & f. & a.* spiritualist
spiritisme *m.* spiritualism
spiritualiser *vt.* to spiritualize
spiritualisme *m.* spiritualism
spiritualiste *m. & f. & a.* spiritualist
spiritualité *f.* spirituality
spirituel *a.* witty; religious; spiritual
spiritueux *a.* alcoholic, spiritous
spleen *m.* boredom, bitter melancholy
splendeur *f.* splendor
splendide *a.* splendid
spoliateur *m.* despoiler; **—** *a.* despoiling
spolier *vt.* to despoil
spongieux *a.* spongy
spontané *a.* spontaneous
spontanéité *f.* spontaneity
sporadique *a.* sporadic
sportif *a.* sportive, sporting; **—** *m.* sports-

man
sportivité *f.* sportsmanship; loyalty
spot *m.* spotlight
spoutnik *m.* sputnik, satellite
sprinter *vi.* to sprint
spumeux *a.* foamy, frothy
squale *m.* shark
squame *f.* skin scale
squameux *a.* scaley
square *m.* small public square
squelette *m.* skeleton
stabilisateur *m.* stabilizer; — *a.* stabilizing
stabaliser *vt.* to stabilize
stabilité *f.* stability
stable *a.* stable
staccato *adv.* staccato
stade *m.* stadium
stage *m.* preparatory period, development stage; probationary period
stagiaire *a.* preparatory, probationary; — *m. & f.* probationer; apprentice
stagnant *a.* stagnant
stagnation *f.* stagnation
stagner *vi.* to stagnate
stalactite *f.* stalactite
stalagmite *f.* stalagmite
stalle *f.* choir stall; stall
stance *f.* stanza
stand *m.* display, stand; grandstand
standard *m.* standard; switchboard
standardisation *f.* standardization
standardiser *vt.* to standardize
standardiste *m. & f.* switchboard operator
standing *m.* standard of living; level of luxury
stase *f.* blood stagnation
station *f.* stop; station; resort; position
stationnaire *a.* stationary
stationnement *m.* parking; — interdit no parking
stationner *vt. & vi.* to park; stand
station-service *f.* service station
statique *f.* statics; — *a.* static
statisticien *m.* statistician
statistique *f.* statistics; — *a.* statistical
statuaire *m.* statuary (person); — *f.* statuary (art)
statuer *vt.* to decree; enact
statuette *f.* statuette
statu quo *m.* status quo
stature *f.* stature, height
statut *m.* statute, ordinance
statutaire *a.* statutory
stéatite *f.* soapstone
steeple *m.* steeplechase
stèle *f.* stele, monument, stone
stellaire *a.* stellar
sténo *m. & f.* stenographer; — dactylo stenographer-typist

sténographe *m. & f.* stenographer
sténographie *f.* stenography
sténographier *vt.* to take down in shorthand
sténographique *a.* stenographic
sténopé *m.* pinhole camera
sténotype *f.* stenotype machine
sténotypie *f.* stenotypy
stentor *m.* stentor; voix de — stentorian voice
stère *m.* cubic meter
stéreographique *a.* stereographic
stéreophonie *f.* stereophonic sound, stereophonic music
stéreophonique *a.* stereophonic
stéréoscope *m.* stereoscope; stereo camera
stéréoscopique *a.* stereoscopic
stéréotype *a.* stereotyped
stéréotyper *vt.* to stereotype
stéréotypie *f.* stereotyping
stérile *a.* sterile, barren
stérilisateur *m.* sterilizer
stérilisation *f.* sterilization
stériliser *vt.* to sterilize
stérilité *f.* sterility
sternum *m.* breastbone, sternum
stéthoscope *m.* stethoscope
stick *m.* hockey stick; walking stick
stigmate *m.* scar; stigma; stigmata
stigmatiser *vt.* to stigmatize, brand
stilligoutte *f.* medicine dropper
stimulant *a.* stimulating; — *m.* stimulant
stimulation *f.* stimulation
stimuler *vt.* to stimulate
stipendiaire *a.* hired
stipendier *vt.* to hire
stipulation *f.* stipulation
stipuler *vt.* to stipulate
stockage *m.* stocking up
stocker *vt.* to stock up, stockpile
stoïcien *a.* stoical
stoïcisme *m.* stoicism
stoïque *a.* stoic
stoppage *m.* repair
stopper *vi. & vt.* to stop; repair a stocking
store *m.* blind, shutter, venetian blind, curtain; windowshade, awning, metal curtain
strabisme *m.* crossed eyes
strangulation *f.* strangulation
strapontin *m.* folding seat
strass *m.* paste jewels
stratagème *m.* strategem
stratège *m.* strategist
stratégie *f.* strategy
stratégique *a.* strategic
stratification *f.* stratification
stratifier *vt.* to stratify
stratosphère *f.* stratosphere
stratosphérique *a.* stratospheric

stratus *m.* stratus cloud
streptococcie *f.* streptococcus infection
streptocoque *m.* streptococcus
streptomycine *f.* streptomycin
strette *f.* (mus.) stretta, fugue passage
strict *a.* strict, severe; exact
strident *a.* shrill, strident, harsh
strié *a.* streaked, striate(d)
strier *vt.* to streak
strige *f.* vampire
strontium *m.* strontium; — 90 strontium 90
strophe *f.* stanza
structure *f.* structure
strychnine *f.* strychnine
stuc *m.* stucco
studieux *a.* studious
studio *m.* studio; studio apartment
stupéfaction *f.* stupefaction
stupéfait *a.* stupefied, nonplussed
stupéfiant *a.* stupefying; — *m.* stupefactive
stupéfier *vt.* to stupify
stupeur *f.* stupor
stupide *a.* stupid; stupefied
stupidité *f.* stupidity
stuquer *vt.* to cover with stucco
stygien *a.* Stygian
style *m.* stylus; style
styler *vt.* to style
stylet *m.* stiletto
styliser *vt.* to stylize
styliste *m. & f.* stylist
stylo(graphe) *m.* fountain pen
suaire *m.* shroud
suave *a.* smooth, suave
suavité *f.* suavity, sweetness
subalterne *a. & m. & f.* subaltern
subconscience *f.* subconscious
subdiviser *vt.* to subdivide
subdivision *f.* subdivision, secondary division
subéreux *a.* corky
subir *vt.* to undergo, submit to
subit *a.* sudden
subjectif *a.* subjective
subjectivité *f.* subjectivity
subjonctif *m.* (gram.) subjunctive mood
subjuguer *vt.* to subjugate
sublimation *f.* sublimation
sublime *a.* sublime
sublimé *m.* sublimate
sublimer *vt.* to sublimate
subliminal *a.* subliminal
sublimité *f.* sublimity
submerger *vt.* to submerge
submersible *a.* submersible
submersion *f.* submersion
subodorer *vt.* to smell from afar
subordination *f.* subordination

subordonné *a. & m.* subordinate
subordonner *vt.* to subordinate
suborner *vt.* to suborn, bribe, tamper with
subreptice *a.* surreptitious, furtive
subrogé *a.* replacement, substitute
subroger *vt.* to replace
subséquent *a.* subsequent
subside *m.* subsidy
subsidiaire *a.* subsidiary
subsistance *f.* subsistence
subsister *vi.* to subsist, last
substantiel *a.* substantial
substantif *m.* noun
substantivement *adv.* as a noun
substituer *vt.* to substitute
substitut *m.* substitute
substrat(um) *m.* substratum
subterfuge *m.* subterfuge
subtil *a.* subtle, thin, sharp
subtiliser *vt.* to refine, make subtle; — *vi.* to be subtle
subtilité *f.* subtlety
subtropical *a.* subtropical
suburbain *a.* suburban
subvenir *vi.* to relieve, assist
subvention *f.* subsidy
subventionner *vt.* to subsidize
subversif *a.* subversive
subversion *f.* subversion
subvertir *vt.* to subvert, overthrow
suc *m.* juice, sap; cellular liquid
succéder *vi.* to follow
succès *m.* success, issue
successeur *m.* successor
successif *a.* successive
succession *f.* inheritance; estate; succession
succinct *a.* succinct
succion *f.* sucking
succomber *vi.* to succumb
succulence *f.* succulence
succulent *a.* succulent, juicy
succursale *f.* branch-office; regional office
sucer *vt.* to suck
sucette *f.* lollipop, sucker; child's pacifier
suçoir *m.* sucker
sucre *m.* sugar
sucré *a.* sugared; sweet
sucrer *vt.* to sugar, sweeten
sucrerie *f.* sugar factory; -s *pl.* candy
sucrier *m.* sugar bowl; sugar manufacturer; — *a.* sugary
sud *m.* south; — -est *m.* southeast; — -ouest *m.* southwest
Sud-Africain *m. & a.* South African
Sud-Américain *m. & a.* South American
sudiste *m.* southerner
Suède *f.* Sweden; — *m.* suede
Suédois *m. & a.* Swedish
suée *f.* sweating

suer *vt. & vi.* to perspire, sweat
sueur *f.* sweat, perspiration
suffire *vi.* to suffice, be sufficient
suffisamment *adv.* sufficiently
suffisance *f.* sufficiency
suffisant *a.* sufficient, conceited
suffixe *f.* suffix
suffocant *a.* suffocating
suffocation *f.* suffocation
suffoquer *vt. & vi.* to suffocate
suffrage *m.* suffrage, vote
suffragette *f.* suffragette
suggérer *vt.* to suggest
suggestif *a.* suggestive
suggestion *f.* suggestion
suicide *m.* act of suicide
suicidé *m.* person who commits suicide
suicider *v.,* se — to commit suicide
suie *f.* soot
suif *m.* tallow, suet
suint *m.* grease, lanolin
suintement *m.* oozing
suinter *vi.* to leak, ooze; trickle
Suisse *f.* Switzerland; — *m. & a.* Swiss; — *m.* beadle; porter; Swiss guard; **petit** — cream cheese
Suissesse *f.* Swiss woman
suite *f.* consequence; series; set; continuation; train, attendants; **à la** — de after, behind; **de** — without stopping; **par** — **de** as a result of; **tout de** — immediately
suivant *m.* follower; **-e** *f.* servant; — *a.* following, subsequent, next; — *prep.* according to
suivi *a.* connected, coherent; popular
suivre *vt. & vi.* to follow
sujet *m.* subject; reason; **au** — **de** about; — *a.* subject, exposed; — **à** apt to
sujétion *f.* subjection
sulfate *m.* sulfate
sulfure *m.* sulfide
sulfurer *vt.* to combine with sulfur
sulfureux *a.* sulfurous
sulfurique *a.* sulfuric
sultanat *m.* sultanate
sultane *f.* sultana
sunnite *m. & f.* orthodox Moslem
superbe *a.* superb; proud, haughty
supercarburant *m.* high-octane gas, ethyl
supercherie *f.* fraud, deceit
superfétation *f.* redundancy
superficie *f.* superficies, surface, area
superficiel *a.* superficial; shallow
superfin *a.* superfine
superflu *a.* superfluous
superfluité *f.* superfluity
supérieur *a.* superior, upper, higher; — *m.* superior
supériorité *f.* superiority
superlatif *a.* superlative

superposer *vt.* to place on top of one another
supersonique *a.* supersonic
superstitieux *a.* superstitious
superstition *f.* superstition
superstructure *f.* superstructure
superviser *vt.* to supervise
supin *a.* supine
supination *f.* supine position
supplanter *vt.* to supplant
suppléant *m.* substitute, assistant
suppléer *vt. & vi.* to supply, make up; substitute for; — **à** to remedy
supplément *m.* supplement, addition, supplemental charge; second helping
supplémentaire *a.* supplementary, additional
supplication *f.* supplication
supplice *m.* torture; punishment; death penalty
supplicier *vt.* to execute; torture; cause to suffer
supplier *vt.* to implore
supplique *f.* petition
support *m.* prop; assistance
supportable *a.* bearable
supporter *vt.* to bear, tolerate, support
supposé *a.* supposed, pretended; — **que** *conj.* supposing that
supposer *vt.* to suppose
supposition *f.* supposition
suppositoire *m.* suppository
suppôt *m.* supporter, upholder, partisan
suppression *f.* suppression, elimination, cancellation
supprimer *vt.* to suppress, cancel, eliminate; conceal
suppuration *f.* festering, suppuration
suppurer *vi.* to form pus
supputation *f.* calculation, evaluation
supputer *vt.* to calculate, evaluate
suprématie *f.* supremacy
suprême *a.* supreme; crowning; — *m.* chicken in cream sauce
sur *prep.* on, upon, over, in, by, near, about, towards
sur *a.* sharp tasting
sur- *prefix* super-, over-
sûr *a.* sure, certain
surabondance *f.* superabundance
surabondant *a.* superabundant
surabonder *vi.* to be superabundant
suractivité *f.* hyperactivity
surajouter *vt.* to add on
suralimenter *vt.* to overfeed, oversupply
suranné *a.* superannuated, old, obsolete
surcharge *f.* surcharge; excess load, overload; word written over another word
surcharger *vt.* to overload; surcharge; supercharge; write over another word

surchauffer *vt.* to overheat
surchoix *m.* first choice, first quality
surclasser *vt.* to outclass
surcontrer *vt.* to redouble (at bridge)
surcroît *m.* addition, increase, surplus; de — extra
surdi-mutité *f.* deafness and dumbness
surdité *f.* deafness
sureau *m.* elder tree
surélever *vt.* to raise, raise excessively
surenchère *f.* higher bid
surenchérir *vt.* to outbid
surestimer *vt.* to overvalue
suret *a.* sharp, somewhat sour
sûreté *f.* surety, security, safety
Sûreté *f.* security police
surévaluer *vt.* to overvalue
surexcitable *a.* overexcitable
surexcitation *f.* overexcitement
surexciter *vt.* to overexcite
surexposer *vt.* (phot.) overexpose
surexposition *f.* (phot.) overexposure
surface *f.* surface
surfaire *vt.* to overvalue, overcharge; overpraise
surfiler *vt.* to weave in and out
surfin *a.* superfine
surgeon *m.* offshoot
surgir *vt.* to arise, rise up; reach port
surhausser *vt.* to elevate; exaggerate
surhomme *m.* superman
surhumain *a.* superhuman
surimposer *vt.* to superimpose
surimposition *f.* superimposing; (phot.) double exposure
surintendance *f.* superintendence
surintendant *m.* superintendent; -e *f.* superintendent; morale officer
surir *vi.* to sour, become acid
surjeter *vt.* to overcast
sur-le-champ *adv.* immediately, instantly
surlendemain *m.* the second day after
surmenage *m.* overwork, overactivity
surmener *vt.* to overwork
sur-moi *m.* superego
surmonter *vt.* to surmount; overcome
surmulet *m.* red mullet
surnager *vi.* to float on the surface; survive, remain
surnaturel *a.* supernatural
surnom *m.* surname
surnombre *m.* excess
surnommer *vt.* to name, give a surname to
surnuméraire *a. & m. & f.* supernumerary
suroît *m.* southwest wind; sou'wester hat; jacket
surpaye *f.* extra pay
surpayer *vt.* to pay dearly for, overpay
surpasser *vt.* to surpass; exceed

surpeuplé *a.* overpopulated
surpeuplement *m.* overpopulation
surplis *m.* surplice
surplomb *m.* overhang; en — overhanging
surplomber *vt.* to overhang
surplus *m.* surplus; au — moreover
surprendre *vi.* to surprise
surpris *a.* surprised
surprise *f.* surprise
surproduction *f.* overproduction
surréalisme *m.* surrealism
surréaliste *m. & f.* surrealist; — *a.* surrealistic
sursaturer *vt.* to supersaturate
sursaut *m.* start; jump; en — *adv.* suddenly
sursauter *vi.* to somersault; jump, start
surseoir *vt.* to suspend
sursis *m.* suspension, delay; avec — with sentence suspended
surtaxe *f.* surtax
surtaxer *vt.* to overtax
surtension *f.* hypertension
surtout *adv.* especially; — *m.* overcoat
surveillant *m.* inspector, overseer
surveille *f.* second day previous
surveiller *vt. & vi.* to oversee, superintend, watch over
survenir *vi.* to come unexpectedly; happen unexpectedly
survenue *f.* unexpected arrival
survie *f.* survival; afterlife
survivance *f.* survival
survivre *vi.* to survive
survoler *vt.* to fly over
survolté *a.*, lampe -e *f.* photoflood lamp
sus *prep.* upon; en — besides, in addition
susceptibilité *f.* susceptibility
susceptible *a.* susceptible, likely; — d'accidents accident-prone
susciter *vt.* to create, cause
susdit *a.* aforementioned
susmentionné *a.* aforementioned
susnommé *a.* aforenamed
suspect *a.* suspected, suspicious
suspecter *vt.* to suspect
suspendre *vt.* to suspend, hang; put off
suspendu *a.* suspended, hanging; pont — suspension bridge
suspens *a.* suspended; en — in suspense
suspension *f.* suspension; hanging; ceiling fixture; points de — *m. pl.* elipsis
suspensoir *m.* suspensory
suspicion *f.* suspicion
sustentateur *m.* sustainer; — *a.* sustaining
sustenter *vt.* to sustain
susurrement *m.* murmer, buzz
susurrer *vt.* to murmer, buzz
suturer *vt.* to suture

suzerain *a.* paramount; — *m.* suzerain
svastike *m.* swastika
svelte *a.* svelte, slender
sveltesse *f.* slenderness, slimness
S.V.P.: s'il vous plaît please
sycophante *m.* sycophant, deceiver
syllabaire *m.* spelling book
syllabe *f.* syllable
syllabique *a.* syllabic
syllogisme *m.* syllogism
sylvestre *a.* sylvan
sylviculture *f.* forestry
symbiotique *a.* (biol.) symbiotic
symbolique *a.* symbolic(al)
symbolisme *m.* symbolism
symboliste *a. & m.* symbolist
symétrie *f.* symmetry
symétrique *a.* symmetrical
sympathie *f.* sympathy, feeling; liking
sympathique *a.* sympathetic; likeable
sympathiser *vi.* to sympathize
symphonie *f.* symphony
symphonique *a.* symphonic
symposion *m.* symposium
symptomatique *a.* symptomatic
symptôme *m.* symptom
synchrone *a.* synchronized
synchronisation *f.* synchronization
synchroniser *vt.* to synchronize
syncope *f.* faint; syncope; syncopation; tomber en — to faint
syncoper *vt.* to syncopate
syndic *m.* syndic, chief, mayor; receiver of a business in receivership
syndical *a.* union, trade union
syndicalisme *m.* trade unionism
syndicaliste *a. & m. & f.* unionist
syndicat *m.* syndicate; trade union
syndiquer *vt.* to syndicate; unionize; se — to join a union
synecdoque *f.* synecdoche
synode *m.* synod
synonyme *a.* synonymous; — *m.* synonym
synonymie *f.* synonymy
synoptique *a.* synoptic
syntaxe *f.* syntax
syntaxique *a.* syntactical
synthèse *f.* synthesis
synthétique *a.* synthetic; synthesizing
synthétiser *vt.* to synthesize
syntonisation *f.* (rad.) tuning
syphilitique *a. & m. & f.* syphilitic
Syrie *f.* Syria
Syrien *m. & a.* Syrian
systématique *a.* systematic
systématiser *vt.* to systematize
système *m.* system
systole *f.* systole

T

ta *a. f.* your
tabac *m.* tobacco
tabagie *f.* smoke-filled room
tabatière *f.* snuffbox
tabellion *m.* notary
tabernacle *m.* tabernacle
table *f.* table; board; list; — de jeu card table; mettre la — to set the table; — des matières table of contents; — volante end table
tableau *m.* picture, painting; blackboard; — de bord (auto.) dashboard; (elec.) switchboard
tablée *f.* group at table
tablette *f.* tablet, notebook; shelf; slab; bar; — de cheminée mantel
tablier *m.* apron; dashboard; bridge roadway
tabou *m. & a.* taboo
tabouret *m.* stool; footstool
tabulaire *a.* tabular
tabulateur *m.* tabulator, tab key
tache *f.* spot, stain; blemish
tâche *f.* task; job
tacher *vt.* to spot, stain
tâcher *vi.* to endeavor, try
tâcheron *m.* pieceworker; taskmaster
tacheté *a.* spotted, speckled
tacheter *vt.* to speckle
tachymètre *m.* tachometer, speedometer
tacite *a.* tacit
tact *m.* touch; tact
tacticien *m.* tactician
tactique *a.* tactical; — *f.* tactics
taffetas *m.* taffeta
taie *f.,* — d'oreiller pillowcase
taillable *a.* subject to head tax
taillade *f.* slash
taillader *vt.* to slash
taillandier *m.* maker of cutting tools
taillant *m.* cutting edge
taille *f.* cut, cutting, trimming; height; size; waist; figure; head tax; cutting edge; tenor; new growth
taille-crayons *m.* pencil sharpener
taille-douce *f.* engraving
taille-ongles *m.* nail clippers
tailler *vt.* to cut, trim; sharpen
taillerie *f.* gem cutting
tailleur *m.* tailor; cutter; lady's suit
tailleuse *f.* dressmaker, cutter
taillis *m.* copse
tailloir *m.* platter, meat-chopping block; (arch.) abacus
tain *m.* tinfoil; silver on a mirror; glace sans — *f.* plate glass
taire *vt.* to conceal, say nothing about, hush up; se — to stop talking, be si-

lent; keep silent
talaire *a.* ankle-length (dress)
talc *m.* talc; talcum powder
talé *a.* bruised (of fruit)
talent *m.* talent, capacity
talentueux *a.* talented
talion *m.* retaliation
talisman *m.* talisman
talon *m.* heel; tub; pile, deck (at cards); keel; foot
talonner *vt.* to tread on with the heel; to follow close upon; — *vi.* to go aground
talonnette *f.* heel reinforcement; heel lift
talonnières *f. pl.* talaria, Mercury's heel wings
talquer *vt.* to spread with talcum
talus *m.* slope; embankment; **en** — at an angle
tamarin *m.* tamarind
tamarinier *m.* tamarind tree
tamaris *m.* tamarisk
tambour *m.* drum; drummer; cylinder; section of a column; spool; eardrum; embroidery hoop; — **de basque** tambourine; — **de frein** brake drum; **sans** — **ni trompette** quietly
tambourin *m.* tambourine; bongo drum, long narrow drum
tambourinaire *m.* drummer
tambouriner *vi.* to drum
tambour-major *m.* drum major
tamis *m.* sieve
tamisage *m.* sifting
Tamise *f.* Thames
tamiser *vt. & vi.* to sift; filter; sieve
tampon *m.* bung, stopper; stamp pad; surgical sponge; (rail.) buffer
tamponnement *m.* collision; (rail.) bump
tamponner *vt.* to plug; collide with; (rail.) to bump
tam-tam *m.* tom-tom; gong
tan *m.* bark used to tan leather
tancer *vt.* to repi ·mand
tandem *m.* tandem carriage, tandem bicycle
tandis que *conj.* whereas, while
tangage *m.* pitch of a boat
tangent *a.* tangeant; –e *f.* tangent
Tanger Tangiers
tango *m.* tango; — *a.* yellow-orange
tanguer *vi.* (naut.) to pitch
tanière *f.* den, lair
tannage *m.* tanning; dressing
tanné *a.* tan, tanned
tanner *vt.* to tan (leather)
tannerie *f.* tannery
tanneur *m.* tanner
tan(n)in *m.* tannin
tannique *a.* tannic
tan-sad *m.* extra saddle of a motorcycle

tant *adv.* so much, so many; — **soit peu** somewhat; — **pis** so much the worse; — **mieux** so much the better; — **s'en faut** far from it; — **que** as long as; **en** — **que** as
tantale *m.* tantalum; tantalus
tantaliser *vt.* to tantalize
tante *f.* aunt
tantinet *m.* small amount, mite
tantôt *adv.* soon, presently; just now; — . . . — sometimes . . . sometimes
taon *m.* horsefly, gadfly
tapage *m.* noise, din
tapageur *a.* noisy; showy; — *m.* noisemaker
tape *f.* slap, tap, pat
tapé *a.* dried (fruit)
tape-à-l'œil *a.* gaudy
tapecul *m.* jolting vehicle
taper *vt.* to tap, slap; typewrite
tapette *f.* tap, light tap; swatter
tapin *m.* drummer
tapinois, en — *adv.* secretly
tapioca *m.* tapioca
tapir *m.* tapir
tapir *v.*, **se** — to squat, crouch, cower
tapis *m.* carpet; cloth; — **roulant** conveyor belt; **sur le** — under discussion; — **vert** gambling table
tapisser *vt.* to paper, hang
tapisserie *f.* tapestry; wallpaper; **faire** — be a wallflower
tapissier *m.* upholsterer; paper hanger; tapestry maker
taponner *vt.* to stopper
tapoter *vt.* to pat, rap; strum
taquet *m.* wedge, block
taquin *a.* teasing
taquiner *vt.* to tease; tantalize
taquinerie *f.* teasing
tarabiscoter *vt.* to overadorn, overornament
taraud *m.* threading tool
tarauder *vt.* to thread, make a thread
taraudeuse *f.* threading machine
tard *adv.* late
tarder *vi.* to delay; be long in; **il me tarde (de)** I am anxious (to)
tardif *a.* tardy, late; backward
tare *f.* defect, taint; (com.) depreciation
tarentelle *f.* tarentella
tarentule *f.* tarantula
tarer *vt.* to damage; **tarnish**
targette *f.* slide bolt
targuer *v.*, **se** — **(de)** to pride oneself (on)
tarière *f.* auger; borer (of an insect)
tarif *m.* tariff; price list, rate; fare
tarifer *vt.* to set the price of
tarir *vt. & vi.* to dry up
tarissement *m.* drying up, exhausting

tarse *m.* instep
tarsier *m.* tarsus
tartane *f.* (naut.) tartan, small fishing boat
tarte *f.* tart
tartine *f.* slice of bread and butter, bread and jam
tartiner *vt.* to spread
tartre *m.* tartar
tartufe *m.* hypocrite
tas *m.* heap, pile
tasse *f.* cup
tasseau *m.* bracket, brace; lug; lathe
tasser *vt.* to compress, pack; se — to sink, settle; crowd together
tâter *vt.* to feel, handle
tâtonner *vi.* to grope; (fig.) to fumble
tâtonneur *a.* groping
tâtons, à — *adv.* gropingly
tatou *m.* armadillo
tatouage *m.* tattoo
tatouer *vt.* to tattoo
taudis *m.* hovel; — *pl.* slums
taupe *f.* mole
taupinière *f.* molehill
taure *f.* heifer
taureau *m.* bull
tauromachie *f.* bullfighting
taux *m.* rate, set price
tavelage *m.* fruit bruise, spot
taveler *vt.* to bruise, spot
taverne *f.* tavern
tavernier *m.* tavern keeper
taxatif *a.* taxable
taxe *f.* tax, duty, rate, charge; toll
taxer *vt.* to tax, regulate; — de to accuse; lettre taxée *f.* postage-due letter
taxi *m.* taxicab
taxidermie *f.* taxidermy
taximètre *m.* meter of a taxi
taxiphone *m.* telephone booth
Tchécoslovaque *m. & f. & a.* Czechoslovakian
Tchécoslovaquie *f.* Czechoslovakia
tchèque *a.* Czech
te *pron.* you, to you, yourself
té *m.* T-shape; T-square
technicien *m.* technician
technicité *f.* technical nature, technical complexity
technique *a.* technical; — *f.* technique
technologie *f.* technology
teck *m.* teakwood
teckel *m.* dachshund
teigne *f.* moth; dandruff, scaliness; (coll.) scurvy fellow
teigneux *a.* scurvy
teindre *vt.* to dye, stain
teint *m.* dye; complexion
teinte *f.* tint

teinter *vt.* to tint
teinture *f.* dye; dyeing; tinting; tincture; slight knowledge
teinturerie *f.* dye shop; dyeing
teinturier *m.* dyer
tel *a.* such, like; — que such as, like; — quel just as it is; — *pron.* such a one
télécommandé *a.* remote-controlled
télécommunication *f.* long-distance communication
télégramme *m.* telegram; — sous-marin cablegram
télégraphe *m.* telegraph
télégraphie *f.* telegraphy; — sans fil wireless
télégraphier *vt. & vi.* to telegraph
télégraphique *a.* telegraphic
télégraphiste *m. & f.* telegrapher; telegram messenger
téléguidage *m.* radio control
téléguider *vt.* to control by radio
téléimprimeur *m.* teleprinter, teletype machine
télémécanique *f.* remote control
télémètre *m.* range finder
téléobjectif *m.* telephoto lens
télépathie *f.* telepathy
téléphérage *m.* aerial transport
téléphérique *m.* cable car
téléphone *m.* telephone; coup de — phone call
téléphoner *vt. & vi.* to telephone
téléphonique *a.* telephonic; cabine — *f.* phone booth
téléphoniste *m. & f.* telephonist, telephone operator
téléphotographie *f.* wire photo-transmission
télescopage *m.* telescoping, collision
télescope *m.* telescope
télescoper *vt.* to telescope, crash into
téléscripteur *m.* teletype machine
téléski *m.* ski lift
téléspectateur *m.* TV viewer
télétype *m.* teletype machine
télévisé *a.* televized
téléviser *vt.* to televize
téléviseur *m.* television set
télévision *f.* television; appareil de — television set
tellement *adv.* so, in such a manner
tellière *m.* foolscap paper
téméraire *a.* rash, bold
témérité *f.* rashness, boldness
témoignage *m.* testimony, evidence
témoigner *vt. & vi.* to testify; show
témoin *m.* witness
tempe *f.* (anat.) temple of the head
tempérament *m.* temperament
tempérant *a.* temperate

température *f.* temperature
tempéré *a.* temperate, moderate
tempérer *vt.* to temper, moderate
tempête *f.* tempest, storm
tempêter *vi.* to storm, fume
tempétueux *a.* stormy; tempestuous
temple *m.* protestant church; temple
temporaire *a.* temporary
temporal *a.* (anat.) relating to the temple of the head
temporel *a.* temporal; — *m.* temporals, church income; temporal power
temporisateur *a.* delaying, postponing
temporisation *f.* delay, postponement
temporiser *vt.* to delya, postpone
temps *m.* time; weather; tense; à — in time; avant le — prematurely; de — en —, de — à autre from time to time; de tout — always; en même — together, at the same time; entre — meanwhile
tenable *a.* tenable
tenace *a.* tenacious; clinging; stubborn
ténacité *f.* tenacity
tenaille *f.* pincers
tenancier *m.* tenant operator *or* director of rented property
tenant *a.*, séance –e forthwith; — *m.* defender, supporter; –s *pl.* details, particulars; –s et aboutissants contiguous lands
tendance *f.* tendency
tendancieux *a.* tendentious; suggestive; prejudiced
tendeur *m.* spreader; shoe tree
tendoir *m.* clothesline
tendon *m.* tendon
tendre *vt. & vi.* to stretch out; hold out; hang; tend, lead; paper a room; — *a.* tender, soft; affectionate; — *m.* tenderness; love
tendresse *f.* tenderness, affection
tendreté *f.* tenderness of meat
tendron *m.* shoot; (coll.) very young girl; –s *pl.* cartilage
tendu *a.* stretched, strained, tight
ténèbres *f. pl.* darkness; (fig.) ignorance
ténébreux *a.* dark, gloomy
teneur *f.* tenor, literal text; — *m.* keeper
ténia *m.* tapeworm
tenir *vt. & vi.* to hold; have; keep; hold out, endure; — à to value, be anxious to, be determined, want; se — to remain, be, stand, stay; contain oneself
tennis *m.* tennis; tennis court
tenon *m.* bolt
ténor *m.* tenor
ténoriser *vi.* to sing tenor
tension *f.* tension, tenseness; pressure
tentacule *m.* tentacle

tentateur *m.* temptor; — *a.* tempting
tentation *f.* temptation
tentative *f.* attempt
tentatrice *f.* temptress
tente *f.* tent
tente-abri *f.* shelter tent
tenter *vt.* to tempt; try
tenture *f.* wallpaper; hanging(s)
tenu *a.* kept; obliged; firm
ténu *a.* tenuous, thin
tenue *f.* holding, keeping; behavior; dress, clothes, uniform
ténuité *f.* tenuousness
ter *adv.* thrice, three times; B, third entrance (house numbers)
térébenthine *f.* turpentine
térébrant *a.* boring, piercing
tergiversation *f.* hesitation, beating about the bush
tergiverser *vi.* to hesitate, beat about the bush
terme *m.* term, limit; end; rental period, quarter
terminaison *f.* ending
terminer *vt.* to terminate, end
terminologie *f.* terminology
terminus *m.* terminal point, end of the line, terminus
termite *m.* termite
termitière *f.* termite's nest
terne *a.* dull, leaden; colorless
ternir *vt.* to tarnish, dull
ternissure *f.* tarnished spot; tarnishing
terrain *m.* ground; playing field
terrasse *f.* terrace; sidewalk in front of a café
terrassement *m.* earth removal; ditch-digging
terrasser *vt.* to throw down; embank; dismay
terrassier *m.* ditchdigger, excavation worker
terre *f.* earth, ground, land; property; — à — earthy, common; ventre à — at full speed
terreau *m.* compost
terre neuve *m.* Newfoundland dog
Terre-Neuve *f.* Newfoundland
terre-neuvien *a.* of Newfoundland; — *m.* Grand Banks fishing boat; Grand Banks fisherman
terre-plein *m.* platform; terre-plein; terrace
terrer *vt.* to put dirt around a plant; se — to live in the ground; hide
Terre-Sainte *f.* Holy Land
terrestre *a.* terrestrial, earthly
terreur *f.* terror, dread
terreux *a.* earthen; earth-colored; earthy
terrien *a.* earth-inhabiting, ground-living;

propriétaire — landed proprietor
terrier *m.* lair, burrow
terrifier *vt.* to terrify
terrine *f.* earthenware pot; casserole; potted meat
territoire *m.* territory
terroir *m.* soil, land
terroriser *vt.* to terrorize
terrorisme *m.* terrorism
terroriste *m.* terrorist
tertiaire *a.* tertiary
tertio *adv.* thirdly
tertre *m.* hillock, knoll
tes *a. pl.* your
tesson *m.* potsherd, pottery fragment
test *m.* testa; test
testacé *a.* testaceous; — *m.* testacean
testament *m.* will, testament
testamentaire *a.* testamentary
testateur *m.* maker of a will
tester *vi.* to make one's will; — *vt.* to test
testicule *m.* testicle
testimonial *a.* testimonial
tétanos *m.* tetanus, lockjaw
têtard *m.* polliwog, tadpole
tête *f.* head; mind; chief, leader; top; signe de — *m.* nod; avoir mal à la — to have a headache
tête-à-queue *m.* sharp full turn of a vehicle
tête-à-tête *m.* private conversation, intimate meeting; love seat
tête-bêche *adv.* upside-down
tétée *f.* act of suckling
téter *vt. & vi.* to suck, feed at the breast
tétin *m.* nipple
tétine *f.* udder; nipple of a nursing bottle
tétraèdre *m.* tetrahedron
tétralogie *f.* tetralogy
tette *f.* teat, dug
têtu *a.* stubborn, headstrong
Teuton *m.* Teuton; — *a.* teutonic
texte *m.* text
textile *a.* textile
textuel *a.* textual
texture *f.* texture
thaï *a.* Thai; — *n.* Thai language
Thaïlande *f.* Thailand
thé *m.* tea
théâtral *a.* theatrical
théâtre *m.* theater
thébaïde *f.* solitude
théier *m.* tea plant
théière *f.* teapot
thématique *a.* thematic
thème *m.* theme; translation into a foreign language
théocrate *m.* theocrat
théocratique *a.* theocratic
théologal *a.* theological

théologie *f.* theology
théologien *m.* theologian
théologique *a.* theological
théorème *m.* theorem
théoricien *m.* theorist
théorie *f.* theory
théorique *a.* theoretical
théosophie *f.* theosophy
thérapeute *m.* therapist
thérapeutique *a.* therapeutic
thermal *a.* thermal; station —e hot springs resort
thermes *m. pl.* hot springs resort; Roman baths
thermique *a.* thermic, thermal
thermite *f.* thermite
thermodynamique *f.* thermodynamics
thermo-électrique *a.* thermoelectric
thermogène *a.* warming, irritating
thermographe *m.* recording thermometer
thermomètre *m.* thermometer
thermométrique *a.* thermometric
thésauriser *vi.* to hoard
thésauriseur *m.* hoarder
thèse *f.* thesis; argument
thiamine *f.* thiamine
thomiste *m.* Thomist
thon *m.* tuna
thonier *m.* tuna boat
thoracique *a.* thoracic
thorax *m.* thorax
thorium *m.* thorium
thrombose *f.* thrombosis
thuriféraire *m.* incense bearer; (fig.) flatterer
thym *m.* thyme
thymus *m.* thymus
thyroïde *a.* thyroid
tiare *f.* tiara
Tibet *m.* Tibet
Tibétain *m. & a.* Tibetan
tic *m.* tic, twitch; mania
ticket *m.* ration ticket; ticket; — modérateur patient's share of payment for health insurance
tiède *a.* lukewarm, tepid
tiédeur *f.* lukewarmness
tiédir *vt. & vi.* to make tepid, grow tepid
tien *pron.*, le —, la —e yours
tierce *f.* (eccl.) tierce (also, in fencing); triplet, three of a kind (at cards); (mus.) third
tiers *m.* third part; un — one third
tiers-point *m.* point of an arch; triangular file; triangular sail
tige *f.* tree trunk, stem; stalk; shaft
tignasse *f.* matted hair
tigre *m.* tiger; -sse *f.* tigress
tigré *a.* striped, tiger-striped
tillac *m.* (naut.) deck

tilleul *m.* lime tree, linden tree

timbale *f.* (mus.) kettledrum; mold, ring mold; food cooked in a ring mold; metal goblet; **-s** *pl.* timpani

timbalier *m.* tympanist

timbrage *m.* stamping

timbre *m.* stamp; bell; timbre; stamp bureau

timbré *a.* stamped; sonorous; (coll.) crazy; **papier —** paper with imprinted revenue stamp

timbre-poste *m.* postage stamp

timbre-quittance *m.* revenue stamp

timbrer *vt.* to stamp

timbreur *m.* stamper

timide *a.* timid

timidité *f.* timidity

timonerie *f.* steerage

timonier *m.* helmsman; wheel horse

timoré *a.* timorous

tin *m.* (naut.) block, support

tine *f.* water cask

tinette *f.* large bucket, cask

tintamarre *m.* noise, uproar

tinter *vt.* & *vi.* to ring, tinkle; tingle

tintinnabuler *vi.* to tinkle

tique *f.* (ent.) tick

tiqueté *a.* spotted

tir *m.* shooting, firing; rifle range; shooting gallery; **— à la cible** target shooting

tirage *m.* drawing, pulling; printing

tiraillement *m.* sniping, shooting; spasm; friction

tirailler *vt.* & *vi.* to snipe, shoot at intervals; pull in two directions

tirailleur *m.* sharpshooter

tirant *m.* (naut.) draft; bootstrap; drawstring

tire *f.* pull, tug; **vol à la —** pocket picking

tiré *a.* drawn; tired; **— à quatre épingles** dapper, neat; **— par les cheveux** farfetched, unlikely

tire-botte *m.* bootjack

tire-bouchon *m.* corkscrew

tire-bouton *m.* buttonhook

tire-clou *m.* claw hammer

tire-d'aile, à **— à** *adv.* rapidly, with rapid flapping of wings

tire-fond *m.* French railway spike; ceiling ring for light fixture

tirelire *f.* coin bank

tirer *vt.* & *vi.* to draw, pull; extract; derive; shoot; stick out; draw, trace; draw off, print; (phot.) print; (naut.) draw, have a draft of; deliver; **se — d'affaire** to get along, manage

tire-sou *m.* penny pincher, petty profiteer

tiret *m.* hyphen, dash

tirette *f.* drawstring, cord; table leaf

tireur *m.* drawer; shooter; fortune teller

tireuse *f.* (phot.) printing box

tiroir *m.* drawer

tisane *f.* infusion, tea

tison *m.* hot coal, ember

tisonner *vi.* to stir the fire

tisonnier *m.* poker

tissage *m.* weaving

tisser *vt.* to weave

tisserand *m.* weaver

tisseur *m.* weaver

tissu *m.* fabric

tissu-éponge *m.* terry cloth

tissure *f.* weave

titan *m.* titan

titane *m.* titanium

titanesque, titanique *a.* titanic

titillation *f.* titillation, tickling

titiller *vt.* & *vi.* to titillate, tickle

titrage *m.* quantitive analysis

titre *m.* title; quality, right; deed; headline; **-s** *pl.* degree, credentials; **-s flamboyants** banner headlines; **à — de** *prep.* as, in the capacity of; **à juste —** *adv.* deservedly, rightly

titrer *vt.* to title

tituber *vi.* to titubate, stagger

titulaire *m.* & *f.* & *a.* titular

toaster *vi.* to make a toast

toasteur *m.* toaster

toboggan *m.* toboggan; slide, chute

toc *m.* (coll.) imitation (of valuable objects); **en —** false, fake

toge *f.* toga; robe

tohu-bohu *m.* tumult, disorder

toi *pron.* you

toile *f.* cloth; curtain; painting, canvas; **— cirée** oilcloth; **— d'araignée** cobweb; **— de fond** backdrop

toilette *f.* toilet, comfort station; dress; dressing table

toise *f.* toise (6½ feet, 2 meters); measuring scale

toisé *m.* measuring

toiser *vt.* to measure; evaluate; disdain

toison *f.* fleece; **— d'or** golden fleece

toit *m.* roof

toiture *f.* roofing

tokai *m.* Tokay wine

tôle *f.* sheet iron

tolérable *a.* tolerable

tolérance *f.* tolerance

tolérant *a.* tolerant

tolérantisme *m.* religious tolerance

tolérer *vt.* to tolerate

tôlerie *f.* sheet metal trade; sheet metal factory

tôlier *m.* sheet metal worker

tollé *m.* outcry

tomaison *f.* volume number

tomate *f.* tomato

tombal *a.* tomb; **pierre —e** tombstone
tombe *f.* tomb
tombeau *m.* tomb, grave, gravestone
tombée *f.* fall
tomber *vi.* to fall, fall down; — *vt.* to fell
tombereau *m.* cart
tombola *f.* lottery
tome *m.* volume
ton *a.* your; — *m.* tune, note; tone; style
tonalité *f.* tonality; tone control
tondaison *f.* shearing
tondeur *a.* shearing
tondeuse *f.* shearing machine; lawn mower; hair clippers
tondre *vt.* to shear, clip; mow
tondu *a.* shorn, fleeced
tonicité *f.* tonicity, tone
tonifier *vt.* to tone; invigorate
tonique *a. & m.* tonic
tonitruant *a.* thundering
tonnage *m.* tonnage
tonnant *a.* thundering
tonne *f.* metric ton
tonneau *m.* cask
tonnelet *m.* small cask, keg
tonnelier *m.* cooper
tonnelle *f.* arbor; tunnel vault; hunting net
tonnellerie *f.* cooperage
tonner *vi.* to thunder; (fig.) to speak with fervor
tonnerre *m.* thunder
tonsure *f.* tonsure
tonsurer *vt.* to tonsure
tonte *f.* shearing
tonture *f.* clipping
tonus *m.* muscle tone
topaze *f.* topaz
toper *vi.* to shake hands in agreement
topinambour *m.* Jerusalem artichoke
topique *a.* topic, topical; — *m.* topic
topographe *m.* topographer
topographie *f.* topography
topographique *a.* topographical
toponymie *f.* study of place names
toquade *f.* whim
toque *f.* cap, bonnet
toquer *v.*, **se — de** to fall in love with
torche *f.* torch
torcher *vt.* to wipe
tochère *f.* torchere, torch holder, candelabrum
torchis *m.* mortar of adobe and straw
torchon *m.* cleaning cloth, rag
torchonner *vt.* to wipe
tordant *a.* very funny
tordeur *m.* twister
tordeuse *f.* twisting machine
tordre *vt.* to twist, wring
tore *m.* (arch) tore, torus, twisted column

toréador *m.* bullfighter
toréer *vi.* to fight bulls
toréro *m.* bullfighter
tornade *f.* tornado
toron *m.* cable strand
torpeur *f.* torpor
torpide *a.* torpid
torpillage *m.* torpedoing
torpille *f.* torpedo; bomb; mine
torpiller *vt.* to torpedo
torpilleur *m.* torpedo boat
torque *f.* coil; twist of tobacco
torréfacteur *m.* roaster
torréfaction *f.* roasting
torréfier *vt.* to roast; grill; scorch
torrentiel *a.* torrential
torrentueux *a.* torrentuous
torride *a.* torrid
tors *a.* twisted; crooked
torsade *f.* twisted braid
torse *m.* torso, trunk
torsion *f.* twisting
tort *m.* wrong, injury, harm; **à —** wrongly; **à — et à travers** helter skelter, indiscriminately; **avoir —** to be wrong; **faire — à** to harm
torticolis *m.* stiff neck
tortillage *m.* twisting
tortillard *m.* interurban train
tortillement *m.* twisting
tortiller *vt. & vi.* to twist
tortionnaire *m.* torturer; — *a.* torturing
tortu *a.* crooked, twisted
tortue *f.* turtle, tortoise
tortueux *a.* tortuous; winding
torturer *vt.* to torture
torve *a.* threatening
Toscan *m. & a.* Tuscan
Toscane *f.* Tuscany
tôt *adv.* soon
total *a. & m.* total; whole
totaliser *vt.* to total
totalitaire *a.* totalitarian
totalitairisme *m.* totalitarianism
totalité *f.* totality
toton *m.* top (toy)
touage *m.* towing
touchant *a.* touching, moving; — *prep.* relating to, concerning
touche *f.* (mus.) stop, key; touch, stroke; assay; touchstone; goad
touche-à-tout *m.* busybody
toucher *vt. & vi.* to touch, feel; play a musical instrument; cash, receive money; — *m.* touch, sense of touch
toucheur *m.* animal driver
toue *f.* tow, towing
touer *vt.* to tow
touffe *f.* tuft; cluster
touffeur *f.* stifling heat

touffu *a.* tufted, thick; full, luxuriant
touiller *vt.* to stir up
toujours *adv.* always; still
toundra *f.* tundra
toupet *m.* tuft of hair; toupee
toupie *f.* top (toy)
toupiller *vi.* to spin like a top
toupillon *m.* tuft
tour *m.* turn, turning; excursion, trip, circuit; lathe; trick; — *f.* tower; castle (chess); — **de contrôle** (avi.) control tower
tourbe *f.* peat, turf; crowd, throng
tourbière *f.* peat bog
tourbillon *m.* whirlwind
tourbillonnement *m.* whirling
tourbillonner *vi.* to whirl
tourelle *f.* turret
tourie *f.* demijohn
tourisme *m.* tourism; **agence de** — travel bureau
touriste *m.* tourist
touristique *a.* tourist, of tourist interest
tourment *m.* torment
tourmente *f.* tempest, storm
tourmenter *vt.* to torment, torture
tourmenteur *m.* tormentor; — *a.* tormenting
tournailler *vi.* to turn about
tournant *m.* turning, turning point, curve; roundabout way; — *a.* turning
tourné *a.* turned; spoiled; **bien** — well-shaped
tourne-à-gauche *m.* wrench
tournebroche *m.* spit for roasting
tourne-disque *m.* record player, turntable
tournedos *m.* filet steak
tournée *f.* round, circuit; journey
tournemain, en un — *adv.* in a moment
tourner *vt. & vi.* to turn, turn over, turn out, go around; produce (movie), film; play a role
tournesol *m.* heliotrope
tourneur *m.* lathe man; — *a.* whirling, turning
tournevis *m.* screwdriver
tourniquet *m.* turnstile
tournoi *m.* tournament
tournoiement *m.* rotation, whirling
tournoyer *vi.* to turn, whirl
tournure *f.* turn; shape, figure; expression
tourte *f.* tart; pie
tourtière *f.* tart pan, pie pan
Toussaint *f.* All-Saints'-Day
tousser *vi.* to cough
toussoter *vi.* to cough intermittently
tout *m.* whole, all; **du** — not at all; — *a. & pron.* all, whole, any, every; — *adv.* all, any, wholly, quite; — **à coup** suddenly; — **à fait** entirely; — **à l'heure**

in a little while; a little while ago; — **de suite** immediately
toute-épice *f.* allspice
toutefois *conj.* yet, however
toute-présence *f.* omnipresence
toute-puissance *f.* omnipotence
tout-puissant *a.* omnipotent
toux *f.* cough; coughing
toxicologie *f.* toxicology
toxicomane *m.* drug addict
toxicomanie *f.* drug addiction
toxine *f.* toxin
toxique *m. & a.* poison
trabe *f.* flagstaff
trac *m.* stage fright
traçage *m.* tracing
tracas *m.* bustle, fuss
tracasser *vt.* to trouble, worry
tracasserie *f.* annoyance, worry
trace *f.* trace, mark, footstep
tracé *m.* outline, draft
tracement *m.* tracing
tracer *vt.* to trace, outline
trachéal *a.* tracheal
trachée (artère) *f.* trachea
trachéen *a.* trachial
tract *m.* tract, pamphlet
tractation *f.* treatment, procedure
tracteur *m.* tractor
traction *f.* traction; — **avant** *f.* small front-wheel-drive auto
tradition *f.* tradition
traditionalisme *m.* traditionalism
traditionaliste *m. & f.* traditionalist; — *a.* traditionalistic
traditionnel *a.* traditional
traducteur *m.* translator; — **juré** official translator
traduction *f.* translation
traduire *vt.* to translate; transfer
traduisible *a.* translatable
trafic *m.* traffic, trade
trafiquant *m.* dealer
trafiquer *vi.* to traffic, trade, deal
tragédie *f.* tragedy
tragédien *m.* tragedian, tragic actor
tragi-comédie *f.* tragi-comedy
tragique *a.* tragic
trahir *vt.* to betray, reveal
trahison *f.* treason, treachery
train *m.* (rail.) train; rate, pace; attendants; bustle, noise; rear, hind part; front, forepart; — **d'atterrissage** (avi.) landing gear; undercarriage; — **avant** (auto.) front assembly; — **arrière** rear assembly; — **de marchandises** freight train; — **de voyageurs** passenger train; — **de plaisir** excursion train; — **express** ordinary express; — **omnibus** local train; — **poste** mail train; — **rapide**

fast express; — **de maison** housekeeping; — **de vie** way of life; — **des équipages** (army) transportation corps; **en** — **(de)** in spirits; in the act of; busy; — **mixte** combination freight and passenger train

traînage *m.* dragging

traînard *m.* straggler; slow poke (U.S. coll.)

traînasser *vi.* to loiter; — *vt.* to drag out

traîne *f.* train of a dress; seine; dragging; **à la** — in tow

traîneau *m.* sled; seine

traînée *f.* powder train; trail

traîner *vt. & vi.* to drag, drag out; loiter

traire *vt.* to milk

trait *m.* arrow, shaft, dart, bolt; line, leash; stroke; gulp; feature; trait; — **d'union** hyphen; — **d'esprit** witticism

traitable *a.* easy to deal with, tractable; treatable

traite *f.* trade, trading

traité *m.* treaty, agreement; treatise

traitement *m.* treatment; salary

traiter *vt. & vi.* to treat, negotiate; — **de** to call, style

traiteur *m.* caterer

traître *m.* traitor; — **(traîtresse)** *a.* traitorous, treacherous

traîtrise *f.* treachery

trajectoire *f.* trajectory

trajet *m.* distance, journey; passage, crossing

tramer *vt.* to plot

tramontane *f.* north wind; **perdre la** — to lose one's bearings

tranchant *a.* sharp; decisive; — *m.* blade, cutting edge

tranche *f.* slice; fore edge of a book; series; rim, edge; **doré sur** — gilt-edged

tranchée *f.* trench; -s *pl.* colic; labor pains

tranchelard *m.* kitchen knife

tranche-montagne *m.* swaggerer

trancher *vt. & vi.* to slice; cut off; decide, determine

tranchoir *m.* chopping block

tranquille *a.* tranquil; quiet; still; calm

tranquilliser *vt.* to quiet, calm

tranquillité *f.* tranquility, quiet

transalpin *a.* transalpine

transat *m.* deck chair

Transat *f.* French Line

transatlantique *a.* transatlantic; — *m.* ocean liner; deck chair

transbordement *m.* transshipping

transborder *vt.* to transship

transbordeur *m.* transshipper; transporter; — *a.* transporting; **pont** — transporter bridge, bridge which carries passengers on a moving platform

transcendence *f.* transcendency

transcendant *a.* transcendent

transcendantal *a.* transcendental

transcontinental *a.* transcontinental

transcripteur *m.* transcriber

transcription *f.* transcription

transcrire *vt.* to copy; transcribe

transe *f.* apprehension; trance

transept *m.* transept

transfèrement *m.* transfer of a prisoner

transférer *vt.* to transfer

transfert *m.* transfer

transfiguration *f.* transfiguration

transfigurer *vt.* to transfigure

transformable *a.* transformable

transformateur *m.* transformer

transformation *f.* transformation; conversion

transformer *vt.* to transform

transfuge *m.* fugitive, deserter

transfuser *vt.* to transfuse; give a transfusion

transfusion *f.* transfusion

transgresser *vt.* to transgress against

transgresseur *m.* transgressor; trespasser

transgression *f.* transgression

transi *a.* numb, benumbed

transiger *vi.* to make concessions

transir *vt. & vi.* to chill, numb; be chilled

transistor *m.* transistor

transiter *vt. & vi.* to transit in bond

transitif *a.* (gram.) transitive

transition *f.* transition

transitoire *a.* transitory

translation *f.* removal; transfer

translucide *a.* translucid

transmetteur *m.* transmitter; — *a.* transmitting

transmettre *vt.* to transmit; forward

transmissible *a.* transmissible

transmission *f.* transmission; transmittal

transmu(t)able *a.* transmutable

transmuer *vt.* to transmute

transmutabilité *f.* transmutability

transocéanique *a.* transoceanic

transparaître *vi.* to be visible through, to be guessed

transparence *f.* transparency

transpercer *vt.* to pierce

transpiration *f.* perspiration

transpirer *vt.* to perspire

transplantation *f.* transplanting

transplanter *vt.* to transplant

transport *m.* transport; ecstasy, rapture

transportable *a.* transportable

transportation *f.* transfer of a prisoner

transporter *vt.* to transport, excite, upset

transporteur *a.* transporting; — *m.* transporter

transposer *vt.* to transpose

transposition *f.* transposition
transsonique *a.* of the speed of sound
transsuder *vt.* to transsude
transvasement *m.* decanting
transvaser *vt.* to decant
transversal *a.* transversal
transvider *vt.* to empty the contents from one vessel into another
trapèze *m.* trapezoid; trapeze; trapezium
trapézoïdal *a.* trapezoidal
trappe *f.* trap; trap door; pitfall
Trappe, la — *f.* Trappist order; Trappist monastery
trappeur *m.* trapper
trappiste *m.* trappist
trapu *a.* short and fat
traquenard *m.* snare, trap
traquer *vt.* to flush (game); pursue
traqueur *m.* tracker
traumatique *a.* traumatic
traumatisme *m.* traumatism
travail (*pl.* travaux) *m.* work; travaux forcés *m. pl.* penal servitude
travailler *vt. & vi.* to work, toil
travailleur *m.* laborer, workman
travailliste *m.* laborite
travée *f.* (arch.) bay of a vault
travers *m.* breadth; à —, au — across; en — across, sideways; de — crosswise
traverse *f.* traverse, crossarm; crossroad, short cut; (rail.) tie; obstacle
traversée *f.* voyage, crossing
traverser *vt.* to cross
traversier *a.* transverse; transversal
traversin *m.* bolster; cross bar
travesti *a.* costumed as the opposite sex; costumed
travestir *vt.* to disguise; travesty
travestissement *m.* disguise, travesty
trayon *m.* teat, dug
trébuchant *a.* stumbling; espèces sonnantes et -es *f. pl.* hard cash
trébucher *vi.* to stumble; trip; — *vt.* to weigh
trébuchet *m.* snare, trap; balance, scales
tréfilage *m.* drawing of wire
tréfiler *vt.* to draw wire
trèfle *m.* clover; cloverleaf; clubs (at cards)
tréfonds *m.* mineral rights; secret hasis
treillage *m.* trellis
treille *f.* vine growing on a trellis
treillisser *vt.* to trellis, interweave
treize *a.* thirteen
treizième *a. & m.* thirteenth
tremble *m.* aspen
tremblement *m.* trembling, shaking; — de terre earthquake
trembler *vi.* to tremble
trembloter *vi.* to shiver

trémie *f.* loading device
trémousser *vt.* to stir up
trempe *f.* temper of iron; character; soaking
trempée *f.* tempering
tremper *vt. & vi.* to dip, soak; temper iron
tremplin *m.* trampoline; diving board; (fig.) stepping stone
trentaine *f.* about thirty
trente *a.* thirty
trentenaire *m.* thirtieth anniversary; — *a.* thirty-year old
trentième *m. & a.* thirtieth
trépaner *vt.* to trepan
trépas *m.* death
trépasser *vi.* to die
trépidant *a.* terror stricken
trépidation *f.* trepidation
trépied *m.* trivet; tripod
trépigner *vi.* to stamp on the ground
très *adv.* very
trésor *m.* treasure; treasury
trésorerie *f.* treasury
trésorier *m.* treasurer
tressaillement *m.* start, leap, shudder
tressaillir *vi.* to start; leap, thrill
tressauter *vi.* to jump, start
tresser *vt.* to braid, twist
tréteau *m.* platform; (theat.) the stage
treuil *m.* windlass
trève *f.* truce
tri *m.* sorting, choosing
triage *m.* choice; sorting
triangle *m.* triangle
triangulaire *a.* triangular
tribord *m.* (naut.) starboard
tribordais *m.* starboard watch
tribu *f.* tribe
tribulation *f.* tribulation
tribune *f.* tribune; gallery, stands; parliament; de la — parliamentary
tribut *m.* tribute; retribution
tributaire *m. & a.* tributary
tricher *vt. & vi.* to cheat
tricherie *f.* cheating
tricheur *m.* cheater
trichine *f.* trichina
trichinose *f.* trichinosis
trichromie *f.* (print.) three-color process
tricolore *a. & m.* tricolor
tricorne *m.* three-cornered hat
tricot *m.* knit fabric, tricot; knit ware
tricotage *m.* knitting, knitted work
tricoter *vt.* to knit
tricoteur *m.* knitter
trictrac *m.* backgammon
tricycle *m.* tricycle
tridimensionnel *a.* three-dimensional
trièdre *a.* three-sided
triennal *a.* triennial; three-year

trier *vt.* to pick, sort

trieur *m.* sorter

trigonométrie *f.* trigonometry

trigonométrique *a.* trigonometric

trilatéral *a.* three-sided

trille *m.* trill

triller *vi.* to trill

trilogie *f.* trilogy

trimestre *m.* quarter, three months

trimestriel *a.* quarterly

trimoteur *a.* trimoter

tringle *f.* rod; curtain rod

Trinité *f.* Trinity; Trinidad

trinquer *vi.* to toast, clink glasses

triomphal *a.* triumphal

triomphateur *a.* triumphant

triomphe *m.* triumph

triompher *vi.* to triumph

triparti(te) *a.* tripartite

tripatouiller *vt.* to tamper with a literary work; mishandle, butcher

triplace *a.* three-seater

triple *a.* triple; treble

triplex *m.* safety glass

triplicata *m.* second copy, second carbon

tripoli *m.* Tripoli; rottenstone

triporteur *m.* bicycle delivery truck

tripot *m.* gambling house, disorderly house

tripotage *m.* mess; intrigue; influence peddling; shady dealings

tripoter *vt.* to misuse, speculate with

triptyque *m.* triptych; international automobile documents

trisaïeul *m.* great-great-grandfather

trisannuel *a.* three-year; triannual

trisection *f.* trisection

trisme, trismus *m.* lockjaw

triste *a.* sad

tristesse *f.* sadness

triturer *vt.* to crush, grind

trivial *a.* trivial; vulgar

trivialité *f.* triviality; vulgar expression

troc *m.* barter

troène *m.* privet

troglodyte *m.* troglodyte, cave dweller

trognon *m.* fruit *or* vegetable core, stalk

trois *a.* three; –ième *a. & m.* third

trolleybus *m.* trolleybus, trackless trolley

trombe *f.* waterspout; **arriver en** — to arrive unexpectedly

tromblon *m.* blunderbuss

trombone *m.* trombone; trombone player; (coll.) paper clip

trompe *f.* hunting horn; elephant's trunk; — d'Eustache Eustachian tube

trompe-la-mort *m. & f.* unexpectedly recovered invalid

trompe-l'œil *m.* deceptively real painting; vain appearance, surface glitter

tromper *vt.* to deceive, delude; **se** — to be

mistaken

tromperie *f.* deceit, cheat

trompeter *vt.* to trumpet, cry

trompette *f.* trumpet; — *m.* trumpet player

trompettiste *m.* trumpeter

trompeur *a.* deceitful

tronc *m.* trunk, stump, stem; poor box; — de cône truncated cone

troncature *f.* truncation

tronçon *m.* stump, piece, fragment

tronçonner *vt.* to cut to pieces

trône *m.* throne

trôner *vi.* to reign supreme

tronqué *a.* cut short, cut off, cut down, truncated

tronquer *vt.* to truncate, curtail

trop *adv.* too, too much, too many

trophée *m.* trophy

tropicalisé *a.* packed for the tropics

tropique *m.* tropic; — du Cancer Tropic of Cancer; — du Capricorne Tropic of Capricorn; — *a.* tropical

trop-perçu *m.* overcharge, overpayment

trop-plein *m.* overflow

troquer *vt.* to barter

troqueur *m.* barterer

trotte *f.* distance, way

trotte-menu *a.* short-stepping

trotter *vi.* to trot, trot along

trotteur *m.* trotter

trotteuse *f.* watch's second hand; fast walker

trottin *m.* errand boy

trottiner *vi.* to trot about

trottinette *f.* scooter

trottoir *m.* sidewalk, pavement

trou *m.* hole

troubadour *m.* troubadour

trouble *m.* confusion; uneasiness; — *a.* cloudy, dim; confused

trouble-fête *m.* kill-joy, wet blanket

troubler *vt.* to disturb, upset; confuse; **se** — to become overcast; become confused

trouée *f.* hole, opening

trouer *vt.* to make a hole, perforate

troupe *f.* troop, company

troupeau *m.* flock, herd

troupier *m.* soldier

troussage *m.* trussing of poultry

trousse *f.* bundle; case, kit; truss

troussé *a.* built, turned

trousseau *m.* bunch of keys; trousseau; layette

trousser *vt.* to tuck, turn up; finish off polish off

troussis *m.* tuck

trouvable *a.* findable

trouvaille *f.* find; godsend

trouver *vt.* to find; think; **se —** to be, be found; feel; happen

trouvère *m.* troubadour of Northern France

Troyen *m. & a.* Trojan

truand *m.* beggar, thief

truanderie *f.* beggars, vagrants; begging

truc *m.* trick; knack; thing, gadget

trucage *m.* faking; special effects (movies); camouflage; counterfeit

truchement *m.* go-between

truc(k) *m.* (rail.) flat-car

truculence *f.* truculence

truculent *a.* truculent

truelle *f.* trowel; fish server

truellée *f.* trowelful

truffe *f.* truffle; nose of a dog

truffer *vt.* to stuff with truffles

truffier *a.* of truffles, truffled; **cochon —** pig trained to hunt truffles

truffière *f.* truffle patch

truie *f.* female pig, sow

truisme *m.* truism

truite *f.* trout

trumeau *m.* pier glass; mirror surmounted by a picture; picture surmounting a mirror; panel between two windows

truquage *m.* falsifying; false aging; special effects (movies)

truquer *vt. & vi.* to fake

truqueur *m.* faker

trust *m.* trust, cartel

truster *vt.* to monopolize

tsar *m.* czar; **–ine** *f.* czarina

tsé-tsé *f.* tsetse fly

T.S.F. *f.* radio

tu *pron.* you

tube cathodique *m.* cathode-ray tube

tuber *vt.* to tube

tubercule *m.* tuber, tubercle

tuberculeux *a.* tuberculous, tubercular

tuberculose *f.* tuberculosis

tubéreuse *f.* tuberose

tubereux *a.* tuberous

tubulaire *a.* tubular

tubulé *a.* tubular, tubulated

tudesque *a.* German

tue-mouches *a.*, **papier —** flypaper; **tapette —** fly swatter

tuer *vt.* to kill

tuerie *f.* massacre

tue-tête, à — *adv.* at the top of one's voice

tueur *m.* killer

tuffeau *m.* chalk

tuilerie *f.* tile factory

tuilier *m.* tilemaker

tularémie *f.* tularemia

tulipe *f.* tulip

tuméfaction *f.* swelling

tuméfier *vt.* to grow, swell

tumescent *a.* tumescent

tumeur *f.* tumor, swelling

tumulaire *a.* tumular, pertaining to a grave

tumulte *m.* tumult

tumultueux *a.* tumultuous

tungstène *m.* tungsten

tunique *f.* tunic; envelope, covering

Tunisie *f.* Tunisia

Tunisien *m. & a.* Tunisian

tunnel *m.* tunnel

turbine *f.* turbine

turboréacteur *m.* turbojet

turbot *m.* turbot

turbulence *f.* turbulence

turbulent *a.* turbulent

turc (turque) *m. & f.* Turk; **—** *a.* Turkish

turf *m.* race track; racing

turfiste *m.* follower of horse races

turlupin *m.* punster, poor joker

turlupinade *f.* pun, poor joke

turlutaine *f.* mania

Turquie *f.* Turkey

turquoise *f.* turquoise

tutélaire *a.* tutelary, guardian

tutelle *f.* guardianship

tuteur *m.*, **tutrice** *f.* guardian; plant support, stake

tuteurer *vt.* to prop up, put on stakes

tutoiement *m.* use of familiar address

tutu *m.* ballet skirt

tuyau *m.* tube, pipe; hose; (coll.) tip, information

tuyautage *m.* pipes, pipe system; pleating

tuyauter *vt.* to pleat; (coll.) to inform

tuyauterie *f.* pipes, pipe system

tuyère *f.* furnace vent

tympan *m.* eardrum; panel between mouldings, tympanum

tympaniser *vt.* to decry; annoy; cry out

type *m.* type; fellow, chap, individual

typhique *a.* typhous; typhoid; **—** *m. & f.* typhus victim; typhoid victim

typhoïde *a.* typhoid

typhoïdique *a.* typhoid

typhon *m.* typhoon

typhus *m.* typhus

typification *f.* standardization

typique *a.* typical

typographe *m.* typographer, printer

typographie *f.* typography

typographique *a.* typographical

tyran *m.* tyrant

tyrannie *f.* tyranny

tyrannique *a.* tyrannical

tyranniser *vt.* to tyrannize

Tyrol *m.* Tyrol

Tyrolien *m. & a.* Tyrolean

tzigane *m. & f. & a.* Gypsy

U

ubiquité *f.* ubiquity
ulcération *f.* ulceration
ulcère *m.* ulcer; sore
ulcérer *vt.* to ulcerate
ultérieur *a.* ulterior; later
ultimatum *m.* ultimatum
ultime *a.* final, last, ultimate
ultimo *adv.* lastly
ultra-sonore *a.* supersonic
ultra-violet *a.* ultraviolet
ululement *m.* hooting
ululer *vi.* to hoot
un (une) *a.* a, an; one
unanime *a.* unanimous
uni *a.* united; even; plain
unification *f.* unification
unifier *vt.* to unify
uniforme *m. & a.* uniform
uniformément *a.* uniformly
uniformiser *vt.* to standardize; make uniform
uniformité *f.* uniformity
unilatéral *a.* unilateral
unioniste *m.* unionist
unique *a.* only, sole; unique
unir *vt.* to unite, join, level; **s'—** à join forces with; marry
unisson *m.* unison; agreement
unitaire *a.* unitarian
unitarien *m.* Unitarian
unité *f.* unity; unit
univers *m.* universe
universalité *f.* universality
universel *a.* universal
universitaire *a.* university, academic; **cité —** university dormitories
université *f.* university
uranium *m.* uranium
urbain *a.* urban
urbanisme *m.* city planning
urbaniste *m.* city planner
urbanité *f.* urbaneness
urée *f.* urea
urémie *f.* uremia
urémique *a.* uremic
uretère *m.* ureter
urgence *f.* urgency; **d'—** immediately
urgent *a.* urgent; **cas —** *m.* emergency
urinaire *a.* urinary
urinal *m.* urinal
uriner *vi.* to urinate
urinoir *m.* urinal
urique *a.* uric
urne *f.* urn; ballot box
us *m. pl.* customs, usage
usage *m.* use; practice, custom
usagé *a.* used
usager *m.* user

usé *a.* worn, worn out, threadbare; frayed
user *vt. & vi.* to wear out; consume; use; **s'—** to wear out; be spent; decay; **— de** make use of
usine *f.* factory, works, mill
usiner *vt.* to tool, machine
usinier *a.* industrial; **— m.** industrialist
usité *a.* used, in use
ustensile *m.* utensil
usuel *a.* usual, ordinary
usure *f.* usury; erosion; wear and tear
usurier *m.* usurer, money-lender
usurpateur *m.* usurper; **— a.** encroaching; usurping
usurpation *f.* usurpation
usurper *vt.* to usurp
ut *m.* (mus.) C, do
utérin *a.* uterine; of the same mother by different fathers
utérus *m.* uterus
utile *a.* useful; profitable; convenient
utilisable *a.* usable, utilizable
utilisation *f.* use, utilization
utiliser *vt.* to utilize; make use of
utilitaire *a.* utilitarian, useful
utilité *f.* utility
utopie *f.* utopia
uval *a.* grape
uvulaire *a.* uvular
uvule *f.* uvula

V

va *interj.* go ahead; **— pour cent francs** a hundred francs is acceptable
vacance *f.* vacancy; **–s** *pl.* holidays, vacation; **grandes —s** summer vacation
vacant *a.* vacant; tenantless
vacarme *m.* uproar, din
vacation *f.* court hearing; **–s** *pl.* suspension of court
vaccin *m.* vaccine
vaccination *f.* vaccination
vacciner *vt.* to vaccinate, inoculate
vache *f.* cow; cowhide
vacher *m.* cowherd
vacherie *f.* cowbarn
vachette *f.* calfskin
vacillation *f.*, **vacillement** *m.* vacillation
vaciller *vi.* to vacillate, reel, waver
vacuité *f.* emptiness
vade-mecum *m.* constant companion or accompaniment
va-et-vient *m.* seesaw; swinging motion; coming and going
vagabond *m. & a.* vagabond
vagabondage *m.* vagabonding, roving
vagabonder *vi.* to rove
vagir *vi.* to cry, wail
vagissement *m.* cry, wail of an infant

vague *f.* wave; — *a.* vague, indefinite
vaguemestre *m.* (mil.) regimental mail clerk
vaguer *vi.* to wander, rove
vaillamment *adv.* valiantly
vaillance *f.* valor, bravery
vaillant *a.* valiant, courageous; brave
vain *a.* vain; **en** — *adv.* uselessly
vaincre *vt.* to vanquish; conquer
vainqueur *a.* conquering, victorious; — *m.* conqueror, victor
vair *m.* fur, squirrel's fur
vairon *m.* minnow; — *a.* wall-eyed; having eyes unmatched in color
vaisseau *m.* vessel, ship; church nave
vaisselier *m.* china cupboard
vaisselle *f.* dishes, tableware
val *m.* valley, vale
valable *a.* valid
Valence *f.* Valencia
valence *f.* valence; Valencia orange
valenciennes *f.* Valenciennes lace
valériane *f.* valerian
valet *m.* valet; jack (at cards); clamp
valétudinaire *a.* sickly
valeur *f.* value, worth; valor; **-s** *pl.* securities, stocks
valeureux *a.* valorous
valgus *a.* bow-legged
valide *a.* valid; able-bodied
valider *vt.* to validate; authenticate
valise *f.* suitcase, valise; — **diplomatique** diplomatic pouch
vallée *f.* valley
vallon *m.* small valley
vallonné *a.* valleyed
valoir *vt. & vi.* to be worth, be of value; produce, yield; — **mieux** to be better; **faire** — to make the most of; **à** — on account
valorisation *f.* valuation
valse *f.* waltz
valser *vi.* to waltz
valve *f.* valve; scallop shell
valvulaire *a.* valvular
valvule *f.* valve, valvule
vampire *m.* vampire; vampire bat; (fig.) leech, bloodsucker
van *m.* winnowing basket; van
vanadium *m.* vanadium
vandale *m.* vandal
vandalisme *m.* vandalism
vanille *f.* vanilla
vanillé *a.* vanilla-flavored
vanilline *f.* vanillin, artificial vanilla
vanité *f.* vanity
vaniteux *a.* vain, conceited
vannage *m.* winnowing
vanne *f.* sluice
vanner *vt.* to winnow

vannerie *f.* basketry; basket making
vanneur *m.* winnower
vannier *m.* basketmaker; basket seller
vannure *f.* chaff
vantail *m.* leaf, panel
vantard *m.* boaster; — *a.* boasting, boastful
vantardise *f.* boasting
vanter *vt.* to praise, extol; **se** — to boast, brag
vanterie *f.* boasting
vapeur *f.* vapor, steam; gas, fumes; **à toute** — at full steam; full speed ahead; — *m.* (naut.) steamer
vaporeux *a.* vaporous, nebulous
vaporisateur *m.* vaporizer, atomizer, sprayer
vaporisation *f.* vaporizing, atomizing
vaporiser *vt.* to vaporize, atomize
vaquer *vi.* to be vacant; not to be in session; — **à** *vt.* to take care of, busy oneself with, pay attention to
varech *m.* seaweed
varenne *f.* game preserve, warren
vareuse *f.* blazer, jacket, middy blouse
variabilité *f.* variability
variable *a.* variable
variante *f.* variant
varice *f.* varicose vein
varicelle *f.* chicken pox
varier *vt. & vi.* to vary; variegate; fluctuate
variété *f.* variety
variole *f.* smallpox
variolé *a.* pockmarked
varioleux *a.* concerning smallpox; — *m.* smallpox victim
variqueux *a.* varicose
varlet *m.* squire; clamp
varlope *f.* jointing plane (tool)
varloper *vt.* to plane
Varsovie *f.* Warsaw
varus (vara) *a.* knock-kneed; pigeon-toed
vasculaire *a.* vascular
vase *m.* vase, receptacle; — *f.* slime, mud
vaseux *a.* muddy, slimy; (coll.) tired, lazy
vasistas *m.* transom
vaso-constricteur *a.* vaso-constrictor
vaso-dilateur *a.* vaso-dilator
vaso-moteur *a.* vasomotor
vasque *f.* basin of a fountain
vaste *a.* vast
Vatican *m.* Vatican; **Cité du** — Vatican City
vaticane *a.* Vatican
vaticiner *vi.* to prophesy, vaticinate
va-tout *m.* all or nothing (gambling)
vaudeville *f.* musical comedy; comedy
vaudevilliste *m.* musical comedy author
vaudou *m.* voodoo

vau-l'eau, à — adv. adrift, with the current
vaurien m. good-for-nothing
vautour m. vulture
vautrer v., se — to wallow, sprawl
veau m. calf; veal; calfskin
vecteur m. (avi.) vector
vedette f. (theat.) star; speedboat; cavalry sentinel; (fig.) prominent position
végétal a. vegetable
végétarien m. & a. vegetarian
végétation f. vegetation; growth, tumor
végéter vi. to vegetate
véhémence f. vehemence
véhément a. vehement
véhicule m. vehicle
vehiculer vt. to transport, cart
veille f. staying up; watch, lookout; vigil; wakefulness; eve, day before
veillée f. watching, vigil, wake; social evening
veiller vt. & vi. to stay up, stay awake; watch, watch over
veilleur a. watchman
veilleuse f. night light; pilot light
veinard m. (coll.) lucky person; — a. lucky
veine f. vein, lode; luck
veiner vt. to vein; grain, streak, marble
veineux a. veined; veinous; veining; venal
veinule f. small vein
vêlage, vêlement m. calving
vêler vi. to calve
vélin m. vellum
velléitaire a. fanciful
velléité f. fancy, desire
véloce a. rapid, lively
vélocipède m. bicycle
vélodrome m. cycling arena
vélomoteur m. light motorcycle
velot m. sheepskin
velours m. velvet
velouté a. velvety; soft, downy; — m. creamed soup
velouter vt. to make like velvet
veloutine f. velveteen
velu a. hairy
vélum m. velum; awning; circus tent
venaison f. venison
vénal a. venal; bought, mercenary
vénalité f. venality
venant a. arriving; — m. comer; à tout — to the first comer
vendable a. sellable
vendange f. vintage, vine harvest
vendanger vt. to harvest (grapes)
vendangeur m. grape harvester; vintner
vendeur m. seller, salesperson
vendre vt. to sell; (fig.) betray; à — for sale

vendredi m. Friday; — saint Good Friday
vendu a. sold; in the pay of
venelle f. small street
vénéneux a. poisonous
vénérable a. venerable
vénération f. veneration
vénérer vt. to venerate
vénerie f. hunting; hunting with a pack of hounds
vénérien a. venerial
veneur m. master of the hunt; master of the hounds
vengeance f. vengeance, revenge
venger vt. to avenge; se — to be revenged, take vengeance
vengeur m. avenger; — a. avenging
véniel a. venial; slight
venimeux a. venimous
venin m. venom, poison
venir vi. to come; occur; reach; faire — to send for; — à (faire quelque chose) to happen to (do something); — de to have just
Venise f. Venice
Vénitien m. & a. Venetian
vent m. wind; coup de — m. gust of wind; faire du — to be windy; sous le — leeward; avoir — de get wind of
ventail m. visor of a helmet
vente f. sale; en — being sold
venteaux m. pl. vents
venter vi. to blow; be windy
venteux a. windy
ventilateur m. electric fan; ventilator
ventilation f. ventilation
ventiler vt. to ventilate
ventis m. pl. blown-down trees
ventosité f. gas in the stomach
ventouse f. suction cup; sucker; cup for bloodletting
ventouser vt. to cup, bleed
ventral a. ventral
ventre m. belly, stomach, womb; à plat — lying face down; bas — abdomen
ventriculaire a. ventricular
ventricule m. ventricle
ventrière f. bellyband
ventriloque m. ventriloquist
ventriloquie f. ventriloquism
ventru a. fat, pot-bellied, paunchy
venu a. received; successful; arrived; — m. comer; le premier — anyone; bien — welcome; mal — unwelcome
venue f. coming, arrival; advent
vénusté f. charm, beauty, elegance
vêpres f. pl. vespers
ver m. worm; maggot; — solitaire tapeworm
véracité f. veracity
véranda f. porch, veranda

verbalisation *f.* report, minutes
verbaliser *vi.* to prepare a detailed report
verbe *m.* verb; word
verbeux *a.* verbose, wordy
verbiage *m.* verbosity, wordiness
verdâtre *a.* greenish
verdeur *f.* greenness; tartness; vigor youth
verdict *m.* verdict
verdir *vt.* to make green; — *vi.* to become green
verdoyant *a.* verdant, green
verdoyer *vi.* to be verdant
verdunisation *f.* chlorination
verduniser *vt.* to chlorinate
verdure *f.* greenness; greens; verdure
véreux *a.* wormy; lowdown; no-good; false
verge *f.* rod, switch, whip; penis
vergé *a.* lined, corded with same material
verger *m.* orchard
vergeter *vt.* to whisk clean; stripe with strokes of a rod
vergette *f.* whisk; little rod
vergeture *f.* lash mark, whip mark
vergeure *f.* lines in the substance of cloth, paper
verglacé *a.* covered with freezing rain
verglas *m.* glazed frost; freezing rain
vergne *m.* alder tree
vergogne *f.* shame
vergue *f.* (naut.) yard
véridique *a.* veracious
vérifiable *a.* verifiable, checkable
vérificateur *m.* verifier
vérification *f.* verification, checking
vérifier *vt.* to verify; check
vérin *m.* jack, hoist
véritable *a.* true, genuine
vérité *f.* truth
verjus *m.* juice of green grapes, verjuice
vermeil *a.* vermilion-colored; ruby-colored; — *m.* gilt
vermiculaire *a.* vermiform; wormlike
vermiforme *a.* vermiform
vermifuge *m.* worm medicine
vermillon *m.* vermilion
vermine *f.* vermin
vermineux *a.* caused by intestinal worms; covered with vermin, buggy
vermisseau *m.* small worm
vermouler *v.*, **se** — to become worm-eaten
vermoulu *a.* worm-eaten
vermoulure *f.* worm hole
vermouth *m.* vermouth
vernaculaire *m.* & *a.* vernacular
vernier *m.* vernier, slide rule
verni *a.* varnished; **cuir** — *m.* patent leather
vernir *vt.* to varnish; polish
vernis *m.* varnish, polish, glaze

vernissage *m.* varnishing; premier, opening of an art show
vernisser *vt.* to glaze
vernisseur *m.* glazer
vérole *f.* syphilis; **petite** — smallpox
verrat *m.* boar, pig
verre *m.* glass; lens; crystal; — **à vitre** sheet glass; — **de sûreté** safety glass
verrerie *f.* glassware
verrière *f.* stained glass window; glass covering a picture
verroterie *f.* glass bibelots, glass figurines
verrou *m.* bolt
verrouiller *vt.* to bolt
verrue *f.* wart
verrugueux *a.* warty, covered with warts
vers *m.* verse; line; — *pl.* poetry, verses; **-s blancs** blank verse; **-s libres** lines of different lengths; **-s libres modernes** free verse
vers *prep.* toward(s); about
versage *m.* pouring; tilling of a fallow field
versant *m.* slope
versatile *a.* versatile; changeable, fickle
versatilité *f.* versatility; fickleness
verse *f.*, **il pleut à** — it's pouring;
versé *a.* versed
versement *m.* payment, installment
verser *vt.* & *vi.* to pour; shed; pay; overturn
verseur *m.* pourer, server
verseuse *f.* straight-handled coffee pot
versicolore *a.* many-colored
versificateur *m.* versifier
versifier *vt.* & *vi.* to versify
version *f.* version; translation from a foreign language to one's own language
vert *a.* green; unripe; tart; fresh; lively, young, active; **langue -e** *f.* slang
vert-de-gris *m.* verdigris
ver-de-grisé *a.* covered with verdigris
vertébral *a.* vertebral
vertèbre *f.* vertebra
vertébré *a.* & *m.* vertebrate
vertical *a.* vertical; **-e** *f.* vertical line
verticalité *f.* verticalness
verticille *m.* whorl
verticillé *a.* in a whorl
vertige *m.* dizziness, giddiness
vertigineux *a.* dizzy, giddy
vertigo *m.* staggers (horses); whim, caprice
vertu *f.* virtue
vertueux *a.* virtuous
vertugadin *m.* farthingale
verve *f.* zest, life, spirit
verveine *f.* verbena
vervelle *f.* band, leg band on birds
verveux *a.* lively, spirited

vésanie *f.* insanity
vésical *a.* vesical
vesicant *a.* blistering, blister-forming
vésicatoire *a.* blistering, vesicatory
vésicule *f.* vesicle; bladder
vespasienne *f.* street urinal
vespéral *a.* evening
vesse-de-loup *m.* puffball mushroom
vessie *f.* bladder
vestale *f.* vestal virgin
veste *f.* jacket
vestaire *m.* checkroom
vestibule *m.* vestibule, entrance hall
vestimentaire *a.* clothing
veston *m.* suit coat; — **intérieur** smoking jacket
Vésuve *m.* Vesuvius
vêtement *m.* article of clothing
vétéran *a.* veteran
vétérinaire *m.* veterinarian; — *a.* veterinary
vétille *f.* trifle
vétilleux *a.* picayune, interested in trifles
vêtir *vt.* to clothe; **se** — to get dressed
vêture *f.* investiture, taking the habit, taking the veil
vétuste *a.* old, worn
vétusté *f.* oldness, age, deterioration
veuf *m.* widower
veule *a.* weak; awkward
veulerie *f.* weakness, lack of energy
veuvage *m.* widowhood
veuve *f.* widow
vexation *f.* vexation
vexatoire, vexatéure *a.* vexing
vexer *vt.* to vex
viabilité *f.* viability, ability to live; good condition
viable *a.* viable, durable
viaduc *m.* viaduct
viager *a.* lifelong; **rente** –**ère** life annuity
viande *f.* meat, flesh
vibrant *a.* vibrating; vibrant
vibration *f.* vibration
vibratoire *a.* vibratory
vibrer *vi.* to vibrate
vibreur *m.* vibrator
vibrion *m.* microbe
vicaire *m.* curate; vicar
vice *m.* vice; fault, imperfection
vice-amiral *m.* vice-admiral
vice-chancelier *m.* vice chancellor
vice-consul *m.* vice-consul
vice-consulat *m.* vice-consulate; vice-consulship
vicennal *a.* of 20 years' duration
vice-présidence *f.* vice-presidency
vice-président *m.* vice-president
vice-recteur *m.* university vice-president
vice-roi *m.* viceroy

vice-versa *adv.* vice versa
vichy *m.* Vichy water; **toile de** — cotton or cotton-rayon cloth
viciable *a.* corruptible; spoilable
viciateur *a.* corrupting
viciation *f.* spoiling; corruption; fouling
vicier *vt.* to vitiate, invalidate; corrupt; spoil
vicieux *a.* vicious; defective
vicinal *a.* local; parochial
vicinalité *f.* local character
vicissitude *f.* vicissitude
vicomte *m.* viscount; **–sse** *f.* vicountess
victime *f.* victim
victoire *f.* victory
victorien *a.* Victorian
victorieux *a.* victorious
victuailles *f. pl.* victuals
vidage *m.* emptying
vidange *m.* emptying; **en** — being emptied, opened
vidanger *vt.* to empty
vide *m.* void, vacuum, emptiness; — *a.* empty, void, vacant
vide-bouteille *m.* roadhouse
vide-cave *m.* cellar pump, sump pump
vide-citron *m.* fruit reamer
vide-gousset *m.* pickpocket
videlle *f.* darn; fruit pitter; pastry cutter
vide-ordures *m.* incinerator chute
vide-poches *m.* nightstand
vide-pomme *m.* apple corer
vider *vt.* to empty; leave; clean, dress; finish, settle; core; bore; gut; exhaust
vidimer *vt.* to certify as exact
vidoir *m.* dump
viduité *f.* widowhood
vie *f.* life, lifetime; **à** — for life
vieillard *m.* old man
vieille *f.* old woman
vieilleries *f. pl.* old things, old ideas
vieillesse *f.* old age
vieillir *vt. & vi.* to age; grow old
vieillot *a.* oldish, old-looking
vièle *f.* viol
vielle *f.* hurdy-gurdy
vieller *vi.* to play the hurdy-gurdy
Vienne *f.* Vienna
Viennois *m. & a.* Viennese; **–e** *f.* filled doughnut
vierge *f. & a.* virgin
vieux (vieil, vieille) *a.* old
vif *a.* live, alive, living; quick, lively
vif-argent *m.* quicksilver
vigie *f.* (naut.) lookout; watch tower
vigilamment *adv.* vigilant
vigilance *f.* vigilance
vigile *f.* vigil, eve; — *m.* night watchman
vigne *f.* vine, vineyard
vigneron *m.* vine grower, vintner

vignette *f.* engraving, cut; vignette; poster stamp, seal
vignoble *m.* vineyard, vines
vigoreux *a.* vigorous, sharp
vigogne *f.* vicuna
vigueur *f.* vigor, power
vil *a.* vile; mean; low, paltry
vilain *a.* villanous; ugly; base
vilebrequin *m.* brace, drill; cam shaft
vilenie *f.* vileness, low act, dastardly deed
vilipender *vt.* to vilify, decry, scorn
villa *f.* summer house, country house
village *m.* village
villageois *m.* villager
villanelle *f.* kind of pastoral poetry; kind of dance
ville *f.* town, city; en — downtown; diner en — to dine out
villégiateur *m.* vacationer
villégiature *f.* vacation
villégiaturer *vi.* to vacation
villeux *a.* hairy
villosité *f.* villosity; roughness; hairiness
vin *m.* wine
vinaigre *m.* vinegar
vinaigrer *vt.* to flavor with *or* add vinegar
vinaigrerie *f.* vinegar works
vinaigrette *f.* oil and vinegar sauce
vinaigrier *m.* vinegar cruet; vinegar manufacturer; vinegar seller
vinasse *f.* residue after distillation; poor wine
vindicatif *a.* vindicative
vindicte *f.* prosecution
viner *vt.* to fortify wine
vineux *a.* wine-producing; tasting of wine, winey; strong with alcohol
vingt *a.* twenty; -ième *m. & a.* twentieth
vingtaine *f.* score, about twenty
vinicole *a.* wine-growing
viniculture *f.* wine making; vine growing
vinification *f.* wine-making
vinylique *a.* vinyl
viol *m.* rape
violacé *a.* purplish
violateur *m.* violator
violation *f.* violation, breach
violâtre *a.* purplish
viole *f.* viol; viola
violemment *adv.* violently
violence *f.* violence
violenter *vt.* to force, do violence to
violer *vt.* to violate, rape
violet *a.* purple; — te *f.* violet (flower)
violine *f.* red violet, red purple; violine
violon *m.* violin, violinist; (coll.) jail
violoncelle *m.* cello; cellist
violoncelliste *m.* cellist
violoneux *m.* fiddler
violoniste *m. & f.* violinist

vipère *f.* viper
vipérin *a.* viperine
virage *m.* curve, turn; turning; (phot.) fixing; fixing-bath
virago *f.* virago, tomboy
viral *a.* virus
virement *m.* transfer; transfer payment
virer *vi.* to turn about; change; — de bord to tack, turn about; — *vt.* to transfer funds; (phot.) to fix
virevolte *f.* rapid movement back and forth
virevolter *vi.* to move back and forth
virginité *f.* virginity
virgule *f.* comma; point et — *m.* semicolon
viril *a.* virile
virilité *f.* virility
virole *f.* ferrule, ring
viroler *vt.* to attach a ferrule to
virtualité *f.* virtuality; potentiality
virtuel *a.* virtual; potential
virtuose *m. & f.* virtuoso
virtuosité *f.* virtuosity
virulence *f.* virulence
virulent *a.* virulent
vis *f.* screw; escalier à — circular staircase; pas de — thread of a screw
visa *m.* visa; certification, authentification
visage *m.* face
vis-à-vis *adv.* opposite; face to face
viscéral *a.* visceral
viscère *m.* viscera
viscose *f.* viscose
viscosité *f.* viscosity
visé *a.* certified
visée *f.* aim, end, design
viser *vt. & vi.* to aim, view; visa; certify; authenticate; — à to aim for
viseur *m.* aimer; viewer; — de bombardement bomb sight
visibilité *f.* visibility
visible *a.* visible, discernible; evident
visière *f.* visor
vision *f.* vision
visionnaire *a.* visionary
visionneuse *f.* slide viewer; film editor
visite *f.* visit; search; inspection; rendre — à to visit
visiter *vt.* to inspect; visit
vison *m.* mink
visqueux *a.* viscous
vissage *m.* screwing
visser *vt.* to screw
visserie *f.* nuts, bolts, and screws; manufacture of screws
visuel *a.* visual
vital *a.* vital
vitalisme *m.* vitalism
vitalité *f.* vitality
vitamine *f.* vitamin

vite *a. & adv.* quick(ly); fast

vitesse *f.* quickness, rapidity; — **relative** air speed

viticole *a.* wine-producing, grape-growing

viticulteur *m.* grape grower

viticulture *f.* vine growing

vitrage *m.* glazing; windows

vitrail (*pl.* **vitraux**) *m.* stained glass window

vitre *f.* pane of glass, window

vitrer *vt.* to glaze; install windows in

vitrerie *f.* glazing, glass trade

vitreux *a.* vitrous, glassy, glasslike

vitrier *m.* glazier, glassworker

vitrifiable *a.* vitrifiable

vitrifier *vt.* to vitrify

vitrine *f.* store window

vitriol *m.* vitriol, sulphuric acid

vitrioler *vt.* to throw acid in the face of

vitupération *f.* vituperation

vitupérer *vt.* to vituperate

vivace *a.* long-lived, perennial

vivacité *f.* vivacity, vivaciousness

vivandier *m.* clerk, seller in an army canteen

vivant *a.* lively; alive; lifelike; **langue –e** modern language; — *m.* living person; — *pl.* the living

vivat *m.* cheer; —! *interj.* bravo!

vivement *adv.* bridly, vigorously, quickly

viveur *m.* playboy, rake

vivier *m.* fishpond

vivifiant *a.* animating

vivifier *vt.* to animate, recreate, make come alive

vivipare *a.* viviparous

vivisection *f.* vivisection

vivoter *vi.* to live from hand to mouth, eke out one's existence

vivre *m.* food; **–s** *pl.* provisions, food

vivre *vi.* to live

vlan! *interj.* bang!, slam!

vocable *m.* word, term

vocabulaire *m.* vocabulary; vocabulary list

vocalisation *f.* vocalization; vocalizing; vocal exercise

vocaliser *vi.* to do a vocal exercise

vocalisme *m.* vowel system

vocatif *m.* vocative case

vocation *f.* vocation

vocifération *f.* vociferation

vociférer *vi.* to vociferate

vœu *m.* vow, wish

vogue *f.* fashion, popularity

voguer *vi.* to sail, wander

voici *adv.* here is, here are

voie *f.* way, means, road; wheelbase; (anat.) canal; trail; **–s de fait** assault and battery; **être en — de** to be on the way to, be in the act of; **— ferrée** railroad

voilà *adv.* there is, there are

voile *m.* veil; — *f.* sail

voiler *vt.* to veil; **se** — to become bent, bow

voilette *f.* small veil on a hat

voilier *m.* sailing ship

voilure *f.* sails, canvas; (avi.) wings

voir *vt. & vi.* to see

voire *adv.* indeed, verily, even

voirie *f.* highway department; dump, sewer

voisin *m.* neighbor; — *a.* neighboring

voisinage *m.* neighborhood, vicinity

voisiner *vi.* to visit with the neighbors

voiturage *m.* trucking, hauling

voiture *f.* carriage, coach; automobile; — **commune** carpool

voiturer *vt.* to haul, cart

voiturier *m.* hauler

voix *f.* voice; vote; **à haute** — loudly; **à** — **basse** in a whisper

vol *m.* flight; robbery, theft; **à — d'oiseau** bird's-eye view

volage *a.* flighty, fickle

volaille *f.* poultry

volailler *m.* poultry store, poultry dealer; poultry yard

volant *a.* flying, winged; **pont** — *m.* movable bridge; **table –e** *f.* end table, light table; — *m.* steering wheel; balance wheel; flounce, ruffle; shuttlecock; badminton

volatil *a.* volatile

volatile *m.* bird; winged creature

volatilisation *f.* volatilization

volatiliser *vt.* to volatilize; **se** — (coll.) to disappear, get out

vol-au-vent *m.* filled patty shell

volcan *m.* volcano

volcanique *a.* volcanic

volcaniser *vt.* to vulcanize

vole *f.* grand slam; **faire la** — to take all the tricks (at cards)

volée *f.* flight of birds, flying; volley; class, rank; **à la** — in flight

voler *vt. & vi.* to rob, steal; fly; — **à l'aveuglette** blind flying; — **sans visibilité** blind flying

volerie *f.* petty theft

volet *m.* shutter; (avi.) flap

voleter *vi.* to fly about

voleur *m.* thief, robber

volière *f.* bird cage, aviary

volige *f.* scantling, board

volleyeur *m.* volley ball player

volontaire *a.* voluntary; — *m.* volunteer

volontariat *m.* (mil.) enlistment (as contrasted to the draft)

volonté *f.* will; willingness; **payable à —** payable at will

volontiers *adv.* willingly, gladly

voltaïque *a.* voltaic

voltaire *m.* high-backed chair

volte-face *f.* about face

voltiger *vi.* to fly about

voltigeur *m.* trapeze or equestrian performer

voltmètre *m.* voltmeter

volubile *a.* volubilate, spiraling

volubilité *f.* volubility, fluency

volumineux *a.* voluminous

volupté *f.* voluptuousness

voluptueux *a.* voluptuous

volute *f.* spiral, curl, scroll

vomir *vt. & vi.* to vomit

vomissement *m.* vomiting; vomit

vomitif *a.* vomitive; — *m.* emetic

vorace *a.* voracious, ravenous

voracité *f.* voraciousness

vos *a. pl.* your

votation *f.* voting

votif *a.* votive

votre *a* your

vôtre *pron.*, **le —, la —** yours

vouer *vt.* to devote; consecrate; pledge

vouloir *vt. & vi.* to wish; intend; **— bien** to be willing; **— dire** to mean; **en — à** to hold a grudge against; **— m.** will

voulu *a.* intentional; desired

vous *pron.* you

voussoir, vousseau *m.* stone of an arch, wedge-shaped stone

voussure *f.* curve of an arch, a vault

voûte *f.* vault, arched roof

voûté *a.* vaulted; crooked; round-shouldered

voûter *vt.* to vault, cover with vaulting; bend

voyage *m.* trip, journey, tour; **— à forfait** prepaid tour

voyager *vi.* to travel; migrate (birds)

voyageur *m.* traveller; passenger; **commis — m.** traveling salesman

voyant *a.* showy, gaudy; **— m.** sight, target; **— m.** seer

voyelle *f.* vowel

voyou *m.* scum, cad, hoodlum (U.S. coll.)

**vrac, en — ** *adv.* in disorder; unpacked

vrai *a.* true, real

vraisemblable *a.* likely, probable

vraisemblance *f.* verisimilitude

vrille *f.* tendril of a vine; gimlet

vriller *vt.* to pierce with a gimlet; **— vi.** ascend in spiral; twist

vrombir *vt.* to rumble

vrombissement *m.* rumble

vu *a.* seen; **— prep.** in view of, considering; **— que** *conj.* considering that

vue *f.* sight; view

vulcanisation *f.* vulcanization

vulcaniser *vt.* to vulcanize

vulcanite *f.* vulcanite

vulgaire *a.* common

vulgarisateur *a.* popularizing; **— m.** popularizer

vulgarisation *f.* popularizing; **ouvrage de — m.** work for popular consumption

vulgariser *vt.* to popularize

vulgarité *f.* vulgarity

vulnérable *a.* vulnerable

vulnéraire *a.* vulnerary

vultueux *a.* flushed of face

vulve *f.* vulva

W

wagon *m.* railway car

wagon-bar *m.* club car

wagon-lit *m.* sleeping car

wagon-poste *m.* mail car

wagon-réservoir *m.* tank car

wagon-restaurant *m.* dining car

wagon-salon *m.* parlor car

wagonnet *m.* cart, handcart

warrant *m.* warrant, guarantee

warranter *vt.* to warrant

wattman *m.* motorman of a streetcar

X

xénophobie *f.* xenophobia

xérophagie *f.* xerophagy

xérophile *adv.* xerophilous

xérophyte *a.* xerophyte

xylographie *f.* wood engraving

xylophone *m.* xylophone

Y

y *adv.* there, here; **il — a** there is, there are; **vous — êtes** you are right, that's it; **— pron.** to it, to them

yachting *m.* yachting

yack *m.* yak

yaourt, yogourt *m.* yoghurt

yeuse *f.* ilex, holly oak

yeux *m. pl.* eyes

yole *f.* yawl

Yougoslave *m. & f. & a.* Yugoslavian

Yougoslavie *f.* Yugoslavia

youyou *m.* sampan, small boat

Z

zazou *m.* bobby-soxer, teen-ager

zèbre *m.* zebra

zébu *m.* zebu

zélateur *a.* zealous
zèle *m.* zeal, warmth; **avec —** zealously
zélé *a.* zealous
zénith *m.* zenith
zéro *m.* cipher, nought, zero
zeste *m.* citrous peel; **–r** *vt.* to peel
zézaiement *m.* lisp
zézayer *vt. & vi.* to lisp
zibeline *f.* sable; sable fur
zigzag *m.* zigzag; **—** *m. & a.* (coll.) drunk
zigzaguer *vi.* to zigzag
zinc *m.* zinc; (coll.) bar, counter
zinguer *vt.* to zinc-plate

zingueur *m.* zinc worker
zinnia *m.* zinnia
zinzolin *m.* red-violet
zircon *m.* zircon
zodiaque *m.* zodiac
zona *f.* (med.) shingles
zoologie *f.* zoology
zoologique *a.* zoological; **parc —** zoo
zoologiste *m.* zoologist
zoonose *f.* zoonosis
zostère *f.* seaweed
zouave *m.* North African trooper
zut! *interj.* curses!

English-French

A

a, an *art.* un, une
Aachen *n.* Aix-la-Chapelle
aback, to be taken — être surpris
abandon *vt.* abandonner; to — oneself to s'abandonner à; –ed *a.* dissolu; –ment *n.* abandon *m.*
abase *vt.* avilir; –ment *n.* avilissement, abaissement *m.*
abate *vi.* diminuer, se calmer, s'apaiser; baisser; –ment *n.* diminution *f.*
abbess *n.* abbesse *f.*
abbey *n.* abbaye *f.*
abbot *n.* abbé *m.*
abbreviate *vt.* abréger
abbreviation *n.* abréviation *f.*
ABC *n.* abc *m.*; abécédaire *m.*
abdicate *vt. & vi.* abdiquer
abdication *n.* abdication, renonciation *f.*
abdomen *n.* abdomen, bas-ventre *m.*
abduct *vt.* enlever; –ion *n.* enlèvement *m.*; –or *n.* ravisseur *m.*
aberration *n.* égarement *m.*, aberration *f.*
abet *vt.* encourager; soutenir
abeyance *n.* attente *f.*; in — en suspens
abhor *vt.* abhorrer; –rence *n.* horreur *f.*; –rent *a.* répugnant
abide *vi.* demeurer, rester; — *vt.* supporter; — by respecter
abiding *a.* permanent, constant
ability *n.* habileté, capacité *f.*; to the best of one's — de son mieux
abject *a.* bas, abject, vil; –ion *n.* bassesse, abjection *f.*
abjuration *n.* abjuration *f.*
abjure *vt.* abjurer
ablative *n.* ablatif *m.*
ablaze *a.* en flammes
able *a.* capable; to be — pouvoir; savoir;

être à même de
able-bodied *a.* propre au service; en bonne santé
ablution *n.* ablution *f.*
ably *adv.* bien, habilement
abnegate *vt.* renier, renoncer à
abnegation *n.* abnégation *f.*, renoncement *m.*
abnormal *a.* anormal; –ity *n.* anormalité *f.*
aboard *adv.* à bord; to go — s'embarquer; to take — embarquer; all —! *interj.* à bord!; en voiture!
abode *a.* demeure, habitation *f.*; domicile *m.*
abolish *vt.* abolir
abolition *n.* abolissement *m.*, abolition *f.*; –ist *n.* abolitionniste, antiesclavagiste *m. & f.*
A-bomb *n.* bombe atomique *f.*
abominable *a.* abominable
abominate *vt.* avoir en abomination
abomination *n.* abomination *f.*
aboriginal *a.* aborigène
abort *vi.* avorter; –ion *n.* avortement *m.*; –ive *a.* avorté, manqué
abound *vi.* abonder; –ing *a.* abondant
about *adv.* çà et là; à peu près, environ; come — arriver; bring — causer; be — to être sur le point de; — *prep.* autour de, près de; parmi, par; vers; au sujet de; sur le point de
about-face *n.* volte-face *f.*
above *adv.* en haut, là-haut, plus haut; — *prep.* au-dessus de, plus haut que; — all surtout; over and — en outre
aboveboard *a.* franc, légitime
above-mentioned *a.* ledit, susdit
abrade *vt.* frotter, user en frottant

abrasion *n.* abrasion *f.*, frottement *m.*
abrasive *a.* abrasif, qui use en frottant;
— *n.* émeri *m.*; abrasif *m.*
abreast *adv.* à côté l'un de l'autre; au courant; two — par deux
abridge *vt.* abréger
abridgment *n.* abrégé *m.*; résumé *m.*
abroad *adv.* à l'étranger; to get — se répandre
abrogate *vt.* abroger
abrogation *n.* abrogation, revocation *f.*
abrupt *a.* abrupte, précipité, brusque; —ness *n.* brusquerie *f.*; précipitation *f.*
abscess *n.* abcès *m.*
abscond *vi.* échapper, disparaître; —ing *n.* évasion, fuite *f.*
absence *n.* absence *f.*; leave of — congé *m.*
absent *a.* absent; — *vt.*, to — one's self s'absenter; —ee *n.* absent (de son poste) *m.*; —eeism *n.* absentéisme *m.*
absent-minded *a.* distrait; —ness *n.* distraction *f.*
absolute *a.* absolu; —ly *adv.* tout à fait; absolument
absolute altitude *n.* (avi.) altitude absolue *f.*
absolution *n.* absolution *f.*
absolve *vt.* absoudre; dégager
absorb *vt.* absorber; —ent *a.* & *n.* absorbant *m.*; —ent cotton coton hydrophile *m.*
abstain *vi.* s'abstenir
abstemious *a.* abstinent, sobre, modéré
abstention *n.* abstention, abstinence *f.*
abstinence *n.* abstinence, privation volontaire *f.*; day of — jour maigre *m.*
abstract *n.* résumé, sommaire *m.*; — *vt.* résumer, abréger; faire abstraction de; — *a.* abstrait; —ion *n.* abstraction *f.*; —ionism *n.* (art) abstractionnisme *m.*
abstruse *a.* abstrus; —ness *n.* complexité *f.*
absurd *a.* absurde; —ity *n.* absurdité *f.*
abundance *n.* abondance *f.*
abundant *a.* abondant
abuse *n.* abus, outrage *m.*; — *vt.* abuser (de), tromper; injurier
abusive *a.* abusif, injurieux; —ness *n.* grossièreté *f.*; abus *m.*
abut *vi.* buter (contre); aboutir (à); —ment *n.* butée, culée *f.*
abysmal *a.* sans fond; profond
abyss *n.* abîme, gouffre *m.*
Abyssinia *n.* Abyssinie *f.*
academic *a.* académique; universitaire; — freedom *n.* franchise académique *f.*
academy *n.* académie, école *f.*
accede *vi.* accéder
accelerate *vt.* accélérer; précipiter; — *vi.* s'accélérer

acceleration *n.* accélération *f.*
accelerator *n.* accélérateur *m.*
accent *vt.* accentuer, souligner, donner de l'emphase à; — *n.* accent, accent tonique *m.*; —uate *vt.* accentuer; —uation *n.* accentuation *f.*
accept *vt.* accepter; agréer; —able *a.* acceptable; —ance *n.* acceptation, réception *f.*; —ation *n.* acception, signification *f.*
access *n.* accès *m.*, entrée *f.*; —ible *a.* accessible, abordable; —ibility *n.* accessibilité *f.*; —ion *n.* avènement *m.*; acquisition *f.*; —ory *n.* & *a.* complice *m.*; accessoire *m.*
accident *n.* accident *m.*; by — par hasard; —al *a.* accidentel, fortuit; —ally *adv.* par hasard, fortuitement
accident-prone *a.* susceptible d'accidents
acclaim *vt.* acclamer, applaudir; — *n.* acclamation *f.*, applaudissements *m.* *pl.*
acclamation *n.* acclamation *f.*
acclimate *vt.* acclimater
accommodate *vt.* accommoder, régler; pourvoir; loger; recevoir; obliger
accommodating *a.* accommodant, serviable, obligeant, complaisant
accommodation *n.* adaptation *f.*; accommodement *m.*; arrangement *m.*, convenance, commodité *f.*; logement *m.*
accompaniment *n.* accompagnement *m.*
accompany *vt.* accompagner
accomplice *n.* complice *m.* & *f.*
accomplish *vt.* accomplir, exécuter, achever; —ed *a.* accompli, habile, expert; —ment *n.* accomplissement, talent *m.*
accord *n.* accord *m.*, union *f.*; convention *f.*; consentement *m.*; of one's own — de son propre gré, de plein gré; with one accord d'un commun accord; — *vt.* accorder; —ance *n.* conformité *f.*; in —ance with selon; —ing *prep.*, —ing to d'après; selon; —ingly *adv.* conformément
accost *vt.* aborder, accoster
account *n.* compte, calcul *m.*; valeur, considération *f.*; importance *f.*; raison *f.*; rapport, récit *m.*; on — (com.) à valoir; on — of à cause de; on no — d'aucune façon; to take into — tenir compte de; to keep -s tenir des comptes; — book *n.* livre de comptes *m.*; — *vt.* compter, calculer; estimer; rendre compte de, rendre raison de, être responsable; —able *a.* responsable; —ant *n.* comptable *m.*; —ing *n.* comptabilité *f.*
accoutrement *n.* équipement *m.*; ornement *m.*
accredit *vt.* croire; accréditer; —ed *a.*

approuvé, agréé
accrue *vi.* accroître; résulter
accumulate *vi.* s'accumuler; — *vt.* amasser
accumulation *n.* accumulation *f.*, entassement *m.*
accuracy *n.* exactitude, justesse *f.*
accurate *a.* exact, juste; **-ly** *adv.* exactement, avec justesse; **-ness** *n.* précision, justesse *f.*
accusation *n.* accusation *f.*
accusative *n.* accusatif *m.*
accuse *vt.* accuser; **-d** *n.* accusé *m.*; **-r** *n.* accusateur *m.*
accustom *vt.* accoutumer, habituer; **to become -ed** s'habituer, s'accoutumer; **-ed** *a.* accoutumé, habituel
ace *n.* as *m.*; expert *m.*; champion *m.*
acetate *n.* acétate *m.*
acetone *n.* acétone *f.*
acetylene *n.* acétylène *m.*
ache *n.* mal *m.*, douleur *f.*; — *vi.* faire mal, souffrir; **my head -s** j'ai mal à la tête
achievable *a.* réalisable
achieve *vt.* atteindre; achever, exécuter; **-ment** *n.* réalisation *f.*; fait, exploit *m.*
aching *n.* peine *f.*; — *a.* douloureux
acid *n. & a.* acide *m.*; — **test** épreuve déterminante *f.*; **-ity** *n.* acidité *f.*
acidulate *vt.* aciduler
acknowledge *vt.* reconnaître; avouer; — **receipt** accuser réception; **-d** *a.* reconnu
acknowledgment *n.* reconnaissance *f.*, aveu, *m.*; concession *f.*; accusé de réception *m.*
acme *n.* sommet *m.*; apogée *f.*; comble *m.*
acorn *n.* gland *m.*
acoustic *a.* acoustique; **-s** *n. pl.* acoustique *f.*
acquaint *vt.* informer, faire savoir; **be -ed with** connaître; **become -ed with** connaître, faire la connaissance de; **-ance** *n.* connaissance *f.*
acquiesce *vi.* acquiescer; **-nce** *n.* soumission *f.*; **-nt** *a.* soumis, consentant
acquire *vt.* acquérir, obtenir
acquisition *n.* acquisition *f.*
acquisitive *a.* capable d'acquérir; qui aime acquérir
acquit *vt.* acquitter, absoudre; **-tal** *n.* acquittement *m.*
acre *n.* acre *f.* (= 40.5 ares); arpent, demi-hectare *m.*
acreage *n.* superficie *f.*, terrain, arpentage *m.*
acrid *a.* âcre; **-ity, -ness** *n.* âcreté *f.*
acrimonious *a.* acrimonieux
acrimony *n.* acrimonie *f.*
acrobat *n.* acrobate *m.*; **-ic** *a.* acrobatique; **-ics** *n.* acrobatie *f.*

across *adv.* de travers; — *prep.* à travers, au travers de; — **the street** de l'autre côté de la rue, en face; **come** — rencontrer; **go** — traverser, passer, franchir
act *n.* acte *m.*, action *f.*, fait, exploit *m.*; loi *f.*; **be in the** — **of** être en train de; **put on an** — faire semblant; **Acts** (eccl.) Actes des apôtres *m. pl.*; — *vt.* agir, opérer; faire; se comporter; — *vt.* jouer, représenter; — **on** suivre; agir d'après; **-ing** *a.* provisoire; intérimaire; **-ing** *n.* (theat.) jeu *m.*; **-ing** *a.* par intérim; **-or** *n.* acteur *m.*; **-ress** *n.* actrice *f.*
actin *n.* (chem.) actinium *m.*
actinic *a.* actinique
action *n.* action *f.*, fait *m.*; bataille *f.*; procès *m.*; **out of** — hors de service; (mil.) hors de combat; **take** — agir
activate *vt.* activer; mettre en marche
activator *n.* (chem.) activeur *m.*
active *a.* actif, agile; vif
activity *n.* activité, vivacité *f.*
actual *a.* réel, véritable, vrai; **-ity** *n.* réalité *f.*; **-ly** *adv.* réellement, véritablement
actuate *vt.* mettre en action; actionner; animer
acuity *n.* acuité *f.*
acumen *n.* finesse *f.*
acute *a.* aigu, pointu; subtil; fin; intense; **-ness** *n.* aiguité *f.*; acuité *f.*
A.D. (Anno Domini) de l'ère chrétienne
adage *n.* adage, proverbe *m.*
adamant *a.* inflexible
adapt *vt.* adapter, accommoder; **-able** *a.* adaptable, applicable; **-ability** *n.* qualité de pouvoir s'adapter *f.*; **-ation** *n.* adaptation *f.*
add *vt.* ajouter, joindre; **to** — **up** additionner; se résumer; **-ing machine** *n.* machine à calculer *f.*
adder *n.* vipère *f.*
addict *vt.* adonner, vouer; — *n.* toxicomane *m.*; **-ion** *n.* manie, disposition *f.*, penchant *m*
addition *n.* addition *f.*, accroissement *m.*; **in** — en outre, en sus; **-al** *a.* additionnel, supplémentaire; de plus
addled *a.* fou; gâté
address *n.* adresse *f.*; allocution *f.*, discours *m.*; plaidoyer *m.*; dextérité, habileté *f.*; — **book** carnet d'adresses *m.*; — *vt.* adresser; parler à; **-ee** *n.* destinataire *m. & f.*
addressograph *n.* machine à adresser
adenoids *n. pl.* adénoïdes *m. pl.*
adept *a.* habile; adepte; **-ness** *n.* habileté *f.*
adequacy *n.* suffisance *f.*
adequate *a.* suffisant; **-ness** *n.* suffisance *f.*

adhere *vi.* adhérer, s'attacher; –nce *n.* adhésion *f.*; –nt *n.* partisan *m.*

adhesion *n.* adhérence, adhésion *f.*

adhesive *a.* adhérent; collant; — *n.* colle *f.*; timbre-poste *m.*; — tape *n.* sparadrap *m.*; –ness *n.* adhésion *f.*

ad infinitum *adv.* à l'infini

adipose *a.* adipeux

adjacent *a.* adjacent, voisin, contigu

adjective *n. & a.* adjectif *m.*

adjoin *vt.* être contigu à, avoisiner; donner sur; –ing *a.* contigu

adjourn *vt.* ajourner, remettre; lever, clore (une séance); –ment *n.* ajournement *m.*; suspension *f.*

adjudicate *vt.* adjuger

adjudge *vt.* adjuger, condamner

adjunct *n.* accessoire *m.*, appartenance *f.* adjoint *m.*

adjust *vt.* ajuster, arranger, régler; corriger; mettre à point; –able *a.* réglable; –ment *n.* réglement *m.*; réglage *m.*; adjustage *m.*; correction

adjutant *n.* adjudant major *m.*; — general général chef des archives militaires *m.*

ad-lib *vi. & vt.* improviser

adman *n.* (com.) publicitaire *m.*

administer, administrate *vt.* administrer, gouverner, gérer

administration *n.* administration *f.*, gouvernement *m.*

administrative *a.* administratif

administrator *n.* administrateur *m.*

admiral *n.* amiral *m.*; rear — contreamiral *m.*; –ty *n.* ministère de la marine *m.*

admire *vt.* admirer; –r *n.* admirateur *m.*

admiring *a.* admiratif

admission *n.* admission, réception *f.*; confession *f.*, aveu *m.*; — charge entrée *f.*, tarif *m.*

admit *vt.* admettre; permettre; avouer; reconnaître; laisser entrer; –tance entrée *f.*; no –tance entrée interdite; –ted *a.* avoué, reconnu; –tedly *adv.* reconnu comme; de son propre aveu

admonish *vt.* exhorter; admonester

admonition *n.* exhortation *f.*; admonestation *f.*

ado *n.* bruit *m.*, céremonies *f. pl.*; difficulté, peine *f.*

adolescent *n. & a.* adolescent *m. & a.*

adopt *vt.* adopter; –ed *a.* adoptif, d'adoption; –ion *n.* adoption *f.*; –ive *a.* adoptif, d'adoption

adorable *a.* adorable

adoration *n.* adoration *f.*

adore *vt.* adorer; –r *n.* adorateur *m.*; soupirant *m.*

adorn *vt.* orner, décorer; parer; embellir;

–ment *n.* ornement *m.*; ornementation *f.*; parure *f.*

adrenalin *n.* adrénaline *f.*

Adriatic Sea *n.* Mer Adriatique *f.*

adrift *adv.* à la dérive

adroit *a.* adroit; habile; –ness *n.* adresse, dextérité *f.*

adulate *vt.* aduler

adulation *n.* adulation *f.*

adulatory *a.* adulateur

adult *n. & a.* adulte *m. & f.*

adulterate *vt.* adultérer; couper; falsifier, corrompre

adulteration *n.* falsification *f.*; adultération *f.*

adulterer, adulteress *n.* adultère *m. & f.*

adultery *n.* adultère *m.*

advance *n.* avance *f.*, avancement *m.*, approche *f.*; progrès *m.*; — guard avant-garde *f.*; in — d'avance, préalablement; — *vt.* avancer; faire avancer, pousser; approcher; — *vi.* s'avancer; –d *a.* avancé; –ment *n.* avancement *m.*

advantage *n.* avantage *m.*, supériorité *f.*; to take — of profiter de; abuser de; turn to one's — mettre à profit; –ous *a.* avantageux; profitable

advent *n.* venue *f.*, avènement *m.*; Avent *m.*

adventure *n.* aventure *f.*, accident, hasard *m.*; — *vt.* risquer; –r *n.* aventurier *m.*; –some *a.* aventureux

adventurous *a.* aventureux

adverb *n.* adverbe *m.*; –ial *a.* adverbial

adversary *n.* adversaire *m.*

adverse *a.* adverse, contraire; défavorable; –ly *adv.* au contraire; d'une façon défavorable

adversity *n.* adversité *f.*

advertise *vt.* annoncer; — *vi.* faire de la publicité; –ment *n.* annonce

advertising *n.* publicité *f.*; réclame *f.*; annonces *f. pl.*

advice *n.* conseil *m.*; avis *m.*; piece of — conseil *m.*; on the — of sur l'avis de; take someone's — suivre le conseil de quelqu'un

advisability *n.* convenance, opportunité *f.*

advisable *a.* prudent, judicieux; convenable; opportun

advise *vt. & vi.* conseiller; — against déconseiller; –r, advisor *n.* conseiller *m.*

advisory *a.* consultatif

advocacy *n.* appui *m.*; soutien *m.*

advocate *n.* défenseur *m.*; avocat *m.*; — *vt.* soutenir; défendre

Aegean Sea *n.* Mer Egée *f.*

aegis *n.* égide *f.*

aeon *n.* éternité *f.*; éon *m.*

aerate *vt.* aérer; gazéifier

aeration *n.* aération *f.*

aerial *a.* aérien; — *n.* antenne *f.*; — **photography** *n.* photographie aérienne *f.*

aerodynamics *n. pl.* aérodynamique *f.*

aeromedicine *n.* médecine de l'aviation *f.*

aeronaut *n.* aéronaute *m.*; **-ics** *n. pl.* aéronautique *f.*

aerosol *n.* aérosol *m.*; bombe, vaporisateur à insecticide *f.*

aerospace *n.* espace interplanétaire *m.*

aerothermodynamics *n.* aérothermodynamique *f.*

aesthetic *a.* esthétique; **-s** *n.* esthétique *f.*

afar *adv.* loin; **from** — de loin

affability *n.* affabilité *f.*

affable *a.* affable, gracieux

affair *n.* affaire *f.*; **love** — liaison *f.*; **foreign** **-s** affaires étrangères *f. pl.*

affect *vt.* affecter; émouvoir, toucher; feindre; **-ation** *n.* affectation *f.*; **-ed** *a.* affecté; **-ing** *a.* touchant

affection *n.* affection *f.*; tendresse *f.*; **-ate** *a.* affectueux, tendre; affectionné

affiance *vt.* fiancer

affidavit *n.* déclaration *f.*, affidavit *m.*

affiliate *vt.* affilier

affiliation *n.* affiliation *f.*; relation *f.*

affinity *n.* affinité *f.*; rapport *m.*

affirm *vt.* affirmer; **-ation** *n.* affirmation *f.*; **-ative** *n.* affirmative *f.*; **-ative** *a.* affirmatif

affix *vt.* fixer, apposer, attacher

afflict *vt.* affliger; **-ion** *n.* affliction *f.*

affluence *n.* affluence, opulence *f.*; abondance *f.*

affluent *a.* abondant, riche; — *n.* affluent *m.*

afford *vt.* pouvoir se payer, se permettre; fournir

affront *n.* affront *m.*, insulte *f.*; — *vt.* affronter; insulter

afghan *n.* couverture *f.*

afire, aflame *adv.* en flammes, en feu

afloat *adv.* à flot, flottant

afoot *adv.* à pied, sur pied, en train

aforementioned, aforesaid *a.* précité, susdit

afraid *a.* éffrayé; **to be** — avoir peur

Africa *n.* Afrique *f.*; **-n** *a. & n.* africain *m.*; **North** — *n.* Afrique du Nord *f.*; **North** **-n** *n. & a.* Nord-Africain *m.*

aft *adv.* à l'arrière

after *adv.* après, plus tard; derrière; — *prep.* après; derrière; à la suite de; d'après; à la poursuite de; — **all** après tout; enfin; **be** — chercher; **day** — **tomorrow** après-demain; **take** — tenir de; **time** — **time** bien des fois; — *conj.* après que; — *a.* arrière, d'arrière, futur, untérieur

afterbirth *n.* arrière-faix, délivre *m.*

aftereffect *n.* résultat *m.*; suite *f.*; répercussion *f.*; contre-coup *m.*

afterglow *n.* lueur (qui subsiste) *f.*

afterlife *n.* vie future *f.*

aftermath *n.* regain *m.*; conséquences, suites *f. pl.*

afternoon *n.* après-midi *m. & f.*

aftertaste *n.* arrière-goût *m.*

afterthought *n.* réflexion après coup *f.*

afterwards *adv.* après

again *adv.* encore, de nouveau; — **and** — sans cesse; **now and** — de temps en temps, de temps à autre; **once** — encore une fois; **then** — d'autre part

against *prep.* contre; vers, sur; — **the grain** à contre-poil; — **the will** à contrecœur; **come up** — se heurter contre; **as** — comparé à

agape *adv.* bouche bée

agar-agar *n.* gélase *f.*

agate *n.* agate *f.*; (print.) corps 5.5 *m.*

age *n.* âge *m.*; génération *f.*; vieillesse *f.*; **under** — *a.* mineur; **of** — majeur; **over** — *a.* trop vieux, périmé; **to be ten years of** — avoir dix ans; — *vi.* vieillir; **-d** *a.* âgé; **middle** **-d** *a.* d'un certain âge

agency *n.* agence *f.*; intermédiaire *m. & f.*; entremise *f.*; action *f.*

agenda *n.* ordre du jour, programme *m.*

agent *n.* agent *m.*

agglomeration *n.* agglomération *f.*

agglutination *n.* agglutination *f.*

aggrandizement *n.* agrandissement *m.*

aggravate *vt.* aggraver; agacer

aggravating *a.* aggravant; agaçant

aggravation *n.* aggravation *f.*; provocation *f.*, agacement *m.*

aggregate *n.* masse *f.*, rassemblement *m.*; **in the** — dans l'ensemble; — *a.* collectif

aggregation *n.* rassemblement *m.*, réunion *f.*

aggression *n.* agression *f.*

aggressive *a.* agressif; entreprenant; **-ness** *n.* caractère agressif *m.*; entreprise *f.*

aggressor *n.* agresseur *m.*

aghast *a.* stupéfait

agile *a.* agile, leste

agility *n.* agilité, légèreté *f.*

agitate *vt.* agiter, remuer; troubler; — *vi.* faire de l'agitation

agitation *n.* agitation *f.*, trouble *m.*

agitator *n.* agitateur *m.*; (pol.) fauteur *m.*

aglow *a.* incandescent, luisant

agnostic *n. & a.* agnostique *m. & f.*; **-ism** *n.* agnosticisme *f.*

ago *adv.* il y a; passé; **long** — il y a longtemps

agog *a.* en train; en émoi

agonize *vi.* agoniser; — *vt.* torturer; **-ed** *a.* d'angoisse

agonizing *a.* angoissant; atroce

agony *n.* agonie *f.*; angoisse *f.*

agrarian *a.* agraire

agree *vi.* convenir; se mettre d'accord; tomber d'accord; être d'accord; s'accorder; **-d** *a.* convenu; d'accord; **-able** *a.* agréable; consentant; **be -able** vouloir bien; **-ment** *n.* accord *m.*; acte *m.*; contrat *m.*; entente *f.*; **be in -ment** être d'accord

agricultural *a.* agricole

agriculture *n.* agriculture *f.*

agriculturist *n.* agriculteur *m.*

agronomy *n.* agronomie *f.*

aground *adv.* à la côte; **to run —** s'échouer

ahead *adv.* en avant; **get — réussir; go —** continuer, persévérer; aller en avant; **straight —** tout droit

aid *n.* aide, assistance *f.*, secours *m.*; aide *m.*; — *vt.* aider, assister, secourir

ail *vt.* chagriner, causer de la peine; **what -s you?** qu'avez-vous?; **-ing** *a.* souffrant; **-ment** *n.* maladie *f.*, mal *m.*

aileron *n.* aileron *m.*

aim *n.* visée *f.*; but *m.*; objet, dessein *m.*; **-less** *a.* sans but; — *vt.* viser, diriger; mettre en joue; (cannon) pointer

air *n.* air *m.*; chant *m.*; (of a person) mine *f.*; apparence *f.*, aspect *m.*; **on the —** (radio) en train d'être radio-diffusé; à la radio; **give oneself -s, put on -s** se donner des airs; **in the open —** en plein air, à la belle étoile; **— base** terrain d'aviation *m.*; **— blast** coup de vent *m.*; **— brake** frein à air comprimé *m.*; **— chamber** chambre à air *f.*; **— corps** aviation *f.*; **— cushion** matelas pneumatique *m.*; **— force** aviation *f.*; **— freight** frêt aérien; *m.* **— gun** fusil à air comprimé *m.*; **— hole** évent, soupirial *m.*; **— letter** aérogramme *m.*; **— passage** route aérienne *f.*; passage aérien *m.*; **— pocket** trou d'air *m.*; **— power** forces aériennes *f. pl.*; **— pressure** pression atmosphérique *f.*; **— pump** pompe à air *f.*; **— raid** raid (aérien) *m.*; **— shaft** puits d'aérage *m.*; **— valve** soupape à air *f.*; — *vt.* aérer; exhiber, montrer; **-ily** *adv.* légerement; **-iness** *n.* abondance d'air et d'espace dans une pièce *f.*; légèreté *f.*; **-ing** *n.* promenade *f.*; aération *f.*; aérage *m.*; ventilation *f.*; **-y** *a.* aéré; exposé à l'air; léger; chimérique

air age *n.* époque de l'espace *f.*

airborne *a.* porté par les airs; **— troops**

parachutistes *m. pl.*

airbrake *n.* aérofrein *m.*

airbrush *n.* pinceau pneumatique *m.*

air-condition *vt.* climatiser; **-ing** *n.* climatisation *f.*

air-cooled *a.* refroidi par air

aircraft *n.* avion *m.*; **— carrier** *n.* porteavions *m.*

airfield *n.* terrain d'aviation *m.*; aérodrome *m.*

air letter *n.* aérogramme *m.*

airlift *n.* pont aérien *m.*

airline *n.* ligne aérienne *f.*; **-r** *n.* avion pour passagers *m.*

airmail *n.* poste aérienne *f.*; — *adv.* & *a.* par avion

airman *n.* aviateur, soldat de l'air *m.*

airplane *n.* avion *m.*

airport *n.* aéroport, aérodrome *m.*

airship *n.* dirigeable *m.*

air speed *n.* vitesse relative *f.*

airstrip *n.* petit aérodrome *m.*; piste d'atterrissage *f.*

air terminal *n.* aérogare *f.*

airtight *a.* étanche, hermétique

airway *n.* route aérienne *f.*; ligne aérienne *f.*

aisle *n.* passage *m.*

ajar *a.* entr'ouvert

akimbo *adv.* les mains sur les hanches

akin *a.* parent; allié

alabaster *n.* albâtre *m.*

alacrity *n.* vivacité, gaieté *f.*; empressement *m.*

alarm *n.* alarme, épouvante *f.*; réveil *m.*; alerte *f.*; **— signal,** avertisseur *m.*; **sound an —** sonner l'alarme; **— bell** *n.* tocsin *m.*; **— clock** *n.* réveille-matin, réveil *m.*; — *vt.* alarmer; **-ing** *a.* inquiétant; **-ist** *n.* alarmiste *m.*

Albania *n.* Albanie *f.*

albatross *n.* albatros *m.*

albeit *adv.* quoique, bien que

albino *n.* albinos *m.*

album *n.* album *m.*

albumen *n.* (egg) albumine *f.*; (bot.) albumen *m.*

alchemist *n.* alchimiste *m.*

alchemy *n.* alchimie *f.*

alcohol *n.* alcool *m.*; **-ic** *n.* & *a.* alcoolique *m.* & *f.*; **-ism** *n.* alcoolisme *m.*

alcove *n.* alcôve *f.*; niche *f.*

alderman *n.* conseiller municipal *m.*

alert *a.* alerte, éveillé; vif; — *n.* alerte *f.*; **on the —** en éveil; sur le qui-vive; — *vt.* avertir, prévenir; alerter; **-ness** *n.* état d'éveil *m.*, vigilance *f.*; vivacité *f.*

Aleutian Islands *n. pl.* Aléoutiennes *f. pl.*

Alexandria *n.* Alexandrie *f.*

alga (algae) *n.* (*pl.*) algue *f.*

algebra *n.* algèbre *m.*; –ic *a.* algébrique

Algeria *n.* Algérie *f.*; –n *a.* & *n.* algérien *m.*

alias *n.* faux nom *m.*; — *adv.* autrement dit

alien *n.* & *a.* étranger *m.* & *a.*; –ate *vt.* aliéner; –ist *n.* médecin aliéniste *m.*

alight *vi.* descendre, mettre pied à terre; (birds) s'abattre; — *a.* allumé, illuminé

align *vt.* aligner; –ment *n.* alignement *m.*

alike *a.* semblable; pareil; — *adv.* également, de même

alimentary *a.* alimentaire

alimony *n.* pension alimentaire *f.*

alive *a.* vivant; gai; en vie; be — with foisonner de, fourmiller de; grouiller de; dead or — mort ou vif

alkali *n.* alcali *m.*; –ne *a.* alcalin; –ze *vt.* alcaliser

alkaloid *n.* alcaloïde *m.*

all *n.* tout *m.*; — *a.* tout, tous *m. pl.*; — *adv.* tout; entièrement; — aboard! en voiture!; — along tout le temps; — but presque; — clear (mil.) fin d'alerte; il n'y a personne; — day toute la journée; — in (coll.) fatigué, épuisé; — in — somme toute; — of a sudden tout à coup; — of us nous tous; — over (*adv.*) partout; (coll.) fini; — right (*adv.*) bien, pas mal; eh bien; alors; honnête; — set tout prêt; — the better tant mieux; — the same tout de même; — together tous ensemble; above — surtout; at — hours à toute heure; by — means certainement; mais oui; not at — pas du tout, point du tout; on — fours à quatre pattes; once and for — une fois pour toutes; one — (sports) un à un; one and — tout le monde

allay *vt.* apaiser, calmer; modérer, tempérer; dissiper

allegation *n.* allégation *f.*

allege *vt.* alléguer; citer; –d *a.* allégué; présumé

allegiance *n.* obéissance *f.*; fidélité *f.*

allegoric(al) *a.* allégorique

allegory *n.* allégorie *f.*

allergen *n.* (med.) allergène *m.*

allergic *a.* allergique

allergy *n.* allergie *f.*

alleviate *vt.* alléger; soulager; apaiser

alleviation *n.* soulagement *m.*

alley *n.* ruelle *f.*; blind — cul-de-sac *m.*

alliance *n.* alliance *f.*; parenté *f.*

allied *a.* allié; parent; voisin

alligator *n.* alligator *m.*; — pear poire d'avocat *f.*

all-night *a.* ouvert toute la nuit; de toute la nuit

allocate *vt.* attribuer; distribuer, allouer

allocation *n.* (com.) allocation *f.*; attribution *f.*

allot *vt.* accorder, attribuer; –ment *n.* allocation *f.*; part, portion *f.*; (mil.) délégation de solde *f.*

allow *vt.* permettre; laisser; autoriser; allouer; avouer; — for avoir égard à; — oneself se permettre; –able *a.* permis; –ance *n.* argent de poche *m.*; allocation *f.*; indulgence *f.*; part *f.*; make –ances for faire la part de; tenir compte de; –ing for vu, eu égard à

alloy *n.* alliage *m.*; — *vt.* allier

all-powerful *a.* tout-puissant

all-purpose *a.* à tout faire; universel

all-round *a.* universel, varié, complet

All Saints' Day *n.* la Toussaint *f.*

allspice *n.* toute épice *f.*; piment *m.*

all-time *a.* de tous les temps

allude *vi.* faire allusion

allure *vt.* séduire, attirer

alluring *a.* attrayant, séduisant

allusion *n.* allusion *f.*

allusive *a.* figuré, fait par allusion

alluvial *a.* alluvien

ally *n.* allié *m.*; — *vt.* allier

almanac *n.* almanach *m.*

almighty *a.* tout-puissant

almond *n.* amande *f.*; — tree *n.* amandier *m.*

almost *adv.* presque; à peu près

alms *n. pl.* aumône, charité *f.*

aloft *adv.* en haut, en l'air

alone *a.* seul; let me —! laissez-moi tranquille!; — *adv.* seulement

along *adv.* de compagnie; avec; en avant; — *prep.* le long de; get — with s'accomoder avec; s'entendre; go — suivre, longer; go — with accompagner

alongside *prep.* le long de; — *adv.* bord à bord; come — aborder

aloof *a.* à l'écart, distant; –ness réserve *f.*; désintéressement *m.*

aloud *adv.* à haute voix

alpaca *n.* (zool.) alpaca *m.*; (material) alpaga *m.*

alphabet *n.* alphabet *m.*; –ical *a.* alphabétique; –ize *vt.* alphabétiser

alpine *a.* alpin; alpestre

Alps *n.* Alpes *f. pl.*

already *adv.* déjà

Alsace *n.* Alsace *f.*

Alsatian *a.* & *n.* alsatien *m.*

also *adv.* aussi, également, encore

altar *n.* autel *m.*

alter *vt.* altérer; changer; modifier; — *vi.* s'altérer; changer; –ation *n.* changement *m.*; altération *f.*; modification *f.*

alternate *a.* alternatif, alternant, alterné;

(rhyme) croisé; — *n.* suppléant, remplaçant *m.*; **-ly** *adv.* tour à tour, alternativement; — *vi.* alterner; — *vt.* faire alterner

alternating *a.* alternant; — **current** courant alternatif *m.*

alternation *n.* alternation *f.*; alternance *f.*

alternative *n.* alternative *f.*, choix *m.*; — *a.* alternatif

although *conj.* quoique, bien que; encore que

altimeter *n.* altimètre *m.*

altitude *n.* élévation, hauteur *f.*; altitude *f.*

altogether *adv.* entièrement, tout à fait

altruism *n.* altruisme *m.*

altruist *n.* altruiste; **-ic** *a.* altruiste

alum *n.* alun *m.*

aluminum *n.* aluminium *m.*

alumnus *n.* ancien élève *m.*

always *adv.* toujours

A.M. (ante meridiem) du matin

amalgam *n.* amalgame *m.*; **-ate** *vt.* amalgamer; **-ation** *n.* almagamation, fusion, union *f.*

amass *vt.* amasser

amateur *n.* nonprofessionnel, amateur *m.*; **-ish** *a.* gauche, inexpérimenté

amatory *a.* amoureux, d'amour, sentimental

amaze *vt.* étonner, émerveiller; **-ment** *n.* étonnement *m.*

amazing *a.* étonnant

amazon *n.* amazone *f.*

ambassador *n.* ambassadeur *m.*; **-ship** *n.* ambassade *f.*

amber *n.* ambre *m.*

ambidextrous *a.* ambidextre

ambiguity *n.* ambiguïté *f.*

ambiguous *a.* ambigu; confus; équivoque; **-ness** *n.* ambiguïté *f.*

ambition *n.* ambition *f.*

ambitious *a.* ambitieux

amble *vi.* aller doucement; (horses) ambler; — *n.* amble *m.*

ambling *a.* à l'amble

ambrosia *n.* ambroisie *f.*

ambulance *n.* ambulance *f.*

ambulatory *a.* ambulatoire; ambulant

ambush *n.* embuscade *f.*; guet-apens *m.*; **in** — en embuscade, embusqué; à l'affût; — *vt.* embusquer

ameliorate *vt.* améliorer: — *vi.* s'améliorer

amelioration *n.* amélioration *f.*

amen *interj.* amen; (prayer books) ainsi soit-il

amenable *a.* docile, traitable; responsable

amend *vt.* amender, corriger; — *vi.* s'amender; se corriger; **-ment** *n.* amendement *m.*

amends *n. pl.* compensation *f.*, dédommagement *m.*; **to make** — faire amende honorable

amenity *n.* aménité *f.*; **amenities** civilités *f. pl.*; commodités *f. pl.*

America *n.* Amérique *f.*; **North** — Amérique du Nord *f.*; **South** — Amérique du Sud *f.*; **Central** — Amérique Centrale *f.*; **-n** *a.* & *n.* américain *m.*; — **plan** (hotels) prix qui comprend chambre et trois repas *m.*, pension complète *f.*

Americanize *vt.* américaniser

amiability *n.* amabilité *f.*

amiable *a.* aimable; **-ness** *n.* amabilité *f.*

amicability *n.* cordialité, amabilité *f.*

amicable *a.* amical, bienveillant

amidships *adv.* par le travers

amid(st) *prep.* au milieu de, parmi

amiss *adv.* mal, en mal, mal à propos; **take** — prendre en mauvaise part

amity *n.* amitié *f.*

ammeter *n.* ampère-mètre *m.*

ammonia *n.* ammoniaque *f.*; — **gas** *n.* ammoniaque *m.*

ammunition *n.* cartouches *f. pl.*; munitions *f. pl.*

amnesia *n.* amnésie *f.*

amnesty *n.* amnistie *f.*; — *vt.* amnistier

amoeba *n.* amibe *f.*

among(st) *prep.* parmi, entre

amoral *a.* amoral

amorous *a.* amoureux

amorphous *a.* amorphe

amortization *n.* amortissement *m.*

amortize *vt.* amortir

amount *n.* montant, total *m.*; somme, quantité *f.*; — *vi.*, **to** s'élever à revenir à; valoir

amour *n.* amourette *f.*; intrigue *f.*

amperage *n.* ampérage *f.*

ampere *n.* ampère *m.*

ampersand *n.* symbole typographique pour *et m.*

amphibian, amphibious *a.* amphibie

amphitheater *n.* amphithéâtre *m.*

ample *a.* ample, large; **-ness** *n.* ampleur, étendue *f.*

amplification *n.* amplification *f.*

amplifier *n.* amplificateur *m.*

amplify *vt.* amplifier, augmenter

amplitude *n.* largeur *f.*; étendue *f.*; amplitude *f.*

amply *adv.* amplement

amputate *vt.* amputer

amputation *n.* amputation *f.*

amputee *n.* amputé *m.*

amuck *adv.* comme un furieux

amulet *n.* amulette *f.*

amuse *vt.* amuser, divertir; — **onself** s'amuser; **-ment** *n.* amusement *m.*;

divertissement *m.*; –ment park fête foraine *f.*
amusing *a.* amusant; divertissant
an *art.* un, une
anachronism *n.* anachronisme *m.*
anachronistic *a.* anachronique
anaconda *n.* boa (de l'Amérique du Sud) *m.*
anal *a.* anal
analgesic *a. & n.* analgésique *m.*
analogical *a.* analogique
analogous *a.* analogue
analogy *n.* analogie *f.*
analysis *n.* analyse *f.*
analyst *n.* analyste *m.*
analytic(al) *a.* analytique
analyze *vt.* analyser
anarchist *n.* anarchiste *m. & f.*
anarchy *n.* anarchie *f.*
anathema *n.* anathème *m.*; –tize *vt.* anathémiser
anatomical *a.* anatomique
anatomist *n.* anatomiste *m.*
anatomy *n.* anatomie *f.*
ancestor *n.* ancêtre, aïeul *m.*; –s *pl.* aïeux *m. pl.*
ancestral *a.* ancestral; héréditaire
ancestry *n.* lignée *f.*; aïeux *m. pl.*
anchor *n.* ancre *f.*; cast — jeter l'ancre; weigh — lever l'ancre; ride at — être à l'ancre; — *vt.* ancrer; — *vi.* jeter l'ancre; –age *n.* ancrage, mouillage *m.*
anchovy *n.* anchois *m.*
ancient *a.* antique; ancien; –ness *n.* ancienneté *f.*
and *conj.* et; (both) — . . . . — et . . . . et; — so on et ainsi de suite
Andalusia *n.* Andalousie *f.*
Andes *n.* Andes *f. pl.*
andiron *n.* chenet *m.*
Andorra *n.* Andorre *f.*
androgen *n.* (biol.) androgène *m.*
anemia *n.* anémie *f.*
anemic *a.* anémique
anemometer *n.* anémomètre *m.*
aneroid *a.* anéroïde
anesthesia *n.* anesthésie *f.*
anesthetic *n.* anesthétique *m.*
anesthetist *n.* anesthésiste *m.*
anesthetize *vt.* anesthésier
anew *adv.* de nouveau; encore; à neuf
angel *n.* ange *m.*; –ic *a.* angélique
anger *n.* colère *f.*; — *vt.* mettre en colère
angle *n.* angle *m.*; coin *m.*; (coll.) point de vue *m.*; — iron cornière *f.*; — *vi.* pêcher à la ligne; –r *n.* pêcheur (à la ligne) *m.*
angleworm *n.* ver de terre *m.*
Anglican *a.* anglican
Anglicism *n.* anglicisme *m.*

Anglicize *vt.* angliciser
angling *n.* pêche à la ligne *f.*
Anglo-Saxon *a. & n.* anglo-saxon *m.*
Angola *n.* Angola *m.*
angora *n.* angora *m.*
angry *a.* fâché, irrité; become — se mettre en colère; be — with être fâché contre
anguish *n.* angoisse *f.*
angular *a.* anguleux; –ity *n.* angularité *f.*
aniline *n.* aniline *f.*
animal *n. & a.* animal *m.*
animate *vt.* animer; encourager; —, –d *a.* animé
animation *n.* animation *f.*
animosity *n.* animosité *f.*
animus *n.* animosité *f.*
anise *n.* anis *m.*
ankle *n.* cheville *f.*; turn one's — se fouler la cheville
anklet *n.* chaussette courte *f.*; bracelet de cheville *m.*
annals *n. pl.* annales *f. pl.*
anneal *vt.* recuire, tempérer
annex *n.* annexe *f.*; — *vt.* annexer; –ation *n.* annexion *f.*
annihilate *vt.* annihiler, anéantir
annihilation *n.* anéantissement *m.*
anniversary *n.* anniversaire *m.*
annotate *vt.* annoter
annotation *n.* annotation *f.*
annotator *n.* annotateur *m.*
announce *vt.* annoncer; –ment *n.* annonce *f.*; faire-part *m.*; avis *m.*; –r *n.* speaker *m.*
annoy *vt.* ennuyer, troubler, gêner; –ance *n.* ennui *m.*; –ing *a.* ennuyeux
annual *n.* annuaire *m.*; plante annuelle *f.*; — *a.* annuel
annuity *n.* rente *f.*; life — rente viagère *f.*
annul *vt.* annuler, casser; –ment *n.* annulation *f.*; (marriage) dissolution *f.*
Annunciation *n.* Annonciation *f.*
anode *n.* anode *f.*
anodyne *n.* remède anodin *m.*
anoint *vt.* oindre; consacrer, sacrer; –ing *n.* onction *f.*
anomalous *a.* anomal, hétéroclite
anomaly *n.* anomalie *f.*
anon *adv.* bientôt, tout à l'heure
anonymity *n.* anonymat *m.*
anonymous *a.* anonyme
another *a.* un autre; encore un; one — l'un l'autre; les uns les autres — *pron.* autrui
answer *n.* réponse, réplique *f.*; raison *f.*; solution *f.*; — *vt.* répondre; réfuter; — for être responsable de; répondre de –able *a.* responsable
ant *n.* fourmi *f.*

antagonism *n.* antagonisme *m.*
antagonist *n.* antagoniste *m.*; –ic *a.* antagoniste; opposé
antagonize *vt.* contrarier, opposer
antarctic *a.* & *n.* antarctique *m.*
anteater *n.* fourmilier *m.*
antecedence *n.* antécédence *f.*; priorité *f.*
antecedent *n.* & *a.* antécédent *m.*
antechamber *n.* antichambre *f.*
antedate *vt.* précéder; antidater
antediluvian *a.* antédiluvien
antelope *n.* antilope *f.*
antenna *n.* antenne *f.*
anterior *a.* antérieur
anteroom *n.* vestibule *m.*, salle d'attente *f.*
anthem *n.* antienne *f.*; hymne *m.*
anthill *n.* fourmilière *f.*
anthology *n.* anthologie, chrestomathie *f.*
anthracite *n.* anthracite *m.*
anthrax *n.* charbon *m.*
anthropological *a.* anthropologique
anthropologist *n.* anthropologiste *m.*
anthropology *n.* anthropologie *f.*
anthropomorphous *a.* anthropomorphe
antiaircraft *a.* antiavion
antibiotic *n.* & *a.* antibiotique *m.*
antibody *n.* anticorps *m.*
antic *n.* singerie, gambade *f.*
anticipate *vt.* anticiper; devancer, aller au-devant de; prévenir
anticipation *n.* anticipation *f.*; prévision *f.*
anticipatory *a.* par anticipation
anticlerical *a.* anticlérical
anticlimax *n.* dénouement décevant *m.*
antidote *n.* antidote *m.*
anti-electron *n.* anti-électron *m.*
antifreeze *n.* antigel *m.*
antihistamine *n.* antihistamine *f.*
anti-particle *n.* (phy.) antiparticule *f.*
antipathy *n.* antipathie *f.*
antiphony *n.* contre-chant *m.*
antiproton *n.* antiproton *m.*
antiquarian, antiquary *n.* antiquaire *m.*
antiquated *a.* suranné, vieilli
antique *n.* antiquité *f.*; — *a.* ancien
antiquity *n.* antiquité *f.*
antisemitism *n.* antisémitisme *m.*
antiseptic *n.* & *a.* antiseptique *m.*
antisocial *a.* antisocial
antisubmarine *a.* anti-sousmarin
antitank *a.* antichar
antithesis *n.* antithèse *f.*
antitoxin *n.* antitoxine *f.*
antitrust *a.* anticartel
antler *n.* andouiller *m.*
antonym *n.* antonyme *m.*
Antwerp *n.* Anvers *m.*
anus *n.* anus *m.*
anvil *n.* enclume *f.*

anxiety *n.* anxiété, inquiétude *f.*
anxious *a.* inquiet, soucieux: désireux; be — to tenir à; avoir hâte de
any *adj.* du, de la, des; quelque; (ne . . .) aucun; n'importe quel; tout; — *pron.* en; (ne . . .) aucun; n'importe lequel
anybody *pron.* (ne . . .) personne; quelqu'un; n'importe qui; le premier venu
anyhow *adv.* n'importe comment; en tout cas
anyone *pron.* (ne . . .) personne; quelqu'un; n'importe qui; le premier venu
anything *pron.* (ne . . .) rien; quelque chose; n'importe quoi, quoi que ce soit; not for — pour rien au monde
anyway *adv.* n'importe comment; en tout cas
anywhere *adv.* n'importe où, où que ce soit, partout; quelque part, (ne . . .) nulle part
aorta *n.* aorte *f.*
apart *adv.* à part, séparément; — from en dehors de; come — se défaire; take — démonter; tell — distinguer (entre)
apartment *n.* appartement *m.*; — building *n.* immeuble d'habitation *f.*
apathetic *a.* apathique
apathy *n.* apathie *f.*
ape *n.* singe *m.*; — *vt.* singer, imiter
aperture *n.* ouverture *f.*
apex *n.* sommet *m.*, pointe *f.*
aphasia *n.* aphasie *f.*
aphorism *n.* aphorisme *m.*
aphoristic *a.* aphoristique
aphrodisiac *a.* aphrodisiaque
apiary *n.* rucher *m.*
apiece *adv.* par pièce, par tête, chacun
apish *a.* de singe; bouffon
aplomb *n.* aplomb *m.*
Apocalypse *n.* apocalypse *f.*
apocalyptic(al) *a.* apocalyptique
apocryphal *a.* apocryphe
apogee *n.* apogée *m.*
apologetic *a.* d'excuse; apologétique
apologist *n.* apologiste *m.*
apologize *vi.* s'excuser
apology *n.* excuses *f. pl.*; (defense) apologie *f.*
apoplectic *a.* apoplectique
apoplexy *n.* apoplexie *f.*
apostasy *n.* apostasie *f.*
apostate *a.* & *n.* apostat *m.*
apostle *n.* apôtre *m.*
apostolic *a.* apostolique
apostrophe *n.* apostrophe *f.*
apothecary *n.* pharmacien *m.*
appall *vt.* effrayer, consterner; –ing *a.* épouvantable
apparatus *n.* appareil *m.*
apparel *n.* vêtements, habits *m. pl.*

apparent *a.* apparent, visible; évident; (of heirs) présomptif; **-ly** *adv.* apparemment, évidemment

apparition *n.* apparition *f.*

appeal *n.* appel *m.*; charme, attrait *m.*; — *vt.* faire appel (à); se reporter (à); être séduisant; (law) interjeter appel; **-ing** *a.* séduisant, attrayant; sympathique

appear *vi.* apparaître, paraître; sembler; **-ance** *n.* apparition *f.*; aspect *m.*; air *m.*; apparence *f.*; — (book) parution *f.*; **to all -ances** apparemment

appease *vt.* apaiser, calmer; **-ment** *n.* apaisement *m.*

appellate *a.* d'appel; — **court** cour d'appel *f.*

append *vt.* apposer, ajouter; **-age** *n.* dépendance *f.*, accessoire *m.*

appendicitis *n.* appendicite *f.*

appendix *n.* appendice *m.*; (anat.) appendice *m.*

appertain *vi.* appartenir (à), concerner

appetite *n.* appétit *m.*

appetizer *n.* amuse-gueule, hors-d'œuvre *m.*; (drink) apéritif *m.*

appetizing *a.* appétissant

applaud *vt.* applaudir

applause *n.* applaudissements *m. pl.*

apple *n.* pomme *f.*; — **brandy** calvados *m.*; — **core** trognon de pomme *m.*; — **dumpling** *n.* chausson *m.*; — **orchard** *n.* pommeraie *f.*; — **pie** tarte aux pommes *f.*; — **tree** *n.* pommier *m.*; **baked** — pomme cuite *f.*

apple-pie order, in — impeccable; tout ce qu'il y a de mieux

applesauce *n.* compote de pommes *f.*

appliance *n.* appareil *m.*; application *f.*

applicability *n.* applicabilité *f.*

applicant *n.* pétitionneur, solliciteur *m.*; candidat, postulant *m.*

application *n.* application *f.*; demande *f.*; emploi, usage *m.*; attention *f.*; — **blank** *n.* formule *f.*

applied *a.* appliqué; — **arts** arts industriels *m. pl.*

apply *vt.* appliquer; employer; — **for** solliciter; — **to** s'adresser à

appoint *vt.* fixer, nommer, désigner; **-ed** *a.* désigné, dit, convenu; **-ee** *n.* fonctionnaire nommé *m.*; **-ment** *n.* rendez-vous *m.*; nomination *f.*; équipement *m.*

apportion *vt.* répartir, partager; **-ment** *n.* répartition *f.*, partage *m.*

apposite *a.* convenable, à propos

appraisal *n.* évaluation, estimation, expertise *f.*

appraise *vt.* priser, évaluer, estimer

appraiser *n.* estimateur, commissaire-priseur *m.*

appreciable *a.* appréciable; sensible

appreciably *adv.* sensiblement

appreciate *vt.* apprécier, évaluer; comprendre, se rendre compte de

appreciation *n.* appréciation *f.*; évaluation, estimation *f.*; augmentation de valeur *f.*

appreciative *a.* reconnaissant; sensible

apprehend *vt.* appréhender; saisir; redouter

apprehension *n.* appréhension, crainte *f.*

apprehensive *a.* craintif, inquiet; **become** — **about** redouter

apprentice *n.* apprenti *m.*; — *vt.* mettre en apprentissage; **-ship** *n.* apprentissage *m.*

apprise *vt.* apprendre; informer

approach *n.* approche *f.*, accès, abord *m.*; — *vt.* approcher; s'approcher de; **-able** *a.* abordable

appropriate *vt.* approprier; — **to oneself** s'approprier; — *a.* approprié, convenable; à propos; **-ness** *n.* convenance, justesse *f.*

appropriation *n.* affectation *f.*; appropriation *f.*

approval *n.* approbation *f.*; **on** — (envoi) au choix, à condition

approve *vt.* approuver; **-r** *n.* approbateur *m.*

approving *a.* approbateur

approximate *vt.* approcher; s'approcher de; — *a.* approximatif

approximation *n.* approximation *f.*

appurtenance *n.* dépendance *f.*, accessoire *m.*

apricot *n.* abricot *m.*; — **tree** *n.* abricotier *m.*

April *n.* avril *m.*; — **Fool's Day** premier avril *m.*; — **fool's joke** poisson d'avril *m.*

apron *n.* tablier *m.*; **he is tied to his mother's** — **strings** il est pendu aux jupes de sa mère

apropos *a.* à propos

apt *a.* apte; propre, enclin à; prompt, porté à; à propos; **-ness** *n.* aptitude, convenance *f.*

aptitude *n.* aptitude, disposition *f.*; talent *m.*

aqualung *n.* aquapoumon *m.*

aquamarine *n.* aigue-marine *f.*

aquaplane *n.* aquaplane *m.*

aquarium *n.* aquarium *m.*

aquatic *n.* aquatique

aqueduct *n.* aqueduc *m.*

aquiline *a.* aquilin

Arab *n.* Arabe *m. & f.*; **-ia** *n.* Arabie *f.*; **Saudi -ia** *n.* Arabie Soudite *f.*; **-ian** *a. & n.* arabe *m.*; **-ic** *a. & n.* arabe *m.*

arable *a.* labourable

arbiter *n.* arbitre *m.*

arbitrary a. arbitraire
arbitrate vt. arbitrer, déterminer, juger
arbitration n. arbitrage m.
arbitrator n. arbitre m.
arbor n. berceau m.; tonnelle, treille f.
arbutus n. aubépine f.
arc n. arc m.; — **light** arc voltaïque m.
arch n. arche f. voûte f.; arc m.; **fallen** —**es** pied bot m.; — vt. voûter; arrondir — a. espiègle; -**ed** a. cintré; voûté
archaeologist n. archéologue m.
archaeology n. archéologie f.
archaic a. archaïque
archaism n. archaïsme m.
archangel n. archange m.
archbishop n. archevêque m.
archduchess n. archiduchesse f.
archduke n. archiduc m.
archer n. archer m.; -**y** n. tir à l'arc m.
archetype n. archétype, prototype m.
archipelago n. archipel m.
architect n. architecte m.; -**ural** a. architectural; -**ure** n. architecture f.
archives n. pl. archives f. pl.
archivist n. archiviste m. & f.
archway n. voûte f.
arctic a. arctique
arc-weld vt. souder à l'arc
ardent a. ardent, violent; -**ly** adv. ardemment
ardor n. ardeur f.
arduous a. ardu; rude; difficile; -**ness** n. difficulté f.
area n. région f.; surface f.; superficie f.; aire f.; zone f.
area code number n. code de district m.
arena n. arène f.; arènes f. pl.
Argentina n. Argentine f.
Argentine n. & a. Argentin m.
argon n. argon m.
arguable a. discutable
argue vt. discuter; soutenir; démontrer; — vi. discuter, disputer; argumenter
argument n. argument m.; discussion f.; -**ation** n. argumentation f.; -**ative** a. disposé à argumenter
aria n. air m.
arid a. aride; -**ity** n. aridité f.
arise vi. s'élever; provenir, résulter
aristocracy n. aristocratie f.
aristocrat n. aristocrate m.; -**ic** a. aristocratique
Aristotle n. Aristote m.
arithmetic n. arithmétique f.; -**al** a. arithmétique; -**ian** n. arithméticien m.
ark n. arche f.; — **of the covenant** arche d'alliance f.; **Noah's** — arche de Noé f.
arm n. bras m.; arme f.; — **in** — bras dessus, bras dessous; **bear** —**s** porter les armes; **be up in** —**s** être en rébellion;

fold one's —**s** croiser les bras; **small** —**s** armes portatives f. pl.; — vt. armer; s'armer; -**s** n. pl. armoiries f. pl.
armada n. armada f.
armadillo n. tatou m.
armament n. armement m.
armature n. armature f.
armband n. brassard m.
armchair n. fauteuil m.
Armenia n. Arménie f.
armful n. brassée f.
armhole n. entournure f.
armistice n. armistice m., trève f.
armor n. armure f.; blindage m., cuirasse f.; — **plate** plaque de blindage f.; — vt. blinder, cuirasser; -**ed** a. blindé; -**er** n. armurier m.; -**ial** a. armorial; d'armoiries; -**y** n. arsenal m.; fabrique d'armes
armor-plated a. blindé, cuirassé
armpit n. aisselle f.
arm-rest n. accoudoir m.
army n. armée f.
aroma n. arome m.; -**tic** a. aromatique
around prep. autour de; — adv. autour, à la ronde; quelque part; (approximation) à peu près. environ
arouse vt. soulever; éveiller; exciter
arraign vt. (law) accuser; -**ment** n. accusation f.
arrange vt. arranger, mettre en ordre; ranger; régler; disposer; -**ment** n. arrangement m.; disposition f.; (mus.) adaptation f.
array n. ordre de bataille m.; rang m., rangée f.; étalage m.; parure f.; — vt. ranger
arrears n. pl. arriéré m.; **be in** — avoir de l'arriéré
arrest n. arrestation f.; arrêt m.; **place under** — mettre aux arrêts; — vt. arrêter
arrival n. arrivée f.
arrive vi. arriver; parvenir; — **at** arriver à; gagner, atteindre
arrow n. flèche f.
arrowhead n. pointe de flèche f.
arson n. crime d'incendie volontaire m.
art n. art m.; habileté f.; artifice m.; -**s and crafts** arts et métiers m. pl.; **the fine** —**s** les beaux-arts; -**ful** a. habile; artificieux; fait avec art; -**isan** n. artisan m.; -**ist** n. artiste m.; peintre m.; -**istic** a. artistique; -**istry** n. art m.; -**less** a. sans art, simple; -**lessness** n. ingenuité, candeur, naïveté f.
arterial a. artériel
arteriosclerosis n. artériosclérose f.
artery n. artère f.
artesian a. artésien
arthritic a. arthritique

arthritis *n.* arthrite *f.*
artichoke *n.* artichaut *m.*
article *n.* article *m.*; condition, stipulation *f.*
articulate *vt.* articuler; énoncer; — *a.* articulé
articulation *n.* articulation *f.*
artifice *n.* artifice *m.*
artificial *a.* artificiel; factice; **-ity** caractère artificiel *m.*
artillery *n.* artillerie *f.*; **-man** *n.* artilleur
Aryan *n. & a.* Aryen *m.*
as *conj.* comme; aussi; que; selon que; suivant, tandis que; puisque; — **far** — jusqu'à; — **far** — **I am concerned** quant à moi; — **for** quant à; — **good** — aussi bon que; — **is** tel quel; — **of** en date du; — **well** — aussi bien que; comme; — **if** comme si; — **it were** pour ainsi dire; — **regards** en ce qui concerne; — **soon** — aussitôt que; — **though** comme si; — **yet** jusqu'ici; **act** — servir de; agir en
asbestos *n.* asbeste, amiante *m.*
ascend *vi. & vt.* monter; — *vt.* s'élever; **-ancy, -ent** *n.* ascendant *m.*
ascension *n.* ascension *f.*
ascent *n.* montée *f.*; ascension *f.*
ascertain *vt.* s'assurer de; prouver; constater, reconnaître; s'informer, vérifier; **-able** *a.* vérifiable, reconnaissable
ascetic *n.* ascète *m.*; — *a.* ascétique; **-ism** *n.* ascétisme *m.*
ascribable *a.* imputable
ascribe *vt.* attribuer, imputer
aseptic *n. & a.* aseptique *m.*
ash *n.* cendres *f. pl.*; (bot.) frêne *m.*; — **tray** cendrier *m.*; **Ash Wednesday** mercredi des cendres *m.*; **-en** *a.* couleur de cendre
ashamed *a.* honteux; **be** — avoir honte
ash-blond *a.* blond cendré
ashore *adv.* à terre; **go** — débarquer
Asia *n.* Asie *f.*; — **Minor** Asie Mineure *f.*; **-n, -tic** *n. & a.* Asiatique *m.*
aside *adv.* de côté, à part; à l'écart; — **from** à part; **lay, put, set** — mettre de côté; **to turn** — (se) détourner; — *n.* aparté *m.*
asinine *a.* d'âne
ask *vt.* demander; réclamer; — **a question** poser une question; — **for** demander; demander à voir
askance *adv.* obliquement, de travers
askew *adv.* de biais
asleep *adv.* endormi; **be** — dormir, être endormi; **fall** — s'endormir
asp *n.* aspic *m.*
asparagus *n.* asperges *f. pl.*
aspect *n.* aspect *m.*, mine *f.*, air *m.*

aspen *n.* tremble *m.*
asperity *n.* aspérité, âpreté *f.*
aspersion *n.* aspersion *f.*; diffamation *f.*
asphalt *n.* asphalte *m.*; bitume *m.*; — *vt.* asphalter
asphyxia *n.* asphyxie *f.*; **-te** *vt.* asphyxier
aspic *n.* gelée *f.*
aspirant *n.* candidat, aspirant, *m.*
aspirate *vt.* aspirer; — *a.* aspiré
aspiration *n.* aspiration *f.*, désir ardent *m.*
aspire *vi.* souhaiter ardemment; prétendre (à); aspirer (à)
aspirin *n.* aspirine *f.*
aspiring *a.* qui aspire; ambitieux
ass *n.* âne *m.*, ânesse *f.*
assail *vt.* assaillir, attaquer; **-able** *a.* attaquable; **-ant** *n.* assaillant *m.*
assassin *n.* assassin *m.*; **-ate** *vt.* assassiner; **-ation** *n.* assassinat *m.*
assault *n.* assaut *m.*; attaque *f.*; atteinte *f.*; viol *m.*; — **and battery** menaces et voies de fait *f. pl.*; — *vt.* assaillir; attaquer; violer
assay *n.* essai, examen *m.*; — *vt.* essayer, éprouver; **-er** *n.* essayeur *m.*; **-ing** *n.* essai *m.*
assemblage *n.* assemblage *m.*; réunion *f.*
assemble *vt.* assembler, rassembler; — *vi.* s'assembler, se rassembler
assembly *n.* assemblée, réunion *f.*; assemblage, montage *m.*; — **line production** fabrication en série *f.*
assemblyman *n.* député *m.*
assent *n.* consentement *m.*; assentiment *m.*; — *vi.* consentir (à); — **to** approuver
assert *vt.* affirmer, maintenir, défendre; revendiquer; faire valoir; **-ion** *n.* affirmation *f.*; **-ive** *a.* assuré; **-iveness** *n.* assurance *f.*
assess *vt.* taxer, imposer, évaluer; **-ment** *n.* répartition *f.* (d'impôts); évaluation *f.*; cote *f.*; **-or** *n.* contrôleur-répartiteur *m.*
asset *n.* bien *m.*; **-s** *pl.* actif *m.*; avoir *m.*
assiduity *n.* assiduité *f.*
assiduous *a.* assidu; **-ly** *adv.* assidûment; **-ness** *n.* assiduité *f.*
assign *vt.* assigner, désigner; attribuer; **-ment** *n.* attribution, désignation *f.* (school) devoir *m.*
assimilate *vt.* assimiler; — *vi.* s'assimiler
assimilation *n.* assimilation *f.*
assist *vt.* aider, secourir; **-ance** *n.* aide *f.*, secours *m.*; **-ant** *n. & a.* assistant, adjoint *m.*
assizes *n. pl.* assises *f. pl.*
associate *n. & a.* associé, adjoint *m.*; — *vt.* associer; — *vi.* s'associer; — **with** fréquenter
association *n.* association, alliance *f.*;

union, société *f.*

assort *vt.* assortir; **–ment** *n.* assortiment *m.*

assuage *vt.* apaiser, soulager

assume *vt.* présumer, supposer; se charger de; prendre; **–d** *a.* d'emprunt; feint; supposé

assuming *a.* prétentieux; **— (that)** en supposant que

assumption *n.* présomption *f.*; (eccl.) Assomption *f.*

assurance *n.* assurance, confiance *f.*; promesse *f.*

assure *vt.* assurer, garantir; **–dly** *adv.* assurément

asterisk *n.* astérisque *m.*

astern *adv.* à l'arrière, en arrière

asteroid *n.* astéroïde *m.*

asthma *n.* asthme *m.*; **–tic** *a.* asthmatique

astigmatic *a.* astigmate

astigmatism *n.* astigmatisme *m.*

astonish *vt.* étonner; **–ing** *a.* étonnant; **–ment** *a.* étonnement *m.*

astound *vt.* étonner, ahurir, stupéfier

astraddle *adv.* à califourchon

astray *a. & adv.* égaré; **go — ** s'égarer; **lead — ** égarer

astride *adv.* à califourchon

astringency *n.* astringence *f.*

astringent *n. & a.* astringent *m.*

astrologer *n.* astrologue *m.*

astrological *a.* astrologique

astrology *n.* astrologie *f.*

astronaut *n.* astronaute *m.*

astronomer *n.* astronome *m.*

astronomical *a.* astronomique

astronomy *n.* astronomie *f.*

astute *a.* fin, rusé; **–ness** *n.* finesse, astuce *f.*

asunder *adv.* à part l'un de l'autre

asylum *n.* asile, refuge *m.*; hospice *m.*; **insane, lunatic — ** asile d'aliénés *f.*

asymmetric(al) *a.* asymétrique

at *prep.* à, dans; en; sur; après; contre; **— all** du tout; **— all costs** à tout prix; **— all events** en tout cas; **— first** d'abord; **— home** à la maison; **— large** libre; **— last** enfin; **— least** au moins; **— length** in extenso; à la longue; **— once** tout de suite; **— peace** en paix; **— pleasure** à loisir; **— your house** chez vous; **— sea** en pleine mer; **— stake** en jeu; **— times** à moments; **— war** en guerre; **— will** à volonté; **— work** au travail; **— your service** à votre service

atavistic *a.* atavique

Athenian *a. & n.* athénien *m.*

Athens *n.* Athènes

atheism *n.* athéisme *m.*

atheist *n.* athée *m.*; **–ic** *a.* athée

athlete *n.* athlète *m.*; **–'s foot** favus (du pied) *m.*

athletic *a.* athlétique; **–s** *n. pl.* athlétisme *m.*

Atlantic Ocean *n.* Océan Atlantique *m.*

atmosphere *n.* atmosphère *f.*; ambiance *f.*

atmospheric *a.* atmosphérique

atom *n.* atome *m.*; **–(ic) bomb** bombe atomique *f.*; **–ic** *a.* atomique; **–ic pile** réacteur atomique *m.*

atomizer *n.* vaporisateur *m.*

atone *vi. & vt.*; **— (for)** expier; racheter; **–ment** *n.* expiation *f.*

atonic *a.* atone; (anat.) atonique

atop *adv.* en haut, au sommet

atrocious *a.* atroce

atrocity *n.* atrocité *f.*

atrophy *n.* atrophie *f.*; **— ** *vi.* s'atrophier

attach *vt.* attacher, fixer; saisir; **be –ed to** se rattacher à; **–ment** *n.* attachement *m.*; accessoire *m.*

attaché *m.* attaché *m.*; **— case** mallette *f.*, porte-documents *m.*

attack *n.* attaque *f.*, assaut *m.*; crise *f.*, accès *m.*; **— ** *vt.* attaquer, assaillir; **–er** *n.* attaquant *m.*

attain *vt.* atteindre, obtenir; **— ** *vi.* parvenir (à); **–able** *a.* qu'on peut atteindre; **–ment** *n.* talent *m.*, connaissance *f.*; réalisation *f.*

attar *n.* essence (de rose) *f.*

attempt *n.* essai *m.*; tentative *f.*, effort *m.*; **— ** *vt.* tenter, essayer; **–ed** *a.*, **–ed murder** tentative d'assassinat *f.*

attend *vt.* assister à; servir, soigner; **— to** s'occuper de; se charger de; **–ance** *n.* assistance *f.*; présence *f.*; **–ant** *n.* serviteur, aide *m.*; **–ant** *a.* attenant, qui accompagne

attention *n.* attention *f.*; (mil.) garde à vous *m.*; **attract — ** se faire remarquer; **pay — ** faire attention

attentive *a.* attentif; prévenant; **–ness** *n.* attention *f.*

attenuate *vt.* atténuer

attenuation *n.* atténuation *f.*

attest *vt.* attester, certifier; **–ation** *n.* attestation, certification *f.*

attic *n.* mansarde *f.*; comble *m.*

attire *n.* vêtement, habillement *m.*, parure *f.*; **— ** *vt.* vêtir, parer

attitude *n.* attitude, posture *f.*

attorney *n.* avocat *m.*; avoué *m.*; **district — ** procureur *m.*; notaire *m.*; **— general** ministre de la justice *m.*; **power of — ** procuration *f.*

attract *vt.* attirer; entraîner; séduire; **–ion** *n.* attraction *f.*, attrait *m.*; **–ive** *a.* séduisant; attrayant; attractif; **–ive-**

ness *n.* attrait, charme *m.*

attributable *a.* attribuable, imputable

attribute *vt.* attribuer, imputer; — *n.* attribut *m.*

attribution *n.* attribution *f.*

attributive *a.*, — adjective adjectif qualificatif *m.*

attrition *n.* attrition *f.*; usure *f.*

attune *vt.* accorder

auburn *n. & a.* châtain clair *m.*

auction *n.* vente aux enchères *f.*; — *vt.* vendre aux enchères; —eer *n.* commissaire-priseur *m.*; crieur *m.*

audacious *a.* audacieux

audacity *n.* audace *f.*; hardiesse *f.*

audible *a.* distinct (à l'oreille)

audience *n.* auditoire *m.*, assistance *f.* audience *f.*

audiology *n.* audiologie *f.*

audiometer *n.* audiomètre *m.*

audit *n.* vérification de comptes *f.*; — *vt.* vérifier; visiter (un cours universitaire); —or *n.* vérificateur *m.*; (school) visiteur *m.*

audio *a.* (coll.) qui se rapporte au son radiodiffusé d'une émission télévisée

audition *n.* audition *f.*; ouïe *f.*

auditorium *n.* salle *f.*

auditory *a.* auditif

auger *n.* tarière *f.*

augment *vt.* augmenter; — *vi.* s'accroître; —ation *n.* augmentation *f.*; —ative *a.* augmentatif

augur *vt.* augurer; — *n.* augure *m.*

August *n.* août *m.*

august *a.* auguste

aunt *n.* tante *f.*

aura *n.* émanation *f.*; souffle *m.*

aural *a.* de l'oreille

aureomycin *n.* auréomycin *m.*

auricle *n.* auricule *f.*; (anat.) oreillette *f.*

auspices *n. pl.* auspices *m. pl.*

auspicious *a.* propice, favorable

austere *a.* austère, sévère

austerity *n.* austérité *f.*

Australia *n.* Australie *f.*; —n *n. & a.* Australien *m.*

Austria *n.* Autriche *f.*; —n *n. & a.* Autrichien *m.*

authentic *a.* authentique; vrai, véritable; conforme; —ate *vt.* vérifier, certifier, viser; —ity *n.* authenticité *f.*

author *n.* auteur *m.*; —ess *n.* femme auteur *f.*; —ship *n.* paternité (littéraire) *f.*

authoritarian *a. & n.* autoritaire *m.*

authoritative *a.* autoritaire; —ness *n.* autorité *f.*

authority *n.* autorité *f.*; mandat, pouvoir *m.*; on good — de bonne source

authorization *n.* autorisation *f.*

authorize *vt.* autoriser

autobiographer *n.* autobiographe *m.*

autobiographical *a.* autobiographique

autobiography *n.* autobiographie *f.*

autocade *n.* défieé des voitures *m.*

autocrat *n.* autocrate *m.*; —ic *a.* autocratique

autogiro *n.* hélicoptère *m.*

autograph *n.* autographe *m.*; — *vt.* signer

automatic *a.* automatique; — tracking *n.* poursuite automatique *f.*

automation *n.* automation *f.*

automaton *n.* automate *m.*

automobile *n.* automobile *f.*

automotive *a.* automobile

autonomous *a.* autonome

autumn *n.* automne *m.*; —al *a.* automnal

auxiliary *n. & a.* auxiliaire, assistant *m.*

avail *n.* utilité *f.*, secours *m.*; — *vt.* servir; — oneself of se servir de, profiter de; —able *a.* disponible; utilisable; —ibility *n.* disponibilité *f.*

avaricious *a.* avare

avenge *vt.* venger; —r *n.* vengeur *m.*

avenue *n.* avenue *f.*; boulevard *m.*

aver *vt.* affirmer

average *n.* moyenne *f.*; on the — en moyenne; — *vt.* calculer la moyenne; — *vi.* atteindre une moyenne de (vitesse, distance, consommation); — *a.* moyen

averse *a.* contraire, opposé

aversion *n.* aversion *f.*; répugnance *f.*

avert *vt.* détourner, écarter

aviator *n.* aviateur *m.*

avid *a.* avide; —ity *n.* avidité *f.*

avocado *n.* poire d'avocat *f.*

avocation *n.* occupation *f.*; distraction *f.*, délaissement *m.*

avoid *vt.* éviter; —able *a.* évitable; —ance *n.* action d'éviter *f.*

avow *vt.* avouer, confesser; —al *n.* aveu *m.*

await *vt.* attendre

awake *vi.* se réveiller; s'éveiller; — *a.* éveillé; —n *vt.* éveiller, réveiller; —ning *n.* réveil *m.*

award *n.* jugement *m.*; récompense *f.*, prix *m.*; — *vt.* décerner; adjuger

aware *a.* conscient, au courant; —ness *n.* conscience *f.*

awash *a.* à fleur d'eau; surnageant

away *a.* absent; loin; — *adv.* au loin, loin; go — s'en aller; take — enlever; send — renvoyer; right — tout de suite

awe *n.* crainte *f.*, respect *m.*; — *vt.* effrayer, impressionner

awe-inspiring, awesome *a.* impressionnant

awe-struck *a.* effrayé, impressionné

awful *a.* terrible; affreux; imposant

awhile *adv.* un peu, un moment

awkward *a.* gauche; maladroit; (situation) gênant; **—ness** *n.* maladresse *f.*

awl *n.* alène *f.*, poinçon *m.*

awning *n.* tente *f.*; abri *m.*; store *m.*

awry *adv.* de travers

ax, axe *n.* hache *f.*

axiom *n.* axiome *m.*; **—atic** *a.* axiomatique

axis *n.* axe *m.*

axle *n.* essieu *m.*; arbre *m.*

ay, aye *n.* & *adv.* oui *m.*; **—** *adv.* toujours

Azores *n.* Açores *f. pl.*

azure *n.* azur *m.*; **—** *a.* azuré, d'azur

B

B.A.: Bachelor of Arts *n.* bachelier ès lettres *m.*

babble *n.* babil *m.*; **—** *vi.* bavarder, parler avec incohérence; babiller, murmurer; **—r** *n.* babillard *m.*

babbling *a.* babillard; (brook) murmurant; **—** *n.* babil *m.*

babe *n.* bébé *m.*

babel *n.* tumulte *m.*; confusion *f.*

baboon *n.* babouin *m.*

babushka *n.* fichu (porté à la tête) *m.*

baby *n.* bébé *m.*; **—** *a.* de bébé; **— carriage** *n.* landau *m.*, poussette *f.*; **— grand piano** piano à, queue *m.*; **—hood** première enfance *f.*; **—ish** *a.* enfantin; **—** *vt.* traiter d'enfant; amadouer

baccalaureate *n.* baccalauréat *m.*

bachelor *n.* célibataire, garçon *m.*; (educ.) bachelier *m.*; **—hood** *n.* célibat *m.*; **—'s-button** *n.* (bot.) bluet *m.*; **—'s degree** baccalauréat *m.*

bacillus *n.* bacille *m.*

back *n.* dos *m.*, derrière *f.*; dossier *m.*; verso *m.*; fond *m.*; revers *m.*; **— to** dos à dos; **behind one's —** à l'insu de; **— talk** (coll.) impertinence, réponse, impertinente *f.*; **turn one's —** tourner le dos; **—** *a.* de derrière; dorsal; **— door** porte de derrière *f.*; **— number** numéro ancien (d'un journal) *m.*; **— payment** arriéré *m.*; **— seat** siege de derrière *m.*; **— stairs** escalier de service *m.*; **-street** ruelle *f.*; **—** *adv.* en arrière, à l'arrière; de retour; en retour; **— and forth** de long en large; (in) **— of** derrière; **bring —** rapporter; **come —** revenir; **give —** rendre; go **—** retourner; **go —** on ne pas tenir (la parole donnée); **—** *vt.* soutenir, subventionner, seconder; parier pour; mettre un dos à; servir de dos (fond) à; **—** *vi.* reculer; faire reculer; aller (faire aller) en marche arrière; **— down, — out** se

dédire; se soustraire (à); **— up** reculer; **-er** *n.* soutien *m.*; **-ing** *n.* appui *m.*; subvention *f.*

backbite *vt.* calomnier

backboard *n.* dossier *m.*

backbone *n.* épine dorsale *f.*

backbreaking *a.* dur; éreintant

backdrop *n.* toile de fond *f.*

backfire *n.* (engine) contre-allumage *m.*; (firefighting) contre-feu *m.*; **—** *vi.* pétarder; (fig.) retomber

backgammon *n.* trictrac *m.*

background *n.* fond *m.*

backhanded *a.* donné avec le revers de la main; (fig.) immoral

backlash *n.* contre-coup *m.*

backlog *n.* accummulation de travail *f.* (qui reste à faire)

backpedal *vi.* contre-pédaler; (fig.) reculer

backslide *vi.* retomber

backstage *adv.* dans les coulisses

backstroke *n.* brasse (sur le dos) *f.*

backtrack *vi.* rebrousser chemin

backward *adv.* en arrière, à la renverse; **—** *a.* arriéré; **-ness** *n.* retard *m.*

backwash *n.* remous *m.*

backwoodsman *n.* homme des forêts, homme des frontières *m.*

bacon *n.* lard *m.*; bacon *m.*

bacteria *n. pl.* bactéries *f. pl.*

bacteriologist *n.* bactériologiste *m.*

bacteriology *n.* bactériologie *f.*

bad *a.* mauvais, méchant; grave, sérieux; **from — to worse** de mal en pire; **too —** dommage; **— debt** mauvaise créance *f.*; **-ly** *adv.* mal; gravement; **want -ly** avoir grande envie de

badge *n.* plaque *f.*; insigne *m.*

badger *n.* blaireau *m.*; **—** *vt.* harceler

badminton *n.* badminton *m.*

baffle *vt.* confondre, déjouer

bag *n.* sac *m.*; **sleeping —** sac de couchage *m.*; **be left holding the —** être dupé; **—** *vt.* mettre en sac; (hunting) prendre; faire une poche; **-gy** *a.* qui font une poche

bagful *n.* sachée *f.*

baggage *n.* bagage *m.*; **to be off bag and —** plier bagage; **— car** fourgon *m.*; **— check** bulletin des bagages *m.*; **excess —** excédent de bagages *m.*

Bahamas *n.* Bahamas *m. pl.*

bagpipe *n.* cornemuse *f.*

bail *n.* caution *f.*; **be out on —** être libre sous caution; **put up —** se porter caution (pour); **—** *vt.* cautionner; **— out** (law) se porter caution pour; (avi.) sauter en parachute; (naut.) écoper

bailiff *n.* huissier *m.*; bailli *m.*

bailiwick *n.* bailliage *m.*; rayon *m.*

bait *n.* appât *m.*, amorce *f.*; — *vt.* amorcer;
appâter, leurrer; harceler
bake *vt. & vi.* cuire au four; faire le pain,
boulanger; **half -d** prématuré, pas assez
mûri; **-r** *n.* boulanger *m.*; **-r's dozen**
treize; **-ry** *n.* boulangerie *f.*
baking *n.* cuisson au four *f.*; — **powder**
levure chimique *f.*; — **soda** bicarbonate
de soude *m.*
balance *n.* balance *f.*; équilibre *m.*; solde
d'un compte *m.*; — **sheet** *n.* bilan *m.*;
— *vt.* peser, balancer; équilibrer; —
vi. hésiter; **-d** *a.* équilibré
balancing *n.* balancement *m.*; équilibre
m.; (com.) solde *m.*
balcony *n.* balcon *m.*; galerie *f.*
bald *a.* chauve; nu; **-ness** *n.* calvitie *f.*
bale *n.* balle *f.* paquet *m.*; — *vt.* emballer
balearic *a.* baléare
baleful *a.* triste; fatal, funeste
balk *vt.* désappointer, frustrer; — *vi.*
regimber; hésiter; reculer; **-y** *a.* rétif:
hésitant, récalcitrant
Balkans *n.* Balkans *m. pl.*
ball *n.* balle, boule *f.*, ballon *m.*; globe
m.; bal *m.*; — **bearing** bille *f.*; roulement à billes *m.*; **masked** — bal
masqué
ballad *n.* romance, chanson populaire *f.*
ballast *n.* lest *m.*; (rail.) ballast *m.*; —
vt. lester; (rail.) empierrer
ballerina *n.* danseuse *f.*; **prima** — première danseuse *f.*
ballistic *a.* balistique; **-s** *n.* balistique *f.*
— **missile** *n.* projectile balistique *m.*
balloon *n.* ballon *m.*; aérostat *m.*; **-ist** *n.*
aérostier *m.*
ballot *n.* scrutin *m.*; bulletin de vote *m.*;
— **box** urne *f.*; — *vi.* voter; **-ing** *n.*
vote, scrutin *m.*
ballroom *n.* salle de danse *f.*
ballyhoo *n.* publicité extravagante *f.*
balm *n.* baume *m.*; (fig.) soulagement *m.*;
-y *a.* balsamique; (coll.) loufoque
balsam *n.* baume *m.*
Baltic Sea *n.* Mer Baltique *f.*
bamboo *n.* bambou *m.*
ban *vt.* empêcher, interdire; — *n.* interdiction *f.*
banal *a.* banal; **-ity** *n.* banalité *f.*
banana *n.* banane *f.*; — **tree** bananier *m.*
band *n.* lien *m.*; ruban *m.*; bande *f.*;
clique *f.*; musiciens *m. pl.*; musique,
fanfare *f.*; (mus.) (coll.) orchestre *m.*;
military — musique militaire *f.*; —
vt. entourer de bandes, bander; marquer de bandes; — **together** se grouper
bandbox *n.* carton de modiste *m.*
bandage *n.* pansement *m.*; — *vt.* panser
bandleader *n.* chef d'orchestre *m.*

bandstand *n.* kiosque *m.*
bandwagon *n.* char des victorieux *m.*;
majorité victorieuse *f.*; **climb, jump on**
the — suivre la majorité
bandy *vt.* discuter
bane *n.* poison *m.*; ruine *f.*; **-ful** *a.* funeste,
nuisible
bang *n.* coup *m.*, tape *f.*; — *vt.* rosser;
fermer avec bruit; —! pan!
bangle *n.* bijou, bracelet *m.*
bangs *n. pl.* frange *f.* (de cheveux)
banish *vt.* bannir, exiler; **-ment** *n.*
bannissement, exil *m.*
banister *n.* rampe *f.*
bank *n.* digue *f.*; bord, rivage *m.*; banc
m.; banque *f.*; — *vt.* terrasser; déposer
(de l'argent dans une banque); (avi.)
virer; — **on** compter sur; **-er** *n.*
banquier *m.*; **-ing** *n.* actions de
banque *f. pl.*
bankbook *n.* carnet de banque *m.*
bank note *n.* billet de banque *m.*
bankrupt *a.* en faillite; — *n.* banqueroutier *m.*; **go** — faire banqueroute; — *vt.*
réduire à la faillite; **-cy** *n.* banqueroute
f.
banner *n.* bannière *f.*
banquet *n.* banquet, festin *m.*; — *vi.*
banqueter
bantamweight *n.* poids bantam *m.*
banter *n.* raillerie, plaisanterie *f.*; — *vt.*
railler, plaisanter
baptism *n.* baptême *m.*; **-al** *a.* de baptême,
baptismal
baptistry *n.* baptistère *m.*
baptize *vt.* baptiser
bar *n.* barre, barrière *f.*; (mus.) mesure *f.*;
barreau *m.*; (fig.) empêchement *m.*;
obstacle *m.*; **candy** — *n.* tablette *f.*;
bar *m.*; **be admitted to the** — être reçu
avocat; **prisoner at the** — prisonnier
devant le banc des accusés *m.*; — *vt.*
empêcher, interdire; barrer; excepter;
-red *a.* barré, à barreaux; **-ring** *prep.*
sauf
barb *n.* barbillon *m.*; **-ed** *a.* pointu; **-ed**
wire fil de fer barbelé *m.*
Barbados *n.* Barbade *f.*
barbarian *n. & a.* barbare *m.*
barbaric *a.* barbare
barbarous *a.* barbare; **-ness** *n.* barabarie
f.
barbecue *vt.* faire rôtir en entier; griller
à la sauce piquante; — *n.* pique-nique
m., grillade (faite en plein air) *f.*
barber *n.* coiffeur *m.*; — **shop** salon de
coiffure *m.*
barbiturate *n. & a.* barbiturique *m.*
bard *n.* barde, poète *m.*
bare *a.* nu, découvert; simple; — *vt.*

mettre à nu; –ly *adv.* à peine; juste
bareback *adv.* à nu
barefaced *a.* impudent, effronté
barefoot(ed) *a.* nu-pieds
bareheaded *a.* nu-tête
barelegged *a.* nu-jambes
bargain *n.* marché, contrat *m.*; bonne affaire *f.*; — counter rayon des marchandises soldées *m.*; — *vt. & vi.* marchander
barge *n.* chaland *m.*; péniche *f.*; — *vi.* entrer sans façons
baritone *n.* baryton *m.*
barium *n.* baryum *m.*
bark *n.* écorce *f.*; barque *f.*, bateau *m.*; (dog) aboiement *m.*; — *vi.* aboyer; –er aboyeur *m.*; sideshow –er barnum *m.*
barley *n.* orge *f.*
barmaid *n.* fille de comptoir *f.*
barn *n.* grange *f.*; écurie, étable *f.*
barnacle *n.* barnache *f.*
barnstorm *vi.* aller en tournée
barnyard *n.* cour, basse-cour *f.*
barometer *n.* baromètre *m.*
barometric *a.* barométrique
baron *n.* baron *m.*; –ess *n.* baronne *f.*; –et *n.* baronnet *m.*; –y *n.* baronnie *f.*
barracks *n.* caserne *f.*
barrage *n.* barrage *m.*
barrel *n.* baril *m.*, barrique *f.*; tonneau *m.*; (gun) canon *m.*; — organ orgue de barbarie *m.*; — *vt.* mettre en tonneau
barren *a.* stérile; –ness *n.* stérilité *f.*
barricade *n.* barricade *f.*; — *vt.* barricader
barrier *n.* barrière *f.*
barroom *n.* cabaret *m.*
barrow *n.* brouette *f.*
bartender *n.* barman *m.*
barter *vt.* échanger; — *n.* échange *m.*
basal metabolism *n.* métabolisme basique *m.*
basalt *n.* basalte *m.*
base *n.* base *f.*, piédestal *m.*; — *a.* bas, vil; — *vt.* baser; –ness *n.* bassesse *f.*
baseball *n.* baseball *m.*
basement *n.* cave *f.*
bash *vt.* (coll.) cogner, assommer
bashful *a.* timide; –ness *m.* timidité *f.*
basic *a.* fondamental; basique; — English *n.* anglais basique *m.*
basil *n.* (spice) basilic *m.*
basilica *n.* basilique *f.*
basin *n.* bassin *m.*; bol *m.*; cuvette *f.*
basis *n.* base *f.*, fondement *m.*
bask *vt.* se chauffer (au soleil)
basket *n.* panier *m.*, corbeille *f.*; wastepaper — *n.* panier *m.*
Basque *n. & a.* Basque *m. & f.*
bas-relief *n.* bas-relief *m.*
bass *n.* (fish) bar *m.*; (mus.) basse *f.*; —

clef clef de fa *f.*; — drum grosse caisse *f.*; — horn basse *f.*; — viol contrebasse *f.*; — *a.* de basse; bas, grave
bassinette *n.* barcelonnette *f.*
bassoon *n.* basson *m.*
basswood *n.* tilleul (d'Amérique) *m.*
bastard *n. & a.* bâtard *m.*; –ize *vt.* abâtardir, avilir
baste *vt.* (cooking) arroser; (sewing) faufiler
basting *n.* (cooking) arrosage *m.*; (sewing) faufilure *f.*
bastion *n.* bastion *m.*
bat *n.* chauve-souris *f.*; bâton *m.*; (baseball) batte *f.*; be at — tenir la batte; go to — for (coll.) appuyer; — *vt.* tenir la batte; battre; without –ting an eye sans battre l'œil; (fig.) impassible; –ter *n.* joueur qui tient la batte
batch *n.* fournée *f.*; lot *m.*
bath *n.* bain *m.*; shower — douche *f.*
bathe *vt.* baigner; — *vi.* se baigner; –r *n.* baigneur *m.*
bathhouse *n.* établissement de bains *m.*
bathing *n.* bain *m.*, baignade *f.*; — beach plage *f.*; — suit costume de bain *m.*; — trunks slip de bain, caleçon de bain *m.*
bath mat *n.* descente de bain *f.*
bathrobe *n.* peignoir *m.*
bathroom *n.* salle de bain *f.*
bathtub *n.* baignoire *f.*
baton *n.* bâton (de chef d'orchestre) *m.*
battalion *n.* bataillon *m.*
batter *n.* pâte *f.*; — *vt.* battre; renverser
battering-ram *n.* bélier *m.*
battery *n.* batterie *f.*; pile *f.*; (law) voies de fait *f. pl.*
battle *n.* bataille *f.*, combat *m.*; — *vi.* livrer combat; lutter, se battre
battle-ax *n.* hache d'armes; (coll.) harpie *f.*
battlefield *n.* champ de bataille *m.*
battlement *n.* créneau *m.*
battleship *n.* cuirassé *m.*
bauble *n.* babiole, bagatelle *f.*
Bavaria *n.* Bavière *f.*; –n *a. & n.* bavarois *m.*
bawl *vi.* brailler, crier; — out réprimander
bay *n.* laurier *m.*; baie *f.* (sea) golfe *m.*; at — aux abois; — window *n.* fenêtre en saillie *f.*; (coll.) bedaine *f.*; — *vi.* aboyer; — *a.* bai
bayberry *n.* baie *f.*; (tree) laurier *m.*
bayonet *n.* baïonnette *f.*; — *vt.* blesser à coups de baïonnette
bayou *n.* anse *f.*
bazaar *n.* bazar *m.*; vente de charité *f.*
bazooka *n.* (mil.) fusil à fusées antichar *m.*

be *vi.* être, exister; devoir; **so — it** ainsi soit-il; **–ing** *n.* être *m.*; **for the time –ing** pour le moment

beach *n.* rivage *m.*; plage *f.*; grève *f.*; — *vt.* échouer

beachcomber *n.* vagabond des plages *m.*

beachhead *n.* débarquement *m.*; (mil.) tête de pont *f.*

beacon *n.* signal, phare *m.*

bead *n.* grain (de collier) *m.*; perle *f.*; **–s** *n. pl.* (eccl.) chapelet *m.*

beak *n.* bec *m.*; pic *m.*

beaker *n.* verre à expériences *m.*

beam *n.* (arch.) poutre *f.*; (naut.) bau *m.*; travers *m.*; (light) rayon *m.*; (rad.) signal *m.*; — *vi.* rayonner; sourire; **–ing** *a.* radieux; rayonnant

bean *n.* haricot *m.*; **kidney —** haricot de Soissons *m.*; **lima —** fève *f.*; **navy —** haricot *m.*; **string —** haricot vert *m.*

bean pole *n.* perche à fèves *f.*

bear *n.* ours *m.*; (stock market) baissier *m.*; **–ish** *a.* brutal, d'ours; (stocks) favorable à la baisse

bear *vt.* porter; supporter; — *vt.* porter; souffrir; **— a grudge against** en vouloir à; **— down** appuyer; **— in mind** tenir présent à l'esprit; **— witness** témoigner; **–able** *a.* supportable; **–er** *n.* porteur *m.*; **–ing** *n.* mine *f.*; (mech.) roulement *m.*; **get one's –ings** s'orienter; **have –ing on** avoir à faire avec; **lose one's –ings** se perdre

beard *n.* barbe *f.*; **–ed** *a.* barbu; **–less** *a.* imberbe; sans barbe

beast *n.* animal *m.*; bête *f.*; **— of burden** bête de somme *f.*; **–liness** *n.* bestialité, brutalité *f.*; **–ly** *a.* brutal, bestial

beat *n.* coup *m.*; battement *m.*; ronde *f.*; — *vt. & vi.* frapper, battre; vaincre; **— a path** frayer un chemin; **— around the bush** éviter la matière à traiter, esquiver; **— back,** — **off** repousser; **— up** battre sévèrement; **that –s me** je n'y comprends rien; **–er** *n.* pilon, battoir, batteur *m.*; **–ing** *n.* battement *m.*; raclée *f.*; défaite *f.*

beatify *vt.* béatifier

beatitude *n.* béatitude *f.*

beatnik *n.* bohémien *m.*

beau *n.* beau, galant *m.*

beautician *n.* coiffeur *m.*, coiffeuse *f.*

beautiful *a.* beau (belle)

beautify *vt.* embellir

beauty *n.* beauté *f.*; **— salon,** — **shop** salon de beauté *m.*; **— spot** tache de beauté *f.*

beaver *n.* castor *m.*

becalm *vt.* accalminer, déventer

because *conj.* parce que; **— of** *prep.* à cause de

beck *n.* signe de tête *m.*; **be at one's — (and call)** être aux ordres de quelqu'un

beckon *vi.* faire un signe

become *vi.* devenir; — *vt.* convenir à; **what has — of him?** qu'est-ce qu'il est devenu?

becoming *a.* convenable, joli

bed *n.* lit *m.*; **to go to —** se coucher; **to put to —** coucher; **flower —** plate-bande *f.*; **folding —** lit escamotable *m.*; **four-poster —** lit à quenouilles *m.*; **mineral —** gisement *m.*; **oyster —** parc d'huîtres *m.*; **road —** encaissement *m.*; — *vt.* coucher; **— down** coucher; se coucher

bedbug *n.* punaise *f.*

bedding *n.* literie *f.*

bedeck *vt.* parer, orner

bedevil *vt.* ensorceler, harceler

bedfellow *n.* camarade de lit *m.*

bed head *n.* chevet *m.*

bedjacket *n.* liseuse *f.*

bedlam *n.* tumulte *m.*

bedpan *n.* bassin de lit *m.*

bedpost *n.* pied de lit *m.*

bedraggled *a.* crotté; échevelé

bedridden *a.* alité

bedrock *n.* roche de fond *f.*

bedroom *n.* chambre à coucher *f.*

bedside *n.* bord du lit *m.*

bedspread *n.* dessus de lit *m.*

bedspring *n.* sommier *m.*

bedstead *n.* bois de lit *m.*

bedtime *n.* heure de coucher *f.*

bee *n.* abeille *f.*; **spelling —** concours d'orthographe *m.*

beef *n.* bœuf *f.*; **— tea** consommé *m.*; **roast —** rosbif, rôti de bœuf *m.*

beefsteak *n.* biftek, steak *m.*

beehive *n.* ruche *f.*

beekeeper *n.* apiculteur *m.*

beeline *n.* route la plus courte *f.*

beer *n.* bière *f.*

beeswax *n.* cire d'abeille *f.*

beet *n.* betterave *f.*; **— sugar** sucre de betterave *m.*; **sugar —** betterave à sucre *f.*

beetle *n.* scarabée *m.*; coléoptère *m.*

beetle-browed *a.* à sourcils épais

befall *vi.* arriver, survenir

befit *vt.* convenir à, être propre à; **–ting** *a.* convenable

befog *vt.* obscurcir

before *adv.* avant, auparavant; en avant; **the day —** la veille *f.*; **the evening —** la veille au soir *f.*; — *prep.* avant; devant; **the day — yesterday** l'avant-veille *f.*; **— conj.** avant que

beforehand *adv.* d'avance, préalablement

auparavant

befoul *vt.* souiller, salir

befriend *vt.* venir en aide à; traiter en ami

beg *vt.* mendier; prier, supplier; — *vi.* mendier; **I — of you!** je vous en prie!, de grâce!; **–gar** *n.* mendiant, gueux *m.*; **–ging** *n.* mendicité *f.*

beget *vt.* engendrer

begin *vt. & vi.* commencer; débuter; se mettre à; **to — with** tout d'abord; **–ner** *n.* commençant, débutant *m.*; novice *m. & f.*; **–ning** *n.* commencement, début *m.*, origine *f.*; **in the –ning** au commencement

begrudge *vt.* envier; donner à contre-cœur

begrudgingly *adv.* à contre-cœur

beguile *vt.* tromper; charmer

behalf *n.* faveur, part *f.*; **on — of** au nom de, de la part de

behave *vi.* se conduire, se comporter; être sage

behavior *n.* conduite, tenue *f.*, comportement *m.*

behead *vt.* décapiter; **–ing** *n.* décapitation *f.*

behest *n.* ordre *m.*; demande *f.*

behind *adv.* derrière, par derrière; en retard; **be —** être en retard; **fall —** traîner en arrière; **— prep.** derrière; en arrière de

behold *vt.* voir, contempler

behoove *vt.* convenir

belabor *vt.* rosser, battre; trop insister sur

belated *a.* attardé; tardif

belch *vi.* éructer; **— n.** éructation *f.*

beleaguer *vt.* cerner; investir

belfry *n.* beffroi, clocher *m.*

Belgian *a. & n.* belge *m. & f.*

Belgian East Africa *n.* Ruanda-Urundi *m.*

Belgium *n.* Belgique *f.*

belie *vt.* démentir

belief *n.* croyance, foi *f.*; **to the best of my —** autant que je sache

believable *a.* croyable

believe *vt. & vi.* croire, penser; **make —** faire semblant; **–r** *n.* croyant *m.*

belittle *vt.* déprécier

bell *n.* cloche, clochette *f.*; (house) sonnette *f.*; **— vt.** attacher un grelot à

bellboy, bellhop *n.* chasseur *m.*; garçon d'hôtel *m.*

belle *n.* beauté *f.*

bell glass, bell jar *n.* cloche (de verre) *f.*

belligerent *a. & n.* belligérant *m.*

bellow *vi.* beugler, mugir; **— n.** beuglement, mugissement *m.*

bellows *n. pl.* soufflet *m.*

bellpull *n.* cordon de sonnette *m.*

bell tower *n.* campanile, clocher *m.*

bellwether *n.* sonnailler *m.*

belly *n.* ventre *m.*; **–ful** *n.* rassasiement, soûl *m.*

bellyband *n.* (horse) sous-ventrière; (baby) brassière *f.*

belong *vi.* appartenir (à), être (à); faire partie (de); **–ings** *n. pl.* biens, effets *m. pl.*

beloved *a.* bien-aimé, chéri

below *adv.* en bas, (au) dessous; ci-dessous, ci-après; **— prep.** au dessous de, sous

belt *n.* ceinture *f.*; zone *f.*; **transmission —** courroie *f.*; **— vt.** ceindre, entourer; **–ed** *a.* à ceinture; **–ing** *n.* ceinture *f.*

bemoan *vt.* déplorer

bench *n.* banc *m.*, banquette *f.*; (law) siège *m.*; magistrature *f.*

bend *n.* courbure *f.*; courbe *f.*; coude, tournant *m.*; **— vt. & vi.** courber; plier, fléchir; tourner; **— down** se courber, se baisser

bends *n. pl.* (coll.) mal des caissons *m.*

beneath *adv.* en bas, (au-) dessous; **— prep.** au-dessous de, sous

benedictine *n.* (monk) bénédictin *m.*; (liqueur) bénédictine *f.*

benediction *n.* bénédiction *f.*

benefaction *n.* bienfait *m.*

benefactor *n.* bienfaiteur *m.*

benefactress *n.* bienfaitrice *f.*

beneficence *n.* bienfaisance *f.*

beneficent *a.* bienfaisant

beneficial *a.* avantageux, profitable; salutaire

beneficiary *n.* bénéficiaire *m. & f.*

benefit *n.* avantage, profit *m.*; bénéfice *m.*; **— vt.** être avantageux, profiter à; bénéficier

benevolence *n.* bienveillance *f.*; bienfait *m.*

benevolent *a.* bienveillant; charitable; bienfaisant; **–ly** *adv.* avec bienveillance

benign *a.* bénin, bénigne

benignant *a.* bienveillant; bénin

bent *n.* penchant *m.*; inclination *f.*; **— a.** courbé; fléchi; résolu, déterminé

benumb *vt.* engourdir

benzine *n.* benzine *f.*

bequeath *vt.* léguer

bequest *n.* legs *m.*

berate *vt.* gronder

bereave *vt.* priver; **–d** *a. & n.* affligé *m.*; **–ment** *n.* deuil *m.*

Bermuda *n.* Bermudes *m. pl.*

berry *n.* baie *f.*; raisin *m.*; grain *m.*

berserk *a.* forcené, affolé

berth *n.* couchette *f.*; emplacement *m.*

beseech *vt.* supplier; **–ing** *a.* suppliant

beset *vt.* assiéger, assaillir
beside *prep.* à côté de, auprès de; **be —** oneself être hors de soi; être transporté; **–s** *adv.* en outre, d'ailleurs, en plus
besiege *vt.* assiéger; **–r** *n.* assiégeant *m.*
besmear *vt.* barbouiller, enduire
besmirch *vt.* souiller, salir
best *a.* le meilleur, la meilleure; **— man** témoin *m.*; **do one's —** faire de son mieux; **get the — of it** l'emporter; avoir le dessus; **make the — of** s'accomoder de; **— adv.** le mieux; **at —** pour dire le mieux; **— vt.** l'emporter sur
bestial *a.* bestial; **–ity** *n.* bestialité *f.*
bestow *vt.* donner, accorder; conférer; **–al** *n.* don *m.*, donation *f.*
best seller *n.* livre à gros tirage *m.*
bet *n.* pari *m.*, gageure *f.*; **— vt.** parier; **–ting** *n.* paris *m.* *pl.*; **–tor** *n.* parieur *m.*
beta particle *n.* particule bêta *f.*
betray *vt.* trahir; révéler; **–al** *n.* trahison *f.*; révélation *f.*; **–er** *n.* traître *m.*; traîtresse *f.*
betroth *vt.* fiancer; **–al** *n.* fiançailles *f.* *pl.*
better *a.* meilleur; supérieur; **— adv.** mieux; **so much the — tant mieux; be —** aller mieux; **get —** guérir; s'améliorer; **get the — of** l'emporter sur; **it is —** il vaut mieux; **think — of** se raviser; **— vt.** améliorer; **— vi.** s'améliorer; **–ment** *n.* amélioration *f.*
between *prep.* entre; **— (us)** entre nous
bevel *adj.* en biseau; **— vt.** couper en biseau, biaiser; **–ed** *a.* coupé en biseau
beverage *n.* breuvage *m.*, boisson *f.*
bevy *n.* troupe, bande *f.*; (quail) volée *f.*
bewail *vt.* pleurer, regretter
beware *vi.* se garder de, se méfier de
bewilder *vt.* confondre, égarer; **–ed** *a.* confondu, abasourdi; **–ment** *n.* abasourdissement, trouble *m.*
bewitch *vt.* ensorceler, enchanter; **–ing** *a.* enchanteur; ravissant
beyond *adv.* au delà; **— prep.** au delà de; **be —, go —** dépasser; **it is — me** je n'y comprends rien; **— (a) doubt** hors de doute; **— n.** au-delà *m.*
B-girl *n.* entremetteuse *f.*
biannual *a.* semi-annuel
bias *n.* biais *m.*; penchant *m.*; prévention *f.*, préjugé *m.*; **on the —** en biais, de biais; **— vt.** prévenir; **–ed** *a.* prédisposé, partial
bib *n.* bavette *f.*
Bible *n.* Bible *f.*
biblical *a.* biblique
bibliographer *n.* bibliographe *m.*
bibliography *n.* bibliographie *f.*
bicarbonate *n.* bicarbonate *m.*; **— of soda** bicarbonate de soude *m.*

biceps *n.* biceps *m.*
bicker *vi.* se quereller, disputer; **–ing** *a.* querelleur; **–ing** *n.* querelle(s) *f.* (*pl.*)
bicuspid *n.* prémolaire *f.*
bicycle *n.* bicyclette *f.*; vélo *m.*; **— vi.** faire de la bicyclette; aller à bicyclette
bicycling *n.* cyclisme *m.*
bicyclist *n.* cycliste *m.* & *f.*
bid *n.* enchère, offre *f.*; (cards) demande *f.*; **— vt.** commander, ordonner; dire; offrir; (cards) demander; **— vi.** faire une offre; **–der** *n.* offrant, enchérisseur *m.*; **–ding** *n.* commandement ordre *m.*; enchères *f.* *pl.*
bide *vt.* attendre
biennial *a.* bisannuel
bier *n.* cercueil *m.*
bifocal *a.* bifocal
big *a.* gros, grand; **get –(ger)** grossir; grandir; **talk —** faire l'important; **–ness** *n.* grosseur *f.*; grandeur *f.*; **— wheel** (coll.) gros bonnet *m.*
bigamist *n.* bigame *m.* & *f.*
bigamy *n.* bigamie *f.*
Big Dipper *n.* Grande Ourse *f.*
bigot *n.* sectaire *m.* & *f.*; fanatique *m.* & *f.*; bigot *m.*, bigote *f.*; **–ed** *a.* fanatique; étroit; **–ry** *n.* fanatisme *m.*; étroitesse *f.*
bike *n.* bécane *f.*, vélo *m.*
bilateral *a.* bilatéral
bilge *n.* sentine *f.*; **— water** eau de cale *f.*
bilingual *a.* bilingue
bilious *a.* bilieux
bilk *vt.* tromper, escroquer
bill *n.* (bird) bec *m.*; (com.) facture, note *f.*; (restaurant) addition *f.*; affiche *f.*, placard *m.*; (law) projet de loi *m.*; **— of fare** carte *f.*; **— of lading** connaissement *m.*; **— of sale** facture *f.*, acte de vente *m.*; **post no –s** défense d'afficher; **— vt.** facturer
billboard *n.* panneau d'affichage *m.*; enseigne *f.*
billet *n.* billet, logement *m.*; **— vt.** loger, cantonner
billfold *n.* portefeuille *m.*
billiard ball *n.* bille *f.*
billiards *n.* *pl.* billard *m.*
billion *n.* milliard *m.*
billionaire *n.* milliardaire *m.*
billow *n.* vague *f.*, flot *m.*; **— vi.** ondoyer; **–y** *a.* onduleux, ondoyant
billy (stick) *n.* bâton d'agent de police *m.*
billy goat *n.* (coll.) bouc *m.*
bimonthly *a.* bimensuel
bin *n.* huche *f.*; coffre *m.*
binary *a.* binaire
binaural *a.* stéréophonique
bind *vt.* lier; relier; obliger; bander; attacher; **–er** lieur *m.*; relieur *m.*;

−ery *n.* atelier de reliure *m.*; −ing *a.* obligatoire; (med.) astringent; −ing *n.* reliure *f.*

binoculars *n. pl.* jumelle(s) *f. pl.*

binomial *a.* & *n.* binôme *m.*

biochemistry *n.* biochimie *f.*

biogenetics *n.* biogénétique *f.*

biogenesis *n.* biogenèse *f.*

biographer *n.* biographe *m.*

biographical *a.* biographique

biography *n.* biographie *f.*

biological *a.* biologique; — **warfare** guerre bactériologique *f.*

biologist *n.* biologiste *m.*

biology *n.* biologie *f.*

biophysical *a.* biophysique

bipartisan *a.* (pol.) dit d'une politique approuvée par les deux partis

biped *n.* bipède *m.*

birch *n.* bouleau *m.*; verge *f.*

bird *n.* oiseau *m.*; — **cage** *n.* cage *f.*

bird's-eye view *n.* vue à vol d'oiseau *f.*

birth *n.* naissance *f.*; **give — to** donner naissance à, donner le jour à, mettre au monde; — **certificate** acte de naissance *m.*; — **control** *n.* limitation sur la natalité *f.*; — **rate** natalité *f.*

birthday *n.* anniversaire *m.*

birthmark *n.* tache, envie *f.*

birthplace *n.* lieu de naissance *m.*

birthright *n.* droit de naissance *m.*

biscuit *n.* biscuit *m.*; (genre de) petit pain *m.* (à la levure chimique)

bisect *vt.* couper en deux

bishop *n.* évêque *m.*; (chess) fou *m.*; −ric *n.* évêché *m.*

bit *n.* (bridle) mors *m.*; (drill) mèche *f.*; morceau, bout, brin *m.*; **a — (of)** un peu (de); — **by —** peu à peu, petit à petit

bitch *n.* chienne *f.*; (coll.) garce *f.*

bite *n.* bouchée *f.*; morsure, piqûre *f.*; (fishing) touche *f.*; — *vt.* mordre, piquer

biting *a.* mordant, piquant

bitter *a.* amer; aigre, âpre; acerbe; −ness *n.* amertume *f.*; acrimonie *f.*, rancune *f.*

bittersweet *a.* aigre-doux

bituminous *a.* bitumineux; — **coal** houille *f.*

biweekly *a.* bihebdomadaire; — *adv.* deux fois par mois

black *a.* noir; sombre; — **eye** œil poché *m.*; — **and blue** (tout) meurtri; — **market** marché noir *m.*; — **sheep** brebis galeuse *f.*; — *n.* noir *m.*; **in — and white** par écrit; **in the —** (com.) bénéficiaire; — *vi.* & *vt.* noircir; −**en** *vt.* noircir; obscurcir; calomnier; −**ish** *a.* noirâtre; −**ness** *n.* noirceur *f.*; obscurité *f.*

blackball *vt.* blackbouler

blackberry *n.* mûre *f.*; mûre de ronce *f.*; (bush) mûrier sauvage *m.*, ronce *f.*

blackbird *n.* merle *m.*

blackboard *n.* tableau noir *m.*

blackguard *n.* goujat, vaurien *m.*

blackhead *n.* point noir *m.*

blackjack *n.* assommoir *m.*; (cards) vingt-et-un *m.*

black list *n.* index *m.*, liste des personnes interdites *f.*; — *vt.* boycotter, interdire

blackmail *n.* chantage *m.*; — *vt.* faire chanter

blackout *n.* obscurcissement *m.*; blackout, camouflage des lumières *m.*

blacksmith *n.* forgeron *m.*

bladder *n.* vessie *f.*

blade *n.* lame *f.*; brin (d'herbe) *m.*; (mech.) aile, ailette, pale *f.*; (man) gaillard *m.*

blamable *a.* blâmable, coupable

blame *n.* blâme *m.*; reproches *m. pl.*; faute *f.*; — *vt.* blâmer, reprocher; s'en prendre (à); −less *a.* innocent, irréprochable; −worthy *a.* blâmable

blanch *vt.* blanchir; — *vi.* pâlir

bland *a.* doux; affable; narquois; −ness *n.* douceur *f.*

blandish *vt.* flatter; −ment *n.* flatterie *f.*

blank *a.* blanc (blanche); — *n.* blanc, vide *m.*; lacune *f.*; formule *f.*

blanket *n.* couverture *f.*; — *a.* général; — *vt.* envelopper, couvrir

blare *vi.* sonner; — *n.* sonnerie *f.*; bruit *m.*

blaspheme *vt.* & *vi.* blasphémer; −r *n.* blasphémateur *m.*

blasphemous *a.* blasphémateur; blasphématoire

blasphemy *n.* blasphème *m.*

blast *n.* bouffée *f.*; souffle *m.*; jet *m.*; charge *f.*; coup *m.*; **full —** (fig.) en pleine activité; — **furnace** haut fourneau *m.*; — *vt.* détruire; faire sauter; foudroyer; −ing *n.* abattage à la poudre *m.*

blatant *a.* vulgaire; criant

blaze *n.* flamme *f.*, incendie *m.*; feu *m.*; — *vi.* flamber; flamboyer; — **a trail** tracer un chemin; frayer un chemin

blazer *n.* jacquette *f.*, veston *m.*

blazing *a.* en feu, embrasé; flambant

bleach *vt.* blanchir; — *n.* blanchiment *m.*; eau de Javel *f.*

bleachers *n.* gradins *m. pl.*

bleak *a.* froid, désert, triste, morne; −ness *n.* tristesse *f.*; nudité *f.*

bleary *a.* chassieux; larmoyant

bleat *vi.* bêler; −ing *n.* bêlement *m.*

bleed *vt.* & *vi.* saigner; −ing *a.* saignant; −ing *n.* saignement *m.*; saignée *f.*

blemish *n.* tache *f.*; défaut *m.*; — *vt.* tacher; souiller

blend *n.* mélange *m.*; — *vt.* mêler, mélanger

bless *vt.* bénir; **-ed** *a.* saint; bienheureux; béni; **-ing** *n.* bénédiction *f.*

blight *n.* influence néfaste *f.*; (agr.) rouille *f.*; — *vt.* flétrir, frustrer, anéantir

blimp *n.* dirigeable *m.*

blind *a.* aveugle; — **alley** cul-de-sac *m.*; — **flying** *n.* vol sans visibilité, vol à l'aveuglette *m.*; — **person** aveugle *m.* & *f.*; **-ly** *adv.* aveuglément; — *vt.* aveugler; éblouir; — *n.* store *m.*; jalousie, persienne *f.*; (fig.) feinte *f.*, subterfuge *m.*; **-ness** *n.* cécité *f.*; (fig.) aveuglement *m.*

blindfold *n.* bande *f.*; — *vt.* bander les yeux; **-(ed)** *a.* & *adv.* les yeux bandés

blink *n.* clignotement *m.*; — *vi.* cligner, clignoter, battre (des yeux); **-er** *n.* feu clignotant *m.*; (horses) œillère *f.*

bliss *n.* félicité *f.*; **-ful** *a.* heureux, bienheureux; **-fullness** *n.* béatitude, félicité *f.*

blister *n.* ampoule *f.*; cloque *f.*; boursouflure *f.*; — *vi.* se couvrir d'ampoules

blithe *a.* gai, heureux

blizzard *n.* tourmente de neige *f.*

bloat *vt.* & *vi.* enfler, bouffir; **-ed** *a.* enflé; congestionné

blob *n.* pâté (d'encre) *m.*; goutte *f.*

block *n.* bloc *m.*; pâté de maisons *m.*; (com.) tranche *f.*; (toy) cube *m.*; — *vt.* bloquer, barrer; — **up** boucher; murer

blockade *n.* blocage *m.*; — *vt.* bloquer

blockhead *n.* sot, imbécile *m.*

blood *n.* sang *m.*; parenté *f.*; race *f.*; — **bank** réserve de sang *f.*; — **donor** donneur de sang *m.*; — **orange** sanguin; — **plasma** plasma du sang *m.*; — **platelet** (med.) plaquette sanguine *f.*; — **poisoning** septicémie *f.*; — **pressure** tension artérielle *f.*; **high** — **pressure** hypertension *f.*; — **stream** cours du sang *m.*; — **vessel** vaisseau sanguin *m.*; **in cold** — de sang-froid

bloodhound *n.* limier *m.*

bloodshed *n.* effusion de sang *f.*; carnage *m.*

bloodshot *a.* injecté de sang; éraillé

bloodstain *n.* tache de sang *f.*; **-ed** *a.* taché de sang

bloodthirsty *a.* sanguinaire *m.*

blood type *n.* groupe sanguin

blood-type *vt.* classer selon le groupe sanguin

bloody *a.* sanglant

bloom *n.* fleur *f.*; épanouissement *m.*; **in** — en fleur, épanoui; — *vi.* fleurir; **-ing**

a. fleurissant, florissant; **-ing** *n.* fleuraison, floraison *f.*

bloomers *n. pl.* (sorte de) culotte de femme *f.*

blooper *n.* (coll.) gaffe, bévue *f.*

blossom *n.* fleur *f.*; — *vi.* fleurir

blot *n.* tache d'encre *f.*; pâté *m.*; — *vt.* tacher; sécher; — *vi.* boire; **-ter** *n.* buvard *m.*; **-ting paper** papier buvard *m.*

blotch *n.* pustule *f.*; tache *f.*; **-y** *a.* brouillé; tacheté

blouse *n.* blouse *f.*; corsage *m.*

blow *n.* coup *m.*; **at a** — d'un coup; **come to -s** en venir aux coups; — *vi.* souffler; — **one's nose** se moucher; — **away** emporter; — **out** (auto.) éclater; — **over** passer; — **up** éclater, sauter; (coll.) se mettre en colère; (phot.) agrandir; **-er** *n.* ventilateur *m.*

blowout *n.* (auto.) crevaison *f.*

blowpipe *n.* chalumeau *m.*

blowtorch *n.* lampe à braser *f.*

blubber *n.* graisse de baleine *f.*; — *vi.* pleurnicher

bludgeon *n.* assommer, rouer de coups; — *n.* assommoir *m.*; massue, matraque *f.*

blue *a.* bleu; (fig.) triste, mélancolique; — **cheese** espèce de fromage genre roquefort *m.*; — **chips** (stocks) premières valeurs *f.*; — *n.* bleu *m.*; azur *m.*; **light** — bleu clair; **navy** — bleu marine; **-s** *n.* mélancolie *f.*; (mus.) blues *m. pl.*; — *vt.* & *vi.* bleuir

blueberry *n.* airelle myrtille *f.*

bluebird *n.* oiseau bleu *m.*

blue-eyed *a.* aux yeux bleus

blueprint *n.* négatif, bleu *m.*; plan *m.*

bluff *a.* escarpé; — *n.* falaise *f.*; à-pic *m.*; bluff *m.*; — *vt.* bluffer

bluing, blueing *n.* bleu *m.*

bluish *a.* bleuâtre

blunder *n.* bévue, gaffe *f.*; — *vi.* faire une bévue, gaffer; — **into** se heuter contre; **-ing** *a.* maladroit

blunt *a.* émoussé; brusque; — *vt.* émousser

blur *n.* tache *f.*; ternissure *f.*; — *vt.* barbouiller; brouiller; rendre indistinct

blurb *n.* annonce publicitaire *f.*

blurt *vt.*, — **out** laisser échapper

blush *n.* rougeur *f.*; — *vi.* rougir

bluster *vi.* tempêter, tonner; — *n.* fracas, tapage *m.*; emportement *m.*

boar *n.* cochon mâle, verrat *m.*; **wild** — sanglier *m.*

board *n.* planche *f.*; table *f.*; tableau *m.*; (chess) tablier *m.*; commission *f.*; **ironing** — planche à repasser *f.*; **room and** — pension *f.*; — **of directors** conseil d'administration *m.*; **on** — à bord; — *vi.* être en pension, prendre la pension; — *vt.* s'embarquer; monter dans; — **up** boucher; **-er** *n.* pensionnaire *m. & f.*; (schools) interne *m. & f.*

boardinghouse *n.* pension *f.*

boardwalk *n.* promenade (faite de planches) au bord de la mer *f.*

boast *n.* vanterie *f.*; — *vi.* se vanter (de); **-ful** *a.* arrogant, vantard; **-ing** *n.* jactance *f.*

boat *n.* bateau *m.*; barque *f.*; canot *m.*; embarcation *f.*; **-ing** *n.* canotage *m.*; **to go -ing** faire du canotage, canoter

boat hook *n.* gaffe *f.*

boathouse *n.* hangar, garage *m.*

boatload *n.* batelée *f.*

boatman *n.* batelier *m.*

boat race *n.* régate *f.*

boatswain *n.* maître d'équipage *m.*

bob *vi.* s'agiter, danser; **-bed** *a.* coupé court

bobbin *n.* bobine *f.*

bobby pin *n.* épingle à cheveux *f.*

bobby-socks *n. pl.* chaussettes courtes *f. pl.*

bobby-soxer *n.* zazou *m.*

bobsled, bobsleigh *n.* bob *m.*

bode *vt. & vi.* présager

bodily *a.* corporel, physique; — *adv.* corporellement; en corps

body *n.* corps *m.*; cadavre *m.*; substance *f.*; — (auto.) carrosserie *f.*

bodyguard *n.* garde du corps *m.*

bog *n.* marécage *m.*; fondrière *f.*; — *vt.* enliser; — (**down**) *vi.* s'enliser

bogus *a.* faux, fausse; simulé

Bohemia *n.* Bohême; **-n** *a. & n.* bohémien *m.*

boil *n.* ébullition *f.*; (med.) furoncle, clou *m.*; — *vi.* bouillir, bouillonner; — *vt.* faire bouillir; **-er** *n.* chaudière *f.*; **-ing** *a.* bouillant; **-ing** *n.* ébullition *f.*, bouillonnement *m.*; **-ing point** point d'ébullition *m.*

boilermaker *n.* chaudronnier *m.*

boisterous *a.* bruyant, débordant; **-ly** *adv.* bruyamment

bold *a.* audacieux, téméraire; hardi; effronté; **-ness** *n.* audace, témérité, hardiesse, effronterie *f.*

boldface (type) *n.* caractères gras *m. pl.*

bold-faced *a.* effronté

Bolivia *n.* Bolivie *f.*

boll weevil *n.* hélothis *m.*

Bolshevik *a. & n.* bolchevique *m. & f.*

bolster *n.* traversin *m.*; — *vt.* soutenir

bolt *n.* verrou, pêne *m.*; rouleau, coupon *m.*; coup de foudre *m.*; **screw** — boulon *m.* (à écrou); **thunder** — fuite *f.*; — *vt.* verrouiller; (food) gober; — *vi.* dé-

camper

bomb *n.* bombe *f.*; — **shelter** abri-voûte *m.*; — *vt.* bombarder; **-er** *n.* bombardier *m.*; **-ing** *n.* bombardement *m.*

bombardier *n.* bombardier *m.*

bombardment *n.* bombardement *m.*

bombast *n.* boursouflage *m.*; enflure *f.*; **-ic** *a.* boursouflé; enflé

bombproof *a.* à l'épreuve des bombes

bombshell *n.* (fig.) sensation *f.*

bombsight *n.* viseur de bombardement, appareil de visée *m.*

bonanza *n.* aubaine *f.*; trouvaille *f.*

bond *n.* lien *m.*; obligation *f.*; (com.) bon *m.*; titre *m.*; **in** — (com.) à l'entrepôt; — *vt.* (com.) entreposer, mettre à l'entrepôt; **-age** *n.* esclavage *m.*; servitude *f.*

bondholder *n.* obligataire *m. & f.*

bondsman *n.* (law) répondant *m.*

bone *n.* os *m.*; (fish) arête *f.*; **have a** — **to pick** avoir maille à partir; — *vt.* désosser; **-less** *a.* désossé, sans os, sans arêtes

bonfire *n.* feu de joie *m.*

bonnet *n.* bonnet, chapeau *m.*

bonus *n.* boni *m.*; prime *f.*; gratification *f.*

bony *a.* osseux; décharné

booby *n.* nigaud *m.*; — **prize** prix qu'on donne au plus mauvais joueur *m.*; — **trap** attrape-nigaud *m.*

book *n.* livre *m.*; bouquin *m.*; livret *m.*; carnet *m.*; **telephone** — annuaire *m.*; — **ends** serre-livres *m. pl.*; — **review** compte rendu *m.*; — *vt.* louer, réserver; **-ing** *n.* réservation *f.*; (theat.) location *f.*

bookbinder *n.* relieur *m.*

bookcase *n.* bibliothèque *f.*; étagère *f.*

bookkeeper *n.* comptable *m. & f.*

bookkeeping *n.* comptabilité *f.*

booklet *n.* livret *m.*; opuscule *m*; brochure *f.*

bookmark *n.* signet *m.*

bookmobile *n.* bibliobus *m.*

bookseller *n.* libraire *m. & f.*

bookshelf *n.* étagère *f.*, rayon (de bibliothèque) *m.*

bookshop, bookstore *n.* librairie *f.*

bookworm *n.* ciron *m.*; (fig.) bibliomane, mangeur de livres *m.*

boom *n.* barrage *m.*; (naut.) bout-dehors, tangon, mât de charge *m.*; (avi.) longeron *m.*; retentissement *m.*; (com.) boom *m.*; vogue *f.*; **sonic** — grondement du son *m.*; — *vi.* retentir, gronder; (com.) être en hausse, prospérer; **-ing** *a.* (com.) florissant

boomerang *n.* boumerang *m.*; — *vi.* revenir vers soi; réagir sur soi

boon n. don m., faveur f.

boor n. rustre m.; goujat m.; -ish a. grossier, rustre; -ishness n. grossièreté, rusticité f.

boost n. relèvement m. aide f.; — vt. soulever par derrière; faire du battage, de la réclame pour; (elec.) survolter; -er n. réclamiste m.; (elec.) survolteur m.; -er rocket fusée de lancement, fusée porteuse f.; -er shot (med.) piqûre de rappel f.; -ing n. battage m., réclame f.

boot n. botte, bottine f.; to — adv. en sus; — vt. botter

bootee n. chausson de bébé m.

bootblack n. cireur m.

booth n. tente f.; cabine f.

bootie n. chausson de bébé m.

bootleg a. de contrebande; — vt. faire la contrebande (de l'alcool); -ger n. contrebandier m.; -ging n. contrebande

booty n. butin m.

border n. bord m., bordure f.; frontière f.; galon m.; — vi. border; — on toucher; approcher

borderline n. frontière f.; — a. limite

bore n. trou m.; calibre m.; (person) raseur m.; ennui m.; — vt. percer; sonder; ennuyer, raser; -dom n. ennui

boric a. borique

boring a. ennuyant, ennuyeux; (coll.) assommant

born, to be — naître; — a. né

boron n. bore m.

borough n. bourg m.

borrow vt. emprunter; -er n. emprunteur m.

bosom n. sein m.; poitrine f.; (fig.) giron m.

boss n. chef, patron m.; — vt. diriger, régenter; -y a. autoritaire

botanical a. botanique

botanist n. botaniste m.

botany n. botanique f.

botch vt. saboter; ravauder; mal faire

both a. les deux; — pron. tous les deux; — . . . and et . . . et

bother n. ennui m.; — vt. déranger; ennuyer, gêner; -some a. importun

bottle n. bouteille f.; bocal m.; — brush n. goupillon m.; nursing — biberon m.; — vt. mettre en bouteille; — up embouteiller

bottleneck n. goulot m.; embouteillage m.

bottling n. mise en bouteilles f.

bottom n. fond m.; bas m.; dessous m.; at — au fond; — dollar dernier sou m.; -less a. sans fond

bough n. rameau m.

boulder n. bloc, rocher m.

bounce n. bond, rebond m.; — vi.

rebondir; — vt. faire rebondir; (coll.) flanquer à la porte; -r n. (coll.) agent, souteneur m.

bound n. bornes, limites f. pl.; bond, saut m.; out of -s hors des limites; défendu; — vi. borner, limiter; sauter, bondir; — a. lié; engagé, obligé; — for en route pour; -less a. sans bornes; illimité

boundary n. borne, limite f.; frontière f.

bounteous, bountiful a. bienfaisant; généreux

bounty n. bonté, munificence f.; prime, subvention f.

bouquet n. bouquet m.

bout n. (sport) match, assaut m.; épreuve f.

bovine a. bovin

bow n. arc m.; (mus.) archet m.; (saddle) arçon m.; (ribbon) nœud m.; révérence f.; inclinaison f.; (naut.) avant m.; — tie nœud papillon m.; — vi. s'incliner; — vt. courber

bowels n. pl. entrailles f. pl.

bower n. tonnelle f., berceau m.

bowie-knife n. couteau-poignard m.

bowl n. bol m.; (spoon) cuilleron m.; (pipe) fourneau m.; (stadium) stade m.; — vt. jeter, lancer; — vi. jouer aux boules; (U.S.) jouer aux quilles; — over renverser; -er n. joueur (de boules, de quilles) m.; chapeau melon m.; -ing n. jeu de boules m.; -ing pin n. quille f.

bowlegged a. arqué, bancal; to be — avoir les jambes arquées

bowman n. archer m.

bowsprit n. beaupré m.

bowstring n. corde d'arc f.; cordon m.

box n. boîte f.; coffre, coffret m.; carton m.; caisse f.; cabine f.; (theat.) loge, baignoire f.; — on the ear claque f.; — camera détective m.; — office bureau de location m.; — vt. mettre en boîte; emboîter, encartonner; claquer; — vt. & vi. (sports) boxer; -er n. boxeur m.; -ing n. boxe f.

boxcar n. wagon de marchandises m.

boy n. garçon, enfant m.; gamin m.; — scout scout, éclaireur m.; -hood n. enfance f.; -ish a. d'enfant, de garçon; enfantin

boycott n. boycottage m.; — vt. boycotter

brace n. attache f., lien m.; écharpe f.; paire f.; vilebrequin m.; — vt. ancrer; fortifier

bracer n. tonique m.; brassard m.

bracing n. tonique

bracket n. console f.; (print.) crochet m.

brackish a. saumâtre

brad n. clou (sans tête) m.

brag n. vanterie f., jactance f.; — vi. se

vanter; –gart *n.* vantard, fanfaron *m.*

braid *n.* tresse *f.*; galon *m.*; passementerie *f.*; — *vt.* tresser; galonner; passementer

brain *n.* cerveau *m.*, cervelle *f.*; **rack one's** — se creuser la cervelle; **–storm** inspiration *f.*; — *vt.* casser la tête à; **–less** *a.* stupide, sans intelligence; **–y** *a.* intelligent

brainwashing *n.* (coll.) indoctrination idéologique (imposée aux prisonniers politiques ou de guerre) *f.*

brake *n.* frein *m.*; — *vt.* freiner, serrer les freins

brakeman *n.* (rail.) serre-frein *m.*

bramble *n.* ronce *f.*

bran *n.* son *m.*

branch *n.* branche *f.*; succursale *f.*; embranchement *m.*; — *v.*, — **off** s'embrancher, se bifurquer; — **out** se ramifier

brand *n.* brandon, tison *m.*; fer chaud *m.*; flétrissure *f.*; (com.) marque *f.*; — *vt.* marquer au fer chaud, flétrir; **–ing iron** *n.* fer (à flétrir) *m.*

brandish *vt.* brandir

brand-new *a.* tout neuf

brandy *n.* eau-de-vie *f.*

brash *a.* impertinent, insolent

brass *n.* cuivre jaune, laiton *m.*; airain *m.*; (mus.) cuivre *m.*

brassiere *n.* soutien-gorge *m.*

brat *n.* (coll.) gosse, marmot *m.*

bravado *n.* bravade *f.*

brave *a.* brave, courageux; — *vt.* braver; **–ry** *n.* bravoure *f.*

brawl *n.* bagarre *f.*; querelle *f.*; — *vi.* brailler; se quereller

brawn *n.* muscles *m. pl.*; **–y** *a.* musclé

bray *n.* braîment *m.*; — *vi.* braire

braze *vt.* braser; souder

brazen *a.* d'airain; impudent, effronté

brazier *n.* chaudronnier *m.*

Brazil *n.* Brésil *m.*; **–ian** *a. & n.* brésilien *m.*

breach *n.* brèche *f.*; rupture *f.*; infraction, violation *f.*; — **of promise** manque de parole *m.*; — **of trust** abus de confiance *m.*; — *vt.* ouvrir une brèche; battre en brèche

bread *n.* pain *m.*; — **crumbs** chapelure *f.*; — *vt.* paner, gratiner

breadbasket *n.* corbeille à pain *f.*; (coll.) estomac *m.*

breadboard *n.* planche à pain *f.*

breadth *n.* largeur *f.*

breadwinner *n.* gagne-pain *m.*; soutien de famille *m.*

break *n.* rupture, ouverture *f.*; cassure, fracture *f.*; lacune *f.*; interruption *f.*; répit, battement *m.*; — **of day** pointe du jour *f.*; aube *f.*; — *vt.* briser, casser, rompre; amortir; ruiner; — **one's word** manquer de parole; — **in** enfoncer; rompre; interrompre; — **into** entrer de force; cambrioler; — **open** forcer, enfoncer; — **out** éclater; s'échapper; — **through** percer; — **up** disperser; fragmenter; diviser; **–able** *a.* fragile; **–age** *n.* fracture *f.*; casse *f.*; **–er** *n.* (naut.) brisant *m.*

breakdown *n.* arrêt *m.*; épuisement *m.*; (auto) panne *f.*

breakfast *n.* petit déjeuner *m.*

breakthrough *n.* découverte scientifique ou technologique *f.*

breakwater *n.* brise-lames *m.*; digue *f.*

breast *n.* sein *m.*; mamelle *f.*; poitrine *f.*; — *vt.* affronter

breastbone *n.* sternum *m.*

breastplate *n.* cuirasse *f.*

breastwork *n.* parapet *m.*

breath *n.* haleine *f.*, souffle *m.*; **out of** — essoufflé, à bout de souffle; **–e** *vt. & vi.* respirer, souffler; **–ing** *n.* respiration *f.*, souffle *m.*; **–ing space** répit *m.*; **–less** *a.* essoufflé, haletant

breech *n.* (gun) culasse *f.*; **–es** *n. pl.* culotte *f.*, pantalon *m.*

breed *n.* race *f.*; — *vt.* engendrer, produire; élever, faire de l'élevage; — *vi.* se reproduire; **–ing** *n.* éducation *f.*; élevage *m.*; **–er** *n.* éleveur *m.*; reproduction *f.*; manières *f. pl.*; savoir-vivre *m.*

breeze *n.* brise *f.*; vent *m.*

breezy *a.* venteux; jovial

brethren *n. pl.* frères *m. pl.*

brevity *n.* brièveté *f.*

brew *n.* breuvage *m.*; brassage *m.*; infusion *f.*; — *vt.* brasser; — *vi.* s'infuser; **–er** *n.* brasseur *m.*; **–ery** *n.* brasserie *f.*; **–ing** brassage *m.*

bribe *n.* pot-de-vin *m.*; — *vt.* corrompre, suborner; **–ry** *n.* corruption *f.*

brick *n.* brique *f.*; — *vt.* briqueter

brickbat *n.* briquaillon *m.*; **hurl –s at** (fig.) lapider

bricklayer *n.* maçon *m.*

brickyard *n.* briqueterie *f.*

bridal *a.* nuptial

bride *n.* épousée *f.*; future *f.*

bridegroom *n.* marié *m.*; futur *m.*

bridesmaid *n.* demoiselle d'honneur *f.*

bridge *n.* pont *m.*; (naut.) passerelle *f.*; (cards) bridge *m.*; — *vt.* construire un pont sur; — **a gap** combler une lacune

bridgehead *n.* (mil.) point d'appui *m.*

bridle *n.* bride *f.*; frein *m.*; — **path** piste *f.*; — *vt.* brider; maîtriser

brief *a.* bref; court; concis; **–ly** en résumé;

— *n.* résumé, abrégé *m.*; dossier *m.*;
— *vt.* mettre au courant; –ing *n.* mise
au courant *f.*; –ness *n.* brièveté *f.*; –s
n. pl. sous-vêtement court *m.*
brief case *n.* serviette *f.*
brig *n.* brick *m.*; prison navale *f.*
brigadier general *n.* général de brigade *m.*
brigantine *n.* brigantin *m.*
bright *a.* clair; brillant; lumineux;
éclatant; vif; –en *vt.* faire briller; –en
vi. s'éclaircir; –ness *n.* éclat *m.*;
clarté *f.*; vivacité *f.*; intelligence *f.*
Bright's disease *n.* néphrite albumineuse
f.
brilliance, brilliancy *n.* éclat *m.*, splendeur
f.
brilliant *a.* brillant, éclatant; –ly *adv.*
brillamment
brilliantine *n.* brillantine *f.*
brim *n.* bord *m.*; — *vi.* déborder; –ful,
–ming *a.* débordant
brimstone *n.* soufre *m.*
brine *n.* saumure *f.*
bring *vt.* apporter, amener; — about
causer, opérer; — along amener; —
back ramener; rapporter; — down
descendre; faire crouler; — in introduire; — out sortir; faire ressortir;
— together réunir; — up éduquer,
élever; monter; –ing *n.*, –ing up éducation *f.*
brink *n.* bord *m.*
briny *a.* salé, amer, saumâtre
brisk *a.* actif; vif; rapide; vivifiant; –ness
n. vivacité; activité *f.*
brisket *n.* poitrine *f.*
bristle *n.* soie *f.*; poil *m.*; — *vi.* se hérisser
bristling *a.* hérissé
Britain *n.*, Great — Grande Bretagne *f.*
British *a.* britannique; anglais
Brittany *n.* Bretagne *f.*
brittle *a.* fragile, cassant; –ness *n.* fragilité
f.
broad *a.* large; grand; général; — daylight
plein jour *m.*; — jump saut (en longueur)
m.; –en *vt.* élargir; –en *vi.* s'élargir;
–ness *n.* largeur *f.*
broadcast *n.* radiodiffusion, émission *f.*;
— *vt.* radiodiffuser, émettre; répandre;
–ing *n.* radiodiffusion *f.*; –er *n.* (instrument) émetteur *m.*; (person) micro-
phoniste *m.*
broadcloth *n.* popeline *f.*
broad-minded *a.* aux idées larges;
tolérant
broadside *n.* bordée *f.*; côté *m.*; (print.)
placard *m.*
brocade *n.* brocart *m.*; –d *a.* de brocart
broccoli *n.* brocoli *m.*
brochure *n.* brochure *f.*

brogue *n.* accent *f.* (irlandais) *m.*; patois
m.; (shoe) brogue *f.*
broil *vt. & vi.* griller; –er gril *m.*
broke *a.* (coll.) fauché
broken *a.* brisé, cassé, rompu
broker *n.* agent *m.*; courtier *m.*; (stock)
agent de change *m.*; –age *n.* courtage *m.*
bromide *n.* bromure *m.*
bromine *n.* brome *m.*
bronchi, bronchia *n. pl.* bronches *f. pl.*
bronchial *a.* bronchique
bronchitis *n.* bronchite *f.*
bronco *n.* cheval sauvage (américain) *m.*
brooch *n.* broche, épingle *f.*
brood *n.* couvée *f.*; — hen couveuse *f.*;
— mare poulinière *f.*; — *vi.* couver;
rêver (noir)
brook *n.* ruisseau *m.*; — *vt.* souffrir
broom *n.* balai *m.*
broomstick *n.* manche à balai *m.*
broth *n.* bouillon, consommé *m.*
brothel *n.* bordel *m.*
brother *n.* frère *m.*; –hood *n.* fraternité,
confrérie *f.*; –ly *a.* fraternel; –ly *adv.*
fraternellement
brother-in-law *n.* beau-frère *m.*
brow *n.* front *m.*; sourcil *m.*; to knit one's
— froncer les sourcils
browbeat *vt.* intimider
brown *a.* brun; marron; châtain; bruni; —
paper papier d'emballage *m.*; — sugar
cassonade *f.*; — *n.* brun *m.*; — *vt.*
dorer; brunir; rissoler; –ish *a.* brunâtre
browse *vt. & vi.* brouter; butiner (dans),
feuilleter
bruise *n.* meurtrissure *f.*; bleu *m.*; — *vt.*
meurtrir; –r *n.* costaud, fort, boxeur *m.*
brunette *n.* brune *f.*
brunt *n.* choc *m.*
brush *n.* brosse *f.*; (paint) pinceau *m.*;
(elec.) balai *m.*; (bot.) brousse *f.*; — *vt.*
brosser; — against frôler; — aside
écarter; — up (on) repasser, rafraîchir
brushwood *n.* broussailles *f. pl.*; brindilles
f. pl.
Brussels *n.* Bruxelles; — sprouts choux de
Bruxelles *m. pl.*
brutal *a.* brutal; –ity *n.* brutalité *f.*;
–ize *vt.* abrutir
brute *n.* brute *f.*; — *a.* brutal; sauvage
brutish *a.* brutal; –ness *n.* brutalité *f.*
bubble *n.* bulle *f.*; — gum gomme à
bulles *f.*, bubble-gum *m.*; — *vi.*
bouillonner; — over déborder
buccaneer *n.* boucanier *m.*
buck *n.* daim, chevreuil *m.*; (coll.) dollar
m.; — *a.*, — private (mil.) simple soldat
m.; — teeth dents saillantes *f. pl.*
bucket *n.* seau *m.*

buckle n. boucle, agrafe f.; — vt. boucler, agrafer; — vi. arquer, gauchir; — **down** s'appliquer

buckram n. bougran m.

buckshot n. gros plomb m.

buckskin n. peau de daim f.

buckwheat n. sarrasin m.; — **cakes** n. pl. crêpes de sarrasin f. pl.

bud n. bouton, bourgeon m.; — vi. boutonner; bourgeonner; **–ding** a. en bouton; en germe; en herbe

Buddhism n. bouddhisme m.

Buddhist n. bouddhiste m.

buddy n. copain m.

budge vi. bouger; reculer

budget n. budget m.; **–ary** a. budgétaire

buff a. & n. couleur chamois f.; — vt. polir, émeuler

buffalo n. buffle m.; bison m.

buffer n. (rail.) tampon m.; (polishing) brunissoir m.

buffet vt. frapper, jeter çà et là

buffoon n. bouffon m.; **–ery** n. bouffonnerie f.

bug n. insecte m.; (coll.) idée fixe f.

bugaboo, bugbear n. croque-mitaine m.

buggy n. buggy, boghei m.; **baby —** landau m., poussette f.

bugle n. (mil.) cor de chasse; clairon m.; **–r** n. clairon m.

build vt. bâtir, construire m.; **–er** n. entrepreneur, constructeur m.; (fig.) fondateur m.; **–ing** n. bâtiment, édifice m.; maison f.; construction f.

buildup n. construction; (med.) consolidation f.

bulb n. bulbe f., oignon m.; (elec.) ampoule f.; lampe f.; **–ous** a. bulbeux

bulge n. bosse, protubérance f.; bombement, renflement m.; — vi. faire une bosse, bomber; **–ing** a. bombé; protubérant; bourré

bulk n. masse, quantité f.; volume m.; **in —** en volume, en bloc, en gros; en quantité; **–y** a. volumineux; gros

bulkhead n. cloison f.

bulldoze vt. intimider; **–r** n. bulldozer m.

bullet n. balle f.

bulletin n. bulletin m.; communiqué m.; **— board** tableau d'affichage m.

bulletproof a. à l'épreuve des balles

bullfight n. course de taureaux f.; **–er** n. toréador m.

bullfrog n. grosse grenouille f.

bullion n. or en lingot m.; argent en lingot m.

bullock n. bœuf m.

bull's-eye n. (target) noir, centre m.; (window) œil-de-bœuf m.

bully n. brutal, tyrant m.; —vt. brutaliser, malmener

bulwark n. rempart m.

bumblebee n. bourdon m.

bump n. bosse f.; choc m.; cahot m.; — vt. cogner; — vi. se cogner; **–er** n. (auto.) pare-choc(s); (rail.) tampon m.; **–er** a., **–er crop** récolte magnifique f.; **–y** a. cahoteux

bumpkin n. rustre, lourdaud m.

bun n. petit pain m.; chignon m.

bunch n. botte f., bouquet m.; grappe f.; (keys) trousseau m.; bande f., groupe m.; — vt. grouper; — vi. se serrer

bunco n. mystification, escroquerie f.; tricherie f.

bundle n. paquet m.; liasse f.; ballot m.; — vt. empaqueter, mettre en paquet

bung n. bondon m.; — vt. bondonner

bungle vt. rater; gâcher; **–r** n. maladroit, gâcheur m.

bungling a. gauche, maladroit; — n. maladresse f.

bunion n. oignon (au pied) m.

bunk n. couchette f.; (coll.) balivernes f. pl.; — vi. se coucher

bunker n. soute f.; (golf) banquette f.

Bunsen burner n. bec Bunsen m.

bunting n. drapeaux m. pl.; étamine f.; (bird) bruant m.

buoy n. (naut.) bouée f.; — vt. faire flotter; soutenir; **–ancy** n. flottabilité f.; **–ant** a. flottable

burden n. fardeau m., charge f.; (mus.) refrain m.; **beast of —** bête de somme f.; — vt. charger; **–some** a. onéreux

bureau n. bureau m.; secrétaire m.; commode f.

bureaucracy n. bureaucratie f.

bureaucrat n. bureaucrate, rond-de-cuir m.; **–ic** a. bureaucratique

burgess, burgher n. bourgeois, citoyen m.

burglar n. cambrioleur m.; — **alarm** signalisateur antivol m.; **–ize** vt. cambrioler; **–y** n. cambriolage m.

Burgundy n. Bourgogne f.; — **wine** bourgogne m.; vin de bourgogne m.

burial n. enterrement m.

burlap n. toile d'emballage f.

burlesque a. burlesque; — n. burlesque m.; parodie f.; variété f.; — vt. parodier

burly a. solide, costaud

Burma n. Birmanie f.

burn n. brûlure f.; — vt. & vi. brûler; **–er** n. bec de gaz m.; brûleur m.; **–ing** a. brûlant; embrasé; en feu

burnish vt. brunir, polir

burro n. âne, baudet m.

burrow n. terrier m.; — vt. creuser; — vi. se terrer

bursar n. économe (d'une université) m.

burst n. explosion f.; éclat m.; jet m.;
— vi. éclater, exploser; crever; — out
laughing éclater de rire; — into tears
se mettre à pleurer
bury vt. enterrer, inhumer
bus n. autobus, autocar, car m.
busboy n. garçon de restaurant (chargé
d'enlever le couvert) m.
bush n. buisson m.; arbuste, arbrisseau m.
-y a. buissonneux; touffu
bushel n. demi-boisseau m. (= 36 litres)
bushing n, garniture f.; fourrure f.; paroi
intérieur m.
busily adv. d'un air affairé; activement
business n. affaire(s) f. (pl.); it's none
of your — cela ne vous regarde pas
businesslike a. capable, sérieux
businessman n. commerçant, homme
d'affaires m.
bust n. (sculpture) buste m.; gorge,
poitrine f.
bustle n. remue-ménage, affairement m.;
— vi. se remuer, s'affairer
bustling a. affairé
busy a. occupé, affairé; — vt., — oneself
with s'occuper à
busybody n. officieux m.
but conj. mais; toutefois; — prep. sauf,
excepté; sinon
butcher n. boucher m.; — shop boucherie
f.; — vt. massacrer, égorger; -y n.
massacre m., tuerie f.
butler n. maître d'hôtel m.
butt n. bout m.; (gun) crosse f.; (cigarette)
mégot m.; (of a remark) plastron m.;
(blow) coup de tête m.; — end gros
bout m.; — vt. & vi. buter (contre);
donner des coups de la tête (contre);
— in intervenir sans façon
butter n. beurre m.; — dish beurrier m.;
— vt. beurrer; — up (coll.) flatter; —
fat gras de beurre m.
butterfingered a. maladroit
butterfly n. papillon m.
buttermilk n. petit lait m.; babeurre m.
buttock n. fesse f.
button n. bouton m.; — vt. boutonner
buttonhole n. boutonnière f.; — vt.
interpeller, prendre à part, aborder
buttonhook n. tire-bouton m.
buttress n. arc-boutant m.; contrefort m.;
— vt. arc-bouter
buxom a. plantureux
buy vt. acheter; -er n. acheteur
buzz n. bourdonnement m.; — saw scie
circulaire f.; — vi. bourdonner; -er
n. sonnerie f.
buzzard n. busard m.; vautour m.
by prep. par; près de; en; — adv. là; par
là; close — tout près; — and — tout à

l'heure; to stand — être là
bygone a. d'autrefois, passé
bylaws n. pl. ordonnances f. pl.; règle-
ments m. pl.
by-line n. signature de journaliste f.
bypass n. contournement m., déviation f.;
— vt. contourner, dévier, éviter
byplay n. jeu muet m.
by-product n. dérivé, sous-produit m.
bystander n. assistant, spectateur m.
byway n. chemin obscur m.
byword n. proverbe m.
Byzantine a. byzantin; — Empire Bas-
Empire m.

C

cab n. taxi m.; fiacre m.; cabine f.; —
driver n. chauffeur de taxi m.
cabal n. cabale f.; — vi. cabaler; -istic a.
cabalistique
cabaret m. boîte de nuit f.
cabbage n. chou m.
cabin n. case, cabane f.; (naut.) cabine f.;
— boy mousse m.; — class deuxième
classe f.
cabinet n. cabinet m.; conseil des ministres m.
cabinetmaker n. ébéniste m.
cable n. câble m.; chaîne f.; — vt. câbler
cable car n. funiculaire m.; téléférique m.
cablegram n. câblogramme m.
cable length n. encablure f.
caboose n. (train) fourgon de queue m.
cabstand n. taxiplace f.
cackle n. caquet m.; — vi. caqueter
cacophony n. cacophonie f.
cad n. mufle m.
cadaver n. cadavre m.
caddie, caddy n. (golf) caddie, cadet m.
cadence n. cadence f., rythme m.
cadet n. cadet m.; élève-officier m.
Cadiz n. Cadix
cadmium n. cadmium m.
cæsarian a. césarienne
café n. café, restaurant m.; — curtains
demi-rideaux m. pl.
cafeteria n. self-service, libre-service m.
caffein n. caféine f.
cage n. cage f.; — vt. mettre en cage; encager
cagey a. (coll.) malin, rusé, fin
Cairo n. Le Caire
caisson n. caisson m.
cajole vt. cajoler, enjôler
cajoling a. cajoleur
cake n. gâteau m.; pâtisserie f.; croûte f.;
— of soap pain de savon m.; — vi. s'agglutiner, se prendre; faire croûte

calabash n. calebasse f.
calamitous a. calamiteux, désastreux
calamity n. calamité f.; malheur m.; désastre m.
calcify vt. calcifier; — vi. se calcifier
calcimine n. chaux f.
calcite n. calcaire m.
calcium n. calcium m.
calculate vt. calculer; compter
calculating a. calculateur
calculation n. calcul m.
calculator n. machine à calculer f.
calculus n. calcul, cacul infinitésimal m.
caldron n. chaudron m.
calendar n. calendrier m.
calf n. veau m.; (of the leg) mollet m.
calfskin n. veau m., peau de veau f.
caliber, calibre n. calibre m.
calibrate vt. calibrer; graduer
calipers n. pl. compas à calibrer m.
calisthenics n. pl. callisthénie f.
calk, caulk vt. calfater
call n. appel m.; cri m.; visite f.; **curtain — rappel** m.; **telephone — coup de téléphone** m.; — vt. appeler; crier; convoquer; — vi. faire une visite; (naut.) faire escale; — **for** venir chercher; demander; — **off** rompre; — **up** donner un coup de téléphone; (mil.) mobiliser; **-ing** n. vocation, profession f., métier m.; **-ing card** carte de visite f.
call girl n. prostituée f.
callous a. calleux; insensible, dur
callow a. jeune, inexpérimenté
callus n. callosité f.
calm vt. calmer; tranquilliser; — **down** vt. pacifier; — **down** vi. se calmer; — a. calme, tranquille; —, **-ness** n. calme m.; tranquillité f.
calorie, calory n. calorie f.
calumny n. calomnie, diffamation f.
caluminate vt. calomnier
calvary n. calvaire m.
calve vi. vêler
calyx n. calice m.
cam n. came f.; **-shaft** arbre de distribution m.
Cambodia n. Cambodge m.
cambric n. batiste f.
camel n. chameau m.
cameo n. camée m.
camera n. appareil (photographique) m.; **movie — caméra** m.
cameraman n. photographe m.
Cameroons n. pl. Cameroun m.
camouflage n. camouflage m.; — vt. camoufler
camp n. camp m.; — **bed lit de sangle** m.; — **chair chaise pliante** f.; — vi. camper, faire du camping

campaign n. campagne f.; — vi. faire une campagne; **-er** n. ancien combattant, vétéran m.
camphor n. camphre m.
campus n. parc d'une université m.
camshaft n. arbre à cames m.
can n. boîte f.; bidon m.; — **opener ouvre-boîtes** m.; — vi. pouvoir; savoir; — vt. mettre en boîtes, conserver; **-ned** a. conservé; **-ned goods conserves** f. pl.; **-ned music musique enregistrée** f.; **-nery conserverie** f.
Canadian n. & a. Canadien m.
canal n. canal m. (pl. canaux); **-ize** vt. canaliser
canary n. serin m.
cancel vt. annuler; rescinder; infirmer; rapporter; biffer; **-lation** n. annulation f.; oblitération f.
cancer n. cancer m.; **-ous** a. cancéreux
candelabrum n. candélabre m.
candid a. sincère; franc (franche); — **camera** n. petit appareil pour photographies impromptues m.
candidacy n. candidature f.
candidate n. candidat, aspirant m.
candied a. confit, glacé, candi
candle n. bougie f.; chandelle f.; (eccl.) cierge f.: — **power bougie** f.
candlestick n. chandelier, bougeoir m.
candor n. franchise, sincérité f.
candy n. confiserie f., sucreries f. pl.; — vt. glacer, faire candir
cane n. canne f.; jonc m.; bâton m., badine f.; — **sugar sucre de canne** m.; **sugar — canne à sucre** f.; — vt. battre, bâtonner; (chair) canner
canine a. canin, de chien; — **tooth canine**, œillère f.
canister n. boîte f.; (mil.) mitraille f.
canker n. chancre m.; (fig.) plaie f.; — vt. ronger corrompre
cannibal n. cannibale, anthropophage m. & f.; **-ism** n. cannibalisme m., anthropophagie f.; **-istic** a. cannibale
cannon n. canon m.; — **ball** n. boulet de canon m.; — **shot** n. coup de canon m.
canoe n. canoë m.; pirogue f.; — vi. faire du canoë; pagayer; **to go -ing faire du canoë; -ist** n. canotier m.
canon n. canon m., règle f.; (person) chanoine m.; — **law** n. droit canon m.; **-ize** vt. canoniser
canopy n. dais, baldaquin m.; marquise f.
cant n. inclinaison f.; (arch.) pan coupé m.; argot, jargon m.; hypocrisie f.; — vt. incliner; **-ing** a. hypocrite
cantaloupe n. cantaloup m.
cantankerous a. revêche, acariâtre
cantata n. cantate f.

canteen *n.* cantine *f.*; bidon *m.*

canter *n.* petit galop *m.*; — *vi.* aller au petit galop

canto *n.* chant *m.*

canton *n.* canton *m.*

canvas *n.* toile *f.*; canevas *m.*; **-back duck** *n.* canard américain *m.*

canvass *vt.* solliciter; faire une tournée électorale; (com.) faire la place; **-er** *n.* solliciteur *m.*; placier *m.*; **-ing** *n.* sollicitation *f.*

canyon *n.* cañon *m.*, gorge *f.*

cap *n.* bonnet *m.*, casquette *f.*; toque *f.*; chapeau *m.*; capuchon *m.*; — **and gown** costume académique *m.*; — *vt.* coiffer; capsuler; couronner; (shell) amorcer

capability *n.* capacité *f.*; faculté *f.*

capable *a.* capable; habile; susceptible

capacious *a.* spacieux, vaste, ample

capacity *n.* capacité *f.*; intelligence, aptitude *f.*; contenance *f.*

capacitate *vt.* rendre capable

cape *n.* cap, promontoire *m.*; pèlerine, cape *f.*; manteau *m.*

Cape of Good Hope Cap de Bonne Espérance *m.*

caper *n.* cabriole *f.*; (bot.) câpre *f.*; — *vi.* faire des cabrioles

capillary *a.* capillaire

capital *a.* capital (*pl.* capitaux); — **punishment** peine capitale *f.*; — *n.* capital, fonds *m.*; (city) capitale *f.*; (letter) majuscule *f.*; (arch.) chapiteau *m.*; **-ism** *n.* capitalisme *m.*; **-ist** *n.* capitaliste *m.* & *f.*; **-ize** *vt.* écrire avec une majuscule; capitaliser

Capitol *n.* Capitole *m.*; — *a.* capitolin

capitulate *vi.* capituler

capitulation *n.* capitulation *f.*

capon *n.* chapon *m.*

caprice *n.* caprice *m.*, lubie *f.*

capricious *a.* capricieux

capsize *vi.* chavirer; capoter; — *vt.* faire chavirer

capsizing *n.* chavirement, capotage *m.*

capstan *n.* cabestan *m.*

capsule *n.* capsule *f.*

captain *n.* capitaine *m.*; chef *m.*; (sports) chef d'équipe *m.*; — *vt.* commander, diriger, conduire; **-cy** *n.* grade de capitaine *m.*; direction *f.*, commandement *m.*

caption *n.* rubrique *f.*; sous-titre *m.*; (law) arrestation *f.*

captious *a.* captieux, pointilleux

captivate *vt.* captiver, fasciner, charmer

captivating *a.* captivant; séduisant, charmant

captive *a.* captif; — *n.* captif, prisonnier *m.*

captivity *n.* captivité *f.*

captor *n.* preneur, ravisseur *m.*

capture *n.* prise *f.*; capture *f.*; — *vt.* prendre; capturer

car *n.* auto, automobile, voiture *f.*; (rail.) wagon *m.*; — **pool** système coopératif de voyager entre la maison et le travail en employant des voitures particulières *m.* used — *n.* voiture d'occasion *f.*

caramel *n.* caramel *m.*; caramel mou *m.*

caravan *n.* caravane *f.*; roulotte *f.*

caravansary *n.* caravansérail *m.*

caraway *n.* carvi, cumin *m.*

carbide *n.* carbure *m.*

carbine *n.* carabine *f.*

carbohydrate *n.* hydrate de carbone *m.*

carbolic *a.* phénique; — **acid** phénol *m.*

carbon *n.* carbone *m.*; — **copy** double *m.*, copie *f.*; — **dioxide** anhydride carbonique *m.*; — **14** (chem.) carbone 14 *m.*; — **monoxide** oxyde de carbone *m.*; — **paper** papier carbone *m.*

carborundum *n.* carborundum *m.*

carbuncle *n.* carboncle *m.*; (stone) escarboucle *f.*

carburetor *n.* carburateur *m.*

carcass *n.* cadavre, corps *m.*; carcasse *f.*

carcinogen *n.* (med.) carcinogénique *m.*

card *n.* carte *f.*; index — fiche *f.*; (coll.) original *m.*; (racing) programme *m.*; **dance** — carnet de bal *m.*; **deck of -s** jeu de cartes *m.*; — **index** fichier, classeur *m.*; — **sharp** *n.* tricheur *m.*; — **table** table de jeu *f.*; — *vt.* carder, peigner

cardboard *n.* carton *m.*

cardiac *a.* cardiaque

cardigan *n.* gilet *m.*

cardinal *a.* cardinal, fondamental; pourpre; — *n.* cardinal *m.*

cardiogram *n.* cardiogramme *m.*

cardiology *n.* cardiologie *f.*

care *n.* souci *m.*; attention *f.*; soins *m. pl.*; sollicitude *f.*; préoccupation *f.*; **take —** not to se garder de, prendre garde de; **take —** of se charger de; arranger; soigner; — *vi.* se soucier; se préoccuper; **I don't —** cela m'est égal; — **for** soigner; aimer; **-ful** *a.* soigneux; attentif; prudent; **-ful!** faites attention!; **-fully** *adv.* soigneusement, avec soin; attentivement; **-fulness** *n.* soin *m.*, attention *f.*; **-less** *a.* négligent; insouciant; **-lessly** *adv.* négligemment; **-lessness** *n.* négligence *f.*; inattention *f.*; insouciance *f.*

careen *vi.* donner de la bande

career *n.* carrière *f.*

carefree *a.* sans souci; insouciant

caress *n.* caresse *f.*; — *vt.* caresser; **-ing** *a.* caressant

caret *n.* signe d'omission *m.*

caretaker n. concierge m. & f.; intendant m.; gardien m.; — **government** régime intérimaire m.

carfare n. prix d'un billet, tarif, billet de tramway m.

cargo n. cargaison f.; chargement m.; — **ship** cargo m.

Caribbean Sea n. mer des Caraïbes f.

caricature n. caricature f.; — vt. caricaturer

caricaturist n. caricaturiste m.

caries n. carie f.

carmine n. carmin m.; — a. carmin; carminé

carnage n. carnage m.

carnal a. charnel; sexuel; sensuel; — **sin** péché de la chair m.

carnation n. (bot.) œillet m.; — a. & n. (color) incarnat m.

carnival n. carnaval m.; fête foraine f.

carnivorous a. carnivore; carnassier

carol n. chant m.; **Christmas —** noël m.; — vt. & vi. chanter

carom n. carambolage m.; — vi. caramboler

carouse vi. faire la bombe

carp n. carpe f.; — vi. critiquer, trouver à redire, épiloguer; -**ing** a. pointilleux; -**ing** n. critique pointilleuse f.

carpenter n. charpentier m.; menuisier m.

carpentry n. charpenterie f.

carpet n. tapis m.; — **sweeper** balayeuse f.; **lay a —** poser un tapis; — vt. recouvrir d'un tapis; -**ed** a. (re)couvert d'un tapis; tapissé; -**ing** n. tapis m.

carpool n. voiture commune f.

carport n. garage ouvert m.; remise f.

carriage n. voiture f.; port m., maintien m.; (gun) affût m.; (typewriter) chariot m.; — **entrance** porte cochère f.

carrier n. porteur m.; voiturier m.; — **pigeon** pigeon voyageur m.; **aircraft —** porte-avions m.; **letter —** facteur m.; **luggage —** porte-bagages m.

carrion n. charogne f.

carrot n. carotte f.

carry vt. porter; emporter; vendre, avoir; conduire; pousser; adopter; (math.) retenir; — **away** (emotion) entraîner, transporter; — **forward** avancer; reporter; — **off** enlever; emporter; réussir; — **on** continuer; soutenir; se comporter; — **out** exécuter; remplir; **be carried** être voté; **be carried away** (fig.) être entraîné; s'emporter; — n. portée f., trajet m.; -**ing** n. port, transport m.

carryall n. charrette, carriole f.

cart n. charrette f.; tombereau m.; — vt. charrier; -**age** n. charriage, transport m.; -**er** n. camionneur m.; charretier m.;

voiturier m.

Cartesian a. cartésien

Carthusian a. & n. chartreux m.; chartreuse f.

cartilage n. cartilage m.

cartographer n. cartographe m

cartography n. cartographie f.

carton n. carton m.; boîte f.

cartoon n. caricature f.; (movies) dessin animé m.; -**ist** n. caricaturiste m.

cartridge n. cartouche f.; (record-player) cellule de lecture f.

cartwheel n. roue f.; **do -s** faire les roues

cartwright n. charron m.

carve vt. découper; graver, sculpter; tailler

carving n. découpage m.; gravure, sculpture f.; — **knife** n. couteau à découper m.; — **set** service à découper m.

cascade n. cascade, chute d'eau f.; — vi. cascader

case n. cas m.; (law) cause f.; caisse f.; colis m.; écrin m.; trousse f.; étui m.; boîte f.; (glass) vitrine f.; (med.) malade m. & f.; (typ.) casse f.; (watch) boîtier m.; **in any —** en tout cas; **upper —** haut de casse m.; — vt. encaisser; envelopper; (coll.) observer, épier

casehardened a. aciéré, cimenté; (person) endurci

casement window n. croisée f.

cash n. argent comptant m.; espèces f. pl.; — **box** n. caisse f.; cassette f.; — **on delivery** contre remboursement; — **register** caisse enregistreuse f.; — vt. toucher, escompter

cashew n. noix d'acajou f.

cashier n. caissier m., caissière f.; — vt. casser; -**'s check** chèque bancaire m.

cashmere n. cachemire m.

casing n. enveloppe f.; chemise f.

cask n. tonneau, fût m., barrique f.

casket n. cassette f.; cercueil m.

Caspian Sea n. Mer Caspienne f.

cassava n. cassave f.

cassock n. soutane f.

cast n. jet m.; coup m.; coulée f.; moulage m.; (theat.) distribution f.; — vt. lancer, jeter; fondre; mouler; couler; (theat.) distribuer; — **lots** tirer au sort; — **aside** mettre de côté; — **off** rejeter; (naut.) abattre; — vt. mettre à la porte; exorciser; — a. moulé; coulé; — **iron** fonte (de fer) f.; -**ing** n. fonte f., moulage m.; jet m.; pièce de fonte f.

castanet n. castagnette f.

castaway n. naufragé m.

caster n. roulette f.

castigate vt. châtier, corriger

castigation n. châtiment m., correction f.

Castile n. Castille f.; — **soap** savon blanc

m.
castle *n.* château *m.*; château fort *m.*;
(chess) tour *f.*; — *vt.* (chess) roquer
castoff *a.* jeté, rejeté; vieux; — *n.* rejeté *m.*
castor oil *n.* huile de ricin *f.*
castrate *vt.* châtrer *m.*
castration *n.* castration *f.*
casual *a.* accidentel, fortuit; indifférent;
désinvolte; insouciant; **–ly** *adv.* par hasard, fortuitement; négligemment
casualty *n.* blessé *m.*; mort *m.*; accidenté
m.
cat *n.* chat *m.*, chatte *f.*; **let the — out of
the bag** vendre la mèche; **–ty** *a.* can-
canier, méchant
cataclysm *n.* cataclysme *m.*; **–ic** *a.* cata-
clysmique
catacombs *n. pl.* catacombes *f. pl.*
catalepsy *n.* catalepsie *f.*
cataleptic *a.* cataleptique
catalog, catalogue *n.* catalogue *m.*; prix-
courant *m.*; liste *f.*; — *vt.* cataloguer
Catalonia *n.* Catalogne *f.*
catalyst *n.* catalyseur *m.*
catalytic *a.* catalyseur, catalytique
catapult *n.* catapulte *f.*; lance-pierres *m.*;
— *vt.* lancer
cataract *n.* cataracte *f.*
catastrophe *n.* catastrophe *f.*
catcall *n.* huée *f.*; sifflet *m.*
catch *n.* prise *f.*; (door) loquet *m.*; (clothing) agrafe *f.*; (buckle) ardillon *m.*;
(fishing) pêche *f.*; attrape *f.*; — *vt.* attraper; saisir; prendre; surprendre; accrocher; — *vi.* prendre, s'engager; s'accrocher; — **on** réussir, prendre; comprendre; — **up with** rattraper; — **cold**
s'enrhumer; — **fire** s'enflammer, prendre feu; **–ing** *a.* contagieux; communicatif; **–y** *a.* entraînant, facile à retenir
catchall *n.* sac ou panier pour recevoir
tout *m.*; catégorie qui comporte un mélange de choses *f.*
catechism *n.* catéchisme *m.*
categorical *a.* catégorique
category *n.* catégorie *f.*
cater *vi.* pourvoir, approvisionner; **–er** *n.*
approvisionneur, pourvoyeur *m.*; **–ing**
n. approvisionnement *m.*
cater-cornered, catty-cornered *a.* diagona
caterpillar *n.* chenille *f.*
catfish *n.* loup marin *m.*
catgut *n.* corde de boyau *f.*
cathartic *a.* cathartique, purgatif
cathedral *n.* cathédrale *f.*
catheter *n.* cathéter *m.*
cathode *n.* cathode *f.*
cathode-ray tube *n.* tube cathodique *m.*
catholic *a.* universel; éclectique
Catholic *n. & a.* (eccl.) catholique *m. & f.*;

–ism *n.* catholicisme *m.*
catkin *n.* (bot.) chaton *m.*
catnap *n.* petit somme *m.*
catnip *n.* cataire *f.*
cat's-paw *n.* (fig.) dupe *f.*
catsup *n.* sauce tomaille *f.*
cattle *n.* bétail *m.*; bêtes *f. pl.*; bestiaux
m. pl.
cattleman *n.* éleveur de bétail *m.*
catwalk *n.* coursive *f.*
caucus *n.* réunion *f.* (d'une clique politique)
cauliflower *n.* chou-fleur *m.*
cause *n.* cause *f.*; raison *f.*; sujet *m.*; procès *m.*; **have –(to)** avoir lieu (de); — *vt.*
causer; faire; occasionner
causeway *n.* chaussée *f.*
caustic *a.* caustique; mordant
cauterize *vt.* cautériser
caution *n.* prudence, précaution *f.*; circonspection *f.*; avertissement *m.*; — *interj.*
attention! — *vt.* avertir
cautious *a.* prudent; circonspect; **–ly** *adv.*
prudemment; avec circonspection
cavalcade *n.* cavalcade *f.*
cavalier *n.* cavalier *m.*; — *a.* cavalier,
désinvolte
cavalry *n.* cavalerie *f.*
cave *n.* grotte *f.*, souterrain *m.*; caverne *f.*,
antre *m.*; — **man** troglodyte *m.*; — *vi.*,
— **in** s'effondrer
cavern *n.* caverne *f.*; **–ous** *a.* caverneux
cavil *vi.* ergoter, chicaner
cavity *n.* cavité *f.*; creux *m.*; trou *m.*;
(tooth) carie *f.*
cavort *vi.* gambader, caracoler
caw *vi.* croasser; —, **–ing** *n.* croassement
m.
cease *vt. & vi.* cesser; (s')arrêter; — **fire**
cesser le feu; — **fire** *n.* trêve *f.*; **–less** *a.*
incessant, continuel; sans arrêt; **–lessly**
adv. sans cesse
cedar *n.* cèdre *m.*
cede *vt. & vi.* céder
cedilla *n.* cédille *f.*
ceiling *n.* plafond *m.*; (avi.) ciel, plafond
m.; — **price** prix maximum *m.*
celebrate *vt.* fêter; célébrer; commémorer;
–ed *a.* célèbre, renommé
celebration *n.* fête *f.*; commémoration *f.*;
célébration *f.*
celebrity *n.* célébrité *f.*; vedette *f.*
celery *n.* céleri *m.*
celestial *a.* céleste; — **mechanics** *n.*
mécanique céleste *f.*
celibacy *n.* célibat *m.*
celibate *a. & n.* célibataire *m. & f.*
cell *n.* cellule *f.*; cachot *m.*; (pol.) noyau
m.; (elec.) élément *m.*; pile *f.*
cellar *n.* cave *f.*; sous-sol *m.*

cello, 'cello *n.* violoncelle *m.*

cellophane *n.* cellophane *f.*

cellular *a.* cellulaire

celluloid *n.* celluloïd *m.*

cellulose *a.* celluleux; — *n.* cellulose *f.*

Celt *n.* Celte *m. & f.*; **-ic** *a.* celte; celtique; **-ic** *n.* celtique

cement *n.* ciment *m.*; cément *m.*; — *vt.* cimenter; cémenter; consolider

cemetery *n.* cimetière *m.*

cenotaph *n.* cénotaphe *m.*

censer *n.* (eccl.) encensoir *m.*

censor *n.* censeur *m.*; — *vt.* interdire; supprimer; **-ing**, **-ship** *n.* censure *f.*; contrôle *m.*

censurable *a.* blâmable, censurable

censure *n.* censure *f.*; blâme *m.*; — *vt.* censurer, blâmer

census *n.* recensement *m.*

cent *n.* cent *m.*; sou, liard *m.*; **per** — pour cent

centennial *a. & n.* centenaire *m.*

center *n.* centre *m.*; milieu *m.*; foyer *m.*; — *vt.* centrer; placer au centre; — *vi.* se concentrer

centerpiece *n.* surtout, milieu *m.*

centigrade *a.* centigrade

centigram *n.* centigramme *m.*

centimeter *n.* centimètre *m.*

centipede *n.* centipède *m.*; myriapode *m.*; mille-pattes *m.*

central *a.* central; **-ization** *n.* centralisation *f.*; **-ize** *vt.* centraliser

Central America *n.* Amérique Centrale *f.*

centrifugal *a.* centrifuge

centrifuge *n.* centrifugeuse *f.*

centripetal *a.* centripète

century *n.* siècle *m.*; — **old** *a.* séculaire

cereal *a. & n.* céréale *f.*

cerebellum *n.* cervelet *m.*

cerebral *a.* cérébral; — **palsy** *n.* paralysie cérébrale *f.*

cerebrum *n.* cerveau *m.*

ceremonial *a.* cérémonial, de cérémonie; — *n.* cérémonial *m.*

ceremonious *a.* cérémonieux

ceremony *n.* cérémonie *f.*; **stand on** — faire des façons; **without** — sans façon(s)

certain *a.* certain, sûr; **make** — s'assurer; **-ly** *adv.* certainement, assurément; parfaitement; certes; **-ty** *n.* certitude *f.*

certificate *n.* certificat *m.*; attestation *f.*; acte *m.*; titre *m.*; diplôme *m.*; **birth** — acte de naissance *m.*

certification *n.* certification, attestation *f.*

certified *a.* certifié; — **check** chèque visé *m.*; — **public accountant** expert-comptable diplômé *m.*

certify *vt.* certifier; attester; authentiquer,

homologuer, légaliser; constater; diplômer

certitude *n.* certitude *f.*

cessation *n.* cessation *f.*

cesspool *n.* fosse d'aisance *f.*

Ceylon *n.* Ceylan *m.*

chafe *vt.* échauffer; frotter; frictionner; irriter; — *vi.* s'énerver, s'irriter

chaff *n.* paille menue *f.*; balle *f.*; (coll.) raillerie *f.*; — *vt.* railler, persifler

chafing *n.* écorchement, frottement *m.*; irritation *f.*; — **dish** réchaud de table *m.*

chagrin *n.* chagrin *m.*; mortification *f.*; dépit *m.* **to be -ed** être mortifié

chain *n.* chaîne *f.*; chaînette *f.*; enchaînement *m.*, — **gang** chaîne de forçats *f.*; — **smoker** fumeur à la file *m.*; — **reaction** réaction en chaîne *f.*; — **stitch** point de chaînette *m.*; — **store** succursale *f.*; — **stores** grand magasin à succursales *m.*; société coopérative *f.*; — *vt.* enchaîner; attacher

chair *n.* chaise *f.*; siège *m.*; fauteuil *m.*; (academic) chaire *f.*

chairman *n.* président *m.*; **-ship** *n.* présidence *f.*

chalice *n.* calice *m.*

chalk *n.* craie *f.*; (geol.) calcaire *m.* (billiards) blanc *m.*; **French** — *n.* talc *m.*; — *vt.*, marquer à la craie; — **up** marquer; attribuer; **-y** *a.* crayeux

challenge *n.* défi *m.*; (mil.) qui-vive *m.*, interpellation *f.*; (sports) challenge *m.*; — *vt.* défier; interpeller; provoquer; disputer, mettre en doute

challenging *a.* de défi; provocateur; provocant; (coll.) très intéressant

chamber *n.* chambre *f.*; salle *f.*, pièce *f.*; — **music** musique de chambre *f.*

chamberlain *n.* chambellan *m.*

chambermaid *n.* femme de chambre *f.*

chameleon *n.* caméléon *m.*

champ *vt. & vi.* mâcher, ronger

champagne *n.* (vin de) champagne *m.*

champion *n.* champion, recordman *m.*; — *vt.* défendre, soutenir; **-ship** *n.* championnat *m.*

chance *n.* hasard *m.*, chance *f.*; sort *m.*; accident *m.*; occasion *f.*; risque *m.*; **by** — par hasard; **off** — chance moyenne; **take a** — encourir un risque; — *vt.* risquer; — *vi.* venir à; — *a.* fortuit; de rencontre

chancellor *n.* chancelier *m.*; ministre *m.*

chandelier *n.* lustre *m.*

change *n.* changement *m.*; monnaie *f.*; revirement *m.*; — **of address** changement de domicile *m.*; **for a** — comme distraction; — **of clothes** vêtements de rechange *m. pl.*; — *vt.* changer; échanger;

donner la monnaie; transformer; modifier; — **clothes** changer de vêtements; — **the subject** changer de sujet; — **color** changer de visage; — *vi.* (se) changer; tourner; **-ability** *n.* mobilité *f.*; variabilité *f.*; **-able** *a.* mobile; variable; **-less** *a.* immuable; éternel

changing *a.* changeant; — *n.* changement *m.*; — **of the guard** relève *f.*

channel *n.* canal *m.*; lit *m.*; chenal *m.*; conduit *m.*; rigole *f.*; voie *f.*; — *vt.* canneler; creuser des rigoles

chant *n.* chant *m.*; (eccl.) psalmodie *f.*; — *vt.* chanter; (eccl.) psalmodier

chanty *n.* chanson (de bord) *f.*

chaos *n.* chaos *m.*

chaotic *a.* chaotique

chap *n.* type, individu *m.*

chap *vt.* crevasser, gercer; — *n.* crevasse, gerçure *f.*; **-ped hands** des crevasses aux mains

chapel *n.* chapelle *f.*; oratoire *m.*

chaplain *n.* aumônier *m.*

chapter *n.* chapitre *m.*; bureau régional ou local d'une société *m.*

char *vt.* carboniser; — *vi.* se carboniser

character *n.* caractère *m.*; marque *f.*; lettre *f.*; personnage *m.*; sujet *m.*; type *m.*; — **actor** acteur de genre *m.*; **be in** — s'accorder, s'harmoniser; **-istic** *a.* caractéristique; **-istic** *n.* trait *m.*; **-istically** *adv.* d'une manière caractéristique; **-ization** *n.* caractérisation *f.*; **-ize** *vt.* caractériser, dépeindre

charcoal *n.* charbon de bois *m.*; (art) fusain *m.*; — **burner** *n.* charbonnier *m.*

charge *n.* prix *m.*; charge *f.*; soin *m.*; accusation; devoir *m.*; fonction *f.*; (of a judge) résumé *m.*; **free of** — gratis; exempt de frais; **take** — **of** se charger de; — **account** compte courant *m.*; — *vt.* charger; accuser; imputer; débiter; demander; porter; **-able** *a.* accusable; imputable; **-r** *n.* cheval de bataille *m.*; (elec.) chargeur *m.*

chariot *n.* char *m.*

charitable *a.* charitable

charity *n.* charité *f.*; aumônes *f. pl.*; bienfaisance *f.*

Charley horse *n.* crampe musculaire, raideur musculaire *f.* (comme résultat d'un exercice violent)

charm *n.* charme, sortilège *m.*; porte-bonheur *m.*; breloque *f.*; — *vt.* charmer, enchanter; ensorceler; **-ing** *a.* charmant

chart *n.* carte *f.*; diagramme *m.*; — *vt.* dresser la carte de; **-er** *n.* charte *f.*; privilège *m.*; (naut.) affrètement *m.*; **-er member** membre fondateur *m.*; **-er** *vt.* accorder une charte à; (naut.) affré-

ter; **-ered** *a.* à charte; privilégié; affrété

chase *n.* chasse, poursuite *f.*; — *vt.* chasser; poursuivre; (gold) ciseler; (metal) repousser; (gem) enchâsser; — **away** chasser; **-r** *n.* chasseur *m.*; pousse-café *m.*; boisson (d'ordinaire) non-alcoolique prise après un verre de whisky *f.*

chasm *n.* gouffre *m.*; chasme *m.*; abîme *m.*

chassis *n.* châssis *m.*

chaste *a.* chaste; pudique; pur; **-n** *vt.* châtier

chastise *vt.* châtier, corriger; **-ment** *n.* châtiment *m.*

chastity *n.* chasteté, pureté *f.*

chat *n.* causerie *f.*; — *vi.* causer, jaser; **-ty** *a.* causeur

chattel *n.* bien mobilier *m.*

chatter *n.* bavardage *m.*; caquetage *m.*; — *vi.* bavarder, caqueter, jaser; claquer; **-ing** *n.* (teeth) claquement *m.*; (people) bavardage *m.*; (birds) caquetage *m.*

chatterbox *n.* bavard, babillard *m.*

chauffeur *n.* chauffeur *m.*

chauvinism *n.* chauvinisme *m.*

cheap *a.* bon marché; (coll.) honteux; **-en** *vt.* baisser le prix de; **-er** *a.* meilleur marché; **-ly** *adv.* bon marché; **-ness** *n.* bon marché, bas prix *m.*; qualité inférieure *f.*; médiocrité *f.*

cheat *n.* tricheur, escroc *m.*; trompeur *m.*; — *vt.* tricher; tromper; frauder; **-ing** *n.* tricherie *f.*; tromperie *f.*

check *n.* chèque *m.*; billet, bulletin, ticket *m.*; contrôle *m.*; vérification *f.*; arrêt *m.*; frein *m.*; (chess) échec *m.*; carreau *m.*; — **list** liste de contrôle *f.*; — *vt.* vérifier; contrôler; arrêter; freiner; retenir, refouler; (chess) faire échec; (baggage) faire enregistrer; — *vi.* s'arrêter; hésiter; — **off** pointer; — **in** (hotel) s'inscrire dans le registre d'un hôtel; — **out** quitter l'hôtel; **-ed** *a.* (material) à carreaux; **-er** *n.* contrôleur *m.*; **-ing** *n.* contrôle *m.*; vérification *f.*; enregistrement *m.*; **-ing account** compte en banque *m.*

checkbook *n.* carnet de chèques *m.*

checkerboard *n.* damier *m.*

checkered *a.* à carreaux, quadrillé; — **career** vie mouvementée *f.*

checkers *n. pl.* dames *f. pl.*

checkmate *n.* échec et mat *m.*; — *vt.* faire échec et mat à

checkroom *n.* vestiaire *m.*; consigne *f.*

checkup *n.* examen *m.*; vérification *f.*

cheddar *n.* cheddar *m.*

cheek *n.* joue *f.*; (coll.) impertinence *f.*, toupet *m.*; **-bone** *n.* pommette *f.*

cheep *vi.* piauler; —, **-ing** *n.* piaulement *m.*

cheer *n.* humeur, disposition *f.*; encouragement *m.*; ban *m.*; acclamation *f.*; — *vt.*

encourager; égayer; acclamer; — **up** se
ragaillardir; — **up!** courage!; –**ful** *a.* de
bonne humeur, gai, égayant; –**fully** *adv.*
gaiement; volontiers, de bon cœur: –**ing**
a. réjouissant; encourageant; –**ing** *n.*
acclamation *f.*; –**less** *a.* triste, morne
cheerleader *n.* étudiant qui organise et
dirige les bans aux événements sportifs
m.
cheese *n.* fromage *m.*
cheesecake *n.* pâtisserie au **fromage** *f.*;
(phot.) (coll.) cheesecake *m.*
cheesecloth *n.* gaze *f.*
chef *n.* chef de cuisine *m.*
chemical *a.* chimique; — *n.* produit chimique *m.*
chemist *n.* chimiste *m.*; –**ry** *n.* chimie *f.*
cherish *vt.* chérir; nourrir, caresser
cherry *n.* cerise *f.*; — **orchard** cerisaie *f.*;
— **tree** cerisier *m.*; — *a.* cerise, vermeil;
wild — merise *f.*
cherub *n.* chérubin *m.*; –**ic** *a.* chérubique
chess *n.* échecs *m.* *pl.*
chessboard *n.* échiquier *m.*
chessman, chesspiece *n.* pièce *f.*
chest *n.* poitrine *f.*; coffret *m.*, caisse *f.*;
— **of drawers** commode *f.*
chestnut *n.* châtaigne *f.*; marron *m.*; (tree)
châtaignier, marronnier *m.*; — *a.* châtain, châtaigne
cheviot *n.* cheviote *f.*
chew *vt.* mâcher; (tobacco) chiquer; (fig.)
méditer; — *n.* morceau *m.*; –**ing** *n.* mas-
tication *f.*; –**ing gum** gomme à mâcher
f.; chewing-gum *m.*
chicanery *n.* chicane, chicanerie *f.*
chicken *n.* poulet *m.*; **spring** — poussin *m.*;
— **pox** *n.* varicelle *f.*
chick-pea *n.* pois chiche *m.*
chicory *n.* chicorée *f.*; endive *f.*
chide *vt.* reprocher; gronder
chief *n.* chef *m.*; patron *m.*; — **of staff** chef
de l'état-major *m.*; — **justice** président
du tribunal *m.*; — *a.* principal; en chef;
–**ly** *adv.* surtout; principalement
chieftain *n.* chef *m.*
chiffon *n.* chiffon *m.*, gaze *f.*
chilblain *n.* engelure *f.*
child *n.* enfant *m.* & *f.*; **with** — enceinte;
–**ish** *a.* enfantin, d'enfant; puéril; –**ishness** *n.* puérilité *f.*
childbirth *n.* accouchement *m.*
childhood *n.* enfance *f.*
Chile *n.* Chili *m.*
chill *n.* froid *m.*; coup de froid *m.*; froidure
f.; refroidissment *m.*; frisson *m.*; **take
the** — **off** (faire) tiédir; — *vt.* glacer,
refroidir; réfrigérer; faire frissonner; –**ed**
a. glacé; –**iness** *n.* froideur *f.*; fraîcheur
f.; –**ing** *a.* glacial; –**y** *a.* frais, froid; feel

–**y** avoir froid; **be** –**y** (behavior) être
froid
chime *n.* carillon *m.*; — *vt.* & *vi.* carillonner; — **in** intervenir
chimerical *a.* chimérique
chiming *n.* carillonnement *m.*; sonnerie *f.*
chimney *n.* cheminée *f.*; — **sweep** *n.* ramoneur *m.*; — **sweeping** *n.* ramonage *m.*
chimpanzee *n.* chimpanzé *m.*
chin *n.* menton *m.*
China *n.* Chine *f.*
china *n.* porcelaine *f.*
Chinese *a.* & *n.* chinois *m.*
chink *n.* fente, crevasse *f.*
chip *n.* copeau, éclat *m.*; brisure *f.*; fragment *m.*; (cards) jeton *m.*; — *vt.*
ébrécher; enlever un copeau (un fragment) à; — *vi.* s'écailler; — **in** contribuer, cotiser
chipmunk *n.* tamias *m.*
chipper *a.* gai, heureux
chiropodist *n.* pédicure *m.*
chiropracter *n.* chiropracteur *m.*
chirp *n.* gazouillement *m.*; grésillement
m.; chant *m.*; — *vi.* pépier, gazouiller;
grésiller
chisel *n.* ciseau *m.*; — *vt.* ciseler
chitchat *n.* conversation *f.*; bavardage *m.*
chivalrous *a.* chevaleresque, de chevalerie
chivalry *n.* chevalerie *f.*
chive *n.* ciboulette *f.*
chloride *n.* chlorure *m.*
chlorinate *vt.* chlorurer
chlorination *n.* chloruration *f.*
chlorine *n.* chlore *m.*
chloroform *n.* chloroforme *m.*; — *vt.*
chloroformer, chloroformiser
chlorophyll *n.* chlorophylle *f.*
chock-full *a.* bondé, comble; bourré
chocolate *n.* chocolat *m.*
choice *n.* choix *m.*; alternative *f.*; préférence *f.*; — *a.* de choix
choir *n.* chœur *m.*
choke *n.* (auto.) étrangleur *m.*; — *vt.* & *vi.*
suffoquer, étouffer, étrangler; boucher;
— **back** refouler; –**r** *n.* foulard *m.*;
(necklace) collier court *m.*
choking *n.* étranglement, étouffement *m.*;
suffocation *f.*
choleric *a.* colérique
cholesterol *n.* cholestérol *m.*
choose *vt.* choisir; élire; préférer; opter;
vouloir
choosing *n.* choix *m.*
choosy *a.* (coll.) difficile à plaire
chop *n.* côtelette *f.*; coup de hache *m.*;
lick one's –**s** se lécher les babines; —
vi. hacher; couper; — *vi.* clapoter; —
down abattre; — **off** trancher, couper;
–**ped meat** viande hachée *f.*; –**per** *n.*

couperet, hachoir *m.*; **-py** *a.* clapoteux
chopsticks *n. pl.* baguettes *f. pl.*, bâton-
nets *m. pl.*
chord *n.* accord *m.*
chore *n.* devoir *m.*; corvée *f.*; **-s** *n. pl.*
travaux de ménage *m. pl.*
choreography *n.* chorégraphie *f.*
chorister *n.* choriste *m.*; enfant de chœur
m.
chortle *vi.* glousser
chorus *n.* chœur *m.*; refrain *m.*; — *vt.*
répéter en chœur
chosen *a.* choisi, élu
Christ *n.* Le Christ, Jésus-Christ *m.*
christen *vt.* baptiser; **-ing** *n.* baptême *m.*
Christendom *n.* chrétienté *f.*
Christian *n. & a.* chrétien *m.*; — **name**
prénom *m.*, nom de baptême *m.*; **-ity**
n. christianisme *m.*
Christmas *n.* Noël *m.*; Merry — joyeux
Noël; — **card** carte de Noël *f.*; — **carol**
chant de Noël *m.*; — Eve la veille de
Noël *f.*; — **presents** cadeaux de Noël
m. pl.
chromatic *a.* chromatique
chrome *n.* acier chromé *m.*; chromage *m.*
chromium *n.* chrome *m.*; chromium *m.*
chromosome *n.* chromosome *m.*
chronic *a.* chronique; continuel, constant
chronicle *n.* chronique *f.*; **-r** *n.* chroniqueur *m.*
chronological *a.* chronologique; in —
order chronologiquement, par ordre des
dates
chronometer *n.* chronomètre *m.*
chrysalis *n.* chrysalide *f.*
chrysanthemum *n.* chrysanthème *m.*
chubby *a.* rondelet; joufflu
chuck *vt.* jeter, lancer; flanquer; — *n.*
petite tape sous le menton *f.*; — **steak**
steak coupé à l'épaule du bœuf *m.*
chuckle *n.* petit rire *m.*; — *vi.* rire tout
bas
chum *n.* copain *m.*; camarade *m.*; **-my** *a.*
copain; intime, familier
chunk *n.* (gros) morceau *m.*
church *n.* église *f.*; (Protestant) temple
m.; — **service** office *m.*
churchman *n.* ecclésiastique *m.*
churchyard *n.* cimetière *m.*
churlish *a.* grossier; mal élevé
churn *n.* baratte *f.*; — *vt.* battre, baratter
chute *n.* glissière *f.*; couloir, conduit *m.*;
coulisse *f.*, coulisseau *m.*
cicada *n.* cigale *f.*
Cicero *n.* Cicéron *m.*
cider *n.* cidre *m.*
cigar *n.* cigare *m.*; — **store** bureau de
tabac *m.*
cigarette *n.* cigarette *f.*; — **butt** mégot

m.; — **holder** porte-cigarettes *m.*; —
lighter *n.* allume-cigarette *m.*
cinch *n.* (saddle) sangle *f.*; (coll.) quelque
chose de très facile
cinder *n.* cendre *f.*; — **track** piste cendrée
f.
cinnamon *n.* cannelle *f.*
cipher *n.* chiffre *m.*; (math.) zéro *m.*; —
vt. chiffrer
circle *n.* cercle *m.*; milieu, monde *m.*; —
vt. entourer, ceindre; faire le tour de;
—*vi.* tournoyer
circuit *n.* circuit *m.*; détour *m.*; tournée
f.; short — court-circuit *m.*; — breaker
n. coupe-circuit *m.*; **-ous** *a.* détourné
circular *a.* circulaire; — *n.* feuille publicitaire *f.*; **-ize** *vt.* prospecter
circulate *vi.* circuler; — *vt.* faire circuler
circulation *n.* circulation *f.*; (newspaper)
tirage *m.*
circumcise *vt.* circoncire; **-d** *a.* circoncis
circumcision *n.* circoncision *f.*
circumference *n.* circonférence *f.*; périphérie *f.*
circumflex *a. & n.* circonflexe *m.*
circumnavigate *vt.* faire le tour de
circumnavigation *n.* circumnavigation *f.*
circumscribe *vt.* circonscrire; limiter
circumscription *n.* circonscription *f.*
circumspect *a.* circonspect, prudent; **-ion**
n. circonspection, prudence *f.*
circumstance *n.* circonstance(s) *f.* (*pl.*);
cas *m.*; incident *m.*; détail *m.*; situation *f.*; pompe, cérémonie *f.*
circumstantial *a.* circonstanciel; circonstancié, détaillé; accidentel; — **evidence** preuves indirectes *f. pl.*
circumvent *vt.* circonvenir
circus *n.* cirque *m.*
cirrus *n.* cirrus *m.*, (coll.) queue de vache
f.
cistern *n.* citerne *f.*; réservoir *m.*
citadel *n.* citadelle *f.*
citation *n.* citation *f.*
cite *vt.* citer; assigner
citizen *n.* citoyen *m.*; citadin *m.*; fellow
— concitoyen *m.*; **-ry** *n.* citoyens *m. pl.*;
-ship *n.* nationalité *f.*; droit de cité *m.*
citric *a.* citrique
citron *n.* cédrat *m.*
citrus *n. & a.* citron *m.*
city *n.* ville *f.*; cité *f.*; — **hall** hôtel de
ville *m.*
civet *n.* civette *f.*
civic *a.* civique; **-s** *n. pl.* instruction
civique *f.*
civil *a.* civil; courtois, poli; — **defense** *n.* défense civile *f.*; — **disobedience** désobéissance civile *f.*; —
rights droits civils *m. pl.*; — **service**

administration publique *f.*; fonction de l'Etat *f.*; **–ian** *a. & n.* civil *m.*; **–ian life** civil *m.*; **–ity** *n.* civilité *f.*; politesse *f.*; **–ization** *n.* civilisation *f.*; **–ize** *vt.* civiliser

clad *a.* vêtu, habillé, couvert

claim *n.* prétention *f.*; titre *m.*; réclamation, revendication *f.*; (prospecting) concession *f.*; **—** *vt.* prétendre; réclamer, revendiquer; demander; faire valoir; soutenir; **–ant** *n.* prétendant *m.*; réclamant, revendicateur *m.*; demandeur *m.*

clairvoyant *a. & n.* voyant *m.*; clairvoyant *m.*

clam *n.* palourde *f.*

clamber *vi.* grimper; **— over, — up** escalader

clamminess *n.* moiteur froide *f.*

clammy *a.* humide, moite; collant

clamor *n.* clameur *f.*, bruit *m.*; **—** *vi.* vociférer; **— for** réclamer; **–ous** *a.* bruyant

clamp *n.* crampon *m.*; main de fer *f.*; agrafe *f.*; attache *f.*; **—** *vt.* fixer, attacher

clan *n.* clan *m.*; **–nish** *a.* de clan; **–nishness** *n.* étroitesse *f.*, esprit de corps étroit *m.*

clandestine *a.* clandestine

clang *n.* son métallique, résonnement *m.*; **–or** son métallique, résonnement (des cloches) *m.*

clap *n.* battement *m.*; coup *m.*; applaudissements *m. pl.*; **—** *vt.* battre (des mains); taper, donner une tape à; **—** *vi.* applaudir; **–per** *n.* battant *m.*; applaudisseur *m.*; claqueur *m.*; **–pers** (theat.) claque *f.*; **–ping** *n.* applaudissements *m. pl.*

claret *n.* (vin de) bordeaux *m.*

clarify *vt.* éclaircir, clarifier

clarinet *n.* clarinette *f.*

clarion *n.* clairon *m.*

clarity *n.* clarté *f.*

clash *n.* choc *m.*; conflit *m.*; dispute *f.*; (color) disparate *f.*; **—** *vi.* se heurter, s'opposer; s'entre-choquer; faire disparate

clasp *n.* agrafe *f.*; fermoir *m.*; fermeture *f.*; étreinte *f.*; **hand—** serrement de mains *m.*; **— knife** couteau pliant *m.*; **—** *vt.* agrafer; étreindre, serrer; tenir

class *n.* classe *f.*; cours *m.*; genre *m.*, sorte *f.*; catégorie *f.*; type *m.*; caste *f.*; **lower —** prolétariat *m.*; **middle —** bourgeoisie *f.*; **—** *vt.* classer; **–ic** *a. & n.* classique *m.*; **–ical** *a.* classique; **–ics** *n.* classiques *m. pl.* humanités *f. pl.*; **–ification** *n.* classement *m.*; classifica-

tion *f.*; **–ified** *a.* classé; **–ified advertisement** petite annonce *f.*; **–ified information** document(s) déclaré(s) secret(s) par le gouvernement *m.* (*pl.*); **–ify** *vt.* classer, classifier; **–y** *a.* chic

classmate *n.* camarade de classe *m.*

classroom *n.* salle de classe *f.*

clatter *n.* bruit, cliquetis *m.*; **—** *vi.* faire du bruit

clause *n.* clause *f.*; article *m.*; (gram.) proposition *f.*

clavicle *n.* clavicule *f.*

claw *n.* griffe *f.*, serre *f.*; pince *f.*; (hammer) panne fendue *f.*; **—** *vt.* griffer, déchirer

clay *n.* argile *f.*; glaise *f.*; **— pipe** pipe en terre *f.*; **— pit** argilière, glaisière *f.*; **–ey** *a.* argileux

clean *a.* propre; net; **—** *adv.* net; tout à fait; **—** *vt.* nettoyer; faire; récurer; (fish) vider; (streets) balayer; **— out** curer; ranger; (person) mettre à sec; **— up** nettoyer; se laver, se débarbouiller; **–er** *n.* nettoyeur *m.*; **–ing** *n.* nettoyage *m.*; **dry –ing** nettoyage à sec; **–liness** *n.* propreté *f.*; netteté *f.*

cleanse *vt.* nettoyer; purifier, écurer; assainir

cleansing *n.* nettoyage *m.*; curage *m.*

clear *a.* clair; net; dégagé; libre; certain; (property) franc d'hypothèque; **all —** (civil defense) fin d'alerte *f.*; **keep — of** éviter; **—** *vt.* éclaircir; clarifier; franchir; dégager; déblayer; liquider; faire un bénéfice; (com.) solder; (land) défricher; (customs) dédouaner; **— away** écarter, enlever; **— oneself** se disculper; **— the table** desservir; enlever le couvert; **— up** éclaircir; **—** *vi.* s'éclaircir; se dégager; **— out** filer; **–ance** *n.* jeu *m.*; espace *m.*; **–ance sale** vente de soldes *f.*; **–ing** *n.* (forest) éclaircie *f.*; dégagement *m.*; (banking) compensation de chèques *f.*; **–ing house** comptoir de règlement *m.*; **–ly** *adv.* clairement, nettement; clair; évidemment; **–ness** *n.* clarté *f.*; netteté *f.*

clear-cut *a.* net

clearheaded *a.* lucide; perspicace

clear-sighted *a.* clairvoyant

cleat *n.* taquet *m.*

cleavage *n.* fendage *m.*; scission *f.*

cleave *vt.* fendre; **—** *vi.* se fendre; s'attacher, adhérer; **–r** *n.* couperet *m.*

cleft *n.* fente, crevasse *f.*; **—** *a.*, **— palate** palais fendu *m.*

clemency *n.* clémence *f.*; (weather) douceur *f.*

clement *a.* clément; doux

clench *vt.* serrer, crisper

clergy *n.* clergé *m.*; **-man** *n.* ecclésiastique *m.*; pasteur *m.*

clerical *a.* clérical, de copiste; — **error** faute de copiste *f.*; — **work** travail de bureau *m.*

clerk *n.* commis *m.*; employé de bureau *m.*; (court) greffier *m.*; (eccl.) clerc *m.*

clever *a.* habile; adroit; fort; intelligent; **-ness** *n.* habileté *f.*; adresse *f.*; intelligence *f.*

cliché *n.* cliché *m.*

click *n.* clic, cliquet, cliquetis *m.*; clappement *m.*; — *vt.* & *vi.* cliqueter; claquer; — *vi.* (coll.) réussir; aller ensemble

cliff *n.* falaise *f.*; escarpement *m.*

climate *n.* climat *m.*

climatic *a.* climatique, climatérique

climax *n.* point culminant *m.*; comble *m.*

climb *n.* montée *f.*; ascension *f.*; — *vt.* & *vi.* monter, gravir; grimper; — **down** descendre; **-er** *n.* grimpeur *m.*; (bot.) plante grimpante *f.*; **mountain -er** alpiniste *m.* & *f.*; **-ing** *a.* grimpant; **-ing** *n.* montée *f.*; escalade *f.*; **mountain -ing** alpinisme *m.*

clinch *n.* crampon, rivet *m.*; (boxing) corps-à-corps *m.*; — *vt.* river; — *vi.* se prendre corps-à-corps; **-er** *n.* argument sans réplique *m.*

cling *vi.* adhérer; coller; s'attacher, s'accrocher alberge, pavie *f.*

clinic *n.* clinique *f.*; **-al** *a.* clinique

clink *n.* tintement (de verres) *m.*; — *vi.* tinter; — *vt.* trinquer; **-er** *n.* mâchefer *m.*

clip *n.* agrafe, griffe, attache, pince *f.*; attache-papiers *m.*; (rifle) chargeur *m.*; — *vt.* couper; tondre; découper; agrafer, pincer, attacher; **-per** *n.* (naut., avi.) clipper *m.*; **-pers** *m. pl.* tondeuse *f.*; **-ping** *n.* coupe *f.*; coupure *f.*; tondage *m.*

clique *n.* coterie *f.*

cloak *n.* manteau *m.*; (fig.) voile *m.*; — **and dagger** *a.* de cape et d'épée; — *vt.* (fig.) masquer

cloakroom *n.* vestiaire *m.*; (rail.) consigne *f.*

clock *n.* horloge, pendule *f.*; **alarm —** réveil *m.*; **one o'—** une heure; **two o'—** deux heures; **twelve o'—** (noon) midi *m.*, (midnight) minuit *m.*; — *vt.* chronométrer

clockwise *a.* dextrorsum; à droite

clockwork *n.* mouvement, rouage *m.*; **like —** comme sur des roulettes

clod *n.* motte *f.*; (person) rustre *m.*

clog *n.* entrave *f.*; galoche *f.*; — *vt.*

entraver; boucher; — *vi.* se boucher

cloister *n.* cloître *m.*; — *vt.* cloîtrer

close *n.* fin *f.*; bout *m.*; clôture *f.*; — *vt.* fermer; terminer; clore; serrer; — *vi.* se fermer; se terminer; — **down** fermer; — **up** boucher; se serrer; — *a.* renfermé; intime; proche; serré; étroit; **at — quarters** de près; **have a — call** l'échapper belle; — *adv.* (de) près; — **by** tout près; **-d** *a.* fermé; (theat.) relâche; **-d shop** usine où la main-d'œuvre est tout à fait syndiquée *f.*; **-ly** *adv.* étroitement; attentivement; **-ness** *n.* proximité *f.*; intimité; exactitude *f.*; réserve *f.*; (weather) lourdeur *f.*

close-cropped *a.* coupé ras

closefisted *a.* ladre, avare

close-fitting *a.* collant

closemouthed *a.* peu communicatif

closet *n.* placard *m.*; armoire *f.*; — *vt.*, **be -ed** être enfermé

close-up *n.* vue prise de près *f.*; — *n.* (movies) gros plan *m.*

closing *n.* fermeture *f.*; clôture *f.*; — *a.* final, dernier

closure *n.* clôture, fermeture *f.*

clot *n.* caillot *m.*; embolie *f.*; — *vi.* se coaguler; se cailler; se figer

cloth *n.* étoffe *f.*; drap *m.*; tissu *m.*; toile *f.*; **-e** *vt.* habiller, vêtir, revêtir; **-es** *n. pl.* vêtements, habits *m. pl.*; effets *m. pl.*; **-ier** *n.* drapier *m.*; **-ing** *n.* vêtements *m. pl.*

clothesbrush *n.* brosse à habits *f.*

clothes closet *n.* garde-robe *f.*

clothes hanger *n.* cintre *f.*

clothesline *n.* étendoir *m.*

clothespin *n.* pince *f.*; épingle à lingne *f.*

cloud *n.* nuage *m.*; nue, nuée *f.*; voile *m.*; — *vt.* voiler, obscurcir; troubler; — **up** se voiler, se couvrir; **-less** *a.* sans nuages; **-y** *a.* nuageux; couvert; trouble

cloudburst *n.* averse, trombe *f.*

clout *n.* linge *m.*; (coll.) claque *f.*

clove *n.* clou de girofle *m.*; — **of garlic** gousse d'ail *f.*

cloven *a.*, — **hoof** pied fourchu *m.*

clover *n.* trèfle *m.*

clown *n.* clown, pitre *m.*; fou *m.*; bouffon *m.*; — *vi.* faire le clown

cloy *vt.* rassasier

club *n.* club, cercle *m.*, société *f.*; cénacle *m.*; (weapon) massue *f.*; (cards) trèfle *m.*; — *vt.* assommer, frapper; — *vi.* se réunir, se cotiser

clubfoot *n.* pied bot *m.*

clubhouse *n.* pavillon *m.*

clubroom *n.* salle de réunion *f.*

club steak *n.* aloyau de bœuf *m.*

cluck *vi.* glousser

clue *n.* indice *m.*; piste *f.*; clef *f.*; indication *f.*

clump *n.* bouquet *m.*; massif *m.*; bloc *m.*; pas lourd *m.*; — *vi.* se grouper; marcher d'un pas lourd

clumsiness *n.* maladresse *f.*; gaucherie *f.*

clumsy *a.* maladroit, gauche

cluster *n.* bouquet *m.*; massif *m.*; groupe *m.*; (grapes) grappe *f.*; — *vt.* grouper; — *vi.* se grouper

clutch *n.* griffe, patte *f.*; (auto.) embrayage *m.*; let in the — embrayer; release the — débrayer; in the —es of sous la patte de; — *vt.* saisir; — at se raccrocher à

clutter *n.* désordre *m.*; encombrement *m.*; — *vt.*, — up mettre en désordre; encombrer

coach *n.* voiture *f.*; carrosse *m.*; (rail.) wagon *m.*; (sports) entraîneur *m.*; — *vt.* entraîner; (theat.) faire répéter

coachhouse *n.* remise *f.*

coachman *n.* cocher *m.*

coagulant *n.* coagulant *m.*

coagulate *vt. & vi.* (se) figer, (se) coaguler

coagulation *n.* coagulation *f.*

coal *n.* charbon *m.*; houille *f.*; — gas gaz d'éclairage *m.*; — mine mine de houille *f.*; houillère *f.*; — miner mineur *m.*; — mining exploitation de la houille *f.*

coalesce *vi.* s'unir, se combiner; fusionner; —nce *n.* coalescence, fusion *f.*

coalition *n.* bloc *m.*; coalition *f.*

coarse *a.* grossier; gros; rude; —ness *n.* grossièreté *f.*; rudesse *f.*; grosseur *f.*; gros grain *m.*

coarse-grained *a.* à gros grain; à gros fil

coast *n.* côte *f.*, rivage *m.*; littoral *m.*; — guard *n.* gardes-côte *m. pl.*; — guardsman garde-côte *m. s.*; — *vi.* descendre en roue libre; —ing *n.* descente en roue libre *f.*; (naut.) cabotage *m.*

coaster *n.* dessous *m.*

coat *n.* habit *m.*; veston *m.*; pardessus, manteau *m.*; (paint) couche *f.*; (animal) robe *f.*; — of arms armes, armoiries *f. pl.*; — of mail cotte de mailles *f.*; — hanger *n.* porte-vêtements *m.*; —room *n.* vestiaire *m.*; — *vt.* couvrir, enduire; —ed *a.* enduit, couvert, recouvert; —ed tongue langue chargée *f.*; —ing *n.* enduit *m.*; couche *f.*; (anat.) paroi *f.*

coauthor *n.* coauteur, collaborateur *m.*

coax *vt.* câliner, cajoler, enjôler; —ing *a.* câlin, cajoleur; —ing *n.* cajolerie *f.*

coaxial *a.* coaxial; — cable *n.* câble coaxial *m.*

cobalt *n.* cobalt *m.*; — bomb bombe au cobalt *f.*

cobbler *n.* savetier, cordonnier *m.*

cobblestone *n.* caillou, galet *m.*

cobweb *n.* toile d'araignée *f.*

cocaine *n.* cocaïne *f.*

cock *n.* coq *m.*; robinet *m.*; (weapons) chien *m.*; crow of the — chant du coq *m.*; — *vt.* armer; dresser; (hat) retrousser; —iness *n.* suffisance *f.*; —y *a.* suffisant

cockade *n.* cocarde *f.*

cock-and-bull *a.*, — story coq-à-l'âne *m.*

cockeyed *a.* de travers, de biais; insensé

cockfight *n.* combat de coqs *m.*

cockpit *n.* cockpit *m.*; carlingue *f.*

cockroach *n.* blatte *f.*, cafard *m.*

cocktail *n.* cocktail *m.*; apéritif *m.*

cocoa *n.* cacao *m.*

coconut *n.* noix de coco *f.*; — palm cocotier *m.*

cocoon *n.* cocon *m.*

cod *n.* morue *f.*

C.O.D. contre remboursement

coddle *vt.* gâter, dorloter, choyer

code *n.* code *m.*; chiffre *m.*; — *vt.* chiffrer

codfish *n.* morue *f.*

codicil *n.* codicille *m.*

codification *n.* codification *f.*

codify *vt.* codifier

cod-liver oil *n.* huile de foie de morue *f.*

coeducational *a.* mixte

coefficient *n.* coefficient *m.*

coerce *vt.* contraindre, forcer

coercion *n.* contrainte *f.*; coercition *f.*

coercive *a.* coercitif

coeval *a.* contemporain

coexist *vi.* coexister; —ence *n.* coexistence *f.*

coffee *n.* café *m.*; black — café nature, café noir; — bean grain de café *m.*; — cup tasse à café *f.*; — grinder, — mill moulin à café *m.*; — grounds marc de café *m.*; — plantation *n.* caféière *f.*

coffeepot *n.* cafetière *f.*

coffer *n.* coffre *f.*

cofferdam *n.* bâtardeau *m.*

coffin *n.* cercueil *m.*

cog *n.* dent *f.*; — *vt.* denter

cogency *n.* force, puissance *f.*

cogent *a.* puissant

cogitate *vi.* réfléchir, méditer

cogitation *n.* réflexion, méditation *f.*

cognac *n.* cognac *m.*

cognizance *n.* connaissance *f.*

cognizant *a.* instruit

cogwheel *n.* roue dentée *f.*

cohabit *vi.* cohabiter

cohere *vi.* adhérer, se tenir; —nce *n.* cohérence *f.*; —nt *a.* cohérent; —ntly *adv.*

avec cohérence
cohesion *n.* cohésion *f.*
cohesive *a.* cohésif
cohort *n.* cohorte *f.*
coif *n.* (headdress of a nun) cornette *f.*
coil *n.* pli *m.*, repli, rouleau *m.*; anneau *m.*; (elec.) bobine *f.*, enroulement *m.*; — *vt.* rouler, bobiner; enrouler; — *vi.* serpenter; s'enrouler, boucler
coin *n.* pièce *f.*; monnaie *f.*; espèces *f. pl.*; — **collector** numismate *m.*; — *vi.* battre (monnaie), frapper; inventer; **-age** *n.* monnayage *m.*; monnaie *f.*
coincide *vi.* coïncider; s'accorder; **-nce** *n.* coïncidence *f.*
coke *n.* coke *m.*
colander *n.* passoire *f.*
cold *a.* froid; indifférent, insensible; **be** — (person) avoir froid; (weather) faire froid; **grow** — se refroidir; — **cream** crème de beauté *f.*; — **cuts** charcuterie *f.*; assiette anglaise *f.*; — **feet** (coll.) trac *m.*, peur *f.*; — **storage** entrepôt frigorifique *m.*; — *n.* froid; (med.) rhume *m.*; **catch (a)** — attraper un rhume, s'enrhumer; **have a** — être enrhumé; **-ness** *n.* froideur *f.*
cold-blooded *a.* (animal) à sang froid; insensible; prémédité
coleslaw *n.* salade de choux *f.*
colic *n.* colique *f.*
Coliseum *n.* Colisée *m.*
colitis *n.* colite *f.*
collaborate *vi.* collaborer
collaboration *n.* collaboration *f.*
collaborator *n.* collaborateur *m.*
collapse *n.* effondrement, écroulement *m.*; débâcle *f.*; chute *f.*. affaissement *m.*., prostration *f.*; — *vi.* s'effondrer, s'écrouler; s'affaisser
collapsible *a.* pliant; démontable
collar *n.* col *m.*; collet *m.*; collier *m.*; (mech.) anneau *m.*; **detachable** — faux col *m.*; — *vt.* saisir; colleter
collarbone *n.* clavicule *f.*
collate *vt.* collationner
collateral *a.* collatéral; — *n.* garantie *f.*
colleague *n.* collègue *m.*; confrère *m.*
collect *vt.* rassembler; recueillir; collectionner; — **oneself** se reprendre; — *vi.* s'assembler, se rassembler; **-ed** *a.* recueilli; calme; **-ion** *n.* recueil *m.*; collection *f.*; (taxes) perception *f.*; (postal) levée *f.*; assemblage *m.*; **-ive** *a.* collectif, commun; **-ivity** *n.* collectivité *f.*; **-or** *n.* (tickets) contrôleur *m.*; (taxes) percepteur *m.*; collectionneur *m.*; receveur *m.*; encaisseur *m.*; collecteur *m.*
collective bargaining *n.* discussion entre les patrons et les ouvrers *f.*

college *n.* collége *m.* (établissement d'enseignement supérieur aux États-Unis)
collegiate *a.* collégial; de collège
collide *vi.* entrer en collision; se heurter
collision *n.* collision *f.*, choc *m.*; (naut.) abordage *m.*; (rail.) tamponnement *m.*
colloquial *a.* familier; vulgaire; **-ism** *n.* expression familière *f.*
collusion *n.* collusion *f.*; complicité *f.*
Colombia *n.* Colombie *f.*
colon *n.* (gram.) deux points *m. pl.*; (anat.) côlon *m.*
colonel *n.* colonel *m.*
colonial *a.* colonial
colonization *n.* colonisation *f.*
colonize *vt.* coloniser; **-r** *n.* colonisateur *m.*
colony *n.* colonie *f.*
color *n.* couleur *f.*; coloris *m.*; teint *m.*; **-s** *n. pl.* (mil., naut.) drapeau, pavillon *m.*; **be off** — être pâle; **lose** — devenir pâle; — *vt.* colorer; colorier; imager; — *vi.* se colorer; rougir; **-ation** *n.* coloration *f.*; **-ed** *a.* coloré, colorié; de couleur; en couleurs; **-ing** *n.* coloris *m.*; coloration *f.*; teint *m.*; **-ful** *a.* coloré; **-less** *a.* incolore; sans couleur
color-blind *a.* daltonien
color blindness *n.* daltonisme *m.*
colorcast *n.* émission de télévision transmise en couleurs *f.*
color television *n.* télévision en couleurs *f.*
colossus *n.* colosse *m.*
colt *n.* poulain *m.*
column *n.* colonne *f.*; (newspaper) rubrique *f.*; **-ist** *n.* journaliste *m.*; chroniqueur *m.*
comatose *a.* comateux
comb *n.* peigne *m.*; carde *f.*; (cock) crête *f.*; — *vt.* peigner; — *vi.* se peigner; **one's hair** se peigner les cheveux; — **out** démêler; éliminer
combat *n.* combat *m.*; — *vt.* combattre; **-ant** *n.* combattant *m.*; **-ive** *a.* combatif
combination *n.* combinaison *f.*; combiné, mélange *m.*
combine *n.* cartel *m.*, combinaison *f.*; (agr.) machine qui bat et qui vanne le grain en même temps; faucheuse-batteuse *f.*; — *vt.* combiner; joindre; — *vi.* se combiner, s'unir; **-d** *a.* réuni
combustible *a.* combustible, inflammable
combustion *n.* combustion *f.*; **spontaneous** — inflammation spontanée *f.*
come *vi.* venir, arriver; advenir; — **about** arriver, se passer; (naut.) virer de bord; — **across** tomber sur, rencontrer; — **after** suivre; succéder à; — **again** revenir; — **along** venir, arriver; accompagner; — **apart** se défaire; — **back**

revenir; — before précéder; — between intervenir, s'interposer; — by passer; obtenir; — down descendre; tomber; baisser; se résumer; — for venir chercher; — forward s'avancer; — home rentrer, revenir; — in entrer; arriver; — off se détacher; avoir lieu; réussir; — out sortir; paraître, se découvrir; débuter; — through traverser, passer par; pénétrer; — to reprendre connaissance; — together se réunir, s'assembler; — up monter; — upon tomber sur, rencontrer; — now! allons!

comeback n. retour à la célébrité m.; riposte f.

comedian n. comique m.; comédien m.

comedy n. comédie f.

come on n. (coll.) leurre m., attrape f.

comet n. comète f.

comfort n. confort m.; consolation f., soulagement m.; — vt. consoler, soulager; bien-être m.; aise, aisance f.; **be –able** a. (things) confortable; (persons) être bien, être à l'aise; **–er** n. consolateur m.; couverture piquée f.; **–ing** a. réconfortant, de consolation

comfort index n. relation entre humidité et température f.

comfort station n. toilette f.

comic a. comique; — **opera** n. opéra bouffe, opéra comique m.; — n. comique; comédien m.; **–al** a. comique, drôle

coming a. qui vient; prochain; futur; — n. venue, arrivée f.; avènement m.; — **out** n. début m.; sortie f.; parution f.; apparition f.

comma n. virgule f.

command n. commandement, ordre m.; gouvernement m.; disposition f.; maîtrise, connaissance f.; **have at one's —** avoir à sa disposition; **be at someone's —** être aux ordres de quelqu'un; — vt. commander, ordonner; inspirer; dominer; **–ant** n. commandant m.; **–eer** vt. réquisitionner; **–er** n. commandant m.; **–ing** a. imposant; d'autorité; **–ing officer** n. commandant m.; **–ment** n. commandement m.

commander-in-chief n. commandant en chef m.

commando n. commando m.

commemorate vt. commémorer, célébrer

commemoration n. commémoration f.; **in —** of en mémoire de

commence vt. & vi. commencer; **–ment** n. commencement m.; (school) distribution des prix f.; réception (d'un grade universitaire) f.

commend vt. louer; recommander, confier; **–able** a. louable; **–ation** n. louange f.

commensurate a. proportionné

comment n. commentaire m.; remarque f.; — vi. faire des observations; critiquer; commenter; **–ary** n. commentaire m.; reportage m.; **–ator** n. commentateur m.; speaker, reporter m.

commercial a. commercial, de commerce; — n. annonce publicitaire f.; **–ize** vt. commercialiser

commingle vt. mêler (ensemble); — vi. se mêler

commiserate vt. & vi.; — **with** avoir de la compassion pour

commiseration n. commisération, compassion f.

commissary n. (mil.) grand magasin à l'usage des militaires et de leurs familles m.

commission n. commission, charge f.; pourcentage, pot de vin m.; perpétration f.; — vt. commissioner; charger; (naut.) armer (un vaisseau); (painting) commander; **–er** n. commissaire m.; membre d'une commission m.; directeur m.; préfet m.

commit vt. commettre; confier; engager; — **to prison** envoyer en prison; — **to memory** apprendre par cœur; **–ment** n. engagement m.; **–tal** n. perpétration f.; mise en prison f.

committee n. comité m.; commission f., conseil m.

commodious a. spacieux, ample

commodity n. produit m.; denrée f.; marchandise f.

common a. commun; ordinaire; courant; vulgaire; — **stock** action(s) ordinaire(s) f. (pl.); — n. terrain commun m.; **in — en** commun; **–er** n. bourgeois m.; homme du peuple m.; **–ness** n. banalité f.; fréquence f.; **House of C–s** Chambre des Communes f.

commonplace a. banal; — n. lieu commun m.; banalité f.

commonwealth n. république f.; état m.

commotion n. commotion, agitation, confusion f.; bruit m.

communal a. communal

commune n. commune f.; — vi. s'entretenir

communicable a. communicable; contagieux

communicant n. (eccl.) communiant m.; informateur m.

communicate vt. & vi. communiquer; (eccl.) communier

communication n. communication f.

communicative a. communicatif

communion n. communion f.

communism n. communisme m.

communist n. communiste m. & f.; –ic a. communiste
community n. communauté f.; voisinage m.; société f.
commutation n. commutation f.; — **ticket** carte d'abonnement au chemin de fer f.
commutator n. (elec.) commutateur m.
commute vt. commuer; — vi. voyager régulièrement entre la maison dans la banlieue et le bureau en ville; –r n. habitant de banlieue qui travaille en ville m.
compact a. serré, compact; — n. pacte, accord m.; convention f.; (cosmetics) poudrier m.; –ness n. compacité f.; concision f.
companion n. compagnon m., compagne f.; –able a. sociable; –ship n. camaraderie f.; compagnie f.
company n. compagnie f.; assemblée f.; monde m.; (com.) société f.; (theat.) troupe f.; (naut.) équipage m.; **keep someone** — tenir compagnie à quelqu'un; **part** — (with) se séparer (de)
comparable a. comparable
comparative a. comparé; comparatif; relatif; –ly adv. relativement; par comparaison
compare vt. comparer; –d to en comparaison de; auprès de
comparison n. comparaison f.; **in** — **with** en comparaison de; auprès de
compartment n. compartiment m.; case f.
compass n. boussole f.; (mech.) compas m.; portée f.; — vt. entourer; comploter
compassion n. compassion f.; –ate a. compatissant
compatibility n. compatibilité, convenance f.
compel vt. contraindre, forcer; obliger; imposer, inspirer; –ling a. puissant, irrésistible; compulsif
compendium n. abrégé m.; manuel m.; recueil m.
compensate vt. compenser, dédommager; rémunérer; — **for** compenser; remplacer
compensation n. compensation f.; honoraires m. pl.; dédommagement m.
compensatory a. compensateur
compete vi. concourir; — **with** faire concurrence à
competence, competency n. compétence f.
competent a. compétent; capable
competition n. concurrence, compétition f.; concours m.; rivalité f.
competitor n. concurrent m.
compilation n. compilation f.
compile vt. compiler; –r n. compilateur m.
complacence, complacency n. complai-

sance f.; suffisance f.
complacent a. complaisant; suffisant
complain vi. se plaindre; faire des réclamations; –ant n. plaignant m.
complaint n. complainte f.; réclamation f.; (med.) mal m.; **cause for** — n. grief m.
complaisant a. complaisant, obligeant
complement n. complément m.; (mil.) effectif m.; — vt. compléter; –ary a. complémentaire
complete vt. compléter; achever; remplir; — a. complet, entier; achevé, terminé; parfait, accompli
completion n. accomplissement, achèvement m.
complex a. complexe; — n. complexe m.; **inferiority** — complexe d'infériorité m.; –ity n. complexité f.
complexion n. complexion f.; teint m.; caractère, aspect m.
compliance n. complaisance f.; acquiescement m.; conformité f.; **in** — **with** conformément à
compliant a. complaisant, obligeant; soumis
complicate vt. compliquer, embrouiller; –d a. compliqué
complication n. complication f.
complicity n. complicité f.
compliment n. compliment m.; flatterie f.; **to pay a** — faire un compliment; — vt. complimenter; flatter; –ary a. complimenteur; gratuit
comply vi. se soumettre; se conformer; obéir, accéder
component n. partie constituante f.; composant m.; — a. composant; — **parts** éléments constitutifs m. pl.
compose vt. composer; arranger; calmer; — **oneself** se calmer; –d a. tranquille, calme; **be** –d **of** se composer de; –r n. compositeur m.
composite a. & n. composé m.
composition n. composition f.; rédaction f., thème m.; constitution f.; composé m.
compositor n. compositeur, typographe m.
compost n. engrais, compost m.
composure n. tranquillité f.; sang-froid m.
compound n. composé m.; (mil.) enceinte f.; — vt. composer, arranger; — a. composé; — **interest** intérêts composés m. pl.; — **number** n. nombre composé m.
comprehend vt. comprendre
comprehensible a. compréhensible
comprehension n. compréhension f.
comprehensive a. compréhensif; étendu; d'ensemble

compress *n.* compresse *f.*; — *vt.* comprimer; condenser; –ion *n.* compression *f.*
comprise *vt.* comprendre, contenir; comporter; renfermer; be –d of se composer de
compromise *n.* compromis *m.*; accomodement *m.*; — *vi.* faire un compromis; transiger; — *vt.* compromettre
compromising *a.* compromettant
comptometer *n.* machine à calculer *f.*
comptroller *n.* comptable *m.*; vérificateur *m.*
compulsion *n.* contrainte *f.*
compulsory *a.* forcé, obligatoire
compunction *n.* remords *m.*, componction *f.*
computation *n.* calcul *m.*
compute *vt.* compter, calculer, computer
comrade *n.* camarade *m.*; –ship *n.* camaraderie *f.*
con *n.* contre *m.*; pros and –s le pour et le contre; — *vt.* étudier; (naut.) gouverner
concave *a.* concave, creux
conceal *vt.* cacher, dissimuler; masquer; voiler; dérober; recéler; –ment *n.* dissimulation *f.*; (law) recel *m.*
concede *vt.* concéder, accorder, admettre
conceit *n.* vanité *f.*; amour-propre *m.*; –ed *a.* vaniteux, vain
conceivable *a.* concevable, imaginable
conceive *vt. & vi.* concevoir; — of imaginer
concentrate *vt.* concentrer
concentration *n.* concentration *f.*; — **camp** camp de concentration *m.*
concentric *a.* concentrique
concept *n.* concept *m.*; –ion *n.* conception *f.*; idée *f.*
concern *n.* affaire, cause *f.*; intérêt, égard *m.*; inquiétude *f.*, trouble *m.*; importance *f.*; compagnie, société anonyme *f.*; maison *f.*; — *vt.* regarder, concerner; inquiéter; toucher, intéresser; –ed *a.* inquiet; intéressé; as far as I am —ed quant à moi; –ing *prep.* touchant, au sujet de, concernant; en ce qui concerne
concert *n.* concert *m.*; in — de concert; (mus.) à l'unisson; — *vt.* concerter; –ed *a.* concerté
concertmaster *n.* premier violon *m.*; chef d'orchestre *m.*
concession *n.* concession *f.*; –naire *n.* concessionnaire *m. & f.*
concessive *a.* concessif
conciliate *vt.* concilier, réconcilier
conciliator *n.* conciliateur *m.*; –y *a.* conciliatoire, conciliant
concise *a.* concis, succinct; –ness *n.* concision *f.*

conclave *n.* conclave *m.*, assemblée *f.*
conclude *vt.* conclure, terminer, achever; — *vi.* conclure, se terminer
concluding *a.* final, dernier
conclusion *n.* conclusion *f.*; fin *f.*; décision *f.*; in — pour conclure
conclusive *a.* concluant, décisif; –ly *adv.* d'une manière décisive
concoct *vt.* préparer, combiner; confectionner, composer; –ion *n.* breuvage *m.*, boisson *f.*; mélange *m.*; confectionnement *m.*
concomitant *a.* concomitant
concord *n.* accord *m.*, harmonie *f.*; concorde *f.*; –ance *n.* concordance *f.*; –ant *a.* concordant, d'accord
concourse *n.* concours *m.*, foule *f.*; place publique *f.*
concrete *a.* concret; — *n.* béton *m.*; reinforced — béton armé *m.*; — **mixer** malaxeur *m.*, bétonnière *f.*; –ly *adv.* d'une manière concrète
concur *vi.* concourir; s'accorder, être d'accord; –rence *n.* accord *m.*; approbation *f.*; simultanéité *f.*; –rent *a.* concourant; simultané
concussion *n.* ébranlement *m.*, secousse *f.*; brain — *n.* commotion cérébrale *f.*
condemn *vt.* condamner; censurer; –ation *n.* condamnation *f.*; censure *f.*
condense *vt.* condenser; abréger; — *vi.* se condenser; –r *n.* condenseur *m.*; condensateur *m.*
condescend *vi.* condescendre, daigner; –ing *a.* condescendant
condescension *n.* condescendance *f.*
condiment *n.* assaisonnement, condiment *m.*
condition *n.* condition *f.*, état, rang *m.*; stipulation *f.*; on — that à condition que, pourvu que; — *vt.* conditionner; habituer, accoutumer; –al *a. & n.* conditionnel *m.*; –ed *a.* conditionné; habitué
condolence *n.* condoléance *f.*
condone *vt.* pardonner; permettre, approuver
conducive *a.* contribuant, contributif; favorable
conduct *n.* conduite *f.*, comportement *m.*; — *vt.* conduire; mener, diriger; — oneself se comporter; –ion *n.* conduction *f.*; –ive *a.* conducteur *m.*; –ivity *n.* conductivité *f.*; –or *n.* conducteur *m.*; (train, bus) contrôleur, receveur *m.*; (mus.) chef d'orchestre *m.*
conduit *n.* conduit, tuyau *m.*
cone *n.* cône *m.*; ice cream — glace en cornet *f.*; pine — pomme de pin *f.*

confection n. confiserie f.; **–er** n. confiseur m.; **–ery** n. confiserie f.
confederacy n. confédération f.
confederate n. & a. confédéré m.; complice m.; — vi. se confédérer
confer vt. conférer; — vi. consulter; **–ence** n. consultation, conférence f.; (sport) groupement (d'équipes) m.
confess vt. confesser, avouer; — vi. se confesser; **–ion** n. confession f.; aveu m.; (eccl.) confesse, confession f.; **–ional** n. confessionnal m.; **–ional** a. confessionnel; **–or** n. confesseur m.
confidant n. confident m.; confidente f.
confide vt. confier; — vi. se confier (à), se fier (à); **–nt** a. assure, confiant; **–nt** n. confident m.; **–ntial** a. confidentiel; particulier.
confidence n. confiance f.; **have — in** avoir confiance en
confiding a. confiant
configuration n. configuration f.
confine n. confins m. pl., frontière f.; — vt. enfermer, renfermer; **— oneself to** se borner à; **–ment** n. emprisonnement m.; accouchement m., couches f. pl.
confirm vt. confirmer, assurer; corroborer; **–ation** n. confirmation f.; **–ed** a. invétéré, endurci
confiscate vt. confisquer, saisir
conflagration n. incendie m., conflagration f.
conflict n. conflit m.; — vi. être en contradiction; se heurter; **–ing** a. contradictoire; opposé
confluence n. confluent m.
conform vt. rendre conforme; conformer; — vi. se conformer; obéir, se soumettre; **–ation** n. conformation f.; **–ity** n. conformité f.; **in –ity with** conformément à
confound vt. confondre; **—!** interj. diable!; **–ed** a. sacré
confraternity n. confraternité f.; confrérie f.
confront vt. confronter; faire face à, affronter; **–ation** n. confrontation f.
confuse vt. confondre, troubler; brouiller; embrouiller; **–d** a. confondu; confus; embrouillé; trouble; **–dly** adv. confusément
confusion n. confusion f.; désordre m.
congeal vt. geler, congeler; coaguler; figer; — vi. geler; se congeler; se figer
congenial a. sympathique, agréable
congenital a. congénital, inné; de naissance
congest vt. congestionner; encombrer; **–ed** a. congestionné; encombré; (traffic) embouteillé; **–ion** n. congestion f.;

encombrement m.
conglomerate vt. conglomérer; — vi. se conglomérer; — a. congloméré
congratulate vt. féliciter
congratulation n. félicitation f.
congratulatory a. de félicitations
congregate vt. rassembler; — vi. s'assembler, se rassembler
congregation n. congrégation f.; assistance f.; rassemblement m.; **–al** a. de congrégation; (eccl.) indépendant; **–alist** a. & n. congrégationaliste m.
congress n. congrès m.; assemblée f.; réunion f.; **–man** n. député m.; **–ional** a. parlementaire
congruent a. congruent; conforme
congruity n. congruité f.; conformité f.
congruous a. conforme
conifer n. conifère m.
conjecture n. conjecture f.; — vt. & vi. conjecturer
conjugate vt. conjuguer; — a. conjugué
conjugation n. conjugaison f.
conjunction n. conjonction f.
conjunctive a. conjonctif
conjuncture n. conjoncture f.
conjure vt. conjurer; comploter; évoquer; — vi. conjurer, faire de la sorcellerie; **–r** n. sorcier m.
connect vt. joindre, lier; unir, réunir, rattacher, relier; — vi. se joindre, s'unir; se réunir, se lier; **–ed** a. suivi; connexe; **–ing rod** n. bielle f.; **–ion** n. connexion f.; liaison f., rapport m., correspondance f.; **in –ion with** à propos de, au sujet de
connive vi. conniver
connoisseur n. connaisseur m.
connotation n. connotation, signification f.
connote vt. signifier (en delà du sens littéral)
connubial a. conjugal
conquer vt. & vi. conquérir, vaincre; **–ing** a. conquérant, triomphant, victorieux; **–or** n. vainqueur m.; conquérant m.
conquest n. conquête, victoire f.
consanguinity n. consanguinité f.; parenté f.
conscience n. conscience f.
conscience-stricken a. pris de remords
conscientious a. consciencieux; **— objector** n. réformé de guerre m. (pour cause de convictions religieuses); **–ness** n. conscience f.; assiduité f.
conscionable a. juste, raisonnable
conscious a. conscient; **be — (awareness)** avoir conscience; (physical state) avoir la connaissance; **–ly** adv. sciemment; **–ness** n. connaissance f.; conscience f.;

sentiment *m.*; **lose** **–ness** perdre connaissance; **regain** **–ness** reprendre connaissance

conscript *n.* conscrit *m.*, recrue *f.*; — *a.* conscrit; — *vt.* recruter, enrôler; **–ion** *n.* conscription *f.*, enrôlement *m.*

consecrate *vt.* consacrer; bénir; **–d** *a.* consacré, béni, saint

consecration *n.* consécration *f.*; dévouement *m.*; sacre *m.*

consecutive *a.* consécutif, successif; de suite; **–ly** *adv.* de suite, consécutivement

consensus *n.* accord *m.*; orientation de l'opinion générale *f.*

consent *n.* consentement *m.*; accord *m.*; — *vi.* consentir (à)

consequence *n.* conséquence *f.*; importance *f.*; suite *f.*; **by —**, **in —** par conséquent

consequent *a.* conséquent; **–ial** *a.* important; consécutif, conséquent; **–ly** *adv.* conséquemment, par conséquent

conservation *n.* conservation, garde *f.*

conservative *n.* & *a.* conservateur *m.*

conservatory *n.* serre *f.*; (mus.) conservatoire *m.*

conserve *vt.* préserver, conserver; **–s** *n. pl.* conserves, confitures *f. pl.*

consider *vt.* considérer, regarder; estimer; penser; avoir égard à; — *vi.* réfléchir; **–able** *a.* considérable; **–ate** *a.* attentif, prévenant, soucieux; **–ateness** *n.* égards *m. pl.*; **–ation** *n.* considération *f.*; importance *f.*; égard *m.*; **be under –ation** être à l'étude; **take into –ation** tenir compte de; **–ing** *prep.* vu, étant donné

consign *vt.* consigner; livrer; **–ee** *n.* consignataire *m.*; **–ment** *n.* livraison *f.*; expédition *f.*; **on –ment** en consignation; **–or** *n.* consignateur *m.*

consist *vi.* consister; être composé (de); **–ency** *n.* consistance, substance *f.*; suite *f.*; **–ent** *a.* consistant; conséquant; d'accord; **–ently** *adv.* conséquemment

consistory *n.* consistoire *m.*

consolable *a.* consolable

console *n.* console *f.*; — *vt.* consoler; **–r** *n.* consolateur *m.*

consolidate *vt.* consolider; unifier; réunir; — *vi.* se consolider

consolidation *n.* consolidation *f.*; unification *f.*

consoling *a.* consolateur, consolant

consonance *n.* consonance *f.*; accord *m.*

consonant *n.* consonne *f.*; — *a.* consonant; conforme (à), d'accord

consort *n.* compagnon *m.*; époux *m.*, épouse *f.*; — *vi.* s'associer; — **with**

fréquenter

conspicuous *a.* apparent, frappant; **become —** se signaler, se faire remarquer

conspiracy *n.* conspiration *f.*

conspirator *n.* conspirateur *m.*

conspire *vi.* conspirer, comploter

constable *n.* constable *m.*; agent de police *m.*; connétable *m.*

constabulary *n.* police, gendarmerie *f.*

constancy *n.* constance *f.*; fidélité *f.*

constant *a.* constant, ferme; continuel; fidèle; — *n.* constante *f.*; **–ly** *adv.* constamment; continuellement

consternation *n.* consternation *f.*

constipate *vt.* constiper

constipation *n.* constipation *f.*

constituency *n.* circonscription (électorale) *f.*; électeurs *m. pl.*

constituent *a.* constituant; — *n.* constituant, composant *m.*; électeur *m.*

constitute *vt.* constituer

constitution *n.* constitution *f.*; tempérament *m.*; **–al** *a.* constitutionnel; **–al** *n.* promenade *f.*; **–ality** *n.* conformité (à la constitution) *f.*

constrain *vt.* contraindre, forcer; **–ed** *a.* contraint, forcé; **–t** *n.* contrainte, force *f.*; retenue *f.*

constrict *vt.* resserrer, contracter; gêner; **–ion** *n.* constriction *f.*; resserrement *m.*; **–or** *n.* constricteur *m.*; **boa –or** boa (constricteur) *m.*

construct *vt.* construire, bâtir; **–ion** *n.* construction *f.*; interprétation *f.*; **under —** en construction; **–ive** *a.* constructif; **–or** *n.* constructeur *m.*

construe *vt.* expliquer, interpréter

consul *n.* consul *m.*; **–ar** *a.* consulaire; **–ate** *n.* consulat *m.*

consult *vt.* consulter; — *vi.* délibérer, se consulter; demander conseil; **–ant** *n.* conseiller, consultant *m.*; **–ation** *n.* consultation *f.*; **–ing** *a.* consultant; conseil

consume *vt.* consumer; brûler; épuiser; dévorer; consommer; **–r** *n.* consommateur *m.*

consummate *vt.* consommer; terminer; — *a.* consommé, parfait, achevé

consummation *n.* consommation *f.*, achèvement *m.*; couronnement, comble *m.*

consumption *n.* consommation *f.*; (med.) phthisie *f.*

consumptive *a.* & *n.* phthisique, poitrinaire *m.* & *f.*

contact *n.* contact *m.*; rapport *m.*; **— lens** verre de contact *m.*; — *vt.* se mettre en relations avec; entrer en communication avec; parler à; écrire à

contagious *a.* contagieux; communicatif; **-ness** *n.* contagiosité *f.*

contain *vt.* contenir; comporter, comprendre; retenir; **-er** *n.* contenant *m.*; boîte *f.*

contaminate *vt.* contaminer, corrompre

contamination *n.* contamination *f.*

contemplate *vt.* contempler; méditer envisager; — *vi.* contempler; méditer

contemplation *n.* contemplation *f.*; méditation *f.*; recueillement *m.*

contemplative *a.* contemplatif

contemplator *n.* contemplateur *m.*

contemporaneous, contemporary *a. & n.* contemporain *m.*

contempt *n.* mépris, dédain *m.*; — **of court** *n.* contumace *f.*; **hold in** — mépriser; **-ible** *a.* méprisable; **-ibly** *adv.* d'une manière méprisable; **-uous** *a.* dédaigneux; **-uously** *adv.* avec mépris

contend *vi.* disputer, combattre; — *vt.* prétendre, soutenir

content *n.* contentement *m.*; contenu *m.*; **-s** *n. pl.* contenu *m.*; **table of -s** table des matières *f.*; **to one's heart's** — à volonté; — *a.* content, tranquille; — *vt.* contenter; **be -(ed) with** se contenter de; **-ment** *n.* contentement *m.*

contention *n.* contention, dispute *f.*; prétention *f.*; **bone of** — pomme de discorde *f.*

contentious *a.* litigieux, querelleur

contest *vt.* disputer; contester; — *n.* concours *m.*; dispute *f.*; combat *m.*; **-able** *a.* contestable; **-ant** *n.* concurrent *m.*; **-ation** *n.* contestation *f.*

context *n.* contexte *m.*

contiguity *n.* contiguïté *f.*

contiguous *a.* contigu

continence *n.* continence *f.*

continent *n. & a.* continent *m.*; **-al** *a.* continental

contingency *n.* contingence *f.*; éventualité *f.*; cas imprévu *m.*

contingent *a.* contingent; éventuel, accidentel; imprévu; **be** — **on** dépendre de; — *n.* contingent

continual *a.* continuel; **-ly** *adv.* continuellement, sans cesse

continuance, continuation *n.* continuation *f.*; suite *f.*

continue *vt. & vi.* continuer; **to be -d** à suivre

continuity *n.* continuité, suite *f.*

continuous *a.* continu

contort *vt.* tordre; **-ed** *a.* tordu, contorsionné; **-ion** *n.* contorsion *f.*; **-ionist** *n.* contorsionniste *m. & f.*

contour *n.* contour *m.*; profil *m.*

contraband *n.* contrebande *f.*

contraceptive *n.* préservatif *m.*

contract *n.* contrat, pacte *m.*; acte *m.*; entreprise *f.*; — *vt.* contracter; crisper; prendre, entreprendre; — *vi.* se contracter; faire un contrat; s'engager; entreprendre, mettre à l'entreprise; **-ing** *n.* entreprise *f.*; **-ion** *n.* contraction *f.*; **-or** *n.* entrepreneur *m.*; adjudicataire *m.*; **-ual** *a.* de contrat, contractuel

contradict *vt.* contredire; démentir; **-ion** *n.* contradiction *f.*; **-ory** *a.* contradictoire

contrail *n.* (avi.) sillage de fumée *m.*

contraption *n.* machin, appareil *m.*

contrapuntal *a.* en contrepoint

contrariness *n.* contrariété *f.*

contrariwise *adv.* au contraire

contrary *n.* contraire, opposé; **on the** — au contraire; — *a.* contraire; — **to** contrairement à

contrast *n.* contraste *m.*; — *vi.* contraster; — *vt.* opposer, faire contraster; **-ing** *a.* opposé, en contraste

contravene *vt.* contrevenir à

contravention *n.* contravention *f.*

contribute *vt. & vi.* contribuer; collaborer

contribution *n.* contribution *f.*; apport *m.*

contributor *n.* collaborateur *m.*; contribuant *m.*; **-y** *a.* contribuant, contributif

contrite *a.* contrit, pénitent

contrivance *n.* projet *m.*; appareil *m.*; invention *f.*

contrive *vt.* inventer, projeter, essayer; combiner; — *vi.* parvenir à; s'arranger

control *n.* contrôle *m.*; autorité, direction *f.*; empire *m.*; **-s** *n. pl.* commandes *f. pl.*; — **stick** *n.* (avi.) manche à balai *m.*; — **tower** *n.* (avi.) tour de contrôle *f.*; — *vt.* contrôler; diriger; commander; — **oneself** se maîtriser; se retenir; **-lable** *a.* gouvernable; maîtrisable

controller *n.* comptable *m.*; contrôleur *m.*

controversial *a.* de controverse, discutable

controversy *n.* controverse *m.*, polémique *f.*

controvert *vt.* disputer; controverser; **-ible** *a.* controversible

contumely *n.* outrage *m.*, insulte *m.*; honte *f.*

contuse *vt.* contusionner

convalesce *vi.* guérir; se remettre; **-nce** *n.* convalescence *f.*; **-nt** *a.* convalescent

convection *n.* convection *f.*

convene *vt.* assembler, réunir, convoquer; — *vi.* s'assembler, se réunir

convenience *n.* aise, commodité *f.*; convenance *f.*; **at your earliest** — aussitôt que possible; **at your own** — quand il vous plaira; **-s** *pl.* confort *m.*

convenient *a.* commode, aisé

convent *n.* couvent *m.*

convention *n.* rassemblement, congrès *m.*; convention *f.*; bienséance *f.*; contrat *m.*; **-al** *a.* conventionnel; ordinaire, normal

converge *vi.* converger; **-nce** *m.* convergence *f.*; **-nt** *a.* convergent

converging *a.* convergent

conversant *a.* familier; versé (dans)

conversation *n.* conversation *f.*, entretien *m.*; **-al** *a.* de conversation

converse *n.* & *a.* converse *f.*; réciproque *f.*; — *vi.* causer, s'entretenir; **-ly** *adv.* réciproquement

convert *n.* converti *m.*; — *vt.* convertir; changer, transformer; — *vi.* se convertir; **-er** *n.* convertisseur *m.*; **-ibility** *n.* convertibilité *f.*; **-ible** *a.* (auto) décapotable; convertible; convertissable

convex *a.* convexe

convey *vt.* transporter; communiquer; transmettre; **-ance** *n.* voiture *f.*; moyen de transport *m.*; transmission *f.*; **-er**, **-or** *n.* transporteur *m.*; courroie *f.*; tapis roulant *m.*

convict *n.* condamné *m.*; forçat *m.*; — *vt.* convaincre, condamner; **-ion** *n.* condamnation *f.*; conviction *f.*

convince *vt.* convaincre, persuader

convincing *a.* convainquant

convivial *a.* sociable, joyeux

convocation *n.* convocation, assemblée *f.*

convoke *vt.* convoquer

convolution *n.* circonvolution *f.*

convoy *n.* convoi *m.*, escorte *f.*; — *vt.* escorter, convoyer

convulse *vt.* convulsionner; ébranler; **-d** *a.* convulsé

convulsive *a.* convulsif

coo *vi.* roucouler; **-ing** *n.* roucoulement *m.*

cook *n.* cuisinier *m.*; cuisinière *f.*; chef *m.*; — *vi.* faire la cuisine; — up (coll.) comploter; **-er** *n.* réchaud *m.*; cuisinière *f.*; **-ery** *n.* cuisine; **-ing** *n.* cuisine *f.*; **-ing utensils** batterie de cuisine *f.*; **-book** *n.* livre de cuisine *m.*

cookie, cooky *n.* gâteau sec, biscuit, petit four *m.*

cool *n.* frais *m.*, fraîcheur *f.*; — *a.* frais (fraîche); indifferent; tranquille; — *vt.* & *vi.* refroidir; — off se refroidir; — one's heels attendre; **-er** *n.* frigorifique *m.*; (coll.) prison *f.*; **-ing** *a.* rafraîchissant; **-ing** *n.* refroidissement *m.*; **-ness** *n.* frais *m.*; indifférence *f.*; froideur *f.*; clame, sang-froid *m.*

cooling-off period (com.) *n*, trêve *f.*, arrangée pour empêcher une grève

coop *n.* cage *f.*, poulailler *m.*; fly the — s'évader; — up *vi.* enfermer

co-op *n.* (coll.) entreprise coopérative *f.*

cooper *n.* tonnelier *m.*; **-age** *n.* tonnellerie *f.*

co-operate *vi.* coopérer, collaborer

co-operation *n.* coopération *f.*

co-operative *n.* entreprise coopérative *f.*; — *a.* coopératif

co-ordinate *vt.* coordonner; — *a.* co-ordonné; — *n.* coordonné *m.*

co-ordination *n.* coordination *f.*

coot *n.* foulque *f.*

cope *vi.* combattre, lutter, se tirer d'affaire

copier *n.* copiste *m.* & *f.*; imitateur *m.*

coping *n.* faîte *m.*; — saw porte-scies *m.*

copious *a.* copieux, abondant; **-ly** *adv.* copieusement; **-ness** *n.* abondance *f.*

copilot *n.* copilote *m.*

copper *n.* cuivre *m.*; monnaie de cuivre *f.*; (coll.) flic *m.*; — *a.* de cuivre, en cuivre; — *vt.* cuivrer

copperhead *n.* (variété de) serpent vénéneux *m.*; partisan du sud *m.* (guerre de sécession, USA)

copperplate *n.* gravure sur cuivre *f.*; plaque de cuivre *f.*

coppersmith *n.* chaudronnier *m.*

copse *n.* taillis *m.*

copulate *vi.* s'accoupler

copulation *n.* copulation *f.*

copulative *a.* copulatif

copy *n.* copie, reproduction *f.*; exemplaire *m.*; numéro *m.*; **-book** *n.* cahier *m.*; **-cat** *n.* imitateur, singe *m.*; — writer (com.) rédacteur d'annonces publicitaires *m.*; rough — brouillon *m.*; — *vt.* copier; imiter; **-ist** *n.* copiste *m.*

copyright *n.* copyright, droit d'auteur *m.*; — *vt.* déposer; **-ed** *a.* dont tous les droits sont réservés

coquette *n.* coquette *f.*

coquettish *a.* coquet

cord *n.* corde *f.*; cordon *m.*, ficelle *f.*; stère *m.*, mesure *f.* (pour le bois: 128 pieds³); — *vt.* corder; ligoter; **-age** *n.* cordage *m.*; **-ed** *a.* à cordes; côtelé

cordial *a.* cordial; — *n.* liqueur *f.*, digestif *m.*; **-ity** *n.* cordialité *f.*

Cordoba *n.* Cordoue *f.*

cordovan *n.* cuir de Cordoue *m.*

corduroy *n.* velours (rayé) *m.*

core *n.* cœur, intérieur *m.*; noyau *m.*; (apple) trognon *m.*; — *vt.* vider

corespondent *n.* coaccusé *m.*

cork *n.* liège, bouchon (de liège) *m.*; — *vt.* boucher; **-age** *n.* débouchage *m.*

corkscrew *n.* tire-bouchon *m.*

cormorant *n.* cormorant *m.*

corn *n.* maïs *m.*; (foot) cor *m.*; — cob *n.* épi de maïs; **-crib** *n.* dépôt de maïs *m.*; — pone *n.* (sorte de) polenta *f.*; —

popper appareil pour faire éclater le maïs *m.*; — *vt.* saler; **–ed beef** bœuf salé *m.*; **–starch** *n.* fécule de maïs *f.*; amidon *m.*

cornea *n.* cornée *f.*

corner *n.* coin, angle *m.*; **extrémité** *f.*; tournant, virage *m.*; — *vt.* attraper; acculer; (com.) accaparer

cornerstone *n.* pierre angulaire *f.*; pierre de refend *f.*

cornice *n.* corniche *f.*

Cornish *a.* cornouaillais

cornucopia *n.* corne d'abondance *f.*

Cornwall *n.* Cornouailles *m.*

corolla *n.* corolle *f.*

corollary *n.* corollaire *m.*

corona *n.* couronne *f.*

coronation *n.* couronnement, sacre *m.*

coronet *n.* petite couronne *f.*

corporal *n.* caporal *m.*; — *a.* corporel (eccl.) corporal

corporate *a.* incorporé

corporation *n.* société anonyme *f.*; (coll.) ventre *m.*, bedaine *f.*

corporeal *a.* corporel, matériel

corps *n.* corps, corps d'armée *m.*

corpse *n.* cadavre *m.*; corps *m.*

corpsman *n.* (mil.) infirmier *m.*

corpulence *n.* corpulence *f.*

corpulent *a.* corpulent

corpuscle *n.* corpuscule, *m.*

corral *n.* enclos *m.*; — *vt.* mettre dans l'enclos

correct *vt.* corriger; châtier, punir; retoucher; — *a.* correct; exact; bienséant; **–ion** *n.* correction *f.*; **–ive** *a.* correctionnel; correctif; **–ly** *adv.* correctement, exactement; **–ness** *n.* correction *f.*; exactitude *f.*

correlate *vi.* correspondre; — *vt.* marquer la corrélation

correlation *n.* corrélation *f.*

correlative *a.* corrélatif, réciproque

correspond *vi.* correspondre; **–ence** *n.* correspondance *f.*; **–ent** *n.* correspondant *m.*; **–ing** *a.* correspondant; conforme

corridor *n.* couloir, corridor *m.*

corroborate *vt.* corroborer

corroboration *n.* corroboration *f.*

corroborator *n.* témoin *m.*

corrode *vt.* corroder, ronger; — *vi.* se corroder

corrosion *n.* corrosion *f.*

corrugate *vt.* rider, froncer, plisser; **–ed iron** tôle ondulée *f.*

corrupt *vt.* corrompre, gâter, séduire; suborner; — *a.* corrompu; **–ible** *a.* corruptible; **–ion** *n.* corruption *f.*

corsage *n.* fleur *f.*, bouquet *m.* (porté au corsage)

Corsica *n.* Corse *f.*; **–n** *a. & n.* corse *m. & f.*

cortex *n.* substance corticale *f.*

cortisone *n.* cortisone *m.*

corundum *n.* corindon *m.*

cosmetic *n.* cosmétique *m.*; fard *m.*; — *a.* cosmétique

cosmic *a.* cosmique; — **ray** rayon cosmique *m.*

cosmopolitan *n. & a.* cosmopolite *m.*

Cossack *n.* Cosaque *m.*

cost *n.* prix *m.*, frais *m. pl.*, dépense *f.*; — **price** prix de revient *m.*; — **of living** coût de la vie *m.*; **whatever the** — coûte que coûte; — *vi.* coûter; **–liness** *n.* (haut) prix *m.*; cherté *f.*; **–ly** *a.* cher; coûteux

Costa Rica *n.* Costa Rica *m.*

costume *n.* costume *m.*; **–r** *n.* costumier *m.*

cot *n.* lit de sangle *m.*

cote *n.* pigeonnier, colombier *m.*

cottage *n.* cabane, chaumière *f.*; villa *f.*; — **cheese** lait caillé, fromage blanc *m.*

cotton *n.* coton *m.*; **absorbent** — coton hydrophile *m.*; — **batting** coton cardé *m.*; ouate *f.*; — **flannel** *n.* flanelle de coton *f.*; — **goods** cotonnades *f. pl.*; — **mill** filature de coton *f.*

couch *n.* lit *m.*; divan *m.*; canapé *m.*; — *vt.* coucher; — *vi.* se tapir

cougar *n.* couguar *m.*

cough *n.* toux *f.*; — **drop** pastille *f.*; — *vi.* tousser; **–ing** *n.* toux *f.*

council *n.* conseil *m.*; concile *m.*; **city** — conseil minucipal *m.*; **–or** *n.* conseiller *m.*

counsel *n.* conseil, avis *m.*; consultation *f.*; avocat *m.*; — *vt. & vi.* conseiller; **–or** *n.* conseiller *m.*; avocat *m.*

count *n.* nombre, compte *m.*; (title) comte *m.*; — *vi.* compter; — **on** compter su :; **–er** *n.* compteur *m.*; jeton *m.*; contre *m.*; comptoir *m.*; **Geiger –er** *n.* compteur de Geiger *m.*; **–er** *adv.* contre; **–er** *a.* contraire; **–less** *a.* innombrable

count-down *n.* (coll.) longue vérification finale avant de lancer un projectile dans l'espace

countenance *n.* contenance *f.*, visage *m.*; air, regard *m.*; — *vt.* soutenir, favoriser; approuver; encourager

counter *vt.* opposer, agir contre; riposter

counteract *vt.* contrebalancer

counterattack *n.* contre-attaque *f.*; — *vt.* contre-attaquer

counterbalance *vt.* contre-balancer; — *n.* contre-poids *m.*

countercharge *n.* contre-accusation *f.*

counterclockwise *adv.* au sens inverse des aiguilles d'une montre

counterfeit *n.* contrefaçon, fausse monnaie

f.; — *vt.* contrefaire; –ing *n.* contrefait; –er *n.* contrefaiteur, faux-monnayeur *m.*

counterintelligence *n.* contre-espionnage *m.*

countermand *vt.* contremander; décommander

countermarch *n.* contremarche *f.*

counteroffensive *n.* contre-offensive *f.*

counterpane *n.* courtepointe *f.*

counterpart *n.* contre-partie *f.*; pendant *m.*

counterpoint *n.* contre-point *m.*

counterreformation *n.* contre-réforme *f.*

counterrevolution *n.* contre-révolution *f.*

countershaft *n.* contre-arbre *m.*

countersign *n.* contre-seing *m.*; (mil.) mot d'ordre *m.*; — *vt.* contresigner

countersink *vt.* fraiser; — *n.* fraise *f.*

countertenor *n.* haute-contre *f.*

counterweight *n.* contre-poids *m.*

countess *n.* comtesse *f.*

country *n.* pays *m.*; contrée, compagne *f.*; **native** — patrie *f.*; **–man** *n.* compatriote *m.*; compagnard *m.*

countryside *n.* paysage *m.*; région *f.*

county *n.* comté, département, canton *m.*; — **seat** chef-lieu *m.*

coupe *n.* coupé *m.*

couple *n.* couple *m.*, paire *f.*; — *vt.* coupler; accoupler; embrayer; grouper; — *vi.* s'accoupler

coupling *n.* accouplement *m.*; couplage *m.*; attelage *m.*

coupon *n.* coupon *m.*; (com.) bon-prime *m.*

courage *n.* courage *m.*; **–ous** *a.* courageux

courier *n.* courrier *m.*

course *n.* course, carrière *f.*; cours *m.*; plat, service *m.*; chemin *m.*, route *f.*; terrain *m.*; (naut.) cap *m.*; **as a matter of** — comme affaire routinière; **in due** — en temps voulu; **in the** — **of time** avec le temps; **of** — bien entendu; **give a** — faire un cours; **take a** — suivre un cours; — *vi.* courir

court *n.* cour *f.*; cour de justice *f.*, tribunal *m.*; (sport) terrain *m.*; — *vt.* faire la cour (à), courtiser

courteous *a.* poli, courtois; **–ness** *n.* politesse *f.*

courtesan *n.* courtisane *f.*

courtesy *n.* courtoisie, politesse *f.*

courthouse *n.* palais de justice *m.*

courtier *n.* courtisan *m.*; homme de la cour *m.*

court-martial *n.* conseil de guerre *m.*; — *vt.* traduire en conseil de guerre

courtroom *n.* salle du tribunal *f.*

courtship *n.* cour *f.*

courtyard *n.* cour (de maison) *f.*

cousin *n.* cousin *m.*, cousine *f.*; **first** — cousin germain *m.*

cove *n.* crique *f.*; abri *m.*; anse *f.*

covenant *n.* contrat, accord *m.*

cover *n.* couvert *m.*, enveloppe *f.*; couverture *f.*; couvercle *m.*; abri *m.*, protection *f.*; prétexte *m.*; — **charge** couvert *m.*; **take** — se mettre à l'abri; **under separate** — sous pli séparé; — *vt.* couvrir; recouvrir; cacher; parcourir; (newspaper) assurer un reportage; **–age** *n.* reportage *m.*; assurance *f.*; (insurance) *n.* couverture d'assurance *f.*; **–ing** *n.* couverture *f.*

coverlet *n.* (bed) couvre-lit *m.*, (foot) couvre-pieds *m.*

covert *a.* couvert, caché

covet *vt. & vi.* convoiter; désirer ardemment; **–ous** *a.* cupide, désireux; avide; **–ousness** *n.* convoitise, cupidité *f.*

covey *n.* couvée, volée *f.*

cow *n.* vache *f.*; — *vt.* intimider

coward *n.* lâche *m.*; **–ice** *n.* lâcheté *f.*; **–ly** *a.* lâche

cowboy *n.* vacher, cow-boy *m.*

cower *vi.* s'accroupir, se tapir

cowhide *n.* vache, peau de vache *f.*

cowl *n.* capuchon *m.*; capot *m.*; **–ing** *n.* capuchonnement *m.*; capotage *m.*

cowlick *n.* épi de cheveux *m.*

co-worker *n.* collaborateur *m.*

cowslip *n.* primevère *f.*

coxcomb *n.* fat, petit-maître *m.*

coxwain *n.* patron de chaloupe *m.*; barreur *m.*

coy *a.* modeste; réservé; **–ness** *n.* modestie, timidité, réserve *f.*

coyote *n.* (genre de) loup *m.*

coziness *n.* confortable *m.*

C.P.A.: Certified Public Accountant comptable diplômé *m.*

crab *n.* crabe *m.*; tourteau *m.*; personne désagréable *f.*; — **(apple)** pomme sauvage *f.*; — *vi.* se plaindre, être désagréable; **–by** *a.* désagréable, grognon, revêche

crack *n.* fente *f.*; craquement, bruit *m.*; fêlure *f.*; — **of dawn** pointe du jour *f.*; — *a.* expert, de premier ordre; — *vi.* se fendre; — *vt.* fendre; — **a joke** faire une plaisanterie; **–down** (coll.) devenir très stricte; **–ed** *a.* fendu; (coll.) fou; **–er** *n.* biscuit *m.*; **–ling** *n.* friton *m.*; craquement *m.*

crackle *vi.* craqueter, pétiller; — *n.* craquement *m.*

crackpot *n.* (coll.) original, excentrique, tapé *m.*

crack-up *n.* collision *f.*; accident *m.*;

écrasement *m.*; écroulement *m.*; accident d'avion *m.*

cradle *n.* berceau *m.*; — *vt.* bercer

craft *n.* métier *m.*, profession *f.*; artifice *m.*, fourberie *f.*; barque *f.*, vaisseau *m.*; **-iness** *n.* ruse *f.*; **-y** *a.* rusé

craftsman *n.* artisan *m.*

crag *n.* rocher escarpé *m.*; **-ged**, **-gy** *a.* escarpé

cram *vt.* fourrer; farcir; — *vi.* (coll.) étudier à la dernière heure; bûcher

cramp *n.* crampe *f.*; — *vt.* gêner, entraver; **-ed** *a.* serré; gêné

cranberry *n.* airelle *f.*; — **sauce** compote d'airelles *f.*

cranial *a.* cranien

cranium *n.* crâne *m.*

crank *n.* manivelle *f.*; (coll.) excentrique *m.*; — *vt.* tourner la manivelle (de); **-iness** *n.* irritabilité, mauvaise humeur *f.*; **-y** *a.* irritable, de mauvaise humeur

crankcase *n.* carter *m.*

crankshaft *n.* arme de manivelle, arbremanivelle *m.*

cranny *n.* fente, crevasse *f.*; coin *m.*; niche *f.*

crape *n.* crêpe *m.*

crash *n.* craquement, fracas *m.*; écrasement *m.*; (com.) krach *m.*; — *vt.* briser, fracasser; — *vi.* retentir

crash-landing *n.* (avi.) atterrissage violent *m.* (exécuté par le pilote dans un cas urgent)

crass *a.* grossier

crate *n.* emballage à claire-voie *m.*; — *vt.* emballer

crater *n.* cratère *m.*

cravat *n.* foulard *m.*; cravate *f.*

crave *vt.* implorer, solliciter; désirer

craven *a.* lâche *m.*

craving *n.* désir ardent *m.*; soif *f.*

crawfish, crayfish *n.* écrevisse *f.*

crawl *vi.* ramper; se traîner; **be -ing with** fourmiller de; — *n.* rampement *m.*; (swimming) crawl *m.*

crayon *n.* couleur *f.*; crayon (de pastel) *m.*; — *vt.* crayonner

craze *n.* manie *f.*; vogue *f.*; — *vt.* rendre fou

craziness *n.* folie *f.*

crazy *a.* fou (folle); —, **(funny)**, **bone** *n.* nerf du coude *m.*; — **quilt** courte-pointe multicolore *f.*

creak *vi.* crier, craquer; — *n.* cri *m.*; **-y** *a.* criard

cream *n.* crème *f.*; meilleur, élite *m.*; **whipped** — crème fouettée *f.*; — **cheese** fromage à la crème, fromage blanc *m.*; — **puff** chou à la crème *m.*; — *vt.* mélanger (beurre et sucre); **-ery** *n.*

crèmerie, laiterie *f.*; **-y** *a.* crémeux

crease *n.* pli, faux pli *m.*; — *vt.* plisser, faire un faux pli; — *vi.* se plisser

create *vt.* créer, produire; inventer

creation *n.* création *f.*; invention *f.*

creative *a.* créateur, inventif

creator *n.* créateur *m.*

creature *n.* créature *f.*; être *m.*; (animal) bête *f.*

credence *n.* créance, foi *f.*

credentials *n. pl.* lettres de créance *f. pl.*, documents, papiers *m. pl.*

credibility *n.* crédibilité *f.*

credible *a.* croyable, digne de foi

credit *n.* crédit *m.*; foi, croyance *f.*; témoignage *m.*; influence *f.*; **to be a** — to faire honneur à; — *vt.* croire, ajouter foi à; donner à crédit; porter au crédit de; **-able** *a.* estimable; **-or** *n.* créditeur *m.*

credulity *n.* crédulité *f.*

credulous *a.* crédule; **-ness** *n.* crédulité *f.*

creed *n.* croyance *f.*; profession de foi *f.*

creek *n.* ruisseau *m.*; crique *f.*

creel *n.* panier de pêche *m.*

creep *vi.* ramper; se traîner; **-er** *n.* (bot.) plante rampante *f.*; **-y** *a.* (coll.) mystérieux

cremate *vt.* incinérer

cremation *n.* incinération *f.*

Creole *n.* Louisianais *m.* (d'origine française ou espagnole)

creosote *n.* créosote *f.*; — *vt.* créosoter

crepe *n.* crêpe *m.*; — **paper** papier crêpe *m.*

crepitation *n.* crépitation *f.*

crescent *a.* & *n.* croissant *m.*

cress *n.* cresson *f.*

crest *n.* crête *f.*; cimier *m.*; sommet *m.*; **-ed** *a.* huppé; à crête

crestfallen *a.* abattu, decouragé, penaud

Crete *n.* Crète *f.*

crevice *n.* crevasse, fente *f.*

crew *n.* troupe, bande *f.*; équipage *m.*; équipe *f.*

crib *n.* mangeoire, crèche, étable *f.*; petit lit *m.*; (grain) coffre *m.*; — *vt.* copier; **-bing** *n.* (coll.) emploi frauduleux d'un aide-mémoire pour réussir à un examen *m.*

cricket *n.* grillon *m.*; (sports) cricket *m.*

crier *n.* crieur *m.*

Crimea *n.* Crimée *f.*

criminal *n.* & *a.* criminel *m.*

criminologist *n.* criminaliste *m.*

criminology *n.* criminologie *f.*

crimp *vt.* friser; gaufrer; — *n.* (coll.) obstacle *m.*

crimson *n.* & *a.* cramoisi *m.*

cringe *vi.* ramper, s'abaisser

cringing *a.* craintif; servile; — *n.* crainte *f.*; servilité *f.*

crinkle *n.* pli *m.*; — *vt.* froisser, plisser

cripple *n.* estropié *m.*; — *vt.* estropier; paralyser

crisis *n.* crise *f.*

crisp *a.* croustillant; vif; brusque; frais; –ness *n.* qualité croustillante *f.*; netteté *f.*

crisscross *a.* en zigzag; en quinconce; — *vt. & vi.* aller en zigzag, (s')entrecroiser

criterion *n.* critérium, critère *m.*

critic *n.* critique *m.*; –al *a.* critique; –ism *n.* critique *f.*; –ize *vt.* critiquer; blâmer

croak *vi.* coasser; (coll.) crever; — *n.* coassement *m.*

Croatia *n.* Croatie *f.*

crochet *n.* ouvrage au crochet *m.*; — *vt.* faire au crochet; — *vi.* faire du crochet

crock *n.* pot de terre *m.*; –ery *n.* poterie *f.*

crocodile *n.* crocodile *m.*

crone *n.* vieille femme *f.*

crony *n.* copain *m.*

crook *n.* crochet *m.*; courbure *f.*; (eccl.) crosse *f.*; (coll.) escroc, malfaiteur, filou *m.*; — *vt.* courber; — *vi.* se courber; –ed *a.* courbé; tortueux; (coll.) malhonnête, filou; –edness *n.* nature tortueuse *f.*

croon *vi.* chantonner doucement; chanter d'une maniere sentimentale; –er *n.* chanteur dont la voix est douce et sentimentale *m.*

crop *n.* récolte, moisson *f.*; (bird) jabot *m.*; (whip) manche *m.*; — *vt.* couper court; — up apparaître, –per, share –er *n.* métayer *m.*

cross *n.* croix *f.*; mélange, croisement *m.*; — *a.* fâché; contraire; — purpose opposition *f.*; — reference renvoi *m.*; — section coupe *f.*; — *vt. & vi.* traverser; croiser; — out rayer; –ing *n.* traversée *f.*; passage *m.*; level –ing (rail.) passage à niveau *m.*; pedestrian –ing passage clouté *m.*

crossbill *n.* bec-croisé *m.*

crossbow *n.* arbalète *f.*; –man *n.* arbalétrier *m.*

crossbreed *n.* personne de race croisée *f.*; — *vt.* croiser la race

cross-check *vt.* vérifier tous les éléments de

cross-country *a.* à travers campagne

crosscut *a.* qui coupe en travers

cross-examination *n.* contre-interrogatoire *m.*

cross-eyed *a.* louche

cross fire *n.* feu croisé *m.*

cross-legged *a.* les jambes croisées

cross-purposes *n. pl.* malentendu *m.*

crossroad *n.* carrefour *m.*; chemin de traverse *m.*

crosswise, crossways *a.* en travers

crossword puzzle *n.* mots croisés *m. pl.*

crotch *n.* entre-jambes *m.*

crotchety *a.* irritable, désagréable, revêche; capricieux

crouch *vi.* se baisser, s'accroupir; — *n.* accroupissement *m.*; (boxing) crouch *m.*

croup *n.* croupion *n.*; (med.) croup *m.*; croupe (d'un cheval) *f.*

crouton *n.* croûton *m.*

crow *n.* corneille *f.*; chant du coq *m.*; as the — flies à vol d'oiseau; — *vi.* chanter; se vanter

crowd *n.* foule, presse *f.*; (coll.) bande, côterie *f.*; — *vt.* encombrer; — *vi.* se presser, s'assembler en foule; –ed *a.* bondé

crown *n.* couronne *f.*; sommet *m.*; forme (d'un chapeau) *f.*; — prince prince héritier *m.*; — *vt.* couronner, sacrer; –ing *a.* suprême; –ing *n.* couronnement *m.*

crow's-foot *n.* patte-d'oie *f.*

crow's-nest *n.* (naut.) vigie *f.*

crucial *a.* crucial, décisif

crucible *n.* creuset *m.*

crucifix *n.* crucifix *m.*; –ion *n.* crucifixion *f.*

cruciform *a.* cruciforme, en forme de croix

crucify *vt.* crucifier

crude *a.* cru; rude; brut; fruste; grossier; — oil pétrole brut *m.*; –ness *n.* crudité *f.*; grossiereté *f.*; rudesse *f.*

crudity *n.* crudité *f.*

cruel *a.* cruel; –ty *n.* cruauté *f.*

cruet *n.* burette *f.*, huilier, vinaigrier *m.*

cruise *n.* croisière *f.*; — *vi.* faire une croisière; –r *n.* croiseur *m.*

cruller *n.* beignet *m.*

crumb *n.* mie, miette *f.*; bread –s chapelure *f.*; — *vt.* paner; –ed *a.* pané

crumble *vt.* émietter; — *vi.* s'écrouler; crouler; s'émietter

crumbling *n.* écroulement *m.*

crumple *vt.* froisser

crunch *vt.* croquer; — *vi.* craquer

crupper *n.* croupe *f.*

crusade *n.* croisade *f.*; –er *n.* croisé *m.*

crush *n.* écrasement *m.*; choc *m.*; foule *f.*; (coll.) amourette *f.*; — *vt.* écraser; opprimer; –ing *a.* écrasant; accablant; –ing *n.* écrasement *m.*

crust *n.* croûte *f.*; incrustation *f.*; — *vt.* encroûter; –y *a.* couvert d'une croûte; vieux, maussade

crustacean *n.* crustacé *m.*

crutch *n.* béquille *f.*

crux *n.* crise *f.*; point central *m.*
cry *n.* cri *m.*; **a far — from** bien eloigné de; **—** *vt.* crier; **—** *vi.* pleurer; crier, s'écrier; **–ing** *n.* pleurs *f. pl.*; cri *m.*
crybaby *n.* pleurnicheur *m.*
cryogenics *n.* cryogénique *f.*
crypt *n.* crypte *f.*; **–ic** *a.* secret; énigmatique
cryptography *n.* cryptographie *f.*
crystal *n.* cristal *m.*; (of a watch) verre *m.*; **—** *a.* de cristal; **–line** *a.* cristallin; **–lize** *vt.* cristaliser; **–lization** *n.* crystallisation *f.*
C.S.T.: Central Standard Time heure du centre (des USA)
cub *n.* petit d'un animal *m.*; (scout) louveteau *m.*; **— reporter** reporter débutant *m.*
cubbyhole *n.* case *f.*
cube *n.* cube *m.*; **—** *vt.* cuber
cubic *a.* cube; cubique
cubicle *n.* cabine *f.*
cuckoo *n.* coucou *m.*; **—** *a.* (coll.) fou
cucumber *n.* concombre *m.*
cud, to chew the **—** ruminer
cuddle *vt.* serrer, presser; **—** *vi.* se serrer
cudgel *n.* massue *f.*; **—** *vt.* rosser; **— one's brains** se casser la tête
cue *n.* (billiards) queue *f.*; (theat.) réplique *f.*; **—** *vt.* donner la réplique
cuff *n.* (blow) coup *m.*; (shirt) manchette *f.*; (trousers) revers *m.*; **— links** boutons de manchette *m. pl.*; **—** *vt.* battre, talocher
culinary *a.* de cuisine, culinaire
cull *vt.* cueillir; choisir; trier
culminate *vi.* culminer
culmination *n.* point culminant *m.*
culottes *n. pl.* pantalon court de femme *m.*
culpability *n.* culpabilité *f.*
culpable *a.* coupable
culprit *n.* coupable *m.*
cult *n.* culte *m.*
cultivate *vt.* cultiver
cultivation *n.* cultivation, culture *f.*
cultivator *n.* cultivateur *m.*
cultural *a.* culturel
culture *n.* culture *f.*; **–d** *a.* cultivé
culvert *n.* ponceau *m.*
cumbersome *a.* embarrassant, incommode
cumulative *a.* cumulatif
cuneiform *a.* cunéiforme
cunning *n.* ruse *f.*, artifice *m.*; **—** *a.* adroit; rusé; (coll.) délicieux, charmant
cup *n.* tasse *f.*; coupe *f.*; (med.) ventouse *f.*
cupboard *n.* armoire *f.*; placard *m.*
cupcake *n.* petit gâteau *m.*
Cupid *n.* Cupidon *m.*

cupidity *n.* cupidité *f.*
cupola *n.* coupole *f.*
cur *n.* chien hargneux *m.*
curable *a.* guérissable
curate *n.* vicaire, curé *m.*
curative *a.* curatif
curator *n.* conservateur *m.*
curb *n.* frein *m.*; restreinte *f.*; bordure (de trottoir) *f.*; **—** *vt.* restreindre; brider
curbstone *n.* bordure (de trottoir) *f.*
curd *n.* lait caillé *m.*; **–le** *vt.* cailler; **–le** *vi.* se cailler
cure *n.* cure *f.*; guérison *f.*, traitement *m.*; **—** *vt.* guérir; mariner, saler; préparer, travailler
cure-all *n.* panacée *f.*
curfew *n.* couvre-feu *m.*
curio *n.* bibelot *m.*
curiosity *n.* curiosité *f.*
curious *a.* curieux
curl *n.* boucle (de cheveux) *f.*; (fig.) ondulation *f.*; **—** *vt. & vi.* friser; **— up** enrouler; **–y** *a.* frisé, en boucles
curlicue *n.* parafe *m.*
currant *n.* groseille *f.*; **black —** cassis *m.*
currency *n.* circulation *f.*, cours *m.*, continuité *f.*; papier-monnaie *m.*
current *n.* courant *m.*; **alternating —** courant alternatif *m.*; **direct —** courant continu *m.*; **—** *a.* courant
curriculum *n.* cours d'études *m.*
curry *n.* cari *m.*; **— powder** cari *m.*; **—** *vt.* étriller; **— favor (with)** chercher à s'insinuer dans les bonnes grâces (de)
curse *n.* malédiction *f.*; **—** *vt.* maudire; **—** *vi.* jurer
cursing *n.* jurons *m. pl.*
cursory *a.* précipité; léger
curt *a.* court, brusque; **–ness** *n.* brusquerie *f.*
curtail *vt.* écourter; retrancher; **–ment** *n.* restriction *f.*
curtain *n.* rideau *m.*; **— call** rappel *m.*; **— raiser** lever de rideau *m.*; **— rod** monture *f.* (pour rideaux); **—** *vt.* garnir de rideaux
curtsy *n.* révérence *f.*; **—** *vi.* faire la révérence
curvature *n.* courbure *f.*
curve *n.* courbe *f.*; virage *m.*; **—** *vt.* courber; **—** *vi.* se courber; **–d** *a.* courbe, courbé
cushion *n.* coussin *m.*; **—** *vt.* rembourrer; amortir
custard *n.* flan *m.*; crème *f.*
custodian *n.* gardien *m.*
custody *n.* garde *f.*; emprisonnement *m.*
custom *n.* coutume, habitude *f.*; **–s** *pl.* douane *f.*; **–ary** *a.* habituel, ordinaire;

-er *n.* client *m.*; (coll.) type *m.*
custom-built, custom-made *a.* fait sur commande, fait sur mesure
customhouse *n.* douane *f.*
cut *n.* coupure *f.*; coupe *f.*; morceau *m.*, tranche *f.*; (print.) gravure *f.*; baisse *f.*; **short — raccourci** *m.*; **— vt.** couper, tailler; trancher; baisser; (prices) réduire; (records) enregistrer; (teeth) faire; **— across** traverser; **— class** sécher un cours; **— down** faucher, abattre; **— out** découper; (coll.) cesser; **— short** couper court (à); **— up** couper en petits morceaux; découper; (coll.) faire la noce; **— a.** coupé; taillé; tranché; baissé; **— and dried** décidé, fixé; **— glass** cristal taillé *m.*; **-ting** *a.* tranchant; mordant; cinglant; **-ting** *n.* coupe *f.*; découpage *m.*; coupon *m.*; coupure *f.*
cutaneous *a.* cutané
cutaway *n.* frac *m.*
cutback *n.* réduction de la force ouvrière d'une usine *f.*
cute *a.* joli, délicieux
cuticle *n.* pellicule *f.*, épiderme *m.*
cutlass *n.* coutelas *m.*
cutlery *n.* coutellerie *f.*
cutlet *n.* (with bone) côtelette *f.*; (without bone) escalope *f.*
cutoff *n.* interrupteur *m.*; soupape *f.*; bifurcation *f.*; chemin plus court *m.*
cutout *n.* (elec.) coupe-circuit *m.* coupure *f.*
cut-rate *a.* à prix réduit
cutthroat *n.* coupe-gorge *m.*; **— a.** acharné
cwt. : hundredweight *n.* un demi quintal *m.*
cyanide *n.* cyanure *m.*
cybernetics *n.* cybernétique *f.*
cycle *n.* cycle *m.*; **— vi.** aller à bicyclette; pédaler
cyclist *n.* cycliste *m. & f.*
cyclotron *n.* cyclotron *m.*
cylinder *n.* cylindre *m.*
cylindrical *a.* cylindrique
cymbal *n.* cymbale *f.*
cynic *n.* cynique *n.*; **-al** *a.* cynique; **-ism** *n.* cynisme *m.*
cypress *n.* cyprès *m.*
Cyprus *n.* Chypre *f.*
cyst *n.* kyste *m.*; sac *m.*
Czar *n.* tsar *m.*; **-ina** *n.* tsarine *f.*
Czech *a. & n.* tchèque *m. & f.*
Czechoslovakia *n.* Tchécoslovakie *f.*

D

D.A.: District Attorney procureur *m.*
dab *n.* éclaboussure *f.*; tache *f.*; petit coup, petit morceau *m.*; **— vt.** éclabous-

ser; tacher; tamponner
dabble *vi.* s'occuper en amateur
Dacron (trademark) *n.* dacron *m.*
dactyl *n.* dactyle *m.*; pied de trois syllabes dont la première accentuée *m.*
dad, daddy *n.* papa *m.*
daffodil *n.* asphodèle *m.*
daft *a.* idiot, fou
dagger *n.* poignard *m.*
daily *n.* quotidien *m.*; **— a.** journalier, quotidien; **— adv.** tous les jours; quotidiennement;
daintiness *n.* délicatesse *f.*
dainty *n.* friandise *f.*; **— a.** délicat
dairy *n.* laiterie *f.*; **— farm** vacherie *f.*; **— industry** industrie laitière *f.*
dairyman *n.* laitier, crémier *m.*
daisy *n.* marguerite *f.*
dale *n.* val *m.*
dalliance *n.* affaire *f.*; flirtage *m.*
dally *vi.* badiner, perdre son temps, s'amuser
Dalmatia *n.* Dalmatie *f.*
dam *n.* barrage *m.*; (zool.) mère *f.*; **— vt.** barrer
damage *n.* dommage *m.*; dégats *m. pl.*; avarie *f.*; **— vt.** endommager, avarier
damaging *a.* nuisible
damascene *vt.* damasquiner
Damascus *n.* Damas *m.*
damask *n.* damas *m.*
dame *n.* dame *f.*; (coll.) femme *f.*
damn *vt.* damner, condamner; **—! interj.** zut!; **-able** *a.* damnable; **-ation** *n.* damnation *f.*; **-ed** *a.* damné; (coll.) sacré
damp *n.* humidité *f.*; **— a.** humide; **-en** *vt.* humidifier; humecter; étouffer; **-er** *n.* registre *m.*; étouffoir *m.*; **-ness** *n.* humidité *f.*
damsel *n.* demoiselle *f.*
damson *n.* prune de damas *f.*
dance *n.* danse *f.*; bal *m.*; dancing *m.*; **— hall,** salle de danse *f.*; dancing *m.*; **— vi.** danser; **-er** *n.* danseur *m.*, danseuse *f.*
dandelion *n.* pissenlit *m.*
dander *n.* colère *f.*
dandle *vt.* bercer, dorloter
dandruff *n.* pellicules *f. pl.*
dandy *n.* dandy *m.*; **— a.** (coll.) épatant
Dane, Danish *a. & n.* Danois *m.*
danger *n.* danger *m.*; **-ous** *a.* dangereux, périleux; **-ously** *adv.* dangereusement
dangle *vi.* être suspendu; pendre, pendiller; **— vt.** suspendre
dank *a.* humide, moite
dapper *a.* vif; élégant
dapple *a.* pommelé, bigarré; **— vt.** tacheter
dare *n.* défi *m.*; **— vt.** donner le défi (à); provoquer; oser; risquer; **— vi.** oser

daredevil *n.* casse-cou *m.*
daring *a.* hardi; audacieux; — *n.* audace *f.*
dark *a.* sombre, obscur; noir; (color) foncé;
— **horse** candidat obscur *m.*; — *n.* obscurité, nuit *f.*; **-en** *vi.* faire nuit; **-en** *vt.* noircir; **-ness** *n.* nuit *f.*; obscurité *f.*
Dark Ages *n.* Moyen-Âge *m.*
darkroom *n.* chambre noire *f.*
darling *n.* favori *m.*, favorite *f.*, chéri *m.*, chérie *f.*; — *a.* chéri, favorite
darn *vt.* raccommoder; repriser; — *n.* raccommodage *m.*; reprise *f.*; —! *interj.* zut!; **-ing** *n.* raccommodage *m.*; **-ing needle** *n.* aiguille à repriser *f.*; demoiselle *f.*
dart *n.* dard, trait *m.*; — *vt.* darder, lancer; jeter; — *vi.* voler comme un trait
dash *n.* trait *m.*; petit brin, grain *m.*; course *f.*; ruée *f.*; (gram.) tiret *m.*; — *vt.* jeter; plonger; précipiter; éclabousser; — *vi.* se briser, se heurter; se ruer; — **off** esquisser; **-ing** *a.* élégant
dastard *n.* lâche *m.*; **-ly** *a.* lâche
data *n.* données *f. pl.*
date *n.* date *f.*; époque *f.*; (bot.) datte *f.*; (coll.) rendez-vous *m.*; **up to** — à la page; — *vt. & vi.* dater; **-d** *a.* vétuste, démodé
dative *n.* datif *m.*
daub *vt.* barbouiller; enduire; peinturer; — *n.* barbouillage *m.*; enduit *m.*
daughter *n.* fille *f.*
daughter-in-law *n.* belle-fille *f.*
daunt *vt.* intimider, abattre; **-less** *a.* intrépide
davenport *n.* divan, canapé *m.*
davit *n.* (naut.) davier *m.*
dawdle *vi.* muser; flâner; **-r** *n.* traînard *m.*
dawdling *a.* musard, flâneur; — *n.* musarderie, flânerie *f.*
dawn *n.* aube, aurore *f.*, point du jour *m.*; — *vi.* paraître, naître; poindre
day *n.* jour *m.*; journée *f.*; **a** — par jour; **by the** — à la journée; **carry the** — vaincre; — **after** lendemain *m.*; — **after** — d'un jour à l'autre; — **before** yesterday avant-hier; — **by** — au jour le jour; jour par jour; **every** — tous les jours; **every other** — tous les deux jours; **from** — **to** — au jour le jour; **on the following** — le lendemain; — **laborer** manœuvrier *m.*; — **nursery** garderie d'enfants *f.*; — **school** externat *m.*; — **shift** équipe du jour *f.*
daybreak *n.* pointe du jour *f.*; aube *f.*
daydream *n.* rêverie *f.*; — *vi.* faire des châteaux en Espagne
daylight *n.* jour *m.*; — **saving time** *n.* heure d'été *f.*
daytime *n.* jour *m.*, journée *f.*

daze *vt.* éblouir; étourdir; — *n.* éblouissement *m.*, étourdissement *m.*
dazzle *vt.* éblouir
dazzling *a.* éblouissant
d.c.: direct current courant continu *m.*
deacon *n.* diacre *m.*
deactivate *vt.* déactiver
dead *a.* mort, sans vie; sourd; — **body** *n.* cadavre *m.*; — **calm** calme plat *m.*; — **center** point mort *m.*; — **end** impasse *f.*, cul-de-sac *m.*; — **heat** manche à manche; — **letter** rebut *m.*; — **line** *n.* experation d'un délai *f.*; — **reckoning** route estimée *f.*; — **shot** bon tireur *m.*; — **silence** silence total *m.*; — **weight** poids inerte *m.*; **-wood** *n.* bois mort *m.*; coulée d'un navire *f.*; **the** — *n.*; les morts *m. pl.*; — *adv.* tout à fait, entièrement; **-en** *vt.* assourdir; amortir; **-ly** *a.* mortel; vénéneux
dead line *n.* heure-limité *f.*
deadlock *n.* impasse *f.*
Dead Sea *n.* (la) Mer Morte *f.*
deaf *a.* sourd; insensible; **stone** — complètement sourd; — **and dumb** sourd-muet; **-en** *vt.* rendre sourd; **-ening** *a.* assourdissant; **-ness** *n.* surdité *f.*
deaf-mute *n.* sourd-muet *m.*
deal *n.* quantité, partie *f.*; (cards) donne *f.*; affaire *f.*; **a great** —, **a good** — beaucoup; — *vt.* (cards) donner, distribuer; — *vi.* avoir affaire, traiter; **-er** *n.* commerçant *m.*; (cards) donneur *m.*; **-ings** *n. pl.* affaires *f. pl.*
dean *n.* doyen *m.*
dear *a.* cher; coûteux; bien aimé; **-ly** *adv.* cher, chèrement; **-ness** *n.* cherté *f.*
dearth *n.* rareté *f.*; pénurie *f.*
death *n.* mort *f.*, trépas *m.*; — **rate** mortalité *f.*; **at** —'**s door** à deux doigts de la mort; **-blow** *n.* coup de mort *m.*; — **penalty** *n.* peine capitale *f.*; — **warrant** ordre d'exécution *m.*; **put to** — exécuter, mettre à mort; **-less** *a.* immortel; **-ly** *a.* mortel
deathbed *n.* lit de mort *m.*
deathtrap *n.* coupe-gorge *m.*
debar *vt.* exclure, priver
debase *vt.* abaisser, avilir; falsifier; **-ment** *n.* avilissement *m.*
debatable *a.* contestable
debate *n.* débat *m.*, dispute *f.*; — *vt. & vi.* débattre; disputer
debauch *vt.* débaucher; **-ery** *n.* débauche *f.*; libertinage *m.*
debenture *n.* reconnaissance, obligation *f.*
debilitate *vt.* débiliter, affaiblir
debility *n.* débilité *f.*
debit *n.* débit *m.*; — *rt.* débiter
debonair *a.* élégant, gai

debris n. débris m. pl.

debt n. dette f.; **to run, get into —** faire des dettes; **-or** n. débiteur m.

debunk vt. démentir

debut n. début m.; **-ante** n. débutante f.

decade n. décade f., dix ans m. pl.

decadence n. décadence f.

decamp vi. décamper. filer

decant vt. décanter; **-er** n. carafe f.

decapitate vt. décapiter

decay n. déclin m., décadence f.; (teeth) carie f.; **—** vi. tomber en ruine; pourrir

decease n. décès m.; **—** vi. déceder; **-d** a. décédé

deceit n. tromperie f.; **-ful** a. trompeur

deceive vt. tromper; **-r** n. trompeur m.

deceleration n. décélération f.

December n. décembre m.

decency n. décence, bienséance f.

decent a. décent, convenable. bienséant

decentralization n. décentralisation f.

decentralize vt. décentraliser

deception n. tromperie f.

deceptive a. trompeur

decide vt. décider, résoudre; juger; **—** vi. se décider; **-ed** a. marqué; résolu; **-edly** adv. notablement: décidément

decimal a. décimal; **—** point virgule f.

decimate vt. décimer

decimation n. décimation f.

decipher vt. déchiffrer; **-able** a. déchiffrable

decision n. décision f.; résolution f.; jugement m.; parti m.; **to come to a —** prendre une décision

decisive a. décisif

deck n. tillac, pont, gaillard m.; (cards) jeu m.; **—** chair transat m.; **—** vt. parer, orner

declaim vt. & vi. déclamer; haranguer

declamation n. déclamation f.

declamatory a. déclamatoire

declaration n. déclaration f.; constatation f.

declare vt. déclarer; **-d** a. déclaré, avoué

declension n. déclinaison f.

decline n. déclin m., décadence f.; **—** vt. refuser; décliner; **—** vi. déchoir; baisser; pencher

declivity n. déclivité f.

decode vt. déchiffrer

decompose vt. décomposer; **—** vi. se décomposer, pourrir

decomposition n. décomposition f.

decompression n. décompression f.

deconsecrate vt. séculariser

deconsecration n. sécularisation f.

decontaminate vt. décontaminer

decontrol vt. libérer du contrôle

decorate vt. décorer, orner

decoration n. décoration f.; décor m.

decorative a. décoratif

decorator n. décorateur m.

decorous a. convenable, comme il faut

decorum n. décorum m., décence f.

decoy n. leurre m.; **—** vt. leurrer

decrease n. diminution f.; amoindrissement m.; **—** vt. & vi. diminuer; (s')amoindrir

decreasing a. diminuant; **-ly** adv. de moins en moins

decree n. décret, édit m.; arrêt, arrêté m.; jugement m.; **—** vt. & vi. décréter

decrepit a. décrépit; **-ude** n. décrepitude f.

decry vt. décrier

dedicate vt. dédier; dévouer; consacrer

dedication n. dédicace, dédication f.

dedicatory a. dédicatoire

deduce vt. déduire, inférer

deduct vt. déduire; **-ion** n. déduction f.; retranchement m., remise f.; **-ive** a. déductif

deed n. action f., acte, fait, exploit m.; (law) titre m.; **—** vt. transférer un titre

deem vt. & vi. juger, penser

deep a. profond; grave; (color) foncé; **—** n. mer f.; ciel m.; **-en** vt. approfondir; obscurcir; **-en** vi. s'approfondir; devenir plus foncé; **-ness** n. profondeur f.

Deepfreeze (trademark) n. frigorifique f.

deep-rooted, deep-seated a. enraciné

deep-sea a., **—** fishing grande pêche f.

deface vt. défigurer, détériorer, mutiler; **-ment** n. défiguration, mutilation f.

defalcate vi. détourner de l'argent

defalcation n. détournement d'argent m.

defamation n. diffamation f.

defamatory a. diffamatoire

defame vt. diffamer; **-r** n. diffamateur m.

default n. défaut m., faute f.; **—** vi. manquer; faire défaut

defeat n. défaite, déroute f.; **—** vt. vaincre, battre, défaire; **-ist** a. & n. défaitiste m. & f.

defect n. défaut m.; vice m.; **—** vt. faire défection; **-ion** n. défection f.; **-ive** a. défectueux; vicieux

defend vt. défendre, protéger; **-ant** n. accusé m.; **-er** n. defenseur m.

defense n. défense, protection f.; **-less** a. sans défense

defensible a. défensible

defensive n. défensive f.; **—** a. défensif

defer vt. & vi. différer, remettre; déférer (à); **-ence** n. déférence f., respect m.; **in -ence to** par respect pour; **-ential** a. respectueux; **-ment** n. délai m.; (army) réformation temporaire f.

defiance n. défi m.; **in —** of au mépris de

defiant a. résistant, combattant; de défi

deficiency *n.* défaut *m.*, insuffisance *f.*
deficient *a.* défectueux, imparfait
deficit *n.* déficit *m.*
defile *n.* defilé *m.*; — *vt.* souiller; — *vi.* défiler; -ment *n.* souillure, tache *f.*
definable *a.* définissable
define *vt.* définir; délimiter
definite *a.* défini, exact, précis; -ly *adv.* décidément, nettement; -ness *n.* netteté *f.*
definition *n.* définition *f.*
deflate *vt.* dégonfler
deflation *n.* dégonflement *m.*; (com.) déflation *f.*
deflect *vt.* détourner; défléchir; -ion *n.* déclinaison *f.*; déflexion *f.*
deforest *vt.* déboiser; -ation *n.* déboisement *m.*
deform *vt.* défigurer, déformer; -ation *n.* déformation *f.*; -ed *a.* difforme, déformé; -ity *n.* difformité *f.*
defraud *vt.* frauder, tromper; -er *n.* fraudeur *m.*
defray *vt.* défrayer, couvrir
defrost *vt.* dégivrer; -er *n.* dégivreuse *f.*
deft *a.* adroit, preste; -ness *n.* adresse, prestesse, dextérité *f.*
defunct *a.* défunt
defy *vt.* défier, braver
degeneracy *n.* dégénération *f.*
degenerate *vi.* dégénérer; — *a.* & *n.* dégénéré *m.*
degeneration *n.* dégénération *f.*
degradation *n.* dégradation *f.*
degrade *vt.* dégrader, avilir
degrading *a.* dégradant
degree *n.* degré *m.*; qualité, condition *f.*, ordre, rang *m.*; (educ.) titre *m.*; in some — dans une certaine mesure; third — (coll.) cuisinage *m.*; by -s peu à peu, petit à petit
dehumidifier *n.* déshydratant *m.*
dehydrate *vt.* dessécher, déshydrater
deification *n.* déification *f.*
deify *vt.* déifier
deign *vi.* daigner
deist *n.* déiste *m.*
deity *n.* déité, divinité *f.*
deject *vt.* affliger, décourager; abattre; -ed *a.* découragé; abattu; -ion *n.* découragement *m.*; abattement *m.*
delay *n.* délai, retard *m.*; — *vt.* retarder; remettre, différer; — *vi.* retarder; tarder, s'attarder
delectable *a.* délectable
delegate *n.* délégué *m.*; — *vt.* déléguer
delegation *n.* délégation *f.*
delete *vt.* rayer, enlever, éliminer, supprimer, effacer
deletion *n.* rature *f.*; suppression *f.*

deliberate *vi.* délibérer; — *a.* délibéré; prémédité; voulu, calculé; réfléchi; -ly *adv.* avec préméditation; exprès; posément
deliberation *n.* délibération *f.*
delicacy *n.* délicatesse *f.*; friandise *f.*
delicate *a.* délicat; fin; friand; tendre; doux; faible
delicatessen *n.* charcuterie *f.*
delicious *a.* délicieux
delight *n.* délice *m.*, délices *f.* pl., plaisir *m.*; joie *f.*; charme *m.*; — *vt.* réjouir, divertir; ravir; — *vi.* prendre plaisir (à); -ed *a.* ravi, enchanté; -ful *a.* charmant; ravissant; délicieux
delimit *vt.* délimiter
delineate *vt.* tracer, dessiner, décrire
delineation *n.* délinéation, esquisse *f.*
delinquency *n.* délit *m.*
delinquent *n.* délinquant *m.*
delirious *a.* en délire; be — délirer
delirium *n.* délire *m.*; — tremens delirium tremens *m.*
deliver *vt.* livrer; remettre, rendre; délivrer; (med.) accoucher; prononcer; s'acquitter de; distribuer; -ance *n.* délivrance *f.*; -er *n.* livreur *m.*; libérateur *m.*; -y *n.* livraison *f.*; (mail) distribution *f.*; (speech) débit *m.*; (med.) accouchement *m.*; (letter) general -y poste restante *f.*; special -y (letter) lettre exprès *f.*
Delphi *n.* Delphes *f.*; -c *a.* de Delphes
delude *vt.* tromper, abuser
deluge *n.* déluge *m.*; — *vt.* inonder
delusion *n.* tromperie, illusion *f.*
delusive *a.* trompeur
delve *vt.* creuser, fouir
demagogue *n.* démogogue *m.*
demand *n.* demande, requête *f.*; in great — très recherché; on — à présentation; — *vt.* réclamer, exiger
demarcate *vt.* délimiter
demarcation *n.* démarcation *f.*
demean *vt.*, — oneself se comporter; se dégrader; -or *n.* conduite, tenue *f.*
demented *a.* aliéné
demerit *n.* démérite *m.*; mauvaise note *f.*
demigod *n.* demi-dieu *m.*
demilitarization *n.* démilitarisation *f.*
demilitarize *vt.* démilitariser
demise *n.* mort *f.*, décès *m.*
demitasse *n.* café noir *m.*
demobilization *n.* démobilisation *f.*
demobilize *vt.* démobiliser
democracy *n.* démocratie *f.*
democrat *n.* démocrate *m.*; -ic *a.* démocratique
demolish *vt.* démolir, abattre
demolition *n.* démolition *f.*

demonstrability *n.* démontrabilité *f.*
demonstrable *a.* démontrable
demonstrate *vt.* démontrer; — *vi.* manifester
demonstration *n.* démonstration *f.*; (pol.) manifestation *f.*
demonstrative *a.* démonstratif
demonstrator *n.* démonstrateur *m.*; (pol.) manifestant *m.*
demoralization *n.* démoralisation *f.*
demoralize *vt.* démoraliser
demote *vt.* dégrader
demotion *n.* dégradation *f.*
demur *n.* hésitation *f* ; — *vi.* différer; hésiter
demure *a.* sobre; modeste
den *n.* caverne *f.*, repaire *m.*; étude *f.*
denaturalize *vt.* dénaturaliser
denature *vt.* dénaturer
deniable *a.* niable, reniable
denial *n.* dénégation *f.*, refus *m.*
denim *n.* étoffe croisée de coton *f.*
denizen *n.* habitant *m.*
Denmark *n.* Danemark *m.*
denominate *vt.* dénommer
denomination *n.* dénomination *f.*; culte *m.*; -al *a.* sectaire, confessionnel
denominator *n.* dénominateur *m.*
denote *vt.* dénoter, désigner
denouement *n.* dénouement *m.*
denounce *vt.* dénoncer, accuser
dense *a.* dense; épais; stupide
density *n.* densité *f.*; épaisseur *f.*
dent *n.* renfoncement *m.*; coche *f.*; — *vt.* laisser une coche, bosseler
dental *a.* dentaire, dental; — brace *n.* rectificateur dentaire *m.*
dentate *a.* denté
dentifrice *n.* dentifrice *m.*
dentist *n.* dentiste *m.*
denture *n.* dentier *m.*, fausses dents *f. pl.*
denude *vt.* dénuer, dépouiller; dénuder
denunciation *n.* dénonciation *f.*
denunciatory *a.* dénonciateur
deny *vt.* nier; dénier; désavouer, renoncer, refuser
deodorant *n.* désodorisant *m.*
deodorize *vt.* désodoriser; -r *n.* désodorisateur
depart *vi.* partir, s'en aller; -ed *a.* mort, défunt; -ure *n.* départ *m.*
department *n.* département *m.*; comptoir, rayon *m.*; — store grand magasin *m.*; -al *a.* départemental
depend *vi.* dépendre (de); résulter (de); se reposer, se fier; -able *a.* digne de confiance; -ence, -ency *n.* dépendance *f.*; -ent *a.* dépendant; -ent *n.* personne dépendante *f.*; be -ent on dépendre de
depict *vt.* dépeindre, décrire

depilation *n.* épilation *f.*
depilatory *a. & n.* dépilatoire *m.*
deplete *vt.* épuiser
depletion *n.* épuisement *m.*
deplorable *a.* déplorable, lamentable
deplore *vt.* déplorer, pleurer, plaindre
depolarization *n.* dépolarisation *f.*
depopulate *vt.* dépeupler
deport *vt.* déporter; (se) comporter; -ation *n.* déportation *f.*; -ment *n.* comportement *m.*
depose *vt.* déposer; mettre bas; attester
deposit *n.* dépôt, gage *m.*; (geol.) gisement *m.*; (com.) arrhes *f. pl.*; — *vt.* déposer; -ion *n.* déposition *f.*; -or *n.* déposant *m.*; -ory *n.* dépôt *m.*
depot *n.* dépôt *m.*; (rail.) gare *f.*
deprave *vt.* dépraver, corrompre
depravity *n.* corruption *f.*; perversité *f.*
deprecate *vt.* s'opposer (à); désapprouver
depreciate *vt.* déprécier; dénigrer; — *vi.* perdre sa valeur
depreciation *n.* dépréciation *f.*
depredation *n.* déprédation *f.* pillage *m.*
depress *vt.* déprimer, abaisser; -ed *a.* abattu, déprimé; -ing *a.* attristant; -ion *n.* dépression *f.*; crise financière *f.*; abattement *m.*
deprivation *n.* privation *f.*
deprive *vt.* priver; destituer
depth *n.* profondeur *f.*, abîme *m.*; milieu, cœur, fort *m.*; hauteur, obscurité *f.*; get out of one's — perdre fond; — bomb, — charge bombe sous-marine *f.*
deputation *n.* députation, délégation *f.*
depute *vt.* déléguer, députer
deputize *vt.* députer
deputy *n.* délégué *m.*; adjoint *m.*; député *m.*
derail *vt.* faire dérailler; be -ed dérailler; -ment *n.* déraillement *m.*
derange *vt.* troubler, déranger; -ment *n.* dérèglement *m.*; dérangement *m.*
derby *n.* (racing) derby *m.*; (hat) chapeau melon *m.*
derelict *n.* vaisseau abandonné *m.*; personne abandonnée *f.*; clochard *m.*; — *a.* abandonné; -ion *n.* abandon *m.*; renoncement *m.*
deride *vt.* railler, se moquer de
derision *n.* dérision *f.*; risée *f.*
derisive *a.* dérisoire
derivation *n.* dérivation *f.*; source *f.*
derivative *n.* dérivé *m.*
derive *vt. & vi.* dériver; — *vi.* provenir, procéder
dermatitis *n.* dermite *f.*
dermatologist *n.* dermatologiste *m.*
derogate *vi.* déroger
derogatory *a.* dérogatoire

derrick n. grue f., derrick m.

descend vi. descendre; be —ed from descendre de; —ant, —ent n. descendant m.

descent n. descente f.; descendance f.

describable a. descriptible a.

describe vt. décrire, dépeindre

description n. description f.

descriptive a. descriptif

desecrate vt. profaner

desecration n. profanation f.

desegregate vt. ôter la ségrégation

desegregation n. intégration f.

desensitize vt. rendre insensible; désensibiliser

desert n. désert m.; — vt. déserter; abandonner; —er n. déserteur m.; —ion n. désertion f.

deserts n. pl. dû m.; punition f.; récompense f.

deserve vt. mériter

deserving a. méritoire, digne

desiccate vt. dessécher; — vi. se dessécher

desiccation n. dessiccation f.; dessèchement m.

design n. dessein m.; intention f.; plan m.; (art) dessin m.; — vt. dessiner; destiner; —er n. dessinateur m.; —ing a. intrigant; —ing n. dessin m.

designate vt. désigner, indiquer, distinguer

desirability n. avantage m.

desirable a. désirable, souhaitable

desire n. désir m., envie f.; — vt. désirer; souhaiter

desirous a. désireux

desist vi. cesser; s'abstenir

desk n. bureau m.; pupitre m.; chaire f.

desolate vt. désoler, dépeupler; — a. désert, dépeuplé; désolé

desolation n. désolation f.

despair n. désespoir f.; — vi. désespérer (de); —ing a. désespéré

despatch n. expédition, diligence f.; dépêche f.; — vt. dépêcher, expédier

desperado n. risque-tout m.; hors-la-loi m.

desperate a. désespéré

desperation n. désespoir m.

despicable a. méprisable, bas

despise vt. dédaigner, détester, mépriser

despite prep. en dépit de, malgré

despoil vt. dépouiller

despondency n. abattement m.

despondent a. désolé; abattu; désespéré

despot n. despote, tyran m.; —ic a. despotique; —ism n. despotisme m.

dessert n. dessert, entremets m.

destine vt. destiner

destiny n. destinée f., destin m.

destitute a. abandonné, dans la misère; destitué

destitution n. dénûment m., misère f.; des-

titution f.

destroy vt. détruire; —er n. destructeur m.; (navy) destroyer m.

destruction n. destruction f.

destructive a. destructif; —ness n. caractère destructif m., nature destructive f.

desuetude n. désuétude f.

desultory a. décousu, sans suite

detach vt. détacher, séparer; —able a. détachable; —ed a. détaché; séparé; désintéressé; —ment n. détachement m.

detail n. détail m.; — vt. détailler

detain vt. détenir, retenir

detect vt. repérer, découvrir; distinguer; —ion n. découverte f.; —ive n. détective m.; —or n. détecteur, appareil récepteur m.

detention n. retard m., détention f.; arrêt m.; retenue f.; emprisonnement m.

deter vt. détourner, décourager; —rent n. empêchement m.

detergent n. & a. détersif, détergent m.

deteriorate vt. détériorer; — vi. se détériorer

deterioration n. détérioration f.

determinable a. déterminable

determinate a. déterminé, défini

determination n. détermination, décision f.

determinative a. déterminatif, déterminant

determine vt. & vi. déterminer, fixer, décider; —d a. résolu

detest vt. détester; —able a. détestable

dethrone vt. détrôner; —ment n. détrônement m.

detonate vi. détoner; — vt. faire détoner

detonation n. détonation f.

detonator n. détonateur m.

detour n. déviation f.; détour m.; — vi. dévier, se détourner

detract vi., — from diminuer; —or n. détracteur m.

detrain vi. débarquer, descendre (du train)

detriment n. détriment m., perte f.; —al a. nuisible, préjudiciable

devaluate vt. dévaluer

devaluation n. dévaluation f.

devalue vt. dévaluer

devastate vt. dévaster

devastating a. accablant; dévastateur

develop vt. développer; — vi. se développer; exploiter; contracter; —er n. développeur m.; révélateur m.; —ment n. développement m.; exploitation f.

deviate vi. dévier, s'égarer, dériver

deviation n. déviation f., égarement m.

device n. appareil m.; moyen m.; ruse f.; devise f., emblème m.

devil n. diable m.; — vt. accommoder au

poivre; –ish *a*. diabolique; espiègle; –try *n*. espièglerie *f*.

devil-may-care *a*. insouciant

devious *a*. détourné; dévié; –ness *n*. détours *m. pl.*

devise *vt*. inventer, imaginer

devoid *a*. vide, dénué

devolve *vi*. échoir; — *vt*. déléguer

devote *vt*. dévouer, dédier, consacrer; –ed *a*. dévoué

devotee *n*. amateur *m*.

devotion *n*. dévotion *f*.; dévouement *m*.; –al *a*. de dévotion

devour *vt*. dévorer

devout *a*. dévot; pieux; –ness *n*. dévotion, piété *f*.

dew *n*. rosée *f*.

dewlap *n*. fanon *m*.

dexterity *n*. dextérité, adresse *f*.

dexterous *a*. adroit; habile

dextrin *n*. dextrine *f*.

dextrose *n*. glucose *f*., dextrose *m*.

diabetes *n*. diabète *m*.

diabetic *a*. diabétique

diabolic(al) *a*. diabolique

diacritic(al) *a*.; — **mark** *n*. marque diacritique *f*.

diadem *n*. diadème *m*.

diaeresis *n*. tréma *m*.

diagnose *vt*. diagnostiquer

diagnosis *n*. diagnostic *m*.

diagnostic *a*. diagnostique

diagonal *n*. diagonale *f*.; — *a*. diagonal

diagram *n*. diagramme *m*.; figure *f*.; schéma *m*.; –matic *a*. schématique

dial *n*. cadran *m*.; — **telephone** téléphone automatique *m*.; — *vt*. composer (un numéro)

dialect *n*. dialecte *m*.

dialog(ue) *n*. dialogue *m*.

diameter *n*. diamètre *m*.

diametrical *a*. diamétral

diamond *n*. diamant *m*.; (cards) carreau *m*.; (sport) terrain de baseball *m*.; (print.) corps 4, 5 *m*.

diapason *n*. diapason *m*.

diaper *n*. couche *f*.

diaphanous *a*. diaphane

diaphragm *n*. diaphragme *m*.

diarrhea *n*. diarrhée *f*.

diary *n*. journal *m*.

diathermy *n*. diathermie *f*.

diatom *n*. diatomée *m*.

diatribe *n*. diatribe *f*.

dice *n. pl.* dés *m. pl.*; — *vt*. couper en cubes; — *vi*. jouer aux dés

dickey, dicky *n*. faux plastron de chemise *m*.

dictaphone *n*. dictaphone *m*.

dictate *n*. règle *f*., précepte *m*.; — *vt*. dic-

ter, prescrire, déclarer

dictation *n*. dictée *f*.

dictator *n*. dictateur *m*.; –ial *a*. dictatorial; –ship *n*. dictature *f*.

diction *n*. diction *f*., style *m*.

dictionary *n*. dictionnaire *m*.

dictum *n*. dicton *m*.; (law) opinion *f*.

didactic *a*. didactique; –s *n. pl.* didactique *f*.

die *n*. dé *m*.; (coin) coin *m*.; (mech.) matrice *f*.

die *vi*. mourir; — **away**, — **down**, — **out** s'eteindre, se mourir

diesel engine *n*. diesel *m*.

diet *n*. nourriture *f*.; diète *f*., régime *m*.; — *vi*. être au régime; –etic *a*. diététique; –etics *n*. diététique *f*.

differ *vi*. différer; –ence *n*. différence *f*.; différend *m*.; –ent *a*. différent; autre; –ential *n*. différentiel; –entiate *vt*. différencier; –entiation *n*. différenciation *f*.

difficult *a*. difficile; –y *n*. difficulté *f*.; inconvénient *m*.; embarras *m*.

diffidence *n*. timidité, hésitation *f*.; défiance *f*.

diffident *a*. timide, hésitant

diffract *vt*. diffracter; –ion *n*. diffraction *f*.

diffuse *vt*. diffuser, répandre; — *a*. diffus; –r *n*. diffuseur *m*.

dig *vt*. creuser; — **up** déterrer; — *n*. (coll.) insulte *f*.; remarque sarcastique *f*.; –ging *n*. excavation *f*.; fouilles *f. pl.*

digest *vt. & vi*. digérer; résumer; — *n*. résumé, digest *m*.; –ible *a*. digestible; –ion *n*. digestion *f*.; –ive *a*. digestif

digit *n*. doigt *m*.; chiffre *f*.; –al *a*. digital; –al computer *n*. calculatrice digitale *f*.

digitalis *n*. digitale *f*.

dignified *a*. plein de dignité, digne

dignify *vt*. rendre digne, honorer

dignitary *n*. dignitaire *m*.

dignity *n*. dignité *f*.

digress *vi*. faire une digression; –ion *n*. digression *f*.

dike *n*. digue *f*.

dilapidate *vt*. dilapider; –d *a*. délabré

dilapidation *n*. délabrement *m*., dilapidation *f*.

dilate *vt*. dilater; — *vi*. se dilater

dilation *n*. dilation *f*.

dilatory *a*. dilatoire

dilemma *n*. dilemme *m*.

diligent *a*. diligent, assidu

dill *n*. aneth *m*.

dilute *vt*. délayer, diluer; –d *a*. dilué

dim *vt*. obscurcir; (lights) baisser; — *a*. obscur; pâle; sceptique; –mers *n. pl.* (headlights) feux de croisement *m. pl.*; –ness *n*. obscurité *f*.

dime *n*. pièce de dix cents *f*.; — **novel** roman populaire *m.*; — **store** (coll.) magasin à prix unique *m.*

dimension *n.* dimension, étendue *f.*

diminish *vt. & vi.* diminuer, amoindrir

diminution *n.* diminution, réduction *f.*

diminutive *a.* diminutif

dimple *n.* fossette *f.*

din *n.* bruit, tintamarre, vacarme *m.*; — *vt.* étourdir; **to — something into some-one** étourdir quelqu'un à force de répéter quelque chose

dine *vi.* dîner; **–r** *n.* dîneur *m.*; (rail.) wagon-restaurant *m.*; **–tte** *n.* petite salle à manger *f.*

dinghy *n.* youyou, canot *m.*

dinginess *a.* couleur sombre *f.*; pauvreté *f.*

dingy *a.* terne, sale

dining *a.*, **— car** *n.* wagon-restaurant *m.*; **— room** *n.* salle à manger *f.*

dinner *n.* dîner *m.*; **— jacket** smoking *m.*

dinosaur *n.* dinosaurien *m.*

dint *n.* coup *m.*, force *f.*; **by — of** à force de

diorama *n.* diorama *m.*

dioxide *n.* bioxyde *m.*

dip *vt. & vi.* tremper, plonger; **— *n.*** plongeon *m.*; baisse *f.*; (road) cassis *m.*; (coll.) bain (de mer) *m.*; **–per** *n.* louche *f.*, cuiller à pot *f.*; **Big Dipper** Grande Ourse *f.*

diphtheria *n.* diphthérie *f.*

diphthong *n.* diphtongue *f.*

diploma *n.* d.plôme *m.*

diplomacy *n.* diplomatie *f.*

diplomat *n.* diplomate *m.*; **–ic** *a.* diplomatique; **–ist** *n.* diplomate *m.*

dire *a.* terrible, affreux; néfaste

direct *a.* direct; droit; exact; juste; **— current** courant continu *m.*; **— *vt.*** mener; conduire; régler; indiquer; **–ion** *n.* direction *f.*; sens *m.*; **–ion finder** *n.* radiogoniomètre *m.*; **–ion indicator** *n.* (avi.) flèche *f.*; signalisateur de direction *m.*; **–ions** *n. pl.* renseignements *m. pl.*; **–ive** *n.* directif *m.*, ordre *m.*; **–or** *n.* directeur *m.*; (theat.) régisseur *m.*; **–ory** *n.* annuaire *m.*; almanach *m.*; **–ly** *adv.* sans détours, sans s'arrêter

direful *a.* épouvantable; catastrophique

dirge *n.* chant funèbre *m.*

dirk *n.* dague *f.*, poignard *m.*

dirt *n.* saleté, crasse *f.*; **–iness** *n.* saleté *f.*; **–y** *a.* sale, crasseux; méchant, vilain; **–y** *vt.* salir, souiller

disability *n.* incapacité, impuissance *f.*

disable *vt.* rendre incapable, estropier; **–d** *a.* mutilé; frappé d'incapacité

disabuse *vt.* désabuser, détromper

disadvantage *n.* désavantage *m.*; inconvénient *m.*; **–ous** *a.* désavantageux, défavorable

disaffect *vt.* aliéner, déranger; **–ion** *n.* désaffection *f.*

disagree *vi.* différer; ne pas être d'accord; ne pas convenir; **–able** *a.* désagréable; facheux; **–ment** *n.* désaccord *m.*; différend *m.*; discordance *f.*

disallow *vt. & vi.* désapprouver, rejeter, interdire

disappear *vi.* disparaître; **–ance** *n.* disparition *f.*

disappoint *vt.* décevoir, désappointer; **–ed** *a.* déçu; **–ment** *n.* déception *f.*

disapprobation, disapproval *n.* désapprobation *f.*

disapprove *vt.* désapprouver

disarm *vt.* désarmer; **–ament** *n.* désarmement *m.*

disarrange *vt.* déranger; **–ment** *n.* dérangement, désordre *m.*

disarray *n.* désordre *m.*, désarroi *m.*

disaster *n.* désastre, malheur *m.*, catastrophe *f.*

disastrous *a.* désastreux

disavow *vt.* désavouer; **–al** *n.* désaveu *m.*

disband *vt.* licencier, congédier; **— *vi.*** se disperser

disbar *vt.* expulser (un avocat)

disbelief *n.* incrédulité *f.*

disbelieve *vt.* ne pas croire

disburse *vt.* débourser, dépenser; **–ment** *n.* déboursement *m.*

disc *n.* disque *m.*; **— jockey** *n.* joueur de disques (à la T.S.F.) *m.*

discard *n.* chose rejetée *f.*; carte écartée *f.*; **— *vt.*** écarter; jeter

discern *vt.* discerner, distinguer; apercevoir; **–ible** *a.* perceptible; **–ing** *a.* judicieux, pénétrant; **–ment** *n.* discernement *m.*

discharge *n.* décharge *f.*; déchargement *m.*; (med.) suppuration *f.*; (mil.) démobilisation *f.*; **— *vt.*** décharger; démobiliser; licencier, renvoyer (d'un poste); **— *vi.*** (med.) suppurer

disciplinarian *n.* homme fort sur la discipline *m.*

disciplinary *a.* disciplinaire

discipline *n.* discipline *f.*; **— *vt.*** discipliner

disclaim *vt.* désavouer, renier; **–er** *n.* désaveu public *m.*

disclose *vt.* découvrir, révéler

disclosure *n.* révélation *f.*

discolor *vt.* décolorer; **— *vi.*** se décolorer; **–ation** *n.* décoloration *f.*

discomfort *n.* malaise *m.*; gêne, incommodité *f.*; **— *vt.*** incommoder

disconcert *vt.* déconcerter, déranger

disconnect *vt.* désunir séparer, détacher

disconsolate *a.* insonsolable, désolé

discontent *n.* mécontentement *m.*; **— *vt.***

mécontenter; —, **-ed** *a.* mécontent

discontinuation *n.* cessation *f.*; discontinuité *f.*; discontinuation *f.*

discontinue *vt.* discontinuer, interrompre

discord, discordance *n.* discorde, dissension *f.*

discordant *a.* dissonant; discordant

discount *n.* escompte, rabais *m.*; — *vt.* escompter, rabattre; **-able** *a.* escomptable

discountenance *vt.* désapprouver, décontenancer

discount house *n.* braderie *f.*

discourage *vt.* décourager; **-ment** *n.* découragement *m.*

discouraging *a.* décourageant

discourse *n.* discours, entretien *m.*

discourteous *a.* impoli; **-ness** *n.* impolitesse *f.*; incivilité *f.*

discourtesy *n.* incivilité *f.*; impolitesse *f.*

discover *vt.* découvrir; divulguer; **-er** *n.* découvreur *m.*; **-y** *n.* découverte *f.*

discredit *n.* discrédit *m.*; — *vt.* discréditer

discreet *a.* discret; **-ness** *n.* discrétion *f.*

discrepancy *a.* différence *f.*; manque de conformité *m.*; désaccord *m.*

discretion *n.* discrétion *f.*; **-ary** *a.* discrétionnaire

discriminate *vt.* discerner, distinguer, séparer; — *a.* distinct; plein de discernement; **-ly** *adv.* avec discernement

discriminating *a.* éveillé, judicieux, fin

discrimination *n.* distinction *f.*; discernement *m.*

discursive *a.* décousu; discursif

discuss *vt.* discuter, examiner; **-ion** *n.* discussion *f.*; examen *m.*

disdain *n.* dédain, mépris *m.*; — *vt.* dédaigner, mépriser; **-ful** *a.* dédaigneux

disease *n.* maladie *f.*, mal *m.*; **-d** *a.* malade

disembark *vt.* & *vi.* débarquer; **-ation** *n.* débarquement *m.*

disembody *vt.* désincorporer

disembowel *vt.* éventrer

disenchant *vt.* désenchanter; **-ment** *n.* désenchantement *m.*

disencumber *vt.* débarrasser, dégager

disengage *vt.* dégager, débarrasser; — *vi.* se dégager; **-ment** *n.* dégagement *m.*

disentangle *vt.* débrouiller, démêler; **-ment** *n.* dégagement *m.*

disentomb *vt.* exhumer

disfavor *n.* défaveur, disgrâce *f.*

disfiguration *n.* difformité *f.*

disfigure *vt.* défigurer, déformer; **-ment** *n.* difformité *f.*

disfranchise *vt.* empêcher de voter; ôter le suffrage à

disgrace *n.* disgrâce, défaveur; honte *f.*;

— *vt.* disgracier; déshonorer; **-ful** *a.* honteux

disguise *n.* déguisement *m.*; dissimulation *f.*; — *vt.* déguiser

disgust *n.* dégoût *m.*, aversion *f.*; — *vt.* dégoûter; **-ing** *a.* dégoûtant

dish *n.* assiette *f.*; (food) mets, plat *m.*; (coll.) goût *m.*, préférence *f.*; — *vt.*, — **up** servir; **side** — *n.* entremets *m.*

dishcloth, dishrag *n.* lavette *f.*, torchon de cuisine *m.*

dishearten *vt.* décourager

dishevel *vt.* écheveler

dishonest *a.* malhonnête; **-y** *n.* malhonnêteté *f.*

dishonor *n.* déshonneur *m.*; — *vt.* déshonorer; **-able** *a.* déshonorant

dishpan *n.* bassine à vaisselle *f.*

dishwasher *n.* (person) laveur de vaiselle, plongeur *m.*; (machine) laveuse de vaisselle *f.*

disillusion *vt.* désillusionner; désabuser; —, **-ment** *n.* désillusionnement *m.*

disincline *vt.* indisposer, éloigner

disinfect *vt.* désinfecter; **-ant** *n.* désinfectant *m.*; **-ion** *n.* désinfection *f.*

disinherit *vt.* déshériter

disintegrate *vt.* désagréger; — *vi.* se désagréger

disintegration *n.* désintégration, désagrégation *f.*

disinterested *a.* désintéressé

disjoint *vt.* disloquer, démembrer; **-ed** *a.* décousu; démembré

disk *n.* disque *m.*; — **jockey** joueur de disques à la T.S.F. *m.*

dislike *n.* aversion *f.*, dégoût *m.*, répugnance *f.*; — *vt.* ne pas aimer; désapprouver

dislocate *vt.* disloquer; déplacer

dislodge *vt.* déplacer; faire sortir

disloyal *a.* déloyal; perfide; **-ty** *n.* déloyauté, perfidie *f.*

dismal *a.* triste, sombre, sinistre, morne

dismantle *vt.* démonter, désassembler; dépouiller, dégarnir

dismay *n.* épouvante, frayeur *f.*; découragement *m.*; — *vt.* épouvanter; décourager

dismember *vt.* démembrer; **-ment** *n.* démembrement *m.*

dismiss *vt.* renvoyer, congédier; **-al** *n.* renvoi *m.*; (law) acquittement *m.*

dismount *vi.* descendre de cheval, mettre pied à terre

disobedience *n.* désobéissance *f.*

disobedient *a.* désobéissant

disobey *vt.* désobéir

disoblige *vt.* désobliger

disorder *n.* confusion *f.*, désordre *m.*; in-

disposition *f.*; — *vt.* mettre en désordre, déranger; **-ly** *a.* déréglé; désordonné

disorganization *n.* désorganisation *f.*

disorganize *vt.* désorganiser

disown *vt.* désavouer, renoncer

disparage *vt.* déprécier, dénigrer; **-ment** *n.* dénigrement *m.*; blâme *m.*

disparity *n.* disparité, inégalité, différence *f.*

dispassionate *a.* sans passion, calme

dispatch *n.* dépêche *f.*; envoi *m.*; promptitude *f.*; — *vt.* dépêcher; expédier

dispel *vt.* disperser, dissiper

dispensary *n.* dispensaire *m.*; pharmacie *f.*

dispensation *n.* dispensation *f.*; dispense *f.*

dispense *vt.* dispenser, distribuer; — **with** se passer de; **-r** *n.* dispensateur *m.*; pharmacien *m.*

dispersal *n.* dispersion *f.*

disperse *vt.* disperser, dissiper; distribuer

dispirited *a.* abattu, découragé

displace *vt.* déplacer; **-d person** sinistré *m.*; **-ment** *n.* déplacement *m.*

display *n.* exposition *f.*; étalage *m.*; — *vt.* exposer; étaler; montrer, révéler

displease *vt.* & *vi.* déplaire

displeasing *a.* déplaisant

displeasure *n.* déplaisir *m.*, mécontentement *m.*

disport *vi.* s'amuser, folâtrer

disposable *a.* qu'on peut jeter; disponible

disposal *n.* disposition *f.*; résolution *f.*; vente *f.*; cession *f.*; **bomb** — désobusage *m.*

dispose *vt.* disposer, diriger, arranger; — **of** se défaire de; jeter; **-ed** *a.* porté

disposition *n.* disposition *f.*; caractère *m.*

dispossess *vt.* déposséder; **-ion** *n.* dépossession *f.*; expropriation *f.*

disprove *vt.* réfuter

disputable *a.* disputable; contestable

dispute *n.* dispute; querelle *f.*; — *vt.* & *vi.* disputer

disqualification *n.* incapacité, non-admissibilité, inéligibilité *f.*

disqualify *vt.* rendre inéligible

disquiet *n.* inquiétude *f.*; — *vt.* inquiéter, troubler; agiter

disquisition *n.* dissertation, recherche *f.*, examen *m.*

disregard *n.* indifférence *f.*; mépris *m.*; — *vt.* négliger; mépriser; **-ful** *a.* indifférent, négligent; dédaigneux

disreputable *a.* honteux, déshonorant; suspect

disrepute *n.* disgrâce *f.*, déshonneur *m.*

disrespect *n.* manque de respect *m.*, incivilité *f.*; **-ful** *a.* incivil, impoli; irrespectueux

disrobe *vt.* déshabiller; — *vi.* se déshabiller

disrupt *vt.* rompre; troubler; **-ion** *n.* rupture *f.*; dislocation *f.*

dissatisfaction *n.* mécontentement *m.*

dissatisfied *a.* mécontent

dissatisfy *vt.* mécontenter, déplaire (à)

dissect *vt.* disséquer; **-ion** *n.* dissection *f.*

dissemble *vt.* & *vi.* dissimuler

disseminate *vt.* semer, répandre

dissemination *n.* dissémination *f.*

disseminator *n.* propagateur *m.*

dissension *n.* dissension, discorde *f.*

dissent *n.* dissentiment *m.*; désaccord *m.*; — *vi.* différer; **-er** *n.* dissident *m.*

dissertation *n.* dissertation *f.*; thèse *f.*

disservice *n.* mauvais office, tort *m.*

dissidence *n.* dissidence, discorde *f.*

dissident *a.* dissident

dissimilar *a.* dissemblable; **-ity** *n.* dissemblance *f.*

dissimulation *n.* dissimulation *f.*

dissipate *vt.* dissiper; dépenser

dissipation *n.* gaspillage *m.*, dissipation *f.*; dispersion *f.*; débauche *f.*

dissociate *vt.* dissocier

dissociation *n.* dissociation *f.*; séparation *f.*

dissolute *a.* dissolu; débauché; **-ness** *n.* débauche *f.*

dissolution *n.* dissolution *f.*

dissolve *vt.* dissoudre; fondre; — *vi.* se dissoudre

dissonance *n.* dissonance *f.*

dissonant *a.* dissonant

dissuade *vt.* dissuader, déconseiller, détourner

distance *n.* distance *f.*, éloignement *m.*; respect *m.*; réserve *f.*; **at a** — à distance; **in the** — au loin; **keep at a** — se tenir à distance

distant *a.* éloigné; lointain; reculé; réservé; vague; distant; **-ly** *adv.* de loin

distaste *n.* dégoût, déplaisir *m.*; aversion *f.*; **-ful** *a.* désagréable

distemper *n.* maladie de chiens *f.*; (painting) détrempe *f.*

distend *vt.* dilater; distendre

distil(l) *vt.* distiller; **-late** *n.* produit de la distillation *m.*; **-lation** *n.* distillation *f.*; **-lery** *n.* distillerie *f.*

distinct *a.* distinct; différent; clair, net; **-ion** *n.* distinction *f.*; **-ive** *a.* distinctif; **-ness** *n.* séparation *f.*; netteté, clarté *f.*

distinguish *vt.* distinguer; **-able** *a.* visible, apparent; qui peut être distingué; **-ed** *a.* distingué

distort *vt.* tordre, contourner, défigurer; **-ion** *n.* contorsion *f.*; déformation *f.*

distract *vt.* distraire, détourner; troubler; **-ed** *a.* distrait; troublé; **-ion** *n.* distraction *f.*; folie *f.*

distraught *a.* distrait

distress *n.* détresse *f.*; misère *f.*; malheur *m.*; — *vt.* affliger, désoler

distribute *vt.* distribuer; répartir

distribution *n.* distribution *f.*; répartition *f.*

distributor *n.* distributeur, répartiteur *m.*; détaillant *m.*

district *n.* district *m.*; région *f.*; quartier *m.*; (pol.) circonscription *f.*; — attorney procureur *m.*

distrust *n.* méfiance, défiance *f.*; — *vt.* se méfier, se défier (de); –ful *a.* méfiant, défiant

disturb *vt.* déranger; troubler; inquiéter; agiter; –ance *n.* dérangement *m.*; trouble *m.*; émeute *f.*; bruit *m.*

disunite *vt.* désunir

disuse *n.* désuétude *f.*

ditch *n.* fossé *m.*; to the last — jusqu'au bout, jusqu'à la dernière extrémité

ditto *n.* ditto, idem *m.*

ditty *n.* chanson *f.*, refrain *m.*

divagate *vi.* divaguer

dive *n.* plongeon *m.*; (naut.) plongée *f.*; (avi.) pique *m.*; (coll.) gargote *f.*, bastringue *m.*; — *vi.* plonger; piquer; –r *n.* (sports) plongeur *m.*; (deep-sea) scaphandrier *m.*

dive bomber *n.* bombardier à piqué *m.*

dive-bombing *n.* bombardement à piqué *m.*

diverge *vi.* diverger; –nce *n.* divergence *f.*; –nt *a.* divergent

diverging *a.* divergent

diverse *a.* divers, différent, varié

diversification *n.* diversification *f.*

diversify *vt.* diversifier, varier

diversion *n.* diversion *f.*; divertissement *m.*; –ary *a.* de diversion

diversity *n.* diversité *f.*

divert *vt.* détourner; divertir, amuser

divest *vt.* dépouiller, dessaisir

divide *vt.* diviser; partager; séparer; désunir; — *vi.* se diviser; se partager; –r *n.* diviseur *m.*; –s *n. pl.* compas *m.*

dividend *n.* dividende *m.*

divination *n.* divination, prédiction *f.*

divine *a.* divin; — *vt.* deviner; — *n.* prêtre, ecclésiastique *m.*; –r *n.* devin *m.*

diving board *n.* plongeoir, tremplin *m.*

diving suit *n.* scaphandre *m.*

divining rod *n.* baguette divinatoire *f.*

divinity *n.* divinité *f.*; dieu *m.*; théologie *f.*

division *n.* division *f.*; partage *m.*; répartition *f.*; désunion *f.*; –al *a.* divisionnaire; de division

divisor *n.* diviseur *m.*

divorce *n.* divorce *m.*; to get a — divorcer;

— *vt.* divorcer; (fig.) séparer

divot *m.* (golf) motte *f.*

divulge *vt.* divulguer

dizziness *n.* vertige, étourdissement *m.*

dizzy *a.* vertigineux; feel — avoir le vertige; make — étourdir

do *vt.* faire; rendre, accomplir; servir, suffire; how — you — (je suis) enchanté de faire votre connaissance; have to — with avoir rapport à, avoir à voir à; — away with tuer; abolir; supprimer; — up emballer, ficeler; — without se passer de; –er *n.* faiseur *m.*; –ing *n.* fait *m.*; –ings *n. pl.* activités *f.*; remue-ménage *m.*; –ne *a.* fait; fini, terminé; cuit; well –ne (food) bien cuit

docility *n.* docilité *f.*

dock *n.* (law) banc des accusés *m.*; quai *m.*; bassin *m.*; dock *m.*; dry — bassin de radoub *m.*; — *vi.* entrer au bassin; arriver; — *vt.* supprimer; diminuer; (law) banc des accusés *m.*

dockyard *n.* chantier de construction maritime *m.*

doctor *n.* docteur *m.*; médecin *m.*; — *vt.* (coll.) falsifier, truquer; –al *a.* doctoral; –ate *n.* doctorat *m.*

document *n.* document *m.*; acte, titre *m.*; — *vt.* documenter; –ary *a. & n.* documentaire *m.*; –ation *n.* documentation *f.*

dodder *vi.* trembloter; –ing *a.* tremblotant; branlant

dodge *n.* esquive *f.*; mouvement de côte *m.*; (coll.) truc *m.*; ruse *f.*; — *vt. & vi.* esquiver, éviter

doff *vt.* ôter

dog *n.* chien *m.*, chienne *f.*; — days canicule *f.*; — races courses de lévriers *f. pl.*; — show exposition canine *f.*; go to the –s se debaucher, se ruiner; — *vt.* filer; marcher sur les pas de; poursuivre; –ged *a.* tenace, obstiné

dogcart *n.* charrette (anglaise) *f.*

dog-eared *a.* corné

dogfight *n.* combat aérien *m.*

dog sled *n.* traineau à chiens *m.*

dog tag *n.* (mil.) plaque d'identité *f.*

dogtrot *n.* petit-trot *m.*

doily *n.* napperon *m.*

doldrums *n. pl.* cafard *m.*; (naut.) calmes *m. pl.*; be in the — avoir le cafard

dole *n.* aumône *f.*; chômage *m.*; — *vt.*, — out distribuer; –ful *a.* triste; douloureux

doll *n.* poupée *f.*

dolorous *a.* douloureux

dolphin *n.* dauphin *m.*

dolt *n.* sot, benêt *m.*

domain *n.* domaine *m.*

dome *n.* dôme *m.*

domestic *a.* domestique; de ménage, de

famille; intérieur; — *n.* servante *f.*; –ate *vt.* apprivoiser, domestiquer

domicile *n.* domicile *m.*

dominance *n.* prédominance *f.*

dominant *a.* dominant

dominate *vt.* dominer; commander

domination *n.* domination *f.*

domineering *a.* tyrannique, autoritaire

Dominica *n.* Dominique *f.*

dominican *a.* & *n.* dominicain *m.*

Dominican Republic *n.* Dominicaine *f.*

dominion *n.* domination *f.*; dominion *m.*

domino *n.* domino *m.*

don *vt.* mettre, revêtir

donate *vt.* donner, faire un don de

donkey *n.* âne *m.*, baudet *m.*; — **engine** petit-cheval *m.*

donor *n.* donneur *m.*

doom *n.* condamnation *f.*; destin; mort *f.*; — *vt.* condamner

doomsday *n.* dernier jugement *m.*

door *n.* porte *f.*; (vehicle) portière *f.*; **out of –s** en plein air, dehors; **front** — porte d'entrée; **open the** — **to** (fig.) rendre possible

doorbell *n.* sonnette *f.*

doorknob *n.* bouton de porte *m.*

doorman *n.* portier *m.*

doormat *n.* essuie-pieds *m.*

doorpost *n.* montant de porte *m.*

doorstep *n.* seuil, pas *m.*

doorway *n.* porte *f.*; encadrement de porte *m.*

dope *n.* enduit *m.*; laque *f.*; narcotique *m.*; (coll.) idiot, imbécile *m.*; (coll.) renseignements *m. pl.*; — **fiend** toxicomane *m.* & *f.*; — **habit** toxicomanie *f.*; — *vt.* enduire; doper; narcotiser; stupéfier

dormancy *n.* repos, sommeil *m.*

dormant *a.* endormi, assoupi

dormer window *n.* lucarne *f.*

dormitory *n.* dortoir *m.*

dormouse *n.* loir *m.*

dorsal *a.* dorsal

dose *n.* dose *f.*; — *vt.* doser; médicamenter

dot *n.* point *m.*; **on the** — à l'heure tapante; **six o'clock on the** — six heures précises; — *vt.* mettre un point sur; pointiller; **–ted line** ligne en pointillé *f.*

dotage *n.* radotage *m.*

dotard *n.* vieillard, radoteur *m.*

dote *vi.* radoter; — **on** aimer à la folie

doting *a.* radoteur; sénile; extravagant

double *a.* double; en deux; duplicata; — **bass** contrebasse *f.*; — **bed** grand lit, lit à deux personnes *m.*; — **boiler** bain-marie *m.*; — **entry** en partie double; — **feature** deux grands films (au même programme); — **talk** *n.* non-sens *m.*; — *n.* double; **–s** *n. pl.* (tennis) double *m.*;

— *vt.* doubler, redoubler; — *vi.* doubler; — **back** faire un crochet; — **up** se plier; se tordre

double-barrelled *a.* à deux coups

double-breasted *a.* croisé

double-cross *vt.* tromper; trahir; — *n.* tromperie *f.*; trahison *f.*

double-dealing *n.* duplicité *f.*

double-edged *a.* à deux tranchants

double-faced *a.* hypocrite

double-header *n.* (sports) deux matchs au même programme *m. pl.*

double-jointed *a.* désarticulé

double-lock *vt.* fermer à double tour

doublet *n.* pourpoint *m.*

double time *n.* pas de gymnastique *m.*; salaire double *m.*; vitresse doublée *f.*

doubly *adv.* doublement

doubt *n.* doute *m.*; **beyond a** — à n'en pas douter; **no** — sans doute; **without a** — sans (aucun) doute; — *vt.* douter (de); **–er** *n.* douteur *m.*; **–ful** *a.* douteux; indécis; suspect; **–less** *a.* sans doute

dough *n.* pâte *f.*; (coll.) fric *m.*

doughboy *n.* (coll.) poilu *m.*

doughnut *n.* beignet *m.*

doughty *a.* vaillant, preux

dour *a.* sévère, austère

douse *vt.* tremper; arroser; (lights) éteindre

dove *n.* colombe *f.*

Dover *n.* Douvres

dovetail *vt.* assembler en queue d'aronde; — *vi.* se raccorder; se réunir; — *n.* queue d'aronde *f.*

dowager *n.* douairière *f.*

dowdy *a.* gauche, mal mis

dowel *n.* cheville *f.*; goujon *m.*

down *adv.* en bas; à bas; descendu; (price) baissé; (sun) couché; — **there** là-bas; — **under** aux antipodes; — **payment** acompte *m.*; **go** — descendre; **fall** — tomber à terre; **be** — **and out** être décavé; être ruiné; **ups and –s** vicissitudes *f. pl.*; — **with** *adv.* à bas; — *vt.* descendre, abattre; battre; — *n.* duvet *m.*; **–y** *a.* duveteux; velouté

downbeat *n.* (mus.) accent principal *m.*; premier accent *m.*

downcast *a.* abattu

downfall *n.* chute *f.*; **–en** *a.* déchu, ruiné; tombé

downgrade *n.* descente *f.*; déclin *m.*; — *vt.* déclasser

downhearted *a.* abattu

downhill *adv.* en descendant; vers le bas, en pente

downpour *n.* déluge *m.*; averse *f.*

downright *a.* absolu, véritable; — *adv.* tout à fait

downstairs *adv.* en bas; **go —** descendre (l'escalier); **—** *n.* rez-de-chaussée *m.*
downstream *adv.* en aval
downtown *adv.* en ville; **—** *n.* centre de la ville *m.*
downtrodden *a.* opprimé
downturn *n.* (com.) baisse *f.*
downward(s) *adv.* en descendant; de haut en bas
dowry *n.* dot *f.*
doze *n.* somme *m.*; **—** *vi.* sommeiller, somnoler; **— off** s'assoupir
dozen *n.* douzaine *f.*; **by the —** à la douzaine
D.P.: Displaced Person *n.* sinistré *m.*
drab *a.* terne; gris; brun
draft, draught *n.* courant d'air *m.*; tirage *m.*; ébauche *f.*; conscription *f.*; (com.) mandat, effet *m.*; traite, lettre de change *f.*; (food & drink) coup, trait *m.*, gorgée *f.*; **— board** (mil.) commission locale des conscriptions *f.*; **— horse** cheval de trait *m.*; **beer on —** bière au tonneau, bière à la pompe *f.*; **rough —** ébauche *f.*; **sight —** effet à vue *m.*; **—** *vt.* rédiger; lever, enrôler; **-ee** *n.* recrue *f.*, conscrit *m.*; **-ing** *n.* dessin industriel *m.*
draftsman *n.* dessinateur *m.*
drag *vt. & vi.* traîner; entraîner; tirer; draguer; **—** *vi.* traîner; **— down** entraîner; **— out** tirer; faire traîner
dragnet *n.* drague, seine *f.*; filet *m.*
drain *n.* tranchée *f.*, canal *m.*; égout *m.*; tuyau d'écoulement *m.*; (med.) drain *m.*; **—** *vt.* faire couler; vider; drainer; épuiser; **—** *vi.* s'écouler, s'égoutter; **-age** *n.* écoulement *m.*; drainage *m.*
drainpipe *n.* tuyau d'écoulement *m.*
dram *n.* drachme *f.*; petit verre *m.*
drama *n.* drame *m.*; théâtre *m.*; **-tic** *a.* dramatique; **-tics** *n. pl.* art dramatique *m.*; **-tist** *n.* dramaturge, auteur dramatique *m.*; **-tize** *vt.* dramatiser
drape *vt.* draper, tendre; **—** *n.* marchand de drap, drapier *m.*; **-ery** *n.* draperie *f.*; **-s** *n. pl.* rideaux *m. pl.*
drastic *a.* drastique
draw *n.* tirage *m.*; loterie *f.*; (sports) partie nulle *f.*; **—** *vt.* tirer; attirer; dessiner; (bow) bander, tendre; (water) puiser; (sports) faire partie nulle; **— aside** prendre à l'écart; **— away** s'éloigner; **— back** retirer; reculer; **— blood** faire saigner; **— lots** tirer au sort; **— near** approcher; s'approcher de; **— off** soutirer; **— out** faire parler, prolonger, traîner; **— up** relever; approcher; aligner; rédiger; (vehicle) s'arrêter; **-er** *n.* tireur *m.*; dessinateur *m.*; (furniture) tiroir *m.*; **chest of —s** commode *f.*; **pair of —ers** *n. pl.* caleçon *m.*; **-ing** *n.* tirage *m.*; dessin *m.*; **mechanical —ing** dessin industriel *m.*; **-ing board** planche à dessin *f.*; **-ing card** (coll.) attrait *m.*, attraction *f.*; **-ing room** salon *m.*; **-n** *a.* tiré
drawback *n.* désavantage, inconvénient *m.*
drawbridge *n.* pont-levis *m.*
drawl *n.* voix traînante *f.*
dray *n.* haquet *m.*
dread *n.* terreur, crainte, peur *f.*; **—** *vt.* redouter, craindre; **-ful** *a.* redoutable, terrible; épouvantable
dreadnought *n.* bâtiment de ligne *m.*
dream *n.* rêve, songe *m.*; rêverie, songerie *f.*; **—** *vt. & vi.* rêver; songer; **— up** (coll.) imaginer, inventer; **-er** *n.* rêveur *m.*, rêveuse *f.*; **-y** *a.* rêveur, songeur; (coll.) épatant
dreariness *n.* tristesse *f.*
dreary *a.* triste, morne
dredge *n.* drague *f.*; **—** *vt. & vi.* draguer; **-r** *n.* dragueur *m.*; (machine) drague *f.*
dregs *n. pl.* lie *f.*
drench *vt.* mouiller, tremper
Dresden *n.* Dresde *f.*; **— china** porcelaine de Saxe *f.*
dress *n.* robe *f.*; toilette *f.*, costume *m.*; habillement *m.*; mise, tenue *f.*; **evening —** tenue de soirée *f.*; **— circle** premier balcon *m.*; **— rehearsal** répétition générale *f.*; **— suit** habit de cérémonie *m.*; **—** *vt.* habiller, vêtir; (med.) panser; (cooking) garnir; **—** *vi.* s'habiller; **— hair** coiffer; **— windows** faire l'étalage; **get -ed** s'habiller; **— up** parer; **-er** *n.* commode *f.*; **-ing** *n.* toilette *f.*; (med.) pansement *m.*; (cooking) assaisonnement *m.*; sauce *f.*; farce *f.*; **-ing gown** peignoir *m.*, robe de chambre *f.*; **-ing room** (theat.) loge *f.*; cabinet de toilette *m.*; **-ing table** toilette *f.*; **-y** *a.* élégant, chic
dressmaker *n.* couturier *m.*, couturière *f.*
dribble *n.* bave *f.*; (sports) dribbling *m.*; **—** *vi.* dégoutter; baver; **—** *vt.* dribbler
dried *a.* séché, sec; en poudre
drift *n.* dérive *f.*; sens *m.*, direction *f.*; (snow) amoncellement *m.*; **—** *vi.* dériver; se laisser aller; s'amonceler; **-er** *n.* (coll.) vagabond *m.*
driftwood *n.* bois flotté *m.*
drill *n.* mèche *f.*, perforateur *m.*; vilebrequin *m.*; perceuse *f.*; (mil.) exercice *m.*; **—** *vt.* percer, perforer; forer; instruire; faire faire l'exercice à; (dent.) buriner; **—** *vi.* faire l'exercice; s'exercer
drillmaster *n.* maître de gymnastique *m.*
drink *n.* boisson *f.*; breuvage *m.*; boire *m.*;

have a — prendre quelque chose (à boire); — *vt.* boire; prendre (quelque chose); — **up** boire; vider le verre; **–able** *a.* potable; **–er** *n.* buveur *m.*; alcoolique *m. & f.*; **–ing** *n.* boire *m.*; alcoolisme *m.*; **–ing fountain** *n.* robinet *m.*

drip *n.* goutte *f.*; dégouttement *m.*; — *vi.* dégoutter, s'égoutter; — *vt.* laisser tomber; **–ping** *a.* trempé; (faucet) qui pleure; **–ping** *n.* dégouttement *m.*; **–pings** *n. pl.* graisse *f.*

drip-coffee *n.* café-filtre *m.*

drip-dry *a.* qui n'a pas besoin d'être repassé

dripolator *n.* filtre à café *m.*

drive *n.* promenade *f.*; propulsion *f.*; énergie *f.*; initiative *f.*; transmission *f.*; (mil.) offensive *f.*; (fund-raising) campagne *f.*; (golf) crossée *f.*; **go for a** — faire une promenade (en auto); — *vt.* conduire; chasser; pousser; forcer; réduire; surmener; (nail) enfoncer; — **a bargain** conclure un marché; — **(someone) crazy** rendre fou; — **along** rouler; — **away** chasser; partir, démarrer; — **back** repousser; reconduire; — **in** enfoncer; entrer; — **on** continuer sa route; — **out** chasser; sortir; **–r** *n.* chauffeur *m.*; conducteur *m.*; **–r's license** permis de conduire *m.*

drivel *vi.* baver; radoter; — *n.* bave *f.*; bêtises *f. pl.*

driveway *n.* allée d'entrée pour autos *f.*

driving *a.* véhément; battant; qui pousse; — **force** force motrice *f.*; — *n.* conduite *f.*

drizzle *n.* pluie fine, bruine *f.*; — *vi.* bruiner

drogue *n.* (avi.) parachute de traînage *m.*

droll *a.* drôle

drone *n.* faux-bourdon *m.*; bourdonnement *m.* (engine) vrombissement *m.*; (avi.) avion sans pilote *m.*

drool *n.* bave *f.*; — *vi.* baver

droop *vi.* languir, s'affaisser; se pencher; s'abaisser

drop *n.* goutte *f.*; pastille *f.*; baisse *f.*; perte *f.*; boîte aux lettres *f.*; — **hammer** marteau-pilon *m.*; — *vt.* laisser tomber; baisser; déposer; omettre; supprimer; abandonner; — *vi.* tomber, se laisser tomber; baisser; — **in** entrer en passant; — **off** tomber, se détacher; — **kick** *n.* coup tombé, drop-kick *m.*

dropout *n.* qui renonce à l'école

dropsy *n.* hydropisie *f.*

dross *n.* scorie, écume *f.*

drought *n.* sécheresse *f.*

drove *n.* troupeau *m.*; foule *f.*; **–r** *n.* bouvier *m.*

drown *vt.* noyer; — *vi.* se noyer; — **out** couvrir; **–ing** *n.* asphyxie *f.*

drowse *vi.* somnoler, s'assoupir

drowsiness *n.* somnolence *f.*

drowsy *a.* assoupi, somnolent

drudge *n.* esclave *m. & f.*; souffre-douleur *m. & f.*; — *vi.* piocher, travailler sans cesse; **–ry** *n.* corvée *f.*; travail pénible *m.*

drug *n.* drogue *f.*; narcotique *m.*; — *vt.* donner un narcotique à; **–gist** *n.* pharmacien *m.*

drugstore *n.* pharmacie *f.*

druid *n.* druide *m.*

drum *n.* tambour *m.*, caisse *f.*; tonneau *m.*; gonne *f.*, bidon *m.*; — **major** tambour major *m.*; **play the** — battre du tambour; — *vi.* battre du tambour; tambouriner; — **into** fourrer; — **up** faire du recrutement; **–mer** *n.* tambour *m.*

drumstick *n.* baguette (de tambour) *f.*; (coll.) cuisse *f.*; pilon *m.*

drunk *a.* ivre, soûl, gris; **get** — s'enivrer, se soûler, se griser; — *n.* ivrogne *m.*; **–ard** *n.* ivrogne *m.*; **–en** *a.* d'ivresse; **–enly** *adv.* en ivrogne; **–enness** *n.* ivresse, ivrognerie *f.*

dry *a.* sec *m.*, sèche *f.*; tari; aride; simulé; — **cell** *n.* pile sèche *f.*; — **cleaner** nettoyeur à sec *m.*; — **cleaning** nettoyage à sec *m.*; — **dock** cale sèche *f.*; bassin de radoub *m.*; — **goods** mercerie *f.*; articles de nouveauté *m. pl.*; — **ice** bioxide de carbone solidifié *m.*; glâce sèche *f.*; — **land** terre firme *f.*; — **wash** ruisseau desséche *m.*; — **rot** carie sèche *f.*; — **run** répétition *f.*, exercice simulé *m.*; **run** — se tarir; — *vt.* sécher, faire sécher, essorer; (dishes) essuyer; — *vi.* sécher, se *n.* séchoir *m.*; essoreuse *f.*; **–ness** *n.* sécheresse *f.*; aridité *f.*

dual *a.* double; **–ism** *n.* dualisme *m.*; **–ity** *n.* dualité *f.*

dub *vt.* donner l'accolade à; (films) post-synchroniser, doubler; enduire (de graisse)

dubious *a.* douteux, incertain, de doute; **–ness** *n.* doute *m.*, incertitude *f.*

duchess *n.* duchesse *f.*

duchy *n.* duché *m.*

duck *n.* cane *f.*, canard *m.*; (motion) esquive *f.*; (fabric) coutil *m.*; **white –s** (pants) pantalon blanc *m.*; — *vi.* se baisser, esquiver; plonger; — *vt.* plonger, baisser; **–ing** *n.* plongeon, bain *m.*; **–ling** *n.* caneton *m.*, canette *f.*

duct *n.* conduit *m.*; canal *m.*; canalisation *f.*; voie *f.*; **–less** *a.* (anat.) (glands) endocrines; à sécrétion interne

due *a.* dû; échu, échéant, payable; juste; (coll.) prêt; — **to** par suite de; **fall** —

venir à échéance; — *adv.* franc, droit; — *n.* dû *m.*; **give someone his —** rendre justice à quelqu'un; **-s** *n. pl.* cotisation *f.*

duel *n.* duel *m.*; — *vi.* se battre en duel; **-ing** *n.* duel *m.*; **-ist** *n.* duelliste *m.*

duenna *n.* duègne *f.*

duet *n.* duo *m.*

duffel bag *n.* sac, fourre-tout *m.*

duffer *n.* maladroit *m.*

dug *n.* mamelle *f.*

dugout *n.* pirogue *f.*, canot *m.*; abri *m.*

duke *n.* duc *m.*; **-dom** *n.* duché *m.*

dulcet *a.* doux (douce)

dull *a.* sourd; lent; lourd; ennuyeux; triste; (point) émoussé; (color) terne; — *vt.* émousser; amortir; ternir; **become —** s'émousser; (senses) s'engourdir; **-ness** *n.* lenteur *f.*; émoussement *m.*; ennui *m.*; tristesse *f.*; monotonie *f.*; **-ard** *n.* lourdaud, sot *m.*

duly *adv.* dûment, justement

dumb *a.* muet, (muette); (coll.) stupide; **deaf and —** sourd-muet; **play —** (coll.) feindre l'innocence, faire l'innocent; **-ness** *n.* mutisme *m.*; (coll.) stupidité *f.*

dumbbell *n.* haltère *m.*; (coll.) idiot *m.*

dumb-waiter *n.* monte-plats *m.*

dumfound *vt.* abasourdir, ébahir, confondre

dummy *n.* mannequin *m.*; prête-nom *m.* (cards) mort *m.*; — *a.* faux (fausse)

dump *n.* décharge publique *f.*; — **truck** camion à benne basculante *m.*; **be in the -s** être mélancolique, avoir le cafard; — *vt.* décharger; jeter à terre; **-y** *a.* trapu; gros, lourd

dumpling *n.* dumpling *m.*, boulette *f.*; **apple —** chausson *m.*; **potato —** gnocchi *m.*

dun *vt.* poursuivre (un débiteur)

dunderhead *n.* imbécile, idiot *m.*

dung *n.* fumier *m.*; fiente, crotte *f.*

dungarees *n. pl.* treillis *m.*; bleus *m. pl.*; pantalon de marin *m.*

dungeon *n.* cachot *m.*

Dunkirk *n.* Dunkerque *f.*

duodecimo *n.* (print.) in-douze *m.*

duplex *a.* duplex, double; — *n.* maison à deux familles *f.*; appartement à deux étages *m.*

duplicate *a.* double; — *n.* double, duplicata *m.*, copie *f.*; — *vt.* reproduire

duplication *n.* duplication, reproduction *f.*

duplicity *n.* duplicité *f.*

durability *n.* durabilité *f.*

duration *n.* durée *f.*

duress *n.* contrainte *f.*

during *prep.* pendant, durant

dusk *n.* crépuscule *m.*; **-y** *a.* sombre, obscur, noirâtre

dust *n.* poussière *f.*; poudre *f.*; — **jacket** chemise *f.*, protège-livres *m.*; — *vt.* épousseter; **-er** *n.* (feather) plumeau *m.*; (cloth) chiffon *m.*; (garment) housse *f.*; **-ing** *n.* époussetage *m.*; **-y** *a.* poussiéreux; (re)couvert de poussière

dustpan *n.* ramasse-poussière *m.*; pelle *f.*

Dutch *a. & n.* hollandais; néerlandais *m.*; — **oven** rôtissoire *f.*; — **treat** (coll.) repas, pris ensemble, où chacun paye sa part *m.*

dutiable *a.* taxable

dutiful *a.* respectueux

duty *n.* devoir *m.*; droit *m.*, taxe *f.*; fonctions *f. pl.*; (mil.) service *m.*, garde *f.*; **be on —** être de service; **liable to —** soumis aux droits de douane

duties (custom) *n.* droits de douane *m. pl.*

duty-free *a.* exempt de droits

dwarf *n.* nain *m.*; — *a.* nain; rabougri; — *vt.* rabougrir; rapetisser

dwell *vi.* demeurer, habiter; rester; — **on** appuyer sur; **-er** *n.* habitant *m.*; **-ing** *n.* demeure *f.*, habitation *f.*; maison *f.*; logis *m.*

dwindle *vi.* diminuer; s'affaiblir

dye *n.* teinture *f.*, teint *m.*; teinte *f.*; colorant *m.*; — *vt.* teindre; **-ing** *n.* teinture *f.*, teintage *m.*; **-r** *n.* teinturier *m.*

dyed-in-the-wool *a.* endurci, convaincu

dying *a.* mourant; moribond

dynamic *a.* dynamique; **-s** *n. pl.* dynamique *f.*

dynamite *n.* dynamite *f.*; — *vt.* dynamiter, faire sauter

dynastic *a.* dynastique

dynasty *n.* dynastie *f.*

dysentery *n.* dysenterie *f.*

dyspepsia *n.* dyspepsie *f.*

E

each *a.* chaque; — *pron.* chacun, *m.*, chacune *f.* — **other** l'un l'autre

eager *a.* ardent; empressé; impatient; avide; âpre; vif; **-ness** *n.* ardeur *f.*, empressement *m.*

eagle *n.* aigle *m.*; **-t** *n.* aiglon *m.*

eagle-eyed *a.* aux yeux d'aigle

ear *n.* oreille *f.*; (corn) épi *m.*; — **specialist** auriste *m.*; **have a good —** (for music) avoir de l'oreille; **keep one's -s open** se tenir aux écoutes

earache *n.* mal d'oreille(s) *m.*; **have an —** avoir mal à l'oreille

earl *n.* comte *m.*; **-dom** *n.* comté *m.*

early *a.* matinal; premier; précoce; prématuré; — *adv.* de bonne heure; tôt; d'avance; **as — as** dès

earmark *vt.* marquer (à l'oreille); — **for**

destiner à; — vt. (fig) spécialiser des fonds

earmuff n. couvre-oreille m.

earn vt. gagner; mériter; **–ings** n. pl. salaire m.; gages m. pl.; profit m.

earnest a. sérieux; pressant; — n., **in** — sérieusement; **be in** — être sérieux; — **money** arrhes f. pl.

earphone n. écouteur m.

earring n. boucle d'oreille f.

earshot n. portée de voix f.

ear-splitting a. à (vous) fendre les oreilles

earth n. terre f.; monde m.; sol m.; terrier m.; **scorched** — terre brûlée; **where on** — . . .? où diable . . .?; **–en** a. de terre; **–ly** a. terrestre; moindre; **–y** a. terreux; grossier

earthenware n. poterie f.

earthquake n. tremblement de terre m.; séisme m.

ease n. aise f.; repos m.; tranquilité f.; facilité f.; loisir m.; **at** — tranquille; (mil.) au repos; **at one's** — à l'aise; — vt. calmer, tranquiliser; adoucir; modérer; soulager; — **up** relentir

easel n. chevalet m.

easily adv. facilement; sans effort, sans difficulté; doucement

easiness n. facilité f.; insouciance f.; douceur f.

east n. est m.; orient, levant m.; — a. oriental, de l'est; — adv. à l'est; vers l'est; — **of** à l'est de; **–erly** a. d'est; **–erly** adv. vers l'est; **–ern** a. de l'est, oriental

Easter n. Pâques m.

eastward adv. vers l'orient

easy a. facile; aisé; tranquille; simple; — **chair** fauteuil m.; — **mark** (coll.) jobard m.; **go** — **on** ménager; **take it** — (coll.) se reposer; se calmer

easygoing a. insoucient; peu exigeant

eat vt. & vi. manger; — **away** ronger; — **up** consumer; — **one's heart out** se faire de la bile; **–ing** n. manger m.; cuisine f.

eaves n. pl. avant-toit m.

eavesdrop vi. écouter à la porte; **–per** n. écouteur m.

ebb n. reflux m.; baisse f.; déclin m.; — **and flow** flux et reflux; — **tide** marée descendante f.; — vi. refluer, baisser; décliner

ebullience n. ébullition f.; bouillonnement m.

ebullient a. bouillonnant; débordant

eccentric a. & n. excentrique m.; (person) original m.; **–ity** n. excentricité, originalité f.

ecclesiastic a. & n. ecclésiastique m.

echo n. écho m.; — vt. répéter; — vi. faire écho; retentir

eclipse n. éclipse f.; — vt. éclipser

eclogue n. églogue f.

economic a. économique; **–al** a. économique; (person) économe; **–s** n. pl. économie politique f.

economist n. économiste m.

economize vt. économiser, faire des économies

economy n. économie f.

ecstasy n. transport m.; ravissement m.; extase f.

ecstatic a. extatique

Ecuador n. Equateur m.

eczema n. eczéma m.

eddy n. tourbillon m.; — vt. tourbillonner

edge n. bord m.; fil, tranchant m.; lisière f.; **on** — nerveux, énervé; — vt. border; — **away** s'écarter peu à peu

edgewise adv. de côté; **get a word in** — glisser un mot

edging n. bord m.; bordure f.

edible a. comestible; bon à manger

edict n. édit m.

edification n. édification f.

edifice n. édifice

edify vt. édifier

Edinburgh n. Edimbourg m.

edit vt. éditer, rédiger; **–ing** n. rédaction f.; préparation f.; **–ion** n. édition f.; **–or** n. éditeur m.; rédacteur m.; **–orial** n. article de tête, article de fond m.; **–orial** a. de la rédaction

educate vt. élever, instruire; **–d** a. cultivé; instruit

education n. enseignement m.; éducation, instruction f.; **–al** a. éducatif; d'enseignement

educator n. éducateur m.

eel n. anguille f.

eerie a. étrange, mystérieux

effable a. qui peut être exprimé

efface vt. effacer; **–ment** n. effacement m.

effect n. effet m.; résultat m.; influence f.; **go into** — entrer en vigueur; **have an** — **on** affecter; **in** — en fait; effectivement; **put into** — mettre à exécution; **take** — prendre; faire effet; — vt. réaliser, effectuer; **–ive** a. efficace; en vigueur; **–iveness** n. efficacité f.; **–ual** a. efficace

effeminate a. efféminé

effervescent a. effervescent

effete a. stérile, épuisé

efficacious a. efficace

efficacy n. efficacité f.

efficiency n. efficacité f.; capacité f.; rendement m.

efficient a. efficace; effectif; capaple

effigy n. effigie f.

effort n. effort m.; travail m.; initiative f.;

–less *a.* sans effort; **–lessness** *n.* aise, simplicité *f.*

effrontery *n.* effronterie, impudence *f.*

effusion *n.* effusion *f.*, épanchement *m.*

effusive *a.* démonstratif; **be — in** se répandre en

egg *n.* œuf *m.*; **fried —** œuf sur le plat; **hard-boiled —** œuf dur; **scrambled —** œuf brouillé; **soft-boiled —** œuf à la coque; **— cup** coquetier *m.*; **— white** blanc d'œuf *m.*; **— yolk** jaune d'œuf *m.*; **— vt.**, **— on** encourager, pousser

egg beater *n.* fouet *m.*

eggplant *n.* aubergine *f.*

egg-shaped *a.* ovoïde; en forme d'œuf

eggshell *n.* coquille d'œuf *f.*

ego *n.* moi *m.*; **–ism** *n.* culte du moi *m.*; égoïsme *m.*; **–tism** *n.* égotisme *m.*; **–tist** *n.* égoïste *m. & f.*

egress *n.* sortie *f.*, issue *f.*

egret *n.* aigrette *f.*

Egypt *n.* Egypte *f.*; **–ian** *a.* egyptien

Egyptology *n.* Egyptologie *f.*

eiderdown *n.* édredon *m.*

eight *a. & n.* huit; **— ball** *n.* (billiards) huit *m.*; **to be behind the — ball** être dans une situation difficile; **–een** *a. & n.* dix-huit; **–eenth** *a.* dix-huitième; **–h** *a.* huitième; **–ieth** *a. & n.* quatre-vingtième; **–y** *a. & n.* quatre-vingts

either *a. & pron.* l'un ou l'autre, n'importe lequel ; chaque, chacun; ni l'un ni l'autre; **— conj.** ou, soit; ou que, soit que; **— adv.** non plus

ejaculate *vt.* crier, s'écrier

eject *vt.* jeter; expulser; **–ion** *n.* expulsion *f.*

eke *vt.*, **— out** ménager

elaborate *a.* compliqué; orné, minutieux, travaillé; recherché; **— vt.** élaborer; **–ness** *n.* élaboration *f.*

elaboration *n.* élaboration *f.*

elapse *vi.* s'écouler

elastic *a. & n.* élastique *m.*; **–ity** *n.* élasticité *f.*; souplesse *f.*

elate *vt.* transporter; ravir

elation *n.* fierté *f.*; transport *m.*; joie *f.*

elbow *n.* coude *m.*; **rub –s with** coudoyer; **— vt.** coudoyer; **— one's way through** se frayer un passage à travers

elder *a.* aîné, plus âgé; **— n.** aîné *m.*; ancien *m.*; (bot.) sureau *m.*; **–ly** *a.* d'un certain âge, d'âge, âgé

eldest *a.* aîné

elect *vt.* élire; choisir; **— n.** élus *m. pl.*; **–ion** *n.* élection *f.*; **–ioneering** *n.* propagande électorale *f.*; **–ive** *a.* électif; facultatif; **–or** *n.* électeur *m.*; **–oral** *a.* électoral; **–orate** *n.* corps électoral *m.*; votants *m. pl.*

electric *a.* électrique; **— bulb** *n.* lampe, ampoule *f.*; **— eye** cellule photo-électrique *f.*; **— meter** compteur de courant *m.*; **— razor** rasoir électrique *m.*; **–al** *a.* électrique; **–al engineer** *n.* ingénieur électricien *m.*; **–al engineering** *n.* technique électrique *f.*; **–ian** *n.* électricien *m.*; **–ity** *n.* électricité *f.*

electrify *vt.* électriser; électrifier

electrocardiograph *n.* électrocardiographe *m.*

electrocute *vt.* électrocuter

electrocution *n.* électrocution *f.*

electrode *n.* électrode *f.*

electrodynamics *n.* électrodynamique *f.*

electrolysis *n.* électrolyse *f.*

electrolyte *n.* électrolyte *m.*

electromagnet *n.* électro-aimant *m.*

electron *n.* électron *m.*; **— microscope** microscope électronique *m.*

electronic *a.* électronique

electroplate *vt.* plaquer à l'électricité

electroscope *n.* électroscope *m.*

elegance *n.* élégance *f.*

elegant *a.* élégant, gracieux

elegy *n.* élégie *f.*

element *n.* élément *m.*; facteur *m.*; **–s** *n. pl.* rudiments *m. pl.*; **–al** *a.* des éléments; élémentaire; **–ary** *a.* élémentaire; **— school** école primaire *f.*

elephant *n.* éléphant *m.*; **–ine** *a.* éléphantin

elevate *vt.* élever; **–d** *a.* élevé; haut; (railroad) aérien

elevation *n.* élévation *f.*; hauteur, altitude *f.*; hausse *f.*

elevator *n.* ascenseur *m.*; (grain) silo *m.*; (avi.) gouvernail *m.*; (freight) monte-charges *m.*

eleven *a. & n.* onze; **–th** *a. & n.* onzième

eleventh hour *a.* de dernière heure

elf *n.* lutin *m.*; **–in, –ish** *a.* des lutins

elicit *vt.* tirer, obtenir; découvrir

elide *vt.* élider

eligibility *n.* éligibilité, admissibilité *f.*

eligible *a.* éligible; acceptable; admissible

eliminate *vt.* éliminer, supprimer

elimination *n.* élimination *f.*

elision *n.* élision *f.*

elite *n.* élite *f.*

ellipsis *n.* ellipse *f.*; (punctuation) points de suspension *m. pl.*

elliptic(al) *a.* elliptique

elm *n.* orme *m.*

elocution *n.* élocution, diction *f.*; **–ist** *n.* déclamateur *m.*

elongate *vt.* allonger; **— vi.** s'allonger

elongation *n.* allongement, prolongement *m.*

elope *vi.* s'enfuir (avec un amant)

eloquence *n.* éloquence *f.*

eloquent *a.* éloquent; **–ly** *adv.* éloquemment

else *a.* autre, d'autre; **anyone** — tout autre; **no one** — personne d'autre; **nothing** — rien d'autre; **nowhere** — nulle partailleurs; **someone** — un autre; **something** — autre chose; **somewhere** — ailleurs, autre part; — *adv.* autrement; **or** — ou bien

elsewhere *adv.* ailleurs, autre part

elucidate *vt.* éclaircir, élucider

elude *vt.* échapper à, se soustraire à; esquiver

elusive *a.* évasif; insaisissable

Elysian *a.* élyséen; — **Fields** *n. pl.* Champs Elysées *m. pl.*

emaciated *a.* amaigri, décharné, émacié

emanate *vi.* émaner

emanation *n.* émanation *f.*

emancipate *vt.* émanciper; affranchir

emancipation *n.* émancipation *f.*, affranchissement *m.*

emasculate *vt.* émasculer, châtrer

embalm *vt.* embaumer; parfumer; **–er** *n.* embaumeur *m.*; **–ing** *n.* embaumement *m.*

embank *vt.* remblayer; endiguer; **–ment** *n.* digue *f.*; levée *f.*; (road) remblai *m.*; (river) berge *f.*

embargo *n.* embargo *m.*; — *vt.* mettre un embargo sur

embark *vt.* embarquer; — *vi.* s'embarquer; **–ation** *n.* embarquement *m.*

embarrass *vt.* embarrasser, déconcerter; **–ed** *a.* embarrassé, gêné; **–ing** *a.* embarrassant, gênant; **–ment** *n.* confusion *f.*; embarras *m.*, gêne *f.*

embassy *n.* ambassade *f.*

embellish *vt.* embellir, orner; agrémenter; enjoliver; **–ment** *n.* embellissement *m.*, décoration *f.*

embers *n. pl.* braise *f.*

embezzle *vt.* s'approprier, détourner; **–ment** *n.* détournement *m.*; **–r** *n.* escroc, detourneur de fonds *m.*

embitter *vt.* aigrir; **–ed** *a.* aigri

emblazon *vt.* embellir

emblem *n.* emblème *m.*; insigne *m.*; devise *f.*; **–atic** *a.* éblématique

embodiment *n.* personnification *f.*; incarnation *f.*

embody *vt.* personnifier; incarner; incorporer

embolism *n.* embolisme *m.*

emboss *vt.* graver en relief; repousser

embrace *n.* étreinte *f.*; embrassement *f.*; — *vt.* étreindre; embrasser; comprendre, comporter

embroider *vt.* broder; **–y** *n.* broderie *f.*

embroil *vt.* brouiller, embrouiller

embryo *n.* embryon *m.*; **–logy** *n.* embryologie *f.*; **–nic** *a.* embryonnaire, en germe

emend *vt.* corriger; **–ation** *n.* correction *f.*

emerge *vi.* sortir; surgir; apparaître

emergency *n.* cas urgent, cas d'urgence *m.*; — **brake** frein de secours *m.*; — **exit** sortie de secours *f.*

emeritus *a.* honoraire; en retraite

emery *n.* émeri *m.*

emetic *n. & a.* émétique *m.*

emigrant *n.* émigrant *m.*; émigré *m.*

emigrate *vt.* émigrer

emigration *n.* émigration *f.*

eminence *n.* éminence *f.*; grandeur, distinction *f.*; élévation *f.*

eminent *a.* éminent; **–ly** *adv.* éminemment

emissary *n.* émissaire *m.*

emission *n.* émission *f.*

emit *vt.* émettre; répandre

emotion *n.* émotion *f.*; attendrissement *m.*; **–al** *a.* émotionnable; **–alism** *n.* émotivité *f.*

empanel *vt.* dresser (la liste des jurés)

emperor *n.* empereur *m.*

emphasis *n.* accentuation, force *f.*

emphasize *vt.* appuyer sur; accentuer; souligner

emphatic *a.* emphatique

emphysema *n.* emphysème *m.*

empire *n.* empire *m.*

empiric(al) *a.* empirique

employ *n.* service, emploi *m.*; — *vt.* employer; occuper; **–ee** *n.* employé *m.*; **–er** *n.* patron *m.*; directeur *m.*; **–ment** *n.* emploi, travail *m.*; place, situation *f.*; occupation *f.*; **–ment agency** bureau de placement *m.*

emporium *n.* magasin, marché *m.*

empower *vt.* autoriser

empress *n.* impératrice *f.*

emptiness *n.* vide *m.*

empty *a.* vide; vain; creux; libre, inoccupé; — *vt.* vider; — *vi.* se vider; se déverser

empty-handed *a. & adv.* les mains vides

emulate *vt.* rivaliser, imiter

emulation *n.* émulation *f.*

emulator *n.* émule, émulateur *m.*

emulsify *vt.* émulsionner

emulsion *n.* émulsion *f.*

enable *vt.* rendre capable (de), mettre à même (de)

enact *vt.* décréter, arrêter; jouer, représenter; **–ment** *n.* décret *m.*; loi *f.*; établissement *m.*

enamel *n.* émail *m.* (*pl.* émaux); laque *f.*; vernis *m.*; — *vt.* émailler; vernir

enamored (with) *a.* amoureux, épris (de)

encamp *vt. & vi.* camper; **–ment** *n.* camp,

campement *m.*

encase *vt.* encaisser, enfermer; recouvrir

enchant *vt.* enchanter, charmer; ensorceler; **–er** *n.* enchanteur *m.*; **–ing** *a.* charmant, ravissant; enchanteur; **–ment** *n.* enchantement *m.*; ensorcellement *m.*; **–ress** *n.* enchanteresse *f.*

encircle *vt.* encercler; entourer

enclose *vt.* entourer; joindre; envoyer

enclosure *n.* clos, enclos *m.*; enceinte, clôture *f.*; action de clore *f.*; (letter) pièce jointe *f.*

encompass *vt.* envelopper; entourer; comporter

encore *n.* bis *m.*; répétition *f.*; **—** *adv.* bis

encounter *n.* rencontre *f.*; **—** *vt.* rencontrer; essuyer; affronter

encourage *vt.* encourager; **–ment** *n.* encouragement *m.*

encouraging *a.* encourageant

encroach *vi.* empiéter; abuser; **–ment** *n.* empiétement; usurpation *f.*

encumber *vt.* encombrer, embarrasser; gêner

encumbrance *n.* charge *f.*; embarras *m.*

encyclopedia *n.* encyclopédie *f.*

end *n.* bout *m.*, fin *f.*; conclusion *f.*; extrémité *f.*; terme *m.*; but *m.*; **in the —** à la longue; à la fin; **on — de** suite; sur bout, debout; **put an — to** mettre fin à; **en finir avec; to no —** en vain; **—** *vt.* finir, terminer, conclure, achever; **—** *vi.* finir, se terminer; **— (up) by** finir par; **–ing** *n.* fin *f.*; terminaison, conclusion *f.*; **–less** *a.* sans fin; éternel; infini; sans bornes; continuel; **–lessly** *adv.* sans cesse, sans fin

endanger *vt.* mettre en danger, risquer; compromettre

endear *vt.* faire aimer, rendre cher à; **–ing** *a.* tendre, affectueux; **–ment** *n.* tendresse *f.*, charme *m.*

endeavor *n.* effort *m.*, tentative *f.*; **—** *vi.* s'efforcer de, tâcher de

endive *n.* endive, chicorée *f.*

endorse *vt.* endosser; appuyer; souscrire à; **–ment** *n.* endos, endossement *m.*; approbation *f.*; appui *m.*; **–r** *n.* endosseur *m.*

endow *vt.* doter, fonder; **–ment** *n.* dotation, fondation *f.*; don *m.*

endurable *a.* supportable

endurance *n.* résistance, endurance *f.*; durée *f.*; **— test** épreuve d'endurance *f.*

endure *vt.* supporter, endurer; **—** *vi.* durer

enduring *a.* durable; endurant, patient

enema *n.* lavement *m.*

enemy *n. & a.* ennemi *m.*

energetic *a.* énergique

energize *vt.* activer, stimuler, donner de l'énergie à

energy *n.* énergie, force *f.*; **atomic —** énergie atomique *f.*

enervate *vt.* énerver

enfold *vt.* envelopper; embrasser

enforce *vt.* mettre en vigueur; appuyer; faire valoir; faire observer; appliquer; **–ment** *n.* mise en vigueur *f.*; application *f.*; exécution *f.*

engage *vt.* engager; occuper; retenir; fiancer; embaucher; **— in conversation** entrer en conversation avec; **–d** *a.* fiancé; **become –d** se fiancer; **be –d in** s'occuper de; faire; **–ment** *n.* fiançailles *f. pl.*; (mil.) combat *m.*; action *f.*; rendez-vous *m.*; promesse *f.*, engagement *m.*

engaging *a.* séduisant, charmant, engageant

engender *vt.* engendrer

engine *n.* machine *f.*; moteur *m.*; locomotive *f.*; **fire — pompe** *f.*; **— room** (naut.) chambre des machines *f.*

engineer *n.* ingénieur; (rail., naut.) mécanicien *m.*; (mil.) soldat du génie *m.*; **chemical — ingénieur chimiste** *m.*; **electrical — ingénieur électricien** *m.*; **mechanical — ingénieur mécanicien** *m.*; **—** *vt.* manigancer, diriger; machiner; **–ing** *n.* génie *m.*; **electrical –ing** technique électrique *f.*; **mechanical –ing** industrie mécanique *f.*; **–s** (mil.) génie *m.*

England *n.* Angleterre *f.*

English *a. & n.* anglais (print.) corps 14 *m.*; **— Channel La Manche** *f.*; (print.) **Old — gothique**

engrave *vt.* graver; **–r** *n.* graveur *m.*

engross *vt.* absorber, occuper

engulf *vt.* engouffrer; engloutir

enhance *vt.* rehausser; relever; augmenter

enigma *n.* énigme *f.*; **–tic** *a.* énigmatique

enjoin *vt.* enjoindre, ordonner, prescrire

enjoy *vt.* jouir de; prendre plaisir à, goûter; **— oneself** s'amuser, se divertir; **–able** *a.* agréable; excellent; **–ment** *n.* jouissance *f.*; plaisir *m.*

enlarge *vt.* agrandir; élargir; **—** *vi.* s'agrandir, s'élargir; **–ment** *n.* agrandissement *m.*; élargissement *m.* (med.) hypertrophie *f.*; **–r** *n.* agrandisseur, amplificateur *m.*

enlighten *vt.* éclairer; **–ment** *n.* éclaircissements *m. pl.*; (hist., lit.) lumière(s) *f. (pl.)*

enlist *vt.* enrôler; **—** *vi.* s'enrôler, s'engager; **–ed** *a.*, **— man** simple soldat *m.*; **–ment** *n.* enrôlement, engagement *m.*

enliven *vt.* animer, égayer

enmity *n.* inimitié *f.*

ennoble *vt.* anoblir

enormity *n.* énormité *f.*

enormous *a.* énorme; **–ness** *n.* énormité *f.*

enough *a. & adv.* assez (de); de quoi; be — suffire; **that's** — cela suffit

enrich *vt.* enrichir; **–ment** *n.* enrichissement *m.*

enrage *vt.* faire enrager; mettre en colère

enrapture *vt.* ravir, transporter

enroll *vt.* enrôler; inscrire; immatriculer; **–ment** *n.* enrôlement *m.*; inscription *f.*; immatriculation *f.*; — *vi.* s'inscrire

ensemble *n.* ensemble *m.*; série *f.*, jeu *m.*

enshrine *vt.* enchâsser

ensign *n.* enseigne *f.*, drapeau *m.*; pavillon *m.*; (naval officer) enseigne *m.*

enslave *vt.* asservir, rendre esclave; **–ment** *n.* asservissement, esclavage *m.*

ensnare *vt.* prendre au piège, attraper

ensue *vi.* s'ensuivre; résulter

ensuing *a.* suivant

entail *vt.* occasionner; entraîner; comporter

entangle *vt.* embrouiller; empêtrer; **–ment** *n.* embrouillement *m.*; embarras *m.*

enter *vt. & vi.* entrer (dans); pénétrer (dans); (vehicle) monter (dans); inscrire; porter; s'engager

enterprise *n.* entreprise *f.*

enterprising *a.* entreprenant

entertain *vt.* amuser, divertir; régaler; éprouver; nourrir, chérir; **–er** *n.* acteur, comédien, exécutant *m.*; **–ing** *a.* amusant, divertissant; **–ment** *n.* amusement, divertissement *m.*; spectacle *m.*

enthrall *vt.* captiver, ravir

enthrone *vt.* mettre sur le trône; **–ment** *n.* intronisation *f.*

enthusiasm *a.* enthousiasme *m.*

enthusiast *n.* (sports) enragé *m.*; enthousiaste *m. & f.*; **–ic** *a.* enragé, passionné; enthousiaste

entice *vt.* attirer, séduire; entraîner; **–ment** *n.* attrait, appât *m.*; tentation, séduction *f.*

enticing *a.* séduisant, attrayant

entire *a.* entier; tout; complet; **–ly** *adv.* entièrement; tout à fait; absolument; **–ty** *n.* totalité *f.*; **in its** — en entier; intégralement; totalement

entitle *vt.* intituler; donner le droit; **be –d to** avoir droit à; avoir le droit de

entity *n.* entité *f.*

entomb *vt.* enterrer; **–ment** *n.* sépulture *f.*; enterrement *m.*

entomologist *n.* entomologiste *m.*

entrain *vi.* prendre le train, entrer dans le train

entrance *n.* entrée *f.*

entrance *vt.* ensorceler; extasier, transporter

entrancing *a.* enchanteur

entrant *n.* inscrit *m.*

entreat *vt.* supplier, prier; **–ing** *a.* suppliant; **–y** *n.* prière, supplication *f.*

entrench *vt.* retrancher

entrust *vt.* confier; charger; remettre

entry *n.* entrée *f.*; début *m.*; inscription *f.*; article *m.*; — **blank** feuille d'inscription *f.*; **single (double)** — **bookkeeping** comptabilité en partie simple (double) *f.*

entwine *vt.* entrelacer, enlacer

enumerate *vt.* énumérer, dénombrer

enumeration *n.* énumération *f.*, dénombrement *m.*

enunciate *vt.* prononcer, articuler; énoncer

enunciation *n.* énonciation, articulation *f.*

envelop *vt.* envelopper; entourer; **–ment** *n.* enveloppement *m.*; action de cerner

envelope *n.* enveloppe *f.*; **in an** — sous enveloppe, sous pli; **window** — enveloppe à panneau transparent *f.*

enviable *a.* digne d'envie

envious *a.* envieux, d'envie

environment *m.* milieu *m.*; ambiance *f.*

environs *n. pl.* environs, alentours *m. pl.*

envoy *n.* envoyé *m.*

envy *n.* envie *f.*; **green with** — dévoré d'envie; — *vt.* porter envie à, envier

enzyme *n.* enzyme *f.*

eon *n.* éternité *f.*

epaulet *n.* épaulette *f.*

ephemeral *a.* éphémère, fugitif

epic *a.* épique; — *n.* épopée *f.*, poème épique *m.*

epicure *n.* gourmet, gastronome *m.*; **–an** *a. & n.* épicurien *m.*

epidemic *a.* épidémique; — *n.* épidémie *f.*

epidermis *n.* épiderme *m.*

epiglottis *n.* épiglotte *f.*

epigram *n.* épigramme *f.*; **–matic** *a.* épigrammatique

epigraph *n.* épigraphe *f.*

epileptic *a. & n.* épileptique *m. & f.*

epilogue *n.* épilogue *m.*

episcopal *a.* épiscopal; **–ian** *n. & a.* épiscopalien *m.*

episode *n.* épisode *m.*

epistle *n.* épître *f.*

epitaph *n.* épitaphe *f.*

epithet *n.* épithète *f.*

epitome *n.* abrégé *m.*; épitomé *m.*

epitomize *vt.* abréger

epoch *n.* époque *f.*

Epsom salts *n. pl.* sels anglais, sels d'Epsom *m. pl.*

equal *a.* égal (*pl.* égaux); **be — to (doing)** être à même de (faire); avoir la force de; — *n.* égal *m.*; pair *m.*; pareil *m.*; sembla-

ble *m*.; — *vt*. égaler; –itarian *a*. & *n*.
égalitaire *m*. & *f*.; –ity *n*. égalité *f*.;
–ization *n*. égalisation *f*.; –ize *vt*.
égaliser, compenser
equanimity *n*. égalité d'âme, tranquillité
d'esprit *f*.
equate *vt*. égaliser; mettre en équation
equation *n*. équation *f*.
equator *n*. équateur *m*.; –ial *a*. de l'équateur, équatorial
Equatorial Africa *n*. Afrique Équatoriale
f.
equestrian *a*. équestre; — *n*. cavalier *m*.;
écuyer *m*.
equidistant *a*. équidistant
equilateral *a*. équilatéral
equilibrium *n*. équilibre *m*.
equine *a*. de cheval
equinox *n*. équinoxe *m*.
equip *vt*. munir; équiper; monter; outiller;
armer; –ment *n*. outillage *m*.; matériel
m.; armement *m*.; équipement *m*.
equitable *a*. équitable, juste
equity *n*. équité, justice *f*.
equivalence *n*. équivalence *f*.
equivalent *a*. & *n*. équivalent *m*.
equivocate *vi*. équivoquer; tergiverser
equivocation *n*. équivocation *f*.
era *n*. ère, époque *f*.
eradicate *vt*. déraciner; extirper
eradication *n*. déracinement *m*.; extirpation *f*.
erase *vt*. effacer; raturer; –r *n*. grattoir
m.; gomme à effacer *f*.; (blackboard)
chiffon *m*.
erasure *n*. rature *f*.; grattage *m*.; suppression *f*.
ere *prep*. avant; — *conj*. avant que
erect *a*. droit; debout; — *vt*. ériger, édifier,
construire; dresser; –ile *a*. érectile; –ion
n. construction *f*.; dressage *m*.; érection
f.; –or *n*. constructeur *m*.; –or set *n*.
mécano *m*.
ermine *n*. hermine *f*.
erode *vt*. éroder
erosion *n*. érosion *f*.
erosive *a*. érosif; corrosif
erotic *a*. érotique
err *vi*. faire erreur, se tromper; s'égarer;
errer; pécher; –or *n*. faute, erreur *f*.;
clerical –or faute de copiste *f*.; typographical –or faute d'impression *f*.
errand *n*. message *m*., commission *f*.;
course *f*.; — boy commissionnaire *m*.;
— girl coursière *f*.
errant *a*. errant, vagabond; knight —
chevalier errant *m*.
erratic *a*. irrégulier; désordonné; erratique; excentrique
erroneous *a*. erroné; –ly *adv*. par erreur

erstwhile *a*. d'autrefois; d'antan
erudite *a*. érudit, savant
erudition *n*. érudition *f*.
erupt *vi*. faire irruption; –ion *n*. irruption
f.
escalator *n*. escalier roulant *m*.
escallop *vt*. cuire au four et à la crème
escapade *n*. escapade, aventure *f*.
escape *n*. évasion *f*.; fuite *f*.; échappement
m.; have a narrow — l'échapper belle;
make one's — se sauver, s'echapper; —
vt. échapper à; éviter; — *vi*. se sauver,
s'echapper, s'évader; –e *n*. évadé *m*.
eschew *vt*. éviter; s'abstenir de
escort *n*. escorte *f*.; compagnon *m*.; — *vt*.
escorter; accompagner
Eskimo *a*. & *n*. Esquimau *m*.
esophagus *n*. œsophage *m*.
especially *adv*. particulièrement; surtout
espionage *n*. espionnage *m*.
espousal *n*. adoption; adhérence *f*.
essay *n*. essai *m*.; — *vt*. essayer; –ist *n*.
essayiste *m*. & *f*.
essential *a*. essentiel, indispensable; — *n*.
essentiel *m*.
EST: Eastern Standard Time heure de
l'est *f*. (USA)
establish *vt*. établir, fonder; –ment *n*.
établissement *m*.; fondation *f*.; maison
f.
estate *n*. domaine *m*.; biens *m*. *pl*.; succession *f*.; terre, propriété *f*.; état *m*.,
condition *f*.; real — biens immeubles,
biens-fonds *m*. *pl*.; propriété (immobilière) *f*.; real — agency agence de
location *f*.
esteem *n*. estime *f*.; — *vt*. estimer
esthetic *a*. esthétique; –s *n*. esthétique *f*.
estimable *a*. estimable
estimate *n*. évaluation, appréciation *f*.;
calcul *m*.; (com.) devis *m*.; — *vt*.
évaluer, apprécier; estimer
estimation *n*. avis, jugement *m*.
Estonia *n*. Estonie *f*.
estrange *vt*. aliéner; éloigner
etch *vt*. graver à l'eau-forte; –er *n*. aquafortiste *m*.; –ing *n*. eau-forte *f*.
eternal *a*. éternel
eternity *n*. éternité *f*.
ether *n*. éther *m*.; –eal *a*. éthéré, céleste,
aérien
ethical *a*. moral
ethics *n*. *pl*. éthique, morale *f*.
Ethiopia *n*. Ethiopie *f*.
ethnological *a*. ethnologique
ethnology *n*. ethnologie *f*.
ethyl *n*. éthyle *m*.
etiquette *n*. étiquette *f*., cérémonial *m*.
etymological *a*. étymologique
etymology *n*. étymologie *f*.

eucalyptus *n.* eucalyptus *m.*
Eucharist *n.* Eucharistie *f.*
eugenics *n. pl.* eugénisme *m.*, eugénique *f.*
eulogize *vt.* faire l'éloge de
eulogy *n.* panégyrique, éloge *m.*
eunuch *n.* eunuque *m.*
euphemism *n.* euphémisme *m.*
euphemistic *a.* euphémique
euphonious *a.* euphonique, mélodieux
euphony *n.* euphonie *f.*
Europe *n.* Europe; **-an** *a. & n.* européen (Européenne)
Eustachian tube *n.* trompe d'Eustache *f.*
euthanasia *n.* euthanasie *f.*
evacuate *vt.* évacuer
evacuation *n.* évacuation *f.*
evacuee *n.* évacué *m.*
evade *vt.* éviter; éluder; se soustraire à; tourner
evaluate *vt.* évaluer
evaluation *n.* évaluation *f.*
evangelic(al) *a.* évangélique; protestant
evangelist *n.* évangéliste *m.*
evangelize *vt.* évangéliser; prêcher
evaporate *vi.* s'évaporer; — *vt.* faire évaporer; **-d milk** lait condensé *m.* (non sucré)
evaporation *n.* évaporation *f.*
evasion *n.* évitement *m.*; échappatoire *f.*; détour *m.*
evasive *a.* évasif
eve *n.* veille *f.*; **Christmas —** la veille de Noël *f.*
even *a.* égal, *pl.* égaux; uni; uniforme; régulier; (number) pair; **— bet** pari égal *m.*; **— temper** humeur égale *f.*; **get — with** se venger de; — *adv.* même; encore; seulement; jusque; **— now** à l'instant même; même aujourd'hui; **— so** quand même; cependant; **— then** déjà; **— though** même, quand même; — *vt.* égaliser; aplanir; rendre égal; **-ly** *adv.* également; régulièrement; **-ness** *n.* égalité *f.*; régularité *f.*
evening *n.* soir *m.*, soirée *f.*; **good —** bonsoir; bonjour; **in the —** le soir; **all —** toute la soirée; **every —** tous les soirs; **the — before** la veille au soir *f.*; **— clothes** tenue de soirée *f.*
event *n.* événement *m.*; cas *m.*; **in any —**, **at all —s** en tout cas, dans tous les cas; quoi qu'il arrive; **in the — that** dans le cas où; **-ful** *a.* mémorable; mouvementé; **-ual** *a.* éventuel; final; **-uality** *n.* éventualité *f.*; **-ually** *adv.* par la suite, en fin de compte
ever *adv.* jamais; toujours; **— since** depuis (que)
evergreen *a.* toujours vert; — *n.* arbre vert *m.*

everlasting *a.* éternel; sempiternel; vivace; inusable
evermore *adv.* pour toujours
every *a.* chaque, tout; **— day** tous les jours; **— other day** tous les deux jours; **— now and then** de temps en temps; de temps à autre
everybody *pron.* tout le monde, chacun
everyday *a.* quotidien; de tous les jours; **in — use** d'usage courant
everyone *pron.* tout le monde, chacun
everything *pron.* tout
everywhere *adv.* partout
evict *vt.* évincer, expulser; **-ion** *n.* éviction *f.*
evidence *n.* évidence *f.*; preuve *f.*; déposition *f.*, témoignage *m.*; signe *m.*, marque *f.*; **give —** déposer, témoigner; — *vt.* manifester, démontrer
evident *a.* évident; **-ly** *adv.* évidemment
evil *a.* mauvais; malin; méchant; néfaste; — *n.* mal (*pl.* maux); **-ness** *n.* méchanceté *f.*
evil-minded *a.* malveillant, malintentionné
evince *vt.* montrer, démontrer
eviscerate *vt.* éventrer, vider
evisceration *n.* éviscération *f.*
evocation *n.* évocation *f.*
evocative *a.* évocateur
evoke *vt.* évoquer
evolution *n.* évolution *f.*; développement *m.*; **-ary** *a.* évolutionnaire
evolve *vt.* développer; élaborer; — *vi.* évoluer, se développer; se dérouler
ewe *n.* brebis *f.*
ewer *n.* aiguière *f.*
exact *a.* exact; précis; juste; — *vt.* exiger; **-ing** *a.* exigeant; **-ly** *adv.* exactement; précisément; justement; au juste; **-ness** *n.* exactitude *f.*
exaggerate *vt.* exagérer
exalt *vt.* élever; exalter; **-ation** *n.* exaltation *f.*
examination *n.* examen *m.*; inspection *f.*; (competitive) concours *m.*; **fail an —** échouer à un examen; **pass an —** réussir à un examen, être reçu à un examen; **take an —** passer un examen
examine *vt.* examiner; inspecter; vérifier; interroger; visiter; **-r** *n.* examinateur *m.*; inspecteur *m.*
example *n.* exemple *m.*; précédent *m.*; **for —** par exemple; **set an —** donner l'exemple
exasperate *vt.* exaspérer, irriter
exasperation *n.* exaspération, irritation *f.*
excavate *vt.* excaver, creuser; faire des fouilles
excavation *n.* excavation *f.*; fouille *f.*

excavator *n.* (hand labor) terrassier *m.*; (archaeology) personne qui fait des fouilles *f.*; (machine) excavateur *m.*

exceed *vt. & vi.* dépasser; –ingly *adv.* très, extrêmement

excel *vi.* exceller; — *vt.* surpasser; –lence *n.* excellence *f.*; –lency *n.* Excellence *f.*; –lent *a.* excellent; –lently *adv.* excellement

excelsior *n.* copeaux d'emballage *m. pl.*

except *prep.* sauf, excepté; à l'exception de; à part; — *vt.* excepter; –ing *prep.* sauf; –ion *n.* exception *f.*; be an –ion faire exception; –ional *a.* exceptionnel

excerpt *n.* extrait *m.*; — *vt.* extraire

excess *n.* excès *m.*; excédent *m.*; to — trop loin; — weight surpoids *m.*; –ive *a.* excessif; immodéré; –ively *adv.* à l'excès, trop

exchange *n.* échange *m.*; change *m.*; in — for en échange de; rate of — taux du change, cours du change *m.*; stock — bourse *f.*; — *vt.* échanger; –able *a.* échangeable

excise *n.* contributions indirectes *f. pl.*; — *vt.* retrancher, exciser

excitable *a.* émotionnable

excite *vt.* exciter; stimuler; enflammer; surexciter; (curiosity) piquer; get –d s'agiter; –ment *n.* agitation, sensation *f.*; surexcitation *f.*

exciting *a.* émouvant, passionnant; excitant, stimulant; épatant

exclaim *vt.* s'écrier

exclamation *n.* exclamation *f.*

exclamatory *a.* exclamatif

exclude *vt.* exclure

excluding *prep.* à l'exclusion de; sans compter

exclusion *n.* exclusion *f.*

exclusive *a.* exclusif; fermé; de choix; — of sans; — rights exclusivité *f.*; –ness *n.* exclusivité *f.*, caractère exclusif *m.*

excommunicate *vt.* excommunier

excrete *vt.* excréter; sécréter

excruciating *a.* affreux

excursion *n.* excursion *f.*; voyage *m.*; randonnée *f.*; promenade *f.*; voyage à forfait, voyage en groupe *m.*

excusable *a.* excusable, pardonnable

excuse *n.* excuse *f.*; prétexte *m.*; — *vt.* excuser, pardonner; dispenser

execrate *vt.* exécrer

execration *n.* exécration *f.*

execute *vt.* exécuter; effectuer

execution *n.* exécution *f.*; –er *n.* bourreau *m.*

executive *a. & n.* exécutif *m.*; — *a.* de direction, de la direction

executor *n.* exécuteur testamentaire *m.*

exemplary *a.* exemplaire; modèle

exemplify *vt.* servir d'example à; donner un example de

exempt *a.* exempt, dispensé; — *vt.* exempter; dispenser; –ion *n.* exemption, dispense *f.*

exercise *n.* exercice *m.*; devoir *m.*; –s *pl.* cérémonies *f. pl.* — *vt.* exercer; pratiquer; (animals) promener; — *vi.* s'entraîner

exert *vt.* exercer; to — oneself faire des efforts; –ion *n.* effort *m.*

exhalation *n.* exhalaison *f.*

exhale *vt.* exhaler; — *vi.* s'exhaler

exhaust *n.* échappement *m.*; — fan ventilateur aspirant *m.*; — pipe tuyau d'échappement *m.*; — *vt.* épuiser; éreinter; tarir; aspirer; –ed *a.* épuisé; –ible *a.* épuisable; –ing *a.* épuisant; –ion *n.* épuisement *m.*; –ive *a.* approfondi; –less *a.* inépuisable

exhibit *n.* exposition *f.*; envoi, objet *m.*; étalage *m.*; — *vt.* exhiber, exposer, montrer; –or *n.* exposant *m.*

exhibition *n.* exposition, démonstration *f.*; étalage *m.*; –ism (psychology) exhibitionnisme *m.*; –ist *n.* exhibitionniste *m. & f.*

exhilarate *vt.* vivifier

exhilarating *a.* vivifiant

exhilaration *n.* joie de vivre *f.*

exhort *vt.* exhorter; –ation *n.* exhortation *f.*

exhumation *n.* exhumation *f.*

exhume *vt.* exhumer

exigency *n.* exigence *f.*; nécessité *f.*, besoin *m.*

exigent *a.* exigeant; urgent

exile *n.* exil *m.*; (person) exilé *m.*; — *vt.* exiler, bannir

exist *vi.* exister; subsister, vivre; être; –ence *n.* existence *f.*; vie *f.*; –ent *a.* existant, actuel; –ing *a.* actuel; présent; existant

existential *a.* existentiel; –ism *n.* existentialisme *m.*; –ist *a. & n.* existentialiste *m. & f.*

exit *n.* sortie *f.*; — *vi.* sortir

exodus *n.* exode *m.*; sortie *f.*

exonerate *vt.* exonérer

exoneration *n.* exonération *f.*

exorbitant *a.* exorbitant

exotic *a.* exotique; — fuel (avi.) combustible exotique *m.*

expand *vt.* élargir, développer; dilater, détendre; — *vi.* se développer, se dilater; se détendre

expanse *n.* étendue *f.*

expansion *n.* développement *m.*; dilation *f.*; expansion *f.*; — band, — bracelet

bracelet extensible *m.*

expansive *a.* expansif; **-ness** *n.* expansivité *f.*; nature expansive *f.*

expatriate *vt.* expatrier; — *n.* expatrié *m.*

expatriation *n.* expatriation *f.*

expect *vt.* attendre; s'attendre à; compter (sur); espérer; **what do you —?** que voulez-vous?; **-ancy** *n.* attente *f.* **-ant** *a.* expectant, qui attend; **-ation** *n.* espérance *f.*; prévision *f.*; attente *f.*; probabilité *f.*

expectorate *vi.* expectorer, cracher

expediency *n.* opportunité *f.*

expedient *a.* opportun, convenable; — *n.* expédient *m.*

expedite *vt.* expédier, hâter, accélérer; **-r** *n.* expéditeur *m.*

expedition *n.* expédition *f.*; **-ary** *a.* expéditionnaire

expeditious *a.* expéditif

expel *vt.* expulser; chasser

expend *vt.* dépenser; consommer; employer; **-able** *a.* non-essentiel; qui peut être abandonné; **-iture** *n.* dépense *f.*

expense *n.* dépense *f.*, frais *m. pl.*; dépens *m.*

expensive *a.* cher, coûteux; **be —.coûter** cher; **-ness** *n.* cherté *f.*; prix (élevé) *m.*

experience *n.* expérience *f.*; épreuve *f.*; pratique *f.*; habitude *f.*; — *vt.* éprouver; **-d** *a.* expérimenté

experiment *n.* expérience *f.*; essai *m.*; — *vi.* expérimenter; faire des expériences; **-al** *a.* expérimental; **-er** *n.* expérimentateur *m.*; **-ing** *n.* expérimentation *f.*

expert *a.* expert; — *n.* expert *m.*; spécialiste *m.*; connaisseur *m.*; **-ness** *n.* habileté *f.*; adresse *f.*

expiation *n.* expiation *f.*

expiration *n.* expiration *f.*; terme *m.*; déchéance *f.*; échéance *f.*

expire *vt.* exhaler, expirer; — *vi.* expirer, mourir; déchoir

explain *vt.* expliquer, éclaircir; **-able** *a.* explicable; justifiable

explanation *n.* explication *f.*

explanatory *a.* explicatif

expletive *a. & n.* explétif *m.*

explicable *a.* explicable

explicit *a.* explicite; clair, précis; **-ly** *adv.* explicitement

explode *vt.* faire éclater; discréditer; — *vi.* éclater, sauter; exploser

exploit *n.* exploit *m.*; — *vt.* exploiter; **-ation** exploitation *f.*

exploration *n.* exploration *f.*

explorative, exploratory *a.* exploratoire

explore *vt.* explorer; **-r** *n.* explorateur *m.*

explosion *n.* explosion *f.*

explosive *a.* explosible; — *n.* explosif *m.*;

-ness *n.* explosibilité *f.*

exponent *n.* interprète *m.*; (math.) exposant *m.*

export *n.* exportation *f.*; — *vt.* exporter; **-ation** *n.* exportation *f.*; **-er** *n.* exportateur *m.*

expose *vt.* exposer; mettre à nu; étaler; dévoiler; **-d** *a.* exposé; à nu

exposition *n.* exposition *f.*; interprétation *f.*

expostulate *vi.* faire des remontrances

exposure *n.* exposé *m.*; froid *m.*; exposition *f.*; scandale *m.*; (phot.) pose *f.*; **— meter** cellule photo-électrique *f.*

express *a.* exprès, formel; — *n.* (rail.) express, rapide *m.*; exprès *m.*; — *vt.* exprimer; témoigner; envoyer par exprès; **-ible** *a.* exprimable; **-ion** *n.* expression *f.*; mot *m.*; phrase *f.*; **-ionless** *a.* impassible; **-ive** *a.* expressif; **-iveness** *n.* nature expressive *f.*; **-ly** *adv.* expressément, formellement

expressway *n.* autostrade *f.*

expropriate *vt.* exproprier

expropriation *n.* expropriation *f.*

expulsion *n.* expulsion *f.*

expurgate *vt.* expurger

expurgation *n.* expurgation *f.*

exquisite *a.* exquis

extemporaneous *a.* impromptu; improvisé; **-ly** *adv.* d'abondance; à l'impromptu

extemporize *vt.* improviser; — *vi.* parler d'abondance

extend *vt. & vi.* étendre, allonger; prolonger; tendre; proroger; — *vi.* s'étendre, s'allonger; se prolonger

extension *n.* extension *f.*; prolongation *f.*; délai *m.*; annexe *f.*; (table) allonge *f.*; (telephone) poste *m.*; **— cord** prolongateur *m.*; **— ladder** échelle à coulisse *f.*

extensive *a.* vaste; considérable; étendu; **-ly** *a.* beaucoup, très loin, très profondément

extent *n.* étendue *f.*; **to a certain —** dans une certaine mesure

extenuating *a.* atténuant

exterior *a. & n.* extérieur *m.*

exterminate *vt.* exterminer

extermination *n.* extermination *f.*

exterminator *n.* exterminateur *m.*

external *a.* extérieur; (med.) externe

extinct *a.* éteint; **-ion** *n.* extinction *f.*

extinguish *vt.* éteindre; **fire -er** extincteur *m.*

extol *vt.* exalter

extort *vt.* extorquer; arracher; **-ion** *n.* extorsion *f.*; **-ionist** *n.* extorqueur *m.*

extra *a.* supplémentaire; de plus; —

charge(s) supplément *m.*; — **pay** surpaye *f.*; — *adv.* non compris, en plus;
extra; — *n.* supplément *m.*; (newspaper) édition speciale *f.*
extract *n.* extrait *m.*; morceau *m.*; — *vt.*
extraire; (tooth) arracher; **-ion** *n.* extraction *f.*; arrachement *m.*; origine *f.*;
-or *n.* extracteur, forceps *m.*
extracurricular *a.* en sus du programme
d'études
extradite *vt.* extrader
extradition *n.* extradition *f.*
extraneous *a.* étranger
extraordinary *a.* extraordinaire, remarquable
extrasensory *a.* clairvoyant; — **percep-**
tion *n.* clairvoyance *f.*
extravagance *n.* extravagance *f.*; prodigalité *f.*
extravagant *a.* extravagant; dépensier;
outré
extravaganza *n.* grand spectacle *m.*
extreme *a.* extrême; exceptionnel; —
penalty dernier supplice *m.*; — *n.*
extrème; **go to –s** pousser (les choses)
à l'extrême
extremist *n.* extrémiste *m. & f.*
extremity *n.* extrémité *f.*; bout *m.*
extricate *vt.* dégager
extrovert *n.* extroverti *m.*
exuberance *n.* exubérance *f.*
exuberant *a.* exubérant
exude *vt. & vi.* exsuder
exult *vi.* exulter, triompher; se réjouir;
–ant *a.* exultant, triomphant; **–ation** *n.*
exultation *f.*; triomphe *m.*
eye *n.* œil *m.* (*pl.* yeux); (needle) chas *m.*;
black — œil poché *m.*; **catch the** — **of**
attirer l'attention de; **electric** — cellule
photo-électrique *f.*; **keep an** — **on** surveiller; ne pas quitter des yeux; **open**
someone's –s (fig.) désabuser; **see** —
to — voir du même œil; **shut one's –s**
to (fig.) être aveugle sur; — *vt.* mesurer
(des yeux); toiser; regarder
eyebrow *n.* sourcil *m.*; **knit one's –s**
froncer le sourcil
eyeful *n.* vue *f.*
eyeglasses *n. pl.* lunettes *f. pl.*
eyelash *n.* cil *m.*
eyelet *n.* œillet *m.*
eyelid *n.* paupière *f.*
eye opener *n.* révélation *f.*
eyeshade *n.* visière *f.*; abat-jour *m.*
eyesight *n.* vue *f.*; portée de vue *f.*
eyestrain *n.* fatigue des yeux *f.*; les yeux
fatigués *m. pl.*
eyetooth *n.* canine, œillère *f.*
eyewash *n.* collyre *m.*; (coll.) la poudre
aux yeux

F

fable *n.* fable *f.*, apologue *m.*; légende *f.*;
-d *a.* fabuleux, légendaire
fabric *n.* tissu *m.*; étoffe *f.*; fabrique *f.*;
édifice *m.*; **-ate** *vt.* fabriquer, inventer;
-ation *n.* fabrication, invention *f.*;
-ator *n.* fabricateur *m.*; menteur *m.*
fabulous *a.* fabuleux
facade *n.* façade *f.*
face *n.* visage *m.*, figure *f.*; face *f.*; mine
f.; physionomie *f.*; aspect *m.*; surface
f.; façade *f.*; (watch) cadran *m.*; —
card figure *f.*; — **cream** crème de beauté
f.; — **lifting** ridectomie *f.*; — **powder**
poudre de riz *f.*; — **towel** serviette de
toilette *f.*; — **to** — en présence; —
value valeur nominale *f.*; **fall on one's**
— tomber à plat ventre; **in the** — **of** en
présence de; contre; **lose** — perdre
l'honneur; **make a** — faire une grimace;
on the — **of** it au premier aspect; **save**
— sauver les apparences; — *vt.* faire
face à; affronter; confronter; donner
sur; revêtir, mettre un revers à; **-d** *a.*
revêtu, à revers
facet *n.* aspect *m.*; (gem) facette *f.*; **-ed**
a. à facettes
facetious *a.* facétieux; **-ness** *n.* facétie *f.*;
plaisanterie *f.*
facial *a.* facial
facile *a.* facile, trop facile, simple
facilitate *vt.* faciliter
facility *n.* facilité *f.*; installation *f.*
facing *n.* revers, parement *m.*
fact *n.* fait *m.*; réalité *f.*; **in** — en fait; de
fait; **as a matter of** — en effet; à vrai
dire; **the** — **is** c'est que; **-ual** *a.* des
faits
factor *n.* facteur *m.*; élément *m.*; (com.)
agent *m.*; **safety** — coefficient de
sûreté *m.*
factory *n.* fabrique, usine *f.*
faculty *n.* faculté *f.*; membres de la
faculté *m. pl.*; corps enseignant *m.*
fad *n.* marotte *f.*; mode *f.*, cri *m.*
fade *vi.* se faner, se flétrir; se déteindre;
— *vt.* décolorer; — **away** s'évanovir;
s'effacer
fade-out *n.* fondu *m.*; (movies) disparition
graduelle *f.*
fail *vi.* manquer, faire défaut; baisser;
faiblir; échouer; rater; — *vt.* refuser; —
n., **without** — sans remise, sans faute;
-ing *n.* défaut, faible *m.*; faiblesse *f.*;
-ing *prep.* à défaut de; **-ure** *n.* défaut
m., manque *m.*; insuccès *m.*; échec *m.*;
fiasco *m.*; (person) raté *m.*; (com.)
faillite *f.*
faint *a.* faible; pâle; léger; vague, indis-

tinct; — *n.* évanouissement *m.*; — *vi.* s'évanouir; **–ness** *n.* faibless *f.*; malaise *m.*

fainthearted *a.* timide

fair *n.* foire *f.*; exposition *f.*; — *a.* juste, équitable; passable; beau; blond; — **ball** *n.* vraie balle, bonne balle *f.*; — **play** franc jeu, jeu loyal *m.*; — **weather** beau temps *m.*; **–ly** *adv.* impartialement; loyalement; passablement; assez; **–ness** *n.* impartialité, équité *f.*; blancheur *f.*; **–ground** *n.* parc des expositions *m.*

fair-minded *a.* impartial; **–ness** *n.* impartialité *f.*

fairway *n.* terrain de golf *m.*; (naut.) chenal *m.*

fairy *n.* fée *f.*; — *a.* de fée, féerique; **–land** *n.* royaume des fées *m.*; **–like** *a.* féerique; — **tale** *n.* conte de fées *m.*

faith *n.* foi *f.*; fidélité *f.*; confiance *f.*; **good** — bonne foi, loyauté *f.*; honneur *m.*; **–ful** *a.* fidèle, loyal; exact; **–fulness** *n.* fidélité, loyauté *f.*; exactitude *f.*; **–less** *a.* sans foi; déloyal; infidèle

fake *a.* (coll.) faux; — *n.* faux *m.*; truc *m.*; trucage *m.*; — *vt.* truquer; feindre; **–r** *n.* truqueur *m.*; simulateur *m.*

fall *n.* chute *f.*; baisse, descente *f.*; échec *m.*; déchéance *f.*; automne *m.* or *f.*; **–s** *pl.* chute d'eau *f.*; — *vi.* tomber; baisser; descendre; échoir; capituler; s'écrouler; — **back** tomber en arrière; reculer; — **back on** avoir recours à; — **behind** rester en arrière; se laisser distancer; — **for** (coll.) tomber amoureux de; se laisser prendre par; — **in** s'effondrer; (mil.) former les rangs; — **into someone's hands** tomber entre les mains de quelqu'un; — **into a trap** donner dans un piège; — **off** tomber de; baisser; diminuer; — **out** tomber; (mil.) quitter les rangs; se brouiller; — **over** tomber à la renverse; buter contre; — **through** échouer; — **upon** se jeter à; attaquer; **–ing** *a.* qui tombe, tombant

fallacious *a.* fallacieux; **–ness** fausseté *f.*

fallacy *n.* erreur *f.*; sophisme *m.*

fallibility *n.* faillibilité *f.*

fallible *a.* faillible

fall-out *n.* poussière radioactive *f.*

fallow *a.* en friche

false *a.* faux (fausse); postiche, artificiel; simulé; — **alarm** fausse alerte *f.*; — **bottom** double fond *m.*; — **teeth** fausses dents *f. pl.*; dentier *m.*; **–ly** *adv.* à faux, faussement; **–hood** *n.* mensonge *m.*; **–ness** *n.* fausseté *f.*

falsetto *n.* fausset *m.*; — *a.* de fausset

falsification *n.* falsification *f.*

falsify *vt.* falsifier; fausser

falsity *n.* fausseté *f.*

falter *vi.* hésiter; chanceler; défaillir; **–ing** *a.* hésitant; chancelant

fame *n.* renom *m.*, renommée *f.*; **–d** *a.* renommé, célèbre

familiar *a.* familier; intime; **be** — **with** connaître; **–ity** *n.* familiarité *f.*; intimité *f.*; connaissance *f.*; **–ize** *vt.* familiariser; habituer

family *n.* famille *f.*; — **man** père de famille *m.*; — **tree** arbre généalogique *m.*

famished *a.* affamé

famous *a.* célèbre, fameux, renommé

fan *n.* éventail *m.*; ventilateur *m.*; amateur *m.*; enragé *m.*; — *vt.* éventer

fanatic *a. & n.* fanatique *f.*; **–ism** *n.* fanatisme *m.*

fancier *n.* amateur *m.*

fanciful *a.* imaginaire; capricieux; fantaisiste

fancy *a.* de fantaisie; — *n.* fantaisie, imagination *f.*; idée *f.*; caprice *m.*; — *vt.* s'imaginer, se figurer

fancy-free *a.* libre, gai

fanfare *n.* sonnerie, fanfare *f.*

fang *n.* croc *m.*; crochet *m.*

fantastic *a.* fantastique

fantasy *n.* fantaisie *f.*

far *a.* lointain, distant, éloigné; — *adv.* loin; beaucoup; — *prep.* loin de; — **and wide** partout; — **from it** tant s'en faut; **as** — **as** *prep.* jusqu'à; **as** — **as** *conj.* autant que; **as** — **as I am concerned** quant à moi; **by** — de beaucoup; **so** — jusqu'ici; **thus** — jusqu'ici

faraway *a.* éloigné, distant

farcical *a.* de farce, burlesque

fare *n.* prix, tarif *m.*; chère, alimentation *f.*, manger *m.*; client *m.*; **full** — place entière *f.*; **half** — demi-place *f.*; — *vi.* aller

farewell *n.* adieu

farfetched *a.* tiré par les cheveux

far-flung *a.* étendu, dispersé; vaste

farm *n.* ferme *f.*; (sports) stage préparatoire *m.*; — *vt.* cultiver; **–er** *n.* fermier *m.*; **–ing** *n.* agriculture *f.*

farm hand *n.* ouvrier agricole *m.*

farmhouse *n.* ferme, maison de ferme *f.*

farmyard *n.* cour, basse-cour *f.*

far-off *a.* lointain, distant, éloigné

far-reaching *a.* important, sérieux, de conséquence

farseeing *a.* clairvoyant; perspicace

farsighted *a.* presbyte; clairvoyant

farther *a.* plus éloigné; — **back** antérieur; — *adv.* plus loin; — **back** plus en arrière

farthest *a.* le plus éloigné; — *adv.* le plus loin

fascinate *vt.* fasciner, séduire

fascinating *a.* séduisant

fascination *n.* fascination *f.*

fascism *n.* fascisme *m.*

fasciste *a.* & *n.* fasciste *m.* & *f.*

fashion *n.* mode, vogue *f.*; façon, manière *f.*; coutume, habitude *f.*; **after a — tant** bien que mal; **in —** à la mode, en vogue; **out of —** démodé; **— vt.** confectionner; faire; façonner; **–able** *a.* à la mode, en vogue; élégant

fashion plate (coll.) élégant *m.*, élégante *f.*

fast *n.* jeûne *m.*; **— day** jour maigre *m.*; **— vi.** jeûner; **— a.** rapide; solide, ferme; fermé; (clock) en avance; **— adv.** vite, rapidement; solidement, ferme; bon

fasten *vt.* attacher; fixer; agrafer; **— vi.** s'attacher, se fixer; **–er** *n.* attache, agrafe *f.*; fermoir *m.*; bouton *m.*; **–ing** *n.* attache, fermeture

fastidious *a.* délicat; difficile; **–ness** *n.* goût difficile *m.*, goût délicat *m.*

fat *a.* gras; gros; riche; **— n.** gras *m.*; graisse *f.*; **–ness** *n.* corpulence *f.*; embonpoint *m.*; **–ten** *vt.* engraisser; **–tening** *a.* engraissant; **–ty** *a.* graisseux; adipeux

fatal *a.* fatal; mortel; **–ism** *n.* fatalisme *m.*; **–ist** *n.* fataliste *m.* & *f.*; **–ity** *n.* fatalité *f.*; accident mortel *m.*

fate *n.* destin, sort *m.*; **–d** *a.* destiné, voué **–ful** *a.* fatal

father *n.* père *m.*; **–'s day** fête des pères *f.*; **— vt.** engendrer; **–hood** *n.* paternité *f.*; **–less** *a.* sans père; **–ly** *a.* paternel

father-in-law *n.* beau-père *m.*

fatherland *n.* patrie *f.*

fathom *n.* brasse *f.*; **— vt.** sonder; pénétrer; **–able** *a.* compréhensible, pénétrable **–less** *a.* sans fond

fatigue *n.* fatigue *f.*; (mil.) corvée *f.*; **–s** *pl.* (mil.) bleus *m. pl.*, tenue de corvée *f.*; **— vt.** fatiguer, lasser

fatuity *n.* stupidité, sottise *f.*

fatuous *a.* stupide, sot

faucet *n.* robinet *m.*

fault *n.* défaut *m.*; faute *f.*; travers *m.*; (geol.) faille *f.*; **at —** en défaut; **find —** trouver à redire; blâmer; **to a —** à l'excès; **–iness** *n.* imperfection *f.*; incorrection *f.*; **–less** *a.* irréprochable; sans défaut; **–y** *a.* défectueux; erroné

faultfinder *n.* épilogueur *m.*; mécontent *m.*

favor *n.* faveur *f.*; service *m.*; grâce *f.*; partialité *f.*; protection *f.*; **be in — of** tenir pour; **be in — with** jouir de la faveur de; **in — of** pour; en faveur de; **show —** favoriser; **— vt.** favoriser, préférer; être pour; avantager; ressembler (à); **–able** *a.* favorable; avantageux; propice; **–ite** *a.* & *n.* favori *m.* (favorite

f.); **–itism** *n.* favoritisme *m.*

fawn *n.* faon *m.*; **— a.** fauve; **— vi., — upon, — over** flatter, cajoler, caresser, câliner

fear *n.* peur, crainte *f.*; **for — of** de peur de, de crainte de; **— vt.** craindre, avoir peur de, redouter; **–ful** *a.* peureux; terrible, effrayant; **–less** *a.* sans peur, intrépide; **–some** *a.* redoutable

feasibility *n.* practicabilité, possibilité *f.*

feasible *a.* faisable, practicable

feast *n.* banquet, festin *m.*; **— day** fête *f.*; **— vt.** régaler; **— vi.** se régaler

feat *n.* fait, exploit *m.*

feather *n.* plume *f.*, **–s** *pl.* plumage *m.*; **— duster** *n.* plumeau *m.* **— vt.** emplumer; empenner; (avi.) mettre en drapeau; (oars) ramener à plat; **–ed** (avi.) en drapeau; **–y** *a.* plumeux

featherbed *n.* lit de plumes, édredon *m.*; **–ding** *n.* pratique des syndicats d'employer plus d'ouvriers qu'il ne faut *f.*

featherbrained *a.* sot, idiot

featherweight *n.* poids (de) plume *m.*

feature *n.* trait *m.*; caractéristique *f.*; spécialité *f.*; **— film** grand film *m.*; **double —** deux grands films *m. pl.*; **— vt.** distinguer, marquer, caractériser; **–d** *a.* à traits

February *n.* février *m.*

fecund *a.* fécond; **–ity** *n.* fécondité *f.*

federal *a.* fédéral

federate *vt.* fédérer; **— vi.** se fédérer

federation *n.* fédération *f.*

fee *n.* honoraires *m. pl.*; cachet *m.*; droit *m.*; frais *m. pl.*

feeble *a.* débile; faible; **–ness** *n.* faiblesse, débilité *f.*

feeble-minded *a.* d'esprit faible

feed *n.* pâture, nourriture *f.*; alimentation *f.*; **— vt.** nourrir, donner à manger; approvisionner; alimenter; **— vi.** manger; paître; **–er** *n.* appareil d'alimentation *m.*; **–er (line)** *n.* (bus, train) ligne secondaire (qui alimente les grandes lignes) *f.* **–ing** *n.* alimentation *f.*

feedback *n.* rétroaction *f.*

feel *n.* tact *m.*; touche *f.*; **— vt.** sentir; éprouver; toucher, tâter, palper; croire, penser; **— for** être plein de pitié pour; **— like** avoir envie de; **–er** *n.* antenne *f.*; **put, send out a –er** tâter le terrain; **–ing** *n.* sensation *f.*; sentiment *m.*; **–ings** *n. pl.* sensibilité *f.*

feign *vt.* feindre, simuler

feint *n.* feinte *f.*; **— vi.** feinter

felicitate *vt.* rendre heureux; féliciter

felicitation *n.* félicitation *f.*

felicity *n.* félicité *f.*

feline *a.* félin

fell *vt.* abattre; — *a.* cruel, féroce
fellow *n.* homme *m.*; gars *m.*; type *m.*; compagnon *m.*; boursier *m.*; membre *m.*; — **citizen** concitoyen *m.*; — **countryman** compatriote *m.*; — **creature**, — **man** semblable *m.*; — **traveler** compagnon de voyage *m.*; (pol.) communisant *m.*; — **worker** compagnon, confrère *m.*; **-ship** *n.* bourse *f.*; camaraderie *f.*
felon *n.* criminel *m.*; **-ious** *a.* criminel; **-y** *n.* crime *m.*
felt *n.* feutre *m.*
female *a.* femelle; féminin, de femme; — *n.* femelle *f.*; femme *f.*
feminine *a.* féminin
femininity *n.* fémininité *f.*
femur *n.* fémur *m.*
fence *n.* clôture *f.*; barrière *f.*; (coll.) receleur *m.*; — *vt.* clôturer; — *vi.* faire de l'escrime; **-r** *n.* escrimeur *m.*
fencing *n.* clôture *f.*; (sport) escrime *m.*; — **master** maître d'armes *m.*; — **match** assaut d'armes *m.*; — **school** salle d'armes *f.*
fend *vt.*, — **off** parer; — *vi.*, — **for oneself** se défendre, se tirer d'affaire
fender *n.* (auto.) aile *f.*; garde-boue *m.*
fennel *n.* fenouil *m.*
ferment *n.* ferment *m.*, fermentation *f.*; — *vt.* faire fermenter; cuver; — *vi.* fermenter, travailler; **-ation** *n.* fermentation *f.*
fern *n.* fougère *f.*
ferocious *a.* féroce; **-ness** *n.* férocité *f.*
ferocity *n.* férocité *f.*
ferret *n.* furet *m.*; — *vi.* fureter; — **out** dénicher
ferric *a.* ferrique
ferrous *a.* ferreux; de fer
ferry *n.* bac, passage *m.*; — *vt.* transborder, passer en bac; transporter
fertile *a.* fertile, fécond
fertility *n.* fertilité, fécondité *f.*
fertilization *n.* fertilisation *f.*; pollinisation *f.*
fertilize *vt.* fertiliser; amender; **-r** *n.* engrais *m.*
fervency *n.* ferveur *f.*
fervent *a.* fervent; **-ly** *adv.* ardemment
fervid *a.* ardent, chaud
fervor *n.* ferveur, ardeur *f.*, zèle *m.*
fester *vi.* suppurer; **-ing** *n.* suppuration *f.*
festival *n.* fête *f.*, festival *m.*
festive *a.* de fête
festivity *n.* fête *f.*; réjouissance *f.*
festoon *vt.* festonner; — *n.* feston *m.*
fetch *vt.* aller chercher, apporter; rapporter; **-ing** *a.* séduisant
fête *vt.* fêter

fetid *a.* fétide; **-ness** *n.* fétidité *f.*
fetish *n.* fétiche *m.*
fetter *n.* lien *m.*; **-s** *n. pl.* fers *m. pl.*, chaînes *f. pl.*; — *vt.* enchaîner; entraver
fettle *n.* condition *f.*
feud *n.* querelle *f.*; vendetta *f.*
feudal *a.* féodal; **-ism** *n.* féodalité *f.*
fever *n.* fièvre *f.*; **-ish** *a.* fiévreux, fébrile; **-ishness** *n.* fièvre *f.*
few *a.* peu de; rares; peu nombreux; **a** — *a.* quelques; — *pron.* peu; quelques-uns; **-er** *a.* moins de; moins nombreux
fiat *n.* autorisation *f.*; décret *m.*
fib *n.* petit mensonge *m.*; — *vi.* mentir; **-ber** *n.* menteur *m.*
fiber *n.* fibre *f.*; nature *f.*
fibroid *a.* fibroïde; — *n.* fibrome *m.*
fibrous *a.* fibreux
fickle *a.* volage, inconstant; **-ness** *n.* inconstance *f.*
fiction *n.* fiction *f.*; ouvrage d'imagination *m.*; **-al** *a.* d'imagination, romanesque
fictitious *a.* fictif, imaginaire
fiddle *n.* violon *m.*; — *vt.* jouer du violon; bricoler, tripoter; **-r** *n.* (joueur de) violon *m.*
fidelity *n.* fidélité, loyauté *f.*; exactitude *f.*; **high** — haute fidélité *f.*
fidget *vi.* se trémousser; s'inquiéter; — **with** tripoter; **-y** *a.* nerveux
field *n.* champ *m.*; terrain *m.*; théâtre *m.*; — **artillery** artillerie de campagne *f.*; — **day** fête *f.*; — **glasses** jumelles *f. pl.*; — **gun** pièce de campagne *f.*; — **hospital** ambulance *f.*; hôpital mobile *m.*; — **marshal** *n.* maréchal *m.*; — **mouse** mulot *m.*; **-er** *n.* (sports) chasseur *m.*
fiend *n.* démon, monstre *m.*; **-ish** *a.* diabolique, infernal; **-ishness** *n.* caractère diabolique *m.*
fierce *a.* féroce; acharné; **-ness** *n.* férocité *f.*; acharnement *m.*
fieriness *n.* ardeur *f.*
fiery *a.* ardent, enflammé; fougueux
fifteen *a.* quinze; **-th** *a.* quinzième
fifth *a.* cinquième
fiftieth *a.* cinquantième
fifty *a.* cinquante
fifty-fifty *a. & adv.* moitié-moitié
fig *n.* figue *f.*; — **leaf** (art) feuille de vigne *f.*; — **tree** figuier *m.*
fight *n.* bataille *f.*, combat *m.*; lutte *f.*; dispute *f.*; match de boxe *m.*; — *vi.* se battre, combattre; lutter; boxer; — *vt.* se battre avec, combattre; — **off** résister, repousser; **-er** *n.* combattant *m.*; boxeur *m.*; **-ing** *n.* combat *m.*; boxe *f.*
figment *n.* fiction, invention *f.*
figurative *a.* figuratif; figuré
figure *n.* taille *f.*; forme, figure *f.*; person-

nage *m.*; chiffre *m.*; — of speech métaphore *f.*; figure de rhétorique; — *vt.*
figurer, représenter; estimer, calculer;
— on compter sur; se trouver; — out
calculer; déchiffrer; -d *a.* à dessein,
décoré

figurehead *n.* prête-nom *m.*; (naut.)
figure de proue *f.*

Figi *n.* Fiji *m.*

filament *n.* filament *m.*; fil *m.*

filch *vt.* voler, chiper

file *n.* classeur *m.*; dossier *m.*; fichier *m.*;
(tool) lime *f.*; — card *n.* fiche *f.*; —
clerk *n.* archiviste *m.* & *f.*; in single —
à la file indienne; — *vt.* classer, ranger;
limer; — by défiler (devant)

filial *a.* filial

filibuster *n.* obstruction *f.*; (hist.) flibustier *m.*

filigree *n.* filigrane *m.*

filing *n.* classement *m.*; limage *m.*; —
cabinet classeur *m.*; — **clerk** archiviste
m. & *f.*; -s *n.* *pl.* limaille *f.*

fill *n.* suffisance *f.*; — *vt.* remplir, emplir;
charger; combler; occuper; (order)
exécuter; — *vi.* se remplir, s'emplir;
(sail) s'enfler; — in remplir; remblayer;
insérer; — out remplir; -er *n.* remplissage *m.*; remplisseur *m.*; papier (pour
un cahier) *m.*; -ing *a.* rassasiant; -ing
n. remplissage *m.*; (dent.) plombage
m.; -ing station poste d'essence *m.*,
station-service *f.*

fillet *n.* filet *m.*; — *vt.* lever les filets

filly *n.* pouliche *f.*

film *n.* pellicule *f.*; film *m.*; couche *f.*;
-strip film (à projection) fixe *m.*; — *vt.*
filmer; -y *a.* voilé; transparent

filter *n.* filtre *m.*; (phot.) écran *m.*; — *vt.*
& *vi.* filtrer; -able *a.* filtrant; — tip *n.*
bout filtrant *m.*

filth *n.* saleté *f.*; corruption *f.*; ordure *f.*;
obscénité *f.*; -y *a.* sale; immonde

filtrate *n.* filtrat *m.*

filtration *n.* filtration *f.*

fin *n.* nageoire *f.*

final *a.* final, dernier; définitif; -e *n.*
finale *m.*; -ist *n.* finaliste *m.* & *f.*; -ity *n.*
finalité *f.*; irrévocabilité *f.*; -ly *adv.*
finalement; enfin

finance *n.* finance *f.*; — *vt.* financer

financial *a.* financier

financier *n.* financier *m.*

financing *n.* financement *m.*

find *n.* trouvaille *f.*; découverte *f.*; — *vt.*
trouver, découvrir; retrouver; appren-
dre; (law) apprendre, — out apprendre,
savoir, découvrir; se renseigner; -er *n.*
trouveur *m.*; détecteur *m.*; (law) inventeur *m.*; -ings *n.* conclusions *f.* *pl.*

fine *n.* amende *f.*; — *a.* fin; raffiné; beau;
excellent; menu; affilé; — **arts** beaux-
arts *m.* *pl.*; -ly *adv.* finement; menu;
bien; -ness *n.* excellence *f.*; élégance *f.*;
— *vt.* frapper d'une amende, condamner
à une amende

finery *n.* parure *f.*

finesse *n.* finesse *f.*; — *vt.* faire une
impasse

finger *n.* doigt *m.*; — **bowl** rince-doigts
m.; **ring** — annulaire *m.*; — *vt.* manier;
-ing *n.* maniement *m.*; touche *f.*

fingernail *n.* ongle *m.*

fingerprint *n.* empreinte digitale *f.*; — *vt.*
prendre les empreintes digitales de

finicky *a.* méticuleux; difficile

finis *n.* fin *f.*

finish *n.* fin *f.*; achevé *m.*; finesse *f.*; — *vt.*
finir, terminer, achever; — *vi.* finir, se
terminer; -ed *a.* fini; accompli, achevé;
-er *n.* polisseur *m.*; -ing *n.* achèvement
m.; photo -ing développement et tirage
m.; -ing *a.* dernier, final

finite *a.* fini, limité

Finland *n.* Finlande *f.*

Finn *n.* Finlandais *m.*; -ish *a.* & *n.* finlandais, Finnois

fire *n.* feu *m.*; incendie *m.*; **catch** — prendre feu; — **alarm** avertisseur *m.*; — **department** pompiers, sapeurs-pompiers
m. *pl.*; — **drill** exercices de sauvetage
(en cas d'incendie) *m.* *pl.*; — **engine**
pompe à incendie; — **escape** échelle de
sauvetage *f.*; — **extinguisher** extincteur *m.*; — **insurance** assurance contre
l'incendie *f.*; **light a** — faire du feu; on
— en feu, en flammes; **set** — **to** mettre
le feu à; — *vt.* mettre le feu à; enflammer; (ceramics) cuire; (weapon) tirer,
faire feu; décharger; (employment)
congédier, licencier; mettre à la porte

firearms *n.* *pl.* armes à feu *f.* *pl.*

fireboat *n.* bateau-pompe *m.*

firebox *n.* poste avertisseur d'incendie *m.*

firebrand *n.* brandon, tison *m.*; rebelle *m.*

firebug *n.* (coll.) incendiaire *m.*

fire chief *n.* commissaire des pompiers *m.*

firecracker *n.* pétard *m.*

firefighter *n.* pompier *m.*

fireless cooker *n.* marmite norvégienne *f.*

fireplace *n.* cheminée *f.*; feu *m.*; foyer *m.*

fireplug *n.* bouche d'incendie *f.*

fireproof *a.* à l'épreuve du feu, ignifuge

fireside *n.* coin du feu *m.*

firetrap *n.* bâtiment inhabitable, bâtiment qui invite l'incendie *m.*

firewood *n.* bois de chauffage *m.*

fireworks *n.* *pl.* feux d'artifice *m.* *pl.*

firing *n.* (furnace) chauffage *m.*; (ceramics) cuite *f.*; (mil.) feu, tir *m.*; (em-

ployment) renvoi *m.*; — **line** traîne de combat *f.*; — **pin** aiguille *f.*

firm *n.* maison *f.*, établissement *m.*; — *a.* ferme; fixe; solide; résolu; — *adv.*, **stand** — tenir bon; **–ness** *n.* fermeté *f.*

first *a.* premier; — **aid** premiers soins *m.* *pl.*; — **aid kit** trousse de pansement *f.*; — **aid station** poste de secours *m.*; — **night** (theat.) première *f.*; **in the** — **place** en premier lieu; d'abord; — *adv.* premièrement, d'abord; plûtot

first-class *a.* de choix, de première qualité; (travel) de première classe

firsthand *a.* de première main

first-rate *a.* excellent, supérieur; de première qualité

fish *n.* poisson *m.*; — *vt. & vi.* pêcher; **–erman** *n.* pêcheur *m.*; **–ery** *n.* pêcherie *f.*; **–ing** *n.* pêche *f.*; **–ing reel** *n.* moulinet *m.*; **–ing rod** canne à pêche *f.*; **–ing tackle** appareil de pêche *m.*; **–y** *a.* de poisson; véreux; louche

fishbone *n.* arête *f.*

fishbowl *n.* aquarium *m.*

fishhook *n.* hameçon *m.*

fishmonger *n.* marchand de poisson *m.*

fishpond *n.* vivier *m.*

fission *n.* fission *f.*, désintégration *f.*

fissionable *a.* désintégrable, fissile

fissure *n.* fente *f.*

fist *n.* poing *m.*; **shake a** — **at** menacer du poing; **–ful** *n.* poignée *f.*

fisticuffs *n. pl.* boxe *f.*

fistula *n.* fistule *f.*

fit *a.* bon, propre; capable; digne; — **to drink** potable; — **to be seen** présentable; **see** — trouver bon; — *n.* attaque *f.*, accès *m.*; crise *f.*; convulsion *f.*; **coughing** — quinte de toux *f.*; — *vt.* aller (à); ajuster; préparer; munir; — *vi.* aller; — **in (with)** s'accorder, être en harmonie (avec); — **out** équiper; **–ful** *a.* irrégulier; **–ness** *n.* aptitude *f.*; bonne santé *f.*; **–ter** *n.* essayeur *m.*; **–ting** *a.* convenable, bienséant; à propos; **–ting** *n.* garniture *f.*; montage, ajustage *m.*; essayage *m.*; **–tings** *n. pl.* garniture *f.*; armement *m.*

five *a.* cinq

fix *n.* (coll.) mauvais pas, embarras *m.*; — *vt.* fixer; préparer; arrêter; réparer; — **up** arranger; **–ed** *a.* fixe; **–edness, –ity** *n.* fixité *f.*; **–ings** *n. pl.* (coll.) accessoires *m. pl.*; garniture *f.*; **–ture** *n.* meuble à demeure *m.*

fizz *vi.* pétiller; — *n.* pétillement *m.*

fizzle *vi.* avorter, ne pas aboutir; — *n.* (coll.) avortement, insuccès *m.*

flabbiness *n.* mollesse, flaccidité *f.*

flabby *a.* mou (molle), flasque

flaccid *a.* flasque

flag *n.* drapeau *m.*; pavillon *m.*; — *vi.* traîner, se ralentir; — **stop** *n.* arrêt sur demande *m.*; **–pole** *n.* hampe de drapeau *f.*

flagellate *vt.* flageller

flagellation *n.* flagellation *f.*

flagging *n.* dallage *m.*; — *a.* traînant, languissant

flagon *n.* flacon *m.*

flagrancy *n.* énormité *f.*

flagrant *a.* flagrant

flagship *n.* amiral, vaisseau amiral *m.*

flagstone *n.* dalle *f.*; dallage *m.*

flail *n.* fléau *m.*

flair *n.* flair *m.*

flake *n.* flocon *m.*; éclat *m.*, paillette *f.*; — *vi.* tomber en flocons; — **off** se feuilleter, s'écailler

flaky *a.* floconneux; feuilleté

flame *n.* flamme *f.*; feu *m.*; ardeur, passion *f.*; — **thrower** lance-flammes *m.*; — *vi.* flamber; s'enflammer

flange *n.* rebord, boudin *m.*, saillie *f.*

flank *n.* flanc, côté *m.*; — *vt.* flanquer; (mil.) prendre en flanc

flannel *n.* flanelle *f.*; **–ette** *n.* flanelle de coton *f.*

flap *n.* battement *m.*; (avi.) volet, aileron *m.*; — *vt. & vi.* battre

flare *n.* flamme *f.*, feu *m.*; fusée éclairante *f.*; (skirt) évasement *m.*; — *vi.* flamboyer; s'évaser; — **up** s'enflammer

flash *n.* éclair *m.*; (coll.) ostentation *f.*, faste *m.*; — **adapter** (phot.) prise de flash *f.*; — **attachment** (phot.) flash *m.*; **in a** — en un clin d'œil; — **in the pan** feu de paille *m.*; — *vi.* jeter des éclairs, éclater; — *vt.* projeter; faire étinceler; faire parade de; **–ing** *a.* clignotant; **–ing** *n.* clignotement *m.*; **–y** *a.* fastueux, vaniteux

flash back *n.* rappel *m.*

flash bulb *n.* ampoule flash *f.*

flash gun *n.* flash *m.*

flashlight *n.* torche, lampe *f.*

flask *n.* flacon *m.*; gourde *f.*; fiole *f.*

flat *a.* plat, uni; aplati; net; fade, insipide; (mus.) bémol; — **broke** *a.* complètement fauché; — **refusal** refus net *m.*; — **tire** crevaison *f.*; **fall** — manquer (son effet); — **on one's face** (tomber) à plat ventre; — *n.* plat *m.*; appartement *m.*; (mus.) bémol *m.*; (theat.) châssis *m.*; **–ten** *vt.* aplatir

flat-bottomed *a.* à fond plat

flatcar *n.* wagon en plate-forme *m.*

flat-footed *a.* aux pieds plats

flatiron *n.* fer à repasser *m.*

flatter *vt.* flatter; **–er** *n.* flatteur *m.*; **–ing**

a. flatteur; **–y** *n.* flatterie *f.*

flattop *n.* (coll.) porte-avions *m.*; **cheveux** taillés en brosse *m. pl.*

flaunt *vt.* étaler, faire étalage de

flavor *n.* goût *m.*, saveur *f.*; parfum *m.*; — *vt.* assaisonner, parfumer; **–ing** *n.* assaisonnement *m.*; **–less** *a.* insipide

flaw *n.* défaut *m.*; imperfection *f.*; tache *f.*; **–less** *a.* sans défaut; sans tache

flax *n.* lin *m.*; **–en** *a.* de lin; blond

flay *vt.* écorcher, fouetter

flea *n.* puce *f.*

fleck *n.* particule; tache *f.*; — *vt.* tacheter

fledgling *n.* oisillon *m.*; novice *m. & f.*

flee *vt. & vi.* fuir; s'enfuir (de)

fleece *n.* toison *f.*; — *vt.* (coll.) plumer, tondre

fleecy *a.* moutonneux, moutonné; floconneux; laineux

fleet *n.* flotte *f.*; — *a.* au pied léger; rapide; — *vi.* s'enfuir; **–ing** *a.* passager; fugitif; **–ness** *n.* vitesse *f.*

fleet-footed *a.* au pied léger

Flemish *a. & n.* flamand *m.*

flesh *n.* chair *f.*; corps *m.*; **— color** carnation *f.*; couleur de chair *f.*; **— wound** blessure légère *f.*; **–y** *a.* charnu

flex *vt.* fléchir

flexibility *n.* flexibilité *f.*; souplesse *f.*

flexible *a.* flexible, pliant, souple

flick *n.* chiquenaude *f.*; tour de main *m.*; — *vt.* taper

flicker *n.* petite lueur *f.*; tremblotement *m.*; battement *m.*; — *vi.* vaciller, trembloter; scintiller

flier *n.* prospectus *m.*; (train) rapide *m.*; (stocks) spéculation au hasard *f.*

flight *n.* fuite *f.*; vol *m.*; volée *f.*; **— pattern** *n.* dessin de vol *m.*; disposition *m.*; **— plan** *n.* plan de vol, projet de vol *m.*; **— of stairs** escalier *m.*; **put to —** mettre en fuite; **–iness** *n.* légèreté, inconstance *f.*; **–y** *a.* volage; frivole

flimsiness *n.* légèreté, pauvreté *f.*

flimsy *a.* léger, peu solide; pauvre

flinch *vi.* reculer; broncher

fling *n.* jet *m.*; essai *m.*, tentative *f.*; (coll.) noce, débauche *f.*; — *vt.* jeter, lancer; — *vi.* se précipiter

flint *n.* silex *m.*; pierre à briquet *f.*

flintlock *n.* fusil à pierre *m.*

flip *vt.* tourner, renverser; — *n.* renversement *m.*; — *a.* léger, cavalier

flippancy *n.* légèreté *f.*; désinvolture *f.*

flippant *a.* léger; désinvolte

flipper *n.* nageoire *f.*

flirt *n.* coquette *f.*; — *vi.* flirter; **–ation** *f.* flirt, flirtage *m.*

flit *vi.* voltiger

float *n.* flot, radeau *m.*; (parade) char bas de cortège *m.*; — *vi.* flotter; nager; faire la planche; — *vt.* flotter; **— a loan** émettre un emprunt; **–ing** *a.* flottant; libre; **–ing** *n.* flottement *m.*; (swimming) planche *f.*; émission *f.*

flock *n.* troupeau *m.*; troupe *f.*; bande, foule *f.*; — *vi.* s'assembler, s'attrouper; faire foule

floe *n.* glaçon flottant *m.*, banquise *f.*

flog *vt.* fouetter, flageller; **–ging** *n.* coups de fouet *m. pl.*; flagellation *f.*

flood *n.* inondation *f.*, déluge *m.*; flux *m.*; flot *m.*; **— tide** marée montante *f.*; — *vt.* inonder; irriguer, noyer; — *vi.* déborder; (auto) se noyer

floodgate *n.* vanne *f.*; porte d'écluse *f.*

floodlight *n.* projecteur, phare *m.*

floor *n.* plancher, parquet *m.*; étage *m.*; fond *m.*; **— ground** rez-de-chaussée *m.*; **tiled —** carrelage *m.*; **have the —** avoir la parole; — *vt.* parqueter; terrasser; **–ing** *n.* plancher, parquetage *m.*

floorwalker *n.* chef de rayon (d'un grand magasin) *m.*

flop *n.* échec, fiasco *m.*; — *vi.* échouer; s'affaler, s'effondrer

floral *a.* florale, *pl.* floraux

florid *a.* fleuri; flamboyant; rubicond

florist *n.* fleuriste *m. & f.*

floss *n.* duvet *m.*; (metal) floss *m.*; **–y** *a.* duveteux

flotilla *n.* flottille *f.*

flounce *n.* volant *m.*; — *vt.* garnir de volant

flounder *n.* carrelet *m.*; — *vi.* se débattre; patauger

flour *n.* farine *f.*; — *vt.* fariner; **–y** *a.* farineux

flourish *n.* fioriture *f.*; parafe *m.*; fanfare *f.*; brandissement *m.*; — *vi.* fleurir, prospérer; — *vt.* brandir; **–ing** *a.* florissant; prospère

flout *vi.* se moquer de; **–ing** *n.* moquerie *f.*

flow *n.* flux, courant *m.*; écoulement *m.*; affluence *f.*; cours *m.*; — *vi.* couler, s'écouler; circuler; se répandre; abonder; **— into** déboucher dans, se verser dans; **–ing** *a.* coulant; flottant; fleuri; gracieux; fluide

flower *n.* fleur *f.*; élite *f.*; **— shop** boutique de fleuriste *f.*; — *vi.* fleurir; **–ed** *a.* à fleurs; **–ing** *a.* fleuri, en fleur; **–ing** *n.* fleuraison *f.*; **–y** *a.* fleuri

flowerbed *n.* platebande *f.*

flu *n.* grippe *f.*

fluctuate *vi.* fluctuer; varier; osciller; flotter

fluctuating *a.* variable

fluctuation *n.* fluctuation *f.*

flue *n.* tuyau *m.*

fluency n. facilité f.

fluent a. coulant, facile; **-ly** adv. couramment

fluff n. duvet m.; peluches f. pl.; — vt. lainer; (coll.) louper; **-y** a. pelucheux

fluid a. fluide; — n. fluide, liquide m.; **-ity** n. fluidité f.

flunkey n. laquais m.

fluorescence n. fluorescence f.

fluorescent a. fluorescent

fluoride n. fluorure m.

fluorine n. fluor m.

fluoroscope n. fluoroscope m.

flurry n. risée f.; agitation f.; **snow —** rafale de neige f.

flush n. chasse d'eau f.; éian m.; éclat m.; rougeur f.; (cards) flush m.; — vi. rougir; — vt. donner une chasse; (hunting) faire lever; — a. à fleur; de niveau; (coll.) en fonds **-ed** a. qui rougit: empourpré; ivre

fluster vt. agiter; — vi. s'agiter

flute n. flûte f.; (arch.) cannelure f.; **-d** a. flûté; cannelé

fluting n. striure f.; cannelure f.

flutist n. flûtiste m. & f.

flatter n. voltigement m.; flottement m.; (wings) battement m.; (heart) palpitation f.; — vt. agiter; battre; — vi. flotter, s'agiter; battre; palpiter

flux n. flux m.; fondant m.

fly n. mouche f.; vol m.; (trousers) braguette f.; — **fishing** pêche à la mouche f.; **on the —** en vol; — vi. voler; aller en avion; aller à toute vitesse; fuir; — vt. faire voler; piloter; — **into a rage** s'emporter; — **off the handle** sortir de ses gonds; — **away** s'envoler; **-er, flier** n. aviateur m.; pilote m.; **-ing** a. volant; **-ing boat** hydravion m.; **-ing buttress** arc-boutant m.; **-ing saucer** soucoupe volante f.; **-ing** n. aviation f., vol m.

flyleaf n. garde f.

flypaper n. papier attrape-mouches m.

flyweight n. poids mouche m.

flywheel n. volant m.

F.M.: Frequency Modulation n. modulation de fréquence f.

foal n. poulain m.; — vi. mettre bas

foam n. écume f.; mousse f.; — **rubber** n. mousse de caoutchouc f.; — vi. écumer; mousser; **-y** a. écumeux; mousseux

F.O.B.; free on board rendu à bord

fob n. régence f.; ornement (sur une chaîne de montre) m.; (pocket) gousset m.

focus n. foyer m.; **in —** au point; — vt. concentrer; mettre au point; — vi. converger; **-ing** n. mise au point f.

fodder n. fourrage m.

foe n. ennemi, adversaire m.

foetus n. foetus m.

fog n. brouillard m., brume f.; — vt. embrumer; embrouiller; voiler; **-gy** a. brumeux; brouillé; **it's -gy** il fait du brouillard

foghorn n. sirène (de brume) f.

foible n. faible m.

foil n. feuille, lame f.; tain m.; (fencing) fleuret m.; — vt. déjouer; faire manquer

foist vt. imposer; insérer

fold n. pli, repli m.; (sheep) parc m.; — vt. plier, replier; — **one's arms** se croiser les bras; — vi. se plier; (coll.) échouer, sombrer; **-er** n. chemise f.; dossier m.; prospectus m.; **-ing** a. pliant; **-ing bed** lit pliant, lit escamotable m.; **-ing chair** chaise pliante f.; **-ing door** porte brisée f.

foliage n. feuillage m.

folio n. folio m.; feuille f.; in-folio m.

folk n. gens m. pl.; peuple m.; — **music** musique populaire f.; — **song** chanson populaire f.; **-s** (coll.) famille f., parents m. pl.

follicle n. follicule m.

follow vt. suivre; poursuivre; succéder à; se conformer; comprendre; — vi. suivre; s'ensuivre; — **up** suivre, poursuivre; **-er** n. disciple m.; partisan m.; **-ing** a. qui suit; suivant; **-ing** n. (pol.) parti m.; partisans m. pl.; **-ing the leader** adv. à la queue leu leu

folly n. folie f.; sottise f.

foment vt. fomenter

fond a. tendre, affectueux; friand; **be —** **of** aimer (bien); être amateur de; **-ness** n. affection f.; goût m.

fondle vt. caresser

font n. fontaine f.; (eccl.) fonts baptismaux m. pl.; (printing) fonte f.

food n. nourriture f.; aliment m.; manger m.; vivres m. pl.; cuisine f.

fool n. sot m.; fou (folle); niais m.; imbécile m. & f.; dupe f.; — vt. duper; berner; **-ery** n. bouffonnerie f.; **-ing** n. duperie f.; dissipation f.; **no -ing** sans blague **-ish** a. fou (folle); insensé; bête; ridicule; **-ishness** n. folie f.; sottise f.

foolhardiness n. témérité f.

foolhardy a. téméraire; imprudent

foolproof a. indétraquable

foolscap n. papier ministre m.

foot n. pied m.; patte f.; base f.; bas m.; — **locker** petite malle f.; — **soldier** soldat d'infanterie m.; **on —** à pied; **set — on** mettre pied sur; **-ing** n. équilibre m.; **lose one's -ing** perdre pied

foot-and-mouth disease n. fièvre aphteuse f.

footbridge n. passerelle f.

footfall n. pas m.
foothills n. pl. contreforts m. pl.
foothold n., get a — prendre pied
footlights n. pl. rampe f.
foot-loose a. libre; sans entraves
footman n. valet de pied, laquais m.
footnote n. note f., renvoi m.
footpath n. sentier m.
footprint n. trace f.; empreinte (de pas) f., pas m.
foot race n. course à pied f.
footsore a. aux pieds meurtris
footstep n. pas m.
footstool n. tabouret m.
foot warmer n. chaufferette f.
footwear n. chaussures f. pl.
footwork n. jeu de pieds m.
fop n. petit-maître m.
for conj. car; — prep. pour; comme; contre; à; de; pendant; depuis; — example par exemple; — sale à vendre; as — quant à; what — pour quoi faire; pourquoi
forage vi. fourrager; — n. fourrage m.
foray n. incursion f.
forbear vt. & vi. s'abstenir; –ance n. abstention f.
forbid vt. défendre, interdire; God —! à Dieu ne plaise!; –den a. défendu; –ding a. sinistre, sombre
force n. force f.; contrainte f.; énergie f.; effort m.; puissance f.; in — en vigueur; police — la police f.; — vt. forcer; obliger; contraindre; arracher; enfoncer; — one's way into pénétrer de force dans; — back repousser; –d a. forcé; obligé; –ful a. énergique; puissant
forceps n. pl. pince f.
forcibly adv. de force, par force
ford n. gué m.; — vt. traverser à gué
fore n. (naut.) avant m.; to the — en vue; — ! interj. (golf) gare devant!
forearm n. avant-bras m.; — vt. prémunir, avertir
forebode vt. présager; pressentir
forecast n. prévision f.; weather — prévisions météorologiques f. pl.; — vt. prédire, prévoir
forecastle n. gaillard d'avant m.
foreclose vt. saisir
foreclosure n. saisie f.
forefather n. aïeul m.
forefinger n. index m.
forefront n. premier rang m.
forego vt. renoncer à; –ing a. précédent, antérieur; –ne a. décidé, déterminé; –ne conclusion n. parti pris m.
foreground n. premier plan m.
forehead n. front m.
foreign a. étranger; — trade commerce

extérieur m.; –er n.; étranger m., étrangère f.
foreleg n. jambe de devant f.
foreman n. contremaître m.; chef d'équipe m.; (jury) chef m.
foremast n. mât de misaine m.
foremost a. premier; — adv., first and — tout d'abord
forenoon n. matinée f.
forerunner n. précurseur m.
foresee vt. prévoir; entrevoir
foreshadow vt. présager; –ing n. présage, pressentiment m.
foreshorten vt. raccourcir
foresight n. prévoyance f.; prévision f.
forest n. forêt f.; — ranger (garde) forestier m.; –ry n. sylviculture f.
forestall vt. anticiper, devancer
foretell vt. prédire
forethought n. prévoyance f.; préméditation f.
forever adv. pour toujours, à jamais
forewarn vt. avertir, prévenir
foreword n. avant-propos m.; préface f., avis au lecteur m.
forfeit n. amende f.; gage m.; forfait m.; — vt. être déchu de; perdre; –ure n. confiscation, forfaiture f.
forge n. forge f.; atelier de forge m.; — vt. forger; contrefaire, falsifier; –r n. forgeron m.; faussaire m. & f.; –ry n. contrefaçon, falsification f.; faux m.
forget vt. oublier; –ful a. oublieux; –fulness n. manque de mémoire m.; oubli m.
forget-me-not n. myosotis m.
forgivable a. pardonnable
forgive vt. pardonner; –ness n. pardon m.
forgiving a. indulgent, généreux
fork n. fourchette f.; fourche f.; bifurcation f.; tuning — diapason m.; — vi. fourcher; se bifurquer; — over, — out (coll.) payer, donner de l'argent –ed a. fourchu
forlorn a. abandonné, délaissé; désespéré
form n. forme f.; figure f.; formalité f.; ton m.; formule f.; bulletin m.; classe f.; — letter lettre circulaire f.; good — bon ton m.; matter of — formalité f.; — vt. former; faire; façonner; organiser; — vi. se former; –ation n. formation f.; organisation f.; –less a. informe; amorphe
formal a. formel; cérémonieux; –ity n. formalité f.; cérémonie f.
formaldehyde n. aldéhyde formique f.
former a. ancien; précédent; premier; — pron., the — celui-là, celle-là; –ly adv. autrefois, jadis; anciennement
formidable a. formidable

formula *n.* formule *f.*
formulate *vt.* formuler
forsake *vt.* abandonner
forswear *vt.* abjurer, répudier
fort *n.* forteresse *f.*; fort *m.*
forte *n.* fort *m.*
forth *adv.* en avant; **and so —** et ainsi de suite
forthcoming *a.* à venir, à paraître
forthright *a.* direct
forthwith *adv.* sur-le-champ
fortieth *a.* quarantième
fortification *n.* fortification *f.*
fortify *vt.* fortifier; renforcer
fortitude *n.* force d'âme *f.*
fortnight *n.* quinze jours *m. pl.*; quinzaine *f.*; **–ly** *a.* tous les quinze jours
fortress *n.* forteresse *f.*
fortuitous *a.* fortuit; **–ly** *adv.* par hasard; **–ness** *n.* fortuité *f.*
fortunate *a.* fortuné, heureux; **–ly** *adv.* heureusement
fortune *n.* fortune *f.*; hasard *m.*; sort *m.*; **— hunter** coureur de dots *m.*; aventurier *m.*; **–teller** diseur (diseuse) de bonne aventure *m. & f.*; tireur (tireuse) de cartes *m. & f.*; **–telling** bonne aventure *f.*; cartomancie *f.*
forty *a.* quarante
forward *a.* en avant; de devant; avancé; effronté; **–(s)** *adv.* en avant; à l'avant; **–pass** *n.* (football) passe en avant *f.*; **—** *vt.* faire suivre; envoyer, expédier; avancer; **–ness** *n.* présomption *f.*, empressement *m.*
fossil *n. & a.* fossile *m.*; **–ize** *vi.* se fossiliser
foster *vt.* nourrir, élever; encourager, développer; **— brother** frère adoptif *m.*; frère de lait *m.*; **— child** enfant adopté *m.*; nourrisson *m.*; **— mother** mère adoptive *f.*; mère nourricière *f.*
foul *a.* immonde; infect; vicié; gros; sale; (sport) hors jeu; **— ball** *n.* balle hors jeu *f.*; **— play** jeu déloyal *m.*; malveillance *f.*; **—** *n.* faute *f.*; coup déloyal *m.*; **—** *vt.* embarrasser; engager; salir, crasser; **–mouthed** *a.* grossier
found *vt.* fonder, établir; **–ation** *n.* fondation *f.*, établissement *m.*; fondement *m.*; base *f.*; assise *f.*; **–er** *n.* fondateur *m.*
founder *vi.* sombrer
foundling *n.* enfant trouvé *m.*
foundry *n.* fonderie *f.*
fount(ain) *n.* fontaine *f.*; jet d'eau *m.*; source *f.*; **— pen** stylo *m.*
fountainhead *n.* source, origine *f.*
four *a.* quatre; **on all –s** à quatre pattes; **–teen** *a.* quatorze; **–teenth** *f.* quatorzième; **–th** *a.* quatrième; (fraction) quart *m.*

four-engined *a.* quadrimoteur
four-footed *a.* quadrupède
four-poster *n.* lit à colonnes *m.*
foursome *n.* (golf) partie double *f.*
fowl *n.* volaille *f.*
fox *n.* renard *m.*; **— terrier** *n.* fox *m.*; **–y** *a.* rusé
foxhole (mil.) *n.* trou *m.*, tranchée individuelle *f.*
foyer *n.* foyer, vestibule *m.*
fracas *n.* dispute, bagarre *f.*
fraction *n.* fraction *f.*; **–al** *a.* fractionnaire; fractionné
fracture *n.* fracture *f.*; **set a —** réduire une fracture; **—** *vt.* fracturer; casser
fragility *n.* fragilité *f.*
fragment *n.* fragment, morceau *m.*; éclat *m.*; **–ary** *a.* fragmentaire
fragrance *n.* parfum *m.*
fragrant *a.* parfumé
frail *a.* frêle, fragile; faible, délicat; **–ty** *n.* faiblesse *f.*; fragilité *f.*
frame *n.* cadre *m.*; taille *f.*; châssis *m.*; armature *f.*; (film) image *f.*; **— of mind** disposition *f.*; **—** *vt.* encadrer; former; projeter; (coll.) monter une accusation contre; **–r** *n.* encadreur *m.*; (fig.) créateur *m.*
framework *n.* charpente *f.*; organisation *f.*; systeme *m.*
framing *n.* encadrement *m.*
France *n.* France *f.*
franchise *n.* franchise *f.*; privilège *m.*; droit de vote *m.*; exclusivité *f.*
Franciscan *n.* franciscain *m.*
frank *a.* franc (franche); **–ly** *adv.* franchement; **–ness** *n.* franchise *f.*
Frank *n.* Franc *m.*; **–ish** *a.* franc
frankfurter *n.* saucisse de Francfort *f.*
frantic *a.* frénétique; effréné
fraternal *a.* fraternel
fraternity *n.* fraternité *f.*; société de collégiens *f.*
fraternize *vt.* fraterniser
fraternizing *n.* fraternisation *f.*
fraud *n.* fraude *f.*; tromperie *f.*; imposteur *m.*; **–ulent** *a.* frauduleux
fraught *a.* plein, riche
fray *n.* combat *m.*; bagarre *f.*; **—** *vi.* s'érailler
freak *n.* monstre *m.*; curiosité *f.*; **— of chance** jeu du hasard *m.*; **–ish** *a.* monstrueux, bizarre
freckle *n.* tache de rousseur *f.*; **–d** *a.* taché de rousseur
free *a.* libre; gratuit; franco; libéral; franc; exempt; dégagé; **— and easy** désinvolte, dégagé; **— for all** lutte pour tous *f.*; **— hand** carte blanche *f.*; **— speech** libre parole *f.*; **— ticket** billet

de faveur *m.*; — **trade** libre échange *m.*; — **will** (phil.) libre arbitre *m.*; **of one's own** — will de son propre gré; — *vt.* libérer; affranchir; élargir; dégager; **–dom** *n.* liberté *f.*; franchise *f.*; **–dom of speech** franc-parler *m.*

free-for-all *n.* bagarre *f.*; mêlée *f.*

freehand *a.* (art) à main levée

freemason *n.* franc-maçon *m.*; **–ry** *n.* franc-maçonnerie *f.*

freethinker *n.* libre penseur *m.*

freeway *n.* autostrade *f.*

freeze *vt.* geler, congeler, glacer; — *vi.* prendre; se figer; **–r** *n.* frigorifique *m.*

freezing *n.* congelation *f.*; — *a.* très froid; **it's** — il gèle

freight *n.* cargaison *f.*, fret *m.*; — **train** train de marchandises *m.*; — *vt.* fréter; **–er** *n.* cargo *m.*

French *a. & n.* français *m.*; — **fried potatoes** pommes (de terre) frites *f. pl.*; — **door** *n.* porte vitrée à petits carreaux *f.*; — **dressing** *n.* sauce à l'huile (pour la salade) *f.*; — **horn** cor (d'harmonie) *m.*; — **toast** tranche de pain frite *f.*, pain perdu *m.*; — **window** porte-fenêtre *f.*; — *n.* français *m.*, langue française *f.*; **–man** *n.* Français *m.*; **–woman** *n.* Française *f.*

frenzy *n.* frénésie, fureur *f.*

frequency *n.* fréquence *f.*; — **modulation** *n.* modulation de fréquence *f.*

frequent *a.* fréquent; **–ly** *adv.* fréquemment; — *vt.* fréquenter; **–er** *n.* habitué *m.*

fresco *n.* fresque *f.*

fresh *a.* frais (fraîche); pur; vert; nouveau; impudent, effronté; — **air** grand air, plein air *m.*; — **water** eau douce *f.*; **–en** *vt.* rafraîchir; **–ness** *n.* fraîcheur *f.*; effronterie *f.*

freshman *n.* étudiant de première année *m.*

fresh-water *a.* d'eau douce

fret *n.* (mus.) touche, touchette *f.*; agitation *f.*; — *vi.* se faire du mauvais sang; **–ful** *a.* agité; irritable

friar *n.* moine *m.*

fricassee *n.* fricassée *f.*

friction *n.* friction *f.*, frottement *m.*; désaccord *m.*

Friday *n.* vendredi *m.*; **Good** — *a.* vendredi saint *m.*

fried *a.* frit; — **eggs** œufs sur le plat *m. pl.*

friend *n.* ami *m.*; amie *f.*; intime *m. & f.*; **make –s** se lier d'amitié; **–less** *a.* sans amis; **–liness** *n.* amitié, amabilité *f.*; **–ly** *a.* amical; d'amitié; sympathique; **–ship** *n.* amitié *f.*

frieze *n.* frise *f.*

frigate *n.* frégate *f.*

fright *n.* peur *f.*; épouvante *f.*; **–en** *vt.* effrayer, épouvanter, faire peur à; **–ened** *a.* apeuré; **be –ened** avoir peur; **–ening** *a.* effrayant; **–ful** *a.* épouvantable, effroyable; affreux, terrible

frigid *a.* froid; glacial; **–ity** *n.* frigidité *f.*

frill *n.* ornement *m.*; jabot *m.*; dentelle *f.*

fringe *n.* frange *f.*; bord *m.*, bordure *f.*; marge *f.*; — **benefit** avantage en dehors du salaire offert aux employés par la direction *m.* — *vt.* franger

frisk *vi.* sauter, bondir; — *vt.* (coll.) fouiller; **–y** *a.* vif

fritter *n.* beignet *m.*; friture *f.*; — *vt.*, — **away** gaspiller

frivolity *n.* frivolité *f.*

frivolous *a.* frivole

fro *adv.* en arrière; **go to and** — aller et venir

frock *n.* robe *f.*; — **coat** *n.* redingote *f.*

frog *n.* grenouille *f.*; **–man** *n.* homme-grenouille *m.*

frolic *n.* gaieté *f.*; fantaisie, folie *f.*; — *vi.* folâtrer; **–some** *a.* folâtre

from *prep.* de, par, dès, depuis, d'après

front *n.* façade *f.*; devant *m.*; (coll.) prête-nom *m.*; **in** — **of** devant; — *a.* de devant; premier; — *vi.* donner, faire face; **–al** *a.* frontal; **–age** *n.* façade *f.*; largeur (du côté de la rue, de la mer) *f.*

frontier *n.* frontière, limite *f.*

frontispiece *n.* frontispice *m.*

frost *n.* givre *m.*; — *vt.* glacer, couvrir de fondant; **–ed** *a.* givré; (cake) glacé; **–ed glass** verre dépoli *m.*; **–ing** *n.* fondant; **–y** *a.* couvert de givre

frostbite *n.* engelure *f.*

frostbitten *a.* gelé

froth *n.* écume, mousse *f.*; — *vi.* écumer, mousser; **–y** *a.* mousseux

frown *n.* froncement des sourcils *m.*; — *vi.* froncer les sourcils; — **on** désapprouver

frozen *a.* gelé, glacé, congelé

frugal *a.* frugal; **–ity** *n.* frugalité *f.*

fruit *n.* fruit *m.*; produit *m.*; — **seller** fruitier *m.*; — **stand** fruiterie *f.*; — *a.* fruitier; **–ful** *a.* fécond; **–less** *a.* stérile; vain

fruition *n.* maturation *f.*; jouissance *f.*

frustrate *vt.* frustrer, annuler; refouler

frustration *n.* refoulement *m.*

fry *n.* (fish) frai *m.*; friture *f.*; — *vt.* frire, faire frire; **–ing** *n.* friture *f.*; **–ing pan** *n.* poêle à frire *f.*

fuel *n.* carburant *m.*; aliment *m.*; — **gauge** indicateur d'essence *m.*; — **oil** gas-oil *m.*; — **tank** réservoir à essence

fugitive n. & a. fugitif m.

fulcrum n. point fixe m.; point d'appui m.

fulfil vt. accomplir, remplir; acquitter; réaliser; **-ment** n. accomplissement m.; réalisation f.

full a. plein; rempli; complet, comble; entier; at — speed à toute vitesse; — dress grande tenue f.; — blast en pleine activité; — house (poker) main pleine f.; — moon pleine lune f.; in — en entier; in — swing en activité, en train; **-ness** n. plénitude f.; ampleur f.; abondance f.; **-y** adv. tout à fait, entièrement

fullback n. arrière m.

full-blooded a. de race pur; robuste

full-blown a. en pleine fleur

full-fledged a. qui a tous ses titres

full-grown a. mûr

full-length a. en pied

fulminate vi. fulminer

fumble n. action maladroite f.; — vi. agir maladroitement; — vt. laisser tomber

fumbling a. maladroit

fume n. fumée, vapeur f.; — vt. & vi. fumer; être en colère

fumigate vi. faire des fumigations

fumigation n. fumigation f.

fuming a. fulminant

fun n. amusement m., gaieté f.; for — pour le sport; have — s'amuser; make — of se moquer de; **-ny** a. drôle; rigolo; amusant, comique; bizarre

function n. fonction f.; faculté f.; — vi. fonctionner, aller, marcher; — as servir de; **-al** a. fonctionnel; **-ary** n. fonctionnaire m.

fund n. fond, bien m.; réserve f.; **-s** pl. fonds m. pl.; argent m.

fundamental a. fondamental; de fond; **-s** n. pl. principes m. pl.

funeral n. funérailles, obsèques f. pl.; — director entrepreneur de pompes funèbres m.; — home, — parlor entreprise de pompes funèbres f.

funereal a. funèbre, lugubre, triste

fungicide a. & n. fongicide m.

fungus n. fongus m.

funicular a. & n. funiculaire m.

funnel n. entonnoir m.

fur n. fourrure f.; pelleterie f.; — coat manteau de fourrure m.; **-red** a. à fourrure; **-rier** n. fourreur, pelletier m.; **-ry** a. à fourrure, fourré

furbish vt. fourbir, polir

furious a. furieux; **-ly** adv. furieusement

furl vt. ployer; (naut.) ferler, serrer

fur-lined a. doublé de fourrure

furlong n. furlong m.

furlough n. congé m., permission f.; on — en permission; — vt. donner un congé (à)

furnace n. fourneau m.; (fig.) fournaise f.

furnish vt. fournir; meubler, garnir; **-ed** a. meublé, garni; **-ings** n. pl. mobilier m.; ameublement m.

furnisher n. fournisseur m.

furniture n. mobilier m.; meubles m. pl.; piece of — meuble m.

furor n. fureur f.; tumulte m.

furrow n. sillon m.; ride f.; guéret m.; — vt. sillonner; rider

further vt. avancer, aider; — adv. de plus, en outre; plus avant, au delà, plus loin; — a. supplémentaire, additionnel; without — ado sans plus de cérémonie; **-ance** n. avancement m.

furthermore adv. d'ailleurs, de plus

furthest a. le plus éloigné; — adv. le plus loin

furtive a. furtif; **-ly** adv. à la dérobée

fury n. furie, frénésie, rage, fureur f.

fuse vt. fondre; fusionner; — vi. fondre; se fusionner; — n. mèche f.; (elec.) fusible m.

fuselage n. fuselage m.

fusillade n. fusillade f.

fusion n. fusion, fonte f.

fuss n. fracas, embarras, bruit m.; — vi. se plaindre; causer de l'embarras; se donner de la peine; **-y** a. difficile, délicat; regardant

futile a. futile, frivole, vain

futility n. futilité, frivolité f.

future n. avenir m.; (gram.) futur m.; in the — à l'avenir; **-s** n. pl. (stocks) valeurs négociées à terme f. pl.; — a. futur

futurity n. futur, avenir m.

fuzz n. duvet, poil m.; **-y** a. duveté, couvert de poil; vague

G

gab n. langue f.; bavardage m.; have the gift of — avoir la langue bien pendue; — vi. bavarder; **-by** a. bavard

gable n. pignon, gable m.

gad vi., — about courir çà et là

gadget n. machin, outil m.; truc m.

Gaelic a. & n. gaélique m.

gaff n. harpon, crochet m.

gag n. bâillon m.; (coll.) blague f.; — vt. bâillonner; — vi. avoir envie de vomir

gaiety n. gaieté, joie f.

gaily adv. gaiement

gain vt. gagner; prendre; — weight prendre du poids; — n. gain, profit m.; **-ful** a. profitable

gainsay vt. contredire; nier

gait *n.* démarche, allure *f.*

gaiter *n.* guêtre *f.*

gala *n.* gala *m.*; — *a.* de gala

galaxy *n.* galaxie *f.*

gale *n.* gros vent *m.*

gall *n.* bile *f.*; rancune, malice *f.*; (coll.) toupet *m.*; — **bladder** vésicule biliaire *f.*; –**stones** calculs biliaires *m. pl.*; — *vt.* vexer, irriter

gallant *n. & a.* vaillant, brave *m.*; élégant, galant *m.*; –**ry** *n.* vaillance *f.*; galanterie *f.*

galleon *n.* galion *m.*

gallery *n.* galerie *f.*; corridor *m.*

galley *n.* galère *f.*; (print.) épreuve *f.*, placard *m.*; (naut.) cuisine *f.*; — **slave** *n.* galérien, forçat *m.*

Gallic *a.* gaulois; –**ism** *n.* gallicisme *m.*

gallivant *vi.* vagabonder, aller et venir, courir

gallop *n.* galop *m.* — *vi.* galoper; aller au galop

gallows *n.* gibet *m.*, potence *f.*

galore *adv.* en abondance, à profusion

galoshes *n. pl.* galoches *f. pl.*

galvanization *n.* galvanisation *f.*; zingage *m.*

galvanize *vt.* galvaniser

gamble *vi.* jouer; — *vt.*, — **away** perdre en jouant; — *n.* aventure *f.*; entreprise hasardeuse *f.*; –**r** *n.* joueur *m.*

gambling *n.* jeu *m.*; — **house** maison de jeu *f.*; tripot *m.*

gambol *n.* gambade *f.*; — *vi.* gambader

game *n.* divertissement, jeu *m.*; (sports) partie *f.*, match *m.*; (hunting) gibier *m.*; — **warden** garde champêtre *m.*; — *a.* brave, intrépide; blessé; estropié

gamecock *n.* coq de combat *m.*

gamekeeper *n.* garde-chasse *m.*

gamma *n.* gamma *m.*; — **globulin** globule gamma *m.*; — **ray** rayon gamma *m.*

gang *n.* troupe, bande *f.*; — *vi.* se grouper; — **up on** attaquer en masse

ganglion *n.* ganglion *m.*

gangplank *n.* passerelle *f.*

gangrene *n.* gangrène *f.*; — *vi.* se gangrener

gangrenous *a.* gangreneux

gangway *n.* passage *m.*; (naut.) passeavant *m.*

gantlet, gauntlet *n.* gantelet *m.*; (mil.) baguettes *f. pl.*; **run the** — courir les baguettes

gap *n.* ouverture, fente, brèche *f.*; lacune *f.*; trou *m.*

gape *vi.* bâiller; rester bouche bée

gaping *a.* béant

garage *n.* garage *m.*; — *vt.* garer; — **man** *n.* garagiste *m.*

garb *n.* vêtement *m.*; costume *m.*; — *vt.* vêtir, habiller

garbage *n.* ordures *f. pl.*; — **can**, — **pail** boîte à ordures, poubelle *f.*

garble *vt.* transformer, mutiler

garden *n.* jardin *m.*; — *vi.* jardiner; –**er** *n.* jardinier *m.*; –**ing** *n.* jardinage *m.*

gardenia *n.* camélia *m.*

gargle *n.* gargarisme *m.*; —*vt.* se gargariser

gargoyle *n.* gargouille *f.*

garish *a.* voyant, criard

garland *n.* guirlande *f.*; — *vt.* guirlander

garlic *n.* ail *m.*; **clove of** — gousse d'ail *f.*

garment *n.* vêtement *m.*

garner *vt.* amasser

garnish *n.* garniture *f.*, ornement *m.*; — *vt.* garnir, parer, orner

garnishee *vt.* saisir (par saisie-arrêt)

garotte *n.* garotte *f.*; — *vt.* garotter

garret *n.* mansarde *f.*; grenier *m.*

garrison *n.* garnison *f.*; — *vt.* mettre en garnison

garrulous *a.* babillard, bavard, loquace

garter *n.* jarretière, jarretelle *f.*; support-chaussettes *m.*; — **snake** *n.* couleuvre à collier *f.*

gas *n.* gaz *m.*; essence *f.*; — **heater** réchaud à gaz *m.*; — **jet** bec de gaz *m.*; — **main** conduit à gaz *m.*; — **mask** masque à gaz *m.*; — **meter** compteur à gaz *m.*; — **station** poste d'essence *m.*, station-service *f.*; — **stove** cuisinière à gaz *f.*; — **tank** réservoir à essence *m.*; — *vt.* gazer; –**eous** *a.* gazeux; –**ify** *vt.* gazéifier; –**sy** *a.* gazeux

Gascony *n.* Gascogne *f.*

gash *n.* coupure *f.*; entaille *f.*; — *vt.* couper; entailler

gasket *n.* garniture *f.*; obturateur de joint *m.*; (naut.) garcette *f.*

gaslight *n.* éclairage au gaz *m.*; bec de gaz *m.*

gasoline *n.* essence *f.*; — **tank** réservoir à essence; — **station** poste d'essence *m.*

gasp *n.* halètement *m.*; souffle *m.*; (hiccup) hoquet *m.*; **last** — dernière extrémité *f.*; — *vi.* haleter; –**ing** *a.* haletant; –**ing** *n.* halètement *m.*

gastric *a.* gastrique

gastritis *n.* gastrite *f.*

gastronomy *n.* gastronomie *f.*

gasworks *n.* usine à gaz *f.*

gate *n.* porte *f.*, portail *m.*, grille, barrière *f.*

gatehouse *n.* loge de garde *f.*

gatekeeper *n.* portier *m.*

gateway *n.* portail *m.*; (fig.) entrée *f.*

gather *vt.* cueillir; ramasser; assembler, réunir; froncer; conclure; — *vi.* s'assembler; s'accumuler; — *n.* froncis *m.*, fronce *f*.; –er *n*. ramasseur *m*.; –ing *n*. rassemblement *m*., réunion *f*.; cueillette, récolte *f*.

gaudy *a*. voyant, criard

gauge *n*. jauge *f*.; calibre *m*.; indicateur *m*.; largeur *f*.; — *vt*. jauger; mesurer; calibrer

Gaul *n*. (person) Gaulois *m*.; (country) Gaule *f*.

gaunt *a*. maigre, décharné

gauntlet *n*. gantelet *m*.; **run the** — courir les baguettes

gauze *n*. gaze *f*.

gavel *n*. marteau *m*.

gawk *vi*. regarder fixement; –y *a*. gauche

gay *a*. gai, joyeux

gaze *n*. yeux *m*. *pl*., regard, regard fixe *m*.; — *vi*., — **at** contempler, regarder fixement

gazetteer *n*. dictionnaire géographique *m*.

gear *n*. accoutrement, appareil, habillement *m*.; (mech.) engrenage *m*.; (auto) vitesse *f*.; **shift** –s changer de vitesse; **throw out of** — disloquer; débrayer; — *vt*. embrayer; gréer; — *vi*. (coll.) se préparer

gearshift *n*. changement de vitesse *m*.

gelatin *n*. gélatine *f*.

geld *vt*. châtrer; –ing *n*. cheval hongre *m*.

gem *n*. pierre précieuse *f*., bijou *m*.

gender *n*. genre *m*.

gene *n*. gène *m*.

genealogy *n*. généalogie *f*.

general *n*. général *m*.; — **staff** état-major *m*.; **brigadier** — général de brigade *m*.; **major** — général de division *m*.; **lieutenant** — général de corps d'armée *m*.; — **of the armies** maréchal *m*.; **in** — en général, généralement; — *a*. général; — **delivery** poste restante *f*.; –**ity** *n*. généralité *f*.; –**ization** *n*. généralisation *f*.; –**ize** *vi*. généraliser; –**ly** *adv*. en général, généralement; –**ship** *n*. tactique *f*.

generate *vt*. engendrer, produire; générer

generator *n*. générateur *m*., génératrice *f*.

generic *a*. générique

generosity *n*. générosité *f*.; libéralité *f*.

generous *a*. généreux; libéral

genesis *n*. genèse *f*.

genetics *n*. eugénique *f*.

Geneva *n*. Genève

genial *a*. agréable, affable, aimable; –ity *n*. amabilité, affabilité *f*.

genie *n*. génie *m*.

genitals *n*. *pl*. parties génitales *f*. *pl*.

genitive *n*. génitif *m*.

genius *n*. génie *m*.

Genoa *n*. Gênes *f*.

genteel *a*. honnête, poli; civil; élégant

gentile *n*. gentil *m*.

gentility *n*. politesse *f*.; élégance *f*.

gentle *a*. doux; –ness *n*. douceur *f*.

gentleman *n*. gentilhomme *m*.; homme honorable *m*.; monsieur *m*.; –'s **agreement** contrat verbal *m*.

gently *adv*. doucement, avec soin

gentry *n*. haute bourgeoisie *f*.; petite noblesse *f*.

genuflection *n*. génuflexion *f*.

genuine *a*. véritable, réel; authentique; –ness *n*. réalité, authenticité *f*.

genus *n*. genre *m*.

geodesic *a*. géodésique

geodesic dome *n*. dôme géodésique *m*.

geographic(al) *a*. géographique

geography *n*. géographie *f*.

geological *a*. géologique

geologist *n*. géologue *m*.

geology *n*. géologie *f*.

geometric(al) *n*. géométrique

geometry *n*. géométrie *f*.; **plane** — géométrie plane *f*.; **solid** — géométrie dans l'espace *f*.

geophysics *n*. géophysique *f*.

geopolitics *n*. géopolitique *f*.

geriatrics *n*. gérontologie *f*.

germ *n*. germe *m*.; microbe *m*.

German *a*. allemand; — **measles** rubéole *f*.

germane *a*. à propos

Germanic *a*. germanique; allemand

Germany *n*. Allemagne *f*.

germicide *n*. microbicide *m*.

germinate *vi*. germer, pousser

gerrymander *vt*. (pol.) truquer (une élection); — *n*. truquage (électoral) *m*.

gerund *n*. gérondif *m*.

gestation *n*. gestation *f*.

gesticulate *vi*. gesticuler

gesticulation *n*. gesticulation *f*.

gesture *n*. geste, signe *m*.; — *vi*. faire un signe; faire des gestes

get *vi*. devenir, se faire; aller, se mettre; — *vt*. obtenir, avoir, gagner, acquérir, s'emparer de, recevoir; atteindre; chercher, aller chercher; attraper; (coll.) comprendre; — **about** sortir; se répandre; — **a kick out of** (coll.) prendre plaisir à; — **along** circuler; procéder; se tirer d'affaire; — **a move on** (coll.) se dépêcher; — **around** contourner; aller partout; sortir; — **at** atteindre; vouloir dire; — **away** s'en aller; s'échapper; s'evader; se sauver; — **away with** s'en aller avec; échapper (sans être puni) —; **down** descendre; (coll.) décourager; — **even with** se venger sur; — **in**, — **into** entrer dans; — **in someone's hair** ennuyer, irriter; — **it over with** (coll.) en finir; — **off** descendre (de);

enlever; se tirer d'affaire, s'échapper; — on monter (sur); mettre; continuer; vieillir; — on with continuer; — out sortir; enlever, éliminer; — over passer; se remettre (de); faire comprendre; — rid of se défaire de; — the better de; triompher de; — through traverser, passer par; finir; — to arriver à; avoir l'occasion de; — together rassembler; se réunir; — up monter; se lever; arranger, dresser; — well se remettre, guérir

getaway n. démarrage m.; fuite f.

get-together n. réunion f.; soirée f.

geyser n. geyser m.

Ghana n. Ghana m.

ghastliness n. horreur f.

ghastly a. horrible, terrible, pâle, affreux

Ghent n. Gand m.

gherkin n. cornichon m.

ghost n. esprit, fantôme m.; ombre f.; — town ville abandonnée f.; — writer rédacteur secret m.; -ly a. de fantôme

ghoul n. goule f.

G.I. n. soldat; — a. fourni par l'armée

giant a. & n. géant m.

gibberish n. jargon m.

gibbet n. gibet m., potence f.

gibe n. raillerie, moquerie f.; — vt. & vi. railler, se moquer de

giblets n. pl. abattis m.

giddiness n. vertige, étourdissement m.; légèreté f.

giddy a. étourdi; frivole, léger

gift n. cadeau m.; don m.; talent m.; -ed a. doué

gig n. cabriolet m.; (naut.) canot m.

gigantic a. gigantesque

giggle vi. pousser des petits rires; — n. petit rire m.

giggling n. petits rires m. pl.

gigolo n. gigolo m.

gild vt. dorer; -ed a. doré; -ing n. dorure f.

gills n. pl. ouïes, branchies f. pl.

gilt n. dorure f.; — a. doré

gilt-edged a. doré sur tranche; d'excellente qualité; très sûr

gimlet n. perçoir m., vrille f.

ginger n. gingembre m.; — ale, — beer soda au gingembre m.; -ly adv. doucement, avec soin

gingerbread n. (genre de) pain d'épices m.

gingersnap n. gâteau sec au gingembre m.

gingham n. guingan m.

gird vt. ceindre, attacher; -er n. poutre f.

girdle n. gaine f., (garment) gaine f.; ceinture f.; — vt. ceindre, ceinturer

girl n. jeune fille f.; fille f.; — scout éclaireuse f.; -hood n. jeunesse f. (de jeune fille); -ish a. de jeune fille

girth n. sangle f.; circonférence f.; tour de la taille m.

gist n. fond m., substance f.

give vt. donner, présenter; — vi. donner; — account rendre compte; — away donner; révéler; — evidence témoigner; — in se rendre; — off émettre; — out distribuer; se rendre, s'épuiser; — over remettre; — up se rendre; — way faire place, reculer; — n. élasticité f.; — and take compromis m., concession mutuelle f.; -n a. donné, fixé; vu, étant donné; -n name prénom m.; -r n. donneur, donateur m.

give-and-take n. donnant donnant, libre échange m.

giving n. don m., donation f.

gizzard n. gésier m.

glacial a. glacial

glacier n. glacier m.

glad a. content; heureux; bien aise; joyeux; -den vt. réjouir; contenter; -ly adv. volontiers, avec plaisir; -ness n. contentement m.; joie f.

glade n. clairière f.

gladiator n. gladiateur m.

gladiolus n. glaïeul m.

glamor n. éclat, charme m.; -ous a. éclatant, ravissant

glance n. coup d'œil m.; at a — d'un coup d'œil; — vi. jeter un coup d'œil; — off ricocher

glancing a. oblique

gland n. glande f.; -ular a. glandulaire, glanduleux

glare n. lumière éblouissante f.; regard féroce m.; — vi. éblouir, briller; regarder d'un œil terrible

glaring a. éblouissant; évident; menaçant

glass n. verre m.; glace f., miroir m.; vitre f.; télescope m.; lorgnon m.; baromètre m.; cut — cristal taillé m.; magnifying — loupe f.; pane of — carreau m.; vitre f.; stained — verre de couleur m.; — blowing soufflage (du verre) m.; -es n. pl. lunettes f. pl.; -y a. vitreux, de verre; -ful n. verre m.

glassware n. verrerie f.

glaucoma n. glaucome m.

glaze n. vernis m.; dorure f.; fondant m.; glace f.; — vt. glacer; vernir; (glass) vitrer

glazier n. vitrier m.

gleam n. rayon m., clarté f.; lueur f.; reflet m.; — vi. rayonner, briller; (re)-luire; -ing a. luisant; rayonnant

glean vt. glaner; recueillir

glee n. joie, allégresse f.; chanson (à plus de deux voix) f.; — club chœur m.; -ful joyeux

glib *a.* coulant, glissant; délié

glide *vi.* couler, glisser, planer; — *n.* glissement *m.*; –**r** *n.* planeur *m.*

glimmer *n.* lueur (faible) *f.*; — *vi.* jeter une faible lueur, reluire

glimpse *vi.* apercevoir; entrevoir; — *n.* aperçu *m.*

glint *n.* étincellement *m.*; lueur *f.*; reflet *m.*; — *vi.* étinceler

glisten *vi.* briller, reluire, étinceler

glitter *vi.* étinceler, reluire; — *n.* éclat, lustre *m.*

gloaming *n.* crépuscule *m.*, brune *f.*

gloat *vi.*, triompher de; — **over** se réjouir de

global *a.* global

globe *n.* globe *m.*; sphère *f.*

globetrotter *n.* grand voyageur *m.*

globular *a.* globuleux

globule *n.* globule *m.*

gloom *n.* obscurité *f.*; tristesse *f.*; –**y** *a.* lugubre, triste, morne

glorify *vt.* glorifier

glorious *a.* glorieux, illustre

glory *n.* gloire *f.*; — **(in)** *vi.* se glorifier, s'enorgueillir (de)

gloss *n.* lustre, éclat *m.*; vernis *m.*; glose *f.*; — *vt.* gloser; rendre éclatant; — **over** mettre en ordre; fausser; –**iness** *n.* poli, lustre, brillant *m.*; –**y** *a.* poli; éclatant; brillant

glossary *n.* glossaire *m.*

glottal *a.*, — **stop** coup de glotte *m.*

glottis *n.* glotte *f.*

glove *n.* gant *m.*; — **store,** — **shop** ganterie *f.*; — *vt.* ganter

glow *n.* lueur *f.*; — *vi.* luire, briller; –**ing** *a.* rayonnant; luisant; rouge; chaleureux

glower *vi.* froncer le sourcil, regarder en menaçant

glowworm *n.* ver luisant *m.*

glucose *n.* glucose *m.*

glue *n.* colle *f.*; — *vt.* coller

glum *a.* sombre, mélancolique; –**ness** *n.* tristesse, mélancolie *f.*

glut *n.* abondance *f.*; satiété *f.*; — *vt.* rassasier; (com.) inonder

glutton *n.* glouton, gourmand *m.*; –**ous** *a.* glouton; –**y** *n.* gourmandise *f.*

glycerine *n.* glycérine *f.*

gnarled *a.* noueux

gnash *vt.* grincer (des dents)

gnat *n.* moucheron *m.*

gnaw *vt.* ronger; –**ing** *a.* rongeur; –**ing** *n.* rongement *m.*

go *n.* énergie *f.*; essai *m.*; succès *m.*; **have a** — **at** essayer; **make a** — of réussir à; **no** — échec *m.*; **on the** — actif; — *vi.* aller; s'en aller; marcher, fonctionner; — **against** s'opposer à; — **ahead** aller

au-devant, prévenir; continuer; — **astray** s'égarer; — **at** attaquer, approcher; — **away** s'en aller; — **back on** ne pas tenir (la parole donnée); — **by** agir selon; passer; croiser; — **down** descendre; tomber; — **for** aller chercher; (coll.) aimer; — **in for** participer à; faire; — **into** entrer dans; — **off** partir; s'en aller; — **on** continuer; se passer; — **out** sortir; — **over** se convertir; franchir; examiner; — **through** traverser; — **to it!** allez-y; — **under** succomber; submerger; — **with** accompagner; — **without** se passer de; **let** — **of** lâcher; –**ing** *a.* actif; courant; –**ing** *n.* départ *m.*; allée *f.*

goad *n.* aiguillon *m.*; — *vt.* aiguillonner, piquer, exciter

go-ahead *a.*, — **signal** signal d'aller en avant *m.*; permission d'agir *f.*

goal *n.* but *m.*

goalie, goalkeeper *n.* but *m.*

goat *n.* chèvre *f.*; bouc *m.*

goatee *n.* barbiche *f.*

gobble *vi.* gober; — **up** avaler; –**r** *n.* dinde *f.*; dindon *m.*

go-between *n.* entremetteur *m.*; intermédiaire *m.* & *f.*

goblet *n.* coupe *f.*

goblin *n.* lutin *m.*

God, god *n.* Dieu, dieu *m.*; — **forbid!** à Dieu ne plaise!; — **willing** plût à Dieu; **thank** — grâce à Dieu; –**less** *a.* imple; –**like** *a.* de dieu; –**liness** *n.* piété, dévotion *f.*; –**ly** *a.* pieux; de dieu

goddaughter *n.* filleule *f.*

goddess *n.* déesse *f.*

godfather *n.* parrain *m.*

God-fearing *a.* élevé dans la crainte de Dieu; craignant Dieu

Godforsaken *a.* perdu

godmother *n.* marraine *f.*

godsend *n.* aubaine *f.*

godson *n.* filleul *m.*

Godspeed *n.* succès *m.*

goggles *n. pl.* lunettes (d'aviateur) *f. pl.*

goiter *n.* goitre *m.*

gold *n.* or *m.*; — **brick** *n.* lingot d'or *m.*; — **dust** poussière d'or *f.*; — **leaf** or en feuille *m.*; — **rush** ruée vers l'or *f.*; — **standard** étalon d'or *m.*; –**en** *a.* d'or; –**en mean** juste milieu *m.*

goldfish *n.* poisson rouge *m.*

gold-plated *a.* plaqué d'or

goldsmith *n.* orfèvre *m.*

golf *n.* golf *m.*; — **course,** — **links** golf *m.*; — **club** club *m.*; — *vi.* jouer au golf; –**er** *n.* golfeur *m.*

gondola *n.* gondole *f.*

gondolier *n.* gondolier *m.*

gonorrhoea *n.* gonorrhée *f.*

good *a.* bon; valable; sage; for — pour toujours; **have a — time** s'amuser; **in — time** bien à temps; **it's no —** ça ne vaut pas la peine; ça ne vaut rien; **make —** réussir; indemnifier; **that's very — of you** c'est bien aimable à vous; **— morning** bonjour; **— afternoon** bonjour; **— evening** bonsoir; bonjour; **— night** bonsoir; (before retiring) bonne nuit; **— turn** service *m.*; bonne action *f.*; **— will** bonne volonté *f.*; (com.) clientèle *f.*; **— n.** bien *m.*; **—s** *pl.* biens *m. pl.*; possessions *f. pl.*; produits *m. pl.*; tissu *m.*; **—!,** —for you! *interj.* très bien!; bravo!, à la bonne heure!; **—ly** *a.* considérable; **—ness** *n.* bonté *f.*; **for —ness' sake** pour l'amour de Dieu; **my —ness** mon Dieu

good-by(e) *n.* adieu *m.*; **— interj.** adieu; au revoir

good-for-nothing *n.* vaurien *m.*

Good Friday *n.* vendredi saint *m.*

goodhearted *a.* charitable

good-humored *a.* de bonne humeur

goodies *f. pl.* (coll.) friandises *f. pl.*

good-looking *a.* beau (belle), joli

good-natured *a.* aimable, paisible; accomodant, obligeant

goon *n.* (coll.) terroriste professionnel *m.*

goose *n.* oie *f.*; **— flesh, — pimples** chair de poule *f.*; **— step** pas d'école *m.*, pas de l'oie *m.*

gooseberry *n.* groseille verte *f.*

gopher *n.* (genre de) rongeur *m.*

gore *n.* sang *m.*; pointe *f.*; piqûre *f.*; **— vt.** percer, piquer

gorge *n.* gorge *f.*; **— vi.** se gorger

gorgeous *a.* splendide; fastueux

gory *a.* ensanglanté, sanglant

gosling *n.* oison *m.*

gospel *n.* évangile *m.*

gossamer *n.* toile d'araignée *f.*; gaze *f.*; **— a.** ténu

gossip *n.* commère, causeuse *f.*; commérage *m.*; **— vi.** bavarder; faire des commérages

Gothic *a.* gothique; (arch.) ogival

gouge *n.* gouge *f.*; **— vt.** arracher; gouger

goulash *n.* ragoût *m.*

gourd *n.* calebasse *f.*; gourde *f.*

gourmet *n.* gourmet *m.*

gout *n.* goutte *f.*

govern *vt. & vi.* gouverner; diriger, régler; **—ess** *n.* institutrice *f.*; gouvernante *f.*; **—ment** *n.* gouvernement *m.*; **—mental** *a.* gouvernemental; **—or** *n.* gouverneur, préfet *m.*; **—orship** *n.* poste de gouverneur *m.*

gown *n.* robe *f.*; **—ed** *a.* en robe

grab *vt.* saisir, se saisir de; **— n.,** **— bag** sac à surprises *m.*

grace *n.* grâce, faveur *f.*, bienfait *m.*; (before meals) bénédicité *m.*; **— vt.** orner, honorer; **—ful** *a.* gracieux; **—fulness** *n.* grâce *f.* **—less** *a.* sans grâce

grace note (mus.) note d'agrément *f.*

gracious *a.* gracieux; favorable; **— interj.** mon Dieu; **—ness** *n.* grâce *f.*; bienveillance *f.*

grade *n.* grade, rang *m.*; pente *f.*; montée *f.*; (educ., mark) note *f.*; (educ., class) classe *f.*; **— crossing** passage à niveau *m.*; **— school** école primaire *f.*; **— vt.** niveler; évaluer; noter; graduer

gradient *a. & n.* montée, descente *f.*

gradual *a.* graduel

graduate *vt.* graduer; décerner un diplôme; **— vi.** recevoir un diplôme; **— n.** verre gradué *m.*; (educ.) étudiant diplômé *m.*; ancien élève *m.*

graduation *n.* graduation *f.*; décernement d'un diplôme *m.*; réception d'un diplome *f.*

graft *vt.* greffer; **— n.** greffe *f.*; (pol.) pot-de-vin *m.*; corruption *f.*

graham wheat *n.* blé entier *m.*; **— bread** *n.* pain bis *m.*

grain *n.* grain, blé *m.*; (wood) grain *m.*; **— alcohol** *n.* alcool ordinaire *n.*; **— elevator** *n.* élévateur à grain *m.*; **against the —** à rebrousse-poil; **— vt.** grainer, veiner

gram *n.* gramme *m.*

grammar *n.* grammaire *f.*; **— school** école primaire *f.*; **—ian** *n.* grammairien *m.*

grammatical *a.* grammatical

Granada *n.* Grenade *f.*

granary *n.* grenier *m.*

grand *a.* grand; sublime; illustre; **— jury** jury d'accusation *m.*; **— larceny** grand larcin *m.*; **— opera** opéra *m.*; **— piano** piano à queue *m.*; **— slam** (cards) grand chelem *m.*

grandchild *n.* petit-enfant *m.*

granddaughter *n.* petite-fille *f.*

grandee *n.* grand *m.*

grandeur *n.* grandeur *f.*

grandfather *n.* grand-père, aïeul *m.*

grandiose *a.* grandiose

grandiloquent *a.* pompeux, emphatique

grandmother *n.* grand'mère *f.*

grandnephew *n.* petit-neveu

grandniece *n.* petite-nièce *f.*

grandparents *n.* grands-parents *m. pl.*

grandson *n.* petit-fils *m.*

grandstand *n.* gradins *m. pl.*, tribune *f.*

grange *n.* ferme, métairie *f.*; grange *f.*

granite *n.* granit *m.*

grant *n.* concession *f.*; (educ.) bourse *f.*;

subvention *f.*; — *vt.* accorder; décerner; octroyer; reconnaître; **take for** —ed supposer, présumer

granular *a.* granulaire

granulate *vt.* granuler; —ed **sugar** sucre en poudre *m.*

grape *n.* raisin *m.*; —**shot** (mil.) mitraille *f.*; **bunch of** —s *n.* grappe de raisin(s) *f.*

grapefruit *n.* grappefruit *m.*, pamplemousse *m.*

graph *n.* courbe *f.*; —**ology** *n.* graphologie *f.*; — *vt.* représenter en courbe; —**ic** *a.* graphique; vivant

graphite *n.* graphite *m.*; mine de plomb *f.*

grapple *vi.* lutter; — **with** (fig.) s'attaquer à

grasp *n.* prise *f.*; connaissance *f.*; **(with)in one's** — entre ses mains; à sa portée; — *vt.* prendre, saisir; comprendre; —**ing** *a.* avide

grass *n.* herbe *f.*, gazon *m.*; **blade of** — brin d'herbe *m.*; —**y** *a.* couvert d'herbe

grasshopper *n.* sauterelle, cigale *f.*

grass roots *a.* populaire, du peuple

grate *n.* grille *f.*, treillis *m.*; foyer *m.*; gril *m.*; — *vt.* râper; (sound) grincer; — *vi.* choquer, ennuyer; —**r** *n.* râpe *f.*

grateful *a.* reconnaissant; —**ness** *n.* reconnaissance *f.*

gratification *n.* gratification, récompense *f.*; satisfaction *f.*

gratified *a.* content, satisfait

gratify *vt.* gratifier, récompenser; satisfaire; —**ing** *a.* agréable

grating *n.* grille *f.*; (sound) grincement *m.*; — *a.* ennuyant, choquant

gratis *adv.* gratuitement, gratis

gratitude *n.* reconnaissance *f.*

gratuitous *a.* gratuit

gratuity *n.* gratification *f.*; pourboire *m.*

grave *n.* fosse *f.*, tombeau *m.*; — *a.* grave; sérieux; — *vt.* graver; —**ness** *n.* gravité *f.*

gravedigger *n.* fossoyeur *m.*

gravel *n.* gravier *m.*; (med.) gravelle *f.*

gravestone *n.* pierre tombale *f.*

graveyard *n.* cimetière *m.*

gravitate *vi.* graviter

gravitation *n.* gravitation *f.*

gravity *n.* gravité *f.*

gravy *n.* sauce *f.*; — **boat** saucière *f.*

gray *a.* gris; —**ish** *a.* grisâtre; **turn** — (hair) grisonner

gray-haired *a.* aux cheveux gris

graze *vt.* faire paître; effleurer, raser; — *vi.* paître

grazing, grazing ground *n.* pâturage *m.*

grease *n.* graisse *f.*; — *vt.* graisser; — **cup** *n.* godet graisseur *m.*

grease gun *n.* graisseur *m.*

grease paint *n.* fard *m.*; crayon gras *m.*

greasy *a.* graisseux; gras

great *a.* grand; gros; éminent; **a** — **deal, a** — **many** beaucoup; **to a** — **extent** en grande partie; —**ly** *adv.* grandement, fort, beaucoup; —**ness** *n.* grandeur *f.*; pouvoir *m.*; force *f.*

greatcoat *n.* capote *f.*

great-grandchild *n.* arrière-petit-fils *m.*, arrière-petite-fille *f.*

great-grandfather *n.* arrière-grand-père *m.*

great-grandmother *n.* arrière-grand'mère *f.*

Grecian *a.* grec (grecque)

Greece *n.* Grèce *f.*

greed *n.* avidité, cupidité *f.*; —**iness** *n.* cupidité *f.*; —**y** *a.* avide, cupide

Greek *n. & a.* Grec (Grecque)

green *a.* vert; frais, récent; jeune; novice; — **light** (coll.) voie libre *f.*; — **thumb** (coll.) capacité de cultiver un jardin avec succès; — *n.* vert *m.*; verdure *f.*; (golf) pelouse d'arrivée *f.*; —s *n. pl.* légumes verts *m. pl.*; —**ery** *n.* verdure *f.*; —**ish** *a.* verdâtre; —**ness** *n.* vert *m.*; verdeur *f.*; verdure *f.*

green-eyed *a.* aux yeux verts; (coll.) jaloux

greengage *n.* reine-claude *f.*

greenhouse *n.* serre *f.*

Greenland *n.* Groënland *m.*; **Greenland** *m.*

greet *vt. & vi.* saluer; —**ing** *n.* salut *m.*

gregarious *a.* grégaire, qui vit en troupe

Gregorian *a.* grégorien

grenade *n.* grenade *f.*

grenadine *n.* grenadine *f.*

grid *n.* gril *m.*; grillage *m.*; — **line** ligne de quadrillage *f.*

griddle *n.* poêle plate sans bords *f.*

gridiron *n.* gril *m.*; terrain de football *m.*

grief *n.* chagrin, regret *m.*, affliction, douleur *f.*

grief-stricken *a.* accablé, affligé (de douleur)

grievance *n.* grief, tort *m.*; abus *m.*

grieve *vt.* chagriner, affliger; — *vi.* se chagriner, s'affliger, se désoler

grievous *a.* grave, affligeant; horrible

grill *n.* gril *m.*; **mixed** — grillade *f.*; — *vt.* cuire sur le gril; faire **griller**; (coll.) cuisiner

grim *a.* renfrogné, hideux, effrayant; sérieux; lugubre

grimace *n.* grimace *f.*; — *vi.* grimacer

grime *n.* crasse *f.*; saleté; poussière de charbon *f.*

grimy *a.* noirci, sale; (face) barbouillé

grin *n.* sourire *m.*; — *vi.* sourire

grind *vt.* moudre; broyer; aiguiser; — *n.*

(coll.) tâche désagréable *f.*; broiement *m.*; –er *n.* broyeur *m.*; **organ** –er joueur d'orgue de Barbarie *m.*; –ing *n.* meulage *m.*; (sound) grincement *m.*

grindstone *n.* pierre à aiguiser *f.*; meule *f.*

grip *n.* empoignement *m.*; griffe *f.*; prise *f.*; levier *m.*; pouvoir *m.*; valise *f.*; — *vt.* saisir; serrer; fasciner; –ping *a.* fascinant; passionnant

gripe *n.* plainte, réclamation *f.*; — *vi.* se plaindre, faire des réclamations

grisly *a.* horrible, hideux

grist *n.* blé à moudre *m.*; profit *m.*

gristle *n.* cartilage *m.*

gristly *a.* cartilagineux

grit *vt.* se grincer (les dents); — *n.* grès *m.*; sable *m.*, poussière sablonneuse *f.*; (coll.) courage *m.*; –s *n. pl.* (food) gruau *m.*; –ty *a.* sablonneux

grizzled *a.* grisonnant

grizzly *a.* grisonnant; — bear ours gris *m.*

groan *n.* gémissement *m.*; — *vi.* gémir, soupirer; –ing *n.* gémissement *m.*

grocer *n.* épicier *m.*; marchand de comestibles *m.*; –y *n.* épicerie *f.*; magasin d'alimentation *m.*; –ies *n. pl.* épicerie *f.*; alimentation *f.*; provisions *f. pl.*

grog *n.* grog *m.*; –gy *a.* étourdi, ébloui; ivre, gris

groin *n.* aine *f.*; (arch.) arête *f.*

groom *n.* palefrenier *m.*; marié *m.*; — *vt.* soigner; (horse) panser

groove *n.* rainure *f.*; sillon *m.*; — *vt.* rainer, rainurer

grope *vi.* tâtonner, aller à tâtons

groping *a.* tâtonnant; — *n.* tâtonnement *m.*; –ly *adv.* à tâtons

gross *n.* grosse *f.*; — *a.* gros, épais; grossier; rude, brut; –ness *n.* grossièreté *f.*; –ly *adv.* grossièrement, fortement

grotesque *a.* grotesque

grotto *n.* grotte *f.*

grouch *n.* personne maussade *f.*; — *vi.* se plaindre; –y *a.* maussade

ground *n.* terrain, champ *m.*; terre *f.*; pays *m.*; lieu *m.*; raison *f.*; (elec.); –s *n. pl.* lie *f.*; raison, cause *f.*; prise de terre *f.*; — **floor** rez-de-chaussée *m.*; — *vt.* mettre à terre; garder à terre; établir une prise de terre; fonder; –ing *n.* (elec.) mise à terre *f.*; (avi.) période dans laquelle on refuse la permission de voler *f.*; –less *a.* sans fondement; — **breaking** premiers coups de pioche faits au début d'une entreprise de construction *m. pl.*

groundwork *n.* fondement *m.*; travail préliminaire *m.*

group *n.* groupe *m.*; cercle *m.*; — *vt.* grouper; — *vi.* se grouper; –ing *n.* groupement *m.*

grouse *n.* coq de bruyère *m.*; — *vi.* grogner, ronchonner

grove *n.* bocage, bosquet *m.*

grovel *vi.* ramper; se vautrer

grow *vt.* cultiver; faire pousser; — *vi.* croître, pousser; grandir; augmenter; s'élargir, se développer; devenir, se faire; — **from** prendre racine dans; prendre naissance dans; — **old** vieillir; — **up** grandir, mûrir; –er *n.* cultivateur *m.*; –ing *a.* croissant; grandissant; –ing *n.* croissance *f.*; culture *f.*; développement *m.*; –th *n.* croissance *f.*, poussée *f.*; développement *m.*; (med.) excroissance *f.*; tumeur *f.*

growl *n.* grondement *m.*; — *vi.* gronder

grub *n.* larve *f.*; ver *m.*; (coll.) soupe, nourriture *f.*; — *vi.* piocher; bêcher; creuser; –by *a.* sale

grudge *n.* rancune *f.*; envie *f.*; **bear a —against**, have a — **against** en vouloir à; — *vt.* refuser; envier

grudgingly *adv.* à contre-cœur

gruel *n.* gruau *m.*, bouillie *f.*

grueling *a.* écrasant, épuisant

gruesome *a.* lugubre, terrifiant

gruff *a.* refrogné, brusque; –ness *n.* brusquerie *f.*

grumble *vi.* grogner, grommeler

grumbling *a.* grognon; — *n.* grognonnement *m.*

grumpy *a.* maussade

grunt *n.* grognement *m.*; — *vi.* grogner

Guadeloupe *n.* Guadeloupe *f.*

guarantee *n.* garant *m.*; garantie, caution *f.*; — *vt.* garantir; –d *a.* (com.) avec garantie

guarantor *n.* garant *m.*

guard *n.* (person) garde *m.*; garde, protection *f.*; **advance** — avant-garde *f.*; **on** — en garde, prévenu; (mil.) en faction, de faction; — *vt.* garder, protéger; — **against** se protéger contre; –ed *a.* voilé, circonspect; –ian *n.* tuteur *m.*; tutrice *f.*; –ian *a.* gardien; –ianship *n.* tutelle *f.*; –rail *n.* garde-fou, parapet *m.*

guardhouse *n.* corps-de-garde *m.*; guérite *f.*; prison militaire *f.*

Guatemala *n.* Guatémala *m.*

guava *n.* goyave *f.*

gubernatorial *a.* de gouverneur

guerila *n.* partisan *m.*; — **warfare** guerre de guerillas, guerre de partisans *f.*

guess *n.* conjecture *f.*; — *vt. & vi.* deviner, conjecturer; — *vt.* croire, penser, estimer

guesswork *n.* conjecture *f.*

guest *n.* hôte, convive, invité *m.*

guffaw *n.* gros rire *m.*

Guiana *n.* Guyane *f.*

guidance *n.* conseils *m. pl.*; **gouverne** *f.*; orientation *f.*

guide *n.* guide, conducteur *m.*; exemple *m.*; — *vt.* guider, conduire, mener; **–d** *a.*, **–d missile** engin téléguidé *m.*

guidebook *n.* guide *m.*

guidepost *n.* poteau indicateur *m.*, borne *f.*

guiding *a.* directeur

guild *n.* société, compagnie *f.*

guile *n.* fourberie, tromperie, ruse *f.*; artifice *m.* **–ful** *a.* rusé; **–less** *a.* simple, sans artifice

guillotine *n.* guillotine *f.*; — *vt.* guillotiner

guilt *n.* crime *m.*, culpabilité, faute *f.*; **–less** *a.* innocent; **–y** *a.* coupable

guinea *n.* guinée *f.*; — **hen** *n.* poule de Guinée *f.*; — **pig** cochon d'Inde *m.*; sujet d'une expérience *m.*

Guinea *n.* Guinée *f.*

guise *n.* manière, *f.*; extérieur *m.*; **in the — of** sous la forme de; sous l'apparence de

guitar *n.* guitare *f.*

gulch *n.* ravin *m.*

gulf *n.* golfe *m.*; gouffre *m.*

Gulf Stream *n.* Gulf-Stream *m.*

gull *n.* mouette *f.*

gullet *n.* gosier *m.*, gorge *f.*

gullibility *n.* crédulité *f.*

gullible *a.* facile à duper, crédule

gully *n.* ravin *m.*

gulp *n.* gorgée *f.*; trait *m.*; — *vt.* avaler (avec avidité)

gum *n.* gomme *f.*; (anat.) gencive *f.*; **chewing —** chewing gum *m.*; — **tree** gommier *m.*; — *vt.* gommer; **–med** *a.* gommé **–my** *a.* gommeux

gumdrop *n.* pâte de fruits *f.*; loukoum *m.*

gumption *n.* esprit *m.*, cervelle, initiative *f.*

gun *n.* fusil *m.*; arme à feu *f.*; canon *m.*; pistolet *m.*; revolver *m.*; **–ner** *n.* canonnier *m.*; **–nery** *n.* tir *m.* — **barrel** canon *m.*

gunboat *n.* canonnière *f.*

gunfire *n.* fusillade, canonnade *f.*; coups de feu *m. pl.*

gunman *n.* gangster *m.*; bandit *m.*

gunny sack *n.* sac de serpillière *m.*

gunpowder *n.* poudre à canon *f.*

gunshot *n.* coup de fusil, coup de canon *m.*; portée de fusil, portée de canon *f.*

gunsmith *n.* armurier *m.*

gunwale *n.* plat-bord *m.*

gurgle *vi.* glousser; glou-glouter; murmurer; — *n.* gloussement *m.*; glou-glou *m.*; murmure *m.*

gush *n.* écoulement, flux *m.*; jaillissement *m.*; — *vi.* jaillir; ruisseler; **–er** *n.* puits à pétrole *m.* (dont le pétrole jaillit à flots); **–ing** *a.* jaillissant; chaleureux

gust *n.* bouffée de vent *f.*; **–y** *a.* orageux

gusto *n.* goût *m.*; entrain *m.*

gut *n.* boyau, intestin *m.*; **–s** *pl.* (coll.) toupet *m.*; courage *m.*; — *vt.* vider, étriper; détruire, laisser en ruines

gutter *n.* gouttière *f.*, ruisseau *m.*; (coll.) rue *f.*

guttersnipe *n.* gamin *m.*

guttural *a.* guttural

guzzle *vt. & vi.* boire avidement

gym, gymnasium *n.* gymnase *m.*

gymnastic *a.* gymnastique; **–s** *n. pl.* gymnastique *f.*

gynecologist *n.* gynécologue *m.*

gynecology *n.* gynécologie *f.*

gypsum *n.* gypse *m.*

gypsy *n.* Bohémien *m.*, (fig.) bohème *m. & f.*; — *a.* bohémien, de bohème

gyrate *vi.* tourner

gyration *n.* gyration, giration *f.*

gyrocompass *n.* gyro-compas *m.*

gyroscope *n.* gyroscope *m.*

H

haberdasher *n.* marchand de vêtements pour hommes *m.*; **–y** *n.* vêtements d'homme *m. pl.*

habit *n.* habitude, coutume *f.*; disposition *f.*; habit, habillement, vêtement *m.*; **break oneself of the — of** se déshabituer de; **get into the — of** s'habituer à; **–ual** *a.* habituel; **–ually** *adv.* d'habitude, d'ordinaire; **–uate** *vt.* habituer, accoutumer

habitation *n.* demeure, habitation *f.*

hack *n.* (blow) entaille *f.*; (cab) fiacre *m.*; (writer) écrivassier *m.*; — *vt. & vi.* hacher, donner des coups de hache

hackneyed *a.* banal, trivial

haddock *n.* merluche *f.*

hag *n.* sorcière *f.*; furie *f.*

haggard *a.* hagard, farouche

haggle *vi.* marchander

Hague *n.*, **The —** La Haye *f.*

hail *n.* grêle *f.*; — *vt.* saluer; héler; — *vi.* (weather) grêler; — **from** être originaire de; — *interj.* salut!

hailstone *n.* grêlon *m.*

hailstorm *n.* tempête de grêle *f.*

hair *n.* cheveu *m.*, cheveux *m. pl.*; poil *m.*; fil *m.*; **split –s** couper les cheveux en quatre; **–less** *a.* chauve, sans cheveux; sans poil; **–y** *a.* poilu; velu; chevelu

hairbrush *n.* brosse à cheveux *f.*

haircut *n.* coupe (des cheveux) *f.*

hairdo *n.* coiffure *f.*

hairdresser *n.* coiffeur *m.*, coiffeuse *f.*; —'s salon de coiffure *m.*

hairpin *n.* épingle à cheveux *f.*; — **turn** lacet *m.*

hair-raising *a.* terrifiant

hairsplitting *n.* ergoterie *f.*

Haiti *n.* Haïti *f.*

hale *a.* sain, vigoureux

half *n.* moitié *f.*; demi *m.*; — *a.* demi; — **a dozen** une demi-douzaine *f.*; — **an hour** une demi-heure *f.*; — **fare** demi-place *f.*; — *adv.* à demi, à moitié

half-breed *n.* métis *m.*

halfhearted *a.* (fait) sans enthousiasme

half-hour *n.* demi-heure *f.*

half-light *n.* pénombre *f.*

half-mast *n.*, **at** — en berne

half-moon *n.* demi-lune *f.*

half note (mus.) blanche *f.*

half-turn *n.* demi-révolution *f.*

halfway *adv.* à mi-chemin

half-wit *n.* idiot *m.*; niais *m.*; **-ted** *a.* faible d'esprit; idiot; niais

halibut *n.* flétan *m.*

halitosis *n.* mauvaise haleine *f.*

hall *n.* vestibule *m.*; corridor *m.*; couloir *m.*; salle *f.*

hallmark *n.* marque, estampille *f.*

hallow *vt.* consacrer, bénir; **All Hallows** *n.* la Toussaint *f.*

Halloween *n.* veille de la Toussaint *f.*

hallucinate *vt.* halluciner

hallway *n.* corridor *m.*; couloir *m.*

halo *n.* halo *m.*, auréole *f.*

halt *n.* halte *f.*; arrêt *m.*; — *vi.* halter, faire halte; s'arrêter; —! halte!; **-ing** *a.* hésitant; **-ingly** *adv.* en hésitant

halter *n.* corde *f.*; licou *m.*

halve *vt.* diviser en deux (parties)

ham *n.* jambon *m.*; (coll.) cabotin *m.*; radio amateur *m.*; — **and eggs** œufs au jambon *m. pl.*

Hamburg *n.* Hambourg

hamburger *n.* viande hâchée *f.*; sandwich à la viande hâchée *m.*

hamlet *n.* hameau *m.*

hammer *n.* marteau *m.*; (gun) chien *m.*; — *vt.* marteler; forger; travailler

hammock *n.* hamac *m.*

hamper *n.* panier *m.*; — *vt.* embarrasser, gêner

hamstring *n.* tendon du jarret *m.*; — *vt.* couper le jarret à; rendre inactif, rendre incapable d'action

hand *n.* main *f.*; (watch) aiguille *f.*; (worker) ouvrier *m.*; (help) coup de main *m.*; (applause) applaudissements *m. pl.*; (writing) écriture *f.*; (measure) palme *f.*; (cards) jeu *m.*, partie *f.*; (naut.) matelot *m.*; **at** — sous la main;

at first — de première main; **be on** — être présent; (com.) être en caisse; **by** — à la main; **change** —s changer de possesseur; **from** — **to** — de main en main; **get out of** — échapper au contrôle; —s **down** sans peine; —s **off!** *interj.* n'y touchez pas!; —s **up!** *interj.* haut les mains!; **in** — en main; **lend a** (helping) — donner un coup de main; — **of God** doigt de Dieu *m.*; **on** — disponible; **old** — vétéran *m.*; **on the one** — d'un côté; **on the other** — de l'autre côté, d'autre part; **shake** —s (with) serrer la main (à); **upper** — dessus *m.*; — *vt.* donner; livrer; présenter; — **down** prononcer (un jugement); transmettre; — **in** remettre; — **out** distribuer; — **over** céder; — **up** passer en haut; **-iness** *n.* habileté *f.*; **-y** *a.* habile; utile

handbag *n.* sac à main *m.*

handball *n.* pelote *f.*

handbill *n.* affiche *f.*, prospectus *m.*

handbook *n.* manuel *m.*

handclasp *n.* poignée de main *f.*

handcuff *vt.* mettre les menottes à; (fig.) lier les mains à, empêcher d'agir; —s *n. pl.* menottes *f. pl.*

handful *n.* poignée *f.*

handicap *n.* handicap *m.*; incapacité *f.*; — *vt.* handicaper; incapaciter

handicraft *n.* métier *m.*; artisanat *m.*

handiwork *n.* travail à la main *m.*; ouvrage *m.*

handkerchief *n.* mouchoir *m.*

handle *n.* manche *m.*, anse *f.*; queue (d'une poêle) *f.*; poignée *f.*; — *vt.* manier, traiter; diriger

handle bar *n.* guidon *m.*

handling *n.* maniement *m.*; manutention *f.*; traitement *m.*; direction *f.*

handmade *a.* fait à la main

handout *n.* aumône *f.*

hand-picked *a.* soigneusement choisi

handrail *n.* rampe *f.*

handshake *n.* poignée de main *f.*

handsome *a.* beau, élégant; généreux; **-ness** *n.* beauté *f.*; générosité *f.*

hand-to-hand *adv.* corps à corps

hand-to-mouth *a.* au jour le jour

handwriting *n.* écriture *f.*

handwritten *a.* manuscrit

handyman *n.* bricoleur, homme à tout faire *m.*

hang *vt.* pendre; suspendre; tapisser; — *vi.* être pendu; être suspendu; être en suspens; balancer; dépendre; — **around** fréquenter; flâner; — **on** se cramponner; subsister; — **out** (coll.) se rassembler; demeurer; — **up** pendre;

(telephone) raccrocher; — *n.*, get the — of comprendre; s'habituer à, se faire à; **-er** *n.* portemanteau *m.*; **-ing** *n.* tenture *f.*; (human beings) pendaison *f.*

hangar *n.* hangar *m.*

hangdog *a.* honteux, contrit

hangman *n.* bourreau *m.*

hangnail *n.* envie *f.*

hangout *n.* repaire, lieu fréquenté *m.*; rendez-vous *m.*

hang-over *n.* gueule de bois *f.*

hank *n.* botte *f.*; écheveau *m.*

hanker *vi.* soupirer (après); **-ing** *n.* désir, souhait *m.*, envie *f.*

hansom *n.* cabriolet de place *m.*

haphazard *n.* chance *f.*; — *a.* fortuit, accidentel

hapless *a.* malheureux, infortuné

happen *vi.* arriver, avoir lieu, se passer; **-ing** *n.* événement *m.*

happiness *n.* bonheur *m.*, félicité *f.*

happy *a.* heureux; content; propice

happy-go-lucky *a.* sans souci

harangue *vt.* haranguer; — *vi.* faire un discours; — *n.* discours *m.*, harangue *f.*

harass *vt.* tourmenter; harceler; **-ment** *n.* harcèlement *m.*

harbinger *n.* avant-coureur *m.*

harbor *n.* port *m.*; — *vt.* héberger; entretenir; — **master** *n.* capitaine de port *m.*

hard *a.* dur; difficile; **drive a — bargain** conclure un marché très avantageux; — **and fast** établi, inébranlable; — **cash** espèces sonnantes et trébuchantes *f. pl.*; — **cider** cidre fermenté *m.*; — **coal** anthracite *m.*; — **labor** travaux forcés *m. pl.*; — **liquor** *n.* alcool *m.*; whisky *m.*; — **luck** guigne *f.*; **be — of hearing** avoir l'oreille dure; — **to please** exigeant; regardant; — **up** pauvre; — *adv.* fort; dur; ferme; fixement; **try — bien essayer;** **—en** *vt.* durcir; **—en** *vi.* se durcir; **-ly** *adv.* à peine; **ne . . . . guère;** presque; **-ness** *n.* dureté *f.*; difficulté *f.*; **-ship** *n.* difficulté, pénurie *f.*

hard-earned *a.* bien gagné

hardhearted *a.* dur, sans compassion

hardihood *n.* hardiesse, audace *f.*

hardiness *n.* hardiesse *f.*

hardly *adv.* à peine; — **ever** presque jamais

hardtack *n.* biscuit de mer *m.*

hardware *n.* quincaillerie *f.*; — **store** quincaillerie *f.*

hardwood *n.* bois dur *m.*

hard-working *a.* industrieux, assidu

hardy *a.* hardi, brave, courageux; robuste

harebrained *a.* écervelé

harelip *n.* bec de lièvre *m.*

harem *n.* harem, sérail *m.*

hark *vt. & vi.* écouter; **—l** *interj.* écoutez!

harlequin *n.* arlequin *m.*

harlot *n.* prostituée *f.*

harm *n.* tort, mal *m.*; dommage *m.*; malheur *m.*; — *vt.* faire du mal à; **-ful** *a.* dangereux; nuisible; **-less** *a.* innocent; sans danger

harmonica *n.* harmonica *m.*

harmonious *a.* harmonieux

harmonize *vt.* rendre harmonieux; accorder; — *vi.* être d'accord, s'accorder

harmony *n.* harmonie *f.*

harness *n.* harnais *m.*; — *vt.* (en)harnacher; (fig.) maîtriser

harp *n.* harpe *f.*; — **on** revenir sur, rabâcher; **-ist** *n.* joueur de harpe *m.*, harpiste *m. & f.*

harpoon *n.* harpon *m.*; — *vt.* harponner

harpsichord *n.* clavecin *m.*

harpy *n.* harpie *f.*

harrow *n.* herse *f.*; — *vt.* herser; torturer; **-ing** *a.* terrifiant

harry *vt.* harceler

harsh *a.* rude; âpre; sévère; dur; **-ness** *n.* sévérité *f.*; rudesse *f.*

harum-scarum *a.* écervelé

harvest *n.* moisson, récolte *f.*; — *vt.* moissonner; **-er** *n.* moissonneur *m.*; (machine) moissonneuse *f.*

has-been *n.* (coll.) personne qui n'est plus en vue *f.*; vedette qui n'est plus à la mode *f.*

hash *n.* hachis *m.*; (fig.) gâchis *m.*; — *vt.* hacher

hasp *n.* loquet *m.*; moraillon *m.*

hassock *n.* pouf *m.*

haste *n.* hâte, diligence *f.*; **in — à la hâte; -n** *vi.* se dépêcher; **-n** *vt.* dépêcher, hâter

hastily *adv.* à la hâte; précipitamment; trop vite; sans trop y penser

hastiness *n.* hâte, précipitation *f.*

hasty *a.* hâtif; prompt, précipité

hat *n.* chapeau *m.*; **opera — chapeau claque** *m.*; **top — chapeau haut de forme** *m.*; **-less** sans chapeau; (woman) en cheveux; **-ter** *n.* chapelier *m.*

hatband *n.* ruban (de chapeau) *m.*

hatbox *n.* carton de modiste *m.*; (luggage) étui à chapeau *m.*

hatch *n.* couvée *f.*; guichet *m.*; (naut.) panneau *m.*; — *vt. & vi.* couver; tramer

hatchet *n.* hachette *f.*

hate *n.* haine *f.*; — *vt.* haïr, détester; **-ful** *a.* haïssable

hatpin *n.* épingle à chapeau *f.*

hat rack *n.* porte-chapeaux *m.*

hatred *n.* haine, détestation *f.*

haughtiness *n.* hauteur *f.*, orgueil *m.*

haughty *a.* hautain, orgueilleux

haul *n.* action de tirer *f.*; trait *m.*; (coll.) coup *m.*; — *vt.* tirer, traîner, haler

haunch *n.* hanche *f.*

haunt *n.* lieu fréquenté *m.*; retraite *f.*; — *vt.* hanter, fréquenter, visiter; –ed *a.* fréquenté par des revenants; –ing *a.* obsédant

Havana *n.* La Havane *f.*

have *vt.* avoir, posséder; contenir; — on porter, être vêtu de; — something done faire faire quelque chose; — to devoir; avoir à

haven *n.* port, havre *m.*

haversack *n.* havresac *m.*

havoc *n.* ravage, dégât *m.*

Hawaii *n.* Hawaï *m.*

hawk *n.* faucon *m.*; épervier *m.*; — *vi.* chasser au faucon; — *vt.* colporter; –er *n.* colporteur *m.*

hawk-eyed *a.* aux yeux d'épervier, qui a la vue bonne

hawser *n.* haussière *f.*, grelin *m.*

hay *n.* foin *m.*; — fever fièvre des foins *f.*

hayloft *n.* grange à foin *f.*

haymaker *n.* faneur *m.*; (coll.) coup très fort *m.*

haystack *n.* tas de foin *m.*, meule de foin *f.*

hazard *n.* hasard, risque *m.*; chance *f.*; — *vt.* hasarder, risquer; –ous *a.* hasardeux; dangereux

haze *n.* brouillard *m.*, brume *f.*; — *vt.* (coll.) berner

hazy *a.* nébuleux, sombre; vague; (weather) brumeux

he *pron.* il, lui; celui; ce

head *n.* tête *f.*; chef *m.*; sommet *m.*; source *f.*; (beer) mousse *f.*; titre *m.*; at the — en tête; by a — à une tête de distance; come to a — mûrir; suppurer; atteindre le point culminant; from — to foot des pieds à la tête; go to one's — monter à la tête de quelqu'un; — first tête première; — of hair chevelure *f.*; — over heels pêle-mêle; — or tail pile ou face; I can't make — or tail of it je n'y comprends goutte; keep one's — rester tranquille; lose one's — perdre la tête; out of one's — fou; put –s together prendre conseil; take it into one's — avoir l'idée de; — *a.* premier; en chef; de tête; — *vt.* diriger, commander; — off prévenir; détourner; –ing *n.* titre *m.*; –less *a.* sans tête

headache *n.* mal de tête *m.*; (coll.) souci *m.*

headband *n.* bandeau *m.*

headdress *n.* coiffure *f.*

headland *n.* cap, promontoire *m.*

headlight *n.* phare, feu de route *m.*

headline *n.* titre, en-tête *m.*

headlong *adv.* précipitamment; — *a.* précipité

headmaster *n.* proviseur *m.*; principal *m.*

head-on *adv.* face à face; de front

headphone *n.* écouteur *m.*

headpiece *n.* coiffure *f.*

headquarters *n.* quartier géneral *m.*, état-major *m.*; police — commissariat *m.*

headrest *n.* appui-tête *m.*

headsman *n.* bourreau *m.*

headstone *n.* pierre tombale *f.*

headstrong *a.* têtu, obstiné

headwaiter *n.* maître d'hôtel *m.*

headwater(s) *n.* (*pl.*) source(s) d'un fleuve *f.* (*pl.*)

headway *n.* progrès *m.*; make — progresser

head wind *n.* vent contraire *m.*

heal *vt.* guérir; — *vi.* guérir, se guérir, se remettre; –ing *n.* guérison *f.*

health *n.* santé *f.*; –ful *a.* sain; salubre; –y *a.* sain, salutaire; salubre

heap *n.* tas, amas *m.*; foule *f.*; — *vt.* entasser; amasser; combler

hear *vt.* entendre; ouïr; entendre dire; apprendre, savoir; — of, — about entendre parler de; –ing *n.* audience *f.*; audition *f.*; (sense) ouïe *f.*; oreille *f.*; hard of –ing dur d'oreille

hearken *vi.* écouter

hearsay *n.* ouï-dire, bruit *m.*

hearse *n.* corbillard *m.*

heart *n.* cœur *m.*; centre *m.*; milieu *m.*; fond *m.*; courage *m.*; at — au fond; broken — chagrin *m.*; by — par cœur; have the — avoir le courage; sick at — chagrin, désolé; to one's –'s content à volonté; — and soul corps et âme; — attack (med.) crise cardiaque *f.*; — trouble maladie de cœur *f.*; –en *vt.* encourager; réjouir; –ily *adv.* sincèrement; ardemment; –iness *n.* sincérité *f.*; cordialité *f.*; –less *a.* sans cœur; cruel; –y *a.* sincère; généreux; cordial; chaleureux; copieux; en bonne santé

heartache *n.* souffrance *f.*; chagrin *m.*

heartbeat *n.* pouls, battement de cœur *m.*

heartbreaking *a.* navrant

heartbroken *a.* désolé, navré, chagrin

heartburn *n.* dyspepsie *f.*

heartfelt *a.* qui vient du cœur

hearth *n.* foyer, âtre *m.*

heart-rending *a.* désolant, navrant, affligeant

heartsick *a.* désolé, chagrin

heart-to-heart *a.* intime; sérieux; — *adv.* à cœur ouvert

heat *n.* chaleur *f.*; chaud *m.*; ardeur *f.*; animosité *f.*; (sports) course *f.*, manche *f.*; **dead** — partie nulle *f.*; **in** — en chaleur; **prickly** — démangeaison, éruption (due à la chaleur) *f.*; — **wave** période de chaleur *f.*; — *vt.* chauffer; — *vi.* chauffer; s'échauffer; — **up** chauffer, réchauffer; **-ed** *a.* chauffé; chaud; **-er** *n.* réchaud *m.*; radiateur *m.*; **water -er** chauffe-eau *m.*; **-ing** *n.* chauffage *m.*; **-ing pad** chauffe-corps *m.*

heath *n.* bruyère *f.*

heathen *n. & a.* païen *m.*

heat-resistant *a.* à l'épreuve de la chaleur, calorifuge; isolant

heatstroke *n.* insolation *f.*

heave *n.* soulèvement *m.*; soupir *m.*; secousse *f.*; — *vt.* lever, soulever, pousser; lancer, jeter; — *vi.* se soulever; s'enfler; palpiter

heaven *n.* ciel *m.*; **-s!** *interj.* ciel!; **-ly** *a.* céleste, divin

heavily *adv.* lourdement; fortement; avec difficulté

heaviness *n.* pesanteur *f.*; poids *m.*; langueur *f.*, ennui *m.*

heavy *a.* pesant, lourd; gros; (phy.) grave

heavyweight *n.* poids-lourd *m.*

Hebrew *a. & n.* hébreu *m.*

heckle *vt.* taquiner, se moquer (de); interrompre; ennuyer; **-r** *n.* critique moqueur *m.*

hectic *a.* agité

hectograph *n.* appareil à polycopier *m.*; — *vt.* polycopier

hedge *n.* haie *f.*; — *vt.* entourer d'une haie; — *vi.* reculer, hesiter

hedgerow *n.* haie *f.*

hedging *n.* indécision *f.*; hésitation *f.*

hedonist *n.* hédoniste *m. & f.*

heed *n.* soin *m.*, attention *f.*; — *vt.* prendre garde, observer, écouter; **-ful** *a.* attentif; **-less** *a.* inattentif; négligent

heel *n.* talon *m.*; (coll.) goujat *m.*; **take to one's -s** prendre la fuite; — *vt.* mettre des talons (à); — *vi.* (naut.) pencher

hefty *a.* robuste, fort

heifer *n.* génisse *f.*

height *n.* hauteur, élévation *f.*; altitude *f.*; sommet *m.*; grandeur *f.*; **-en** *vt.* rehausser; perfectionner, embellir; accentuer

heinous *a.* odieux; atroce

heir *n.* héritier *m.*; — **apparent** héritier présomptif *m.*; **-ess** *n.* héritière *f.*

heirloom *n.* bijou ou meuble de famille *m.*

helibus *n.* navette hélicoptère *f.*

helicopter *n.* hélicoptère *m.*

heliport *n.* héliport *m.*

helium *n.* hélium *m.*

hell *n.* enfer *m.*; **-ish** *a.* infernal, diabolique

Hellenic *a.* hellène; hellénique

hello *interj.* bonjour; (telephone) âllô

helm *n.* casque *m.*; (naut.) gouvernail *m.*; timon *m.*; **-sman** *n.* timonier *m.*

helmet *n.* casque *m.*

help *n.* aide *f.*, secours *m.*; employés *m. pl.*; **—!** *interj.* au secours!; — *vt.* aider, secourir; — **oneself** se défendre; (food) se servir; — **out** donner un coup de main; **I cannot — it** ce n'est pas de ma faute; **-er** *n.* aide *m.*; **-ful** *a.* utile, secourable; **-ing** *n.* portion *f.*; **-ing** *a.* utile; **-less** *a.* sans secours; impuissant

helpmate *n.* aide *m. & f.*; épouse *f.*

helter-skelter *adv.* en désordre, pêle-mêle

hem *n.* ourlet, bord *m.*; — *vt. & vi.* ourler, border; — **in** *n.* cerner, entourer

hemisphere *n.* hémisphère *f.*

hemoglobin *n.* hémoglobine *f.*

hemophilia *n.* hémophilie *f.*

hemorrhage *n.* hémorrhagie *f.*

hemorrhoids *n. pl.* hémorrhoïdes *f. pl.*

hemp *n.* chanvre *m.*; **-en** *a.* de chanvre

hemstitch *vt.* ourler à jour

hen *n.* poule *f.*

hence *adv.* d'ici; donc, pour cette raison, par conséquent

henceforth *adv.* désormais, dorénavant

henchman *n.* bras droit, partisan *m.*

hencoop *n.* cage à poules *f.*

henhouse *n.* poulailler *m.*

henna *n.* henné *m.*

henpeck *vt.* maîtriser; harceler; **-ed** *a.*, **-ed husband** mari docile, mari harcelé sans cesse par sa femme *m.*

heptagonal *a.* heptagone; heptagonal

her *a.* son, sa, ses; — *pron.* elle; la; **lui**; **-s** *pron.* le sien, la sienne; à elle

herald *n.* héraut *m.*; avant-coureur *m.*; — *vt.* annoncer; **-ic** *a.* héraldique; **-ry** *n.* blason *m.*

herb *n.* herbe *f.*; **-age** *n.* herbage *m.*

herbaceous *a.* herbacé

herbivorous *a.* herbivore

herd *n.* troupeau *m.*, troupe *f.*; foule *f.*; — *vi.* vivre en troupeau; — *vt.* grouper, mener; élever (des animaux); **-er** *n.* berger *m.*; **-sman** *n.* berger *m.*

here *adv.* ici; — **below** ici-bas; — **comes** voici; — **is** voici; — **lies** ci-gît; **-'s to you** à votre santé; **that's neither — nor there** ça n'a rien à faire

hereabouts *adv.* aux environs, près d'ici

hereafter *adv.* à l'avenir, désormais; ci-dessous; — *n.* avenir *m.*, vie future *f.*

hereby *adv.* par ce moyen
hereditary *a.* héréditaire
heredity *n.* hérédité *f.*
herein *adv.* ci-inclus; ici
heresy *n.* hérésie *f.*
heretic *n.* hérétique *m. & f.*; –al *a.* hérétique
heretofore *adv.* jusqu'ici
herewith *adv.* ci-joint
heritage *n.* héritage *m.*
hermetic *a.* hermétique; –ally *adv.* hermétiquement
hermit *n.* hermite *m.*; –age *n.* hermitage *m.*
hernia *n.* hernie *f.*
hero *n.* héros *m.*; –ic *a.* héroïque; –ics *n. pl.* héroïsme ostentatoire *m.*; –ine *n.* héroïne *f.*; –ism *n.* héroïsme *m.*
heroin *n.* héroïne *f.*
herring *n.* hareng *m.*; smoked — hareng saur *m.*
herringbone *n.* point de chausson *m.*
herself *pron.* elle-même; se
hesitancy *n.* hésitation *f.*
hesitant *a.* hésitant
hesitate *vi.* hésiter
hesitation *n.* hésitation *f.*
heterodox *a.* hétérodoxe
heterogeneous *a.* hétérogène
hew *vt.* couper, tailler
hexagon *n.* hexagone *m.*; –al *a.* hexagonal
hexameter *n.* hexamètre *m.*
heydey *n.* meilleure période *f.*; fleur *f.*
hiatus *n.* hiatus *m.*; lacune *f.*
hibernate *vi.* hiberner
hibernation *n.* hibernation *f.*
hiccup, hiccough *n.* hoquet *m.*; — *vi.* avoir le hoquet
hide *n.* peau *f.*; cuir *m.*
hide *vt.* cacher; — *vi.* se cacher; de dérober
hide-and-seek *n.* cache-cache *m.*
hidebound *a.* étroit; conservateur
hideous *a.* hideux; effroyable; horrible; atroce; –ness *n.* horreur *f.*; laideur *f.*; atrocité *f.*
hide-out *n.* retraite *f.*, abri *m.*; cachette *f.*
hiding *n.*, in — caché; — place cachette *f.*
hierarchy *n.* hiérarchie *f.*
hieroglyph *n.* hiéroglyphe *m.*; –ics *n. pl.* hiéroglyphes *m. pl.*
hi-fi *a.* (coll.) de haute fidélité; — *n.* radio-phonographe de haute fidélité *m.*
high *a.* haut, élevé; sublime; grand; fort; gros; (meat) avancé; (wind) violent; (coll.) saoul, gris; — and dry échoué; abandonné; leave — and dry abandonner; — and low partout; — and mighty hautain; act — and mighty le prendre de haut; — jump saut en hauteur *m.*; — noon plein midi *m.*; — priest grand

prêtre *m.*; — school école secondaire *f.*; — seas haute mer *f.*; — sign signal *m.*; — stakes gros jeu *m.*; — voltage haute tension *f.*; — water marée haute *f.*; in — spirits joyeux, gai; it is — time il est bien temps; — *adv.* haut, en haut; — *n.* record *m.*; –er *a.* plus haut, plus élevé; superiéur; –ly *adv.* très, fort; think very –ly of avoir une très bonne opinion de; estimer beaucoup; –ness *n.* hauteur *f.*; élévation *f.*; (title) Altesse *f.*
high-and-low *adv.* de tous côtés
highball *n.* whisky à l'eau, cognac à l'eau *m.*, fine à l'eau *f.*
highborn *a.* de haute naissance
highboy *n.* chiffonnier *m.*
highbrow *a.* (coll.) intellectuel, de l'élite; hautain
high-class, high-grade *a.* de (première) qualité, supérieur
high-flown *a.* ampoulé
high-frequency *a.* à haute fréquence
highhanded *a.* arbitraire
highland *m.* pays montagneux *m.*; montagnes *f. pl.*; –er *n.* montagnard *m.*
highlight *n.* clou *m.*; — *vt.* mettre en vedette
high-minded *a.* magnanime
high-pitched *a.* aigu
high-powered *a.* de haute puissance; fort, puissant
high-pressure *a.* à haute pression; insistant
high-priced *a.* cher, coûteux
high-sounding *a.* beau, impressionnant (mais vide)
high-spirited *a.* joyeux, gai; fougueux
high-strung *a.* nerveux
high-test *a.* (gasoline) très raffinné
highway *n.* route *f.*; grand'route *f.*; grand chemin *m.*
highwayman *n.* voleur des grands chemins *m.*
hijack *vt.* (coll.) arrêter (un camion) sur la route et en voler les marchandises; –ing *n.* vol à main armée (d'un camion) sur la route *m.*
hike *n.* longue promenade à pied *f.*; — *vi.* faire de longues promenades à pied; — *vt.* (coll.) hausser, augmenter
hiking *n.* longue(s) promenade(s) à pied *f.* (*pl.*)
hilarious *a.* gai, joyeux
hilarity *n.* gaieté *f.*
hill *n.* colline, côte *f.*, coteau *m.*; pente *f.*; montée *f.*; descente *f.*; –y *a.* montagneux
hillbilly *n.* (coll.) montagnard du Sud des États-Unis *m.*
hillock *n.* petite colline *f.*; butte *f.*

hillside n. (flanc de) coteau m.
hilt n. poignée, garde f., manche m.
him pron. lui; le
himself pron. lui-même; se
hind n. biche f.
hind a. postérieur, de derrière; — legs pattes de derrière f. pl.; –quarters n. arriére-train m.
hinder vt. empêcher; embarasser; troubler
hindmost a. dernier
hindrance n. empêchement, obstacle m.
hindsight n. expérience acquise après l'événement f., conscience de qu'on autrait dû faire f.
Hindu a. & n. hindou m.
hinge n. gond m.; pivot m.; charnière f.; — vi. tourner; dépendre
hint n. suggestion, insinuation f.; avis m.; demi-mot m.; soupçon m.; give a —, drop a — donner un bienveillant avis; take a — accepter un conseil; know how to take a — entendre à demi-mot; — vt. suggérer, donner à entendre
hinterland n. arrière-pays m.
hip n. hanche f.
hire n. louage m.; location f.; for — à louer; — vt. louer; employer
hireling n. mercénaire m.; laquais m.
hirsute a. velu, poilu
his a. son, sa, ses; — pron. le sien, la sienne; à lui
Hispanic a. hispanique
hiss a. & vi. siffler; — n. sifflement m.; –ing n. sifflement(s) m. (pl.)
histology n. histologie f.
historian n. historien m.
historic(al) a. historique
history n. histoire f.
histrionic a. de comédien, de la scène; –s n. pl. art du théâtre m.
hit n. coup m.; atteinte f.; succès m., réussite f.; be a —, make a — réussir; — vt. frapper, atteindre; se heurter contre; — it off s'entendre, se trouver d'accord; — the ceiling (coll.) se mettre en colère; — the jackpot (coll.) gagner le prix; faire fortune d'un seul coup; — the spot plaire, satisfaire; rafraîchir
hitch n. saccade f.; entrave f., obstacle m., condition f.; (naut.) nœud m.; (coll.) période de service militaire f.; — vt. atteler, attacher
hitchhike vi. faire de l'autostop
hither adv. ici; — a. qui est de ce côté
hitherto adv. jusqu'ici
hit-or-miss a. & adv. à tout hasard
hive n. ruche f.
hives n. pl. (med.) éruption allergique f.
hoarfrost n. gêlée blanche f.
hoarse a. enroué, rauque; –ness n.

enrouement m.
hoary a. blanc; blanchi; gris
hoax n. mystification f.; — vt. mystifier
hobble vi. clocher, boiter; — vt. lier, attacher (par les pieds)
hobby n. distraction, marotte f.
hobbyhorse n. cheval d'enfant, cheval de bois m.
hobgloblin n. lutin m.
hobnail n. caboche f.
hobnob vi., — with frequenter, s'associer avec
hobo n. chemineau, vagabond m.
hock n. jarret m.; vin du Rhin m.; in — (coll.) en gage; — shop (coll.) mont de piété m.; — vt. mettre en gage
hockey n. hockey m.
hocus-pocus n. jonglerie f., tour de passe-passe m.
hod n. hotte, auge f.; — carrier aide-maçon m.
hodgepodge n. salmigondis m.; mélange m.
hoe n. houe, binette f.; — vt. houer, sarcler
hog n. cochon, porc, pourceau m.
hogshead n. barrique f.
hoist vt. lever, guinder; — n. poulie, grue f.
hold n. prise f.; appui m.; pouvoir m.; (naut.) cale f.; get — of, take — of prendre, saisir, se saisir de; — vt. tenir; prendre; avoir; retenir; détenir; maintenir, soutenir; arrêter; estimer, penser, croire; — vi. tenir; — back retenir; — forth discourir; — good être valable; — no water être défectueux; — off hésiter, attendre; — on tenir; subsister; — one's own tenir ferme; se défendre; — one's tongue se taire; — out against résister à; –over continuer, remettre; — together tenir; — true être vrai; — up retarder; voler (à main armée); — with être du même avis que; approuver; souffrir, supporter; –er n. propriétaire m. & f.; détenteur m.; (cigarettes) porte-cigarette m.; –ing n. possession f.; tenue f.
holdup n. vol à main armée m.
hole n. trou m.; orifice m.; (coll.) mauvais pas m.; — vt. trouer, percer
holiday n. jour de fête m., fête f.; jour férié m.
holiness n. sainteté f.
Holland n. Hollande f.
hollow n. creux, trou m.; cavité f.; — a. creux; enfoncé; peu sincère; (sound) sourd; — vt. creuser; évider
hollow-cheeked a. aux joues creuses
holly n. houx m.

hollyhock n. rose trémière f.
holster n. fourreau de pistolet m.; gaine f.
holy a. saint; béni, sacré; — **water** eau bénite f.
Holy Week n. semaine sainte f.
homage n. hommage m.
home n. maison f.; logis m., demeure f.; foyer m.; intérieur m.; patrie f.; **at** — chez soi; à la maison; **make oneself at** — se mettre à l'aise, faire comme chez soi; — a. de (la) famille; familial; — **economics** n. économie domestique f.; — **rule** autonomie f.; –**stretch** dernière étape f.; — **team** locaux m. pl.; — **town** ville natale f.; — adv. à la maison, chez soi; **strike** — frapper juste
homeland n. patrie f.; pays m.
homelike a. familial, comme à la maison
homeliness n. laideur f.
homely a. laid
homemade a. fait à la maison
homemaker n. femme d'intérieur f.; épouse f.
homesick a. qui a le mal du pays; –**ness** n. mal du pays m.
homespun a. filé à la maison; grossier
homestead n. maison, propriété f.
homeward(s) adv. à la maison, vers la maison
homework n. devoirs à faire à la maison m. pl.
homicidal a. homicide, meurtrier
homicide n. homicide m.
homily n. homélie f.
homing pigeon n. pigeon voyageur m.
hominy n. gruau de maïs m.
homogeneous a. homogène
homogenize vt. homogénéiser
homologous a. homologue
homonym n. homonyme m.
homosexual a. homoseuxuel
Honduras n. pl. Honduras m. pl.
hone vt. affiler; (razor) repasser
honest a. honnête; sincère; loyal; –**y** n. honnêteté, probité f.; sincérité f.
honey n. miel m.; douceur f.; (coll.) chérie f.; –**ed** a. emmielé, couvert de miel; mielleux, onctueux; –**bee** abeille, mouche à miel f.
honeycomb n. rayon de miel n.; — vt. veiner
honeydew melon n. melon espagnol m.
honeymoon n. lune de miel f.
honk n. bruit de klaxon m.; cornement m.; — vi. klaxonner, corner
honor n. honneur m.; dignité f.; **word of** — parole d'honneur f.; — vt. honorer; –**able** a. honorable; –**able mention** m. accessit; –**ary** a. honoraire; –**ary degree** grade honoris causa m.; –**ed** a. honoré;

honorable
hood n. chaperon m.; capuchon m.; (auto) capote f.; (coll.) gangster m.; –**ed** a. à capuchon
hoodwink vt. tromper; mystifier
hoof n. sabot m.
hoofbeat n. pas de cheval m.
hook n. crochet m.; crampon m.; hameçon m.; — **and eye** agrafes f. pl.; —, **line, and sinker** tout à fait; **by** — **or by crook** n'importe comment; — vt. accrocher; prendre; — vi. s'accrocher; — **up** accrocher; –**ed** a. crochu; fait au crochet; pris
hookup n. chaîne f.
hooky n., **play** — faire l'école buissonière
hoop n. cercle m.; cerceau m.; — **skirt** jupe à panier f.
hoot n. huée f.; **owl's** — ululement m.; — vi. huer; ululer
hop n. saut, bond m.; (bot.) houblon m.; (avi.) escale, étape f.; — vi. sauter, sautiller
hope n. espérance f., espoir m.; — vi. espérer; –**ful** a. qui a de l'espoir; prometteur; –**less** a. sans espoir, désespéré; (person) incorrigible
hopper n. trémie f.
hopscotch n. marelle f.
horde n. horde, troupe f.
horizon n. horizon m.; –**tal** a. horizontal
hormone n. hormone f.
horn n. corne f.; cor m.; (auto) klaxon m.; **draw in one's** –**s** (fig.) rentrer les cors; –**ed** a. cornu, à cornes; –**ed owl** duc m.; –**y** a. de corne
hornpipe n. cornemuse f.; danse des matelots f.
horn-rimmed a. en corne
horoscope n. horoscope m.
horrible a. horrible, terrible
horrid a. horrible; affreux
horrify vt. horrifier
horror n. horreur f.
horror-stricken a. épouvanté
hors d'œuvre n. hors-d'œuvre m.
horse n. cheval m.; cavalerie f.; — **chestnut** marron d'Inde m.; — **race** course de chevaux f.; — **racing** courses de chevaux f. pl.; — **sense** (coll.) bon sens m.; **get on one's high** — monter sur ses grands chevaux; **ride a** — monter (à cheval)
horsefly n. taon m.
horsehair n. crin m.
horseman n. cavalier; –**ship** équitation f.
horsepower n. cheval-vapeur m.
horse-radish n. raifort m.
horseshoe n. fer (à cheval) m.
horsewhip n. cravache f.; — vt. fouetter

horsewoman *n.* cavalière, amazone *f.*
horticulture *n.* horticulture *f.*; jardinage *m.*
horticulturist *n.* horticulteur *m.*
hose *n.* bas *m. pl.*; tuyau *m.*; (garden) tuyau d'arrosage *m.*; — *vt.* arroser
hosiery *n.* bonneterie *f.*; bas *m. pl.*
hospitable *a.* hospitalier
hospital *n.* hôpital *m.*; –ization insurance assurance médicale *f.*
hospitality *n.* hospitalité *f.*
host *n.* hôte *m.*; armée *f.*; (eccl.) hostie *f.*; –ess *n.* hôtesse *f.*
hostage *n.* otage *m.*
hostel *n.* hôtel *m.*, auberge *f.*; youth — auberge de la jeunesse *f.*
hostility *n.* hostilité *f.*
hot *a.* chaud; ardent, violent; échauffé; be — être chaud; (person) avoir chaud; (weather) faire chaud; — air bavardage *m.*; — dog saucisse de Francfort *f.*; — water (coll.) situation difficile *f.*
hotbed *n.* couche *f.*; (fig.) centre, foyer *m.*
hot-blooded *a.* fougueux
hotel *n.* hôtel *m.*
hothouse *n.* serre chaude *f.*
hot plate *n.* réchaud, chauffe-assiette *m.*
hot rod *n.* (coll.) vieille auto dont la puissance a été fortement augmentée *f.*
hot-tempered *a.* colérique
hot-water bottle *n.* bouillotte *f.*
hot-water heater *n.* chauffe-eau *m.*
hound *n.* chien de chasse *m.*; — *vt.* persécuter, poursuivre, harceler
hour *n.* heure *f.*; by the — à l'heure; half an — demi-heure *f.*; per — à l'heure; for –s pendant des heures; –hand petite aiguille *f.*; –ly *adv.* toutes les heures
hourglass *n.* sablier *m.*
house *n.* maison, habitation *f.*; ménage *f.*; logis *m.*; (legislature) chambre *f.*; private — maison particulière *f.*; keep — tenir maison, tenir le ménage; — *vt.* loger, arbitrer
houseboat *n.* bateau-maison *m.*
housebreaker *n.* cambrioleur *m.*
housebreaking *n.* cambriolage *m.*, effraction *f.*
housebroken *a.* (animals) dressé
housecoat *n.* peignoir *m.*
housefly *n.* mouche (commune) *f.*
houseful *n.* pleine maison *f.*
household *n.* famille *f.*, ménage *m.*; — *a.* de ménage, de la maison, de famille
housekeeper *n.* femme de menage *f.*
housekeeping *n.* ménage *f.*
housemaid *n.* bonne *f.*

house physician *n.* médecin interne *m.*
housetop *n.* toit *m.*
housewarming *n.* pendaison de la crémaillère *f.*
housewife *n.* mère de famille, ménagère *f.*
housework *n.* travail de ménage *m.*
housing *n.* logement *m.*; boîte *f.*; enchâssure *f.*; (machinery) housse, monture *f.*;
hovel *n.* taudis *m.*
hover *vi.* voltiger; rôder; hésiter
how *adv.* comment; comme; (in exclamations) que, comme; — about (doing) si nous faisions . . . .; — are you? comment-allez-vous? ; comment ça va?; — do you do enchanté; — much, — many combien de; — often? combien de fois?; — old are you? quel âge avez-vous?
however *adv.* cependant, pourtant, toutefois; quelque . . . . que
howitzer *n.* obusier *m.*
howl *vi.* hurler; — *n.* hurlement *m.*
hub *n.* moyeu *m.*; (fig.) centre *m.*
hubbub *n.* tumulte *m.*, remue-ménage *m.*
hubcap *n.* couvre-moyeu *m.*
huckleberry *n.* airelle *f.*
huckster *n.* revendeur *m.*; agent de publicité *m.*
huddle *n.* groupe, tas *m.*; — *vi.* se grouper, se réunir; –d *a.* blotti; entassé
hue *n.* couleur, teinte *f.*; cri *m.*; — and cry cri de haro *m.*
huff *n.* accès de colère, emportement *m.*; –y *a.* brusque; irrité, arrogant
hug *n.* étreinte *f.*; — *vt.* étreindre; embrasser, serrer; rester près de; longer, raser
huge *a.* vaste; énorme, immense; –ness *n.* énormité, immensité *f.*
Huguenot *n.* Huguenot *m.*
hulk *n.* (person) pataud *m.*; (ship) carcasse *f.*; –ing *a.* gros, lourd
hull *n.* (bot.) cosse, coque *f.*; (ship) coque *f.*; — *vt.* écosser
hullabaloo *n.* tumulte, brouhaha *m.*
hum *n.* bourdonnement *m.*; ronflement *m.*; — *vi.* bourdonner; ronfler; (song) chantonner
human *n. & a.* humain *m.*; –e *a.* humain; humanitaire; –ism *n.* humanisme *m.*; –ist *n.* humaniste *m.*; –itarian *a. & n.* humanitaire *m.*; –ity *n.* humanité *f.*; –ize *vt.* rendre humain; –kind *n.* genre humain *m.*
humble *vt.* humilier, abattre; — *a.* humble, modeste; –ness *n.* humilité *f.*
humbly *adv.* modestement; avec humilité
humbug *n.* charlatan *m.*; blague, duperie *f.*
humdrum *a.* banal; ennuyeux
humerus (anat.) humérus *m.*

humid *a.* humide, moite; **–ifier** *n.* humidificateur *m.*; **–ify** *vt.* humidifier; **–ity** *n.* humidité *f.*; **–or** *n.* boîte à tabac *f.*
humiliate *vt.* humilier
humiliation *n.* humiliation *f.*
humility *n.* humilité *f.*
hummock *n.* tertre *m.*
humor *n.* humeur *f.*, disposition du caractère *f.*; humour, comique, esprit *m.*; **bad** — mauvaise humeur *f.*; — *vt.* ménager, accéder (aux lubies d'une personne); **–ist** *n.* humoriste *m.*; **–ous** *a.* comique, spirituel; humoristique
hump *n.* bosse *f.*
hunch *n.* bosse *f.*; (coll.) pressentiment *m.*; — *vi.* s'accroupir
hunchback *n.* bossu *m.*; **–ed** *a.* bossu
hundred *n.* cent *m.*, centaine *f.*; — *a.* cent; **–fold** *adv.* au centuple; **–th** *a.* centième
hundredweight *n.* quintal *m.* (50 kilogrammes)
Hungarian *a.* & *n.* hongrois *m.*
Hungary *n.* Hongrie *f.*
hunger *n.* faim *f.*; — *vi.* avoir faim
hungrily *adv.* avidement
hungry *a.* affamé; **be** — avoir faim
hunk *n.* (coll.) gros morceau *m.*
hunt *n.* chasse *f.*; poursuite *f.*; recherches *f. pl.*; — *vi.* chasser; — **for** chasser; chercher; **–er** *n.* chasseur *m.*; chercheur *m.*; **–ing** *n.* chasse *f.*; **–ress** *n.* chasseresse *f.*; **–sman** *n.* chasseur *m.*
hurdle *n.* claie *f.*; haie *f.*; barrière *f.*; **–s** *pl.* (sports) course d'obstacle *f.*; — *vi.* faire une course à la haie
hurdy-gurdy *n.* vielle *f.*; orgue de Barbarie *f.*
hurl *vt.* lancer, jeter; précipiter; — **back** repousser, refouler
hurly-burly *n.* tohu-bohu, tintamarre *m.*
hurrah *interj.* & *n.* hourra *m.*
hurricane *n.* ouragan *m.*
hurried *a.* pressé, rapide
hurry *n.* hâte, précipitation *f.*; **to be in a** — être pressé; **there is no** — cela ne presse pas; — *vt.* presser, hâter; — *vi.* se dépêcher, se hâter; — **away** s'en aller vite; — **back** revenir vite; retourner vite; — **on** se presser, continuer rapidement; — **over** venir vite; aller vite; — **up** se dépêcher
hurt *n.* mal *m.*, blessure *f.*; tort, dommage *m.*; — *vt.* faire tort à; faire mal à; blesser; — *a.* blessé; **–ful** *a.* nuisible
hurtle *vi.* se précipiter
husband *n.* mari, époux *m.*; — *vt.* ménager; cultiver; **–ry** *n.* agriculture *f.*; élevage *m.*
hush *n.* silence *m.*; — *vt.* faire taire; — *vi.* se taire; — *interj.* chut!

husk *n.* cosse, gousse, peau *f.*; — *vt.* écosser
husky *n.* chien arctique, chien esquimau *m.*; — *a.* gros, costaud; fort; (voice) enroué
hussy *n.* gueuse, coquine *f.*; effrontée *f.*
hustle *n.* (coll.) énergie, activité *f.*; ambition *f.*; — *vt.* presser, pousser; — *vi.* se presser; **–r** *n.* (coll.) débrouillard *m.*
hut *n.* hutte, cabane *f.*
hutch *n.* huche *f.*
hybrid *a.* & *n.* hybride *m.*
hydrant *n.* bouche à eau, bouche d'incendie *f.*
hydraulic *a.* hydraulique; **–s** *n.* hydraulique *f.*
hydrocarbon *n.* hydrocarbone *m.*
hydrochloric *a.* chlorhydrique
hydrodynamic *a.* hydrodynamique; **–s** *n.* hydrodynamique *f.*
hydroelectric *a.* hydroélectrique
hydrogen *n.* hydrogène *f.*; — **bomb** bombe à hydrogène *f.*; — **peroxide** *n.* eau oxygénée *f.*
hydrolysis *n.* hydrolyse *f.*
hydrophobia *n.* hydrophobie *f.*
hydroplane *n.* hydravion *m.*
hydroponics *n. pl.* culture de légumes dans une solution aqueuse *f.*
hydrostatics *n. pl.* hydrostatique *f.*
hydrotherapy *n.* hydrothérapie *f.*
hygiene *n.* hygiène *f.*
hygienic *a.* hygiénique
hymn *n.* hymne *m.*
hyperbola *n.* (math.) hyperbole *f.*
hypercritical *a.* critique à l'excès
hypergolic *a.* hypergolique
hypersensitive *a.* excessivement sensible
hypersonic *a.* hypersonique
hypertension *n.* hypertension *f.*
hypertrophy *n.* hypertrophie *f.*
hyphen *n.* trait d'union *m.*; **–ate** *vt.* écrire avec un trait d'union
hypnosis *n.* hypnose *f.*
hypnotic *a.* hypnotique
hypnotism *n.* hypnotisme *m.*
hypnotize *vt.* hypnotiser
hypo *n.* (phot.) fixateur *m.*
hypochondria *n.* hypocondrie *f.*; **–c** *n.* hypocondriaque *m.*
hypocrisy *n.* hypocrisie *f.*
hypocrite *n.* hypocrite *m.*
hypocritical *a.* hypocrite
hypodermic *a.* hypodermique; — **syringe** *n.* seringue à injections *f.*
hypotension *n.* (med.) hypotension *f.*
hypotenuse *n.* hypoténuse *f.*
hypothesis *n.* hypothèse *f.*
hypothetic *a.* hypothétique

hysteria n. hystérie f.
hysterical a. hystérique
hysterics n. pl. hystérie f.; crise de nerfs f.

I

I pron. je; moi
ice n. glace f.; — **cream** glace(s) f. (pl.); — **water** eau glacée; — **age** n. période glaciaire f.; — vt. glacer; refroidir; frapper; –d a. glacé
ice bag n. sac à glace m.
icebound a. pris dans la glace
icebox n. glacière
icebreaker n. brise-glace m.
ice-cream cone n. glace en cornet f.
Iceland n. Islande f.; –ic a. & n. islandais m.
iceman n. glacier m.
ichthyology n. ichtyologie f.
icicle n. glaçon m.
iciness n. froideur f.
icing n. fondant m.
icon n. icone f.
iconoclasm n. iconoclasme m.
iconoclast n. iconoclaste m.; –ic a. iconoclaste
icy a. glacé; glissant
idea n. idée f.; notion f.
ideal n. & a. idéal m.; –ism n. idéalisme m.; –ist n. idéaliste m. & f.; –istic a. idéaliste; –ize vt. idéaliser
identical a. identique
identification n. identification f.; — **card**, — **papers** carte d'identité f.
identify vt. identifier
identity n. identité f.
ideological a. idéologique
ideology n. idéologie f.
idiocy n. idiotisme m., idiotie f.
idiom n. idiome m.; idiotisme m. -atic a. idiomatique
idiosyncrasy n. idiosyncrasie f.
idiot n. idiot, benêt m.; –ic a. idiot
idle vi. être oisif, fainéanter; (engine) tourner au ralenti; — **away** perdre; — a. inoccupé; au repos; paresseux, oisif; vain; perdu; –ness n. oisiveté f.; –r n. flâneur m.; paresseux m.
idol n. idole f.; –ater n. idolâtre m.; –atrous a. idolâtre; –atry n. idolatrie f.; –ize vt. idolâtrer, adorer
idyl(l) n. idylle f.; –lic a. idyllique
i.e.: id est c'est-à-dire
if conj. si; — **not** sinon; — **so** dans ce cas
igneous a. ignée
ignite vt. allumer, incendier; — vi. prendre feu
ignition n. allumage m.; — **switch** contacteur du démarreur m.

ignominious a. ignominieux
ignominy n. ignominie f.
ignoramus n. ignorant m.
ignorance n. ignorance f.
ignorant a. ignorant; **be** — **of** ignorer
ignore vt. dédaigner, ne pas faire attention à; ne pas tenir compte de
ilium n. (anat.) ilion m.
ilk n. espèce f., genre m.
ill n. mal, malheur m.; — a. malade, souffrant; mauvais; mal; **become** — tomber malade; — **at ease** mal à l'aise; — **health** mauvaise santé; — adv. mal; –ness n. maladie f.
ill-advised a. mal conseillé
ill-bred a. mal élevé
ill-considered a. (fait) sans réflexion
ill-disposed a. mal disposé
illegal a. illégal; illicite; –ity n. illégalitè f.
illegible a. illisible
illegitimate a. illégitime
ill-fated a. malheureux
ill feeling n. rancune f.
ill-founded a. mal fondé
ill-gotten a. mal acquis
ill-humored a. maussade; de mauvaise humeur
illicit a. illicite, défendu
illiteracy n. analphabétisme m.
illiterate a. illettré
ill-mannered a. impoli
ill-natured a. maussade
illogical a. illogique
ill-starred a. malheureux; de mauvaise augure
ill-timed a. inopportun, déplacé
illuminate vt. illuminer, éclairer
illumination n. illumination f.; éclairage m.
illumine vt. illuminer
illusion n. illusion f.
illustrate vt. illustrer; expliquer, éclaircir
illustration n. illustration f.; gravure f.; explication f., éclaircissement m.
illustrative a. explicatif
illustrator n. dessinateur m.; illustrateur m.
illustrious a. illustre, célèbre
ill will n. mauvaise volonté f.
image n. image f.; portrait m.; –ry n. images f. pl.
imaginable a. imaginable, concevable
imaginary a. imaginaire, idéal
imagination n. imagination f.
imaginative a. imaginatif
imagine vt. imaginer; s'imaginer; inventer; se figurer
imbecile n. & a. imbécile, idiot m.
imbecility n. imbécillité f.
imbibe vt. absorber; boire, imbiber

imbue *vt.* imprégner, pénétrer
imitate *vt.* imiter
imitation *n.* imitation *f.*; (comm.) contre-façon *f.*; — *a.* simili-; imitatif; factice
imitative *a.* imitatif
imitator *n.* imitateur *m.*
immaculate *a.* immaculé; impeccable
immanent *a.* immanent
immaterial *a.* immatériel; qui n'a rien à faire, qui n'a aucun rapport
immature *a.* vert, pas mûr
immaturity *n.* immaturité *f.*
immeasurable *a.* immesurable; incommensurable
immediate *a.* immédiat; urgent; **–ly** *adv.* tout de suite; aussitôt; immédiatement
immemorial *a.* immémorial, très-ancien
immense *a.* immense, vaste; **–ly** *adv.* énormément
immensity *n.* immensité *f.*
immerse *vt.* immerger, plonger
immersion *n.* immersion *f.*
immigrant *n.* immigrant *m.*
immigrate *vi.* immigrer
immigration *n.* immigration *f.*
imminence *n.* imminence *f.*
imminent *a.* imminent
immobility *n.* immobilité *f.*
immobilize *vt.* immobiliser
immoderate *a.* immodéré
immodest *a.* immodeste, impudique; **–y** *n.* immodestie *f.*
immolate *vt.* immoler
immolation *n.* immolation *f.*
immoral *a.* immoral; **–ity** *n.* immoralité *f.*
immortal *a.* immortel; **–ity** *n.* immortalité *f.*; **–ize** *vt.* immortaliser
immovable *a.* immobile; inébranlable; (fig.) insensible
immune *a.* immunisé
immunity *n.* immunité *f.*; exemption *f.*
immunization *n.* immunisation *f.*
immunize *vt.* immuniser
immutability *n.* immutabilité *f.*
immutable *a.* immuable, invariable
imp *n.* diablotin *m.*; petit drôle *m.*; **–ish** *a.* espiègle
impact *n.* impact *m.*, collision *f.*; choc *m.*
impair *vt.* détériorer, affaiblir, diminuer; endommager
impale *vt.* empaler
impalpable *a.* impalpable
impart *vt.* donner, communiquer
impartial *a.* impartial; **–ity** *n.* impartialité *f.*
impassable *a.* impraticable; insurmontable
impassibility *n.* insensibilité *f.*
impassioned *a.* passionné
impassive *a.* insensible; impassible; **–ness** *n.* insensibilité *f.*; impassibilité *f.*
impatience *n.* impatience *f.*
impatient *a.* impatient; **–ly** *adv.* impatiemment
impeach *vt.* accuser; **–able** *a.* susceptible d'être accusé; attaquable; douteux; **–ment** *n.* accusation *f.*
impecunious *a.* indigent
impeccable *a.* impeccable
impedance *n.* impédance *f.*
impede *vt.* empêcher, arrêter, entraver
impediment *n.* empêchement, obstacle *m.*
impel *vt.* pousser, forcer
impend *vi.* menacer, être imminent; **–ing** *a.* imminent
impenetrability *n.* impénétrabilité *f.*
impenetrable *a.* impénétrable
imperative *a.* impératif; — *n.* impératif *m.*
imperceptible *a.* imperceptible, insensible
imperfect *a.* imparfait; **–ion** *n.* imperfection *f.*
imperial *a.* impérial; **–ism** *n.* impérialisme *m.*; **–ist** *n.* impérialiste *m.*; **–istic** *a.* impérialiste
imperil *vt.* mettre en danger
imperious *a.* impérieux, exigeant
impermeable *a.* imperméable
impersonal *a.* impersonnel
impersonate *vt.* personnifier; contrefaire, se déguiser en
impersonation *n.* personnification *f.*; rôle *m.*; représentation *f.*
impertinence *n.* impertinence *f.*
impertinent *a.* impertinent, insolent; sans aucun rapport
imperturbable *a.* imperturbable
impervious *a.* impénétrable, inaccessible; étanche
impetuosity *n.* impétuosité *f.*
impetuous *a.* impétueux
impetus *n.* impulsion, force motrice *f.*
impiety *n.* impiété *f.*
impinge *vt.* heurter; — **on** enfreindre
impious *a.* impie
implacability *n.* implacabilité *f.*
implacable *a.* implacable
implant *vt.* implanter; imprimer; — *n.* implantation *f.*; (med.) greffe *f.*
implement *n.* outil, ustensile *m.*; — *vt.* exécuter, réaliser; complémenter; rendre effectif
implicate *vt.* impliquer
implication *n.* implication *f.*
implicit *a.* implicite; absolu
implied *a.* implicite
implore *vt.* implorer, supplier
imploring *a.* suppléant
imply *vt.* impliquer
impolite *a.* impoli; **–ness** *n.* impolitesse *f.*
imponderable *a.* impondérable
import *n.* importation *f.*; importance *f.*;

sens *m.*, valeur *f.*; — **duty** douane *f.*; — *vi.* importer; –**ation** *n.* importation *f.*; –**er** *n.* importateur *m.*; –**ing** *n.* importation *f.*

importance *n.* importance *f.*; **be of** — importer

important *a.* important; **be** — importer

importunate *a.* importun

importune *vt.* importuner

impose *vt.* imposer; — **upon** gêner, abuser de, en imposer à

imposing *a.* imposant; splendide, magnifique

imposition *a.* imposition *f.*; tromperie *f.*; impôt *m.*

impossibility *n.* impossibilité *f.*

impossible *a.* impossible

impostor *n.* imposteur *m.*

imposture *n.* imposture *f.*; tromperie *f.*

impotence *n.* impuissance *f.*; impotence *f.*

impotent *a.* (med.) impotent; impuissant; faible

impound *vt.* confisquer; mettre en fourrière (un animal)

impoverish *vt.* appauvrir

impracticability *n.* impossibilité *f.*

impracticable *a.* impraticable

impractical *a.* peu pratique

imprecate *vt.* maudire

imprecation *n.* malédiction *f.*

impregnable *a.* imprenable

impregnate *vt.* imprégner; féconder

impresario *n.* imprésario *m.*

impress *n.* empreinte, impression *f.*; — *vt.* imprimer, empreindre, graver; impressionner; enrôler par force; –**ion** *n.* impression *f.*; –**ionable** *a.* impressionnable; –**ive** *a.* impressionnant

impressionism *n.* impressionnisme *m.*

impressionist *n.* impressionniste *m.*; –**ic** *a.* impressionniste

imprint *vt.* empreindre, imprimer, graver; — *n.* empreinte *f.*

imprison *vt.* emprisonner; –**ment** *n.* emprisonnement *m.*; prison *f.*

improbability *n.* improbabilité *f.*, invraisemblance *f.*

improbable *a.* improbable; invraisemblable

impromptu *a. & n.* impromptu *m.*

improper *a.* impropre; inconvenant

impropriety *n.* impropriété *f.*; inconvenance *f.*

improve *vt.* améliorer, perfectionner; — *vi.* s'améliorer, faire des progrès; –**ment** *n.* amélioration *f.*; perfectionnement *m.*

improvidence *n.* imprévoyance *f.*

improvident *a.* imprévoyant

improvisation *n.* improvisation *f.*

improvise *vt. & vi.* improviser

imprudence *n.* imprudence *f.*

imprudent *a.* imprudent

impudence *n.* impudence *f.*; effronterie, insolence *f.*

impudent *a.* impudent; effronté, insolent

impugn *vt.* attaquer; contester

impulse *n.* impulsion, incitation *f.*; mouvement *m.*

impulsive *a.* impulsif; –**ly** *adv.* par impulsion; d'un mouvement naturel

impunity *n.* impunité *f.*

impure *a.* impur; souillé

impurity *n.* impureté *f.*

impute *vt.* imputer, attribuer

in *prep.* en, dans; à; sous; sur; — *adv.* dedans; (pol.) au pouvoir; **be** — (at home) être chez soi, être la; — *n.* (coll.) entrée *f.*

inability *n.* incapacité *f.*

inaccessibility *n.* inaccessibilité *f.*

inaccessible *a.* inaccessible

inaccuracy *n.* inexactitude *f.*

inaccurate *a.* inexact

inaction *n.* inaction *f.*

inactive *a.* inactif

inactivity *n.* inactivité *f.*

inadequacy *n.* insuffisance *f.*

inadequate *a.* insuffisant

inadmissible *a.* inadmissible

inadvertence *n.* inadvertance *f.*

inadvertent *a.* négligeant; fait par mégarde; –**ly** *adv.* par mégarde

inadvisibility *n.* inopportunité *f.*

inalienable *a.* inaliénable

inane *a.* idiot, stupide

inanimate *a.* inanimé

inapplicable *a.* inapplicable

inappropriate *a.* inopportun; pas convenable; impropre

inarticulate *a.* inarticulé

inasmuch as *conj.* vu que, attendu que

inattention *n.* inattention, négligence *f.*,

inattentive *a.* inattentif

inaudible *a.* imperceptible

inaugurate *vt.* inaugurer

inauguration *n.* inauguration *f.*

inauspicious *a.* peu propice

inborn, inbred *a.* inné

incalculable *a.* incalculable

incandescence *n.* incandescence *f.*

incandescent *a.* incandescent

incantation *n.* incantation *f.*

incapability *n.* incapacité, impuissance *f.*

incapable *a.* incapable

incapacitate *vt.* rendre incapable

incapacity *n.* incapacité *f.*

incarcerate *vt.* incarcérer

incarceration *a.* emprisonnement *m.*

incarnation *n.* incarnation *f.*

incase *vt.* encaisser, enfermer

incautious *a.* négligent, imprudent

incendiary *n. & a.* incendiaire *m.*

incense *n.* encens *m.*; — *vt.* encenser; exaspérer; –d *a.* irrité

incentive *n.* motif *m.*; encouragement *m.*; ambition *f.*

inception *n.* début, commencement *m.*

incessant *a.* incessant, continuel; –ly *adv.* sans cesse

inch *n.* pouce *m.*

incidence *n.* incidence *f.*

incident *n.* incident *m.*; — *a.* accidentel, casuel; –al *a.* accidentel, fortuit; accessoire; –ally *adv.* par hasard; accessoirement; incidamment; à propos

incinerate *vt.* incinérer

incinerator *n.* four (à brûler les ordures) *m.*; incinérateur *m.*

incipient *a.* naissant, commençant

incise *vt.* inciser

incision *n.* incision *f.*

incisive *a.* incisif; pénétrant

incisor *n.* incisive *f.*

incite *vt.* inciter, exciter; –ment incitation, excitation *f.*

incivility *n.* incivilité *f.*

inclemency *n.* inclémence, intempérie *f.*

inclement *a.* inclément, rigoureux, dur

inclination *n.* inclination *f.*, penchant *m.*, inclinaison *f.*

incline *n.* pente *f.*; rampe *f.*; — *vt. & vi.* incliner, pencher; s'incliner; être porté à

include *vt.* renfermer, comprendre

including *prep.* y compris

inclusive *a.* inclus; y compris

incognito *n. & adv.* incognito *m.*

incoherence *n.* incohérence *f.*

incoherent *a.* incohérent

incombustible *a.* incombustible

income *n.* revenu *m.*, rentes *f. pl.*; — tax *n.* impôt sur le revenu *m.*

incoming *a.* rentrant; nouveau

incommensurable *a.* incommensurable

incommode *vt.* incommoder

incommunicable *a.* incommunicable

incommunicado *a.* sans communication

incommutable *a.* incommuable

incomparable *a.* incomparable

incompatibility *n.* incompatibilité *f.*

incompatible *a.* incompatible

incompetence *n.* incompétence *f.*; incapacité *f.*

incompetent *a.* incompétent; incapable

incomplete *a.* incomplet, inachevé

incomprehensible *a.* incompréhensible

inconceivable *a.* inconcevable

inconclusive *a.* inconcluant, peu concluant

incongruity *n.* inconguité *f.*

incongruous *a.* incongru

inconsequent *a.* inconséquent; –ial *a.* in-conséquent

inconsiderable *a.* insignifiant

inconsiderate *a.* inconsidéré

inconsistency *n.* incompatibilité, inconsistance, incongruité *f.*

inconsistent *a.* inconsistant, incompatible

inconsolable *a.* inconsolable

inconspicuous *a.* peu remarquable, peu en vue

inconstancy *n.* inconstance *f.*

incontestable *a.* incontestable

incontinence *n.* incontinence *f.*

incontinent *a.* incontinent

incontrovertible *a.* indisputable; incontestable

inconvenience *n.* incommodité *f.*; dérangement *m.*; — *vt.* troubler, déranger

inconvenient *a.* inopportun; incommode

incorporate *vt.* incorporer; — *vi.* s'incorporer; –d *a.* incorporé; (com.) anonyme

incorporation *n.* incorporation *f.*

incorrect *a.* incorrect; inexact

incorrigible *a.* incorrigible

incorruptible *a.* incorruptible

increase *n.* accroissement *m.*; augmentation *f.*; — *vt.* augmenter; accroître; redoubler; — *vi.* (s')augmenter; s'accroître

increasing *a.* augmentant, croissant; –ly *adv.* de plus en plus

incredible *a.* incroyable

incredulity *n.* incrédulité *f.*

incredulous *a.* incrédule

increment *n.* augmentation *f.*; accroissement, surcroît *m.*

incriminate *vt.* inculper, incriminer

incrust *vt.* incruster

incubate *vt. & vi.* couver

incubation *n.* incubation *f.*

incubator *n.* couveuse *f.*

incubus *n.* cauchemar, incube *m.*

inculcate *vt.* inculquer

inculpate *vt.* inculper

incumbent *n.* bénéficier *m.*; titulaire *m.*; — *a.* obligatoire; be — on incomber à

incur *vt.* encourir, s'attirer

incurable *a.* incurable

incursion *n.* irruption *f.*

indebted *a.* endetté; redevable; obligé; reconnaissant; –ness *n.* obligation *f.*

indecency *n.* indécence *f.*

indecent *a.* indécent

indecision *n.* indécision *f.*

indecisive *a.* indécis

indeed *adv.* en vérité, vraiment, réellement; en effet

indefatigable *a.* infatigable

indefensible *a.* indéfendable, insoutenable

indefinable *a.* vague; indéfinissable

indefinite *a.* indéfini

indelible *a.* indélébile, ineffaçable

indelicate *a.* indélicat, grossier

indemnify *vt.* indemniser, dédommager

indemnity *n.* indemnité *f.*, dédommagement *m.*

indent *vt.* denteler; renfoncer; faire un alinéa; –ation *n.* dentelure *f.*; renforcement *m.*; alinéa *m.*

indenture *n.* contrat d'apprentissage *m.*; — *vt.* mettre en apprentissage

independence *n.* indépendance *f.*

independent *a.* indépendant

indescribable *a.* indescriptible

indestructible *a.* indestructible

indeterminable *a.* indéterminable

indeterminate *a.* indéterminé, indécis

index *n.* table des matières *f.*; index *m.*; — finger index *m.*; — *vt.* cataloguer, classer; faire l'index de

India *n.* Inden *f.*, Indes *f. pl.*

Indian *n. & a.* Indien *m.*; — giver (coll.) homme qui veut qu'on lui rende le cadeau qu'il a fait *m.*; — Summer période de beau temps; qui suit la première gelée *f.*

indicate *vt.* indiquer

indication *n.* indication *f.*, indice *m.*

indicative *n. & a.* indicatif *m.*

indicator *n.* indicateur *m.*; aiguille *f.*

indict *vt.* accuser; –ment *n.* acte d'accusation *m.*

Indies *n. pl.* Indes *f. pl.*; East — Indes orientales; West — Antilles *f. pl.*

indifference *n.* indifférence *f.*

indifferent *a.* indifférent

indigence *n.* indigence *f.*

indigenous *a.* indigène

indigent *a.* indigent

indigestible *a.* indigeste

indignant *a.* indigné

indignity *n.* indignité, injure *f.*, affront *m.*

indigo *n.* indigo *m.*

indiscernible *a.* imperceptible

indiscreet *a.* indiscret

indiscretion *n.* indiscrétion *f.*; imprudence *f.*

indiscriminate *a.* sans discernement, sans distinction; indistinct, confus

indispensable *a.* indispensable

indispose *vt.* indisposer; rendre malade

indisposition *n.* indisposition, maladie *f.*

indisputable *a.* indisputable, incontestable

indistinct *a.* indistinct; vague

indistinguishable *a.* indistinct; imperceptible

individual *n.* individu *m.*; — *a.* individuel; –ism *n.* individualisme *m.*; –ity *n.* individualité *f.*

indivisible *a.* indivisible, inséparable

Indo-China *n.* Indochine *f.*

indoctrinate *vt.* indoctriner

Indo-European *a. & n.* indo-européen, aryen *m.*

indolent *a.* indolent

indomitable *a.* indomptable

Indonesia *n.* Indonésie *f.*

indoor *a.* d'intérieur; –s *adv.* à l'intérieur

indorse *vt.* endosser; –ment *n.* endos, endossement *m.*; (fig.) approbation *f.*; –r *n.* endosseur *m.*

induce *vt.* induire, persuader, engager, causer; –ment *n.* encouragement, motif *m.*

induct *vt.* installer; mobiliser; –ion *n.* induction *f.*; mobilisation *f.*; –ive *a.* (elec.) inducteur; inductif

indulge *vt.* avoir de l'indulgence pour; tolérer; — *vi.* s'abandonner (à); se laisser aller; — in se livrer à; se permettre; –nce *n.* indulgence *f.*; –nt *a.* indulgent

industrial *a.* industriel; — psychology *n.* psychologie industrielle *f.*; –ism *n.* industrialisme *m.*; –ist *n.* industriel *m.*; –ization *n.* industrialisation *f.*; –ize *vt.* industrialiser

industrious *a.* industrieux, assidu

industry *n.* industrie *f.*

inebriate *n.* ivrogne *m.*; — *vt.* saouler, enivrer; –d *a.* ivre, saoul

ineffable *a.* ineffable, inexprimable

ineffective, ineffectual *a.* inefficace, inutile; –ness *n.* inefficacité *f.*

inefficacious *a.* inefficace

inefficacy *n.* inefficacité *f.*

inefficiency *n.* inefficacité *f.*

inefficient *a.* inefficace

ineligible *a.* inéligible

inept *a.* inepte; incapable; –itude, –ness *n.* ineptie *f.*; inaptitude *f.*

inequality *n.* inégalité *f.*

inequitable *a.* inéquitable

inert *a.* inerte, inactif; –ia *n.* inertie *f.*

inescapable *a.* inévitable

inestimable *a.* inestimable

inevitable *a.* inévitable

inexact *a.* inexact

inexcusable *a.* inexcusable

inexhaustible *a.* inépuisable

inexpensive *a.* bon marché, pas cher

inexperienced *a.* inexpérimenté

inexplicable *a.* inexplicable

inexpressible *a.* inexprimable

inextricable *a.* inextricable

infallibility *n.* infaillibilité *f.*

infallible *a.* infaillible

infamous *a.* infâme, honteux

infamy *n.* infamie *f.*

infancy *n.* première enfance *f.*

infant *n.* bebé *m.*; –icide *n.* infanticide *m.*;

–ile *a.* enfantin; –ile paralysis *n.* polio-miélite *m.*; paralysie infantile *f.*

infantry *n.* infanterie *f.*; –man *n.* soldat d'infanterie *m.*

infatuate *vt.* infatuer; become –d s'engouer

infatuation *n.* engouement *m.*

infect *vt.* infecter; contagionner; –ion *n.* infection *f.*; contagion *f.*; –ious *a.* contagieux; infectieux

infer *vt.* inférer; –ence *n.* déduction, conclusion *f.*

inferior *n.* inférieur *m.*; — *a.* inférieur; subalterne, subordonné; –ity *n.* infériorité *f.*; — complex complexe d'infériorité *m.*

infernal *a.* infernal, d'enfer

inferno *n.* enfer *m.*

infest *vt.* infester

infidel *n.* infidèle *m.*; –ity *n.* infidélité *f.*

infiltrate *vi.* s'infiltrer (dans)

infinite *a.* infini

infinitesimal *a.* infinitésimal

infinitive *n.* infinitif *m.*

infinity *n.* infinité *f.*; infini *m.*

infirm *a.* infirme; irrésolu; –ary *n.* infirmerie *f.*; –ity *n.* infirmité *f.*

inflame *vt.* enflammer; irriter; — *vi.* s'enflammer

inflammable *a.* inflammable

inflammation *n.* inflammation *f.*

inflammatory *a.* inflammatoire; (fig.) incendiaire

inflate *vt.* gonfler; enfler; hausser

inflation *n.* gonflement *m.*; (finance) inflation *f.*

inflect *vt.* fléchir; (gram.) décliner, conjuguer; –ion *n.* inflexion *f.*

inflexibility *n.* inflexibilité *f.*

inflexible *a.* inflexible

inflict *vt.* infliger, imposer; –ion *n.* infliction *f.*

influence *n.* influence *f.*; (coll.) piston, bras long *m.*; — *vt.* influencer

influential *a.* influent

influenza *n.* grippe *f.*

influx *n.* flux *m.*, affluence *f.*

inform *vt.* faire savoir; faire part à; avertir; renseigner; informer, instruire; — against dénoncer; –ant *n.* accusateur, dénonciateur; informateur *m.*; source *f.* (d'un renseignement); –ation *n.* renseignements *m. pl.*; piece of –ation renseignement *m.*; –ed *a.* instruit; –er *n.* dénonciateur *m.*

informal *a.* sans cérémonie; non-officiel; –ity *n.* manque de cérémonie *m.*

infraction *n.* violation, infraction *f.*

infrared *a.* infra-rouge

infrequent *a.* rare

infringe *vt.* enfreindre, violer; –ment *n.* infraction *f.*

infuriate *vt.* rendre furieux

infuse *vt.* infuser; inspirer

infusion *n.* infusion *f.*; inspiration *f.*

ingenious *a.* ingénieux, inventif

ingenuity *n.* génie *m.*; ingéniosité *f.*

ingenuous *a.* ingénu, naïf, candide; –ness *n.* ingénuité *f.*; naïveté, candeur *f.*

inglorious *a.* inglorieux; honteux

ingrained *a.* inné; enraciné

ingrate *n.* ingrat *m.*

ingratiate *vt.* mettre en faveur; — oneself se mettre en faveur; s'insinuer

ingratitude *n.* ingratitude *f.*

ingredient *n.* ingrédient *m.*

ingress *n.* entrée *f.*

ingrown *a.* retourné; tourné en dedans; — toenail ongle incarné *m.*

inhabit *vt.* habiter; –able *a.* habitable; –ant *n.* habitant *m.*

inhale *vt.* inspirer, aspirer

inharmonious *a.* inharmonieux

inherent *a.* inhérent

inherit *vt.* hériter; –ance *n.* héritage *m.*; –ance tax *n.* impôt de succesion *m.*

inhibit *vt.* prohiber; refouler; –ion *n.* prohibition *f.*; refoulement *m.*

inhospitable *a.* inhospitalier

inhuman *a.* inhumain; –ity *n.* inhumanité *f.*

inhume *vt.* inhumer, enterrer

inimical *a.* ennemi, hostile

inimitable *a.* inimitable

iniquitous *a.* inique, injuste *f.*

iniquity *n.* iniquité, injustice *f.*

initial *n.* initiale *f.*; — *a.* initial; — *vt.* parapher

initiate *vt.* initier; commencer

initiation *n.* initiation *f.*; commencement *m.*

initiative *n.* initiative *f.*; énergie *f.*

initiator *n.* initiateur *m.*

inject *vt.* injecter; piquer; –ion *n.* injection *f.*; piqûre *f.*

injudicious *a.* injudicieux

injunction *n.* injonction *f.*

injure *vt.* faire tort à, injurier; nuire; blesser

injurious *a.* injurieux; nuisible

injury *n.* injustice *f.*; tort *m.*; mal *m.*; blessure *f.*

injustice *n.* injustice, iniquité *f.*

ink *n.* encre *f.*; — blot pâté d'encre *m.*; India — encre de Chine *f.*; — *vt.* couvrir d'encre; –y *a.* couvert d'encre; très obscur, noir foncé

inkling *n.* pressentiment, soupçon *m.*

ink pad *n.* tampon à impression *m.*

inkwell *n.* encrier *m.*

inlaid *a.* marqueté, parqueté
inland *n. & a.* intérieur *m.*; — *adv.* vers l'intérieur
in-laws *n. pl.* parents par alliance *m. pl.*; beaux-parents *m. pl.*
inlay *vt.* marqueter; incruster; — *n.* marqueterie, incrustation *f.*
inlet *n.* anse *f.*; débouché *m.*; admission *f.*
inmate *n.* pensionnaire *m.*; prisonnier *m.*
inmost, innermost *a.* le plus intérieur; le plus intime
inn *n.* auberge *f.*
innate *a.* inné
inner *a.* intérieur; — tube chambre à air *f.*; –most *a.* le plus intime
inning *n.* (baseball) période *f.*
innkeeper *n.* aubergiste *m.*
innocence *n.* innocence *f.*
innocent *a. & n.* innocent *m.*
innocuous *a.* innocent, inoffensif
innovate *vi.* innover
innovation *n.* innovation *f.*
innuendo *n.* allusion, insinuation *f.*
innumerable *a.* innombrable
inoculate *vt.* inoculer; vacciner
inoffensive *a.* inoffensif
inoperative *a.* inefficace
inopportune *a.* mal à propos, inopportun
inordinate *a.* déréglé; irrégulier; démesuré
inorganic *a.* inorganique
inquest *n.* enquête judiciaire *f.*
inquire *vi.* s'enquérir, s'informer; demander (un avis); s'adresser
inquiry *n.* enquête, recherche *f.*, examen *m.*
inquisitive *a.* curieux; –ness *n.* curiosité *f.*
inquisitor *n.* inquisiteur *m.*
inroad *n.* incursion, invasion *f.*
insane *a.* insensé, fou; aliéné; — asylum asile des aliénés *m.*; maison de fous *f.*
insanity *n.* folie, démence *f.*
insatiability *n.* insatiabilité *f.*
insatiable *a.* insatiable
inscribe *vt.* inscrire; dédier
inscription *n.* inscription *f.*; (book) dédicace *f.*
insect *a.* insecte *m.*; –icide *n. & a.* insecticide *m.*
insecure *a.* mal assuré, peu sûr
insecurity *n.* insécurité, incertitude *f.*, danger *m.*
insensible *a.* insensible
insensitive *a.* insensible
inseparable *a.* inséparable
insert *vt.* insérer, introduire; — *n.* insertion *f.*; –ion *n.* insertion; introduction *f.*
inset *vt.* insérer (un cliché, un texte, dans un autre cliché, un autre texte); — *n.* objet inséré *m.*; hors-texte *m.*
inside *n.* intérieur *m.*; dedans *m.*; — out

à l'envers; –s *pl.* entrailles *f. pl.*; — *a.* intérieur; — of (time) en moins de; — track (coll.) avantage *m.*; — *adv.* à l'intérieur, vers l'intérieur; — *prep.* dans, à l'intérieur de; –r *n.* personne de la maison *f.*; initié *m.*
insidious *a.* insidieux
insight *n.* intuition *f.*; goût, jugement *m.*; aperçu *m.*
insignia *n. pl.* insignes *m. pl.*
insignificance *n.* insignifiance *f.*
insignificant *a.* insignifiant; peu important, sans importance
insincere *a.* peu sincère; faux, trompeur
insincerity *n.* manque de sincérité *m.*
insinuate *vt.* insinuer, suggérer, laisser entendre, donner à entendre
insinuating *a.* insinuant
insinuation *n.* insinuation *f.*
insipid *a.* insipide; fade; –ity *n.* insipidité *f.*; fadeur *f.*
insist *vi.* insister, persister; — on persister à; tenir à; — that insister pour que; –ence *n.* insistence *f.*; –ent *a.* insistant
insole *n.* semelle intérieure *f.*
insolence *n.* insolence *f.*
insolubility *n.* insolubilité *f.*
insoluble *a.* insoluble; irrésoluble
insolvency *n.* insolvabilité *f.*
insolvent *a.* insolvable
insomnia *n.* insomnie *f.*
insomuch as *conj.* dans la mesure que; à un tel pointe que
inspect *vt.* inspecter, surveiller, examiner; visiter; –ion *n.* inspection *f.*; visite *f.*; –or *n.* inspecteur *m.*
inspiration *n.* inspiration *f.*; respiration *f.*
inspire *vt.* inspirer, respirer
instability *n.* instabilité *f.*
install *vt.* installer; –ation *n.* installation *f.*
installment *n.* mensualité *f.*, versement, paiement, acompte *m.*
instance *n.* sollicitation *f.*; circonstance *f.*; for — par exemple
instant *n.* moment, instant *m.*; — *a.* immédiat, instantané; (dates) courant; –ly *a.* immédiatement; tout de suite; à l'instant; –aneous *a.* instantané
instead *adv.* à sa place; — of *prep.* au lieu de
instep *n.* cou-de-pied *m.*
instigate *vt.* instiguer, exciter, provoquer
instigator *n.* instigateur *m.*
instill *vt.* instiller; inculquer
instinct *n.* instinct *m.*; –ive *a.* instinctif
institute *n.* institut *m.*; — *vt.* instituer, établir, fonder
institution *n.* institution *f.*
instruct *vt.* instruire, enseigner; –ion *n.* enseignement *m.*; –ions *n. pl.* instruc-

tions *f. pl.*; ordres *m. pl.*; –ive *a.* instructif; –or *n.* professeur *m.*

instrument *n.* instrument *m.*; outil *m.*; (law) acte *m.*; –al *a.* instrumental; be –al in contribuer à, jouer un rôle dans; –alist *n.* instrumentiste *m.*; –ation *n.* instrumentation *f.*

insubordinate *n.* insubordonné

insubordination *n.* insubordination *f.*

insufferable *a.* intolérable, insupportable

insufficiency *n.* insuffisance *f.*

insufficient *a.* insuffisant

insular *a.* insulaire

insulate *vt.* isoler

insulator *n.* isolateur *m.*

insulin *n.* insuline *f.*

insult *n.* insulte *f.*; — *vt.* insulter

insuperable *a.* insurmontable

insupportable *a.* insupportable

insurable *a.* assurable

insurance *n.* assurance *f.*; **group** — assurance par groupe *f.*; **life** — assurance sur la vie; **fire** — assurance contre l'incendie; — **policy** police d'assurance *f.*

insure *vt.* assurer

insurgent *n. & a.* insurgé, révolté *m.*

insurmountable *a.* insurmontable

insurrection *n.* insurrection *f.*

intake *n.* adduction *f.*; robinet d'adduction *m.*; prise, entrée, admission *f.*

intangibility *n.* intangibilité *f.*

integer *n.* nombre entier *m.*

integral *n.* (math.) intégrale *f.*; — *a.* intégral, entier

integrate *vt.* intégrer

integration *n.* intégration *f.*

integrity *n.* intégrité, probité *f.*

intellect *n.* intellect *m.*; –ual *a. & n.* intellectuel *m.*

intelligence *n.* intelligence *f.*; nouvelle *f.*, avis, rapport *m.*

intelligent *a.* intelligent

intelligible *a.* intelligible, clair

intemperance *n.* intempérance *f.*

intemperate *a.* immodéré

intend *vi.* se proposer, compter, penser; avoir l'intention de; — *vt.* destiner; –ed *a.* projeté; voulu; –ed *a. & n.* fiancé *m.*, fiancée *f.*

intense *a.* intense, véhément; fort; –ness *n.* intensité *f.*

intensify *vt.* renforcer; intensifier

intensity *n.* intensité *f.*

intensive *a.* intensif

intent *a.* absorbé; appliqué, attentif; déterminé; **with** — **to** dans l'intention de; — *n.* intention *f.*; –ion *n.* intention *f.*; –ional *a.* intentionnel; voulu; –ionally *adv.* exprès, à dessein; –ness *n.* atten-

tion *f.*

inter *vt.* enterrer, ensevelir; –ment *n.* enterrement *m.*

interact *vi.* réagir réciproquement

interbreed *vt.* croiser deux espèces

intercede *vi.* intercéder

intercept *vt.* intercepter; capter; –ion *n.* interception *f.*; captation *f.*

interchange *n.* échange *m.*; communication *f.*; alternance *f.*; — *vt.* échanger; –able *a.* interchangeable

interdepartmental *a.* interdépartemental

interdict *n.* (eccl.) interdit *m.*; — *vt.* interdire; –ion *n.* interdiction *f.*

interest *n.* intérêt *m.*; profit *m.*; participation *f.*; **compound** — intérêts composés *m. pl.*; **rate of** — taux de l'intérêt *m.*; **take an** — **in** s'intéresser à; — *vt.* intéresser; –ed *a.* intéressé, d'intérêt; be –ed in s'intéresser à

interfere *vi.* intervenir; se mêler; s'interposer; — **with** gêner; –nce *n.* intervention *f.*; (rad.) brouillage *m.*

interim *a.* intérimaire; — *adv.* entre temps; en attendant; — *n.* intérim *m.*

interior *n. & a.* intérieur *m.*

interjection *n.* interjection *f.*

interlace *vt.* entrelacer

interlinear *a.* interlinéaire

interlining *n.* doublure intermédiaire *f.*

interlock *vi.* s'entrecroiser, s'entrelacer; –ing *a.* qui s'entrecroisent; — *vt.* (rail.) enclencher

interloper *n.* intrus *m.*

interlude *n.* intermède *m.*

intermarriage *n.* intermariage *m.*

intermarry *vi.* se marier les uns avec les autres

intermediary *a. & n.* intermédiaire *m.*

intermediate *a.* intermédiaire; moyen

interminable *a.* interminable

interminably *adv.* sans fin

intermingle *vt.* entremêler; — *vi.* se mêler, s'entremêler

intermission *n.* entr'acte *m.*

intermittent *a.* intermittent; –ly *adv.* par intervalles

intern *vt.* interner; — *n.* interne des hôpitaux *m.*; –ment *n.* internement *m.*; –ship *n.* internat *m.*

internal *a.* interne, intérier; intestin

international *a.* international

interplanetary *a.* interplanétaire

interpolate *vt.* interpoler, intercaler

interpolation *n.* interpolation *f.*

interpret *vt.* interpréter; expliquer; –ation *n.* interprétation *f.*; –er *n.* interprète *m. & f.*

interrelated *a.* en relation mutuelle

interrelation *n.* corrélation *f.*

interrogate *vt.* interroger, questionner

interrogation *n.* interrogation *f.*; interrogatoire *m.*; — **point** point d'interrogation *m.*

interrogative *a.* interrogatif

interrupt *vt.* interrompre; **–er** *n.* (elec.) interrupteur *m.*; coupe-circuit *m.*; **–ion** *n.* interruption *f.*

interscholastic *a.* interscolaire

intersect *vt.* entrecouper, intersecter; — *vi.* se couper, se croiser, s'intersecter; **–ion** *n.* intersection *f.*; (roads) carrefour *m.*; croisement *m.*; coin *m.*

intersperse *vt.* entremêler

interstate *a.* entre les états; — **commerce** commerce dans lequel les marchandises sont transportées au delà des frontières de l'etat *m.*

interurban *a.* interurbain

interval *n.* intervalle *m.*; **at –s** par intervalles

intervene *vi.* intervenir; arriver; (time) s'écouler

interview *n.* entrevue *f.*; interview *m.*; entretien *m.*; — *vt.* interviewer

interwoven *a.* entrelacé, entremêlé

intestate *a.* intestat

intestine *n.* intestin *m.*

intimacy *n.* intimité *f.*

intimate *a.* intime; étroit; — *n.* intime *m.* & *f.*; — *vt.* donner à entendre; suggérer

intimation *n.* suggestion *f.*

intimidate *vt.* intimider

intimidation *n.* intimidation *f.*

into *prep.* dans, en; entre

intolerable *a.* intolérable; insupportable

intolerance *n.* intolérance *f.*

intolerant *a.* intolérant

intonation *n.* ton *m.*, intonation *f.*

intone *vt.* entonner

intoxicate *vt.* enivrer; griser; **–d** *a.* ivre; gris

intoxicating *a.* enivrant

intoxication *n.* ivresse *f.*; enivrement *m.*

intractable *a.* intraitable

intransitive *a.* intransitif

intravenous *a.* dans les veines, intraveineux

intrepid *a.* intrépide; **–ity** *n.* intrépidité, hardiesse *f.*

intricacy *n.* complexité *f.*

intricate *a.* compliqué

intrigue *n.* intrigue *f.*; — *vt.* & *vi.* intriguer; **–r** *n.* intrigant *m.*

intriguing *a.* intrigant; très intéressant; qui intrigue; — *n.* intrigues *f. pl.*

intrinsic *a.* intrinsèque

introduce *vt.* présenter; introduire

introduction *n.* présentation *f.*; introduction *f.*; (book) avant-propos *m.*

introductory *a.* préliminaire; d'introduction

introspection *n.* introspection *f.*

introspective *a.* introspectif

introvert *n.* introverti *m.*; **–ed** *a.* introverti, recueilli

intrude *vi.* s'ingérer; s'infiltrer; — **on** déranger; **–r** *n.* intrus *m.*

intrusion *n.* intrusion *f.*; importunité *f.*

intrust *vt.* confier

intuition *n.* intuition *f.*

intuitive *a.* intuitif; **–ly** *adv.* par intuition

inundate *vt.* inonder

inundation *n.* inondation *f.*

inure *vt.* accoutumer, habituer; endurcir

invade *vt.* envahir; **–r** *n.* envahisseur *m.*

invalid *n.* & *a.* (health) malade; infirme; valétudinaire *m.* & *f.*; **–ate** *vt.* invalider; vicier; infirmer

invalid *a.* invalide; **–idate** *vt.* invalider, déclarer de nul effet

invaluable *a.* inestimable

invariable *a.* invariable

invariably *adv.* invariablement

invasion *n.* invasion *f.*, envahissement *m.*; violation *f.*

invective *n.* invective *f.*

inveigh *vi.* invectiver

inveigle *vt.* séduire, entraîner, enjôler

invent *vt.* inventer; **–ion** *n.* invention *f.*; **–ive** *a.* inventif; **–iveness** *n.* don d'invention *m.*; imagination *f.*; **–or** *n.* inventeur *m.*

inventory *n.* inventaire *m.*; — *vt.* faire l'inventaire de

inverse *a.* inverse; — *n.* inverse, contraire *m.*

inversion *n.* (gram.) inversion *f.*; renversement *m.*

invert *vt.* renverser; invertir

invertebrate *n.* & *a.* invertébré *m.*

invest *vt.* (money) placer, mettre; (mil.) investir; **–ment** *n.* placement, investissement *m.*; **–or** *n.* actionnaire *m.* & *f.*; rentier *m.*

investigate *vt.* faire une enquête sur; examiner, étudier

investigation *n.* enquête, investigation *f.*; étude *f.*

investigator *n.* investigateur *m.*; agent *m.*

inveterate *a.* invétéré, acharné; implacable

invigorate *vt.* fortifier; vivifier

invigorating *a.* fortifiant, vivifiant

invincibility *n.* invincibilité *f.*

invincible *a.* invincible

inviolable *a.* inviolable

invisibility *n.* invisibilité *f.*

invisible *a.* invisible

invite *vt.* inviter; provoquer
inviting *a.* attrayant, invitant; séduisant
invocation *n.* invocation *f.*
invoice *n.* facture *f.*; — *vt.* facturer
invoke *vt.* invoquer; évoquer
involuntarily *adv.* involontairement
involuntary *a.* involontaire
involve *vt.* envelopper; compliquer; engager; impliquer; entraîner; nécessiter; —ed *a.* compliqué; embrouillé; engagé; impliqué
invulnerable *a.* invulnérable
inward *a.* interne, intérieur; vers l'intérieur; —ly *adv.* en dedans; à l'intérieur; —s *adv.* vers l'intérieur
iodide *n.* iodure *m.*
iodine *n.* iode *m.*; tincture of — teinture d'iode *f.*
ion *n.* ion *m.*; —ization *n.* ionisation *f.*; —osphere ionosphère *f.*; —ize *vt.* ioniser
I.O.U. *n.* reconnaissance de dette *f.*
Iran *n.* Iran *m.*; —ian *a.* & *n.* iranien *m.*
Iraq *n.* Irak *m.*; —i *a.* & *n.* irakien *m.*
irascible *a.* irascible
irate *a.* en colère
ire *n.* colère *f.*; courroux *m.*
Ireland *n.* Irlande *f.*
iridescence *n.* iridescence *f.*
irisdescent *a.* iridescent, irisé
Irish *a.* & *n.* Irlandais *m.*; —man *n.* Irlandais; —woman *n.* Irlandaise *f.*
irk *vt.* ennuyer; —some *a.* ennuyeux
iron *n.* fer *m.*; (laundry) fer à repasser *m.*; cast — fer de fonte *m.*; curling — fer à friser *m.*; — curtain rideau de fer *m.*; — lung poumon de fer *m.*; — ore minerai de fer *m.*; pig — fonte en saumon *f.*; scrap — ferraille *f.*; wrought — fer forgé *m.*; —s *n. pl.* fers *m. pl.*, chaînes *f. pl.*; — *a.* de fer; — *vt.* repasser, donner un coup de fer à; — out faire disparaître; aplanir; —ing *n.* repassage *m.*
ironclad *a.* cuirassé; (fig.) parfait, qui ne peut être démenti
ironic(al) *a.* ironique
irony *n.* ironie *f.*
irradiate *vt.* rayonner, illuminer, éclairer
irrational *a.* déraisonnable; irrationnel
irreconcilable *a.* implacable; irréconciliable; inconciliable
irrecoverable *a.* irréparable
irreducible *a.* irréductible
irrefutable *a.* incontestable, irréfutable, irrécusable
irregular *a.* irrégulier; —ity *n.* irrégularité *f.*
irrelevance *n.* inapplicabilité *f.*
irrelevant *a.* inapplicable, hors de propos, non pertinent
irreligious *a.* irréligieux

irremediable *a.* irremédiable
irremovable *a.* inamovible
irreparable *a.* irréparable
irreplaceable *a.* qui ne peut être remplacé
irrepressible *a.* irréprimable
irreproachable *a.* irréprochable
irresistible *a.* irrésistible
irresolute *a.* irrésolu
irrespective *a.* indépendent; — *adv.*, — of sans égard à; sans tenir compte de
irresponsibility *n.* irresponsabilité *f.*
irresponsible *a.* irréfléchi, étourdi
irretrievable *a.* irrémédiable
irreverence *n.* irrévérance *f.*
irreverent *a.* irrévérent; irrévérencieux
irreversible *a.* irrévocable
irrevocable *a.* irrévocable
irrigate *vt.* irriguer; arroser
irrigation *n.* irrigation *f.*
irritability *n.* irritabilité *f.*
irritable *a.* irritable
irritant *n.* irritant *m.*
irritate *vt.* irriter, agacer
irritating *a.* irritant, agaçant
irritation *n.* irritation *f.*
isinglass *n.* colle de poisson *f.*
island *n.* île *f.*; îlot *m.*; —er *n.* insulaire *m.* & *f.*
isle *n.* île *f.*
isolate *vt.* isoler; —ed *a.* isolé, écarté
isolation *n.* isolement *m.*; solitude *f.*; —ism (pol.) politique d'isolement *f.*
isometrics *n.* isométrique *f.*
isosceles *a.* isocèle
isotope *n.* isotope *m.*
Israel *n.* Israël *m.*; —i *a.* & *n.* israëlien *m.*; —ite *a.* & *n.* israélite *m.* & *f.*
issue *n.* question *f.*; publication *f.*; émission *f.*; délivrance *f.*; numéro *m.*; issue, sortie *f.*; résultat *m.*; fin *f.*; enfants *m. pl.*; — *vt.* publier; émettre; lancer; donner; délivrer; — *vi.* sortir, provenir
Istanbul *n.* Istamboul *m.*
isthmus *n.* isthme *m.*
it *pron.* il, elle; ce, cela; le, la
Italian *a.* & *n.* italien *m.*
italicize *vt.* mettre en italique
italics *n. pl.* italique *m.*
itch *n.* démangeaison *f.*; — *vi.* démanger
item *n.* article, détail *m.*; question *f.*; news — fait divers *m.*; —ize faire la liste de
iterate *vt.* réitérer
itinerant *a.* ambulant
itinerary *n.* itinéraire *m.*
its *a.* son, sa, ses
itself *pron.* se; lui-même, elle-même, soi-même
ivory *n.* ivoire *m.*; — *a.* d'ivoire; — tower tour d'ivoire *f.*

J

jab *n.* coup de pointe *m.*; (boxing) coup sec *m.*; — *vt.* piquer

jabber *vi.* bavardage *m.*; jacasserie *f.*; jacasser; —; –ing *n.* baragouinage *m.*

jack *n.* cric, lève-roue *m.*; (cards) valet *m.*; — *vt.*, — (up) soulever; augmenter; — rabbit *n.* lapin de plaine *m.*

jackass *n.* âne, baudet *m.*

jacket *n.* veston *m.*; veste *f.*; jaquette *f.*; (book) chemise, couverture *f.*

jack-in-the-box *n.* diable *m.*, boîte à surprise *f.*

jackknife *n.* couteau de poche *m.*

jack-o'-lantern *n.* feu follet *m.*

jack pot *n.* gros lot; hit the — (coll.) gagner le prix; faire fortune d'un seul coup

jade *n.* jade *m.*; (person) coquine *f.*; –d *a.* fatigué, éreinté

jag *vt.* ébrécher; — *n.* dent de scie *f.*

jagged *a.* dentelé, ébréché; –ness *n.* dentelure *f.*

jail *n.* prison *f.*; — *vt.* mettre en prison; –er *n.* gardien *m.*

jam *n.* confiture *f.*; presse *f.*; (traffic) embouteillage *m.*; — *vt.* presser, serrer; fourrer, enfoncer; coincer; (radio) brouiller; — *vi.* se coincer; (gun) s'enrayer

jamboree *n.* (coll.) grande réunion *f.*

jangle *vi.* cliqueter, s'entre-choquer; — *vt.* faire entre-choquer; –d *a.* agacé

janitor *n.* concierge, portier *m.*

January *n.* janvier *m.*

Japan *n.* Japon *m.*; –ese *a.* & *n.* japonais *m.*

jar *n.* bocal *m.*, pot *m.*; choc *m.*, secousse *f.*; — *vt.* choquer; agacer; — *vi.* être en désaccord; — on choquer, crisper

jaundice *n.* jaunisse *f.*

jaunt *n.* excursion, sortie *f.*; –y *a.* désinvolte; vif

Java *n.* Java *m.*; –nese *n.* & *a.* Javanais *m.*

javelin *n.* javeline *f.*, javelot *m.*

jaw, jawbone *n.* mâchoire *f.*

jaywalker (coll.) *n.* piéton imprudent *m.* (qui traverse la rue en dehors du passage clouté)

jealous *a.* jaloux; –y *n.* jalousie *f.*

jeans *n.* pantalon de coutil *m.*

jeep *n.* jeep *f.*

jeer *vi.* se moquer; — at railler; siffler; se moquer de; –ing *a.* railleur; –ing *n.* raillerie *f.*

jellied *a.* en gelée

jelly *n.* gelée *f.*; — *vt.* faire prendre en gelée; — *vi.* se prendre en gelée

jeopardize *vt.* compromettre; mettre en péril

jeopardy *n.* péril, danger *m.*

jerk *n.* saccade, secousse *f.*; — *vt.* tirer (d'un coup sec); — *vi.* se mouvoir par saccades; –ed beef bœuf séché *m.*; –y *a.* coupé, saccadé

jersey *n.* tricot *m.*; (sports) maillot *m.*

jest *n.* plaisanterie *f.*; — *vi.* plaisanter; –er *n.* bouffon *m.*

Jesus Christ *n.* Jésus-Christ *m.*

jet *n.* jet *m.*; brûleur, bec *m.*; (motor) réacteur *m.*; (mineral) jais *m.*; — plane avion à réaction *m.*; — propulsion propulsion à réaction *f.*

jet-black *a.* noir comme du jais

jet-propelled *a.* à réaction

jettison *vt.* jeter

jetty *n.* jetée *f.*

Jew *n.* Juif *m.*; –ish *a.* juif *m.*, juive *f.*

jewel *n.* bijou, joyau *m.*; (watch) rubis *m.*; –er *n.* bijoutier, joaillier *m.*; –ry *n.* bijouterie, joaillerie *f.*

jib *n.* (naut.) foc *m.*

jibe *vi.* s'accorder; être d'accord

jig *n.* gigue *f.*; — *vi.* danser une gigue

jigger *n.* chique *f.*; (drink measure) deux doigts *m. pl.*

jigsaw *n.* scie à chantourner *f.*; — puzzle jeu de patience *f.*

jilt *vt.* abandonner

jingle *n.* tintement *m.*; — *vi.* tinter; — *vt.* faire tinter

jitters *n. pl.* (coll.) nervosité *f.*; crise de nerfs *f.*

jive *n.* jive *m.*

job *n.* emploi *m.*; poste *m.*, situation *f.*; travail *m.*; métier *m.*; — lot lot de soldes; — work travail à la pièce *m.*; –ber *n.* revendeur *m.*; –less *a.* sans travail, désœuvré; –less *n.* chômeurs *m. pl.*

jockey *n.* jockey *m.*; — *vt.* & *vi.* manœuvrer

jocose *a.* plaisant, badin

jocular *a.* rieur, facétieux

jocund *a.* enjoué, jovial

jodhpurs *n. pl.* pantalon d'équitation *m.*

jog *n.* secousse *f.*; petit trot *m.*; — *vi.* aller au petit trot

join *vt.* & *vi.* joindre, unir, réunir; ajouter; relier; (club) entrer dans; — *vi.* se joindre, s'unir; — in prendre part; — up s'engager; –er *n.* (carpentry) menuisier *m.*

joint *n.* joint *m.*, jointure *f.*; articulation *f.*; out of — disloqué; — *a.* commun; collectif, combiné; — account compte conjoint, compte en participation *m.*; — heir cohéritier *m.*; –ly *adv.* en commun; ensemble; conjointement

joist *n.* solive *f.*

joke *n.* blague, plaisanterie *f.*; **practical** — mystification *f.*; **play a** — on mystifier; jouer un tour a; — *vi.* plaisanter; **-r** *n.* plaisant, farceur *m.*; (cards) joker *m.*; **practical -r** mauvais plaisant *m.*

joking *a.* moqueur; **-ly** *adv.* en plaisantant; — *n.* plaisanterie *f.*

jolly *a.* gai, enjoué

jolt *n.* cahot *m.*, secousse *f.*; — *vt.* cahoter, secouer

Jordan *n.* (river) Jourdain *m.*; (country) Jordanie *f.*

jostle *vt.* bousculer, coudoyer, serrer

jot *n.* iota *m.*; — *vt.*, — **down** prendre note de, noter; **-tings** *n. pl.* notes *f. pl.*

jounce *vt.* secouer

journal *n.* journal *m.*; **-ese** *n.* (coll.) jargon des journaux *m.*; **-ism** *n.* journalisme *m.*; **yellow -ism** *n.* journalisme sensationnel *m.*; **-ist** *n.* journaliste *m. & f.*; **-istic** *a.* journalistique

journey *n.* voyage *m.*; — *vi.* voyager; **-man** *n.* ouvrier, compagnon *m.*

joust *vi.* jouter; — *n.* joute *f.*

jovial *a.* jovial; **-ity** *n.* jovialité, joie *f.*

jowl *n.* joue, bajoue *f.*

joy *n.* joie *f.*; **-ful** *a.* joyeux; **-fully** *adv.* joueusement; **-less** *a.* triste; **-ous** *a.* joyeux

jubilant *a.* joyeux, réjoui; triomphant

jubilate *vt.* jubiler

jubilee *n.* jubilé *m.*

Judaism *n.* judaïsme *n.*

judge *n.* juge *m.*; arbitre *m.*; connaisseur *m.*; **be a good** — **of** s'y connaître en; — *vt.* juger; estimer, mesurer

judgment *n.* jugement *m.*; arrêt *m.*, sentence *f.*; avis *m.*, opinion *f.*; — **day** jugement dernier *m.*

judicial *a.* judiciare; juridique

judiciary *a.* judiciaire; — *n.* magistrature *f.*

judicious *a.* judicieux

jug *n.* cruche *f.*, pot, broc *m.*; — *vt.* mettre en pot; **-ged hare** *n.* civet de lièvre *m.*

juggle *vi.* jongler; **-r** *n.* jongleur, bateleur *m.*

jugular *a.* jugulaire

juice *n.* jus, suc *m.*

juiciness *n.* succulence *f.*

juicy *a.* juteux, succulent; fondant

jukebox *n.* grand tourne-disque à sous, jukebox *m.*

julep *n.* julep *m.*; **mint** — boisson au whisky et à la menthe *f.*

July *n.* juillet *m.*

jumble *n.* confusion *f.*; — *vt.* brouiller

jumbo *a.* énorme

jump *n.* saut, bond *m.*; saute *f.*; (racing) obstacle *m.*; **broad** — saut en longueur *m.*; **high** — saut en hauteur *m.*; — *vi.* sauter, bondir; — *vt.* sauter, faire sauter; attaquer; — **at** saisir; — **the gun** devancer; commencer prématurément; — **the track** dérailler; **-er** *n.* sauteur *m.*; (clothes) casaquin *m.*; (elec.) connexion volante *f.*; **-iness** *n.* agitation, nervosité *f.*; **-ing** *a.* sautant, sautillant; actif; **-ing jack** pantin *m.*; **-ing** *n.* saut *m.*; **-y** *a.* nerveux, irritable

jump rope *n.* corde à sauter *f.*

junction *n.* jonction *f.*; bifurcation *f.*; carrefour *m.*; — **point** connexion *f.*

juncture *n.* jointure *f.*; moment *m.*

June *n.* juin *m.*

jungle *n.* jungle *f.*

junior *a.* plus jeune, cadet; (in names) fils; (mil.) subalterne; — **college** établissement qui ne fait que les deux premières années des études universitaires *m.*; — **high school** établissement qui ne fait que les deux premières années des études secondaires *m.*

juniper *n.* genièvre *m.*

junk *n.* débris, rejets *m. pl.*; (naut.) jonque *f.*; — *vt.* mettre au rancart

junket *n.* voyage fait aux frais de l'Etat *m.*

junta *n.* junte *f.*

juridical *a.* juridique

jurisdiction *n.* juridiction *f.*; **-al** *a.* juridictionnel

jurisprudence *n.* jurisprudence *f.*

jurist *n.* juriste *m.*

juror *n.* juré, membre du jury *m.*

jury *n.* jury *m.*, jurés *m. pl.*; — **box** banc des jurés *m.*

just *a.* juste; équitable; — *adv.* justement, juste; au juste; précisément; tout simplement; — **as** au moment où; — **now** tout à l'heure; actuellement, pour le moment; **-ly** *adv.* justement; avec justice

justice *n.* justice *f.*; (person) juge, magistrat *m.*

justifiable *a.* justifiable, légitime

justification *n.* justification *f.*

justify *vt.* justifier; motiver

jut *vi.*, — **(out)** faire saillie; — **out over** surplomber

juvenile *a.* juvénile; puéril; — **delinquent** accusé mineur *m.*; — *n.* jeune *m. & f.*

juxtaposition *n.* juxtaposition *f.*; **in** — juxtaposé

K

kale *n.* chou frisé *m.*

kaleidoscope *n.* kaléidoscope *m.*

Kashmir n. Cachemire m.

kayak n. kayac m.

keel n. quille f.

keen a. vif; ardent; aigu; fin; **—ness** n. finesse f.; ardeur f.; acuité f.

keep n. (castle-) donjon m.; **board and —** nourriture f.; **for —s** pour de bon; **—** vt. garder; tenir; entretenir, maintenir; retenir; empêcher; conserver, préserver; **—** vi. se tenir, rester; continuer; se conserver; **— an eye on** ne pas perdre de vue; **— from** s'abstenir de; empêcher de; s'empêcher de; **— in** retenir; rester dedans; rester à la maison; **— off** ne pas toucher (à); éloigner; **— on** garder; avancer; continuer; **— out** empêcher d'entrer; ne pas se mêler; rester dehors; **— quiet** rester tranquille; ne pas parler; se taire; **— up** maintenir, entretenir; faire veiller; **— waiting** faire attendre; **—er** n. garde, gardien m.; **—ing** n. garde f.; **in —ing with** en accord avec

keepsake n. souvenir m.

keg n. tonnelet, barillet m.

kelp n. soude de varech f.

ken n. savoir m., compréhension f.

kennel n. niche f.; chenil m.

kerchief n. fichu m.

kernel n. grain m.

kerosene n. kérosène m.

kettle n. bouilloire, marmite f.

kettledrum n. timbale f.

key n. clé, clef f.; (piano) touche f.; **— industry** n. industrie-clef f.; **— ring** porte-clefs m.; **sending —** manipulateur m.; **— word** mot-clé m.; **master —** passe-partout m.

keyboard n. clavier m.

keyhole n. trou de serrure m.

keynote n. (mus.) tonique f.; (fig.) point principal m.

keystone n. clef de voûte f.

khaki n. khaki m.

kick n. coup de pied m.; (coll.) frisson m.; (gun) recul m.; **—** vt. donner un coup de pied à; (sports) botter; **— vi.** donner un coup de pied; regimber; reculer; **—back** n. ristourne f.; **— out** mettre à la porte; chasser à coups de pied

kickoff n. coup d'envoi m.

kid n. chevreau m., chevrette f.; (coll.) gosse m. & f.; **— gloves** gants de chevreau m. pl.; **handle with — gloves** ménager; **—** vt. (coll.) plaisanter, faire marcher; **no —ding!** (coll.) sans blague!

kidnap vt. enlever, voler; **—per** n. kidnapper, ravisseur m.; **—ping** n. kidnapping, enlèvement, vol m.; rapt m.

kidney n. rein m.; (food) rognon m.; **— bean** haricot de Soissons m.

kidney-shaped a. réniforme

kidskin n. peau de chevreau f.

kill vt. tuer; (animal) abattre; (fig.) supprimer; **—er** n. assassin, meurtrier m.; tueur m.; **—ing** n. meurtre m.; tuerie f., massacre m.; (coll.) coup m.

kill-joy n. rabat-joie m.

kiln n. four m.

kilocycle n. kilocycle m.

kilogram n. kilo, kilogramme m.

kilometer n. kilomètre m.

kilometric a. kilométrique

kilowatt n. kilowatt m.

kilowatt-hour n. kilowatt-heure m.

kilt n. kilt m.

kilter n. bon ordre m.; **out of —** détraqué, déréglé

kin n. parents m. pl.; famille f.; **next of —** le plus proche parent m.; **—ship** n. parenté f.

kind n. genre m., espèce f., sorte f.; **nothing of the —** rien de la sorte; **payment in —** paiement en nature m.; **—** a. bon; aimable; bienveillant; **—liness** n. bonté, bienveillance f.; **—ly** a. bon, bienveillant; **—ness** n. bonté, bienveillance f.; prévenance f.; service m.

kindergarten n. jardin d'enfants m.; école maternelle f.

kindhearted a. bon, bienveillant

kindle vt. allumer, enflammer; susciter; **—** vi. s'allumer, s'enflammer

kindling (wood) n. petit bois m.

kindred a. de la même famille; de la même nature; **— souls** âmes sœurs f. pl.

kinescope n. tube à rayons cathodiques m.

kinetic a. cinétique; **—s** n. pl. cinétique f.

king n. roi m.; (checkers) dame f.; **—dom** n. royaume m.; règne m.; **—ly** a. de roi royal

king-size a. grand, (plus) long

kink n. nœud m.; coque f.; faux pli m.; **—** vi. se nouer; **—y** a. crépu

kinsfolk n. parents m. pl., famille f.

kinsman n. parent m.

kinswoman n. parente f.

kiosk n. kiosque m.

kiss n. baiser m.; **—** vt. embrasser; (hand) baiser

kit n. trousseau m., trousse f.; nécessaire m.

kitchen n. cuisine f.; **-ette** n. petite cuisine f.; **— police (K.P.)** n. (mil.) corvée de cuisine f.; **— range** n. cuisinière f.; **— utensils** batterie de cuisine f.

kite n. cerf-volant m.; **fly a —** lancer un cerf-volant

kith *n.* parents, amis *m. pl.*

kitten *n.* chaton, petit chat *m.*; **–ish** *a.* enjoué, folâtre

kleptomania *n.* kleptomanie *f.*; **–c** *n.* kleptomane *m. & f.*

knack *n.* don *m.*, habileté *f.*; coup *m.*; flair *m.*

knapsack *n.* sac *m.*

knave *n.* coquin, fripon *m.*; **–ry** *n.* friponnerie *f.*

knead *vt.* pétrir, travailler

knee *n.* genou *m.*; **on one's –s** à genoux, agenouillé

kneecap *n.* rotule *f.*

knee-deep *a.* jusqu'aux genoux

knee-high *a.* à la hauteur du genou

kneel *vi.* s'agenouiller, se mettre à genoux; **–ing** *a.* à genoux, agenouillé

knell *n.* glas *m.*; **death — glas funèbre** *m.*

knickers, knickerbockers *n.* (*pl.*) culotte *f.*; knickerbockers *m. pl.*

knicknack *n.* bibelot, colifichet *m.*

knife *n.* couteau *m.*; **— grinder** rémouleur *m.*; **—** *vt.* poignarder

knight *n.* chevalier *m.*; (chess) cavalier *m.*; **—** *vt.* armer chevalier, faire chevalier; **–hood** *n.* chevalerie *f.*; **–ly** *a.* chevaleresque

knight-errant *n.* chevalier errant *m.*; **–ry** *n.* chevalerie errante *f.*

knit *vt.* tricoter; lier, joindre; **— one's brows** froncer les sourcils; **–ted** *a.* tricoté, en tricot; **–ing** *n.* tricot *m.*; tricotage *m.*; union *f.*; **–ing needle** aiguille à tricoter *f.*

knob *n.* bouton *m.*; bosse *f.*

knock *n.* coup *m.*; (engine) cognement *m.*; **— out** knock-out *m.*; **—** *vt.* frapper, cogner; heurter; (coll.) trouver à redire; **—** *vi.* (engine) cogner; **–down** renverser; abattre; **— off** (coll.) finir; cesser de travailler; **— out** knockouter; supprimer; **–er** *n.* (door) marteau *m.*; **–ing** *n.* coups *m. pl.*

knock-kneed *a.* cagneux

knoll *n.* monticule, tertre, mamelon *m.*

knot *n.* nœud *m.*; groupe *m.*; **overhand —** nœud simple *m.*; **reef —** (naut.) nœud marin *m.*; **slip–** nœud coulant *m.*; **tie a —** faire un nœud; **—** *vt.* nouer; **—** *vi.* se nouer; **–ted** *a.* à nœuds; **–ty** *a.* noueux; **–ty question** question épineuse *f.*

knothole *n.* trou de nœud *m.*

know *vt.* savoir; connaître; apprendre; **as far as I —** autant que je sache; **–ing** *a.* fin; (look) entendu; **–ingly** *adv.* sciemment; **–n** *a.* connu

know-how *n.* connaissances techniques *f. pl.*; savoir-faire *m.*

knowledge *n.* science *f.*; savoir *m.*; connaissance(s) *f.* (*pl.*); **not to my —** pas que je sache; **without my —** à mon insu; **–able** *a.* intelligent

knuckle *n.* articulation du doigt *f.*; (animal) manche *m.*

Koran *n.* Coran *m.*

Korea *n.* Corée *f.*

kosher *a.* cawcher, kascher, cacher

kowtow *vi.* se prosterner; **—** *vt. & vi.* saluer à la chinoise

L

label *n.* étiquette *f.*; **—** *vt.* étiqueter

labial *a.* labial; **— n.** labiale *f.*

labor *n.* travail *m.*; labeur *m.*; ouvriers *m. pl.*; main-d'œuvre *f.*; (med.) couches *f. pl.*; **hard —** travail disciplinaire *m.*; **— union** syndicat ouvrier *m.*; **—** *vi.* travailler; élaborer; **–er** *n.* travailleur, ouvrier *m.*; manœuvre *m.*; **–ious** *a.* laborieux, pénible

laboratory *n.* laboratoire *m.*

laborsaving *a.* qui économise le travail

lace *n.* dentelle *f.*; (shoe) lacet, cordon *m.*; **—** *vt.* lacer; entrelacer

lacerate *vt.* lacérer; déchirer

laceration *n.* lacération; déchirure *f.*

lack *n.* manque, défaut *m.*, absence *f.*; **for —** of faute de; **—** *vt. & vi.* manquer (de); **–ing** *a.* qui manque; dépourvu de; insuffisant

lackadaisical *a.* apathique; languissant

lackey *n.* laquais *m.*

laconic *a.* laconique

lacquer *n.* lacque, vernis *m.*; **—** *vt.* laquer

lacrimose *a.* larmoyant

lactate *vi.* sécréter du lait

lactation *n.* lactation *f.*

lactic *a.* lactique

lactose *n.* lactose *f.*

lad *n.* garçon, jeune homme *m.*

ladder *n.* échelle *f.*

lading *n.* chargement *m.*; **bill of —** connaissement *m.*

ladle *n.* louche *f.*; puisoir *m.*; **—** *vt.*, **— out** servir

lady *n.* dame *f.*; **ladies and gentlemen** mesdames et messieurs, (coll.) messieurs-dames; **young —** jeune fille, demoiselle *f.*

ladylike *a.* de dame; comme il faut

lag *n.* retard, décalage *m.*; **—** *vi.* traîner, rester en arrière

lager *n.* bière blonde *f.*

laggard *n.* traînard *m.*; **—** *a.* tardif

lagoon *n.* lagune *f.*; (atoll) lagon *m.*

laid *a.* posé, laissé; (paper) couché

laid up *a.* malade; en panne

lair *n.* repaire *m.*, tanière *f.*

laity *n.* laïques *m. pl.*

lake *n.* lac *m.*

lamb *n.* agneau *m.*; — **chop** côtelette d'agneau *f.*; — *vi.* agneler

lame *a.* boiteux; estropié; (excuse) faible, pauvre; — *vt.* rendre boiteux; estropier; **-ness** *n.* boitement *m.*; faiblesse *f.*

lament *n.* lamentation, complainte *f.*; — *vt.* pleurer; **-able** *a.* déplorable, lamentable; **-ation** *n.* lamentation *f.*; **-ed** *a.* regretté

laminate *vt.* laminer

lamp *n.* lampe *f.*

lampoon *n.* libelle *m.*, satire *f.*; — *vt.* lancer des satires contre; **-er** *n.* libelliste, satiriste *m.*

lamppost *n.* réverbère *m.*

lamp shade *n.* abat-jour *m.*

lance *n.* lance *f.*; — *vt.* inciser, percer; **-r** *n.* lancier *m.*; **-t** *n.* lancette *f.*, bistouri *m.*

land *n.* terre *f.*; terrain *m.*; pays *m.*; — *vt.* débarquer; (plane) atterrir; (fish) amener à terre; (coll.) gagner, remporter; — *vi.* débarquer; atterrir; — **on one's feet** retomber sur ses pieds; **-ed** *a.* foncier; qui possède des terres; **-ing** *n.* débarquement *m.*; atterrissage *m.*; (stair) palier *m.*; **-ing barge, -ing craft** *n.* péniche de débarquement *f.*; **-ing field** *n.* terrain d'atterrissage *m.*; **-ing strip** *n.* piste d'atterrissage *f.*

landfall *n.* atterrage *m.*; aubaine *f.*

landlady *n.* propriétaire *f.*; aubergiste *f.*

landlord *n.* propriétaire *m.*; aubergiste *m.*

landlubber *n.* marin d'eau douce *m.*

landmark *n.* repère *m.*; point coté *m.*; monument *m.*

land office *n.* bureau du cadastre *m.*; **do a — business** faire des affaires inouïes, avoir un chiffre d'affaires énorme

landowner *n.* propriétaire foncier *m.*

landscape *n.* paysage *m.*; — **garden** *n.* jardin à l'anglaise *m.*; — **gardener** *n.* jardiniste *m.*; — **painter** *n.* paysagiste *m.*

landslide *n.* glissement de terre *m.*; (pol.) victoire écrasante *f.*

landward *adv.* vers la terre

lane *n.* ruelle *f.* passage *m.*; route *f.*

language *n.* langue *f.*; langage *m.*

languid *a.* languissant, langoureux; **-ness** *n.* langueur *f.*

languish *vi.* languir; **-ing** *a.* languissant, langoureux

languor *n.* langueur *f.*; **-ous** *a.* langoureux

lanky *a.* grand et maigre

lanolin *n.* lanoline *f.*

lantern *n.* lanterne *f.*; fanal *m.*; **Chinese —**

lanterne vénitienne *f.*; — **slide** *n.* diapositive de projection *f.*

lantern-jawed *a.* aux joues creuses

lanyard *n.* garant *m.*

Laos *n.* Laos *m.*

lap *n.* genoux *m. pl.*; (sports) circuit, tour *m.*, étape *f.*; — *vt.* boucler; dépasser; — *vi.* (waves) clapoter; — **up** laper; gober

lapel *n.* revers *m.*

lapidary *a. & n.* lapidaire *m.*

Lapland *n.* Laponie *f.*

lapse *n.* laps *m.*; délai *m.*; intervalle *m.*; lapsus *m.*, faute *f.*; — *vi.* manquer; périmer; tomber; **-d** *a.* périmé; déchu; caduc

larboard *n.* bâbord *m.*

larceny *n.* larcin, vol *m.*

lard *n.* saindoux, lard *m.*; — *vt.* larder

larder *n.* garde-manger *m.*

large *a.* grand, gros; fort; nombreux; **grow -(r)** grandir, grossir; **-ly** *adv.* en grande partie; — *n.*, **at —** libre, en liberté; **-ness** *n.* grandeur *f.*; grosseur *f.*; étendue *f.*

large-scale *a.* à grande échelle, de grande échelle; de grande envergure

lariat *n.* lasso *m.*

larva *n.* larve *f.*

laryngitis *n.* laryngite *f.*

larynx *n.* larynx *m.*

lascivious *a.* lascif; **-ness** *n.* lascivité *f.*

lash *n.* coup de fouet *m.*; — *vt.* fouetter; cingler; attacher, lier; **-ing** *n.* coups de fouet *m. pl.*, flagellation *f.*; (rope) ligne d'amarrage *f.*

lass *n.* jeune fille *f.*

lassitude *n.* lassitude *f.*

last *a.* dernier; — **night** hier soir; cette nuit; — **week** la semaine passée; **la — semaine** dernière; **next to —** l'avant-dernier; — *n.* dernier; bout *m.*, fin *f.*; **at —** enfin; — *vi.* durer; **-ing** *a.* durable; **-ly** *adv.* en dernier lieu

latch *n.* loquet *m.*; — *vt.* fermer à demi-tour; — **on to** (coll.) saisir

latchkey *n.* clef *f.*, passe-partout *m.*

late *a.* en retard; tard; tardif; récent; (deceased) feu; **of —** depuis peu; — *adv.* en retard; tard; **-ly** *adv.* récemment, depuis peu; **-ness** *n.* heure avancée *f.*; arrivée tardive *f.*; **-r** *a.* plus récent; ultérieur; **-r** *adv.* plus tard, après; **-st** *a.* le plus récent, le plus nouveau, dernier

latent *a.* latent, caché

lateral *a.* latéral

lath *n.* latte *f.*

lathe *n.* tour *m.*

lather *n.* mousse de savon *f.*; — *vt.* savonner; — *vi.* mousser

Latin *a. & n.* latin *m.*; — **America** Amérique latine *f.*

latitude *n.* latitude *f.*; (fig.) liberté *f.*

latrine *n.* latrines *f. pl.*

latter *a.* dernier; **the** — celui-ci; celle-ci

latter-day *a.* moderne

lattice *n.* treillis, treillage *m.*

Latvia *n.* Lettonie, Latvie *f.*; **–n** *a. & n.* letton *m.*; (language) lette *m.*

laud *vt.* louer; **–able** *a.* louable; **–atory** *a.* élogieux

laugh *n.* rire *m.*; — *vi.* rire; — **at** rire de; — **to oneself** rire tout bas; — **off** se moquer de, traiter à la légère; **–able** *a.* ridicule, risible; **–ing** *a.* riant; rieur; **it is no –ing matter** il n'y a pas de quoi rire; **–ing gas** *n.* gaz hilarant *m.*; **–ingstock** *n.* risée *f.*; **–ter** *n.* rires *m. pl.*

launch *n.* chaloupe *f.*; — *vt.* lancer; **–ing** *n.* lancement *m.*; mise à l'eau *f.*

launching pad *n.* plate-forme de lancement *f.*

launder *vt.* blanchir

laundress *n.* blanchisseuse *f.*

laundry *n.* blanchisserie *f.*; linge à blanchir *m.*; **–man** *n.* blanchisseur *m.*

lava *n.* lave *f.*

lavatory *n.*; lavabo; lavoir; cabinet de toilette *m.*

lavender *a. & n.* lavande *f.*

lavish *a.* prodigue; somptueux; — *vt.* prodiguer; **–ness** *n.* prodigalité *f.*; somptuosité *f.*

law *n.* loi *f.*; droit *m.*; **civil** — droit civil *m.*; **lay down the** — to faire la loi a; **–ful** *a.* légal, permis; légitime; valide; **–less** *a.* sans loi; désordonné; **–lessness** *n.* désordre *m.*; anarchie *f.*

law-abiding *a.* respectueux des lois

lawbreaker *n.* transgresseur de la loi *m.*

lawmaker *n.* législateur *m.*

lawn *n.* pelouse *f.*; gazon *m.*

lawn mower *n.* tondeuse *f.*

lawsuit *n.* procès *m.*

lawyer *n.* avocat, avoué *m.*

lax *a.* relâché; négligent, inexact; **–ity** *n.* relâchement *m.*; inexactitude *f.*

laxative *a. & n.* laxatif *m.*

lay *n.* lai *m.*, chanson *f.*; (land) configuration *f.*; — *a.* laï, laïque; — *vt.* placer, mettre, coucher, poser; (egg) pondre; (bet) parier; — **aside**, — **away** mettre de côté; — **before** présenter à, soumettre à; — **by** mettre de côté; — **down** déposer; imposer, décréter; — **in** se faire une provision de; — **off** (labor) congédier; (coll.) laisser tranquille; — **on** appliquer; — **out** disposer, étaler; (money) débourser; — **siege to** assiéger; — **up** mettre hors de service;

tenir au lit, tenir enfermé; **–er** *n.* couche *f.*; (hen) pondeuse *f.*

layman *n.* laïque *m.*

layoff *n.* renvoi d'ouvriers en masse *m.*

layout *n.* disposition *f.*; dessin, schéma de montage *m.*; plan *m.*

layover *n.* arrêt en cours de route *m.* (pour attendre une correspondance)

laziness *n.* paresse *f.*

lazy *a.* paresseux; fainéant

lead *n.* (mineral) plomb *m.*; (pencil) mine de plomb *f.*; (naut.) sonde *f.*; — **pencil** crayon à mine de plomb; — **poisoning** saturnisme *m.*; **–en** *a.* de plomb; pesant

lead *n.* exemple *m.*, direction *f.*; (theat.) premier rôle *m.*; (elec.) câble de canalisation *m.*; (journalism) article de fond *m.*; **take the** — prendre le pas; — *vt.* conduire, mener; guider; commander, diriger; porter, entraîner; — *vi.* conduire; aboutir; — **away** emmener; entraîner; — **off** commencer, être le premier; emmener; — **on** encourager; — **up to** amener à; **–er** *n.* conducteur, chef *m.*; (pol.) leader *m.*; (film) amorce *f.*; **–erless** *a.* sans chef; **–ership** *n.* direction *f.*, commandement *m.*; **–ing** *a.* principal; important; premier; **–ing man**, **–ing lady** premier rôle *m.*; vedette *f.*; **–ing question** question tendancieuse *f.*

leaf *n.* feuille *f.*; (book) feuillet *m.*; (door) battant *m.*; (table) rallonge *f.*; **turn over a new** — faire peau neuve; — *vt.*, — **through** feuilleter; **–age** *n.* feuillage *m.*; **–let** *n.* feuille *f.*; annonce *f.*; **–y** *a.* touffu, couvert de feuilles

league *n.* ligue *f.*; (measurement) lieue *f.*; (sports) groupement *m.*, association *f.*; **in** — **with** d'intelligence avec; — *vi.*, — **together** se liguer

leak *n.* fuite, perte *f.*; écoulement *m.*; (naut.) voie d'eau *f.*; — *vi.* fuir, couler; (naut.) faire eau; — **out** (rumor) s'ébruiter; **–age** *n.* fuite, perte *f.*; **–y** *a.* qui fuit, qui coule

leakproof *a.* étanche

lean *vi.* s'appuyer; (se) pencher; s'adosser; incliner; — *vt.* appuyer; adosser; — **back** se pencher en arrière, se renverser; — **out** se pencher à; **–ing** *a.* penchant, penché; **–ing** *n.* inclination, tendance *f.*, penchant *m.*

lean *a.* maigre; décharné; — *n.* maigre *m.*; **–ness** maigreur *f.*

lean-to *n.* abat-vent *m.*; remise *f.*

leap *n.* saut *m.*; — **year** année bissextile *f.*; — *vt. & vi.* sauter

leapfrog *n.* saute-mouton *m.*

learn *vt.* apprendre; savoir; **–ed** *a.* instruit, savant; **–ing** n. science, érudition f.; savoir m.

lease n. bail m.; — vt. louer; donner à bail; prendre à bail

leash n. laisse, attache f.

least a. moindre; plus petit; — n. le moins m.; **at** — au moins; du moins; **not in the** — pas du tout; — adv. le moins

leather n. cuir m.; — a. en cuir, de cuir; — **goods** maroquinerie f.; **–ette** n. simili-cuir m.; **–y** a. (food) coriace; comme de cuir

leave n. congé m.; permission f.; — **of absence** congé m.; — vt. laisser; quitter; partir de; — vi. partir; s'en aller; — **behind** laisser; oublier; — **out** omettre

leaven n. levain m.; — vt. faire lever

leave-taking n. adieux m. pl.

leaving n. départ m.; **–s** n. pl. restes m. pl.; reliefs m. pl.

Lebanon n. Liban m.

lecherous a. lascif, débauché; **–ness** n. lasciveté f.

lecture n. conférence f.; — vi. faire une conférence; — vt. (coll.) sermonner; **–er** n. conférencier m.

ledge n. rebord m.; corniche f.

ledger n. registre, grand livre m.

lee, leeward a. sous le vent; — n. côté sous le vent m.

leek n. poireau m.

leer n. œillade f.; — vi., — **at** lancer des œillades à

lees n. pl. lie f.

leeway n. (naut.) dérive; (coll.) liberté f.; (plus de) **temps** m.; (plus de) place f.

left a. & n. gauche f.; — adv. à gauche; **on the** —, **to the** — à gauche; **–ist** n. partisan de la gauche m.

left-handed a. gaucher

leg n. jambe f.; patte f.; (fowl) cuisse f.; (lamb) gigot m.; (object) pied m.; **pull someone's** — faire marcher quelqu'un; **–ged** a. à jambes

legacy n. legs m.

legal a. légal; juridique; **–ity** n. légalité f.; **–ize** vt. légaliser, authentiquer

legatee n. légataire m. & f.

legation n. légation f.

legend n. légende f.; **–ary** a. légendaire

legerdemain n. tour d'adresse m.

leggings n. pl. jambières f. pl.

Leghorn n. Livourne f.

leghorn n. paille d'Italie f.; poule blanche f.

legibility n. lisibilité f.

legible a. lisible

legion n. légion f.; **–ary** n. légionnaire m.

legislate vi. faire des lois

legislation n. législation f.

legislator n. législateur m.

legislature n. législature f.

legitimacy n. légitimité f.

legitimize vt. légitimiser

legume n. légume m.

leisure n. loisir m.; **at** — à loisir, à tête reposée; **–ly** a. posé, mesuré; **in a –ly manner** sans se presser

lemon n. citron m.; — (tree) citronnier m.; **–ade** n. citron pressé m.; (lemon drink) citronnade f.; (carbonated) limonade f.; — **squeezer** n. presse-citron m.

lend vt. prêter; **–er** n. prêteur m.; **–ing** n. prêt m.; (com.) prestation f.

lend-lease n. prêt-bail m.

length n. longueur f.; bout, morceau m.; (fabric) coupon m.; (pipe) tronçon m.; **at** — longuement; en détail; enfin; **–en** vt. allonger, rallonger, prolonger; — vi. s'allonger; augmenter; **–y** a. long, prolixe

lengthwise adv. en long, en longueur

leniency n. clémence f.; indulgence f.

lenient a. clément; indulgent

lens n. lentille f., verre m.; (phot.) objectif m.; — **speed** n. ouverture relative f.

Lent n. Carême m.; **–en** a. de Carême

lentil n. lentille f.

leprosy n. lèpre f.

leprous a. lépreux

lesion n. lésion f.

less a. moindre; moins (de); — adv. moins (de); **–en** vt. amoindrir; diminuer; — vi. diminuer; **–er** a. moindre; petit

lessee n. locataire m. & f.

lesson n. leçon f.; exemple m.

lessor n. bailleur m.

lest conj. de peur que, de crainte que

let vt. & vi. laisser; permettre; louer; — **go of** lâcher; — **in** laisser entrer; — **off** laisser partir; tirer, décharger; — **out** laisser sortir; faire sortir; — **up** laisser monter; ralentir, devenir moins sévère

lethargic a. léthargique

lethargy n. léthargie f.

letter n. lettre f.; caractère m.; **capital** — majuscule f.; — **box** boîte aux lettres; — **carrier** facteur m.; — **of credit** n. lettre de crédit f.; — **opener** ouvre-lettres m.; — vt. marquer avec des lettres; **–ing** n. lettrage m.; inscription f.

letterhead n. en-tête (de papier à écrire) m.

letter-perfect a. impeccable, parfait dans tous les détails

letterpress n. (print.) typographie f.

lettuce *n.* laitue *f.*
letup *n.* relâche *m.*
Levantine *n. & a.* Levantin *m.*
levee *n.* levée *f.*; (reception) lever *m.*, réception *f.*
level *n.* niveau *m.*; palier *m.*; **on a — with** de niveau avec; à la hauteur de; égal à; **— a.** égal; à niveau; **— with** à ras de, à fleur de; **— vt.** niveler; égaliser
levelheaded *a.* pondéré, sensé
lever *n.* levier *m.*; **–age** *n.* force de levier *f.*, bras de levier *m.*
levity *n.* légèreté *f.*
levy *n.* levée *f.*; impôt *m.*; **— vt.** lever, imposer
lewd *a.* lascif, impudique; débauché; **–ness** *n.* lascivité, luxure *f.*
lexicography *n.* lexicographie *f.*
lexicon *n.* lexique *m.*
liability *n.* responsabilité *f.*; **liabilities** *pl.* passif *m.*; dettes, obligations *f. pl.*
liable *a.* responsable; passible (de); sujet (à)
liar *n.* menteur *m.*
libel *n.* diffamation *f.*; libelle *m.*; **— vt.** diffamer; **–ous** *a.* diffamatoire
liberal *a.* libéral; généreux; large; ample; **— n.** libéral *m.*; **–ism** *n.* libéralisme *m.*; **–ity** *n.* générosité *f.*; **–ly** *adv.* libéralement; généreusement
liberal-minded *a.* large d'esprit
liberate *vt.* libérer
liberation *n.* libération *f.*
liberator *n.* libérateur *m.*
Liberia *n.* Libéria *m.*
libertine *n.* libertin *m.*
liberty *n.* liberté *f.*; **at —** libre; en liberté; **take the — of** se permettre de
librarian *n.* bibliothécaire *m. & f.*
library *n.* bibliothèque *f.*; **circulating —** cabinet de lecture *m.*
Libya *n.* Libye *f.*
license *n.* permis *m.*, permission *f.*; patente *f.*; autorisation *f.*; licence *f.*; **driver's —** permis de conduire *m.*; **— number** *n.* (auto) immatriculation *f.*; numéro matricule *m.*; **— plate** *n.* plaque d'immatriculation *f.*; **— vt.** accorder un permis à
licentious *a.* licencieux; **–ness** *n.* licence *f.*, dérèglement *m.*
licit *a.* licite
lick *n.* coup de langue *m.*; **— vt.** lécher; (coll.) battre, rosser; **— one's chops** se lécher les babines
licorice *n.* réglisse *f.*
lid *n.* couvercle *m.*; (eye) paupière *f.*
lie *n.* mensonge *m.*; (of land) disposition, configuration *f.*; **— vi.** mentir; (position) être couché; se trouver, être; **—**

down se coucher; **— still** rester tranquille; **here –s** ci-gît
lie detector *n.* machine à déceler le mensonge *f.*
lien *n.* hypothèque *f.*
lieutenant *n.* lieutenant *m.*; **— commander** lieutenant de vaisseau *m.*; **— general** lieutenant de division *m.*; **second —** sous-lieutenant *m.*
life *n.* vie *f.*; existence *f.*; vivant *m.*; biographie *f.*; animation *f.*; **come to —** s'animer; **for —** à vie, à perpétuité; **it's a matter of — and death** il y va de la vie; **— annuity** rente viagère *f.*; **— insurance** assurance sur la vie, assurance-vie *f.*; **–less** *a.* sans vie; still nature morte
life belt *n.* ceinture de sauvetage *f.*
lifeblood *n.* sang *m.*; (fig.) vie, âme *f.*
lifeboat *n.* canot de sauvetage *m.*
lifeguard *n.* surveillant de plage *m.*
life jacket *n.* ceinture de sauvetage *f.*
lifelong *a.* de toute la vie
life preserver *n.* appareil de sauvetage *m.*; bouée *f.*; brassière de sauvetage *f.*
lifesaving *n.* sauvetage *m.*
life-size *a.* en grand; de grandeur normale
lifetime *n.* vie *f.*; vivant *m.*; espace d'une vie *m.*
lift *n.* haussement *m.*, levée *f.*; (elevator) ascenseur *m.*; (shoe) talon *m.*; **give a — to** conduire, faire monter (dans une auto); encourager; rafraîchir; animer; **ski —** télésiège *m.*; **— vt.** lever; soulever; élever; (coll.) plagier; **— vi.** s'élever
ligament *n.* ligament *m.*
light *n.* lumière *f.*; lueur *f.*; jour *m.*; lampe *f.*; feu *m.*; phare *m.*; **electric —** bulb ampoule *f.*; **— wave** onde lumineuse *f.*; **by the — of** à la lumière de, au clair de; **bring to —** mettre au jour; **come to —** se révéler; **throw — on** éclairer; **— vt.** allumer; éclairer, illuminer; **— vi.** s'allumer; s'éclairer; **— a.** clair; blond; (weight) léger; **–en** *vt.* alléger; soulager; hausser; **–er** *n.* briquet *m.*; (naut.) péniche *f.*; **–ing** *n.* éclairage *m.*; allumage *m.*; **–ly** *adv.* légèrement; à la légère; **–ness** *n.* légèreté *f.*
light-fingered *a.* fripon, voleur
light-footed *a.* agile
lightheaded *a.* étourdi
lighthearted *a.* au cœur léger; gai
lighthouse *n.* phare (marin) *m.*
light meter *n.* (phot.) luxmètre, photomètre, posemètre *m.*
lightning *n.* foudre *f.*; éclair *m.*; **flash of —** éclair *m.*; **— rod** paratonnerre *m.*;

forked — foudre en zigzag *f.*
lightship *n.* bateau-phare *m.*
lightweight *n.* poids léger; — *a.* leger
light-year (ast.) année-lumière *f.*
likable, likeable *a.* sympathique, aimable, agréable
like *a.* pareil, semblable; tel; — *prep.* comme; what is he —? comment est-il?; what is the weather —? quel temps fait-il?; — *n.* semblable *m.* & *f.*; goût *m.*; — *vt.* aimer; trouver; vouloir; –lihood *n.* probabilité, vraisemblance *f.*; chance *f.*; –ly *a.* probable, vraisemblable; –ly *adv.* probablement; –n *vt.* comparer; –ness *n.* ressemblance *f.*; image *f.*, portrait *m.*
likewise *adv.* de même, autant; aussi
liking *n.* goût *m.*; gré *m.*; penchant *m.*
limb *n.* membre *m.*; branche *f.*; (math.) limbe *m.*
limber *a.* souple, flexible
limelight *n.* projecteur *m.*; in the — (très) en vue
limestone *n.* calcaire *m.*; pierre à chaux *f.*
limit *n.* limite, borne *f.*; — *vt.* limiter, borner; restreindre; –ation *n.* limitation *f.*; –ed *a.* borné, limité; restreint; –less *a.* sans bornes
limp *n.* boitement, clochement *m.*; — *vi.* boiter, clocher; — *a.* mou; souple; –ing *a.* boiteux; –ly *adv.* mollement; sans énergie; –ness *n.* mollesse *f.*
limpid *a.* limpide, clair; –ity *n.* limpidité, clarté *f.*
linden *n.* tilleul *m.*
line *n.* ligne *f.*; trait *m.*; forme *f.*; rangée, queue, file *f.*; (of a poem) vers *m.*; métier *m.*; compagnie *f.*; stand in — faire la queue; — *vt.* ligner, régler; border; (clothes) doubler; (brakes) rapetasser; — up aligner; faire la queue; –age *n.* lignée *f.*; –al *a.* linéal, en ligne directe; –ar *a.* linéaire; –d *a.* doublé
lineman *n.* poseur de lignes *m.*; (football) arbitre de touche *m.*; (tennis) arbitre de lignes *m.*; (railroad) garde-ligne *m.*
linen *n.* toile de lin *f.*; linge *m.*, lingerie *f.*; — closet lingerie *f.*
liner *n.* (ship) paquebot *n.*; garniture, bande de remplissage *f.*
line-up *n.* queue, file *f.*; disposition *f.*
linger *vi.* s'attarder; traîner; –ing *a.* lent; prolongé
lingual *a.* lingual
lingerie *n.* linge *m.*
linguist *n.* linguiste *m.* & *f.*; –ic *a.* linguistique; –ics *n. pl.* linguistique *f.*
liniment *n.* liniment *m.*

lining *n.* doublure *f.*; (brake) garniture *f.*; (hat) coiffe *f.*
link *n.* chaînon *m.*; anneau *m.*; lien *m.*; — *vt.* enchaîner; lier, relier
linoleum *n.* linoléum *m.*
linotype *n.* linotype *f.*
linseed *n.* graine de lin *f.*; — oil *n.* huile de lin *f.*
lint *n.* charpie *f.*
lintel *n.* linteau *m.*
lip *n.* lèvre *f.*; bord *m.*; — reading lecture sur les lèvres *f.*
lipstick *n.* rouge à lèvres *m.*
liquefaction *n.* liquéfaction *f.*
liquefy *vt.* liquéfier; — *vi.* se liquéfier
liqueur *n.* liqueur *f.*
liquid *n.* liquide *m.*; — *a.* liquide; — assets valeurs disponibles *f. pl.*; — hydrogen *n.* hydrogène liquide *m.*; –ate *vt.* liquider; –ation *n.* liquidation *f.*
liquor *n.* boisson alcoolique *f.*; alcool *m.*
Lisbon *n.* Lisbonne *f.*
lisp *n.* zézayement *m.*; — *vt.* & *vi.* zézayer; zozoter
list *n.* liste *f.*; état *m.*; (naut.) bande, gîte *f.*; (fabric selvage) lisière *f.*; — price *n.* prix marqué *m.*; — *vt.* faire une liste de; cataloguer; — *vi.* (naut.) donner de la bande
listen *vt.* écouter, prêter l'oreille, faire attention; –er *n.* auditeur *m.*; –ing *n.* écoute *f.*
listless *a.* apathique, insouciant
litany *n.* litanies *f. pl.*
liter *n.* litre *m.*
literacy *n.* capacité de lire et d'écrire *f.*
literal *a.* littéral; sans imagination; –ly à la lettre, au pied de la lettre; littéralement
literary *a.* littéraire
literate *a.* qui sait lire et écrire
literature *n.* littérature *f.*; (com.) prospectus *m. pl.*
lithe *a.* agile, souple
lithograph *n.* lithographie *f.*; — *vt.* lithographier; –er *n.*; –ic *a.* lithographique; lithographe *m.*; –y *n.* lithographie *f.*
Lithuania *n.* Lithuanie *f.*
litigate *vt.* & *vi.* plaider
litigation *n.* litige, procès *m.*
litmus *n.* tournesol *m.*; — paper *n.* papier de tournesol *m.*
litter *n.* civière, litière *f.*; encombrement *m.*; détritus, débris *m. pl.*; (of an animal) portée *f.*; — *vt.* mettre en désordre; joncher; –ed *a.* encombré
little *a.* petit; peu de; a — un peu de; — *adv.* peu; — *n.* peu *m.*; — by — peu à peu, petit à petit; –ness *n.* petitesse *f.*

liturgy *n.* liturgie *f.*

live *a.* vivant, en vie; (coal) ardent; (wire) en charge; (television) en direct; — broadcast *n.* émission transmise en direct *f.*; -lihood *n.* vie *f.*; gagne-pain *m.*; -liness *n.* vivacité *f.*; vie *f.*; animation *f.*; -ly *a.* vif (vive); animé, -n *vt.*, -n up animer

live *vi.* vivre, exister; demeurer, habiter; durer

liver *n.* foie *m.*

livery *n.* livrée *f.*; — stable *n.* écurie de chevaux de louage *f.*

livestock *n.* bétail *m.*, bestiaux *m. pl.*

livid *a.* livide; plombé

living *a.* vivant, en vie; vif; — room salon *m.*; — wage salaire vital *m.*; — *n.* vie *f.*; make a — gagner de quoi vivre, gagner sa vie; standard of — niveau de vie *m.*

load *n.* fardeau *m.*; charge *f.*; poids *m.*; — *vt.* charger; accabler; — *vi.* prendre charge; -ing *n.* chargement *m.*

loaf *n.* pain *m.*; — *vi.* fainéanter; flâner; -er *n.* fainéant *m.*; flâneur *m.*

loam *n.* terre grasse *f.*

loan *n.* prêt *m.*; emprunt *m.*; — shark *n.* usurier *m.*; — *vt.* prêter

loath *a.* fâché, peu enclin

loathe *vt.* détester, abhorrer

loathing *n.* dégoût *m.*

loathsome *a.* dégoûtant, repoussant

lobby *n.* vestibule *m.*; — *vi.* chercher à faire valoir l'influence (sur la législature); -ist *n.* agent, représentant (d'un groupe cherchant à faire valoir son influence) *m.*

lobe *n.* (anat.) lobe *m.*; (rad) écran du radar *m.*

lobster *n.* homard *m.*; spiny — langouste *f.*

local *a.* local; régional; -e *n.* scène *f.*; lieu *m.*; -ity *n.* localité *f.*; région *f.*; voisinage *m.*; -ize *vt.* localiser; -ly *adv.* localement; dans la région; dans le voisinage

locate *vt.* trouver, découvrir, localiser; situer; be -d se trouver, être situé

location *n.* situation *f.*; lieu, endroit *m.*

lock *n.* serrure *f.*; (rifle) platine *f.*; (dam) écluse *f.*; air — sas *m.*; écluse pneumatique *f.*; pick a — crocheter une serrure; under — and key sous clef; — *vt.* fermer à clef; enfermer; — *vi.* s'enrayer; s'enclencher; -er *n.* armoire *f.*; compartiment *m.*

locket *n.* médaillon *m.*

lockjaw *n.* trisme *m.*

lock nut *n.* contre-écrou *m.*

locksmith *n.* serrurier *m.*

lockup *n.* prison *f.*

locomotion *n.* locomotion *f.*

locomotive *a.* locomotif; — *n.* locomotive *f.*

locus *n.* (math.) lieu *m.*

lode *n.* filon *m.*, veine *f.*

lodge *n.* cabane *f.*; pavillon *m.*; loge *f.*; — *vt.* loger; — a complaint porter plainte; — *vi.* se loger; -r *n.* pensionnaire *m. & f.*

lodging *n.* logement *m.*

loft *n.* grenier *m.*; soupente *f.*; atelier *m.*

loftiness *n.* élévation, hauteur *f.*

lofty *a.* élevé, haut; sublime

log *n.* bûche *f.*; (naut.) livre de loch *m.*, journal de navigation *m.*; — cabin cabane de bois *f.*; — *vt. & vi.* exploiter (une forêt); -ger *n.* bûcheron *m.*

loganberry *n.* ronce-framboise *f.*

logarithm *n.* logarithme *m.*

loggerhead *n.*, be at -s être aux prises

logic *n.* logique *f.*; -al *a.* logique

logistics *n. pl.* approvisionnement, ravitaillement *m.*

loin *n.* (beef) aloyau *m.*; (veal) longe *f.*; -s *pl.* reins *m. pl.*

loiter *vi.* flâner; rôder; -er *n.* flâneur *m.*; rôdeur *m.*; -ing *n.* flânerie *f.*; vagabondage *m.*

loll *vi.* flâner, s'étaler; pendre

London *n.* Londres

lone *a.* seul, solitaire; -liness *n.* solitude *f.*; -ly *a.* solitaire; isolé; -some *a.* seul, solitaire

long *a.* long (longue); -shot (coll.) concurrent qui a peu de chance de gagner; a — time longtemps; in the — run à la longue; — *adv.* longtemps; as — as tant que; be — in tarder à; how long? (depuis) combien de temps; depuis quand; — *vi.*, — for avoir envie de; soupirer après; brûler de; -ing *n.* désir *m.*, envie *f.*

long-distance *a.* à longue distance; — call communication interurbaine *f.*; — operator inter *m.*

longevity *n.* longévité *f.*

long-faced *a.* triste, à triste mine

longhand *n.* écriture ordinaire *f.*; — *a.* non-dactylographié, écrit à main

longitude *n.* longitude *f.*

longitudinal *a.* longitudinal

long-legged *a.* aux jambes longues

long-lived *a.* à longue vie; à longue durée

long-lost *a.* perdu depuis longtemps

long-playing *a.* microsillon, à longue durée; — record disque microsillon *m.*

longshoreman *n.* docker, débardeur *m.*

long-standing *a.* de longue date

long-suffering *a.* endurant, patient

long-winded *a.* de longue haleine; intarissable, interminable

look *n.* regard *m.*; coup d'œil *m.*; air, aspect *m.*, apparence *f.*; — *vt.* regarder; avoir l'air, paraître; — **like** ressembler à; — **after** s'occuper de; soigner; veiller sur; — **at** regarder; — **away** détourner les yeux; — **for** chercher; — **into** étudier, examiner; — **out** prendre garde; — **over** parcourir; — **up** lever les yeux; se ranimer; consulter; (person) rechercher; –**ing** *a.*, –**ing glass** miroir *m.*, glace *f.*

lookout *n.* (person) guetteur *m.*, (naut.) vigie *f.*; **be on the** — guetter; être sur le qui-vive

loom *n.* métier à tisser *m.*; — *vi.* paraître; sortir; surgir

loop *n.* boucle *f.*; œil *m.*; attache *f.*; — *vt. & vi.* boucler

loophole *n.* meurtrière *f.*; (fig.) échappatoire *f.*

loose *a.* détaché; défait; branlant; dégagé; lâche; relâché; dissolu; **be at — ends** être sans occupation; **come —** se détacher, se dégager, se défaire; — *vt.* lâcher, libérer; –**n** *vt.* relâcher; dénouer; dégager; — *vi.* se défaire, se relâcher, se dégager; –**ness** *n.* relâchement *m.*; jeu *m.*

loose-leaf *a.* à feuilles mobiles

loot *n.* butin *m.*; — *vt.* piller; –**ing** *n.* pillage, sac *m.*

lop *vt.* élaguer, couper

lope *n.* galop lent *m.*; pas lent *m.*; — *vi.* aller doucement

lopsided *a.* déversé, déséquilibré

loquacious *a.* loquace

lord *n.* seigneur *m.*; châtelain *m.*; lord *m.*; — *vt.*, — **it** faire l'important; –**ly** *a.* noble; hautain; –**ship** *n.* seigneurie *f.*

Lord *n.* Seigneur; Dieu *m.*; **in the year of Our** — en l'an de grâce; –**'s Prayer** *n.* patenôtre *f.*; oraison dominicale *f.*

lore *n.* science *f.*, savoir *m.*

lose *vt.* perdre, égarer; — **oneself in** s'absorber dans; — **one's temper** s'emporter; — **one's way** se perdre, s'égarer; — **sight of** perdre de vue; –**r** *n.* battu, perdant *m.*; **bad** –**r** mauvais joueur *m.*

loss *n.* perte *f.*; privation *f.*; **be at a —** to avoir de la peine à; ne pas savoir

lot *n.* sort *m.*, fortune *f.*; (portion) lot *m.*, quantité *f.*; (land) terrain *m.*; **a — (of)** beaucoup (de); **draw –s** tirer au sort

lottery *n.* loterie *f.*

loud *a.* fort, haut; bruyant; (color) criard; — *adv.* à haute voix; –**ness** *n.* bruit *m.*; force *f.*

loud-speaker *n.* haut-parleur *m.*

lounge *n.* hall, salon *m.*; foyer *m.*; **chaise — chaise longue** *f.*; — *vi.* flâner; s'étendre

louver *n.* bande, grille *f.*, cloison *m.*; –**ed** *a.* à bandes, cloisonné

lovable *a.* aimable

love *n.* amour *m.*; tendresse, affection *f.*; (person) ami *m.*, amie *f.*; amour *m. & f.*; (tennis) rien, zéro *m.*; **be in — (with)** être amoureux (de), être épris (de); **fall in — (with)** tomber amoureux (de), s'éprendre (de); — **affair** liaison *f.*; — **letter** billet doux *m.*; — **song** romance, chanson d'amour *f.*; — *vt.* aimer; adorer; –**less** *a.* sans amour; –**liness** *n.* beauté *f.*; –**ly** *a.* beau (belle); charmant, ravissant; –**r** *n.* amant *m.*; amoureux *m.*; amateur *m.*

love-making *n.* cour *f.*

lovesick *a.* féru d'amour

loving *a.* aimant, affectueux; — **cup** trophée *f.*

low *a.* bas; vil; peu élevé; (dress) décolletée; (spirits) abattu; (sound) grave; — *adv.* bas; — *n.* niveau le plus bas *m.*; –**er** *a.* inférieur; plus bas; –**er** *vt.* baisser; abaisser; rabaisser; descendre; –**li**-**ness** *n.* humilité *f.*; –**ly** *a.* petit, humble, modeste; –**ness** *n.* petitesse *f.*; faiblesse *f.*; (action) bassesse *f.*; (spirits) abattement *m.*

low *n.* (cow) meuglement *m.*; — *vi.* meugler

lowboy *n.* commode basse *f.*

low-cut *a.* décolleté

lowland *n.* plaine basse *f.*; –**s** *pl.* terres basses *f. pl.*

low-pitched *a.* grave

low-pressure *a.* à basse pression

low-priced *a.* pas cher, bon marché

low-spirited *a.* triste, abattu

low-water mark *n.* niveau des basses eaux

loyal *a.* fidèle; loyal; –**ist** *n.* loyaliste *m. & f.*; –**ty** *n.* fidélité *f.*

lozenge *n.* pastille *f.*; lozenge *f.*

lubricant *n.* lubrifiant *m.*

lubricate *vt.* lubrifier, graisser

lubrication *n.* lubrification *f.*, graissage *m.*

lucid *a.* lucide; –**ity** *n.* lucidité *f.*

luck *n.* chance *f.*; hasard *m.*; **bad —** malheur *m.*; malchance *f.*; **good —** bonheur *m.*; bonne chance *f.*; **stroke of —** coup de veine *m.*; –**ily** *adv.* heureusement, par bonheur; –**less** *a.* infortuné, malheureux; –**y** *a.* fortuné; **be –y** avoir de la chance; (object) porter bonheur

lucrative *a.* lucratif

ludicrous *a.* risible; ridicule; absurde; –**ness** *n.* ridicule *m.*

lug *vt.* traîner; — *n.* saillie, oreille, cosse,

lamelle, patte *f.*
luggage *n.* bagages *m. pl.*
lugubrious *a.* lugubre
lukewarm *a.* tiède; **–ness** *n.* tiédeur *f.*
lull *n.* moment de calme *m.*; accalmie *f.*; — *vt.* bercer, endormir; — *vi.* se calmer
lullaby *n.* berceuse *f.*
lumber *n.* bois de charpente *m.*; — *vi.* se traîner; **–ing** *a.* lourd, lent
lumberjack *n.* bûcheron *m.*
lumberjacket *n.* gros blouson *m.*, canadienne *f.*
lumberyard *n.* dépôt de bois de charpente, chantier de bois *m.*
luminary *n.* luminaire *m.*
luminescence *n.* luminescence *f.*
luminous *a.* lumineux
lump *n.* morceau *m.*; bloc *m.*; motton *m.*; (throat) serrement *m.*; — **sum** somme grosse *f.*; prix à forfait *m.*; — *vt.* mettre en bloc; — **together** réunir ensemble; **–y** *a.* grumeleux
lunacy *n.* folie *f.*; aliénation, démence *f.*
lunar *a.* lunaire
lunatic *a.* fou; de fou; — *n.* aliéné, fou, dément *m.*
lunch *n.* déjeuner, lunch *m.*; — *vi.* déjeuner; **–eon** *n.* déjeuner, lunch *m.*
lunchtime *n.* heure du déjeuner *f.*
lung *n.* poumon *m.*; **iron —** poumon d'acier *m.*
lunge *n.* mouvement en avant *m.*; — *vi.* se jeter en avant
lurch *n.* embarras *m.*; embardée *f.*, cahot *m.*; titubation *f.*; — *vi.* embarder; marcher en titubant
lure *n.* leurre *m.*, piège *m.*; (fig.) attrait, appel *m.*; — *vt.* leurrer; attirer, séduire; — **away** détourner
lurid *a.* sensationnel, éblouissant, choquant
lurk *vi.* se cacher; rôder; **–ing** *a.* caché
luscious *a.* succulent
lush *a.* surabondant; plein de sève *n.*
lust *n.* convoitise *f.*; concupiscence *f.*; désir *m.*; luxure *f.*; soif *f.*; — *vi.* désirer ardemment; — **after** convoiter; **–ful** *a.* luxurieux; **–y** *a.* robuste, vigoureux
luster, lustre *n.* éclat, lustre, brillant *m.*
lustrous *a.* éclatant, lustré
lute *n.* luth *m.*
Luxembourg *n.* Luxembourg *m.*
luxuriant *a.* luxuriant
luxuriate *vi.* croître avec abondance; s'abandonner, vivre dans l'abondance
luxurious *a.* luxueux; somptueux; **–ness** *n.* luxe *m.*
luxury *n.* luxe *m.*
lye *n.* lessive *f.*

lying *a.* menteur; (position) couché, étendu; — *n.* mensonge *m.*
lying-in hospital *n.* (hospice de la) maternité *f.*
lymph *n.* lymphe *f.*; **-atic** *a.* lymphatique
lynch *vt.* lyncher; **–ing** *n.* lynchage *m.*
Lyons *n.* Lyon
lyre *n.* lyre *f.*
lyric(al) *a.* lyrique

M

M.A.: Master of Arts licencié ès lettres *m.*
macadam *n.* macadam *m.*
macaroni *n.* macaronis *m. pl.*
macaroon *n.* macaron *m.*
mace *n.* masse *f.*; (bot.) macis *m.*, fleur de muscade *f.*
macerate *vt.* macérer
mach *n.* mach, la vitesse du son *f.*
machination *n.* machination *f.*, complot *m.*, intrigue *f.*
machine *n.* machine *f.*; (pol.) organisation *f.*; — **gun** mitrailleuse *f.*; — **tool** machine-outil *f.*; — *vt.* usiner; **–ry** *n.* machines *f. pl.*; mécanisme *m.*
machine-gun *vt.* mitrailler
machine shop *n.* atelier de construction de machines *m.*
machinist *n.* machiniste, mécanicien *m.*
mackerel *n.* maquereau *m.*
mad *a.* fou, aliéné; insensé; furieux; enragé; **go —** devenir fou; **–den** *vt.* rendre fou; exaspérer; **–ly** *adv.* follement; furieusement; **love –ly** aimer éperdument; **–ness** *n.* folie *f.*; démence *f.*; rage *f.*
Madagascar *n.* Madagascar *m.*
madam *n.* madame *f.*
madcap *n. & a.* fou, insensé *m.*
made *a.* fait; confectionné; fabriqué
Madeira *n.* Madère *f.*
made-to-order, made to measure *a.* fait sur mesure, fait sur commande
made-up *a.* maquillé; inventé; fait; factice
madhouse *n.* maison de fous *f.*
madman *n.* fou, aliéné *m.*
madonna *n.* madone *f.*
madrigal *n.* madrigal *m.*
maestro *n.* maître *m.*
magazine *n.* revue *f.*, périodique *m.*; (mil.) magasin, dépôt *m.*; (camera) chargeur *m.*; **powder —** poudrière *f.*
maggot *n.* asticot *m.*
magic *n.* magie *f.*; —, **-al** *a.* magique; **–ian** *n.* magicien *m.*
magistrate *n.* magistrat *m.*; juge *m.*
magnanimity *n.* magnanimité *f.*
magnanimous *a.* magnanime
magnate *n.* magnat *m.*
magnesia *n.* magnésie *f.*

magnesium *n.* magnésium *m.*

magnet *n.* aimant *m.*; –ic *a.* magnétique, d'aimant, aimanté; –ic (recording) tape *n.* ruban magnétique *m.*; –ic speaker *n.* haut-parleur électro-magnétique *m.*; –ism *n.* magnétisme *m.*; –ize *vt.* magnétiser

magneto *n.* magnéto *m.*; –hydrodynamics *n.* hydrodynamique magnétique, magnétohydrodynamique *f.*

magnification *n.* amplification *f.*, grossissement *m.*

magnificence *n.* magnificence *f.*

magnificent *a.* magnifique

magnify *vt.* grossir, amplifier; –ing glass *n.* verre grossissant *m.*, loupe *f.*

magnitude *n.* grandeur *f.*; magnitude *f.*

maid *n.* servante, bonne *f.*; fille *f.*; old — vieille fille *f.*; –en *n.* jeune fille *f.*; vierge *f.*; –en *a.* de jeune fille, de demoiselle; –en speech discours de début *m.*

mail *n.* courrier *m.*; poste *f.*; (armor) maille *f.*; — *vt.* mettre (une lettre) à la poste; expédier; — order *n.* commande par la poste *f.*

mailbox *n.* boîte aux lettres *f.*

mailman *n.* facteur *m.*

mail-order house *n.* établissement de vente par correspondance *m.*

mailplane *n.* avion postal *m.*

maim *vt.* estropier, mutiler

main *n.* (water) canalisation maîtresse *f.*; océan *m.*, mer *f.*; in the — en général; — *a.* principal, essentiel; grand; le plus important; — office (com.) siège social *m.*; — thing essentiel *m.*; –ly *adv.* principalement

mainland *n.* continent *m.*; terre firme *f.*

mainspring *n.* grand ressort, ressort principal *m.*

mainstay *n.* point d'appui *m.*; appui principal *m.*

maintain *vt.* maintenir, soutenir; entretenir; garder; défendre; prétendre; subvenir aux besoins de

maintenance *n.* entretien *m.*; maintien *m.*; pension alimentaire *f.*; ménage *m.*

majestic *a.* majestueux; –ally *adv.* majestueusement

majesty *n.* majesté *f.*

major *n.* commandant *m.*; (age) majeur *m.*; — general général de division *m.*; — *a.* majeur, plus grand; — *vi.* (school) se spécialiser; –ity *n.* majorité *f.*; la plus grande partie *f.*

make *n.* marque *f.*; fabrication *f.*; — *vt.* faire; fabriquer; façonner; créer; construire; confectionner; (with adjective) rendre; causer; nommer; (cards) battre; (money) gagner; — a living gagner son pain; — for se diriger vers; (naut.) mettre le cap sur; favoriser; — fun of se moquer de; — good réussir; — it (coll.) réussir, y arriver; — off filer, décamper; — over céder, transmettre; — out faire; (list) dresser; (check) écrire, tirer; comprendre; déchiffrer; distinguer; — up regagner; préparer; inventer; se maquiller; se réconcilier; –r *n.* fabricant *m.*; faiseur *m.*

Majorca *n.* Majorque *f.*

Maker *n.* Créateur *m.*

make-believe *n.* semblant *m.*; land of — pays des chimères *m.*; — *vt.* faire semblant

makeshift *a.* improvisé; de fortune

make-up *n.* maquillage, fard *m.*; composition *f.*

making *n.* fabrication *f.*; confection *f.*; construction *f.*; composition *f.*; création *f.*; have the –s avoir tout ce qu'il faut; in the — en train de se faire; — up préparation, composition *f.*; compensation *f.*; réconciliation *f.*

maladjusted *a.* mal adapté, inadapté

maladjustment *n.* ajustement défectueux *m.*

malady *n.* maladie *f.*

Malay *a. & n.* malais *m.*; –a *n.* Malaisie *f.*

malcontent *a. & n.* mécontent *m.*

male *a. & n.* mâle *m.*

malefactor *n.* malfaiteur *m.*

malevolence *n.* malveillance *f.*

malevolent *a.* malveillant

malfeasance *n.* malfaisance *f.*

malformation *n.* malformation *f.*

malformed *a.* malformé

malice *n.* méchanceté *f.*; malice *f.*; with — aforethought avec préméditation

malicious *a.* méchant; malveillant; rancunier; –ness *n.* malice, malveillance *f.*

malign *a.* pernicieux; — *vt.* diffamer, calomnier; –ancy *n.* malignité *f.*; –ant *a.* malin (maligne)

mall *n.* mail *m.*

malleability *n.* malléabilité *f.*

malleable *a.* malléable, forgeable

mallet *n.* maillet *m.*

malnutrition *n.* sous-alimentation *f.*

malodorous *a.* malodorant

malpractice *n.* malversation *f.*

malt *n.* malt *m.*; –ed milk *n.* boisson composée de lait et de crème glacée, parfumée au malt *f.*

Malta *n.* Malte *f.*

Maltese *a. & n.* maltais *m.*

maltreat *vt.* maltraiter; –ment *n.* mauvais traitement *m.*

mama, mamma *n.* maman *f.*

mammal *n.* mammifère *m.*; –ian *a.* des

mammifères

mammary *a.* mammaire

mammoth *n.* mammouth *m.*; — *a.* géant

man *n.* homme *m.*; mari *m.*; ouvrier *m.*; domestique *m.*; (chess) pièce *f.*; (sports) joueur *m.*; **dead** — mort *m.*; **old** — vieillard *m.*; **to a** —, **to the last** — jusqu'au dernier; — *vt.* armer, équiper, garnir; **–hood** *n.* âge d'homme *m.*; **–kind** *n.* humanité *f.*, homme, genre humain *m.*; **–liness** *m.* virilité *f.*; **–ly** *a.* d'homme; viril

manacles *n. pl.* menottes *f. pl.*

manage *vt.* diriger, conduire; gérer, arranger; faire; savoir; arriver à; **–able** *a.* maniable, traitable; **–ment** *n.* direction, conduite *f.*; gérance *f.*; administration *f.*; **–r** *n.* directeur, gérant, administrateur *m.*; chef *m.*

managing *a.* directeur, gérant

Manchukuo *n.* Mandchoukouo *m.*

Manchuria *n.* Mandchourie *f.*

mandate *n.* mandat *m.*; commandement *m.*

mandatory *a.* obligatoire, mandatif

mandible *n.* mandibule *f.*

mandolin *n.* mandoline *f.*

mane *n.* crinière *f.*

man-eater *n.* mangeur d'hommes *m.*

maneuver *n.* manœuvre *f.*; — *vt.* manœuvrer

manganese *n.* manganèse *m.*

mange *n.* gale (de chien) *f.*

manger *n.* mangeoire, crèche *f.*

mangle *n.* calandre *f.*; — *vt.* mutiler, déchirer; (laundry) calandrer

mangy *a.* galeux

manhandle *vt.* malmener; manutentionner

manhole *n.* trou de visite *m.*, bouche d'égout *f.*

mania *n.* manie *f.*; **–c** *n.* fou *m.*, folle *f.*; **–cal** *a.* maniaque

manicure *n.* manucure *m.*; — *vt.* soigner les ongles (mains), se faire les ongles (mains)

manicurist *n.* manucure *f.*

manifest *a.* manifeste, évident; — *n.* manifeste *m.*; — *vt.* manifester; montrer; témoigner; **–ation** *n.* manifestation *f.*; **–o** *n.* manifeste *m.*

manifold *a.* varié, divers, multiple, nombreux; (engine) tubulure *f.*

manikin *n.* mannequin *m.*

Manila *n.* Manille *f.*

manila *n.* manille *f.*; — **paper** papier bulle *m.*

manipulate *vt.* manipuler; tripoter

manipulation *n.* manipulation *f.*; tripotage *m.*

manipulator *n.* manipulateur *m.*

manna *n.* manne *f.*

manner *n.* manière *f.*; façon *f.*; espèce, sorte *f.*, genre *m.*; air, maintien *m.*; **in a** — of speaking pour ainsi dire; **in such a** — that de manière que, de sorte que; **in this** — de cette façon, de cette manière; **–s** *pl.* manières *f. pl.*; politesse *f.*; mœurs *f. pl.*; **–ism** *n.* affectation *f.*, maniérisme *m.*; **–ly** *a.* poli; bien élevé

man-of-war *n.* vaisseau de guerre *m.*

manor *n.* château seigneurial *m.*; seigneurie *f.*

man power *n.* main-d'œuvre *f.*; (mil.) effectifs *m. pl.*

mansard *n.* toit en mansarde *m.*

mansion *n.* hôtel (particulier) *m.*; château *m.*

manslaughter *n.* homicide involontaire *m.*

mantel *n.* manteau de cheminée *m.*; dessus de cheminée *m.*

mantle *n.* manteau *m.*, pèlerine *f.*; (fig.) voile *m.*; (heraldry) lambrequin *m.*; — *vt.* voiler, couvrir

manual *a.* manuel, de manœuvre; à bras, à main; — **training** *n.* apprentissage manuel *m.*; — *n.* manuel *m.*

manufacture *n.* fabrication *f.*; — *vt.* fabriquer, manufacturer; **–r** *n.* fabricant, manufacturier, industriel *m.*

manufacturing *n.* fabrication *n.*; — *a.* industriel

manure *n.* fumier *m.*; engrais *m.*; — *vt.* fumer, engraisser

manuscript *n.* manuscrit *m.*

Manx *n. & a.* Mannois *m.*

many *a. & n.* beaucoup (de); bien des; un grand nombre (de); maint; pas mal (de); **as** — autant (de); **how** — combien (de); **so** — tant (de); **too** — trop (de)

many-sided *a.* à plusieurs côtés; à de multiples reflets; polygone

map *n.* carte *f.*; plan *m.*; — **maker** cartographe *m.*; — **making** cartographie *f.*; **road** — carte routière *f.*; — *vt.* tracer une carte de; — **out** arranger, projeter, préparer; **–ping** *n.* cartographie *f.*; action de tracer une carte *f.*

mar *vt.* gâter, troubler

maraschino *n.* marasquin *m.*

marauder *n.* maraudeur *m.*; malandrin *m.*

marble *n.* marbre *m.*; bille *f.*; — *a.* en marbre; — *vt.* marbrer; **–d** *a.* marbré

march *n.* marche *f.*; pas *m.*; — *vi.* marcher; — **in** entrer; — **by** défiler; — *vt.* faire marcher; **–ing** *n.* marche *f.*; **–ing** *a.* en marche

March *n.* mars *m.*

marchioness *n.* marquise *f.*

mare *n.* jument *f.*

margin n. marge f.; bord m.; (stock) acompte m.; **-al** a. marginal

margin release n. (typewriter) déclanchemarge m.

marimba n. xylophone m.

marine a. marin; maritime; — n. marine f.; soldat d'infanterie marine m.; **merchant — marine** marchande f.; **-r** n. marin m.

marital a. marital; matrimonial

maritime a. maritime

marjoram n. marjolaine f.

mark n. marque f.; signe m.; preuve f.; témoignage m.; trace f.; tache f.; but m.; (school) note f.; **question —** point d'interrogation m.; — vt. marquer; indiquer; (cards) maquiller, piper; (school) noter, coter; — **down** (com.) démarquer; solder; noter; — **off** mesurer; — **time** marquer le pas; — **up** défigurer; couvrir de taches; hausser le prix de; **-ed** a. marqué; sensible

marked-down a. soldé

market n. marché m.; halle f.; — **place** place du marché f.; — **price** prix courant m.; **on the —** en vente; — vt. lancer sur le marché; — vi. faire son marché; **-able** a. vendable; **-ing** n. marché

marksman n. bon tireur m.; **-ship** n. adresse au tir f.

markup n. bénéfice, profit m.

marmalade n. marmelade f.

marmoset n. marmouset m.

marmot n. marmotte f.

maroon a. & n. marron m.; — vt. abandonner (dans une île); isoler

marquee n. marquise f.

marquetry n. marqueterie f.

marquis n. marquis m.

marriage n. mariage m.; **by —** par alliance; **give (away) in —** donner en mariage; — **certificate** acte de mariage m.; **-able** a. en d'âge à (se) marier, nubile

married a. marié; conjugal; **get —** se marier; — **couple** ménage m.

marrow n. moelle f.

marry vt. se marier (avec), épouser; — **into** s'allier à; — **off** marier

Marseilles n. Marseille

marsh n. marais, marécage m.; **-y** a. marécageux

marshal n. maréchal m.; maître es cérémonies m.; — vt. ranger; rassembler

marshmallow n. guimauve f.

marsupial n. marsupial m.

mart n. marché m.; entrepôt m.

martinet n. homme fort sur la discipline m.

Martinique n. Martinique f.

martyr n. martyr m.; **-dom** n. martyre m.

marvel n. merveille f.; — vi. s'étonner, s'émerveiller; **-ous** a. merveilleux; **-ously** à merveille, merveilleusement

Marxist a. & n. marxiste

marzipan n. massepain m.

mascara n. rimmel m.

mascot n. mascotte f.

masculine a. masculin; mâle; viril; — n. masculin m.

masculinity n. masculinité f.

mash n. mâche f.; pâtée f.; purée f.; — vt. brasser, broyer; mettre en purée; -ed a. en purée; **-ed potatoes** purée de pommes de terre f.

mask n. masque m.; — vt. masquer; cacher

mason n. maçon m.; franc-maçon m.; **-ic** a. maçonnique; **-ry** n. maçonnerie f.; franc-maçonnerie f.

masquerade n. mascarade f.; bal masqué m.

Mass n. (eccl.) Messe f.; **High —** Grandmesse, Messe haute f.; **Requiem —** Messe des morts f.; **hear —** assister à la Messe; — **book** missel m.

mass n. masse f.; multitude, foule f.; — **meeting** réunion en masse; — **production** fabrication en série, construction en série f.; **-ive** a. massif; en masse: — vi. se masser, se réunir, se rassembler: — vt. rassembler, réunir

massacre n. massacre m.; — vt. massacrer

massage n. massage m.; (head) friction f.; — vt. masser; malaxer

masses pl. foule f.; peuple m.

mast n. mât m.; pylône m.

master n. maître m.; chef, patron m.; (duplicator) cliché n.; — **key** passe-partout m.; — **of arts** licencié ès lettres m.; — **stroke** coup de maître m.; — vt. maîtriser, dompter; apprendre à fond; **-ful** a. autoritaire; **-ly** a. de maître; **-y** n. maîtrise f.; connaissance f.

mastermind n. chef, organisateur, cerveau m.; — vt. diriger, organiser

masterpiece n. chef d'œuvre m.

masticate vt. mâcher, mastiquer

mastiff n. mâtin m.

mastoid a. mastoïde

mat n. natte f., paillasson m.; picture — passe-partout m.; **place —** dessous m.; — vt. natter; — vi. s'emmêler; **-ted** a. emmêlé

match n. allumette f.; mariage m.; (colors) assortiment m.; (sports) match m.; partie f.; égal, pareil m.; — vt. égaler; assortir; — vi. s'assortir; **-ing, to —** a. assorti; **-less** a. sans pareil, sans égal; incomparable

matchbox n. boîte à allumettes f.

matchmaker *n.* marieur *m.*, marieuse *f.*

mate *n.* époux *m.*, épouse *f.*; compagnon *m.*, compagne *f.*; mâle *m.*, femelle *f.*; (chess) échec et mat *m.*; (naut.) officier *m.*; first — second *m.*; — *vt.* accoupler; (chess) faire échec et mat; — *vi.* s'accoupler

material *a.* matériel; pertinent, important; — *n.* matière *f.*, matériaux *m. pl.*; étoffe *f.*, tissu *m.*; sujet *m.*; -ism *n.* matérialisme *m.*; -istic *a.* matérialiste; matériel; -ize *vi.* se matérialiser; se réaliser; -ly *adv.* matériellement; sensiblement

maternal *a.* maternel

maternity *n.* maternité *f.*; — hospital *n.* (hospice de la) maternité *f.*

mathematical *a.* mathématique

mathematician *n.* mathématicien *m.*

mathematics *n. pl.* mathématiques *f. pl.*

matriarch *n.* femme chef d'une famille *f.*

matriculate *vt.* immatriculer

matriculation *n.* immatriculation *f.*

matrimonial *a.* matrimonial; conjugal

matrimony *n.* mariage *m.*; vie conjugale *f.*

matrix *n.* matrice *f.*; moule *f.*

matron *n.* matrone *f.*; intendante *f.*; -ly *a.* domestique, en femme mariée, d'un certain âge

matter *n.* matière *f.*; sujet *m.*; chose, affaire *f.*; question *f.*; as a — of fact à vrai dire; en effet; — of course chose qui va de soi *f.*; — of form formalité *f.*; — in hand chose dont il s'agit *f.*; what is the —? qu'y a-t-il?, qu'avez-vous?; what is the — with him? qu'a-t-il?; — *vi.* importer; it does not — n'importe

matter-of-course *a.* qui va sans dire

matter-of-fact *a.* positif, pratique, calme

matting *n.* natte *f.*; ouate *f.*

mattress *n.* matelas *m.*; (spring) sommier *m.*

mature *a.* mûr, d'âge mûr; (bond) échu; — *vt.* mûrir; — *vi.* mûrir; arriver à échéance

maturity *n.* maturité *f.*; échéance *f.*

maudlin *a.* excessivement sentimental

maul *vt.* meurtrir, malmener

Mauritania *n.* Mauritanie *f.*

Mauritius *n.* (île) Maurice *f.*

mausoleum *n.* mausolée *m.*

maverick *n.* bœuf non marqué au fer *m.*; solitaire, sauvage *m.*

maxim *n.* maxime *f.*, dicton *m.*

maximum *a. & n.* maximum *m.*

may *vi.* pouvoir; it — be il se peut

May *n.* mai *m.*; — Day le premier mai *m.*

mayhem *n.* mutilation *f.*; (fig.) ravage, dégat *m.*

maybe *adv.* peut-être

mayor *n.* maire *m.*; président du conseil

municipal *m.*

maypole *n.* arbre du premier mai *m.*

maze *n.* labyrinthe *m.*

M.C.: Master of Ceremonies maître des cérémonies *m.*

me *pron.* me, moi

meadow *n.* pré *m.*; prairie *f.*; — lark *n.* étourneau *m.*

meager, meagre *a.* maigre; pauvre; peu nombreux

meal *n.* repas *m.*; farine *f.*; -y *a.* farineux

mealtime *n.* heure du repas *f.*

mean *a.* bas, vil, méprisable; sale, vilain; mesquin; misérable; (math.) moyen; — *n.* milieu; (math.) moyenne *f.*; -s *pl.* moyen *m.* (*pl.*); ressources *f. pl.*; by all -s (mais) certainement; by no -s pas du tout; en aucune façon; by -s of au moyen de; -ness *n.* vilenie, mesquinerie *f.*; bassesse *f.*; petitesse *f.*; médiocrité *f.*

mean *vt.* vouloir dire, signifier; avoir l'intention de; -ing *n.* sens *m.*, signification *f.*; -ingful *a.* significatif; -ingless *a.* dépourvu de sens

meander *vi.* serpenter; — *n.* méandre *m.*

meantime *adv. & n.*; in the — sur ces entrefaites; dans l'intervalle

meanwhile *adv.* sur ces entrefaites

measles *n. pl.* rougeole *f.*

measurable *a.* mesurable

measurably *adv.* sensiblement; modérément

measure *n.* mesure *f.*; démarche *f.*; in some — en partie; — *vt.* mesurer; métrer; avoir; -d *a.* compté; modéré; -less *a.* vaste, sans bornes; -ment *n.* mesure *f.*; mesurage *m.*

meat *n.* viande *f.*; nourriture *f.*; (fig.) moelle *f.*; -ball *n.* boulette de viande *f.*; -less *a.* (eccl.) maigre; -y *a.* charnu

meat market *n.* boucherie *f.*

Mecca *n.* Mecque *f.*

mechanic *n.* mécanicien *m.*; (auto) garagiste *m.*; -al *a.* mécanique; automatique; -al engineer *a.* ingénieur mécanicien *m.*; -al engineering *n.* mécanique *f.*; -s *n. pl.* mécanique *f.*

mechanism *n.* mécanisme *m.*; appareil *m.*

mechanize *vt.* mécaniser

medal *n.* médaille *f.*; -lion *n.* médaillon *m.*

meddle *vi.* se mêler (de), s'occuper (de); -some *a.* qui se mêle de tout

medial *a.* moyen, médial

median *a.* médian

mediate *vi.* s'interposer; servir de médiateur

mediation *n.* médiation *f.*

mediator *n.* médiateur *m.*; arbitre *m.*

medical *a.* médical; — school école de médecine *f.*

medicare *n.* programme d'assurance contre la maladie pour les personnes âgées *m.*

medicate *vt.* médicamenter

medicine *n.* médicine *f.*; médicament *m.*

medicine chest *n.* pharmacie *f.*

medicine dropper *n.* compte-gouttes *m.*

medicine man *n.* médecin indien, sorcier indien *m.*

medieval *a.* médiéval; du moyen-âge

mediocre *a.* médiocre

mediocrity *n.* médiocrité *f.*

meditate *vt. & vi.* méditer

meditation *n.* méditation *f.*

meditative *a.* méditatif

Mediterranean *n.* Méditerranée *f.*

medium *n.* moyen *m.*; milieu *m.*; intermédiare *m.*; organe *m.*; (spiritualist) médium *m.*; — *a.* moyen; (cooking) à point

medium-sized *a.* de grandeur moyenne, de taille moyenne

medley *n.* mélange *m.*; (color) bigarrure *f.*; (mus.) pot-pourri *m.*

medulla *n.* moelle *f.*

meek *a.* humble, doux; timide; **–ness** *n.* humilité, douceur *f.*

meet *vt.* rencontrer; retrouver; croiser; faire la connaisance de; — *vi.* se rencontrer; se joindre; se réunir; **go to** — aller au-devant de, aller à la rencontre de; **make both ends** — joindre les deux bouts; **until we** — **again** au revoir; — **with** éprouver, essuyer; **–ing** *n.* réunion *f.*, meeting *m.*; rencontre *f.*; **–ing place** rendez-vous *m.*

megaphone *n.* mégaphone *m.*

melancholy *a.* mélancolique; — *n.* mélancolie *f.*

meld *n.* (cards) combinaison *f.*; — *vi.* annoncer

mellow *a.* doux (douce); mûr; moelleux; — *vt.* adoucir; mûrir; — *vi.* s'adoucir; mûrir; **–ness** *n.* moelleux *m.*; maturité *f.*; mollesse *f.*

melodious *a.* mélodieux; **–ness** *n.* mélodie *f.*

melodrama *n.* mélodrame *m.*; **–tic** *a.* mélodramatique

melody *n.* air *m.*; mélodie *f.*

melon *n.* melon *m.*

melt *vt.* fondre; — *vi.* (se) fondre; **–ing** *a.* fondant; **–ing** *n.* fonte, fusion *f.*; **–ing point** point de fusion *m.*; **–ing pot** creuset *m.*

member *n.* membre *m.*; partie *f.*; (pol.) représentant, député *m.*; **–ship** *n.* nombre des membres *m.*; qualité de membre *f.*; membres *m. pl.*

membrane *n.* membrane *f.*; tunique *f.*

memento *n.* souvenir, mémento *m.*

memo *n.* mémo, mémorandum *m.*

memoir *n.* mémoire *m.*; **–s** *pl.* mémoires *m. pl.*

memorable *a.* mémorable

memorandum *n.* mémorandum, mémo *m.*; — **pad** bloc-notes *m.*

memorial *a.* commémoratif; — *n.* monument commémoratif *m.*; **–ist** *n.* auteur de mémoires *m.*

memorize *vt.* apprendre par cœur

memory *n.* mémoire *f.*; souvenir *m.*; **commit to** — apprendre par cœur

menace *n.* menace *f.*; — *vt.* menacer

menagerie *n.* ménagerie *f.*

mend *n.* raccommodage *m.*, reprise *f.*; **on the** — en voie de guérison; — *vt.* raccommoder; réparer; — *vi.* se remettre; **–able** *a.* réparable; **–ing** *n.* raccommodage *m.*

mendicant *a. & n.* mendiant *m.*

menial *a.* bas, servile; — *n.* domestique, laquais *m.*

meningitis *n.* méningite *f.*

menopause *n.* ménopause *f.*

menstruation *n.* menstruation *f.*

mental *a.* mental; de tête; de l'esprit; — **hospital** maison de santé *f.*; asile d'aliénés *m.*; **–ity** *n.* mentalité *f.*

mention *n.* mention *f.*; — *vt.* mentionner; faire mention de; citer; **don't** — **it** il n'y a pas de quoi; de rien; **not to** — sans parler de

mentor *n.* mentor, guide *m.*

menu *n.* carte *f.*, menu *m.*

mercantile *a.* mercantile, commercial

mercenary *a. & n.* mercenaire *m.*

mercerize *vt.* merceriser

merchandise *n.* marchandise *f.*

merchant *n.* marchand *m.*; commerçant, négociant *m.*; — **marine** marine marchande *f.*

merchantman *n.* vaisseau marchand *m.*

merciful *a.* miséricordieux; clément

merciless *a.* impitoyable

mercurial *a.* mercuriel, ardent, vif

mercurochrome *n.* mercurochrome *m.*

mercury *n.* mercure *m.*

Mercury-switch *n.* interrupteur à mercure *m.*

mercury-vapor lamp *n.* lampe à vapeur de mercure *f.*

mercy *n.* miséricorde *f.*; clémence, grâce, merci *f.*; pitié *f.*; **be at someone's** — être à la merci de; **have** — **on** avoir pitié de

mere *a.* seul; simple; pur; **–ly** *adv.* seulement, (tout) simplement

merge *vt.* fondre, fusionner; — *vi.* se fon-

dre; fusionner; s'amalgamer
meridian *n.* méridien *m.*; **-al** *a.* méridional
merit *n.* mérite *m.*; **-s** *pl.* le pour et le contre; — *vt.* mériter; **-orious** *a.* méritoire
mermaid *n.* sirène *f.*
merrily *adv.* joyeusement
merriment *n.* gaieté, réjouissance *f.*
merry *a.* joyeux, gai
merry-go-round *n.* manège (de chevaux de bois) *m.*
mesa *n.* plateau élevé *m.*
mesh *n.* maille *f.*; engrenage *m.*, prise *f.*; — *vt.* engrener, endenter; — *vi.* être en prise, engrener
mesmerism *n.* mesmérisme *m.*
mesmerize *vt.* hypnotiser
mesotron *n.* électron lourd, méson *m.*
mess *n.* désordre *m.*; saleté *f.*; gâchis *m.*; (mil.) soupe *f.*, mess *m.*; **-y** *a.* sale; en désordre
message *n.* message *m.*; mot *m.*; communication *f.*
messenger *n.* messager *m.*; commissionnaire *m.*; courrier *m.*
Messiah *n.* Messie *m.*
mess hall *n.* (mil.) salle de mess *f.*, réfectoire *m.*; (navy) carré des officiers *m.*
mess kit *n.* gamelle *f.*
Messrs. MM. *n.* *pl.* messieurs *m.* *pl.*
metabolism *n.* métabolisme *m.*
metal *n.* métal; **-lic** *a.* métallique; **-lurgy** *n.* métallurgie *f.*
metamorphosis *n.* métamorphose *f.*
metaphor *n.* métaphore *f.*; **-ical** *a.* métaphorique
metaphysical *a.* métaphysique
metaphysics *n.* *pl.* métaphysique *f.*
metatarsal *a.* métatarsien
mete *vt.* distribuer
meteor *n.* météore *m.*; **-ic** *a.* météorique; rapide; **-ite** *n.* aérolithe *m.*; **-ological** *a.* météorologique; **-ologist** *n.* météorologiste, météo *m.*; **-ology** *n.* météorologie *f.*
meter *n.* mètre *m.*; compteur *m.*
methane *n.* méthane *m.*
method *n.* méthode *f.*; procédé *m.*; **-ical** *a.* méthodique
methyl *n.* méthyle *m.*; **-ate** *vt.* méthyler
meticulous *a.* méticuleux
metric *a.* métrique; **-al** *a.* métrique; en vers, mesuré
metronome *n.* métronome *m.*
metropolis *n.* métropole *f.*
metropolitan *a.* métropolitain
mettle *n.* courage, coeur *m.*
mew *vi.* miauler
Mexican *a. & n.* mexicain *m.*
Mexico *n.* Mexique *m.*
mezzanine *n.* entresol *m.*

microbe *n.* microbe *m.*
microbiology *n.* microbiologie *f.*
microcircuit *n.* microcircuit *m.*
microcosm *n.* microcosme *m.*
microfilm *n.* microfilm *m.*; — *vt.* microfilmer
microgroove *n.* microsillon *m.*
micrometer *n.* micromètre *m.*
micron *n.* micron *m.*
microörganism *n.* micro-organisme *m.*
microphone *n.* microphone *m.*
microphysics *n.* microphysique *f.*
microscope *n.* microscope *m.*; **electron** — microscope électronique *m.*
microscopic *a.* microscopique
microwave *n.* onde ultracourte *f.*
mid *a.* du milieu, moyen
midday *n.* midi *m.*
middle *n.* milieu *m.*; centre *m.*; **in the** — of au milieu de; en train de; — *a.* moyen central; du milieu; — **class** bourgeoisie *f.*
Middle Ages *n.* *pl.* Moyen-Âge *m.*
middle-aged *a.* d'un certain âge
middle-class *a.* bourgeois
middleman *n.* intermédiaire *m.*; revendeur *m.*; entremetteur *m.*
middleweight *n.* poids moyen *m.*
middling *a.* moyen; médiocre
middy blouse *n.* blouse de matelot *f.*
midget *n.* nain *m.*, naine *f.*
midland *a.* intérieur, de l'intérieur
midnight *n.* minuit *m.*
midriff *n.* diaphragme *m.*; tour de ceinture *m.*
midshipman *n.* aspirant de marine, midship *m.*
midst *n.*, **in the** — of au milieu de; parmi; en train de
midway *adv.* à mi-chemin, à mi-distance; — *n.* allée centrale *f.*; fête foraine *f.*
midwife *n.* sage-femme *f.*
mien *n.* mine *f.*, air *m.*
might *n.* puissance, force *f.*; **-y** *a.* puissant, fort; grand; **-y** *adv.* (coll.) très, fort
migraine *n.* migraine *f.*
migrant *n.* nomade *m.*
migrate *vi.* émigrer
migration *n.* migration *f.*
migratory *a.* migrateur, de passage
mild *a.* doux (douce); léger; (climate) tempéré; **-ness** *n.* douceur *f.*
mildew *n.* moisissure *f.*; chancissure *f.*
mile *n.* mille *m.*; **-age** *n.* milles *m.* *pl.*; distance en milles *f.*; kilométrage *m.*
milestone *n.* borne *f.*
militarism *n.* militarisme *m.*
military *a.* militaire; — *n.* militaires *m.* *pl.*
militate *vi.* militer
militia *n.* milice *f.*; garde nationale *f.*;

–man *n.* milicien *m.*

milk *n.* lait *m.*; **bottle of** — carafe de lait *f.*; — **of magnesia** magnésie *f.*; — **sugar** *n.* sucre de lait *m.*; lactine *f.*; — **tooth** dent de lait *f.*; — *vt.* traire; exploiter; **–y** *a.* laiteux

milkmaid *n.* laitière *f.*

milkman *n.* laitier *m.*

milkweed *n.* laiteron *m.*

Milky Way *n.* voie lactée *f.*

mill *n.* moulin *m.*; fabrique, usine *f.*; — *vt.* moudre; fraiser; laminer; meuler; usiner; canneler; — *vi.* se presser; fourmiller; **–er** *n.* meunier *m.*

millennium *n.* millénaire *m.*; (eccl.) millénium *n.*

milligram *n.* milligramme *m.*

millimeter *n.* millimètre *m.*

milliner *n.* modiste *f.*; **–y** *n.* modes *f. pl.*; **–y shop** magasin de modes *m.*

million *n.* million *m.*; **–aire** *n.* millionnaire *m. & f.*; **–th** *a.* millionième

millrace *n.* canal de moulin *m.*

millstone *n.* meule *f.*

milt *n.* laite, laitance *f.*

mime *n.* mime *m.*; — *vi.* mimer

mimeograph *n.* machine à polycopier *f.*; — *vt.* polycopier

mimic *n.* imitateur *m.*; — *vt.* imiter, mimer; **–ry** *n.* imitation; mimique *f.*

minaret *n.* minaret *m.*

mince *vt.* hacher; **not to** — **one's words** parler sans phrases; **–d** *a.* haché; **–d meat** hachis *m.*

mincemeat *n.* mincemeat *m.*

mind *n.* esprit *m.*; âme *f.*; intelligence *f.*; mémoire *f.*; — **reader** personne qui lit dans la pensée des autres *f.*; **bear in** — ne pas oublier; **be of one** — être d'accord; **bring to** — rappeler; **change one's** — changer d'avis; **have a** — **to** avoir envie de; **have in** — avoir en vue; **make up one's** — se décider, prendre le parti (de); **peace of** — tranquillité d'esprit *f.*; **state of** — état d'âme *m.*; — *vt.* garder, surveiller; faire attention à; s'occuper de; ne pas vouloir; **I don't** — cela m'est égal; je veux bien; **never** — n'importe; ne vous inquiétez pas; **–ful** *a.* attentif

mine *n.* mine *f.*; — **field** champ de mines *m.*; — *pron.* le mien *m.*; — *a.* à moi; — **layer** *n.* poseur de mines *m.*; — **shaft** puits *m.*; — **sweeper** *n.* dragueur de mines, balayeur de mines *m.*; — *vt.* fouiller; (coal) exploiter; (mil.) miner; **–r** *n.* mineur *m.*

mineral *a. & n.* minéral *m.*; — **water** eau minérale *f.*; boisson gazeuse *f.*; **–ogist** *n.* minéralogiste *m.*; **–ogy** minéralogie *f.*

–ngle *vi.* se mêler, se mélanger

miniature *n.* miniature *f.*; — *a.* en miniature

miniaturization *n.* reproduction en miniature

minimize *vt.* réduire au minimum

minimum *a. & n.* minimum *m.*

mining *n.* exploitation des mines, industrie minière *f.*; (naut.) pose des mines *f.*

minion *n.* mignon *m.*; (print.) corps 7 *m.*

minister *n.* ministre *m.*; pasteur *m.*; — *vi.*, — **to someone's needs** subvenir aux besoins de

ministry *n.* (administration) ministère; (eccl.) le saint ministère; (pol.) gouvernement *m.*

mink *n.* vison *m.*

minnow *n.* vairon *m.*

minor *a.* petit, mineur, peu important; — *n.* mineur *m.*; **–ity** *n.* minorité *f.*

minstrel *n.* ménestrel *m.*; chanteur, musicien *m.*

mint *n.* monnaie *f.*; (bot.) menthe *f.*; — *vt.* frapper, battre

minuet *n.* menuet *m.*

minus *prep.* moins; (coll.) sans; — *n.* moins *m.*; — *a.* négatif

minute *n.* minute *f.*; instant, moment *m.*; note *f.*; **any** — à tout moment; — **hand** grande aiguille *f.*; **–s** *pl.* notes *f. pl.*, procès-verbal *m.*; — *a.* menu, minuscule; moindre; minutieux

minx *n.* coquine *f.*

miracle *n.* miracle *m.*; — **play** *n.* miracle *m.*; — **worker** thaumaturge, faiseur de miracles *m.*

miraculous *a.* miraculeux

mirage *n.* mirage *m.*

mire *n.* boue, fange *f.*; — *vi.* s'enfoncer dans la boue; s'embourber

mirror *n.* miroir *m.*, glace *f.*; **rear-view** — rétroviseur *m.*

mirth *n.* gaieté, joie *f.*

misadventure *n.* mésaventure *f.*

misalliance *n.* mésalliance *f.*

misanthrope *n.* misanthrope *m.*

misanthropic *a.* misanthrope

misapprehension *n.* méprise *f.*, malentendu *m.*

misappropriation *n.* détournement *m.*

misbehave *vi.* se comporter mal, se conduire mal

misbehavior *n.* mauvaise conduite *f.*

miscalculate *vt.* mal calculer; — *vi.* se tromper

miscalculation *n.* mécompte *m.*, erreur de calcul *f.*

miscarriage *n.* (med.) fausse couche *f.*; avortement, insuccès *m.*; — **of justice** erreur judiciaire *f.*

miscarry *vi.* (med.) faire une fausse couche; avorter, manquer, échouer

miscellaneous *a.* divers, varié

miscellany *n.* mélanges *m. pl.*

mischief *n.* espièglerie *f.*; mauvais tour *m.*; mal *m.*; malice *f.*

mischievous *a.* espiègle, malicieux; méchant

misconception *n.* idée fausse *f.*

misconduct *n.* mauvaise conduite *f.*; mauvaise administration *f.*

misconstrue *vt.* mésinterpréter; mal prendre

miscount *n.* erreur d'addition *f.*

miscreant *n.* mécréant *m.*

misdeal *n.* (cards) maldonne *f.*; — *vt.* faire maldonne

misdeed *n.* méfait *m.*

misdemeanor *n.* délit *m.*

misdirect *vt.* mal diriger; mal renseigner

miser *n.* avare *m.*; -ly *a.* avare

miserable *a.* misérable; malheureux

misery *n.* misère *f.*; souffrance *f.*

misfire *vi.* rater

misfit *n.* vêtement manqué *m.*; (person) raté *m.*; déchu *m.*

misfortune *n.* malheur *m.*, infortune *f.*

misgiving *n.* appréhension, hésitation *f.*; doute *m.*

misguide *vt.* mal guider, égarer

mishap *n.* contretemps *m.*, mésaventure *f.*; accident *m.*

misinform *vt.* mal renseigner

misinterpret *vt.* mal interpréter; -ation *n.* fausse interprétation *f.*

misjudge *vt.* mal juger; méconnaître

mislay *vt.* égarer

mislead *vt. ir.* égarer, tromper; -ing *a.* trompeur

mismanage *vt.* mal conduire, mal administrer; -ment *n.* mauvaise administration *f.*

mismatch *vt.* mal assortir

misnomer *n.* faux nom *m.*; nom mal approprié *m.*

misplace *vt.* mal placer; déplacer; perdre

misprint *n.* faute d'impression *f.*

mispronounce *vt.* mal prononcer

misquote *vt.* citer à faux

misrepresent *vt.* mal représenter; travestir; -ation *n.* faux rapport *m.*, fausse déclaration *f.*

misrule *n.* désordre m.; mauvaise administration *f.*

miss *n.* mademoiselle *f.*; jeune fille, demoiselle *f.*

miss *n.* coup manqué, coup raté *m.*; — *vt.* manquer, rater; ne pas trouver; ne pas avoir; ne pas saisir; regretter; -ing *a.* absent; disparu; qui manque

misshapen *a.* difforme; déformé

missile *n.* projectile *m.*; (rocket) engin *m.*; guided — engin téléguidé *m.*; intercontinental — engin intercontinental *m.*

mission *n.* mission *f.*; -ary *a. & n.* missionnaire *m.*

misspell *vt.* mal épeler; -ing *n.* faute d'orthographe *f.*

misstate *n.* mal énoncer; annoncer à faux; -ment rapport inexact *m.*

misstep *n.* faux pas *m.*

mist *n.* brume *f.*; buée *f.*; voile *m.*; -y *a.* brumeux; vague

mistake *n.* faute, erreur *f.*; méprise *f.*; by — par erreur; **make a** — faire une faute; se tromper; — *vt.* se tromper; mal comprendre; -n *a.* erroné; dans l'erreur

mister, Mr. *n.* monsieur *m.*

mistranslation *n.* erreur de traduction *f.*; contre-sens *m.*

mistress *n.* maîtresse *f.*

mistrust *n.* méfiance, défiance *f.*; — *vt.* se méfier de; -ful *a.* méfiant

misunderstand *vt.* mal comprendre; mal interpréter; se méprendre; méconnaître; -ing *n.* malentendu; quiproquo *m.*

misuse *n.* abus *m.*; mauvais usage *m.*; — *vt.* faire mauvais usage

mite *n.* mite *f.*; brin *m.*, miette *f.*

mitigate *vt.* atténuer, mitiger; adoucir

mitigating *a.* atténuant

mitre *n.* onglet *m.*; (eccl.) mitre *f.*; — *vt.* tailler à onglet

mitten *n.* mitaine *f.*

mix *vt.* mêler, mélanger; confondre; composer; malaxer; — *vi.* se mêler, se mélanger; aller (bien) ensemble; — *a.* mêlé; mixte; assorti; -er *n.* agitateur *m.*; malaxeur, mixer *m.*; -ture *n.* mélange *m.*; mixture *f.*, (med.) potion *f.*

moan *n.* gémissement *m.*; — *vi.* gémir; — *vt.* dire en gémissant

moat *n.* fossé *m.*

mob *n.* foule, cohue *f.*; populace *m.*; canaille *f.*; — *vt.* faire foule autour de; — *vi.* s'ameuter; s'attrouper

mobile *a.* mobile; changeant; — **unit** *n.* groupe mobile *m.*

mobility *n.* mobilité *f.*

mobilization *n.* mobilisation *f.*

mobilize *vt.* mobiliser

moccasin *n.* mocassin *m.*

mocha *n.* moka *m.*

mock *a.* faux; factice; feint; d'imitation; (as prefix); simili-; — **tortoise-shell** *a.* écaille imitation *f.*; — **trial** *n.* simulacre de procès *m.*; — *vt.* se moquer de, railler; imiter; -ery *n.* moquerie, raillerie *f.*; -ing *a.* moqueur, railleur

modal *a.* modal

mode *n.* mode *m.*; manière *f.*; (fashion)

mode *f.*
model *n.* modèle *m.*; patron *m.*; maquette *f.*; (person) modèle *n.* & *f.*; — *a.* modèle; — *vt.* modeler; (clothes) exposer, montrer; **–ing** *n.* modelage *m.*
moderate *vt.* modérer; tempérer; — *vi.* se modérer; — *a.* modéré; raisonnable, mesuré; modique
moderation *n.* modération *f.*; mesure *f.*
moderator *n.* président, arbitre *m.*
modern *a.* moderne; — languages langues vivantes *f. pl.*; **–istic** *a.* moderne; **–ize** *vt.* moderniser
modest *a.* modeste; pudique; **–y** *n.* modestie *f.*; pudeur *f.*
modicum *n.* petite quantité *f.*; un peu *m.*
modification *n.* modification *f.*
modify *vt.* modifier
modulate *vt.* & *vi.* moduler
modulation *n.* modulation *f.*
module *n.* module *m.*
Mohammedan *a.* & *n.* mahométan *m.*; **–ism** *n.* mahométisme *m.*
moist *a.* humide, moite; mouillé; **–en** *vt.* mouiller, humecter, moitir; **–ness** *n.* humidité *f.*; moiteur *f.*; **–ure** *n.* humidité *f.*
molar *a.* & *n.* molaire *f.*
molasses *n.* mélasse *f.*
mold *n.* moule *m.*, matrice *f.*; moisissure *f.*, moisi *m.*; — *vt.* mouler; pétrir; — *vi.* moisir; **–er** *vi.* tomber en poussière; **–iness** *n.* moisissure *f.*; **–ing** *n.* moulage *m.*; moulure *f.*; **–y** *a.* moisi
mole *n.* grain de beauté *m.*
molecular *a.* moléculaire; — biology *n.* biologie moléculaire *f.*
molecule *n.* molécule *f.*
molehill *n.* taupinière *f.*
moleskin *n.* molesquine *f.*
molest *vt.* molester
mollify *vt.* apaiser
mollusk *n.* mollusque *m.*
molt *vi.* muer; **–ing** *a.* en mue; **–ing** *n.* mue *f.*
molten *a.* fondu
molybdenum *n.* molybdène *m.*
moment *n.* moment, instant *m.*; importance *f.*; (fig.) heure *f.*; at the — en ce moment, pour le moment; cf — important; **–ary** *a.* momentané; **–ous** *a.* très important
momentum *n.* force vive *f.*, moment *m.*; vitesse *f.*
Monacan *a.* & *n.* monégasque *m.*
Monaco *n.* Monaco *m.*
monarch *n.* monarque *m.*; **–ic** *a.* monarchique; **–ist** *n.* monarchiste *m.*; **–y** *n.* monarchie *f.*
monastery *n.* monastère *m.*
monastic *a.* monastique

Monday *n.* lundi *m.*
monetary *a.* monétaire
money *n.* argent *m.*; (school) pion *m.*; monnaie *f.*; espèces *f. pl.*; counterfeit — fausse monnaie *f.*; — belt ceinture à porte-monnaie *f.*; — box caisse *f.*; — order mandat-poste *m.*; **–ed** *a.* riche, opulent
Mongol *n.* Mongol *m.*; **–ia** *n.* Mongolie *f.*; **–ian** *a.* mongol, mongolique
mongrel *n.* bâtard *m.*; métis *m.*
monitor *vt.* contrôler, écouter; — *n.* moniteur *m.*; (school) pion *m.*; détecteur *m.*; contrôleur *m.*; **–ing** *n.* écoute *f.*; contrôle *f.*
monk *n.* moine, religieux *m.*
monkey *n.* singe *m.*; guenon *f.*; — wrench clé anglaise *f.*
monochromatic *a.* monochrome
monochrome *n.* monochrome
monogamous *a.* monogame
monogamy *n.* monogamie *f.*
monogram *n.* chiffre, monogramme *m.*
monograph *n.* monographie *f.*
monolithic *a.* monolithe
monologue *n.* monologue *m.*
monomania *n.* monomanie *f.*; **–c** *n.* monomane *m.* & *f.*
monoplane *n.* monoplan *m.*
monopolistic *a.* de monopole, monopoleur
monopolize *vt.* monopoliser; accaparer
monopoly *n.* monopole *m.*
monorail *n.* monorail *m.*
monosyllabic *a.* monosyllabique
monotonous *a.* monotone
monotony *n.* monotonie *f.*
monoxide *n.* protoxyde *m.*; carbon — sous-oxyde de carbone *m.*
monsoon *n.* mousson *f.*
monster *n.* monstre *m.*
monstrance *n.* (eccl.) ostensoir *m.*
monstrosity *n.* monstruosité *f.*; monstre *m.*; enormité *f.*
monstrous *a.* monstrueux; **–ness** *n.* monstruosité *f.*
month *n.* mois *m.*; by the — au mois; **–'s** pay mois *m.*; once a — une fois par mois, mensuellement; **–ly** *a.* mensuel; **–ly** payment mensualité *f.*; **–ly** *adv.* une fois par mois, mensuellement
monument *n.* monument *m.*; **–al** *a.* monumental
moo *vi.* meugler, beugler
mood *n.* disposition, humeur *f.*; (gram.) mode *m.*; **–iness** *n.* humeur changeante *f.*; **–y** *a.* d'humeur changeante; maussade
moon *n.* lune *f.*; — *vi.* musarder
moonbeam *n.* rayon de lune *m.*
moonlight *n.* clair de lune *m.*
moon-struck, moon-stricken *a.* lunatique
moor *n.* bruyère, lande *f.*; — *vt.* amarrer;

— *vi.* s'amarrer; **–ing** *n.* amarrage *m.*; (rope) amarre *f.*

Moor *n.* Maure *m.*, Mauresque *f.*; **–ish** *a.* mauresque, maure, des Maures

moors *n. pl.* landes *f. pl.*, bruyère *f.*

moot *a.* discutable; — **court** *n.* procés simulé *m.*

mop *n.* guipon *m.*; — **of hair** tignasse *f.*; — *vt.* nettoyer avec un guipon; essuyer; éponger

mope *vi.* rêver; s'ennuyer

moral *a.* moral; — *n.* morale, moralité *f.*; **–s** *pl.* moralité *f.*; **–ist** *n.* moraliste *m. & f.*; **–ity** *n.* moralité *f.*; bonnes mœurs *f. pl.*; **–ize** *vi.* moraliser; **–ly** *adv.* moralement

morass *n.* marais *m.*

morbid *a.* morbide; maladif

more *a.* plus de; encore de, encore un; d'autres; — *n.* davantage; — *adv.* plus; davantage; **all the —** d'autant plus; — **and —** de plus en plus; **once —** encore une fois; **no —** ne . . . plus (de)

moreover *adv.* d'ailleurs, du reste

mores *n. pl.* mœurs *f. pl.*

moribund *a.* moribond

Mormon *n.* Mormon *m.*

morning *n.* matin *m.*; matinée *f.*; **good —** bonjour; **in the —** le matin; (clock time) du matin; **the next —** le lendemain matin *m.*

Moroccan *a. & n.* marocain *m.*

Morocco *n.* Maroc *m.*; — **leather** maroquin *m.*; — **leather goods** maroquinerie *f.*

moron *n.* idiot *m.*

morose *a.* morose; **–ness** *n.* morosité *f.*

morphology *n.* morphologie *f.*

Morse code *n.* alphabet Morse *m.*

morsel *n.* morceau *m.*

mortal *a.* mortel; fatal; à mort; — *n.* mortel *m.*; **–ity** *n.* mortalité *f.*; **–ly** *adv.* mortellement; à mort

mortar *n.* mortier *m.*; enduit *m.*

mortgage *n.* hypothèque *f.*; — *vt.* hypothéquer

mortician *n.* entrepreneur de pompes funèbres *m.*

mortification *n.* mortification *f.*; gangrène *f.*

mortify *vt.* mortifier; humilier; — *vi.* se mortifier; se gangrener

mortuary *a.* mortuaire; — *n.* morgue *f.*

mosaic *n.* mosaïque *f.*; — *a.* en mosaïque

Moscow *n.* Moscou *m.*

Moslem *a. & n.* mahométan, musulman *m.*

mosque *n.* mosquée *f.*

mosquito *n.* moustique *m.*; — **net** *n.* moustiquaire *f.*

moss *n.* mousse *f.*; **–y** *a.* moussu

most *a.* la plupart de; le plus de; — *n.* le plus *m.*; la plupart; — *adv.* le plus; très; **–ly** *adv.* pour la plupart

moth *n.* mite *f.*; papillon de nuit *m.*; **phalène** *f.*; **–y** *a.* mité

mothball *n.* boule de naphtaline *f.*

moth-eaten *a.* mité

mother *n.* mère *f.*; maman *f.*; — **tongue** langue maternelle *f.*; — *vt.* dorloter; **–hood** *n.* maternité *f.*; **–less** *a.* sans mère; **–ly** *a.* maternel

mother-in-law *n.* belle-mère *f.*

mother-of-pearl *n.* nacre *f.*

motion *n.* mouvement *m.*; signe *m.*; (debate) motion, proposition *f.*; — **picture** film *m.*; — **pictures** *n. pl.* cinéma *m.*; **set in —** mettre en marche, mettre en mouvement; — *vt. & vi.* faire signe; **–less** *a.* immobile

motion-picture *a.* cinématographique; du cinéma; — **camera** *n.* caméra *m.*

motivate *vt.* motiver

motive *a.* moteur (motrice); — *n.* motif, mobile *m.*

motley *a.* bigarré, bariolé

motor *a.* moteur (motrice); automobile; — *n.* moteur *m.*; **–cade** *n.* défilé de voitures *m.*; — **launch** *n.* chaloupe à moteur *m.*; — *vi.* aller en auto; **–ist** *n.* automobiliste *m. & f.*; **–ize** *vt.* motoriser

motorbike *n.* cyclomoteur *m.*

motorboat *n.* canot automobile *m.*, vedette *f.*

motorcade *n.* défilé (d'autos) *m.*

motorcycle *n.* moto, motocyclette *f.*

motorman *n.* wattman *m.*

mottle *vt.* marbrer; tacheter; **–d** *a.* marbré

motto *n.* devise *f.*

mound *n.* monticule *m.*, tertre *m.*; tas *m.*

mount *n.* mont *m.*, montagne *f.*; montage *m.*; armement *m.*; (horse) monture, monte *f.*; — *vt.* monter (sur); gravir; armer; — *vi.* monter; monter à cheval; — **up** croître; **–ed** *a.* à cheval; monté; **–ing** *n.* montage *m.*; garniture *f.*

mountain *n.* montagne *f.*; — *a.* des montagnes; montagneux; (person) montagnard; — **range** chaîne de montagnes; — **climber** *n.* alpiniste *m. & f.*; — **climbing** *n.* alpinisme *m.*; **–eer** *n.* alpiniste *m. & f.*; **–ous** *a.* montagneux

mountebank *n.* charlatan *m.*

mourn *vt. & vi.* pleurer, déplorer; **–er** *n.* affligé *m.*; personne qui est en deuil *f.*; **–ful** *a.* funèbre, lugubre; **–ing** *a.* en deuil; **–ing** *n.* deuil *m.*, affliction *f.*

mouse *n.* souris *f.*; — **trap** *n.* souricière *f.*

moustache, mustache *n.* moustache *f.*

mouth *n.* bouche *f.*; gueule *f.*; ouverture *f.*;

(river) embouchure *f*.; — organ harmonica *m*.; — **wash** dentifrice *m*.; — *vt*. & *vi*. déclamer; **-ful** *n*. bouchée *f*.
mouthpiece *n*. embouchure *f*.; bec, bocal *m*.
movable *a*. mobile; mobilier
move *n*. mouvement *m*.; (household) déménagement *m*.; (chess) coup *m*.; — *vt*. bouger, remuer; pousser; mouvoir; émouvoir, toucher; attendrir; déménager; (debate) proposer; (chess) jouer; — *vi*. bouger; se mouvoir, se déplacer; jouer; — **off** s'éloigner; — **on** continuer son chemin; — **out** déménager; **-ment** *n*. mouvement *m*.; transport *m*.; déplacement *m*.; **-r** *n*. moteur *m*.; déménageur *m*.
moving *a*. en marche, en mouvement; moteur, motrice; attendrissant; émouvant; — *n*. déménagement *m*.
mow *vt*. faucher; (lawn) tondre; **-er** *n*. faucheuse *f*.; (lawn) tondeuse *f*.; (person) faucheur *m*.
Mrs.: Mistress, Mme. *n*. madame *f*.
much *a*. beaucoup (de); bien (de); — *adv*. beaucoup; bien; **as** — autant (de); **how** — combien de; **so** — tant (de); **too** — trop (de); **very** — beaucoup
mucilage *n*. mucilage *m*., colle *f*.
muck *n*. fange *f*.; crotte *f*.
mucous *a*. muqueux
mucus *n*. mucus *m*.
mud *n*. boue *f*.; fange *f*.; vase *f*.; **-dy** *a*. boueux, fangeux, vaseux; (liquid) trouble
muddle *n*. confusion *f*.; — *vt*. brouiller, embrouiller
mudguard *n*. garde-boue *m*.
muff *n*. manchon *m*.; — *vt*. rater, louper, gâcher
muffin *n*. galette *f*.; (sorte de) brioche *f*.
muffle *vt*. envelopper; emmitoufler; étouffer; **-r** *n*. cache-nez *m*.; (auto) pot d'échappement *m*.
mufti *n*. tenue de ville *f*.; **in** — en civil
mug *n*. pot *m*., chope *f*.
muggy *a*. chaud et humide; lourd
mulatto *n*. mulâtre *m*., mulâtresse *f*.
mule *n*. mulet *m*., mule *f*.; **-teer** *n*. muletier *m*.
mulish *a*. obstiné, entêté
mull *vt*. (wine) chauffer avec des épices: — (coll.) méditer, ruminer; **-ed wine** vin chaud, vin chauffé *m*.
mullet *n*. (fish) mulet *m*.; **red** — rouget *m*.
multicolored *a*. multicolore
multigraph *n*. multigraphe *m*., machine à imprimer *f*.
multimillionaire *n*. multimillionaire, milliardaire *m*. & *f*.

multiple *a*. & *n*. multiple *m*.
multiple sclerosis *n*. sclérose multiple *f*.
multiplication *n*. multiplication *f*.
multiplicity *n*. multiplicité *f*.
multiply *vt*. multiplier; — *vi*. se multiplier
multitude *n*. multitude *f*.; foule *f*.
mumble *vt*. & *vi*. marmotter; marmonner
mummify *vt*. momifier
mummy *n*. momie *f*.
mumps *n*. oreillons *m*. *pl*.
munch *vt*. mâcher, mâchonner, croquer
mundane *a*. du monde, mondain
municipal *a*. municipal; **-ity** *n*. municipalité *f*.
munificence *n*. munificence *f*.
munificent *a*. munificent, généreux
munitions *n*. *pl*. munitions *f*. *pl*.
murder *n*. meurtre *m*.; assassinat *m*.; — *vt*. assassiner; **-er** *n*. meurtrier, assassin *m*.; **-ous** *a*. meurtrier, assassin
murky *a*. brouillé; ténébreux
murmur *n*. murmure *m*.; — *vt*. & *vi*. murmurer, parler à voix basse
Murphy-bed *n*. (trademark) lit escamotable *m*.
muscatel *n*. muscat *m*.
muscle *n*. muscle *m*.
muscle-bound *a*. aux muscles raides
muscular *a*. musculaire; musculeux, musclé; **-ity** *n*. constitution musculaire *f*.
muse *n*. muse *f*.; — *vi*. méditer, rêver
museum *n*. musée *m*.
mush *n*. polenta *f*.; **-y** *a*. mollet, mou; (fig.) sentimental
mushroom *n*. champignon *m*.; — *vi*. faire champignon
music *n*. musique *f*.; — **box** boîte à musique *f*.; **-al** *a*. de musique; musical; mélodieux; **-al comedy** *n*. opérette *f*.; **-ale** *n*. soirée musicale *f*.; **-ian** *n*. musicien *m*., musicienne *f*.
musing *n*. méditation, rêverie *f*.
musket *n*. mousquet *m*.; **-eer** *n*. mousquetaire *m*.
muskmelon *n*. cantaloup *m*.
muskrat *n*. rat musqué *m*.
muslin *n*. mousseline *f*.
muss *n*. désordre *m*.; — *vt*. mettre en désordre; froisser
mussel *n*. moule *f*.
must *n*. nécessité *f*.; — *vt*. devoir; falloir; **I** — je dois; il me faut, il faut que je . . . .
must *n*. moisi *m*.; **-iness** *n*. relent *m*.; odeur de moisi *f*.; **-y** *a*. de moisi, de relent; qui sent le renfermé
mustard *n*. moutarde *f*.; — **gas** *n*. gaz moutarde *m*.; — **pot** *n*. moutardier *m*.; — **plaster** *n*. cataplasme *m*.; sinapisme *m*.

muster *n.* revue *f.*; assemblée *f.*; rassemblement *m.*; — *vt.* rassembler; (mil.) passer en revue

mustiness *n.* moisi *m.*; renfermé *m.*

mutability *n.* mutabilité *f.*

mutable *a.* changeant, instable

mutant *n.* mutante *f.*

mutation *n.* changement *m.*

mute *a.* muet (muette); — *n.* muet *m.*, (mus.) sourdine *f.*; — *vt.* amortir, assourdir; **–d** *a.* en sourdine; **–ness** *n.* mutisme *m.*

mutilate *vt.* mutiler, estropier

mutilation *n.* mutilation *f.*

mutineer *n.* mutin *m.*; revolté *m.*

mutinous *a.* mutin; séditieux

mutiny *n.* mutinerie *f.*; — *vi.* se mutiner

mutter *vt.* & *vi.* marmotter, marmonner

mutton *n.* mouton *m.*

mutual *a.* réciproque, mutuel; commun; — **aid** *n.* entr'aide *f.*

muzzle *n.* museau *m.*; muselière; (gun) bouche *f.*; — *vt.* museler

my *pron.* mon, ma, mes; —! *interj.* tiens!; **–self** *pron.* me; moi; moi-même

myopia *n.* myopie *f.*

myopic *a.* myope

myriad *n.* myriade *f.*

mysterious *a.* mystérieux; **–ness** *n.* mystère *m.*

mystery *n.* mystère *m.*

mystic *a.* mystique; occulte; — *n.* mystique *m.* & *f.*; **–al** *a.* mystique; **–ism** *n.* mysticisme *m.*

mystify *vt.* mystifier

myth *n.* mythe *m.*; **–ical** *a.* mythique; **–ological** *a.* mythologique; **–ology** *n.* mythologie *f.*

N

nab *vt.* arrêter, saisir, pincer

nacelle *n.* (avi.) nacelle *f.*

nag *n.* bidet *m.*; — *vt.* & *vi.* gronder, quereller; **–ging** *a.* grondeur, querelleur; agaçant

nail *n.* clou *m.*; (finger) ongle *m.*; — **file** lime à ongles *f.*; — *vt.* clouer; clouter

naive *a.* naïf

naked *a.* nu; découvert; **–ness** *n.* nudité *f.*

name *n.* nom *m.*; réputation *f.*, renom *m.*; **by** — de nom; **Christian** —, **first** — prénom, nom de baptême *m.*; **family** — nom, nom de famille *m.*; **maiden** — nom de demoiselle *m.*; **nick** — sobriquet *n.*; **my** — **is** je m'appelle; — *vt.* nommer; citer; **be –d** s'appeler, se nommer; **–less** *a.* sans nom; anonyme; **–ly** *adv.* c'est-à-dire; à savoir

name plate *n.* plaque; étiquette, marque *f.*

namesake *n.* homonyme *m.*

nap *n.* somme *m.*; (cloth) poil, duvet *m.*; — *vi.* sommeiller

nape *n.* nuque *f.*

naphtha *n.* naphte *m.*

napkin *n.* serviette *f.*; — **ring** *n.* rond de serviette *m.*

narcotic *a.* & *n.* narcotique, stupéfiant *m.*

narrate *vt.* raconter, narrer

narration *n.* narration *f.*

narrator *n.* narrateur *m.*

narrow *a.* étroit; borné; faible; **have a —** **escape** l'échapper belle; — *vt.* borner, rétrécir; — *vi.* devenir plus étroit; se rétrécir; **–ness** *n.* étroitesse *f.*

narrow-minded *a.* borné, à l'esprit étroit; **–ness** *n.* étroitesse d'esprit *f.*

narrows *n.* détroit *m.*

nasal *a.* nasal; nasillard; **–ize** *vt.* nasaliser

nasty *a.* désagréable; vilain, sale; mauvais; méchant

natal *a.* natal, de naissance

nation *n.* nation *f.*; pays *m.*; **–al** *a.* national; de la nation; **–alism** *n.* nationalisme *m.*; **–alist** *n.* nationaliste *m.* & *f.*; **–ality** *n.* nationalité *f.*; **–alization** *n.* nationalisation *f.*; **–alize** *vt.* nationaliser

nationwide *a.* national, de toute la nation, à travers toute la nation, à travers le pays

native *n.* natif *m.*, native *f.*; indigène *m.* & *f.*; originaire *m.* & *f.*; — *a.* natal; de naissance; indigène, originaire; inné, naturel; — **land** patrie *f.*; pays natal *m.*; — **language** langue maternelle *f.*

nativity *n.* nativité *f.*

natural *a.* naturel; inné; de la nature; — *n.* (mus.) bécarre *m.*; **–ism** *n.* naturalisme *m.*; **–ist** *n.* naturaliste *m.* & *f.*; **–ization** *n.* naturalisation *f.*; **–ize** *vt.* naturaliser; **–ly** *adv.* naturellement; de nature; **–ness** *n.* naturel *m.*

nature *n.* nature *f.*; naturel *m.*; tempérament *m.*; genre *m.*, sorte, espèce *f.*; **by** — de nature; par tempérament; **from** — (art) d'après nature; — **study** *n.* histoire naturelle *f.*

naughty *a.* méchant, mauvais; espiègle

nausea *n.* nausée *f.*; mal au cœur *m.*; **–te** *vt.* écœurer; **–ting** *a.* écœurant, nauséabond

nauseous *a.* nauséabond

nautical *a.* nautique, marin

naval *a.* naval; de marine

nave *n.* nef *f.*

navel *n.* nombril *m.*

navigable *a.* navigable

navigate *vi.* naviguer; — *vt.* naviguer, gouverner

navigation *n.* navigation *f.*

navigator n. navigateur m.
navy n. marine f.; flotte f.; — bean n. haricot m.; — blue a. bleu foncé, bleu marine m.; — yard arsenal maritime m.
Nazi a. & n. nazi m.; -sm n. nazisme m.
near a. proche; — adv. près; proche; — prep. près de; auprès de; — vt. s'approcher de; -ly adv. à peu près; presque; près de; -ness n. proximité f.
nearby adv. tout près
nearsighted a. myope
neat a. soigné; rangé; net (nette); sec; -ness n. (bon) ordre m.; netteté f.
nebula n. nébuleuse f.
nebulous a. nébuleux
necessary a. nécessaire; indispensable; if — au besoin, s'il le faut; it is — il faut
necessitate vt. nécessiter
necessity n. nécessité f.; besoin m.
neck n. cou m.; (bottle) goulot m.; (dress) encolure f.; (land) langue f.
neckband n. collet de chemise m.
necklace n. collier m.; parure f.
necktie n. cravate f.
neckwear n. cravates f. pl.; foulards m. pl.
necromancy n. nécromancie f.
nectar n. nectar m.; -ine n. brugnon m.
need n. besoin m.; nécessité f.; indigence f.; — vt. avoir besoin de; falloir, manquer; -less a. inutile; -iness n. indigence f.; -y a. nécessiteux; indigent
needle n. aiguille f.
needlework n. ouvrage à l'aiguille m.
nefarious a. infâme
negation n. négation f.
negative a. négatif; — n. négative f.; (phot.) négatif m.; (gram.) négation f.
neglect n. négligence f.; inattention f.; — vt. négliger; omettre; -ed a. négligé; à l'abandon; -ful a. négligent
negligee n. négligé m.
negligence n. négligence f.
negligent a. négligent
negligible a. négligeable
negotiable a. négociable
negotiate vt. négocier; conclure; surmonter
negotiation n. négociation f.; in — with en pourparlers avec
negotiator n. négociateur m.
Negress n. négresse f.
Negro a. & n. nègre m.
neigh n. hennissement m.; — vi. hennir
neighbor n. voisin m.; (fig.) autrui m.; prochain m.; -hood n. voisinage m.; quartier m.; environs, alentours m. pl.; -ing a. voisin, proche; -ly a. amical
neither conj. ni; — adv. ni; non plus; — pron. ni; — . . . . nor ni . . . . ni
neon n. néon m.; — a. au néon; — sign n.

enseigne au néon f.
neophyte n. néophyte m.
nephew n. neveu m.
nepotism n. népotisme m.
nerve n. nerf m.; sang-froid m.; (coll.) toupet m.; — cell n. cellule nerveuse f.; — center n. centre nerveux m.; — fibre n. fibre nerveuse f.
nerve-racking a. énervant
nervous a. nerveux; irrité; énervé; inquiet; -ness n. nervosité f.; inquiétude f.; — system n. système nerveux m.
nest n. nid m.; nichée f.; — egg nichet m.; bas de laine m.; — vi. (se) nicher; -le vi. se nicher; se serrer
net n. filet m.; réseau m., tulle m.; — vt. prendre au filet; (com.) rapporter net; — a. net
Netherlands n. pl. Hollande f.; Pays-Bas
nettle n. ortie f.; — vt. piquer, irriter
network n. réseau m.; système m.
neuralgia n. névralgie f.
neuritis n. névrite f.
neurologist n. nevrologue m.
neurology n. névrologie f.
neurosis n. névrose f.
neurotic a. & n. névrotique, névrosé m.
neuter a. neutre
neutral a. & n. neutre; — n. (auto.) point mort m.; -ity n. neutralité f.; -ize vt. neutraliser
neutron n. neutron m.
never adv. jamais, ne . . . jamais; — mind n'importe
never ending a. perpétuel, éternel, sans fin
nevertheless conj. néanmoins, cependant, pourtant, toutefois; quand même
new a. nouveau (nouvelle); neuf (neuve); -ly adv. récemment, fraîchement; -ness n. nouveauté f.; inexpérience f.; -s pl. nouvelles f. pl.; piece of -s nouvelle f.
newborn a. nouveau-né
New Caledonia n. Nouvelle Calédonie f.
newcomer n. nouveau venu m.
Newfoundland n. Terre-Neuve f.
New Hebrides n. Nouvelles Hébrides f. pl.
newlywed n. nouveau marié m., nouvelle mariée f. -s nouveaux mariés m. pl.
New Orleans n. La Nouvelle Orléans f.
newsboy n. crieur de journaux m.
newscast n. bulletin d'informations, journal parlé m.; -er n. rédacteur de journal parlé m.
newspaper n. journal m.
newsprint n. papier de journal m.
newsreel n. actualités f. pl.
newsstand n. kiosque m.
newsworthy a. d'actualité
New Year n. nouvel an m.; -'s Day jour de l'an m.

New Zealand *n.* Nouvelle Zélande *f.*; — *a.* néo-zélandais

New Zealander *n.* Néo-Zélandais *m.*

next *a.* prochain; voisin; d'à côté; suivant; — **day** lendemain *m.*; — **door** à côté; dans la maison voisine; — **morning** lendemain matin *m.*; — *adv.* après; ensuite, puis; — *n.* suivant *m.*; — *prep.* auprès de, à côté de

nibble *vt.* & *vi.* grignoter; mordre; — *n.* grignotement, petit morceau *m.*

Nicaragua *n.* Nicaragua *m.*

nice *a.* gentil (gentille); aimable; agréable; sympathique; bon; **–ly** *adv.* gentiment; agréablement; bien; **–ty** *n.* finesse *f.*; minutie *f.*

nick *n.* coche, encoche, entaille *f.*; **in the** — **of time** à pic; juste à point; — *vt.* encocher, entailler

nickel *n.* nickel *m.*; pièce de cinq cents *f.*

nickel-plated *a.* nickelé

nickname *n.* sobriquet *m.*

niece *n.* nièce *f.*

Nigeria *n.* Nigérie *f.*

niggardly *a.* mesquin, chiche

nigh *a.* proche, près; **well** — à peu près; — *adv.* presque; de près

night *n.* nuit *f.*; soir *m.*; **at** — la nuit *f.*; **by** — de nuit; **good** — bonsoir; (before retiring) bonne nuit; **last** — hier soir; cette nuit; **the** — **before** la veille au soir; — **club** *n.* boîte de nuit *f.*, cabaret *m.*; — **letter** télégramme de nuit (sans priorité) *m.*; — **light** veilleuse *f.*; — **watchman** veilleur de nuit *m.*; **–ly** *a.* & *adv.* tous les soirs

nightblindness *n.* nyctalopie *f.*

nightcap *n.* bonnet de nuit *m.*; (coll.) boisson alcoolique prise avant de se coucher *f.*

nightfall *n.* tombée de la nuit *f.*; **at** — à la nuit tombante

nightgown *n.* chemise de nuit *f.*

nightmare *n.* cauchemar *m.*

nightshirt *n.* chemise de nuit *f.*

nighttime *n.* nuit *f.*

nihilist *n.* nihiliste *m.*

nil *n.* nul, zéro *m.*

Nile *n.* Nil *m.*

nimble *a.* leste, agile

nimbus *n.* nimbe *m.*; (cloud) nimbus *m.*

nincompoop *n.* sot, niais *m.*

nine *a.* neuf; **–teen** *a.* dix-neuf; **–teenth** *a.* dix-neuvième; **–tieth** *a.* quatre-vingt-dixième; **–ty** *a.* quatre-vingt-dix

ninth *a.* neuvième

nip *n.* pincement *m.*; morsure *f.*; goutte *f.*; — *vt.* pincer; piquer; mordre; — **in the bud** étouffer dans le germe; **–per** *n.* pince *f.*

nipple *n.* mamelon *m.*; (bottle) tétine *f.*

niter, nitre *n.* nitre, salpêtre *m.*

nitrate *n.* nitrate, azotate *m.*

nitric *a.* nitrique, azotique

nitrocellulose *n.* nitrocellulose *f.*

nitrogen *n.* azote *m.*

nitroglycerin *n.* nitroglycérine *f.*

nitrous *a.* nitreux, azoteux

no *adv.* non; — *a.* pas de; aucun, nul; **ne** .... **pas**; peu; **by** — **means** pas du tout; en aucune façon; **in** — **way en aucune façon**; — **one** personne; — **smoking** défense de fumer; — *n.* non *m.*; voix contre *f.*

nobility *n.* noblesse *f.*

noble *a.* noble; grand; — *n.* noble *m.*; **–ness** *n.* noblesse *f.*; grandeur *f.*

nobleman *n.* noble *m.*

noblewoman *n.* femme noble *f.*

nobly *adv.* noblement; superbement

nobody *pron.* personne; — *n.* nullité *f.*

nocturnal *a.* nocturne

nod *n.* signe de tête *m.*; inclination de tête *f.*; — *vt.* faire un signe de tête; incliner la tête

node *n.* nœud *m.*

nodule *n.* nodule *m.*

noise *n.* bruit *m.*; fracas, vacarme *m.*; son *m.*; **make** — faire du bruit; **–less** *a.* sans bruit; **–lessly** *adv.* sans bruit; silencieusement

noisily *adv.* bruyamment

noisiness *n.* grand bruit, tumulte *m.*

noisome *n.* infect, dégoûtant

noisy *a.* bruyant

nomad *n.* nomade *m.* & *f.*; **–ic** *a.* nomade

nomenclature *n.* nomenclature *f.*

nominal *a.* nominal; de nom

nominate *vt.* nommer, désigner; proposer

nomination *n.* nomination *f.*

nominative *a.* & *n.* nominatif *m.*

nominee *n.* candidat *m.*

nonacceptance *n.* refus *m.*, non-acceptation *f.*

nonaggression *n.* non-agression *f.*

nonattendance *n.* absence *f.*

nonchalant *a.* nonchalant

noncompliance *n.* refus d'acquiescer *m.*

noncombatant *n.* non-combattant *m.*

noncommissioned *a.* sans brevet; — **officer** gradé, sous-officier *m.*

noncommittal *a.* qui n'engage à rien

nonconductor *n.* non-conducteur *m.*

nonconformist *a.* & *n.* dissident *m.*

nondescript *a.* hétéroclite; inclassable

none *pron.* aucun, nul; personne; rien; — **too soon** juste à temps, juste à point

nonentity *n.* nullité *f.*

nonessential *a.* non-essentiel, peu essentiel

nonexistent *a.* non-existent, fictif

nonintervention *n.* non-intervention *f.*

nonobservance *n.* inobservance *f.*

nonpareil *a.* sans pareil

nonpayment *n.* non-payement *m.*

nonplussed *a.* confus, étourdi

nonresistance *n.* obéissance passive *f.*

nonsectarian *a.* sans esprit sectaire; sans prévention religieuse

nonsense *n.* non-sens *m.*, absurdité *f.*

nonsensical *a.* absurde

nonstop *a. & adv.* sans arrêt; (avi.) sans escale

nonsupport *n.* non-support *m.*

nonunion *a.* non-syndiqué

noodle *n.* nouille *f.*

nook *n.* coin, recoin, enfoncement *m.*

noon *n.* midi *m.*; **-day** *a.* de midi

noose *n.* corde *f.*; (trap) lacs, nœud coulant *m.*

nor *conj.* ni; **neither** . . . . — ni . . . . ni

Nordic *a.* nordique

norm *n.* norme *f.*; **-al** *a.* normal; ordinaire; **-al school** *n.* école normale *f.*; **-alcy** *n.* normalité *f.*; **-ally** *adv.* normalement; d'ordinaire

Norman *a. & n.* normand *m.*; **-dy** *n.* Normandie *f.*

Norse *a.* norvégien *m.*; **-man** *n.* Norvégien *m.*

north *n.* nord *m.*; — *a.* nord, du nord; septentrional; — *adv.* au nord, vers le nord; **-erly** *a.* au nord, vers le nord; **-ern** *a.* du nord; septentrional

North America *n.* Amérique du Nord *f.*

northeast *a. & n.* nord-est *m.*; — *adv.* vers le nord-est

North Pole *n.* pôle du nord *m.*

northward *a.* au nord, du nord; **-s** *adv.* vers le nord

northwest *a. & n.* nord-ouest *m.*; — *adv.* vers le nord-ouest

Norway *n.* Norvège *f.*

Norwegian *a. & n.* norvégien *m.*

nose *n.* nez *m.*; (animals) museau *m.*; (ballistics) cône *m.*; **blow one's** — se moucher; **hold one's** — se boucher le nez; **lead by the** — mener par le bout du nez

nosebleed *n.* saignement du nez *m.*

nose dive *vi.* piquer du nez; — *n.* piquage du nez *m.*; piqué *m.*

nostalgia *n.* nostalgie *f.*

nostril *n.* narine *f.*; (horse) naseau *m.*

nostrum *n.* panacée *f.*

not *adv.* pas; point; ne . . . . pas; — **at all** pas du tout; — **including** sans compter; — **that** ce n'est pas que

notability *n.* notabilité *f.*

notable *a.* notable; remarquable; considérable; éminent; — *n.* notable *m.*

notably *adv.* notamment

notary *n.* notaire *m.*

notation *n.* notation *f.*

notch *n.* encoche, entaille *f.*; — *vt.* encocher, entailler

note *n.* note *f.*; annotation *f.*; remarque *m.*; billet, mot *m.*, lettre *f.*; renom *m.*; son *m.*; (mus.) caractère *m.*; (piano) touche *f.*; **make a** — of prendre note de; **take —s** prendre des notes; — *vt.* noter, constater, remarquer; **-d** *a.* éminent, distingué; remarquable;

notebook *n.* cahier, carnet *m.*; **loose-leaf** — *n.* cahier à feuilles mobiles *m.*; — **filler** *n.* feuilles mobiles *f. pl.*

noteworthy *a.* digne d'attention

nothing *n.* rien *m.*; ne . . . . rien; rien de; zéro *m.*; — **but** rien que; — **else** rien d'autre; **-ness** *n.* néant *m.*

notice *n.* avis, avertissement *m.*; délai *m.*; affiche *f.*; annonce *f.*; attention *f.*; revue *f.*; **at short** — du jour au lendemain; **à court délai**; à l'instant; **give** — (to employee) donner son congé à; (to employer) donner sa démission; **take** — of faire attention à; tenir compte de; **until further** — jusqu'à nouvel avis; — *vt.* observer, remarquer, tenir compte de; **-able** *a.* qui se voit; perceptible, sensible

notification *n.* notification, faire-part *m.*

notify *vt.* notifier, faire savoir

notion *n.* notion, pensée, opinion *f.*; **-s** *pl.* mercerie *f.*

notoriety *n.* notoriété, évidence *f.*

notorious *a.* notoire; fameux; **-ness** *n.* notoriété *f.*

notwithstanding *prep. & adv.* nonobstant; — *conj.* bien que

nougat *n.* nougat *m.*

nought *n.* rien, néant *m.*; zéro *m.*

noun *n.* nom, substantif *m.*

nourish *vt.* nourrir; **-ment** *n.* nourriture *f.*; **-ing** *a.* nutritif

novel *n.* roman *m.*; — *a.* nouveau, neuf; **-ist** *n.* romancier *m.*; **-ty** *n.* nouveauté *f.*

November *n.* novembre *m.*

novena *n.* neuvaine *f.*

novice *n.* novice *m.*

novitiate *n.* noviciat *m.*

novocaine *n.* novocaïne *f.*

now *adv.* à présent, maintenant; **by —** à l'heure qu'il est; **just —** pour le moment; — **and then,** — **and again** de temps; **until —** jusqu'ici; — *interj.* or; eh bien; tiens

nowadays *adv.* de nos jours

nowhere *adv.* nulle part

noxious *a.* nuisible; pernicieux

nozzle *n.* lance *f.*, bec *m.*
nuance *n.* nuance *f.*
nuclear *a.* nucléaire
nucleic *a.* nucléique
nucleus *n.* noyau *m.*
nude *a.* nu
nudge *n.* coup de coude *m.*; — *vt.* pousser légèrement (du coude)
nudism *n.* nudisme *m.*
nudist *n.* nudiste *m. & f.*
nudity *n.* nudité *f.*
nugget *n.* pépite *f.*
nuisance *n.* incommodité *f.*; ennui *m.*
null *a.* nul, non valide; **–ification** *n.* annulation *f.*; **–ify** *vt.* annuler
numb *vt.* engourdir; — *a.* engourdi; **–ness** *n.* engourdissement *m.*
number *n.* nombre *m.*, quantité *f.*; numéro *m.*; chiffre *m.*; — *vt.* numéroter; **–ing** *n.* numérotage, calcul *m.*; **–ing** *a.* au nombre de; **–ing machine** *n.* numéroteur *m.*; **–less** *a.* innombrable
numeral *n.* chiffre *m.*; — *a.* numéral
numerator *n.* numérateur *m.*
numerical *a.* numérique
numerous *a.* nombreux
numskull, numbskull *n.* sot, lourdaud *m.*
nun *n.* nonne, religieuse *f.*; **–nery** *n.* couvent (de femmes) *m.*
nuncio *n.* (eccl.) nonce *m.*
nuptial *a.* nuptial; **–s** *n. pl.* noces *f. pl.*
nurse *n.* infirmière *f.*; garde-malade *f.*; **male —** infirmier *m.*; **wet —** nourrice *f.*; — *vt.* nourrir (au sein); soigner; — *vi.* téter; **–ry** *n.* chambre d'enfants *f.*; (bot.) pépinière *f.*; **–ry school** jardin d'enfants *m.*, école maternelle *f.*
nursemaid *n.* nourrice *f.*
nursing *n.* profession d'infirmière *f.*; tétée *f.*; **— bottle** biberon *m.*
nursling *n.* nourrisson *m.*
nurture *vt.* nourrir, élever
nut *n.* noix *f.*; (mech.) écrou *m.*; **a hard — to crack** un problème épineux; **–s, –ty** *a.* (coll.) fou
nutcracker *n.* casse-noisettes *m.*
nutmeg *n.* muscade *f.*
nutrient *n.* aliment *m.*; **–a** nutritif
nutriment *n.* nourriture *f.*, aliment *m.*
nutrition *f.* nutrition *f.*; nourriture *f.*, aliment *m.*
nutritious *a.* nourrissant
nutshell *n.* coquille de noix *f.*; **in a —** en un mot
nymph *n.* nymphe *f.*

O

oaf *n.* sot, benêt *m.*
oar *n.* rame *f.*, aviron *m.*; **–sman** *n.* rameur *m.*

oasis *n.* oasis *f.*
oat(s) *n.* avoine *f.*; **sow one's wild —** jeter sa gourme
oath *n.* serment, jurement *m.*
oatmeal *n.* bouillie d'avoine *f.*
obdurate *a.* endurci; obstiné
obedience *n.* obéissance *f.*
obedient *a.* obéissant
obeisance *n.* salut *m.*, révérence *f.*
obelisk *n.* obélisque *m.*
obese *a.* obèse
obesity *n.* obésité *f.*
obey *vt.* obéir à; — *vi.* obéir
obituary *n.* notice nécrologique *f.*
object *n.* objet *m.*, matière *f.*, sujet *m.*; (gram.) complément d'objet *m.*
object *vt.* objecter; **–ion** *n.* objection *f.*; **–ionable** *a.* désagréable; **–ive** *n.* objectif *m.*; — *a.* objectif; **–ivity** *n.* objectivité *f.*; **–or** *n.* objecteur *m.*; **conscientious –or** objecteur de conscience *m.*
obligation *n.* obligation *f.*
obligatory *a.* obligatoire
oblige *vt.* obliger; contraindre; **— someone to do something** obliger quelqu'un à faire quelque chose; **be –d to do something** être obligé de faire quelque chose
obliging *a.* obligeant
oblique *a.* oblique
obliterate *vt.* oblitérer, effacer
obliteration *n.* rature *f.*; oblitération *f.*
oblivion *n.* oubli *m.*
oblivious *a.* oublieux
oblong *a.* oblong
obnoxious *a.* nuisible, coupable, désagréable, dégoûtant
obscene *a.* obscène
obscenity *n.* obscénité *f.*
obscure *vt.* obscurcir; — *a.* obscur
obscurity *n.* obscurité *f.*
obsequious *a.* obséquieux
observable *a.* remarquable, appréciable
observance *n.* observation *f.*; observance *f.*; pratique *f.*
observant *a.* observateur, attentif; respectueux
observation *n.* observation *f.*
observatory *n.* observatoire *m.*
observe *vt.* observer; remarquer; fêter; **–r** *n.* observateur *m.*
observing *a.* observateur
obsess *vt.* obséder; **–ion** *n.* obsession *f.*
obsolescence *n.* désuétude *f.*
obsolescent *a.* qui tombe en désuétude
obsolete *a.* désuet, inusité, vieilli; **become —** tomber en désuétude
obstacle *n.* obstacle *m.*
obstetrician *n.* accoucheur *m.*
obstetrics *n. pl.* obstétrique *f.*
obstinacy *n.* opiniâtreté *f.*

obstinate *a.* obstiné
obstreperous *a.* déréglé, insoumis, bruyant, turbulent
obstruct *vt.* encombrer, obstruer; mettre obstacle à; **–ion** *n.* obstacle, empêchement *m.*, opposition *f.*; **–ive** *a.* embarrassant, obstructif
obtain *vt.* obtenir; **–able** *a.* trouvable, disponible
obtrusive *a.* importun
obtuse *a.* obtus
obviate *vt.* obvier à
obvious *a.* clair, évident; **–ly** *adv.* évidemment; **–ness** *n.* évidence *f.*
occasion *n.* occasion *f.*, incident *m.*; besoin *m.*; motif *m.*, cause *f.*; — *vt.* occasionner, causer; **–al** *a.* occasionnel, casuel; intermittent; **–ally** *adv.* de temps en temps
occident *n.* occident *m.*; **–al** *a.* occidental
occult *a.* occulte; **–ism** *n.* occultisme *m.*
occupancy *n.* prise de possession *f.*; habitation *f.*
occupant *n.* occupant, possesseur, habitant *m.*
occupation *n.* occupation *f.*, emploi *m.*; possession *f.*; **–al** *a.* du métier; **–al therapy** *n.* thérapie rééducative *f.*
occupier *n.* occupant *m.*
occupy *vt.* occuper, employer; habiter; prendre possession de; **be occupied with** s'occuper de
occur *vi.* arriver; avoir lieu; venir (à l'esprit); **–ence** *n.* événement *m.*
ocean *n.* océan *m.*; **–ic** *a.* océanique
Oceania *n.* Océanie *f.*
o'clock *adv.* **it is one** — il est une heure; **it is two** — il est deux heures
octagon *n.* octogone *m.*; **–al** *a.* octogonal
octane *a. & n.* (gasoline) octane *m.*
octet *n.* octuor *m.*
October *n.* octobre *m.*
ocular *a.* oculaire
oculist *n.* oculiste *m.*
odd *a.* singulier, étrange; (numbers) impair; **–ity** *n.* singularité, bizarrerie *f.*; **–s** *n. pl.* inégalité *f.*; avantage *m.*; chances *f. pl.*; **–s and ends** restes *m. pl.*, pièces diverses *f. pl.*; **be at –s** être brouillé
ode *n.* ode *f.*
odious *a.* odieux
odium *n.* haine *f.*
odor *n.* odeur *f.*; bouquet *m.*
odorous *a.* parfumé
of *prep.* de
off *a.* éloigné; loin, loin de; distant; — *adv.* au loin; à distance; **— and on** de temps en temps; **be —** partir, démarrer; **come —** tomber, se détacher; réussir; **go —** s'en aller; réussir, se passer; **put —** re-

mettre; **right —**, **straight —** (coll.) tout de suite; **set —** mettre en valeur; **take — enlever**; (avi.) décoller; **take — on** satiriser; **turn —** (lights) éteindre; (road) bifurquer **— prep.** de, de dessus, éloigné de; à une petite distance de; (naut.) au large; **— limits** défendu; défense d'entrer; **— the record** non-officiel
offal *n.* rebuts *m. pl.*; ordures *f. pl.*
off-color *a.* salé, risqué
offend *vt. & vi.* offenser, irriter; **–er** *n.* offenseur *m.*; **–ing** *a.* offensant, fautif
offense *n.* offense *f.*; faute *f.*; crime *m.*
offensive *a.* offensant, injurieux; — *n.* offensive *f.*
offer *vt. & vi.* offrir, présenter; — *n.* offre *f.*; **–ing** *n.* offrande *f.*; **–tory** *n.* offertoire *m.*; quête *f.*
offhand *a.* cavalier, improvisé; — *adv.* cavalièrement, sans préparation
office *n.* bureau *m.*; office *m.*; fonction, charge *f.*; **–r** *n.* officier *m.*; (police) agent *m.*; **— seeker** *n.* candidat à un poste, intrigant *m.*
official *n.* employé *m.*; fonctionnaire *m.*; officier *m.*; **–ese** *n.* jargon officiel *m.*
officiate *vi.* administrer; officier
officious *a.* officieux
offing *n.* large *m.*; **in the —** en vue
offset *n.* compensation *f.*; (print.) offset *m.*; — *vt.* contrebalancer
offshoot *n.* rejeton *m.*
offshore *adv.* vers la haute mer, en s'éloignant de la côte; — *adj.* éloigné de la côte
off side *adv.* hors des limites; de l'autre côté; hors jeu
offspring *n.* descendants *m. pl.*; lignée *f.*; rejeton *m.*
off stage *adv.* dans les coulisses
often *adv.* souvent; **how —** combien de fois
ogle *vt.* lorgner, regarder fixement
ogre *n.* ogre *m.*; **–ss** *n.* ogresse *f.*
oh! *interj.* oh!; ah!; hélas!; ouf!; aïe!
ohm *n.* ohm *m.*
oil *n.* huile *f.*; pétrole *m.*; **crude —** pétrole brut *m.*; **mineral —** huile minérale *f.*; **— paint, — painting** *n.* peinture à l'huile *f.*; **— well** *n.* puits à pétrole *m.*; **— slick** *n.* couche d'huile *f.*; — *vt.* huiler; **–y** *a.* huileux; **— can** *n.* broc à huile *m.*
oilcloth *n.* toile cirée *f.*
ointment *n.* onguent, baume *m.*
okra *n.* quingombo *m.*
old *a.* vieux, ancien; **become —**, **grow —** vieillir; **how — are you?** quel âge avez-vous?; **I am ten years —** j'ai dix ans; **— hand** vétéran *m.*; **— maid** vieille fille *f.*;

—ish *a.* plutôt vieux; —ness *n.* âge *m.*; vieillesse *f.*; ancienneté *f.*

old-fashioned *a.* démodé

old-line *a.* de vieille famille; qui remonte très loin

old-time *a.* du bon vieux temps

oleomargarine *n.* margarine *f.*

olfactory *a.* olfactif

oligarchy *n.* oligarchie *f.*

olive *n.* olive *f.*; (tree) olivier *m.*; — oil huile d'olive *f.*; — *a.* de couleur olive

Olympiad *n.* olympiade *f.*

Olympian *a.* olympien

Olympic *a.* olympique; —s *n. pl.* jeux olympiques *m. pl.*

omelet *n.* omelette *f.*

omen *n.* présage, augure *m.*

ominous *a.* de mauvais augure

omission *n.* omission *f.*

omit *vt.* omettre; négliger; oublier

omnibus *n.* omnibus *m.*; anthologie *f.*

omnipotence *n.* toute-puissance *f.*

omnipotent *a.* tout-puissant

omnipresence *n.* ubiquité *f.*; présence universelle *f.*

omnipresent *a.* présent en tous lieux

omniscient *a.* omniscient

omnivorous *a.* omnivore

on *prep.* sur; à; dans; — *adv.* en avant; and so — et ainsi de suite

once *adv.* une fois; autrefois; at — tout de suite; — and for all une fois pour toutes; — upon a time (il était) une fois

oncoming *a.* à venir, qui vient; approchant; hardi

one *a.* un, une; — *pron.* on; — another l'un l'autre, les uns les autres; — by — un à un; —'s son, sa, ses

one-eyed *a.* borgne

one-horse *a.* à un cheval; (fig.) provincial, insignifiant

onerous *a.* onéreux

oneself *pron.* soi, soi-même; se

one-sided *a.* à un seul côté; partial; —ness *n.* partialité *f.*

onetime *a.* ancien, d'autrefois

one-track *a.* à une voie; (fig.) borné

one-way *a.* à sens unique; — ticket billet simple, aller *m.*

onion *n.* oignon *m.*

onionskin (paper) *n.* papier pelure *m.*

onlooker *n.* spectateur *m.*

only *a.* seul; unique; — *adv.* ne . . . que; seulement

onomatopoeia *n.* onomatopée *f.*

onrush *n.* ruée *f.*; attaque *f.*

onset *n.* assaut, *m.*, attaque *f.*; début, commencement *m.*

onslaught *n.* attaque *f.*, assaut *m.*

on-the-job *a.* (coll.) *à* sur place

onto *prep.* sur; à; dans

onus *n.* fardeau, poids *m.*, charge *f.*

onward *adv.* en avant

ooze *n.* vase, bourbe *f.*; — *vi.* filtrer; suinter; s'écouler

opalescent *a.* opalescent

opaque *a.* opaque; —ness *n.* opacité *f.*

open *vt.* ouvrir; commencer; découvrir; — *vi.* s'ouvrir; — *a.* ouvert; franc, sincère; — house réception *f.*; — shop entreprise qui emploie des ouvriers syndiqués et non syndiqués; —er *n.*, can —er ouvre-boîtes *m.*; —ing *n.* ouverture *f.*; (theat.) première *f.*; débouché *m.*; —ness *n.* franchise *f.*

open-air *n.* en plein air; à la belle étoile

open-eyed *a.* les yeux écarquillés

openhanded *a.* généreux

openhearted *a.* franc

open-minded *a.* large d'esprit

openmouthed *a.* étourdi, abasourdi; bouche bée

openwork *n.* ouvrage à jour

opera *n.* opéra *m.*; — glasses jumelles de théâtre *f. pl.*; — hat chapeau claque; — house *n.* opéra *m.*; —atic *a.* d'opéra

operate *vi.* opérer, agir; — *vt.* faire marcher

operating room *n.* amphithéâtre *m.*

operation *n.* opération *f.*; have an — être opéré; —al *a.* en état de marche

operator *n.* opérateur *m.*

opiate *n.* opiat *m.*

opine *vt.* opiner

opinion *n.* opinion *f.*, sentiment *m.*; avis *m.*; in my — à mon avis; —ated *a.* opiniâtre

opium *n.* opium *m.*

opossum *n.* opossum *m.*

opponent *n.* antagoniste, adversaire *m.*

opportune *a.* opportun; à propos; —ness *n.* opportunité *f.*

opportunism *n.* opportunisme *m.*

opportunist *n.* opportuniste *m.*

opportunity *n.* occasion *f.*

oppose *vt.* & (*vi.*) s'opposer

opposite *a.* & *n.* opposé *m.*

opposition *n.* opposition, résistance *f.*

oppress *vt.* opprimer; —ion *n.* oppression *f.*; —ive *a.* oppressif; —or *n.* oppresseur *m.*

opprobrium *n.* opprobre *m.*

optic *a.* optique, visuel; —al *a.* optique; —ian *n.* opticien *m.*; —s *n.* optique *f.*

optimism *n.* optimisme *m.*

optimist *n.* optimiste *m.* & *f.*; —ic *a.* optimiste

optimum *a.* le meilleur

option *n.* option *f.*, choix *m.*; —al *a.* facultatif

optometry *n.* optométrie *f.*

opulence *n.* opulence *f.*
opulent *a.* opulent
opus *n.* composition musicale *f.*
or *conj.* ou, **either** . . . — ou . . . ou;
 — **else** ou bien
oral *a.* oral; par la bouche; **–ly** *adv.* oralement, par la bouche; — **contraceptive** *n.*
 préservatif oral *m.*
orange *n.* orange *f.*; (tree) oranger *m.*; —
 a. orangé, couleur orange
orangutan *m.* orang-outan *m.*
orate *vi.* pérorer
oration *n.* discours *m.*; harangue *f.*; (funeral) oraison *f.*
orator *n.* orateur *m.*; **–ical** *a.* oratoire
orb *n.* orbe *m.*, sphère *f.*; globe *m.*
orbit *n.* orbite *f.*; — *vi.* décrire une courbe
 orbitale, décrire une orbite
orchard *n.* verger *m.*
orchestra *n.* orchestre *m.*; — **seat** fauteuil
 d'orchestre *m.*; **–l** *a.* orchestral; **–te** *vt.*
 orchestrer; **–tion** *n.* orchestration *f.*
orchid *n.* orchidée *f.*
ordain *vt.* ordonner; établir; sacrer
ordeal *n.* épreuve *f.*
order *n.* ordre, rang *m.*; commande *f.*; précepte, commandement *m.*; billet *m.*;
 mandat *m.*; décoration *f.*; (com.) demande *f.*; **money** — mandat-poste *m.*;
 call to — rappeler à l'ordre; **in** — **to**
 pour; **in** — en règle; par rang; **in** — **that**
 pour que, afin que; **in alphabetical** —
 par ordre alphabétique; **in chronological**
 — par ordre de date; **make to** — faire
 sur commande; **on** — commandé; **out**
 of — détraqué, déréglé; déplacé; — *vt.*
 ordonner; commander; régler, disposer;
 –liness *n.* bon ordre *m.*; **–ly** *n.* ordonnance *f.*; **–ly** *a.* bien réglé, régulier; ordonné; rangé
ordinal *a.* ordinal
ordinance *n.* ordonnance *f.*; règlement
 municipal *m.*
ordinarily *adv.* d'ordinaire, d'habitude
ordinary *a.* ordinaire; — *n.* ordinaire *m.*;
 out of the — peu ordinaire; extraordinaire
ordnance *n.* service des munitions *m.*
ore *n.* minerai *m.*
organ *n.* organe *m.*; (mus.) orgue *m.*; —
 loft *n.* tribune d'orgue *f.*; — **pipe** *n.* tuyau d'orgue *m.*; — **stop** *n.* jeu d'orgue
 m.; **–ic** *a* organique; **–ism** *n.* organisme
 m.; **–ist** *n.* organiste *m.*
organdy *n.* organdi *m.*
organ-grinder *n.* joueur d'orgue de barbarie *m.*
organization *n.* organisation *f.*
organize *vt.* organiser; — *vi.* s'organiser;
 –r *n.* organisateur *m.*

orgy *n.* orgie *f.*
orient *n.* orient *m.*; — *vt.* orienter; **–al** *a.*
 oriental; **–ate** *vt.* orienter; **–ation** *n.*
 orientation *f.*
orifice *n.* orifice *m.*, ouverture *f.*
origin *n.* origine, source *f.*; commencement
 m.; **–al** *a.* original; originaire; (eccl.)
 originel **–al** *n.*; original *m.*; **–ality** *n.* originalité *f.*; **–ally** *adv.* originalement;
 –ate *vt.* produire, faire naître; **–ate** *vi.*
 provenir, naître; **–ator** *n.* initiateur,
 auteur *m.*
ornament *n.* ornement *m.*; décoration *f.*;
 — *vt.* orner, parer; ornementer; **–al** *a.*
 ornemental; **–ation** *n.* ornementation *f.*
ornate *a.* orné; fleuri
ornithology *n.* ornithologie *f.*
orphan *n.* orphelin *m.*, orpheline *f.*; — *a.*
 orphelin; **–age** *n.* orphelinat *m.*
orthodontist *n.* orthodentiste *m.*
orthodox *a.* orthodoxe; **–y** *n.* orthodoxie *f.*
orthography *n.* orthographe *f.*
orthopedic *a.* orthopédique
orthopedist *n.* orthopédiste *m.*
oscillate *vi.* osciller
oscillation *n.* oscillation *f.*
osmosis *n.* osmose *f.*
ossification *n.* ossification *f.*
ossify *vt.* ossifier; — *vi.* s'ossifier
ostensible *a.* ostensible, visible; soi-disant,
 prétendu
ostentation *n.* ostentation *f.*; parade *f.*
ostentatious *a.* fastueux
osteopathy *n.* malaxion médicale, osteo-
 pathie *f.*
ostracism *n.* ostracisme *m.*
ostracize *vt.* ostraciser
other *pron.* autre; **each** — l'un l'autre; —
 a. autre; **every** — **day** tous les deux
 jours; — *adv.* autrement; **–s** *pron.* d'autres; autrui
otherwise *adv.* autrement
ottoman *n.* pouf *m.*
ought *vt.* devoir; — *vi.* falloir; — *n.* zéro
 m.; — *pron.* rien, quoi que ce soit
ounce *n.* once *f.* (30 grammes)
our *a.* notre, (*pl.* nos); **–s** *pron.* le nôtre,
 la nôtre, les nôtres
ourselves *pron.* nous-mêmes, nous
oust *vt.* déloger; évincer
out *adv.* dehors, au dehors; sorti; (book)
 paru; (flower) épanoui, en fleur; (tide)
 bas; (sports) hors jeu; — *a.* de dehors,
 extérieur; détaché; — **of** *prep.* hors de;
 en dehors de; dans; de; sur; **–er** *a.* extérieur; **–s** *n. pl.*, **ins and –s** coins et re-
 coins *m. pl.*; **at –s, on the –s** brouillé(s)
out-and-out *a.* entier, complet; achevé
outbid *vt.* enchérir sur
outboard *n.* hors-bord *m.*

outbreak *n.* éruption *f.*
outbuilding *n.* annexe, dépendance *f.*
outburst *n.* explosion *f.*; accès *m.*
outcast *a.* exilé *m.*; rebut *m.*
outclass *vt.* surpasser; surclasser
outcome *n.* résultat *m.*; issue *f.*
outcry *n.* cri *m.*, clameur *f.*
outdated *a.* périmé; suranné
outdistance *vt.* dépasser, surpasser
outdo *vt.* l'emporter sur
outdoor *a.* du dehors; **–s** *adv.* au dehors, en plein air
outfit *n.* équipement *m.*; nécessaire *m.*; garde-robe *m.*; costume et accessoires *m. pl.*; — *vt.* équiper
outflank *vt.* déborder
outflow *n.* écoulement *m.*
outgoing *a.* sortant, partant; sociable, cordial, communicatif; sympathique
outgrow *vt.* surpasser en croissance; devenir trop grand pour; **–th** *n.* excroissance *f.*; résultat *m.*
outguess *vt.* deviner mieux que; l'emporter sur
outhouse *n.* dépendance *f.*
outing *n.* excursion *f.*; piquenique *m.*
outlandish *a.* bizarre
outlast *vt.* surpasser en durée; survivre à
outlaw *n.* proscrit *m.*; hors-la-loi *m.*; — *vt.* proscrire
outlay *n.* dépense *f.*; déboursés *m. pl.*
outlet *n.* sortie *f.*; issue *f.*; (com.) débouché *m.*
outline *n.* contour *m.*; silhouette *f.*; esquisse *f.*; plan *m.*; — *vt.* dessiner les contours de; silhouetter; esquisser; dresser un plan de
outlive *vt.* survivre à
outlook *n.* perspective *f.*, point de vue *m.*
outlying *a.* éloigné, extérieur
outmaneuver *vt.* tourner (l'ennemi); manœuvrer plus habilement que
outmoded *a.* démodé
outnumber *vt.* surpasser en nombre
out-of-date *a.* périmé, démodé
out-of-doors *adv.* au dehors
out-of-print *a.* épuisé
out-of-the-way *a.* caché, obscur
outpatient *n.* malade ambulant *m.* (traité à l'hôpital sans être hospitalisé)
outpoint *vt.* battre aux points
outpost *n.* avant-poste *m.*
outpouring *n.* effusion *f.*, épanchement *m.*
output *n.* production, chiffre de production *f.*; puissance *f.*
outrage *n.* outrage *m.*; — *vt.* outrager; **–ous** *a.* scandaleux; outrageux
outrank *vt.* surpasser de rang
outrider *n.* piqueur *m.*
outright *adv.* sur-le-champ, tout de suite;

(com.) à forfait; parfaitement; franchement; — *a.* parfait, complet
outrun *vt.* dépasser à la course, distancer
outset *n.* commencement, début *m.*
outshine *vt.* surpasser en éclat; dépasser
outside *n.* dehors *m.*, surface *f.*, extérieur *m.*; — *adv.* au dehors; dehors; en dehors, à l'extérieur; — *a.* du dehors, extérieur; — *of prep.* sauf; en dehors de; hors de; **–r** *n.* étranger *m.*
outskirts *n.* banlieue *f.*; environs *m. pl.*
outspoken *a.* franc
outspread *a.* étendu
outstanding *a.* éminent, remarquable; (com.) non-payé
outstare *vt.* décontenancer
outstay *vt.* rester plus longtemps que; — one's welcome rester plus longtemps qu'on ne le veut
outstretch *vt.* étendre
outstrip *vt.* dépasser, surpasser
outward *a.* extérieur; — *adv.* au dehors; — **bound** en destination pour l'étranger; **–ly** *adv.* à l'extérieur; **–s** *adv.* en dehors; vers l'extérieur
outwear *vt.* user; ne plus avoir besoin (d'un vêtement)
outweigh *vt.* peser plus que; l'emporter sur
outwit *vt.* surpasser en finesse; tromper, duper
oval *a. & n.* ovale *m.*
ovary *n.* ovaire *m.*
ovate *a.* ové
oven *n.* four *m.*; (fig.) fournaise *f.*; **Dutch** — cuisinière *f.*
over *prep.* sur, au-dessus de; par-dessus; plus de; pendant; — *adv.* au-delà; de l'autre côté; fini, passé; de nouveau; — **again** une fois de plus; **all** — partout; — **and above** par dessus; — **and** — (again) sans s'arrêter; — **there** là-bas; **–ly** *adv.* trop, à l'exces
overabundant *a.* surabondant
overage *a.* trop vieux
over-all *a.* complet
overalls *n.* cotte à bretelles *f.*; bleus *m. pl.*
overawe *vt.* impressionner, épouvanter
overbalance *vt.* l'emporter sur; renverser; peser plus que
overbearing *a.* arrogant, impérieux
overboard *adv.* à la mer
overburden *vt.* surcharger
overcast *vt.* obscurcir; surjeter; couvrir; — *a.* couvert (de nuages), sombre
overcharge *n.* prix exorbitant *m.*; surtaxe *f.*; — *vt.* surcharger, accabler; faire payer trop cher
overcoat *n.* pardessus *m.*
overcome *vt.* dompter, vaincre, maîtriser; — *a.* accablé

overconfidence *n.* suffisance *f.*

overconfident *a.* confiant à l'excès

overcooked *a.* trop cuit

overcrowd *vt.* encombrer, bonder

overdeveloped *a.* trop développé; (phot.) trop poussé

overdo *vt.* trop faire, outrer; — *vi.* se surmener; **–ne** *a.* trop cuit

overdose *n.* dose trop forte *f.*

overdraw *vt.* excéder son crédit, tirer à découvert

overdrive *vt.* surmener; — *n.* (auto) quatrième vitesse qui économise l'essence *f.*

overdue *a.* en retard; échu

overeat *vi.* trop manger

overestimate *vt.* surestimer

overexcite *vt.* surexciter

overexertion *n.* surmenage *m.*

overexposure *n.* excès d'exposition *m.*; (photo.) excès de pose *m.*

overfeed *vt.* surnourrir, suralimenter

overflow *n.* inondation *f.*; trop-plein *m.*; débordement ; — *vi.* déborder; surabonder; **–ing** *a.* débordant

overgrown *a.* excessivement accru, énorme; (with weeds) couvert

overgrowth *n.* couverture *f.*

overhang *vt.* surplomber; menacer

overhaul *vt.* réparer; réfectionner; — *n.* réparation *f.*; revision *f.*

overhead *adv.* au-dessus de la tête, en haut; — *n.* frais généraux *m. pl.*

overhear *vt.* entendre; surprendre

overheat *vt.* surchauffer

overindulge *vt.* gâter; **–nce** *n.* excès d'indulgence *m.*; abus *m.*

overjoyed *a.* ravi; transporté de joie, au comble de la joie

overland *a. & adv.* par voie de terre

overlap *vt. & vi.* recouvrir, chevaucher; — *n.* recouvrement, chevauchement

overload *vt.* surcharger; surmener; — *n.* surcharge *f.*

overlook *vt.* passer sous silence, négliger, mépriser; donner sur

overlord *n.* suzerain *m.*

overnight *adv.* toute la nuit; pour (toute) la nuit; jusqu'au lendemain; — *a.* de nuit

overpass *vt.* passer au-delà, franchir; — *n.* passage supérieur *m.*; pont-route *m.*

overpayment *n.* paiement en trop *m.*

overpopulate *vt.* surpeupler

overpower *vt.* dominer, opprimer, accabler; **–ing** *a.* accablant; irrésistible

overproduction *n.* surproduction *f.*

overrate *vt.* évaluer trop haut; surestimer

overreach *vt.* dépasser; — oneself aller trop loin, se duper

override *vt.* fouler; l'emporter sur

overripe *a.* trop mûr

overrule *vt.* casser, annuler

overrun *vt.* envahir, ravager

oversea *a.* d'outre-mer; **–s** *adv.* outre-mer

oversee *vt.* surveiller; **–r** *n.* inspecteur, surveillant, intendant *m.*

overshadow *vt.* ombrager; éclipser

overshoe *n.* galoche *f.*

overshoot *vt.* dépasser

oversight *n.* méprise, erreur, inadvertance *f.*

oversleep *vi.* dormir trop longtemps

overstate *vt.* exagérer; **–ment** *n.* exagération *f.*

overstep *vt.* dépasser

oversupply *n.* excédent *m.*, abondance *f.*

overt *a.* manifeste; ouvert

overtake *vt.* dépasser, surpasser; rattraper; arriver à

overtax *vt.* surtaxer; surmener

overthrow *n.* renversement *m.*; défaite *f.*; — *vt.* renverser; détruire, défaire

overtime *n.* heures de travail supplémentaires *f. pl.*

overtone *n.* note harmonique *f.*

overtrick *n.* (cards) levée en plus *f.*

overtrump *vt.* surcouper

overture *n.* ouverture *f.*

overturn *vt.* renverser; — *vi.* se renverser

overvalue *vt.* trop estimer, surestimer

overview *n.* vue, perspective *f.*

overweight *n.* excédant (de poids) *m.*; surpoids *m.*; — *a.* obèse; (baggage) en excédent; qui pèse trop

overwhelm *vt.* accabler, écraser; combler; **–ing** *a.* irrésistible; accablant

overwork *vi.* se surmener; — *vt.* surmener; trop employer; — *n.* excès de travail *m.*; surmènage *m.*

overwrought *a.* surmené; excédé

overzealous *a.* trop zélé

oviparous *a.* ovipare

ovum *n.* œuf *m.*

owe *vt.* devoir

owing *a.* dû; — to *prep.* à cause de, en raison de, par suite de

own *vt.* posséder; reconnaître, avouer; **–er** *n.* possesseur, propriétaire *m.*; **–ership** *n.* possession, propriété *f.*

own *a.* propre; my — à moi; le mien

ox *n.* bœuf *m.*

oxalic *a.* oxalique

oxide *n.* oxyde *m.*

oxidize *vt.* oxyder; — *vi.* s'oxyder

oxygen *n.* oxygène *m.*; — tent tente à oxygène *f.*

oyster *n.* huître *f.*; — bed banc d'huîtres *m.*; — plant salsifis *m.*

ozone *n.* ozone

P

pace *n.* pas *m.*; allure *f.*; (horse) amble *m.*;
keep — rester aux côtés (de quelqu'un);
rester à la page; — *vi.* aller au pas,
faire les cent pas; — **off** mesurer (au
pas); **-r** *n.* cheval qui va à l'amble *m.*
pacemaker *n.* entraîneur *m.*
pacific *a.* pacifique; **-ation** *n.* pacification *f.*, apaisement *m.*
Pacific Ocean *n.* Océan Pacifique *m.*
pacifist *n.* pacifiste *m.* & *f.*
pacify *vt.* pacifier, apaiser
pack *n.* paquet, ballot *m.*; fardeau *m.*;
(cards) jeu *m.*; bande, meute *f.*; —
animal *n.* bête de somme *f.*; — horse *n.*
cheval de bât *m.*; — *vt.* & *vi.* emballer,
empaqueter; fourrer; (earth) tasser;
faire (une valise); — **off** envoyer; — **up**
faire ses valises; **-age** *n.* colis, emballage *m.*; **-er** *n.* emballeur *m.*; **-ing** *n.*
emballage *m.*; action de faire les valises
f.; (mech.) garniture *f.*; **-ing case** caisse
d'emballage *f.*; **-ing house** abattoir *m.*
packet *n.* paquet *m.*
packsaddle *n.* bât *m.*
pact *n.* pacte, contrat *m.*
pad *n.* (paper) bloc *m.*; tampon *m.*; —
vt. rembourrer, ouater; gonfler; — *vi.*
aller doucement, aller à pas sourds;
-ding *n.* remplissage *m.*, ouate *f.*
paddle *n.* rame *f.*; pagaie *f.*; — **wheel** roue
à aubes *f.*; — *vt.* & *vi.* pagayer, ramer;
(coll.) fesser
paddock *n.* enclos *m.*; paddock *m.*
padlock *n.* cadenas *m.*; — *vt.* cadenasser
pagan *n.* & *a.* païen *m.*; **-ism** *n.* paganisme
m.
page *n.* page *f.*; (court) page *m.*; (messenger) chasseur *m.*; (book) (left) verso
(right) recto *m.*; — *vt.* chercher; crier
(le nom d'une personne), faire appeler (par un chasseur); (print.) paginer
pageant *n.* spectacle, défilé *m.*, parade *f.*;
-ry *n.* faste *m.*, pompe, parade *f.*
pagination, paging *n.* (print.) pagination
f.
pail *n.* seau *m.*
pain *n.* peine, douleur *f.*; mal *m.*; **be in** —
souffrir; **take great –s to** se donner de
la peine pour; — *vt.* peiner, donner de
la peine à; faire mal à; **-ful** *a.* pénible;
douloureux; **-less** *a.* sans douleur
painstaking *a.* soigné; laborieux; assidu
paint *n.* couleur *f.*; peinture *f.*; — *vt.*
peindre; dépeindre; **-er** *n.* peintre *m.*;
(naut.) amarre *f.*; **house –er** peintre en
bâtiments *m.*; **-ing** *n.* peinture *f.*;
tableau *m.*
paintbrush *n.* pinceau *m.*

pair *n.* paire *f.*; couple *m.*; — *vt.* apparier;
assortir; — **off** s'apparier
paisley *n.* châle écossais *m.*
pajamas *n.* pyjama *m.*
Pakistan *n.* Pakistan *m.*
palace *n.* palais *m.*
palatable *a.* agréable au goût
palate *n.* palais *m.*
palatial *a.* semblable à un palais; somptueux, magnifique
palatinate *n.* palatinat *m.*
Palatine *n.* Palatin *m.*
palaver *n.* verbiage *m.*; palabre *f.*
pale *n.* pieu *m.*; enceinte *f.*; **beyond the**
— inaccessible; — *a.* pâle, blême; — *vi.*
pâlir, blêmir; **-ness** *n.* pâleur *f.*
paleography *n.* paléographie *f.*
paleolithic *a.* paléolithique
Palestine *n.* Palestine *f.*
palette *n.* palette *f.*
palfrey *n.* palefroi *m.*
palisade *n.* palissade *f.*
pall *n.* poêle *m.*; — *vi.* affaiblir; devenir
insipide
pallbearer *n.* porteur d'un cercueil *m*
pallet *n.* petit lit, grabat *m.*
palliate *vt.* pallier
palliative *a.* & *n.* palliatif *m.*
pallid *a.* pâle, blême
pallor *n.* pâleur *f.*
palm *n.* (tree) palmier *m.*; (leaf) palme *f.*;
(hand) paume *f.*; — *vt.* empaumer,
escamoter; — **off** faire accepter (une
chose pour ce qu'elle n'est pas)
Palm Sunday *n.* Dimanche des Rameaux *m.*
palmist *n.* chiromancier *m.*; **-ry** *n.* chiromancie *f.*
palpitate *vi.* palpiter
palpitation *n.* palpitation *f.*
palsied *a.* paralysé
palsy *n.* paralysie *f.*
paltry *a.* méprisable, bas, pauvre, mesquin
pamper *vt.* dorloter, choyer
pamphlet *n.* pamphlet *m.*; brochure *f.*,
dépliant *m.*; **-eer** *n.* pamphlétaire *m.*
pan *n.* poêle, casserole *f.*; cuvette *f.*; —
vt. (gold) laver; (coll.) critiquer; — **out**
(coll.) arriver; réussir
panacea *n.* panacée *f.*
Panama *n.* Panama *m.*
Pan-American *a.* pan-américain
pancake *n.* crêpe *f.*; — **landing** atterrissage à plat *m.*
panchromatic *a.* panchromatique
pancreas *n.* pancréas *m.*
pandemonium *n.* pandémonium *m.*
pander *n.* maquereau *m.*; — *vi.* faire le
maquereau
pane *n.* carreau (de vitre), panneau *m.*

panegyric *a.* panégyrique
panel *n.* panneau *m.*; jury *m.*; — *vt.* diviser en panneaux; lambrisser; –ing *n.* lambris *m.*; boiserie *f.*; –ist *n.* membre du jury *m.*
pang *n.* angoisse *f.*
panhandle *n.* queue de poêle *f.*; — *vt.* (coll.) mendier; –r *n.* (coll.) mendiant *m.*
panic *n.* panique *f.*; — *vt.* terrifier, affoler; –ky *a.* (coll.) affolé; inquiet
panic-stricken *a.* pris de panique; terrifié
panoply *n.* panoplie *f.*
panorama *n.* panorama *m.*
panoramic *a.* panoramique
pant *n.* halètement *m.*; — *vi.* palpiter; haleter; –ing *n.* halètement *m.*
pantaloons *n. pl.* pantalon *m.*
pantheism *n.* panthéisme *m.*
pantheist *n.* panthéiste *m.*
pantheon *n.* panthéon *m.*
panther *n.* panthère *f.*
pantomimist *n.* (actor) pantomime, mime *m.*
pantry *n.* office *f.*; garde-manger *m.*
pants *n. pl.* pantalon *m.*
pap *n.* mamelle *f.*; bouillie *f.*; pulpe *f.*
papacy *n.* papauté *f.*
papal *a.* papal
paper *n.* papier *m.*; journal *m.*; écrit *m.*; article *m.*; communication *f.*; **blotting** — papier buvard *m.*; **carbon** — papier carbone *m.*; **toilet** — papier hygiénique; — **bag** sac *m.*; — **boy** crieur, vendeur de journaux *m.*; — **clip** attache *f.*; — **cutter,** — **knife** coupe-papier *m.*; — **money** papier-monnaie *m.*; — *vt.* tapisser (de papier peint)
paperback *n.* livre broché, livre bon marché *m.*
paperhanger *n.* colleur *m.*
paperweight *n.* presse-papiers *m.*
papier-mâché carton-pâte *m.*; papier-mâché *m.*
papist *n.* papiste *m.*
paprika *n.* paprika; piment hongrois *m.*
Papua *n.* Papouasie *f.*
papyrus *n.* papyrus *m.*
par *n.* valeur égale *f.*; pair *m.*; niveau *m.*
parable *n.* parabole *f.*; — *vt.* réprésenter par un parabole
parabola *n.* parabole *f.*
parachute *n.* parachute *m.*; — *vt. & vi.* parachuter
parachutist *n.* parachutiste *m.*
parade *n.* défilé *m.*; — *vi.* défiler; faire la parade; — *vt.* faire parade de
paradise *n.* paradis *m.*
paradox *n.* paradoxe *m.*; –ical *a.* para-

doxal
paraffin *n.* paraffine *f.*; — **oil** pétrole *m.*
paragraph *n.* paragraphe, alinéa *m.*
parallel *n.* parallèle *f.*; ressemblance *f.*; — *vt.* mettre en parallèle, comparer; — *a.* parallèle; –ism *n.* parallélisme *m.*
parallelogram *n.* parallélogramme *m.*
paralysis *n.* paralysie *f.*
paralytic *a.* paralytique
paralyze *vt.* paralyser
paramedic *n.* parachutiste du corps médecin *m.*
paramilitary *a.* paramilitaire
paramount *a.* supérieur, éminent
paramour *n.* amant, *m.*, amante *f.*
paranoia *n.* paranoïa *f.*
parapet *n.* parapet *m.*
paraphernalia *n.* attirail *m.*; équipement *m.*; outillage *m.*; effets, bagages *m. pl.*
paraphrase *vt.* paraphraser; — *n.* paraphrase *f.*
paraplegia *n.* paraplégie *f.*
parapsychology *n.* parapsychologie *f.*
parasite *n.* parasite *m.*; pique-assiette *m.*
parasitic *a.* parasite
parasol *n.* parasol *m.*, ombrelle *f.*
parboil *vt.* bouillir (avant de rôtir)
parcel *n.* paquet, colis *m.*; parcelle, quantité *f.*; — **post** *n.* colis postal *m.*; — *vt.* morceler, parceller
parch *vt.* brûler légèrement, griller; dessécher
parchment *n.* parchemin *m.*
pardon *n.* pardon *m.*, grâce *f.*; — *vt.* pardonner; gracier; –able *a.* pardonnable
pare *vt.* peler; rogner
paregoric *a. & n.* parégorique *m.*
parent *n.* père *m.*, mère *f.*; –s *pl.* parents *m. pl.*; –age *n.* parenté, parentage *m.*, naissance *f.*; –al *a.* paternel, maternel; –hood *n.* parenté *f.*
parenthesis *n.* parenthèse *f.*
parenthetical *a.* entre parenthèses
parfait *n.* glace mêlée de sirop de fruits *f.*
paring *n.* rognure, pelure, écorce *f.*; — **knife** éplucheuse *f.*
Paris *n.* Paris *m.*; –ian *a. & n.* parisien *m.*
parish *n.* paroisse *f.*; — *a.* paroissial; –ioner *n.* paroissien *m.*
parity *n.* parité *f.*
park *n.* parc *m.*; — *vt. & vi.* stationner; –ing *n.* stationnement *m.*; **no** –ing stationnement interdit; –ing **light** feu de position, feu de stationnement *m.*
parkway *n.* boulevard *m.*; autostrade *f.*
parlance *n.* langage *m.*
parley *n.* pourparler *m.*; — *vi.* discuter; (mil.) parlementer
parliament *n.* parlement *m.*; –ary *a.* parlementaire

parlor *n.* petit salon *m.*; (convents, schools) parloir *m.*; **funeral** — établissement de pompes funèbres *m.*; — **car** voiture-salon *f.*

Parnassian *a. & n.* parnassien *m.*

parochial *a.* (eccl.) paroissial; communal

parody *n.* parodie *f.*; — *vt.* parodier

parole *n.* parole *f.*; liberté provisoire *f.*; — *vt.* libérer provisoirement

paroxysm *n.* paroxysme *m.*

parquet *n.* parquet *m.*; (theat.) orchestre *m.*

parry *vt.* parer, éviter; — *n.* parade *f.*

parse *vt.* (gram.) expliquer (une phrase), faire l'analyse (d'une phrase)

parsimonious *a.* parcimonieux

parsimony *n.* parcimonie *f.*

parsley *n.* persil *m.*

parsnip *n.* panais *m.*

parson *n.* curé *m.*; prêtre *m.*; **-age** *n.* presbytère *m.*; cure *f.*; maison du curé *f.*

part *n.* partie, part, portion *f.*; parti, rôle *m.*; (hair) raie *f.*; **for my** — pour ma part; quant à moi; **in** — en partie; partiellement; **in great** — en grande partie; **the greater** — la plupart; **be** — **of** faire partie de; **play a** — jouer un rôle; **take** — **in** prendre part à; **take someone's** — prendre le parti de; **spare** — pièce détachée *f.*; pièce de rechange *f.*; — *adv.* en partie; moitié; — *vt.* diviser; séparer; — *vi.* se séparer; se diviser; se quitter; **-ing** *n.* départ *m.*; séparation *f.*: **-ly** *adv.* en partie, partiellement

partake *vi.* avoir part, participer, prendre part

partial *a.* (prejudiced) partial; (part) partiel; **-ity** *n.* partialité *f.*

participant *n.* participant *m.*

participate *vi.* participer

participation *n.* participation *f.*

participial *a.* (gram.) participial

participle *n.* (gram.) participe *m.*

particle *n.* (gram.) particule *f.*; parcelle *f.*, brin, atome *m.*

particular *n.* particularité *f.*, détail *m.*; particulier *m.*; — *a.* particulier; singulier; exigeant, regardant, pointilleux; **in** — notamment, en particulier; **-ity** *n.* particularité *f.*; **-ize** *vt.* particulariser, spécifier; **-ly** *adv.* en particulier, particulièrement

partisan *n.* partisan *m.*; — *a.* de parti

partition *n.* partition, division *f.*; cloison *f.*; (pol.) partage *m.*; — *vt.* diviser (par une cloison), cloisonner

partitive *a.* partitif

partner *n.* associé *m.*; compagnon *m.*;

partenaire *m.* (*& f.*); **silent** — associé commanditaire *m.*; **-ship** *n.* association *f.*; **go into** — **with** s'associer avec

part owner *n.* copropriétaire *m. & f.*

part-time *a.*, — **work** emploi partiel *m.*

party *n.* parti *m.*; partie *f.*; intérêt *m.*; individu *m.*; soirée *f.*, divertissement *m.*, fête *f.*; **be (a)** — **to** prendre part à, participer à; être complice de; **give someone a** — fêter quelqu'un; — **line** ligne téléphonique utilisée par plusieurs abonnés *f.*; doctrine (d'un parti politique) *f.*

pass *n.* passage étroit, défilé *m.*; situation *f.*, état *m.*; billet gratuit *m.*; laissez-passer *m.*; passe *f.*; **come to** — se passer, arriver; — *vt.* passer; dépasser, doubler; croiser; voter; — *vi.* passer; se passer; (education) être reçu (à un examen), réussir (à); — **away** décéder; — **by** passer (par); — **judgment** prononcer un jugement; — **off** faire passer; — **on** procéder; décéder; — **out** se pâmer; perdre connaissance; — **over** laisser passer, négliger; **-able** *a.* passable; praticable; **-ing** *n.* passage *m.*; mort *f.*; **-ing** *a.* passager; passant; **by-** *n.* bec-allumeur *m.*; route d'évitement *f.*

passage *n.* passage *m.*; couloir *m.*

passageway *n.* corridor, passage *m.*

passbook *n.* livret de banque *m.*

passenger *n.* passager *m.*; voyageur *m.*

passer-by *n.* passant *m.*

passion *n.* passion *f.*; **-ate** *a.* passionné

passive *a. & n.* passif *m.*; **-ness** *n.* passivité *f.*

passkey *n.* passe-partout *m.*

Passover *n.* Pâque *f.*

passport *n.* passeport *m.*

password *n.* mot d'ordre *m.*

past *n. & a.* passé *m.*; — *prep.* plus loin que; devant; hors de; au delà de; — *adv.*, **go** — passer

paste *n.* colle *f.*; pâte *f.*; (jewels) strass *m.*; — *vt.* coller

pasteboard *n.* carton *m.*

pasteurization *n.* pasteurisation *f.*

pasteurize *vt.* pasteuriser; **-d** *a.* pasteurisé

pastiche *n.* pastiche *m.*; — *vt.* pasticher

pastime *n.* passe-temps *m.*

pastor *n.* pasteur *m.*; **-al** *n.* pastorale *f.*; — *a.* pastoral

pastry *n.* pâtisserie *f.*; — **cook** *n.* pâtissier *m.*; — **shop** pâtisserie *f.*

pasturage *n.* pâturage *m.*

pasture *n.* pâture *f.*; pré *m.*; pâturage *m.*; — *vi.* paître; — *vt.* faire paître

pasty *a.* blême; pâteux

pat *n.* petit coup *m.*, tape *f.*; rondelle *f.*;

petit morceau (de beurre) *m.*; — *vt.*
frapper légèrement, taper; — *a.* convenable, propre, tout prêt
patch *n.* pièce *f.*, morceau *m.*; (eye) tampon *m.*; (face) mouche *f.*; terrain, plant
m., plantation *f.*; — *vt.* rapiécer, raccommoder
patchwork *n.* rapiéçage *m.*; travail à la
pièce *m.*
pate *n.* tête *f.*
patella *n.* (anat.) rotule *f.*
patent *n.* brevet *m.*; — *a.* breveté; évident, patent; — **leather** *n.* cuir verni;
— *vt.* faire breveter
paternal *a.* paternel
paternity *n.* paternité *f.*
path *n.* sentier, chemin *m.*; route *f.*
pathetic *a.* pathétique
pathfinder *n.* explorateur *m.*
pathological *a.* pathologique
pathology *n.* pathologie *f.*
pathos *n.* pathétique *m.*; pathos *m.*
pathway *n.* sentier *m.*
patience *n.* patience *f.*
patient *n.* malade *m.*; — *a.* patient; endurant; **be** — patienter
patina *n.* patine *f.*
patriarch *n.* patriarche *m.*
patrician *a. & n.* patricien *m.*
patrimony *n.* patrimoine *m.*
patriot *n.* patriote *m.*; **–ic** *a.* patriotique;
–ism *n.* patriotisme *m.*
patrol *n.* patrouille *f.*; — *vi.* faire la ronde;
— *vt.* surveiller
patrolman *n.* agent de police (qui fait la
ronde) *m.*
patron *n.* patron, protecteur *m.*; — **saint**
patron *m.*, patronne *f.*; **–age** *n.* patronage *m.*; clientèle *f.*; **–ize** *vt.* patronner; donner son clinetèle à; traiter avec
condescendance
patter *vi.* bavarder; piétiner; faire du
bruit; — *n.* bavardage *m.*; bruit *m.*
pattern *n.* patron, modèle *m.*
paucity *n.* manque *m.*, disette *f.*
paunch *n.* panse *f.*; bedaine *f.*
pauper *n.* pauvre *m.*, pauvresse *f.*
pause *n.* pause *f.*; — *vi.* faire une pause;
s'arrêter; hésiter
pave *vt.* paver; frayer; (fig.) préparer;
–ment *n.* pavé *m.*; pavage *m.*
pavilion *n.* pavillon *m.*
paving *n.* pavage *m.*; pavé *m.*
paw *n.* patte *f.*; — *vt. & vi.* frapper du
pied; griffer; caresser avec la patte
pawl *n.* cliquet *m.*
pawn *n.* (chess) pion *m.*; gage *m.*; **–broker**
n. prêteur sur gages *m.*; **–shop** *n.*
mont-de-piété *m.*; — **ticket** *n.* reconnaissance de mont-de-piété *f.*; — *vt.*

engager, mettre en gage
pay *n.* solde *f.*; salaire *m.*; — *vt.* payer;
acquitter; — **attention** prêter attention; — **a visit** rendre visite, faire
visite; — **back** rembourser; — **for**
payer; — **off** payer; réussir; — **up**
solder; **–able** *a.* payable; **–day** *n.* jour
de paie *m.*; **–load** *n.* poids utile *m.*;
–master *n.* trésorier, payeur *m.*; **–ment**
n. paiement *m.*; versement, acompte *m.*;
–roll *n.* feuille de paie, liste de paie *f.*
pea *n.* pois *m.*; — **shooter** sarbacane *f.*;
soup potage Saint-Germain *m.*; — purée
de pois; — **soup fog** (coll.) brouillard
épais
peace *n.* paix *f.*; **justice of the** — juge de
paix *m.*; **–ful** *a.* paisible, tranquille;
–fulness *n.* paix, tranquillité *f.*; —
offering *n.* sacrifice expiatoire, cadeau
de réconciliation *m.*
peace-loving *a.* pacifique
peacemaker *n.* conciliateur *m.*
peach *n.* pêche *f.*; (tree) pêcher *m.*
peak *n.* pic, sommet *m.*, cime *f.*; pointe *f.*;
— *a.* meilleur; premier; **–ed** *a.* en
pointe; (hat) à visière
peal *n.* carillon *m.*; bruit *m.*; coup *m.*; —
vt. faire retentir; — *vi.* retentir; gronder
peanut *n.* arachide, cacahuète *f.*; — **brittle**
caramel aux arachides *m.*; — **butter**
crème d'arachides *f.*
pear *n.* poire *f.*; (tree) poirier *m.*
peasant *n.* paysan *m.*; **–ry** *n.* paysans
m. pl.
peat *n.* tourbe *f.*
pebble *n.* caillou *m.*
pebbly *a.* caillouteux
pecan *n.* pacane *f.*; (tree) pacanier *m.*
peccadillo *n.* peccadille *f.*
peck *n.* coup de bec *m.*; (measure) peck
m. (= 9 litres); — *vt. & vi.* becqueter,
picoter
pectoral *a. & n.* pectoral *m.*
peculiar *a.* particulier, singulier, unique;
–ity *n.* singularité *f.*
pecuniary *a.* pécuniaire
pedagogical *a.* pédagogique
pedagogue *n.* pédagogue *m.*
pedagogy *n.* pédagogie *f.*
pedal *n.* pédale *f.*; — *vi.* pédaler
pedant *n.* pédant *m.*; **–ic** *a.* pedant; **–ry** *n.*
pédanterie *f.*
peddle *vt.* colporter; **–r** *n.* colporteur *m.*
pedestal *n.* piédestal *m.*
pedestrian *n.* piéton *m.*
pediatrician *n.* pédiatre *m.*
pedigree *n.* généalogie *f.*; lignage *m.*;
pedigree *m.*; **–d** *a.* de race, pur-sang
pediment *n.* fronton *m.*

pedlar *n.* colporteur *m.*
pedometer *n.* podomètre *m.*
peek *n.* aperçu *m.*; coup d'œil *m.*; — *vi.* regarder furtivement
peekaboo *n.* cache-cache *m.*
peel *n.* pelure *f.*; peau *f.*; écorce *f.*; — *vt.* peler, éplucher
peep *n.* regard furtif *m.*; cri (d'un poussin) *m.*; pépiement *m.*; — *vi.* regarder furtivement; crier, pépier
peephole *n.* judas *m.*
peer *n.* pair *m.*; — *vi.* regarder longuement; –age *n.* pairie *f.*; –less *a.* incomparable, sans pareil
peevish *a.* bourru, maussade; –ness *n.* mauvaise humeur *f.*
peg *n.* cheville *f.*; (tent) piquet *m.*; — *vt.* cheviller
pegleg *n.* jambe de bois *f.*
pejorative *a.* péjoratif
pellagra *n.* pellagre *f.*
pellet *n.* boulette *f.*; grain de plomb *m.*, balle *f.*
pell-mell *adv.* pêle-mêle
pelt *n.* peau, fourrure *f.*; — *vt.* assaillir; battre
pelvic *a.* pelvien
pelvis *n.* bassin *m.*
pen *n.* plume *f.*; stylographe, stylo *m.*; (cattle) enclos *m.*; (poultry) poulailler; **ballpoint** — stylo à bille *m.*; — **name** nom de plume *m.*; — *vt.* écrire; — **in**, — **up** enfermer
penal *a.* pénal; –ize *vt.* punir; (sport) pénaliser
penalty *n.* pénalité, peine, punition, amende *f.*
penance *n.* pénitence *f.*
pencil *n.* crayon *m.*; — **sharpener** taille-crayons *m.*; — *vt.* dessiner au crayon
pendant *n.* pendant *m.*, pendeloque *f.*
pending *a.* pendant, indécis; — *prep.* en attendant
pendulum *n.* pendule *m.*
penetrate *vt. & vi.* pénétrer
penetrating *a.* pénétrant
penetration *n.* pénétration *f.*; sagacité *f.*
penholder *n.* porte-plume *m.*
penicillin *n.* pénicilline *f.*
peninsula *n.* péninsule *f.*; –r *a.* péninsulaire
penis *n.* pénis *m.*
penitence *n.* pénitence *f.*
penitent *a. & n.* pénitent *m.*
penitentiary *n.* prison *f.*
penknife *n.* canif *m.*
penmanship *n.* écriture *f.*
pennant *n.* banderole, flamme *f.*
penniless *a.* sans le sou
penny *n.* sou *m.*

pension *n.* pension *f.*; retraite *f.*; allocation *f.*; — *vt.*, — **off** mettre à la retraite; –er *n.* pensionnaire, retraité *m.*
pensive *a.* pensif
pentagon *n.* pentagone *m.*; –al *a.* pentagonal
pentameter *n.* pentamètre *m.*
penthouse *n.* appartement (aménagé au sommet d'un grand bâtiment) *m.*
pent-up *a.* (emotion) refoulé; enfermé
penumbra *n.* pénombre *f.*
penurious *a.* parcimonieux; pauvre
penury *n.* indigence, pénurie *f.*
people *n.* peuple *m.*; gens *m. pl.*; parents *m. pl.*; public *m.*; — *vt.* peupler
pepper *n.* poivre *m.*; poivron, piment *m.*; — *vt.* poivrer; (fig.) saupoudrer; –y *a.* poivré
peppercorn *n.* grain de poivre *m.*
peppermint *n.* menthe poivrée *f.*
pepsin *n.* pepsine *f.*
peptic *a.* digestif, gastrique
per *prep.* par, pour; — **cent** pour cent
perambulator *n.* voiture d'enfant *f.*
perceivable *a.* perceptible
perceive *vt.* apercevoir, sentir, voir
per cent *n.* pour cent *m.*
percentage *n.* pourcentage *m.*
perceptibility *n.* perceptibilité *f.*
perceptible *a.* perceptible
perception *n.* perception *f.*
perceptive *a.* perceptif
perch *n.* (fish) perche *f.*; perchoir *m.*; — *vt. & (vi.)* (se) percher
perchance *adv.* par hasard
percolate *vt. & vi.* filtrer
percolator *n.* cafetière (à l'américaine) *f.*
percussion *n.* percussion *f.*, coup *m.*; — **cap** *n.* capsule *f.*
perdition *n.* perdition *f.*; ruine *f.*
peremptory *a.* péremptoire, absolu
perennial *a.* perpétuel; (bot.), vivace; –ly *adv.* éternellement; tout le temps
perfect *vt.* perfectionner, achever, compléter; — *a.* parfait; complet; –ion *n.* perfection *f.*
perfidious *a.* perfide
perfidy *n.* perfidie *f.*
perforate *vt.* perforer, percer
perforation *n.* perforation *f.*
perforce *adv.* forcément
perform *vt. & vi.* exécuter, accomplir, faire; réussir; –ance *n.* accomplissement *m.*, exécution *f.*; ouvrage *m.*; exploit, fait *m.*, action *f.*; représentation *f.*; –er *n.* exécutant, artiste, acteur *m.*
perfume *n.* parfum *m.*; — *vt.* parfumer; –r *n.* parfumeur *m.*
perfunctory *a.* superficiel, négligent

perhaps *adv.* peut-être
pericardium *n.* péricarde *m.*
perigee *n.* périgée *m.*
peril *n.* péril, danger *m.*; –ous *a.* dangereux
perimeter *n.* périmètre *m.*
period *n.* période *f.*; époque *f.*; âge *m.*; terme *m.*; (punctuation) point *m.*; –ic(al) *a.* périodique; –ical *n.* périodique *f.*
peripatetic *a.* péripatétique; ambulant
peripheral *a.* périmétrique
periphery *n.* périphérie *f.*
periphrasis *n.* périphrase *f.*
periscope *n.* périscope *m.*
perish *vi.* périr; –able *a.* périssable
peristalsis *n.* mouvement péristaltique *m.*
peritoneum *n.* péritoine *m.*
peritonitis *n.* péritonite *f.*
perjure *vt.* parjurer; –d *a.* parjure; –er *n.* parjure *m.*
perjury *n.* parjure *m.*
perk *vi.* se rengorger; — up se ranimer; –y *a.* animé, vif
permanent *a.* permanent; — wave *n.* ondulation permanente, indéfrisable *f.*; –ly *adv.* d'une manière permanente
permanganate *n.* permanganate *m.*
permeable *a.* perméable
permeate *vt.* passer à travers, pénétrer, saturer
permeation *n.* pénétration *f.*
permissible *a.* admissible, tolérable
permissive *a.* qui permet; indulgent
permit *n.* permis *m.*; — *vt.* permettre; laisser
permutation *n.* permutation *f.*
pernicious *a.* pernicieux
peroration *n.* péroraison *f.*
peroxide *n.* peroxyde *m.*; peroxyde d'hydrogène *m.*
perpendicular *a. & n.* perpendiculaire *m.*
perpetrate *vt.* commettre, faire
perpetration *n.* perpétration *f.*
perpetrator *n.* auteur *m.*
perpetual *a.* perpétuel; sans cesse, sans fin
perpetuate *vt.* perpétuer
perpetuation *n.* perpétuation *f.*
perplex *vt.* embarrasser; confondre; embrouiller; –ity *n.* perplexité *f.*, embarras *m.*
perquisite *n.* casuel, émolument *m.*
persecute *vt.* persécuter
persecution *n.* persécution *f.*
persecutor *n.* persécuteur *m.*
perseverance *n.* persévérance *f.*
persevere *vi.* persévérer
persevering *a.* persévérant
Persia *n.* Perse *f.*; –n *a. & n.* persan *m.*;

–n Gulf Golfe Persique *m.*
persimmon *n.* plaqueminier *m.*
persist *vi.* persister; –ence, –ency *n.* persistance *f.*; –ent *a.* persistant
person *n.* personne *f.*; individu *m.*; personnalité *f.*; –able *a.* bien fait; aimable, sociable; –age *n.* personnage *m.*; personne *f.*; –al *a.* personnel; particulier; –ality *n.* personnalité *f.*; –ification *n.* personnification *f.*; –ify *vt.* personnifier
perspective *n.* perspective *f.*; — *a.* perspectif
perspicacity *n.* perspicacité *f.*
perspiration *n.* transpiration, sueur *f.*
perspire *vi.* transpirer, suer
persuade *vt.* persuader, convaincre
persuasion *n.* persuasion, conviction *f.*
persuasive *a.* persuasif
pert *a.* vif, pétulant, impertinent
pertain *vi.* appartenir, concerner
pertinence *n.* convenance, propriété *f.*; justesse *f.*
pertinent *a.* pertinent, convenable; juste, à propos
perturb *vt.* troubler, perturber; –ation *n.* perturbation *f.*, trouble *m.*
Peru *n.* Pérou *m.*
perusal *n.* lecture *f.*, examen *m.*
peruse *vt.* lire, parcourir
pervade *vt.* pénétrer
pervasive *a.* pénétrant
perverse *a.* pervers; têtu
perversion *n.* perversion *f.*
perversity *n.* perversité *f.*; méchanceté *f.*
pervert *vt.* pervertir, dépraver; — *n.* perverti *m.*
pervious *a.* perméable
pessimism *n.* pessimisme *m.*
pessimist *n.* pessimiste *m.*; –ic *a.* pessimiste
pest *n.* fléau *m.*; personne gênante *f.*; –er *vt.* gêner, ennuyer
pestilence *n.* peste *f.*
pestilent *a.* pestilentiel
pestle *n.* pilon *m.*
pet *n.* favori *m.*; animal favori *m.*; — name petit nom *m.*; — *vt.* caresser
petal *n.* pétale *m.*
petition *n.* pétition, supplication *f.*; demande *f.*; requête *f.*; — *vt.* pétitionner, supplier; demander à; réclamer à; –er *n.* demandeur *m.*; pétitionnaire *m. & f.*
petrel *n.* pétrel *m.*
petrify *vt. & (vi.)* (se) pétrifier
petroleum *n.* pétrole *m.*
petticoat *n.* jupon *m.*
pettiness *n.* petitesse *f.*
petty *a.* petit, inférieur; chétif; — cash

petite caisse *f.*; — **officer** (navy) sous-officier *m.*
petulance *n.* pétulance *f.*
petulant *a.* pétulant
pew *n.* banc d'église *m.*
pewter *n.* étain *m.*
phalanx *n.* phalange *f.*
phantom *n.* fantôme *m.*
Pharaoh *n.* Pharaon *m.*
Pharisee *n.* Pharisien *m.*
pharmaceutic(al) *a.* pharmaceutique
pharmacist *n.* pharmacien *m.*
pharmacy *n.* pharmacie *f.*
pharynx *n.* pharynx *m.*
phase *n.* phase *f.*
phenol *n.* phénol *m.*
phenomenal *a.* phénoménal
phenomenon *n.* phénomène *m.*
Philadelphia *n.* Philadelphie *f.*
philander *vi.* courir; **–er** *n.* coureur *m.*
philanthropic *a.* philanthropique
philanthropist *n.* philanthrope *m.*
philatelic *a.* philatélique
philatelist *n.* philateliste *m.*
philharmonic *a.* philharmonique
Philippines *n.* Philippines *f. pl.*
Philistine *n.* Philistin *m.*
philologist *n.* philologue *m.*
philology *n.* philologie *f.*
philosopher *n.* philosophe *m.*
philosophic(al) *a.* philosophique
philosophize *vi.* philosopher
philosophy *n.* philosophie *f.*
phlegm *n.* flegme *m.*; **–atic** *a.* flegmatique
phobia *n.* phobie *f.*
Phoenicia *n.* Phénicie *f.*; **–n** *a. & n.* phénicien *m.*
phone *n.* téléphone *m.*; — *vi.* téléphoner
phonetic *a.* phonétique; **–s** *n.* phonétique *f.*
phonic *a.* phonique
phosphate *n.* (chem.) phosphate *m.*
phosphide *n.* phosphure *m.*
phosphorescence *n.* phosphorescence *f.*
phosphoric *a.* phosphorique
phosphorus *n.* phosphore *m.*
photoelectric *a.* photo-électrique
photoengraving *n.* photogravure *f.*
photoflash lamp *n.* lampe éclair *f.*
photograph *n.* photographie *f.*; — *vt.* photographier; **–er** *n.* photographe *m.*; **–ic** *a.* photographique; **–y** *n.* photographie *f.*
photostat *n.* photocopie *f.*
photosynthesis *n.* photosynthèse *f.*
phrase *n.* phrase, expression *f.*; locution *f.*; — *vt.* exprimer, rédiger
phraseology *n.* phraséologie *f.*
phrenetic *a.* frénétique
phrenology *n.* phrénologie *f.*

physic *n.* médicament *m.*; purgatif *m.*; médecine *f.*; **–s** *n.* physique *f.*; **–al** *a.* physique; matériel
physician *n.* médecin *m.*
physicist *n.* physicien *m.*
physiognomy *n.* physionomie *f.*
physiological *a.* physiologique
physiologist *n.* physiologiste *m.*
physiology *n.* physiologie *f.*
physiotherapy *n.* physicothérapie *f.*
physique *n.* physique *m.*
pianist *n.* pianiste *m. & f.*
piano *n.* piano *m.*; **baby grand** — piano à demi-queue *m.*; **grand** — piano à queue; **upright** — piano droit *m.*
Picardy *n.* Picardie *f.*
picayune *a.* mesquin
piccolo *n.* piccolo, octavin *m.*
pick *n.* pioche *f.*; — *vi.* piquer, becqueter; — *vt.* cueillir, glaner, ramasser; éplucher, trier; choisir; — **out** choisir; — **up** ramasser; acheter à bon marché; retrouver; relever; apprendre; **–ings** *n. pl.* épluchures *f. pl.*, petits morceaux *m. pl.*; profit *m.*
pickaback *adv.* sur le dos
pickax(e) *n.* pioche *f.*
pickerel *n.* brocheton *m.*
picket *n.* piquet *m.*; pieu *m.*; (striker) piquet de grève, débaucheur *m.*; — **fence** palis *m.*; — *vt.* entourer de débaucheurs
pickle *n.* cornichon *m.*; (coll.) difficulté *f.*; mauvais pas *m.*; — *vt.* conserver au vinaigre
picklock *n.* crochet *m.*
pickpocket *n.* pickpocket *m.*
pickup *n.* (radio, television, or phonograph) pick-up *m.*; (coll.) fille, personne rencontrée dans la rue *f.*; (auto) accélération *f.*
picnic *n.* pique-nique *m.*; — *vi.* piqueniquer
picot *n.* picot *m.*; — *vt.* picoter
pictorial *a.* pittoresque, illustré
picture *n.* tableau *m.*; peinture *f.*; image *f.*; film *m.*; — **tube** *n.* kinescope *m.*; — *vt.* peindre; représenter
picturesque *a.* pittoresque
piddling *a.* insignifiant, mesquin
pidgin *a.*, — **English** jargon anglo-oriental *m.*
pie *n.* tarte *f.*
piebald *a.* pie
piece *n.* pièce *f.*, morceau *m.*; bout *m.*; partie *f.*; — *vt.* raccommoder, rapiécer; — **together** joindre, unir, réunir
piecemeal *a.* séparé, divisé; — *adv.* par petits morceaux
piecework *n.* travail à la pièce *m.*

pied *a.* pie, bigarré

pier *n.* môle *m.*; pilier, pied-droit *m.*; pile *f.*

pierce *vt. & vi.* percer, pénétrer

piercing *a.* pénétrant; aigu

piety *n.* piété, dévotion *f.*

pig *n.* cochon *m.*; porc *m.*; **buy a — in a poke** acheter chat en poche; **— iron** fer en fonte *m.*; **-gish** *a.* semblable à un cochon; glouton

pigeon *n.* pigeon *m.*; **clay —** pigeon artificiel *m.*; **homing —** pigeon voyageur *m.*

pigeon-breasted *a.* (qui a) la poitrine en saillie

pigeonhole *n.* case *f.*

pigheaded *a.* têtu, entêté; **-ness** *n.* entêtement *m.*, obstination *f.*

pigment *n.* pigment *m.*; couleur *f.*; **-ation** *n.* pigmentation *f.*

pigmy *n.* pygmée *m.*

pigpen, pigsty *n.* étable à cochons *f.*

pigskin *n.* peau de porc *f.*; (coll.) ballon de football *m.*

pigtail *n.* tresse *f.*

pike *n.* pique *f.*; pointe *f.*; (fish) brochet *m.*; (coll.) autostrade *f.*

pilaster *n.* pilastre *m.*

pilchard *n.* sardine *f.*

pile *n.* pieu, pilotis *m.*; monceau, tas *m.*; bûcher *m.*; édifice *m.*; duvet *m.*; (coll.) fortune *f.*; **—** *vt.* entasser; amonceler; amasser; **—** *vi.*, **— up** s'entasser

piles *n. pl.* hémorroïdes *f. pl.*

pilfer *vt.* voler, chiper; **-age, -ing** *n.* petits vols *m. pl.*

pilgrim *n.* pèlerin *m.*; **-age** *n.* pèlerinage *m.*

pill *n.* pilule *f.*

pillar *n.* pilier *m.*

pillbox *n.* boîte à pilules *f.*; (mil.) réduit en béton armé *m.*

pillory *n.* pilori *m.*; **—** *vt.* mettre au pilori

pillow *n.* oreiller *m.*; **—** *vt.* reposer, coucher

pillowcase *n.* taie d'oreiller *f.*

pilot *n.* pilote *m.*; **—** *vt.* piloter; **— light** *n.* veilleuse *f.*

pimento *n.* piment *m.*

pimple *n.* bouton *m.*, pustule *f.*

pimply *a.* boutonneux

pin *n.* épingle *f.*; (bowling) quille *f.*; **— money** argent de poche *m.*; **safety —** épingle de sûreté *f.*; **—** *vt.* épingler; fixer, attacher

pinafore *n.* bavette *f.*; sarrau *m.*

pincers *n. pl.* pinces, tenailles *f. pl.*

pinch *n.* pince *f.*; prise *f.*; difficulté *f.*, embarras *m.*; **—** *vt. & vi.* pincer; serrer; **-ed** *a.* tiré; à l'étroit

pinch-hit *vi.* (coll.); **— for** remplacer, suppléer (provisoirement)

pincushion *n.* pelote à épingles *f.*

pine *n.* pin *m.*; **—** *vi.* languir, soupirer

pineapple *n.* ananas *m.*

pinhole *n.* trou d'épingle *m.*; (phot.) sténopé *m.*

pinion *n.* pignon *m.*; **—** *vt.* lier

pink *n.* (bot.) œillet *m.*; rose (couleur) *f.*; **— of condition** en parfaite santé *f.*; **—** *a.* rose; **—** *vt.* denteler, découper

pinnacle *n.* pinacle, sommet *m.*; couronnement *m.*

pinpoint *vt.* localiser, mettre au net

pint *n.* demi-litre *m.*; pinte *f.*

pinwheel *n.* roue à fuseaux *f.*

pioneer *n.* pionnier *m.*

pious *a.* pieux

pip *n.* (bot.) pépin *m.*; signal *m.*

pipe *n.* tuyau *m.*; pipe *f.*; **—** *vt.* jouer; faire passer par un tuyau; **-r** *n.* joueur de flute *m.*; **-line** *n.* conduite *f.*; pipeline *m.*

pipecleaner *n.* cure-pipe *m.*

piping *n.* passe-poil *m.*; tuyauterie *f.*; **—** *a.* maladif; **— hot** tout chaud

piquant *a.* piquant

pique *n.* pique *f.*; **—** *vt.* piquer, irriter

piracy *n.* piraterie *f.*; (literature) plagiat *m.*

pirate *n.* pirate *m.*; **—** *vi.* commettre un plagiat; pirater

pirouette *n.* pirouette *f.*; **—** *vi.* pirouetter

pistachio *n.* pistache *f.*

pistol *n.* pistolet *m.*

piston *n.* piston *m.*; **— rod** *n.* tige du piston *f.*

pit *n.* fosse *f.*; trou *m.*; carrière *f.*, tombeau *m.*; (theat.) parterre; creux *m.*; **—** *vt.* opposer; grêler, marquer de trous

pitch *n.* poix *f.*; degré, point *m.*; hauteur *f.*; portée *f.*; (mus.) ton *m.*; **—** *vt.* poisser; fixer, planter, ranger; jeter, lancer; paver; obscurcir; **—** *vi.* tomber; (naut.) tanguer; **— (in)** se mettre au travail; **-er** *n.* cruche *f.*; (sport) joueur qui lance la balle *m.*

pitchblende *n.* pechblende *f.*

pitchfork *n.* fourche *f.*

pitch pipe *n.* diapason *m.*

piteous *a.* piteux, pitoyable

pitfall *n.* piège *m.*

pith *n.* moelle *f.*; **-y** *a.* plein de moelle

pitiable *a.* digne de pitié

pitiful *a.* déplorable, pitoyable; méprisable

pitiless *a.* impitoyable

pittance *n.* pitance, portion *f.*

pitter-patter *n.* bruit de la pluie sur un

toit *m.*

pituitary *a.* pituitaire

pity *n.* pitié, compassion *f.*; **it is a —**
c'est dommage; **to take — on** prendre
en pitié; — *vt.* plaindre, avoir pitié de

pivot *n.* pivot *m.*; — *vi.* pivoter

pixie *n.* lutin *m.*, fée *f.*

placard *n.* placard *m.*, affiche *f.*; — *vt.*
afficher

placate *vt.* apaiser

place *n.* place *f.*; lieu *m.*; endroit *m.*; rang
m.; emploi *m.*; demeure *f.*; position *f.*;
in — of au lieu de; **out of —** déplacé;
take — avoir lieu; — *vt.* placer, mettre; **-ment** *n.* mise *f.*; position *f.*;
— kick *n.* (football) coup placé, coup
d'envoie *m.*

placer *n.* (mining) placer *m.*; placeur *m.*

placid *a.* paisible, calme, placide; **-ity** *n.*
placidité *f.*, calme *m.*

plagiarism *n.* plagiat *m.*

plagiarize *vt.* plagier

plague *n.* peste, contagion *f.*; tourment
m.; — *vt.* tourmenter

plaid *n.* tartan, plaid, tissu écossais *m.*

plain *n.* plaine *f.*; — *a.* plat, uni, simple,
sincère, franc; clair; laid; **-ness** *n.*
simplicité, franchise *f.*; laideur *f.*

plainsman *n.* homme des plaines *m.*

plaintiff *n.* demandeur *m.*

plaintive *a.* plaintif

plait *n.* pli *m.*, tresse *f.*; — *vt.* plisser;
tresser

plan *n.* plan, dessin *m.*; projet *m.*; — *vt.*
projeter; dresser le plan de; compter;
avoir l'intention de

plane *n.* plan *m.*; (tool) rabot *m.*; (avi.)
avion *m.*; — *vt.* raboter; — *a.* plan,
plat; **— tree** *n.* platane *m.*

planet *n.* planète *f.*; **-ary** *a.* planétaire;
-arium *n.* planétaire *m.*

plank *n.* planche *f.*; — *vt.* planchéier;
-ing *n.* planchéiage *m.*, planches *f. pl.*

plant *n.* plante *f.*; plant *m.*; (industry)
usine *f.*; — *vt.* planter; établir; **— louse**
n. puceron *m.*; **-er** *n.* planteur *m.*

plantain *n.* plantain *m.*

plantation *n.* plantation *f.*

plasma *n.* plasma *m.*; **—physics** *n.* physique
plasmatique *f.*

plaster *n.* plâtre *m.*; emplâtre *m.*; — *vt.*
plâtrer; adhesive **—** emplâtre resineux;
sparadrap *m.*; mustard **—** sinapisme
m.; **-board** *n.* panneau de plâtre et de
papier *m.*; **— of Paris** *n.* gypse *m.*;
plâtre fin *m.*; **-er** *n.* plâtrier *m.*; **-ing** *n.*
plâtrage *m.*

plastic *a.* plastique; — *n.* matière plastique *f.*; **-ity** *n.* plasticité *f.*

plat *n.* plan *m.*, carte *f.*

plate *n.* (metal) plaque *f.*; (dish) assiette *f.*;
(flatware) argenterie *f.*; (food) plat *m.*;
(teeth) dentier *m.*; (engraving) gravure
f.; — *vt.* plaquer, laminer; étamer; argenter; **— glass** glâce (sans tain) *f.*

plateau *n.* plateau, massif *m.*

plateful *n.* assiettée *f.*

platform *n.* plate-forme *f.*; (rail.) quai *m.*;
(politics) programme politique *m.*

platinum *n.* platine *m.*

platitude *n.* platitude *f.*

platonic *a.* platonique

platoon *n.* peloton *m.*

platter *n.* plat *m.*

plaudit *n.* applaudissement *m.*

plausibility *n.* plausibilité *f.*

plausible *a.* plausible

play *n.* jeu *m.*; (theat.) pièce *f.*; **— on**
words calembour *m.*; — *vi.* jouer; — *vt.*
jouer; faire; **— a trick on** jouer un tour
à; **— on** abuser de; **— tennis** jouer au
tennis; **— the piano** jouer du piano; —
up to courtiser; flatter; **-er** *n.* joueur
m.; (theat.) acteur, comédien *m.*; **-er**
piano piano à rouleau *m.*; **-ful** *a.*
badin, espiègle; **-ing** *n.* jeu *m.*; **-ing**
cards cartes à jouer *f. pl.*; **-ing field** terrain *m.*

playboy *n.* luron, libertin *m.*; homme riche
qui fréquente les boîtes de nuit *m.*

playgoer *n.* habitué du théâtre *m.*

playground *n.* terrain de jeu *m.*, cour de
récréation *f.*

playhouse *n.* théâtre *m.*

playmate *n.* camarade de jeu *m.*

plaything *n.* jouet *m.*

playwright *n.* auteur dramatique *m.*

plea *n.* défense *f.*; excuse *f.*; prières *f. pl.*

plead *vi.* plaider; — *vt.* défendre; alléguer,
prétexter; **-ing** *n.* prières *f. pl.*; (law)
plaidoirie *f.*

pleasant *a.* agréable; **-ness** *n.* agrément,
charme *m.*; **-ry** *n. pl.* plaisanterie *f.*

please *vt. & vi.* plaire à, être agréable,
contenter; — *interj.* s'il vous plaît;
as you — comme il vous plaira; **if you
—** s'il vous plaît; **— be seated** veuillez
vous asseoir; **-d** *a.* content, heureux; **-d
to meet you** enchanté de faire votre
connaissance

pleasing *a.* agréable, charmant

pleasurable *a.* agréable

pleasure *n.* plaisir, gré *m.*; **with —** avec
plaisir, volontiers

pleat *n.* pli, pli creux *m.*; — *vt.* plisser,
mettre en plis

plebeian *a. & n.* plébéien *m.*

plebiscite *n.* plébiscite *m.*

pledge *n.* gage *m.*; caution *f.*; toast *m.*;
vœu *m.*, promesse *f.*; — *vt.* engager;

promettre

plenary *a.* plein, complet, parfait

plenipotentiary *n. & a.* plénipotentiaire *m.*

plentiful *a.* abondant

plenty *n.* abondance *f.*; **have — of** ne pas manquer de, avoir beaucoup de

plethora *n.* pléthore *f.*

pleurisy *n.* pleurésie *f.*

plexus *n.* plexus *m.*

pliability *n.* souplesse, flexibilité *f.*

pliable, pliant *a.* flexible, pliable; docile

pliers *n. pl.* pince *f.*

plight *n.* condition *f.*, état *m.*; **— vt.** engager

plod *vi.* piocher; marcher avec peine; **-der** *n.* piocheur *m.*

plop *n. & interj.* pouf, plouf *m.*; **— vi.** faire plouf

plot *n.* morceau de terre *m.*; plan, complot *m.*; intrigue *f.*; **— vt. & vi.** comploter, conspirer, machiner; inventer; **-ter** *n.* conspirateur *m.*; **-ting** *n.* machinations *f. pl.*

plow, plough *n.* charrue *f.*; bouvet *m.*; **gang —** charrue polysoc *f.*; **— vt.** labourer; sillonner; **-ing** *n.* labourage *m.*; **-man** *n.* laboureur *m.*

plowshare *n.* soc de charrue *m.*

pluck *n.* action intrépide *f.*; courage *m.*; fressure (d'un animal) *f.*; **— vt.** arracher; (feathers) plumer; cueillir; **-y** *a.* courageux

plug *n.* tampon *m.*, cheville *f.*; piston *m* ; bouchon *m.*; prise (de courant) *f.*; fiche *f.*; **spark — bougie** *f.*; **— vt.** boucher; cheviller; tamponner; **— away** *vi.* (coll.) persévérer; **— in** mettre la fiche dans (la prise)

plum *n.* prune *f.*; (tree) prunier *m.*

plumb *n.* plomb *m.*; sonde *f.*; **— line** *n.* niveau *m.*; fil à plomb *m.*; **— vt.** mettre à plomb; **— adv.** à plomb; **-er** *n.* plombier *m.*; **-ing** *n.* installation sanitaire *f.*

plume *n.* plume *f.*, panache *m.*; plumet *m.*; **— vt.** orner d'une plume; lisser

plummet *n.* plomb *m.*, sonde *f.*; **— vi.** tomber

plump *vi.* s'enfler; tomber lourdement; soutenir (une candidature); **— a.** dodu, potelé, planturcux; **-ness** *n.* embonpoint *m.*

plunder *n.* pillage, butin *m.*; **— vt.** piller, spolier

plunge *vt.* plonger; **—· vi.** se plonger; (se) jeter; **-r** *n.* plongeon *m.*; piston *m.*; (person) risque-tout *m.*

pluperfect *n.* plus-que-parfait *m.*

plural *n. & a.* pluriel *m.*; **-ity** *n.* pluralité *f.*

plus *prep.* plus

plush *n.* peluche *f.*; **— a.** (coll.) somptueux, élégant

plutocracy *n.* plutocratie *f.*

plutocrat *n.* ploutocrate *m.*

plutonium *n.* plutonium *m.*

ply *n.* épaisseur *f.*; **— vt.** se servir de; accabler, offrir

plywood *n.* bois contreplaqué *m.*

P.M. de l'après-midi, du soir

pneumatic *a.* pneumatique

pneumonia *n.* pneumonie *f.*; fluxion de poitrine *f.*

poach *vt.* pocher; **— vi.** piller; braconner; **-er** *n.* braconnier *m.*

pocket *n.* poche *f.*; (billiards) blouse *f.*; **— book** livre de poche *m.*; **-knife** couteau de poche *m.*; **— vt.** empocher; blouser; avaler (un affront)

pocketbook *n.* (ladies) sac *m.*

pock-marked *a.* grêlé

pod *n.* cosse, écale *f.*

poem *n.* poème *m*

poet *n.* poète *m.*; **-ic(al)** *a.* poétique; **-ics** *n.* art poétique *m.*; **-ry** *n.* poésie *f.*

poignancy *n.* piquant *m.*

poignant *a.* piquant; douloureux, aigu

point *n.* pointe *f.*; cap *m.*; point, moment *m.*; degré *m.*; lieu *m.*; but *m.*; sujet *m.*, idée *f.*; (math.) virgule *f.*; **— blank** directement, de but en blanc; **— of departure** point de départ *m.*; **— of view** point de vue *m.*; **in — of** fact en fait; **make a — of** faire un devoir de; **to the — à** propos; **to the — of** jusqu'à; **— vt.** pointer; aiguiser, affiler; **— out** montrer, signaler; **— up** (coll.) souligner; **-ed** *a.* pointu; piquant, mordant; marqué; **-er** *n.* (dog) chien d'arrêt *m.*; aiguille *f.*; baguette *f.*; **-less** *a.* sans pointe; sans but, sans raison

poise *vt.* tenir suspendu; tenir prêt; **— vi.** se tenir suspendu, se tenir prêt; **— n.** sang-froid, savoir-faire *m.*; équilibre *m.*; **-d** *a.* bien équilibré, suave, imperturbable

poison *n.* poison *m.*; **— vt.** empoisonner; **-ing** *n.* empoisonnement *m.*; **-ous** *a.* empoisonné; venimeux; (plants) vénéneux

poke *n.* coup de poing *m.*; (coll.) sac *m.*; **— vi.** fouiller; **— vt.** donner un coup de poing à; taper; (head) passer; (fire) tisonner; **-r** *n.* tisonnier *m.*; (game) poker *m.*

Poland *n.* Pologne *f.*

polar *a.* polaire; **-ity** *n.* polarité *f.*; **-ize** *vt.* polariser

pole *n.* pôle *m.*; perche *f.*; timon *m.*; poteau *m.*; **— vault** saut à la perche *m.*

Pole *n.* Polonais *m.*

polecat *n.* putois *m.*

polemic *n.* polémique *f.*

police *n.* police *f.*; — chief, chief of — *n.* commissaire de police *m.*; — court *n.* tribunal de police *m.*; — dog berger allemand *m.*; — headquarters, — station commissariat de police *m.*; — *vt.* surveiller, policer

policeman *n.* agent de police *m.*

policewoman *n.* femme-agent de police *f.*

policy *n.* politique *f.*; ruse *f.*; police *f.*; plan *m.*; insurance — police d'assurance *f.*

polio(myelitis) *n.* poliomyélite *f.*

polish *n.* poli *m.*; élégance *f.*; — *vt.* polir; vernir; cirer

Polish *a. & n.* polonais *m.*

polite *a.* poli; courtois; -ness *n.* politesse *f.*; courtoisie *f.*

politic *a.* politique; prudent, judicieux; -al *a.* politique; -s *n.* politique *f.*

politician *n.* politicien *m.*

polka *n.* polka *f.*; — dot *n.* rond de couleur *m.*; pois *m.*

poll *n.* liste électorale *f.*; enquête *f.*; voix *f.*, vote *m.*; -s *n. pl.* urnes *f. pl.*; — tax *n.* capitation *f.*; — *vt.* consulter; voter

pollen *n.* pollen *m.*

pollinate *vt.* féconder

polling booth *n.* isoloir; bureau de scrutin *m.*

pollute *vt.* polluer; souiller

pollution *n.* pollution *f.*; souillure *f.*

polo *n.* polo *m.*; — shirt maillot *m.*

poltroon *n.* poltron, lâche *m.*

polygamous *a.* polygame

polygamy *n.* polygamie *f.*

polyglot *n. & a.* polyglotte *m.*

polygon *n.* polygone *m.*; -al *a.* polygone

polygraph *n.* polygraphe *m.*

polymer chemistry *n.* chimie polymère *f.*

Polynesia *n.* Polynésie *f.*; -n *a. & n.* polynésien *m.*

polyp *n.* polype *m.*

polyphonic *a.* polyphonique

polyphony *n.* polyphonie *f.*

polysyllabic *a.* polysyllabe

polysyllable *n.* polysyllabe *m.*

polytechnic *a.* polytechnique

pomade *n.* pommade *f.*

pomegranate *n.* grenade *f.*; (tree) grenadier *m.*

pommel *n.* pommeau *m.*; — *vt.* rosser

pomp *n.* pompe *f.*, éclat *m.*, faste *m.*; -ous *a.* pompeux; ampoulé; suffisant; -ousness *n.* suffisance *f.*; emphase *f.*

pompadour *n.* coiffure à la Pompadour *f.*

pompom *n.* (mil.) canon-mitrailleuse *m.*

pond *n.* étang *m.*; vivier *m.*; mare *f.*

ponder *vt. & vi.* peser; méditer; –able *a.* pondérable; -ous *a.* pesant

pontiff *n.* pontife *m.*

pontifical *a.* pontifical

pontificate *n.* pontificat *m.*; — *vi.* parler ex-cathedra; pontifier

pontoon *n.* ponton *m.*

pony *n.* poney *m.*; (educ.) traduction *f.* (utilisée par un élève pour éviter de traduire lui-même)

pony tail *n.* (hair) queue de cheval *f.*

poodle *n.* caniche *f.*

pool *n.* étang *m.*; mare *f.*; (swimming) piscine *f.*; (game) billard (à blouses) *m.*; (betting) poule *f.*; exploitation en commun *f.*; dépôt *m.*; — *vt.* mettre en commun, exploiter en commun; — room *n.* salle de billard *f.*

poop *n.* poupe *f.*; (coll.) potins *m. pl.*

poor *a.* pauvre; indigent; mauvais; inférieur; — *n.* pauvres *m. pl.*; -ness *n.* pauvreté *f.*; infériorité *f.*

poorhouse *n.* maison de charité *f.*, refuge *m.*

pop *n.* petit coup *m.*; (coll.) père *m.*; (beverage) soda *m.*, boisson gazeuse; — *vi.* éclater; — *vt.* faire éclater; — in (coll.) entrer en passant; — up arriver; apparaître; — *interj.* crac!

popcorn *n.* maïs éclaté *m.*

Pope *n.* pape *m.*; (Greek Church) pope *m.*

popgun *n.* canonnière *f.*

poplar *n.* peuplier *m.*

poplin *n.* popeline *f.*

populace *n.* populace *f.*

popular *a.* populaire; à la mode; -ity *n.* popularité *f.*; -ize *vt.* populariser

populate *vt.* peupler

population *n.* population *f.*

populous *a.* populeux

porcelain *n.* porcelaine *f.*

porch *n.* porche, portique *m.*, véranda *f.*

porcine *a.* de porc

porcupine *n.* porc-épic *m.*

pore *n.* pore *m.*; — *vi.* avoir les yeux fixés; — over dévorer; méditer; être absorbé dans

pork *n.* porc *m.*; — chop côtelette de porc *f.*; -er *n.* porc, cochon *m.*

pornographic *a.* pornographique

pornography *n.* pornographie *f.*

porosity *n.* porosité *f.*

porous *a.* poreux

porphyry *n.* porphyre *m.*

porpoise *n.* marsouin *m.*

porridge *n.* bouillie *f.*

port *n.* port *m.*; (gun opening) sabord *m.*; (wine) porto *m.*; (side) bâbord *m.*; (hole) hublot *m.*; — *vt.* (arms) porter; (naut.) mettre à bâbord

portable *a.* portatif
portage *n.* portage *m.*
portal *n.* portail *m.*, porte *f.*
portend *vt.* présager
portent *n.* présage *m.*; −ous *a.* de mauvais augure
porter *n.* portier *m.*; porteur, portefaix *m.*
porterhouse *n.* châteaubreant *m.*
portfolio *n.* portefeuille *m.*; carton *m.*
portico *n.* portique *m.*
portion *n.* portion, part, partie *f.*; dot *m.*; — *vt.* partager; doter
portliness *n.* embonpoint *m.*
portly *a.* corpulent
portrait *n.* portrait *m.*; — painter portraitiste *m.*
portray *vt.* peindre, dépeindre, décrire; −al *n.* portrait *m.*; peinture *f.*; description *f.*
Portugal *n.* Portugal *m.*
Portuguese *a. & n.* portuguais *m.*
pose *n.* pose, attitude *f.*; — *vt.* poser; proposer; — as se faire passer pour; confondre (avec)
position *n.* position, situation *f.*; attitude, posture *f.*; thèse *f.*; in a — to à même de; in — en place; — *vt.* situer
positive *n.* positif *m.*; — *a.* positif; certain, sûr, assuré; affirmatif; vrai; −ly *adv.* positivement; certainement
positivism *n.* positivisme *m.*
positron *n.* positron *m.*
posse *n.* force publique d'un comté; milice *f.*
possess *vt.* posséder; jouir de; avoir; disposer de; be −ed of posséder; −ion *n.* possession *f.*; −ive *a.* possessif; −or *n.* possesseur *m.*
possibility *n.* possibilité *f.*; moyen *m.*; éventualité *f.*
possible *a.* possible; éventuel; if — si (c'est) possible
possibly *adv.* peut-être
post *n.* poste *f.*; courrier *m.*; poste, emploi *m.*; poteau *m.*; pilier *m.*; pieu (x) *m.* (*m. pl.*) (mil.) (lieu de) garnison *f.*; — office bureau de poste *m.*; — *vt.* afficher; mettre à la poste; — no bills défense d'afficher; −al *a.* postal; −er *n.* affiche *f.*
postage *n.* affranchissement *m.*; — due letter lettre taxée *f.*; — meter compteur d'affranchissement *m.*; — stamp timbre-poste *m.*
post card *n.* carte postale *f.*
postdate *vt.* postdater
posterior *a.* postérieur; — *n.* postérieur, derrière *m.*
posterity *n.* postérité *f.*
postgraduate *n.* étudiant *m.* (qui poursuit des études au-delà du baccalauréat)
posthaste *adv.* promptement, en grande diligence; en grand hâte
posthumous *a.* posthume
postilion *n.* postillon *m.*
postman *n.* facteur *m.*
postmark *n.* oblitération *f.*
postmaster *n.* receveur des postes *m.*
post-mortem *n.* (med.) autopsie *f.*; — *a. & adv.* après décès
postpaid *a.* port payé; — *adv.* franco
postpone *vt.* remettre, différer; −ment *n.* ajournement *m.*
postscript, P.S. *n.* post-scriptum *m.*
postulate *n.* postulat *m.*; — *vt.* poser, postuler
posture *n.* posture, attitude; pose *f.*
postwar *a.* d'après-guerre
pot *n.* pot *m.*; −herb herbe potagère *f.*; — roast estouffade *f.*; take −luck courir la fortune du pot; — *vt.* mettre en pot
potable *a.* potable
potash *n.* potasse *f.*
potato *n.* pomme de terre *f.*; baked — pomme au four *f.*; boiled — pomme à l'anglaise *f.*; fried −es (pommes) frites *f.*; mashed −es purée de pommes *f.*; sweet — patate *f.*; — masher pressepurée *m.*
potbellied *a.* ventru
potency *n.* puissance, force *f.*
potent *a.* puissant, fort; −ate *n.* potentat *m.*; −ial *a.* virtuel, potentiel, latent; −iality *n.* potentialité *f.*
potholder *n.* poignée pour les pots chauds *f.*
potion *n.* breuvage *m.*; philtre *m.*
potshot *n.* coup tiré sans viser *m.*
potter *n.* potier *f.*; −y *n.* poterie *f.*
pouch *n.* poche, pochette *f.*; bourse *f.*
poultice *n.* cataplasme *f.*
poultry *n.* volaille *f.*; — yard *n.* basse-cour *f.*
pounce *vi.* fondre, se précipiter
pound *n.* livre *f.*; livre sterling *f.*; (animal) fourrière *f.*; — *vt.* piler, broyer; −age *n.* (taux de) poids *m.*
pour *vt.* verser, épancher; — *vi.* pleuvoir à verse; couler rapidement; se précipiter avec violence; — off décanter; — out verser; épancher; sortir en foule
pout *vi.* bouder, faire la moue; — *n.* moue *f.*
poverty *n.* pauvreté, indigence *f.*; misère *f.*
poverty-stricken *a.* dans la misère
powder *n.* poudre *f.*; — puff houppe *f.*; — *vt.* pulvériser; poudrer, saupoudrer; −y *a.* poudreux

power *n.* pouvoir *m.*, puissance, faculté, force *f.*; autorité *f.*; **-ful** *a.* puissant; **fort**; **-less** *a.* impuissant; **-lessness** impuissance *f.*

powwow *n.* réunion, conférence *f.*; — *vi.* se réunir

practicability *n.* praticabilité *f.*

practicable *a.* praticable, faisable

practical *a.* pratique; — joke canular *m.*, farce *f.*; — nurse infirmière non-diplômée *f.*; **-ly** *adv.* en pratique; presque

practice *n.* pratique *f.*, habilité *f.*; expérience *f.*; coutume *f.*; habitude *f.*; méthode *f.*; clientèle *f.*; — *vt.* pratiquer; exercer; répéter; — *vi.* s'exercer; **-d** *a.* expérimenté; habile

practitioner *n.* praticien *m.*; **general** — médecin non-spécialisé *m.*

pragmatic *a.* pragmatique

prairie *n.* prairie *f.*; — dog *n.* marmotte des prairies *f.*

praise *n.* louange *f.*; éloge *m.*; — *vt.* louer; célébrer; **-worthy** *a.* louable, méritoire

praline *n.* bonbon au praliné *m.*

prance *vi.* piaffer; se pavaner; se cabrer

prancing *a.* fringant; — *n.* action de se cabrer *f.*

prank *n.* folie *f.*; farce *f.*, tour *m.*

prate *vi.* caqueter, jaser

prattle *n.* babil *m.*; — *vi.* babiller, jaser

pray *vt.* & *vi.* prier; **-er** *n.* prière *f.*; **Lord's -er** *n.* patenôtre, oraison dominicale *f.*

preach *vt.* & *vi.* prêcher; **-er** *n.* prédicateur *m.*; prêcheur *m.*; ministre *m.*; **-ing** *n.* prédication *f.*

preamble *n.* préambule *m.*

prearrange *vt.* arranger au préalable

precarious *a.* précaire

precaution *n.* précaution *f.*; **-ary** *a.* préventif

precede *vt.* précéder, devancer; préfacer; **-nce** *n.* préséance *f.*; priorité *f.*; **-nt** *n.* précédent *m.*

preceding *a.* précédent

precept *n.* précepte *m.*; **-or** *n.* précepteur *m.*

precinct *n.* borne, limite *f.*; circonscription électorale *f.*

precious *a.* précieux; **-ness** *n.* valeur *f.*

precipice *n.* précipice *m.*

precipitate *n.* précipité *m.*; — *vt.* précipiter; hâter; — *vi.* (se) précipiter; — *a.* précipité

precipitation *n.* précipitation *f.*

precipitous *a.* précipité, rapide; escarpé

precise *a.* précis, exact; scrupuleux; **-ly** *adv.* précisément; avec précision; **-ness** *n.* précision *f.*

precision *n.* précision *f.*

preclude *vt.* exclure; empêcher

precocious *a.* précoce; **-ness** *n.* précocité *f.*

precocity *n.* précocité *f.*

preconceive *vt.* concevoir d'avance; **-d** *a.* préconçu

preconception *n.* préconception *f.*

precursor *n.* précurseur *m.*; avant-coureur *m.*

predatory *a.* rapace; de rapine

predecessor *n.* prédécesseur, devancier *m.*

predestination *n.* prédestination *f.*

predestine *vt.* prédestiner

predetermine *vt.* prédéterminer, déterminer d'avance

predicament *n.* mauvais pas *m.*; situation difficile *f.*

predicate *n.* prédicat *m.*; attribut *m.*; — *vt.* affirmer

predict *vt.* prédire; **-ion** *n.* prédiction *f.*

predilection *n.* prédilection, partialité *f.*

predispose *vt.* prédisposer

predisposition *n.* prédisposition *f.*

predominance *n.* ascendant *m.*; prédomination *f.*

predominant *a.* prédominant

predominate *vi.* prédominer

pre-eminence *n.* prééminence *f.*

pre-eminent *a.* prééminent

pre-emption *n.* préemption *f.*

preen *vt.* lisser, ajuster; — oneself faire des grâces

pre-established *a.* pré-établi

pre-existent *a.* pré-existant

prefabricate *vt.* préfabriquer

preface *n.* préface *f.*; — *vt.* préfacer

prefatory *a.* préliminaire

prefect *n.* préfet *m.*; **-ure** *n.* préfecture *f.*

prefer *vt.* préférer; présenter, apporter; **-able** *a.* préférable; **-ence** *n.* préférence *f.*; **-ential** *a.* privilégié; **-red** *a.* préféré; **-red stock** action de priorité *f.*

prefix *n.* préfixe *m.*; — *vt.* mettre devant

pregnant *a.* enceinte

preheat *vt.* faire chauffer au préalable

prehensile *a.* préhensile

prehistoric *a.* préhistorique

prejudge *vt.* préjuger

prejudice *n.* préjugé *m.*; prévention *f.*; — *vt.* être préjudiciable pour; prévenir; **be -d** avoir des préjugés

prejudicial *a.* préjudiciable

preliminary *a.* & *n.* préliminaire *m.*

prelude *n.* prélude *m.*; — *vt.* préluder

premature *a.* prématuré

premedical *a.* qui prépare la médecine; qui précède les cours de médecine

premeditate *vt.* préméditer; **-d** *a.* prémédité, réfléchi

premeditation *n.* préméditation *f.*

premier *n.* premier ministre *m.*; (France) président du conseil *m.*

première *n.* première, générale *f.*

premise *n.* prémisse *f.*; –s *pl.* locaux *m. pl.*; — *vt.* poser

premium *n.* prime *f.*; récompense *f.*; at a — à prime; en prime

premonition *n.* prémonition *f.*

prenatal *a.* prénatal

preoccupation *n.* préoccupation *f.*

preoccupy *vt.* préoccuper

preordain *vt.* préordonner, ordonner d'avance

prepaid *a.* payé d'avance; franc de port; — *adv.* franco

preparation *n.* préparation *f.*; –s *pl.* préparatifs *m. pl.*

preparatory *a.* préparatoire, préliminaire; — school lycée *m.*, école secondaire *f.*

prepare *vt.* préparer; apprêter; — *vi.* se préparer, s'apprêter; — for préparer

prepay *vt.* payer d'avance; envoyer franco; –ment *n.* paiement d'avance *m.*; affranchissement *m.*

preponderance *n.* prépondérance *f.*

preponderant *a.* prépondérant

preposition *n.* préposition *f.*; –al *a.* prépositif, prépositionnel

prepossess *vt.* pénétrer, préoccuper; –ed *a.* pénétré, imprégné; –ing *a.* prévenant, engageant

preposterous *a.* absurde; déraisonnable; –ness *n.* absurdité *f.*

prerequisite *n.* nécessité préalable *f.*; condition nécessaire *f.*; cours obligatoire *m.*

prerogative *n.* prérogative *f.*

presage *n.* présage *m.*; — *vt.* présager; augurer

prescience *n.* prescience *f.*

prescribe *vt.* prescrire; (med.) ordonner; — *vi.* (med.) faire une ordonnance; faire la loi

prescription *n.* (law) prescription *f.*; (med.) ordonnance *f.*

presence *n.* présence *f.*; — of mind sangfroid *m.*, présence d'esprit *f.*; in the — of en présence de

present *n.* (time) présent *m.*; (gift) cadeau *m.*; at — à present, actuellement, en ce moment; –s *pl.* (law) présentes *f. pl.*; — *vt.* présenter, offrir; — *a.* présent; actuel, courant; –able *a.* présentable; –ation *n.* présentation *f.*: –ly *adv.* tout à l'heure; à présent

present-day *a.* d'aujourd'hui

presentiment *n.* pressentiment *m.*

preservation *n.* préservation *f.*; conservation *f.*

preservative *a. & n.* préservatif *m.*

preserve *n.* conserve *f.*; refuge (pour animaux) *m.*; réserve *f.*; — *vt.* préserver; conserver; mettre en conserve

preside *vi.* présider

presidency *n.* présidence *f.*

president *n.* président *m.*; –ial *a.* présidentiel

press *n.* presse *f.*; force *f.*; (clothing) armoire *f.*; imprimerie *f.*; in — sous presse; — *vt.* presser, (se) serrer; appuyer; exprimer; harceler; insister; (iron) repasser; –ing *a.* pressant; –ing *n.* repassage *m.*

pressure *n.* pression *f.*; presse *f.*; urgence *f.*; blood — tension artérielle *f.*; high blood — hypertension *f.*; — cooker marmite norvégienne *f.*; autoclave *m.*; — group groupe organisé pour influencer les autres; un bloc de politique

pressurize *vt.* maintenir la pression atmosphérique (dans)

prestige *n.* prestige *m.*

presumable *a.* présumable

presumably *adv.* à ce qu'il paraît, vraisemblablement

presume *vt.* présumer, supposer

presuming *a.* présomptueux

presumption *n.* présomption *f.*

presumptive *a.* présomptif

presumptuous *a.* présomptueux; –ness *n.* présomption *f.*

presuppose *vt.* présupposer

pretend *vi.* faire semblant (de); — *vt.* feindre, simuler; –er *n.* prétendant *m*

pretense *n.* prétention *f.*; prétexte *m.*

pretension *n.* prétention *f.*

pretentious *a.* prétentieux; –ness *n.* prétention *f.*

preterit *n.* (gram.) prétérit, passé *m.*

preternatural *a.* surnaturel

pretext *n.* prétexte *m.*; on the — of sous prétexte de

prettiness *n.* gentillesse, élégance *f.*; beauté *f.*

pretty *a.* joli; gentil; — *adv.* assez

pretzel *n.* bretzel *m.*

prevail *vi.* prévaloir; régner; –ing *a.* régnant, courant; commun, ordinaire

prevalence *n.* étendue, généralité *f.*

prevalent *a.* dominant, répandu, général

prevaricate *vi.* prévariquer; tergiverser

prevaricator *n.* prévaricateur *m.*

prevent *vt.* prévenir; empêcher (de); –able *a.* évitable; –ion *n.* prévention *f.*; empêchement *m.*; –ive *a. & n.* préventif *m.*

preview *n.* examen préliminaire *m.*; (film) avant-première *f.*; — *vt.* examiner d'avance

previous *a.* préalable; précédant; antérieur; –ly *adv.* auparavant

prewar *a.* d'avant-guerre

prey *n.* proie *f.*; **fall — to** être en proie à; — *vi.* piller, ronger; — **on** tourmenter; attaquer, piller

price *n.* prix *m.*, valeur *f.*; — **control** prix dirigé *m.*; **sale —** prix de vente *m.*; prix de réclame *m.*; –**list** prix-courant *m.*; **at any —** à tout prix; — *vt.* évaluer, mettre le prix à; demander le prix de; –**less** *a.* sans prix, inestimable

prick *n.* piqûre *f.*; — *vt.* piquer, percer; éperonner; tourmenter; **to — up one's ears** dresser les oreilles; –**ly** *a.* piquant; –**ly heat** lichen *m.*; –**ly pear** fruit de cactus *m.*

pride *n.* orgueil *m.*; fierté *f.*; — *vt.*, — **oneself on** s'enorgueillir de, se vanter de

priest *n.* prêtre *m.*; –**hood** *n.* prêtrise *f.*; sacerdoce *m.*; –**ly** *a.* de prêtre; sacerdotal

prig *n.* fat *m.*; prude *m.*; –**gish** *a.* pédant, fat

prim *a.* réservé; soigné; guindé

primacy *n.* primaute *f.*

primarily *adv.* surtout, principalement

primary *a.* primaire, primitif; principal

prime *n.* perfection *f.*; élite *f.*; fleur, force *f.*, printemps *m.*; (math.) nombre premier *m.*; — *vt.* amorcer; préparer; — *a.* premier; de meilleure qualité; principal; — **minister** premier ministre *m.*

primer *n.* premier livre, abécédaire *m.*; amorce *f.*; **great –er** (print.) corps 18 *m.*; **long –er** (print.) corps 10 *m.*

primeval *a.* primitif, vierge

priming *n.* amorce *f.*; préparation *f.*

primitive *a.* primitif; –**ness** *n.* rudesse *f.*

primordial *a.* primordial

primp *vi.* se parer

prince *n.* prince *m.*; –**ly** *a.* princier

princess *n.* princesse *f.*

principal *n.* chef *m.*; directeur *m.*; proviseur *m.*; — *a.* principal, premier

principality *n.* principauté *f.*

principle *n.* principe *m.*

print *n.* empreinte, impression; caractères d'impimerie *m. pl.*; (phot.) épreuve *f.*; **out of —** épuisé; — *vt.* imprimer; (phot.) tirer (des épreuves); écrire en caractères d'imprimerie; –**ed matter** imprimés *m. pl.*; –**er** *n.* imprimeur *m*: –**er's devil** apprenti imprimeur *m*: –**er's ink** encre d'imprimerie *f.*; –**ing** *n.* impression; (phot.) tirage *m.*; –**ing press** presse (à imprimer) *f.*; — **shop** *n.* imprimerie *f.*

prior *a.* antérieur; — **to** avant; –**ity** *n.* priorité *f.*; — *n.* (eccl.) prieur *m.*; –**y** *n.* prieuré *m.*

prism *n.* prisme *m.*; –**atic** *a.* prismatique

prison *n.* prison *f.*; –**er** *n.* prisonnier *m.*

pristine *a.* primitif, ancien

privacy *n.* secret, isolement *m.*, retraite, solitude *f.*; intimité *f.*

private *n.* simple soldat *m.*; — *a.* privé, particulier; secret, retiré; — **house** maison particulière *f.*

privateer *n.* corsaire *m.*; –**ing** *n.* course *f.*

privilege *n.* privilège *m.*; prérogative *f.*; — *vt.* privilégier

privy *a.* privé, particulier; secret; — *n.* cabinets *m. pl.*

prize *n.* prix *m.*; récompense *f.*; prise *f.*; lot *m.*; — **fight** *n.* partie de boxe *f.*; — *vt.* évaluer, faire cas de; — **fighter** *n.* boxeur *m.*

pro *prep. & adv.* pour; — **and con** pour et contre; — *n.* professionnel *m.*

probability *n.* probabilité *f.*; vraisemblance *f.*

probable *a.* probable; vraisemblable

probate *n.* (law) vérification, homologation *f.*; — *vt.* valider (un testament)

probation *n.* épreuve *f.*; noviciat *m.*; sursis (avec surveillance) *m.*; –**ary** *a.* d'épreuve

probe *n.* sonde *f.*; — *vt.* sonder

problem *n.* problème *m.*; –**atical** *a.* problématique

procedure *n.* procédé *m.*; procédure *f.*

proceed *vi.* procéder; provenir, poursuivre; continuer; –**ings** *n. pl.* procédure *f.*; délibérations *f. pl.*; –**s** *n. pl.* produit, revenu *m.*

process *n.* progrès, cours *m.*; procédé *m.*; procès *m.*; — *vt.* traiter; developper; –**ion** *n.* procession *f.*; cortège *m.*

proclaim *vt.* proclamer, déclarer

proclamation *n.* proclamation *f.*, édit *m.*

proclivity *n.* inclination *f.*, penchant *m.*

procrastinate *vi.* temporiser, s'attarder, hésiter

procrastinator *n.* temporisateur *m.*

procreate *vt.* procréer

procreation *n.* procréation *f.*

proctor *n.* avoué *m.*; censeur *m*: surveillant *m.*; pion *m.*

procurable *a.* qui peut se procurer

procure *vt.* procurer; –**ment** *n.* aquisition *f.*; ravitaillement *m.*; –**r** *n.* entremetteur *m.*

prod *n.* aiguillon *m.*; — *vt.* piquer; aiguillonner; pousser

prodigal *a. & n.* prodigue *m.*; –**ity** *n.* prodigalité *f.*

prodigious *a.* prodigieux

prodigy *n.* prodige *m.*

produce *n.* produit *m.*; denrées *f. pl.*; — *vt.* produire; faire, fabriquer; exhiber; (theat.) monter; –**r** *n.* producteur *m.*;

(theat.) directeur *m.*

product *n.* produit *m.*; **–ion** *n.* production *f.*; fabrication *f.*; produit *m.*; **–ive** *a.* productif; **–ivity** *n.* productivité *f.*

profane *vt.* profaner; — *a.* profane; blasphématoire

profanity *n.* juron *m.*; emploi de jurons *m.*; impiété *f.*

profess *vt.* professer, faire profession de; **–ed** *a.* déclaré; (eccl.) profès; **–edly** *adv.* ouvertement; **–ion** *n.* profession *f.*; metier *m.*; **–ional** *n.* professionnel *m.*; **–ional** *a.* professionnel; de carrière, de métier; **–or** *n.* professeur *m.*; **–orial** *a.* professoral; **–orship** *n.* professorat *m.*; chaire de professeur *f.*

proffer *n.* offre, proposition *f.*; — *vt.* proposer, offrir

proficiency *n.* capacité *f.*; connaissance *f.*; niveau *m.*

proficient *a.* habile; capable; ayant atteint un niveau déterminé

profile *n.* profil *m.*; — *vt.* profiler

profit *n.* profit, gain, avantage *m.*; produit, revenu *m.*; bénéfice *m.*; — *vt. & vi.* profiter; être utile; — **by** profiter de; **–able** *a.* profitable, avantageux; **–eer** *vi.* gagner des bénéfices démesurés; **–eer** *n.* profiteur *m.*; **–eering** *n.* mercantilisme *m.*; **–less** *a.* sans profit; — **sharing** *n.* participation aux bénéficies *f.*

profligate *n. & a.* débauché *m.*

profound *a.* profond; **–ly** *adv.* profondément

profundity *n.* profondeur *f.*

profuse *a.* prodigue; abondant; **–ness** *n.* profusion *f.*; **–ly** *adv.* excessivement

profusion *n.* profusion *f.*; abondance *f.*; prodigalité *f.*

progenitor *n.* ancêtre *m.*

progeny *n.* progéniture *f.*; lignée *f.*

prognosis *n.* (med.) prognose *f.*, pronostic *m.*

prognostic *n.* pronostic *m.*; **–ate** *vt.* prognostiquer; **–ation** *n.* prognostication *f.*, pronostic *m.*

program *n.* programme *m.*; — *vt.* établir un programme pour

progress *n.* progrès *m.*; **in** — en cours, en voie; — *vi.* faire des progrès; **–ion** *n.* progression *f.*; **–ive** *a.* progressif; (pol.) progressiste

prohibit *vt.* prohiber; défendre; interdire; **–ion** *n.* prohibition, défense *f.*; **–ive** *a.* prohibitif

project *n.* projet, dessein *m.*; — *vt.* projeter; — *vi.* saillir; **–ile** *n.* projectile *m.*; **–ion** *n.* projection *f.*; saillie *f.*; **–or** *n.* projecteur *m.*

proletarian *a.* prolétaire, prolétarien; —

n. prolétaire *m. & f.*

proletariat *n.* prolétariat *m.*

prolific *a.* prolifique, fertile

prologue *n.* prologue *m.*

prolong *vt.* prolonger; **–ation** *n.* prolongation *f.*, prolongement *m.*

promenade *n.* promenade *f.*; bal *m.*; — *vi.* se promener

prominence *n.* proéminence *f.*; éminence *f.*

prominent *a.* proéminent; éminent; prononcé; (qui est) très en vue; **–ly** *adv.* très en vue

promiscuous *a.* mêlé; confus; au hasard; libre, sans contrainte

promise *n.* promesse *f.*; espérances *f. pl.*; avenir *m.*; **break a** — manquer de parole; — *vt. & vi.* promettre

promissory *a.* qui contient une promesse; — **note** *n.* billet à ordre *m.*

promontory *n.* promontoire *m.*

promote *vt.* promouvoir, avancer; élever; encourager; **–r** *n.* homme d'affaires *m.*, animateur *m.*; auteur *m.*; promoteur *m.*

promotion *n.* promotion *f.*; avancement *m.*; publicité, réclame *f.*

prompt *vt.* souffler; suggérer; — *a.* prompt; immédiat; **–er** *n.* souffleur *m.*; **–ly** *adv* promptement; ponctuellement; immédiatement, sur-le-champ; à l'heure; **–ness** *n.* promptitude *f.*

promulgate *vt.* promulguer, publier

promulgation *n.* promulgation *f.*

prone *a.* couché le visage contre terre; — **to** enclin à, susceptible de

prong *n.* fourchon *m.*; dent *f.*; **–ed** *a.* à fourchons, à dents

pronominal *a.* pronominal

pronoun *n.* pronom *m.*

pronounce *vt.* prononcer; articuler; **–able** *a.* prononçable; **–d** *a.* prononcé, marqué; **–ment** *n.* déclaration *f.*

pronunciation *n.* prononciation *f.*

proof *n.* preuve *f.*; épreuve *f.*; épreuves *f. pl.*; essai *m.*; — *a.* à l'épreuve (de); impénétrable

proofread *vt.* corriger les epreuves de; **–er** *n.* correcteur *m.*; **–ing** *n.* correction *f.*

prop *n.* appui, soutien *m.*; étai *m.*; (theat.) accessoire *m.*; — *vt.* appuyer, soutenir; étayer

propaganda *n.* propagande *f.*

propagandist *n.* propagandiste *m.*

propagate *vt.* propager; répandre; — *vi.* se propager, se reproduire

propagation *n.* propagation *f.*; dissémination *f.*

propel *vt.* pousser en avant; **–lant** *n.* propulseur *m.*; **–ler** *n.* hélice *f.*

propensity *n.* penchant *m.*, inclination *f.*

proper *a.* propre; bon; convenable; comme il faut; exact; **-ly** *adv.* proprement; correctement; comme il faut

property *n.* propriété, qualité *f.*; possession *f.*; (theat.) accessoire *m.*

prophecy *n.* prophétie *f.*

prophesy *vt. & vi.* prophétiser

prophet *n.* prophète *m.*; **-ic** *a.* prophétique

prophylactic *a.* prophylactique

prophylaxis *n.* prophylaxie *f.*

propinquity *n.* proximité *f.*

propitiate *vt.* rendre propice; apaiser

propitious *a.* propice, favorable

proponent *n.* partisan *m.*

proportion *n.* proportion *f.*; mesure *f.*; **in — as** à mesure que; **in — to** en proportion de, proportionné à; **—** *vt.* proportionner; **-al** *a.* proportionnel; **-ate** *a.* proportionné; **-ed** *a.* proportionné

proposal *n.* proposition, offre *f.*; plan, projet *m.*; demande (en mariage) *f.*

propose *vt.* proposer; avoir l'intention de; **—** *vi.* se déclarer, faire une déclaration, faire une demande en mariage

proposition *n.* proposition *f.*; offre *f.*

propound *vt.* proposer, offrir; poser

proprietary *a.* de propriété, de propriétaire

proprietor *n.* propriétaire *m. & f.*

propriety *n.* convenance *f.*, décorum *m.*; à-propos *m.*, opportunité *f.*

propulsion *n.* propulsion *f.*

prorate *vt.* répartir

prosaic *a.* prosaïque

proscenium *n.* (theat.) avant-scène *f.*

proscribe *vt.* proscrire, interdire

proscription *n.* proscription *f.*; interdiction *f.*

prose *n.* prose *f.*

prosecute *vt.* poursuivre

prosecution *n.* poursuite *f.*

prosecutor *n.* procureur *m.*; plaignant *m.*

proselyte *n.* prosélyte *m. & f.*

prospect *n.* perspective *f.*; vue *f.*, aspect *m.*; **—** *vi.* prospecter; (min.) faire des recherches; **-ive** *a.* à venir; **-or** *n.* prospecteur *m.*

prospectus *n.* prospectus *m.*

prosper *vi.* prospérer, réussir; **-ity** *n.* prospérité *f.*; **-ous** *a.* prospère

prostitute *n.* prostituée *f.*; **—** *vt.* prostituer

prostrate *vt.* renverser, abattre; prosterner; accabler; **—** *a.* prosterné; (med.) prostré; **-d** *a.* abattu

prostration *n.* prosternation *f.*; abattement *m.*; (med.) prostration *f.*

protagonist *n.* protagoniste *m.*

protect *vt.* protéger, défendre; sauvegarder; patronner; **-ion** *n.* protection,

défense *f.*; sauvegarde *f.*; abri *m.*; patronage *m.*; **-ive** *a.* protecteur; préservatif; **-or** *n.* protecteur *m.*; protectrice *f.*; **-orate** *n.* protectorat *m.*

protein *n.* protéine *f.*

protest *n.* protestation *f.*; représentation *f.*; **under —** sous réserve; **—** *vt. & vi.* protester; **-ation** *n.* protestation *f.*

protocol *n.* protocole *m.*

proton *n.* proton *m.*

protoplasm *n.* protoplasme *m.*

prototype *n.* prototype, archétype *m.*

protozoa *n. pl.* protozoaires *m. pl.*

protract *vt.* prolonger; traîner; **-ion** *n.* prolongation *f.*; relevé *m.*; **-or** *n.* (math.) rapporteur *m.*

protrude *vi.* s'avancer, faire saillie; **—** *vt.* pousser dehors

protruding *a.* saillant; en saillie; débordant

protrusion *n.* protubérance, saillie *f.*

protuberance *n.* protubérance *f.*

proud *a.* orgueilleux, fier; superbe

provable *a.* démontrable

prove *vt.* prouver; éprouver; démontrer; vérifier; **—** *vi.* se trouver; se montrer

provender *n.* provende *f.*; fourrage *m.*; nourriture *f.*

proverb *n.* proverbe *m.*; **-ial** *a.* proverbial

provide *vt.* pourvoir, fournir, munir; **—** *vi.* (se) pourvoir; **-d** *a.* muni, pourvu; **-d that** *conj.* pourvu que; **-r** *n.* pourvoyeur, fournisseur *m.*

provident *a.* prévoyant; **-ial** *a.* providentiel

provincial *a.* provincial; de province; **—** *n.* provincial *m.*

provision *n.* clause *f.*, article *m.*; disposition *f.*; **-s** *pl.* comestibles, vivres *m. pl.*; **—** *vt.* approvisionner, ravitailler; **-al** *a.* provisoire

proviso *n.* condition *f.*

provisory *a.* provisoire

provocation *n.* provocation *f.*; défi *m.*

provocative *a.* provocateur; provocant

provoke *vt.* provoquer; exciter; inciter; irriter; contrarier; défier

provoking *a.* contrariant, irritant

provost *n.* prévôt *m.*

prow *n.* proue *f.*

prowess *n.* prouesse *f.*; vallance *f.*

prowl *vi.* rôder; **-er** *n.* rôdeur *m.*; (inside) cambrioleur *m.*

proximity *n.* proximité *f.*

proxy *n.* procuration *f.*; mandat, mandataire *m.*; délégué *m.*

prude *n.* prude *f.*; **-ry** *n.* pruderie *f.*

prudence *n.* prudence *f.*

prudent *a.* prudent, judicieux
prudish *a.* prude; **-ness** *n.* pruderie *f.*
prune *n.* pruneau *m.*; — *vt.* tailler; élaguer
pruning *n.* taille *f.*; élagage *m.*; — **hook** ébranchoir *m.*; — **knife** sécateur *f.*; — **shears** sécateur *m.*
pry *vt.* soulever; forcer; — *vi.* fouiller (dans); fureter; — *n.* levier *m.*; **-ing** *a.* curieux
psalm *n.* psaume *m.*
Psalter *n.* psautier *m.*
pseudonym *n.* pseudonyme *m.*
psychiatric *a.* psychiatrique
psychiatrist *n.* psychiatre *m.*
psychiatry *n.* psychiatrie *f.*
psychic *a.* psychique
psychoanalist *n.* psychanalyste *m.*
psychological *a.* psychologique
psychologist *n.* psychologue *m.*
psychology *n.* psychologie *f.*
psychopathic *a.* psychopathique
psychosomatic *a.* psychosomatique
ptomaine *n.* ptomaïne *f.*; — **poisoning** intoxication alimentaire *f.*
puberty *n.* puberté *f.*
public *n.* public, peuple *m.*; **in** — en public, publiquement; — *a.* public, publique; **make** — publier, rendre public; — **holiday** fête légale; — **library** bibliothèque municipale *f.*; — **official** fonctionnaire *m.*; — **school** école municipale *f.*; — **spirit** civisme *m.*; — **works** travaux publics; **-ation** *n.* publication *f.*
publicity *n.* publicité *f.*; réclame *f.*
publicize *vt.* publier; faire de la réclame pour
publish *vt.* publier; **just -ed** vient de paraître; **-er** *n.* éditeur *m.*; **-ing** *n.* publication *f.*; **-ing house** maison d'édition *f.*
puck *n.* (sport) palet; lutin *m.*
pucker *n.* pli *m.*; ride *f.*; fronce *f.*; — *vt.* plisser; rider; — *vi.* (se) froncer
puddle *n.* flaque d'eau *f.*; — *vt.* corroyer
pudgy *a.* rondelet; replet
puerile *a.* puéril
Puerto Rico *n.* Porto-Rico *m.*
puff *n.* bouffée *f.*; souffle *m.*; (clothes) bouffant; **powder** — houppe *f.*; — **pastry** pâte feuilletée *f.*; — *vt.* gonfler; fumer; — *vi.* souffler; haleter; **-iness** *n.* boursouflure *f.*; bouffissure *f.*; **-y** *a.* bouffi; boursouflé
pug *n.* (dog) carlin *m.*; — **nose** *n.* nez épaté *m.*
pugilism *n.* pugilat *m.*, boxe *f.*
pugilist *n.* pugiliste, boxeur *m.*
pugnacious *a.* batailleur
pull *n.* traction *f.*; attraction *f.*; appel

m.; poignée *f.*; (coll.) influence *f.*, piston, bras long *m.*; — *vt.* tirer; traîner; — **apart** déchirer; séparer; — **off** enlever; remporter; — **out** tirer, sortir; — **through** guérir; se tirer d'affaire; — (oneself) **together** se reprendre; — **up** remonter; hisser; hausser; s'arrêter; se ranger
pullet *n.* poulette, poularde *f.*
pulley *n.* poulie *f.*; — **block** *n.* moufle *f.*
Pullman *n.* (rail.), — **car** voiture Pullman *f.*; wagon-lit, wagon-salon *m.*
pulmonary *a.* pulmonaire
pulp *n.* pulpe *f.*; pâte *f.*; chair *f.*; **-y** *a.* charnu; pulpeux
pulpit *n.* chaire *f.*
pulsate *vi.* palpiter, vibrer, (se) battre
pulsation *n.* pulsation *f.*, battement *m.*
pulse *n.* pouls *m.*; battement *m.*, pulsation *f.*
pulverization *n.* pulvérisation *f.*
pulverize *vt.* pulvériser; atomiser
pumice *n.* ponce *f.*
pummel *vt.* battre (de coups de poing)
pump *n.* pompe *f.*; (shoe) escarpin *m.*; **air** — pompe à air; — **room** chambre des pompes; buvette *f.*; — *vt.* pomper; — **up** gonfler; faire monter
pumpkin *n.* citrouille *f.*, potiron *m.*
pun *n.* calembour *m.*
punch *n.* poinçon *m.*; perçoir *m.*; emporte-pièce *m.*; coup de poing *m.*; (drink) punch *m.*; — *vt.* poinçonner; percer; donner un coup de poing à; **-ing bag** punching *m.*
Punch and Judy show *n.* guignol *m.*
punctilious *a.* pointilleux
punctual *a.* exact, ponctuel; **-ity** *n.* ponctualité, exactitude *f.*
punctuate *vt.* ponctuer
punctuation *n.* ponctuation *f.*
puncture *n.* piqûre, perforation *f.*; (tire) crevaison *f.*; (med.) ponction *f.*; — *vt.* perforer, crever; ponctionner
puncture-proof *a.* increvable
pungency *n.* odeur forte *f.*; saveur *f.*
pungent *a.* piquant, âcre; mordant
puniness *n.* chétiveté *f.*
punish *vt.* punir, châtier; corriger; **-able** *a.* punissable; **-ment** *n.* punition *f.*; châtiment *m.*; peine *f.*; **capital** — peine capitale *f.*
punitive *a.* punissant; pénal
punt *n.* (sports) coup de volée *m.*; (boating) bateau plat *m.*, plate *f.*
puny *a.* chétif; faible
pup, puppy *n.* petit chien, jeune chien *m.*
pupa *n.* chrysalide *f.*
pupil *n.* (anat.) pupille *f.*; élève *m. & f.*
puppet *n.* marionnette *f.*; pantin *m.*; —

show théâtre de marionnettes *m.*
purchase *n.* achat *m.*, acquisition *f.*, emplette *f.*; prise *f.*, point d'appui *m.*; — *vt.* acheter; **-r** *n.* acheteur *m.*
purchasing agent *n.* acheteur *m.*
pure *a.* pur; **-ly** *adv.* purement; absolument; tout à fait
purgation *n.* purgation *f.*
purgative *a. & n.* purgatif *m.*
purgatory *n.* purgatoire *m.*
purge *n.* purgatif *m.*; purgation *f.*; — *vt.* purger; purifier; épurer
purging *n.* purgation *f.*
purification *n.* purification *f.*; épuration *f.*
purifier *n.* épurateur *m.*
purify *vt.* purifier; épurer
purist *n.* puriste *m. & f.*
puritan *a. & n.* puritain; **-ical** *a.* de puritain
purity *n.* pureté *f.*
purloin *vt.* voler
purple *a. & n.* violet *m.*; (fig.) pourpre *f.*; royal —, imperial — pourpre *f.*
purport *n.* sens *m.*; portée *f.*; — *vt.* avoir la prétention de
purpose *n.* but, objet, dessein *m.*; intention *f.*; fin *f.*; détermination *f.*; for the — of dans le but de; on — exprès; to no — en vain; **-ful** *a.* avisé; réflechi; **-ly** *adv.* exprès; à dessein
purr *vi.* ronronner; **-ing** *n.* ronron *m.*
purse *n.* bourse *f.*; porte-monnaie *m.*; sac à main *m.*; — *vt.* pincer (les lèvres); **-r** *n.* commissaire *m.*
pursuant *adv.* conformément
pursue *vt.* poursuivre; suivre; **-r** *n.* poursuivant *m.*
pursuit *n.* poursuite *f.*; recherche *f.*; profession *f.*; occupation *f.*; in — of à la poursuite de; (fig.) à la recherche de
purvey *vt.* fournir; **-or** *n.* fournisseur, pourvoyeur *m.*
push *n.* poussée, impulsion *f.*; effort *m.*; — button poussoir, pressoir *m.*; — *vt.* pousser; bousculer; presser; — back repousser; **-ing** *a.* entreprenant, ambitieux
pushcart *n.* charrette à bras *f.*
pushover *n.* quelque chose de tres facile *m.*; adversaire facile à vaincre *m.*
pusillanimous *a.* pusillanime
puss(y) *n.* minette *f.*
pustule *n.* pustule *f.*
put *vt.* mettre, poser, placer; — to bed coucher; — away ranger; serrer; (money) mettre de côté; — back remettre; retarder; — down déposer, poser; supprimer; noter; — in faire; (naut.) entrer; — in order ranger; — off remettre; ajourner; différer; — on

mettre; enfiler; (shoes) chausser; — on the light(s) allumer; — on weight prendre du poids; — out tendre; mettre à la porte; (light) éteindre; contrarier; publier; — oneself out se déranger; — together assembler; — up construire, bâtir; poser; proposer; loger, descendre; — up with souffrir de; se résigner à
putrefaction *n.* putréfaction *f.*
putrefy *vi.* se putréfier, pourrir
putrid *a.* putride
putty *n.* mastic *m.*; — knife spatule *f.*; — *vt.* mastiquer
puzzle *n.* énigme *f.*; casse-tête *m.*; crossword — mots croisés *m. pl.*; jigsaw — patience *f.*; — *vt.* confondre; embarrasser; — *vi.* se casser la tête
pylon *n.* pylône *m.*
pygmy *n.* pygmée *m.*
pyorrhea *n.* pyorrhée *f.*
pyramid *n.* pyramide *f.*
pyre *n.* bûcher *m.*
Pyrenees *n. pl.* Pyrénées *f. pl.*
pyrotechnic *a.* pyrotechnique; **-s** *n. pl.* pyrotechnie *f.*

Q

quack *n.* charlatan *m.*; (sound) couin-couin *m.*; — *vi.* faire couin-couin; **-ery** *n.* charlatanisme *m.*
quadrangle *n.* cour carrée *f.*; (math.) quadrilatère *m.*
quadrangular *a.* quadrangulaire
quadrant *n.* quart, quadrant, secteur *m.*
quadratic *a.*, — equation équation du second degré *f.*
quadrilateral *a.* quadrilatéral, quadrilatère; — *n.* quadrilatère *m.*
quadruped *a. & n.* quadrupède *m.*
quadruple *a.* quadruple; **-ts** *n. pl.* quatre enfants nés de la même couche *m. pl.*
quaff *vt.* boire (d'un seul trait)
quagmire *n.* fondrière *f.*
quail *n.* caille *f.*; — *vi.* fléchir
quaint *a.* pittoresque; suranné; **-ness** *n.* pittoresque *m.*
quake *vi.* trembler
qualification *n.* qualité *f.*, titre *m.*; capacité *f.*; réserve, condition *f.*
qualified *a.* capable; brevcté; diplômé; conditionnel
qualify *vt.* qualifier; modifier; — *vi.* être reçu; se qualifier; **-ing** *a.* qualificatif; (sports) éliminatoire
qualitative *a.* qualitatif
quality *n.* qualité *f.*; — *a.* de qualité, de première qualité
qualm *n.* scrupule, remords; soulèvement de cœur *m.*; **-ish** *a.* qui a mal au cœur;

–ishness *n.* nausée *f.*

quandary *n.* incertitude *f.*; impasse *f.*

quantitative *a.* quantitatif

quantity *n.* quantité *f.*

quarantine *n.* quarantaine *f.*; — *vt.* mettre en quarantaine

quarrel *n.* querelle, dispute *f.*; — *vi.* se disputer, se quereller; se brouiller; –some *a.* querelleur

quarry *n.* carrière *f.*; proie *f.*; — *vt.* exploiter une carrière

quart *n.* litre *m.* 1 qt. (dry)´ = 0.95 litre (sec); 1 qt. (liquid) = 1.06 litres (liquides)

quarter *n.* (fraction) quart *m.*; quartier *m.*; trimestre *m.*; côté *m.*; (money) vingt-cinq cents *m. pl.*; a — after, a — past et quart; a — to moins le quart, moins un quart; — of an hour quart d'heure *m.*; –s *pl.* quartiers *m. pl.*, appartement, logement *m.*; (naut.) poste *m.*; — *vt.* diviser en quatre; écarteler; loger, cantonner; –ly *a.* trimestriel; –ly *adv.* par trimestre

quarter-deck *n.* gaillard arrière *m.*

quartermaster *n.* (mil.) intendant général *m.*

quartet *n.* quatuor *m.*

quasar *n.* objet quasi-stellaire *m.*

quash *vt.* étouffer; casser

quaver *vi.* trembloter; — *n.* tremblement *m.*; (mus.) trémolo *m.*; croche *f.*

queen *n.* reine *f.*; (cards) dame *f.*; — *vt.* faire la reine; (chess) damer; –ly *a.* de reine; royale

queer *a.* bizarre; étrange; drôle; original; –ness *n.* bizarrerie, étrangeté *f.*; — *vt.* gâter, gâcher

quell *vt.* étouffer, réprimer

quench *vt.* éteindre; étouffer; étancher; — one's thirst se désaltérer

query *n.* question *f.*; — *vt.* s'informer

quest *n.* recherche *f.*; quête *f.*; in — of à la recherche de

question *n.* question *f.*; demande *f.*; doute *m.*; — mark point d'interrogation *m.*; ask a — poser une question, faire une question; in — en question; out of the — impossible; without — sans aucun doute; — *vt.* interroger, questionner; mettre en doute; –able *a.* douteux; contestable; problématique; –er *n.* interrogateur *m.*; –ing *a.* interrogateur; –ing *n.* interrogation *f.*; interrogatoire *m.*

quibble *n.* chicane *f.*; argutie *f.*; — *vi.* chicaner; ergoter

quibbling *n.* chicane *f.*

quick *n.* vif *m.*; — *a.* rapide; vif, vive; prompt; agile; be —! dépêchez-vous!;

–ly *adv.* vite, rapidement; vivement; –en *vt.* accélérer, presser, hâter; animer, vivifier; –en *vi.* s'accélérer; s'animer; –ness *n.* rapidité, vitesse *f.*; vivacité *f.*; promptitude *f.*

quick-acting *a.* à action rapide

quick-freeze *vt.* congeler

quicklime *n.* chaux vive *f.*

quicksand *n.* sable mouvant *m.*

quicksilver *n.* vif-argent, mercure *m.*

quick-tempered *a.* emporté; qui s'emporte facilement

quick-witted *a.* éveillé, vif; à l'esprit prompt

quiescence *n.* quiétude *f.*

quiescent *a.* en repos

quiet *n.* tranquillité *f.*, calme *m.*; silence *m.*; repos *m.*; — *a.* tranquille, calme; silencieux; intime; simple; be —, keep — se taire; — *vt.* calmer, apaiser; faire taire; — (down) se calmer, s'apaiser; –ly *adv.* tranquillement; silencieusement, sans bruit; doucement; –ness *n.* tranquillité *f.*, calme *m.*; repos *m.*; paix *f.*; –ude *n.* quiétude *f.*

quill *n.* plume *f.*; tuyau *m.*

quilt *n.* couverture piquée *f.*; courtepointe *f.*; édredon *m.*; — *vt.* contrepointer, piquer; –ed *a.* piqué, contrepointé

quintessence *n.* quintessence *f.*

quintuple *a.* quintuple; –ts *n. pl.* cinq enfants nés de la même couche

quip *n.* repartie *f.*

quire *n.* main de papier *f.*

quirk *n.* habitude particulière *f.*; idiosyncrasie *f.*

quisling *n.* quisling, traître *m.*

quit *vt.* quitter, démissionner; — *vi.* cesser, s'arrêter; –s *a.* quitte; –ter *n.* lâcheur *m.*

quite *adv.* tout à fait; complètement, entièrement

quiver *n.* frémissement, tremblement *m.*; (archery) carquois *m.*; — *vi.* frémir, trembler; trembloter

quixotic *a.* visionnaire

quiz *n.* petit examen *m.*; — *vt.* examiner, interroger

quorum *n.* quorum *m.*

quota *n.* quote-part *f.*; contingentement *m.*

quotation *n.* citation *f.*; (com.) cote *f.*, cours *m.*; — marks guillements *m. pl.*

quote *vt.* citer; faire un prix; coter

quotient *n.* quotient *m.*

R

rabbi *n.* rabbin *m.*

rabbit *n.* lapin *m.*

rabble *n.* canaille, populace *f.*

rabid *a.* enragé; furieux

rabies *n.* rage, hydrophobie *f.*

race *n.* course *f.*; (breed) race *f.*, sang *m.*; **human** — race humaine *f.*; humanité *f.*; **homme** *m.*; **foot** — course à pied *f.*; **horse** — course de chevaux *f.*; **boat** — régate *f.*; — **horse** cheval de course *m.*; — **track** *n.* champ de courses *m.*; piste *f.*; — *vi.* faire une course; courir; lutter de vitesse; — *vt.* lutter de vitesse avec; faire courir; (engine) emballer; **-r** *n.* coureur *m.*; auto de course *f.*

racing *n.* courses *f. pl.*

racist *n.* raciste *m.*

rack *n.* (luggage) porte-bagages *m.*; filet *m.*; (coat) porte-manteau *m.*; (torture) chevalet *m.*; — *vt.* torturer, tourn enter; — **one's brains** se creuser l'esprit

racket *n.* raquette *f.*; bruit, vacarme, tapage *m.*; (slang) métier, genre d'affaires *m.*, affaire louche *f.*; **-eer** *n.* gangster *m.*

racy *a.* savoureux

radar *n.* radar *m.*

radial *a.* radial

radiance *n.* rayonnement *m.*; éclat *m.*

radiant *a.* rayonnant; radieux

radiate *vi.* rayonner; — *vt.* émettre

radiation *n.* (phy.) radiation *f.*; rayonnement *m.*; — **sickness** maladie de radiation *f.*

radiator *n.* radiateur *m.*

radical *a. & n.* radical *m.*; **-ism** *n.* radicalisme *m.*

radicle *n.* (bot.) radicelle *f.*; radicule *f.*

radio *n.* radio *f.*; T.S.F. (télégraphie sans fil) *f.*; — *vt.* envoyer (un message) par radio; — **operator** radio *m.*; — **set** poste de T.S.F. *m.*; — **station** poste émetteur *m.*

radiobroadcast *n.* radiodiffusion *f.*; — *vt.* radiodiffuser, transmettre; **-er** *n.* appareil émetteur *m.*; (person) speaker *m.*, speakerine *f.*; annonceur *m.*; **-ing** *n.* radio-émission, radiophonie *f.*

radioactive *a.* radio-actif

radioastronomy *n.* radio-astronomie *f.*

radio frequency *n.* radio-fréquence *f.*

radiogram *n.* radiogramme *m.*

radiology *n.* radiologie *f.*

radiosensitive *a.* radiosensible

radiotherapy *n.* radiothérapie *f.*

radish *n.* radis *m.*

radium *n.* radium *m.*

radius *n.* rayon *m.*; **within a** — **of** dans un rayon de

raffle *n.* tombola *f.*

raft *n.* radeau *m.*; (coll.) grand nombre *m.*

rafter *n.* chevron *m.*

rag *n.* chiffon *m.*; lambeau *m.*; — **doll** pou-

pée de chiffons *f.*; **-s** *pl.* guenilles *f. pl.*, haillons *m. pl.*; **-ged** *a.* en haillons; inégal; désordonné

ragamuffin *n.* gamin *m.*; va-nu-pieds *m.*

rage *n.* fureur *f.*; rage *f.*; manie *f.*; **fly into a** — s'emporter; — *vi.* être furieux; faire rage

raging *a.* furieux

ragout *n.* ragoût *m.*

ragpicker *n.* chiffonnier *m.*

ragweed *n.* jacobée *f.*

raid *n.* raid *m.*; incursion *f.*; razzia *f.*; (police) descente *f.*; — *vt.* faire un raid à; razzier; faire une descente dans; **-er** *n.* maraudeur *m.*; attaquant *m.*

rail *n.* rail *m.*; rampe *f.*; balustrade *f.*; garde-fou *m.*; barreau *m.*; grille *f.*; **by** — par chemin de fer *m.*; **third** — rail de contact *m.*; **-ing** *n.* barrière *f.*; balustrade *f.*; garde-fou *m.*

rail *vi.*, — **at** s'en prendre à; crier contre

raillery *n.* raillerie *f.*

railroad, railway *n.* chemin de fer; — **track** voie *f.*; — **station** gare *f.*

rain *n.* pluie *f.*; **in the** — sous la pluie; — *vi.* pleuvoir; **it's -ing** il pleut; **-y** *a.* pluvieux; des pluies

rainbow *n.* arc-en-ciel *m.*

raincoat *n.* imperméable *m.*

rainfall *n.* pluie, précipitation *f.*

rain forest *n.* forêt pluvieuse *f.*

rainproof *a.* imperméable

rain water *n.* eau de pluie *f.*

raise *vt.* lever, soulever; hausser; relever; élever; cultiver; (salary) augmenter; — **a cry** pousser un cri

rake *n.* râteau *m.*, râtissoire *f.*; (person) roué *m.*; — *vt.* râteler, ratisser; — **off** prélever

rally *n.* ralliement *m.*; réunion *f.*; (sports) reprise *f.*; retour *m.*; — *vt.* rallier; — *vi.* se rallier; (mil.) se reformer; (med.) se remettre; (sports) se reprendre

ram *n.* (animal) bélier *m.*; pilon *m.*; — *vt.* heurter; enfoncer; (naut.) éperonner

ramble *n.* balade, promenade *f.*; — *vi.* errer, rôder; battre la compagne; parler sans suite

rambling *a.* vagabond; sans suite; — *n.* vagabondage *m.*; radotage *m.*

ramification *n.* ramification *f.*

ramify *vi.* se ramifier

ramp *n.* rampe *f.*; pont *m.*

rampage *n.* furie, folie *f.*; — *vi.* déclamer, divaguer

rampant *a.* rampant; **be** — s'étaler; se répandre

rampart *n.* rempart *m.*

ramshackle *a.* délabré

ranch *n.* grosse ferme d'élevage *f.*; ranch

m.; **-er** *n.* fermier *m.*; propriétaire de ranch *m.*

rancid *a.* rance; **-ness** *n.* rancidité *f.*

rancor *n.* rancune *f.*

random *n.* at — au hasard; à tort et à travers; — *a.* fait au hasard

range *n.* portée *f.*; étendue *f.*; champ *m.*; gamme *f.*; distance *f.*; (mountains) chaîne *f.*; (kitchen) cuisinière *f.*; — **finder** télémètre *m.*; **in** — ¿ portée; **out of** — hors de portée; — *vt.* ranger; — *vi.* s'étendre; errer; s'échelonner; **-r** *n.* (garde) forestier *m.*

rank *n.* rang *m.*; classe *f.*; (mil.) grade *m.*; — **and file** la troupe *f.*; — *vi.* se ranger; être classé; — *a.* fétide; luxuriant; criant; parfait; **-ing** *a.* premier; en chef

ransack *vt.* piller, saccager; fouiller

ransom *n.* rançon *f.*; — *vt.* rançonner; racheter

rant *vi.* extravaguer

rap *n.* coup *m.*; (coll.) sou *m.*; — *vt.* frapper; donner sur

rapacious *a.* rapace; **-ly** *adv.* avec rapacité; **-ness** *n.* rapacité *f.*

rape *n.* viol *m.*; — *vt.* violer

rapid *a.* rapide; **-ly** *adv.* rapidement, vite; **-ity** *n.* rapidité *f.*; **-s** *n. pl.* rapides *m. pl.*

rapid-fire *a.* à tir rapide

rapier *n.* rapière *f.*

rapt *a.* absorbé; ravi; **-ure** *n.* transport *m.*; ravissement *m.*; extase *m.*; **-urous** *a.* d'extase

rare *a.* rare; (meat) saignant **-ness** *n.* rareté *f.*

rarefaction *n.* raréfaction *f.*

rarefied *a.* raréfié

rarefy *vt.* raréfier

rarity *n.* rareté; chose rare *f.*; objet rare *m.*

rascal *n.* coquin, fripon *m.*; **-ity** *n.* coquinerie *f.*

rash *n.* éruption *f.*; — *a.* irréfléchi; téméraire; **-ness** *n.* témérité *f.*

rasp *n.* (tool) râpe *f.*; grincement *m.*; — *vt.* râper; racler; — *vi.* grincer; **-ing** *a.* grinçant; âpre

raspberry *n.* framboise *f.*

rat *n.* rat *m.*; — **poison** mort aux rats *f.*; **-trap** ratière *f.*; **smell a** — se douter de quelque chose

ratchet *n.* cliquet, rochet *m.*

rate *n.* taux *m.*; cours *m.*; tarif *m.*; prime *f.*; vitesse *f.*; allure *f.*; **at any** — en tout cas, dans tous les cas; **at the** — of au taux de; à la vitesse de; sur le pied de; **birth** — natalité *f.*; **death** — mortalité *f.*; — **of exchange** cours du change *m.*; — **of interest** taux de l'intérêt *m.*; — *vt.* classer; considérer; estimer, évaluer; —

vi. être classé; se ranger

rather *adv.* plutôt; assez; **I would** — . . . j'aimerais mieux . . . , **je préfère-rais** . . .

ratification *n.* ratification *f.*

ratify *vt.* ratifier

rating *n.* classement *m.*, classification *f.*; estimation *f.*

ratio *n.* proportion *f.*; rapport *m.*

ration *n.* ration *f.*; — *vt.* rationner; **-ing** *n.* rationnement *m.*

rational *a.* raisonnable; raisonné; (math.) rationnel; **-ize** *vt.* rationaliser

rattle *n.* cliquetis *m.*; tapotis *m.*; (child's) hochet *m.*, hochette *f.*; (snake) sonnette *f.*; (med.) râle *m.*; — *vi.* cliqueter; trembler; (med.) râler; — *vt.* faire cliqueter; agiter; — **off** dire rapidement; — **on** continuer à parler; **-r** *n.* serpent à sonnettes *m.*

rattlesnake *n.* serpent à sonnettes *m.*

raucous *a.* rauque

ravage *n.* ravage *m.*; — *vt.* ravager

ravaging *a.* ravageur

rave *vi.* extravaguer; délirer; s'extasier

ravel *vt.* emmêler

ravenous *a.* vorace

ravine *n.* ravin *m.*; défilé *m.*

ravish *vt.* ravir; violer; **-ing** *a.* ravissant

raw *a.* cru; vert; inexperimenté; **-ness** *n.* crudité *f.*; inexpérience *f.*

rawhide *n.* cuir vert *m.*

ray *n.* rayon *m.*; (fish) raie *f.*

rayon *n.* rayonne *f.*

raze *vt.* raser

razor *n.* rasoir *m.*; — **blade** lame de rasoir; *f.*; **safety** — rasoir de sûreté *m.*

re *n.*, **in** — au sujet de

reach *n.* étendue *f.*; allonge *f.*; portée *f.*; **out of** — hors de portée; **within** — à la portée de; — *vt.* arriver à, atteindre; parvenir; — *vi.* s'étendre; — **out** tendre la main

react *vi.* réagir; **-ion** *n.* réaction *f.*; **-ionary** *a. & n.* réactionnaire *m. & f.*

read *vt.* lire; étudier; parcourir; (meter) relever; **-able** *a.* lisible; **-er** *n.* lecteur *m.*, lectrice *f.*; livre de lecture *m.*; (child's) livre de lectures, abécédaire *m.*; **-ing** *n.* lecture *f.*; interprétation *f.*; observation *f.*; façon de lire *f.*; (meter) relevé *m.*; **-ing room** salle de lecture *f.*

readily *adv.* volontiers; facilement

readiness *n.* promptitude *f.*; bonne volonté *f.*; facilité *f.*; **in** — prêt

readjust *vt.* rajuster; **-ment** *n.* rajustement *m.*

ready *a.* prêt; prompt, facile; **get** — se préparer, se disposer, s'apprêter

ready-made *a.* tout fait; de confection

reaffirm *vt.* réaffirmer
reagent *n.* réactif *m.*
real *a.* réel; vrai, véritable; naturel; — estate propriété immobilière *f.*; biens immeubles *m. pl.*; –ism *n.* réalisme *m.*; –ist *n.* réaliste *m. & f.*; –istic *a.* réaliste; –ity *n.* réalité *f.*; réel *m.*; –ization *n.* connaissance, conception *f.*; réalisation *f.*; –ize *vt.* se rendre compte de; réaliser; –ly *adv.* vraiment; réellement; sans blague
realm *n.* royaume *m.*
realtor *n.* agent immobilier *m.*
ream *n.* rame *f.*; — *vt.* aléser
reanimate *vt.* ranimer
reap *vt.* moissonner; cueillir, recueillir; –er *n.* (person) moissonneur *m.*; (machine) moissonneuse *f.*; –ing *n.* moisson *f.*
reappear *vi.* reparaître; –ance *n.* réapparition *f.*
rear *n.* arrière *m.*; derrière *m.*; — *a.* postérieur; d'arrière; — admiral contre-amiral *m.*; — guard arrière-garde *f.*; — *vt.* élever; — *vi.* se cabrer
rearm *vt.* réarmer; –ament *n.* réarmement *m.*
rearrange *vt.* rarranger, arranger; –ment *n.* nouvel arrangement *m.*
rearview *a.*, — mirror rétroviseur *m.*
reason *n.* raison *f.*; argument *m.*; sujet, lieu *m.*; cause *f.*; have — to avoir lieu de; avoir sujet à; it stands to — c'est évident; listen to — entendre raison; — (why) pourquoi *m.*; — *vi.* raisonner; — *vt.* arguer, discuter; –able *a.* raisonnable; modéré; –ing *n.* raisonnement *m.*
reassemble *vt.* rassembler; remonter; — *vi.* se rassembler
reassurance *n.* promesse *f.*; encouragement *m.*
reassure *vt.* rassurer
reawaken *vt. & (vi.)* (se) réveiller
rebate *n.* rabais *m.*; escompte *m.*; ristourne *f.*; — *vt.* diminuer
rebel *n.* rebelle, révolté, insurgé *m.*; — *vt. & (vi.)* (se) révolter, (s')insurger, (se) soulever; –lion *n.* révolte *f.*; –lious *a.* rebelle
rebind *vt.* relier de nouveau
rebirth *n.* renaissance *f.*
rebound *n.* ricochet *m.*; rebondissement *m.*; — *vi.* rebondir
rebroadcast *vt.* (radio) diffuser de nouveau
rebuff *n.* refus *m.*; — *vt.* repousser; refuser
rebuild *vt.* rebâtir, reconstruire
rebuke *n.* réprimande *f.*; — *vt.* réprimander, blâmer
recalcitrance *n.* récalcitrance *f.*
recalcitrant *a.* récalcitrant; réfractaire
recall *n.* révocation *f.*; rappel *m.*; — *vt.*

rappeler; se souvenir de
recant *vt.* rétracter; — *vi.* se rétracter; chanter la palinodie
recap *vt.* rechaper
recapitulation *n.* récapitulation *f.*
recapture *vt.* reprendre; — *n.* reprise *f.*
recede *vi.* reculer; s'éloigner; (forehead) fuir
receipt *n.* reçu *m.*; recette *f.*; réception *f.*; récépissé *m.*, quittance *f.*, accusé de réception *m.*; acknowledge — accuser réception; — *vt.* acquitter
receivable *a.* recevable; bills — effets à recevoir *m. pl.*
receive *vt.* recevoir; (welcome) accueillir; –r *n.* destinataire *m. & f.*; (law) administrateur *m.*; (stolen goods) receleur *m.*; (phone) récepteur *m.*
receiving *n.* réception *f.*; — station poste récepteur *m.*
recent *a.* récent, nouveau; –ly *adv.* récemment
receptacle *n.* réceptacle *m.*
reception *n.* réception *f.*; accueil *m.*; –ist *n.* employé de bureau chargé de recevoir les clients *m.*
receptive *a.* réceptif
recess *n.* (school) récréation *f.*; (court) vacances *f. pl.*; enfoncement *m.*; recoin *m.*; embrasure *f.*; –ion *n.* recul *m.*; régression *f.*; crise financière *f.*; –ional *n.* hymne de sortie *m.*; –ive *a.* régressif, récessif — *vt.* encastrer, enfoncer
recipe *n.* recette *f.*
recipient *n.* bénéficiaire *m. & f.*; destinataire *m. & f.*
reciprocal *a.* réciproque; mutuel; inverse
reciprocate *vt.* payer de retour; — *vi.* retourner un compliment, rendre la pareille
reciprocity *n.* réciprocité *f.*
recital *n.* récitation *f.*; récit *m.*; (mus.) récital *m.*
recitation *n.* récitation *f.*
recite *vt.* réciter, déclamer; (school) répondre (à une question)
reckless *a.* insouciant; imprudent
reckon *vt.* compter; calculer; juger; — *vi.* compter; calculer; — with compter avec; –ing *n.* calcul, compte *m.*; estime *f.*
reclaim *vt.* réformer; (land) défricher; mettre en valeur
reclamation *n.* réforme *f.*; défrichement *m.*; mise en valeur *f.*; réclamation *f.*
recline *vt.* appuyer, coucher; — *vi.* être couché; être étendu
recognition *n.* reconnaissance *f.*
recognizable *a.* reconnaissable
recognizance *n.* (law) caution personnelle

f.

recognize *vt.* reconnaître; donner la parole à

recoil *n.* recul *m.*; contre-coup *m.*; détente *f.*; — *vi.* reculer; se détendre

recollect *vt.* se rappeler; se souvenir de; **–ion** *n.* souvenir *m.*

recommence *vt. & vi.* recommencer

recommend *vt.* recommander; **–ation** *n.* recommandation *f.*

recompense *n.* récompense *f.*; dédommagement *m.*; — *vt.* récompenser; dédommager

reconcilable *a.* conciliable

reconcile *vt.* réconcilier, racommoder; concilier; mettre d'accord; — **oneself to** se résigner à

reconciliation *n.* réconciliation *f.*; conciliation *f.*

recondition *vt.* rénover; mettre à neuf

reconnaissance *n.* reconnaissance *f.*

reconnoiter *vt.* reconnaître; — *vi.* faire une reconnaissance

reconquer *vt.* reconquérir

reconsider *vt.* reviser; considérer de nouveau; revenir sur

reconstitute *vt.* reconstituer

reconstruct *vt.* rebâtir, reconstruire; **–ion** *n.* reconstruction *f.*

record *n.* registre *m.*; note *f.*; procès-verbal *m.*; document *m.*; dossier *m.*; (sports) record *m.*; (phonograph) disque *m.*; **off the** — non-officiel; **–s** *pl.* archives *f. pl.*; — *vt.* enregistrer; rapporter; graver; faire une note de; **–er** *n.* enregistreur *m.*; archiviste *m.*; machine à enregistrer *f.*; **tape –er** magnétophone *m.*; **–ing** *n.* enregistrement *m.*

record-breaking *a.* qui bat le record; surpassant le record

recount *vt.* raconter

re-count *vt.* recompter

recoup *vt. & (vi.)* (se) dédommager; (se) rattraper (sur); rembourser, dédommager (de)

recourse *n.* recours *m.*

recover *vt.* retrouver, regagner; (loss) réparer, reprendre; recouvrer; (oneself) revenir à soi; — *vi.* guérir, se remettre (de); **–y** *n.* guérison *f.*; recouvrement *m.*; reprise *f.*

re-cover *vt.* recouvrir

recreation *n.* récréation *f.*; divertissement *m.*

recrimination *n.* récrimination *f.*

recruit *n.* recrue *f.*; — *vt.* (mil.) recruter; racoler; **–ing** *n.* recrutement *m.*

rectal *a.* rectal

rectangle *n.* rectangle *m.*

rectangular *a.* rectangulaire

rectification *n.* rectification *f.*

rectifier *n.* (elec.) redresseur, rectificateur *m.*

rectify *vt.* rectifier; réparer, corriger; (elec.) redresser

rectilinear *a.* rectiligne

rectitude *n.* rectitude, droiture *f.*

rector *n.* recteur *m.*; curé *m.*; **–y** *n.* presbytère *m.*

recumbent *a.* couché

recuperate *vi.* se remettre, se rétablir; guérir

recuperation *n.* rétablissement *m.*; guérison *f.*

recur *vi.* se reproduire; revenir; **–rence** *n.* retour *m.*; (med.) récidive *f.*; **–rent** *a.* recurrent; qui revient; **–ring** *a.* recurrent; périodique

red *n.* rouge *m.*; **in the** — en déficit; — *a.* rouge; (hair) roux (rousse); pourpre; — **tape** paperasserie *f.*; **see** — voir rouge; **turn** — rougir; **–den** *vi.* rougir; (sky) rougeoyer; **–dish** *a.* rougeâtre; **–ness** *n.* rougeur *f.*; (hair) rousseur *f.*

red-blooded *a.* robuste, vigoureux

redcap *n.* porteur (de gare) *m.*

redecorate *vt.* repeindre; refaire

redeem *vt.* racheter; amortir; dégager; **–able** *a.* rachetable; **–er** *n.* rédempteur *m.*

redemption *n.* rachat *m.*; amortissement *m.*; (eccl.) rédemption *f.*

red-eyed *a.* aux yeux éraillés

red-haired *a.* roux (rousse), aux cheveux roux

red-handed *a.* en flagrant délit

redhead *n.* personne aux cheveux roux *f.*; **–ed** *a.* roux (rousse), aux cheveux roux

red-hot *a.* (chauffé au) rouge

rediscover *vt.* retrouver

redistribute *vt.* redistribuer

red-letter *a.*, — **day** jour mémorable *m.*

redolence *n.* odeur *f.*, parfum *m.*

redolent *a.* parfumé, odorant; — **of** qui sent

redouble *vt. & vi.* redoubler; (cards) surcontrer

redoubtable *a.* redoutable

redound *vi.* contribuer

redress *n.* réparation *f.*; — *vt.* réparer

redskin *n.* peau-rouge *m.*

reduce *vt.* réduire; diminuer; abaisser; — *vi.* maigrir

reducible *a.* réductible

reduction *n.* réduction *f.*; diminution *f.*; baisse *f.*

redundancy *n.* redondance *f.*

redundant *a.* redondant

reduplicate *vt.* redoubler

re-echo *vi.* résonner, retentir

reed *n.* roseau *m.*; (mus.) anche *f.*

reef *n.* récif, écueil *m.*; (naut.) ris *m.*; — *vt.* prendre un ris dans

reek *n.* odeur *f.*; relent *m.*; — *vi.* sentir; suer; -ing *a.* qui sent

reel *n.* bobine *f.*, dévidoir *m.*; (fishing) moulinet *m.*; — *vt.* bobiner, dévider; — *vi.* chanceler, tournoyer; tituber; — off réciter, énumérer rapidement

re-elect *vt.* réélire; -ion *n.* réélection *f.*

re-enact *vt.* reproduire

re-enlist *vi.* se rengager

re-enter *vt.* rentrer (dans)

re-entry *n.* rentrée *f.*

re-establish *vt.* rétablir; -ment *n.* rétablissement *m.*

re-examination *n.* nouvel examen *m.*

re-examine *vt.* examiner de nouveau

refashion *vt.* refaire, refaçonner

refasten *vt.* rattacher

refectory *n.* réfectoire *m.*

refer *vt.* soumettre; renvoyer; — *vi.* se rapporter; se reporter; faire allusion; parler; -ence *n.* référence *f.*; renvoi *m.*; appel *m.*; rapport *m.*; -ence work ouvrage à consulter *m.*

referee *n.* arbitre *m.*; — *vt.* arbitrer

refill *n.* rechange *m.*; pièce de rechange *f.*; — *vt.* remplir

refine *vt.* raffiner; purifier; -d *a.* raffiné; cultivé, distingué; -ment *n.* raffinage *m.*; raffinement *m.*; -ry *n.* raffinerie *f.*

refit *vt.* remonter; (naut.) réarmer

reflect *vt.* refléter; réfléchir; — *vi.* réfléchir; méditer; se dire; faire du tort; -ion *n.* réflexion *f.*, réfléchissement *m.*; reflet *m.*; image *f.*; -or *n.* réflecteur *m.*

reflex *a.* & *n.* réflexe *m.*; -ive *a.* (gram.) réfléchi

reforestation *n.* reboisement *m.*

reform *n.* réforme *f.*; — *vt.* réformer, corriger; — *vi.* se réformer, se corriger; -ation *n.* réforme *f.*; réformation *f.*; -atory *n.* maison de correction *f.*; -er *n.* réformateur *m.*

re-form *vt.* reformer; — *vi.* se reformer

refract *vt.* réfracter; -ion *n.* refraction *f.*; -ory *a.* réfractaire; insoumis

refrain *n.* (mus.) refrain *m.*; — *vi.* s'abstenir, se retenir

refresh *vt.* refraîchir; -ing *a.* rafraîchissant; -ment *n.* rafraîchissement *m.*; boisson *f.*; quelque chose à boire (ou à manger) *m.*

refrigerate *vt.* réfrigérer, refroidir; frigorifier

refrigeration *n.* réfrigeration *f.*; frigorification *f.*

refrigerator *n.* glacière *f.*, frigidaire *m.*

refuel *vi.* faire le plein d'essence

refuge *n.* refuge *m.*; abri *m.*; take — se réfugier; -e *n.* réfugié, sinistré *m.*

refulgence *n.* éclat *m.*

refund *n.* remboursement *m.*; — *vt.* rembourser; -able *a.* remboursable

refurnish *vt.* remonter

refusal *n.* refus *m.*; first — première offre *f.*

refuse *n.* rebut *m.*; — *vt.* refuser; ne pas vouloir

refutation *n.* réfutation *f.*

refute *vt.* réfuter

regain *vt.* regagner; reprendre; — consciousness reprendre connaissance

regal *a.* royal; -ia *n.* insignes *m. pl.*

regale *vt.* régaler

regard *n.* attention *f.*, égard *m.*; estime *f.*; in — to en ce qui concerne; out of — for par égard pour; with — to quant à; have no — for ne pas estimer; faire peu de cas de; show — témoigner de l'estime; -s *pl.* amitiés *f. pl.*; give my -s to faites mes amitiés à; — *vt.* regarder, considérer; -ing *prep.* en ce qui concerne; quant à; à l'égard de; -less *a.* sans regarder; sans se soucier; -less *adv.* en tout cas; quand même

regatta *n.* régate *f.*

regency *n.* régence *f.*

regenerate *vt.* régénérer; — *vi.* se régénérer; — *a.* régénéré

regeneration *n.* régénération *f.*

regenerator *n.* régénérateur *m.*

regent *n.* régent *m.*

regime, regimen *n.* régime *m.*

regiment *n.* régiment *m.*; -al *a.* du régiment; -ation *n.* régimentation *f.*; — *vt.* réglementer

region *n.* région *f.*; -al *a.* régional

register *n.* registre *m.*; compteur *m.*; cash — caisse enregistreuse *f.*; — *vt.* enregistrer; inscrire; immatriculer; (letter) recommander; (trademark) déposer; — *vi.* s'inscrire; s'immatriculer

registrar *n.* archiviste, secrétaire; teneur de registres *m.*

registration *n.* enregistrement *m.*; inscription *f.*; (school, auto) immatriculation *f.*

registry *n.* secrétariat *m.*; bureau d'enregistrement *m.*

regress *vi.* régresser; -ion *n.* régression *f.*

regret *n.* regret *m.*; — *vt.* regretter; être désolé; -ful *a.* plein de regrets; -fully *adv.* avec regret; -table *a.* regrettable; à regretter

regroup *vt.* regrouper

regular *a.* régulier; ordinaire; habituel; (officer) de carrière; (coll.) vrai; -ity *n.* régularité; -ize *vt.* régulariser; -ly *adv.* régulièrement; d'ordinaire, d'habitude

regulate vt. régler
regulation n. règlement m.; ordonnance f.
regulator n. régulateur m.
regurgitate vt. régurgiter; — vi. regorger
rehabilitate vt. réhabiliter
rehabilitation n. réhabilitation f.
rehearsal n. répétition f.
rehearse vt. répéter
reheat vt. réchauffer
reign n. règne m.; — vi. régner; –ing a. régnant
reimburse vt. rembourser; –ment n. remboursement m.
rein n. bride, rêne, guide f.; — vt. brider
reincarnation n. réincarnation f.
reincorporate vt. réincorporer
reinforce vt. renforcer; appuyer; –d a. renforcé; –d concrete béton armé m.; –ment n. renforcement m.; –ments n. pl. renfort m.
reinstate vt. réintégrer, rétablir; –ment n. réintégration f.
reinsurance n. réassurance, contre-assurance f.
reinsure vt. réassurer
reissue vt. émettre de nouveau; publier de nouveau
reiterate vt. réitérer
reiteration n. réitération f.
reject n. pièce de rebut f.; — vt. rejeter; refuser; –ion n. rejet m.; refus m.
rejoice vt. réjouir; — vi. se réjouir (de)
rejoin vt. rejoindre; retrouver; — vi. répondre, répliquer; –der n. réplique f.
rejuvenate vt. & vi. rajeunir
rekindle vt. rallumer; ranimer
relapse n. rechute f.; — vi. rechuter, avoir une rechute; retomber (dans)
relate vt. raconter; relater; rapporter; — vi. avoir rapport (à), se rapporter; –d a. apparenté; parent; allié
relation n. (narrative) récit m.; rapport m.; relation f.; (relative) parent m.; –ship n. rapport m.; relation f.; parenté f.; in — to à l'égarde de
relative a. relatif; — n. parent m.; humidity n. humidité relative f.; — to au sujet de
relativity n. relativité f.
relax vt. détendre, relâcher; — vi. se détendre, se relâcher; –ation n. détente f.; repos m.; relâchement m.
relay n. relais m.; relève f.; — race course à relais f.; — vt. relayer
re-lay vt. reposer, poser de nouveau
release n. libération f.; élargissement m. déclencheur m.; (document) quittance f., acquit m.; — vt. libérer; élargir; lâcher; déclencher; acquitter
relegate vt. reléguer, remettre

relent vi. revenir sur; s'adoucir; –less a. impitoyable, implacable; –lessness n. implacabilité f.
relevance n. à propos m.
relevant a. à propos, pertinent; qui se rapporte à
reliability n. régularité f.; honnêteté f.
reliable a. sûr; digne de confiance
reliance n. confiance f.
reliant a., be — on dépendre de; avoir confiance en
relic n. relique f.; –s pl. restes m. pl.
relief n. soulagement m.; aide f.; secours m.; assistance publique f.; relief m.; — map carte en relief
relieve vt. soulager; aider, secourir; relever; dégager
relight vt. rallumer
religion n. religion f.; culte m.
religious a. religieux; dévot; pieux; –ly adv. religieusement; scrupuleusement
reline vt. redoubler; (brakes) regarnir
relinquish vt. renoncer; délaisser; abandonner
relish n. goût m.; assaisonnement, condiment m.; entremets m.; — vt. goûter, savourer
reload vt. recharger
relocate vt. reloger, changer de place
relocation n. relogement m.
reluctance n. regret m.; répugnance f.; hésitation f.; (elec.) reluctance f.
reluctant a. hésitant; peu disposé; –ly adv. à regret; à contre-cœur
rely vi., — on compter sur
remain vi. rester; demeurer; se tenir; –s n. pl. restes m. pl.; vestiges m. pl. –der n. reste m.; (book) solde d'édition m.
remake vt. refaire
remand n. renvoi m.; — vt. renvoyer
remark n. remarque f., observation f.; attention f.; — vt. remarquer, observer, constater; — vi. faire une remarque; –able a. remarquable
remarry vi. se remarier
remediable a. rémédiable
remedial a. réparateur; curatif
remedy n. remède m.; recours m.; — vt. remédier
remember vt. se souvenir de; se rappeler
remembrance n. souvenir m.; mémoire f.
remind vt. rappeler; faire penser; faire souvenir; –er n. rappel m.; souvenir m.; mémento m.
reminiscence n. réminiscence f.; souvenir m.
reminiscent a. qui rappelle
remiss a. négligent; –ion n. rémission f.; remise f.; –ness n. négligence f.
remit vt. remettre, envoyer; pardonner;

−tance *n.* remise *f.*; envoi *m.*; −ter *n.* remettant *m.*

remnant *n.* reste *m.*; coupon *m.*

remodel *vt.* remodeler

remonstrance *n.* remontrance *f.*

remonstrate *vi.* faire des remontrances; — *vt.* protester

remorse *n.* remords *m.*; −ful *a.* plein de remords; −less *a.* sans remords; sans pitié

remote *a.* lointain, éloigné; reculé; peu probable; −ly *adv.* loin; de loin; −ness *n.* éloignement *m.*

removable *a.* amovible; détachable

removal *n.* enlèvement *m.*; déplacement *m.*; transport *m.*; révocation *f.*

remove *vt.* enlever, écarter; déplacer, transporter; −d *a.* éloigné; loin

remunerate *vt.* rémunérer

remuneration *n.* rémunération *f.*

remunerative *a.* rémunérateur

renaissance *n.* renaissance *f.*

renal *a.* rénal

rename *vt.* renommer, rebaptiser

renascence *n.* renaissance

renascent *a.* renaissant

rend *vt.* déchirer; fendre; faire retentir

render *vt.* rendre; traduire; interpréter; (cooking) fondre; −ing, rendition *n.* rendu *m.*; traduction *f.*; interprétation *f.*

rendezvous *n.* rendez-vous *m.*

renegade *n.* renégat *m.*

renew *vt.* renouveler; (subscription) réabonner; — *vi.* renouer −able *a.* renouvelable; interchangeable; −al *n.* renouvellement *m.*; réabonnement *m.*

renounce *vt.* renoncer à; abandonner; répudier

renovate *vt.* renouveler; rénover; mettre à neuf

renovation *n.* rénovation *f.*

renown *n.* renom *m.*, renommée *f.*; −ed *a.* renommé, célèbre, illustre

rent *n.* (property) loyer *m.*; (clothing) déchirure *f.*; fente, fissure *f.*; (income) *n. pl.* rentes *f.*, revenu *m.*; — *vt.* louer, affermer; — *vi.* se louer; −al *n.* loyer *m.*; −er *n.* locataire *m. & f.*

renunciation *n.* renonciation *f.*, renoncement *m.*; répudiation *f.*

reoccupy *vt.* réoccuper

reopen *vt.* rouvrir; — *vi.* (se) rouvrir; (school) rentrer; −ing *n.* réouverture *f.*; rentrée *f.*

reorder *vt.* commander de nouveau; — *vi.* renouveler une commande

reorganization *n.* réorganisation *f.*

reorganize *vt. & vi.* réorganiser

repair *n.* réparation *f.*; état *m.*; — shop *n.* atelier de réparation *m.*; — *vt.* réparer; raccommoder; — *vi.* aller, se rendre; −ing *n.* réparation *f.*; (clothes) raccommodage *m.*; (mech.) dépannage *m.*

repairman *n.* réparateur *m.*; dépanneur *m.*

reparable *a.* réparable

reparation *n.* réparation; satisfaction *f.*

repartee *n.* repartie *f.*; réplique *f.*

repast *n.* repas, festin *m.*

repatriate *vt.* rapatrier

repave *vt.* repaver

repay *vt.* rembourser; récompenser; rendre; −able *a.* payable, à rembourser; −ment *n.* remboursement *m.*

repeal *n.* révocation, abrogation *f.*; — *vt.* révoquer, (law) abroger

repeat *n.* répétition *f.*; (mus.) reprise *f.*; — *vt.* répéter; réitérer; — *vi.* se répéter; −ed *a.* répété; réitéré; −edly *adv.* à plusieurs reprises; −ing *a.* qui répète

repel *vt.* repousser; répugner à; −lent *a.* répulsif; repoussant; insect −lent *n.* chasse-insectes *m.*; −ling *a.* répulsif

repent *vt. & vi.* se repentir (de); −ance *n.* repentir *m.*; −ant *a.* repenti; repentant

repercussion *n.* répercussion *f.*; contrecoup *m.*

repertoire, repertory *n.* répertoire *m.*

repetition *n.* répétition *f.*; (mus.) reprise *f.*

rephrase *vt.* rédiger de nouveau, dire d'une autre façon

replace *vt.* remplacer; replacer; remettre; −able *a.* remplaçable; interchangeable; −ment *n.* remplacement *m.*; pièce de rechange *f.*; remise *f.*; −ment *a.* de remplacement, de rechange

replate *vt.* replaquer

replenish *vt.* remplir; se réapprovisionner (de); −ing, −ment *n.* recharge *f.*

replete *a.* rempli, plein

replica *n.* réplique *f.*; copie *f.*

reply *n.* réponse *f.*; réplique *f.*; — *vt. & vi.* répondre, répliquer

report *n.* rapport *m.*; compte-rendu *m.*; procès-verbal *m.*; bruit *m.*, rumeur *f.*; (firearms) détonation *f.*; weather — bulletin météorologique *m.*; — *vt.* rapporter; rendre compte de; signaler; dire; −er *n.* reporter, journaliste *m.*; −ing *n.* reportage *m.*

repose *n.* repos *m.*; calme *m.*, tranquillité *f.*; — *vi.* (se) reposer

repository *n.* dépôt *m.*

repossess *vt.* reprendre (possession); −ion *n.* rentrée en possession *f.*

reprehensible *a.* blâmable, répréhensible

represent *vt.* représenter; symboliser; jouer; −ation *n.* représentation *f.*; −ative *a.* représentatif; −ative *n.* représentant *m.*; député *m.*; House of Representatives Chambre des Représentants

f.
repress *vt.* réprimer; refouler; **-ed** *a.* réprimé; refoulé; **-ion** *n.* répression *f.*
reprieve *n.* commutation *f.*; sursis, répit *m.*; — *vt.* accorder une commutation à
reprimand *n.* réprimande *f.*; — *vt.* réprimander
reprint *n.* réimpression *f.*; tirage à part; tiré à part; *m.*; — *vt.* réimprimer; tirer à part
reprisal *n.* représaille *f.*
reproach *n.* reproche *m.*; beyond — irréprochable; — *vt.* faire des reproches à; **-ful** *a.* plein de reproches
reprobate *n.* vaurien *m.*; roué *m.*; — *vt.* réprouver
reproduce *vt.* reproduire; multiplier; — *vi.* se reproduire; se multiplier
reproduction *n.* reproduction *f.*; copie *f.*
reproof *n.* reproche *m.*, réprimande *f.*
reprove *vt.* réprimander, reprendre, réprouver
reproving *a.* de reproche; réprobateur
republic *n.* république *f.*; **-an** *a.* & *n.* républicain *m.*
republish *vt.* rééditer; republier
repudiate *vt.* répudier, désavouer, renier
repudiation *n.* répudiation *f.*, désaveu *m.*, reniement *m.*
repugnant *a.* répugnant
repulse *vt.* repousser, refouler
repulsion *n.* répugnance *f.*; répulsion *f.*
repulsive *a.* repoussant, dégoûtant, répulsif
repurchase *n.* rachat *m.*; — *vt.* racheter
reputable *a.* honorable, estimable
reputation *n.* réputation *f.*, renom *m.*
repute *n.* réputation *f.*; renom *m.*, renommée *f.*; estime *f.*; **-d** *a.* réputé; attribué; supposé, censé
request *n.* demande *f.*; requête *f.*; sollicitation *f.*; on — sur demande; — *vt.* demander; solliciter; prier
require *vt.* exiger; demander; falloir; **-d** *a.* exigé, demandé; requis, nécessaire, prescrit; voulu; **-ment** *n.* exigence *f.*; besoin *m.*; nécessité *f.*
requisite *a.* requis, nécessaire; — *n.* nécessaire *m.*, chose nécessaire *f.*
requisition *n.* réquisition, demande *f.*; — *vt.* réquisitionner
reroute *vt.* transmettre par une autre route; envoyer par une autre route
rerouting *n.* (telephone) transmission déroutée *f.*
rerun *n.* (TV) répétition *f.*
resaddle *vt.* reseller
resale *n.* revente *f.*
rescind *vt.* rescinder; abroger
rescue *n.* délivrance *f.*; sauvetage *m.*; —

vt. délivrer, sauver; **-r** *n.*, libérateur, sauveur *m.*
research *n.* recherche *f.*; enquête *f.*; investigation *f.*; travaux de recherche *m. pl.*
resemblance *n.* ressemblance *f.*
resemble *vt.* ressembler (à)
resent *vt.* ressentir; s'offenser de; **-ful** *a.* plein de ressentiment; **-ment** *n.* ressentiment *m.*
reservation *n.* réserve *f.*; place louée; chambre retenue *f.*; restriction *f.*; terres réservées *f. pl.*
reserve *n.* réserve *f.*; — power *n.* réserve de puissance *f.*; — *vt.* réserver; louer; retenir; **-d** *a.* réservé; loué; retenu; (person) renfermé
reservoir *n.* réservoir *m.*
reset *vt.* remettre; remonter; recomposer
resettle *vt.* réinstaller; — *vi.* se réinstaller
reside *vi.* résider, demeurer; **-nce** *n.* résidence *f.*; demeure *f.*; domicile *m.*; séjour *m.*; habitation *f.*; maison *f.*; hôtel *m.*; **-nt** *n.* habitant *m.*; résident *m.*; interne *m.*; **-ntial** *a.* d'habitation
residue *n.* résidu *m.*
resign *vt.* résigner; démissionner; — oneself se résigner; **-ation** *n.* démission *f.*; résignation *f.*; **-ed** *a.* résigné
resilience *n.* résilience *f.*; élasticité *f.*; rebondissement *m.*
resiliency *n.* élasticité, résilience *f.*
resilient *a.* élastique
resin *n.* résine *f.*; **-ous** *a.* résineux
resist *vt.* résister; **-ance** *n.* résistance *f.*; (elec.) impédance *f.*; — coil *n.* bobine de résistance *f.*; **-ant** *a.* résistant; **-ible** *a.* résistible; **-or** *n.* (elec.) résistance *f.*
resole *vt.* ressemeler
resolute *a.* résolu, ferme, déterminé; **-ness** *n.* résolution *f.*
resolution *n.* résolution *f.*; décision *f.*; détermination *f.*
resolve *n.* résolution *f.*; — *vt.* résoudre; décider; — *vi.* se résoudre; se décider; **-d** *a.* résolu; décidé
resonance *n.* résonance *f.*, retentissement *m.*
resonant *a.* résonnant; sonore; accordé
resonator *n.* résonateur *m.*
resort *n.* recours *m.*, ressource *f.*; (place) station *f.*; summer — station balnéaire *f.*; — *vi.* avoir recours, recourir
resound *vi.* résonner; retentir; **-ing** *a.* résonnant; retentissant
re-sound *vt.* répéter
resource *n.* ressource *f.*; **-ful** *a.* débrouillard; **-fulness** *n.* ressource *f.*
respect *n.* respect *m.*, estime, considération *f.*; égard *m.*; rapport *m.*; in this —

à cet égard; with — to en ce qui concerne; –s *pl.* hommages, respects *m. pl.*; — *vt.* respecter; estimer, honorer; –ability *n.* respectabilité *f.*; –able *a.* respectable; honorable; convenable, comme il faut; –ful *a.* respectueux; –fully *adv.* respectueusement; –ive *a.* respectif; –ively *adv.* respectivement

respirator *n.* respirateur *m.*; –y *a.* respiratoire

respite *n.* répit, relâche *m.*; délai *m.*

resplendent *a.* resplendissant

respond *vi.* répondre

response *n.* réponse, réplique *f.*; réaction *f.*; accueil *m.*; fonction *f.*, rendement *m.*

responsibility *n.* responsabilité *f.*; charge *f.*; devoir *m.*

responsible *a.* responsable; compétent

responsive *a.* sensible; sympathique; –ness *n.* sensibilité *f.*

rest *n.* repos *m.*; reste *m.*; (support) appui *m.*; (mus.) pause *f.*, whole — pause *f.*, half — demi-pause *f.*, quarter — soupir *m.*; come to — s'arrêter; take a — se reposer; — room lavabo *m.*; — *vt.* reposer; appuyer; — *vi.* se reposer; s'appuyer; peser; –ful *a.* reposant; tranquille; –ive *a.* inquiet; rétif; –less *a.* sans repos; troublé, agité; inquiet; impatient

restate *vt.* énoncer de nouveau; énoncer en d'autres termes

restive *a.* rétif; opiniâtre

restoration *n.* restitution, restauration *f.*

restore *vt.* restituer, restaurer; rendre; remettre; rétablir

restrain *vt.* retenir; contraindre: empêcher; –t *n.* contrainte *f.*; réserve *f.*

restrict *vt.* restreindre; –ed *a.* restreint; limité; –ion *n.* restriction *f.*; –ive *a.* restrictif

result *n.* résultat *m.*; as a — par conséquent; as a — of par suite de; — *vi.* résulter; s'ensuivre; –ant *a.* résultant

resume *vt.* reprendre; se remettre à

resumé *n.* résumé *m.*

resumption *n.* reprise *f.*

resurface *vt.* donner une nouvelle surface à; (road) refaire le revêtement de

resurgent *a.* renaissant

resurrect *vt.* ressusciter; –ion *n.* résurrection *f.*

resuscitate *vt.* ressusciter

resuscitation *n.* retour à la vie *m.*; renaissance *f.*

retail *n.* vente au détail *f.*; détail *m.*; — price prix de détail *m.*; — *vt.* vendre au détail, détailler; –er *n.* marchand au détail; détaillant *m.*

retain *vt.* retenir; garder, conserver; –er

n. avance *f.*; honoraires payés d'avance *m. pl.*; serviteur *m.*; –ing fee *n.* honoraires payés d'avance *m. pl.*; –ing wall *n.* mur de soutènement *m.*

retaliate *vi.* user de représailles

retaliation *n.* représailles *f. pl.*; talion *m.*

retaliatory *a.* de représailles

retard *vt.* retarder; –d *a.* attardé

retch *vi.* vomir

retell *vt.* redire, répéter

retention *n.* conservation *f.*

retentive *a.* tenace; qui retient; –ness *n.* ténacité *f.*

reticence *n.* réticence *f.*

reticent *a.* taciturne

retina *n.* rétine *f.*

retinue *n.* suite *f.*

retire *vi.* se retirer; prendre la retraite; se coucher; se replier; — *vt.* mettre à la retraite; –d *a.* retiré; retraité; en retraite; –ment *n.* retraite *f.*

retiring *a.* réservé; qui prend la retraite; sortant

retort *n.* réplique *f.*; (chem.) cornue *f.*; — *vt. & vi.* répliquer, riposter; renvoyer

retouch *vt.* retoucher

retrace *vt.* retracer; revenir sur

retract *vt.* rétracter; escamoter; se dédire; –able *a.* escamotable; –ion *n.* rétraction *f.*; désaveu *m.*

retread *n.* pneu rechapé *m.*; — *vt.* rechaper

retreat *n.* retraite *f.*; asile *m.*; — *vi.* battre en retraite; se retirer; –ing *a.* qui bat la retraite; (forehead) fuyant

retrench *vt.* restreindre; –ment *n.* réduction *f.*

retribution *n.* récompense *f.*; jugement *m.*

retrieve *vt.* rapporter; retrouver; –r *n.* chien rapporteur *m.*

retroactive *a.* rétroactif; réactif, de réaction

retrograde *a.* rétrograde; — *vi.* rétrograder

retrospect, retrospection *n.* coup d'œil rétrospectif, examen rétrospectif *m.*

return *n.* retour *m.*; profit, revenu *m.*; restitution *f.*; in — en retour; in — for en retour de; en échange de; moyennant; by — mail par retour du courrier; — address adresse de l'expéditeur *f.*; — match match retour *m.*; — ticket billet de retour *m.*; — trip voyage de retour *m.*; — *vi.* revenir; retourner; être de re; tour; rentrer; — *vt.* rendre, restituer-remettre; répondre; rapporter

reunite *vt.* réunir; réconcilier; — *vi.* se réunir; se réconcilier

revamp *vt.* refaçonner, refaire, réorganiser

reveal *vt.* révéler, découvrir; laisser voir; dévoiler; mettre à jour; –ing *a.* révéla-

tour
reveille n. (mil.) diane f.
revel n. divertissement m.; orgie f.; — vi. se divertir; faire bombance; **-ry** n. divertissements m. pl.; bombance f.; orgie f.
revelation n. révélation f.
revenge n. vengeance f.; **take** — se venger (de); — vt. venger; **-ful** a. vengeur, vindicatif
revenue n. revenu m.; rente f.
reverberate vt. retentir; réverbérer
reverberation n. réverbération, répercussion f.
revere vt. révérer, honorer, vénérer; **-nce** n. révérence, vénération f.; **-nd** a. & n. révérend m.; **-nt** a. respectueux
reverie n. rêverie f.
reversal n. revirement m.; inversion f.; renversement m.; (law) réforme f.
reverse a. opposé, contraire; inverse; — side dos m.; envers m.; revers m.; verso m. — n. opposé, contraire, inverse, verso m.; revers m.; verso m.; (auto.) marche arrière f.; — vt. renverser; invertir; retourner; faire marche arrière; (law) réformer, revoquer
revert vi. retourner, revenir
review n. revue f.; révision f.; examen m. compte rendu m.; — vt. reviser; passer en revue; faire le compte rendu de; **-er** n. critique m.
revile vt. injurier, insulter
revisal n. revision f.; (print.) seconde f., (2nd) troisième épreuve d'auteur
revise vt. revoir, reviser; corriger
reviser n. réviseur m.
revision n. révision f.
revisit vt. visiter de **nouveau**, revisiter
revival n. retour à la vie m.; renaissance f.; reprise f.; réveil m.; renouveau m.; **-ist** n. revivaliste m. & f.
revive vt. faire revivre, ressusciter; réveiller; renouveler; ranimer; — vi. reprendre connaissance; ressusciter se ranimer; renaître; reprendre
revocable a. révocable
revocation n. révocation f.
revoke vt. révoquer
revolt n. révolte f.; — vi. se révolter, se rebeller, s'insurger, se soulever; **-ing** a. en révolte; repoussant, révoltant
revolution n. révolution f.; tour m.; **-ary** a. & n. révolutionnaire m. & f.; **-ist** n. révolutionnaire m. & f.; **-ize** vt. révolutionner
revolve vt. faire tourner, retourner; — vi. tourner; **-r** n. révolver m.
revolving a. tournant; pivotant
revulsion n. revirement m.

reward n. récompense f.; — vt. récompenser
rewind vt. rembobiner, réenrouler
reword vt. redire en d'autres termes; rédiger de nouveau
rewrite vt. récrire; refaire, remanier
rhapsody n. rapsodie f.
Rheims n. Reims
Rhenish a. rhénan, du Rhin
rhetoric n. rhétorique f.; **-al** a. de rhétorique; **-ian** n. rhétoricien, rhéteur m.
rheumatic a. rhumatismal; — **fever** n. rhumatisme articulaire m.; — n. rhumatisant m.
rheumatism n. rhumatisme m.
Rhine n. Rhin m.
rhinestone n. faux diamant m.
rhubarb n. rhubarbe f.
rhyme n. rime f.; vers m.; — vi. rimer; — vt. faire rimer; **neither — nor reason** ni rime ni raison
rhythm n. rythme m.; **-mically** adv. avec rythme; **-mical** a. rythmique, rythmé
rib n. côte f.; nervure f.; support m.; — vt. garnir de nervures; (coll.) faire marcher; taquiner; **-bed** a. à nervures, à cotes
ribald a. libertin, obscène; **-ry** n. libertinage m.; langage licencieux m.
ribbon n. ruban m.; bande f.; **tear to -s** déchiqueter; mettre en lambeaux
rice n. riz m.; — **field**, — **paddy** n. rizière — **paper** n. papier de riz m.; — **pudding** n. riz au lait m.
rich a. riche; fertile; gras; somptueux; — n. riches m. pl.; **-es** n. pl. richesse f.; **-ness** n. richesse f.; fertilité f.; somptuosité f.
rickets n. pl. rachitisme m.
rickety a. délabré, boiteux, bancal; (med.) rachitique
rickrack n. passement en zigzag m., bordure f.
ricochet vi. ricocher
rid vt. débarrasser; purger; délivrer; **get — of** se débarrasser de, se défaire de; **-dance** n. débarras m.
riddle n. devinette f.; énigme f.; — vt. cribler
ride n. voyage m., promenade f.; trajet m.; **go for a —** (aller) faire une promenade (en auto) — vi. aller, voyager, se promener; aller à cheval, monter à cheval; — vt. monter; (coll.) ennuyer; harasser; taquiner; **-r** n. personne qui va en auto passager m. & f.; cavalier m.; jockey m.; (law) clause additionnelle f., annexe, allonge f.
ridge n. arête f.; crête f.; ride f.
ridicule n. ridicule m.; risée f.; raillerie,

moquerie *f.*; — *vt.* se moquer de

ridiculous *a.* ridicule; **–ness** *n.* ridicule *m.*

riding *n.* équitation *f.*; — **boots** *n. pl.* bottes *f. pl.*; — **breeches** *n. pl.* culotte de cheval *f.*; — **habit** *n.* amazone *f.*; — **master** maître d'équitation *m.*

RH factor *n.* facteur RH *m.*

Rhodesia *n.* Rhodésie *f.*

rife *a.*, **to be** — sévir

riffraff *n.* canaille *f.*

rifle *n.* fusil *m.*; carabine *f.*; — **range** champ de tir *m.*; — **shot** coup de fusil *m.*; **within** — **shot** à portée de fusil; — *vt.* (guns) rayer; piller; fouiller

rifleman *n.* chasseur, tirailleur, fusilier *m.*

rifling *n.* pillage *m.*; (rifle bore) rayage *m.*

rift *n.* fente, fissure *f.*; (persons) brouille *f.*

rig *n.* (naut.) gréement *m.*; équipement *m.*; voiture *f.*; attelage *m.*; — *vt.* gréer, équiper; installer, monter; (coll.) truquer; **–ging** *n.* gréage *m.*; équipage *m.*; agrès *m. pl.*

right *a.* droit; juste; bon; correct; exact; (watch) à l'heure; **all** — bon; bien; entendu; — **angle** *n.* angle droit *m.*; **be** — avoir raison; **that's** — c'est cela; — **side** endroit, bon côté *m.*; — **side up** à l'endroit; — *adv.* droit; tout; **do** — faire bien; **go** — réussir; aller à droite; — **and left** de tous les côtés; — **away** tout de suite, sur-le-champ; — *n.* droit *m.*; bien *m.*; titre *m.*; droite *f.*; — **and wrong** le bien et le mal; **on the** —, **to the** — à droite; **keep to the** — tenir la droite; serrer à droite; **–s** *n. pl.* droit(s) *m. pl.*; **within one's –s** dans son droit; *vt.* redresser, réparer; rectifier; **–eous** *a.* droit, juste; **–eousness** *n.* droiture *f.*; **–ful** *a.* légitime; **–ist** *n.* partisan de la droite *m.*; **–fully** *adv.* à juste titre; **–ness** *n.* justesse *f.*

rightabout face *n.* demi-tour à droite *m.*; (fig.) revirement *m.*

right-hand *a.* de droite; de la main droite; — **man** bras droit *m.*; **–ed** *a.* droitier

right-of-way *n.* priorité *f.*; (rail.) voie *f.*

right-wing *a.* de droite; **–er** *n.* partisan de la droite *m.*

rigid *a.* rigide; raide; sévère; **–ity** *n.* rigidité *f.*; raideur *f.*; sévérité *f.*

rigmarole *n.* procédure compliquée *f.*; galimatias *m.*

rigor *n.* rigueur *f.*; sévérité *f.*; — **mortis** rigidité cadavérique *f.*; **–ous** *a.* rigoureux; sévère; **–ousness** *n.* rigueur *f.*

rile *vt.* troubler; faire enrager

rim *n.* bord *m.*; (eyeglasses) monture *f.*; — *vt.* border; **–less** *a.* sans monture

rind *n.* peau *f.*; pelure *f.*; écorce *f.*; croûte *f.*

ring *n.* anneau *m.*, bague *f.*; cercle *m.*; alliance *f.*; rond *m.*; groupe *m.*; bande *f.*; arène *f.*; (boxing) ring *m.*; (circuit) enceinte *f.*; sonnerie *f.*; coup de téléphone *m.*; — **finger** annulaire *m.*; **wedding** — alliance *f.*; — *vt.* entourer; sonner; — *vi.* sonner; résonner, retentir; tinter; **–ing** *n.* son *m.*; tintement *m.*; **–er** *n.* (bell) sonnette *f.*; (person) sonneur *m.*; **dead –er** (coll.) jumeau, double *m.*

ringleader *n.* chef, meneur *m.*

ringworm *n.* teigne (tonsurante) *f.*

rink *n.* patinoire *f.*

rinse *vt.* rincer; — *n.* (hair) rinçage *m.*

riot *n.* émeute *f.*; — **squad** police-secours *f.*; — *vi.* s'ameuter; **–ing** *n.* émeutes *f. pl.*; **–ous** *a.* tumultueux; déréglé, dissipé

rip *n.* déchirure *f.*; **–cord** *n.* corde d'ouverture *f.*; — *vt.* découdre, déchirer; — *vi.* se déchirer; — **open** ouvrir en déchirant

ripe *a.* mûr; prêt; **–n** *vt.* (faire) mûrir; **–n** *vi.* mûrir; **–ness** *n.* maturité *f.*

ripple *n.* ride *f.*; gazouillement *m.*; ondulation *f.*; murmure *m.*; — *vt.* rider; — *vi.* se rider; onduler; murmurer; parler

rippling *n.* murmure *m.*; clapotage *m.*; — *a.* murmurant

rise *n.* lever *m.*; hausse *f.*; élévation *f.*; (ground) éminence *f.*; (tide) montée *f.*; — *vi.* se lever; s'élever; monter; se soulever; se dresser; **–r** *n.* contremarche *f.*

rising *a.* levant; montant; en hausse; — *n.* lever *m.*; hausse *f.*

risk *n.* risque, péril *m.*; **run a** — courir un risque; — *vt.* risquer; hasarder; **–y** *a.* hasardeux; (story) risqué

rite *n.* rite *m.*; cérémonie *f.*

ritual *a.* rituel; — *n.* rituel *m.*; rites *m. pl.*; **–istic** *a.* rituel

rival *a. & n.* rival *m.*; émule *m. & f.*; — *vt.* rivaliser avec; **–ry** *n.* rivalité *f.*; émulation *f.*

river *n.* fleuve *m.*; rivière *f.*; **down** — en aval; **up** — en amont

riverside *n.* bord de la rivière *m.*; — *a.* qui s'étend au bord de l'eau; riverain

rivet *n.* rivet *m.*; clou (à river) *m.*; — *vt.* river, riveter; **–er** *n.* (machine) riveteuse *f.*; **–ing** *n.* rivetage *m.*

Riviera *n.* Côte d'Azur *f.*

rivulet *n.* ruisseau *m.*

road *n.* chemin *m.*; route *f.*; voie *f.*; — **map** carte routière *f.*; **on the** — en voyage; en province

roadbed *n.* empierrement *m.*

roadblock *n.* barricade *f.*

roadhouse *n.* cabaret au bord de la route *m.*; auberge *f.*

roadside *n.* bord de la route *m.*

roadster *n.* coupé *m.*

roadway *n.* voie *f.*; chaussée *f.*

roam *vi.* errer, rôder (dans); — *vt.* parcourir, errer çà et là (par); –ing *a.* errant; –er *n.* vagabond *m.*

roar *n.* rugissement *m.*; mugissement *m.*; grondement *m.*; éclat *m.*; — *vi.* rugir; mugir; gronder; éclater; –ing *a.* mugissant, pétillant

roast *a.* & *n.* rôti *m.*; — beef rosbif *m.*; — *vt.* rôtir; griller; (coffee) torréfier; –er *n.* rôtissoire *f.*; (coffee) brûloir *m.*; –ing *n.* cuisson *f.*; (coffee) torréfaction *f.*

rob *vt.* voler; –ber *n.* voleur *m.*; –bery *n.* vol *m.*

robe *n.* robe *f.*; couverture *f.*; — *vt.* vêtir; — *vi.* se vêtir

robot *n.* automate *m.*

robust *a.* robuste, vigoureux; –ness *n.* vigueur, force *f.*

rock *n.* roc, rocher *m.*, roche *f.*, pierre *f.*; — candy *n.* sucre candi *m.*; — crystal cristal de roche *m.*; — garden jardin de rocaille *m.*; — salt sel gemme *m.*; — *vt.* balancer, bercer; — *vi.* balancer; –er *n.* bascule *f.*; (chair) rocking-chair, fauteuil à bascule *m.*; –ing *n.* bercement, balancement *m.*; tremblement *m.*; –y *a.* rocheux; rocailleux

rock-bottom *a.* dernier, le plus bas

rocket *n.* fusée, roquette *f.*; — launcher lance-fusée, lance-roquette *m.*; — motor moteur-fusée, moteur-roquette *m.*

rocketry *n.* science des fusées *f.*

rocking chair *n.* chaise à bascule *f.*, rocking-chair *m.*

Rocky Mountains *n.* *pl.* Montagnes Rocheuses *f.* *pl.*

rod *n.* baguette, verge *f.*; tige *f.*; (measurement) perche *f.*; connecting — bielle motrice *f.*; curtain — tringle *f.*; fishing — canne à pêche *f.*

rodent *a.* & *n.* rongeur *m.*

rodeo *n.* concours d'équitation des cowboys *m.*

Roentgen *n.* röntgen *m.*; — rays *n.* *pl.* rayons X *m.* *pl.*; — tube *n.* tube à rayons X *m.*

rogue *n.* fripon, coquin *m.*

roguish *a.* fripon, malin; –ness *n.* friponnerie, malice *f.*

roil *vt.* troubler

role *n.* rôle *m.*

roll *n.* rouleau *m.*; petit pain *m.*; liste *f.*; roulement *m.*; (naut.) roulis *m.*; call the — faire l'appel; — call appel *m.*; — *vt.* rouler; (metal) laminer; — *vi.* rouler; — over (se) retourner; — up enrouler; (sleeve) retrousser; –er *n.* rouleau *m.*;

(metal) cylindre; –er bearings *n.* *pl.* roulement à rouleaux *m.*; –er coaster *n.* montagnes russes *f.* *pl.*; –er skates patins à roulettes *m.* *pl.*; –ing *a.* roulant; ondulé; –ing *n.* roulement *m.*; roulis *m.*; –ing mill usine de laminage *f.*; –ing pin rouleau *m.*, bille *f.*

roly-poly *a.* dodu, potelé

romaine *n.* romaine *f.*

Roman *a.* & *n.* romain *m.*; — numerals chiffres romains *m.* *pl.*; — type caractères romains *m.* *pl.*; –ic *a.* roman

romance *n.* roman *m.*; aventure sentimentale *f.*; histoire romanesque *f.*; (mus.) romance *f.*; — *vt.* romancer

Romance languages *n.* langues romanes *f.* *pl.*

Romanesque *a.* & *n.* roman *m.*

Romania *n.* Roumanie *f.*; –n *a.* & *n.* roumain *m.*

romantic *a.* romanesque; sentimental; (lit.) romantique; –ism *n.* romantisme *m.*

Romany *n.* les gitanes *m.* *pl.*; langue des gitanes *f.*

romp *vi.* jouer, folâtrer, badiner; — *n.* gamine *f.*; (play) tapage; –ers *m.* *pl.* barboteuse *f.*

rood *n.* quart d'arpent *m.*; crucifix *m.*; — screen *n.* jubé *m.*

roof *n.* toit *m.*; toiture *f.*; — of the mouth dôme du palais *m.*; — *vt.* couvrir; –ing *n.* toiture *f.*; –less *a.* sans toit, sans abri

rook *n.* (chess) tour *f.*; — *vt.* escroquer, (se) rouler, filouter

room *n.* place *f.*; espace *m.*; pièce *f.*; salle *f.*; chambre *f.*; at — temperature chambré; make — for faire place à; — *vi.* vivre en pension, vivre en garni; habiter; –er *n.* pensionnaire *m.* & *f.*; souslocataire *m.* & *f.*; –y *a.* ample; spacieux

roomette *n.* (rail.) cabine de wagon-lits *f.*

roommate *n.* compagnon de chambre *m.*

roost *n.* perchoir, juchoir *m.*; — *vi.* se percher, se jucher; –er *n.* coq *m.*

root *n.* racine *f.*; fond *m.*; source *f.*; — beer (sorte de) boisson gazeuse *f.*; square — racine carrée *f.*; take — prendre racine; — *vt.* enraciner; — for (sports) être partisan de; — out déraciner; extirper; –ed *a.* cloué, figé

rope *n.* corde *f.*; cordage *m.*; cordon *m.*; — *vt.* lier; corder

ropemaker *n.* cordier *m.*

rosary *n.* rosaire *m.*; (eccl.) chapelet *m.*

rose *n.* rose *f.*; (color) rose *m.*; — window (arch.) rosace *f.*; wild — églantine *f.*

rosebud *n.* bouton de rose *m.*

rosebush *n.* rosier *m.*

rose-colored *a.* couleur de rose, rosé; **look through —** glasses voir la vie en rose

rosemary *n.* romarin *m.*

rosin *n.* résine, colophane *f.*

roster *n.* tableau *m.*, liste *f.*

rostrum *n.* tribune *f.*

rosy *a.* couleur de rose; rose, rosé; vermeil

rot *n.* pourriture *f.*; mildiou *m.*; (fig., coll.) blague; sottise *f.* — *vi.* pourrir; se putréfier; se décomposer; (teeth) se carier; **–ten** *a.* pourri; (eggs) gâté; sale; (coll.) de chien; (teeth) carié

rotary *a.* de rotation; rotatif; **— press** *n.* rotative *f.*

rotate *vi.* tourner tournoyer; pivoter; — *vt.* faire tourner; alterner; (crops) varier

rotation *n.* rotation *f.*; (agr.) assolement *m.*; **in —** à tour de rôle

rote *n.* routine *f.*; **by —** par routine; par cœur

rotogravure *n.* rotogravure *f.*

rotund *a.* rond, arrondi; **–ity** *n.* rondeur, rotondité *f.*

rotunda *n.* rotonde *f.*

rouge *n.* fard, rouge *m.*; — *vt.* mettre du rouge

rough *a.* rude; inégal; grossier; brutal; approximatif; **— draft, — sketch** ébauche *f.* croquis *m.*; **— premier jet** *m.*; **— weather** gros temps *m.*; **—, –en** *vt.* rendre rude; **—, –en** *vi.* devenir rude; grossir; **–ly** *adv.* rudement, brutalement; à peu pres, approximativement; **treat –ly** brutaliser, malmener; **–ness** *n.* rudesse *f.*; inégalité *f.*; **–shod, ride –shod over** fouler aux pieds; traiter brutalement

roughage *n.* matières cellulosique *f. pl.*

round *a.* rond, circulaire; (tone) plein; **— numbers** chiffres ronds *m. pl.*; **— table** table ronde *f.*; **— trip** *a. & n.* aller et retour *m.*; **— *n.*** rond, cercle *m.*; tour *m.* tournée *f.*; (mil.) ronde *f.*; salve *f.*; (mus.) canon *m.*; (boxing) round *m.*; — *vt.* arrondir; **— up** *vi.* rassembler; — *adv.* autour de; à la ronde; — *prep.* par, autour de; **–ed** *a.* arrondi; rebondi; **–ness** *n.* rondeur *f.*; **— steak** *n.* bifteck pris dans le jarret *m.*

roundabout *a.* indirect, détourné

roundhouse *n.* (rail.) remise pour locomotives *f.*

round-shouldered *a.* voûté

round-the-clock *a.* jour et nuit

roundup *n.* rassemblement *m.*

rouse *vt.* réveiller, éveiller; remuer; mettre en colère; — *vi.* se réveiller

rousing *a.* entraînant; bon, grand

rout *n.* déroute *f.*; — *vt.* mettre en déroute

route *n.* route *f.*; itinéraire *m.*; direction *f.*

routine *n.* routine *f.*; — *a.* courant

rove *vi.* rôder, errer, vagabonder; — *vt.* parcourir, errer par; **–r** *n.* vagabond *n.*

roving *a.* vagabond, errant

row *n.* rang *m.*, rangée, file, ligne *f.*; (agr.) rayon *m.*; — *vi.* ramer; nager, canoter; — *vt.* conduire à l'aviron; **–er** *n.* rameur *m.*; canotier *m.*; **–ing** *n.* canotage *m.*

rowboat *n.* bateau à rames *m.*

royal *a.* royal (*pl.* royaux); du roi; princier; **–ist** *n.* royaliste *m. & f.*; **–ly** *adv.* royalement; **–ty** *n.* royauté *f.*; redevance *f.*, droits d'auteur *m. pl.*

r.p.m.: revolutions per minute *n.* tours par minute *m. pl.*

rub *n.* frottement *m.*; friction *f.*; difficulté *f.*; — *vt.* frotter; frictionner; — *vi.* (se) frotter; **— down** frictionner; **— out** effacer

rubber *n.* caoutchouc *m.*; gomme *f.*; (cards) robre *m.*; (person) masseur *m.*, masseuse *f.*; **— band** élastique, bracelet de caoutchouc, ruban de caoutchouc *m.*; **— stamp** timbre en caoutchouc, tampon *m.*; **–ize** *vt.* caoutchouter

rubberneck *n. & a.* badaud *m.*; (coll.) touriste *m. & f.*; — *vi.* badauder

rubbish *n.* décombres *m. pl.*, ordures *f. pl.*; rebuts *m. pl.*; débris *m. pl.*; blague, bêtise *f.*; fatras *m.*

rubble *n.* rocaille *f.*; blocaille *f.*

rubric *n.* rubrique *f.*

rudder *n.* gouvernail *m.*

ruddy *a.* rouge, rougeâtre; coloré

rude *a.* impoli, mal élevé; grossier; rude; violent; **–ness** *n.* impolitesse *f.*; grossièreté *f.*; rudesse *f.*

rudiment *n.* rudiment *m.*; **–s** *pl.* éléments, rudiments *m. pl.*; **–ary** *a.* rudimentaire

rue *vt.* regretter, se repentir de; — *n.* rue *f.*; **–ful** *a.* triste; déplorable

ruff *n.* fraise *f.*

ruffian *n.* brute *f.*; bandit, brigand *m.*

ruffle *n.* volant *m.*, ruche *f.*; (fig.) trouble *m.*; (drum) roulement *m.*; — *vt.* troubler; froisser; plisser; rucher

rug *n.* tapis *m.*; **bedside —** descente de lit *f.*

rugged *a.* rude; raboteux; solide; **–ness** *n.* rudesse *f.*; aspérité *f.*

ruin *n.* ruine *f.*; **go to —** tomber en ruine; — *vt.* ruiner; perdre; abîmer; **–ation** *n.* ruine, perte *f.*; **–ed** *a.* abîme; ruiné; en ruines

ruinous *a.* ruineux

rule *n.* règle *f.*; règlement *m.*; autorité *f.*; ordonnance *f.*; décision *f.*; **as a —** en général; en principe; **slide —** règle à calcul *f.*; — *vt.* régler (sur), régir; décider; tracer à la règle; — *vi.* régner; **— out** éliminer, écarter; **–r** *n.* souverain *m.*; roi *m.*; (measuring) règle *f.*, mètre *m.*

rule of thumb *n.* approximation *f.*

ruling *a.* dirigeant; dominant; — *n.* décision, ordonnance *f.*

rum *n.* rhum *m.*; **-runner** *n.* contrebandier d'alcool *m.*

Rumania *n.* Roumanie *f.*; **-n** *a.* & *n.* Roumain

rumble *n.* grondement *m.*; grouillement *m.*; (coll.) bagarre *f.*; — **seat** *n.* banquette arrière *f.*, — *vi.* gronder; grouiller

ruminate *vi.* ruminer; méditer

rummage *n.* choses usagées *f. pl.*, objets usagés *m. pl.*; — **sale** vente d'objets usagés *f.*; — *vt.* fouiller

rumor *n.* bruit *m.*, rumeur *f.*; — *vt.*, **it is -ed that** le bruit court que

rump *n.* croupe *f.*; — **steak** *n.* romsteck *m.*

rumple *vt.* froisser, chiffonner

rumpus *n.* chahut, chamaillis, fracas *m.*

run *n.* course *f.*; cours *m.*, marche *f.*; suite *f.*; parcours, trajet *m.*; libre accès *m.*; durée *f.*; (fish) remonte *f.*; (luck) veine *f.*; (sports) point *m.*; (stocking) échelle *f.*, maille partie *f.*; **first** — *a.* (movies) en exclusivité; **in the long** — à la longue; **on the** — à courir; qui court; qui s'enfuit; — *vi.* courir; fuir, s'enfuir, se sauver; couler; marcher, fonctionner; (eyes) pleurer; (fish) remonter; (material) déteindre; durer; (pol.) être candidat, poser sa candidature; — *vt.* faire courir; courir; diriger; tenir; — **across** rencontrer, tomber sur; — **along** longer; filer, s'en aller; — **an errand** faire une course; — **a red light** brûler un feu rouge; — **a temperature** avoir de la fièvre; — **away** se sauver, s'échapper, s'enfuir; — **away with** enlever; — **down** descendre en courant; couler; délabrer; — **for it** se sauver; — **into** rencontrer; heurter; — **on** continuer; — **out** expirer; s'épuiser; cesser; prendre fin; — **over** écraser; déborder; — **through** parcourir; transpercer; (money) manger, gaspiller; — **up** monter en courant; laisser accumuler; — **up against** se heurter contre, se briser contre; avoir à lutter avec; **-ner** *n.* coureur *m.*; courrier *m.*; galet *m.*; **-ning** *a.* courant; continu, soutenu; de suite; **-ning** *n.* course *f.*; marche *f.*, fonctionnement *m.*; direction *f.*; **-ning board** marchepied *m.*

run-down *a.* épuisé; déchargé; délabré; — *n.* (coll.) résumé *m.*, explication *f.*

rung *n.* traverse *f.*, barreau, échelon *m.*

runner-up *n.* deuxième, accessit *m.*

run-of-the-mill *a.* ordinaire, commun

runt *n.* avorton, nain *m.*

runway *n.* piste *f.*

rupture *n.* rupture *f.*; hernie *f.*; — *vt.* rompre; — *vi.* se rompre; **-d** *a.* rompu; hernié

rural *a.* rural; de la campagne; agreste; champêtre

rush *n.* ruée *f.*; bond *m.*; hâte *f.*; (bot.) jonc *m.*; — **hours** heures d'affluence *f. pl.*; — **order** commande urgente *f.*; — *vi.* se précipiter, s'élancer; se dépêcher; — *vt.* dépêcher; faire (quelque chose) d'urgence

rusk *n.* biscotte *f.*

russet *a.* roussâtre; rustique

Russia *n.* Russie *f.*; U.R.S.S. *f.*; **-n** *a.* & *n.* russe; Soviétique *m.*

rust *n.* rouille *f.*; — *vi.* & *vt.* (se) rouiller; **-y** *a.* rouillé; rouilleux; **-proof** *a.* antirouille; inoxydable

rustic *a.* agreste, rustique; — *n.* compagnard, paysan *m.*; **-ate** *vi.* vivre à la campagne, se faire campagnard

rustle *n.* froissement *m.*; — *vi.* bruire; — *vt.* froisser; faire bruire

rut *n.* ornière *f.*; routine *f.*

rutabaga *n.* rutabaga *m.*

ruthless *a.* impitoyable; brutal; **-ly** *adv.* sans pitié; **-ness** *n.* dureté, cruauté, inhumanité *f.*

rye *n.* seigle *m.*; (drink) whisky de seigle, whisky irlandais *m.*; — **bread** pain de seigle *m.*

S

Saar *n.* Sarre *f.*; **-lander** *n.* Sarrois *m.*

Sabbath *n.* sabbat *m.*; dimanche *m.*

saber, sabre *n.* sabre *m.*

sable *n.* zibeline *f.*; (heraldry) sable *m.*

sabotage *n.* sabotage *m.*; — *vt.* saboter

saccharin *n.* saccharine *f.*

sack *n.* sac *m.*; pillage *m.*; — *vt.* mettre en sac; saccager, piller

sackcloth *n.* toile à sacs *f.*; toile d'emballage *f.*; sac *m.*

sacrament *n.* sacrement *m.*; **-al** *a.* sacramental

sacred *a.* sacré; saint; consacré

sacrifice *n.* sacrifice *m.*, immolation *f.*; offrande *f.*; (com.) vente à perte; — *vt.* sacrifier, immoler; renoncer à; (com.) vendre à perte

sacrificial *a.* sacrificatoire

sacrilege *n.* sacrilège *m.*

sacrilegious *a.* sacrilège

sacristan *n.* sacristan *m.*

sacristy *n.* sacristie *f.*

sacrosanct *a.* sacro-saint

sad *a.* triste; morne; **-den** *vt.* attrister; **-ly** *adv.* tristement; très, fort; **-ness**

S
T
U

n. tristesse *f.*

saddle *n.* selle *f.*; **-bag** *n.* sacoche, musette *f.*; **-cloth** *n.* housse de cheval *f.*; **— horse** *n.* cheval de selle *m.*; **— vt.** seller; charger; **be –d with** avoir sur le dos

safe *n.* coffre-fort *m.*; **— a.** sauf; sûr; à l'abri; sans danger; **— and sound** sain et sauf; **-ly** *adv.* sans danger; sans accident; à coup sûr; **-ness** *n.* sûreté; sécurité *f.*; **-ty** *n.* sûreté, sécurité *f.*; **-ty catch** cran de sûreté; **— pin** épingle de sûreté *f.*; **-ty valve** soupape de sûreté *f.*

safe-conduct *n.* sauf-conduit *m.*

safe-deposit box *n.* (bank) coffre-fort *m.*

safeguard *n.* sauvegarde *f.*; **— vt.** sauvegarder

safekeeping *n.* bonne garde *f.*

safety island *n.* refuge; refuge pour piétons *m.*

safety match *n.* allumette de sûreté *f.*

safety razor *n.* rasoir de sûreté *m.*

saffron *n.* safran *m.*

sag *n.* fléchissement *m.*; flèche *f.*; **— vi.** fléchir, s'affaisser; pendre; **-ging** *a.* fléchissant; (com.) creux

sagacious *a.* sage, intelligent, sagace

sagacity *n.* sagacité *f.*

sage *a.* sage, prudent; **— n.** sage *m.*; philosophe *m.*; (bot.) sauge *f.*

said *a.* ledit, susdit

sail *n.* voile *f.*; toile *f.*; voyage *m.*; promenade à la voile *f.*; **— vt.** naviguer; conduire; **— vi.** aller à la voile; naviguer; voguer; planer; **-ing** *a.*, **-ing ship** voilier *m.*; **-ing** *n.* navigation *f.*; marche *f.*; départ *m.*; **-or** *n.* marin, matelot *m.*

sailboat *n.* bateau à voiles *m.*; canot à voiles *m.*

sailcloth *n.* toile à voile *f.*

saint *n.* saint *m.*, sainte *f.*; **-ed** *a.* saint; canonisé; **-ly** *a.* saint

Saint Helena *n.* Sainte-Hélène *f.*

sake *n.*, **for the — of** pour; pour l'amour de; à cause de; dans l'intérêt de

salaam *n.* salamalec *m.*; **— vi.** faire des salamalecs

salable *a.* qui peut se vendre, qui se vend bien

salacious *a.* lubrique, lascif; **-ness** *n.* lubricité, lasciveté *f.*

salad *n.* salade *f.*; **fruit —** macédoine de fruits *f.*; **— bowl** saladier *m.*; **— dressing** sauce *f.*; huile *f.* et vinaigre *m.*; assaisonnement pour salade *m.*

salaried *a.* aux appointements, salarié

salary *n.* salaire; traitement *m.*, appointements *m. pl.*

sale *n.* vente *f.*; vente de soldes *f.*; solde(s) *m.* (*pl.*); **auction —** vente aux enchères;

for **—** à vendre; **on —** en vente; solde(s); **-s slip** *n.* reçu *m.*

salesclerk *n.* vendeur *m.*, vendeuse *f.*

salesman *n.* vendeur *m.*; représentant *m.*; (commis) voyageur *m.*; **-ship** *n.* art de vendre *m.*

salesroom *n.* salle des ventes *f.*

sales tax *n.* impôt sur la vente *m.*

saleswoman *n.* vendeuse *f.*

salicylic *a.* salicylique

salient *a.* & *n.* saillant

saline *a.* salin

saliva *n.* salive *f.*; **-ry** *a.* salivaire

sallow *a.* jaunâtre, olivâtre

salmon *n.* saumon *m.*; **— trout** *n.* truite saumonée *f.*

saloon *n.* buvette *f.*; café *m.*; bar *m.*

salsify *n.* salsifis *m.*

salt *n.* sel *m.*; **coarse —** gros sel *m.*; **rock —** sel gemme *m.*; **table —** sel blanc *m.*; **-ed** *a.* salé; **— water** *n.* eau de mer *f.*; **— vt.** saler; **-y** *a.* salé; de sel

saltceller, salt shaker *n.* salière *f.*

saltine *n.* biscuit très salé *m.*

saltpetre *n.* salpêtre *m.*

salt-water *a.* salé, d'eau de mer

salubrious *a.* salubre

salutary *a.* salutaire

salutation *n.* salutation *f.*; salut *m.*

salute *n.* salut *m.*; salve *f.*; **— vt.** (guns) salver; (person) saluer

salvage *n.* sauvetage *m.*; récupération *f.*; relevage *m.*; **— vt.** sauver; récupérer; relever

salvation *n.* salut *m.*

salve *n.* onguent, baume *m.*; **— vt.** adoucir, calmer

salvo *n.* salve *f.*

Samaritan *n.* samaritain *m.*

same *a.* même; identique; **all the —** tout de même; quand même; **it's all the — to me** cela m'est égal; **at the — time** en même temps; à la fois; **the — to you** à vous de même; **-ness** *n.* identité *f.*; monotonie *f.*

sample *n.* échantillon *m.*; exemple *m.*; **— vt.** goûter, déguster; essayer; échantillonner; **-r** *n.* (person) échantillonneur *m.*; modèle *m.*

sampling *n.* choix *m.*

sanctify *vt.* consacrer; sanctifier

sanctimonious *a.* confit; béat

sanction *n.* sanction *f.*; consentement *m.*; **— vt.** sanctionner

sanctity *n.* sainteté *f.*

sanctuary *n.* sanctuaire *m.*; asile, refuge *m.*

sand *n.* sable *m.*; **— vt.** sablonner; sabler; poncer; passer au papier de verre; **-y** *a.* sablonneux, sableux, sablé; (hair) blond

roux
sandal *n.* sandale *f.*
sandbag *n.* sac à terre *m.*; — *vt.* protéger par des sacs à terre
sand bar *n.* banc de sable *m.*
sandblast *n.* jet de sable *m.*; — *vt.* décaper
sandbox *n.* boîte à sable *f.*
sandpaper *n.* papier de verre *m.*; — *vt.* poncer, doucir, passer au papier de verre
sand pit *n.* sablière *f.*
sandstone *n.* grès *m.*
sandstorm *n.* tempête de sable *f.*, simoun *m.*
sandwich *n.* sandwich *m.*; — **man** homme-affiches *m.*; — *vt.* intercaler; serrer
sane *a.* sain (d'esprit); raisonnable; sensé
sanforize *vt.* rendre irrétrécissable
sanguinary *a.* sanguinaire
sanitarium *n.* sanatorium *m.*
sanitary *a.* sanitaire; hygiénique
sanitation *n.* système sanitaire *m.*; hygiène *f.*
sanity *n.* santé (d'esprit) *f.*
San Marino *n.* Saint-Marin *m.*
Sanscrit *a. & n.* sanscrit *m.*
sap *n.* sève *f.*; (mil.) sape *f.*; — *vt.* saper, miner; —**per** *n.* sapeur *m.*
sapling *n.* jeune arbre *m.*
Saracen *n. & a.* Sarrasin *m.*
sarcasm *n.* sarcasme *m.*; ironie *f.*
sarcastic *a.* sarcastique
sarcophagus *n.* sarcophage *m.*
Sardinia *n.* Sardaigne *f.*
sash *n.* ceinture *f.*; écharpe *f.*; cadre, (window) châssis *m.*
Satan *n.* Satan *m.*
satanic *a.* satanique
satchel *n.* sacoche *f.*; valise *f.*
sateen *n.* satinette *f.*
satellite *n.* satellite *m.*
satiate *vt.* rassasier (de); — *a.* rassasié
satiation, satiety *n.* satiété *f.*
satin *n.* satin *m.*; — *a.* satiné; de satin; —**y** *a.* satiné
satirical *a.* satirique
satirist *n.* auteur satirique *m.*
satirize *vt. & vi.* satiriser
satisfaction *n.* satisfaction *f.*; contentement *m.*; réparation *f.*; dédommagement *m.*
satisfactory *a.* satisfaisant; acceptable
satisfy *vt. & vi.* satisfaire, contenter; remplir; faire réparation; suffire à; convaincre
saturate *vt.* saturer; tremper; become –d s'imprégner
saturation *n.* saturation *f.*; imprégnation *f.*
Saturday *n.* samedi *m.*

saucedish *n.* saucière *f.*
saucepan *n.* casserole *f.*
saucer *n.* soucoupe *f.*; flying — soucoupe volante *f.*
saucy *a.* impertinent; insolent; effronté
Saudi Arabia *n.* Arabie Soudite *f.*
sauerkraut *n.* choucroute *f.*
saunter *vi.* flâner, aller lentement
sausage *n.* saucisse *f.*; saucisson *m.*; — meat *n.* chair à saucisse *f.*
savage *a.* sauvage; brutal; féroce; — *n.* sauvage *m. & f.*; —**ry** *n.* sauvagerie *f.*; brutalité *f.*; férocité *f.*
save *vt.* sauver; préserver; protéger; réserver, retenir; économiser, mettre de côté; éviter; épargner; — *prep.* sauf, excepté, à l'exception de; hormis; —**r** *n.* sauveur *m.*; sauveteur *m.*; personne économe *f.*
saving *a.* qui sauve; économe; — *n.* sauvetage *m.*; salut *m.*; épargne, économie *f.*; —**s bank** *n.* caisse d'épargne *f.*; —**s bond** *n.* bon d'épargne *m.*
Saviour *n.* Le Sauveur *m.*
savor *n.* saveur *f.*; goût *m.*; —*vt.* savourer; —**y** *a.* savoureux; piquant
saw *n.* scie *f.*; — *vt.* scier
sawdust *n.* sciure (de bois) *f.*
sawhorse *n.* chevalet *m.*
sawmill *n.* scierie *f.*
saw-toothed *a.* en dents de scie
Saxon *n. & a.* Saxon *m.*
say *n.* voix *f.*; mot *m.*, parole *f.*; have one's — dire son mot; — *vt.* dire; parler; faire; réciter; to — nothing of sans parler de; that is to — c'est-à-dire; —**ing** *n.* proverbe, adage, dicton *m.*; it goes without —**ing** cela va de soi
scab *n.* croûte *f.*; gale *f.*; jaune *m.*; — *vi.* former une croûte
scabbard *n.* gaine *f.*, fourreau *m.*
scads *n. pl.* (coll.) des tas *m. pl.*; — of beaucoup de
scaffold *n.* échafaud *m.*; —**ing** *n.* échafaudage *m.*
scalawag *n.* fripon *m.*
scald *n.* échaudure *f.*; — *vt.* échauder; blanchir; —**ing** *n.* échaudage *m.*; — *a.* bouillant, tout bouillant
scale *n.* écaille *f.*; tartre *m.*, incrustation *f.*; (weight) balance *f.*; plat de balance *m.*; (measurement) échelle, graduation, série *f.*; cadran *m.*; règle *m.*; étendue *f.*; (mus.) gamme *f.*; on a large — en grand; — *a.* à l'échelle; — *vt.* écailler; escalader; dessiner à l'échelle; établir à l'échelle; — *vi.* s'écailler; peser
scaling *n.* escalade *f.*; graduation *f.*
scallion *n.* ciboule *f.*
scallop *n.* coquille (Saint-Jacques) *f.*;

pétoncle *m.*; (sewing) dentelure *f.*; feston *m.*; — *vt.* faire cuire en coquille; (sewing) découper, festonner

scalp *n.* épicrâne *m.*; scalpe *m.*; –er *n.* trafiqueur *m.*; — *vt.* scalper; (coll.) vendre des billets à des prix exorbitants

scalpel *n.* scalpel *m.*

scaly *a.* écailleux

scamp *n.* vaurien, garnement *m.*

scamper *vi.* courir vite; se sauver

scan *vt.* scruter; parcourir; (verse) scander; –ner *n.* analyseur *m.*, (radar) antenne tournante *f.*; –ning *a.* analyseur, explorateur

scandal *n.* scandale *m.*; médisance *f.*; –ize *vt.* scandaliser; –ous *a.* scandaleux; diffamatoire

scandalmonger *n.* médisant *m.*

Scandinavia *n.* Scandinavie *f.*; –n *a.* & *n.* scandinave *m. & f.*

scant *a.* à peine rempli; modique

scantily *adv.* à peine; insuffisamment

scanty *a.* insuffisant; étroit; sommaire

scapegoat *n.* bouc émissaire *m.*

scapular *n.* scapulaire *m.*

scar *n.* cicatrice *f.*; — *vi.* se cicatriser

scarce *a.* rare; –ly *adv.* à peine; ne . . . guère; presque (pas)

scarcity *n.* manque *m.*; rareté *f.*; disette *f.*

scare *vt.* épouvanter, effrayer, faire peur à, effarer

scarecrow *n.* épouvantail *m.*

scarf *n.* écharpe *f.*, fichu *m.*; cache-nez *m.*; foulard *m.*

scarlet *a. & n.* écarlate *f.*; — fever scarlatine *f.*

scathing *a.* mordant, acerbe, cinglant

scatter *vt.* disperser; éparpiller, diffuser; — *vi.* se disperser; s'éparpiller; –ed *a.* dispersé; épars; –ing *n.* petit nombre *m.*

scatterbrained *a.* évaporé, écervelé

scavenger *n.* balayeur *m.*

scenario *n.* scénario *m.*

scene *n.* scène *f.*; lieu *m.*; décor *m.*; paysage *m.*; –ry *n.* paysage *m.*; (theat.) décor *m.*

scenic *a.* scénique

scent *n.* odeur *f.*; parfum *m.*, senteur *f.*; piste, trace *f.*; — *vt.* parfumer; flairer; –ed *a.* parfumé

scepter *n.* sceptre *m.*

sceptic *n.* sceptique *m. & f.*; –al *a.* sceptique; –ism *n.* scepticisme *m.*

schedule *n.* horaire *m.*; liste *f.*; tarif *m.*; programme, plan *m.*; –d *a.* dans le programme; be –d devoir

scheme *n.* schéma *m.*; combinaison *f.*; projet, plan *m.*; intrigue, machination *f.*; — *vi.* projeter; intriguer, comploter; –r *n.* intrigant *m.*

scheming *n.* machinations *f. pl.*; — *a.* intrigant

schism *n.* schisme *m.*

schizophrenia *n.* schizophrénie *f.*

scholar *n.* érudit, lettré, savant *m.*; boursier *m.*; –ly *a.* érudit, savant; –ship *n.* bourse *f.*; érudition, science *f.*; savoir *m.*

scholastic *a.* scolaire; (phil.) scolastique; –ism *n.* scolastique *f.*

school *n.* école *f.*; académie *f.*; faculté; classe *f.*; (fish) troupe de poissons *f.*; elementary — école primaire *f.*; high — école secondaire (supérieure) *f.*; private — école libre *f.*; — *vt.* instruire, former; enseigner; –ing *n.* instruction, éducation, enseignement *m.*; formation *f.*; — *a.* scolaire, classique

schoolbook *n.* livre de classe, livre classique *m.*

schoolboy *n.* écolier, élève *m.*

schoolgirl *n.* écolière, élève *f.*

schoolhouse *n.* école *f.*

schoolroom *n.* salle de classe *f.*

schoolteacher *n.* maître, professeur *m.*

schooner *n.* goélette *f.*, schooner *m.*; (glass) chope *f.*

sciatica *n.* sciatique *f.*

science *n.* science *f.*

scientific *a.* scientifique

scientist *n.* homme de science, savant *m.*

scimitar *n.* cimeterre *m.*

scintillate *vi.* étinceler, scintiller

scissors *n. pl.* ciseaux *m. pl.*

sclerosis *n.* sclérose *f.*

scoff *vi.* se moquer; — *vt.* tourner en dérision; –ing *n.* moquerie, raillerie *f.*

scold *vt. & vi.* gronder; — *n.* grondeuse *f.*; –ing *a.* grondeur; –ing *n.* gronderie *f.*; –ingly *adv.* en grondant

scoop *n.* cuiller *f.*; pelle *f.*; main *f.*; (journalism) primeur *f.*; nouvelle(s) *f.* (*pl.*); — *vt.* excaver; ramasser; écoper

scoot *vi.* filer; –er *n.* patinette, trottinette *f.*; motor –er scooter *m.*

scope *n.* portée, étendue *f.*; champ *m.*

scorch *vt.* roussir; brûler; dessécher; — *vi.* roussir; –er *n.* journée d'une chaleur accablante *f.*; –ed *a.* brûlé; –ing *a.* brûlant; torride

score *n.* entaille *f.*; compte *m.*; sujet *m.*; score *m.*, points *m. pl.*, marque *f.*; (mus.) partition *f.*; (number) vingtaine *f.*; — *vt.* entailler, encocher; compter; marquer; blâmer; faire; (mus.) orchestrer

scorn *n.* dédain, mépris *m.*; — *vt. & vi.* dédaigner, mépriser; –ful *a.* dédaigneux

Scot n. Écossais m.

scotch n. scotch, whisky écossais m.; — vt. faire manquer, faire avorter; mettre fin à

Scotch a. & n. écossais m.; — terrier terrier griffon m.

scot-free a. indemne; sans frais

Scotland n. Écosse f.

Scotsman n. Écossais m.

Scottish a. & n. écossais m.

scoundrel n. gredin, scélérat m.

scour vt. récurer; frotter; nettoyer; parcourir; chercher, fouiller; — the country battre la campagne; –ing n. recurage m.; nettoyage m.

scourge n. fléau m.; — vt. fouetter, châtier

scout n. éclaireur m.; boy — boy scout, éclaireur m.; girl — éclaireuse f.; — vi. aller en reconnaissance; — vt. éclairer, reconnaître

scoutmaster n. chef de troupe m.

scow n. chaland m.

scowl n. froncement de sourcils m.; air menaçant m.; — vi. froncer les sourcils, se refrogner

scraggy a. rocailleux; escarpé; maigre

scramble n. mêlée f.; (avi. mil.) alerte d'avions f.; — vi. se bousculer, se battre; — vt. brouiller; –d eggs œufs brouillés m. pl.

scrap n. fragment, petit morceau, bout m.; parcelle f.; (talk) bribes f. pl.; dispute, querelle f.; –s pl. restes m. pl.; — heap tas de ferraille m.; rebut m.; — iron ferraille f.; — vt. mettre au rebut; supprimer, desaffecter; — vi. se battre

scrapbook n. album m.

scrape n. difficulté f., mauvais pas m.; — vt. gratter, racler; érafler; frotter; — vi. gratter, grincer; –r n. grattoir, racloir m.

scratch n. égratignure f.; coup d'ongle m.; rayure f.; grattement, grincement m.; (sports) scratch m.; (coll.) argent, fric m.; — paper n. papier à brouillon m.; start from — partir de zéro; — vt. égratigner; érafler; rayer; gratter; — vi. gratter, grincer

scratch-pad n. bloc-notes m.

scrawl n. griffonnage m.; — vt. griffonner

scrawny a. maigre, décharné

scream n. cri aigu, cri perçant m.; — vt. crier, pousser un cri (perçant), hurler; –ing a. perçant, qui crie

screech n. cri perçant m.; — vi. pousser des cris perçants; — owl n. chat-huant m.

screen n. écran m.; paravent m.; — vt. cacher, masquer: (films) mettre à

l'écran; (sift) passer

screw n. vis f.; (naut.) hélice f.; — vt. visser; serrer; — vi. tourner; — up pincer, grimacer; tortiller

screw driver n. tournevis m.

screw thread n. filet m.

scribble n. griffonnage m.; — vt. griffonner

scribe n. copiste m.; scribe m.; — vt. pointer, tracer; –r n. pointe à tracer f.

scrimmage n. mêlée f.

scrip n. coupons, tickets, bons m. pl.

script n. écriture f.; scénario m.

scriptural a. biblique, scriptural; de l'Ecriture Sainte

Scripture n. Ecriture Sainte f.

scriptwriter n. scénariste m.

scrofula n. scrofules f. pl.

scroll n. rouleau m.; (arch.) volute f.

scrounge vt. récupérer, glaner

scrub n. nettoyage, récurage m.; (bot.) brousse f.; — vt. nettoyer, récurer; laver; –by a. rabougri

scuff n. nuque f.

scruple n. scrupule m.; hésitation f.

scupulous a. scrupuleux; méticuleux, minutieux

scrutinize vt. scruter, examiner

scrutiny n. examen rigoureux m.

scuff vt. frotter, user

scuffle n. mêlée, bagarre f.; — vi. se battre, se bousculer

scullery n. laverie f.; — maid souillon f.

sculptor n. sculpteur m.

sculpture n. sculpture f.; — vt. sculpter

scum n. écume f.; rebut m.

scurry vi. se hâter, courir

scurvy n. scorbut m.

scuttle vt. (naut.) saborder; — vi., — away filer; — n. seau, panier m.

scythe n. faux f.; — vt. faucher

sea n. mer f.; océan m.; at — en mer; désorienté; by the — au bord de la mer; heavy — grosse mer f.; high –s le large m.; on the high –s au grand large; — a. de mer, de la mer; — breeze brise du large f.; — captain capitaine de vaisseau m.; — legs pied marin m.; — level niveau de la mer; — lion otarie f., phoque m.; — urchin oursin m.; — wall digue f.

seaboard n. côte f.; bord de la mer

seacoast n. côte f., littoral m.

seafarer n. marin, matelot m.

seafaring a. marin, de la mer

seafood n. poisson de mer m.; coquillages m.; — pl., fruits de la mer m. pl.

sea-going a. maritime; de haute mer

seal n. sceau m.; cachet m.; (zool.) phoque m.; — vt. sceller; cacheter; fermer; –ing *a.*, — **wax** cire à cacheter *f.*

sealskin *a. & n.* peau de phoque *f.*

seam *n.* couture *f.*; joint *m.*; couche, veine *f.*; — *vt.* couturer; –**less** *a.* sans couture

seaman *n.* marin, matelot *m.*; –**ship** *n.* art de naviguer *m.*

seamstress *n.* couturière *f.*

seaplane *n.* hydravion *m.*

seaport *n.* port de mer *m.*

sea power *n.* puissance maritime *f.*

sear *vt.* dessécher, flétrir; — *a.* fané, sêché

search *n.* recherche *f.*; visite *f.*; — **warrant** mandat de perquisition *m.*; **in** — **of** à la recherche de; — *vt.* chercher (dans); fouiller; (customs) visiter; perquisitionner; sonder; — *vi.* chercher, rechercher; –**ing** *a.* pénétrant; minutieux

searchlight *n.* projecteur, phare *m.*

sea shell *n.* coquillage *m.*, coquille *f.*

seasick *a.* qui a le mal de mer; –**ness** *n.* mal de mer *m.*

seaside *n.* bord de la mer *m.*

season *n.* saison *f.*; temps *m.*; **in** — de saison; **off** — morte-saison *f.*; **out of** — hors de saison, mal à propos; — **ticket** carte d'abonnement *f.*; — *vt.* assaisonner; mûrir; conditionner; tempérer; — *vi.* mûrir; sécher; –**able** *a.* de saison; à propos, –**al** *a.* saisonnier, des saisons; –**ed** *a.* assaisonné; mûr; sec; expérimenté; –**ing** *n.* assaisonnement *m.*; condiment *m.*

seat *n.* siège *m.*; place *f.*; banquette *f.*; fond *m.*; derrière *m.*; centre, foyer *m.*; — **cover** *n.* housse *f.*; — *vt.* asseoir; **be** –**ed** s'asseoir; être assis; –**ing** *n.* places *f. pl.*; disposition des places *f.*; –**ing capacity** nombre de places *m.*

seaward(s) *adv.* vers la mer

seaweed *n.* varech *m.*

seaworthy *a.* en état de tenir la mer

secede *vi.* faire scission, faire sécession

secession *n.* sécession *f.*

seclude *vt.* éloigner, tenir éloigné, tenir retiré; — **oneself** se retirer; –**d** *a.* retiré

seclusion *n.* retraite, solitude *f.*

second *n.* seconde *f.*; instant *m.*; second *m.*; (com.) article de deuxième qualité, deuxième choix *m.*; — *a.* second, deuxième; autre, nouveau; — **floor** premier étage *m.*; — **hand** (watch, clock) trotteuse *f.*; — **lieutenant** sous-lieutenant *m.*; — **nature** seconde nature *f.*; — **sight** clairvoyance *f.*; — *vt.* seconder; (debate) appuyer; –**ary** *a.* secondaire; –**ly** *adv.* en second lieu, deuxièmement

second-class *a.* (rail.) de seconde (classe); de second ordre; de deuxième qualité

secondhand *a.* de seconde main; usagé;

d'occasion; — **dealer** brocanteur *m.*

second-rate *a.* de qualité inférieure; de second ordre; médiocre

secrecy *n.* mystère, secret *m.*; discrétion *f.*

secret *a.* secret; caché; — *n.* secret *m.*; **keep a** — garder un secret; **in** —, –**ly** *adv.* en secret, secrètement; –**ive** *a.* réservé

secretary *n.* secrétaire *m. & f.*; **private** — secrétaire particulier *m.*

secrete *vt.* sécréter; cacher

secretion *n.* sécrétion *f.*

sect *n.* secte *f.*; –**arian** *a. & n.* sectaire *m.*; –**arianism** *n.* esprit sectaire *m.*

section *n.* section *f.*; coupe, tranche *f.*; profil *m.*; division, partie *f.*; (city) quartier *m.*; (store) rayon *m.*; — *vt.* sectionner, diviser en sections; –**al** *a.* en sections; (drawing) en coupe

sector *n.* secteur *m.*

secular *a.* séculier, laïque, profane, temporel; –**ize** *vt.* séculariser

secure *a.* assuré; en sûreté; hors de danger; à l'abri (de); ferme, fixe, solide; — *vt.* obtenir; se procurer; retenir; mettre en sûreté; fixer, assujettir

security *n.* sécurité, sûreté *f.*; (com.) gage, nantissement *m.*, caution *f.*

securities *n. pl.* fonds, titres *m. pl.*, valeurs *f. pl.*; actions *f. pl.*

sedan *n.* voiture à 6 places *f.*; (voiture à) conduite intérieure *f.*; — **chair** *n.* chaise à porteurs *f.*

sedate *a.* posé, composé; –**ness** *n.* calme *m.*, tranquillité *f.*

sedative *a. & n.* sédatif *m.*

sedentary *a.* sédentaire

sediment *n.* sédiment *m.*; lie *f.*; –**ary** *a.* sédimentaire; –**ation** *n.* sédimentation *f.*

sedition *n.* sédition *f.*

seditious *a.* séditieux

seduce *vt.* séduire, dépraver

seduction *n.* séduction *f.*; charme *m.*

seductive *a.* séduisant; –**ness** *n.* séduction *f.*; charmes *m. pl.*

see *n.* (eccl.) siège épiscopale *m.*; — *vt.* voir; apercevoir; observer; regarder; comprendre; envisager; trouver; visiter; **as far as I can** — à ce que je vois; — **fit** trouver bon; — **to it** faire; — **to the door** accompagner à la porte; — **about** s'occuper de; — **off** dire adieu; — **through** pénétrer; persévérer; –**ing** *a.* voyant; –**ing that** vu que, attendu que; –**ing** *n.* vue, vision *f.*; –**ing is believing** voir c'est croire

seed *n.* graine *f.*; semence *f.*; pépin *m.*; (fig.) germe *m.*; — *vt.* semer, ensemencer; **–ling** *n.* jeune plante *f.*; plante semée *f.*; **–y** *a.* d'aspect minable

seek *vt.* chercher, rechercher; demander; essayer, tâcher; — **out** rechercher

seem *vi.* sembler, paraître; avoir l'air; **–ing** *a.* apparent; **–ingly** *adv.* apparemment, en apparence; **–ly** *a.* convenable, bienséant

seep *vi.* suinter; fuir; s'infiltrer; **–age** *n.* suintement *m.*; fuite *f.*; infiltration *f.*

seer *n.* prophète *m.*; visionnaire *m.*

seesaw *n.* bascule *f.*; balançoire *f.*; — *vi.* basculer

seethe *vi.* bouillir, bouillonner; grouiller

segregate *vt.* séparer; mettre à part; — *vi.* se grouper à part

segregation *n.* ségrégation, séparation *f.*

segregationist *n.* ségrégationiste *m.*

seismograph *n.* sismographe *m.*

seize *vt.* saisir; s'emparer de; empoigner; prendre

seizure *n.* saisie, prise *f.*; accès *m.*; attaque *f.*

seldom *adv.* rarement

select *vt.* choisir; — *a.* choisi; de choix; d'élite; **–ion** *n.* choix *m.*; sélection *f.*; recueil *m.*; **–ive** *a.* sélectif; **–ivity** *n.* sélectivité *f.*

selectman *n.* conseiller municipal *m.*

selenium *n.* sélénium *m.*

self *a.* même; — *n.* moi *m.*

self-acting *a.* automatique

self-addressed *a.* adressé par le destinataire

self-apparent *a.* évident; qui va de soi

self-assurance *n.* confiance en soi

self-assured *a.* posé; maître de soi

self-centered *a.* égocentrique

self-confidence *n.* confiance en soi

self-confident *a.* sûr de soi

self-conscious *a.* embarrassé, gêné; **–ness** *n.* embarras *m.*; gêne *f.*

self-contained *a.* réservé, circonspect; (technical) incorporé

self-control *n.* maîtrise de soi *f.*; sang-froid *m.*; **–led** *a.* réservé, maître de soi; (technical) auto-entretenu

self-defense *n.* (law) légitime défense *f.*

self-denial *n.* renoncement *m.*; abnégation *f.*

self-discipline *n.* discipline *f.*

self-educated *a.* autodidacte

self-esteem *n.* amour-propre *m.*

self-evident *a.* évident; qui saute aux yeux

self-explanatory *a.* qui s'explique de soi-même, clair, concis

self-expression *n.* expression de l'individu *f.*

self-governed *a.* autonome

self-government *n.* autonomie *f.*

self-help *n.* efforts personnels *m. pl.*

self-induced *a.* inspiré par l'individu

self-indulgence *n.* indulgence de soi *f.*

self-indulgent *a.* qui ne se refuse rien

selfish *a.* égoïste, intéressé; **–ness** *n.* égoïsme, intérêt *m.*

self-liquidating *a.* qui s'amortit; se liquidant soi-même

self-made *a.* parvenu par ses propres moyens

self-possessed *a.* maître de soi

self-possession *n.* maîtrise de soi *f.*; sang-froid, aplomb *m.*

self-preservation *n.* conservation de soi-même *f.*

self-propelled *a.* autopropulsé

self-propelling *a.* automoteur

self-protection *n.* protection de soi *f.*

self-regulating *a.* à autorégulation

self-reliance *n.* indépendance *f.*

self-reliant *a.* indépendant

self-respect *n.* respect de soi *m.*; amour-propre *m.*

self-restraint *n.* retenue *f.*

self-righteous *a.* qui se croit juste, content de soi

self-sacrifice *n.* abnégation *f.*

selfsame *a.* identique

self-satisfied *a.* suffisant; content de soi

self-service *n. & a.* libre-service *m.*

self-starter *n.* autodémarreur *m.*

self-styled *a.* soi-disant

self-sufficient *a.* suffisant en soi

self-supporting *a.* indépendant, qui gagne sa propre vie

self-taught *a.* autodidacte

sell *vt.* vendre; **–out** vendre tout; épuiser; **–er** *n.* vendeur *m.*, vendeuse *f.*; **–ing** *n.* vente *f.*

seltzer *n.* eau de seltz *f.*

selvage *n.* lisière *f.*

semantic *a.* sémantique; **–s** *n. pl.* sémantique *f.*

semaphore *n.* sémaphore *m.*

semblance *n.* apparence, semblant *m.*

semester *n.* semestre *m.*

semiannual *a.* semi-annuel; **–ly** *adv.* tous les six mois

semiautomatic *a.* semi-automatique

semicircle *n.* demi-cercle *m.*

semicolon *n.* point et virgule *m.*

semifinal *n.* demi-finale *f.*

semimonthly *a.* bimensuel

seminar *n.* séminaire, groupe d'études *m.*

seminary *n.* seminaire *m.*

semiofficial *a.* demi-officiel

Semitic *a.* sémitique

semitransparent *a.* demi-transparent

semitropical *a.* subtropical

senate *n.* sénat *m.*

senator *n.* sénateur *m.*; **–ial** *a.* sénatorial

send *vt.* envoyer; expédier; **— away, —
back** renvoyer; **— for** envoyer chercher;
faire venir; **— in** faire entrer; remettre;
— out lancer; émettre; jeter; **–er** *n.*
expéditeur, envoyeur *m.*; **–ing** *n.* expédition *f.*; envoi *m.*

Senegal *n.* Sénégal *m.*

senile *a.* sénile

senility *n.* sénilité *f.*

senior *a.* aîné; père; supérieur; ancien;
— *n.* aîné *m.*; ancien *m.*; (Amer. college)
étudiant de quatrième année *m.*; **–ity**
n. ancienneté *f.*

sensation *n.* sensation *f.*; impression *f.*;
sentiment *m.*; **–al** *a.* sensationnel;

sense *n.* sens *m.*; sensation *f.*; sentiment
m.; raison *f.*; **common — sens** commun
m.; **make — (out) of** comprendre; **talk
—** parler raison; **— of smell** odorat *m.*;
–s *pl.* sens *m.* *pl.*; raison, tête *f.*; **—** *vt.*
sentir, pressentir; **–less** *a.* insensé, déraisonnable; (unconscious) sans connaissance

sensibility *n.* sensibilité *f.*

sensible *a.* raisonnable, sensé; pratique;
perceptible, sensible

sensitive *a.* sensible; **–ness** *n.* sensibilité *f.*

sensitivity *n.* sensibilité *f.*

sensitize *vt.* sensibiliser; **–ed** *a.* sensible

sensory *a.* sensoriel

sensual *a.* sensuel; voluptueux; **–ity** *n.*
sensualité *f.*

sensuous *a.* voluptueux

sentence *n.* phrase *f.*; (law) sentence *f.*,
arrêt *m.*; peine *f.*; **prison —** peine de
prison; **—** *vt.* condamner

sentiment *n.* sentiment *m.*; opinion *f.*; **–al**
a. sentimental; **–ality** *n.* sentimentalité
f.

sentinel *n.* sentinelle *f.*; factionnaire *m.*

sentry *n.* factionnaire *m.*; sentinelle *f.*

separable *a.* séparable

separate *a.* séparé; distinct; détaché;
particulier, individuel; **—** *vt.* séparer;
détacher, dégager; **—** *vi.* se séparer; se
détacher; se quitter

separation *n.* séparation *f.*

sepia *n.* sépia *f.*

September *n.* septembre *m.*

septic *a.* septique; **— tank** fosse septique *f.*

septicemia *n.* (med.) septicémie *f.*

sepulchral *a.* sépulcral

sepulchre *n.* sépulcre *m.*

sequel *n.* suite *f.*; conséquence *f.*

sequence *n.* suite, série, succession *f.*

sequin *n.* séquin *m.*; (decoration) paillette
f.

Serbia *n.* Serbie *f.*

serenade *n.* sérénade *f.*; **—** *vt.* donner une
sérénade à

serene *a.* serein; calme, tranquille

serenity *n.* sérénité *f.*; calme *m.*; tranquillité *f.*

serf *n.* serf *m.*; **–dom** *n.* servage *m.*

sergeant *n.* sergent *m.*; **— at arms** huissier *m.*; **first —** sergent chef, adjudant *m.*; **master —** adjudant chef *m.*

serial *a.* de série; **— number** numéro de
série; **—** *n.* roman-feuilleton *m.*

series *n.* série, suite *f.*; (mus.) gamme
f.; **in —** en série

serious *a.* sérieux; grave; **–ly** *adv.* sérieusement, gravement; grièvement; **take –ly**
prendre au sérieux; **–ness** *n.* gravité *f.*;
sérieux *m.*

sermon *n.* sermon *m.*; **–ize** *vt.* & *vi.* sermonner

serpent *n.* serpent *m.*; **–ine** *a.* serpentin,
serpentant, sinueux

serrate *a.* en dents de scie

serried *a.* serré, compact

serum *n.* sérum *m.*

servant *n.* domestique *m.* & *f.*; servant *m.*,
servante *f.*; serviteur *m.*; **civil —** fonctionnaire *m.* & *f.*

serve *vt.* servir; desservir; suffire; (time)
faire des années de prison; **—** *vi.* servir;
— as servir de; **–r** *n.* serveur (serveuse)

service *n.* service *m.*; emploi *m.*; administration *f.*; utilité *f.*; (auto.) entretien
m.; dépannage *m.*; (eccl.) office *m.*;
(law) délivrance *f.*; **at your —** à votre
disposition; **be of —** être utile; servir;
— station *n.* station-service *f.*, poste
d'essence *m.*; **—** *vt.* entretenir; **–able** *a.*
utilisable

serviceman *n.* soldat *m.*

servicing *n.* entretien *m.*; dépannage *m.*

servile *a.* servile; bas

servility *n.* servilité *f.*; bassesse *f.*

serving *n.* service *m.*

servitor *n.* serviteur *m.*

servitude *n.* servitude *f.*, esclavage *m.*

servomotor *n.* servo-moteur *m.*

sesame *n.* sésame *m.*

session *n.* séance *f.*; session *f.*; **be in —**
siéger

set *n.* jeu *m.*; série *f.*; ensemble *m.*; collection *f.*; coterie *f.*; (dishes) service
m.; (hair) mise *f.*; (radio) poste *m.*;
(theat.) décor *m.*; scène *f.*; **—** *vt.* poser,
placer, mettre, asseoir; donner; ajuster;
régler; (bone) remettre, réduire; (date)
fixer; (gem) enchâsser; (type) composer; **—** *vi.* se coucher; prendre; se
figer; **— aside** écarter, mettre à part;
— back remettre; retarder; **— forth**
avancer, exposer; partir, se mettre en

443

route; — **out** se mettre en route; — **the table** mettre le couvert; — **up** établir; monter; — **upon** attaquer; — *a.* fixe; figé; réglé; imposé; déterminé; prêt; **-ting** *a.* couchant; **-ting** *n.* coucher *m.*; mise *f.*; réglage *m.*; montage *m.*; prise *f.*; (bone) réduction *f.*; (gem) monture *f.*; (theat.) décor *m.*; (type) composition *f.*; **-ting up** *n.* établissement *m.*; installation *f.*

setback *n.* revers *m.*; recul *m.*

setscrew *n.* vis de serrage *f.*

settee *n.* canapé *m.*

setter *n.* setter, chien d'arrêt *m.*

settle *vt.* arranger; résoudre, décider, déterminer; terminer; établir; coloniser; calmer; — *vi.* s'établir; s'installer; se calmer; déposer, se précipiter; — **down** se ranger; se caser; se calmer; **-ment** *n.* colonie *f.*; paiement *m.*; règlement *m.*; accord *m.*; **-r** *n.* colon *m.*

setup *n.* organisation *f.*; arrangement *m.*; montage *m.*

seven *a. & n.* sept; **-teen** *a. & n.* dix-sept; **-teenth** *a. & n.* dix-septième; **-th** *a. & n.* septième; **-ty** *a. & n.* soixante-dix

seventy-one soixante et onze

seventy-two soixante-douze

sever *vt.* rompre; couper; **-ance** *n.* séparation *f.*

several *a.* plusieurs; divers; différent; séparé

severance *n.* séparation *f.*

severe *a.* sévère; rigoureux; austère

severity *n.* sévérité *f.*; rigueur *f.*; austérité *f.*

sew *vt.* coudre; **-ing** *n.* couture *f.*; ouvrage *m.*; **-ing machine** machine à coudre *f.*

sewage *n.* eaux d'égout *f. pl.*

sewer *n.* égout *m.*

sex *n.* sexe *m.*; **-ual** *a.* sexuel; **-uality** *n.* sexualité *f.*

sextant *n.* sextant *m.*

sextet *n.* sextuor *m.*

sexton *n.* sacristain *m.*

shabby *a.* usé, râpé; minable; mesquin

shack *n.* case, cabane, hutte *f.*

shackle *vt.* enchaîner, entraver; **-s** *n. pl.* fers *m. pl.*

shad *n.* alose *f.*

shade *n.* ombre *f.*; nuance *f.*; (lamp) abat-jour *m.*; (window) store *m.*; — *vt.* ombrager; nuancer; ombrer; **-d** *a.* ombragé; ombré

shadiness *n.* ombre *f.*; ombrage *m.*

shadow *n.* ombre *f.*; — *vt.* ombrager; (person) filer; **-y** *a.* vague; mystérieux

shady *a.* ombreux; ombragé; (coll.) louche

shaft *n.* puits *m.*; (elevator) cage *f.*; arbre *m.*; souche *f.*; manche *m.*; flèche *f.*, trait *m.*; (arch.) tige *f.*; (light) rayon *m.*

shaggy *a.* poilu; touffu; à longs poils

shake *n.* secousse *f.*; — **of the head** hochement de tête *m.*; — *vt.* secouer; agiter; hocher; ébranler; — *vi.* trembler, trembloter; chanceler; — **a fist at** menacer du poing; — **hands with** serrer la main à; — **down** faire tomber; extorquer; — **off** secouer; se défaire de; **-n** *a.* bouleversé, confus; **-r** *n.* (salt) salière *f.*; (cocktail) frappe-cocktail *m.*

shake-up *n.* bouleversement *m.*; renversement *m.*; remaniement *m.*

shaking *a.* tremblant; (voice) ému; — *n.* tremblement *m.*; secouement *m.*

shaky *a.* tremblant; chancelant; faible

shallot *n.* échalote *f.*

shallow *a.* peu profond; superficiel; plat; — **water** hauts-fonds *m. pl.*; **-ness** *n.* manque de profondeur *m.*

sham *a.* feint, simulé, faux; — *n.* feinte *f.*; imposture *f.*; — *vt.* feindre, simuler

shambles *n. pl.* carnage *m.*; désordre *m.*

shame *n.* honte *f.*; **what a** —! quel dommage!; — *vt.* humilier, faire honte à; **-ful** *a.* honteux; **-less** *a.* effronté; honteux; scandaleux

shamefaced *a.* penaud; honteux

shampoo *n.* shampooing *m.*; — *vt.* (se) laver les cheveux, donner un shampooing à

shamrock *n.* trèfle *m.*

shank *n.* (meat) manche *f.*; tibia *m.*

shanty *n.* hutte, cabane, case *f.*

shape *n.* forme *f.*; façon *f.*; **out of** — déformé; — *vt.* façonner, former; tailler; **-less** *a.* informe; **-liness** *n.* jolie taille *f.*; belle forme *f.*; symétrie *f.*; **-ly** *a.* bien fait, bien tourné

share *n.* part, portion *f.*; intérêt *m.*; (com.) action *f.*, titre *m.*, (plow) soc *m.*; — *vt.* partager; avoir part à; — *vi.* participer

sharecropper *n.* métayer *m.*

shareholder *n.* actionnaire *m. & f.*

shark *n.* requin *m.*

sharp *a.* aigu, tranchant, pointu; net, marqué; vif; fin; rusé, malin; piquant; — **turn** tournant brusque *m.*; — *adv.*, **two o'clock** — deux heures précises; — *n.* (mus.) dièse *m.*; **-en** *vt.* tailler; aiguiser; affiler; aviver; **-ener** *n.* aiguisoir *m.*; (pencil) taille-crayons *m.*; **-(er)** *n.* (cards) tricheur *m.*; **-ly** *adv.* sévèrement; vivement; nettement; brusquement; **-ness** *n.* acuité, finesse *f.*; sévérité *f.*; netteté *f.*; piquant *m.*

sharp-edged *a.* affilé, tranchant
sharpshooter *n.* tireur d'élite *m.*
sharp-witted *a.* spirituel
shatter *vt.* fracasser, briser; — *vi.* se fracasser, se briser
shatterproof *a.* incassable; de sécurité
shave *n.* action de raser *f.*; **have a —** se raser; se faire raser; **have a close —** (fig.) l'échapper belle; — *vt.* raser, faire la barbe à; planer; **-r** *n.* barbier *m.*; **electric -r** rasoir électrique *m.*
shaving *n.* action de (se) raser *f.*; (wood) copeau *m.*; — **brush** blaireau *m.*; — **cream** savon à barbe *m.*
shawl *n.* châle, fichu *m.*
she *pron.* elle
sheaf *n.* gerbe *f.*; (papers) liasse *f.*
shear *vt.* tondre; couper; **-s** *n. pl.* ciseaux *m. pl.*; cisailles *f. pl.*; **-ing** *n.* tondaison *f.*; **-ing machine** *n.* tondeuse *f.*
sheath *n.* gaine *f.*; fourreau *m.*; enveloppe *f.*; **-e** *vt.* rengainer; revêtir
shed *n.* hangar *m.*; baraque *f.*; — *vt.* (tears) verser; (skin) jeter; — **light on** éclairer; **-ding** *n.* mue *f.*; perte *f.*
sheen *n.* luisant, lustre *m.*
sheep *n.* mouton *m.*, brebis *f.*; **black —** brebis galeuse *f.*; **-ish** *a.* penaud
sheepskin *n.* peau de mouton *f.*, parchemin *m.*; (coll.) diplôme *m.*
sheer *a.* pur, véritable; à pic
sheet *n.* drap *m.*; (paper) feuille *f.*; (glass) verre à vitres *m.*; (metal) tôle *f.*; (naut.) écoute *f.*; (mus.) feuille de musique *f.*; **-ing** *n.* drap *m.*, toile pour draps *f.*; tôlerie *f.*
shelf *n.* étagère, tablette *f.*, rayon *m.*
shell *n.* (peas, nuts) écaille, cosse *f.*; (egg) coque; (empty egg) coquille *f.*; (earth) écorce *f.*; (shellfish) coquillage *m.*; (cannon) obus *m.*; (gun) cartouche *f.*; **tortoise —, turtle —** écaille *f.*; — *vt.* (nuts) écaler; (peas) écosser; (oysters) ouvrir; (mil.) bombarder
shellac *n.* laque, gomme-laque *f.*; — *vt.* laquer
shellfire *n.* tir à obus *m.*
shellfish *n.* crustacé *m.*
shelter *n.* abri *m.*; asile *m.*; — *vt.* abriter, protéger
shelve *vt.* mettre sur les rayons; classer
shelving *n.* bois à faire des étagères *m.*; toile (papier) à recouvrir les étagères *f.* (*m.*)
shepherd *n.* berger, pâtre *m.*; pasteur *m.*; **-ess** *n.* bergère *f.*; — *vt.* garder; mener
sherbet *n.* sorbet *m.*
sheriff *n.* sheriff, chef de gendarmerie *m.*
sherry *n.* vin de Xérès *m.*
shield *n.* bouclier *m.*; (heraldry) écu *m.*;

(fig.) protection *f.*; (mech.) armature, gaine *f.*; blindage, capot, carter, écran *m.*; — *vt.* protéger; blinder
shift *n.* déplacement *m.*; changement *m.*; (industry) équipe (d'ouvriers) *f.*; (auto.) levier de changement de vitesse *m.*; (typewriter) touche à majuscules *f.*; — *vt.* déplacer; — *vi.* se déplacer; changer; (auto.) changer de vitesse; — **for oneself** se tirer d'affaire; **-less** *a.* faible; incapable; paresseux; **-y** *a.* peu digne de confiance; (eyes) fuyant
shilly-shally *vi.* être indécis; temporiser
shimmer *vi.* scintiller, reluire; — *n.* faible clarté *f.*
shimmy *n.* dandinement des roues avant *m.*; — *vi.* dandiner
shin *n.* tibia, devant de la jambe *m.*; **-ny (up)** *vi.* (coll.) grimper
shine *n.* brillant, poli *m.*; **take a — to** s'éprendre de; — *vt.* polir; (shoes) cirer; — *vi.* luire, reluire, briller; **-r** *n.* (coll.) œil poché *m.*
shingle *n.* bardeau *m.*; (coll.) enseigne (d'un médecin) *f.*
shining *a.* luisant; brillant, éclatant; — *n.* éclat *m.*; splendeur *f.*
ship *n.* vaisseau, navire *m.*; paquebot *m.*; — *vt.* envoyer, expédier; embarquer. (oars) rentrer; **-ment** *n.* cargaison *f.*, chargement *m.*; envoi *m.*, expédition *f.*; **-per** *n.* expéditeur *m.*; **-ping** *n.* envoi *m.*, expédition *f.*; commerce maritime *m.*; **-ping room** *n.* salle d'expédition *f.*
ship-to shore *a.*, — **telephone** liaison radio maritime *f.*
shipwreck *n.* naufrage *m.*; **-ed** *a.* naufragé; — *vi.* faire naufrage
shipyard *n.* chantier de construction *m.*
shirk *vt.* manquer à, éviter
shirr *vt.* froncer
shirt *n.* chemise *f.*; **-ing** *n.* toile à chemises *f.*
shirtmaker *n.* chemisier *m.*
shiver *n.* frisson *m.*; — *vi.* frissonner; **-ing** *a.* qui frossonne; à faire frissonner
shoal *n.* banc de sable *m.*; endroit peu profond *m.*; banc de poissons *m.*
shock *n.* choc *m.*; coup *m.*; secousse *f.*; — **absorber** amortisseur *m.*; — **treatment** électronarcose *f.*; — *vt.* choquer; offenser; **-ing** *a.* choquant; **-proof** *a.* à l'épreuve des secousses (persons) inébranable
shoddy *a.* de mauvaise qualité, inférieur
shoe *n.* chaussure *f.*; soulier *m.*; (wooden) sabot *m.*; (horse) fer *m.*; — **polish** cirage *m.*; — **store** cordonnerie *f.*; (magasin de) chaussures *m.*; — *vt.* chausser; (horse) ferrer

shoehorn *n*. chausse-pied *m*.

shoelace *n*. lacet *m*.

shoemaker *n*. cordonnier *m*.

shoestring *n*. lacet *m*.; on a — (coll.) avec très peu d'argent; — potatoes pommes-allumettes *f. pl.*

shoe tree *n*. forme à chaussures *f*.

shoot *n*. rejeton, scion *m*.; pousse *f*.; partie de chasse *f*.; — *vt*. tirer, lancer; fusiller; — *vi*. s'élancer; se précipiter; bourgeonner, pousser; -ing *n*. tir *m*.; action de tirer *f*.; -ing *a*., -ing star étoile filante *f*.

shop *n*. boutique *f*., magasin *m*.; (industry) atelier *m*.; -keeper *n*. marchand *m*.; boutiquier *m*.; -lifter *n*. voleur à l'étalage *m*.; talk — parler affaires; — window *n*. vitrine, devanture *f*.; -per *n*. acheteur, client *m*.; -ping bag *n*. filet à provisions *m*.; -ping plaza *n*. place marchande *f*.; quartier commerçant *m*.; — *vi*. faire des emplettes; -worn *a*. défraîchi; — for chercher à acheter; go -ping faire des emplettes; faire des courses

shore *n*. rivage *m*., côte *f*.; — leave permission (d'aller à terre) *f*.; — *vt*. étayer

shore line *n*. ligne de côte *f*., littoral *m*.

short *a*. court; bref; concis; serré; — subject *n*. court métrage *m*.; be — of être à court de; manquer de; cut — couper court (à); fall — of rester au-dessous de; — circuit *n*. (elec.) court-circuit *m*.; -age *n*. insuffisance *f*.; -en *vt*. raccourcir; -ening *n*. matière grasse *f*.; -ly *adv*. bientôt; -s *n. pl.* short *m*.; caleçon court *m*.

shortcake *n*. gateau recouvert de fruits frais *m*.

shortchange *vt*. rendre la monnaie insuffisante

short-circuit *vt*. court-circuiter

shortcoming *n*. faiblesse, insuffisance *f*.

shorthand *n*. sténographie *f*.

shorthanded *a. & adv.* avec une insuffisance de personnel

short-lived *a*. de courte durée

shortsighted *a*. myope; peu prévoyant

short-tempered *a*. qui s'emporte facilement

short-term *a*. à courte échéance

short-wave *a*. à ondes courtes

shot *n*. coup de feu *m*.; portée *f*.; plomb *m*.; (med.) piqûre *f*.; (coll.) verre d'alcool *m*.

shotgun *n*. fusil de chasse *m*.; — shell cartouche chargée à plomb *f*.

shoulder *n*. épaule *f*.; — strap bretelle *f*.; — *vt*. mettre sur les épaules; se charger de

shoulder blade *n*. omoplate *f*.

shout *n*. cri *m*.; — *vt. & vi.* crier

shove *n*. coup *m*., poussée *f*.; — *vt*. pousser; bousculer; — off partir; démarrer; (naut.) pousser au large

shovel *n*. pelle *f*.; — *vt*. pelleter

show *n*. spectacle *m*.; étalage *m*.; parade *f*.; — window vitrine *f*.; — *vt*. montrer, faire voir; démontrer; — off étaler, faire parade de; faire valoir; se faire voir; — up révéler, démasquer; (coll.) arriver; paraître; -y *a*. fastueux, voyant

showcase *n*. vitrine *f*.

showdown *n*. explication armée *f*.; moment décisif *m*.

shower *n*. douche *f*.; pluie, averse *f*.; — *vt*. accabler, combler

showman *n*. impresario *m*.; acteur *m*.; -ship *n*. art de présenter *m*.

showroom *n*. salle de vision, salle d'exposition *f*.

shred *n*. morceau *m*., rognure *f*.; — *vt*. couper en petits morceaux

shrew *n*. mégère *f*.; (zool.) musaraigne *f*.; -ish *a*. acariâtre

shrewd *a*. fin; rusé; -ness *n*. finesse, ruse *f*.

shriek *n*. cri perçant *m*.; — *vi*. pousser des cris perçants

shrill *a*. perçant, aigu

shrimp *n*. crevette *f*.

shrine *n*. chapelle *f*.; reliquaire *m*., châsse *f*.

shrink *vi*. se resserrer, se rétrécir, se raccourcir; reculer; -age *n*. rétrécissement *m*.

shrivel *vi*. (se) rider

shroud *n*. linceul, drap mortuaire *m*.; (naut.) hauban *m*.; — *vt*. défendre, protéger; couvrir d'un drap mortuaire

Shrove Tuesday *n*. mardi gras *m*.

shrub *n*. arbrisseau, arbuste *m*.; -bery *n*. verdure *f*.; arbrisseaux *m. pl.*

shrug *n*. haussement d'épaules *m*.; — *vt*. lever, hausser

shuck *vt*. écosser; éplucher; — *n*. cosse *f*.

shudder *n*. frissonnement *m*.; — *vi*. frissonner, frémir; trembler

shuffle *n*. mélange *m*.; mouvement traînant *m*.; — *vt*. mélanger, mêler; battre; — *vi*. traîner les pieds

shuffleboard *n*. jeu de palets *m*.

shuffling *a*. évasif; (gait) qui traîne les pieds; — *n*. battement de cartes *m*.; marche traînante *f*.

shun *vt*. éviter

shunt *vt*. changer de voie; dévier

shut *vt*. fermer, renfermer; — *vi*. se fermer; — down faire cesser; fermer; — in renfermer, garder à l'intérieur; — off fermer, interrompre; — out garder à l'extérieur; — up renfermer; se taire; –ter *n.* volet *m.*; store *m.*; (phot.) obturateur *m.*

shutdown *n.* cessation *f.*; fermeture *f.*

shut-in *n.* malade *m. & f.* (qui ne peut pas quitter la maison)

shuttle *n.* navette *f.*; — *vi.* faire la navette

shuttlecock *n.* volant *m.*

shy *vi.* faire un écart; se jeter de côté; — *a.* réservé; timide; farouche; –ness *n.* réserve, timidité; –en *vt.* rendre manquer de; –ly *adv.* timidement

shyster *n.* avocat malhonnête *m.*

Siam *n.* Siam *m.*; –ese *a. & n.* siamois *m.*

Siberia *n.* Sibérie *f.*; –n *n. & a.* Sibérien *m.*

Sicilian *a. & n.* sicilien *m.*

Sicily *n.* Sicile *f.*

sick *a.* malade; indisposé; dégoûté; get — tomber malade; — *vt.* rendre malade, dégoûter; –en *vi.* tomber malade; –ly *a.* maladif; –ness *n.* mal *m.*; maladie *f.*

sickbed *n.* lit de malade *m.*

sickle *n.* faucille *f.*

sick leave *n.* congé de convalescence *m.*

sickroom *n.* chambre de malade *f.*

side *n.* côté *m.*; flanc *m.*; bord *m.*; parti *m.*; — by — côte à côte; on all –s de tous côtés; on one — d'un côté; — *a.* de côté; oblique; auxiliaire, supplémentaire; — dish entremets *m.*; — *vi.*, — with appuyer, prendre le parti de

sideboard *n.* buffet *m.*, desserte *f.*

side light *n.* détail révélateur, détail intéressant *m.*

side line *n.* distraction *f.*; intérêt secondaire *m.*

sidelong *a.* oblique

side show *n.* exhibition de fête foraine *f.*

side-step *vt.* esquiver, éviter; — *vi.* faire un écart

sideswipe *vt.* prendre en écharpe

sidetrack *vt.* écarter, dévier

sidewalk *n.* trottoir, pavé *m.*

sidewards, sideways, sidewise *adv.* de côté, latéralement

siding *n.* (rail.) voie de garage *f.*

sidle *vi.* approcher latéralement

siege *n.* siège *m.*; lay — to assiéger; raise a — lever un siège

siesta *n.* sieste *f.*

sieve *n.* tamis *m.*; — *vt.* tamiser; trier

sift *vt.* tamiser, passer au tamis; trier; examiner, juger; –er *n.* tamis *m.*

sigh *n.* soupir *m.*; — *vi.* soupirer; pousser un soupir

sight *n.* vue *f.*; vision *f.*; aspect *m.*; specta-

cle *m.*; (gun) mire *f.*; — draft *n.* (com.) effet à vue *m.*; at — à premiere vue; by — (com.) de vue; in — en vue; lose — of perdre de vue; on — à vue; out of — hors de vue; — unseen sans examiner d'avance; — *vt.* apercevoir, remarquer; –less *a.* aveugle

sight-see *vi.* visiter les curiosités; –ing *n.* tourisme *m.*; voyage *m.*; visites *f. pl.*; –r *n.* touriste, visiteur *m.*

sign *n.* signe *m.*, marque *f.*, symbole *m.*; enseigne *f.*, pancarte *f.*; — *vt.* signer; — off cesser d'émettre; — off *n.* (radio) fin de message *f.*; — up enrôler, inscrire; — language *n.* langage par signe *m.*; –post *n.* poteau indicateur *m.*, borne *f.*; –er *n.* signataire *m. & f.*

signal *n.* signal, signe *m.*; — corps *n.* transmissions *f. pl.*; — light *n.* (nav.) fanal *m.*; — lights *n. pl.* feux de route *m. pl.*; — *vt.* signaler; — *a.* signalé, insigne; –ize *vt.* signaler

signature *n.* signature *f.*; (end) fin de message *f.*

signet *n.* cachet *m.*

significance *n.* signification *f.*; importance *f.*

significant *n.* significatif, signifiant

signify *vt.* signifier

silage *n.* fourrage ensilé *m.*

silence *n.* silence *m.*; — *vt.* faire taire; –r *n.* amortisseur *m.*

silent *a.* silencieux; (movies) muet; — partner *n.* commandataire *m.*

silica *n.* silice *f.*; –te *n.* silicate *m.*

siliceous *a.* siliceux

silicone *n.* silicone *m.*

silk *n.* soie *f.*; — *a.* de soie; –en, –y *a.* soyeux

silkworm *n.* ver à soie *m.*

sill *n.* seuil, appui *m.*

silliness *n.* sottise *f.*

silly *a.* sot; niais, simple

silver *n.* argent *m.*; — plate argenterie *f.*; — *a.* d'argent, en argent; argenté; — *vt.* argenter

silver-plated *a.* plaqué d'argent

silversmith *n.* orfèvre *m.*

silverware *n.* argenterie *f.*

similar *a.* semblable; –ity *n.* similarité, ressemblance *f.*; –ly *adv.* de la même façon

simile *n.* comparaison *f.*

similitude *n.* similitude *f.*

simmer *vi.* mijoter; — *vt.* faire mijoter

simper *n.* minauderie *f.*; — *vi.* sourire niaisement

simple *a.* simple, naïf; pur; –ness *n.* simplicité *f.*

simple-minded *a.* simple, idiot

simpleton *n.* niais, sot *m.*

simplicity *n.* simplicité *f.*

simplification *n.* simplification *f.*

simplify *vt.* simplifier

simulate *vt.* feindre, simuler

simultaneous *a.* simultané; **—ness** *n.* simultanéité *f.*

sin *n.* péché *m.*; **mortal —** péché capital *m.*; **original —** péché originel; **—** *vi.* pécher; **—ful** *a.* pécheur; **—ner** *n.* pécheur *m.*

since *conj.* puisque; depuis que; comme; **—** *prep.* depuis; **—** *adv.* depuis

sincere *n.* sincère

sincerity *n.* sincérité *f.*

sine *n.* (math.) sinus *m.*

sinecure *n.* sinécure *f.*

sinew *n.* nerf *m.*; tendon *m.*; **—y** *a.* nerveux; vigoureux

sing *vt. & vi.* chanter; **—er** *n.* chanteur *m.*; cantatrice *f.*; **—ing** *n.* chant *m.*

singe *n.* roussi *m.*; **—** *vt.* brûler légèrement, flamber, roussir

single *a.* seul, particulier, singulier, simple; célibataire; **— file** *adv.* à la file indienne; **—ness** *n.* nature simple *f.*; sincérité *f.*

single-breasted *a.* droit, non croisé

singlehanded *a.* sans aide, seul

single-minded *a.* sincère; qui n'a qu'un seul but

singly *adv.* un à un

singsong *n.* chant monotone *m.*; (fig.) psalmodie *f.*; **—** *a.* monotone, traînant

singular *n. & a.* singulier *m.*; **—ity** *n.* singularité *f.*

sinister *a.* sinistre

sink *n.* évier *m.*; **—** *vi.* couler; s'enfoncer; s'abaisser, succomber; **—** *vt.* enfoncer; creuser; abaisser; perdre; plonger, précipiter; **—er** *n.* (fishline) poids, plomb *m.*; (coll.) beignet *m.*

sinking fund *n.* caisse d'amortissement *f.*

sinuosity *n.* sinuosité *f.*

sinuous *a.* sinueux

sip *n.* petit coup *m.*; gorgée *f.*; **—** *vt.* déguster, siroter

sir *n.* monsieur *m.*; (title) Sir, chevalier

sire *n.* père *m.*; Sire *m.*

siren *n.* sirène *f.*

sirloin *n.* aloyau *m.*

sirup, syrup *n.* sirop *m.*

sister *n.* sœur *f.*; (eccl.) religieuse *f.*; **—ly** *a.* de sœur, comme une sœur

sister-in-law *n.* belle-sœur *f.*

sit *vi.* s'asseoir; demeurer; siéger; être situé; **— down** s'asseoir; **— up** se dresser sur son séant; **—ter** *n.* celui qui est assis *m.*; garde des enfants *f.*; **—ting** *n.* séance *f.*; **—ting room** salon *m.*

sit-down strike *n.* grève sur le tas *f.*

site *n.* site, emplacement *m.*

situate *vt.* localiser; **—d** *a.* situé; sis; **be —d** se trouver

six *a. & n.* six *m.*; **—teen** *n. & a.* seize *m.*; **—teenth** *n. & a.* seizième *m.*; **—th** *a. & n.* sixième *m.*; **—tieth** *a. & n.* soixantième *m.*; **—ty** *a. & n.* soixante *m.*

sizable *a.* de grandeur appréciable, assez grand

size *n.* grandeur, taille *f.*; grosseur *f.*; mesure *f.*; pointure *f.*; colle *f.*; **—** *vt.* encoller; **— up** évaluer; **—d** *a.* de taille, de grandeur

sizing *n.* colle *f.*, collage, encollage *m.*

sizzle *vi.* griller en crépitant

sizzling *a.* crépitant; excessivement chaud

skate *n.* patin *m.*; (fish) raie *f.*; **roller —** patin à roulettes *m.*; **—** *vi.* patiner; **—r** *n.* patineur *m.*

skating *n.* patinage *m.*; **— rink** *n.* patinoire *f.*

skein *n.* écheveau *m.*

skeleton *n.* squelette *m.*; **— key** *n.* passepartout *m.*

skeptic *n.* sceptique *m.*; **—al** *a.* sceptique; **—ism** *n.* scepticisme *m.*

sketch *n.* esquisse *f.*; **—** *vt.* esquisser, ébaucher; **—y** *a.* esquissé, ébauché

sketchbook *n.* album *m.*

skewer *n.* brochette *f.*; **—** *vt.* embrocher

ski *n.* ski *m.*; **—** *vi.* faire du ski; **— jump** *n.* saut à ski *m.*; **— lift** *n.* remonte-pentes, télésiège *m.*

skid *n.* dérapage *m.*; **—** *vi.* déraper

skiff *n.* esquif *m.*

skilful *a.* adroit; habile

skill *n.* habileté *f.*; **—ed** *a.* adroit, habile; **—ed worker** *n.* spécialiste *m. & f.*

skillet *n.* poêle épaisse *f.*

skim *vt. & vi.* écumer, effleurer; (milk) écrémer; **— milk** *n.* lait écrémé *m.*; **—mer** *n.* écumoire *f.*; écrémeur *m.*

skimp *vi.* être frugal, économiser; **— on** lésiner sur; **—y** *a.* frugal, chiche

skin *n.* peau *f.*; pelure *f.*; écorce *f.*; **—flint** *n.* avare *m.*; **— graft** *n.* greffe épidermique *f.*; **—** *vt.* écorcher, dépouiller; dénuder; **—tight** *a.* collant

skin-deep *a.* superficiel

skin-dive *vi.* explorer au scaphandre autonome

skinny *a.* décharné, maigre

skip *n.* saut *m.*; **—** *vt.* sauter

skipper *n.* sauteur *m.*; capitaine *m.*

skipping rope *n.* corde à sauter *f.*

skirmish *n.* escarmouche *f.*; **—** *vi.* escarmoucher

skirt *n.* (dress) jupe *f.*; (forest) bord *m.*; **—** *vt.* contourner

skit *n.* saynète *f.*; scénario *m.*

skittish *a.* ombrageux; capricieux, volage

skulduggery *n.* roublardise *f.*

skulk *vi.* se cacher, rôder

skull *n.* crâne *m.*

skullcap *n.* calotte *f.*

skunk *n.* putois *m.*

sky *n.* ciel *m.*; **–light** *n.* lucarne *f.*; **–line** *n.* silhouette des bâtiments d'une ville *f.*; horizon *m.*; **–rocket** *n.* fusée *f.*; **–rocket** *vi.* (coll.) monter rapidement; **–scraper** *n.* gratte-ciel *m.*; maison démesurément haute *f.*; **–writing** *n.* publicité aérienne *f.*

slab *n.* plaque, dalle *f.*; tranche *f.*

slack *n.* mou *m.*; **–s** *pl.* pantalon *m.*; — *a.* mou; inactif, mort; — *vt.* relâcher; **–en** *vt.* relâcher, détendre; **–en** *vi.* se détendre; **–er** *n.* lâche, paresseux *m.*; embusqué *m.*

slag *n.* crasses *f. pl.*

slain *n. pl.* morts *m. pl.*

slake *vt.* (lime) éteindre; (thirst) apaiser

slam *vt.* fermer avec bruit; — *n.* claquement *m.*; insulte *f.*; (cards) schlem *m.*; **grand —** grand schlem *m.*; **small —** petit schlem *m.*; **make a —** faire schlem

slander *n.* médisance *f.*; — *vt.* colomnier, diffamer; **–er** *n.* calomniateur *m.*; **–ous** *a.* calomniateur, médisant

slang *n.* jargon, argot *m.*

slant *n.* pente *f.*; (coll.) interprétation *f.*; point de vue *m.*; — *vt.* interpréter, préparer, destiner; — *vi.* être en pente; **–ing** *a.* en pente; oblique; de travers; **–wise** *adv.* en biais

slap *n.* claque, tape *f.*; soufflet *m.*; **— in the face** gifle *f.*; — *vt.* taper, claquer; **— in the face** gifler

slapstick *n.* bouffonnerie *f.*; burlesque *f.*

slash *n.* taillade *f.*; baisse, réduction *f.*; — *vt.* balafrer, taillader; réduire

slat *n.* latte *f.*; lamelle *f.*

slate *n.* ardoise *f.*; liste *f.*; (pol.) liste des candidats *f.*; — *vt.* couvrir d'ardoise; destiner

slaughter *n.* carnage, massacre *m.*; abattage *m.*; — *vt.* abattre; massacrer

slaughterhouse *n.* abattoir *m.*

Slav *n.* Slave *m. & f.*; **–ic** *a.* slave; **–onic** *a.* slave

slave *n.* esclave *m. & f.*; **— driver** *n.* (fig.) maître sévère et cruel *m.*; — *vi.* travailler comme un esclave; **–r** *n.* négrier *m.*; **–ry** *n.* esclavage *m.*; **white –ry** prostitution *f.*

slavish *a.* servile; d'esclave

slaw *n.* salade de choux *f.*

slay *vt.* tuer; **–er** *n.* tueur, meurtrier *m.*; **–ing** *n.* meurtre, assassinat *m.*

sled *n.* traîneau *m.*

sledge hammer *n.* marteau à frapper *m.*

sleek *vt.* lisser, polir; — *a.* lisse, poli

sleep *n.* sommeil *m.*; — *vi.* dormir; **go to —** s'endormir; **put to —** endormir; **–er** *n.* dormeur *m.*; voiture-lits *f.*, wagon-lits *m.*; **–iness** *n.* somnolence *f.*; **–ing bag** *n.* sac de couchage *m.*; **–ing car** *n.* wagon-lits, sleeping (-car) *m.*; **–ing room** *n.* chambre à coucher *f.*; **–ing sickness** *n.* maladie du sommeil *f.*; **–less** *a.* sans sommeil, blanc; **–y** *a.* endormi; **be –y** avoir sommeil

sleepwalking *n.* somnambulisme *m.*

sleet *n.* grésil *m.*; — *vi.* grésiller

sleeve *n.* manche *f.*; **–less** *a.* sans manche

sleigh *n.* traîneau *m.*; **— bell** *n.* clochette *f.*, grelot *m.*

sleight *n.* tour d'adresse *m.*; ruse *f.*; **— of hand** paresseux *m.* tour de passe-passe

slender *a.* mince, svelte; chétif

sleuth *n.* détective *m.*

slice *n.* tranche *f.*; — *vt.* trancher

slick *a.* lisse, glissant; — *vt.* lisser; — *n.* (oil) couche d'huile *f.*; — *adv.* d'emblée; **–er** *n.* imperméable *m.*

slide *n.* glissade, glissoire *f.*; coulisse *f.*; (microscope) fiche *f.*; (projection) diapositif *m.*; **— rule** règle à calcul *f.*; — *vt. & vi.* glisser, faire glisser

sliding scale *n.* échelle mobile *f.*

slight *n.* dédain *m.*; — *vt.* dédaigner; manquer à; — *a.* mince, insignifiant; léger

slim *a.* mince, svelte; **–ness** *n.* minceur *f.*

slime *n.* limon *m.*, bourbe *f.*; bave *f.*

sliminess *n.* viscosité *f.*

slimy *a.* visqueux, vaseux; gluant

sling *n.* écharpe *f.*; lancement *m.*; (gun) bretelle *f.*; — *vt.* lancer, jeter

slingshot *n.* lance-pierres *m.*; fronde *f.*

slink *vi.* s'en aller furtivement

slip *n.* glissade *f.*; erreur *f.*; barde *f.*; écoulement *m.*; (bot.) scion *m.*; (undergarment) chemise *f.*; combinaison *f.*; (paper) bout *m.*; **— cover** *n.* housse *f.*; — *vt.* glisser; faire une erreur: — *vi.* glisser; se tromper; faire un faux-pas

slipper *n.* pantoufle *f.*; mule *f.*

slippery *a.* glissant

slipshod *a.* négligé

slit *n.* fente *f.*; — *vt.* fendre

sliver *n.* éclat; — *vi.* éclater

slobber *n.* bave *f.*; — *vi.* baver

sloe *n.* prunelle *f.*; **— gin** *n.* prunelline *f.*

slogan *n.* slogan *m.*

sloop *n.* chaloupe *f.*

slop *n.* rinçure *f.*; eau de vaisselle *f.*; lavasse *f.*; — *vt.* répandre; **–py** *a.* négligé; désordonné; peu soigné; sale

slope *n.* pente, déclivité *f.*; talus *m.*; — *vi.* s'incliner

slot *n.* fente, ouverture *f.*; **— machine** *n.*

machine à sous *f.*

sloth *n.* paresse *f.*; (zool.) paresseux *m.*; **-ful** *a.* paresseux

slouch *vt. & vi.* abaisser la tête; rabaisser le chapeau; se dandiner lourdement; — *n.* attitude affaissée *f.*; — **hat** *n.* chapeau mou *m.*

slough *n.* bourbier *m.*; dépouille *f.*; — *vt.* se dépouiller de

Slovakia *n.* Slovaquie *f.*

slovenly *a.* malpropre; sale

slow *a.* lent; tardif; — *vt.* ralentir; — **down** ralentir; **-ly** *adv.* lentement; **-ness** *n.* lenteur *f.*; (clocks) retard

slow-motion *a.* (films) film tourné au ralenti

sludge *n.* cambouis *m.*; calamine *f.*; dépôt carboné *m.*; boues *f. pl.*

slug *n.* (zool.) limace *f.*; (print., bar) lingot *m.* (token) jeton *m.*; — *vt.* (coll.) assomer

sluggish *a.* indolent; lent; **-ness** *n.* indolence *f.*; lenteur *f.*

sluice *n.* écluse *f.*; **-gate** *n.* porte éclusière *f.*; — *vt.* vanner

slum *n.* quartier misérable *m.*; **go -ming** visiter les quartiers misérables

slumber *n.* sommeil *m.*; — *vi.* sommeiller

slump *n.* chute, baisse *f.*; affaissement *m.*; — *vi.* baisser; s'affaisser; s'enfoncer

slur *n.* tache *f.*; blâme *m.*; (mus.) coulé *m.*; — *vt.* salir; passer légèrement; (mus.) lier les notes

slush *n.* neige à moitié fondue *f.*

sly *a.* fin; rusé; **on the —** en cachette; furtivement

smack *n.* goût *m.*; claque *f.*; (fishing) bâteau de pêche *m.*; — *vt.* claquer; — *vi.* avoir le goût; rappeler

small *n.* partie la plus mince *f.*; — **of the back** reins *m. pl.*; — *a.* petit; léger; menu; — **change** *n.* menue monnaie *f.*; — **fry** enfants *m. pl.*; — **hours** heures matinales *f. pl.*; — **intestine** *n.* intestin grêle *m.*; — **talk** bavardage *m.*; **-ish** *a.* assez petit; **-ness** *n.* petitesse *f.*

smallpox *n.* petite vérole *f.*

small-town *a.* provincial

smart *n.* douleur aiguë *f.*; — *vi.* sentir une cuisante douleur; faire sentir une cuisante douleur; — *a.* intelligent, vif; élégant; **-ness** *n.* intelligence *f.*; élégance *f.*

smash *vt.* briser, écraser; — *n.* fracas *m.*; collision *f.*; grande réussite *f.*

smashup *n.* collision *f.*, accident *m.*

smattering *n.* connaissance superficielle *f.*; notions *f. pl.*

smear *n.* tache *f.*; avilissement *m.*; — *vt.* tacher, barbouiller; avilir; (coll.) ca-

lomnier, diffamer

smell *n.* odeur *f.*; — *vt. & vi.* sentir

smelt *n.* éperlan *m.*

smelt *vt.* fondre; **-er** *n.* fonderie *f.*

smile *n.* sourire *m.*; — *vi.* sourire

smirk *vi.* sourire, minauder

smite *vt.* frapper; enflammer

smith *n.* forgeron *m.*; **-y** *n.* forge *f.*

smithereens *n. pl.* atomes *m. pl.*; **break to — atomiser**

smock *n.* tablier *m.*, blouse *f.*

smoke *n.* fumée *f.*; vapeur *f.*; — *vt. & vi.* fumer; — **house** *n.* fumoir *m.*; **-less** *a.* sans fumée; **-r** *n.* fumeur *m.*

smoke screen *n.* rideau de fumée *m.*

smokestack *n.* cheminée

smoking *n.* action de fumer *f.*; — **car** *n.* wagon des fumeurs *m.*; **no — défense de fumer**

smoking jacket *n.* veston d'intérieur *m.*

smoky *a.* fumeux; enfumé

smolder *vi.* brûler sans flamme

smooth *vt.* unir; lisser; apaiser; flatter; dérider; — *a.* uni; poli, lisse, doux; **-ness** *n.* douceur *f.*; poli, calme *m.*

smooth-spoken, **smooth-tongued** *a.* à langue dorée

smother *vt.* étouffer, suffoquer; couvrir

smudge *n.* barbouillage *m.*; dépôt de suie *m.*; tache; — *vt.* barbouiller

smug *a.* content de sol

smuggle *vt.* faire la contrebande; **-r** *n.* contrebandier *m.*

smuggling *n.* contrebande *f.*

smut *n.* tache de suie *f.*; obscénités *f. pl.*; — *vt.* noircir; **-ty** *a.* taché de suie; grossier

snack *n.* casse-croûte *m.*; goûter *m.*; collation *f.*

snag *n.* bosse *f.*, nœud *m.*; entrave, difficulté *f.*; — *vt.* accrocher

snail *n.* limaçon, escargot *m.*; **at a -'s pace** à pas de tortue

snake *n.* serpent *m.*; — *vi.* onduler

snap *n.* claquement *m.*; bruit sec *m.*; fermoir *m.*; (coll.) quelque chose de facile *m.*, — *vi.* claquer; se briser; — **at** prendre dans les dents; parler sur un ton hargneux; — *vt.* casser, briser; **-per** *n.* fermoir *m.*, fermeture *f.*

snapshot *n.* instantané *m.*

snare *n.* piège *m.*; — *vt.* prendre au piège

snarl *vi.* grogner, gronder; emmêler; — *n.* grognement *m.*; (coll.) embouteillage *m.*

snatch *n.* prise *f.*; accès *m.*; morceau *m.*; — *vt.* saisir, arracher violemment

sneak *n.* lâche *m.*; — *vt.* voler; — *vi.* se glisser; — **thief** *n.* voleur *m.*

sneer *n.* ricanement *m.*, raillerie *f.*; — *vi.* ricaner

sneeze *vi.* éternuer; — *n.* éternuement *m.*

snicker *n.* ricanement *m.*; — *vi.* ricaner

sniff *vi.* renifler; — *n.* reniflement *m.*; respirée *f.*

sniffle *n.* reniflement *m.*; — *vi.* renifler; pleurnicher; -s *n. pl.* reniflement *m.*; rhume de cerveau *m.*

snip *n.* coupure *f.*; petit morceau *m.*; — *vt.* couper; rogner

snipe *n.* bécassine *f.*; — *vi.* tirer; canarder; -r *n.* franc-tireur *m.*

snivel *vi.* pleurnicher

snob *n.* snob; parvenu *m.*; -bish *a.* snob; vulgaire; -bishness *n.* snobisme *m.*; suffisance *f.*

snoop *n.* curieux *m.*; espion *m.*; — *vi.* épier

snooze *n.* petit somme *m.*; — *vi.* somnoler

snore *n.* ronflement *m.*; — *vi.* ronfler

snoring *n.* ronflement *m.*; — *a.* qui ronfle

snorkel *n.* schnorchel *m.*

snort *n.* ébrouement *m.*; — *vi.* s'ébrouer

snout *n.* museau *m.*; groin *m.*

snow *n.* neige *f.*; — *vi.* neiger; -y *a.* neigeux

snowball *n.* boule de neige *f.*

snowbound *a.* bloqué par la neige

snow-capped *a.* couronné de neige

snowdrift *n.* amas de neige *m.*

snowfall *n.* chute de neige *f.*

snowflake *n.* flocon de neige *m.*

snow line *n.* limite des neiges *f.*

snowplow *n.* chasse-neige *m.*

snow slide *n.* avalanche de neige *f.*

snow storm *n.* tempête de neige *f.*

snub *n.* affront *m.*; — nose nez camus *m.*; — *vt.* tourner le dos à

snuff *n.* tabac à priser *m.*; — box tabatière *f.*; — *vt.* éteindre; moucher

snuffle *vi.* renifler

snug *a.* serré; commode, confortable; bien

snuggle *vi.* se serrer

so *adv.* ainsi; si; tellement; tant; aussi; comme cela; de même; alors; and — on et ainsi de suite; — as to pour; — much tant; — that pour que, afin que; de sorte que; — long! au revoir, à bientôt

soak *vt. & vi.* tremper; -ing *a.*, -ing wet trempé, mouillé (jusqu'aux os); -ing *n.* action de tremper *f.*; arrosage *m.*

soap *n.* savon *m.*; — bubble bulle de savon *f.*; -suds mousse de savon *f.*; toilet — savonnette *f.*; — *vt.* savonner; -y *a.* savonneux

soapbox *n.* caisse à savon *f.*; plate-forme improvisée *m.*

soapstone *n.* stéatite *f.*

soar *vi.* prendre l'essor; s'élever

sob *n.* sanglot *m.*; — *vi.* sangloter

sober *a.* sobre; pas ivre; — *vt.* calmer; ramener à la raison

sobriety *n.* sobriété *f.*; modération *f.*

so-called *a.* soi-disant; ainsi nommé

sociability *n.* sociabilité *f.*

sociable *a.* sociable; amical

social *a.* social; sociable; — security assurances sociales *f. pl.*; — service, — work travail d'amélioration sociale *m.*; -ism *n.* socialisme *m.*; -ist *n.* socialiste *m. & f.*; -ite *n.* mondain *m.*, mondaine *f.*; -ize *vt.* socialiser

society *n.* société *f.*; monde *m.*

sociological *a.* sociologique

sociology *n.* sociologie *f.*

sock *n.* chaussette *f.*; coup de poing *m.*; — *vt.* donner un coup de poing à, frapper du poing

socket *n.* douille *f.*; soc. *m.*; (elec.) prise *f.*; (eye) orbite *f.*; (tooth) alvéole *m.*; socle *m.*; — wrench clé à tube *f.*

sod *n.* motte de terre *f.*; gazon *m.*

soda *n.* soude *f.*; soda *m.*; baking —, bicarbonate of — bicarbonate de soude *m.*; — water soda *m.*; eau de Seltz *f.*

sodium *n.* sodium *m.*; — chloride *n.* chlorure de soude *m.*

sofa *n.* sofa, canapé *m.*; — bed *n.* canapé qui se transforme en lit, lit-divan *m.*

soft *a.* mou, doux; tendre, faible, facile, délicat; efféminé; (water) non-calcaire; — coal charbon *m.*; — drink boisson rafraîchissante *f.*, boisson non-alcoolisée *f.*; -en *vt.* amollir, adoucir, attendrir; -ness *n.* douceur *f.*; mollesse *f.*

softball *n.* baseball (jouée avec une balle molle) *m.*

softhearted *a.* sensible; sentimental; compatissant

soft-pedal *vt.* étouffer, adoucir; minimiser

soft-spoken *a.* doux

soggy *a.* humide

soil *n.* souillure *f.*; terre *f.*; sol, terrain *m.*; — *vt.* souiller, salir

sojourn *n.* séjour *m.*; — *vi.* séjourner

sol *n.* (mus.) sol *m.*

solace *n.* consolation *f.*; — *vt.* consoler

solar *a.* solaire; du soleil; — plexus *n.* plexus solaire *m.*; -ium *n.* solarium *m.*

sold *a.*, — out épuisé; complet; tout vendu

solder *n.* soudure *f.*; — *vt.* souder; -ing *n.* soudure *f.*; -ing iron *n.* fer à souder *m.*

soldier *n.* soldat *m.*

sole *n.* (foot) plante du pied *f.*; (shoe) semelle *f.*; (fish) sole *f.*; — *vt.* ressemeler; — *a.* unique, seul

solemn *a.* solennel; -ity *n.* solennité *f.*; -ize *vt.* solenniser

solicit *vt.* solliciter; inviter; -ation *n.* sollicitation *f.*; -or *n.* solliciteur *m.*; (law) avoué *m.*; -ous *a.* plein de sollicitude; -ude *n.* sollicitude *f.*

solid *a.* solide; massif; réel; grave, profond; (color) uni; — *n.* corps solide *m.*; **–arity** *n.* solidarité *f.*; **–ify** *vt.* solidifier; **–ify** *vi.* se solidifier; **–ity** *n.* solidité *f.*; — **geometry** *n.* géométrie dans l'espace *f.*

soliloquy *n.* monologue *m.*

solitaire *n.* solitaire *m.*; (game) patience *f.*

solitary *a.* solitaire; retiré

solitude *n.* solitude *f.*

solo *n.* solo *m.*; **–ist** *n.* soliste *m. & f.*; — *a. & adv.* seul

solstice *n.* solstice *m.*

soluble *a.* dissoluble

solution *n.* solution *f.*

solve *vt.* résoudre

solvency *n.* solvabilité *f.*

solvent *n.* dissolvant *m.*; — *a.* (com.) solvable

Somalia *n.* Somalie *f.*

somber *a.* sombre

some *a.* quelque, un peu de; du, de la; — *pron.* un peu; certains; quelques-uns; les uns; les autres

somebody, someone *pron.* quelqu'un

somehow *adv.* de façon ou d'autre

somersault *n.* culbute *f.*; — *vi.* culbuter

something *pron.* quelque chose

sometime *adv.* un jour, un de ces jours; — *a.* ancien, ci-devant, honoraire

sometimes *adv.* quelquefois, de temps en temps; tantôt

somewhat *adv.* un peu; assez

somewhere *adv.* quelque part; — **else** ailleurs; autre part

somnambulist *n.* somnambule *m. & f.*

somnolent *a.* somnolent

son *n.* fils *m.*

sonata *n.* sonate *f.*

song *n.* chanson *f.*; chant *m.*; **–ster** *n.* chanteur *m.*; **–stress** *n.* chanteuse *f.*

Song of Songs Cantique des Cantiques *f.*

sonic *a.* sonique; — **boom** *n.* grondement sonique *m.*

son-in-law *n.* gendre *m.*

sonorous *a.* sonore

soon *adv.* bientôt, tôt, de bonne heure; **as — as** aussitôt que; **how —?** dans combien de temps?

soot *n.* suie *f.*; **–y** *a.* couvert de suie; fuligineux

soothe *vt.* flatter; apaiser

soothsayer *n.* devin *m.*

sop *n.* morceau trempé *m.*; (fig.) os à ronger; cadeau, présent *m.*; — *vt.* tremper; **–ping** *a.* trempé

sophisticated *·a.* sophistiqué, blasé

sophistication *n.* sophistication *f.*

sophomore *n.* étudiant universitaire de deuxième année *m.*

sophomoric *a.* jeune, inexpérimenté

soporific *n. & a.* soporifique *m.*

sorcerer *n.* sorcier *m.*

sorceress *n.* sorcière *f.*

sorcery *n.* sorcellerie *f.*, sortilège *m.*

sordid *a.* sordide

sore *n.* ulcère *m.*, plaie *f.*; — *a.* douloureux; écorché; violent; **–ness** *n.* mal *m.*; douleur *f.*; sensibilité *f.*

sorority *n.* société d'étudiantes' universitaires *f.*

sorrow *n.* chagrin *m.*, affliction, tristesse *f.*; — *vi.* être affligé; être en deuil; **–ful** *a.* triste, affligé; affligeant; **–fulness** *n.* chagrin *m.*, tristesse *f.*

sorry *a.* affligé; triste; fâché; désolé; **be —** regretter

sort *n.* sorte, espèce, classe, mantière *f.*, genve *m.*; — *vt.* séparer, classer, trier, assortir

so-so *a.* comme ci comme ça

sot *n.* sot, imbécile *m.*; ivrogne *m.*

soul *n.* âme *f.*, esprit *m.*; **–ful** *a.* plein d'émotion; plein d'âme

sound *n.* son, bruit *m.*; (med.) sonde *f.*; (geog.) goulet, détroit *m.*; — *a.* sain, bien portant, vigoureux; — **barrier** *n.* barrière du son *f.*; — **effect** effet sonore *m.*; — **track** piste sonore *f.*; — **truck** camion d'enregistrement *m.*; — **wave** onde sonore *f.*; — *vt. & vi.* sonner; (med.) sonder; **–ing** *n.* sondage *m.*; **–ing** *a.*, **–ing board** table d'harmonie *f.*; **–ing line** ligne de sonde *f.*; **–ness** *n.* solidité *f.*

soundproof *a.* insonore; — *vt.* insonoriser

soup *n.* soupe *f.*, potage *m.*; — **plate** assiette creuse; — **tureen** *n.* soupière *f.*

sour *a.* aigre; acide; — *vt.* rendre acide; aigrir; — *vi.* tourner; s'aigrir; **–ness** *n.* aigreur *f.*

south *n.* sud, midi *m.*; **–east** *n.* sud-est *m.*; **–ern** *a.* méridional, du sud; **–erner** *n.* méridional; **–land** *n.* midi *m.*; **–ward** *adv.* vers le sud; **–west** *n.* sud-ouest *m.*

sovereign *a.* souverain; **–ty** *n.* souveraineté *f.*

Soviet *n.* Soviet *m.*; — *a.* soviétique

sow *n.* truie *f.*; — *vt.* semer, ensemencer; **–er** *n.* semeur *m.*

soybean *n.* soya *m.*

spa *n.* ville d'eau *f.*

space *n.* espace *m.*; distance *f.*, intervalle *m.*; — *vt.* espacer; — **capsule** *n.* astronef *m.*; — **fiction** *n.* fiction interplanétaire *f.*; **–r** *n.* (typewriter) barre d'espacement *f.*

spacious *a.* spacieux, vaste; **–ness** *n.* grandeur, immensité *f.*

spade *n.* bêche *f.*; (cards) pique *m.*; — *vt. & vi.* bêcher

Spain *n.* Espagne *f.*

span *n.* empan *m.*; portée, travée *f.*; durée *f.*; — *vt.* couvrir, traverser
spangle *n.* paillette *f.*
Spaniard *n.* Espagnol *m.*
Spanish *a. & n.* espagnol *m.*
spank *vt.* fesser; —ing *n.* fessée *f.*
spar *n.* espar *m.*; (geol.) spath *m.*; — *vi.* boxer
spare *vt. & vi.* épargner, ménager, traiter avec indulgence; — *a.* maigre; de rechange; disponible; — parts pièces de rechange *f. pl.*; — time loisir *m.*; — tire pneu de rechange *m.*
sparerib *n.* plat de côte *m.*
sparing *a.* rare; frugal; chiche
spark *n.* étincelle *f.*; — plug bougie *f.*
sparkle *vi. & vt.* étinceler
sparkling *a.* étincelant; (drink) mousseux
sparse *a.* épars
Sparta *n.* Sparte *f.*; —n *a. & n.* spartiate *m. & f.*
spasm *n.* spasme *m.*; —odic *a.* spasmodique
spastic *a.* spasmodique, spastique
spat *n.* guêtre *f.*; (coll.) dispute *f.*; — *vi.* se disputer
spatial *a.* de l'espace
spatter *n.* éclaboussure *f.*; — *vt.* éclabousser
spatula *n.* spatule *f.*
spawn *n.* frai *m.*; — *vt. & vi.* frayer; engendrer
spay *vt.* châtrer
speak *vt. & vi.* parler, discourir; prononcer; — out lever la voix; — up parler plus haut; —er *n.* parleur, conférencier *m.*; (organization) président *m.*; (radio) haut-parleur *m.*
spear *n.* lance *f.*; harpon *m.*; épieu *m.*; — *vt.* percer à coups de lance; harponner
spearhead *n.* fer de lance *m.*; pointe *f.*; (mil.) point d'attaque *m.*
special *a.* spécial; particulier; — delivery par exprès; — delivery letter *n.* lettre exprès *f.*; —ist *n.* spécialiste *m. & f.*; —ize *vt.* spécialiser; —ize *vi.* se spécialiser; —ty *n.* spécialité *f.*
species *n.* espèce, sorte *f.*
specific *n. & a.* spécifique *m.*; — gravity *n.* poids spécifique *m.*; —ation *n.* spécification *f.*
specify *vt.* spécifier
specimen *n.* spécimen, modèle *m.*
specious *a.* spécieux
speck *n.* tache *f.*, point *m.*; — *vt.* tacher
speckle *n.* petite tache, bigarrure *f.*; — *vt.* tacheter, moucheter
spectacle *n.* spectacle *m.*; —s *pl.* lunettes *f. pl.*
spectacular *n.* représentation à grand spectacle; — *a.* spectaculaire

spectator *n.* spectateur *m.*
specter *n.* spectre *m.*, apparition *f.*
spectral *a.* spectral
spectroscope *n.* spectroscope *m.*
spectrum *n.* spectre *m.*
speculate *vi.* spéculer; jouer
speculation *n.* spéculation, méditation *f.*
speculator *n.* spéculateur *m.*
speech *n.* discours *m.*; langage *m.*, harangue *f.*; plaidoyer *m.*; figure of — *n.* figure de rhétorique *f.*; —less *a.* interdit; muet
speed *n.* vitesse *f.*; — limit vitesse maxima *f.*; — *vi.* se dépêcher; aller très vite; aller trop vite; — *vt.* dépêcher, hâter; — up intensifier; presser; aller plus vite; -y *a.* rapide; hâtif
speedboat *n.* canot automobile *m.*; vedette *f.*; hors-bord *m.*
speedometer *n.* indicateur de vitesse *m.*; tachymètre *m.*
speed-up *n.* accélération *f.*
speedway *n.* piste d'autos *f.*
spell *n.* charme *m.*; sortilège *m.*; moment *m.*; attaque *f.*, accès *m.*, crise *f.*; — *vt.* épeler, orthographier; remplacer; —er *n.* livre d'orthographe *m.*; —ing *n.* orthographe *f.*; —ing bee concours d'orthographe *m.*
spellbound *a.* charmé, fasciné
spend *vt.* dépenser, employer; consommer; dissiper; épuiser; —er *n.* dépensier, dissipateur *m.*
spendthrift *n.* prodigue *m.*
spent *a.* épuisé; dépensé
sperm *n.* sperme *m.*
spermatozoa *n. pl.* spermatozoïdes *m. pl.*
sperm whale *n.* cachalot *m.*
spew *vt.* vomir
sphere *n.* sphère *f.*
spherical *a.* sphérique
spheroid *n.* sphéroïde *m.*
sphinx *n.* sphinx *m.*
spice *n.* épice *f.*; — *vt.* épicer
spick-and-span *a.* impeccable
spicy *a.* aromatique, épicé
spider *n.* araignée *f.*
spigot *n.* fausset *m.*; robinet *m.*
spike *n.* épi de blé *m.*; pointe *f.*; long clou *m.*, cheville *f.*; — *vt.* clouer
spill *vt.* répandre, renverser
spillway *n.* déversoir *m.*
spin *vt. & vi.* filer; faire tournoyer; — *n.* promenade en auto *f.*; —ning *n.* filature *f.*; —ning jenny jenny *f.*; —ning mill filature *f.*; —ing wheel rouet *m.*
spinach *n.* épinards *m. pl.*
spinal *a.* spinal; — column *n.* colonne vertébrale *f.*; — cord *n.* moelle épinière *f.*
spindle *n.* fuseau *m.*, broche *f.*; pivot *m.*

spine *n.* épine dorsale *f.*; (book) dos *m.*
spinet *n.* épinette *f.*
spinnaker *n.* foc de yacht *m.*
spinster *n.* vieille fille *f.*
spiny *a.* épineux
spiral *a.* spiral; en spirale; — *n.* spirale *f.*
spire *n.* aiguille, flèche (de clocher) *f.*
spirit *n.* esprit *m.*, âme *f.*; courage, feu *m.*; génie *m.*; fantôme *m.*; liqueur spiritueuse *f.*; **in high –s** joie *f.*, abandon *m.*; **low —** abattement *m.*; **raise one's –s** remonter le courage de quelqu'un; — **lamp** *n.* réchaud à alcool *m.*; — **level** *n.* niveau à bulle d'air *m.*; — *vt.* animer, encourager; — **away** enlever; **–ed** *a.* animé, vigoureux; **–less** *a.* inanimé; **–ual** *a.* spirituel; **–ual** *n.* (mus.) chant religieux populaire *m.*; **–ualism** *n.* spiritisme *m.*; **–ualist** *n.* spiritualiste *m.*
spit *n.* (rod) broche *f.*; salive *f.*; — *vt.* embrocher; cracher; **–tle** *n.* crachat *m.*; **–toon** *n.* crachoir *m.*
spite *n.* dépit *m.*, rancune *f.*; **in — of** en dépit de, malgré; — *vt.* contrarier; **–ful** *a.* malicieux, rancunier
spitfire *n.* mégère *f.*; (avi.) spitfire *m.*
splash *n.* éclaboussure *f.*; — *vt.* éclabousser
spleen *n.* rate *f.*; (fig.) spleen *m.*
splendid *a.* splendide; magnifique, brillant
splendor *n.* splendeur *f.*; éclat *m.*
splice *n.* jointure, soudure *f.*; (film) collure *f.*; — *vt.* joindre à onglet; (naut.) épisser
splint *n.* éclisse *f.*
splinter *n.* éclat (de bois) *m.*; — *vt.* briser, fendre; — *vi.* voler en éclats
split *n.* fente *f.*; querelle *f.*; division *f.*; (dance) grand écart *m.*; demi-bouteille *f.*; — *vt.* fendre, briser; — *vi.* se fendre; crever; **–ting** *n.* fendage *m.*; (atom) fissure *f.*; **–ting** *a.* écrasant
splotch *n.* tache *f.*; — *vt.* tacher
splurge *n.* faste, parade *f.*; — *vi.* faire parade; se payer une fête
splutter *vi.* bredouiller
spoil *n.* pillage *m.*; butin *m.*; dépouille *f.*; — *vt.* gâter, abîmer; — *vi.* se gâter; — **for** désirer; **–er** *n.* spoliateur *m.*; **–age** *n.* dégats *m. pl.*; choses gatées *f. pl.*
spoilsport *n.* trouble-fête *m.*
spoke *n.* rais, rayon *m.*
spokesman *n.* porte-parole *m.*
sponge *n.* éponge *f.*; — **bath** *n.* bain anglais *m.*; — **cake** (genre de) gâteau de Savoie *m.*; — *vt.* éponger; — *vi.* (coll.) vivre en parasite; **–r** *n.* pique-assiette *m.*
spongy *a.* spongieux
sponsor *n.* garant *m.*; parrain *m.*; marraine *f.*; (rad.) annonceur *m.*, commanditaire, patron; — *vt.* présenter; payer

les frais; **–ship** *n.* parrainage *m.*; patronage *m.*
spontaneity *n.* spontanéité *f.*
spontaneous *a.* spontané; **–ly** *adv.* spontanément; **–ness** *n.* spontanéité *f.*
spool *n.* rouleau *m.*; bobine *f.*; — *vt.* embobiner
spoon *n.* cuiller, cuillère *f.*; **table–** cuiller à bouche *f.*; **tea–** cuiller à café *f.*; — *vt.* prendre dans une cuiller; **–ful** *n.* cuillerée *f.*
sporadic *a.* sporadique
sport *n.* sport *m.*; divertissement, amusement, jeu *m.*; — *vt. & vi.* faire parade de; se divertir, badiner; **–ing** *a.* juste, équitable; **–ing goods** articles de sport *m. pl.*; **–ive** *a.* sportif; gai; — **shirt** *n.* chemise de sport *f.*
sportsman *n.* sportif *m.*; **–ship** *n.* attitude du sportif *f.*
spot *n.* tache *f.*; lieu *m.*, place *f.*; (ground) coin *m.*; (coll.) pétrin, mauvais pas *m.*; — *vt.* tacher; tacheter; (coll.) marquer; **–less** *a.* sans tache; **–ted** *a.* tacheté; **–ty** *a.* taché, inégal
spotlight *n.* projecteur intensif, spot *m.*
spot welding *n.* soudage par points *m.*
spouse *n.* époux *m.*, épouse *f.*
spout *n.* tuyau de décharge *m.*; jet *m.*; — *vi.* jaillir; — *vt.* faire jaillir; énoncer, dire, prononcer
sprain *n.* foulure, entorse *f.*; — *vt.* se fouler; se donner une entorse à
sprawl *vi.* s'étaler
spray *n.* écume *f.*; vapeur *f.*; rameau *m.*; — *vt. & vi.* vaporiser; couvrir d'écume; **–er** *n.* vaporisateur *m.*
spread *n.* étendue *f.*; rayonnement *m.*; (bed) dessus de lit, couvre-lit *m.*; collation *f.*; — *vt.* répandre, faire rayonner, vulgariser; — *vi.* se répandre, rayonner
sprig *n.* brin *m.*, brindille *f.*
sprightliness *n.* vivacité, gaieté *f.*, feu *m.*
sprightly *a.* vif, gai
spring *a. & n.* (season) printemps *m.*; (water) source *f.*; (mech.) ressort *m.*; (movement) élan, saut *m.*; — *vi.* s'élancer, bondir; — **from** naître de; **–y** *a.* élastique
springboard *n.* tremplin *m.*
springlike *a.* printanier
springtime *n.* printemps *m.*
sprinkle *vt. & vi.* asperger, arroser; (fig.) parsemer; — *n.* légère pluie *f.*; **–r** *n.* arroseur *m.*; arroseur automatique *m.*; pomme d'arrosage *f.*
sprinkling *n.* arrosage *m.*; petite quantité *f.*; connaissance superficielle *f.*, notions *f. pl.*
sprint *n.* course *f.*; sprint *m.*; — *vi.* cou-

rir à toute vitesse; **-er** *n.* coureur rapide *m.*

sprite *n.* esprit, fantôme *m.*

sprocket *n.* (mech.) dent *f.*; galet *m.*; **—wheel** roue dentée *f.*; pignon *m.*

sprout *n.* jet, rejeton *m.*; pousse *f.*; **Brussels —s** choux de Bruxelles *m. pl.*; **—** *vi.* germer, pousser

spruce *vi.*, **— up** se faire beau; **—** *a.* pimpant; bien mis; **—** *n.* sapin *m.*

sprung *a.* déformé

spry *a.* vif, animé, actif; **-ness** *n.* activité, vivacité *f.*

spume *n.* écume *f.*; **—** *vi.* écumer, mousser

spun *a.* filé, en fil

spur *n.* éperon *m.*; aiguillon *m.*; ergot *m.*; stimulant *m.*; hâte *f.*; **on the — of the moment** à l'impromptu; **—** *vt.* éperonner, instiguer, inspirer

spurious *a.* faux, falsifié

spurn *vt.* mépriser, dédaigner

spurt *n.* jet, jaillissement; **—** *vi.* jaillir

sputter *n.* bredouillement *m.*; **—** *vi.* bredouiller, balbutier

sputum *n.* expectorations *f. pl.*

spy *n.* espion *m.*, espionne *f.*; **—** *vt.* épier, espionner; **-glass** *n.* longue-vue *f.*

squab *n.* jeune pigeon *m.*

squabble *n.* querelle *f.*; bagarre *f.*; **—** *vi.* se chamailler

squad *n.* escouade *f.*; équipe *f.*; **rescue —** équipe de secours *f.*

squadron *n.* escadron *m.*; escadre *f.*

squalid *a.* sale, malpropre

squall *n.* cri alarmant *m.*; (weather) rafale *f.*, coup de vent, grain *m.*; **—** *vi.* crier, brailler

squalor *n.* misère, saleté *f.*

squander *vt.* dissiper, gaspiller

square *n.* carré *m.*; équerre *f.*; place *f.*; **—** *vt. & vi.* carrer; régler, ajuster; **—** *a.* carré; convenable; conforme; balancé; juste, honnête; équitable; **— dance** quadrille américain *m.*; **— root** racine carrée *f*

squash *n.* courge, gourde *f.*; foule, presse *f.*; écrasement *m.*; (sport) jeu de paume *m.*; **—** *vt.* écraser

squat *vi.* s'accroupir, se tapir; **—** *a.* accroupi, blotti; **-ter** *n.* colon, squatter *m.*

squawk *n.* cri rauque *m.*; **—** *vi.* crier

squeak *n.* cri perçant *m.*; **—** *vi.* jeter des cris perçants; grincer; **-y** *a.* criard; (mech.) glapissant

squeal *n.* cri (du cochon) *m.*; **—** *vi.* (like a pig) crier; (coll.) manger le morceau, chanter

squeamish *a.* délicat; dégoûté; **-ness** *n.* délicatesse exagérée *f.*

squeegee *n.* essuie-glace *m.*; rouleau en caoutchouc *m.*

squeeze *n.* compression *f.*; serrement *m.*; **—** *vt.* presser, serrer; **— out** exprimer; éliminer; **-r** *n.* presse *f.*; **lemon -r** presse-citrons *m.*

squelch *n.* réplique écrasante *f.*; **—** *vt.* écraser

squib *n.* (fig.) satire *f.*; bon mot *m.*

squint *n.* regard louche *m.*; **—** *vi.* loucher; cligner les yeux

squint-eyed *a.* louche

squire *n.* écuyer *m.*; propriétaire *m.*; cavalier *m.*; **—** *vt.* accompagner

squirm *vi.* se tortiller

squirt *n.* jet *m.*; **—** *vt.* jeter; **—** *vi.* jaillir

squirt gun *n.* seringue *f.*

stab *n.* coup de poignard *m.*; **make a — at** tenter, essayer; **—** *vt.* poignarder

stability *n.* stabilité, constance *f.*

stabilize *vt.* stabiliser; **—** *vi.* devenir stable; **-r** *n.* stabiliseur *m.*

stable *n.* étable, écurie *f.*; **—** *vt.* établer; **—** *a.* stable, fixe; constant, ferme

stack *n.* (hay) meule *f.*; (wood) pile *f.*; tas *m.*; **—** *vt.* entasser; mettre en meule

stadium *n.* stade *m.*

staff *n.* bâton *m.*; état-major *m.*; soutien *m.*; personnel *m.*; (mus.) portée *f.*

stag *n.* cerf *m.*; **— party** soirée pour hommes *f.*; **go —** aller sans compagne

stage *n.* échafaudage *m.*; estrade *f.*; théâtre *m.*, scène *f.*; degré, état *m.*; relais *m.*; journée *f.*; voiture publique *f.*; **—** *vt.* monter; mettre en scène

stagger *vi.* chanceler; hésiter, vaciller; **—** *vt.* ébranler, étonner; échelonner; **-ed** *a.* échelonné

staging *n.* mise en scène *f.*; échafaud *m.*; **— area** *n.* camp temporaire (avant l'embarquement) *m.*

stagnant *a.* stagnant; inactif

stagnate *vi.* être stagnant

stagy *a.* théâtral, artificiel

staid *a.* grave, posé; **-ness** *n.* gravité *f.*

stain *n.* tache, souillure *f.*; honte *f.*; couleur *f.*; **—** *vt.* tacher; teindre; teinter; souiller; **-less** *a.* sans tache; qui ne se tache pas; **-less steel** *n.* acier inoxydible *m.*

stair *n.* marche d'un escalier *f.*; **-s** *n. pl.* escalier *m.*

staircase *n.* escalier *m.*

stairway *n.* cage d'escalier *f.*

stake *n.* poteau *m.*; enjeu *m.*; **—** *vt.* garnir de pieux; mettre en jeu; subventionner

stalactite *n.* stalactite *f.*

stalagmite *n.* stalagmite *f.*

stale *a.* vieux, usé, gâté; rassis; éventé; **–ness** *n.* vieillesse *f.*

stalk *n.* tige, queue *f.*; démarche fière *f.*; — *vi.* marcher fièrement; — *vt.* suivre à la piste

stallion *n.* étalon *m.*

stalwart *a.* vaillant, vigoureux

stamen *n.* étamine *f.*

stamina *n.* force, vigueur *f.*

stammer *vi.* bégayer, balbutier; **–er** *n.* bègue *m.* & *f.*

stamp *n.* poinçon, coin *m.*; empreinte, impression *f.*; cachet *m.*, estampe *f.*; trempe *f.*; **postage** — timbre (-poste) *m.*; — **pad** *n.* tampon *m.*; **revenue** — timbre fiscal *m.*; **rubber** — timbre en caoutchouc *m.*; — *vt.* frapper du pied; broyer; imprimer; timbrer; (mail) affranchir; — **out** éliminer

stampede *n.* ruée *f.*; (cattle) fuite (de bœufs) *f.*; sauve-qui-peut *m.*; — *vi.* fuir; se ruer; — *vt.* provoquer une fuite, effaroucher

stance *n.* attitude *f.*

stanch, staunch *vt.* étancher; — *a.* solide; ferme; sûr

stand *n.* station *f.*; place *f.*; délai *m.*; pause, halte *f.*; résistance *f.*; embarras *m.*; guéridon *m.*, console *f.*, étalage *m.*; stand *m.*; **–s** *pl.* tribune *f.*; — *vi.* se lever; se mettre debout; rester debout; être debout; résister; supporter; — **aside** se tenir à l'écart; — **back** reculer; — **by** se tenir à l'écart; soutenir; se tenir prêt; attendre; — **for** signifier; tolérer; supporter; — **in for** remplacer; — **off** se tenir à l'écart; repousser; — **on** insister sur; — **out** se détacher; — **still** se tenir tranquille; ne pas bouger; — **to** courir le risque de; avoir des chances de; — **up** se lever, se mettre debout; — **up against** opposer; combattre; — **up for** défendre, soutenir, appuyer; **–ing** *n.* position *f.*; durée *f.*; **–ing** *a.* debout; permanent; **–ing room** place debout *f.*; promenoir *m.*

standard *n.* étendard *m.*; pavillon *m.*; étalon *m.*; titre *m.*; modèle *m.*; type *m.*; mesure *f.*; **gold** — étalon d'or *m.*; — **of living** niveau de la vie *m.*; — *a.* normal, ordinaire, classique; — **time** heure normale *f.*; — **works** classiques *m. pl.*; **–ization** *n.* standardisation *f.*; **–ize** *vt.* standardiser

standard-bearer *n.* porte-drapeau, enseigne *m.*; porte-étendard *m.*

stand-by *n.* service de secours *m.*; suppléant *m.*; adjoint *m.*

stand-in *n.* (movies) remplaçant *m.*

standpoint *n.* point d'arrêt *m.*

standstill *n.* point mort *m.*; affaire nulle *f.*

stanza *n.* strophe *f.*

staple *n.* denrée *f.*; matière première *f.*; crampon *m.*; — *a.* établi; principal; — *vt.* fixer (avec des crampons); **–r** *n.* brocheuse *f.*

star *n.* étoile *f.*; astre *m.*; (type) astérisque *m.*; (theat.) vedette *f.*; **shooting** — étoile filante *f.*; — *vt.* étoiler; parsemer; présenter comme vedette; — *vi.* apparaître comme vedette; **–less** *a.* sans étoiles; **–let** *n.* (movies) starlette, starlet *f.*; **–ry** étoilé; brillant

starboard *n.* tribord *m.*

starch *n.* empois *m.*; amidon *m.*; — *vt.* empeser

star-chamber *a.* clandestin

stare *n.* regard fixe *m.*; — *vi.* regarder fixement

stark *a.* & *adv.* fort; vrai, pur; tout-à-fait

starlight *n.* lumière des étoiles *f.*

starlit *a.* étoilé

star-spangled *a.* étoilé, parsemé d'étoiles

start *n.* tressaillement *m.*; saut *m.*; élan *m.*; premier pas *m.*; commencement *m.*; début *m.*; — *vi.* tressaillir; — *vt.* commencer, débuter; se mettre à; se mettre en route; — **out** se mettre en route; **–er** *n.* (auto) démarreur *m.*; **–ing point** *n.* point de départ *m.*

starting gate, starting post *n.* barrière *f.*

startle *vt.* effrayer; faire tressaillir, étonner

startling *a.* étonnant

starvation *n.* inanition *f.*; faim *f.*

starve *vt.* faire mourir de faim, affamer; — *vi.* mourir de faim

state *n.* état *m.*, condition *f.*; rang *m.*, dignité, pompe *f.*; — *vt.* établir, régler; constater, détailler; déclarer; — **house** *n.* parlement *m.*; **–liness** *n.* grandeur *f.*; **–ment** *n.* déclaration *f.*; procès-verbal *m.*; (com.) relevé de compte *m.*

statecraft *n.* politique *f.*

stateroom *n.* cabine *f.*

statesman *n.* homme d'état *m.*; **–ship** *n.* politique *f.*, art de gouverner *m.*

static *n.* (rad.) parasites *m. pl.*; **–s** *n.* statique *f.*; — *a.* statique

station *n.* situation, position, condition *f.*; poste *m.*, place *f.*, emploi *m.*; état, rang *m.*; (rail.) gare *f.*; — **house, police** — commissariat de police *m.*; — *vt.* poster, placer

station agent *n.* chef de gare *m.*

stationary *a.* stationnaire, fixe

stationer *n.* papetier, marchand de papier *m.*; libraire *m.*; **–'s** *n.* papeterie, librairie *f.*; **–y** *n.* papeterie *f.*

Stations of the Cross *n.* calvaire *m.*

statistic *n.* statistique *f.*; **–s** *pl.* statistique *f.*; **–al** *a.* statistique; **–ian** *n.* statisticien *m.*

statuary *n.* (sculptor) statuaire *m.*; (statues) statuaire *f.*

statue *n.* statue *f.*

statuesque *a.* de statue; comme une statue

statuette *n.* statuette *f.*

stature *n.* stature, taille *f.*

status *n.* condition *f.*; rang *m.*; **— quo** *n.* statu quo *m.*

statute *n.* statut *m.*, loi *f.*

statutory *a.* conforme à la loi; défini par la loi

staunch, stanch *a.* loyal, sûr; **–ness** *n.* loyauté, fidélité, force *f.*

stave *n.* douve *f.*; (mus.) portée *f.*; **—** *vi.* **— in** défoncer; **— off** écarter, différer

stay *n.* séjour *m.*; soutien *m.*; **–s** *n.* *pl.* corset *m.* *pl.*; **—** *vt.* arrêter, empêcher; **—** (fig.) principal soutien *m.*; **—** *vi.* rester, demeurer, s'arrêter; attendre, rester immobile; **— up** rester en haut; veiller

stay-at-home *n.* casanier *m.*

stead *n.* place *f.*, lieu *m.*

steadfast *a.* stable, fixe; constant; **–ness** *n.* fermeté, constance *f.*

steadily *adv.* fermement; régulièrement

steadiness *n.* fermeté *f.*; régularité *f.*

steady *vt.* affermir, assurer; **—** *a.* ferme, solide

steak *n.* bifteck, steak *m.*

steal *n.* vol *m.*; **—** *vt.* voler; **—** *vi.* s'échapper; aller doucement, se glisser, aller à la dérobée

stealth *n.* action clandestine *f.*; **by —** à la dérobée; **–ily** *adv.* clandestinement; **–y** *a.* furtif

steam *n.* vapeur *f.*; **— engine** *n.* machine à vapeur *f.*, locomotive *f.*; **— (pressure) cooker** *n.* marmite à vapeur *f.*; **—** *vi.* fumer; naviguer à la vapeur; **—** *vt.* (cooking) cuire à la vapeur

steamboat *n.* vapeur, paquebot *m.*

steampipe *n.* tuyau à vapeur *m.*

steam roller *n.* rouleau à vapeur *m.*

steamship *n.* vapeur, paquebot *m.*

steam shovel *n.* excavateur à vapeur *m.*

steed *n.* coursier, cheval *m.*

steel *n.* acier *m.*; **—** *a.* d'acier; **— mill** *n.* aciérie *f.*; **— wool** *n.* paille de fer, paille d'acier *f.*; **—** *vt.* endurcir; **–works** *n.* aciérie *f.*; **–y** *a.* d'acier

steep *vt.* tremper, infuser; **—** *a.* escarpé; raide; **–ness** *n.* raideur, pente *f.*, escarpement *m.*

steeple *n.* clocher *m.*

steeple jack *n.* ouvrier qui monte sur les clochers *m.*

steer *vt.* gouverner, diriger; conduire; **—** *n.* bœuf *m.*; **–age** *n.* (boat) dernière classe *f.*; **–ing** *a.* de direction; **–ing wheel** *n.* volant *m.*

steersman *n.* timonier *m.*

stein *n.* chope *f.*

stellar *a.* stellaire

stem *n.* tronc *m.*; tige, queue *f.*; pédoncule *m.*; race *f.*; **—** *vt.* opposer, arrêter

stench *n.* puanteur *f.*

stencil *n.* pochoir *m.*; (duplicating machine) stencil *m.*; **—** *vt.* marquer au pochoir

stenographer *n.* sténographe *m.* & *f.*

stenotype, stenotyping *n.* sténotypie *f.*

stentorian *a.* de stentor

step *n.* pas *m.*, marche *f.*; échelon *m.*; marche pied *m.*; **—** *vi.* faire un pas, marcher; **— se mettre à l'écart; — in** entrer; **— out** sortir; **— up** s'approcher; monter; augmenter

stepbrother *n.* beau-frère *m.*

stepchild *n.* beau-fils *m.*, belle-fille *f.*

stepdaughter *n.* belle-fille *f.*

stepfather *n.* beau-père *m.*

stepladder *n.* échelle double *f.*; marche-pied *m.*

stepmother *n.* belle-mère *f.*

steppe *n.* steppe *m.*

steppingstone *n.* marchepied *m.*; moyen de parvenir *m.*

stepsister *n.* belle-sœur *f.*

stepson *n.* beau-fils *m.*

stereophonic *a.* stéréophonique

stereoscope *n.* stéréoscope *m.*

stereotype *n.* cliché *m.*; **—** *vt.* stéréotyper; **—** *a.* stéréotype *m.*

sterile *a.* stérile

sterility *n.* stérilité *f.*

sterilization *n.* stérilisation *f.*

sterilize *vt.* stériliser; **–r** *n.* stérilisateur *m.*

sterling *a.* sterling; vrai, véritable; honnête

stern *n.* poupe *f.*; **—** *a.* sévère; austère; rude; **–ness** *n.* sévérité *f.*

sternum *n.* sternum *m.*

stethoscope *n.* stéthoscope *m.*

stevedore *n.* arrimeur *m.*

stew *n.* étuvée, estouffade *f.*, ragoût *m.*; compote *f.*; **—** *vt.* cuire à l'étuvée

steward *n.* intendant, économe, maître d'hôtel *m.*; **–ess** *n.* (boat) femme de chambre de bord *f.*; (avi.) hôtesse *f.*

stick *n.* bâton *m.*; canne *f.*; **—** *vt.* coller, fixer; percer; **—** *vi.* être collé, s'attacher; **— out** faire saillie; **— to** persévérer dans; **— up** (coll.) voler à main armée; **— up for** défendre; **–er** *n.* vignette (à coller) *f.*; **–y** *a.* collant

stickler *n.* personne meticuleuse *f.*; colle *f.*, problème difficile *m.*

stickpin *n.* épingle à cravate *f.*

stiff *a.* raide; obstiné; gêné, affecté; empesé; — **neck** *n.* torticolis *m.*; —**en** *vt.* raidir; —**en** *vi.* se raidir; –**ness** *n.* raideur *f.*

stifle *vt.* étouffer

stifling *a.* étouffant

stigma *n.* stigmate *m.*; flétrissure *f.*; –**tize** *vt.* stigmatiser

stiletto *n.* poinçon *m.*; stylet *m.*

still *n.* silence *m.*; alambic *m.*; (movies) photographie vue fixe *f.*; — *a.* tranquille, calme; — life nature morte *f.*; — *adv.* encore, toujours; — *vt.* calmer, apaiser; distiller

stillborn *a.* mort-né

stilted *a.* ampoulé; gauche

stilts *n.* échasses *f. pl.*

stimulant *n. & a.* stimulant *m.*

stimulate *vt.* stimuler, piquer

stimulation *n.* stimulation *f.*

stimulus *n.* stimulant *m.*; aiguillon *m.*

sting *n.* piqûre *f.*; remords *m.*; aiguillon *m.*; — **ray** raie, torpille *f.*; — *vt.* piquer; mordre; –**er** *n.* (insects) aiguillon, dard *m.*; –**ing** *a.* piquant, mordant

stinginess *n.* mesquinerie *f.*

stingy *a.* chiche, avare, mesquin

stink *n.* puanteur *f.*; — *vi.* puer; –**er** *n.* (coll.) cochon, chameau *m.*

stint *n.* limite, restreinte *f.*; tache *f.*, travail du jour *m.*; — *vt. & vi.* restreindre, être parcimonieux

stipend *n.* salaire *m.*, appointements *m. pl.*

stipple *vt.* pointiller

stipulate *vi.* stipuler

stipulation *n.* stipulation *f.*

stir *n.* tumulte *m.*, agitation *f.*; — *vt.* remuer, agiter; inciter, animer; faire naître, provoquer; — *vi.* se remuer, se révolter; apparaître; — **up** fomenter; –**ring** *a.* émouvant

stirrup *n.* étrier *m.*

stitch *n.* point *m.*; maille *f.*; (med.) agrafe *f.*; — *vt.* piquer; coudre; brocher; — **up** recoudre, faire un point à

stock *n.* tronc *m.*; bloc *m.*; famille, race *f.*; assortiment *m.*; (cattle) bétail *m.*; (com.) actions *f. pl.*; (bot.) matthiole *f.*; (punishment) pilori *m.*; (inventory) stock, matériel, inventaire *m.*; (theat.) répertoire *m.*; **laughing** — risée *f.*; — **exchange** bourse *f.*; — *a.* classique, banal, d'usage; — *vt.* emmagasiner, garder, tenir; — **up on** s'approvisionner de; –**y** *a.* trapu

stockade *n.* palissade *f.*

stockbroker *n.* agent de change *m.*

stockholder *n.* actionnaire *m. & f.*

stocking *n.* bas *m.*; chaussette *f.*

stockpile *n.* dépôt *m.*; provision *f.*; réserve *f.*; — *vt.* emmagasiner

stockyard *n.* parc à bestiaux *m.*; abattoir *m.*

stodgy *a.* fade; lourd; trapu

stoic *n. & a.* stoïcien *m.*; –**al** *a.* stoïque; –**ism** *n.* stoïcisme *m.*

stoke *vt.* garnir, alimenter; chauffer; –**er** *n.* chauffeur *m.*

stole *n.* étole *f.*

stolid *a.* lourd; flegmatique; –**ness** *n.* flegme *m.*

stomach *n.* estomac *m.*; cœur *m.*; envie *f.*; **turn the** — donner mal au cœur; — *vt.* supporter

stone *n.* pierre *f.*; caillou *m.*; (seed) pépin, noyau *m.*; — *a.* de pierre; — *adv.*, **dead** raide-mort; — **deaf** complètement sourd; — *vt.* lapider; ôter les pépins (de)

stonecutter *n.* tailleur de pierre(s) *m.*

stonemason *n.* maçon *m.*; –**ry** *n.* maçonnerie *f.*

stoneware *n.* grès *m.*

stonework *n.* ouvrage en pierre *m.*; maçonnerie *f.*

stony *a.* pierreux

stool *n.* tabouret *m.*; (med.) selle *f.*; — **pigeon** *n.* (coll.) mouchard *m.*

stoop *n.* inclination *f.*; abaissement *m.*; (arch.) perron *m.*; — *vi.* s'incliner, se baisser

stop *n.* pause *f.*; arrêt *m.*, halte *f.*; obstacle *m.*; (organ) jeu *m.*; (phot.) ouverture du diaphragme *f.*; — **signal** (street) feu rouge *m.*; (auto.) feu stop, signal de freinage *m.*; — *vt.* arrêter, faire cesser; boucher; — *vi.* s'arrêter, cesser; — **in** venir voir, faire visite; — **off**, — **over** interrompre son voyage; –**page** *n.* cessation *f.*; panne *f.*; –**per** *n.* bouchon *m.*; –**per** *vt.* boucher; –**ping** *n.* arrêt *m.*

stopgap *a.* temporaire, provisoire

stop light *n.* feu rouge *m.*; (auto.) feu stop, signal de freinage *m.*

stopover *n.* halte *f.*, séjour *m.*

stop watch *n.* chronographe, compte-secondes *m.*

storage *n.* entreposage, emmagasinage *m.*; frais d'entrepôt *m. pl.*; — **battery** *n.* accumulateur *m.*

store *n.* magasin, dépôt *m.*; quantité *f.*; provisions *f. pl.*; **department** — grand magasin *m.*; **in** —, à venir; en réserve; **set** — **by** faire grand cas de; — *vt.* emmaganiser, mettre en dépôt

storehouse *n.* dépôt, magasin *m.*

storekeeper *n.* commerçant, boutiquier *m.*

storeroom n. magasin m., réserve f.

storied a. historié

storm n. orage m., tempête f.; assaut m.; — coat n. pardessus d'hiver avec col de fourrure m.; — troops troupes d'assaut f. pl.; — window contre-fenêtre f.; fenêtre extérieure utilisée en hiver f.; — vi. tempêter; — vt. assaillir; -ing n. assaut m.; -y a. orageux, violent

story n. histoire f.; récit m.; conte m.; fable f.; mensonge m.; (arch.) étage m.; short — nouvelle f., conte m.

storyteller n. conteur, raconteur m.

stout a. fort; résolu; gros; corpulent; — stout m , bière noire anglaise f.; -ness n. embonpoint m.

stouthearted a. brave, résolu

stove n. poêle m.; (range) cuisinière f.

stovepipe n. tuyau de poêle m.

stow vt. serrer, entasser; (naut.) arrimer; — away serrer; s'embarquer en cachette

stowaway n. passager clandestin m.

straddle vi. écarter les jambes; marcher les jambes écartées; être à califourchon; — vt. être à califourchon (sur); ne pas prendre parti (sur)

straggle vi. rester en arrière; -r n. traînard m.

straight a. droit; direct; franc; honnête, sincere; (beverage) sec; — adv. directement; droit; -way adv. tout de suite; —en vt. redresser; ranger; —en up ranger; se tenir droit; -ness n. droiture f.; rectitude f.; franchise f.

straightforward a. franc, honnête, sincère; loyal

straightway adv. tout de suite, sur-le-champ

strain n. effort m.; tension f.; (med.) entorse f.; manière f.; style m.; trace f.; (music) mélodie f.; — vt. tendre; filtrer; serrer, forcer; se fouler; — vi. s'efforcer; -er n. passoire f.

strait n. détroit m.; défilé m.; gorge f.; embarras m.; — a. étroit; sévère, pénible; -en vt. resserrer

strait-laced a. sévère; prude

strait jacket n. camisole de force f.

strand n. côte f., rivage m.; grève f.; fil m., fibre f.; brin m.; — vt. & vi. échouer

strange a. singulier; étrange; étranger; inconnu; -ness n. étrangeté, singularité f.; -r n. étranger m.; inconnu m.

strangle vt. étrangler

strangle hold n. prise de cou f.; prise inébranlable f.

strangulate vt. étrangler

strangulation n. étranglement m.

strap n. sangle, courroie, bretelle f.; — vt. attacher, lier, boucler; -ping a. solide,

bien découplé

stratagem n. stratagème, artifice m.

strategic a. stratégique

strategist n. stratégiste m.

strategy n. stratégie f.

stratify vt. stratifier

stratosphere n. stratosphère f.

stratum n. couche f.; strate f.

straw n. paille f.; last — comble m.; — vote vote non-officiel qui s'informe de l'opinion publique m.

strawberry n. fraise f.; — bed n. fraisière f.

stray n. bête épave f.; bête égarée f.; — a. égaré; — vi. s'égarer

streak n. raie, bande f.; filet m.; — vt. rayer, bigarrer; -y a. rayé, bariolé

stream n. courant, torrent m.; ruisseau m.; rivière f.; flot m.; jet m.; — vi. couler, ruisseler; briller; -er n. banderole f.; serpentin m.

streamline vt. donner un profil aérodynamique à; caréner; moderniser; -d a. à profil aérodynamique; moderne

street n. rue f.; — floor rez-de-chaussée m.

streetcar n. tramway m.

street sweeper n. balayeur m.; (machine) balayeuse f.

streetwalker n. fille publique f.

strength n. force f.; résistance f.; forces f. pl.; solidité f.; at full — au complet; —en vt. fortifier; — vi. se fortifier

strenuous a. ardu; énergique; -ness n. ardeur f.

streptococcus n. streptocoque m.

streptomycin n. streptomycine f.

stress n. importance f.; violence f.; effort m.; accent tonique m.; — vt. souligner; accentuer; appuyer sur

stretch n. étendue f.; tension f.; at a — d'arrache-pied; — vt. étendre, élargir, allonger; exagérer; — vi. s'étendre, s'élargir, se déployer; -er n. (med.) brancard m.; -ing n. tension f.; allongement m. forcer

strew vt. parsemer, répandre çà et là; joncher

striated a. strié

stricken a. atteint; rayé

strict a. strict; exact; formel; sévère, rigoureux; -ly adv. rigoureusement, strictement; formellement; absolument; -ness n. sévérité, rigueur f.; exactitude f.; -ure n. contraction f.

stride n. enjambée f.; pas m.; — vi. marcher à grands pas

stridency n. stridence f.

strident a. strident

strife n. lutte f.; contestation f.; différend m.

strike n. grève f.; (geol.) découverte

(d'un gisement) *f.*; — *vt.* frapper, heurter, battre; rencontrer, tomber sur; affliger; étonner, épouvanter; lancer, jeter, pousser; choquer, imprimer, graver; marquer; faire; — **a bargain** conclure un marché; — **a match** frotter une allumette; — *vi.* se mettre en grève, (labor) faire la grève, être en grève; — **out** partir, se lancer; — **up** se faire; commencer; —**r** *n.* gréviste *m. & f.*

strikebreaker *n.* (labor) briseur de grève *m.*

striking *a.* frappant

string *n.* corde *f.*, cordon *m.*, ficelle, attache *f.*, fil *m.*; fibre *f.*, tendon, filament *m.*; suite *f.*; — **bean** haricot vert *m.*; — *vt.* mettre des cordes à; corder; bander; enfiler; — **along** (coll.) ménager; accepter (l'avis d'un autre); — **up** pendre; —**ed** *a.* à cordes; —**y** *a.* fibreux

stringency *n.* sévérité, rigueur *f.*

stringent *a.* fort, rigoureux

strip *n.* bande *f.*, ruban *m.*; — *vt.* dépouiller; déshabiller; dégarnir

stripe *n.* raie *f.*; barre *f.*; type *m.*, trempe, sorte *f.*; (mil.) chevron, galon *m.*; — *vt.* rayer; —**d** *a.* rayé, à raies

stripling *n.* jeune homme *m.*; débutant *m.*

strive *vi.* s'efforcer (de), tâcher (de); combattre; lutter

striving *n.* effort *m.*; lutte *f.*

stroke *n.* coup *m.*; trait de plume *m.*; (med.) attaque d'apoplexie *f.*; (swimming) brassée *f.*; — **of luck** coup de veine *m.*; **on the — of** à l'heure sonnante; — *vt.* caresser

stroll *n.* promenade *f.*; — *vi.* se promener; —**er** *n.* promeneur *m.*; voiture d'enfant *f.*; —**ing** *a.* ambulant

strong *a.* fort; vigoureux, robuste; puissant, énergique; solide, ferme; impétueux

strongbox *n.* coffre-fort *m.*

stronghold *n.* place forte *f.*

strontium *n.* strontium *m.*

strop *n.* cuir à repasser *m.*; — *vt.* repasser sur le cuir

structural *a.* de structure, structural

structure *n.* construction *f.*; édifice *m.*; structure *f.*

struggle *n.* combat *m.*, lutte *f.*; — *vi.* s'efforcer (de), se débattre, lutter (contre)

struggling *a.* pauvre; débutant

strum *vt.* gratter

strut *n.* démarche fière *f.*; (arch.) entretoise *f.*; — *vi.* se pavaner; — *vt.* entretoiser

strychnine *n.* strychnine *f.*

stub *n.* tronc, tronçon, chicot *m.*; (cigarette) mégot *m.*; (ticket) volet *m.* sou-

che *f.* — *vt.* cogner; —**by** *a.* trapu, court *m. pl.*

stubble *n.* chaume *f.*; poils de la barbe *m. pl.*

stubbly *a.* couvert de chaume; non-rasé

stubborn *a.* obstiné; entêté, têtu; tenace; —**ness** *n.* obstination *f.*, entêtement *m.*

stucco *n.* stuc *m.*

stuck *a.* coincé, collé

stud *n.* clou *m.*; bouton de plastron *m.*; (arch.) montant *m.*; — **farm** haras *m.*; — **horse** étalon *m.*; — *vt.* clouter, couvrir de clous; couvrir; —**ded** *a.* parsemé, constellé; —**ding** *n.* lattis *m.*

student *n.* étudiant *m.*

studied *a.* étudié, savant; recherché, voulu

studio *n.* atelier, studio *m.*

studious *a.* studieux; diligent

study *n.* étude *f.*; attention *f.*; méditation *f.*; cabinet *m.*; — *vt.* étudier; faire des études de

stuff *n.* matière, étoffe *f.*; (coll.) choses *f. pl.*, machins, ettrucs, rebuts *m. pl.*, — *vt.* fourrer; empailler; (cram) bourrer; (crowd) encombrer; (cooking) farcir; —**ing** *n.* empaillage *m.*; (cooking) farce *f.*; —**y** *a.* moisi, mal aéré; lourd; fastidieux, affecté

stultify *vt.* rendre ridicule; rendre inutile

stumble *n.* faux pas *m.*; — *vi.* trébucher, faire un faux pas; — **on** trouver par accident

stumbling block *n.* pierre d'achoppement *f.*

stump *n.* tronc, tronçon, bout, chicot *m.*; moignon *m.*; (coll.) estrade *f.*; — *vi.* marcher lourdement; faire une tournée de conférences en faveur de quelque chose; — *vt.* laisser sans réponse, maîtriser, triompher de

stun *vt.* étourdir, abasourdir; —**ning** *a.* ravissant; accablant

stunt *n.* tour *m.*, acrobatie *f.*; — *vt.* empêcher de croître; rabougrir; — *vi.* faire des acrobaties

stupefaction *n.* stupéfaction *f.*; stupeur *f.*

stupefy *vt.* hébéter, stupéfier

stupendous *a.* prodigieux, étonnant

stupid *a.* stupide; bête; —**ity** *n.* stupidité *f.*; bêtise, niaiserie *f.*

stupor *n.* stupeur *f.*

sturdiness *n.* force, vigueur, hardiesse *f.*

sturdy *a.* vigoureux, fort, robuste

stutter *vi. & vt.* bégayer, bredouiller; — *n.* bégaiement *m.*; —**er** *n.* bègue *m. & f.*; —**ing** *n.* bégaiement *m.*

sty *n.* étable à cochons *f.*; (med.) orgelet *m.*

style *n.* style *m.*; goût, genre *m.*; manière, façon *f.*; modèle *m.*; chic *m.*, élégance *f.*;

— vt. appeler; donner le titre de; dessiner

stylish a. de bon ton; élégant; **-ness** n. chic, ton m., élégance f.

stylist n. styliste m.; **-ic** n. stylistique f.

stylize vt. styliser

stylus n. style m.

styptic a. hémostitique

suave a. suave

suavity n. suavité, douceur f.

subcommittee n. sous-commission f., sous-comité m.

subconscious a. & n. subconscient m.

subcontract vt. sous-traiter; — n. sous-traite m.; **-or** n. sous-entrepreneur m.

subcutaneous a. sous-cutané

subdivide vt. subdiviser

subdivision n. subdivision f.

subdue vt. subjuguer; vaincre; dompter; amortir; atténuer

subhead, subheading n. sous-titre m.

subject n. sujet m.; — vt. soumettre, subjuguer, exposer; — a. sujet, soumis à; **-ion** n. sujétion f.; soumission f.; **-ive** a. subjectif

subjugate vt. subjuguer, assujettir

subjugation n. subjugation f., assujettissement m.

subjunctive a. & n. subjonctif m.

sublease, sublet vt. sous-louer

sublimate n. & a. sublimé m.; — vt. sublimer

sublimity n. sublimité f.

submarine n. & a. sous-marin m.

submerge vt. submerger; plonger

submersion n. submersion f.; plongée f.

submission n. soumission f.; résignation f.

submissive a. soumis (à); **-ness** n. soumission f.

submit vt. soumettre; — vi. se soumettre

subnormal a. inférieur à la normale

subordinate vt. subordonner, soumettre; — n. & a. subordonné m.

subpoena n. assignation, citation f.; — vt. citer (à comparaître en justice)

subscribe vt. souscrire, s'abonner; consentir; **-r** n. abonné m.

subscription n. souscription f.; abonnement m.; cotisation f.

subsequent a. subséquent, suivant, qui suit; ultérieur

subservience n. utilité f.; subordination f.; dépendance f.; servilité f.

subservient a. subordonné; utile

subside vi. baisser; se calmer, s'apaiser

subsidiary n. & a. auxiliaire m.; subsidiaire m.; filiale f.

subsidize vt. subventionner

subsidy n. subvention f.

subsist vi. subsister, exister; **-ence** n. subsistence, existence f.; allocation f.

subsoil n. sous-sol m.

substance n. substance, matière f.; essentiel, m. corps m.; réalité f.; fortune f.

substantial a. substantiel; essentiel; réel; matériel, fort; solide

substantiate vt. établir; prouver par des faits

substantive n. substantif m.

substation n. sous-station f.

substitute vt. substituer; remplacer, suppléer, — vi. être substitué — n. remplaçant, suppléant m.; factice m.

substitution n. substitution f.; remplacement m.

substratum n. couche inférieure f.

substructure n. substructure f.

subterfuge n. subterfuge, faux-fuyant m.

subterranean a. souterrain

subtitle n. sous-titre m.

subtle a. subtil; fin; **-ty** n. subtilité f.; finesse f.

subtly adv. subtilement; avec finesse

subtract vt. soustraire; **-ion** n. soustraction f.

suburb n. ville de la banlieue f., faubourg m.; **-an** a. faubourien, banlieusard; **-anite** n. banlieusard, faubourien m.; **-ia** n. banlieue f.

subvention n. subvention f.; — vt. subventionner

subversion n. subversion f., renversement m.

subversive a. subversif

subvert vt. subvertir

subway n. passage souterrain m.; (rail.) métro m.

succeed vt. succéder; suivre; — vi. réussir, parvenir, arriver

success n. succès m.; réussite f.; **-ful** a. prospère, heureux, qui a du succès; **-ion** n. succession f.; héritage m.; suite, série f.; in **-ion** de suite; consécutif, successif **-ive** a. successif; **-or** n. successeur m.

succinct a. concis; succinct

succor n. secours m., aide f.; — vt. secourir, aider, assister, seconder

succumb vi. succomber

such a. tel; pareil, semblable; de la sorte; — pron. ceux; tel; — as prep. tel que

suck n. action de sucer f.; — vt. & vi. sucer; téter; **-er** n. (candy) sucette f.; (fish) rémora m.; (animal) suçoir; (octopus) ventouse f.; (bot.) drageon m.; (coll.) nigaud, innocent m.

suckle vt. allaiter

suckling n. nourrisson m.; — **pig** cochon de lait m.

sucrose n. saccharose m.

suction n. aspiration f.; — **pump** pompe

aspirante *f.*

Sudan *n.* Soudan *m.*

sudden *a.* brusque; soudain, subit; **all of a —** tout à coup; brusquement; **-ly** *adv.* soudainement, soudain; tout à coup; brusquement; **-ness** *n.* brusquerie *f.*; rapidité *f.*

suds *n.* mousse de savon *f.*

sue *vt.* poursuivre en justice; supplier, implorer; demander

suede *n.* suède *m.*

suet *n.* suif *m.*

Suez *n.*, **— Canal** Canal de Suez *m.*

suffer *vt.* souffrir; essuyer, subir; supporter; permettre; **—** *vi.* souffrir; **-ance** *n.* tolérance *f.*; **-ing** *a.* souffrant; **-ing** *n.* souffrance *f.*

suffice *vi.* suffire; **—** *vt.* suffire à

sufficiency *n.* suffisance *f.*

sufficient *a.* suffisant; **-ly** *adv.* suffisamment, assez

suffix *n.* suffixe *m.*

suffocate *vt. & vi.* suffoquer, étouffer

suffocation *n.* étouffement *m.*

suffuse *vt.* répandre, remplir

suffusion *n.* suffusion *f.*; épanchement *m.*

sugar *n.* sucre *m.*; **beet —** sucre de betterave *m.*; **brown —** sucre brut *m.*; **cane —** sucre de canne *m.*; **granulated —** sucre en poudre *m.*; **lump —** sucre en morceaux *m.*; **powdered —** sucre de confiseur *m.*; **beet —** betterave à sucre *f.*; **bowl** sucrier *m.*; **cane** canne à sucre *f.*; **mill** moulin à cannes *m.*; **—** *vt.* sucrer; saupoudrer de sucre; **-y** *a.* sucré

suggest *vt.* suggérer, insinuer, inspirer; **-ion** *n.* suggestion *f.*; **-ive** *a.* suggestif; évocateur

suicide *n.* suicide *m.*; **commit —** se suicider

suit *n.* (men's) complet *m.*; (women's) tailleur *m.*; costume *m.*; (request) requête *f.*; (law) procès *m.*; (cards) couleur *f.*; **—** *vt.* convenir à; aller à; **-ability** *n.* convenance *f.*; conformité *f.*; **-able** *a.* à propos; bon; sortable; convenable; **-or** *n.* prétendant *m.*; soupirant *m.*

suitcase *n.* valise *f.*

suite *n.* suite *f.*; train *m.*; (furniture) mobilier *m.*

sulfide *n.* sulfure *m.*

sulfite *n.* sulfite *m.*

sulfur *n.* soufre *m.*; **-ic** *a.* sulfurique; **-ous** *a.* sulfureux

sulk *n.* bouderie *f.*; **—** *vi.* bouder; **-y** *a.* boudeur; maussade; **-iness** *n.* maussaderie *f.*

sulky *n.* voiture légère à deux roues (utilisée aux courses attelées) *f.*

sullen *a.* maussade; chagrin; sombre

sully *vt.* souiller, tacher

sultan *n.* sultan *m.*; **-a** *n.* sultane *f.*

sultry *a.* d'une chaleur étouffante; suffocant

sum *n.* somme *f.*, tout, total *m.*; **in —** total en somme, somme toute; **—** *vt.* additioner; **— up** résumer; **-ming** *n.*, **-ing up** résumé *m.*

summarize *vt.* résumer

summary *n.* sommaire, résumé *m.*; **—** *a.* sommaire

summer *n.* été *m.*; **— resort** station estivale *f.*; **— sausage** saucisson *m.*

summerhouse *n.* pavillon *m.*; villa *f.*

summertime *n.* été *m.*, saison d'été *f.*

summit *n.* sommet *m.*; cime *f.*; comble *m.*; **— conference** conférence au sommet *f.*

summon *vt.* sommer; citer, assigner; ordonner, commander; appeler; convoquer; **-s** *n.* citation, assignation *f.*; appel *m.*

sump *n.* puisard *m.*, fosse *f.*

sumptuous *a.* somptueux; **-ness** *n.* somptuosité *f.*; luxe *m.*, richesse *f.*

sun *n.* soleil *m.*; **— parlor**, **— porch** solarium *m.*; **— visor** abat-jour *m.*; **—** *vt.* exposer au soleil; **— oneself** prendre le soleil; **-ny** *a.* ensoleillé; **it is -ny** il fait du soleil

sun-bathe *vi.* prendre le soleil

sunbeam *n.* rayon de soleil *m.*

sunbonnet *n.* capeline *f.*

sunburn *n.* hâle *m.*; coup de soleil *m.*; **-ed** *a.* hâlé; brûlé (par le soleil); **—** *vt.* bruler, hâler

sundae *n.* coupe (glace, sirop et fruit) *f.*

Sunday *n.* dimanche *m.*

sunder *vt.* séparer, partager

sundial *n.* cadran solaire *m.*

sundown *n.* coucher du soleil *m.*

sundries *n. pl.* diverses choses *f. pl.* (com.) divers *m. pl.*

sundry *a.* divers

sunfast, sunproof *a.* inaltérable au soleil

sunglasses *n. pl.* lunettes contre lessoleil *f. pl.*

sunken *a.* creux; enfoncé

sunlight *n.* soleil *m.*; lumière du soleil *f.*; jour *m.*

sun parlor *n.* (house) solarium *m.*

sunrise *n.* lever du soleil *m.*

sunset *n.* coucher du soleil *m.*

sunshine *n.* soleil *m.*

sunspot *n.* tache solaire *f.*

sunstroke *n.* insolation *f.*

sun tan *n.* hâle *m.*

sup *vi.* souper

superable *a.* surmontable

superabundance *n.* surabondance *f.*

superabundant *a.* surabondant
superannuated *a.* suranné; retraité
superb *a.* superbe
supercargo *n.* subrécargue *m.*
supercharge *vt.* supercompresser; **−er** *n.* supercompresseur *m.*
supercilious *n.* hautain, arrogant; **−ness** *n.* hauteur *f.*
superficial *a.* superficiel
superfine *a.* surfin
superfluous *a.* superflu; inutile
superhighway *n.* autostrade *f.*
superhuman *a.* surhumain
superimpose *vt.* superposer, surimposer
superintend *vt.* surveiller; **−ent** *n.* surintendant *m.*; inspecteur *m.*
superior *a. & n.* supérieur *m.*; **−ity** *n.* supériorité *f.*
superlative *n.* superlatif *m.*; **—** *a.* superlatif, suprême
superman *n.* surhomme *m.*
supermarket *n.* supermarket, grand magasin d'alimentation *m.*
supernatural *a.* surnaturel
supernumerary *n. & a.* surnuméraire *m.*
supersaturate *vt.* sursaturer
supersede *vt.* remplacer; faire supprimer; (law) surseoir à
supersensitive *a.* hypersensible
supersonic *a.* supersonique, ultrasonore
superstition *n.* superstition *f.*
superstructure *n.* édifice *m.*; superstructure *f.*
supervene *vi.* survenir
supervise *vt.* surveiller, diriger
supervision *n.* surveillance *f.*; direction *f.*
supervisor *n.* surveillant; inspecteur *m.*; directeur *m.*
supine *a.* couché sur le dos; **—** *n.* (gram.) supin *m.*
supper *n.* souper *m.*; **have —** souper
Supper, The Last la Sainte Cène *f.*
suppertime *n.* heure du souper *f.*
supplant *vt.* supplanter, remplacer
supple *a.* souple, flexible; **−ness** *n.* souplesse, flexibilité *f.*
supplement *n.* supplément *m.*; **—** *vt.* suppléer à; ajouter à, augmenter; **−al, −ary** *a.* supplémentaire
suppliant *n. & a.* suppliant *m.*
supplicant *n.* suppliant
supplicate *vt.* supplier
supplication *n.* supplication *f.*
supplier *n.* fournisseur *m.*; pourvoyeur, approvisionneur *m.*
supply *n.* fourniture *f.*; provision *f.*; approvisionnement *m.*; (mil.) ravitaillement *m.*; **— and demand** l'offre et la demande; **—** *vt.* approvisionner; fournir, pourvoir; munir

support *n.* soutien, appui, support *m.*; **—** *vt.* soutenir; entretenir; appuyer; assister; souffrir; supporter; faire subsister; **— oneself** gagner sa vie; **−able** *a.* supportable; **−er** *n.* soutien, partisan *m.*; (sport) slip (pour sportif) *m.*; (med.) suspensoire *m.*
suppose *vt.* supposer, imaginer; penser, croire; s'imaginer; **−d** *a.* censé; supposé; présumé; soi-disant; prétendu
suppress *vt.* supprimer; empêcher; étouffer, cacher; refouler, réprimer; **−ion** *n.* répression *f.*; refoulement *m.*
suppurate *vi.* suppurer
supremacy *n.* suprématie, supériorité *f.*
supreme *a.* suprême
Supreme Court *n.* Cour Suprême *f.*; grand tribunal *m.*
surcease *n.* arrêt *m.*, interruption *f.*
surcharge *n.* surcharge *f.*; surtaxe *f.*; **—** *vt.* surcharger
surd *n.* (sound) sourd *m.*; (math.) irrationnel *m.*
sure *a.* sûr, certain; assuré, ferme; **to be —!** assurément! certainement!; **be — to** ne pas manquer de; **make —** s'assurer; **—!** *interj.* mais oui, bien sûr; entendu; **−ly** *adv.* sûrement; assurément
sure-footed *a.* au pied sûr
surety *n.* sûreté *f.*; caution *f.*
surf *n.* brisant, ressac *m.*
surface *n.* surface *f.*; **on the —** (fig.) en apparence; **—** *vt.* mettre une nouvelle surface à; **—** *vi.* revenir à la surface
surfacing *n.* apprêtage; (road) revêtement *m.*
surfboard *n.* aquaplane *m.*
surfeit *n.* satiété *f.*; surabondance *f.*; **—** *vt.* soûler, rassasier; **—** *vi.* se soûler; se gorger
surge *n.* vague *f.*, flot *m.*, houle *f.*; **—** *vi.* s'élever, s'enfler; se soulever
surgeon *n.* chirugien *m.*
surgery *n.* chirurgie *f.*
surgical *a.* chirurgical
surging *a.* houleux
surly *a.* hargneux, maussade, bourru
surmise *n.* conjecture *f.*; **—** *vi.* conjecturer; **—** *vi.* se douter de
surmount *vt.* surmonter
surname *n.* surnom, nom de famille *m.*; **—** *vt.* surnommer
surpass *vt.* surpasser, dépasser; **−ing** *a.* supérieur
surplice *n.* surplis *m.*
surplus *n.* surplus *m.*; excédent *m.*
surprise *n.* surprise *f.*; étonnement *m.*; **—** *vt.* surprendre; étonner; **be −d** s'étonner
surprising *a.* surprenant; étonnant
surrealist *n.* surréaliste *m.*

surrender *n.* reddition *f.*; cession *f.*; — *vi.* se rendre; — *vt.* rendre; céder; renoncer à

surreptitious *a.* subreptice, clandestine

surrogate *n.* délégué *m.*; — **court** cour qui s'occupe des testaments *f.* — *vt.* subroger

surround *vt.* environner, entourer; **–ings** *n. pl.* environs *m. pl.*; milieu *m.*

surtax *n.* surtaxe *f.*; — *vt.* surtaxer

surveillance *n.* surveillance *f.*

survey *n.* coup d'œil *m.*; examen *m.*; inspection *f.*; référendum *m.*; arpentage *m.*; — *vt.* surveiller, examiner, observer; consulter; arpenter; **–ing** *n.* arpentage *m.*; **–or** *n.* arpenteur *m.*

survival *n.* survivance *f.*

survive *vi.* survivre; — *vt.* survivre à

survivor *n.* survivant *m.*

susceptibility *n.* susceptibilité *f.*

suspect *n.* personne suspecte *f.*; — *vt.* soupçonner, se douter de

suspend *vt.* suspendre; **–ers** *n. pl.* bretelles *f. pl.*

suspense *n.* suspens, doute *m.*, incertitude *f.*; cessation *f.*; **in** — en suspens

suspension *n.* suspension *f.*; — **bridge** *n.* pont suspendu *m.*

suspicion *n.* soupçon *m.*; doute *m.*; méfiance, défiance *f.*

suspicious *a.* soupçonneux; suspect; méfiant; **–ness** *n.* méfiance *f.*; doute *m.*

sustain *vt.* soutenir, maintenir, entretenir; subir, essuyer, éprouver; **–ed** *a.* soutenu

sustenance *n.* subsistance *f.*; entretien *m.*

suture *n.* suture *f.*; — *vt.* suturer

swab *n.* faubert *m.*; (cotton) tampon d'ouate *m.*; — *vt.* fauberter; laver, nettoyer

swaddle *vt.* emmailloter

swaddling clothes *n. pl.* maillot *m.*

swagger *vi.* faire le fanfaron, fanfaronner; se pavaner; — **stick** (mil.) bâton d'officier *m.*; **–er** *n.* fanfaron *m.*; **–ing** *a.* important

swallow *n.* (bird) hirondelle *f.*; gorgée *f.*; avalement *m.*; coup *m.*; — *vt.* avaler, engloutir; gober; — **up** engloutir

swamp *n.* marécage, marais *m.*; — *vt.* embourber; engloutir; submerger; inonder; **–y** *a.* marécageux

swan *n.* cygne *m.*; — **dive** saut d'ange, plongeon en nage *m.*

sward *n.* gazon *m.*, pelouse *f.*

swarm *n.* essaim *m.*; fourmillière *f.*; — *vi.* essaimer; fourmiller; grouiller

swarthy *a.* basané; noir, sombre

swashbuckler *n.* fanfaron *m.*

swastika *n.* croix gammée *f.*; svastika *m.*

swatch *n.* échantillon *m.*

swath *n.* andain *m.*, fauchée *f.*

swathe *n.* maillot *m.*, langes *m. pl.*; — *vt.* emmailloter

sway *n.* pouvoir *m.*, domination *f.*; prépondérance *f.*; — *vt.* influencer; balancer; détourner; — *vi.* vaciller; se balancer; s'incliner

sway-backed *a.* ensellé

swear *vi.* jurer; blasphémer; — *vt.* jurer; — **to** certifier, attester; — **in** faire prêter serment à; **–ing** *n.* jurons *m. pl.*; **–ing in** *n.* assermentation *f.*

sweat *n.* sueur, transpiration *f.*; — *vi.* suer, transpirer; bûcher, travailler dur; (wall) suinter; **–shop** *n.* entreprise dont les ouvriers sont surmenés *f.*; **–ing** *n.* transpiration *f.*; (wall) suintement *m.*

sweater *n.* chandail; pull-over; maillot *m.*; tricot *m.*

Swede *n.* Suédois *m.*

Sweden *n.* Suède *f.*

Swedish *a.* suédois

sweep *n.* balayage, coup de balai *m.*; (chimney) ramoneur *m.*; (naut.) aviron *m.*; **at a** —, **at one** — d'un seul coup; **make a clean** — faire table rase; — *vt.* balayer; couvrir; (chimney) ramoner; — **away**, — **off** balayer; emporter; — **out**, — **up** balayer; nettoyer; **–er** *n.* balayeur *m.*; **carpet –er** *n.* balayeuse *f.*, balai méchanique *m.*; **–ing** *n.* action de balayer *f.*; **–ings** *n. pl.* balayures *f. pl.*; **–ing** *a.* général; complet

sweepstake(s) *n.* (*pl.*) sweepstake(s) *m.*; poule(s) *f.*

sweet *a.* doux (douce); savoureux, odorant; sucré; mélodieux; gracieux; tendre; aimable, agréable; gentil; frais; — **potato** patate *f.*; — *n.* bonbon *m.*, confiserie *f.*; sucrerie *f.*; **–en** *vt.* sucrer, **–ening** *n.* sucrage *m.*; sucre *m.*; **–ness** *n.* douceur *f.*

sweetbread *n.* ris de veau *m.*

sweetheart *n.* amoureux *m.*, amoureuse *f.*; ami *m.*, amie *f.*

sweetmeats *n. pl.* confiserie *f.*; sucreries *f. pl.*

swell *n.* élévation *f.*; (sea) houle *f.*; élégant *m.*; — *vt.* enfler, gonfler; augmenter; — *vi.* s'enfler; se gonfler; s'augmenter; accroître; — *a.* (coll.) formidable; épatant; excellent; élégant; **–ing** *n.* enflure *f.*; enflement *m.*; gonflement *m.*

swelter *vi.* étouffer de chaleur; **–ing** *a.* étouffant de chaleur

swerve *vi.* dévier; fléchir; se dérober; — *n.* crochet *m.*, embardée *f.*

swift *n.* martinet *m.*; — *a.* prompt; rapide; léger; **–ly** *adv.* vite, rapidement; **–ness** *n.* vitesse, rapidité *f.*

swift-footed *a.* au pied léger

swill *n.* eaux grasses *f. pl.*

swim *n.* bain de mer *m.*; — *vi.* nager; — *vt.* traverser à la nage; **–mer** *n.* nageur *m.*; **–ming** *a.* (fig.) tournant; noyé; **–ming** *n.* natation *f.*; **–ming pool** piscine *f.*; **–suit** costume de bain *m.*

swindle *n.* escroquerie *f.*; — *vt. & vi.* escroquer; filouter; **–r** *n.* escroc *m.*; filou *m.*

swine *n.* cochon *m.*; porc *m.*

swineherd *n.* porcher *m.*

swing *n.* oscillation *f.*; dandinement *m.*; branle *m.*; escarpolette *f.*; balançoire *f.*; (mus.) swing *m.*; **in full —** en plein travail; en activité; — *vt.* balancer; tourner; basculer; brandir; — *vi.* se balancer; tourner; **–ing** *a.* balançant; rythmé; battant; **–ing door** porte battante *f.*

swipe *n.* coup *m.*; — *vt.* frapper; (coll.) chiper; voler

swirl *n.* tourbillon *m.*; — *vi.* tourbillonner

swish *n.* sifflement *m.*; froissement *m.*; — *vt.* faire siffler; — *vi.* bruire

Swiss *a. & n.* suisse *m.*

switch *n.* baguette *f.*; (rail.) aiguille *f.*; (elec.) interrupteur, bouton *m.*; (coll.) changement *m.*, substitution *f.*; — *vt.* (whip) cingler; agiter; échanger; (rail.) aiguiller; **— off** couper, éteindre; **— on** allumer

switchboard *n.* (phone) standard (téléphonique) *m.*; **— operator** standardiste *m. & f.*

switchman *n.* (rail.) aiguilleur *m.*

Switzerland *n.* Suisse *f.*

swivel *n.* pivot *m.*; **— chair** fauteuil tournant *m.*; — *vi.* pivoter

swollen *a.* enflé, gonflé; (river) en crue

swoon *n.* évanouissement *m.*; — *vi.* s'évanouir

swoop *n.* descente *f.*; attaque *f.*; ruée *f.*; coup *m.*; — *vi.* fondre, s'abattre

sword *n.* épée *f.*; sabre *m.*

swordsman *n.* épéiste *m.*; duelliste *m.*

syllabification *n.* division en syllabes *f.*

syllable *n.* syllabe *f.*

syllabus *n.* sommaire, programme *m.*; syllabus *m.*

sylph *n.* sylphe *m.*; sylphide *f.*

sylvan *a.* sylvestre

symbol *n.* symbole *m.*; **–ic(al)** *a.* symbolique; **–ism** *n.* symbolisme *m.*; **–ize** *vt.* symboliser

symmetrical *a.* symétrique

symmetry *n.* symétrie *f.*

sympathetic *a.* sympathique; compatissant

sympathize *vi.* sympathiser; **— with** avoir de la compassion pour; être partisan de; comprendre, se rendre compte de; **–r** *n.*

partisan *m.*

sympathy *n.* sympathie *f.*; compassion *f.*; condoléances *f. pl.*

symphonic *a.* symphonique

symphony *n.* symphonie *f.*; **— orchestra** orchestre symphonique *m.*

symposium *n.* réunion *f.*; discussion *f.*; banquet *m.*

sympton *n.* symptôme, indice *m.*; **–atic** *a.* symptomatique

synagogue *n.* synagogue *f.*

synchronize *vt.* synchroniser

syncopate *vt.* syncoper

syndicate *n.* syndicat *m.*; — *vt.* faire publier (un écrit) dans plusieurs journaux

synod *n.* synode *m.*

synonym *n.* synonyme *m.*; **–ous** *a.* synonyme

synopsis *n.* résumé *m.*, analyse *f.*

syntax *n.* syntaxe *f.*

synthesis *n.* synthèse *f.*

synthesize *vt.* synthétiser; produire synthétiquement

synthetic *a.* synthétique

syphilis *n.* syphilis *f.*

syphilitic *a.* syphilitique

Syria *n.* Syrie *f.*; **–c** *n.* syriaque *m.*; **–n** *a. & n.* syrien *m.*

syringe *n.* seringue *f.*; — *vt.* seringuer

syrup *n.* sirop *m.*; **–y** *a.* siropeux

system *n.* système, régime *m.*, méthode *f.*; réseau *m.*; **–atic** *a.* systématique; méthodique; **–atize** *vt.* systématiser

T

tab *n.* oreille, oreillette *f.*; touche *f.*; patte *f.*; (coll.) addition *f.*; **keep — on** surveiller, contrôler

table *n.* table *f.*; tableau *m.*; bureau *m.*; liste *f.*; tablette *f.*; tablier *m.*; **set the —** mettre la table; **— of contents** table *f.*; **turn the –s on** faire tourner les chances contre; — *vt.* (a proposition) ajourner; classer

tablecloth *n.* nappe *f.*

tableland *n.* plateau *m.*

tablespoon *n.* cuiller à bouche, cuiller à soupe *f.*; **–ful** *n.* cuillerée à bouche *f.*

tablet *n.* tablette *f.*; plaque *f.*; comprimé *m.*; (paper) bloc *m.*

tableware *n.* service de table *m.*

tabloid *n.* journal de petit format *m.*; journal sensationnel *m.*

taboo, tabu *n. & a.* tabou *m.*; — *vt.* interdire

tabular *a.* en forme de table; tabulaire

tabulate *vt.* disposer en forme de table; classer, cataloguer

tachometer *n.* tachymètre *m.*

tacit *a.* tacite

taciturn *a.* taciturne

tack *n.* petit clou *m.*, broquette *f.*; (naut.) amure *f.*; — *vt.* accrocher, attacher; (naut.) louvoyer; thumb— *n.* punaise *f.*

tackle *n.* attirail *m.*; appareil *m.*; articles *m. pl.*; (sport) action de saisir, de renverser *f.*; block and — moufle *m.*; — *vt.* saisir, renverser; plaquer; chercher à résoudre, aborder

tacky *a.* collant; pas encore sec

tact *n.* tact *m.*; savoir-faire *m.*; —ful *a.* (plein) de tact; —less *a.* sans tact

tactical *a.* tactique

tactics *n. pl.* tactique *f.*

taffeta *n.* taffetas *m.*

tag *n.* étiquette *f.*; — *vt.* attacher une étiquette à; — along *vi.* (coll.) accompagner (sans être invité)

Tahiti *n.* Taïti *m.*

tail *n.* queue *f.*; culée *f.*; (coin) pile *f.*; (shirt) pan *m.*; turn — tourner les talons, se sauver, s'échapper; —light *n.* (auto.) feu rouge arrière *m.*; —s *n. pl.* habit à queue *m.*

tailor *n.* tailleur *m.*; — *vi.* exercer l'état de tailleur; — *vt.* confectionner, façonner, faire

tailor-made *a.* (fait) sur mesure

tail spin *n.* chute en vrille *f.*

taint *n.* souillure, tache *f.*; infection *f.*; — *vt.* gâter; souiller, infecter, corrompre

take *n.* prise *f.*; (coll.) profit *m.*; butin *m.*; — *vt.* prendre; saisir, s'emparer de; tenir; mener, conduire; amener; emporter; louer; accepter, recevoir, admettre; tolérer, souffrir, supporter; penser, croire, supposer; — *vi.* prendre; avoir effet; réussir; — after ressembler à, tenir de; — along emporter; amener; — apart démonter; — away enlever, emporter; emmener; — back reprendre; rapporter, rapporter; — down descendre; — in duper, rouler, tromper; rentrer; recevoir; comprendre, comporter; — off enlever, ôter; partir, filer; (avi.) décoller; — off one's clothes se déshabiller; — on prendre; se charger de, s'occuper de; assumer; (industry) embaucher; — out enlever; sortir; accompagner dehors; — over prendre possession de; prendre la direction de; — to s'habituer à, s'accoutumer à, se faire à; s'adonner à; — up monter; prendre; rétrécir; occuper; étudier; absorber; — an examination passer un examen; — a walk faire une promenade; se promener; — care of se charger de, s'occuper de; prendre soin de; soigner; garder, surveiller; — charge of se charger de; pren-

dre la direction de; — effect entrer en vigueur; produire son effet; — it easy se ménager; — place avoir lieu; — prisoner faire prisonnier; —n *a.* pris; saisi; occupé; be —n ill tomber malade

takeoff *n.* (avi.) décollage *m.*; imitation, satire *f.*

taking *n.* prise *f.*

talcum *n.* talc *m.*

tale *n.* conte *m.*, histoire *f.*

talent *n.* talent *m.*; génie *m.*; flair *m.*; —ed *a.* de talent; doué

talk *n.* conversation *f.*; discours *m.*; causerie *f.*; propos *m. pl.*; paroles *f. pl.*; — *vi.* parler, causer, jaser; raisonner; — *vt.* parler; — over discuter; —ative *a.* bavard; loquace; —ativeness *n.* loquacité *f.*;—er *n.* bavard, causeur *m.*;—ing *a.* parlant; parlé; —ing *n.* conversation *f.*

tall *a.* grand; haut; (coll.) incroyable; —ness *n.* hauteur *f.*; grande taille *f.*

tallow *n.* suif *m.*

tally *n.* compte *m.*; taille *f.*; entaille, coche *f.*; — *vi.* correspondre; — *vt.* pointer, contrôler

talon *n.* serre, griffe *f.*

tambourine *n.* tambourin *m.*

tame *vt.* apprivoiser; dompter; — *a.* apprivoisé, dompté, doux, domestique; abattu, humilié; —ness *n.* docilité *f.*, caractère doux *m.*; —r *n.* apprivoiseur, dompteur *m.*

tamp *vt.* pilonner; bourrer

tamper *vt.* expérimenter (avec); — with se mêler de; altérer; fausser, falsifier

tan *n.* tan *m.*; (sun) hâle *m.*; (color) brun-jaune *m.*; — *vt.* tanner; hâler; (coll.) fesser; —ner *n.* tanneur *m.*; —nery *n.* tannerie *f.*; —ing *n.* tan *m.*

tang *n.* goût âpre *m.*; saveur *f.*

tangent *n.* tangente *f.*; — *a.* tangent, tangentiel

tangerine *n.* mandarine *f.*

tangible *n.* tangible, tactile; sensible; matériel

Tangiers *n.* Tanger *m.*

tangle *vt.* embarrasser, embrouiller; emmêler; — *n.* embrouillement *m.*; embarras *m.*

tank *n.* citerne *f.*; réservoir *m.*; (mil.) tank, char *m.*; gas — réservoir à essence *m.*; — car wagon-citerne *m.*; —er *n.* bâteau-citerne *m.*

tankard *n.* chope *f.*

tannic *a.* tannique

tannin *n.* tanin *m.*

tantalize *vt.* tourmenter, tantaliser, taquiner

tantalizing *a.* qui tantalise; (fig.) ravissant; délicieux; séduisant; provocant tantalum *n.* tantale *m.*

tantamount *a.* équivalent

tantrum *n.* accès de colère *m.*

tap *n.* tape *f.*, coup léger *m.*; cannelle *f.*, robinet *m.*; — dance danse à claquettes *f.*; — water eau du robinet *f.*; on — en vidange; — *vt.* percer; taper; frapper

tap-dance *vi.* danser à la claque

tape *n.* ruban *m.*; bande *f.*; adhesive — sparadrap *m.*; recording — ruban magnétique *m.*; red — paperasseries *f. pl.*; — measure, — line mètre en ruban *m.*; — recorder *n.* magnétophone *m.*; — *vt.* entourer d'un ruban; entourer de sparadrap; enregistrer sur ruban

taper *n.* bougie *f.*; — *vi.* se terminer en pointe; — *vt.* tailler en cône, côner; diminuer; –ed, –ing *a.* conique; en pointe; effilé

tapestry *n.* tapisserie *f.*

tapeworm *n.* ver solitaire *m.*

taproot *n.* racine principale *f.*

taps *n.* (mil.) signal d'éteindre les lumières dans les casernes *m.*

tar *n.* goudron *m.*; matelot *m.*; — *vt.* goudronner; –ry *a.* goudronneux

tarentella *n.* tarentelle *f.*

tardiness *n.* lenteur *f.*; manque de poncualité *m.*

tardy *a.* tardif, lent; en retard

tare *n.* ivraie *f.*; (com.) tare *f.*

target *n.* cible *f.*; but *m.*

tariff *n.* tarif *m.*

tarnish *n.* ternissure *f.*; — *vi.* se ternir

tarpaulin *n.* bâche *f.*; prélart *m.*

tarragon *n.* estragon *m.*

tarry *vi.* tarder, attendre; demeurer

tart *n.* tarte *f.*; — *a.* aigre; acide; mordant, piquant; –ness *n.* aigreur, acidité *f.*

tartar *n.* tartre *m.*

Tartar *a. & n.* tartare *m.*

tartar *n.* (chem.) tartre *m.*; cream of — crème de tartre *f.*

task *n.* tâche, besogne *f.*; travail *m.*; (school punishment) pensum *m.*; take to — réprimander; — force (mil.) groupe chargé d'une mission spéciale *m.*

taskmaster *n.* surveillant tyrannique *m.*

Tasmania *n.* Tasmanie *f.*

tassel *n.* gland *m.*, houppe *f.*

taste *n.* goût *m.*; saveur, odeur *f.*; petit morceau, petit peu *m.*; penchant *m.*; — *vt.* goûter; déguster; sentir; — *vi.* avoir le goût; sentir; –ful *a.* de bon goût; –less *a.* sans goût; fade, insipide; –r *n.* dégustateur *m.*

tastiness *n.* saveur *f.*, goût *m.*

tasty *a.* délicieux; savoureux

tat *vt.* confectionner de la dentelle; faire de la frivolité; –ting *n.* frivolité; tit for

— à bon chat bon rat

tatter *n.* guenille *f.*, lambeau *m.*; –ed *a.* en lambeaux

tattle *vi.* cancaner; commérer; bavarder

tattletale *n.* rapporteur *m.*

tattoo *n.* tatouage *m.* (mil.) retraite *f.*; — *vt.* tatouer; –ing *n.* tatouage *m.*

taunt *n.* insulte *f.*; raillerie *f.*; — *vt.* insulter; tourner en ridicule

taupe *n.* gris-jaune *m.*

taut *a.* raide, tendu; –ness *n.* raideur *f.*

tautology *n.* tautologie *f.*

tavern *n.* cabaret *m.*, auberge *f.*; taverne *f.*; — keeper aubergiste *m.*

tawdry *a.* clinquant; de mauvais goût, vulgaire

tawny *a.* tanné; basané

tax *n.* taxe *f.*, impôt *m.*; contributions *f. pl.*; — collector percepteur *m.*; receveur *m.*; — *vt.* taxer; mettre à l'épreuve; –able *a.* imposable, sujet à la taxe; –ation *n.* taxation *f.*; impôts *m. pl.*

taxpayer *n.* contribuable *m. & f.*

taxi(cab) *n.* taxi *m.*; — *vi.* (avi.) rouler

taxidermist *n.* empailleur *m.*

taxidermy *n.* empaillage *m.*, taxidermie *f.*

taximeter *n.* taximètre *m.*

tea *n.* thé *m.*; to come to — venir prendre le thé; — bag *n.* sachet de thé *m.*; — ball boule à thé *f.*

teach *vt.* enseigner, apprendre; professer; –er *n.* professeur *m.*; instituteur *m.*, institutrice *f.*; maître d'école *m.*; maîtresse d'école *f.*; –er's college école normale *f.*; –ing *n.* enseignement *m.*; –ing staff *n.* corps enseignant *m.*

teacup *n.* tasse à thé *f.*

teakettle *n.* bouilloire *f.*

team *n.* équipe *f.*; (horses) attelage *m.*; — *vt.* atteler; — *vi.*, — (up) with collaborer avec; se joindre à

teamwork *n.* travail d'équipe *m.*, collaboration *f.*

teapot *n.* théière *f.*

tear *n.* larme *f.*; –s *pl.* larmes *f. pl.*, pleurs *m. pl.*; — gas gaz lacrymogène *m.*; –ful en pleurs; larmoyant; –fully *adv.* en pleurant

tear *n.* déchirure *f.*; — *vt.* déchirer; arracher; — *vi.* se déchirer; aller à toute vitesse; — down démolir; — up déchirer

tearoom *n.* salon de thé *m.*; pâtisserie *f.*

tease *vt.* taquiner, tourmenter; — *n.* taquin *m.*; –r *n.* question difficile *f.*

teasing *a.* taquin; raillant; — *n.* taquinerie *f.*; raillerie *f.*

teaspoon *n.* cuiller à café *f.*; –ful *n.* cuillerée à café *f.*

teat *n.* tétin *m.*; mamelon *m.*; tette *f.*

technical *a.* technique; –ity *n.* technicité

f.; détail (technique) *m.*

technician *n.* technicien *m.*

technique *n.* technique *f.*

technological *a.* technologique

technology *n.* technologie *f.*

tedious *a.* ennuyeux, fatigant; **–ness** *n.* ennui *m.*

tedium *n.* ennui *m.*

tee, T *n.* té *m.*; golf — *m.* dé; pointe de départ *m.*; — *vi.*, — **off** commencer

teem *vi.* fourmiller, foisonner, abonder, grouiller; pleuvoir à verse; **–ing** *a.* fécond, fertile

teen-age *a.* adolescent; âgé de 13 à 19 ans; **–r** *n.* adolescent *m.*

teens *n. pl.* numéros de 13 à 19 *m. pl.*; adolescence *f.*

teeth *n.* dents *f. pl.*; **–e** *vi.* faire les dents; **–ing** *n.* dentition *f.*

teeter *vi.* vaciller; se balancer; faillir tomber

teeter-totter *n.* balançoire *f.*

teetotaler *n.* buveur d'eau *m.*

telecast *n.* émission de télévision *f.*

telegram *n.* télégramme *m.*

telegraph *n.* télégraphe *m.*; — *vt.* télégraphier; **–ic** *a.* télégraphique; **–y** *n.* télégraphie *f.*

telelens *n.* téléobjectif *m.*

telemeter *n.* télémetre *m.*

teleological *a.* téléologique

teleology *n.* téléologie *f.*

telepathic *a.* télépathique

telepathy *n.* télépathie *f.*

telephone *n.* téléphone *m.*; dial — téléphone automatique *m.*; — **booth** *n.* cabine téléphonique *f.*; — **directory** *n.* annuaire *m.*; — **exchange** *n.* central téléphonique *m.*; — **operator** *n.* standardiste *m. & f.*; — **receiver** *n.* recepteur *m.*; — *a.* téléphonique; — *vt. & vi.* téléphoner (à)

telephonic *a.* téléphonique

telephony *n.* téléphonie *f.*

teleprinter *n.* télétype, téléscripteur *m.*

telescope *n.* télescope *m.*; longue-vue *f.*; — *vt.* télescoper; — *vi.* se télescoper

telescopic *a.* télescopique

teletypewriter *n.* télétype *m.*

televise *vt.* téléviser

television *n.* télévision *f.*; — **set** téléviseur *m.*

tell *vt.* dire; raconter, conter; apprendre; marquer, indiquer; ordonner; distinguer; savoir; — *vi.* porter; **–er** *n.* conteur, raconteur *m.*; (bank) caissier, payeur *m.*; **fortune —** *n.* diseuse de bonne aventure *f.*; **–ing** *a.* efficace; frappant; **–ing** *n.* récit *m.*, narration *f.*

telltale *a.* révélateur

tellurium *n.* tellure *m.*

temerity *n.* témérité, audace *f.*

temper *n.* caractère *m.*; naturel *m.*; humeur *f.*; irritation *f.*; colère *f.*; (metal) trempe *f.*; **lose one's —** se mettre en colère, s'emporter; — *vt.* tempérer, modérer; adoucir; broyer; tremper; **–ed** *a.* trempé, recuit

tempera *n.* détrempe *f.*

temperament *n.* tempérament *m.*; humeur *f.*, caractère *m.*; **–al** *a.* d'humeur inégale, capricieux

temperance *n.* tempérance, modération *f.*

temperate *a.* tempéré, modéré; **–ness** *n.* modération *f.*; douceur *f.*

temperature *n.* température *f.*; fièvre *f.*

tempest *n.* tempête *f.*, orage *m.*; **–uous** *a.* orageux

temple *n.* temple *m.*; (anat.) tempe *f.*

temporal *a.* temporel; (anat.) temporal

temporary *a.* temporaire, provisoire, intérimaire; passager

temporize *vi.* temporiser; transiger (avec)

tempt *vt.* tenter; **–ation** *n.* tentation *f.*; **–er** *n.* tenteur *m.*; **–ress** *n.* tentatrice *f.*

ten *n. & a.* dix *m.*; **about —** dizaine *f.*; **–th** *n. & a.* dixième *m.*

tenable *a.* tenable

tenacious *a.* tenace

tenacity *n.* ténacité *f.*; entêtement *m.*

tenancy *n.* (law) usufruit *m.*; location *f.*

tenant *n.* tenancier, fermier *m.*; locataire *m. & f.*; — *vt.* tenir à bail; habiter; **–less** *a.* sans habitant

tend *vt.* garder, surveiller; avoir soin de; soigner; — *vi.* tendre; contribuer; **–er** *n.* offre *f.*; (rail.) tender *m.*; **legal –er** monnaie légale *f.*; **–er** *vt.* offrir

tendency *n.* tendance *f.*; disposition *f.*; penchant *m.*, inclination *f.*

tendentious *a.* tendancieux

tender *a.* tendre; affectueux; délicat; sensible; **–ness** *n.* tendresse *f.*; délicatesse *f.*; sensibilité *f.*

tenderfoot *n.* bleu, débutant *m.*

tenderhearted *a.* sensible

tenderloin *n.* filet *m.*

tendril *n.* vrille *f.*

tenement *n.* immeuble d'habitation dans un quartier misérable *m.*

tenet *n.* dogme, principe *m.*

tenor *n.* caractère *m.*; teneur *f.*; (mus.) ténor *m.*

tense *n.* temps *m.*; — *a.* tendu, raide; nerveux; **–ness** *n.* tension *f.*

tensile *a.* de traction; extensible

tension *n.* tension *f.*; traction *f.*; raideur *f.*; voltage *m.*

tent *n.* tente *f.*; — *vi.* camper

tentacle *n.* tentacule *m.*

tentative *a.* d'essai; experimental

tenuous *a.* ténu, insaisissable, mince; **-ness** *n.* ténuité *f.*

tenure *n.* possession, occupation, tenure *f.*

tepid *a.* tiède

term *n.* terme *m.*; limite *f.*; période *f.*; (com.) échéance *f.*; condition, stipulation *f.*; expression *f.*; inscription *f.*; school — semestre *m.*; trimestre *m.*; be on good **-s** with être bien avec; come to **-s** with s'arranger avec; — *vt.* appeler, nommer

terminal *a.* final, terminal; — *n.* terminus *m.*; gare *f.*; (elec.) borne *f.*

terminate *vt.* terminer, mettre fin à; — *vi.* se terminer, finir

termination *n.* fin, limite *f.*, terminaison *f.*

terminology *n.* terminologie *f.*

terminus *n.* terminus *m.*; (railroad) gare *f.*

termite *n.* termite *m.*

tern *n.* sterne *m.*

terrace *n.* terrasse *f.*; — *vt.* terrasser, disposer en terrasse

terra cotta *n.* terre cuite *f.*

terrestrial *a.* terrestre

terrible *a.* terrible, épouvantable; atroce

terrific *a.* terrible; (coll.) formidable; épatant; excellent; **-ally** *adv.* terriblement

terrify *vt.* effrayer, épouvanter, terrifier

territorial *a.* territorial

territory *n.* territoire *m.*

terror *n.* terreur *f.*; épouvante *f.*; effroi *m.*; **-ism** *n.* terrorisme *m.*; **-ist** *n.* terroriste *m.*; **-ize** *vt.* terroriser

terror-stricken *a.* épouvanté

terrycloth *n.* étoffe bouclée *f.*; tissu-éponge *m.*

terse *a.* net; concis; **-ness** *n.* netteté, concision *f.*

tertiary *a.* tertiaire

test *n.* épreuve *f.*; essai *m.*; examen *m.*; test *m.*; — **tube** *n.* éprouvette *f.*; — *vt.* éprouver; mettre à l'épreuve; essayer; examiner; vérifier, contrôler; **-er** *n.* essayeur *m.*; vérificateur *m.*

testament *n.* testament *m.*; **-ary** *a.* testamentaire

testator *n.* testateur *m.*

testicle *n.* testicule *m.*

testify *vt.* témoigner; — *vi.* déposer

testimonial *n.* certificat *m.*, attestation *f.*; témoignage *m.*

testimony *n.* témoignage *m.*, preuve *f.*; déposition *f.*

testiness *n.* irritabilité *f.*

testy *a.* maussade, bourru; irritable

tetanus *n.* tétanos *m.*

tether *n.* attache (des chevaux) *f.*; — *vt.* attacher

tetragonal *a.* tétragone, quadrilatère

tetrahedron *n.* tétraèdre *m.*

tetrameter *n.* tétramètre *m.*

text *n.* texte *m.*; **-ual** *a.* textuel, de texte

textbook *n.* texte *m.*; livre classique *m.*; manuel *m.*

Thailand *n.* Thaïland *m.*

Thames *n.* Tamise *f.*

than *adv.* que, (before numbers) de

thank *vt.* remercier; **-s** *n. pl.* grâces *f. pl.*; remerciments *m. pl.*; **-s!** merci, merci bien, merci beaucoup; je vous remercie; **-fulness** *n.* reconnaissance *f.*; **-less** *a.* ingrat

thanksgiving *n.* action de grâces *f.*

that *a.* ce, cet, cette; — *conj.* que, qui; afin que, pour que, de manière que; — *pron.* cela, ça, ce; — **one** celui-là, celle-là

thatch *n.* chaume *m.*; — *vt.* couvrir de chaume; **-ed** *a.* de chaume

thaw *n.* dégel *m.*; — *vt. & vi.* dégeler

the *art.* le, la, les

theater *n.* théâtre *m.*

theatrical *a.* théâtral, scénique; — *n.* spectacle *m.*

thee *pron.* toi, te

theft *n.* vol, larcin *m.*

their *a.* leur, leurs; **-s** *pron.* le leur; la leur; les leurs; à eux, à elles

theist *n. & a.* théiste *m.*

them *pron.* eux, elles; les; **-selves** *pron.* eux-mêmes, elles-mêmes, se

theme *n.* thème *m.*

then *adv.* alors; après; puis, ensuite; donc, par conséquent; till — jusque là, d'ici là; now and — de temps en temps, de temps à autre

thence *adv.* de là

thenceforth *adv.* dès lors

theocratic(al) *a.* théocratique

theologian *n.* théologien *m.*

theologic(al) *a.* théologique

theology *n.* théologie *f.*

theorem *n.* théorème *m.*

theoretic(al) *a.* théorique; **-ally** *adv.* en principe

theorist *n.* théoricien *m.*

theorize *vi.* théoriser

theory *n.* théorie *f.*

theosophy *n.* théosophie *f.*

therapeutic *a.* thérapeutique; **-s** *n.* thérapeutique *f.*

therapy *n.* traitement *m.*

there *adv.* là; y; here and — çà et là; — is, — are il y a; voilà

thereabouts *adv.* environ

thereafter *adv.* après, ensuite; dès lors

thereby *adv.* par là, ainsi

therefore *adv.* ainsi, donc; aussi

therefrom *adv.* de là, de cela

therein *adv.* là-dedans

thereon *adv.* là-dessus

thereupon *adv.* là-dessus; sur quoi

therm *n.* microthermie *f.*

thermic *a.* thermique

thermodynamics *n.* thermodynamique *f.*

thermometer *n.* thermomètre *m.*

thermos (bottle) *n.* thermos *m.*, bouteille isolante *f.*

thermostat *n.* calorifère *f.*; thermostat *m.*

these *pron. pl.* ceux-ci, celles-ci; — *a.* ces

thesis *n.* thèse *f.*

they *pron.* ils, elles; eux; on

thick *n.* épaisseur *f.*; fort *m.*; — *a.* épais, gros, grand; touffu; trouble; grossier; fréquent; -en *vt. & vi.* épaissir; -ness *n.* épaisseur *f.*; grosseur *f.*

thicket *n.* taillis, fourré *m.*

thickheaded *a.* à la tête dure; bête; idiot

thickset *a.* trapu

thick-skinned *a.* insensible

thick-witted *a.* bête, stupide

thief *n.* voleur *m.*

thieve *vt. & vi.* voler; -ry *n.* vol, larcin *m.*

thievish *a.* voleur

thigh *n.* cuisse *f.*

thimble *n.* dé à coudre; -ful *n.* dé, doigt *m.*

thin *a.* mince, maigre; léger; ténu; (hair) rare; (voice) grêle; — *vt.* amincir; délayer; — *vi.* maigrir; s'amincir; -ly *adv.* à peine; -ness *n.* maigreur, minceur *f.*; légèreté *f.*; rareté *f.*

thine *pron.* à toi; le tien, la tienne

thing *n.* chose *f.*; objet *m.*; article *m.*; affaire *f.*; effet *m.*; créature *f.*, être *m.*; latest — dernier cri *m.*

think *vt. & vi.* penser; croire; trouver; juger; réfléchir; songer; s'imaginer; I — so je pense que oui; — of penser à; — out peser, méditer; — over réfléchir; -able *a.* concevable, imaginable; -er *n.* penseur *m.*; -ing *a.* qui pense; -ing *n.* pensées *f. pl.*

thin-skinned *a.* susceptible, sensible

third *a.* troisième; — *n.* (fraction) tiers *m.*

thirst *n.* soif *f.*; altération *f.*; — *vi.* avoir soif; -y *a.* altéré; avide; be -y avoir soif

thirteen *a.* treize; -th *a.* treizième; treize

thirtieth *a.* trentième

thirty *a.* trente

this *a.* ce, cet, cette; — *pron.* ceci; cela; celui(-ci), celle(-ci)

thong *n.* courroie *f.*; lanière *f.*

thoracic *a.* thoracique

thorax *n.* thorax *m.*

thorium *n.* thorium *m.*

thorn *n.* épine *f.*; -y *a.* épineux

thorough *a.* complet; profondi; approfondi; -ly *adv.* complètement, tout à fait; parfaitement; à fond; -ness *n.* profondeur *f.*; assiduité *f.*

thoroughbred *a.* (horse) de race, pur sang; — *n.* (horse) cheval de race *m.*

thoroughfare *n.* voie, rue *f.*

thoroughgoing *a.* assidu, consciencieux

those *a.* ces; — *pron.* ceux(-là), celles(-là)

thou *pron.* tu; toi

though *conj.* bien que, quoique, encore que; — *adv.* cependant, pourtant

thought *n.* pensée *f.*; réflexion *f.*; idée *f.*; méditation *f.*; intention *f.*; -ful *a.* pensif; prévenant; -fulness *n.* prévenance *f.*; réflexion *f.*; -less *a.* irréfléchi; sans prévenance

thousand *a.* mille; — *n.* (un) millier *m.*; -th *a. & n.* millième *m.*

thrash *vt.* battre, rosser; -ing *n.* raclée, rossée *f.*

thread *n.* fil *m.*; (screw) filet, filetage *m.*; — *vt.* enfiler; fileter

threadbare *a.* râpé; usé

threat *n.* menace *f.*; -en *vt.* menacer; intimider; -ening *a.* menaçant

three *a.* trois

three-act *a.* en trois actes

three-cornered *a.* triangulaire; (hat) tricorne

threefold *a.* triple

three-legged *a.* à trois pieds

three-ply *a.* à trois épaisseurs

threesome *n.* partie de trois *f.*

three-speed *a.* à trois vitesses

three-wheeled *a.* à trois roues

thresh *vt.* battre; -er *n.* (person) batteur *m.*; (machine) batteuse *f.*; -ing *n.* battage *m.*; -ing machine *n.* batteuse *f.*

threshold *n.* seuil, pas *m.*; limite *f.*

thrice *adv.* trois fois

thrift *n.* économie, frugalité *f.*; -iness *n.* économie *f.*; -y *a.* économe, frugal

thrill *n.* frémissement, tressaillement *m.*; émotion *f.*; — *vt.* émouvoir, émotionner; faire frémir; — *vi.* frémir, tressaillir; -er *n.* (coll.) écrit mélodramatique *m.*; -ing *a.* émouvant, passionnant

thrive *vi.* réussir; bien marcher; prospérer

thriving *a.* florissant; prospère

throat *n.* gorge *f.*; gosier *m.*; clear one's — s'éclaircir la voix; have a sore — avoir mal à la gorge; cut- *a.* concurrence ruineuse

throb *vi.* palpiter, battre; — *n.* battement *m.*, pulsation *f.*; -bing *n.* pulsation *f.*, battement *m.*

throes *n. pl.* agonie *f.*; douleurs *f. pl.*

thrombosis *n.* thrombose *f.*

throne *n.* trône *m.*

throng *n.* foule *f.*; — *vi.* affluer, se presser; — *vt.* encombrer

throttle *n.* étrangleur *m.*; — *vt.* étrangler

through *prep.* à travers; par; go — traverser, parcourir; fouiller; — *adv.* à travers; jusqu'au bout; — *a.* direct; (coll.) fini

throughout *prep.* partout (dans)

throw *n.* jet *m.*; coup *m.*; lancée *f.*; lancement *m.*; — *vt.* jeter, lancer; projeter; (horse) démonter; (wrestling) terrasser; — **away** jeter, rejeter; — **back** renvoyer; — **off** jeter; se défaire de; enlever; dépister; — **out** jeter, rejeter; expulser, metter à la porte; (clutch) débrayer; — **up** rejeter, vomir; (hands) lever; abandonner, renoncer à

throwback *n.* retour *m.*

thrust *n.* poussée *f.*; coup, trait *m.*; — *vt.* pousser; enfoncer; fourrer; — *vi.* porter un coup

thruway *n.* autostrade *f.*

thud *n.* bruit sourd *m.*; — *vi.* tomber avec un bruit sourd

thug *n.* bandit, gangster *m.*

thumb *n.* pouce *m.*; — **index** encoches *f. pl.*; — *vt.* manier; — **a ride** (coll.) faire de l'auto-stop; — **through** parcourir, jeter un coup d'œil à

thumbnail *n.* ongle du pouce *m.*; — *a.* petit, miniscule

thumbtack *n.* punaise *f.*

thump *n.* coup (de poing) *m.*; coup sourd *m.*; — *vt.* taper, bourrer, battre

thunder *n.* tonnerre *m.*; foudre *f.*; **clap of** — coup de foudre *m.*; — *vt. & vi.* tonner; **-ing** *a.* tonnant

thunderbolt *n.* coup de foudre *m.*

thundercloud, thunderhead *n.* cumulus à bords blancs *m.*

thunderstorm *n.* orage *m.*

thunderstruck *a.* abasourdi

Thursday *n.* jeudi *m.*

thus *adv.* ainsi; donc; aussi; de cette manière, de cette façon; — **far** jusqu'ici

thwart *n.* (naut.) banc de nage *m.*; — *vt.* faire avorter, contrecarrer

thy *a.* ton, ta, tes

thyme *n.* thym *m.*

thyroid *a.* thyroïde

tiara *n.* tiare *f.*

Tibet *n.* Thibet *m.*

tick *n.* tic-tac *m.*; trait *m.*, marque *f.*; (zool.) tique *f.*; — *vi.* faire tic-tac; marcher, fonctionner; **-er** *n.* télégraphe imprimeur *m.*; (coll.) cœur *m.*; **-ing** *n.* tic-tac *m.*; coutil à matelas *m.*

ticket *n.* billet *m.*; ticket *m.*; bulletin *m.*; **complimentary** — billet de faveur *m.*; **one-way** — billet simple *m.*; **round-trip** — billet d'aller et retour *m.*; **season** — carte d'abonnement *f.*; — **collector** contrôleur *m.*; — **window** guichet *m.*

tickle *vt.* chatouiller; amuser; — *vi.* avoir

des chatouillements; **-r** *n.* question difficile *f.*

tickling *n.* chatouillement *m.*

ticklish *a.* chatouilleux; délicat; difficile

tidal *a.* de la marée; — **wave** vague de fond *f.*

tidbit *n.* friandise, bouchée *f.*

tiddlywinks *n. pl.* jeu de puce *m.*

tide *n.* marée *f.*; (fig.) fortune *f.*; **flood** — marée montante *f.*; **high** — marée haute *f.*; **low** — marée basse *f.*

tidewater *n.* eau de marée *f.*

tidily *adv.* avec soin; avec ordre

tidiness *n.* bon ordre *m.*; propreté *f.*

tidings *n. pl.* nouvelles *f. pl.*

tidy *a.* en bon ordre; ordonné; propre; bien tenu; considérable, assez grand; — *vt.* ranger, arranger; mettre de l'ordre dans

tie *n.* cravate *f.*; nœud *m.*; lien *m.*; liaison *f.*; nombre égal *m.*; égalité *f.*; (rail.) traverse *f.*; — **game** match à égalité *m.*; — **clip** pince à cravate *f.*; — *vt.* lier, attacher, nouer; — *vi.* être à égalité; — **a knot** faire un nœud; — **up** ficeler, attacher; panser; immobiliser

tier *n.* rangée *f.*; gradin, étage *m.*

tie-up *n.* suspension des affaires *f.*; arrêt de la circulation *m.*

tiff *n.* querelle *f.*

tight *a.* serré; collant; tendu; imperméable; étanche; ivre, gris, soûl; avare; — *adv.* fermement; bien; **-s** *n. pl.* maillot *m.*; **-en** *vt.* serrer, reserrer, raidir; **-ly** *adv.* étroitement; fortement; bien; **-ness** *n.* tension *f.*; étroitesse *f.*

tightfisted *a.* avare, ladre

tight-fitting *a.* collant

tight-lipped *a.* aux lèvres serrées; silencieux; impassible

tightrope *n.* corde *f.*; — **artist** funambule *m. & f.*; danseur de corde *m.*

tile *n.* tuile *f.*; carreau *m.*; — *vt.* carreler; **-d** *a.* en tuiles; carrelé

tiling *n.* carrelage *m.*

till *n.* tiroir-caisse *m.*; — *prep.* jusqu'à; à; — *conj.* jusqu'à ce que; — *vt.* labourer, cultiver; **-able** *a.* arable, labourable; **-age** *n.* labour, labourage *m.*; **-er** *n.* laboureur, cultivateur *m.*; (naut.) barre *f.*; **-ing** *n.* labour *m.*

tilt *n.* pente, inclinaison *f.*; joute *f.*; **at full** — à toute vitesse; — *vt. & vi.* pencher, incliner

timber *n.* bois (de construction) *m.*; poutre *f.*; (coll.) étoffe *f.*, calibre *m.*; trempe *f.*; — *vt.* boiser, blinder

timberland *n.* pays boisé *m.*

timbre *n.* timbre *m.*

time *n.* temps *m.*; heure *f.*; époque *f.*; moment *m.*; saison *f.*; âge *m.*; fois *f.*; (mus.) mesure *f.*; **a short — after** peu après; **at all —s** toujours; **at no —** jamais; **at the same —** en même temps; à la fois; d'autre part; **at —s** parfois; **for the —** being pour le moment; **from — to —** de temps en temps, de temps à autre; **in —** à temps; avec le temps; **keep —** suivre la mesure; **on —** à l'heure; **spare —** loisir *m.*; temps disponible *m.*; **what — is it?** quelle heure est-il?; **— exposure** pose *f.*; **— lag** retard *m.*; **— limit** délai *m.*; limite de temps *f.*; **— signal** signal horaire *m.*; **— vt.** régler, mesurer, calculer; chronométrer; **–less** *a.* éternel; **–liness** *n.* à propos *m.*; opportunité *f.*; **–ly** *a.* opportun, à-propos

time-honored *a.* consacré; vénérable

timekeeper *n.* chronométreur *m.*; controlleur

timepiece *n.* montre *f.*; pendule *f.*

timesaver *n.* économiseur de temps *m.*

timetable *n.* horaire, indicateur *m.*

timeworn *a.* vénérable; usé par le temps

timid *a.* timide; peureux; **–ity** *n.* timidité *f.*

timing *n.* réglage *m.*; chronométrage *m.*; calcul *m.*

timpani *n.* timbales *f. pl.*

tin *n.* étain *m.*; fer-blanc *m.*; (baking) plat *m.*; **— can** boîte *f.*; **— plate** ferblanterie *f.*; **— vt.** étamer; **–ny** *a.* d'étain; grêle

tincture *n.* teinture *f.*; **— vt.** teinter, teindre

tinder *n.* mèche de briquet *f.*

tine *n.* fourchon *m.*, dent *f.*

tin foil *n.* feuille d'étain *f.*; papier d'étain *m.*

tinge *n.* teinte *f.*; **— vt.** teindre

tingle *vi.* tinter; picoter; **— n.** tintement *m.*; fourmillement *m.*

tingling *n.* tintement *m.*; fourmillement, picotement *m.*

tinker *n.* chaudronnier *m.*; **— vi.** bricoler; **— (with)** *vt.* rafistoler

tinkle *vi.* tinter; **— n.** tintement *m.*

tinsel *n.* clinquant *m.*; faux brillant *m.*

tinsmith *n.* ferblantier *m.*

tinware *n.* ferblanterie *f.*

tint *n.* teinte *f.*; **— vt.** teinter, colorer

tiny *a.* tout petit; minuscule

tip *n.* bout *m.*, pointe, extrémité *f.*; pourboire *m.*, gratification *f.*; (coll.) tuyau, conseil *m.*; **— vt.** donner un pourboire à; embouter; **— over** renverser; **–ping** *n.* pourboires *m. pl.*

tipple *vi.* boire à l'excès; **–r** *n.* ivrogne *m.*

tipsiness *n.* ivresse *f.*

tipsy *a.* ivre, gris

tiptoe *n.* pointe des pieds *f.*; **on —** sur la pointe des pieds; **— vi.** marcher sur la pointe des pieds

tirade *n.* tirade, diatribe *f.*

tire *n.* pneu *m.*; **flat —** pneu à plat *m.*; crevaison *f.*; **spare —** pneu de rechange; **— vt.** fatiguer, lasser; **— vi.** se fatiguer, se lasser; **–d** *a.* fatigué; las (lasse); **grow –d of** se lasser de; **–dness** *n.* fatigue, lassitude *f.*; **–less** *a.* infatigable, inlassable; **–some** *a.* fatigant; ennuyeux

tissue *n.* tissu *m.*; **— paper** papier de soie *m.*

titanic *a.* titanique

tit for tat, à bon chat bon rat

tithe *n.* dîme *f.*

titillate *vi. & vt.* chatouiller, titiller

title *n.* titre *m.*; droit *m.*; **— vt.** intituler; **–d** *a.* titré; **— n.** (law) titre de propriété; acte *m.*; **— rôle** *n.* premier rôle *m.*

titlist *n.* champion *m.*

titrate *vt. & vi.* titrer

titter *n.* petit rire *m.*; **— vi.** pousser de petits rires

titular *a.* titulaire

to *prep* à; vers; en; chez; jusqu'à; de; pour; **— adv.**, **come —** reprendre connaissance; **go — and fro** aller et venir

toadstool *n.* champignon vénéneux *m.*

toast *n.* pain grillé, toast *m.*; **— vt.** griller; boire à la santé de; **–er** *n.* grille-pain *m.*

toastmaster *n.* celui qui annonce les toasts *m.*, celui qui préside à un banquet *m.*

tobacco *n.* tabac *m.*, **— pouch** *n.* blague à tabac *f.*

toboggan *n.* toboggan *m.*

today *adv.* aujourd'hui; **a week from —** d'aujourd'hui en huit

toddle *vi.* marcher à petits pas; **–r** *n.* enfant qui commence à marcher *m.*

toddy *n.* grog *m.*

to-do *n.* remue-ménage *m.*; bruit, tapage *m.*

toe *n.* orteil, doigt du pied *m.*; (shoe) bout *m.*, pointe *f.*; **— vt.**, **— the line** se conformer, s'aligner

toenail *n.* ongle d'orteil *m.*

toffee *n.* (candy) caramel au beurre *m.*

together *adv.* ensemble; avec; à la fois; de concert; **bring —** rassembler, réunir

toggle *n.* barrette *f.*; cabillot *m.*; **— switch** *n.* levier articulé *m.*

toil *n.* travail, labeur *m.*; **— vi.** travailler, peiner; **–er** *n.* travailleur *m.*; **–some** *a.* pénible

toilet *n.* cabinets *m. pl.*, toilette *f.*; **— paper** papier hygiénique *m.*; **— water** eau de Cologne *f.*

token *n.* jeton *m.*; témoignage, signe *m.*, marque *f.*; **by the same —** de plus; **— of love** gage d'amour *m.*

tolerance *n.* tolérance *f.*

tolerant *a.* tolérant

tolerate *vt.* supporter, tolérer

toleration *n.* tolérance *f.*

toll *n.* taxe *f.*; droit de passage *m.*; (bell) son *m.*, son de cloches; **death** — mortalité *f.*; — **bridge** pont à péage *m.*; — **call** communication interurbaine *f.*; **-gate** barrière *f.*; — **house** péage *m.*; — *vt.* & *vi.* sonner

tomato *n.* tomate *f.*

tomb *n.* tombe *f.*; tombeau *m.*

tomboy *n.* garçon manqué *m.*

tombstone *n.* pierre tombale *f.*

tomfoolery *n.* niganderie *f.*

tomorrow *adv.* demain; **day after** — àpresdemain *m.*; — **morning** demain matin; **week from** — de demain en huit

ton *n.* tonne *f.*; **-nage** *n.* tonnage *m.*, jauge *f.*

tone *m.* ton, accent, son *m.*; voix *f.*; nuance *f.*; — *vt.*, — **down** atténuer, adoucir; **-less** *a.* atone; sans éclat

tongs *n. pl.* pinces, tenailles, pincettes *f. pl.*

tongue *n.* langue *f.*; (buckle) ardillon *m.*; (shoe) languette *f.*; **native** — langue maternelle *f.*

tongue-tied *a.* interdit

tonic *a.* tonique; — *n.* tonique, fortifiant *m.*

tonight *adv.* ce soir; cette nuit

tonsil *n.* amygdale, tonsile *f.*; **-litis** *n.* amygdalite *f.*; **-lectomy** *n.* amygdalotomie *f.*

tonsure *n.* tonsure *f.*; — *vt.* tonsurer

too *adv.* trop; aussi; de plus, d'ailleurs; — **much** trop, trop de

tool *n.* outil, instrument, ustensile *m.*; **-box** coffre à outils *m.*; — *vt.* travailler, usiner; équiper; dorer; **-ing** *n.* usinage *m.*; dorure *f.*

toot *n.* cornement, coup de klaxon *m.*; (naut.) coup de sirène *m.*; — *vt.* corner, donner un coup de klaxon; sonner; — *vi.* corner; sonner

tooth *n.* dent *f.*; — **powder** poudre dentifrice *f.*; **-ed** *a.* denté; dentelé; **-less** *a.* édenté, sans dents

toothache *n.* mal de dents *m.*; **have a** — avoir mal aux dents

toothbrush *n.* brosse à dents *f.*

tooth paste *n.* pâte dentifrice *f.*

toothpick *n.* cure-dents *m.*

top *n.* sommet, haut *m.*, cime *f.*; dessus *m.*; tête *f.*; (toy) toupie *f.*; — *a.* (le) plus haut, supérieur; (floor) dernier; (quality) premier; — **hat** chapeau haut de forme *m.*; — *vt.* surmonter; coiffer; surpasser, dépasser; être à la tête de

topcoat *n.* pardessus *m.*

topflight *a.* excellent, supérieur, premier

top-heavy *a.* trop lourd du haut

topic *n.* sujet *m.*, matière *f.*; **-al** *a.* actuel, d'actualité; topique

topknot *n.* chignon *m.*; (bird) huppe *f.*

topmost *n.* le plus haut, le plus élevé

topographer *n.* topographe *m.*

topography *n.* topographie *f.*

topple *vt.* faire tomber; — *vi.* tomber; branler

top-secret *a.* extrêmement secret

topsoil *n.* terre végétale *f.*

topsy-turvy *a.* & *adv.* sens dessus dessous

tor *n.* pic *m.*

torch *n.* torche *f.*, flambeau *m.*

torchlight *n.* lumière de flambeau *f.*; — **procession** retraite aux flambeaux *f.*

toreador *n.* toréador *m.*

torment *n.* tourment *m.*; torture *f.*, supplice *m.*; — *vt.* tourmenter, torturer; **-or** *n.* tourmenteur *m.*; bourreau *m.*

torn *a.* déchiré

tornado *n.* ouragan *m.*, tornade *f.*

torpedo *n.* torpille *f.*; — **boat** torpilleur *m.*; — **tube** lance-torpille *m.*; — *vt.* torpiller

torpid *a.* engourdi

torpor *n.* torpeur *f.*

torque *n.* couple de torsion *m.*

torrent *n.* torrent *m.*; **in -s** (rain) par torrents, à verse; **-ial** *a.* torrentiel

torrid *a.* torride, brûlant

torso *n.* torse *m.*

tort *n.* (law) dommage *m.*

tortoise-shell *n.* écaille *f.*; — *a.* d'écaille

tortuous *a.* tortueux, sinueux

torture *n.* torture *f.*; supplice, tourment *m.*; — *vt.* torturer, mettre au supplice; **-r** *n.* bourreau *m.*

toss *n.* jet, lancement *m.*; coup *m.*; — *vt.* jeter, lancer; choisir (à pile ou face); hocher; secouer, agiter; (of horse) démonter; — *vi.* (s')agiter, (se) tourner; — **off** faire rapidement; expédier; (drink) lamper; **-ing** *n.* lancement *m.*; agitation *f.*

tossup *n.* chance égale *f.*

tot *n.* petit enfant *m.*

total *a.* total; global; complet; — *n.* total, montant *m.*; — *vt.* & *vi.* totaliser; **-ity** *n.* totalité *f.*; **-ize** *vt.* totaliser

totalitarian *a.* totalitaire

totter *vi.* chanceler; tituber; **-ing** *a.* chancelant; titubant

touch *n.* toucher, tact *m.*; coup *m.*; touche *f.*; contact, rapport *m.*; communication *f.*; soupçon *m.*, pointe *f.*; **in** — **with** en rapport avec, en communication avec; — *vt.* toucher; effleurer; émouvoir; attendrir; — *vi.* se toucher; — **off** déclencher; — up faire des retouches; **–iness** *n.* susceptibilité *f.*; **–ing** *a.* touchant, émouvant, attendrissant; **–y** *a.* qui se pique facilement; susceptible; difficile *m.*

touchdown *n.* touché *m.*

touchstone *n.* pierre de touche *f.*

tough *a.* dur, difficile; fort; tenace; **–en** *vt.* durcir, endurcir; **–ness** *n.* dureté *f.*, difficulté *f.*; force *f.*; ténacité *f.*

tour *n.* voyage *m.*, excursion *f.*; tour *m.*, tournée *f.*; — *vi.* voyager; — *vt.* visiter; **–ist** *n.* touriste *m. & f.*

tournament *n.* tournoi *m.*; concours *m.*

tousle *vt.* ébouriffer

tout *vi.* (coll.) donner des tuyaux; — *n.* pisteur *m.*

tow *n.* remorque *f.*; filasse *f.*; — *vt.* remorquer; **–ing** *n.* remorque *f.*

toward(s) *prep.* vers; envers; pour

towel *n.* serviette *f.*; essuie-mains *m.*; — **rack** porte-serviettes *m.*; — *it.* essuyer; frotter; **–ing** *n.* tissu-éponge *m.*

tower *n.* tour *f.*; pylône *m.*; (church) clocher *m.*; — *vi.* dominer; **–ing** *a.* très haut; énorme

town *n.* ville *f.*; — **hall** hôtel de ville *m.*

township *n.* commune *f.*

townsman *n.* habitant de la ville *m.*

townspeople *n.* habitants de la ville, citoyens *m. pl.*

toxic *a.* toxique

toxicology *n.* toxicologie *f.*

toxin *n.* toxine *f.*

toy *n.* jouet *m.*; joujou *m.*; — **dog** chien de salon *m.*; — *vi.*, — **with** s'amuser avec

trace *n.* trace *f.*; vestige *m.*; trait *m.*; — *vt.* tracer; calquer; **–able** *a.* qu'on peut suivre; attribuable; **–r** *n.* (mil.) traceuse *f.*

trachea *n.* trachée *f.*

tracheotomy *n.* trachéotomie *f.*

tracing *n.* tracé *m.*; calque *m.*; — **paper** papier à calquer *m.*

track *n.* piste, trace *f.*; chemin *m.*, voie *f.*; (rail.) voie ferrée *f.*; rail(s) *m.* (*pl.*); (sports) courses à pied *f. pl.*; (tractor) chenille *f.*; **keep** — **of** ne pas perdre de vue; surveiller; suivre; **on the right** — sur la bonne voie; **throw off the** — dépister; — *vt.* suivre, traquer; — **down** dépister

tract *n.* étendue *f.*; brochure *f.*; (anat.) appareil *m.*

tractable *a.* traitable, docile

traction *n.* traction *f.*

tractor *n.* tracteur *m.*

trade *n.* commerce *m.*; métier *m.*; — **wind** vent alizé *m.*; — *vi.* faire du commerce; — *vt.* échanger; **–r** *n.* commerçant, marchand *m.*

trade-in *n.* reprise en compte *f.*

trademark *n.* marque (de fabrique) *f.*

tradesman *n.* marchand, fournisseur *m.*

trade-union *n.* syndicat (ouvrier) *m.*; **–ism** *n.* syndicalisme *m.*

trading *n.* commerce *m.*; — *a.* commerçant, marchand; commercial

tradition *n.* tradition *f.*

traditional *a.* traditionnel

traffic *n.* circulation *f.*; trafic, commerce *m.*; mouvement *m.*; — **jam** embouteillage *m.*; — **light** feu *m.*; — **manager** chef de mouvement *m.*; — **sign** indicateur *m.*; — **ticket** procès-verbal *m.*, contravention *f.*; — *vi.* trafiquer

tragedian *n.* tragédien *m.*

tragedy *n.* tragédie *f.*

tragic *a.* tragique

tragicomedy *n.* tragicomédie *f.*

trail *n.* trace, piste *f.*; traînée *f.*; sentier *m.*; — *vt.* traquer, suivre à la piste; — *vi.* traîner; ramper; **–er** (auto.) baladeuse *f.*; caravane *f.*; roulotte *f.*; (film) film-annonce *m.*; **–ing** *a.* rampant; qui (se) traîne

train *n.* train *m.*; suite *f.*; série *f.*; (dress) queue *f.*; — *vt.* exercer; former, élever; préparer; (animal) dresser; (sports) entraîner; (cannon) pointer, orienter; — *vi.* s'exercer; s'entraîner; **–ed** *a.* exercé; dressé; **–er** *n.* entraîneur *m.*; dresseur *m.*; **–ing** *n.* formation, éducation *f.*; entraînement *m.*; dressage *m.*; **physical –ing** éducation physique *f.*

trait *n.* trait *m.*

traitor *n.* traître *m.*; **–ous** *a.* traître, perfide

trajectory *n.* trajectoire *f.*

trammel *n.* tramail *m.*; — *vt.* entraver

tramp *n.* pas lourd *m.*; vagabond, chemineau *m.*; — **steamer** cargo, chemineau *m.*; — *vi.* marcher à pas lourds

trample *vt.* fouler (aux pieds); piétiner; écraser

trance *n.* transe, hypnose *f.*; extase *f.*

tranquil *a.* tranquille, calme; paisible; **–ize** *vt.* tranquilliser, calmer; apaiser; **–izer** *n.* calmant *m.*; **–lity** *n.* tranquillité *f.*, calme *m.*

transact *vt.* faire; **–ion** *n.* affaire *f.*; conduite *f.*; opération *f.*

transatlantic *a.* transatlantique

transcend *vt.* aller au delà de; surpasser, dépasser; **–ence, –ency** *n.* transcendance *f.*; **–ent** *a.* transcendant; **–ental** *a.* transcendantal

transcribe *vt.* transcrire; **–r** *n.* transcripteur *m.*

transcript *n.* copie, transcription *f.*; enregistrement *m.*; **–ion** *n.* transcription *f.*; enregistrement *m.*

transfer *n.* transfert *m.*; transport *m.*; correspondance *f.*, bulletin de correspondance *m.*; — *vt.* transférer; transmettre; virer; calquer; — *vi.* faire une correspondance; **–able** *a.* transmissible; mobilier; **–ence** *n.* transfert *m.*

transfigure *vt.* tranfigurer

transfix *vt.* transpercer

transform *vt.* transformer; convertir; métamorphoser; **–ation** *n.* transformation *f.*; conversion *f.*; métamorphose *f.*; **–er** *n.* transformateur *m.*

transfuse *vt.* transfuser

transgress *vt.* transgresser; — *vi.* pécher; **–ion** *n.* violation, transgression *f.*; péché *m.*, faute *f.*; **–or** *n.* transgresseur *m.*; pécheur *m.*, pécheresse *f.*

transient *a.* transitoire, passager, de passage; momentané

transistor *n.* transistor *m.*

transit *n.* transport *m.*; transit *m.*; passage; **–ion** *n.* transition *f.*; passage *m.*; **–ive** *a.* transitif; **–ory** *a.* transitoire, de passage

translate *vt.* traduire

translation *n.* traduction *f.*; version *f.*

translator *n.* traducteur *m.*

translucence *n.* translucidité *f.*

translucent *a.* translucide

transmission *n.* transmission *f.*; transport *m.*; émission *f.*

transmit *vt.* transmettre; transporter; (radio) émettre; **–ter** *n.* émetteur *m.*; transmetteur *m.*

transmute *vt.* transmuer, transformer

transoceanic *a.* transocéanique

transom *n.* vasistas *m.*, imposte *f.*

transparency *n.* transparence *f.*; transparent *m.*; (phot.) diapositive *f.*

transparent *a.* transparent; clair

transpiration *n.* transpiration *f.*

transpire *vt. & vi.* transpirer

transplant *vt.* transplanter; **–ation** *n.* transplantation *f.*

transport *n.* transport *m.*; — *vt.* transporter; **–ation** *n.* transport *m.*

transpose *vt.* transposer

transposition *n.* transposition *f.*

transverse *a.* transversal; en travers

trap *n.* piège *m.*; trappe *f.*; (sink) collecteur *m.*; set a — tendre un piège, dresser un piège; — door trappe *f.*; **–shooting** tir aux pigeons *m.*; — *vt.* prendre au piège; — *vi.* trapper; **–ped** *a.* pris (au piège); **–per** *n.* trappeur *m.*; **–pings** *n. pl.* apparat *m.*, atours *m. pl.*

trapeze *n.* trapèze *m.*

trapezoid *n.* quadrilatère irrégulier *m.*

trash *n.* débris *m. pl.*; camelote *f.*; **–y** *a.* de camelote

traumatic *a.* traumatique

travel *n.* voyage(s) *m.* (*pl.*); — *vi.* voyager, faire un voyage; parcourir; aller, circuler, marcher; **–er** *n.* voyageur *m.*; **–ing** *n.* voyages *m. pl.*; **–ing** *a.* de voyage; **–ing salesman** commis voyageur *m.*

traveler's check *n.* chèque de voyage *m.*

travelogue *n.* conférence avec projections décrivant un voyage *f.*

traverse *n.* traverse *f.*; — *vt.* traverser, passer à travers de

travesty *n.* travestissement *m.*; parodie *f.*; — *vt.* travestir; parodier

trawl *n.* chalut *m.*; — *vi. & vt.* pêcher au chalut; **–er** *n.* chalutier *m.*

tray *n.* plateau *m.*; cuvette *f.*

treacherous *a.* traître, perfide

treachery *n.* trahison, perfidie *f.*

treacle *n.* mélasse *f.*

tread *n.* pas *m.*; (stair) giron *m.*; (tire) chape *f.*, roulement *m.*; — *vi.* marcher; — *vt.* fouler; — **water** nager debout

treadle *n.* pédale *f.*

treadmill *n.* moulin de discipline *m.*

treason *n.* trahison *f.*; **–able** *a.* traître, perfide; de trahison

treasure *n.* trésor *m.*; — *vt.* priser, aimer beaucoup; **–r** *n.* trésorier *m.*

treasury *n.* trésorerie *f.*; trésor *m.*

treat *n.* régal *m.*; plaisir *m.*; — *vt.* régaler; payer; traiter; soigner; — **oneself to** se payer, s'offrir

treatise *n.* traité *m.*

treaty *n.* traité *m.*, convention *f.*, accord *m.*

treble *a.* triple; — **clef** clef de sol *f.*; — *vt.* tripler

tree *n.* arbre *m.*; **family** — arbre généalogique *m.*

trek *n.* voyage *m.*; — *vi.* voyager

trellis *n.* treillis, treillage *m.*

tremble *n.* frisson *m.*, vibration *f.*; — *vi.* trembler, vibrer

trembling *a.* tremblant; — *n.* tremblement *m.*; vibration *f.*

tremendous *a.* énorme; terrible

tremolo *n.* trémolo *m.*

tremor *n.* tremblement, choc *m.*, secousse *f.*; frémissement *m.*

tremulous *a.* tremblotant

trench *n.* tranchée *f.*, fossé *m.*; — **coat** imperméable *m.*

trenchant *a.* tranchant

trencherman *n.* gros mangeur *m.*

trend *n.* tendance *f.*; — *vi.* tendre

trepidation *n.* trépidation *f.*

trespass *n.* (eccl.) péché *m.*, offense *f.*; (law) violation *f.*; — *vi.* pécher; — **on** violer; empiéter; pénétrer sans autorisation dans une propriété; –er *n.* (eccl.)

transgresseur, pécheur *m.*; personne qui commet une violation de propriété *f.*

tress *n.* tresse, boucle *f.*

trestle *n.* tréteau, chevalet *m.*; (rail.) pont (sur chevalets) *m.*

trey *n.* (cards) trois *m.*

triad *n.* triade *f.*

trial *n.* procès *m.*, cause *f.*, jugement *m.*; essai *m.*, épreuve *f.*; — *a.* d'essai, d'épreuve; experimental — **balance** *n.* balance de vérification *f.*

triangular *a.* triangulaire

triangulation *n.* triangulation *f.*

tribal *a.* de tribu

tribe *n.* tribu *f.*

tribesman *n.* membre d'une tribu *m.*

tribulation *n.* tribulation *f.*

tribunal *n.* tribunal *m.*; cour (de justice) *f.*

tribune *n.* (person) tribune *f.*, tribun *m.*

tributary *a.* tributaire; — *n.* affluent, tributaire *m.*

tribute *n.* tribut, hommage *m.*

trice *n.*, **in a** — en un clin d'œil; tout de suite

trick *n.* tour *m.*, ruse *f.*; truc *m.*; habitude, manie *f.*; (cards) levée *f.*; **card** — tour de cartes *m.*; **play a** — **on** jouer un tour à; — *vt.* jouer un tour à; tromper, duper; **–ery** *n.* tricherie *f.*; tromperie *f.*; **–iness** *n.* nature compliquée *f.*; **–y** *a.* compliqué, difficile; rusé

trickle *vi.* ruisseler, dégoutter, couler; — *n.* filet *m.*; petit peu *m.*

trickling *a.* dégouttant

tricolor *n.* drapeau français, drapeau tricolore *m.*

tricycle *n.* tricycle; (com.) triporteur *m.*

triennial *a.* triennal; trisannuel

trifle *n.* bagatelle, vétille *f.*; rien *m.*; — *vi.* jouer; vétiller; s'occuper à des choses peu importantes

trifling *a.* peu important, insignifiant

trigger *n.* gâchette, détente *f.*

trigonometry *n.* trigonométrie *f.*

trill *n.* (mus.) trille *m.*; — *vt.* triller; rouler; — *vi.* faire des trilles

trillion *n.* trillion *m.*

trilogy *n.* trilogie *f.*

trim *n.* ornement *m.*, ornementation *f.*; bon état, bon ordre *m.*; équilibrage *m.*; (hair) coupe *f.*; **in** — en forme; — *a.* soigné; élégant; propre; — *vt.* orner, ornementer, parer; garnir; équilibrer; tailler, couper; (hair) rafraîchir; **–ming** *n.* ornement *m.*, ornementation *f.*; garniture *f.*, garnissage *m.*; parure *f.*; (sewing) passementerie *f.*; taille *f.*; **–mings** *n. pl.* garniture *f.*, accompagnements *m. pl.*; **–ness** *n.* élégance *f.*; belle taille *f.*

Trinidad *n.* Trinité *f.*

trinity *n.* groupe de trois *m.*; (eccl.) Trinité *f.*

trinket *n.* babiole *f.*; bibelot *m.*

trip *n.* voyage *m.*, excursion *f.*; trébuchement, faux pas *m.*; **take a** — faire un voyage; — *vt.* faire trébucher; donner un croc-en-jambe à; — *vi.* trébucher, faire un faux pas

tripe *n.* tripes *f. pl.*; gras-double *m.*; bêtises *f. pl.*; camelote *f.*

triphammer *n.* marteau à bascule *m.*

triple *a.* triple; — *vt.* & *vi.* tripler

triplet *n.* trijumeau *m.*, trijumelle *f.*; (mus.) triolet *m.*; **–s** *n. pl.* trois jumeaux

triplicate *n.* triple, triplicata *m.*; **in** — en triple (exemplaire)

tripod *n.* trépied *m.*; pied (à trois branches) *m.*

triptyque *n.* (auto.) triptyque *m.*

trite *a.* banal; **–ness** *n.* banalité *f.*

triumph *n.* triomphe *m.*; victoire *f.*; succès *m.*; — *vi.* triompher; — **over** triompher de; l'emporter sur; **–al** *a.* de triomphe; triomphal; **–ant** *a.* triomphant; de triomphe

triumvirate *n.* triumvirat *m.*

trivet *n.* trépied *m.*, chevrette *f.*

trivial *a.* trivial; sans importance, insignifiant; léger; **–ity** *n.* insignifiance *f.*

trochaic *a.* trochaïque

troche *n.* (med.) tablette *f.*

Trojan *n.* & *n.* Troyen *m.*

troll *n.* (fishing) moulinet *m.*; — *vi.* pêcher à la cuiller; **–ing** *n.* pêche à la cuiller *f.*

trolley *n.* trolley *m.*, poulie *f.*; (car) tram-way *m.*; chariot *m.*; — **bus** trolley-autobus *m.*

trollop *n.* souillon *f.*

troop *n.* troupe, bande *f.*; — *vi.* aller en troupe; s'attrouper; — **in** entrer en troupe; **–er** *n.* soldat, troupier *m.*

troopship *n.* transport militaire *m.*

trophy *n.* trophée *m.*

tropic *n.* tropique *m.*; **–al** *a.* tropical

trot *n.* trot *m.*; — *vi.* trotter, aller au trot; **–ter** *n.* cheval de trot *m.*

troubadour *n.* troubadour, trouvère *m.*

trouble *n.* difficulté *f.*; peine *f.*; ennui *m.*; trouble *m.*; **be in** — avoir des ennuis, avoir des difficultés; **be worth the** — to valoir la peine de; **take the** — to prendre la peine de; — *vt.* préoccuper, tourmenter, affliger, inquiéter; déranger, ennuyer, incommoder; donner de la peine à; troubler; — *vi.* s'inquiéter; se déranger; **–d** *a.* inquiet; trouble; **–some** *a.* difficile; ennuyeux, incommode

troublemaker *n.* fomentateur, fauteur *m.*

trough *n.* auge *f.*; baquet *m.*; abreuvoir

m.; (wave) creux *m.*

trounce *vt.* écraser; rosser

troupe *n.* troupe *f.*; **–r** *n.* (theater) membre d'une troupe *m.*

trousers *n. pl.* pantalon *m.*

trousseau *n.* trousseau *m.*

trout *n.* truite *f.*

trowel *n.* truelle *f.*; déplantoir *m.*

troy (weight) *n.* poids troy *m.*

Troy *n.* Troie *f.*

truant *n.* élève absent sans permission *m. & f.*

truce *n.* trève *f.*; **flag of —** drapeau parlementaire *m.*

truck *n.* camion *m.*, camionnette *f.*; wagon *m.*; chariot *m.*; affaire *f.*; rapports *m. pl.*; **— driver** camionneur *m.*; **— farm** jardin maraîcher *m.*; **—** *vt.* porter en camion; camionner; **–er** *n.* camionneur *m.* **–ing** *n.* camionnage *m.*

truculent *a.* truculent; féroce

trudge *vi.* marcher lourdement

true *a.* vrai, véritable; fidèle; juste; réel; **—** *adv.* vrai; juste; **come —** se réaliser; **hold —** en être de même; **—** *n.*, **out of —** hors d'aplomb; décentré; faussé; gauchi; **—** *vt.* ajuster; défausser, dégauchir

truism *n.* axiome, truisme *m.*

truly *adv.* vraiment, véritablement; en vérité; fidèlement

trump *n.* atout *m.*; **no —** sans-atout; **—** *vt.* couper; **— up** forger, inventer

trumpet *n.* trompette *f.*; **—** *vi.* sonner de la trompette; (elephant) barrir; **—** *vt. & vi.* proclamer; **–er** *n.* trompette *m.*; trompettiste *m.*

truncate *vt.* tronquer

truncheon *n.* gros bâton *m.*

trundle *n.* roulette *f.*; **—** *vt.* faire rouler; pousser

trunk *n.* (tree) tronc *m.*; (luggage) malle *f.*; (elephant) trompe *f.*; **— line** (rail.) ligne principale *f.*; (telephone) ligne interurbaine *f.*; **–s** *pl.* caleçon; caleçon de bain; cache-sexe *m.*

truss *n.* cintre *m.*; armature *f.*; bandage (herniaire) *m.*; **—** *vt.* armer, renforcer; lier, ligoter

trust *n.* confiance *f.*; crédit *m.*; charge *f.*; garde *f.*; syndicat, trust *m.*; **in —** en dépôt; **on —** à crédit; **—** *vt.* se fier à; confier; espérer; faire crédit à; **—** *vi.* se fier; se confier; **–ed** *a.* de confiance; fidèle; **–ful** *a.* confiant; **–ing** *a.* plein de confiance

trustee *n.* dépositaire *m.*; administrateur *m.*; curateur *m.*; **–ship** *n.* administration *f.*

trustworthiness *n.* fidélité, loyauté *f.*

trustworthy *a.* digne de foi, digne de confiance, fidèle

trusty *a.* fidèle, loyal, sûr

truth *n.* vérité *f.*; vrai *m.*; **in —, to tell the —** à vrai dire; **–ful** *a.* vrai; véridique; **–fulness** *n.* véracité; véridicité *f.*

try *n.* essai *m.*; **—** *vt.* essayer, tenter, tâcher; expérimenter; éprouver; mettre à l'épreuve; faire l'essai de; goûter; (law) juger; **—** *vi.* essayer, tâcher; **— on** essayer; **— out** essayer, mettre à l'épreuve; **–ing** *a.* pénible, dur, difficile; fatigant

tryout *n.* essai *m.*, épreuve *f.*

tryst *n.* rendez-vous *m.*, assignation *f.*

tub *n.* baquet *m.*, cuve *f.*, cuvier *m.*; (bath) baignoire *f.*; bain *m.*; **–by** *a.* boulot; gros

tube *n.* tube, tuyau *m.*; canal, conduit *m.*; (radio) lampe, ampoule *f.*; **inner —** chambre à air *f.*; **test —** éprouvette *f.*; **—** *vt.* tuber

tuber *n.* tubercule *m.*; tuberacée *f.*

tubercular *a.* tuberculeux

tuberculosis *n.* tuberculose *f.*

tuberous *a.* tubéreux

tubing *n.* tube, tuyau *m.*; tuyautage *m.*

tubular *a.* tubulaire; à tubes

tuck *n.* pli, rempli *m.*; troussis *m.*; **—** *vt.* plisser; remplier; raccourcir; rentrer; **— in** (bedding) rentrer; border

Tuesday *n.* mardi *m.*; **Shrove —** mardi gras *m.*

tuft *n.* (hair) touffe *f.*; (bird) houppe *f.*; mèche *f.*; pompon *m.*; flocon *m.*; huppe *f.*; aigrette *f.*; **—** *vt.* former en touffes **–ed** *a.* en touffe, en houppe, huppé

tug *n.* traction *f.*; serrement *m.*; (naut.) remorqueur *m.*; **— of war** lutte (de traction) à la corde *f.*; **—** *vt. & vi.*; tirer; tirailler

tugboat *n.* remorqueur *m.*

tuition *n.* (frais d') instruction *f.*, enseignement *m.*

tumble *n.* chute, culbute *f.*; **—** *vi.* faire une chute, tomber; faire des culbutes; s'agiter; **— into** se jeter dans; **— out of** sauter de; **–r** *n.* acrobate *m. & f.*; verre *m.*; (elec.) culbuteur *m.*; (lock) gorge *f.*

tumble-down *a.* délabré; qui tombe en ruines

tumescent *a.* tumescent

tumor *n.* tumeur *f.*

tumult *n.* tumulte, trouble *m.*; **–uous** *a.* tumultueux; turbulent

tun *n.* fût *m.*; tonne *f.*; (naut.) tonneau

tundra *n.* toundra *f.*

tune *n.* air *m.*; accord *m.*; **in —** (piano) d'accord, (engine) au point; **out of —** désaccordé; **—** *vt.* accorder, mettre d'accord; (radio) syntoniser **— in** accrocher;

accorder; — **up** s'accorder; (engine) mettre au point, régler; **-ful** a. harmonieux, mélodieux; **-r** n. accordeur m.

tungsten n. tungstène m.

tunic n. tunique f.

tuning n. accordage m.; mise au point f., réglage m.; **— fork** diapason m.

Tunis n. Tunis m.

Tunisia n. Tunisie f.

tunnel n. tunnel, souterrain m.; **— vt. & vi.** percer (un tunnel)

turbid a. trouble; **-ity** n. turbidité f.

turbojet n. turboréacteur m.

turbomotor n. turbomoteur m.

turbulence n. turbulence, agitation f.

turbulent a. turbulent, tumultueux

tureen n. soupière f.

turf n. gazon m.; turf m.

turgid a. turgide, enflé, ampoulé; **-ity** n. enflure, emphase f.

Turk n. Turc m., Turque f.; **-ey** n. Turquie f.; **-ish** a. turc, turque; **-ish bath(s)** hammam(s) m. (pl.); **-ish towel** serviette éponge f.

turkey n. dindon m., dinde f.

turmoil n. trouble m., agitation f.

turn n. tour m.; tournure f.; tournant m.; virage m.; service m.; (done) to a — (cuit) au point; **in —** tour à tour, à tour de rôle; **out of —** avant son tour; **— of mind** tour d'esprit m.; **— vt.** tourner, retourner; passer; **— vi.** tourner; se tourner, se retourner; changer, se changer; dépendre; devenir; **— around** tourner; se retourner; **— away** détourner; **— back** rebrousser chemin, retourner sur ses pas; repousser; **— down** retourner; refuser; repousser; baisser; (collar) rabattre; **— in** aller se coucher; **— off** fermer, éteindre, couper; tourner; **— on** ouvrir, allumer; se jeter sur; **— out** mettre dehors; retourner; produire, confectionner, fabriquer; éteindre, fermer, couper; tourner; arriver; paraître; se réunir, se rassembler; **— over** tourner, retourner; donner; capoter; **— up** relever; retrousser; retourner; trouver; arriver, se présenter; **-ing** a. tournant; **-ing** n. rotation f.; changement m.; virage m.; **-ing point** tournant m.; moment critique m.

turncoat n. renégat m.

turnip n. navet m.

turnout n. foule, assemblée f.

turnover n. changement m.; écoulement m.; **apple —** chausson aux pommes m.

turnpike n. grande route à péage f.

turnstile n. tourniquet m.

turntable n. plaque tournante f.; tourne-disques m.

turpentine n. térébenthine f.

turpitude n. turpitude f.

turret n. tourelle f.

turtle n. tortue f.

Tuscany n. Toscane f.

tusk n. défense, grosse dent f.

tussle n. lutte f.; mêlée f.; corps-à-corps m.; **— vi.** lutter

tutelage n. tutelle f.

tutor n. précepteur m.; **— vt.** instruire; donner des leçons particulières à; **-ial** a. individuel; particulier

tuxedo n. smoking m.

TV (television) n. télévision f.

twaddle n. balivernes f. pl.

twang n. son aigu m.; ton nasillard m.; **speak with a —** parler du nez; **— vt.** gratter, pincer; faire résonner; **— vi.** résonner, vibrer

tweak vt. pincer; tirer

tweed n. tweed m., cheviote f.

tweet n. pépiement m.; **— vi.** pépier

tweezers n. pl. pinces f. pl.; (hair) pinces à épiler f. pl.

twelfth a. douzième

twelve a. douze; une douzaine de; **— o'clock** (noon) midi; (midnight) minuit

twentieth a. vingtième

twenty a. vingt

twenty-one a. vingt et un

twice adv. deux fois

twiddle vt. (thumbs) tourner

twig n. brindille f.

twilight n. crépuscule m.

twill n. croisé m.

twin n. jumeau m., jumelle f.; **— beds** lits jumeaux m. pl.

twine n. ficelle f.; **— vt.** tordre; entrelacer; **— vi.** se tordre; s'enlacer

twin-engine (d) a. bimoteur

twinge n. élancement m.; **— vi.** élancer

twinkle n. scintillement m.; pétillement m.; lueur f.; **— vi.** scintiller; pétiller

twinkling n. scintillement m.; **— of an eye** clin d'œil m.

twirl vt. tortiller; (faire) tourner; faire des moulinets avec; **— vi.** tournoyer

twist n. torsion f.; tour m.; coude m.; cordon m.; tortillon m.; (tobacco) rouleau m.; **— of the wrist** tour de poignet m.; **— vt.** tordre; tortiller; **— vi.** se tordre; se tortiller; tourner; serpenter; **— one's ankle** se donner une entorse; **-ed** a. tordu; **-er** n. (coll.) tornade f.; **-ing** a. tortueux

twit vt. railler; taquiner

twitch n. tic m., crispation f.; (pain) élancement m.; **— vt.** crisper, contracter; **— vi.** se crisper, se contracter; avoir un tic

twitter n. gazouillement m.; émotion f.; **—**

vi. gazouiller

two *a.* deux

two-edged *a.* à deux tranchants

two-faced *a.* hypocrite; à deux visages

two-fisted *a.* (coll.) fort, vigoureux

twofold *a.* double

two-handed *a.* à deux mains

two-legged *a.* bipède

two-piece *a.* en deux pièces

two-seater *n.* voiture à deux places *f.*

two-step *n.* pas de deux *m.*

two-way *a.* (street) à deux sens

tycoon *n.* magnat industriel *m.*

type *n.* type *m.*; genre *m.*; (print.) caractère *m.*; set — composer; — *vt.* écrire à la machine, dactylographier, taper

typesetter *n.* compositeur *m.*

typesetting *n.* composition *f.*

typewriter *n.* machine à écrire *f.*

typhoid *a.* typhoïde; — **fever** fièvre typhoïde *f.*

typhoon *n.* typhon *m.*

typhus *n.* typhus *m.*

typical *a.* typique, caractéristique; **-ly** *adv.* d'une manière typique

typify *vt.* être caractéristique de; représenter, symboliser

typist *n.* dactylographe, dactylo *m. & f.*

typographer *n.* typographe *m.*

typographic(al) *a.* typographique

typography *n.* typographie *f.*

tyrannical *a.* tyrannique

tyrannize *vt.* tyranniser; — *vi.* faire le tyran

tyranny *n.* tyrannie *f.*

tyrant *n.* tyran *m.*

U

ubiquitous *a.* qui se trouve partout

udder *n.* mamelle *f.*; pis *m.*

ugliness *n.* laideur *f.*

ugly *a.* laid

ulcer *n.* ulcère *m.*; **-ate** *vt.* ulcérer; **-ation** *n.* ulcération *f.*; **-ous** *a.* ulcéreux

ulna *n.* cubitus *m.*

ulterior *a.* ultérieur; — **motive** arrière-pensée *f.*, motif caché *m.*

ultimate *a.* final; dernier; décisif; **-ly** *adv.* en fin de compte

ultimatum *n.* ultimatum *m.*

ultra *a.* extrême

umbilical *a.* ombilical

umbrage *n.* ombrage *m.*; **take** — s'offenser

umbrella *n.* parapluie *m.*; — **stand** porte-parapluies *m.*

umpire *n.* arbitre *m.*; — *vt.* arbitrer

umpiring *n.* arbitrage *m.*

unabashed *a.* sans être décontenancé

unabated *a.* non-diminué

unabating *a.* soutenu

unable *a.* incapable; impuissant; **be** — ne pas pouvoir

unabridged *a.* intégral, non abrégé

unaccented *a.* sans accent; atone

unacceptable *a.* inacceptable

unaccommodating *a.* peu accommodant; désobligeant

unaccompanied *a.* seul, inaccompagné; (mus.) sans accompagnement

unaccomplished *a.* inaccompli, inachevé; qui manque de talent

unaccountable *a.* inexplicable

unaccounted *a.*, — **for** inexpliqué; disparu, perdu; qui manque

unaccredited *a.* non-accrédité

unaccustomed *a.* peu habitué; inaccoutumé

unacknowledged *a.* non-reconnu; (letter) sans réponse

unacquainted *a.*, **be** — **with** ignorer; ne pas connaître

unaddressed *a.* sans adresse

unadorned *a.* sans parure, sans ornement; pur, simple

unadulterated *a.* naturel, pur, san mélange

unadvisable *a.* peu sage; imprudent

unaffected *a.* sans affectation, sans pose; sans recherche; sincère; réfractaire; qui n'est pas changé

unaffiliated *a.* non-affilié

unaided *a.* sans aide

unalloyed *a.* sans alliage, pur

unalterable *a.* immuable

unaltered *a.* sans changement

unambitious *a.* sans ambition

unanimous *a.* unanime; **-ly** *adv.* unanimement; à l'unanimité

unannounced *a.* sans se faire annoncer

unanswerable *a.* sans réponse, sans réplique

unanticipated *a.* imprévu

unappeased *a.* inapaisé

unappetizing *a.* peu appétissant

unappreciated *a.* inapprecié; méconnu

unappreciative *a.* insensible; qui manque de discernement

unapproachable *a.* inabordable, inaccessible

unarmed *a.* sans armes

unashamed *a.* sans honte; éhonté

unasked *a.* non-demandé; sans être invité

unassailable *a.* inattaquable

unassimilated *a.* inassimilé

unassisted *a.* sans aide

unassuming *a.* sans prétention, modeste

unattached *a.* indépendant; libre; qui n'est pas attaché

unattainable *a.* impossible à atteindre; inaccessible

unattended *a.* seul, sans être accompagné

unattractive *a.* peu attrayant; peu sympathique; laid

unauthorized *a.* sans autorisation, inautorisé

unavailing *a.* inutile

unavoidable *a.* inévitable

unavoidably *adv.* inévitablement

unavowed *a.* inavoué

unaware *adv.* ignorant; **be — of** ignorer; **—s** *adv.* à l'improviste; par inadvertance

unbalance *vt.* déséquilibrer **—d** *a.* instable, non balancé

unbearable *a.* insupportable; intolérable

unbeatable *a.* invincible

unbeaten *a.* non-battu

unbecoming *a.* peu convenable; déplacé; qui ne va pas bien

unbeknown *a.* inconnu; **—** *adv.* à l'insu (de)

unbelievable *a.* incroyable

unbeliever *n.* incrédule *m. & f.*

unbelieving *a.* incrédule

unbend *vt.* détendre; redresser; **—** *vi.* se détendre; se déraidir; **—ing** *a.* ferme, inflexible

unbiased *a.* impartial; sans prévention, sans parti pris

unbidden *a.* sans être invité

unblemished *a.* sans tache; sans défaut

unblock *vt.* désencombrer

unbolt *vt.* déverrouiller

unborn *a.* pas encore né; à venir

unbound *a.* délié; (hair) dénoué; (books) non-relié; **—ed** *a.* illimité, sans bornes; démesuré

unbreakable *a.* incassable; inébranlable

unbridled *a.* débridé; effréné

unbroken *a.* non-cassé, non-brisé; intact; indompté; non-rompu; continu

unbuckle *vt.* déboucler

unburden *vt.* soulager, alléger

unburied *a.* non-enterré; déterré

unbusinesslike *a.* irrégulier; peu organisé

unbutton *vt.* déboutonner

uncalled *a.* non-appelé; **— for** déplacé, mal à propos; immérité

uncanny *a.* mystérieux, étrange; inquiétant

uncared-for *a.* délaissé; à l'abandon

unceasing *a.* continu, incessant; soutenu; **—ly** *adv.* sans cesse

uncensored *a.* non-expurgé

unceremonious *a.* sans façon

uncertain *a.* incertain; douteux; indéterminé; mal assuré; **—ty** *n.* incertitude *f.*

uncertified *a.* non-diplômé

unchain *vt.* déchaîner

unchallenged *a.* indisputé; sans être con-

tredit

unchangeable *a.* immuable, invariable

unchanged *a.* toujours le même; inchangé

unchanging *a.* immuable, invariable

uncharitable *a.* peu charitable

uncharted *a.* qui ne se trouve pas sur la carte

unchecked *a.* sans frein; non verifié

unchivalrous *a.* peu courtois

unchristened *a.* non baptisé

unchristian *a.* peu chrétien; infidèle

uncivil *a.* incivil, impoli; **—ized** *a.* incivilisé; barbare

unclaimed *a.* non-réclamé; **— letter** lettre de rebut *f.*

unclasp *vt.* défaire, dégrafer; desserrer

uncle *n.* oncle *m.*

unclean *a.* malpropre; impur; **—liness** *n.* saleté, malpropreté *f.*

unclench *vt.* desserrer

unclothed *a.* déshabillé, nu, sans vêtements

uncock *vt.* désarmer

uncoil *vt.* dérouler

uncolored *a.* non-coloré; incolore

uncombed *a.* non-peigné, mal peigné

uncomfortable *a.* mal à l'aise, inquiet; incommode; peu confortable; gênant, désagréable

uncommon *a.* peu commun; peu ordinaire; rare

uncommunicative *n.* peu communicatif

uncomplimentary *a.* peu flatteur

uncompromising *a.* intransigeant; absolu

unconcern *n.* indifférence, insouciance *f.*; **—ed** *a.* indifférent, insouciant, dégagé

unconditional *a.* sans condition(s); catégorique; inconditionnel

unconfirmed *a.* non-confirmé

uncongenial *a.* peu sympathique

unconnected *a.* sans rapport; sans suite

unconquerable *a.* invincible; insurmontable

unconquered *a.* non-vaincu; indompté

unconscionable *a.* sans conscience

unconscious *a.* sans connaissance; inconscient; **be —** être sans connaissance; **be — of** ignorer; **—ly** *adv.* inconsciemment; **—ness** *n.* inconscience *f.*; évanouissement *m.*

unconsidered *a.* inconsidéré

unconstitutional *a.* inconstitutionnel

unconstrained *a.* spontané; désinvolte

uncontested *a.* incontesté

uncontrollable *a.* irrésistible, ingouvernable

uncontrolled *a.* sans frein; indépendant

unconventional *a.* original

unconvinced *a.* non-convaincu; sceptique

unconvincing *a.* peu convaincant

uncooked *a.* non-cuit; cru

uncork *vt.* déboucher; **–ed** *a.* sans bouchon; débouché

uncouple *vt.* découpler; débrayer

uncouth *a.* grossier, rude; malappris; **–ness** *n.* rudesse *f.*; grossièreté *f.*

uncover *vt.* découvrir

uncrowned *a.* sans couronne, non-couronné

unction *n.* onction *f.*; **extreme —** extrême-onction *f.*

unctuous *a.* onctueux; grasseux; **–ness** *n.* onctuosité *f.*

uncultivated *a.* inculte; peu cultivé

uncultured *a.* incultivé

uncurbed *a.* sans frein, débridé; libre

uncured *a.* non-guéri

uncut *a.* non-coupé, non-taillé

undamaged *a.* non-endommagé; indemne

undated *a.* sans date, non-daté

undaunted *a.* intrépide

undeceive *vt.* détromper, désabuser, non-trompé

undecided *a.* indécis; hésitant

undecipherable *a.* indéchiffrable

undefeated *a.* invaincu

undefended *a.* sans défense

undefinable *a.* indéfinissable

undefined *a.* indeterminé, indéfini; vague

undelivered *a.* non-délivré; non livré

undemonstrative *a.* réservé, peu démonstratif

undeniable *a.* incontestable, indéniable

undeniably *adv.* incontestablement

under *prep.* sous, au-dessous de; **— lock and key** sous clef; **— repair** en réparation; **— the circumstances** dans les circonstances; **—** *a.* inférieur; de dessous; **—** *adv.* dessous, au-dessous

underage *a.* mineur

underbid *vt.* offrir moins que, demander moins cher que; (cards) demander au-dessous des valeurs

underbrush *n.* broussailles *f. pl.*

undercarriage *n.* dessous, châssis *m.*

undercharge *vt.* accepter trop peu d'argent, ne pas faire payer assez

underclothes, underclothing *n.* vêtements de dessous *m. pl.*, linge *m.*, lingerie *f.*

undercover *a.* secret, clandestin

undercurrent *n.* courant (de fond) *m.*

undercut *vt.* vendre moins cher que; couper

underdeveloped *a.* insuffisamment développé

underdog *n.* opprimé *m.*; concurrent dont les chances sont peu favorables *m.*; perdant probable *m.*

underdone *a.* pas assez cuit

underestimate *vt.* sous-estimer, faire trop peu de cas de

underexposed *a.* (phot.) qui manque de pose

underexposure *n.* (phot.) manque de pose *m.*

underfed *a.* mal nourri, sous-alimenté

undergarment *n.* sous-vêtement *m.*

undergo *vt.* subir; essuyer, éprouver

undergraduate *n.* (America) étudiant de collège *n.*

underground *a.* souterrain; **—** *adv.* sous terre, sous le sol; **—** *n.* (rail.) métro *m.*, chemin de fer souterrain *m.*; (war) résistance *f.*; maquis *m.*

undergrowth *n.* sous-bois *m.*; broussailles *f. pl.*

underhand(ed) *a.* clandestin, secret; sournois; (sports) par en dessous; **—** *adv.* en secret; sous main, sournoisement; par en dessous

underlie *vt.* être au fond de, être à la base de

underline *vt.* souligner

underling *n.* subalterne, subordonné *m.*

underlying *a.* fondamental

undermanned *a.* à court de personnel; à court d'équipage

undermentioned *a.* sous-mentionné

undermost *a.* le plus bas

undermine *vt.* miner, saper; (fig.) détruire

underneath *prep.* sous, au-dessous de; **—** *a.* inférieur; de dessous; **—** *adv.* dessous, au-dessous

undernourished *a.* sous-alimenté, mal nourri

underpaid *a.* mal payé, mal rétribué

underpass *n.* passage souterrain *m.*

underpin *vt.* étayer, étançonner; **–ning** *n.* étayage, étançonnement *m.*

underprivileged *a.* nécessiteux, indigent; déshérité

underrate *vt.* sous-estimer, faire trop peu de cas de; mal juger

undersea *a.* sous-marin

undersecretary *n.* sous-secrétaire *m.*

undersell *vt.* vendre moins cher que, vendre à meilleur marché que

undershirt *n.* gilet, tricot *m.*

undersigned *a.* soussigné

undersized *a.* petit, trop petit; moins grand que les autres

underskirt *n.* jupon *m.*

understand *vt.* comprendre; se rendre compte de; savoir; connaître; s'entendre; **–able** *a.* compréhensible; **that is –able** cela se comprend; **–ing** *a.* qui comprend; sympathique; **–ing** *n.* compréhension, appréhension *f.*; entendement *m.*; intelligence *f.*, jugement *m.*; accord *m.*, entente *f.*; **have an –ing with** être d'intelligence avec; **on the** –ing that à condition que

understate vt. amoindrir; –**ment** n. amoindrissement m.

understood a. compris; entendu, convenu; qui va sans dire

understudy n. doublure f.; — vt. doubler

undertake vt. entreprendre; se charger de; –**r** n. entrepreneur de pompes funèbres m.

undertaking n. entreprise f.; affaire f.

undertone n. ton bas m.; **in an** — à demivoix

undertow n. contre-marée f., ressac m.

undervalue vt. sous-évaluer, sous-estimer; déprécier

underwear n. sous-vêtements m. pl., linge m., lingerie f.

underweight a. qui manque de poids; trop maigre

underworld n. bas-fonds m. pl., enfers m. pl.

underwrite vt. souscrire, garantir; –**r** n. assureur m.; –**rs** n. pl. syndicat de garantie m.

undeserved a. immérité; injuste; –**ly** adv. à tort, injustement

undeserving a. indigne; peu méritant, sans mérite

undesirable a. peu désirable, indésirable

undetected a. inaperçu

undetermined a. indécis, indéterminé

undeterred a. non-découragé

undeveloped a. a. inexploité; non-développé

undeviating a. constant, fidèle; droit

undigested a. mal digéré; indigeste

undignified a. peu digne, qui manque de dignité

undiluted a. pur; concentré; non dilué

undiminished a. non diminué

undiplomatic a. peu diplomatique; indiscret

undiscernible a. imperceptible

undiscerning a. peu pénétrant; sans discernement

undisciplined a. indiscipliné

undiscovered a. inconnu; caché; non-découvert

undiscriminating a. sans goût, sans discernement

undisguised a. non-déguisé; ouvert; –**ly** adv. ouvertement, franchement

undismayed a. non-découragé; sans perdre de courage; sans peur

undisputed a. incontesté, indisputé

undistinguished a. obscur; médiocre

undistinguishable a. indistinguible

undisturbed a. tranquille, paisible, calme; non dérangé

undivided a. indivisé, entier; non-partagé; unanime

undo vt. défaire; dénouer; réparer; –**ing** n. ruine, perte f.

undone a. défait; ruiné; perdu; inaccompli, inachevé

undoubtedly adv. sans (aucun) doute; indubitablement

undraped a. nu

undress n. déshabillé m.; — vt. déshabiller, dévêtir; — vi. se déshabiller, se dévêtir; –**ed** a. déshabillé, dévêtu; (manufacturing) brut, non-preparé; (cooking) au naturel

undrinkable a. impotable, inbuvable

undue a. indû; peu justifié; illégitime

undulate vi. ondoyer, onduler

unduly adv. indûment; trop; à l'excès

undutiful a. peu fidèle à ses devoirs

undying a. immortel

unearned a. non gagné; immérité

unearth vt. déterrer; –**ly** a. sinistre, surnaturel

uneasiness n. inquiétude f.; malaise m.

uneasy a. inquiet; agité; mal à l'aise

uneducated a. qui manque d'instruction

unemotional a. impassible, peu émotionnable

unemployed a. sans travail; désœuvré; — **person** chômeur m.

unemployment n. chômage m.

unencumbered a. non-encombré, non-embarrassé, débarrassé

unending a. interminable, sans fin

unendurable a. insupportable

unenterprising a. peu entreprenant

unenviable a. peu enviable

unequal a. inégal; irrégulier; au-dessous de; –**led** a. sans égal; inégalé

unequivocal a. sans équivôque; clair

unerring a. infaillible

unessential a. non-essentiel

uneven a. inégal; irrégulier; (number) impair; (terrain) accidenté; –**ness** n. inégalité f.

uneventful a. calme, sans incident(s); monotone

unexcelled c. que l'on n'a pas surpassé

unexciting a. ennuyeux; monotone; peu passionnant

unexpected a. inattendu; imprévu; inopiné; inespéré

unexpired a. non-périmé

unexplained a. inexpliqué

unexploded a. non-éclaté

unexplored a. inexploré

unexposed a. (phot.) vierge

unexpurgated a. intégral, non expurgé

unfading a. impérissable

unfailing a. infaillible, certain, sûr

unfair *a.* injuste; inéquitable; **-ness** *n.* injustice *f.*

unfaithful *a.* infidèle; déloyal; inexact; **-ness** *n.* infidélité *f.*; inexactitude *f.*

unfaltering *a.* assuré, ferme

unfamiliar *a.* peu familier; inconnu; be — with ne pas connaître; ignorer; **-ity** *n.* manque de connaissance *f.*; ignorance *f.*

unfashionable *a.* qui n'est pas à la mode; démodé

unfasten *vt.* détacher; défaire

unfathomable *a.* insondable; impénétrable

unfavorable *a.* peu favorable; défavorable; désavantageux; (wind) impropice

unfeasible *a.* impraticable

unfeeling *a.* insensible

unfeigned *a.* non-simulé; franc, sincère

unfettered *a.* libre, sans entraves

unfilled *a.* non-rempli, vide

unfinished *a.* inachevé

unfit *a.* incapable; inapte; impropre; indigne; **-ness** *n.* incapacité *f.*; inaptitude; **-ting** *a.* peu convenable; mal à propos; déplacé

unflagging *a.* infatigable

unflattering *a.* peu flatteur

unflinching *a.* qui ne bronche pas

unfold *vt.* déplier; dérouler; exposer; — *vi.* se dérouler

unforseen *a.* imprévu, inattendu

unforgettable *a.* inoubliable

unforgivable *a.* impardonnable

unforgiving *a.* implacable

unfortified *a.* sans fortifications, non-fortifié, ouvert

unfortunate *a.* infortuné, malheureux; regrettable; **-ly** *adv.* malheureusement, par malheur

unfounded *a.* sans fondement

unfrequented *a.* peu fréquenté; écarté

unfriendliness *n.* manque d'amitié *m.*; hostilité *f.*

unfriendly *a.* peu amical; hostile; mal disposé

unfrock *vt.* défroquer

unfruitful *a.* peu fructueux; inutile

unfulfilled *a.* non-satisfait; inaccompli

unfurl *vt.* déployer; (naut.) déferler

unfurnished *a.* non-meublé

ungainly *a. & adv.* maladroit, gauche

ungenerous *a.* peu généreux

ungentlemanly *a.* mal élevé; peu comme il faut

unglazed *a.* non-glacé; non-verni; mat

ungodliness *n.* impiété *f.*

ungraceful *a.* sans grâce, disgracieux; gauche

ungracious *a.* de mauvaise grâce, malgracieux, mal vu; **-ness** *n.* mauvaise grâce *f.*

ungrammatical *a.* peu grammatical

ungrateful *a.* ingrat, peu reconnaissant; **-ness** *n.* ingratitude *f.*, manque de reconnaissance *m.*

ungratified *a.* non-satisfait; inassouvi

ungrounded *a.* sans fondement

ungrudging *a.* libéral, généreux

unguarded *a.* sans défense; non-gardé; inattentif; indiscret

unguent *n.* onguent *m.*

unhallowed *a.* profane; non-béni

unhampered *a.* libre, qui n'est pas gêné

unhand *vt.* lâcher; **-y** *a.* maladroit, gauche

unhappily *adv.* tristement; malheureusement

unhappiness *n.* chagrin *m.*, tristesse *f.*; malheur *m.*

unhappy *a.* triste; malheureux, infortuné; peu content, mécontent

unharmed *a.* sain et sauf; intact

unhealthiness *n.* insalubrité *f.*

unhealthy *a.* malsain, insalubre; maladif

unheard-of *a.* inouï; inconnu

unheeded *a.* inaperçu; négligé

unheeding *a.* inattentif; insouciant

unhesitating *a.* résolu, qui n'hésite pas; **-ly** *adv.* sans hésitation, sans hésiter

unhindered *a.* sans obstacle, sans empêchement

unhook *vt.* décrocher; dégrafer

unhoped *a.*, — for inespéré

unhorse *vt.* démonter

unhurt *a.* sain et sauf; sans mal; intact

unidentified *a.* non-identifié; inconnu

unification *n.* unification *f.*

uniform *a.* uniforme, régulier; — *n.* uniforme *m.*; costume *m.*; tenue *f.*; **-ity** *n.* uniformité, régularité *f.*; unité *f.*; **-ly** *adv.* uniformément

unify *vt.* unifier

unilateral *a.* unilatéral

unimaginable *a.* inimaginable

unimaginative *a.* qui manque d'imagination

unimpaired *a.* non-altéré, non affaibli, non-diminué; intact

unimpeachable *a.* inattaquable, sûr

unimpeded *a.* sans empêchement

unimportant *a.* peu important, sans importance

unimpressed *a.* impassible, froid; peu impressionné

unimpressive *a.* peu imposant, peu impressionnant; ordinaire, médiocre

uninformed *a.* ignorant; be — ignorer; ne pas connaître

uninhabitable *a.* inhabitable

uninhabited *a.* inhabité

uninitiated *a.* non-initié

uninjured *a.* non-blessé; sain et sauf; sans

mal; intact

uninspired a. sans inspiration

uninsured a. non-assuré

unintelligible a. inintelligible

unintentional a. involontaire; fait par inadvertance

uninterested a. non-intéressé; qui ne s'intéresse pas

uninteresting a. peu intéressant, sans intérêt

uninterrupted a. ininterrompu; suivi

uninvited a. sans être invité; inconvivié

uninviting a. peu engageant; peu appétissant

union n. union f.; (labor) syndicat m.; **−ism** n. syndicalisme m.; **−ist** n. syndicaliste m. & f., syndiqué m.; **−ize** vt. syndicaliser

Union of South Africa n. Union de l'Afrique du Sud f.

unison n. unisson m.; **in** — à l'unisson; de concert

unit n. unité f.; élément m.

Unitarian a. & n. unitarien m.

unite vt. unir; unifier; joindre; — vi. s'unir, se joindre; se confédérer; se combiner; **−d** a. uni; unique; réuni

United Arab Republic n. République Arabe Unie f.

United Nations n. Nations Unies f. pl.

United States n. Etats-Unis m. pl.

unity n. unité f.; concorde f., accord m.

univalent a. monovalent, univalent

universal a. universel

universe n. univers m.

university n. université f.; — a. universitaire

unjust a. injuste

unjustifiable a. injustifiable

unjustified a. non justifié

unkempt a. mal peigné; dépeigné; mal tenu

unkind a. peu aimable; cruel; méchant; **−ly** a. peu aimable; peu favorable; **−ly** adv. cruellement, méchamment; **−ness** n. manque de bienveillance m.; méchanceté f.

unknowing a. ignorant; **−ly** adv. sans le savoir

unknown a. inconnu; ignoré; obscur; — **to** à l'insu de; — n. inconnu m.; (math.) inconnue f.

unknot vt. dénouer, défaire

unlace vt. délacer, défaire

unlawful a. illégal, illicite

unleash vt. lâcher

unleavened a. sans levain; azyme; — **bread** azyme m.

unless conj. à moins que; si

unlettered a. illettré, peu lettré

unlicensed a. non-autorisé; sans patente

unlike a. différent; peu ressemblant; dissemblable; **−lihood** n. improbabilité, invraisemblance f.; **−ly** a. peu probable, invraisemblable

unlimited a. illimité; sans bornes

unload vt. décharger; **−ed** a. déchargé; non chargé; **−ing** n. déchargement m.

unlock vt. ouvrir

unlooked a., — **for** inattendu

unlucky a. malheureux, infortuné; de mauvais augure

unmanageable a. intraitable; indocile

unmanly a. indigne d'un homme; peu viril

unmannerly a. mal élevé, impoli, grossier

unmarked a. non-marqué; sans marque; sans blessure

unmarketable a. invendable

unmarried a. non-marié, célibataire

unmask vt. démasquer; dévoiler

unmatched a. sans égal, incomparable, sans pareil

unmentionable a. dont on ne doit pas parler

unmerciful a. impitoyable

unmerited a. non-mérité, immérité

unmindful a. négligent, oublieux

unmistakable a. clair, évident

unmistakably adv. clairement, évidemment

unmixed a. sans mélange; sans alliage; pur

unmolested a. sans être molesté, sans obstacle

unmoved a. impassible; inflexible

unnamed a. anonyme; sans nom

unnatural a. contre nature; non-naturel; (laugh) forcé

unnavigable a. innavigable

unnecessarily adv. sans nécessité, inutilement

unnecessary a. inutile, superflu, peu nécessaire

unneeded a. dont on n'a pas besoin; peu nécessaire

unneighborly a. de mauvais voisin

unnerve vt. démonter

unnoticed a. inaperçu, inobservé

unobservant a. inattentif, peu observateur

unobserved a. inobservé, inaperçu

unobstructed a. non-encombré, libre

unobtainable a. qui est impossible à obtenir

unobtrusive a. effacé; discret

unoccupied a. libre, disponible; inoccupé; inhabité

unofficial a. non-officiel; non confirmé

unopened a. (letter) non-décacheté

unopposed a. sans opposition

unorthodox a. peu orthodoxe; original

unostentatious *a.* sans faste; simple
unpack *vt.* défaire; dépaqueter
unpaid *a.* non-payé; sans traitement; non-acquitté
unpalatable *a.* désagréable, dégoûtant
unparalleled *a.* sans pareil; sans précédent
unpardonable *a.* impardonnable
unpatriotic *a.* peu patriotique; (person) peu patriote
unpaved *a.* non-pavé
unperceivable *a.* imperceptible
unperceived *a.* inaperçu
unperturbed *a.* peu ému; froid; impassible
unpin *vt.* défaire
unpitying *a.* impitoyable
unplaced *a.* sans place, non-placé
unplayable *a.* injouable
unpleasant *a.* désagréable; déplaisant; peu aimable; **−ness** *n.* chose désagréable *f.*; nature désagréable *f.*
unpleasing *a.* désagréable, peu agréable
unpolished *a.* non-poli; rude, grossier
unpolluted *a.* non-pollué; pur; sain
unpopular *a.* impopulaire; **−ity** *n.* impopularité *f.*
unpracticed *a.* inexpérimenté
unprecedented *a.* sans précédent, sans exemple; inouï
unprejudiced *a.* sans préjugés, sans prévention, impartial
unpremeditated *a.* non-prémédité
unprepared *a.* non-préparé; improvisé; sans préparation
unprepossessing *a.* peu engageant
unpresuming *a.* sans présomption
unpretentious *a.* modeste, sans prétention(s)
unprincipled *a.* sans principes; sans mœurs
unprocurable *a.* impossible à obtenir
unproductive *a.* improductif; stérile
unprofitable *a.* inutile; peu profitable, improfitable; peu lucratif
unpromising *a.* qui ne promet rien; qui s'annonce mal
unprompted *a.* spontané
unpropitious *a.* défavorable, impropice
unprotected *a.* sans protection, non-protégé, sans défense; exposé
unproved *a.* non-prouvé, improuvé; inéprouvé
unprovided *a.* dépourvu; **— for** *a.* sans ressources
unprovoked *a.* non-provoqué, improvoqué
unpublished *a.* non-publié; inédit
unpunished *a.* impuni
unqualified *a.* incapable; incompétent; sans réserve, catégorique
unquenchable *a.* inassouvissable
unquestionable *a.* incontestable, indubitable, indiscutable
unquestioned *a.* incontesté, indisputé
unquestioning *a.* sans question
unravel *vt.* effiler; débrouiller; — *vi.* s'effiler; se débrouiller
unread *a.* non-lu; illettré
unreadable *a.* illisible
unreal *a.* irréel; imaginaire
unreasonable *a.* déraisonnable, peu raisonnable
unrecognizable *a.* méconnaissable
unrecognized *a.* non-reconnu; méconnu
unreconcilable *a.* irréconciliable
unreconciled *a.* irréconcilié
unrecorded *a.* non-enregistré; qui n'est pas mentionné
unredeemed *a.* non-racheté; non dégagé
unrefined *a.* non-raffiné; grossier, peu raffiné
unregistered *a.* non-enregistré; non-inscrit
unrehearsed *a.* spontané; sans répétition(s)
unrelated *a.* sans rapport; non-apparenté
unrelenting *a.* implacable, inflexible
unreliability *n.* inexactitude *f.*; manque de fidélité *m.*
unreliable *a.* peu fidèle; sur lequel on ne peut pas compter
unremitting *a.* soutenu, ininterrompu
unremunerative *a.* peu lucratif, peu rémunérateur
unrepentant *a.* impénitent
unrequited *a.* non-partagé; non récompensé
unreserved *a.* sans réserve, franc; non réservé; complet
unresponsive *a.* peu sensible; impassible; froid
unrest *n.* agitation *f.*; inquiétude *f.*
unrestrained *a.* libre; non-restreint
unrestricted *a.* sans restriction; absolu
unrevenged *a.* non-vengé, invengé
unrewarded *a.* sans récompense
unripe *a.* vert, qui n'est pas mûr
unrivaled *a.* sans rival; sans pareil
unroll *vt.* dérouler; — *vi.* se dérouler
unromantic *a.* peu sentimental; peu romanesque
unruffled *a.* calme; imperturbable
unruly *a.* intraitable, insoumis
unsaddle *vt.* desseller; désarçonner
unsafe *a.* peu sûr; dangereux
unsanitary *a.* non-hygiénique
unsatisfactory *a.* peu satisfaisant
unsatisfied *a.* peu satisfait, mécontent
unsatisfying *a.* peu satisfaisant
unscathed *a.* sans blessure; sain et sauf; intact
unscientific *a.* peu scientifique

unscrew *vt.* dévisser

unscrupulous *a.* peu scrupuleux; sans scrupule

unseal *vt.* desceller; décacheter

unseasonable *a.* hors de saison; mal à propos

unseasoned *a.* non-assaisonné; inexpérimenté; (wood) vert

unseat *vt.* (horseman) démonter, désarçonner; (pol.) invalider

unsecured *a.* mal assujetti; non-garanti

unseeing *a.* aveugle

unseemliness *n.* inconvenance *f.*

unseemly *a.* peu convenable; malséant

unseen *a.* invisible; inaperçu

unselfish *a.* désintéressé; altruiste; **−ness** *n.* désintéressement *m.*

unserviceable *a.* inutilisable

unsettle *vt.* troubler; déranger; **−d** *a.* troublé, inquiet; dérangé; indécis; non colonisé; (bill) non-réglé, impayé

unshakeable *a.* inébranlable, ferme

unshaken *a.* inébranlé, ferme

unshapely *a.* difforme; informe; mal fait

unshaven *a.* non-rasé

unsheathe *vt.* dégainer

unsheltered *a.* sans abri; exposé

unsightly *a.* désagréable à la vue; laid; sale

unsigned *a.* non-signé

unsinkable *a.* insubmersible

unskilful *a.* malhabile, inhabile; maladroit

unskilled *a.* inexpert; inexpérimenté; **—** labor main-d'œuvre *f.*

unsociable *a.* insociable; peu aimable, peu amical

unsoiled *a.* sans tache

unsold *a.* invendu

unsolicited *a.* non-sollicité; spontané

unsolved *a.* non-expliqué; non-résolu

unsophisticated *a.* simple, ingénu; naïf

unsound *a.* malsain, non-sain, maladif; peu solide; mauvais, faible, peu convaincant; **−ness** *n.* manque de solidité *m.*; faiblesse *f.*

unsparing *a.* prodigue; impitoyable; infatigable

unspeakable *a.* inexprimable, indicible

unspecified *a.* non-spécifié

unspoiled *a.* non-gâté

unspoken *a.* non-prononcé; tacite

unsportsmanlike *a.* peu loyal, antisportif

unstable *a.* instable; inconstant

unstained *a.* sans tache; non-teint

unstamped *a.* non-affranchi, sans timbre

unsteadiness *n.* instabilité *f.*; irrésolution *f.*; irrégularité *f.*

unsteady *a.* peu solide, instable; irrésolu; irrégulier; (step) chancelant; (voice) mal assuré

unstrap *vt.* déboucler

unstressed *a.* sans accent; inaccentué

unstring *vt.* (fig.) détraquer

unsubdued *a.* insoumis; indompté

unsubsidized *a.* sans subvention

unsuccessful *a.* manqué, raté; sans succès; non réussi; refusé; **be —** échouer; **−ly** *adv.* sans succès

unsuitable *a.* qui ne convient pas; peu convenable; inopportun; peu fait, inapte; **−ness** *n.* inaptitude *f.*; inopportunité *f.*

unsuited *a.* peu fait, inapte; mal adapté

unsullied *a.* sans tache, sans souillure

unsupported *a.* sans soutien, sans appui

unsurpassed *a.* sans égal, sans pareil

unsuspected *a.* non-suspect; insourçonné

unsuspecting, unsuspicious *a.* sans défiance, sans soupçons; qui ne se doute pas

unsweetened *a.* non-sucré

unswerving *a.* ferme, constant; qui ne s'écarte pas

unsymmetrical *a.* sans symétrie; asymétrique

unsympathetic *a.* peu compatissant; indifférent; peu sympathique

unsystematic *a.* sans méthode; sans système

untainted *a.* non-gâté; non-corrompu

untalented *a.* sans talent(s)

untamed *a.* non-apprivoisé; indompté

untapped *a.* (fig.) inutilisé

untarnished *a.* non-terni; (fig.) sans tache

untenable *a.* insoutenable; intenable

untenanted *a.* inhabité, inoccupé

untested *a.* pas encore mis à l'épreuve; inéprouvé, inessayé

unthinkable *a.* inconcevable, inimaginable

unthinking *a.* irréfléchi

untidiness *n.* désordre *m.*; malpropreté *f.*

untidy *a.* en désordre; négligé; malpropre

untie *vt.* délier, détacher, défaire, dénouer, déficeler

until *prep.* jusqu' à; **—** *conj.* jusqu'à ce que; **wait —** attendre que

untilled *a.* non-labouré; inculte, incultivé

untimely *a.* inopportun, mal à propos; hors de saison; indu; prématuré

untiring *a.* infatigable, inlassable

unto *prep.* à; vers; jusqu'à

untold *a.* non-compté; énorme; incalculable; inouï

untouchable *n.* hors-caste *m.*

untouched *a.* intact; sain et sauf; indifférent; non-discuté

untoward *a.* incommode; malheureux, fâcheux; malséant

untraceable *a.* introuvable

untrained *a.* inexpert, inexpérimenté, inexercé; (animal) non-dressé

untranslatable *a.* intraduisible

untraveled *a.* qui n'a pas beaucoup voyagé; inexploré

untried *a.* non-essayé, inessayé; pas encore mis à l'épreuve

untrimmed *a.* sans ornement, sans garniture; simple

untrodden *a.* non-frayé; inexploré

untroubled *a.* calme, tranquille

untrue *a.* faux (fausse); inexact; infidèle

untrustworthy *a.* qui n'est pas digne de confiance; infidèle; douteux

untruth *n.* mensonge *m.*; **–ful** *a.* menteur; mensonger; faux; **–fulness** *n.* fausseté *f.*

unturned *a.*, leave no stone — faire tout son possible

untutored *a.* illettré, sans instruction

unusable *a.* inutilisable

unused *a.* non-employé; inutilisé; peu habitué

unusual *a.* exceptionnel, rare; peu commun; peu usité; **–ness** *n.* rareté *f.*

unvanquished *a.* invaincu

unvaried *a.* sans variété; monotone; uniforme

unvarnished *a.* non-verni; (fig.) simple, sans fard

unvarying *a.* invariable; uniforme

unveil *vt.* dévoiler; inaugurer; **–ing** *n.* inauguration *f.*

unverified *a.* invérifié; non-corroboré

unversed *a.* peu versé

unvoiced *a.* sourd

unwanted *a.* non-voulu, non-désiré

unwarrantable *a.* injustifiable

unwarranted *a.* peu justifié; déplacé; sans garantie

unwary *a.* imprudent, imprévoyant

unwavering *a.* ferme, résolu, constant

unwearying *a.* infatigable

unwelcome *a.* importun, mal venu; désagréable

unwell *a.* indisposé; souffrant, malade

unwholesome *a.* malsain; insalubre

unwieldy *a.* peu maniable

unwilling *a.* inserviable; qui ne veut pas; be — ne pas vouloir, être peu disposé; **–ly** *adv.* à contre-cœur; **–ness** *n.* mauvaise volonté *f.*

unwind *vt.* dérouler; débobiner

unwise *a.* peu sage, imprudent

unwitting *a.* inconscient; **–ly** *adv.* inconsciemment; sans le savoir

unwonted *a.* inaccoutumé

unworkable *a.* impraticable

unworked *a.* non-travaillé; inexploité

unworldly *a.* d'un autre monde; peu mondain; peu naturel

unworthiness *n.* manque de mérite, peu de mérite *m.*

unworthy *a.* indigne; peu méritoire

unwounded *a.* sans blessure

unwrap *vt.* défaire

unwrinkled *a.* sans rides; uni; lisse

unwritten *a.* non-écrit; oral

unyielding *a.* ferme, inflexible, qui ne cède pas

up *adv.* haut; en haut; debout; relevé; (sun) levé; be — against se heurter à; get — se lever; go — monter; it's — to you (to) c'est à vous (de); speak — parler plus haut; — there là-haut; — to jusqu'à; walk — and down se promener de long en large; **–s** *n. pl.*, **–s and downs** vicissitudes *f. pl.*

upbraid *vt.* reprocher

upbringing *n.* éducation *f.*

upgrade *n.* montée *f.*; be on the — monter; reprendre

upheaval *n.* soulèvement *m.*; bouleversement *m.*

uphill *a.* montant; — *adv.* en montant; go — monter

uphold *vt.* soutenir, maintenir; confirmer

upholster *vt.* tapisser, couvrir; garnir; **–er** *n.* tapisseur *m.*; **–ing, –y** *n.* tapisserie *f.*; garniture *f.*

upkeep *n.* entretien *m.*

upland *n.* haut pays *m.*

uplift *n.* élévation *f.*; — *vt.* soulever, élever

upon *prep.* sur; à; vers; sous; de; en

upper *a.* supérieur; de dessus; (plus) haut, plus élevé; — classes hautes classes *f. pl.*; — hand dessus *m.*; — part dessus *m.*

upper-class *a.* de la haute classe

uppermost *a.* le plus haut, le plus élevé; le plus important; — *adv.* en dessus

upright *a.* droit; vertical, perpendiculaire; debout; honnête, intègre; — *n.* montant *m.*; **–ness** *n.* droiture, intégrité *f.*

uprising *n.* soulèvement *m.*, insurrection *f.*

uproar *n.* chahut, tumulte, vacarme, grand bruit *m.*; **–ious** *a.* tumultueux

uproot *vt.* déraciner; arracher, extirper

upset *n.* désordre *m.*; renversement *m.*; bouleversement *m.*; — *vt.* renverser; bouleverser; troubler, inquiéter, agiter; déranger; démonter; émouvoir; indisposer; — *vi.* se renverser; — *a.* renversé; troublé; ému; bouleversé; dérangé

upshot *n.* issue *f.*, résultat *m.*

upside-down *a.* sens dessus dessous; renversé; bouleversé

upstairs *adv.* en haut; — *n.* étage supérieur *m.*; go — monter (l'escalier) — *a.* d'en haut

upstanding *a.* honnête

upstart *n.* parvenu *m.*

upstream *adv.* en amont

contreplaqué *m.*; (fig.) vernis *m.*; — *vt.* plaquer

venerable *a.* vénérable

venerate *vt.* vénérer

veneration *n.* vénération *f.*

venereal *a.* vénérien

Venetian *a. & n.* vénitien *m.*; — **blind** jalousie *f.*

Venezuela *n.* Vénézuéla *m.*

vengeance *n.* vengeance *f.*; **take** — se venger

vengeful *a.* vindicatif

venial *a.* véniel, pardonnable

Venice *n.* Venise *f.*

venison *n.* venaison *f.*

venom *n.* venin *m.*; **-ous** *a.* venimeux; vénéneux

vent *n.* passage, trou *m.*; soupirail *m.*; lumière *f.*; **give — to** donner libre cours à; — *vt.* décharger

ventilate *vt.* ventiler, aérer

ventilation *n.* ventilation, aération *f.*, aérage *m.*

ventilator *n.* ventilateur *m.*

ventricle *n.* ventricule *m.*

ventriloquist *n.* ventriloque *m. & f.*

venture *n.* enterprise *f.*; — *vt.* hasarder, risquer; oser; **-some** *a.* aventureux; risqué, aventuré

venue *n.* (law) voisinage *m.*, juridiction *f.*

veracious *a.* véridique

veracity *n.* véracité, véridicité *f.*

veranda(h) *n.* véranda *f.*

verb *n.* verbe *m.*; **-al** *a.* verbal; oral; littéral; **-ally** *adv.* verbalement; **-ose** *a.* verbeux, prolixe; **-osity** *n.* verbosité, prolixité *f.*

verbatim *adv.* mot pour mot

verdant *a.* verdoyant, vert

verdict *n.* verdict *m.*; jugement *m.*

verdigris *n.* vert-de-gris *m.*

verge *n.* bord *m.*; bordure *f.*; verge *f.*; **on the — of** sur le point de; à la veille de; — *vi.*, **— on** friser, toucher à

verger *n.* bedeau, sacristain *m.*

verifiable *a.* vérifiable, contrôlable

verification *n.* vérification *f.*

verify *vt.* vérifier; contrôler; confirmer

veritable *a.* véritable

verity *n.* vérité *f.*

vermiform *a.* vermiforme; **— appendix** *n.* appendice du cæcum *m.*

vermilion *n.* vermillon *m.*; **—** *a.* vermeil, vermillon

vermin *n.* vermine *f.*

vernacular *a.* vernaculaire; vulgaire

versatile *a.* varié; souple; versatile

versatility *n.* souplesse *f.*; versatilité *f.*

verse *n.* vers *m.*; strophe *f.*; couplet *m.*; poésie *f.*; (eccl.) verset *m.*; **-d** *a.* versé;

expérimenté

versify *vt.* versifier, mettre en vers

version *n.* version *f.*; interprétation *f.*

versus *prep.* contre

vertebra *n.* vertèbre *f.*; **-l** *a.* vertébral; **-te** *n. & a.* vertébré *m.*

vertex *n.* sommet *m.*

vertical *a.* vertical; **-ness** *n.* verticalité *f.*

vertiginous *a.* vertigineux

vertigo *n.* vertige *m.*

very *adv.* très; bien, fort; **at the — latest** au plus tard; **at the — most** tout au plus; **not — peu**; **— much** beaucoup; — *a.* même; propre; seul; justement

vesicle *a.* vésicule *f.*

Vespers *n.* vêpres *f. pl.*

vessel *n.* vaisseau *m.*; vase *m.*; navire *m.*; instrument *m.*

vest *n.* gilet *m.*; — *vt.* revêtir, investir; **-ed** *a.* dévolu; **-ed interests** droits acquis *m. pl.*

vestal *a.* virginal; **— virgin** *n.* vestale *f.*

vestige *n.* vestige *m.*, trace *f.*

vestigial *a.* qui tient des vestiges

vestment *n.* vêtement *m.*

vest-pocket *a.* de poche; petit

vestry *n.* sacristie *f.*

veteran *n.* vétéran *m.*; ancien combattant *m.*; **—** *a.* expérimenté; de vétéran

veterinarian, veterinary *n.* vétérinaire *m.*

veto *n.* veto *m.*; — *vt.* mettre le veto à; interdire

vex *vt.* vexer, fâcher; **-ation** *n.* vexation *f.*; dépit *m.*, contrariété *f.*, ennui *m.*; **-atious** *a.* contrariant, fâcheux, ennuyeux; **-ed** *a.* vexé, fâché, contrarié

via *prep.* via; par; **— air mail** par avion

viability *n.* viabilité *f.*

viaduct *n.* viaduc *m.*

vial *n.* fiole *f.*

viand *n.* mets *m.*; viande *f.*

vibrate *vi.* vibrer; osciller; **—** *vt.* faire vibrer

vibration *n.* vibration *f.*; oscillation *f.*

vibrator *n.* vibrateur *m.*; oscillateur *m.*; (elec.) vibreur *m.*

vicar *n.* vicaire *m.*; curé *m.*; **-age** *n.* cure *f.*, presbytère *m.*; **— general** *n.* grand vicaire *m.*

vicarious *a.* substitutif; **-ly** *adv.* par substitution; à la place d'un autre

vice *n.* vice *m.*; défaut *m.*

vice-admiral *n.* vice-amiral *m.*

vice-chairman *n.* vice-président *m.*

vice-consul *n.* vice-consul *m.*

vice-president *n.* vice-président *m.*

viceroy *n.* vice-roi *m.*

vicinity *n.* voisinage *m.*; environs, alentours *m. pl.*

vicious *a.* vicieux; hargneux; **— circle** cercle vicieux *m.*

vicissitude *n.* vicissitude *f.*; péripétie *f.*

victim *n.* victime *f.*; **-ize** *vt.* tromper; abuser

victor *n.* vainqueur *m.*; **-ious** *a.* victorieux; **-y** *n.* victoire *f.*

Victorian *a.* victorien

victual *vt.* aprovisionner; **-s** *n. pl.* (coll.) provisions *f. pl.*, vivres *m. pl.*

video *n.* télévision *f.*; — *a.* vidéo, visuel; — **signal** *n.* signal d'image *m.*

vie *vi.* rivaliser; disputer

Vienna *n.* Vienne *f.*

Viennese *a. & n.* viennois

Viet Nam *n.* Viet-Nam *m.*

view *n.* vue *f.*; regard *m.*; perspective *f.*; aperçu *m.*; opinion *f.*, avis *m.*; idée *f.*; **bird's-eye** — vue à vol d'oiseau *f.*; **in** — en vue; **in** — **of** vu; en considération de; **point of** — point de vue *m.*; — *vt.* regarder; voir; envisager; **-er** *n.* spectateur *m.*

viewfinder *n.* viseur *m.*

viewpoint *n.* point de vue *m.*

vigil *n.* veille *f.*; (eccl.) vigile *f.*; **keep a** — veiller; **-ance** *n.* vigilance *f.*; **-ant** *a.* éveillé, alerte, vigilant; **-antly** *adv.* avec vigilance

vigilante *n.* membre d'un comité de surveillance *m.*

vigor *n.* vigueur *f.*; énergie *f.*; **-ous** *a.* vigoureux; robuste; fort

vile *a.* vil, bas; abominable; sale; **-ness** *n.* bassesse *f.*

vilification *n.* dénigrement *m.*

vilify *vt.* diffamer, dénigrer

villa *n.* villa *f.*; maison de campagne *f.*

village *n.* village *m.*; **-r** *n.* villageois *m.*

villain *n.* scélérat *m.*; (theat.) traître *m.*; **-ous** *a.* vil; scélérat; infâme; **-y** *n.* scélératesse, infamie *f.*

vim *n.* vigueur, énergie *f.*

vindicate *vt.* justifier; défendre, soutenir; revendiquer

vindication *n.* justification, défense *f.*; revendication *f.*

vindicator *n.* défenseur *m.*

vindictive *a.* vindicatif; vengeur; **-ness** *n.* esprit de vengeance *m.*

vine *n.* vigne *f.*

vinegar *n.* vinaigre *m.*; — **cruet** *n.* vinaigrier *m.*

vineyard *n.* vigne *f.*, vignoble *m.*

vintage *n.* vendange *f.*; crû *f.*; année *f.*; — **wine** *n.* vin de crû, grand vin, vin de marque *m.*

vintner *n.* vigneron, viticulteur *m.*; marchand en vins *m.*

vinyl *n.* vinyl *m.*; — *a.* vinylique

viola *n.* (mus.) alto *m.*

violate *vt.* violer

violation *n.* violation *f.*; infraction, contravention *f.*

violator *n.* violateur; contravenant *m.*

violence *n.* violence *f.*

violent *a.* violent; fort; **-ly** *adv.* violemment, avec violence

violin *n.* violon *m.*; **-ist** *n.* violoniste *m.&f.*

violincello *n.* violoncelle *m.*

viper *n.* vipère *f.*

virago *n.* mégère *f.*

virgin *a.* vierge; virginal; — *n.* vierge *f.*; **-al** *a.* virginal; **-ity** *n.* virginité *f.*

virile *a.* viril; mâle

virility *n.* virilité *f.*

virtual *a.* vrai; de fait; virtuel; **-ly** *adv.* de fait; virtuellement; presque

virtue *n.* vertu *f.*; qualité *f.*; **by** — **of** en vertu de, en raison de

virtuosity *n.* virtuosité *f.*

virtuoso *n.* virtuose *m. & f.*

virtuous *a.* vertueux

virulence *n.* virulence *f.*

virulent *a.* virulent

virus *n.* virus *m.*

visa *n.* visa *m.*

visage *n.* visage *m.*, figure *f.*

viscid *a.* visqueux

viscosity *n.* viscosité *f.*

viscount *n.* vicomte *m.*; **-ess** *n.* vicomtesse *f.*

viscous *a.* visqueux

vise *n.* étau *m.*

visibility *n.* visibilité *f.*; vue *f.*

visible *a.* visible; visuel

vision *n.* vision *f.*, vue *f.*; apparition *f.*; imagination *f.*; **-ary** *a. & n.* visionnaire *m. & f.*

visit *n.* visite *f.*; — *vt.* rendre visite à; (place) visiter; **-ation** *n.* visite *f.*; apparition *f.*; **-ing** *a.* en visite; de visite; **-or** *n.* visiteur *m.*

visor *n.* visière *f.*; paresoleil *m.*; protège-vue *m.*

vista *n.* vue, perspective, échappée *f.*

visual *a.* visuel; optique; **-ize** *vt.* se représenter

vital *a.* vital, essentiel; — **statistics** état civil *m.*; **-ity** *n.* vitalité *f.*; vie, vigueur *f.*; **-ly** *adv.* d'une manière vitale; (coll.) très, fort, extrêmement; **-s** *n. pl.* parties vitales *f. pl.*

vitamin *n.* vitamine *f.*

vitiate *vt.* vicier, corrompre

vitreous *a.* vitreux

vitrify *vt.* vitrifier; — *vi.* se vitrifier

vitriol *n.* vitriol *m.*; acide sulfurique *m.*; **-ic** *a.* acide; mordant

vituperation *n.* injures, insultes *f. pl.*

vituperative *a.* injurieux

vivacious *a.* vif; enjoué; gai; animé; **–ness** *n.* vivacité *f.*

vivacity *n.* vivacité *f.*; animation *f.*

vivid *a.* vif; vivant; **–ly** *a.* d'une manière vivante; **–ness** *n.* vivacité *f.*; vigueur *f.*; imagination *f.*

vivify *vt.* vivifier, animer

vixen *n.* (zool.) renarde *f.*; femme querelleuse *f.*

viz: videlicet à savoir, c'est-à-dire

vocabulary *n.* vocabulaire *m.*

vocal *a.* vocal; bruyant; **—— cords** cordes vocales *f. pl.*; **–ist** *n.* chanteur *m.*, chanteuse *f.*; **–ization** *n.* vocalisation *f.*; **–ize** *vt.* vocaliser

vocation *n.* vocation *f.*; profession *f.*; métier *m.*; **–al** de(s) métiers; professionnel; **–al school** école des arts et des métiers *f.*

vociferate *vi.* vociférer

vociferation *n.* vocifération *f.*

vociferous *a.* vociférant; criard; **–ly** *adv.* bruyamment

vodka *n.* vodka *m.*

vogue *n.* vogue, mode *f.* **in —— en** vogue, à la mode

voice *n.* voix *f.*; **in a low —— à** voix basse, à mi-voix; **——** *vt.* exprimer; voiser; **–d** *a.* exprimé; voisé; sonore; **–less** *a.* sans voix; non voisé; sourd

void *a.* vide; nul; **null and ——** nul et caduc; **—— of** dénué de; **——** *vt.* vider, évacuer, annuler; **——** *n.* vide *m.*

volatile *a.* volatil; (fig.) vif, léger; volage

volatility *n.* volatilité *f.*

volcanic *a.* volcanique

volcano *n.* volcan *m.*

volition *n.* volonté, volition *f.*; gré *m.*

volley *n.* volée, décharge, salve *f.*; (sports) volée *f.*

volleyball *n.* volleyball *m.*

volt *n.* volt *m.*; **–age** *n.* voltage *m.*, tension *f.*; **high –age** *n.* haute tension *f.*; **–aic** *a.* voltaïque

voltmeter *n.* voltmètre *m.*

volubility *n.* volubilité *f.*

voluble *a.* facile; qui parle avec volubilité

volume *n.* volume *m.*; livre, tome *m.*

volume control *n.* réglage de puissance *m.*

voluminous *a.* volumineux; **–ness** *n.* grosseur, étendue *f.*

voluntarily *adv.* volontairement

voluntary *a.* volontaire; spontané

volunteer *n.* volontaire *m.*; **——** *vt.* offrir volontairement, donner volontairement; **——** *vi.* s'offrir; **——** *a.* de volontaire

voluptuous *a.* voluptueux; **–ly** *adv.* voluptueusement; **–ness** *n.* sensualité *f.*; volupté *f.*

vomit *n.* vomissement *m.*; **——** *vt. & vi.* vomir; **–ing** *n.* vomissement *m.*

voracious *a.* vorace; dévorant; **–ly** *adv.* avec voracité; **–ness** *n.* voracité *f.*

voracity *n.* voracité *f.*

vortex *n.* tourbillon *m.*

votary *n.* adorateur, dévoué *m.*; sectateur *m.*; partisan *m.*

vote *n.* voix *f.*; vote, scrutin *m.*; suffrage *m.*; résolution *f.*; **put to a ——** mettre aux voix; **——** *vt. & vi.* voter, donner sa voix; **–r** *n.* votant, électeur *m.*

voting *n.* vote, scrutin *m.*

votive *a.* votif

vouch *vt. & vi.* affirmer, garantir; **—— for** répondre de; **–er** bon *m.*; fiche *f.*, reçu *m.*; passavant *m.*

vow *n.* vœu *m.*; serment *m.*; **——** *vt. & vi.* vouer; faire vœu; jurer

vowel *n.* voyelle *f.*

voyage *n.* voyage *m.*; **——** *vi.* voyager; **–r** *n.* voyageur *m.*

vulcanite *n.* caoutchouc vulcanisé *m.*

vulcanize *vt.* vulcaniser

vulgar *a.* vulgaire; commun; grossier, de mauvais goût; **–ism** *n.* expression vulgaire *f.*; **–ity** *n.* vulgarité *f.*; grossièreté *f.*; **–ization** vulgarisation *f.*; **–ize** *vt.* vulgariser

Vulgate *n.* Vulgate *f.*

vulnerability *n.* vulnérabilité *f.*

vulnerable *a.* vulnérable

W

wad *n.* liasse *f.*; bourre *f.*; paquet *m.*; **——** *vt.* (garment) ouater; **–ding** *n.* ouate *f.*; bourre *f.*

waddle *n.* dandinement *m.*; **——** *vi.* se dandiner

wade *vi.* marcher dans l'eau; patauger; **—— across** passer à gué

wafer *n.* gaufrette *f.*; (eccl.) hostie *f.*

waffle *n.* gaufre *f.*; **—— iron** *n.* gaufrier *m.*

waft *vt.* transporter; **——** *vi.* flotter

wag *n.* mouvement de la queue *m.*; (person) farceur *m.*; **——** *vt.* remuer, agiter

wage *vt.*, **—— war** faire la guerre; **–(s)** *n. & n. pl.* salaire *m.*; gages *m. pl.*; paye *f.* récompense *f.*

wage earner *n.* salarié, gagne-pain *m.*

wager *n.* pari *m.*, gageure *f.*; **——** *vt.* parier, gager

wagon *n.* charrette *f.*; chariot *m.*; fourgon *m.*

waif *n.* enfant abandonné, enfant sans domicile *m.*

wail *n.* gémissement *m.*, plainte *f.*; **——** *vi.* gémir; se lamenter

wainscoting *n.* lambrissage *m.*; boiserie *f.*

waist *n.* taille, ceinture *f.*; (naut.) embelle *f.*

waistband n. ceinture f.

waistcoat n. gilet m.

waistline n. taille, ceinture f.

wait n. attente f.; **in —** en embuscade, à l'affût; **— vt. & vi.** attendre; **— for attendre; — on** servir; **— up** ne pas se coucher; attendre l'arrivée de quelqu'un (la nuit); **-er** n. garçon m.; **head -er** maître d'hôtel m.; **-ing** n. attente f.; service m.; **-ing game -ing tactics** tactique attentiste f.; **lady in -ing** dame d'honneur f.; **-ing list** n. liste supplémentaire f.; **-ing room** salle d'attente f.; antichambre f.

waitress n. serveuse f.

waive vt. renoncer à; ne pas exiger; ne pas insister sur; **-r** n. abandon m.; désistement m.

wake n. veillée (mortuaire) f.; (naut.) sillage m.; (fig.) traces f. pl., suite f.; **— vi.** se réveiller; **— vt.** réveiller; éveiller; **-ful** a. éveillé, vigilant; **-fulness** n. vigilance f., état de veille m.; **-n** vt. réveiller; éveiller; **— -n** vi. se réveiller; s'éveiller

waking n. veille f.; réveil m.; **— a.** de veille

Wales n. (Pays de) Galles m.

walk n. promenade f.; marche f.; démarche f.; avenue, allée f.; promenoir m.; métier m., profession f.; **go for a —, take a —** faire une promenade, (aller) se promener; **— vi.** marcher; aller à pied; se promener; (horse) aller au pas; **— vt.** faire marcher; promener; (streets) courir; **-er** n. marcheur m.; piéton m.; promeneur m.; **-ing** n. marche f.; promenade(s) f. (pl.)

walkie-talkie n. radio-téléphone portatif m.

walkout n. grève f.

walk-up n. appartement sans ascenseur m.

wall n. mur m., muraille f.; paroi f.; **— bracket** n. console murale f.; **— plug, — socket** n. prise de courant murale f.; **— vt.** murer; **-in, — up** murer; **-ed** a. muré

wallet n. portefeuille m.

walleyed a. qui à l'œil vairon

wallflower n. (fig.) tapisserie f.

wallop n. (gros) coup m.; **— vt.** rosser, frapper; tanner la peau à

wallow vi. se vautrer; se baigner

wallboard n. panneau de fibres de bois m.

wallpaper n. papier peint m.

walnut n. noix f.; (wood, tree) noyer m.

waltz n. valse f.; **— vi.** valser

wan a. pâle, blafard, blème; triste; **-ness** n. pâleur f.

wand n. baguette f.

wander vi. errer; vaguer; s'écarter; divaguer; **-er** n. voyageur, vagabond m.; **-ing** a. errant, vagabond; nomade; in-

cohérent; **-ing** n. vagabondage m.; voyages m. pl.; divagation f.

wanderlust n. désir de voyager m.

wane n. décroissance f., déclin m.; **— vi.** décroître; décliner

wangle vt. resquiller, carotter

waning n. déclin m.

want n. désir m.; besoin m.; défaut, manque m.; indigence f.; **for —** of faute de; **— vi.** manquer; **— vt.** vouloir, désirer; manquer; falloir; avoir besoin de; exiger; demander; **-ed** a. voulu, désiré; recherché par la police; **-ing** a. qui manque, manquant

wanton a. impudique; gratuit; **— n.** femme impudique f.; **-ness** n. libertinage m.; étourderie f.

war n. guerre f.; **cold —** guerre froide f.; **— of nerves** guerre des nerfs f.; **total —** guerre totale f.; **— vi.** faire la guerre; lutter; **-ring a.** en guerre

warble n. gazouillement m.; **— vi.** gazouiller; chanter en gazouillant; **-r** n. fauvette f.; oiseau chanteur m.

ward n. pupille m.; quartier, arrondissement m.; (hospital) salle (d'hôpital) f.; **— vt., — off** prévenir; parer

warden n. directeur de prison m.; gardien m.; **air raid —** chef d'îlot m.

wardrobe n. garde-robe f.; vêtements m. pl.; armoire f.

wardroom n. carré des officiers m.

ware n. articles m. pl.; marchandise f.; **-s** pl. marchandise(s) f. (pl.)

warehouse n. magasin m.; entrepôt, dépôt m.; garde-meuble m.

warfare n. guerre f.

warehouseman n. magasinier m.; garde-magasin m.

warhead n. partie explosible f.

war horse n. cheval de bataille m.; vétéran m.

warily adv. prudemment

wariness n. prudence f.; défiance f.

warlike a. belliqueux; guerrier, martial

warm a. chaud; chaleureux; cordial; généreux; **be — (person)** avoir chaud; (weather) faire chaud; **— vt.** chauffer, réchauffer; **— vi.** se chauffer, se réchauffer; **-ing** n. chauffage m.; **-th** n. chaleur f.; cordialité f.

warm-blooded a. à sang chaud

warmhearted a. généreux

warmonger n. belliqueux m.

warmup n. temps de chauffage m.; répétition f.

warn vt. avertir, prévenir; **-ing** n. avertissement m.

warp n. chaîne f.; (wood) courbure, voilure f.; **— vt.** ourdir; (wood) faire voiler, déjeter; (naut.) touer; (fig.) pervertir, fausser; — *vi.* se déjeter; se déformer; se voiler; –ed *a.* déjeté, voilé; perverti, faussé

warrant *n.* mandat, ordre *m.*; warrant *m.*; garantie *f.*; — **of arrest** mandat d'arrêt *m.*; — **officer** *n.* adjutant *m.*; — *vt.* garantir; certifier; justifier; –ed *a.* garanti; justifié; –y *n.* garantie *f.*

warren *n.* garenne *f.*

warrior *n.* guerrier, soldat *m.*

Warsaw *n.* Varsovie *f.*

warship *n.* navire de guerre *m.*

wart *n.* verrue *f.*

wartime *n.* temps de guerre *m.*

wary *a.* prudent; attentif

wash *n.* lavage *m.*; blanchissage *m.*; lessive *f.*; (art) lavis *m.*; (naut.) sillage *m.*; — *vt.* laver; blanchir; lotionner; — **one's hands** se laver les mains; — *vi.* se laver; — **away** enlever; emporter; — **down** laver; (food) arroser; — **out** laver; rincer; enlever; –able *a.* lavable; –ed *a.* lavé; –ed **out** délavé; raté; –er *n.* laveur *m.*; plongeur *m.*; –ing *n.* lavage *m.*; blanchissage *m.*; linge *m.*; –ing **machine** laveuse méchanique *f.*; –ing **soda** soude *m.*

washbowl *n.* cuvette de lavabo *f.*

washcloth *n.* gant-éponge *m.*, lavette *f.*

washroom *n.* lavabos *m. pl.*; cabinets *m. pl.*

washstand *n.* lavabo *m.*

washtub *n.* cuvier *m.*

waste *n.* gaspillage *m.*; déchets *m. pl.*, rebut *m.*; désert *m.*; — **of time** perte de temps *f.*; –paper papiers *m. pl.*, papiers de rebut *m. pl.*; — **pipe** tuyau d'écoulement *m.*; — *a.* de rebut; — *vt.* gaspiller; (time) perdre; user, consumer; — *vi.* s'user; se perdre; maigrir; –d *a.* gaspillé; perdu; dévasté; –ful *a.* gaspilleur; prodigue; –fulness *n.* gaspillage *m.*; prodigalité *f.*

wastebasket *n.* corbeille (à papiers) *f.*

wastepaper *a.*, — **basket** corbeille (à papiers) *f.*

watch *n.* surveillance *f.*; garde *f.*; (naut.) quart *m.*; bordée *f.*; (timepiece) montre *f.*; **on the** — sur ses gardes, en observation; **be on the** — **for** guetter; — **pocket** gousset de montre *m.*; — *vt.* observer; regarder; veiller (sur); surveiller; assister à; — *vi.* veiller; — **out** être sur ses gardes; faire attention, prendre garde; — **out!** attention!, prenez garde!; — **over** garder; surveiller; –er *n.* observateur *m.*; –ful *a.* attentif; alerte, vigilant; –fulness *n.* vigilance *f.*

watchdog *n.* chien de garde *m.*

watch fire *n.* feu (de bivouac) *m.*

watchmaker *n.* horloger *m.*

watchman *n.* veilleur de nuit *m.*; **garde**, gardien *m.*

watchtower *n.* tour d'observation *f.*

watchword *a.* mot d'ordre *m.*

water *n.* eau *f.*; **by** — en bateau; **cold** — eau fraîche *f.*; **drinking** — eau potable *f.*; **fresh** — eau douce *f.*; **running** — eau courante *f.*; **turn on the** — ouvrir l'eau; **under** — submergé; inondé; — **closet** *m.*; cabinets *m. pl.*; — **color** aquarelle *f.*; — **cure** hydrothérapie *f.*; — **faucet** robinet *m.*; — **front** quartier de la ville qui fait face à l'eau *m.*; — **gauge** hydromètre *m.*; — **glass** verre *m.*; (chem.) silicate de soude *m.*; — **level** niveau d'eau *m.*; — **line** niveau d'eau *m.*; (naut.) flottaison *f.*; — **lily** *n.* lis d'eau *m.*; — **main** conduite principale *f.*; — **polo** waterpolo *m.*; — **power** force hydraulique *f.*; — **softener** adoucisseur d'eau *m.*; — **system** canalisation d'eau *f.*; — **tower** château d'eau *m.*; — **wheel** roue hydraulique *f.*; — *vt.* arroser; diluer; couper; abreuver; — *vi.* larmoyer, pleurer; — **down** atténuer; –ing *n.* irrigation *f.*; arrosage *m.*; dilution *f.*; abreuvage *m.*; (eyes) larmoiement *m.*; –ing **can** arrosoir *m.*; –y *a.* aqueux; larmoyant; (color) déteint

watercress *n.* cresson *m.*

waterfall *n.* chute d'eau, cascade *f.*

waterlog *vt.* imprégner d'eau; –ged *a.* plein d'eau

watermark *n.* (paper) filigrane *m.*; –ed *a* à filigrane

watermelon *n.* pastèque *f.*

waterproof *a.* imperméable; — *vt.* rendre étanche

waterspout *n.* gouttière *f.*; tuyau *m.* trombe *f.*

watertight *a.* étanche

waterway *n.* voie d'eau (navigable) *f.*

waterworks *n. pl.* service des eaux *m.*

watt *n.* watt *m.*; –**age** *n.* wattage *m.*; consommation en watts *f.*

wave *n.* (gesture) geste, salut *m.*; **vague**, onde *f.*; (hair) ondulation *f.*; **permanent** — indéfrisable *f.*; **tidal** — raz de marée *m.*; — *vi.* ondoyer; flotter, se balancer; tournoyer; faire un geste, saluer; — *vt.* agiter; (hair) onduler; –d *a.* ondulé

wave length *n.* longueur d'onde *f.*

waver *vi.* vaciller, chanceler; –ing *n.* vacillation, irrésolution *f.*; –ing *a.* irrésolu, vacillant; — *n.* hésitation, indécision *f.*

wavy *a.* ondoyant; ondulé, onduleux

wax *n* cire *f* · — **paper** papier ciré *m* ; —

vt. cirer; — *vi.* croître, s'accroître; se faire; **–en** *a.* de cire; **–y** *a.* de cire, comme de la cire

way *n.* voie *f.*; chemin *m.*, route *f.*; passage *m.*; moyen, expédient *m.*; manière, façon *f.*; **all the —** jusqu'au bout; **by the —** à propos; **by — of** par; **get out of the —** laisser passer; se ranger; give **—** céder le pas; se ranger; se rompre; (floor) se casser **look the other —** ne pas regarder; détourner les yeux; **lose one's —** se perdre, s'égarer; **make —** faire place (à); **on the —** en route; **out of the —** isolé; **start on one's —** se mettre en route; **the right —** la bonne voie, la bonne route *f.*; **the wrong —** la mauvaise voie, la mauvaise route *f.*; **go the wrong —** se tromper de chemin; prendre la mauvaise route; **under —** en route; en train; **— in** entrée *f.*; **— out** sortie *f.*

wayfarer *n.* voyageur *m.*

waylay *vt.* guetter au passage

wayside *n.* bord de la route *m.*; **leave by the —** abandonner; laisser en arrière

wayward *a.* vagabond; rebelle

we *pron.* nous; on

weak *a.* faible; débile; mou (molle); pauvre; sans vigueur; **–en** *vi.* s'affaiblir; — *vt.* affaiblir; **–ening** *n.* affaiblissement *m.*; **–ling** *n.* faible *m.*; **–ness** *n.* faiblesse *f.*; faible *m.*

weakhearted *a. & adv.* qui manque de courage; sans courage

weak-kneed *a.* irrésolu; aux genoux faibles

weakling *n.* personne **faible** *f.*, homme faible *m.*; homme qui manque de force *m.*

weak-minded *a.* peu intelligent

wealth *n.* bien *m.*, richesses *f. pl.*; **–y** *a.* riche, **opulent**

wean *vt.* sevrer; priver de

weapon *n.* arme *f.*; **–ry** *n.* arsenaux d'un pays *m. pl.*; armement *m.*

wear *n.* usure *f.*; usage *m.*; — *vt.* porter; user; — *vi.* faire de l'usage; s'user; **— away** *vt.* user; ronger; effacer; **— away** *vi.* s'user; **— out** user; fatiguer, epuiser; **–able** *a.* propre à porter; **–ing** *a.* fatigant

weariness *n.* lassitude, fatigue *f.*; ennui *m.*

wearisome *a.* ennuyeux

weary *vt.* fatiguer; ennuyer; — *a.* las, fatigué, ennuyé

weather *n.* temps *m.*; **— bureau** bureau météorologique *m.*; **— forecast** prévisions météorologiques *f. pl.*; **–man** météorologue *m.*; **— report** bulletin météorologique *m.*; **the — is nice** il fait beau; **the — is bad** il fait mauvais; **—**

vt. resister à; user, décolorer

weather-beaten *a.* battu par le vent

weatherproof *a.* à l'épreuve du temps; imperméable

weave *n.* texture *f.*; — *vt.* tisser; entrelacer; mêler, entremêler; **–r** *n.* tisserand *m.*

weaving *n.* tissage *m.*

web *n.* tissu *m.*; (spider) toile d'araignée *f.*; membrane *f.*; **–bed** *a.* palmé

web-footed *a.* aux pieds palmés

wed *vt.* épouser, se marier avec; — *vi.* se marier; **–ding** *n.* mariage *m.*, noces *f. pl.*; **–ding cake** gâteau de noces *m.*; **–ding ring** alliance *f.*

wedge *n.* coin *m.*; — *vt.* fendre; serrer, forcer; coincer; caler; **–d** *a.* en forme de coin; cunéiforme

wedlock *n.* mariage *m.*

Wednesday *n.* mercredi *m.*; **Ash —** mercredi des cendres *m.*

wee *a.* tout petit

weed *n.* mauvaise herbe *f.*; **–s** *pl.* habits de deuil *m. pl.*; — *vt.* sarcler; **— out** sarcler; éliminer; **–er** *n.* sarcleur *m.*; (tool) sarcloir *m.*; **–ing** *n.* sarclage *m.*

week *n.* semaine *f.*; huit jours *m. pl.*; **two –s** quinze jours *m. pl.*; deux semaines *f. pl.*; **a — from today** d'aujourd'hui en huit; **–ly** *a.* hebdomadaire

weekday *n.* jour de la semaine *m.*; jour ouvrable *m.*; — *a.* des jours ouvrables

weekend *n.* fin de semaine *f.*; week-end *m.*

weep *vi.* pleurer; **–er** *n.* pleureur *m.*; **–ing** *n.* pleurs *m. pl.*, larmes *f. pl.*; **–ing willow** saule pleureur *m.*; **–y** *a.* larmoyant

weigh *vt.* peser; soupeser; examiner, considérer; — *vi.* peser; **— anchor** lever l'ancre; **— down** surcharger; **— in** se faire peser; **–ing** *n.* pesée *f.*

weight *n.* poids *m.*, pesanteur *f.*; fardeau *m.*; importance *f.*; force *f.*; **gain —** prendre du poids; **lose —** perdre du poids; maigrir; — *vt.* charger; plomber; **–less** *n.* pesanteur *f.*; importance *f.*; **–lessness** *n.* non-pesanteur *f.*; **–y** *a.* pesant, important

weird *a.* mystérieux, surnaturel

welcome *n.* bon accueil *m.*; bienvenue *f.*; **—** *interj.* soyez le bienvenu; **—** *a.* bienvenu; agréable; **you're —** de rien; ce n'est rien; il n'y a pas de quoi; à votre service; — *vt.* accueillir, faire bon accueil à

weld *n.* soudure *f.*; — *vt.* souder (à chaud); **–er** *n.* soudeur *m.*; **–ing** *n.* soudage *m.*

welfare *n.* bien-être *m.*; **— state** état socialiste *m.*; **— work** bonnes œuvres *f. pl.*; assistance sociale *f.*

well *n.* puits *m.*; — *vi.* sourdre; jaillir —

adv. bien; alors; as —. aussi; as — as aussi bien que; comme; very — très bien; — a. bien; bon; be — aller bien, se porter bien; — interj. eh bien

well-advised a. prudent, sage

well-behaved a. sage; bien élevé

well-being n. bien-être m.

wellborn a. de haute raissance

well-bred a. bien élevé; bien éduqué

well-chosen a. bien choisi

well-earned a. bien mérité

well-educated a. instruit

well-informed a. au courant; bien renseigné; instruit

well-kept a. bien tenu; (secret) bien gardé

well-known a. connu; célèbre; fameux

well-mannered a. bien élevé

well-meaning a. bien intentionné

well off a. aisé; qui a du bien

well-read a. instruit; savant

well-shaped a. bien formé

well-spent a. bien utilisé

well-suited a. to be — to être fait pour

well-to-do a. prospère, riche, aisé

Welsh a. gallois; –man n. Gallois m.

welt n. zébrure f.

welter n. désordre m., confusion f.

welterweight n. poids mi-moyen m.

wen n. loupe f., goître m.

wench n. fille f.; donzelle f.; gaillarde f.

wend vi. aller, poursuivre; — vt. se diriger, poursuivre son chemin

west n. ouest, occident m.; — adv. vers l'ouest; — a. de l'ouest; -erly a. de l'ouest; -ern a. occidental, de l'ouest; –ward adv. vers l'ouest

wet n. humidité f.; — vt. mouiller, humecter, arroser; — a. mouillé, humide, get — se mouiller; **soaking** — mouillé jusqu'aux os; — **blanket** trouble-fête, rabat-joie m.; — **nurse** nourrice f.; –ness n. humidité f.

whack n. coup m.; — vt. battre, rosser

whale n. baleine f.; –r n. baleinier m.; — vi. faire la pêche à la baleine

wharf n. quai m.; embarcadère m.; appontement m.; — vi. amarrer; –age n. quayage m.

what pron. que, qu'est-ce que, qu'est-ce qui; ce qui, ce que; quoi; — a. quel; — **is the matter?** qu'y a-t-il?; — **is the matter with him?** qu'a-t-il?; –'s the **use?** à quoi bon?; — **time is it?** quelle heure est-il?; — interj. quoi; comment

whatever pron. tout ce qui, tout ce que; n'importe quoi; quoi que ce soit; — a. quelconque; quel . . . . que; aucun

whatsoever pron. quoi que ce soit; quelconque

wheat n. froment, blé m.; –en a. de blé

wheedle vt. enjôler, flatter

wheel n. roue f.; **spinning** — rouet m.; **steering** — volant m.; — vt. & vi. rouler, faire tourner –ed a. à roues

wheelbarrow n. brouet m.

wheel base n. distance entre les essieux f.

wheel chair n. fauteuil roulant m., voiture de malade f.

wheelwright n. charron m.

wheeze vi. respirer avec bruit; siffler

wheezing n. respiration sifflante f.

wheezy a. sifflant; asthmatique

whelp n. petit chien m.; — vi. mettre bas

when adv. quand; lorsque; tandis que; où; **since** — depuis quand

whenever adv. quand; n'importe quand; toutes les fois que

where adv. où

whereabouts n. situation f.; où l'on se trouve

whereas conj. puisque, comme; vu que; tandis que

whereby adv. par quoi; par lequel

wherefore adv. pourquoi; — n. les pourquoi m. pl.

wherein adv. en quoi; où; dans lequel

whereof adv. de quoi

whereupon adv. sur quoi; là-dessus

wherever adv. n'importe où; où que; partout où

wherewithal n. de quoi; ce qu'il faut

whet vt. aiguiser; exciter

whether conj. soit que; que; si

whetstone n. pierre à aiguiser f.

which pron. lequel, laquelle; qui, que; — a. quel; quoi; — **one** lequel; — **way** par où; **of** — dont; duquel

whichever a. quel (que); — conj. quoi que; — pron. n'importe lequel

whiff n. souffle m., bouffée f.

while n. temps, espace de temps m.; **a little** — **ago** tout à l'heure; **in a little** — tout à l'heure; **be worth** — valoir la peine; — vt., **to** — **away** tuer (le temps); — conj. pendant que, tandis que; tant que; à mesure que; bien que, quoique

whim n. caprice m., fantaisie f.

whimper vi. pleurnicher; — n. pleurnichement m.; –er n. pleurnicheur m.; –ing n. pleurnichement m.

whimsical a. capricieux; bizarre

whine n. plainte f.; gémissement m.; — vi. se plaindre, geindre, gémir, se lamenter

whining a. plaintif, pleurnicheur; — n. plaintes f. pl., pleurnichement m.; sifflement m.

whinny n. hennissement m.; — vi. hennir

whip n. fouet m.; **riding** — cravache f.; — **hand** avantage, dessus m.; — vt. fouetter; battre, vaincre; **-ped cream**

crème fouettée *f.*; –ping *n.* fouettée *f.*; fouettement *m.*; coups de fouet *m.* *pl.*

whirl *n.* tourbillon *m.*; tournoiement *m.*; — *vt.* faire tourner avec vitesse; — *vi.* tournoyer, pirouetter

whirlpool, whirlwind *n.* tourbillon *m.*

whirr, whir *n.* ronflement *m.*; — *vi.* ronfler

whisk *n.* mouvement brusque *m.*; époussette *f.*; — broom petit balai *m.*; — *vt.* agiter; — away enlever, chasser; enlever; — *vi.* passer rapidement

whisker *n.* poil (de la barbe) *m.*; –s *pl.* barbe *f.*; side –s favoris *m.* *pl.*

whisper *n.* chuchotement *m.*; — *vt.* & *vi.* chuchoter

whistle *n.* sifflet *m.*; sifflement *m.*; — *vt.* & *vi.* siffler

whit *n.* point, iota *m.*

white *a.* blanc (blanche); pâle; pur; turn — blanchir; pâlir; — elephant *n.* (fig.) fardeau *m.*; chose encombrante *f.*; — — heat *n.* incandescence *f.*; — *n.* blanc *m.*; -ness *n.* blancheur *f.*

whitecap *n.* mouton *m.*

white-collar, — worker *a.* & *n.* employé (dans un bureau)

whitefish *n.* merlan *m.*

white-hot *a.* chauffé à blanc, incandescent

whiten *vt.* blanchir

whitewash *n.* blanc de chaux, lait de chaux *m.*; — *vt.* passer au chaux, blanchir à la chaux; (fig.) justifier, donner des apparences légitimes à

whither *adv.* où

whitish *a.* blanchâtre

whittle *vt.* couper, tailler; amenuiser

whiz *n.* sifflement *n.*; (coll.) expert, génie *m.*; — *vi.* siffler; passer très vite

who *pron.* qui, qui est-ce qui; quel

whoever *pron.* qui que; quiconque, celui qui; qui que ce soit

whole *n.* total, tout *m.*; totalité *f.*; entier *m.*; — number *n.* nombre entier *m.*; — note *n.* (mus.) ronde *f.*; on the — pour la plupart; dans l'ensemble; à tout prendre, en somme — *a.* tout, entier, complet; sain

wholehearted *a.* sincère, de tout cœur

wholesale *n.* gros *m.*; — *a.* & *adv.* en gros; — *vt.* vendre en gros; -r *n.* marchand en gros *m.*

wholesome *a.* sain, salutaire

whole-wheat *a.* de blé entire

wholly *adv.* entièrement, complètement, tout cà fait

whom *pron.* que; qui; lequel; of — dont, duquel

whomever *pron.* quiconque, celui que

whoop *n.* huée *f.*; houp *m.*; — *vi.* huer, crier; –ing cough *n.* coqueluche *f.*

whore *n.* prostituée *f.*

whorl *n.* volute *f.*

whose *pron.* dont, de qui, à qui

why *adv.* pourquoi; — *interj.* mais

wick *n.* mèche *f.*

wicked *a.* méchant, scélérat; mauvais; -ness *n.* méchanceté *f.*

wicker *n.* osier *m.*; — *a.* en osier

wicket *n.* guichet *m.*

wide *a.* large; vaste, ample; — *adv.* largement; au loin; far and — partout; — awake *a.* tout à fait éveillé; ouvert; -ly *adv.* largement; très; beaucoup; -n *vt.* élargir; -n *vi.* s'élargir

wide-eyed *a.* abasourdi

wide-felt *a.* ressenti partout

wide-open *a.* ouvert

widespread *a.* répandu

widow *n.* veuve *f.*; — *vt.* rendre veuve; priver; -ed *a.* veuf; -er *n.* veuf *m.*; -hood *n.* veuvage *m.*

width *n.* largeur *f.*

wield *vt.* manier, tenir, porter

wife *n.* femme, épouse *f.*; -ly *a.* de femme, d'épouse

wig *n.* perruque *f.*

wiggle *vt.* manier, tortiller; — *vi.* se tortiller

wigwag *vt.* agiter; signaler par l'emploi de drapeaux

wild *a.* sauvage, farouche; agreste, inculte; irrégulier, dissolu; -s *n.* *pl.* désert *m.*; -ness *n.* férocité *f.*; état sauvage *m.*; fureur *f.*; extravagance *f.*

wildcat *n.* lynx *m.*; — *a.* spéculatif, risqué; — strike grève non autorisée *f.*

wilderness *n.* désert *m.*

wildfire *n.* feu grégeois *m.*; like — extrêmement vite

wild-goose chase *n.* entreprise infructueuse *f.*; démarches inutiles *f.* *pl.*

wile *n.* fourberie, ruse *f.*

wilful *a.* entêté; prémédité; -ly *adv.* à dessein, exprès; avec entêtement; -ness *n.* entêtement *m.*, obstination *f.*

wiliness *n.* astuce *f.*

will *n.* volonté *f.*; disposition *f.*; (law) testament *m.*; at — à volonte; of one's own free — de son plein gré; — *vt.* vouloir; laisser par testament; léguer; -ing *a.* disposé, consentant; be -ing vouloir bien; -ingness *n.* consentement *m.*; bonne volonté *f.*

willow *n.* saule *m.*; weeping — saule pleureur *m.*; -y *a.* svelte, souple

will power *n.* volonté *f.*

willy-nilly *adv.* bon gré mal gré

wilt *vi.* se faner, se flétrir

wily *a.* rusé, fin; malin

wimple *n.* guimpe *f.*

win *vt. & vi.* gagner; acquérir; — **a prize** remporter un prix; — **over** gagner; **–ner** *n.* gagnant *m.*; **–ning** *a.* gagnant; engageant

wince *vi.* broncher; faire une grimace

winch *n.* treuil *m.*

wind *n.* vent *m.*; haleine *f.*; **get one's second** — reprendre haleine; — **instrument** instrument à vent *m.*; — *vt.* essoufler; **–ed** *a.* essoufflé, hors d'haleine; **–y** *a.* venteux; **it is –y** il fait du vent

wind *n.* tour *m.*; tournant *m.*; — *vt.* tourner, tordre; envelopper, entourer; enrouler; — *vi.* tourner, se tordre, serpenter; — **up** remonter; terminer; **–ing** *n.* détour, tournant *m.*; enroulement *m.*; bandage *m.*; **–ing** *a.* sinueux, en lacet; **–ing sheet** *n.* linceul *m.*

windfall *n.* aubaine *f.*

windjammer *n.* voilier *m.*

windlass *n.* treuil, guindeau *m.*

windmill *n.* moulin à vent *m.*

window *n.* fenêtre; croisée *f.*; (ticket) guichet *m.*; (store) vitrine, devanture *f.*; **French** — porte-fenêtre *f.*; **stained-glass** — vitrail *m.*; — **envelope** enveloppe à fenêtre *f.*

window dresser, window trimmer *n.* étalagiste *m.*

window dressing *n.* art de l'étalage *m.*; (coll.) trompe-l'œil *m.*

windowpane *n.* carreau *m.*

window-shopping *n.* lèche-vitrines *m.*

window sill *n.* appui, rebord (de fenêtre) *m.*

windpipe *n.* trachée-artère *f.*; gosier *m.*

windshield *n.* pare-brise *m.*; — **wiper** essuie-glace *m.*

wind-swept *a.* venteux

wind tunnel *n.* tunnel aérodynamique *m.*

windward *a. & adv.* vers le vent, sous le vent

wine *n.* vin *m.*; — **grower** vigneron *m.*

winecellar *n.* cave au vin *f.*

wineglass *n.* verre à vin *m.*

wing *n.* aile *f.*; **–s** *pl.* (theat.) coulisses *f. pl.*; — *vi.* voler, s'envoler; **–ed** *a.* ailé

wingspan, wingspread *n.* envergure *f.*

wink *n.* clin d'œil *m.*; clignement d'œil *m.*; — *vi.* clignoter; cligner de l'œil; fermer les yeux

winnow *vt.* vanner; éplucher

winsome *a.* séduisant

winter *n.* hiver *m.*; — *vi.* hiverner; passer l'hiver; **–ize** *vt.* équiper pour l'hiver

wintergreen *n.* wintergreen *m.*, pyrole *f.*; gaulthérie (du Canada) *f.*; palommier *m.*

wintertime *n.* hiver *m.*, saison d'hiver *f.*

wintry *a.* d'hiver; froid, glacial

wipe *n.* action d'essuyer; — *vt.* essuyer; — **one's nose** se moucher; — **out** détruire, exterminer; effacer

wire *n.* fil (de métal) *m.*; télégramme *m.*; **pull –s** (coll.) arranger les choses, user de l'influence; — *vt.* munir de fils; faire une installation électrique; — *vi.* (coll.) télégraphier; **–less** *a.* san fil; **–less** *n.* radio

wire cutter *n.* coupe-fil *m.*

wire-haired *a.* à poil dur

wire tapping *n.* captation *f.*

wiring *n.* canalisation, pose de fils *f.*

wiry *a.* de fil, de en fil (de metal); (hair) raide; (person) sec

wisdom *n.* sagesse *f.*; — **tooth** dent de sagesse *f.*

wise *n.* manière, façon *f.*; **in no** — d'aucune façon; — *a.* sage; prudent

wish *n.* souhait *m.*; désir *m.*; vœu *m.*; — *vt. & vi.* désirer, vouloir; souhaiter; **–ful** *a.* désireux

wishbone *n.* lunette *f.*

wishy-washy *a.* fade, indifférent

wisp *n.* touffe, poignée *f.*

wistful *a.* pensif; plein de regret

wit *n.* esprit *m.*; bel esprit *m.*; — *vt.* savoir; **to** — à savoir, c'est-à-dire; **–less** *a.* sans esprit; **–tingly** *adv.* à dessein; **–ty** *a.* spirituel

witch *n.* sorcière *f.*; **–craft** *n.* sorcellerie *f.*; sortilège *m.*; — **hunt** *n.* chasse aux sorcières; (pol.) persécution des adversaires *f.*

with *prep.* avec; de; par; parmi; à; malgré

withdraw *vt.* retirer; rappeler; — *vi.* se retirer, s'éloigner; **–al** *n.* retrait, rappel *m.*; retraite *f.*

wither *vt.* flétrir, faner, dessécher; — *vi.* se faner, se dessécher

withhold *vt.* retenir, détenir; empêcher; **–ing** *a.*, **–ing tax** impôt retenu à la source *m.*

within *adv.* dedans, à l'interieur; — *prep.* à l'intérieur de; dans; à portée de; à moins de; avant

without *prep.* sans; hors de; **do** — se passer de; — *adv.* dehors; au dehors, en dehors; — *conj.* sans que

withstand *vt.* résister, s'opposer à

witness *n.* témoin, témoignage *m.*; **to bear** — **to** témoigner de; — *vt.* attester, être temoin de, assister à

witticism *n.* bon mot *m.*

wizard *n.* magicien, sorcier *m.*

wobble *vi.* chanceler, vaciller, tituber; branler

wobbly *a.* vacillant, branlant

woe *n.* douleur *f.*; malheur *m.*; **–ful** *a.* triste, malheureux woman *n.* femme *f.*; **-ly** *a.* féminin; de femme

womb *n.* matrice *f.*; sein, ventre *m.*

wonder *n.* étonnement *m.*, admiration *f.*; miracle *m.*; — *vi.* s'étonner; se demander; **-ful** *a.* merveilleux; **-ment** *n.* étonnement *m.*, admiration *f.*

wonderland *n.* pays des merveilles *m.*

wondrous *a.* merveilleux

wont *n.* coutume, habitude *f.*; **-ed** *a.* accoutumé, habituel

woo *vt.* courtiser; faire la cour à

wood *n.* bois *m.*; forêt *f.*; **-ed** *a.* boisé; **-en** *a.* de bois, en bois; **-en** (fig.) gauche **-y** *a.* ligneux; fibreux; — **alcohol** *n.* alcool méthylique *m.*

wood carving *n.* sculpture sur bois *f.*

woodcut *n.* gravure sur bois *f.*, bois *m.*, xylographie *f.*

woodcutter *n.* bûcheron *m.*

woodland *n.* bois *m.*

woodshed *n.* bûcher *m.*

woodsman *n.* homme des bois *m.*

wood wind *n.* bois *m.*

woodwork *n.* boiseries *f. pl.*; charpenterie *f.*; menuiserie *f.*

woof *n.* trame *f.*

woofer *n.* haut-parleur (pour les sons graves) *m.*

wool *n.* laine *f.*; **steel** — laine d'acier *f.*; **-en** *a.* de laine; **-ens** *n. pl.* étoffes de laine *f. pl.*; **-y** *a.* laineux; touffu

word *n.* mot *m.*; parole *f.*; nouvelle *f.*, renseignement *m.*; recommandation *f.*; in a — en un mot, bref; **send** — **to** faire savoir, avertir, prevenir; **-s** *pl.* dispute *f.*; **have -s** se disputer avec; s'expliquer; — *vt.* exprimer, rédiger; **-iness** *n.* verbosité *f.*; **-ing** *n.* termes *m. pl.*; **-y** *a.* verbeux, prolixe

work *n.* travail *m.*; occupation *f.*; ouvrage *m.*; opération *f.*; œuvre *f.*; besogne, tâche *f.*; **at** — au travail; en jeu; **-s** *pl.* usine *f.*; — *vi.* travailler; (function) marcher, aller; fonctionner; agir; — *vt.* faire travailler; travailler; opérer; accomplir; exploiter; développer; élaborer; — **out** résoudre, trouver; s'arranger; — **up** susciter, causer; **-able** *a.* pratique; réalisable; **-er** *n.* ouvrier, travailleur *m.*; **-ing** *a.* qui travaille; ouvrier; **-ing class** classe ouvrière *f.*; ouvriers *m. pl.*; **-ing** *n.* travail *m.*; marche *f.* fonctionnement *m.*

workbench *n.* établi *m.*

workbook *n.* manuel *m.*

workday *n.* jour ouvrable *m.*

workhouse *n.* hôpital *m.*; maison de travail *f.*; prison municipale *f.*

workman *n.* ouvrier *m.*; **-like** *a.* bien travaillé; **-ship** *n.* fini *m.*, construction *f.*; exécution *f.*

workout *n.* exercice *m.*; essai *m.*

workroom, workshop *n.* atelier *m.*

world *n.* monde, univers *m.*, terre *f.*; milieu *m.*; **a** — **of** pas mal de; — **war** guerre mondiale *f.*; **-liness** *n.* mondanité *f.*; **-ly** *a.* du monde; mondain

world-famous *a.* très connu, célèbre

world-wide *a.* universel

worm *n.* ver *m.*; — *vt.* (coll.) tirer; **-y** *a.* vermoulu

worm-eaten *a.* vermoulu

worn *a.* usé

worry *n.* ennui, souci *m.*; inquiétude *f.*; tracasserie *f.*; chagrin, dépit *m.*, contrariété *f.*; — *vt.* harasser, tourmenter, tracasser; inquiéter; — *vi.* s'inquiéter; se tracasser; **don't** — ne vous inquiétez pas; soyez tranquille

worse *a.* pire, plus mauvais; — *adv.* plus mal, pis; **so much the** — tant pis; **-n** *vt.* aggraver, empirer; **-n** *vi.* s'aggraver, empirer

worship *n.* adoration *f.*, culte *m.*; — *vt.* adorer

worst *n.* pire, pis; **at the** — au pis; — *vt.* vaincre, défaire; l'emporter sur; — *a.* le pire, le plus mauvais; — *adv.* le pis, le plus mal

worsted *n.* laine filée, laine peignée *f.*

worth *n.* valeur *f.*, prix *m.*; mérite *m.*; — *a.* qui vaut; digne de; **be** — valoir; **be** — **the trouble, be** — **while** valoir la la peine; **-iness** *n.* mérite *m.*; **-less** *a.* sans valeur; **-y** *a.* digne; **be -y of** mériter, être digne de

worthwhile *a.* qui vaut la peine

would-be *a.* soi-disant

wound *n.* blessure *f.*; plaie *f.*; — *vt.* blesser; froisser

wraith *n.* apparition *f.*

wrangle *n.* querelle *f.*; — *vi.* se quereller; **-er** *n.* querelleur *m.*; vacher *m.*

wrap *n.* (garment) manteau *m.*; emballage *m.*; — *vt.* emballer; envelopper, entourer; **-per** *n.* emballage *m.*; couverture *f.*; chemise *f.*; robe de chambre *f.*; **-ping** *n.* emballage *m.*, couverture *f.*; **-ping paper** papier d'emballage *m.*

wrath *n.* colère *f.*, courroux *m.*; **-ful** *a.* courroucé

wreak *vt.* exécuter, infliger

wreath *n.* guirlande, couronne *f.*; **-e** *vt.* couronner, enguirlander

wreck *n.* naufrage *m.*; ruine *f.*; accident *m.*; — *vt.* causer un naufrage; causer la destruction de; ruiner; détruire; saboter; **-age** *a.* débris *m. pl.*; décombres *m. pl.*; **-ed** *a.* détruit; naufragé; **-er** *n.*

(auto.) voiture de dépannage *f.*; (house) démolisseur *m.*; –ing *n.* ruine, destruction *f.*

wrench *n.* torsion *f.*; (tool) clé *f.*; **monkey** — clé anglaise *f.*; — *vt.* arracher, tordre; se fouler

wrestle *vi.* lutter; — **with** lutter avec, lutter contre; s'attaquer à; –r *n.* lutteur *m.*

wrestling *n.* lutte *f.*, catch *m.*

wretch *n.* misérable *m.*; malheureux *m.*; –**ed** *a.* misérable; malheureux, méprisable; pitoyable; –**edness** *n.* misère *f.*; malheur *m.*

wriggle *vi.* se tortiller; frétiller; — *vt.* tortiller

wring *vt.* tordre, tortiller; arracher; –**er** *n.* essoreuse *f.*

wrinkle *n.* ride *f.*; faux pli *m.*; (fig.) nouveau tour *m.*; — *vt.* rider; froncer; — *vi.* se rider; –**d** *a.* ridé

wrist *n.* poignet *m.*

wrist watch *n.* montre-bracelet *m.*

writ *n.* assignation *f.*; mandat *m.*

write *vt.* écrire; — *vi.* écrire; être écrivain; — **down** noter; inscrire; — **off** rayer, (com.) amortir; — **out** rédiger; — **up** rédiger, faire le procès-verbal de; –**r** *n.* écrivain *m.*, auteur *m.*

writhe *vi.* se tordre

writing *n.* écrit, ouvrage *m.*; écriture *f.*; **in** — par écrit; — **paper** *n.* papier à écrire *m.*

wrong *n.* tort *m.*; dommage, détriment *m.*, injustice *f.*; **be in the** — avoir tort; — *vt.* faire tort à; — *a.* faux; injuste; impropre; mauvais; mal; **be** — avoir tort; **what's** — qu'y a-t-il; **what's** — **with you** qu'avez-vous; — *adv.* mal; à tort; **do** — faire mal; **to go** — s'égarer; se détraquer, se déranger; –**ful** *a.* injuste; –**ly** *adv.* à tort; **rightly or** –**ly** à tort ou à raison

wrongdoer *n.* malfaiteur *m.*

wrongdoing *n.* mal, crime *m.*

wrought *a.* travaillé, ouvragé; — **iron** fer forgé *m.*

wry *a.* tors, tordu, difforme

X

xenon *n.* xénon *m.*

xerophagy *n.* xérophagie *f.*

xerophilous *a.* xérophile

xerophyte *n.* xérophyte *m.*

X ray *n.* rayon X *m.*; — **picture** *n.* radiogramme *m.*; — **specialist** *n.* radiologiste *m.* & *f.*

xylophone *n.* xylophone *m.*

Y

yacht *n.* yacht *m.*; –**ing** *n.* yachting *m.*

yachtsman *n.* yachtman *m.*

yam *n.* patate *f.*

yank *n.* secousse *f.*; — *vt.* tirer brusquement

Yankee *n.* (coll.) Américain *m.*; habitant du Nord des Etats-Unis *m.*; habitant de la Nouvelle-Angleterre *m.*

yap *n.* aboiement *m.*; jappement *m.*; — *vi.* aboyer; japper

yard *n.* cour *f.*; chantier *m.*; (naut.) vergue *f.*; (rail.) dépôt *m.*; (measure) yard *m.* (= 91 cm.); — **master** *n.* maître de chantier *m.*

yardstick *n.* mètre en bois *m.*

yarn *n.* fil (pour tissage) *m.*; (coll.) histoire *f.*

yawl *n.* yole *f.*

yawn *n.* bâillement *m.*; — *vi.* bâiller; –ing *a.* qui bâille; (fig.) béant

ye *pron.* vous

yea *adv.* oui; vraiment

year *n.* an *m.*, année *f.*; **leap** — année bissextile *f.*; **last** — l'année passée; **school** — année scolaire *f.*; –**ly** *a.* annuel; –**ly** *adv.* annuellement

yearbook *n.* annuaire *m.*

yearling *n.* animal d'un an *m.*

yearn *vi.*, — **for** soupirer après; –**ing** *n.* désir ardent *m.*, aspiration *f.*

yeast *n.* levure *f.*, levain *m.*; **—** levain en cubes *m.*

yell *n.* hurlement *m.*; cri *m.*; — *vi.* hurler; pousser un cri

yellow *n.* jaune *m.*; — *a.* jaune; lâche; infame; **turn** — jaunir; — **fever** fièvre jaune *f.*; — *vt.* & *vi.* jaunir; –**ish** *a.* jaunâtre

yelp *vi.* glapir, japper; — *n.* jappement *m.*

Yemen *n.* Yemen *m.*

yen *n.* désir *m.*

yeoman *n.* yeoman *m.*; hallebardier *m.*

yes *adv.* oui; (after negation) si; — **man** *n.* giroutte *f.*

yesterday *adv.* hier; **day before** — avanthier

yet *adv.* encore; cependant, toutefois; déjà; malgré tout; **as** — jusqu'ici

yield *n.* produit, rendement *m.*; — *vt.* céder; produire, rendre, donner; accorder; procurer; — *vi.* céder; succomber; consentir; –**ing** *a.* complaisant; souple; mou (molle)

yodel *n.* tyrolienne *f.*; — *vi.* chanter une tyrolienne; iouler

yoke *n.* joug, attelage *m.*; couple *m.*; (dress) empiècement *m.*; — *vt.* mettre au joug; subjuguer; accoupler

yokel *n.* provincial, rustique *m.*

yolk *n.* jaune d'œuf *m.*

yon, yonder *a.* qui est là; — *adv.* là-bas

yore *adv.* jadis, autrefois; **in days of — au** temps jadis

you *pron.* vous; tu; toi; on

young *a.* jeune; nouveau; tendre; **-er** *a.* cadet

youngster *n.* jeune personne *f.*, jeune homme *m.*; enfant *m.*

your *a.* votre, vos; ton, ta, tes; **-s** *pron.* le vôtre, la vôtre, les vôtres; à vous; le tien, la tienne; à toi; **-self** *pron.* vous-même, vous; toi-même, toi

youth *n.* jeunesse *f.*; jeune homme *m.*; **-ful** *a.* jeune; de jeunesse; **-fulness** *n.* jeunesse *f.*

yowl *n.* hurlement, jappement *m.*; — *vi.* hurler, japper

Yule *n.* Noël *m.*; — **log** bûche de Noël *f.*

Yuletide *n.* fêtes de Noël *f. pl.*

Z

zany *n.* bouffon *m.*; — *a.* (coll.) niais; fou; capricieux

zeal *n.* zèle *m.*; ardeur *f.*; **-ous** *a.* zélé

zealot *n.* fanatique *m. & f.*

zenith *n.* zénith *m.*; comble *m.*

zero *n.* zéro *m.*; (fig.) rien; — **hour** *n.* (mil.) heure de l'attaque, heure H *f.*

zest *n.* goût *m.*; appétit *m.*; enthousiasme *m.*

zigzag *n.* zigzag *m.*; — *a.* en zigzag; — *vi.* faire des zigzags

zinc *n.* zinc *m.*; — *vt.* zinguer

Zion *n.* Sion *m.*

zip code number *n.* code postale d'arrondissement *m.*

zipper *n.* fermeture éclair *f.*

zircon *n.* zircon *m.*

zither *n.* cithare *f.*

zodiac *n.* zodiaque *m.*

zone *n.* zone *f.*; — *vt.* repartir en zones

zoo *n.* jardin *n.* jardin zoologique, zoo *m.*

zoologist *n.* zoologiste *m.*

zoology *n.* zoologie *f.*

zoom *n.* bourdonnement *m.*; — *vi.* monter verticalement; bourdonner

zoonosis *n.* zoonose *f.*

Zulu *a. & n.* zoulou *m.*

TRAVELER'S CONVERSATION GUIDE
Guide de Conversation pour le Voyage

STATION (OR AIRPORT)

Where do I go through customs?
I have nothing to declare.
All I have are my personal things and a few packages of cigarettes.
I need a porter.
Where is my baggage?
This is not my suitcase. Please look for mine.
This is my baggage.
I checked two trunks.
I'll carry this suitcase.
Are meals included on that flight?

Are the cars air-conditioned?

TAXI

Will you get a taxi for me, please?

Take me to the Hotel ———.
How much is the fare?
Is it very far?
I am in a great hurry
Drive carefully, please.
Stop at the next corner.
Faster, please.
Not so fast.
Slower.
Stop!
Go on.
Go straight ahead.
Turn to your left. (right)
This is for you.

HOTEL

Where is the office?
I have a reservation.
I want a single room with bath.

Have you a two-bed room?
Is it a front room?

I'm going to stay two weeks. (a week)

LA GARE (OU L'AÉROPORT)

Où se trouve la douane?
Je n'ai rien à déclarer.
Je n'ai que des effets personnels et quelques paquets de cigarettes.
J'ai besoin d'un porteur.
Où sont mes bagages?
Cette valise n'est pas à moi. Allez chercher la mienne, s'il vous plaît.
Voici mes bagages.
J'ai fait enregistrer deux malles.
Cette valise, je vais la porter.
Est-ce que le prix du billet comprend les repas?
Est-ce que les wagons sont climatisés?

LE TAXI

Voulez-vous bien me chercher un taxi?
L'Hôtel ———, s'il vous plaît.
Le tarif, c'est combien?
Est-ce que c'est très loin?
Je suis très pressé.
Conduisez avec soin, s'il vous plaît.
Arrêtez (-vous) à la prochaine rue.
Plus vite, s'il vous plaît.
Pas si vite.
Plus lentement.
Arrêtez-vous!
Continuez.
Allez tout droit.
Tournez à gauche. (droite)
Voici pour vous.

L'HÔTEL

Où est le bureau?
J'ai fait réserver une chambre.
Je voudrais une chambre à un lit avec bain.
Avez-vous une chambre à deux lits?
Est-ce que la chambre donne sur la rue?
Je vais rester quinze jours. (huit jours)

Can I pay by the week or by the month?	Est-ce qu'on peut payer par semaine ou par mois?
Do you have anything less expensive?	Avez-vous quelque chose de moins cher?
Are meals included in the price?	Est-ce le prix de la chambre comprend les repas? Combien de repas?
How many?	
What are your meal hours?	A quelle heure sert-on les repas?
Is there a bank near here?	Est-ce qu'il y a une banque près d'ici?
Is there a post office near here?	Est-ce qu'il y a un bureau de poste près d'ici?
Are there towels in the room?	Y a-t-il des serviettes dans la chambre?
Bring me some ice, please.	Apportez-moi de la glace, s'il vous plaît.
Is the water here drinkable?	L'eau ici est potable, n'est pas?
Don't you have any pillows?	N'avez-vous pas d'oreillers?
Please call me at eight o'clock	Je voudrais qu'on m'appelle à huit heures.
Is there laundry service?	Puis-je faire blanchir mon linge ici?
I want this suit pressed.	Pouvez-vous donner un coup de fer à ce complet.
I want this dress cleaned.	Pouvez-vous nettoyer cette robe.
I would like an extra blanket.	Je voudrais une couverture supplémentaire.
Do you have a map of ———?	Avez-vous une carte de ———?
Do you have any stamps?	Avez-vous des timbres?
May I have the bill, please?	La note, s'il vous plaît.
Are taxes and service included?	Taxes et service compris, n'est pas?
Do you accept travelers' checks?	Acceptez-vous les chèques de voyageur?
Will you have my bags taken down, please?	Voulez-vous bien faire descendre mes bagages?

RESTAURANT

LE RESTAURANT

Do you have a table for two?	Avez-vous une table pour deux?
I would like to sit near a window. (outside) (inside)	Je préférerais une table près d'une fenêtre. (sur la terrase) (à l'intérieur)
I'll have the table d'hote dinner.	Le menu régulier (ordinaire), s'il vous plaît.
May I have a menu?	La carte, s'il vous plaît.
May I keep this as a souvenir?	Est-ce que je peux garder cela comme souvenir?
I have no napkin.	Je n'ai pas de serviette.
Bring me some butter, please.	Du beurre, s'il vous plaît.
How do you prefer the steak?	Comment préférez-vous le bifteck?
I prefer it very rare. (medium rare) (medium) (well-done)	Je le préfère saignant. (juste à point) (bien cuit) (très bien cuit)
What do you have for dessert?	Qu'avez-vous comme dessert?
Bring me some more bread please.	Apportez-moi encore du pain, s'il vous plaît.

Coffee with cream, please. (milk)

Un café à la crème, s'il vous plaît. (au lait)

Tea with lemon. (milk)
Un thé au citron, (au lait)

Waiter, the check, please.
Garçon, l'addition, s'il vous plaît.

Where is the washroom?
Où se trouvent les cabinets?

They have fish. (meat, fowl)
Il y a du poisson. (de la viande, de la volaille)

Do you want pork? (beef, veal, lamb, chicken, turkey, duck)
Voulez-vous du porc? (du bœuf, du veau, de l'agneau, du poulet, du dindon, du canard)

I want my eggs fried. (poached, scrambled, soft-boiled, with ham, with bacon)
Je préfère les œufs sur le plat. (pochés, brouillés, à la coque, au jambon, au lard)

A glass of milk, please.
Un verre de lait, s'il vous plaît.

Orange juice and black coffee.
Un jus d'orange et un café noir.

Rolls and butter.
Des petits pains avec du beurre.

Crescent rolls and coffee with milk.
Des croissants et un café au lait.

Continental breakfast. (coffee, rolls, butter and jam)
Un café (déjeuner) complet.

Toast and jam.
Du pain grillé avec de la confiture.

Waiter, I need a glass. (fork, spoon, knife)
Garçon, je n'ai pas de verre. (de fourchette, de cuillère, de couteau)

MONEY

L'ARGENT

Where can I cash a check?
Où puis-je toucher un chèque?

What is the rate of exchange?
Quel est le cours du change?

Here is my passport.
Voici mon passeport.

POST OFFICE

LE BUREAU DE POSTE

I want to send this letter by airmail.
Je veux expédier cette lettre par avion.

How much postage is needed for foreign mail?
Quel est l'affranchissement pour l'étranger?

When will this letter reach the United States by regular mail?
Quand est-ce que cette lettre arrivera au États-Unis, si je l'expédie par courrier ordinaire?

How much is it by regular mail?
Combien est-ce par courrier ordinaire?

I'd like to register this letter.
Je voudrais faire recommander cette lettre.

Are there any letters for me?
Y a-t-il des lettres pour moi?

Is the post office open on Saturday?
Le bureau de poste est-il ouvert le samedi?

RAILROAD

LE CHEMIN DE FER

Where is the ticket window?
Où se trouvent les guichets?

Two first-class (second) tickets to ———.
Deux billets de première (seconde) classe pour ———.

One way.
Aller seulement.

No, round trip.
Non, aller et retour.

Is this the train to ———?
Ce train va à ———?

Does it have Pullman cars?	Y a-t-il des wagons-lits?
I want an upper (lower) berth.	Je veux une couchette supérieure. (inférieure)
I want a one-berth compartment. (two-berth)	Je veux un compartiment individuel. (double)
When do we reach ———?	A quelle heure arrivons-nous à ———?
Are we on time?	Sommes-nous à l'heure?
How late are we?	De combien sommes-nous en retard?
Is there a dining car?	Y a-t-il un wagon-restaurant?
How late do they serve breakfast?	Jusqu'à quelle heure sert-on le petit déjeuner?
When do they start serving lunch?	À quelle heure commence-t-on à servir le déjeuner?
The first service is at noon.	Le premier service est à midi.
The second service is at one-thirty.	Le deuxième service est à une heure et demie.
I'm going to bed.	Je vais me coucher.
Is the berth made up?	Le lit est fait?
Please take down that suitcase.	Voulez-vous bien descendre cette valise?
I feel a draft.	Je sens un courant d'air.
May we turn off the fan?	Si l'on fermait le ventilateur?
May I open the window? (door)	Puis-je ouvrir la fenêtre? (porte)
Have you seen the conductor?	Avez-vous vu le contrôleur?

AUTOMOBILE

L'AUTOMOBILE

Forty liters of gas, please.	Quarante litres d'essence, s'il vous plaît.
Will you please check the oil and water?	Voulez-vous bien vérifier l'huile et l'eau?
Fill the tank.	Faites le plein.
I've run out of gas.	J'ai une panne d'essence.
I have a flat tire.	J'ai un pneu dégonflé.
Can you fix this puncture?	Pouvez-vous réparer cette crevaison?
Check the tires, including the spare.	Vérifiez les pneus, y compris le pneu de rechange.
Add some air if necessary.	Gonflez-les un peu s'il le faut.
Where is the next gas station?	Où se trouve le prochain poste d'essence?
I want to leave the car here overnight.	Je veux laisser l'auto ici jusqu'à demain matin.
Wash it and change the oil.	Lavez-la et vidangez l'huile.
What do you charge for greasing?	Combien pour le graissage?
Is the road in good condition?	Le chemin est en bon état?

PHOTOGRAPHY

LA PHOTOGRAPHIE

Is picture taking permitted?	Est-ce qu'on peut photographier?
May I take my camera into the church? (museum)	Puis-je garder mon appareil photographique dans l'église? (le musée)
What is the fee for taking pictures?	Quelle est la taxe pour photographier?

I need some 620 films. (120, color)

J'ai besoin de quelques pellicules six-neuf, petite bobine. (six-neuf, grosse bobine, en couleur)

Where can I buy camera supplies?

Où puis-je acheter du matériel photographique?

My camera doesn't work. Can you fix it?

Mon appareil ne marche pas. Pouvez-vous le réparer?

Can you have this film developed?

Pouvez-vous faire développer cette pellicule?

I want three prints of each.

Je veux trois épreuves de chaque.

Do you have movie film?

Avez-vous des films cinématographiques?

Do you have flashbulbs?

Avez-vous des lampes flash?

May I have these enlarged?

Puis-je faire agrandir ces clichés?

When will it be ready?

Quand est-ce que ce sera prêt?

Does the price include developing?

Est-ce que le prix comprend la développement?

Will you put in the film?

Voudriez-vous mettre la pellicule?

SHOPPING

LES EMPLETTES

I'm going shopping.

Je vais faire des emplettes. (courses)

Is there a department store near here?

Est-ce qu'il y a un grand magasin près d'ici?

How much is this?

C'est combien?

It's too expensive.

C'est trop cher.

May I see something better?

Puis-je voir quelque chose de meilleure qualité?

May I see some shirts? (gloves, ties, handkerchiefs, socks, stockings)

Je voudrais voir des chemises? (gants, cravates, mouchoirs, chaussettes, bas)

Do you have it in white?

L'avez-vous en blanc?

I prefer solid colors.

Je préfère les couleurs unies.

I'd like to try on this dress.

Je voudrais essayer cette robe.

This suit doesn't look very well on me.

Ce tailleur ne me va pas très bien. (f.)
Ce complet ne me va pas très bien. (m.)

What size?

Quelle taille?

Can you have them sent to the hotel?

Pourrez-vous les faire envoyer à l'hôtel?

I'll take these postal cards.

Je voudrais ces cartes postales.

KINDS OF STORES

LES MAGASINS

Bookstore

Librairie

Department store

Grand magasin

Drugstore (prescriptions, patent medicines only)

Pharmacie

Florist

Fleuriste

General Hardware, (paint, wallpaper)

Marchand de couleurs, Quincaillerie

Jewelry

Bijouterie

Leather goods

Maroquinerie

Perfumery	Parfumerie
Stationery	Papeterie
Tobacco, matches, stamps, bicycle licenses	Bureau de tabac
Watchmaker, watch repairs	Horlogerie
Variety, ten-cent stores	Prisunic, monoprix, uniprix
Bakery (bread, hard rolls)	Boulangerie
Butcher shop (beef, veal)	Boucherie
Dairy products (milk, cream, cheese, butter, margarine)	Laiterie
Delicatessen, pork (some canned goods)	Charcuterie
Fowl, rabbits	Marchand de volaille
General grocery	Grand magasin d'alimentation
Horsemeat	Boucherie chevaline
Pastries (fancy bread and rolls)	Pâtisserie
Pushcarts (usually only one item of fresh produce)	Marchand des quatre saisons
Spices, staples (sometimes fresh vegetables, fruits, and wine)	Épicerie
Vegetables	Marchand de légumes
Wines & Liqueurs (bottled, bulk)	Marchand de vin
Dressmaker, women's clothes	Couturière
Men's ready-made clothes	Vêtements de confection
Shoes	Chaussures
Tailor, men's made-to-order clothes	Tailleur
Women's hats	Modiste
Barber shop	Coiffeur pour hommes
Beauty shop	Coiffeur pour dames

GENERAL EXPRESSIONS — LES EXPRESSIONS ORDINAIRES

Good morning.	Bonjour
I don't speak French. (English)	Je ne parle pas français. (anglais)
I understand it a good deal, but I don't speak it.	Je comprends assez bien, mais je ne parle pas.
Where are you going?	Où allez-vous?
Come here, please.	Venez ici, s'il vous plaît.
I want to show you something.	Je veux vous montrer quelquechose.
Speak slowly, please.	Parlez lentement, s'il vous plaît.
Wait here.	Attendez ici.
I have no time today.	Je n'ai pas le temps aujourd'hui.
What can I do for you?	Qu'y a-t-il pour votre service?
Can you tell me. . . . ?	Pouvez-vous me dire. . . . ?
I think so. (not)	Je crois que oui. (non)
Is there a doctor near here?	Y a-t-il un médecin près ici?
What do you think?	Qu'en pensez-vous?
You know what I mean?	Vous savez ce que je veux dire?
How do you say that in French?	Comment dit-on cela en français?
What is that for?	A quoi est-ce que cela sert?
Do you understand me?	Me comprenez-vous?
I understand you when you speak slowly.	Je vous comprends quand vous parlez lentement.

Sorry, but I don't understand you.	Je regrette, je ne vous comprends pas.
Please repeat that question.	Veuillez répéter la question?
Now I understand.	Maintenant je comprends.
You are too kind.	Vous êtes trop aimable.
Thank you very much.	Merci beaucoup.
You are welcome.	De rien.
How are you?	Comment allez-vous?
Fine, thank you, and you?	Bien, merci, et vous?
Of course	Bien entendu
Right and left	À droite et à gauche
After all	Après tout
Willingly	Volontiers
By force	De force
From time to time	De temps en temps

WEATHER

LE TEMPS

What is the weather like?	Quel temps fait-il?
It is fine weather. (bad, sunny, cold, cool, hot, windy)	Il fait beau. (mauvais, du soleil, froid, frais, chaud, du vent)
It is raining.	Il pleut.
It is snowing.	Il neige.
It is cloudy.	Il y a des nuages.

DIVISIONS OF TIME

TELLING TIME

L'HEURE

What time is it?	Quelle heure est-il?
It is one o'clock. (two)	Il est une heure. (deux heures)
It is 10:15.	Il est dix heures et quart.
It is 10:30.	Il est dix heures et demie.
It is a quarter to eleven.	Il est onze heures moins le quart.
It is 11:20.	Il est onze heures vingt.
It is twenty minutes to eleven.	Il est onze heures moins vingt.
It is noon. (midnight)	Il est midi. (minuit)
It is 2 A.M.	Il est deux heures du matin.
It is 2 P.M.	Il est deux de l'après midi.
The train leaves at 2 P.M.	Le train part à quatorze heures.
It is 6 P.M.	Il est six heures du soir.

DAYS OF THE WEEK

JOURS DE LA SEMAINE

Monday	lundi
Tuesday	mardi
Wednesday	mercredi
Thursday	jeudi
Friday	vendredi
Saturday	samedi
Sunday	dimanche

MONTHS OF THE YEAR

January
February
March
April
May
June
July
August
September
October
November
December

MOIS DE L'ANNÉE

janvier
février
mars
avril
mai
juin
juillet
août
septembre
octobre
novembre
décembre

SEASONS OF THE YEAR

Spring: summer: fall: winter

SAISONS DE L'ANNÉE

printemps: été: automne: hiver

CONVERTING TEMPERATURES

FAHRENHEIT TO CENTIGRADE
Subtract 32° and multiply by 5/9.
50°F = 10°C.   −4°F = −20°C.

CENTIGRADE TO FAHRENHEIT
Multiply by 9/5 and add 32°.
40°C = 104°F.   20°C = 68°F.

CONVERTING METRIC MEASURES

AMERICAN TO FRENCH
1 gallon = 3.785 liters (3.8)
1 pound =   .4536 kilos (.45)
1 inch   = 2.54 centimeters (2.5)
1 yard   =   .9144 meters (.9)
1 mile   = 1.6093 kilometers (1.6)
1 acre   =   .4047 hectares (.4)

FRENCH TO AMERICAN
1 liter   =   .2642 gallons (.26)
1 kilo   = 2.2046 pounds (2.2)
1 centimeter =   .3937 inches (.4)
1 meter   = 1.094 yards (1.1)
1 kilometer =   .6214 miles (.6)
1 hectare   = 2.471 acres (2.5)

The figures in parentheses are approximate equivalents.

To convert American measurements into their approximate French equivalents. or vice versa, multiply as indicated in the examples.

Examples: To determine the approximate number of liters in ten gallons, multiply 3.8 (liters per gallon) × 10 = 38.1 liters.

To determine the approximate number of miles in 14 kilometers, multiply .6 (miles per kilometer) × 14 = 8.4 miles.

FRENCH ROAD SIGNS

French traffic signs, like those in the United States, show typical shapes but some bear symbols while others have only words. The most common are shown on the following pages. The three distinct shapes are triangular, circular, and rectangular.

△ — Triangular signs indicate danger ahead.

○ — Circular signs give explicit instructions.

▢ — Rectangular signs contain specific information.

French traffic proceeds on the right-hand side of the street.

LES SIGNAUX DE LA ROUTE	ROAD SIGNS
Tournant	Curve
Virage	Turn
Virage à Droite (Gauche)	Curve to the Right (Left)
Virages sur . . . km.	Winding Road for . . . Kilometers
Priorité	Right of Way
Prudence	Caution
Pont Coupé	Bridge Out
Passage à Niveau	Level Crossing
Sortie d'École	School Exit
Chaussée Glissante	Slippery Pavement
Chaussée Rétrécie	Narrowing Pavement
Chaussée Déformée	Rough Road, Bumpy Road
Travaux	Road Under Repair
Travaux ralentir	Slow! Construction
Chute de Pierres	Rock Slide, Fallen-rock Zone
Passage à Niveau	Railroad Crossing
Intersection	Crossroads, Side Road
Sens Unique	One-way Street
Sens Obligatoire	One-way Traffic (as indicated)
Serrez à Droite	Keep to the Right
Limite de Vitesse	Speed Limit
Défense de Doubler	No Passing
Entreé Interdite	No Entry
Interdiction de Stationner, Stationnement Interdit	No Stopping
Interdiction de Parquer	No Parking
Parcage Autorisé	Parking Allowed
Stationnement Autorisé Jours Pairs (Impairs)	Parking on Even (Odd) Calendar Dates
Stationnement Pair—Impair	Parking on Even-numbered Side of the Street on Even Calendar Dates: Odd Side on Odd Dates
Stationnement Réglementé	Parking Restricted

Stationnement Réservé aux Cars (Autobus, Taxis, Voitures de Tourisme)	Parking Reserved for Buses (Taxis, Passenger Cars)
Circulation Interdite	No Thoroughfare
Ralentissez	Slow
Deviation	Detour
Interdit à Tous les Véhicules Automobiles	Closed to All Motor Vehicles
Interdit aux Poids Lourds	Closed to Heavy Traffic
Interdit aux Cyclistes	Closed to Cyclists
Fin d'Interdiction de Stationner	End of No Parking Zone
Fin d'Interdiction de Dépasser	End of No Passing Zone
Fin de Sens Unique	End of One-way Traffic, Two-way Traffic Begins
Signaux Sonores Interdits	Use of Horns Forbidden
Vitesse Maximum	Speed Limit
Hauteur Limitée	Low Clearance
Dispositif de Contrôle Obligatoire, Disque Obligatoire	Parking Only with Disk in Window to Indicate Time of Arrival
Zone Bleue	Zone in Which Parking Disk Must be Used
Fin de Chantier	End of Construction Area
Bac	Ferry
Pont Étroit	Narrow Bridge
Poste de Douane	Customs
Hôpital	Hospital
Secours Routier Français	French Highway Aid, Emergency Telephone
Allumez vos Lanternes	Turn on Headlights

I. DANGER SIGNS

CURVE SIGNS

Curve	Left	Right	Dangerous	S-curve

CROSSING SIGNS

Railroad Signs (guarded)	(unguarded)	Dangerous Crossroad	You Have Priority	Right Has Priority

GENERAL SIGNS

Bump or Dip

Hill

Side Road

Narrow Road

Caution

**Slippery
Pavement**

Crosswalk

**Cattle
Crossing**

School

**Men
Working**

Drawbridge

**Stop
Ahead**

Stop

**Yield
Ahead**

Yield

II. DEFINITE INSTRUCTION SIGNS

NO ENTRY SIGNS

**Closed to
Traffic**

No Entry

No Autos

No Motorcycles

No Vehicles

GENERAL SIGNS

**No
Left Turn**

**No
Passing**

**End No Passing
Zone**

**Bicycle
Path**

**No
Bicycles**

50 km. per hr.

**cars 50
trucks 30**

**End
Speed Limit**

No Horns

One Way

**No
Parking**

**Traffic
Circle**

Keep Right

Customs

**Stop—Police
(check-point)**

III. INFORMATIVE SIGNS

Parking

Gas Station

Telephone

Garage

Hospital

THE *NEW CENTURY* DICTIONARIES

VELAZQUEZ SPANISH/ENGLISH DICTIONARY
VEST-POCKET DICTIONARIES
French
German
Italian
Spanish

INSTANT CONVERSATION GUIDES
French
German
Spanish